Red Hat® Fedora™ Linux® Secrets®

Red Hat® Fedora™ Linux® Secrets®

Naba Barkakati

Wiley Publishing, Inc.

Red Hat® Fedora™ Linux® Secrets®

Published by
Wiley Publishing, Inc.
10475 Crosspoint Boulevard
Indianapolis, IN 46256
www.wiley.com

Published by Wiley Publishing, Inc., Indianapolis, Indiana
Published simultaneously in Canada

ISBN-13: 978-0-471-74757-4
ISBN-10: 0-471-74757-2

Manufactured in the United States of America

10 9 8 7 6 5 4 3 2 1

1B/SS/QZ/QV/IN

Library of Congress Cataloging-in-Publication Data

Barkakati, Nabajyoti, 1956-
Red Hat Fedora Linux Secrets / Naba Barkakati.
p. cm.
Includes index.
ISBN-13: 978-0-471-74757-4 (paper/dvd)
ISBN-10: 0-471-74757-2 (paper/dvd)
1. Linux. 2. Operating systems (Computers) I. Title.
QA76.76.O63B3661525 2005
005.4 32—dc22

2005017620

To my wife, Leha, and daughters, Ivy, Emily, and Ashley.

About the Author

Naba Barkakati, an electrical engineer and a successful computer-book author, has experience in a wide variety of systems, ranging from MS-DOS and Windows to UNIX and Linux. He bought his first personal computer—an IBM PC-AT—in 1984 after graduating with a Ph.D. in electrical engineering from the University of Maryland at College Park. While pursuing a full-time career in engineering, Naba dreamed of writing software for the emerging PC software market. As luck would have it, instead of building a software empire like Microsoft, he ended up writing successful computer books. Currently, Naba is a Senior Level Technologist at the Center for Technology and Engineering in the U.S. Government Accountability Office (GAO).

Over the past 17 years, Naba has written more than 25 computer books on a number of topics, ranging from object-oriented programming with C++ to Linux. He has written several best-selling titles, such as *The Waite Group's Turbo C++ Bible, Object-Oriented Programming in C++, X Window System Programming, Visual C++ Developer's Guide, Borland C++ 4 Developer's Guide,* and *Linux Secrets.* His books have been translated into many languages, including Spanish, French, Polish, Greek, Italian, Chinese, Japanese, and Korean. Naba's most recent books are *SUSE Linux 9.3 For Dummies* and *Linux All-in-One Desk Reference For Dummies*, both published by Wiley.

Naba lives in North Potomac, Maryland, with his wife, Leha, and their children, Ivy, Emily, and Ashley.

Credits

Acquisitions Editor
Debra Williams Cauley

Development Editor
Kenyon Brown

Technical Editor
John Kennedy

Copy Editor
Nancy Rapoport

Editorial Manager
Mary Beth Wakefield

Production Manager
Tim Tate

Vice President and Executive Group Publisher
Richard Swadley

Vice President and Publisher
Joseph B. Wikert

Project Coordinator
Erin Smith

Graphics and Production Specialists
Carrie Foster
Denny Hager
Lynsey Osborn

Quality Control Technicians
John Greenough
Carl William Pierce

Permissions Editor
Laura Moss

Media Development Coordinator
Laura Atkinson

Media Development Specialists
Angela Denny
Steve Kudirka
Kit Malone
Travis Silvers

Proofreading and Indexing
TECHBOOKS Production Services

Contents at a Glance

Contents

Acknowledgments

I am grateful to Debra Williams Cauley for giving me the opportunity to write *Red Hat® Fedora™ Linux® Secrets®*. Kenyon Brown guided me through the manuscript review process and kept everything moving. I also really appreciate the thorough copy editing by the wonderful folks at Wiley.

I thank John Kennedy for reviewing the manuscript for technical accuracy and providing many useful suggestions for improving the book's content.

Thanks to everyone at Wiley Publishing, Inc., for transforming my raw manuscript into this well-edited and beautifully packaged book.

Of course, there would be no reason for this book if it were not for Linux. For this, we have Linus Torvalds and the legions of Linux developers around the world to thank. Thanks to the Fedora Project for continuing to develop and enhance the Linux distribution called Fedora Core and for making publicly available the ISO image used to create the DVD-ROM that is bundled with this book.

Finally, and as always, my greatest thanks go to my wife, Leha, and our daughters, Ivy, Emily, and Ashley—it is their love and support that keep me going. Thanks for being there!

Introduction

If you are new to using Linux, you need a practical guide that not only gets you going with the installation and setup of Linux but also shows you how to use Linux for specific functions, such as a Web server or a software development platform. If you want to learn Linux, the practical guide should also include tutorials on how various parts of a Linux system work behind the scenes. *Red Hat Fedora Linux Secrets* is just the book to help you learn Linux and use it productively.

There are many capable Linux distributions that you could use to learn and use Linux. What this book offers is Fedora Core (also referred to as Fedora or Fedora Linux)—the able successor to the venerable Red Hat Linux and the testing ground for Red Hat's commercial Linux offering, Red Hat Enterprise Linux. Fedora Core is a full-fledged Linux distribution with all the desktop and server components you need for every conceivable task you expect a Linux system to do. You have the choice of GNOME and KDE desktops. For productivity applications, Fedora includes the Firefox Web browser, Evolution personal information manager, and the OpenOffice.org office suite. As for servers, Fedora comes with the standard suite of Apache Web server, Tomcat Java application server, Sendmail mail server, Samba Windows server, Bind domain name server, and many more.

Red Hat Fedora Linux Secrets follows the successful model of the "Secrets" series and highlights crucial, less-known facts as "secrets." The focus is on providing insights into the inner workings of Linux—which configuration files control what, which commands to type in what sequence to perform a key task, and so on. In addition to these insights, the book provides all the usual information on many of the applications—such as email, the Web, and news, plus graphics and text utilities—that are included on the book's companion DVD-ROM.

The book's companion DVD-ROM comes with the binaries for the latest release of Fedora as well as all the source code. The DVD-ROM is packed with all the software you need to turn your PC into a powerful Linux desktop and server. The book provides detailed technical information on installing and customizing Linux for use with various types of computers and peripherals.

The unique aspects of *Red Hat Fedora Linux Secrets* are the details of how things work behind the scenes. The book includes tutorials, tips, techniques, shortcuts, and little-known facts about using Linux in various real-world tasks that range from simply learning UNIX commands to setting up a secure, Java-capable Web server for your business.

By reading this book you can:

- Learn how to install and set up Linux from the DVD-ROM included with the book
- Learn how to use various peripherals (video cards, hard disks, and network cards) in Linux
- Learn about dial-up networking (with SLIP and PPP) under Linux
- Get tips, techniques, and shortcuts for specific uses of Linux, such as:
  - Setting up and using Internet services such as Web, Mail, News, FTP (File Transfer Protocol), NFS (Network File System), NIS (Network Information Service), and DNS (Domain Name Service)
  - Setting up a Windows server using Samba

    - Learning UNIX on Linux
    - Learning Perl, shell, and Tcl/Tk programming on Linux
    - Learning Java programming on Linux
- Understand the basics of system and network security
- Learn to perform system and network administration tasks
- Receive many Linux tools and utilities
- Learn about Linux resources that can serve as continuing sources of information in the ever-changing world of Linux
- Learn how to download the latest release of Fedora and burn a DVD-ROM from the downloaded ISO file

Organization of the Book

Red Hat Fedora Linux Secrets contains 26 chapters and 9 appendixes and is organized into 6 parts covering topics such as installation and setup, routine use, networking and server setup, system administration, and programming.

Part I: Setting Up Linux

Part I includes six chapters that introduce you to Linux, guide you through Linux installation, and show you how to configure various types of hardware in Linux. The first chapter provides an overview of Linux in general. The second chapter takes you through the steps needed to install Linux from this book's companion DVD-ROM. The next four chapters explain how to configure the X Window System, printers using the Common Unix Printing System (CUPS), and sound and network components.

Part II: Exploring Linux

This part acquaints you with Linux. The six chapters in this section describe the popular GNU utilities, the GUI desktops—GNOME and KDE, and the applications included with Linux on the companion DVD-ROM. You will also learn how to edit text files, prepare DocBook documentation, and perform basic systems administration functions.

Part III: Internetworking Linux

The seven chapters in Part III focus on connecting the Linux system to the Internet and setting up various Internet services on the system. After describing dial-up networking, the chapters in this part walk you through the setup and configuration of a number of servers including Web, FTP, SMTP (Simple Mail Transfer Protocol for mail), news, DNS, NIS, NFS, and Samba.

Part IV: Managing Linux

The three chapters in Part IV cover systems administration and security. The first chapter in this part, Chapter 20, starts by discussing a number of advanced system administration topics. The next two chapters show you how to install and upgrade software using the Red Hat Package Manager (RPM), how to build software from source files, how to rebuild and install a new kernel, and how to secure the system and the network.

Part V: Programming Linux

The four chapters in Part V turn to the subject of programming in Linux. The first chapter, Chapter 23, covers the basics as well as a number of software development tools and the GNU Public License that affects software developed in Linux. Then, that chapter briefly touches on C and C++ programming. The next two chapters cover scripting using the shell, Perl, and Tcl/Tk. Finally, the last chapter in this section introduces you to writing applet, servlets, and standalone applications using Java.

Part VI: Appendixes

This section includes nine appendixes:

- Appendix A, "Linux Commands," presents alphabetically arranged reference entries for the many commonly used Linux commands.
- Appendix B, "Disk Drives," describes IDE and SCSI disk controllers and lists driver modules needed for specific SCSI controllers.
- Appendix C, "CD and DVD Drives," lists specific types of Linux-supported CD-ROM drives, categorized by interface type.
- Appendix D, "Ethernet Cards," describes the physical setup of an Ethernet LAN and lists the Ethernet cards that Linux supports.
- Appendix E, "Modems and Terminals," explains how to connect, set up, and use modems and terminals in Linux.
- Appendix F, "PC Cards," briefly describes PC Cards that use the PCMCIA interface and the PCMCIA support package for Linux.
- Appendix G, "Linux Resources," lists resources on the Internet where you can obtain the latest information about Linux.
- Appendix H, "Fedora Upgrade Procedure," explains how to download and upgrade your system to the latest Fedora Linux release.
- Appendix I, "About the DVD-ROM," summarizes the contents of the book's companion DVD-ROM.

If you are a new user, you should start by reading Part I, which guides you through installing Linux from the DVD-ROM that accompanies the book (see Appendixes H and I also). If you have specific hardware questions, you should go directly to the relevant appendix (see Appendixes B through F). If you have already installed Linux, you might want to begin with Part II, where you'll learn how to make the most of Linux in everyday use (see Appendix G also). For questions related to Internet services, consult the appropriate chapter in Part III. Part IV gets you going with various systems administration tasks and explains how to maintain system and network security. To learn about programming in specific languages, consult the relevant chapters in Part V. When you need information on a specific Linux command, turn to Appendix A and look for that command in the alphabetically arranged reference entries.

Conventions Used in This Book

Red Hat Fedora Linux Secrets uses a simple notational style. All listings, filenames, function names, variable names, and keywords are typeset in a `monospaced font` for ease of reading. The first occurrences of new terms and concepts are in *italic*. Text you are directed to type is in **boldface**. The output of commands follows the typed command and the output is shown in a `monospaced font`.

Each chapter starts with a short list that highlights the "secrets" you will find in that chapter. The summary at the end of the chapter tells you a bit more about what the chapter covered.

Following in the time-honored tradition of the "Secrets" series, I use icons to help you quickly pinpoint useful information. The icons include the following:

note

The Note icon marks a general interesting fact—something that I thought you'd like to know.

insider insight

The Insider Insight icon marks things that you should know to make your job easier and to work smarter.

caution

The Caution icon highlights potential pitfalls. With this icon, I'm telling you: "Watch out! This could hurt your system!"

cross ref

The Cross-Reference icon points out other chapters in the book for a deeper discussion of a specific topic.

The Secret icon marks facts that explain the inner working of some aspect of Linux and related software. These are details that may not be that well-documented, but are important to know. It's not that no one knows this fact—it's just hard to find; and knowing this fact usually clears up many other questions that you may have. This icon also marks technical information that will be of interest to an advanced user.

About the Companion DVD-ROM

Red Hat Fedora Linux Secrets addresses the needs of new users who want to put Linux to some productive use on their home or office PC. To ensure that readers have everything they need to start using Linux, this book includes a copy of Fedora on the companion DVD-ROM. Fedora is a well-known Linux distribution that's easy to install and is well supported by a community of developers (`http://fedora.redhat.com`).

See Appendix I for a summary description of the contents of the companion DVD-ROM. To learn how to download a newer version of Fedora and burn your own DVD, see Appendix H. As you browse the contents of the DVD-ROM, you'll notice that there is a huge amount of software included in Linux. The long list of software shouldn't overwhelm you. You have to learn to use only what you need. Besides, this book will show you how to install Linux and use most of this software.

If you have enough space (at least 5GB) available on your PC's hard disk (or, better yet, a spare second hard disk) and your PC can boot from the DVD drive, Linux installation can be as simple as plopping the DVD-ROM into the DVD drive, booting the PC, and filling up information in a series of dialog boxes. You don't have to take my word for it—you can see for yourself.

It's time to get started on your Linux adventure. Take out the companion DVD-ROM, turn to Chapter 1, and let the fun begin. Before you know it, you'll be a Linux expert!

I hope you enjoy this book as much as I enjoyed writing it!

Reach Out

The publisher and I would like your feedback. After you have had a chance to use this book, if you want to share any thoughts, please feel free to contact me directly at:

```
naba@ieee.org
```

Part I

Setting Up Linux

An Overview of Linux

Secrets in This Chapter

The world of operating systems changed forever when Linus Torvalds of the University of Helsinki in Finland decided to build a UNIX-like operating system for the PC. What started as a simple task-switching example, with two processes that printed AAAA . . . and BBBB . . . on a dumb terminal, has grown into a full-fledged, multitasking, multiuser operating system that rivals commercially available UNIX systems for Intel 80x86 systems. Many programmers around the world have contributed code and collaborated to bring Linux to its current state. With the release of version 1.0 in March 1994, Linux became an operating system of choice for UNIX enthusiasts, as well as for people looking for a low-cost UNIX platform for a specific purpose, such as developing software or running an Internet host.

This chapter provides a broad-brushstroke picture of Linux and describes how you can get the most out of the built-in capabilities of Linux, such as networking, developing software, and running applications.

After you overcome your initial fear of the unknown and install Linux, you will see how you can use it to turn your PC into a UNIX workstation. The best part is that you can get Linux for free—just download it from one of several Internet sites (for example, you'll find links to many Linux distributions at the Distrowatch.com website at `www.distrowatch.com`). The best way for beginners and experts alike to get started, though, is to buy a book (such as this one) that comes with a Linux distribution on a DVD. This book is your guide to the inner workings of Linux. The next chapter shows how to install Linux, and subsequent chapters describe specific tasks (such as connecting to the Internet or developing software) that you may want to perform with your Linux PC. In addition to many utilities with graphical user interfaces (GUIs), this book provides you the details such as what commands to use and what configuration files to edit.

What Is Linux?

Linux is a freely available UNIX-like operating system that runs on a wide variety of systems. Linus Torvalds and other programmers originally developed Linux for the Intel 80x86 processor. Nowadays, Linux is also available for systems based on other processors, such as those with AMD's 64-bit AMD64 processors, the Motorola 68000 family; Alpha AXPs; Sun SPARCs and UltraSPARCs; Hewlett-Packard's HP PA-RISC; the PowerPC and PowerPC64 processors; and the MIPS R4x00 and R5x00. More recently, IBM has released its own version of Linux for its S/390 and zSeries mainframes. This book covers Fedora Core—a Linux distribution for the Intel 80x86 and Pentium processors (these are known as the IA32 architecture processors, or i386, because they support the instruction set of the 80386 processor). Fedora Core evolved from Red Hat Linux, which was a freely available and popular Linux distribution from Red Hat.

Red Hat, Fedora Project, and Fedora Core

In late September 2003, Red Hat announced the Fedora Project—an open-source project sponsored by Red Hat where the developer community can participate and continue to evolve what used to be the Red Hat Linux product (Red Hat Linux 9 was the last version of that product line). The new Linux distribution from the Fedora Project goes by the name *Fedora Core* (or, simply, Fedora) and the project is expected to have Fedora Core releases every four to six months. Red Hat will continue to participate in the Fedora Project and help prepare the Fedora Core releases, but everything will be done with the involvement of the open source community under a public release schedule. As you might expect, Fedora Core is available freely, just as Red Hat Linux used to be, and you can expect books such as this one to include Fedora Core on DVD or CDs.

Red Hat anticipates that new technologies and enhancements that first appear in Fedora Core will eventually find their way into Red Hat Enterprise Linux—the commercial Linux offering from Red Hat. In this way, the Fedora Project should serve as an incubator and testing ground for future Linux development. This means that by learning what's in Fedora Core, you can keep up with (or, more accurately, stay ahead of) the latest developments in Red Hat Enterprise Linux.

To learn more about the Fedora Project and the latest Fedora Core releases, visit the Fedora Project's home page at `http://fedora.redhat.com`.

Fedora Core is a specific Linux distribution. A *Linux distribution* is essentially a package consisting of the Linux operating system and a collection of applications, together with an easy-to-use installation program. All Linux distributions include the core Linux operating system (the kernel); the X Window System (graphical user interface); one or more graphical desktops, such as GNOME and KDE; and a large selection of applications. Everything comes in ready-to-run binary format, but the source code and documentation are also available. By now, each Linux distribution includes so much software that it comes on multiple CD-ROMs or a DVD-ROM. For example, this book comes with a DVD-ROM containing the full Fedora Core Linux distribution, including the source code.

Some Linux distributions such as Red Hat Enterprise Linux and SUSE Linux are commercial Linux distributions. The GNU (which stands for "GNU's Not UNIX") General Public License that applies to Linux allows for such commercial, for-profit distribution, but requires that the software be distributed in source-code form, and stipulates that anyone can copy and distribute the software in source-code form to anyone else.

Both the Linux kernel and Fedora Core Linux have gone through a number of versions. The version numbers are unrelated, but each has particular significance.

Linux Kernel Version Numbers

After Linux version 1.0 was released on March 14, 1994, the loosely organized Linux development community adopted a version-number scheme. Versions 1.x.y and 2.x.y, where x is an even number, are stable versions. The y number is the *patch level*, which is incremented as problems are fixed. Notice that these version numbers are of the form *Major.Minor.Patch*, where *Major* and *Minor* are integers denoting the major and minor version numbers, and *Patch* is another integer representing the patch level.

Versions 2.x.y with an odd x number are beta releases for developers only; they may be unstable, so you should not adopt these versions for day-to-day use. Developers add new features to these odd-numbered versions of Linux.

At the time of this writing, the latest stable version of the Linux kernel is 2.6.11 (note that information about the latest version of the Linux kernel is available at `www.kernel.org/`). This book's companion DVD-ROM contains the latest version of the Linux kernel as of Spring 2005.

cross ref

If you hear about a later version of Linux or about helpful patches (minor corrections) to the current version, you can obtain the patches and rebuild the kernel by following the instructions in Chapter 21. That chapter also describes how you can download the new kernel from the Fedora Project.

Fedora Core Version Numbers

The Fedora Project assigns the Fedora Core version numbers, such as 3 or 4. Most Linux distributions use version numbers of the form *X.Y*, where *X* is the major version and *Y* the minor version. Nowadays, if the minor version number is zero, it's simply dropped — as in Fedora Core 3 and Fedora Core 4. Unlike with the Linux-kernel version numbers, no special meaning is associated with odd and even minor versions. Each version of a Linux distribution includes specific versions of the Linux kernel and other major components, such as GNOME, KDE, and various applications such as the OpenOffice.org suite.

The Fedora Project releases new versions of Fedora Core on a regular basis — every six months or so. For example, Fedora Core 1 came out in November 2003, Fedora Core 2 in May 2004, Fedora Core 3 in November 2004, and Fedora Core 4 in June 2005. Typically, each new major version of Fedora Core provides significant new features. In each revision, in addition to providing the latest versions of various applications such as OpenOffice.org, Firefox Web browser, Evolution e-mail client, and the GIMP photo manipulation program, the Fedora Project also updates the core components from the kernel to the GNU C Compiler and associated libraries. Often these behind-the-scenes changes to the core operating system provide significant benefits such as support for newer interfaces and a more secure system.

Red Hat's Commercial Linux Products

Red Hat continues to sell its commercial Linux distribution — called Red Hat Enterprise Linux. Red Hat offers four different products, grouped into two categories:

- **Server solutions** include the Red Hat Enterprise Linux AS and the Red Hat Enterprise Linux ES. Red Hat Enterprise Linux AS is meant for corporate database and application servers whereas Red Hat Enterprise Linux ES is for small to mid-range servers such as ones running domain name system (DNS), Web, and FTP. Both server products include all desktop applications. Red Hat Enterprise Linux ES can run on systems with up to two processors and 16GB of memory whereas Red Hat Enterprise Linux AS does not have any limit on the number of processors and amount of memory (except, of course, the limits imposed by the hardware architecture and the Linux kernel — the Linux 2.6 kernel can support 64 processors and access 64GB of memory).
- **Client solutions** include Red Hat Enterprise Linux WS and Red Hat Desktop. Red Hat Enterprise Linux WS is for technical workstations that serve as desktops for power users such as software developers, graphics artists, or someone running other engineering design software. The Red Hat Desktop is available in only 10-unit or 50-unit packs that are meant to be deployed as desktops for individual users throughout an organization. The Red Hat Enterprise Linux WS and Red Hat Desktop are similar products except that the Red Hat Desktop runs on only single-processor systems with up to 4GB of memory whereas Red Hat Enterprise Linux WS supports systems with up to two processors and unlimited memory.

Red Hat sells the Red Hat Enterprise Linux products by annual subscription and plans to support them for seven years.

Under the Hood in Linux Kernel 2.6

Linux kernel 2.6 includes many new features and improvements when compared with its predecessor—the 2.4 kernel. This section highlights some of these improvements. As a user, you may not notice many of these improvements because they work behind the scenes. All you see is a Linux system that simply works great!

Support for a Wider Range of Computer Hardware

For starters, the 2.6 kernel has been redesigned to support computers spanning a wider range of hardware than before—from bare-bones embedded microcontrollers to larger-scale servers with multiple processors.

To support distinct hardware architectures of the same processor family (such as x86), Linux 2.6 uses the concept of a *subarchitecture,* which refers to the processor and the associated bus and other hardware that defines a unique type of computer. For example, most of today's PCs are based on what is called the PC/AT subarchitecture because these PCs are based on the original IBM PC/AT. The 2.6 kernel supports PC/AT machines as well as other x86 subarchitectures, such as the NEC Voyager and the PC-9800 machines. The bottom line is that the 2.6 kernel can run on many variations of the x86-based machines.

Linux 2.6 also supports advanced features of processors such as hyperthreading, which enables a single processor to act as multiple virtual processors at the hardware level.

Better Scalability

The 2.6 kernel provides better scalability for Intel x86 hardware by supporting advanced features such as Intel's Physical Address Extension (PAE), which enables many newer 32-bit x86 systems to access up to 64GB of memory. Linux 2.6 also provides better handling of interrupts for multiprocessor systems through improved support for Intel's Input/Output (I/O) Advanced Programmable Interrupt Controller (APIC).

Internally, the 2.6 kernel raises many internal limits from number of users to the maximum number of open files. For example, the number of unique users and groups has been increased from 65,536 to over 4 billion. The maximum number of open files can now grow as needed. File systems can be as large as 16TB (that's about 16,000 gigabytes!).

Linux 2.6 also increases the limits on the major and minor device numbers, which used to be a maximum of 255 in earlier kernels. These device numbers translate to 255 device types and 255 devices of a single type. In kernel version 2.6, the major device numbers can be up to 4,095 and minor device number can be more than a million. The upshot is that Linux 2.6 can support many more device types and many devices of a single type.

Improved Device Handling

Linux 2.6 has a number of new features for handling devices—especially hot plug devices such as the ones that connect to USB and Firewire interfaces common in today's PCs. First, the kernel uses a new virtual file system called *sysfs* that is meant to hold information about the devices on the system. The sysfs file system mounts on `/sys` and it presents a hierarchical view of all the devices organized by device type, bus, and so on.

Through sysfs, the 2.6 kernel makes available to other applications a lot of information about devices, including the name of a device, resources such as interrupts and I/O ports used by the device, the power status of the device, and so on.

Dynamic Device Files with udev

By using the sysfs capabilities available in the Linux 2.6 kernel, a separate device-handling program called udev can now dynamically add device files when the system boots as well as when a device is added to a system. The udev program is invoked by the `/sbin/hotplug` shell script that runs when any hot plug device such as a USB device is plugged into the computer. udev gives each device a name that stays the same every time that device connects to the system. Fedora Core uses udev to manage the device files in the `/dev` directory. Every time you boot your PC, the udev program runs and creates all the device files in the `/dev` directory.

Other device-handling improvements in Linux 2.6 include features which ensure that device driver modules are not unloaded while still in use and that standardize the way in which device drivers make available information about devices they support. All device driver module filenames now use the `.ko` extension — for *kernel object* — instead of the generic `.o` extension commonly used for object files.

Linux 2.6 also has improved support for many devices such as USB 2.0 and wireless devices. As for storage devices, the Integrated Drive Electronics (IDE) — also called AT Attachment (ATA) — and Small Computer System Interface (SCSI) support was updated in Linux 2.6. For example, IDE CD-recorders are now accessed through the IDE driver instead of a special SCSI-emulation driver that was used in earlier versions of the kernel. The 2.6 kernel also supports the new Serial ATA (SATA) interface that can support data transfer rates of 150MB per second.

For desktop users, an exciting new feature of Linux 2.6 is the new sound system called the Advanced Linux Sound Architecture (ALSA). ALSA includes modular drivers for many sound cards and supports systems with multiple sound cards. ALSA also has new capabilities such as support for audio and MIDI (Musical Instrument Digital Interface) devices that connect to the PC through the USB port. In addition to improved audio support, the 2.6 kernel also includes an upgraded Video4Linux (V4L) subsystem that supports television tuners and video cameras. Linux 2.6 also adds built-in support for Digital Video Broadcasting (DVB) hardware, which, with appropriate software, can be used to make a Linux-based video recording device.

Mandatory access control with Security Enhanced Linux

Linux kernel 2.6 includes the mandatory access control framework provided by Security Enhanced Linux (SELinux), which was developed by the National Security Agency (NSA), a U.S. government agency. SELinux is implemented as a Linux Security Module (LSM) — an extension of the Linux kernel that allows security mechanisms to be easily added to the kernel. You can find more about SELinux at the NSA's website, `www.nsa.gov/selinux/`.

Without SELinux, access control in Linux is based on the user and group ID that owns a process or a file. In this discretionary access control approach, the superuser (`root`) has absolute discretion to access and do anything on the system. In contrast to this approach, SELinux views the system in terms of *subjects* (users or processes) and *objects* (files, devices, any system resources). Subjects can take on different *roles* such as normal user or system administrator. Each subject also has a *domain* and each object has a *type*. SELinux provides fine-grained control over who can access what in a Linux system by defining what domains can access what types and how one domain can transition into another when programs execute.

The mandatory access control rules are defined in the SELinux *security policy*. To support the fine-grained access control, all files need additional attributes called *contexts* that are stored in labels added to the files. Think of the contexts as information about which roles can access and do what with the file. When SELinux is enabled, all files in the file system have to be labeled with the security contexts. Only then can SELinux manage the fine-grained access control.

When you install Fedora Core, you can select the level of access control you want SELinux to enforce. This option appears in the GUI installation screen where you configure the firewall.

note

SELinux can be very helpful in securing your organization's external Web and e-mail servers that are exposed to the Internet and, therefore, subject to attacks. With a well-designed security policy, SELinux can make such Internet-facing servers resistant to damage from attacks, even if an attacker manages to gain superuser privileges. However, the additional effort involved in setting up and running SELinux may not be worthwhile for internal servers not directly connected to the Internet.

Linux as a UNIX Platform

Like other UNIX systems, Linux is a multiuser, multitasking operating system, which means that it enables multiple users to log in and to run more than one program at the same time.

UNIX was developed in the early 1970s at AT&T Bell Laboratories. Its development came on the heels of another operating system called MULTICS; developers are said to have come up with the name UNIX by changing the MULT in MULTICS to UN (meaning one). Bell Laboratories continued to develop UNIX and released several versions: System III, followed by System V Release 1, or SVR1, and SVR2, SVR3, and SVR4.

As it maintained and enhanced UNIX, Bell Laboratories distributed source code to educational institutions. The University of California at Berkeley (UC Berkeley) was one of the schools that received a copy of UNIX and added many new features to the operating system. Eventually, UC Berkeley released its version of UNIX, called Berkeley Software Distribution (BSD) UNIX. The most widely used versions of BSD UNIX are 4.3 and 4.4 (known as 4.4BSD).

By the time 4.4BSD UNIX came out, UC Berkeley realized that there was very little original Bell Laboratories UNIX code in the source code. Soon, several groups wrote new code to replace the small amount of leftover Bell Laboratories code and adapted BSD UNIX to the Intel 386 processor. This resulted in the FreeBSD and NetBSD versions of freely available BSD UNIX for Intel PCs.

Note that UNIX System V, Release 4 — SVR4 — combines all features of System V and BSD UNIX.

POSIX Compliance

Linux is designed to comply with IEEE Std 1003.1 1996 Edition (POSIX). This standard defines the functions that applications written in the C programming language use to access the services of the operating system — for tasks ranging from opening a file to allocating memory. On March 8, 1996, the Computer Systems Laboratory of the National Institute of Standards and Technology (NIST), a U.S. government agency, confirmed that Linux version 1.2.13, as packaged by Open Linux Ltd., conforms to the POSIX standard. To see a list of POSIX-validated products, point your Web browser to `www.nist.gov/itl/div897/ctg/posix/finalreg4.htm`. Note that the NIST POSIX testing program ended on December 31, 1997. Of course, POSIX compliance, while commendable, is not synonymous with a high-quality operating system.

Along with POSIX conformance, Linux includes many features of other UNIX standards, such as the System V Interface Document (SVID) and the Berkeley Software Distribution (BSD) version of UNIX. Linux takes an eclectic approach, picking the most-needed features of several standard flavors of UNIX.

POSIX stands for Portable Operating System Interface (abbreviated as POSIX to make it sound like UNIX). The Institute of Electrical and Electronics Engineers (IEEE) began developing the POSIX standards to promote the portability of applications across UNIX environments. POSIX is not limited to UNIX, however. Many other operating systems, such as Hewlett-Packard OpenVMS and Microsoft Windows NT/2000/XP, implement POSIX — in particular, the IEEE Std. 1003.1 1996 Edition, or POSIX.1, which provides a source-level C-language Application Program Interface (API) to the services of the operating system, such as reading and writing files. POSIX.1 has been accepted by the International Organization for Standardization (ISO) and is known as the ISO/IEC 9945-1:1996 standard.

Incidentally, the term POSIX is used interchangeably with the IEEE 1003 and 2003 family of standards. There are several other IEEE standards besides the 1003 and 2003 family — such as 1224 and 1228 — that also provide APIs for developing portable applications. For the latest information on all IEEE standards, visit the IEEE Standards Home Page at `http://standards.ieee.org/`. To view a list of POSIX standards, visit the IEEE Standards Web page at `http://standards.ieee.org/catalog/olis/posix.html`.

In addition to POSIX (IEEE 1003.1) compliance, Linux supports the IEEE 1003.2 standard, which focuses on the operating system's command interpreter (commonly referred to as the shell) and a standard set of utility programs. If you know UNIX or you've had some exposure to it, you know that UNIX takes a tools-oriented view of the operating system. It provides a tool for almost anything you might want to do, and the shell enables you to combine several tools to perform tasks more complicated than those the basic tools handle. The IEEE 1003.2 standard maintains this tools-oriented view, providing the following features:

- A shell with a specified set of built-in commands and a programming syntax that can be used to write shell programs, or scripts
- A standard set of utility programs — such as sed, tr, and awk — that shell scripts and applications can call. Even the vi editor and the electronic-mail program are part of the standard set. You learn more about these utilities in Chapters 8, 10, and 11.
- A set of C functions, such as `system` and `getenv`, that applications can use to access features of the shell
- A set of utilities, such as Perl and Tcl, for developing shell applications

The default Linux shell is called Bash, which stands for Bourne-Again Shell — a reference to the Bourne shell, which has been the standard UNIX shell since the early days of UNIX. Bash incorporates many of the features IEEE 1003.2 requires and then some. It essentially inherits the features and functionality of the Bourne shell. In case of any discrepancy between the Bourne shell and IEEE 1003.2, Bash follows IEEE 1003.2. For stricter IEEE 1003.2 compliance, Bash even includes a POSIX mode.

All in all, Linux serves as a good platform for learning UNIX because it offers a standard set of UNIX commands (the IEEE 1003.2 standard, as well as the best features of both System V and BSD UNIX).

Linux's support for POSIX and other common UNIX system calls (the functions that applications call) makes it an excellent system for software development. Another ingredient of modern workstation software, the X Window System, is also available in Linux in the form of X.Org X11.

Linux Standard Base

Linux has become important enough that there is now a standard for Linux called the Linux Standard Base, or LSB for short. LSB is a set of binary standards that should help reduce variations among the Linux distributions and promote portability of applications. The idea behind LSB is to provide application binary interface (ABI) so that software applications can run on any Linux (or other UNIX) systems that conform to the LSB standard. The LSB specification references the POSIX standards as well as many other standards such as the C and C++ programming language standards, the X Window System version 11 release 6 (X11R6), and the Filesystem Hierarchy Standard (FHS). LSB version 1.2 (commonly referred to as LSB 1.2) was released on June 28, 2002. LSB 1.3 came out in January 2003 and LSB 2.0 was released on August 30, 2004.

The LSB specification is organized into two parts—a common specification that remains the same across all types of processors and a set of hardware-specific specifications, one for each type of processor architecture. For example, LSB 1.2 has architecture-specific specifications for Intel 32-bit (IA32) and Power PC 32-bit (PPC32) processors. LSB 1.3 adds a specification for the Intel 64-bit (IA64) architecture, in addition to the ones for IA32 and PPC32. LSB 2.0 includes specification for the AMD 64-bit (AMD64) processors.

There is an LSB certification program, and by now a number of Linux systems, such as Red Hat Linux 9, Red Hat Enterprise Linux 3 for x86, SUSE Linux 9.1, and Sun Wah Linux Desktop 3.0 are certified to be LSB 1.3–compliant IA32 runtime environments. Several others such as MandrakeLinux Corporate Server 3.0, SUSE Linux 9.2, and RAYS LX 1.0 (from Sun Wah Linux Limited) are certified as LSB 2.0–compliant IA32 runtime environments. You can expect more distributions to be LSB 2.0 certified in the near future.

To learn more about LSB, visit `www.linuxbase.org/`. The latest list of LSB-certified systems is available at `www.opengroup.org/lsb/cert/cert_prodlist.tpl`.

Linux Desktop

Let's face it — typing cryptic UNIX commands on a terminal is boring. Those of us who know the commands by heart may not realize it, but the installed base of UNIX is not going to increase significantly if we don't make the system easy to use. This is where the X Window System, or X, comes to the rescue.

X provides a standard mechanism for displaying device-independent, bitmapped graphics. In other words, an X application can display its graphic output on many different machines that use different methods to display text, graphics, and images on the monitor. X is also a windowing system, meaning it enables applications to organize their output in separate windows. X uses a client/server architecture and works over the network, so you can run X applications on various systems on the network while the output appears in windows that are managed by an X server running on your system.

Although X provides the mechanism for windowed output, it does not offer any specific look or feel for applications. The look and feel comes from GUIs, such as GNOME and KDE, which are based on the X Window System.

cross ref

The Fedora Core Linux distribution on this book's DVD-ROM comes with the X Window System in the form of X.Org X11 — an implementation of X11R6 (X Window System version 11, release 6, which is the latest release of X) for 80x86 systems. A key feature of X.Org X11 is its support for a wide variety of video cards available for today's PCs. As you learn in Chapter 3, X.Org X11 supports hundreds of PC video cards, ranging from the run-of-the-mill Super Video Graphics Array (SVGA) to accelerated graphics cards such as the ones based on the 3Dfx, ATI, Intel, Matrox, NVIDIA, and S3 video chipsets. However, X.Org X11 may not work well on some generic video cards containing variants of popular chipsets such as S3.

insider insight

Until 2004, XFree86 from the XFree86 Project (`www.xfree86.org`) was the most commonly used X Window System implementation for x86 systems. However, around version 4.4, some changes to the XFree86 licensing terms caused concerns for many Linux and UNIX vendors — they felt that the licensing terms were no longer compatible with the GNU General Public License (GPL). In January 2004, several vendors formed the X.Org Foundation (`www.x.org`) to promote continued development of an open source X Window System and graphical desktop. The first release of X.Org X11 uses the same code as that used by XFree86 4.4, up until the time when the XFree86 license changes precipitated the creation of X.Org Foundation. By now most Linux distributions have switched over to X.Org X11 as the choice for X Window System.

As for the GUI, Linux includes two powerful graphical desktop environments: KDE (K Desktop Environment) and GNOME (GNU Network Object Model Environment). When you install Linux, you can choose which desktop you want or you can install both and switch between the two. GNOME and KDE provide desktops similar to the ones in Microsoft Windows and the Apple Mac OS. GNOME also comes with the Nautilus graphical shell that makes it easy to find files, run applications, and configure your Linux system. With GNOME or KDE, you can begin using your Linux workstation without having to learn UNIX commands. However, if you should ever need to use UNIX commands, all you have to do is open a terminal window and type the commands at the shell prompt.

Linux also comes with many graphical applications that run under X. The most noteworthy programs relate to image display and editing. The first is the GIMP — the GNU Image Manipulation Program — a program with capabilities on par with Adobe Photoshop; the second program is ImageMagick.

Another important aspect of the X Window System is that you can run applications across the network because X uses a client/server architecture. The X server runs at the workstation and controls the display, keyboard, and mouse. Client applications send requests to the X server to receive user input and display output. For example, you might run an X application on a server somewhere on the network but view that application's output and interact with it from your Linux desktop that's running an X-based GUI. In other words, with X, your Linux PC becomes a gateway to all the other systems on the network.

Motif is the dominant GUI in the UNIX marketplace, but it's not packaged with Linux because the Open Software Foundation does not distribute Motif for free. Motif has a look and feel similar to Microsoft Windows and includes the Motif Window Manager (MWM) and the Motif toolkit for programmers. You can download OpenMotif for Linux from `www.motifzone.net/`. In addition to OpenMotif from The Open Group, another option for Motif for Linux is LessTif, a free version of Motif distributed under the GNU General Public License (visit the LessTif home page at `www.lesstif.org` for the latest information on LessTif). Fedora Core comes with OpenMotif and is automatically installed if you select the X Software Development package group during installation.

If you need Motif for a project, using a Linux PC with a copy of OpenMotif installed is an economical way to set up a software-development platform. If you have a consulting business, or if you want to develop X and Motif software at home, Linux is definitely the way to go.

Along with GNOME and KDE, you get two more options for developing GUI applications in Linux. GNOME comes with a toolkit called Gtk+ (GIMP toolkit), and KDE comes with the Qt toolkit. If you do not want to learn Motif, you may want to use Gtk+ or Qt for your GUI applications.

cross ref

Chapter 3 shows you how to set up X Window System. Chapter 8 presents the GNOME and KDE desktops.

Office productivity software — such as word-processing, spreadsheet, and database applications — is an area in which Linux used to be lacking. This situation has changed, though. Linux comes with the OpenOffice.org office-productivity applications. In addition, there are several prominent commercially available office-productivity applications for Linux that are not included on the companion DVD-ROM. Applixware Office is a good example of productivity software for Linux (`www.vistasource.com/`). Another well-known productivity-software package is StarOffice from Sun Microsystems (`www.sun.com/staroffice/`). CrossOver Office, from CodeWeavers (`www.codeweavers.com/site/products`), is a commercially available software package that enables you to install your Microsoft Office applications (Office 97, Office 2000, and Office 2003) in Linux. Furthermore, many existing software packages (designed for UNIX workstations with the X Window System) can be readily ported to Linux, thanks to Linux's support for portable standards such as POSIX and the X Window System.

Linux Networking

Networking refers to all aspects of data exchange within one computer or between two or more computers, ranging from the physical connection to the protocol for the actual data exchange. A network protocol is the method the sender and receiver agree upon for exchanging data across a network.

Different network protocols are used at different levels of the network. At the physical level — at which the data bits travel through a medium, such as a cable — Ethernet and Asynchronous Transfer Mode (ATM) are two commonly used protocols. Application programs don't really work at the physical level, however. Instead, they rely on protocols that operate on blocks of data. These protocols include Novell's Internet Packet Exchange (IPX) and the well-known Transmission Control Protocol/Internet Protocol (TCP/IP).

cross ref

The different levels of network protocols can be represented by a networking model such as the seven-layer Open Systems Interconnection (OSI) reference model, developed by ISO. Chapter 6 includes a discussion of this model.

Standard network protocols such as TCP/IP have been key to the growth of interconnected computers, resulting in local area networks (LANs), as well as wide area networks (WANs). Protocols have enabled these smaller networks to communicate with each other, and we now have interconnected networks that form an internetwork: the Internet.

TCP/IP

The ability to network has been one of the strengths of UNIX since its early days. In particular, the well-known TCP/IP protocol suite has been an integral part of UNIX ever since TCP/IP appeared in BSD UNIX around 1982. By now, TCP/IP is the wide area and local area networking protocol of choice in the global Internet. TCP/IP does not depend on the physical communication media. This media independence enables TCP/IP to work in a wide variety of networks.

Linux supports the TCP/IP protocol suite and includes all common network applications such as Telnet, FTP, and sendmail. At the physical-network level, Linux includes drivers for many Ethernet cards. Token ring is also an integral part of the Linux kernel source; all you have to do is load the token ring driver to enable support for token ring.

cross ref

You might say that Linux's support for TCP/IP — the dominant protocol suite of the Internet — comes naturally. The rapid development of Linux itself would not have been possible without the collaboration of so many developers from Europe, America, and other parts of the world. That collaboration, in turn, has been possible only because of the Internet. Chapters 13 through 19 show you how to set up TCP/IP networking and how to use various servers to offer services such as Web, email, and domain name service.

Linux also includes the Berkeley Sockets programming interface (so named because the Sockets interface was introduced in Berkeley UNIX around 1982), a popular interface for network programming in TCP/IP networks. For those of you with C programming experience, the Sockets interface consists of several C header files and several C functions that you call to set up connections and to send and receive data. Chapter 6 describes Sockets.

You can use the Berkeley Sockets programming interface to develop Internet tools such as Web browsers. Because most TCP/IP programs (including those available for free at various Internet sites) use the Sockets programming interface, it is easy to get these programs up and running on Linux because the operating system includes the Sockets interface.

PPP Dialup Network

Not everyone has an Ethernet connection to the Internet (although a growing number of us are beginning to have high-speed always-on connections to the Internet, thanks to cable modems or DSL). Most of us still connect to the Internet and communicate by using the TCP/IP protocol over a phone line and a modem. To do this, you need access to a server — a system that has an Internet connection and that accepts a dial-in connection from your system.

Commercial outfits known as Internet service providers (ISPs) offer this type of service for a fee. If you don't want to pay for such a connection, find out whether a computer at your place of business provides this access. That option may not be unreasonable, especially if you are doing UNIX software development (for your company) on your Linux PC at home.

When you access the Internet through a server, the server runs the Point-to-Point Protocol (PPP), which works over any serial link, including dial-up connections.

cross ref

Linux supports PPP for dial-up Internet connections. You can also turn your Linux system into a PPP server so that other computers can dial in to your computer and establish a TCP/IP connection over the phone. Chapter 13 explains how to set up a PPP dial-up Internet connection on your Linux system.

Cable/DSL and Wireless Networks

If you have high-speed Internet access through cable modem or DSL (Digital Subscriber Line), you can easily hook up an Ethernet-equipped Linux PC to the Internet. For the most part, the configuration of the Linux PC is the same as that for TCP/IP networking. However, for ISPs that use PPP over Ethernet (PPPoE), you may have to do some additional configuring. Linux includes support for PPPoE.

Linux also supports wireless Ethernet cards that you can use to connect laptop PCs to an existing wired Ethernet local area network (LAN). These wireless Ethernet cards conform to the IEEE 802.11 family of standards, also known as Wi-Fi. If your LAN connects to the Internet through a cable/DSL router and hub, you can extend the LAN by connecting a wireless access point to the hub. Then, any Wi-Fi–equipped laptop or desktop PC can connect to the Internet through the cable or DSL connection.

cross ref

Chapter 13 describes how to configure Linux for a wireless Ethernet network.

File Sharing with NFS

In the Microsoft Windows or Novell NetWare world, you may be familiar with the concept of a file server — a system that maintains important files and allows all other systems on the network to access those files. Storing files on a central server provides for better security and enables convenient backups. Essentially, all PCs on the network share one or more central disks. In Windows and Novell, users see the file server's disk as just another drive, with its own drive letter (such as U). Typically in PC networks, you implement file sharing with Novell NetWare or Microsoft LAN Manager protocols.

File sharing exists in UNIX as well. The Network File System (NFS) provides a standard way for a system to access another system's files over the network. To the user, the remote system's files appear to be in a directory on the local system.

cross ref

NFS is available in Linux; you can share your Linux system's directories with other systems that support NFS. The other systems that access your Linux system's files via NFS do not necessarily have to run UNIX; NFS is available for DOS, Windows, OS/2, and NetWare as well. Therefore, you can use a Linux PC as the file server for a small workgroup of PCs that run DOS and/or Windows. Chapter 19 further explores the use of a Linux PC as a file server. Chapter 19 also explains how to use the Samba package to set up your Linux PC as a server in a Windows network.

Linux System Administration

The term "system administration" refers to tasks that someone must perform to keep a computer system up and running properly. Now that almost all computers are networked, it's necessary to perform another set of tasks to keep the network up and running. All these tasks are collectively called network administration. A site with many computers probably has a full-time system administrator who takes care of all system-administration and network-administration tasks. Really large sites may have separate system-administration and network-administration personnel. If you are running Linux on a home PC or on a few systems in a small company, you are probably both the system administrator and the network administrator.

cross ref

Linux supplies all the basic commands and utilities you need for system and network administration. Chapters 12 and 20 briefly cover some of these commands. Chapter 6 describes some network-administration tools.

GNOME's Nautilus graphical shell comes with many GUI tools that enable you to perform most system-administration and network-administration tasks without having to edit configuration files manually or type cryptic commands. However, you should always learn the key commands and be proficient with a plaintext editor such as vi, for those times when you must use a text-only login and the GUI tools are not available. Additionally, you need to understand the layout of the key configuration files. I cover this type of information throughout this book, even when describing GNOME and KDE, because they too depend on configuration files for correct operation.

System-Administration Tasks

As a system administrator, your tasks typically are the following:

- **Installing, configuring, and upgrading the operating system and various utilities:** You learn how to install Linux and other software packages in Chapter 2. Chapter 3 tells you how to install and configure the X Window System, and Chapter 21 shows you how to upgrade the operating system — the Linux kernel.
- **Adding and removing users:** As shown in Chapter 18, you can use the User Manager graphical tool or the `useradd` command to add a new user after you install Linux. If a user forgets a password, you can change the password from the User Manager or you can use the `passwd` command to change it.
- **Installing new software:** For the typical Linux software, which you get in source-code form, this task involves using tools such as gunzip (to uncompress the software), tar (to unpack the archive), and make (to build the executable programs). For Linux software in Red Hat Package Manager (RPM) files, use the `rpm` command to install the software. Chapter 21 describes RPM.
- **Making backups:** You can use the tar program to archive one or more directories and to copy the archive to a floppy disk (if the archive is small enough) or to a tape (if you have a tape drive). If you have a CD/DVD burner, you can also back up files by burning the files onto a recordable CD or DVD. Chapter 20 covers backing up and restoring files and directories.
- **Managing file systems:** When you want to read an MS-DOS floppy disk, for example, mount that disk's MS-DOS file system on one of the directories of the Linux file system. Use the `mount` command to do this. You can also mount an NT file system (NTFS) after installing a kernel module that supports NTFS. You also want to monitor the file system to ensure that users or some errant process have not filled them up.
- **Monitoring the system's performance:** You have to use a few utilities, such as top (to see where the processor is spending most of its time) and free (to see the amount of free and used memory in the system).
- **Monitoring the system's integrity:** You want to make sure that no one has tampered with key system files. You can use tools such as Tripwire to perform this task. Chapter 22 covers how to maintain system security.
- **Starting and shutting down the system:** Although starting the system typically involves nothing more than powering up the PC, you do have to take some care when you want to shut down your Linux system. Use the `shutdown` command to stop all programs before turning off your PC's power switch. If your system is set up for a graphical login screen, you can perform the shutdown operation by selecting a menu item from the login screen.

Network-Administration Tasks

Typical network-administration tasks are the following:

- **Maintaining the network configuration files:** In Linux (as well as in other UNIX systems), several text files hold the configuration information for the TCP/IP network. You may have to edit these files to make networking work. You may have to edit one or more of the following files: `/etc/hosts`, `/etc/networks`, `/etc/host.conf`, `/etc/resolv.conf`, `/etc/hosts.allow`, `/etc/hosts.deny`, and the scripts in the `/etc/sysconfig/network-scripts` directory. You can either edit these files manually or use the graphical Network Configuration tool to configure them.

- **Setting up PPP:** You may use tools such as `wvdial` to set up and use PPP connections. You can also use the Internet Configuration Wizard to set up PPP connections. Chapter 13 shows you how to work with PPP commands and configuration files.
- **Monitoring network status:** You have to use tools such as `netstat` (to view information about active network connections), `/sbin/ifconfig` (to check the status of various network interfaces), and `ping` (to make sure that a connection is working).
- **Securing Internet services:** If your system is connected to the Internet (or if it is on an internal network), you have to secure the system against anyone who might use one of many Internet services to gain access to your system. Each service — such as email, Web, or FTP — requires running a server program that responds to client requests arriving over the TCP/IP network. Some of these server programs have weaknesses that may enable an outsider to log in to your system — maybe with root privileges. Turn off services you do not need, and edit configuration files to restrict access to those services you are running. Chapter 22 covers network security and how to use commands such as `chkconfig` to turn Internet services on or off.

Windows and Linux

As you probably know, MS-DOS used to be and Microsoft Windows (in its various versions from Windows 95/98 to Windows XP) continues to be the most popular operating system for 80386, 80486, and Pentium PCs. Because Linux started on 80386/80486 PCs, a connection between DOS/Windows and Linux has always existed. Typically, you start the Linux installation with some steps in DOS.

Linux has maintained its connection to DOS/Windows in several ways:

- Linux supports the older MS-DOS file system called FAT (file allocation table), as well as the newer Windows VFAT (long filenames) and FAT32 file systems. From Linux, you can access MS-DOS and Windows files on a hard disk or a floppy disk.
- Linux supports read-only access to the NTFS file system that is used in Windows NT/2000/XP. You can build (or download) and load a driver module to incorporate the NTFS support.
- Linux features a set of tools (called mtools) that manipulates DOS/Windows files from within Linux.

An ongoing project called WINE is developing a free implementation of Windows for the X Window System under UNIX (see `www.winehq.com/`). WINE enables you to run Windows 3.1/95/98/NT/2000/XP programs. WINE works on some versions of UNIX for the Intel x86 systems, including Linux and FreeBSD.

cross ref

Chapter 12 describes how you can access DOS from Linux and explains the use of the mtools utilities.

Software Development in Linux

Of all its potential uses, Linux is particularly well suited to software development. Software-development tools, such as the compiler and libraries, are included because you need them when you rebuild the Linux kernel. If you are a UNIX software developer, you already know UNIX, so you will feel right at home in Linux.

As far as the development environment goes, you have the same basic tools (such as an editor, a compiler, and a debugger) that you might use on other UNIX workstations, such as those from IBM, Sun Microsystems, and Hewlett-Packard (HP). Therefore, if you work by day on one of the mainstream UNIX workstations, you can use a Linux PC at home to duplicate that development environment at a fraction of the cost. Then, you can either complete work projects at home or devote your time to software you write for fun and share on the Internet.

Just to give you a sense of Linux's software-development support, the following is a list of various features that make Linux a productive software-development environment:

- GNU's C compiler, gcc, which can compile ANSI-standard C programs
- GNU's C++ compiler (g++), which supports ANSI-standard C++ features
- The GNU compiler for the Java programming language, `gcj`, as well as everything you need to develop Java applications — applets, client-side applications, and server-side applications (servlets)
- The Eclipse graphical interactive development environment (IDE) for building Java applications
- The GNU debugger, gdb, which enables you to step through your program to find problems and to determine where and how a program has failed. (The failed program's memory image is saved in a file named core; gdb can examine this file.)
- The GNU profiling utility, gprof, which enables you to determine the degree to which a piece of software uses your computer's processor time
- The GNU make utility, which enables you to compile and link large programs
- Concurrent Versions System (CVS) and Revision Control System (RCS), which maintain version information and control access to the source files so that two programmers don't modify the same source file inadvertently
- The GNU Emacs editor, which prepares source files and even launches a compile-link process to build the program
- The Perl scripting language, which you can use to write scripts that tie together many smaller programs with UNIX commands to accomplish a specific task
- The Tool Command Language and its X toolkit (Tcl/Tk), which enable you to prototype X applications rapidly
- The Python language, an interpreted language comparable to Perl and Tcl (the Fedora Core Linux installation program, called anaconda, is written in Python and provided by Red Hat)
- Dynamically linked shared libraries, which allow the actual program files to be much smaller because all the library code that several programs may use is shared, with only one copy being loaded in the system's memory
- POSIX header files and libraries, which enable you to write portable programs

cross ref
Chapter 23 covers software development in Linux. Read Chapters 24 and 25 to learn about Perl and Tcl/Tk programming. Chapter 26 covers Java programming in Linux.

Linux as an Internet On-Ramp

Most likely, you have experienced much of what the Internet has to offer: electronic mail, newsgroups, and the Web. So you may be happy to learn that a Linux system includes everything you need to access the Internet. In fact, your PC can become a first-class citizen of the Internet, with its own Web server on which you can publish any information you want.

Although Linux includes TCP/IP and supporting network software with which you can set up your PC as an Internet host, there is one catch: First, you have to obtain a physical connection to the Internet. Your Linux PC has to be connected to another node (which can be another computer or a networking device, such as a router) on the Internet. This requirement is the stumbling block for many people — an Internet connection costs money, the price proportional to the data-transfer rate.

Many commercial ISPs provide various forms of physical connections to the Internet. In the United States, if you are willing to spend between $15 and $30 a month, you can get an account on a PPP server. Then you can run PPP software on your Linux system, dial in via a modem, and connect to the Internet at data-transfer rates ranging from 28,800 bits per second (bps) to 56,000 bps, depending on your modem.

Although a dial-up connection may be adequate for accessing the Internet, receiving email, and reading news, it may not be adequate if you want to download multimedia files or set up your system to provide information to other people through the Web or FTP (File Transfer Protocol). Besides, your ISP may not allow you to use the dial-up connection to run a Web server. To set up a useful Web server, you need a connection that is available 24 hours a day, because other systems may try to access your system any time of day. For a few hundred dollars a month, you can get a dedicated connection and make your system a permanent presence on the Internet. Other options that offer higher-capacity Internet connections than dial-up modems are cable modems and Digital Subscriber Lines (DSL). You may also opt to run the server at the ISP's facility — something many people do because it's very convenient.

Another requirement for a business — or for anyone who has a few networked PCs — is connecting a local area network (LAN) to the Internet. You can run Linux on one of the PCs and use it as the Internet gateway to accomplish this task. Typically, you have an Ethernet LAN running TCP/IP connected to all of the PCs on the network, including the Linux machine. The Linux PC sets up a PPP connection to the Internet (via a dial-up or dedicated connection). You then set up the Linux PC to act as a gateway between the Ethernet LAN and the Internet so that the PCs on your LAN can access other systems on the Internet.

cross ref
In Chapter 13, you learn to configure your Linux system to access the Internet.

Summary

After you get Linux going on your PC, you can turn your attention to the work you plan to do with it. Whether you want to develop software or set up your PC as an Internet host, you can use Linux wisely if you know its overall capabilities. Accordingly, this chapter provided an overview of various aspects of Linux, ranging from software development to networking and system administration. In the next chapter, I show you how to install Linux from this book's companion DVD-ROM and get started on using Linux.

By reading this chapter, you learned the following:

- Linux is a freely available UNIX-like operating system that runs on a wide variety of systems. Fedora Core is a specific Linux distribution — a package incorporating the Linux operating system and a huge collection of applications, together with an easy-to-use installation program.
- Linux developers use a version-number scheme to help you understand what the various versions of Linux kernel — the core operating system — mean. Kernel versions 2.x.y, where x is an even number, are stable versions. The number represented by y is the patch level, which is incremented as problems are fixed. Versions 2.x.y, where x is an odd number, are beta releases for developers only, because these releases may be unstable.
- POSIX stands for Portable Operating System Interface (abbreviated as POSIX to make it sound like UNIX). The Institute of Electrical and Electronics Engineers (IEEE) began developing the POSIX standards to promote the portability of applications across UNIX environments.
- Many Linux distributions conform to a binary standard called Linux Standard Base (LSB), which promotes compatibility among Linux systems so that applications built for one system can run on all LSB-compliant systems with the same processor architecture.
- This book's Fedora Core Linux distribution comes with X.Org X11 (X Window System Version 11 Release 6 or X11R6), GNOME, and KDE software. After you install X.Org X11 and GNOME or KDE, you have a graphical user interface (GUI) for Linux. In addition, X enables you to run applications across the network — which means that you can run applications on another system on the network and can have the output appear on your Linux PC's display.
- Linux effectively supports TCP/IP networking. TCP/IP is the networking protocol of choice on the Internet. Therefore, a Linux PC is ideal as an Internet host, providing services such as FTP and World Wide Web access. You can also use the Linux PC as your Internet ramp by connecting to an Internet service provider through a dial-up, cable, or DSL connection and running a Web browser to surf the Net. You can configure Linux to support wireless Ethernet network cards.
- The Linux distribution on the companion DVD-ROM also includes Nautilus with many graphical tools that enable you to perform most system-administration and network-administration tasks from a GUI.
- Linux provides all the software development tools you need to write UNIX and X applications. You'll find the GNU C and C++ compiler for compiling source files, make for automating the compiling, the gdb debugger for finding bugs, and Concurrent Versions System (CVS) and Revision Control System (RCS) for managing various revisions of a file. Thus, a Linux PC is the software developer's ideal workstation.

Linux Installation

Chapter 2

Secrets in This Chapter

Linux installation can be either straightforward or complicated, depending on the specific type of hardware in your PC. If your PC is relatively new and the installer detects all the peripherals such as the video card and network interface card correctly, then you can sail through the installation. On the other hand, if your PC has components that Linux does not support, you'd have to perform additional steps to install Linux. Typically, you are more likely to find Linux drivers for common name-brand hardware, but these drivers may not work properly for generic hardware. In all cases, if you decide to keep your existing Microsoft Windows installation and install Linux as a second operating system, you have to go through the trouble of creating the disk partitions for Linux.

You need some specific information about your PC's hardware, such as the type of disk controller, video card, and network card to figure out whether you can install Linux easily or not. The Linux operating system controls the hardware through drivers (software through which the operating system accesses the hardware), so you need to make sure that the current release of Linux includes drivers for your hardware. If your hardware is popular enough, there's a good chance that someone has developed a driver for it. The version of Linux on the companion DVD-ROM supports a wide variety of hardware, so all of your PC's peripherals are probably supported.

In this chapter, you learn how to install Linux from the companion DVD-ROM. The chapter starts with an overview of the entire installation process; then it guides you through the installation process, highlighting the critical parts and providing technical information necessary to complete these installation steps.

cross ref

If you have installed Linux already, Chapter 7 shows you how to get started with Linux.

Understanding the Linux Installation Process

Before starting a big job, I always find it helpful to visualize the entire sequence of tasks I must perform. The process is similar to studying a map before you drive to a place you have never been. Linux installation can be a big job, especially if you run into snags. This section shows you the road map for the installation process. After reading this section, you should be mentally prepared to install Linux.

Here are the general steps for installing Linux:

1. Gather information about your PC's hardware before you install Linux. The Linux operating system accesses and uses various PC peripherals through software components called *drivers*. You have to make sure that the version of Linux you are about to install has the necessary drivers for your system's hardware configuration. Conversely, if you do not have a system yet, look at the list of hardware that Linux supports, and make sure you buy a PC with components that Linux supports.
2. Because most PCs come with Microsoft Windows preinstalled on the hard disk, you have to perform a step known as *partitioning* to allocate parts of your hard disk for Linux's use. If you have a spare hard disk, you should keep Windows on the first hard disk and install Linux on the second hard disk. With a spare second disk, you don't need to worry about partitioning under DOS or Windows. If you have only one hard disk, however, you have to partition that disk into several

parts. Use a part for Windows, and leave the rest for Linux. Use a commercial hard-drive partitioning tool such as PartitionMagic from PowerQuest. If you already have Linux installed or you can boot your PC using Linux (such as a Live CD version on a CD or DVD), then you can also download and use Ntfsresize to resize an NTFS partition. (For more information on Ntfsresize, visit `http://linux-ntfs.sourceforge.net/info/ntfsresize.html`.) You can, of course, install Linux as the sole operating system on a PC; in that case, you can ignore this step and simply let the Linux installation program automatically create the necessary partitions.

3. Boot your PC from the DVD-ROM. Even if your PC normally does not boot from the CD/DVD drive, you can usually press a function key as the PC boots and enter the BIOS setup screen from which you can select the CD/DVD drive as the boot device. You may want to consult your PC's manual to see how you can change the BIOS settings so that the CD/DVD drive is the first boot device on your PC.
4. After the PC boots from the DVD-ROM, you get a `boot:` prompt. If you press Enter, the boot loader loads the Linux kernel and runs anaconda, the Fedora Core Linux installation program. From this point on, you respond to a number of dialog boxes as the anaconda installer takes you through the steps. You have the option of using a text mode or a graphical user interface (GUI). You have to use the text mode if, for some reason, the installer fails to start the X Window System. In addition, you have to type the `linux noprobe` command if the Linux kernel does not detect some of the older hardware, such as the SCSI controller and network adapter installed in your system. When you type the `linux noprobe` command, you have to either provide a driver disk or load the drivers for your SCSI controller and network adapter by selecting them from a list of drivers.
5. Respond to the dialog box that asks you to choose a language to be used during installation. Then select the keyboard layout for your language.
6. Choose whether you want to install a new system or to upgrade an existing installation. For a new installation, you also have to decide whether you want to set up a Personal Desktop, Workstation, Server, or a Custom system. Select a Custom installation for maximum flexibility.
7. Prepare the hard disk partitions on which you plan to install Linux. If you have created space for Linux by reducing the size of an existing Windows partition, you can specify that the installer keep all existing partitions and use existing free space on the hard disk. You can also manually create the Linux partitions using Disk Druid, a graphical partitioning utility. Typically, you need at least two partitions: one for the Linux files and the other for use as the swap partition, which is a form of virtual memory. If you manually create the hard disk partitions, indicate which partition is the swap, and specify the partition on which you want to install Linux (this is called the root partition).
8. Specify options for installing a boot loader — the GNU GRand Unified Bootloader (GRUB) — on your hard disk, so you can boot Linux when you power up your PC after shutting it down. For the GRUB boot loader, you can also enable a password that has to be typed every time the system boots. If you are planning to keep both Windows and Linux on the PC's hard disk, GRUB can boot either one — you get to select the operating system from a GRUB menu after the PC boots.
9. If the initial Linux kernel detects a network card (assuming that you have one installed on your system), the installation program lets you configure the network (the local area network, not the dial-up network). If the Linux kernel does

not detect your network card, you can type the `linux noprobe` command and select your network card from a list. To configure the network, you can either choose to use DHCP — Dynamic Host Configuration Protocol — to get the IP address (a DHCP server provides IP addresses to systems in a network) or specify a number of parameters explicitly, including an IP address, a host name, the IP address of name servers, and a domain name for your Linux system.

10. Configure the firewall and security enhanced Linux (SELinux). You can set the firewall security level for your system by selecting one of three predefined levels of security — high, medium, or none. You can activate or disable SELinux, or set it to warning mode where SELinux prints warning messages, but does not enforce access control policies.
11. Specify the local time zone.
12. Enter a root password. The root user is the superuser — a user who can do anything — in Linux.
13. Select various software package groups to install. Each package represents a part of Linux, from the base operating system to packages such as the GNOME and KDE graphical desktops, the Emacs editor, programming tools, and the X Window System (a graphical windowing system that GNOME and KDE require). Select the package groups you need, and let the installation program do its job.
14. The installation program formats the disk partitions and installs the selected package groups.
15. If you find that Linux does not work properly with one or more of your system components (such as the network card or sound card), you may have to reconfigure the Linux operating system to add support for those system components.

The following sections guide you through the basic installation steps and the initial booting of Linux.

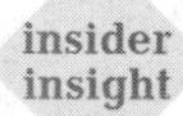

Your PC must have a CD/DVD drive — one that Linux supports — to install Linux from this book's companion DVD-ROM. This should not be a problem because most PCs nowadays come with a CD/DVD drive. Most new PCs have CD/DVD drives that connect to the hard disk controller (called IDE for Integrated Drive Electronics). Any IDE CD/DVD drive works in Linux.

Preparing Your PC for Linux Installation

Before you install Linux, you should prepare your PC for the installation. You can be in either of two situations:

- You already have a PC that runs some version of Microsoft Windows.
- You are about to buy a new PC, and you plan to run Linux on that PC at least some of the time.

If you are about to purchase a PC, you are lucky because you can get a PC configured with peripherals that Linux supports. You may have to ask the PC vendor explicitly for detailed information about hardware, such as the video card, CD/DVD drive, and networking card, to ensure that you can use the peripherals under Linux. Selecting a PC with Linux-supported hardware minimizes the potential for problems when you install Linux.

If you want to install Linux on an existing PC, verify that the latest Linux distribution supports all of the hardware on your PC. In other words, you have to take an inventory of your PC's hardware components and determine whether Linux currently supports all of them.

Checking Your PC's Hardware

Like many other operating systems, Linux supports various types of hardware through device drivers. For each type of peripheral device, such as a networking card or a CD/DVD drive, Linux needs a driver. In fact, each kind of peripheral needs a separate driver. Because Linux is available free (or relatively inexpensively) and because many programmers scattered throughout the world cooperate to develop Linux, you cannot demand support for a specific kind of hardware. You can only hope that someone who can write a Linux driver has the same hardware you do. In all likelihood, that person will write a driver, which eventually will find its way into a version of Linux, and then you can use that hardware under Linux. It may take a while for Linux to support new interfaces.

If you're concerned that your PC may not be able to run Linux, here are some of the key components in your PC that you need to consider before you start the Linux installation:

- **DVD/CD drives:** You must have a DVD/CD-ROM drive and the PC must be able to boot from that drive. The exact model doesn't matter. What matters is how the DVD/CD-ROM drive connects to the PC. Most new PCs have DVD/CD-ROM drives that connect to the hard drive controller (called IDE for Integrated Drive Electronics or ATA for AT Attachment). If you add an external DVD/CD drive, it most likely connects to the USB port. Most IDE/ATA or USB DVD/CD-ROM drives work in Linux.
- **Hard drives:** Any IDE disk drive works in Linux. Another type of hard drive controller is SCSI (Small Computer System Interface), which Linux also supports. To comfortably install and play with Linux, you need about 5GB of hard drive space.
- **Keyboard:** All keyboards work with Linux and the X Window System.
- **Modem:** If you plan to dial out to the Internet, you need a modem that Linux supports. For software-based modems, called soft modems or winmodems, you may have to download a driver from the manufacturer (it may or may not be freely available).
- **Monitor:** The kind of monitor is not particularly critical except that it must be capable of displaying the screen resolutions that the video card uses. The screen resolution is expressed in terms of the number of picture elements (pixels), horizontally and vertically (for example, 1024 × 768). The installer can detect most modern monitors. If it does not detect your monitor, you can select a generic monitor type with a specific resolution such as 1024 × 768. You can also specify the monitor by its make and model (which you can find on the back of the monitor). Chapter 3 further describes X Window System and monitors.
- **Mouse:** The installation program can detect the mouse. All types of mice (such as PS/2 or USB) work with Linux and the X Window System.
- **Network card:** Not all PCs have network cards, but if yours does, the installer can probably detect and use it. If you have problems, try to find the make and model (such as Linksys LNE100TX Fast Ethernet Adapter) so that you can search for information on whether Linux supports that card or not.
- **Processor:** A 400 MHz Pentium II or better is best. The processor speed, expressed in MHz (megahertz) or GHz (gigahertz), is not that important as long as it's over

400 MHz, but the faster the better. Linux can run on other Intel-compatible processors such as AMD, Cyrix, and VIA processors.

- **RAM:** RAM is the amount of memory your system has. As with processing speed, the more RAM, the better. You need 256MB to install both Linux and the X Window System and to comfortably run a GUI desktop.
- **SCSI controller:** Some high-performance PCs have SCSI controllers that connect disk drives and other peripherals to a PC. If your PC happens to have a SCSI controller, you might want to find out the make and model of the controller.
- **Sound card:** If your PC has a sound card and you want to have sound in Linux, you have to make sure it's compatible. You can configure the sound card after successfully installing Linux.
- **Video card:** Linux works fine with all video cards (also known as display adapters) in text mode, but if you want the GUI, you need a video card that works with the X Window System. The installer can detect a supported video card and configure the X Window System correctly. However, if the installer cannot detect the video card, it helps if you know the make and model of your video card.

In addition to this hardware, you also need to find out the make and model of any printer you plan to use in Linux.

cross ref

Appendixes B through F provide more information about whether or not Linux supports your system's unique hardware configuration. In these appendixes, you can also find information about how to get the most from your PC's hardware under Linux.

insider insight

If you plan to install Linux on an empty second hard disk or if you want to install Linux over an existing DOS/Windows partition, you do not have to go through the process of partitioning (dividing) your hard disk. You can skip the next few sections and proceed to "Booting the Linux Installer." Then you can boot Linux from the DVD-ROM and proceed to install Linux.

cross ref

If you are installing Linux on a laptop, please see the "Installing Linux on a Laptop" section for more information.

Repartitioning Your Hard Drive

If your PC has a single hard disk drive, chances are good that you have some version of Microsoft Windows installed on that drive. If your hard drive is at least 10GB, I recommend that you keep Windows installed on your system, even if you want to work mostly in Linux. After all, you may have Windows applications that you paid for and would like to use now and then. Of course, you can also access the Windows files from Linux. You get the best of both worlds if you keep Windows around when you install Linux.

Typically, your PC hard disk is set up as a single large partition, designated by the drive letter C (Windows XP installations often have a hidden first partition and the second partition designated as drive C). Unless you can scrounge up a second hard disk for your PC, or you already have a second disk, your first task is to shrink the existing partition on your one and only hard disk and create free space on the disk for Linux.

You can use PartitionMagic to resize the existing partition on your hard disk. PartitionMagic is a commercial product that can resize hard disk partitions and create new partitions on any version of Microsoft Windows and Linux. In particular, PartitionMagic can resize partitions that contain NTFS file systems used in Windows NT/2000/XP.

With PartitionMagic, the idea is to shrink the existing Windows partition and to create unused disk space for the Linux partition. Later on, during Linux installation, you can choose the installer option to leave the existing Windows partition intact and use the available free space for Linux.

The bottom line is that once you have successfully shrunk the existing Microsoft Windows partition and created a block of unused disk space for Linux, you are past the biggest hurdle in installing Linux while retaining Windows intact.

Repartitioning with PartitionMagic

PartitionMagic, from PowerQuest, can resize and split disk partitions in all Microsoft Windows operating systems. It's a commercial product, so you have to buy it to use it. At the time of this writing, the list price of PartitionMagic 8.0 is $69.95. You can read about it and buy it at `www.powerquest.com/partitionmagic`.

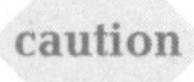

Resizing the disk partition always involves the risk of losing all data on the hard disk. Therefore, before you resize hard disk partitions using a disk partitioning tool such as PartitionMagic, you should back up your hard disk. After making your backup, please make sure that you can restore files from the backup.

When you run PartitionMagic, it shows the current partitions in a window. If you are running Windows XP, you probably have two partitions — one small hidden partition that contains Windows XP installation files and a huge second NTFS partition that serves as the C drive. You have to reduce the size of the existing C drive, which creates unused space following that partition. Then, during Linux installation, the installation program can create new Linux partitions in the unused space.

To reduce the size of the partition, follow these steps:

1. In the partition map in PartitionMagic's main window, right-click the partition and select Resize/Move from the menu (see Figure 2-1). The Resize Partition dialog box appears.

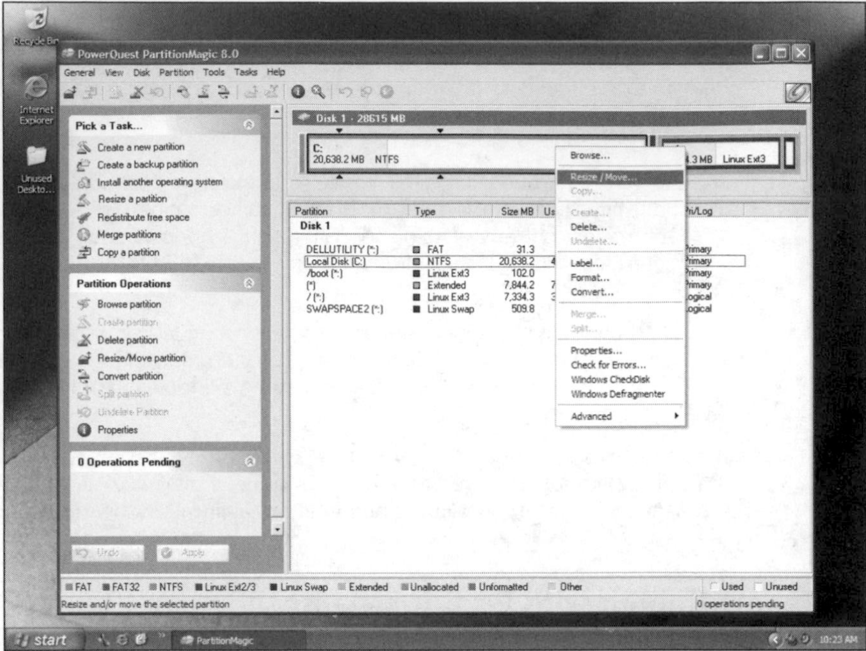

Figure 2-1: Right-Clicking on the Partition to Resize in PartitionMagic 8.0.

2. In the Resize/Move Partition dialog box, click and drag the right edge of the partition to a smaller size. For a large hard disk (anything over 10GB), reduce the Windows partition and leave the rest for Linux. If possible, try to leave 5GB or more for Linux.
3. Click OK and then Apply to apply the changes. After PartitionMagic has made the changes, click OK.
4. Reboot the PC.

You do not have to do anything with the disk space left over after shrinking the partition that used to be the C drive. Later, in the "Partitioning and Using the Hard Disk" section, you learn to use the free disk space to install Linux.

Booting the Linux Installer

The Linux installer runs under Linux; therefore, you need to boot Linux on your PC before you can go through the installation steps. This initial version of Linux comes from the DVD-ROM. The initial Linux operating system, in turn, runs the Linux installer, which prepares the disk partitions and copies all necessary files from the DVD-ROM to the disk.

You can start the initial version of the Linux operating system by booting your PC from the DVD-ROM (this works only if your PC is bootable from the DVD-ROM; most PCs can boot from the DVD-ROM drive, as I explain a little later).

The following sections describe these approaches to booting Linux and initiating the Red Hat installation.

Booting from the Linux DVD-ROM

Most new PCs can boot directly from the DVD-ROM as long as they come with a DVD drive. To do so, you have to go into SETUP as the PC powers up. The exact steps for entering SETUP and setting the boot device depend on the PC, but they typically involve pressing a key such as F2. As the PC powers up, a brief message should tell you what key to press to enter SETUP. Once you are in SETUP, you can designate the CD/DVD-ROM drive as the boot device.

After your PC is set up to boot directly from the CD/DVD-ROM drive, place the Fedora Linux DVD-ROM into the CD/DVD drive, and reboot the PC. The PC should power up and start the Linux kernel from the DVD-ROM. After Linux starts from the DVD-ROM, the Linux installation program begins to run. The section "Installing from the Linux DVD-ROM" describes this process in detail.

Watching the Boot Process during Installation

A few moments after you start the boot process, an initial screen appears — the screen displays a welcome message and ends with a `boot:` prompt. The welcome message tells you that help is available by pressing one of the function keys, F1 through F5.

If you want to read the help screens, press the function key corresponding to the help you want. If you don't press any keys, after a minute the boot process proceeds with the loading of the Linux kernel into the PC's memory. To start booting Linux immediately, press Enter. After the Linux kernel loads, it automatically starts the Linux installation program, which, in turn, starts the X Window System and provides a GUI for the installation.

At the start of the installation, as the Linux kernel begins to run, various messages appear on the screen. These boot messages tell you whether or not the Linux kernel has detected your hardware. The messages typically flash by too quickly for you to follow. Afterward, the screen shows a dialog box with a welcome message and some helpful information about the installation. At this point, you can read the messages about your hardware by pressing Ctrl-Alt-F4 — this switches the display to another virtual screen where all kernel messages appear in a form slightly different from what you see on the main installation screen. In particular, look for a message about the CD/DVD drive, because the kernel has to detect the CD/DVD drive to proceed with the rest of the installation. To return to the graphical installation screen, press Ctrl-Alt-F7.

Installing from the Linux DVD-ROM

After you start the initial version of Linux following the procedures described in the section "Booting the Linux Installer," Linux runs the Linux installation program — called anaconda — from the DVD-ROM. The rest of the installation occurs under the control of the installation program. The installation program uses a GUI. You can go through the installation steps by pointing and clicking with the mouse.

anaconda is the Fedora Core Linux installation program. It runs after the initial Linux kernel boots and shows the text or GUI screens through which you perform the installation. anaconda is written in the Python programming language.

To learn more about anaconda, visit Red Hat's website on anaconda at `http://rhlinux.redhat.com/anaconda/`.

If for some reason anaconda fails to start the X Window System–based graphical interface, press Ctrl-Alt-Del to restart the installation and type **linux text** at the boot prompt to activate the text-mode installer. In text mode, the anaconda installer uses a full-screen text-based interface. Each screen typically presents a dialog box with various elements, such as lists of items from which you select one or more buttons to indicate action. Typically, the buttons are labeled OK and Cancel. The bottom of the screen displays a help message that shows you how to navigate around the text screen.

If, for some reason, the installer fails to detect your IDE CD/DVD drive and prompts you for the type of CD/DVD drive, restart the installation by pressing Ctrl-Alt-Del. When you see the boot prompt, type **linux hd*x*=cdrom** where *x* is a single letter—a, b, c, or d—identifying the IDE interface to which the CD/DVD drive is connected. The letter *a* refers to the master or primary connector of the first IDE controller, and *b* is the slave on the first IDE controller. The letters *c* and *d* refer to the master and slave of the second IDE controller. Thus, if your CD/DVD drive is connected as the master on the second IDE controller, you would type the following at the boot prompt (you call it `cdrom` even if it's a DVD drive):

```
linux hdc=cdrom
```

Monitoring the Installation Process

As the installation progresses, you respond primarily to various dialog boxes, entering information the installation program needs. The installation program displays useful information about a number of virtual consoles—these are screens of text in memory that you can view on the physical screen by pressing the key sequences shown in Table 2-1.

insider insight

You work mostly in the main console—virtual console 7 in GUI installation and 1 in text mode. To switch to another virtual console, press the appropriate keystroke shown in Table 2-1. For example, to view the install log on virtual console 3, press Ctrl-Alt-F3. After you are done viewing the log, press Ctrl-Alt-F7 to return to the GUI console so you can continue with the installation.

Typically, you can get by without ever having to switch to the other screens, but if something goes wrong, you can switch to the install log screen by pressing Ctrl-Alt-F3, where you can get more information about the problem.

Table 2-1: Virtual Consoles Available for Linux Installation

Virtual Console	*Keystroke*	*Description*
1	Ctrl-Alt-F1	This is the main console on which the installation program displays the text-based user interface through which you start the Linux installation and install Linux when you choose text mode.
2	Ctrl-Alt-F2	This console displays a shell prompt from which you can use Linux commands to monitor the progress of installation.
3	Ctrl-Alt-F3	This is the install log. Messages from the installation program appear here.
4	Ctrl-Alt-F4	The Linux kernel displays its messages on this console. After Linux initially boots, you may want to switch to this console to see the kernel messages because they include information about hardware that Linux detects in your PC.
5	Ctrl-Alt-F5	This console shows the output of any other programs run during the installation process.
7	Ctrl-Alt-F7	This is where the anaconda installer displays the X Window System–based graphical user interface.

Understanding the Fedora Core Installation Phases

Installing Fedora Core Linux is a fairly lengthy process that contains the following major phases:

1. **Getting Ready to Install:** After the graphical installation screen appears, choose the language to be used during the installation process. Indicate the type of keyboard. Then specify whether you are installing or upgrading and, if you are installing, the type of installation: workstation, server, or custom. I show a custom system installation in this chapter.
2. **Partitioning and Using the Hard Disk:** This step is to prepare the hard disk space you plan to use for Linux. Select the automatic partition option to let the installation program perform this step, or partition the disk manually using Disk Druid. At minimum, you need two partitions — one to be used as swap area and the other for the Linux root file system (represented by /). The partitions are also formatted before use. Appendix B discusses typical partitioning strategies in an operational Linux system.
3. **Configuring Linux:** In this phase, specify where the GRUB boot loader should be loaded. For GRUB, you can also specify a password that has to be entered to load Linux at system startup. You set up the TCP/IP network, the firewall, and the time zone, and you specify a password for the root — the superuser.
4. **Selecting the Package Groups to Install:** Select which package groups — such as X Window System, GNOME desktop, KDE Desktop, Editors, and Web server — you want to install. Up to this point, you can abort the installation without

writing anything to the hard disk. After you select the package groups, the installation program prepares the hard disk and installs the selected packages on the hard disk.

If all goes well, installing Fedora Core Linux from the companion DVD-ROM on a fast Pentium PC should take approximately an hour (assuming that you select nearly all packages). For example, on a 1 GHz Pentium PC with 256MB RAM and a 6GB disk partition devoted to Linux, the entire installation took about an hour.

Detecting Hardware during Installation

The anaconda installer uses kudzu (a utility program) to probe—attempt to determine the presence of—specific hardware, and tailors the installation steps accordingly. For example, if the installation program detects a network card, the program automatically displays the screens on which you can configure the TCP/IP network. Therefore, you may see some variation in the sequence of steps, depending on your specific hardware configuration.

Kudzu is a configuration program as well as a library of object code that can probe and determine what hardware is installed on your system. The anaconda installation program uses kudzu to detect hardware during installation.

To learn more about kudzu, visit Red Hat's kudzu website at `http://rhlinux.redhat.com/kudzu/`.

The following sections describe each of the Fedora Core installation phases in detail.

Getting Ready to Install

In this phase, you perform the following steps before moving on to disk setup and the actual installation of Linux:

1. A text screen appears with a welcome message and a `boot:` prompt. Press Enter to begin installing in GUI mode or type **linux text** to install in text mode. If you have a SCSI controller or network card that the Linux kernel may not automatically detect, you should type **linux noprobe** to manually install the hardware (in this case, you have to select the hardware from a list or provide a driver disk; see Appendix B for more information on setting up SCSI controllers). Typically, you press Enter to continue the installation in GUI mode.
2. The installation program starts the GUI and displays a list of languages to be used during the installation. The list includes languages such as Chinese, English, French, German, Hindi, Italian, Norwegian, Romanian, Russian, Slovak, Spanish, and Ukrainian. Use your mouse to select the language you want to use for the installation screens, and then click the Next button to continue.

   In the graphical mode installation, each screen has online help available on the left side of the screen. You can read the help message to learn more about what you are supposed to select in a specific screen.
3. The installation program displays a list of keyboard layouts. Select a keyboard layout suitable for your language's character set (for example, U.S. English in the United States).

Note that you can always reconfigure your keyboard after finishing the installation. Simply log in as `root` at a text console (you can get one by pressing, for example, Ctrl-Alt-F2) and type **setup**. This runs a text-mode setup utility that enables you to configure, among other things, the keyboard, the mouse, and the printer.

4. The installation program searches for any existing Fedora Core installation on your PC and then prompts you for the installation type — whether you want to install a new system or upgrade any older Fedora Core installation. If you are performing a fresh installation, you have to select the installation type: Personal Desktop, Workstation, Server, or Custom. The Personal Desktop, Workstation, and Server installations simplify the installation process by selecting software packages in a predefined manner. The Personal Desktop installation creates a Linux system for home, laptop, or desktop use. A graphical environment is installed along with productivity applications.

   A Workstation installation installs graphical environment as well as software development and system administration tools. A Server installation sets up all the Internet servers such as Web server, FTP server, and mail server. By default, the Server installation does not install the graphical environment, but you can always add the packages for the GUI desktops. For maximum flexibility, select the Custom installation, but note that the other installation types can be easier because many choices are already made for you.

The next major phase of installation involves partitioning the hard disk for use in Linux.

Partitioning and Using the Hard Disk

You have to partition and prepare a hard disk before you can install Linux. You usually do not perform this step for PCs running Windows; when you buy your PC from a vendor, the vendor takes care of preparing the hard disk and installing Windows and all other applications on the hard disk. Because you are installing Linux from scratch, however, you have to perform this crucial step yourself. As you see in the following sections, this task is just a matter of following instructions.

When the Linux installation program reaches the disk-partitioning phase, it displays a screen from which you can select a partitioning strategy. The screen gives you the following options for partitioning and using the hard disk:

- **Automatically partition:** This option causes the installation program to create new partitions for installing Linux, based on your installation type, such as workstation or server. You get a chance to customize the partitions before anything is done to the hard disk. This is the option most users choose.
- **Manually partition with Disk Druid:** With this option, you can use the Disk Druid program that lets you partition the disk any way you want and, at the same time, specify which partitions are mounted on which parts of the Linux file system.

From the disk-partitioning strategy screen, select the `Automatically partition` option to have the installer automatically partition the disk for you. The Linux installation program, then displays another screen (see Figure 2-2) that asks you how you want the automatic partitioning to be done.

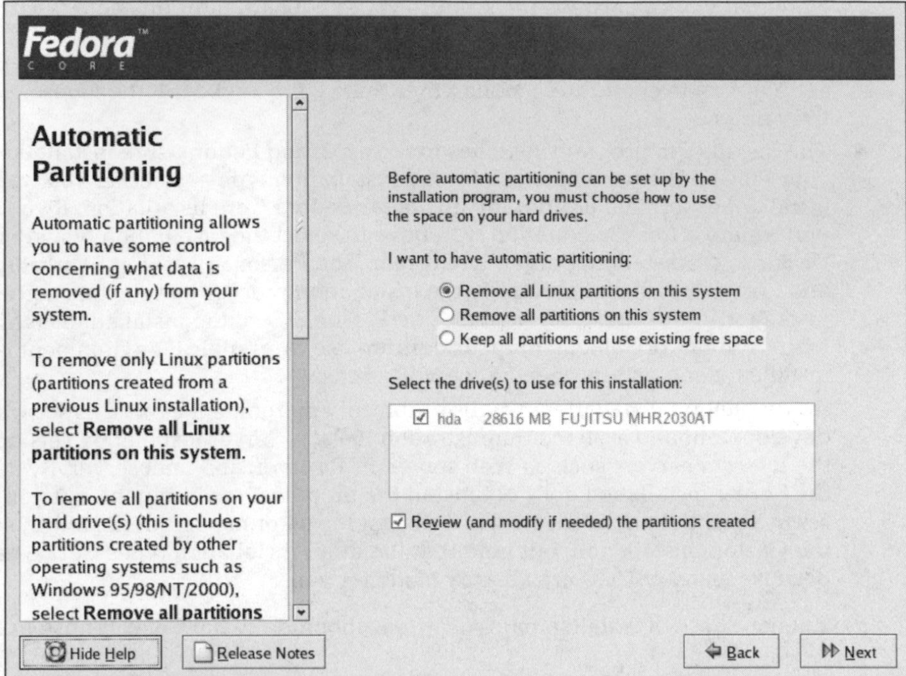

Figure 2-2: Selecting Automatic Partitioning Options during Linux Installation.

As Figure 2-2 shows, you can select from three automatic partitioning options:

- **Remove all Linux partitions on this system:** This option causes the installation program to remove all existing Linux partitions and to create new partitions for installing Fedora Core Linux. You can use this option if you already have Linux installed on your PC and want to wipe it out and install the latest version of Fedora Core Linux.
- **Remove all partitions on this system:** This option is similar to the first option, except that the installation program removes all partitions, including those used by other operating systems such as Microsoft Windows.
- **Keep all partitions and use existing free space:** If you have created space for Linux by using PartitionMagic, select this option to create the Linux partitions using the free space on the hard disk. If you are installing Linux on a new PC after resizing the partition, this is the option to choose.

caution

Do not select the `Remove all partitions on this system` **option if you want to retain any existing Windows partitions.**

Select the appropriate option, and click Next. For example, if you select the first option, the Linux installation program displays a dialog box to confirm your choice and to point out that all data in the existing Linux partitions will be lost. Click Yes to continue. In the next screen (see Figure 2-3) the installer shows the partitions it has prepared. The exact appearance of this screen depends on your hard disk's capacity and its current partitions.

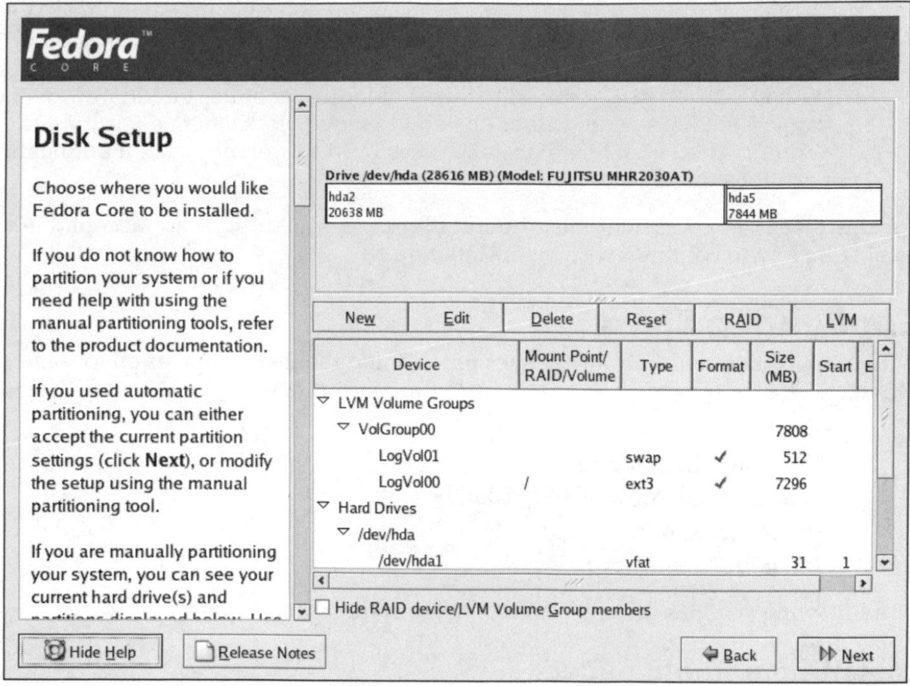

Figure 2-3: Partitions Automatically Created by the Linux Installer.

The screen displays the disk drives and the current partition information for the drives. If you want to accept the partitions as is, click Next to proceed.

caution

If your PC does not have enough memory (typically less than 128MB), the installer asks if it can write the partition table and activate the swap partition. Once you do this, your hard disk partitions will be changed. Click Yes only if you are committed to the new partitions and definitely want to install Linux.

You can also perform specific disk-setup tasks through the six buttons that run across the middle of the screen. Specifically, the buttons perform the following actions:

- **New** lets you create a new partition, assuming there is enough free disk space available to create a partition. When you click this button, another dialog box appears, in which you can fill in information necessary to create a new partition.
- **Edit** lets you alter the attributes of the partition currently highlighted in the partitions list. You make changes to the current attribute in another dialog box that appears when you click the Edit button.
- **Delete** is used to delete the partition currently highlighted in the partitions list.
- **Reset** causes the installation program to ignore any changes you may have made.
- **RAID** is used to set up a RAID (Redundant Array of Independent Disks) device — a technique that combines multiple disks to improve reliability and data transfer rates. There are several types of RAID configurations. You have to select at least two partitions to make a RAID device.

- **LVM** creates a logical volume for Logical Volume Management (LVM), which groups together multiple physical disk partitions into a volume group and manages that volume group in terms of logical extents instead of physical partitions. With LVM, you can easily adjust sizes of logical volumes or add new disk partitions to the file system without having to move files from one partition to another. The Fedora Core installer uses LVM by default when it automatically partitions the hard disk.

For this discussion, I assume that the installer-created partitions are acceptable and that you click Next to continue with the installation.

Configuring Linux

When the installation program finishes partitioning the disk, it moves on to some configuration steps. The typical configuration steps are as follows:

- Install boot loader.
- Configure the network.
- Configure the firewall and SELinux.
- Set the time zone.
- Set the root password.

The following sections describe each of these configuration steps.

Installing a Boot Loader

You can install the GRUB boot loader. GRUB stands for Grand Unified Bootloader; this boot loader program can reside on your hard disk and start Linux when you power up your PC. If you have Microsoft Windows on your hard disk, the installer should detect the Windows partition and configure the boot loader to load Windows as well. You can view the boot loader configuration and edit the settings from the boot loader configuration screen (see Figure 2-4).

The boot loader configuration screen (see Figure 2-4) shows you information about the boot loader to be installed and the partitions from which that the boot loader boots the PC. You also get a chance to change the boot loader or add other partitions that contain non-Linux operating systems.

GRUB is the default boot loader, and it's installed by default in the master boot record (MBR) of the hard disk. If you do not want to the boot loader currently installed on your hard disk, click the "Change boot loader" button near the top of the window. From the dialog box that appears, you can skip the boot loader installation entirely.

caution

If you choose not to install any boot loader during Linux installation, you won't be able to start Linux when you reboot the PC. You will be able to boot only whatever the current boot loader is set up to load.

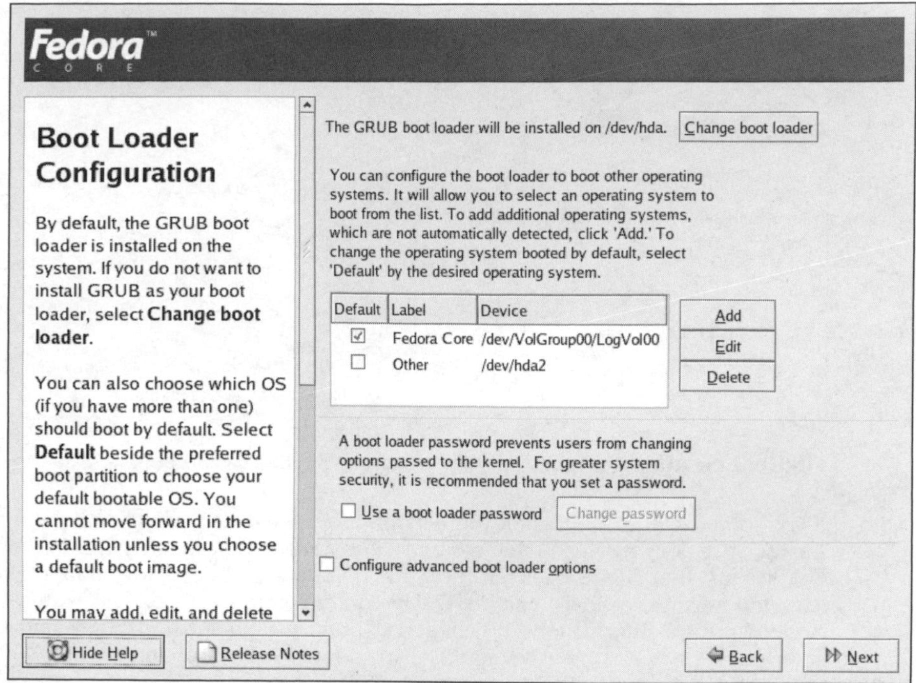

Figure 2-4: Selecting and Configuring a Boot Loader.

In the middle of the boot loader configuration screen, a table lists the disk partitions from which the boot loader can boot the PC. That table lists the Linux partition and any other partitions that may contain another operating system (such as Windows XP or 2000). Each entry in that table is an operating system that the boot loader can load and start. The default operating system is the one with a check mark in the Default column.

You must assign a label to the Windows XP partition that appears in the list of partitions—click that line and enter the label. If there is no label, GRUB will not display that partition as a choice in its boot screen, and you won't be able to boot Windows XP after you finish installing Linux.

If GRUB fails to detect and list an existing Windows XP partition in the list, you should click the Add button and fill in the information about the Windows XP partition, as shown in Figure 2-5. Typically, the Windows XP partition should be the `/dev/hda2` device (the first partition—`/dev/hda1`—is usually a hidden partition that holds files used to install Windows XP).

continues

continued

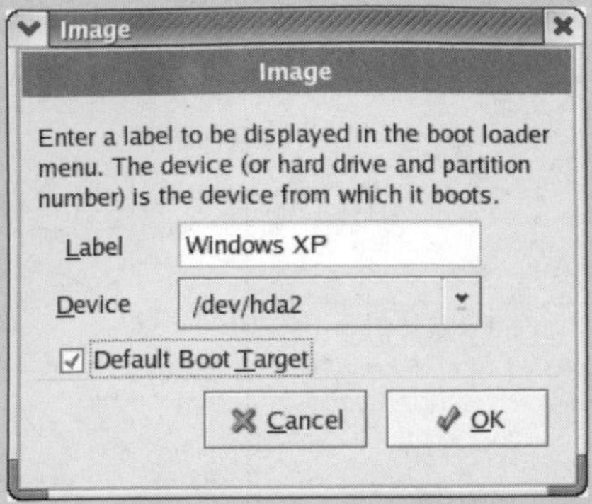

Figure 2-5: Adding a Windows XP Partition to the List of Partitions to Boot.

If you forget to enter a label for the Windows XP partition or add the XP partition to the list, that does not mean that all is lost. The XP partition is still there on the hard disk. It's just that GRUB does not show it as an option to boot from. To fix the problem, you have to manually edit the GRUB configuration file, `/etc/grub.conf`. See Appendix B for information on configuring boot loaders such as GRUB and LILO. After you fix the `/etc/grub.conf` file, you should get the option to boot XP from the initial GRUB screen the next time you reboot the PC.

If you decide to install the GRUB boot loader, consider adding a password for GRUB. Click the "Use a boot loader password" check box and make sure that a check mark appears there. The installer displays a dialog box where you can specify a password for GRUB. With a GRUB password, your system is more secure because no one can boot your system without a password given that GRUB will not load the operating system without the password.

If you select the "Configure advanced boot loader options" check box and click Next, the installer displays the Advanced Boot Loader Configuration screen, as shown in Figure 2-6.

The screen of Figure 2-6 gives you the option to install the GRUB boot loader in one of two locations:

- Master Boot Record (MBR), which is located in the first sector of your PC's hard disk (the C drive)
- First sector of the Linux boot partition

You can also add any necessary boot options in the text field labeled "General kernel parameters." These are options passed to the kernel as the system boots.

You should install the boot loader in the Master Boot Record unless you are using another operating system loader, such as BootMagic or Windows NT/2000/XP Boot Manager. After making your selections for the boot loader, click Next to continue.

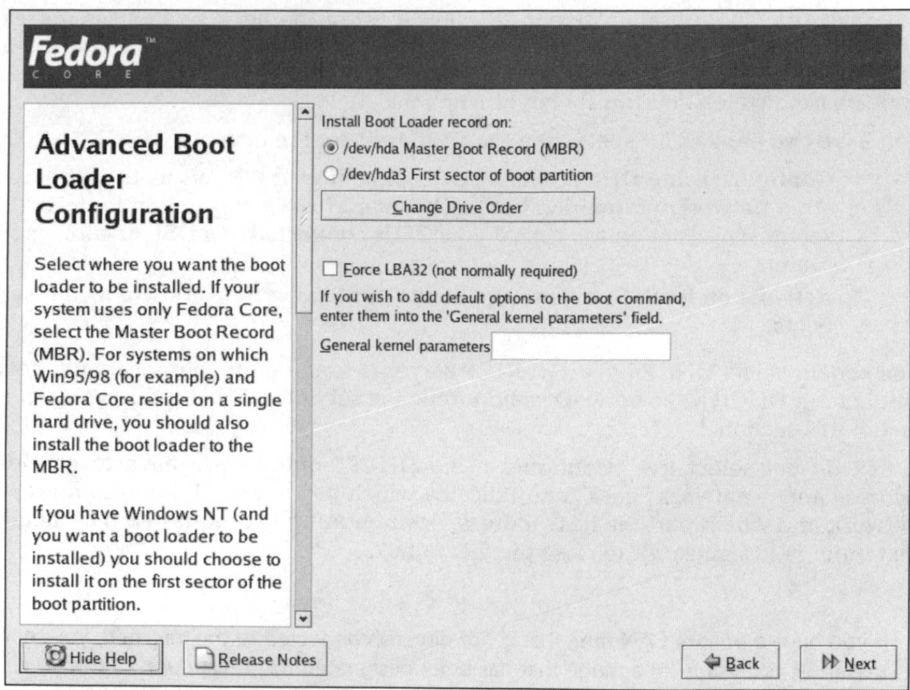

Figure 2-6: Selecting Where to Install Boot Loader and Providing Kernel Options.

cross ref

If you install GRUB in the first sector of the Linux boot partition, then you have to configure the Windows NT/XP boot loader to load Linux. See the "Booting from the Hard Disk" section in Appendix B for more information.

Configuring the Network

Assuming that the Linux kernel has detected a network card, the Linux installation program displays the Network Configuration screen, which enables you to configure the local area network (LAN) parameters for your Linux system.

This step is not for configuring the dial-up networking. You need to perform this step if your Linux system is connected to a TCP/IP LAN through an Ethernet card.

cross ref

If the Linux installer does not detect your network card, you should restart the installation and type **linux noprobe** at the boot prompt. Then, you will be able to select your network card manually. See the "Troubleshooting the Installation" section for more information.

The Network Configuration screen displays a list of the network devices (for example, Ethernet cards) installed in your PC. For each network device, you can indicate how the IP (Internet Protocol) address is set. Click the Edit button next to the list, and a dialog box appears from which you can specify the options.

You have two choices for specifying the IP address for the network card:

- **Configure using DHCP:** Enable this option if your PC gets its IP address and other network information from a Dynamic Host Configuration Protocol (DHCP) server. This is often the case if your PC is connected to a DSL or cable modem router.
- **Activate on boot:** Enable this option to turn on the network when your system boots.

You should select DHCP only if a DHCP server is running on your local area network. If you choose DHCP, your network configuration is set automatically, and you can skip the rest of this section.

If you do not select the "Configure using DHCP" option, you have to provide an IP address and a network mask that indicates which part of the IP address represents the network and which part the host address. After entering the requested parameters in the text input fields, click OK to close the dialog box.

cross ref

If you have a private LAN (one that is not directly connected to the Internet), you may use an IP address from a range that has been designated for private use. Common IP addresses for private LANs are in the range 192.168.0.1 through 192.168.0.254. You will learn more about TCP/IP networking and IP addresses in Chapter 6.

In the rest of the Network Configuration screen, you have to specify how to set the host name. You have two options to set the host name:

- **Automatically via DHCP:** Enable this option to assign a host name automatically using DHCP. (This works only if the DHCP server is configured to assign host names.)
- **Manually:** Use this option to manually specify a host name — type the name in the text field next to the radio button. If you do not assign any host name, your system will have the default host name: `localhost.localdomain`.

After you enter the requested parameters, click the Next button to proceed to the firewall and SELinux configuration step.

Configuring the Firewall and SELinux

In this step, you configure the built-in packet filter that comes with Linux and that enables you to control how various types of IP packets are handled. You can enable or disable the firewall from the Firewall Configuration screen (see Figure 2-7), and customize the firewall to suit your needs. You can also configure mandatory access control by enabling Security Enhanced Linux (SELinux), which is part of the latest Linux kernel.

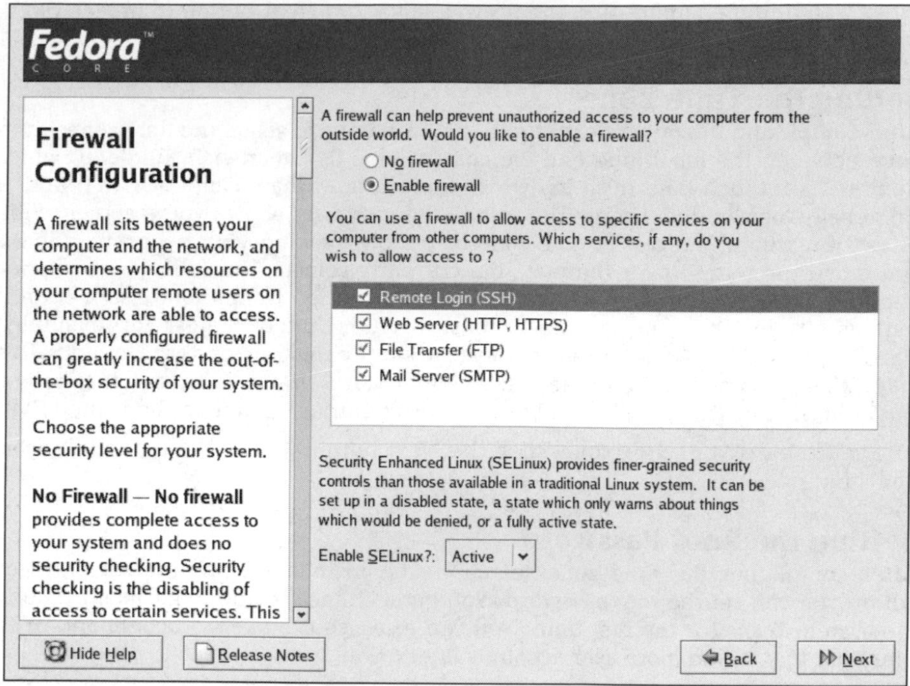

Figure 2-7: Setting up the Packet Filtering Firewall and SELinux Access Control Built into Your System.

The installer offers the following options for firewall:

- **No firewall** means your system accepts connections at all ports and does not perform any security checking. Use this option only if your system runs in a trusted network, if it is already inside a firewall, or if you plan to set up a more elaborate firewall configuration later on (the sooner the better).
- **Enable firewall** means you want to set up a firewall. This means that your system does not accept any connections other than those that you explicitly enable. By default, the system accepts only Domain Name Service (DNS) and DHCP requests. You can then select the services such as Mail and FTP that are allowed to pass through the firewall.

For the SELinux access control configuration, you can choose from a drop-down list one of the following options:

- **Active** means SELinux enforces mandatory access control.
- **Warn** means SELinux prints warning messages, but does not actually enforce the access control policies.
- **Disabled** means SELinux is turned off.

cross ref

If you do not configure the firewall correctly here, you can do so later on by following instructions outlined in Chapter 22.

When you're done configuring the firewall, click the Next button to proceed to the next step.

Setting the Time Zone

After completing the network configuration, you have to select the time zone — the difference between the local time and the current time in Greenwich, England, which is the standard reference time (also known as Greenwich Mean Time, or GMT, and UTC, or Universal Coordinated Time). The installation program shows you a screen with a map view from which you pick a time zone by simply clicking your geographic location. As you move the mouse over the map, the currently selected location's name appears in a text field. If you want, you can also select your location from a long list of countries and regions. If you live on the East Coast of the United States, for example, select USA/Eastern. Of course, the easiest way is to simply click the eastern United States on the map. When you pick a time zone in the United States, the installer automatically enables Daylight Saving Time, which applies to many countries, including the United States.

After you select your time zone, click the Next button to proceed to the next configuration step.

Setting the Root Password

After completing the time zone selection, the installation program displays a screen where you can set the root password. You get a chance to add other user accounts when the system boots for the first time. You can also use the `useradd` command or the User Manager tool to add more user accounts later on.

The root user is the superuser in Linux. Because the superuser can do anything in the system, you should assign a password that you can remember but that others cannot guess easily. Make the password at least eight characters long, include a mix of letters and numbers, and, for good measure, throw in some special characters, such as + or *.

Type the password on the first line, and reenter the password on the next line. Each character in the password appears as an asterisk (*) on the screen. You have to type the password twice, and both entries must match before the installation program accepts it. This ensures that you do not make any typing mistakes.

After you type the root password twice, then click the Next button to continue with the installation.

Selecting the Package Groups to Install

After you complete the key configuration steps, the installation program displays a message about reading package information and, after a short while, shows a screen (see Figure 2-8) with the default packages for the type of installation — personal desktop, desktop, or workstation — that you selected earlier during the installation. You get a different screen if you select custom installation.

In this case, Figure 2-8 shows the default package group selections for a workstation installation that includes the desktop applications, software development tools, and system administration tools. If you want to accept the default selections, click Next. Otherwise, click the radio button labeled Customize software packages to be installed and then click Next.

If you choose to customize the package selections or if you picked the custom installation type earlier, then the installer displays a screen (see Figure 2-9) from which you can select the package groups you want to install.

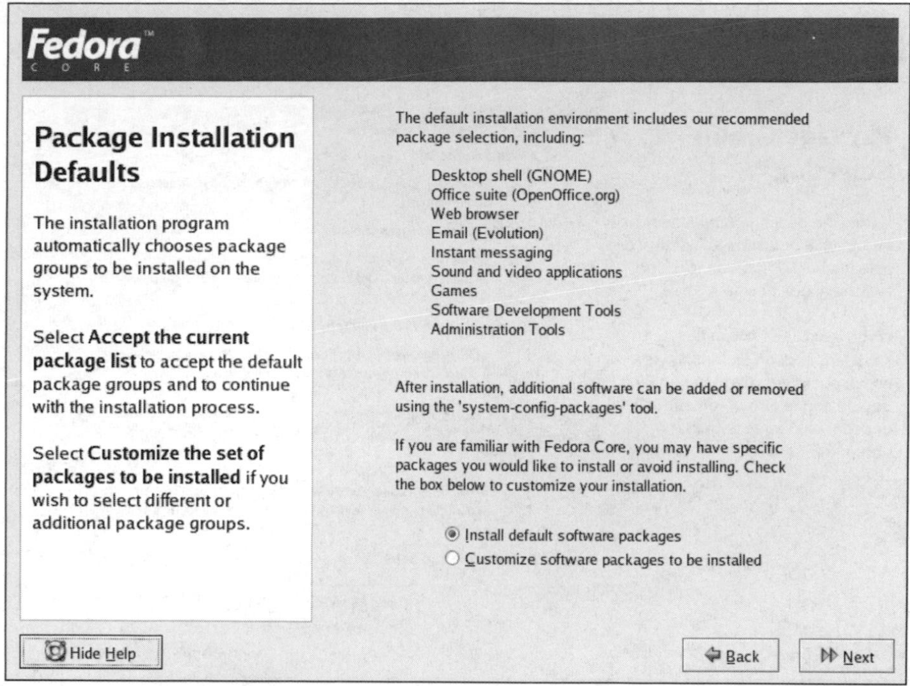

Figure 2-8: Default Package Groups for Selected Installation Type.

After you select the package groups, you can take a coffee break, and the installation program can format the disk partitions and copy all selected files to those partitions.

> **cross ref** Several Linux distributions including Fedora Core and Red Hat Enterprise Linux use special files called *packages* to bundle a number of files that make up specific software. For example, all configuration files, documentation, and binary files for the Perl programming language come in a Red Hat package. You use a special program called Red Hat Package Manager (RPM) to install, uninstall, and get information about packages. Chapter 21 shows you how to use RPM. For now, just remember that a package group is made up of several Red Hat packages (also called RPMs).

As Figure 2-9 shows, the package groups are organized into broad categories such as Desktops, Applications, Servers, and so on. Within each category, each package group is shown with a label, an icon, a brief description, and a check box. To select a package group, you should click on the check box so that a check mark appears in the box. As you select package groups, the installer shows the total disk space needed for the installation.

Some of the package groups are already selected, as indicated by the check marks in the check boxes. You can think of the selected package groups as the minimal set of packages recommended for installation. You can, however, choose to install any or all of the components. Use the mouse to move up and down in the scrolling list and click the mouse on a check box to select or deselect that package group.

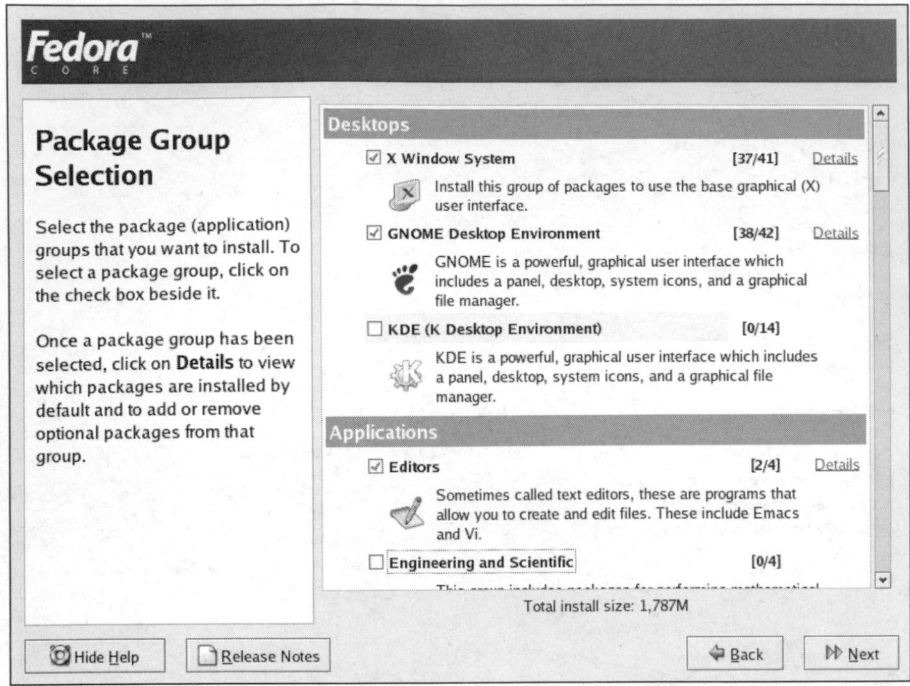

Figure 2-9: Selecting Package Groups to Install.

In an actual production installation of Linux, you should install exactly those package groups that you need. However, when you are trying to learn everything about Linux, you need many different packages. If you have enough disk space (at least 6GB) for the Linux partition, go ahead and select the package group labeled Everything—this installs all the package groups. Being able to install everything makes it easy for you to try out everything. Note that Everything is much more than the package groups that you see listed during installation—Everything includes nearly all the packages on the companion DVD-ROM.

I must repeat that you should install Everything only when you are trying to play with all the packages on a system that is specifically meant for experimenting with Linux. Do not install Everything on a system that will be used for anything critical. Installing everything is likely to open up too many security holes in your system.

Table 2-2 shows the package groups organized by the categories as they appear on the Package Group Selection screen. In addition to these user-selectable package groups, the installation program automatically installs a number of packages needed to run Linux and the applications you select. In other words, even if you do not select any of the package groups, the installation program installs a number of packages needed simply to run the core Linux operating system and a minimal set of utilities.

insider insight

Because each package group is a collection of many different packages, the installation program also gives you the option to select individual packages. If you click the link labeled "Details" that appears next to each package group in the list, the installation program displays a dialog box from which you can select individual packages in that package group. You can do this for any package group in the list.

If you are installing Linux for the first time, you do not need to go down to this level of detail to install specific packages. Simply pick the package groups you think you need from Table 2-2. If you forget something, you can always install additional packages later with the RPM utility program or the graphical Package Management utility, described in Chapter 21. After you have selected the package groups you want, click the Next button to continue with the rest of the installation.

Table 2-2: List of Package Groups in Fedora Core Linux

Package Group	*Description*
Desktops	
X Window System	Packages that make up X.Org X11, the X Window System for Intel x86 systems; includes all fonts, libraries, and GUI tools for configuring X, adding users, configuring printers, and so on.
GNOME Desktop Environment	Packages for the GNOME (GNU Network Object Model Environment) graphical desktop, including the Nautilus graphical shell.
KDE (K Desktop Environment)	Packages for the KDE—K Desktop Environment—another graphical desktop for Linux.
Applications	
Editors	Text editors such as Emacs and vi.
Engineering and Scientific	Packages such as units and gnuplot for performing math and science computations and plotting.
Graphical Internet	Graphical email, Web, chat, and instant messaging clients included in packages such as evolution, firefox, thunderbird, xchat, and gaim.
Text-based Internet	Text-based email, Web, FTP, and news reader clients included in packages such as fetchmail, lynx, mutt, and slrn.
Office/Productivity	Office suites, PDF viewers, and more in packages such as openoffice.org, gnucash, and xpdf.
Sound and Video	Multimedia applications for tasks such as playing audio CDs and burning CD/DVDs in packages such as HelixPlayer, cdda2wav, cdparanoia, cdrecord, dvd+rw-tools, dvgrab, k3b, mkisofs, xcdroast, and xmms.

(continued)

Table 2-2 *(continued)*

Package Group	***Description***
Authoring and Publishing	Tools to create documentation in TeX (pronounced "tech") and DocBook document-formatting system, provided in packages such as docbook-utils, tetex, and xmlto.
Graphics	Packages such as xsane, gimp, ImageMagick, dia, and xfig to scan and manipulate images and draw graphics.
Games and Entertainment	A number of computer games provided in packages such as gnome-games and kdegames.
Servers	
Server Configuration Tools	Fedora Core's custom server configuration tools in packages such as system-config-boot, system-config-httpd, system-config-nfs, system-config-printer, system-config-printer-gui, system-config-samba, system-config-securitylevel, and system-config-services.
Web Server	Packages such as httpd, php, mod_perl, mod_ssl, and php-mysql needed to run the Apache Web server.
Mail Server	Packages such as sendmail, dovecot, and sendmail-cf used to set up a mail server.
Windows File Server	Samba and other supporting packages needed to use the Linux PC as a LAN Manager server.
DNS Name Server	The bind and caching nameserver packages needed to provide Domain Name Service (DNS) on the Linux system.
FTP Server	The vsftpd packages needed to run an FTP server.
PostgreSQL Database	Packages such as postgresql- and postgresql-server that enable you to implement the PostgreSQL database.
MySQL Database	Packages such as mysql, mysql-devel, and mysql-server that enable you to implement the MySQL database.
News Server	The inn package for setting up an Internet News server.
Network Servers	Packages such as dhcp, krb5-server, and ypserv that enable you to run other services such as DHCP (Dynamic Host Configuration Protocol), Kerberos 5, and NIS (Network Information Service).
Legacy Network Servers	Packages such as rsh-server and telnet-server that enable you to run older services such as remote shell and Telnet.
Development	
Development Tools	Software development tools in packages such as gcc, gcc-c++, gcc-gfortran, gdb, make, cvs, rcs, and so on.
X Software Development	Packages such as xorg-x11-devel, Xaw3d-devel, and openmotif-devel needed to develop GUI applications for the X Window System.

Package Group	*Description*
GNOME Software Development	Packages such as gtk2-devel, glade2, libglade2-devel, libgnome-devel, and libbonobo-devel needed to develop GTK+ and GNOME graphical applications.
KDE Software Development	Packages such as PyQt-devel, kdebase-devel, kdelibs-devel, qt-designer, and qt-devel needed to develop QT and KDE graphical applications.
Legacy Software Development	The compat-gcc-32 and compat-libstdc++-296 packages needed to provide compatibility with previous releases of Red Hat Enterprise Linux.
Java Development	Packages such as ant, libgcj-devel, servletapi5, struts11, and tomcat5 needed to develop Java applications, including Java Server applications that can run with Apache Tomcat and Apache Web server.
System	
Administration Tools	Graphical system administration tools in packages such as system-config-date, system-config-keyboard, system-config-kickstart, system-config-language, system-config-lvm, system-config-network, system-config-packages, system-config-rootpassword, system-config-soundcard, system-config-users, system-config-packages, and system-logviewer.
System Tools	System administration and networking tools in packages such as ethereal, gnome-nettool, nmap, openldap-clients, samba-client, and vnc.
Printing Support	Packages such as cups, hal-cups-utils, system-config-printer, and ghostscript needed to print from the system or enable the system to act as a print server.
Miscellaneous	
Everything	Select this item to install all of the package groups plus many more additional packages.
Minimal	Select this to install a minimal system. This can be useful for setting up a Linux system to be used as a router or a firewall.

Completing the Installation

After you complete the key configuration steps and select the package groups to install, the installer displays a screen informing you that installation is about to begin and that a log of the installation will be in the `/root/install.log` file. That file essentially lists all the packages installed in your system. You can review the install log later and move the file to another directory for future reference. The content of the install log depends on the exact packages you choose to install.

The message also tells you that a kickstart file containing the installation options used in this installation is stored in the `/root/anaconda-ks.cfg` file. If you are going to repeat the same installation configuration on many more PCs, you can use this file along with a kickstart installation. See the "Using Kickstart Installation" section for more information.

caution

This is your last chance to abort the installation without doing anything to the hard disk. To abort, simply press Ctrl-Alt-Delete to restart the PC. To proceed with installation, click Next.

After you click Next at this step, the installer formats the disk partitions and installs the packages one by one. As it installs packages, the installation program displays a status screen showing the progress of the installation, including information such as the size of the current package being installed and the estimated time remaining to install.

After installation is complete, the installer ejects the DVD and informs you that installation is complete. Click Exit to reboot your PC.

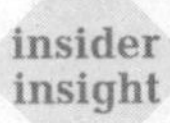

When Fedora Core boots for the first time, a server named `firstboot` runs and gives you an opportunity to perform some initial setup tasks such as setting the date and time and installing any other CDs that you might have.

Troubleshooting the Installation

One common installation problem is that the installer may not detect some key hardware such as the network interface card on your system. The installer takes you through a sequence of installation steps that depends on what hardware the installer detects. For example, if the installer cannot detect the network card, it skips the network configuration step.

Another common installation problem crops up when you restart the PC and, instead of a graphical login screen, you get a text terminal or worse, the system seems to be hung. This means that there is something wrong with the X Window System (or X) configuration.

There is an alternate way to install Linux so that you can force it to configure the network card. You can also troubleshoot any problems with X by reconfiguring X.

If you have problems with the X Window System, your printer, sound, or the network, consult Chapters 3 through 6 for more information. In particular, Chapter 3 shows you how to configure X, and Chapter 4 shows you how to set up printers.

Using Text Mode Installation

The installation program attempts to use a minimal X server to display the GUI mode installation screens. If the program fails to detect a video card, X does not start. If—for this reason or any other reason—it fails to start X, you can always fall back on the text mode installation program.

To use text mode installation, type **linux text** at the `boot:` prompt after you boot the PC from the Linux DVD-ROM. From then on, the basic sequence is similar to that of the graphical installation described previously in this chapter. However, many small details are different. You should be able to respond to the prompts and perform the installation.

In text mode, when the installation program fails to detect the video card, it displays a list of video cards from which you can select one. By selecting the video card, X may work when you install in text mode. If it does not, you can configure X using the information in Chapter 3.

Using the linux noprobe Command

If the Fedora Core installation program does not detect your network card, you can specify the network card manually by typing the `linux noprobe` command at the boot prompt.

Look for any indication of network devices in the messages the Linux kernel displays as it boots. To view these boot messages during installation, press Ctrl-Alt-F4. This switches to a text-mode virtual console on which the messages appear. (A virtual console is a screen of text or graphical information stored in memory that you can view on the physical screen by pressing the appropriate key sequence.)

Another sign of undetected hardware is when the installation program skips a step. For example, if the Linux kernel does not detect the network card, the installation program skips the network configuration step.

To manually install a network card, type **linux noprobe** at the `boot:` prompt in the initial text screen. The installation program then displays a dialog box that gives you the opportunity to add devices. Press Tab to highlight the Add Device button, and then press Enter. The installation program then displays a dialog box that prompts you to select a driver from a list. You can then select the driver for your network card and press Enter.

After you finish adding any network cards, select Done and press Enter. The installation program switches to graphics mode and guides you through the rest of the installation, as described previously in this chapter.

Troubleshooting X at the First Reboot

Sometimes you may run into a curious installation problem. During installation, the X configuration step works fine. But when you reboot the PC for the first time after installation, the graphical login screen does not appear. Instead, the boot process seems to hang just as it starts something called `firstboot`. If this happens to you, see the accompanying Secret for help on troubleshooting the problem.

When the firstboot process runs during the first system startup, it can either be uneventful or an aggravation. If all goes well, firstboot displays a GUI that enables you to perform one-time setups such as date and time configuration as well as install any other CDs. Unfortunately firstboot may get stuck if the X Window System is not working on your system. You have to get around the firstboot process to configure X again and continue with the normal course of events that Fedora planned for you. Here's how you can stop firstboot and configure X to tide you over this problem:

1. Press Ctrl-Alt-F1 to get back to the text-mode boot screen. You see the text display with the boot messages that stop at a line displaying information about firstboot.
2. Press Ctrl-Alt-Del to reboot the PC. The PC starts to boot, and you get to a screen where the GRUB boot loader prompts you to press Enter to boot Linux. (If you have a GRUB password, you have to enter that password before you get to this point.)
3. Press *a* to add an option for use by the Linux kernel. The GRUB boot loader then displays a command line for the Linux kernel and prompts you to add what you want.
4. Type a space followed by the word **single** and then press Enter. The Linux kernel boots in a single-user mode and displays a prompt that looks like the following:

```
sh-3.00#
```

   Now you can configure X.

X uses a configuration file, called `xorg.conf`, to figure out the type of display card, monitor, and the kind of screen resolution you want. The anaconda installer prepares the configuration file, but sometimes the configuration is not correct.

To quickly create a working `xorg.conf` file, follow these steps:

1. Type the following command:

```
/usr/X11R6/bin/X -configure
```

   This causes the X server to run and create a configuration file. The screen goes blank and then the X server exits after displaying some messages. The last line of the message says the following:

```
To test the server, run 'X -config //xorg.conf.new'
```

2. Use a text editor such as vi to edit the `//xorg.conf.new` file and change `/dev/mouse` to `/dev/input/mice` (see Chapter 11 for more information on the vi text editor).
3. Try the new configuration file by typing the command:

```
/usr/X11R6/bin/X -config //xorg.conf.new
```

   If you see a blank screen with an X-shaped cursor, the configuration file is probably working fine.
4. Press Ctrl-Alt-Backspace to kill the X server.
5. Copy the new `xorg.conf` file to the `/etc/X11` directory with the following command:

```
cp //xorg.conf.new /etc/X11/xorg.conf
```

That should provide a working X configuration file. Now, you can reboot the PC by pressing Ctrl-Alt-Del or typing **reboot**.

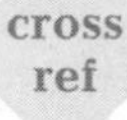

The `xorg.conf` file created by using the `-configure` option of the X server is not displayed at the best resolution possible. To fine-tune the configuration file, you should turn to Chapter 3, where you can learn more about configuring the X Window System and editing the `/etc/X11/xorg.conf` file further.

Resolving Other Installation Problems

I am sure I have not covered all the installation problems that at least someone out there may encounter. There are so many different combinations of components in Intel x86 PCs that there is bound to be some combination of hardware that the installation program cannot handle. This section lists a few known problems. For others, I advise you to go to Google Groups (`http://groups.google.com`) and type in some of the symptoms of the trouble. Assuming that others are running into similar problems, you should get some indication of how to troubleshoot out of your particular predicament.

PC Reboots When You Press Enter at boot prompt

On some PCs when you press Enter at the boot prompt, the initial Linux kernel loads and immediately reboots the PC. This could be due to a bad implementation of Advanced Configuration and Power Interface (ACPI) in the PC's BIOS. To bypass the problem, type **linux acpi=off** at the boot prompt to turn off ACPI. If that does not work, consult Table 2-3 for other boot options that you might want to try.

Problem Installing on Some Sony VAIO Laptops

On some Sony VAIO laptops the Fedora Core installation hangs. If this happens, press Ctrl-Alt-Del to restart the installation. At the boot prompt, type **linux pci=off ide1=0x180,0x386**. (If you need other options such as `acpi=off`, append these options to the same line.) That should enable the installation to continue. If any devices are not detected during installation because of these options, those devices will be detected the next time you reboot the Sony VAIO laptop.

Understanding the Fatal Signal 11 Error

Some people get a fatal signal 11 error during installation. This usually happens past the initial boot screen as the anaconda installer is starting its GUI or text interface. The most likely cause of a signal 11 error during installation is a hardware error related to memory or the cache associated with the CPU (microprocessor).

Signal 11, also known as SIGSEGV (short for Segment Violation Signal), can occur in other Linux applications. A segment violation occurs when a process tries to access a memory location that it is not supposed to access. The operating system catches the problem before it happens and stops the offending process by sending it a signal 11. When it happens during installation, it means that anaconda had an error accessing memory, and the most likely reason is some hardware problem.

A commonly suggested cure for the signal 11 problem is to turn off CPU cache in the BIOS. To do this, you have to enter setup as the PC boots (by pressing a function key such as F2) and then turn off CPU cache from the BIOS setup menus.

continues

continued

If the problem is due to a hardware error in memory (in other words, the result of bad memory chips), you could try swapping the memory modules around in their slots. You may also consider replacing an existing memory module with another memory module, if you have it handy.

You can read more about the signal 11 problem at `www.bitwizard.nl/sig11/`.

Using Boot Commands during Installation

When you boot the PC for installation, either from a boot disk or directly from the DVD-ROM, you get a text screen with the `boot:` prompt. Typically, you press Enter at that prompt or do nothing and the installation begins shortly. You can, however, type quite a variety of commands at the `boot:` prompt. The commands can provide options to the Linux kernel that takes care of the installation and controls various aspects of the installation such as whether the kernel should probe for hardware or whether to use GUI screens for the installation. Some of these commands can be helpful in bypassing problems that you may encounter during installation.

To use these boot commands, you type the word **linux** followed by the boot command. For example, to perform text-mode installation and tell the kernel that your PC has 256MB of memory, you'd type the following at the boot prompt:

```
linux text mem=256M
```

Consult Table 2-3 for a brief summary of the boot commands.

insider insight A few of the boot commands do not require you to type `linux` first. You can simply type text to enter `text-mode` installation.

Table 2-3: Linux Boot Commands for the Fedora Core Linux Installation

Command	*Description*
`allowcddma`	Enables direct memory access (DMA) for CD/DVD drive.
`askmethod`	Prompts you for other installation methods such as installing over the network using NFS, FTP, or HTTP.
`acpi=off`	Turns off support for ACPI (Advanced Configuration and Power Interface), which can sometimes cause problems.
`apic`	Works around a bug commonly encountered in the Intel 440GX chipset BIOS and should be executed only with the installation program kernel.
`apm=allow_ints`	Changes how the laptop can be suspended.
`apm=off`	Disables APM (Advanced Power Management) in case a BIOS has a buggy APM.

Command	Description
apm=power_off	Causes Linux to power off the system (useful for symmetric multiprocessing — SMP — systems that do not shut down by default).
apm=realmode_power_off	Causes APM to work the way it does in Windows 95 instead of how it works in Windows NT (useful if BIOS crashes when trying to shut down the machine).
dd	Prompts for a driver disk during the installation.
dns=IPaddress1, IPaddress2	Causes installer to use the specified comma-separated list of DNS servers during network installation.
display=IP_address:0	Causes installer GUI to appear on the remote system identified by the IP address (make sure that you run the command xhost +*hostname* on the remote system where *hostname* is the host where you are running the installer).
driverdisk	Performs the same function as the dd command.
expert	Enables you to partition removable media and prompts for a driver disk.
gateway=IP Address	Causes installer to use the specified IP address as the gateway for the local area network (used during network installations).
graphical	Forces a GUI install (needed if you want GUI when installing over a network using FTP or HTTP).
ide=nodma	Disables DMA (direct memory access) on all IDE devices and can be useful when you are having IDE-related problems.
ip=dhcp or IP address	Specifies IP address to use for network interface (during network installation); if set to dhcp, IP address is obtained from DHCP server.
isa	Prompts you for the configuration of older ISA — the older IBM-compatible PC architecture — devices.
ks	Configures the Ethernet card using DHCP and then runs a kickstart installation by using a kickstart file from an NFS server identified by the bootServer parameters provided by the DHCP server.
ks=kickstartfile	Runs a kickstart installation by using the kickstart file specified by kickstartfile (see the "Using kickstart Installation" section for the format of the kickstartfile specification).
lowres	Forces the installer GUI to run at a lower resolution (640 × 480).
mediacheck	Prompts you if you want to check the integrity of the DVD image (also called ISO image). This is done by computing the MD5 checksum and comparing that with the official Fedora provided value. It can take a few minutes to check a DVD-ROM.

(continued)

Table 2-3 *(continued)*

Command	***Description***
`mem=`*`xxx`*`M`	Overrides the amount of memory the kernel detects in the PC (some older machines could detect only 16MB of memory, and on some new machines the video card may use a portion of the main memory). Replace *`xxx`* with the number representing the megabytes of memory in your PC.
`method=cdrom` or URL	Specifies the location of the packages (can be `cdrom` for CD/DVD media or `http://`, `ftp://`, `nfs://`, or `hd://` URL where `hd://` URL refers to a disk partition).
`nmi_watchdog=1`	Enables the built-in kernel deadlock detector that makes use of Non Maskable Interrupt (NMI).
`noapic`	Prevents the kernel from using the Advanced Programmable Interrupt Controller (APIC) chip (use this on motherboards known to have a bad APIC).
`nofirewire`	Does not load support for FireWire.
`noht`	Disables hyperthreading (a feature available in some SMP systems).
`nomce`	Disables self-diagnosis checks performed on the CPU by using Machine Check Exception (MCE). On some machines these checks are performed too often and need to be disabled.
`nomount`	Does not automatically mount any installed Linux partitions in rescue mode.
`noparport`	Does not load the modules needed to support parallel port.
`nopass`	Does not pass the keyboard and mouse information to stage 2 of the installation program .
`nopcmcia`	Ignores any PCMCIA controllers in the system.
`noprobe`	Disables automatic hardware detection and instead prompts the user for information about SCSI and network hardware installed on the PC. You can pass parameters to modules by using this approach.
`noshell`	Disables shell access on virtual console 2 (the one you get by pressing Ctrl-Alt-F2) during installation.
`nousb`	Disables the loading of USB support during the installation (may be useful if the installation program hangs early in the process).
`nousbstorage`	Disables the loading of the usbstorage module in the installation program's loader. It may help with device ordering on SCSI systems.
`pci=biosirq`	Causes the kernel to use BIOS settings to route interrupt requests (IRQs).
`pci=noacpi`	Causes the kernel to not use ACPI to route interrupt requests.
`reboot=b`	Changes the way the kernel tries to reboot the PC so that it can reboot even if the kernel hangs during system shutdown.

Command	*Description*
`rescue`	Starts the kernel in rescue mode where you get a shell prompt and can try to fix problems.
`resolution=`*`HHH`*`x`*`VVV`*	Causes the installer GUI to run in the specified video mode (replace *HHH* and *VVV* with standard resolution numbers, such as 640 × 480, 800 × 600, 1024 × 768, and so on).
`selinux=0`	Disables the SELinux kernel extensions.
`serial`	Turns on serial console support during installation.
`skipddc`	Skips the Display Data Channel (DDC) probe of monitors (useful if the probing causes problems).
`text`	Runs the installation program in text mode.
`updates`	Prompts for a floppy disk containing updates (bug fixes).
`vnc`	Starts a VNC (Virtual Network Computing) server so that you can control the GUI installer from another networked system that runs a VNC client.

Learning Other Installation Methods

The Red Hat installer anaconda (used to install Fedora) supports a number of installation methods. The CD/DVD-ROM method is one that you see described in this chapter. The other methods involve installing from different types of servers or even a hard disk partition that holds an exact copy of the Linux CD/DVD-ROMs. These images of a CD/DVD-ROM are known as ISO images.

Here are all the installation methods that anaconda supports:

- **CD-ROM:** This method installs Linux from CD/DVD-ROMs. You can boot from the CD/DVD-ROM. This chapter describes the CD/DVD-ROM installation method in detail.
- **Hard Drive:** If you have copied the Linux ISO images to a local hard drive with either FAT or Linux (ext2 or ext3) file systems, you can use this method to install Linux. You have to boot from a boot CD and then identify the hard drive partition and the directory that contains the ISO images.
- **NFS:** This method installs from ISO images made available on a Network File System (NFS) server on the network. You have to boot the PC with a boot CD and then specify the NFS server and the directory as the source of the ISO images.
- **FTP:** This method installs Linux from ISO images located on an FTP server. You have to boot from a boot CD and then specify the FTP server and the directory that contains the ISO images.
- **HTTP:** In this method, the Linux ISO images are on a Web server and anaconda gets them by using HTTP (the Web server protocol). You have to boot the PC using a boot CD and then identify the Web server directory where the ISO images are located.

Using kickstart Installation

If you need to install Linux on many PCs, you need a way to automate the process so that you do not have to respond to the GUI installer prompts for each PC. kickstart is the answer to this need. It's an automated installation method that enables you to install Linux with very little interaction from you.

The idea behind kickstart is to create a text file with all the installation options and then "kick start" the installation by booting and then providing the kickstart file as input.

Starting a kickstart Installation

Setting aside for the moment how to prepare a kickstart file, I want to briefly explain how you can start a kickstart installation. The common use of kickstart installation is to place the Linux ISO images on a server on the network and then perform kickstart installations at all the PCs. Let's assume that you have the ISO images on a Web server and you want to install over the network using the HTTP installation method, but do this under the control of a kickstart file. Here's what you would do:

1. Prepare a boot CD with the `boot.iso` file (located in the `images` directory of the first Fedora Core CD-ROM).
2. Place the ISO images and the kickstart file on the Web server and make note of the directory where the kickstart file is located.
3. Boot the PC using the boot CD. At the boot prompt, type the following command:

   ```
   linux ks=http://<server>/<pathname of kickstart file>
   ```

   where `<server>` stands for the name of the Web server and `<pathname of kickstart file>` is the complete pathname of the kickstart file. Thus, if the server is `mycompany.com` and the kickstart file's pathname is `/fedora4/ks.cfg`, you type the following at the boot prompt:

   ```
   linux ks=http://mycompany.com/fedora4/ks.cfg
   ```

After that the installation should proceed under the control of the kickstart file.

If the kickstart file is on an NFS server, all you have to do is specify the kickstart file appropriately. The kickstart syntax for NFS is

```
linux ks=nfs:<server>:/<path>
```

Thus, if the NFS server is `someserver.com` and the location of the kickstart file is `/somedir/ks.cfg`, you type the following command at the boot prompt:

```
linux ks=nfs:someserver.com:/somedir/ks.cfg
```

You can also place a kickstart file named `ks.cfg` on a floppy (type **mcopy ks.cfg a:** to copy the file to a floppy), and then install it with the following command at the boot prompt:

```
linux ks=floppy
```

You can also use a very simple form of the kickstart installation command that looks like this:

```
linux ks
```

In this case, the installation program configures the Ethernet card using DHCP and then uses the `bootServer` item from the DHCP response as the NFS server from which to get the kickstart file. The name and location of the kickstart file depends on the bootfile specified by DHCP. If the DHCP server does not specify a bootfile, the installer tries to read the file `/kickstart/A.B.C.D-kickstart`, where `A.B.C.D` is the numeric IP address of the PC on which you are installing Linux.

Preparing the kickstart File

One way to get a kickstart file is to perform the installation on one PC. The Fedora Core installer saves the installation options in the `/root/anaconda-ks.cfg` kickstart file. You can then use this kickstart file to repeat the installation on other PCs. You can also use this kickstart file as a starting point and edit it to create a custom kickstart file suitable for your situation.

Here's a typical anaconda-generated kickstart file:

```
# Kickstart file automatically generated by anaconda.

install
cdrom
lang en_US.UTF-8
langsupport --default=en_US.UTF-8 en_US.UTF-8
keyboard us
xconfig --card "nVidia GeForce 2 Go" --videoram 16384 --hsync 31.5-37.9 --
vsync
50-70 --resolution 800x600 --depth 16 --startxonboot  --defaultdesktop
gnome
network --device eth0 --bootproto dhcp
rootpw --iscrypted $1$w6sf9IrK$V3kGEnTVmuxtohTST49UD/
firewall --enabled
selinux --enforcing
authconfig --enableshadow --enablemd5
timezone America/New_York
bootloader --location=mbr --driveorder=hda --append="rhgb quiet"
... other kickstart options deleted ...

%packages
@ office
@ engineering-and-scientific
@ mysql
@ editors
@ system-tools
@ gnome-software-development
@ text-internet
@ x-software-development
@ legacy-network-server
@ gnome-desktop
@ dialup
.... other package groups...
@ dns-server
@ development-tools
```

```
@ sound-and-video
@ graphical-internet
... other individual packages...
pcmcia-cs
e2fsprogs
lvm2
kernel-devel
grub
kernel

%post
```

As you can see, the file starts with a long list of kickstart options that essentially mirrors the installation steps that you normally go through when you install Linux interactively. After the kickstart options comes a `%packages` section that lists the package groups and individual packages to install. Finally, you see a `%post` section that contains any commands to execute after the installation is complete. For example, you could add commands in the `%post` section to add one or more user accounts.

As this example illustrates, a kickstart file has the following sections, in the exact order shown:

- **Command section:** This section lists all the kickstart options that control various aspects of the installation.
- **%packages section:** This section lists the package groups (with names that have an @ prefix) and individual package names.
- **%pre and %post sections:** These two sections are optional, and they can appear in any order.

The command section of the kickstart file contains, at minimum, all the required options shown in Table 2-4. That table shows all the kickstart options and briefly describes each one.

The package group names listed in the `%package` section are defined in the `Fedora/base/comps.xml` file on the Fedora Core DVD-ROM. The `comps.xml` file uses XML to define the package database. Each package group contains one or more packages. The `comps.xml` file also defines the dependencies for each package — the other packages that a package needs in order to work properly.

The `%pre` section includes commands to be executed immediately after the kickstart file has been processed but before any installation steps are performed. In the `%pre` section, you can place a shell script to perform any preparatory tasks that have to be performed before installation can begin.

The `%post` section contains the commands to be executed after installation is complete. In this section, you can place commands to turn services on or off and add user accounts.

If you have a working Fedora Core system-with a GUI desktop, you can use a GUI tool, called Kickstart Configurator, to create the kickstart file. To use the tool, select Applications ➪ System Tools ➪ Kickstart. You can also start the tool by typing the `system-config-kickstart` **command in a terminal window.**

Table 2-4: kickstart Options

Option	*Optional (O) or Required (R)*	*Description*
`autostep`	O	Similar to `interactive`, except that it goes to the next screen for you. It is used mostly for debugging.
`auth` or `authconfig`	R	Specifies the authentication options. Use one or more of the following arguments after this option: `--enablemd5` (use MD5 encryption for passwords) `--enablenis` (turns on NIS support) `--nisdomain=<nisdomain>` (specifies NIS domain name) `--nisserver=<nisserver>` (specifies the NIS server name) `--useshadow` or `--enableshadow` (turns on shadow passwords) `--enableldap` (turns on LDAP support in `/etc/nsswitch.conf` and requires the nss_ldap package) `--enableldapauth` (enables LDAP as an authentication method) `--ldapserver=<LDAPserver>` (specifies the LDAP server name) `--ldapbasedn=<LDAP-DN>` (specifies LDAP distinguished name) `--enableldaptls` (uses transport layer security during LDAP lookups) `--enablekrb5` (turns on Kerberos 5 for authenticating users) `--krb5realm=<KRBrealm>` (specifies the Kerberos realm) `--krb5kdc=<KDCserver>` (specifies the Key Distribution Center) `--krb5adminserver=<Kadminserver>` (specifies the server running kadmind) `--enablehesiod` (enables Hesiod support for looking up user information) `--hesiodlhs` (specifies the Hesiod left-hand side) `--hesiodrhs` (specifies the Hesiod right-hand side) `--enablesmbauth` (enables authentication of users by an SMB server) `--smbservers=<SMBservers>` (specifies the servers to use for SMB authentication) `--smbworkgroup=<WkGrpName>` (specifies the workgroup name) `--enablecache` (enables the nscd service that caches user information)

(continued)

Table 2-4 *(continued)*

Option	*Optional (O) or Required (R)*	*Description*
bootloader	R	Specifies where the boot loader is installed and, optionally, which boot loader to install. Use one or more of the following arguments after this option: --append=<kernel-params> (specifies kernel parameters) --location=[mbr|partition|none] (tells where to write the boot loader: one of mbr, part, or none) --password=<GRUB-passwd> (specifies the GRUB password) --md5pass=<encrypted-GRUB-pass> (encrypted GRUB password) --useLilo (forces installation of LILO instead of GRUB) --lba32 (when using LILO, force use of LBA32 mode of hard disk access) --upgrade (upgrades existing boot loader configuration)
clearpart	O	Removes partitions from the system before creating new partitions. Use one or more of following arguments after this option: --linux (erases all existing Linux partitions) --all (erases all existing partitions) --drives=<drivenames> (specifies which drives to clear partitions from) --initlabel (initializes the disk label to the default for PC's architecture)
device <type> <moduleName> --opts=<options>	O	Instructs installer to load extra device driver modules. Use the following arguments: <type> (either scsi or eth — for a SCSI or Ethernet card) <moduleName> (the name of the driver module) --opts=<options> (options for the module, these depend on the driver)
deviceprobe	O	Probes the PCI bus for devices and loads modules for all the devices found (assuming that a module is available for the device).
driverdisk	O	Instructs the installer to look for driver disks in the specified disk partition. Use the following arguments: <partition> (disk partition containing the driver disk contents) --type=<fstype> (optional argument that specifies file system type: vfat, ext2, or ext3)

Option	*Optional (O) or Required (R)*	*Description*
`firewall`	O	Configures the firewall based on the arguments: `<securitylevel>` (one of `--high`, `--medium`, or `--disabled`) `--trust=<device>` (trusted network device such as `eth0`) `<incoming>` (one of `--dhcp`, `--ssh`, `--telnet`, `--smtp`, `--http`, `--ftp`) `--port=<portnum:protocol>` (ports allowed through firewall)
`install`	O	Indicates that you want to do a fresh install. Specify the install method with one of the following arguments: `cdrom` (installs from the first CD-ROM drive) `harddrive --partition=<part> --dir=<dirname>` (installs from a directory on hard disk partition) `nfs --server=<servername> --dir=<dir>` (installs from a directory on the NFS server) `url --url http://<server>/<dir>` (installs from a Web server) `url --url ftp://<username>:<password>@<server>/<dir>` (installs from a FTP server)
`interactive`	O	Allows you to view and modify options as kickstart install progresses.
`keyboard`	R	Sets the keyboard type. Here is the list of available keyboards on i386, Itanium, and Alpha machines: `be-latin1`, `be-latin2`, `bg`, `br-abnt2`, `cf`, `cz-lat2`, `cz-us-qwertz`, `de`, `de-latin1`, `de-latin1-nodeadkeys`, `dk`, `dk-latin1`, `dvorak`, `es`, `et`, `fi`, `i-latin1`, `fr`, `fr-latin0`, `fr-latin1`, `fr-pc`, `fr_CH`, `fr_CH-latin1`, `gr`, `hu`, `hu101`, `is-latin1`, `it`, `it-ibm`, `it2`, `jp106`, `no`, `no-latin1`, `pl`, `pt-latin1`, `ro`, `ru`, `ru-cp1251`, `ru-ms`, `ru1`, `ru2`, `ru_win`, `se-latin1`, `sg`, `sg-latin1`, `sk-qwerty`, `slovene`, `speakup`, `speakup-lt`, `trq`, `ua`, `uk`, `us`.
`lang`	R	Sets the language to use during installation. Valid language codes are `cs_CZ`, `da_DK`, `en_US`, `fr_FR`, `de_DE`, `is_IS`, `it_IT`, `ja_JP.eucJP`, `ko_KR.eucKR`, `no_NO`, `pt_PT`, `ru_RU.koi8r`, `sl_SI`, `es_ES`, `sv_SE`, `uk_UA`, `zh_CN.GB18030`, `zh_TW.Big5` .

(continued)

Table 2-4 *(continued)*

Option	*Optional (O) or Required (R)*	*Description*
langsupport	R	Sets the languages to install on the system. Use the same language codes as the ones for the lang option. If you install more than one language, indicate the default with the following argument: --default=<lang> (sets default language)
logvol	O	Creates a logical volume for Logical Volume Management (LVM). Provide the following arguments: <mountpoint> (name of directory where volume is mounted) --vgname=<groupname> (name of volume group) --size=<size> (size in megabytes) --name=<volname> (name of logical volume)
mouse	O	Specifies the mouse type and configures it. Use the following arguments: --device=<devname> (name of mouse device such as psaux or ttyS0) --emulthree (enable emulation of a three-button mouse) <mousetype> (specifies mouse type such as genericps/2 or generic3ps/2)
network	O	Configures the local area network information. For installations over network, the installation uses the first Ethernet card (eth0) and configures it dynamically using DHCP. Use the following arguments to configure your network: --bootproto=<protocol> (one of dhcp, bootp, or static) --device=<netdevice> (Ethernet device name such as eth0 or eth1) --ip=<IPaddress> (the IP address for static addressing) --netmask=<Netmask> (for static addressing) --gateway=<gateway_IP> (default gateway IP address) --nameserver=<nameserver_IP> (primacy nameserver's IP address) --nodns (do not configure any DNS server) --hostname=<hostname> (hostname of the system)

Option	*Optional (O) or Required (R)*	*Description*
part or partition	R	Creates a partition on the hard drive. Use the following arguments to specify details: <mntpoint> (the directory where the partition is mounted or the keyword swap for swap partition) --recommended (use with swap to size the partition automatically) raid.<id> (to use partition in a software RAID device) pv.<id> (to use partition in a logical volume) --size=<megabytes> (size in megabytes) --grow (causes partition to grow up to available space) --maxsize=<maxMB> (maximum size in megabytes) --noformat (do not format partition) --onpart=<partname> (puts partition on already existing device) --usepart=<partname> (puts partition on already existing device) --ondisk=<diskname> (creates partition on the specified disk) --ondrive=<diskname> (creates partition on the specified disk) --asprimary (creates a primary partition) --bytes-per-inode=<numbytes> (number of bytes per inode on the filesystem) --fstype=<filesystem> (name of file system — one of ext2, ext3, swap, or vfat) --start=<startCylinder> (starting cylinder of partition) --end=<endCylinder> (ending cylinder of partition) --badblocks (checks partition for bad blocks)
raid	O	Creates a software RAID device. Use the following arguments: <mntpoint> (the directory where the RAID device is mounted) --level=<RAID_level> (the RAID level to use — 0, 1, or 5) --device=<devname> (name of RAID device such as md0 or md1) --spares=<number> (number of spare drives allocated for the RAID array) --fstype=<filesystemType> (filesystem type — one of ext2, ext3, swap, or vfat) --noformat (does not format the RAID array)

(continued)

Table 2-4 *(continued)*

Option	*Optional (O) or Required (R)*	*Description*
reboot	O	Reboots after the installation is complete.
rootpw	R	Sets the system's root password. Use the following arguments: --iscrypted (password is already encrypted) <password> (the encrypted root password)
selinux	R	Specifies the SELinux setting. Use the following arguments: --enforcing (mandatory access control is enforced) --warning (only warnings generated) --disabled (SELinux access control turned off)
skipx	O	Skips configuration of X Window System.
text	O	Performs the installation in text mode (instead of the default graphical mode).
timezone	R	Sets the system time zone. Use the following arguments: --utc (indicates that hardware clock is set to UTC — Greenwich Mean Time) <timezone> (the time zone name such as America/New_York or EST5EDT)
upgrade	O	Upgrades an existing system rather than installing a fresh system.
xconfig	O	Configures the X Window System. Use the following arguments: --noprobe (does not probe the monitor) --card=<videcardName> (name of video card from list in /usr/share/hwdata/Cards) --videoram=<kilobytes> (amount of video RAM in kilobytes) --monitor=<monitorName> (name of monitor from list in /usr/share/hwdata/MonitorsDB) --hsync=<HSyncRange> (range of horizontal synchronization frequencies in kHz such as --hsync 31.5-69.0) --vsync=<VSyncRange> (range of vertical synchronization frequencies in Hz such as --vsync 55-120) --defaultdesktop=<DesktopName> (GNOME or KDE) --startxonboot (provides a graphical login screen) --resolution=<*HHH*x*VVV*> (default resolution in terms horizontal and vertical pixels such as 640 × 480 or 1024 × 768) --depth=<defaultDepthBits> (default color depth — one of 8, 16, 24, or 32)

Option	Optional (O) or Required (R)	Description
`volgroup`	O	Creates a Logical Volume Management (LVM) group. Use the following arguments: `<name>` (name of logical volume group) `<partition>` (partition to use)
`zerombr`	O	Initializes any invalid partition tables found on disks. Use the following argument: `yes` (destroy disks with invalid partition tables)
`%include`	O	Includes the content of another file into this kickstart file. Use the following arguments: `<pathname>` (the file to include)

Installing Linux on a Laptop

Laptops or so-called notebook computers are more integrated than desktops are; a laptop's video card, monitor, and hard disk are all built into a compact package. In other words, you cannot easily mix and match components with laptops as you do with desktop systems, so you have to make sure that Linux supports all components of your laptop system.

Laptops typically have a PCMCIA adapter where you can plug in many peripherals such as a wireless Ethernet network card or a modem. When installing Linux on a laptop with a CD/DVD-ROM drive, follow the same installation steps as the ones described earlier in this chapter.

Most laptops with Intel Celeron or better processors should be able to run plain Linux without any problems. If you want to install X.Org X11, however, you may have some trouble if X.Org X11 does not support the video card (on a laptop, video circuitry is built into the motherboard) and the pointing device. You can use the VESA driver to get X working on most laptops even if X.Org X11 doesn't natively support the laptop's graphics chipset. Also, nowadays, most laptop pointing devices can at least emulate a standard PS/2 Mouse, so all pointing devices should work with XFree86.

This section barely touches upon the subject of how to run Linux on laptops. Installing Linux on a specific laptop model is a unique experience, and there are simply too many different models to describe here. As users install and run Linux on a variety of laptops, the user community's cumulative experience of Linux on laptops continues to grow. Much of this information is summarized and made available on the Web. For detailed information on how to install and run Linux on laptops, point your Web browser to the Linux on Laptops Home Page: `www.linux-on-laptops.com/`. Another good resource for information on running Linux on laptops is the TuxMobil website at `http://tuxmobil.org/`.

This page includes links to many more Web pages, each documenting the details of how to install and run Linux on a specific laptop model. In particular, you will find out if you have to do anything special to get Linux and X running on your laptop.

PCMCIA

Laptops typically include the PCMCIA (commonly referred to as PC Card) interface through which you can connect many different peripheral devices to the laptop. As this chapter explained earlier, the version of Linux on the companion DVD-ROM supports PCMCIA. The current PCMCIA drivers support most common PCMCIA controllers, including Intel, Cirrus, Vadem, VLSI, Ricoh, and Databook chipsets. See Appendix F for a discussion of specific PC Cards that Linux supports.

Power Management

Another laptop-specific feature is power management, which refers to the capability of a laptop to suspend its activities to conserve battery power. There are two standards for power management — Advanced Power Management (APM) and Advanced Configuration and Power Interface (ACPI). ACPI is a newer standard and it supersedes APM.

Laptops that have APM capability in the BIOS can suspend and resume power-consuming components (such as the display and hard drive), as well as provide information on battery life. ACPI not only provides these power-management features, it can also provide hardware information. Unfortunately, many vendors ship their systems with defective ACPI implementations. On some systems, Linux cannot even boot with ACPI enabled.

The version of Linux on the companion DVD-ROM supports both APM and ACPI, but you can enable only one or the other. ACPI is enabled by default, but if you are having problems with ACPI turned on, you should turn it off with the boot option `acpi=off`.

Sound on Laptops

Many high-end laptops come with built-in sound. Using the sound capabilities under Linux is a straightforward process, provided that you can figure out what type of sound card your laptop has. Chapter 5 covers sound cards in detail.

Red Hat's kudzu program — used in Fedora to probe and detect hardware — should detect your laptop's sound card and set it up correctly. If your sound card is not detected, you can still get it to work by locating the appropriate driver module with the `modprobe` command. To determine the driver, you would need information about the sound card. If sound support is not automatically set up, you should check your laptop's documentation for clues about the make and model of the sound card before you set up sound support.

The bottom line is that you can set up Linux to support sound on a laptop the same way you can for a desktop PC.

X on Laptops

Users have reported success in running Linux together with X.Org X11 on many Celeron and Pentium laptops. Nowadays, laptops support high-resolution LCD screens with capabilities on par with those of desktop PCs. You can configure X to work as long as the laptop's video chipsets are supported by X.org X11.

Most laptops use one of the following types of video chipsets:

- ATI Mobility Radeon 9000/9200/9700/9800, Mobility FireGL 7800/9000
- Intel i810, i830M
- NVidia GeForce2 Go, GeForce4 Go, GeForce Go 6800, GEForceFX Go 5200/5600/5650/5700

- Chips & Technology 655xx series chipset
- NeoMagic NM20xx and NM21xx chipsets

X.Org X11 supports these chipsets. You can learn more about the details of X configuration in Chapter 3.

Summary

Linux is a UNIX-like operating system for Intel 80x86, Pentium, and compatible systems. The DVD-ROM that accompanies this book includes the latest version of the popular Fedora Core Linux distribution. This chapter guides you through the process of installing Fedora Core on your PC. The next chapter turns to another configuration task — how to configure and run the X Window System on your Linux PC. You need X because with it you can have a GUI for Linux.

By reading this chapter, you learned the following:

- Information you should gather about your PC before installing Linux
- The overall process of installing Linux (including the X Window System, GNOME, and KDE) from the companion CD-ROMs
- Steps you may need to perform in Microsoft Windows before installing Linux
- How to boot Linux initially, partition the hard disk, and load the various software packages from the companion DVD-ROM by using the anaconda Linux installer
- How to troubleshoot some common installation problems
- How to perform a kickstart installation
- How to install Linux on laptops

X Window System Setup

Secrets in This Chapter

If you have used Apple Mac OS or Microsoft Windows, you are familiar with the convenience of a graphical user interface (GUI, pronounced gooey). In Linux, the GUI is not an integral part of the operating system. Instead, Linux distributions, such as Fedora Core, typically provide GNOME and KDE as the GUI. GNOME and KDE are, in turn, built on a windowing system called the X Window System, or X. Fedora Core includes a version of X called X.Org X11, which is designed to work with your PC's video card and monitor. The video card and monitor you use do not matter much if you work only with text. But to install X.Org X11, you need detailed information about your video card and monitor.

The companion DVD-ROM contains the X.Org X11 software, which you might have installed on your hard disk during the installation process shown in Chapter 2. At that time, the installation program would have detected your video card and monitor, and configured X.Org X11. This chapter describes the attributes of video cards and monitors and explains the X Window System. It also shows you how to use the system-config-display GUI utility to configure X in case the installer fails to configure X.Org X11 properly on your PC.

Understanding Video Cards and Monitors

The video card or graphics adapter contains the electronics that control the monitor. On most systems, the video card takes the form of a circuit board that plugs into a slot on your PC's motherboard. On many new systems, however, the motherboard itself contains the necessary graphics chipsets.

Raster-Scan Display

All video cards operate on the same principle: They store an image in video memory (also called video RAM or VRAM for short) and generate the appropriate signals to display the image on the monitor's screen.

The monitor is the physical device that contains the display screen where the graphic and text output appears. The display screen is typically a phosphor-coated glass tube on which an electron beam traces the output image. On laptop computers, the display screen is a *liquid crystal display* (LCD). More expensive laptops use active-matrix LCD-display screens.

The image that appears on the monitor is made up of many horizontal lines, known as raster lines. An electron beam in the monitor generates the *raster lines* by sweeping back and forth on a phosphor-coated screen, as illustrated in Figure 3-1.

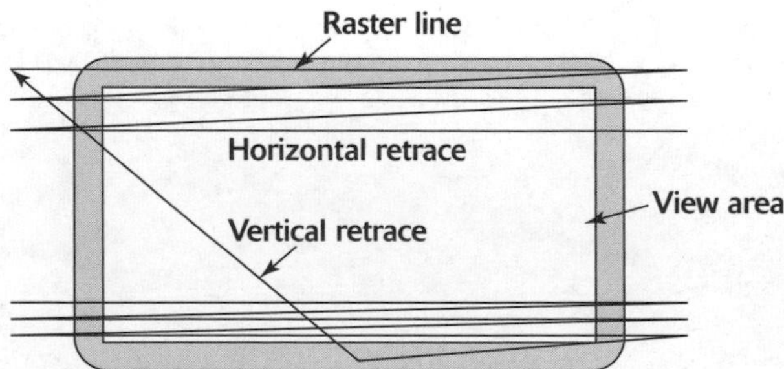

Figure 3-1: A Typical Raster-Scan Display.

The phosphor on the screen glows in proportion to the intensity of the electron beam. The glowing dot on the screen represents a picture element, or pixel. Thus, a line of the image is generated by controlling the intensity of the beam as it scans across the screen. The phosphor fades in a while, but if the lines are redrawn repeatedly, our persistence of vision creates an illusion of a steady image. Most PC monitors redraw an entire screen full of raster lines 50 to 90 times per second.

As Figure 3-1 shows, the electron beam scans an area larger than the actual view area of the display screen, but the electron beam is active only when the beam is in the viewable area. Also, after reaching the end of a line, the beam has to return to the start of the next raster line. This part of the beam's motion is known as the *horizontal retrace*. Similarly, when the beam reaches the bottom of the screen, it has to return to the first line to start another cycle of drawing. This period is known as the *vertical retrace*. The beam's intensity is reduced (the beam is blanked) during horizontal and vertical retrace so that those lines do not appear on the screen.

The video card generates the signals necessary to sweep the electron beam across the display and refresh the display at a rapid rate. There are two types of refreshing: *interlaced* and *noninterlaced*. In an interlaced refresh, each screen is drawn in two steps. First, the electron beam sweeps across the screen, drawing all the odd-numbered raster lines. Then the electron beam goes back to the beginning of the screen and draws all the even-numbered raster lines. Broadcast television uses interlaced refreshing. A noninterlaced refresh involves drawing all raster lines in a single step. Most video cards refresh the screen 60 times or more per second and use a noninterlaced refresh.

Color Display

Color display screens represent any color with a combination of the three primary colors: red (R), green (G), and blue (B). Most color displays use three electron beams, one for each primary color.

The screen in a color display has a repeated triangular pattern of red, green, and blue phosphor dots. Each phosphor dot glows in its color when the electron beam impinges on it. A perforated metal screen, known as a shadow mask, ensures that each electron beam strikes the phosphor of the intended color. The video card varies the intensity of the red, green, and blue electron beams, thereby displaying many colors.

Color Palette and Resolution

Older video cards used a palette of 256 colors, and each pixel's color was stored in an 8-bit value. The actual color (in terms of R, G, B components) that corresponds to a pixel's 8-bit value was determined by consulting a color lookup table or colormap.

Today's high-performance video cards allow three bytes of storage per pixel, so that each pixel's value can directly specify the RGB components that determine that pixel's color. These so-called 24-bit video cards provide true color display but require more video memory to store the entire image.

The resolution of a display screen is expressed in terms of the number of visible dots (pixels) across a raster line and the total raster lines. A common resolution is 640 dots across by 480 lines vertically, which is commonly expressed as 640 × 480. Other common screen resolutions are 800 × 600, 1,024 × 768, and 1,280 × 1,024.

Video RAM

The video card stores the contents of the pixels in random-access memory (RAM), known as video RAM. The number of colors and the display resolution supported by a video card depends on the amount of video RAM. To store the information content of a 256-color 1,024 × 768 display screen, for example, the video card needs 1,024 × 768, or 786,432 bytes of video RAM (because an 8-bit pixel value represents 256 colors and 1 byte = 8 bits). On the other hand, to display 24-bit color at 1,024 × 768 resolution, the video card needs three times as much video RAM: 3 × 786,432 = 2,359,296 bytes, or about 2.3MB of video RAM (because 24 bit = 3 bytes).

Nowadays typical video cards have 16, 32, 64, 128, or even 256MB of video RAM. A video card with 4MB of video RAM can comfortably handle a million-color, 1,024 × 768-resolution display, but video cards need lots of extra RAM for storing other data needed to render realistic three-dimensional graphics and video at a good frame rate (the *frame rate* is the number of times per second the video card can redraw the entire image displayed on the monitor).

Dot clock

You run across the term dot clock when you configure a video card to work with X.Org X11 (the X Window System). This term refers to the rate at which the video card can traverse the raster lines that make up a complete display screen. The value of the dot clock is expressed in terms of the number of dots drawn per second.

To get a rough idea of the dot clock, consider a 640 × 480 display, which has 640 × 480 = 307,200 dots (visible ones, anyway). To produce the appearance of a steady display, these dots should be repainted at least 72 times per second. Thus, the video card has to paint 640 × 480 × 72 = 22,118,400 dots a second. This rate amounts to approximately 22 million dots a second, which is expressed as a dot clock of 22 MHz (1 MHz = a million times per second).

In reality, an even higher dot clock is required for a 640 × 480 display refreshed at 72 Hz (which means 72 times per second) because the electron beam cannot turn around on a dime. As illustrated in Figure 3-1, the electron beam has to traverse a scan line beyond the visible number of dots before it can snap back to the beginning of the next line. The required dot clock for a 640 × 480 display at a 72-Hz refresh rate, for example, is 25.2 MHz.

As you must realize by now, a higher-resolution display requires an even higher dot clock. A 1,024 × 768 display at a 72-Hz refresh rate implies 1,024 × 768 × 72 = 56,623,104 dots per second, at minimum. Thus, you can tell that the dot clock necessary for a 1,024 × 768 display will be somewhat higher than 56.6 MHz.

Older video cards support a fixed set of dot clocks, but many advanced video cards include a programmable dot clock. When a video card has a programmable dot clock, the X server can set the video card to operate at any dot clock that lies in a range of acceptable values. For a video card with a programmable dot clock, however, you may need to specify the name of the chip that controls the dot clock (known as the clock chip).

Importance of Video Card and Monitor

Linux works with any video card/monitor combination in text mode. If a video card and monitor work under Windows, the combination also works under Linux in text mode. The story is different when you install X.Org X11, the X Window System for Linux. Because

X.Org X11 controls the video card directly (MS-DOS typically uses standard predefined modes of the video card and Windows has its own video drivers), getting X.Org X11 running with a specific video card takes more work.

The monitor also is important for X.Org X11. Electrical signals from the video card control the monitor, so the monitor must be compatible with the video card. The output on the monitor is the result of a rapidly moving electron beam that the video card's signals control. A monitor's compatibility with a video card has to do with how fast the video card attempts to move the electron beam on the display screen.

The resolutions a video card/monitor combination supports depend on the amount of video memory on the card and on how fast the monitor's electron beam can move. X.Org X11 gets the necessary information about the monitor and the video card from a special text file named `xorg.conf` in the `/etc/X11` directory.

Understanding the X Window System

The name "X Window System" (*X* for short) is loosely applied to several components that facilitate window-based graphics output (or a graphical interface) on a variety of bitmapped displays. A bitmapped display has two distinct components: a *video monitor* on which the graphics output appears and a *video card* (or *graphics card*) — either a plug-in card or some circuitry built into the system's motherboard — that causes the output to appear on the monitor.

At the heart of X is the *X server* — a process (computer program) running on a computer that has a bitmapped display, a keyboard, and a mouse. Applications — X *clients* — that need to display output do so by communicating with the X server via one of several possible interprocess-communication mechanisms. The communications between the X clients and the X server follow a well-defined protocol: the *X protocol*. In addition to the X server, the clients, and the X protocol, the term X encompasses a library of routines known as *Xlib*, which constitutes the C-language interface to the facilities of the X server.

The development of the X Window System started in 1984 at the Massachusetts Institute of Technology (MIT), under the auspices of the MIT Laboratory for Computer Science and MIT/Project Athena. X had industry support from the beginning because Digital Equipment Corporation (DEC) and IBM were involved in Project Athena. By early 1986, DEC had introduced the first commercial implementation of X running on the VAXstation-II/GPX under the Ultrix operating system: X version 10, release 3 (X10R3). Soon X attracted the attention of other prominent workstation vendors such as Hewlett-Packard, Apollo Computer (which has since merged with Hewlett-Packard), Sun Microsystems, and Tektronix.

Feedback from users of X10 urged project members to start a major redesign of the X protocol. While the design of what would become X version 11 (X11) proceeded, X10R4 was released in December 1986. X10R4 was the last release of X version 10.

continues

continued

In January 1987, during the first X technical conference, 11 major computer vendors announced a joint effort to support and standardize on X11. The first release of X11 — X11R1 — became available in September 1987. To ensure the continued evolution of X under the control of an open organization, the MIT X Consortium was formed in January 1988. Under the leadership of Robert W. Scheifler, one of the principal architects of X, the consortium was a major cause of the success of X. Since then, control of the X Window System has been passed on to the X Consortium, Inc., a not-for-profit corporation.

In March 1988, release 2 of X11 — X11R2 — became available. X11 release 3 — X11R3 — appeared in late October 1988. In January 1990, the MIT X Consortium released X11R4; X11R5 followed in August 1991. X11R6 — the latest release of X — was released in April 1994. Throughout these releases, the X11 protocol has remained unchanged. All enhancements have been made through the X11 protocol's ability to support extensions.

X Server and Clients

When you run X on your system, the X server runs on your computer and controls the monitor, keyboard, and mouse. The server responds to commands that X clients send that open windows and draw in those windows. The X clients may run locally or on remote systems. This arrangement is known as the *client/server model*. As the name implies, the server provides a service that the client requests. Usually, clients communicate with the server through a network, with client and server exchanging data using a protocol that both understand.

You may already have seen the client/server model in action. A *file server*, for example, stores files and allows clients to access and manipulate those files. Another common application, the *database server*, provides a centralized database from which clients retrieve data by sending queries. Similarly, the X display server offers graphics-display services to clients that send X protocol requests to the server.

One major difference exists between the X server and other servers, such as file and database servers. File servers and database servers are usually processes executing on remote machines, but the X server is a process executing on the computer where the monitor is located. The X clients may run locally or on remote systems.

insider insight

In the PC LAN's client/server model, applications are typically stored on a central server. Users access these server-based applications from client PCs. When you run an application from a PC, the application executes in your PC's processor. In the X client/server model, the situation is reversed. The X server runs on your PC and manages the display, keyboard, and mouse. The X clients — graphical applications that display output using X — are the ones that run in the server's processor. In other words, the X server runs in a location you typically associate with the client (as in the client PC in a PC LAN). Keep this distinction in mind when working with the X client/server model.

Graphical User Interfaces and X

An application's user interface determines its appearance (*look*) and behavior (*feel*). When the user interface uses graphic objects, such as windows and menus, we call it a *graphical user interface* (GUI). You can also call a GUI a point-and-click user interface because users generally interact with a GUI by moving the mouse pointer onscreen and clicking the mouse button. To confirm the closing of a file, for example, the user may click the mouse button while the mouse pointer is inside a button labeled OK. By now everyone is so used to GUIs that you'd describe that action of clicking the OK button as "click OK."

GUIs were originally developed at the Xerox Palo Alto Research Center (PARC). Subsequently, Apple Computer made such interfaces popular in its Lisa and Macintosh systems. Today, GUIs are available for most systems. Microsoft Windows is available for most IBM-compatible PCs; Motif, GNOME, and KDE — all built on X — are available for Linux and UNIX systems.

Most GUIs, including Motif, GNOME, and KDE, have three components:

- A window system
- A window manager
- A toolkit

The graphical window system organizes graphics output on the display screen and performs basic text- and graphics-drawing functions. The X Window System is the window system used by all X-based GUIs, such as GNOME and KDE.

The window manager enables the user to move and resize windows. The window manager is also partly responsible for the appearance of the windows because it usually adds a decorative frame to them. The window manager also manages input focus, the mechanism by which the user can select one of several windows onscreen and make that one the current active window (the window with which the user intends to interact). This process is called giving the input focus to a window. For GUIs based on the X Window System, a window manager is an X client, just like any other X application. For example, GNOME comes with the Metacity window manager.

The third component, the toolkit, is a library of routines with a well-defined programming interface. This toolkit is primarily of interest to programmers because it enables them to write applications that use the facilities of the window system and that have a consistent look and feel. For example, GNOME comes with a toolkit named Gtk+ (GIMP toolkit), and KDE comes with the Qt toolkit.

X on Linux

The X Window System for Linux comes from the X.Org Foundation — a non-profit organization whose mission is to maintain and enhance the X Window System code. (You can access the X.Org home page at `www.x.org/`.) As a result, the Linux version of X is called X.Org X11.

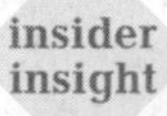

The X server configures the display (number of colors, resolution in terms of number of pixels horizontally and vertically), mouse, and keyboard based on information stored in a configuration file. Linux comes with X.Org X11, which uses a single X server that loads different driver modules to support different video cards. A configuration file — `/etc/X11/xorg.conf` — configures the X server to work on a specific video card and display output in a specific resolution.

To configure X, you must prepare the X configuration file. The configuration file contains information about your video card, monitor, keyboard, and mouse. Fedora Core Linux comes with a GUI utility program called `system-config-display` that enables you to create the `xorg.conf` configuration file.

Setting Up X on Linux

You want to get X set up and going quickly; without it, Linux has no GUI. If you are used to other graphical environments (perhaps on another UNIX workstation or on a PC running Microsoft Windows), you probably want a similar graphical environment on Linux.

If you plan to develop software on your Linux system, chances are good that your software has a graphical component that must be implemented and tested under X. You have to set up and run X to perform this implementation and testing.

No matter what your purpose, if you want to set up X.Org X11, you have to prepare a special configuration file named `xorg.conf` (which must be present in the `/etc/X11` directory) that contains information about your hardware. You can use the system-config-display utility to create the `xorg.conf` file. The next few sections guide you through the process of configuring X.Org X11 and starting X on your Linux PC.

cross ref

You do not have to configure X.Org X11 if you have already successfully installed X during Linux installation, as explained in Chapter 2.

Knowing Your Video Hardware before Configuring X.Org X11

To configure X.Org X11, you must know the hardware that X must access and use. From this chapter's brief introduction to X, you know that the X server controls the following hardware:

- The video card
- The monitor
- The keyboard
- The mouse

The X server needs information about these components to work properly.

The Monitor

X.Org X11 controls the monitor through the video card. This means that an X.Org X11 server can cause a video card to send a wide range of signals to the monitor (to control how fast a raster line is drawn, for example, or how often the entire screen is redrawn). If a video card causes the monitor to perform some task beyond its capabilities (drawing each raster line much faster than it was designed to do, for example), the monitor may actually be damaged. To ensure that the signals from the video card are within the acceptable range for a monitor, X.Org X11 needs information about some key characteristics of the monitor.

At minimum, you have to provide the following information about the monitor:

- The range of acceptable horizontal synchronization frequencies. A typical range might be 30–64 kHz.

- The range of allowable vertical synchronization rates (also known as *vertical refresh rates*), such as 50–90 Hz
- If available, the bandwidth in megahertz, such as 75 MHz

Typically, the monitor's documentation includes all this information. If you bought your PC recently, you may still have the documentation. If you have lost your monitor's documentation, one way to find the information might be to check your Microsoft Windows setup. If your system came with a Windows driver for the display, that driver may display information about the monitor. Another possibility is to visit your computer vendor's website and look for the technical specification of the monitor. I found useful information about my system's monitor on the vendor's website. You can also try searching on a search engine such as Google (`www.google.com/`).

The Video Card

X.Org X11 already provides an X server that loads an appropriate video driver designed to work with a particular video chipset (the integrated circuit chips that generate the signals needed to control the monitor). To select the correct video driver, you have to indicate the video chipset your video card uses.

Even within a family of video cards based on a specific chipset, many configurable parameters may vary from one card to another. Therefore, you also must specify the vendor name and the model of your video card.

At a minimum, you have to provide the following information about the video card:

- Video chipset, such as S3, NVidia GeForce2, or ATI Radeon 9800 Pro
- Vendor name and model, such as Diamond Stealth 64 VRAM, Diamond Viper V550, Number Nine GXE64, or ATI Graphics Xpression
- Amount of video RAM (random access memory), such as 16MB or 32MB.

Most PC vendors indicate only the make and model of the video card in advertisements; ads rarely mention the video chipset. You should ask explicitly about the video chipset and for as much information as the vendor can provide about the video card's model.

insider insight

If you are going to use an old PC to run Linux, you can try to find the video chipset information by opening your computer's case and looking at the video card. The vendor name and model number may be inscribed on the card. For the video chipset, you have to look at the markings on the different chips on the video card and try to guess. For example, if you find a chip with the following markings (only part of the markings are shown here):

```
S3 Trio 64 (GACC 2)
86C764 - P
```

you might then guess that this card uses the S3 chipset. In fact, markings on the chip show the 86C764 number as well (either in the full form or as the number 764). Now, if you can locate the vendor name and model of this card, you may be all set to configure the X server to run properly on your PC.

To learn about video cards supported by the latest version of X.Org X11, 6.8.2, visit `http://xorg.freedesktop.org/X11R6.8.2/doc/manindex4.html` and click on the name of a driver (I briefly summarize the information here, organized by video chipset and card manufacturer):

- **3Dfx:** Voodoo Graphics and Voodoo2 supported by `glide` driver (the `glide` driver needs the Glide library). Voodoo Banshee, Voodoo3, Voodoo4, and Voodoo5 chipsets supported by `tdfx` driver.
- **3Dlabs:** Permedia series (including 1, 2, 2a, 2v, 3, and 4) and GLINT series (including 300SX, 500TX, MX, R3, and R4) with the Gamma, Gamma2, or Delta coprocessor supported by the `glint` driver.
- **Alliance ProMotion:** AT24, AT25, AT3D, AP6420, and AP6422 are supported by the `apm` driver.
- **ARK Logic:** ARK1000PV, ARK2000PV, and ARK2000MT are supported by the `ark` driver.
- **ATI:** All hardware except for Mach8 and some old Mach32 chips is supported by the `ati` driver. ATI Rage 128-based video cards such as ATI Rage Fury AGP 32MB, ATI XPERT 128 AGP 16MB, and the ATI XPERT 99 AGP 8MB are supported by the `r128` driver. The `radeon` driver support all ATI Radeon chipsets (IGP320, IGP330, IGP340, M7, M9, M9+, M10, M11, Mobility 7000 IGP, 7000, 7000 IGP, 7200, 7500, FireGL 7800, 8500, FireGL 8700/8800, 9000, 9000PRO0, 9100, 9100 IGP, 9200, 9200PRO, 9200SE, 9500, 9500PRO, 9600, 9600PRO, 9600SE, 9600TX, 9600XT, 9700, 9700PRO, 9800, 9800PRO, 9800SE, 9800XT, FireGL T2, FireGL X1/Z1). The `radeon` driver supports some of the advanced features such as hardware 3D acceleration only on some Radeon chipsets.
- **Chips and Technologies:** All chipsets (65520, 65525, 65530, 65535, 65540, 65545, 65546, 65548, 64200, 64300, 65550, 65554, 65555, 68554, 69000, and 69030) are supported by the `chips` driver.
- **Cirrus Logic:** The Alpine (5430, 5434-4, 5434-8, 5436, 5446, 5480, 7548, 7555, 7556) and Laguna (5462, 5464, 5464BD, 5465) chipsets are supported by the `cirrus` driver. Other Cirrus Logic chipsets are not supported.
- **Cyrix:** The Cyrix MediaGX, MediaGXi and MediaGXm processors with built-in video are supported by the `cyrix` driver. Note that Cyrix MediaGX processors are now known as National Semiconductors Geode. The `nsc` driver supports the GXLV, SC1200, SC1400, and GX2 chipsets used with the Geode processor family.
- **HP/Compaq/Digital:** DEC 21030 TGA 8 plane and 24 plane chipsets are supported by the `tga` driver. TGA2 (also called PowerStorm 3D30/4D20) cards are not currently supported.
- **IBM:** VGA chipsets (and compatibles) are supported by the `vga` driver. IBM 8514/A and XGA-2 are not supported.
- **Integrated Micro Solutions (IMS):** IMS Twin Turbo 128 and Twin Turbo 3D are supported by the `imstt` driver.
- **Intel:** The i740 is supported by the `i740` driver. Intel i810, i810-DC100, i810e, i815, 830M, 845G, 852GM, 855GM, 865G, and 915G chipsets are supported by the `i810` driver.
- **Matrox:** MGA2064W (Millennium I), MGA1064SG (Mystique), MGA2164W (Millennium II, both PCI and AGP), G100, G200, G400, G450, and G550 are supported by the `mga` driver.
- **Micronix, Inc. (MX):** These chipsets are not supported.

- **NCR:** These chipsets are not supported.
- **NeoMagic:** NeoMagic MagicGraph 128 (NM2070), 128V (NM2090), 128ZV (NM2093), 128ZV+ (NM2097), 128XD (NM2160), 256AV (NM2200), 256AV+ (NM2230), 256ZX (NM2360), and 256XL+ (NM2380) chipsets are supported by the `neomagic` driver.
- **NVIDIA:** Riva 128, 128ZX, TNT, TNT2, GeForce (DDR, 256), Quadro, GeForce2 (GTS, Ultra, MX, Go), Quadro2, GeForce3, Quadro DCC, nForce, nForce2, GeForce4, Quadro4, GeForce FX, and Quadro FX are supported by the `nv` driver.
- **Number Nine:** Imagine 128, Revolution 3D, Revolution IV, Ticket 2 Ride, and Ticket 2 Ride IV are supported by the `i128` driver.
- **Oak Technologies, Inc.:** These chipsets are not supported.
- **Paradise/Western Digital:** These chipsets are not supported.
- **RealTek:** These chipsets are not supported.
- **Rendition/Micron:** Verite 1000, 2100, and 2200 are supported by the `rendition` driver. Note that Diamond Stealth II S220 is the only known card that uses the Verite 2100.
- **S3:** The 964 (revisions 0 and 1), 968, Trio32, Trio64, Trio64, Trio64V+, Trio64UV+, Aurora64V+, Trio64V2, and PLATO/PX chipsets are supported by the `s3` driver when they are used with the IBM RGB 524, Texas Instruments 3025, or an internal TrioDAC RAMDAC chip. The ViRGE, ViRGE/VX, ViRGE/DX, ViRGE/GX, ViRGE/GX2, ViRGE/MX, ViRGE/MX+, Trio3D, and Trio3D/2X are supported by the `s3virge` driver. Savage3D, Savage4, Savage2000, Savage/MX, Savage/IX, ProSavage PM133, ProSavage KM133, Twister (ProSavage PN133), TwisterK (ProSavage KN133), ProSavage DDR, and ProSavage DDR-K are supported by the `savage` driver. Other S3 chipsets are not yet supported.
- **Silicon Graphics, Inc. (SGI):** SGI Indy's Newport cards (also known as XL) are supported by the `newport` driver. These cards are also used in SGI Indigo 2.
- **Silicon Integrated Systems (SiS):** PCI and AGP cards based on SiS 530, 620, 6326, 5597, 5598, 300, 305, 540, 630, 730, 315/H/PRO, 550, 551, 552, 650, 651, M650, 661FX, M661FX, M661MX, 740, 741, 741GX, M741, 330 (Xabre), 760, and M760 are supported by the `sis` driver.
- **Silicon Motion, Inc.:** Lynx, LynxE, Lynx3D, LynxEM, LynxEM+, Lynx3DM, and Cougar3DR chipsets are supported by the `siliconmotion` driver.
- **Sun Microsystems:** Sun BW2 framebuffers are supported by the `sunbw2` driver. Sun CG3 framebuffers are supported by the `suncg3` driver. Sun CG6 framebuffers are supported by the `suncg6` driver. Sun CG14 framebuffers are supported by the `suncg14` driver. Sun FFB framebuffers are supported by the `sunffb` driver. Sun LEO framebuffers are supported by the `sunleo` driver. Sun TCX framebuffers are supported by the `suntcx` driver.
- **Trident Microsystems:** TVGA8900B, TVGA8900C, TVGA8900CL, TVGA9000, TVGA9000i, TVGA9100B, TVGA9200CXr, TVGA8900D, TGUI9440AGi, TGUI9660, TGUI9680, ProVidia 9682, ProVidia 9685, 3DImage975, 3DImage985, Blade3D, Cyber9320, Cyber9382, Cyber9385, Cyber9388, Cyber9397, Cyber9397/DVD, Cyber9520, Cyber9525/DVD CyberBlade/Ai1, CyberBlade/i7, CyberBlade/i1, CyberBlade/DSTN/Ai1, CyberBlade/DSTN/i7, CyberBlade/DSTN/i1, CyberBlade/e4, CyberBladeXP, and BladeXP are supported by the `trident` driver.

- **Tseng Labs:** ET4000AX, ET4000/W32, ET4000/W32i, ET4000/W32p, ET6000, and ET6100 are supported by the `tseng` driver.
- **VIA:** CLE266, CLE3122, CLE3022, KM400, K8M800, VT3204, VT3205, VT7204, and VT7205 chipsets are supported by the `via` driver.

The Mouse

The mouse is an integral part of a GUI because users indicate choices and perform tasks by pointing and clicking. The X server moves an onscreen pointer as you move the mouse. The X server monitors all mouse clicks and sends these mouse-click events to the appropriate X client application — the one whose window contains the mouse pointer.

Although you may have set up the mouse during Linux installation, you still have to provide information about the mouse to the X server. The X.Org X11 X server needs a mouse to start; if the X server cannot access and control the mouse, it won't start.

To specify the mouse, you need to know the following things:

- The mouse type, such as Microsoft, Logitech, BusMouse, or PS/2-style mouse
- The type of connection between your mouse and the system (serial, bus, PS/2-style connector, or USB)
- The mouse's device name. You can leave this as the generic name `/dev/input/mice` because the Fedora installation program sets up a link between `/dev/mouse` and the actual mouse device; the actual device name depends on the type of mouse and where it is connected — the exact serial port for a serial mouse, for example.

You should not have any problem with the mouse as long as the mouse type and device names are correct.

Configuring X.Org X11 Using system-config-display

Fedora Core includes a GUI utility called system-config-display, written in the Python programming language, that enables you to configure X.

The system-config-display utility provides a convenient way to configure X through a GUI that itself uses X. To run it, type **system-config-display** at a shell prompt or, if you are already on the GNOME desktop, select Desktop ➪ System Settings ➪ Display from GNOME's top panel. The utility probes the monitor and video card. Then it starts X (if X is not already running) and displays a window from which you can further configure the settings such as resolution and color.

To probe the monitor, system-config-display uses the Display Data Channel (DDC) — a command interface developed by the Video Electronics Standards Association (VESA) to support plug-and-play setup of monitors. The DDC interface enables bidirectional communication between the computer and the monitor. Older monitors are not fully DDC compliant, and they may not return information needed by display configuration programs such as system-config-display. If it does not get the needed information, system-config-display makes some assumptions about the monitor and shows it as an unknown monitor.

If there is an existing X configuration file — /etc/X11/xorg.conf — system-config-display reads and uses the existing configuration information to start X. If there is no xorg.conf file, system-config-display creates a new file based on information it gathers and your input.

The only problem occurs when the initial probing by system-config-display does not result in good information and you get a blank screen. When this happens, try pressing Ctrl-Alt-Keypad– (Keypad– means the minus key in the numeric keypad) and then waiting for a few moments. This causes the X server (which system-config-display has started) to switch to a lower screen resolution (for example, 800 × 600 instead of 1,024 × 768). Sometimes that's all it takes to get X going. You'll know when X is working because you should see the main window of system-config-display, as shown in Figure 3-2.

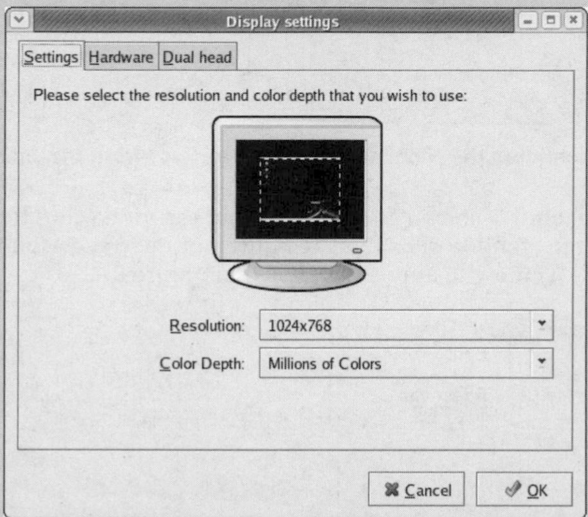

Figure 3-2: Main Window from system-config-display.

The window has three tabs — Settings, Hardware, and Dual head. Initially system-config-display shows the Settings tab. On that tab, the utility shows two drop-down lists that enable you to change the resolution and colors. The initial settings show what system-config-display has been able to determine through its own probing. The Hardware tab enables you to configure the video card and the monitor. If you happen to have two video cards in your PC, you can set up a dual head display from the Dual head tab. If you are happy with everything else, you can change the resolution and colors to different values from the Settings tab.

Clicking the Hardware tab causes system-config-display to display that tab, as shown in Figure 3-3. The Hardware tab enables you to configure the monitor and the video card. Initially, system-config-display shows the current settings for the monitor and the video card.

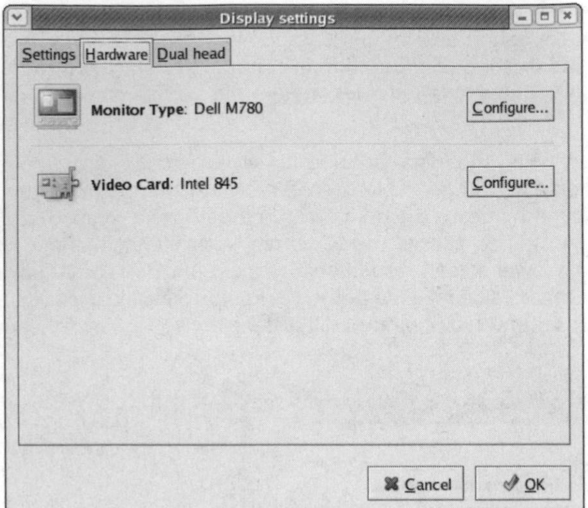

Figure 3-3: You Can Configure the Monitor and the Video Card from the Advanced Tab.

In this example, the monitor is shown as Dell M780 and the video card type is an Intel 845 chipset. To configure the monitor, click the Configure button in the Monitor section of the tab. This causes a new window to appear, as shown in Figure 3-4.

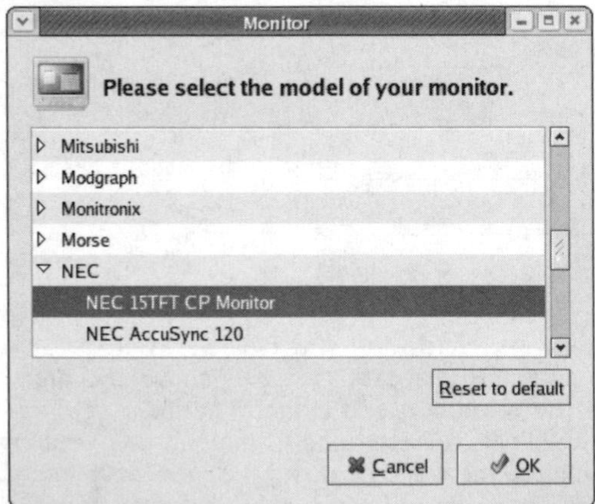

Figure 3-4: Configuring the Monitor in system-config-display.

If you know your monitor's make and model, select it from the list. Otherwise, you can select a generic CRT display or a generic LCD display. When you select a generic monitor, you have to specify the maximum resolution (such as 1,024 × 768) that your monitor can support.

Click OK after selecting the monitor. The window closes, and you get back to the Hardware tab in the system-config-display utility's main window.

Check the video card information. Typically, system-config-display does a good job of detecting the video card. If you need to change the video card information, click the

Configure button next to the video card information (refer to Figure 3-3). This causes system-config-display to display a new window, as shown in Figure 3-5.

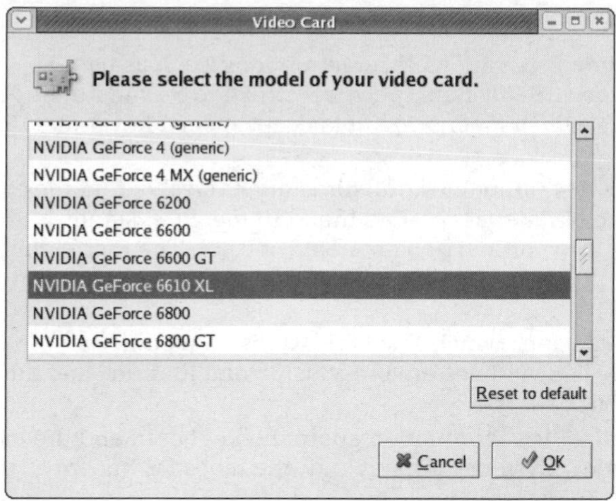

Figure 3-5: Configuring the Video Card in system-config-display.

Initially system-config-display shows the detected video card type. If you want to change the video card type, scroll through the list and pick your video card from the list.

After selecting the video card, click OK to return to the main window of system-config-display. Then, click OK to complete the X configuration. The system-config-display utility writes the configuration to the `/etc/X11/xorg.conf` file and displays a dialog box informing you what has been done.

Click OK to close the dialog box. That completes the X configuration. You can now restart your PC and get the graphical login screen (assuming that the default run level is 5).

Examining the xorg.conf File

The `xorg.conf` file describes your video card, monitor, and mouse to the X server. By default, the X server first looks for the configuration file in the `/etc/X11` directory (`/etc/X11/xorg.conf`), which is where you should save the configuration file.

If you study the `/etc/X11/xorg.conf` file (I refer to this file generically as `xorg.conf`), you see that the configuration file consists of several sections. Each section has the following format:

```
# This a comment
Section "SectionName"
    EntryName  EntryValue
    ...
    ...
    Subsection "SubsectionName"
        EntryName EntryValue
        ...
        ...
    EndSubsection
EndSection
```

Sections consist of a sequence of entries; each entry has a name and a value. A section may contain one or more subsections. A hash mark (#) at the beginning of a line marks a comment line.

The `xorg.conf` file contains one or more of the following sections:

- **ServerFlags:** This section lists various X server options, such as `DontZap` (which means "do not allow the Ctrl-Alt-Backspace keystroke to terminate the X server") and `DontZoom` (which means "do not accept special keystrokes to change screen resolution").
- **Files:** This section lists the pathnames (full directory names) of font files and the file that contains the color database, called the *RGB file*. RGB stands for red, green, and blue — the three primary components of color. The font pathname typically specifies the port number where the X font server provides font information.
- **Module:** This section specifies which X server extension modules and font modules should be loaded. The modules are object code and libraries that add specific functionality to the X server.
- **InputDevice:** This section lists information about the keyboard and the mouse or pointer. (In the X Window System's terminology, the mouse is known as the *pointer*.)
- **Device:** This section describes the characteristics of a video card (or *graphics device*). The configuration file may have more than one `Device` section. The `Driver` entry in the `Device` section specifies the X.Org X11 driver for the video card.
- **Monitor:** This section includes the specifications of a monitor (such as horizontal and vertical synchronization rates) and a list of video modes that the monitor supports. In X.Org X11, a set of VESA modes is defined internally in the server, so for most monitors it isn't necessary to specify any modes explicitly in the `Monitor` section.
- **Screen:** This section describes a combination of a video card and monitor to be used by the X server. This section includes a `Display` subsection with the depth (number of colors) and the modes (supported screen resolutions) in terms of the numbers of horizontal and vertical pixels (for example, 1,024 × 768).
- **ServerLayout:** This section combines one or more `Screen` sections and one or more `InputDevice` sections to specify the complete layout of the display screens and input devices.
- **DRI:** This optional section provides information for the Direct Rendering Infrastructure that enables the X server to use the hardware acceleration capabilities of modern video cards. (To learn more about DRI, consult the DRI documentation online at `http://dri.freedesktop.org/wiki/Documentation`.)

You should not have to learn all the details of these sections, and you need not change the configuration file manually. If you need to edit the configuration file, start with an `xorg.conf` file generated by the system-config-display utility, save a backup copy, and change only what you need.

Three sections in xorg.conf deal with the video card and monitor:

- The Screen section combines a video card and monitor with the video modes to be used by the X server for that screen. Each Screen section typically contains several Display subsections — one for each depth and display mode. The configuration can have multiple Screen sections, one for each display screen, if the system has multiple displays.
- The Device section describes the characteristics of a video card (also known as a graphics device) as well as the driver that X.Org X11 needs to use that video card. The configuration file can have several Device sections, one for each video card, if the system has multiple video cards.
- The Monitor section lists the technical specifications of a monitor, specifically the horizontal and vertical synchronization rates.

As you learned earlier in this chapter, you can create the xorg.conf file by running the system-config-display utility program. If system-config-display correctly detects your video card and monitor, the generated xorg.conf file may work as is. Typically, you run into problems only when you attempt to use the full capabilities of advanced video cards.

Understanding the Screen Section

The X server determines the settings of the video card and the monitor from the Screen section meant for that server. The Screen section specifies the names of a Device (video card) and a Monitor that make up this screen. Following is a Screen section from a typical xorg.conf file:

```
Section "Screen"
    Identifier   "Screen0"
    Device       "Videocard0"
    Monitor      "Monitor0"
    DefaultDepth 24

    Subsection "Display"
        ViewPort  0 0
        Virtual   1024 768
        Depth     16
        Modes     "800x600" "640x480"
    EndSubsection

    Subsection "Display"
        ViewPort  0 0
        Depth     24
        Modes     "1024x768" "800x600" "640x480"
    EndSubsection
    ... other Display subsections ...
EndSection
```

Comment lines start with the hash mark (#). The section's definition is enclosed in the Section . . . EndSection block.

The Identifier line gives a name to this screen. This name is used to refer to the screen in the ServerLayout section. Following the Device and Monitor names are several Display subsections. Each Display subsection applies to a specific Depth (the number of bits of storage per pixel, which also determines the number of colors that can be displayed at a time).

The X server automatically uses the first `Display` subsection in the `Screen` definition, but you can start the server with command-line options that specify a different `Depth`. You can start the X server with a `Depth` of 24 by having the following line in the `[servers]` section of the `/etc/X11/gdm/gdm.conf` file:

```
0=/usr/bin/X11/X -bpp 24
```

The `-bpp` option for the X server program stands for bits per pixel, which is the same as `Depth`. Selecting a value for the `Depth` works, provided that the video card and the monitor are capable of supporting that `Depth`. You can also specify a default depth through the `DefaultDepth` entry in the `Screen` section.

The Modes line in the Display subsection lists the names of video modes that the monitor and video card can support. The names of these modes appear in the Monitor section of the xorg.conf file.

For some video cards, if the card has more memory than is needed to hold the information for all visible pixels in a specific mode, the X server can use the leftover memory to give the appearance of a much larger array of pixels than the 640 × 480 or 1,024 × 768 that a video mode may specify. In other words, you get a large virtual screen from which you can select a smaller area to view. The Virtual line indicates the size of this virtual screen, whereas ViewPort specifies which part of the virtual screen is mapped to the physical display.

Understanding the Device Section

The Device section of the xorg.conf file provides information about the video card. For a video card based on the nVidia GeForce 2 Go chipset, xorg.conf has a Device section that looks like this:

```
Section "Device"
        Identifier  "Videocard0"
        Driver      "nv"
        VendorName  "Videocard vendor"
        BoardName   "nVidia GeForce 2 Go"
EndSection
```

Each line in the section provides some information about the video card. In this case, the Identifier indicates the name assigned to this video card; this identifier is used in the Screen section to refer to this specific video card. If the information is available, the VendorName and BoardName further identify the video card.

For older video cards that do not have a programmable dot clock, an important line in the Device section is the Clocks line. The values in this line indicate the dot clocks that the video card supports. A typical Clocks line looks like this:

```
Clocks    25.2 28.3
```

Nowadays, most video cards do not require the `Clocks` line because the cards have programmable dot clocks. In addition to the `Clocks` line, you can specify one or more flags meant for the X server for the type of video card that you are specifying in the `Device` section.

If your PC has more than one video card, you also need in the `Device` section of the `xorg.conf` file a `BusID` line identifying the location of this particular video card on the bus. For PCI bus video cards, type the `lspci` command to find this information. For example, here's the output from lspci on a PC:

```
00:00.0 Host bridge: Intel Corp. 82845 845 (Brookdale) Chipset Host
Bridge (rev 05)
00:01.0 PCI bridge: Intel Corp. 82845 845 (Brookdale) Chipset AGP
Bridge (rev 05)
00:1d.0 USB Controller: Intel Corp. 82801CA/CAM USB (Hub #1) (rev 02)
00:1d.1 USB Controller: Intel Corp. 82801CA/CAM USB (Hub #2) (rev 02)
00:1e.0 PCI bridge: Intel Corp. 82801BAM/CAM PCI Bridge (rev 42)
00:1f.0 ISA bridge: Intel Corp. 82801CAM ISA Bridge (LPC) (rev 02)
00:1f.1 IDE interface: Intel Corp. 82801CAM IDE U100 (rev 02)
00:1f.3 SMBus: Intel Corp. 82801CA/CAM SMBus (rev 02)
00:1f.5 Multimedia audio controller: Intel Corp. 82801CA/CAM AC'97
Audio (rev 02)
00:1f.6 Modem: Intel Corp. 82801CA/CAM AC'97 Modem (rev 02)
01:00.0 VGA compatible controller: nVidia Corporation NV11 [GeForce2
Go] (rev b2)
02:01.0 Ethernet controller: 3Com Corporation 3c905C-TX/TX-M
[Tornado] (rev 78)
02:04.0 CardBus bridge: 02 Micro, Inc. 0Z6912 Cardbus Controller
```

The first part of the output shows the bus ID of PCi devices. In this case, the ID 01:00.0 refers to the video card. Therefore, the `BusID` line should look like this:

```
BusID      "PCI:01:00:0"
```

Understanding the Monitor Section

The `Monitor` section lists the technical specifications of the monitor: the horizontal synchronization (or *horizontal sync*) frequency and vertical refresh rate. These two critical parameters of your monitor have the following meanings:

- **Horizontal synchronization frequency:** The number of times per second that the monitor can display a horizontal raster line, in kilohertz (kHz), referred to as `HorizSync` in the Monitor section.
- **Vertical refresh rate or synchronization rate:** How many times a second the monitor can display the entire screen, referred to as `VertRefresh` in the Monitor section.

You can get these two values from your monitor's manual.

The horizontal-sync signal occurs at the end of each raster line; this signal moves the electron beam from the end of one line to the beginning of the next raster line. The horizontal-sync frequency is essentially the number of times per second that the monitor can trace a raster line on the display screen. If the monitor can display 480 lines (at 640 × 480 resolution, for example) and repaint the screen 72 times per second (a vertical refresh rate of 72 Hz), the horizontal-sync frequency is at least 480 × 72 = 34,560 times per second = 34,560 Hz = 34.56 kHz. The actual value is higher because the monitor always has to trace more lines than are displayed.

You have to be careful when specifying the values of horizontal sync and vertical refresh rates because the X server uses these values to select the signals sent from the video card. A monitor may be physically damaged if the video card sends signals that are beyond the monitor's specifications.

Most new monitors are multisync and support a range of horizontal-synchronization frequencies (as opposed to a fixed set of values). If you have the monitor's manual, you can specify the range of frequencies for the horizontal sync that the monitor supports.

The `Monitor` section may also include `ModeLine` lines that define video modes suitable for use with the monitor. Typically, a set of VESA standard video modes is defined internally in the X server, so there is no need to define any video modes explicitly in the `Monitor` section, for most monitors.

Following is a typical `Monitor` section (comments show the format of video-mode specification):

```
Section "Monitor"
        Identifier   "Monitor0"
        VendorName   "Monitor Vendor"
        ModelName    "Dell M780"
        DisplaySize  320         240
        HorizSync    30.0 - 85.0
        VertRefresh  50.0 - 160.0
        Option      "dpms"
# Modes can be specified in two formats. A compact one-line
# format, or a multiline format.

# The following two are equivalent

#ModeLine "1024x768i" 45 1024 1048 1208 1264 768 776 784 817 Interlace

#  Mode "1024x768i"
#     DotClock  45
#     HTimings  1024 1048 1208 1264
#     VTimings  768 776 784 817
#     Flags    "Interlace"
#  EndMode

EndSection
```

The `Monitor` section's Identifier field gives a name to this monitor; this name is used in the `Screen` section to refer to this monitor. You should fill in the `HorizSync` and `VertRefresh` lines with information from the monitor's manual.

Computing a ModeLine

Although you can live with the VESA standard video modes defined in the X server, you may sometimes have to add a `ModeLine` manually to get a video mode to work for a specific video card/monitor combination.

You specify a `ModeLine` on a single line with the following syntax:

```
ModeLine "name"  CLK  HRES HSS HSE HTOT  VRES VSS VSE VTOT flags
```

You must fill in all arguments, except the last argument, which is an optional keyword that indicates the type of the mode. The flags field, for example, can be `Interlace` for an interlaced mode (alternate raster lines are drawn through the image each time) or `DoubleScan` (each scan line is doubled). Other flags indicate the polarity of the sync signal. The values can be `+HSync`, `-HSync`, `+VSync`, or `-VSync`, depending on the polarities you are specifying.

The arguments on the `ModeLine` have the following meanings:

- **"name":** The name of this mode, in double quotes. Usually, the resolution of the mode is used as its name. Thus, you'll see mode names such as "640 × 480" and "1024 × 768". These mode names are used in the `Display` subsection of the Screen section.
- **CLK:** The dot clock to be used for this mode. For a video card with a fixed set of dot clocks, the dot clock should be one of the values on the `Clocks` line in the `Device` section of the `xorg.conf` file.
- **HRES HSS HSE HTOT:** The horizontal timing parameters. `HRES` is the horizontal resolution in terms of the number of pixels visible on a raster line. As Figure 3-1 shows, the actual number of pixels on a raster line exceeds the number of visible pixels. `HTOT` is the total pixels on the line. `HSS` is where the horizontal-sync signal begins, and `HSE` is the pixel number where the horizontal-sync signal ends. The horizontal-sync signal moves the electron beam from one line to the next. For a 640 × 480 video mode, these four parameters might be 640 680 720 864. That sequence of numbers expresses that 864 pixels are on the raster lines but that only 640 are visible. The horizontal-sync signal begins at pixel 680 and ends at pixel 864.
- **VRES VSS VSE VTOT:** The vertical timing parameters. `VRES` is the vertical resolution in terms of the number of visible raster lines on the display screen. As Figure 3-1 shows, the actual number of raster lines exceeds the number of visible raster lines. `VTOT` is the total raster lines. `VSS` is the line number where the vertical-sync signal begins, and `VSE` is the line number where the vertical-sync signal ends. The vertical-sync signal moves the electron beam from the bottom of the screen to the beginning of the first line. For a 640 × 480 video mode, these four parameters might be 480 488 491 521.

From a monitor's manual, you can get two key parameters: the vertical refresh rate (in Hz) and the horizontal synchronization frequency (in kHz). The monitor's manual provides these two values as ranges of valid values. The vertical refresh rate is typically between 50 Hz and 90 Hz; the horizontal sync frequency can be anywhere from 30 kHz to 135 kHz. Following are two equations that define the relationship between the dot clock and some of the horizontal and vertical timing parameters on the `ModeLine`:

```
CLK = RR * HTOT * VTOT
CLK = HSF * HTOT
```

In these equations, `RR` is a screen refresh rate within the range of the vertical refresh rate of the monitor, and `HSF` is a horizontal-scan frequency the monitor supports. Remember to convert everything to a common unit (for example, make sure that all values are in Hz) when you apply these formulas.

To define a mode, you can start with a desired refresh rate (`RR`) such as 72 Hz. For a given dot clock, you then can compute the product `HTOT * VTOT` from the first equation. Next, plug in a value for `HSF` within the range of supported horizontal-scan frequencies for the monitor. Because the dot clock is already known, you can compute `HTOT` from the second equation. After you know `HTOT`, you can determine `VTOT` because you have already computed the product of `HTOT * VTOT`.

At this point, you know `HTOT` and `VTOT`. You have to select the arguments `HSS`, `HSE`, `VSS`, and `VSE`, which you need for the `ModeLine`. Unfortunately, figuring out these four parameters requires some trial and error. You can pick the `HRES` and `VRES` values first (`HRES` and `VRES` determine the resolution of the mode). Then, you have to select `HSS` and `HSE` to lie between `HRES` and `HTOT` and ensure that `HSE > HSS`. Similarly, `VSS` and `VSE` should be between `VRES` and `VTOT`; make sure that `VSE > VSS`.

If the display area looks small or not centered, you have to alter the values `HSS`, `HSE`, `VSS`, and `VSE` to tweak the display. One way to correct any minor display problems is to run the xvidtune utility that comes with X.Org X11. If your X display is working but the display does not look as good as you think it should (for example, if it does not fill the whole screen or is skewed to one side), type **xvidtune** in a terminal window. The program prints a few lines of information about the monitor on the terminal window. The xvidtune window and a dialog box appear. If the video chip does not allow modes to be tuned, xvidtune exits with a message informing you so. Otherwise xvidtune displays a warning message (see Figure 3-6) that tells you about the possibility of damaging your monitor and video card if you use the xvidtune program improperly.

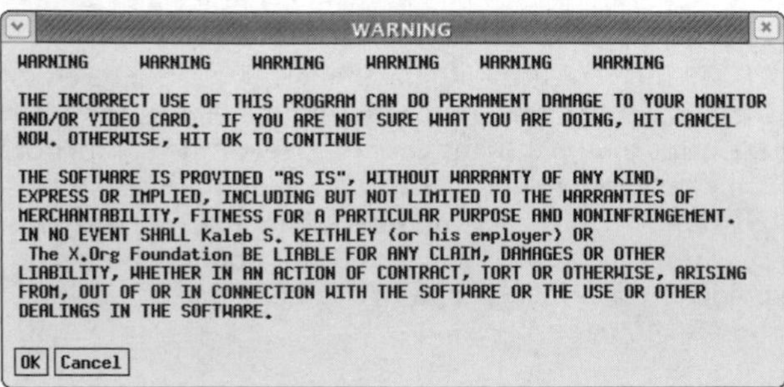

Figure 3-6: Warning Message from xvidtune.

If you decide to proceed, click OK to dismiss the dialog box. You have to interact with xvidtune through its main window, as shown in Figure 3-7.

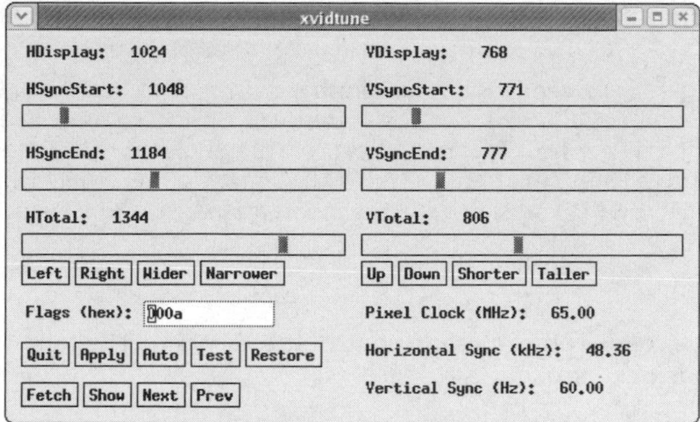

Figure 3-7: Adjust ModeLine Parameters from the Main Window of xvidtune.

Click the Auto button. Then, click the appropriate buttons (Up, Down, Left, Right, Shorter, Taller, Wider, and Narrower) to adjust the display. After each click, the display changes. After you have adjusted the display to your liking, click Show. This prints a `ModeLine` of the following form on the terminal window:

```
"1024x768"     65.00   1024 1048 1184 1344    768  771 777  806 -hsync -vsync
```

The idea is that you can use this `ModeLine` in the `Monitor` section of the `/etc/X11/xorg.conf` file, save the file, and restart the X display (press Ctrl-Alt-Backspace to kill the X server).

If you want to adjust the other video modes, you can click the Next and Prev buttons to switch modes. The effect of these buttons is equivalent to pressing Ctrl-Alt-Keypad+ and Ctrl-Alt-Keypad– (Keypad– means the minus key in the numeric keypad), respectively.

When you are through using xvidtune, click the Quit button to exit the program.

Running X

After you have a complete `xorg.conf` file, your X server should be ready to run. Typically, you have already selected a graphical login option during installation, so that X starts automatically when you reboot your system.

If you are not already running X, you can start the X server from the text console by running the `startx` script, which is a file that contains Linux commands. This script is in the `/usr/X11R6/bin` directory, but that directory should already be in your `PATH` environment variable. Therefore, to run that script, type **startx** at the shell prompt.

The `startx` script looks for another script file, named `.xinitrc`, in your home directory. If `startx` does not find any `.xinitrc` file in your home directory, it runs the `xinit` command with the default script `/etc/X11/xinit/xinitrc`. Notice that unlike the `.xinitrc` file in your home directory, the default script file does not have a period as the first character of its name.

continues

continued

The result of running `startx` depends on the commands in `.xinitrc` in your home directory, if you have one. Otherwise, the result depends on the commands in the `/etc/X11/xinit/xinitrc` file. The net effect of running `/etc/X11/xinit/xinitrc` is to execute the `/etc/X11/xinit/Xclients` script. That script, in turn, starts a GNOME or KDE session with a window manager and several other applications.

There are some special keystrokes you can use to control the X server. The following sections describe these methods of controlling X.

Aborting X Using Ctrl-Alt-Backspace

If you have created a new `xorg.conf` file to try out some new video modes, you can press Ctrl-Alt-Backspace to kill the X server. (In Linux, the term kill refers to exiting a program abnormally. Linux even has a `kill` command that stops errant programs.)

If you have selected the graphical login option, the X server immediately restarts but this time with the configuration options in the new xorg.conf file. If your system is not set up for a graphical login screen, you go back to the text display.

insider insight

If you have enabled the graphical login screen and X does not work properly because of erroneous configuration options in the `xorg.conf` file, press Ctrl-Alt-F1 to get a text-mode login screen. Log in as root, and run `system-config-display` to configure X, carefully selecting the options for monitor, video card, and video mode (resolution and depth). After preparing the new `xorg.conf` file, press Ctrl-Alt-F7 to get back to the graphical login screen, and press Ctrl-Alt-Backspace to kill the X server and to force it to restart with the new configuration options.

Trying Different Video Modes

In your `xorg.conf` file, if you look at the `Screen` section that applies to your X server, you notice several `Display` subsections. Each `Display` subsection lists the video modes supported for a specific depth — the number of bits in each pixel's value. An X server typically supports depths of 16 or 24, which means that each pixel has a 16-bit or 24-bit value and that the server can display up to thousands or millions of distinct colors. The `Display` subsection lists the video modes in terms of the display resolution, which in turn is expressed in terms of the number of pixels horizontally and vertically. For example, here is a partial listing of a `Screen` section of the X configuration file:

```
Section "Screen"
        Identifier "Screen0"
        Device     "Videocard0"
        Monitor    "Monitor0"
        DefaultDepth     24
        SubSection "Display"
                Viewport   0 0
```

```
                Depth     16
                Modes    "800x600" "640x480"
        EndSubSection
        SubSection "Display"
                Viewport   0 0
                Depth     24
                Modes    "640x480" "800x600" "1024x768"
        EndSubSection
    ... other Display subsections ...
EndSection
```

When the X server starts, it configures the video card at the first listed resolution (in this case, 640 × 480, or 640 pixels horizontally by 480 pixels vertically) that corresponds to the first mode shown in the `Modes` entry, as follows:

```
Modes         "640x480" "800x600" "1024x768"
```

You can try the other video modes without having to exit the X server. Press Ctrl-Alt-Keypad+ (Keypad+ means the plus key in the numeric keypad). The X server switches to the next mode—in this case 800 × 600. Press Ctrl-Alt-Keypad+ again, and the X server switches to 1,024 × 768 mode. When you press Ctrl-Alt-Keypad+, the X server cycles forward to the next mode listed in the Modes entry.

Press Ctrl-Alt-Keypad+ several times to make sure that the X server works in all video modes.

To cycle backward to the preceding mode, press Ctrl-Alt-Keypad–. Therefore, if the X server is displaying in 800 × 600 mode and you press Ctrl-Alt-Keypad–, the server switches to 640 × 480 mode.

You can make the X server start in any of the supported modes. If you want the X server to start at the highest-resolution mode, simply change the `Modes` entry in the `Screen` section that corresponds to your X server (the `Driver` entry in the `Screen` section indicates the X server type) to the following:

```
Modes         "1024x768" "800x600" "640x480"
```

This change makes X start in 1,024 × 768 mode, which gives you much more screen area than 640 × 480 mode.

The screen resolutions in the `Modes` entry determine several things:

- The first resolution is the default (the resolution in which the X server starts).
- When you alter screen resolutions, the X server scrolls through them in the order shown in the Modes entry. When you press Ctrl-Alt-Keypad+, the X server changes resolutions in the left-to-right order; the order is reversed when you press Ctrl-Alt-Keypad–.

For example, suppose an application requires you to run the X server in 16-bits-per-pixel mode (also referred to as a 16-bit color depth). To make the X server start with a 16-bit color depth, perform the following steps:

1. Open the `/etc/X11/xorg.conf` file by using your favorite text editor.
2. Locate the `Screen` section.
3. Just before the first Display subsection, insert the following line:

   ```
   DefaultColorDepth 16
   ```

   This forces the X server to use a 16-bit color depth. The server uses the information from the `Display` subsection that specifies `Depth` as 16.
4. Save the `xorg.conf` file.
5. If X is running (and assuming you have enabled the graphical login screen), press Ctrl-Alt-Backspace to stop the X server and force it to restart. It should now use a 16-bit color depth.

Adjusting the Display Settings

After you get X running, you can adjust the display settings — the resolution, color depth, monitor type, and video card — by using the Display Settings utility from the GNOME or KDE desktops. Select Desktop ➪ System Settings ➪ Display and the Display Settings window appears. In fact, this is the same system-config-display utility that you use to configure X initially. From the Settings tab of the Display Settings window you can adjust the resolution and the number of colors (also known as color depth or the bits per pixel).

Summary

Video cards and monitors don't matter much if you use Linux in text mode only. If you want to use the X.Org X11 X Window System, however, you have to pay attention to the video card and monitor. You need X to run graphical desktops such as GNOME and KDE. The X Window System (X) is a popular window system that serves as the basis of GUIs and graphical output on most UNIX workstations. X.Org X11 is a free implementation of X for Intel 80x86 and compatible PCs. X.Org X116 works with a variety of video cards, but you have to configure it to use the appropriate parameters for your video card and monitor. This chapter showed you how to configure and run X on your Linux system.

By reading this chapter, you learned the following:

- In a PC, the video card stores the array of pixels that constitutes the image you see onscreen. The video card converts the pixel values to analog signals that drive the red (R), green (G), and blue (B) electron guns in a monitor. These RGB electron beams, in turn, paint the color image on the phosphor-coated display screen. The combination of the video card and monitor is important to the X Window System because the X server controls the video card directly and because the monitor must be capable of handling the signals the video card generates.
- X Window System is a network-transparent windowing system based on the client/server model. The X server, running on a workstation with a bit-mapped graphics display, manages regions of the screen known as windows, where the output from X client applications appears. The X clients often run on remote systems, but their output appears on the local X display.

- The term graphical user interface (GUI—pronounced *gooey*) describes a user interface that makes use of windows, menus, and other graphical objects, so that users can interact with the application by pointing with the mouse and clicking mouse buttons. From an application developer's point of view, a GUI is a combination of a window manager, a style guide, and a library of routines or a toolkit that can be used to build the user interface.
- X provides the basic functions that can be used to build a GUI. Many GUIs are built upon X, including Motif, GNOME, and KDE. GNOME and KDE are popular GUIs for Linux systems.
- X.Org X11 is the X Window System for Linux PCs; it comes on this book's companion DVD-ROM. When you install Linux from the DVD-ROM, you also install X.Org X11.
- When the X server runs, it consults a configuration file named `xorg.conf` (in the `/etc/X11` directory) to select an appropriate video mode and to configure the video card and monitor for proper operation. Computing the valid video-mode parameters is complicated. As long as you know the technical specification of your monitor (such as horizontal-synchronization frequency and refresh rate), you do not need to compute the video-mode information.
- You configure X.Org X11 as you install Linux. However, you can reconfigure X.Org X116 by running the system-config-display program. This program prompts you for some technical information about your PC's video card, monitor, and mouse.
- You should specify the correct information about your monitor because incorrect information may damage it.
- You can kill the X server by pressing Ctrl-Alt-Backspace. If you have a graphical login screen, this key combination restarts the X server.
- You can switch among different modes (screen resolutions such as 1,024 × 768 and 800 × 600) by pressing special key combinations: Ctrl-Alt-Keypad+ and Ctrl-Alt-Keypad–.

Printer Setup

Secrets in This Chapter

When you set up Linux on a PC, the printer probably is the last thing on your mind. First, you want to get Linux running on the PC; then you may decide to make the modem work to dial up your Internet service provider. When you begin to depend more on Linux, however, you'll want to print documents that you prepare or get from the Internet, and that's when you want to know how to make the printer work with Linux.

As you might guess, physically connecting a printer to the PC's USB port or parallel port is straightforward; that part doesn't depend on the operating system. The software setup for printing is the part that takes some effort. Accordingly, this chapter provides information on setting up the printing environment in Linux.

Configuring CUPS Print Queues

Setting up a printer in Linux involves setting up a queue for the print spooler or scheduler—the process that accepts and sends files for printing and does whatever is needed to get them printed. The queue is essentially a holding place for files that are to be sent to a printer. Before being sent to the printer, however, the files are usually processed to convert them to a form that the printer can understand. For example, to print on a PostScript printer, the files have to be converted to PostScript, which is a page description language (from Adobe Systems Incorporated) that many printers understand.

If you have printed under Microsoft Windows, you may already be familiar with spooling. Spooling refers to the ability to print in the background. When you print from a word processor in Windows, for example, the output first goes to a file on the disk. Then, while you continue working with the word processor, a background process sends that output to the printer.

The Linux printing environment, which consists of several programs described later in this chapter, also supports spooling. The spool directory refers to the directory that contains output files intended for the printer.

Print job refers to what you print with a single print command. The printing environment queues print jobs by storing them in the spool directory. A background process periodically sends the print jobs from the spool directory to the printer.

Linux uses the Common UNIX Printing System (CUPS) for its printing environment. CUPS is a printing system based on the Internet Printing Protocol (IPP)—an application-level protocol for distributed printing using Internet technologies. IPP assumes a client/server model with the client being an application and the server a "Printer"—an abstraction of an output device or a printing service provider. IPP supports a distributed printing environment with the clients and Printer servers communicating over the Internet. You could use an IPP client to print on a printer anywhere on the Internet. The client and Printer exchange data using the HTTP 1.1 protocol. The client application uses IPP to inquire about capabilities of a printer, submit print jobs, and inquire about and cancel print jobs. Because IPP uses HTTP—the same protocol that Web servers use, CUPS configuration directives are similar to those used by the Apache Web server. (Chapter 14 describes the Apache Web server configuration files.)

CUPS has been developed by Easy Software Products and is distributed under the GNU General Public License (GPL), version 2. The CUPS application-programming interface (API) library is distributed under the GNU Library General Public License (LGPL), version 2. For a discussion of GPL and LGPL, see Chapter 23.

You can configure CUPS print queues through the graphical printer configuration tool or by typing the `lpadmin` command in a terminal window (a print queue or printer queue is a mechanism for scheduling printing on a specific printer). You can also manage CUPS print queues through the Web browser. To access the CUPS administration functions, point the Web browser to `http://localhost:631/`.

Your Linux system should have CUPS already installed. That installation also includes documentation on CUPS. To read the CUPS documentation, start the Firefox or Mozilla Web browser and open the file `/usr/share/doc/cups*/documentation.html`. You can also read CUPS documentation from the Internet at `www.cups.org/documentation.php` as well as on your own system at `http://localhost:631/documentation.html`.

For the latest information about CUPS and to read the CUPS Frequently Asked Questions (FAQ), visit the CUPS website at `www.cups.org/`.

At the user level, you can use either System V UNIX commands or Berkeley Software Distribution (BSD) UNIX commands to submit and manage print jobs. Although CUPS supports both BSD and System V-style print commands, it favors the System V print commands such as `lp` to print a file and `lpstat` to check the status of the print queues. As you become more knowledgeable about UNIX (or if you are a UNIX old-timer), you may find this bit of information useful because it tells you the printing commands you can use in Linux. If you don't know anything about System V or BSD UNIX, don't worry; you will learn about the printing commands in the following sections.

Using the Printer Configuration Tool

In Linux, you can configure a printer by using the printer configuration GUI tool. To configure printers with this tool, you must be running GNOME or KDE. From the graphical login screen, log in as `root`, and select Desktop ⇨ System Settings ⇨ Printing from the GNOME or KDE desktop. You can also start the tool by typing the command **system-config-printer** in a terminal window.

The main window of the printer configuration tool appears (see Figure 4-1).

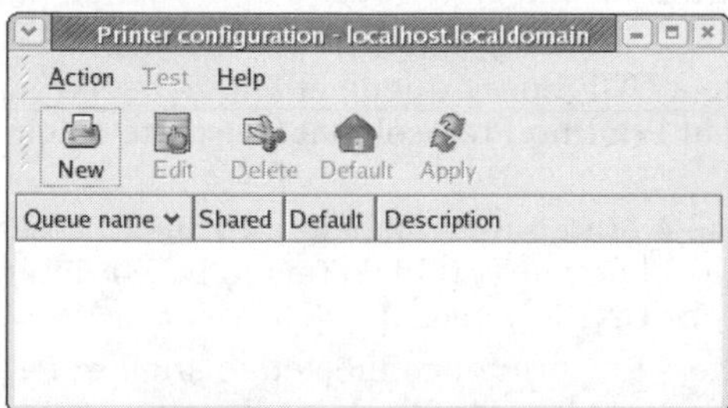

Figure 4-1: The Main Window of the Printer Configuration Tool.

You can create and manage print queues by using the printer configuration tool. Each *print queue* refers to a holding place for files that are to be sent to a specific printer (note that the terms *print queue* and *printer queue* are typically used interchangeably). Thus, a print queue is associated with at least one printer. To add a printer to your Linux system is equivalent to creating a printer queue and associating that queue with the printer.

To add a new printer queue, click the New button on the toolbar. The printer configuration tool displays the Add a new print queue Wizard that takes you through the process of adding a new printer queue. The initial step shows a message that assures you that nothing will be changed until you click the Finish button at the end of all the steps. Click the Forward button to continue. The next screen prompts you for the print queue's name and a short description, as shown in Figure 4-2.

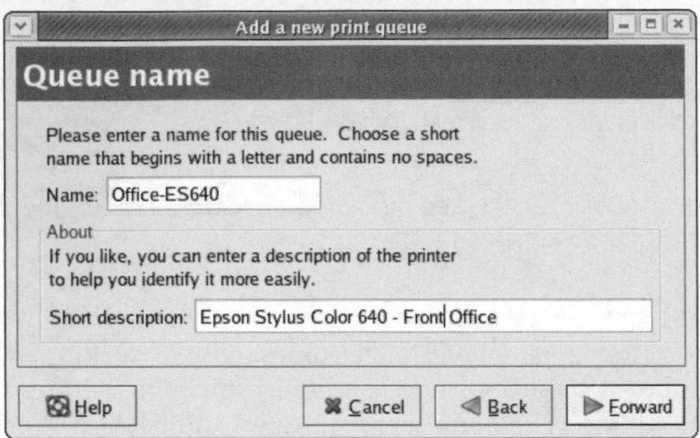

Figure 4-2: Set the Print Queue Name and Description.

Enter a name for the queue and description. You should use some systematic approach when naming the print queue. For example, if I have an HP Laserjet 4 printer on the second floor in Room 210, I might name the queue Room-210-HPLJ4 because this makes it easy to find the printer. Sometimes systems administrators choose cute names such as kermit, piggy, elmo, cookiemonster, and so on, but once you have too many printers, such cute schemes do not work well. It's best to provide a clue about the printer's location as well as the make and model in the print queue's name. After entering the queue name and description, click Forward.

The Queue Type window appears. You have to select a queue type from the drop-down selection box (see Figure 4-3). As the drop-down list shows, you have to select the queue type from the following list:

- **Locally-connected:** Refers to a printer connected directly to the serial, parallel, or USB port of the PC.
- **Networked CUPS (IPP):** Refers to a CUPS print queue at another server on the network. (IPP refers to the Internet Printing Protocol that is used to communicate with the remote CUPS server.)
- **Networked UNIX (LPD):** Refers to a print queue managed by the LPD server on another UNIX system on the local network. (LPD refers to Line Printer Daemon — another print spooler for UNIX systems.)
- **Networked Windows (SMB):** Refers to a printer connected to another PC on the local network and that uses the Server Message Block (SMB) protocol, the underlying protocol in Windows file and print sharing.
- **Networked Novell (NCP):** Refers to a printer connected to a Novell Netware server on the local network.
- **Networked JetDirect:** Refers to a network-connected printer that prints data received at a specific TCP/IP port (typically, port number 9100). HP JetDirect cards use this method of printing.

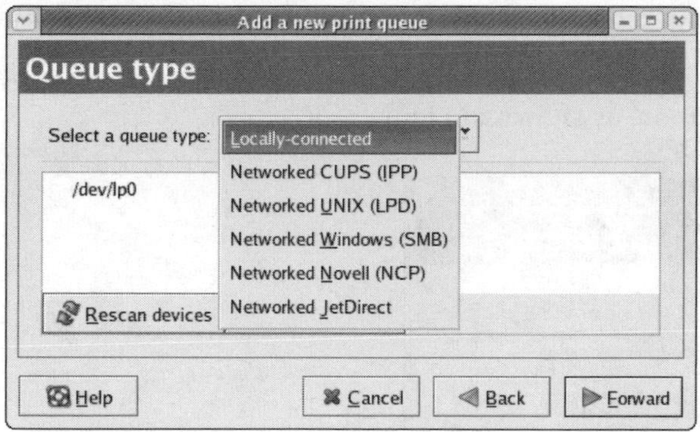

Figure 4-3: Select the Print Queue Type.

Select the print queue type that applies to your configuration. When you select any of the networked print queues, you have to identify the server and remote queue name using the syntax appropriate for that type of queue. For example, if you want to set up a print queue directed at a Windows (SMB) printer, you have to identify the printer by using the following syntax:

```
//WindowsMachine/PrinterName
```

On the other hand, for remote CUPS or LPD queues, you specify the server's hostname and the queue's name (as defined on that remote server).

If you select a locally connected printer, you should see the parallel port device (`/dev/lp0`) listed. If you want to connect the printer to another port (such as serial port or USB), you can click the Custom device button. Then enter the device name (such as `/dev/ttyS0` for the first serial port or `/dev/usb/lp0` for the first USB printer) in the dialog box that appears. After specifying the device, click Forward and the wizard takes you to the next step, where you select a print driver from a list. Click the drop-down list (above the scrolling list) and a list of printer manufacturers appears. Select the printer manufacturer, and the scrolling list displays the names of different printer models from that manufacturer, as shown in Figure 4-4 (for Epson).

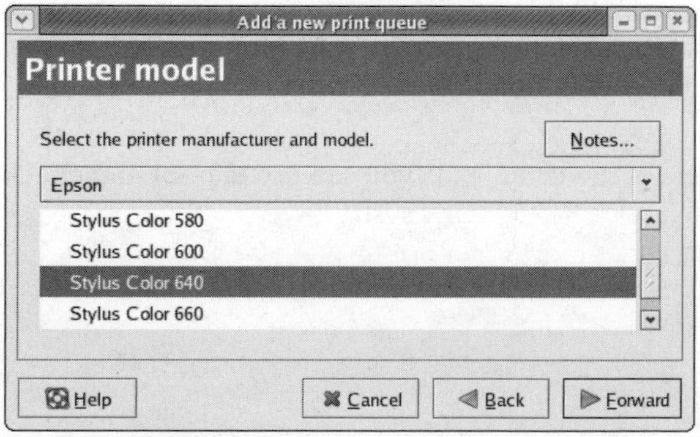

Figure 4-4: Select a Printer Manufacturer and Model.

You can then select your printer model from the list. If you have a PostScript printer, you can simply go to the Generic list (Generic is one of the choices in the manufacturer list) and select PostScript printer. After selecting the print driver, click Forward to continue. This brings you to the final screen, as shown in Figure 4-5.

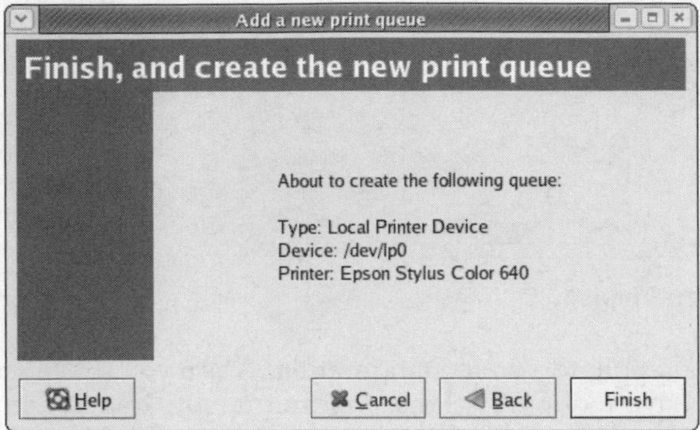

Figure 4-5: Finish Creating the New Print Queue.

This step displays a message that tells you what print queue you are about to create. Click Finish to complete the task.

A dialog box prompts you if you want to print a test page. Click Yes. This applies all the changes and restarts cupsd, the print scheduler daemon that takes care of printing. (A daemon is essentially a background process that runs as long as the system is up.) The printer should print a test page. A message box appears asking you to check the test page. Click OK to dismiss the message box.

Now, the new print queue should appear in the printer configuration window, and you should be able to submit print jobs to this queue. To quit the printer configuration tool select Action ⇨ Quit or close the printer configuration window by clicking the X button in the upper-right corner of the window's frame.

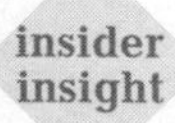

If you did not print a test page when you initially set up the print queue, you can always do so from the Test menu in the printer configuration tool. Click the print queue in the Printer configuration window, and then select Test ⇨ CUPS Test page from the menu to print a test page on the printer.

The next section describes some of the commands you can use to print and check the status of print jobs.

Administering Printers with the CUPS Web Interface

Although you can use the printer configuration tool to configure CUPS printers, there is another way to administer CUPS. You can also administer a CUPS printer through its Web interface. In fact, the Web interface is the method used to configure CUPS printers on non–Red Hat systems because the printer configuration tool is meant for Red Hat and Fedora Linux systems only.

The CUPS scheduler — cupsd — listens on port 631 on your system. Port 631 is assigned to the IPP service. For example, here's what you should get when you search for `ipp` in the `/etc/services` file:

```
grep ipp /etc/services
ipp             631/tcp          # Internet Printing Protocol
ipp             631/ucp          # Internet Printing Protocol
```

When you use a Web browser to connect to port 631 on your system, cupsd displays its Web interface, as shown in Figure 4-6. Note that you have to log in as root in order to perform all the administration tasks shown in Figure 4-6.

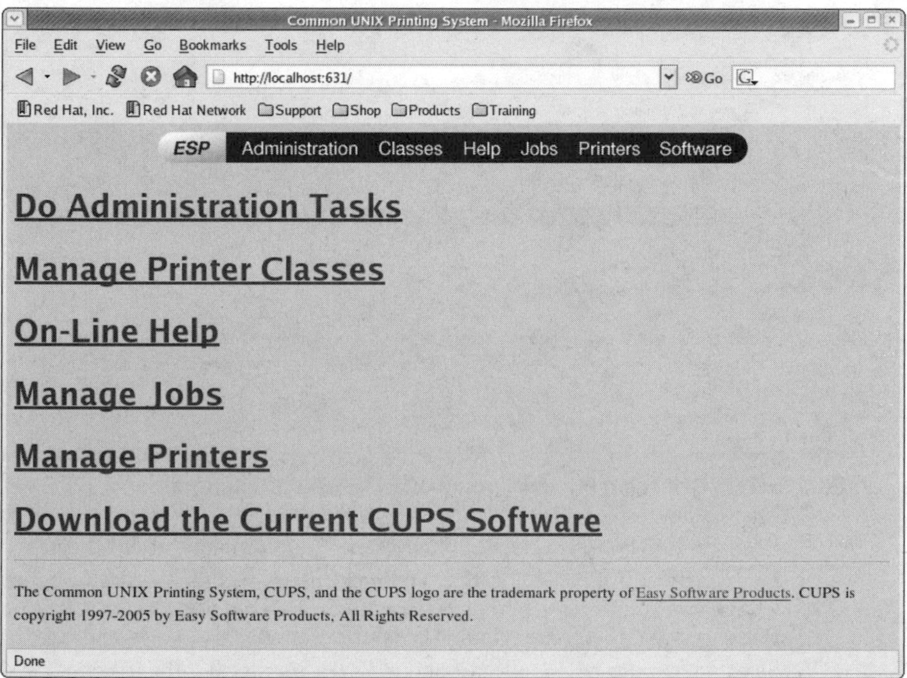

Figure 4-6: Accessing the CUPS Web Interface at Port 631.

You can perform a variety of administration tasks through the links and the buttons on the CUPS Web interface. If you click the Do Administration Tasks link, CUPS displays a new Web page from which you can manage printer classes (explained later in this section), jobs, and printers.

To add a printer through the CUPS Web interface, follow these steps:

1. Start the CUPS Web interface by pointing the Web browser at `http://localhost:631/`. The Web interface appears, as shown in Figure 4-6.
2. Click the Manage Printers link. CUPS displays information about each of the current printers as well as buttons for performing many different tasks (see Figure 4-7). A set of buttons enables you to perform tasks such as print a test page and stop a printer. Additionally, a single Add Printer button enables you to add a printer.

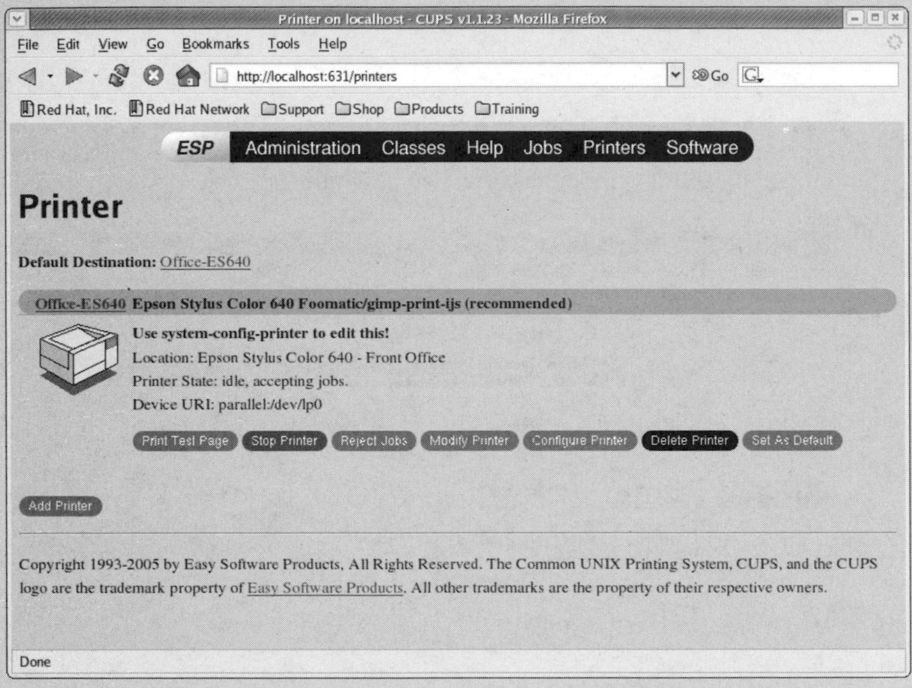

Figure 4-7: Managing Printers through the CUPS Web Interface.

3. Click the Add Printer button. CUPS prompts for information about the new printer.
4. Enter the printer's name, location, and description, and then click Continue. CUPS asks you to select the device from a drop-down list. The list is more extensive than what the printer configuration tool shows.
5. Select printer device, and click Continue. CUPS prompts for the make of the printer. The list is much shorter than what you get from the printer configuration tool.
6. Select the printer make and click Continue. CUPS prompts for the printer model. That list depends on the make you selected.
7. Select the model, and click Continue. CUPS adds the printer by adding the new printer's information to the `/etc/cups/printers.conf` file and creating a PPD file for the printer in the `/etc/cups/ppd` directory (PPD stands for PostScript Printer Description and a PPD is a text file containing information about a printer's capability).

insider insight

A key concept in CUPS is the idea of a class of printers. You can define a class consisting of a number of printers and then send print jobs to the class (instead of individual printers). CUPS then sends the print job to the first available printer in the class. This is a good way to share the printing load among a number of printers. You can print on a class just as you print on an individual printer. For example, if your system has the class `pr5` defined, then you can print the `sample.ps` file on this class with the following `lp` command:

```
lp -d pr5 sample.ps
```

To define a class of printers from the CUPS Web interface point the Web browser to `http://localhost:631/` and then follow these steps:

1. Click Classes on the toolbar in the Web interface. CUPS displays the current classes, if any, and an Add Class button.
2. Click the Add Class button. A dialog box prompts for a user name and password. Enter the root as user name and the root password. CUPS then prompts for information about the class.
3. Enter the following identifying information about the new class:
   - **Name:** The class name, up to 127 printable characters (no embedded spaces)
   - **Location:** Information about where this class of printers is located
   - **Description:** A brief description of this class of printers

   Click Continue. CUPS asks you to select which of the currently defined printers should be members of this class.
4. Click the printers you want to add to the class, and then click Continue. CUPS creates the new class.

When you create a new class, the class definition is added to the `/etc/cups/classes.conf` file. For example, here's the definition of a class named `pr5`:

```
<Class pr5>
Info Printers on 5th Floor
Location 5th Floor
State Idle
Accepting Yes
JobSheets none none
Printer 5N28-hplj4
Printer 5X15-hplj5000
Printer 5Z15-hplj4200
QuotaPeriod 0
PageLimit 0
KLimit 0
</Class>
```

In this case, the `pr5` class contains three printers identified by the `Printer` lines inside the class definition.

Learning the Printing Commands

After you have set up the print queue for a printer on your Linux system, you can type commands in a terminal window to print and check the status of the print queue. The following sections provide an overview of the basic printing commands. You can use either System V or BSD UNIX print commands. Table 4-1 summarizes the two sets of print commands. In addition to these commands, you can use `lpadmin` to manage the printer queues and `lpoptions` to set default options for a print queue.

Table 4-1: System V and BSD Print Commands

Task	*System V Command*	*BSD Command*
Submit a print job	`lp`	`lpr`
Cancel a print job	`cancel`	`lprm`
Check status of a print job	`lpstat`	`lpq`

Printing a File

You can use the `lp` or `lpr` command to print a file. For example, to print the file `rfc1789.txt`, you can type the following `lp` command in a terminal window:

```
lp rfc3966.txt
```

This `lp` command then queues the `rfc3966.txt` file for printing on the default printer. The default printer is identified by the `<DefaultPrinter` *queuename*`>` entry in the CUPS configuration file `/etc/cups/printers.conf` (where *queuename* is the name of the print queue).

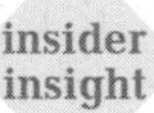

When you use the `lp` command to print a file, `lp` sends that file along with information about the print job to the `cupsd` print scheduler that stores this information in a control file and a data file in the `/var/spool/cups` directory. The `cupsd` scheduler then processes the files according to the file extension (such as `.txt` or `.ps`) and sends them to the printer using its backend interfaces. Thanks to various configuration files, the cupsd scheduler knows what to do to make sure that the file — be it a text file or an image file — gets printed properly.

You can embellish the simple `lp` command with some options. If you have many different print queues defined, you can specify the destination of the print job with the `-d` option. For example, to send a print job to the Hewlett-Packard LaserJet 5000 printer named `Rm5N28hplj5000` you would type the following command (later, in the "Understanding the CUPS Configuration Files" section, you'll see that the print queue name appears in the `/etc/cups/printers.conf` file):

```
lp -d Rm5N28hplj5000  rfc3966.txt
```

If you mistakenly print a large file and want to stop the print job before you waste too much paper, you can use the `lpstat` or `lpq` command to look at the current print jobs and then cancel the large print job. Here is a typical output from the `lpstat` command after I typed the `lp` command to print a file on the queue named `Office-ES640`:

```
lpstat
Office-ES640-2          naba          43008   Sat Apr  2 15:47:12 2005
```

The first field of the output shows the name of the queue with a job number appended to it (that number identifies the print job). You need that job number to cancel the print job.

When I type `lpq` for the same print job, here is the output I get:

```
lpq
Office-ES640 is ready and printing
Rank    Owner   Job     File(s)                         Total Size
active  naba    2       rfc3966.txt                     43008 bytes
```

The `lpq` command also shows the job number and the name of the file that I am printing (`rfc3966.txt`).

To remove a job from the print queue, use the `cancel` or `lprm` command. For example, to remove print job 2, type the following command:

```
cancel 2
```

You can get the same result with the following `lprm` command:

```
lprm 2
```

insider insight

If you are in a hurry and want to cancel all print jobs you have submitted so far, use `cancel` or `lprm` with `-a` as the argument, as follows:

```
cancel -a
```

Specifying Print Options

You can use the `-o` option with the `lp` and `lpr` commands to specify print job options such as paper size, whether to print in landscape orientation, and whether to print a banner page at the start and the end of a print job. For example, suppose that you want to print a file on A4-size paper instead of U.S. letter-size paper that happens to be the default. You can specify this in the print command, as follows:

```
lp -o media=A4 letter.pdf
```

That part — `-o media=A4` — specifies the value of the standard option named media that can set the size, type, and source of the output media (paper or transparency). If you also want a standard banner page at the start of the print job, you can add the `job-sheets` option and specify the type of banner you want:

```
lp -o media=A4 -o job-sheets=standard letter.pdf
```

There is an extensive set of standard options, but some of them work only if your printer supports that option. You can specify these options with the `-o` option of the `lp` command.

Use the lpoptions command to see what options a printer supports. Suppose that you have a print queue named hpdj8 for a HP Deskjet printer. You can query the options it accepts with the following command:

```
lpoptions -p hpdj8 -l
ColorModel/Output Mode: CMYK2 *CMYK Gray
Resolution/Output Resolution: *300dpi 600x300dpi 600dpi
Duplex/Double-Sided Printing: *None DuplexNoTumble DuplexTumble
PageSize/Media Size: *Letter Legal Executive Tabloid A3 A4 A5 B5 EnvISOB5
Env10 EnvC5 EnvDL EnvMonarch
InputSlot/Media Source: *Tray Manual Envelope Auto
MediaType/Media Type: *Plain Bond Special Transparency Glossy
PageRegion/PageRegion: Letter Legal Executive Tabloid A3 A4 A5 B5 EnvISOB5
Env10 EnvC5 EnvDL EnvMonarch
Option1/Duplexer: True *False
```

The first field on each line is the name of the option. The text between the forward slash (/) and the colon (:) is the description of that option. The rest of the lines show the possible values you can specify for that option. The default value is marked with an asterisk (*).

Controlling the Print Queue

To see the names of printers connected to your system, use the lpc status command. On my system, the lpc status command shows the following:

```
lpc status
Office-ES640:
        printer is on device 'parallel' speed -1
        queuing is enabled
        printing is enabled
        no entries
        daemon present
```

Notice that queuing and printing are both enabled for this printer. The last line tells you that the cupsd daemon is running and available to handle print jobs.

You can use the accept and reject commands to enable or disable queuing for a print queue. For example, to stop queuing further print jobs for the Office-ES640 printer, I would type:

```
reject Office-ES640
```

This command disables queuing jobs for this printer. If anyone tries to send a print job using the lp command, the user receives an error message like this:

```
lp: unable to print file: server-error-not-accepting-jobs
```

If you want to allow queuing of print jobs, but want to start or stop the printing, use the enable and disable commands. When you disable printing, users can submit print jobs, but nothing gets printed until you enable printing again. For example, here is the command I use to disable printing on the Office-ES640 printer:

```
disable Office-ES640
```

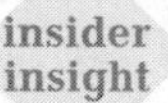

If you are trying to print, but nothing seems to be coming out of the printer, check the printer status with the `lpc status` command and make sure that the daemon is present and that both queuing and printing are enabled. To allow the queuing of print jobs, use the `accept` command and to start printing, use the `enable` command.

Understanding the CUPS Printing System

In Linux, with the CUPS printing system, the user's view of printing is based on the basic printing commands: `lp`, `lpr`, `lpq`, `lprm`, and `lpc status`. A bit more information will help you understand how printing works behind the scenes. As with so many things in Linux, support for the CUPS printing system is all a matter of having the right files in the right places. This becomes apparent after you have configured Linux for networking and have set up dial-in modems, for example. In each case, you have to make sure that several configuration files appear in the correct places. The printing environment has the same requirement: configuration files that specify how printing occurs.

Although nowadays you can use graphical configuration tools to set up services such as printing and dial-up networking, it is useful to know the names of the text-configuration files because you can then fix problems even if you do not have access to a graphical login.

If you have experience with MS-DOS from a long time ago, you might have printed files by simply copying them to the printer port (LPT1, for example). You might think that a similar approach is good enough for Linux. As you see in the next section, such a brute-force approach to copying a file to the physical printer port is not appropriate for a multi-user system such as Linux. You need a way to queue print jobs and to have a separate printing process take care of the printing.

Copying to the Printer: Brute-Force Printing

If you have a printer connected to the `/dev/lp0` parallel port, you can print a text file simply by sending the file to the printer with the following command:

```
cat webstat.txt > /dev/lp0
```

This command indeed produces a printout of the file `webstat.txt`, provided that the following conditions are true:

- You are logged in as `root` (Linux allows only `root` and certain processes direct access to physical devices, such as printers).
- The printer is connected to the `/dev/lp0` port, powered up, and online.

The problem with copying a file directly to the printer device is that the command completes only when the copying (which, in this case, is equivalent to printing) is completed. For a large file, this process can take a while. In fact, if the printer is not turned on, the command appears to hang (if this happens, just press Ctrl-C to abort the command).

Printing the CUPS Way

On a multitasking and multiuser system such as Linux, a better way to print is to spool the data and schedule the printing: send the output to a file, and have a separate process send the output to the printer. That way, you can continue with your work while the printing takes place in the background. In addition, if your system has more than one user, everyone can print on the same printer, without worrying about whether or not the printer is available; the background printing process can take care of all the details.

That's how the CUPS printing environment works. Users use a client program — lp or lpr — to send the files to be printed to a server called cupsd, the printer daemon, over a TCP/IP connection. The cupsd server then queues the files, filters the files (to get them ready for the printer), and sends them to the printer.

Although you typically have only one printer connected to your PC, one advantage of the CUPS printing system is the capability to print on a printer connected to another system on a network. Printing to a remote printer is handled in the same fashion as printing to a local printer; the local cupsd daemon simply sends the files to the remote system's server.

As explained earlier, the user-level programs for spooling a file are lp and lpr. When lp or lpr runs, it sends the data to the cupsd server that manages the specified print queue. Other user-level commands for working with print queues are `lpstat`, `lpq`, `cancel`, `lprm`, and `lpc`. The program that completes the CUPS printing environment is the CUPS scheduler: `cupsd`.

In addition to the commands `lpd`, `lpr`, `lpq`, `lprm`, `cancel`, and `lpc`, the configuration files in the `/etc/cups` directory play a crucial role in the CUPS printing environment. The section "Understanding the CUPS Configuration Files" describes the key configuration files.

A good way to understand CUPS is to take a look at the *CUPS architecture* — the parts that make up CUPS and how they fit together. CUPS is designed around the cupsd print scheduling process that accepts print jobs submitted through printing commands, spools print files, uses filters to convert files to a form acceptable to the printer, and sends the data to printers using backends. Figure 4-8 shows the basic architecture of CUPS.

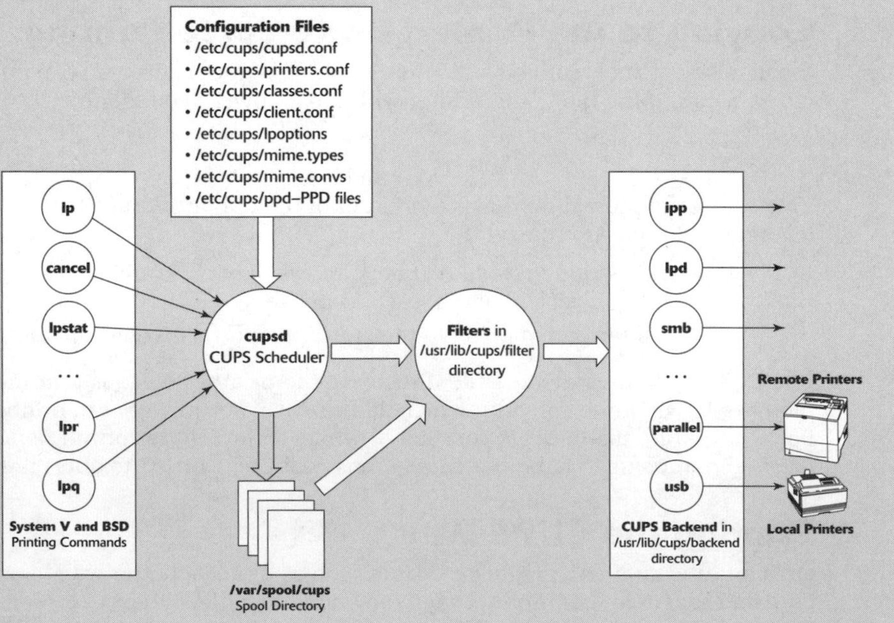

Figure 4-8: The CUPS Architecture.

As Figure 4-8 shows, the major components of CUPS are as follows:

1. **CUPS Scheduler:** cupsd is the scheduling process that acts as an HTTP 1.1 server and handles printing requests sent by clients using the Internet Printing Protocol (IPP). cupsd also acts as a Web server and provides a Web interface for administering CUPS print queues.
2. **Configuration Files:** The configuration files in `/etc/cups` directory control how CUPS works. The "Understanding the CUPS Configuration Files" section further describes these files.
3. **Printing Commands:** System V and BSD printing commands enable you to submit print jobs and check printer status from the command line.
4. **Filters:** The filter programs located in the `/usr/lib/cups/filter` directory convert various input file formats (such as text, PostScript, and image) into output understood by the printer on which the file is being printed. CUPS uses Ghostscript to convert PostScript page description language into output suitable for a specific printer.
5. **Backend:** The backend programs located in the `/usr/lib/cups/backend` directory send the output of the filters to the destination printer. Each backend takes care of sending output to a specific type of connection such as a locally connected parallel printer or a remote Windows printer that communicates with the SMB protocol.

Understanding the CUPS Configuration Files

You can learn a lot about the CUPS configuration files by examining the entries in various configuration files that the printer configuration tool creates when you set up a new print queue. The CUPS configuration files are in the `/etc/cups` directory.

Consider the example of adding a new print queue named `Office-ES640` for an Epson Stylus Color 640 printer that is connected to the parallel port of the PC. Here are the files that contain information about this print queue and the printer model:

- **/etc/printcap:** This file used to be the printer capabilities database and was very important to the LPD print spooler that was popular before CUPS came along (not that I miss LPD; CUPS is much better). CUPS generates single entry in the `/etc/printcap` file for each printer. For example, here is the `/etc/printcap` file that CUPS generates for a print queue named `Office-ES600` (the details of the printer are in the `/etc/cups/printers.conf` file):

```
# This file was automatically generated by cupsd(8) from the
# /etc/cups/printers.conf file.  All changes to this file
# will be lost.
Office-ES640|:rm=localhost.localdomain:rp=Office-ES640:
```

- **/etc/cups/printers.conf:** This is the printer configuration file with entries for each print queue. The information includes the device where the printer is connected and other parameters of the queue. Here is the entry for the Epson Stylus Color 640 printer (that `redhat-config-printer` in the second line is a reference to the old name of the system-config-printer tool):

```
<DefaultPrinter Office-ES640>
Info Created by redhat-config-printer 0.6.x
DeviceURI parallel:/dev/lp0
Location Epson Stylus Color 640 - Front Office
State Idle
Accepting Yes
JobSheets none none
QuotaPeriod 0
PageLimit 0
KLimit 0
</Printer>
```

- **/etc/cups/cupsd.conf:** This is the configuration file for cupsd, the CUPS print scheduler. The syntax of the configuration file is similar to that of Apache httpd, the Web server (see Chapter 14 for a description of Apache httpd configuration). The similarities with the Apache httpd configuration files are to be expected because cupsd is also an HTTP server. Here are the entries in `/etc/cups/cupsd.conf` for the print queue named `Office-ES600`:

```
# Lines below are automatically generated - DO NOT EDIT
<Location /printers/Office-ES640>
Order Deny,Allow
Deny From All
Allow From 127.0.0.1
AuthType None
</Location>
Browsing On
BrowseProtocols cups
BrowseOrder Deny,Allow
BrowseAllow from @LOCAL
Listen 127.0.0.1:631
```

  There are many more directives in the `/etc/cups/cupsd.conf` file that apply to all print queues managed by the cupsd server.

- **/etc/cups/lpoptions:** This file stores the default option settings that apply to all print jobs when you create a print queue as `root`. Note that users can specify other options when they print with the `lp` commands. Here is the `/etc/cups/lpoptions` file with the default options for the `Office-ES600` printer:

```
Dest Office-ES640 page-bottom=86 cpi=12 page-right=57 page-left=57
page-top=72 scaling=100 lpi=7 wrap=true
```

- **/etc/cups/ppd:** This is a directory that contains the PostScript Printer Description (PPD) file for the Epson Stylus Color 600 printer in a file named `Office-ES600.ppd` (the name I had assigned to that print queue). Each PPD file is a text file containing information about the printer capability (similar to the old `/etc/printcap` file in intent, but PPD files have much more detailed information). Here are the first few lines from the PPD file `/etc/cups/ppd/Office-ES640.ppd`:

```
*PPD-Adobe: "4.3"
*%
*% For information on using this, and to obtain the required backend
```

```
*% script, consult http://www.linuxprinting.org/
*%
*% This file is published under the GNU General Public License
... lines deleted...
*FormatVersion: "4.3"
*FileVersion:   "1.1"
*LanguageVersion: English
*LanguageEncoding: ISOLatin1
*PCFileName:    "GIMP-PRI.PPD"
*Manufacturer:  "Epson"
*Product:       "(Stylus Color 640)"
*cupsVersion:   1.0
*cupsManualCopies: True
*cupsModelNumber:  2
*cupsFilter:    "application/vnd.cups-postscript 0 foomatic-rip"
*%pprRIP:        foomatic-rip other
*ModelName:     "Epson Stylus Color 640"
*ShortNickName: "Epson S. Co. 640 gimp-print-ijs"
*NickName:      "Epson Stylus Color 640 Foomatic/gimp-print-ijs
(recommended)"
*PSVersion:     "(3010.000) 550"
*PSVersion:     "(3010.000) 651"
*PSVersion:     "(3010.000) 652"
*PSVersion:     "(3010.000) 653"
*PSVersion:     "(3010.000) 704"
*PSVersion:     "(3010.000) 705"
*PSVersion:     "(3010.000) 800"
*LanguageLevel: "3"
*ColorDevice:   True
*DefaultColorSpace: RGB
*FileSystem:    False
*Throughput:    "1"
*LandscapeOrientation: Plus90
*TTRasterizer:  Type42

*HWMargins: 9 9 9 0
*VariablePaperSize: True
*MaxMediaWidth: 100000
*MaxMediaHeight: 100000
.... many lines deleted ...
```

That should give you an idea of the kind of information stored in PPD files. You don't have to understand or prepare the PPD files manually. CUPS generates the PPD file automatically from descriptions in the Foomatic printer drivers that come with Linux (described later in this chapter).

As this example shows, for each print queue it manages, CUPS needs a considerable amount of information stored in multiple configuration files. So far, I have shown you only the configuration files affected by the definition of a new print queue. It's helpful to know the full extent of the configuration files, understand their purpose, and have a rough idea of what each of these files contain.

CUPS relies on a large number of configuration files to provide a comprehensive printing solution for Linux. Although you do not have to manually edit these configuration files, be aware of what these files are and where they are stored. The key configuration files are located in the `/etc/cups` directory and its subdirectories. Here is a brief summary of the configuration files:

- ***/etc/cups/cupsd.conf:*** The CUPS HTTP server configuration file, used by cupsd, the CUPS scheduler, and the IPP server process. The directives in this file are similar to those used by the Apache httpd (Web server). This means that if you know how to read an Apache httpd configuration file, you can also read and understand `cupsd.conf`. In particular, `cupsd.conf` defines access control for a printer in the same way that Apache httpd defines access control for a directory.
- ***/etc/cups/printers.conf:*** Defines all available print queues. Information about each printer is in a `<Printer PrinterName> ... </Printer>` block. A `<DefaultPrinter>` tag identifies the default printer.
- ***/etc/cups/classes.conf:*** Contains definitions of all printer classes. A *printer class* is a collection of printers. Print jobs sent to a class are forwarded to the first available printer in the class.
- ***/etc/cups/mime.types:*** Lists the supported MIME types, such as text/plain and application/postscript, and the rules for automatically detecting the format of a file. (MIME stands for *Multipurpose Internet Mail Extensions*, which began life as a way to send attachments in a single message file.) The cupsd server uses these rules to determine the type of a file.
- ***/etc/cups/mime.convs:*** Contains the MIME conversion rules to convert a file into a format acceptable to a printer. The conversion is achieved by using filters. Each filter has a relative cost associated with it, and the filtering algorithm selects the set of filters that will convert the file to the needed format with the lowest total cost.
- ***/etc/cups/ppd:*** A directory with the PostScript Printer Description (PPD) files for the printers being managed by CUPS. These PPD files describe the capabilities of all printers, not just PostScript printers. There is one PPD file for each printer. A PPD file for a non-PostScript printer identifies a filter with the `cupsFilter` attribute. CUPS uses that filter to convert a file into a form suitable for sending to the printer. For example, the `cupsFilter` attribute for an Epson Stylus Color 640 printer identifies `foomatic-rip` as the filter, like this:

```
*cupsFilter:    "application/vnd.cups-postscript 0 foomatic-rip"
```

  The `foomatic-rip` filter is located in the `/usr/lib/cups/filter` directory.
- ***/etc/cups/client.conf:*** Specifies the default options for clients (in particular, the default server name and whether encryption is to be used or not). Note that a client is any machine that sends print jobs to another machine for final printing. This means that when your system prints to a local printer, it's a client to the cupsd scheduler running on your system.

Summary

Printing under Linux is simple, provided that the CUPS printing environment is set up properly. You do have to learn a small set of commands to submit a print job and to check the status of pending print jobs. This chapter explained the CUPS printing system from the user's point of view and how to set everything up as a system administrator.

By reading this chapter, you learned the following things:

- Linux comes with the CUPS printing system, which is an open-source implementation of a printing system based on the Internet Printing Protocol (IPP) and integrated with other tools such as Foomatic filter scripts and Ghostscript printer drivers.
- As a user, you print with the `lp` or `lpr` command, check the status of the print queue with `lpq` or `lpstat`, cancel print jobs with `lprm` or `cancel`, and check the printer's status with `lpc status`.
- Behind the scenes, the `lp` command sends the print file and a control file to the cupsd server (the print scheduler daemon), which places the files in a holding directory called the spool directory. Then cupsd processes the spooled print files through filters and sends them to the printer by using backend interface programs.
- You can use the printer configuration tool or the CUPS Web interface (`http://localhost:631/`) to set up printers.
- CUPS relies on a number of configuration files, located in the `/etc/cups` directory, for its operation. This chapter explains these configuration files.

Sound Setup

Secrets in This Chapter

Without a sound card, the PC's built-in speaker can play only a single note; you can't even vary the loudness of the note. Luckily, most PCs nowadays come with a sound card — either a separate card or some sound circuitry built into the motherboards — that greatly improves the sound-output capability of the PC. The sound card is an adapter that plugs into a slot on your PC's motherboard and includes the electronic circuitry needed to play and record sound. You can plug speakers and a microphone into the back of a sound card.

When a microphone is hooked up to the sound card, the card can convert the analog (continuously varying) sound waves into 8-bit or 16-bit numbers, sampling the wave at rates ranging from 4 kHz (4,000 times a second) to 44 kHz (44,000 times a second) and more. Higher sampling rates and a higher number of bits (16) provide better quality, but you need more disk space to store high-quality sound. In addition, the sound card can convert digital sound samples to analog signals you can play on a speaker.

Most sound cards, including the popular Sound Blaster, also support MIDI (Musical Instrument Digital Interface) commands, in addition to recording and playing back waveform sound. MIDI is commonly used to record and play back musical sounds that a synthesizer can create. (Most sound cards have built-in synthesizers and some stand-alone MIDI and audio devices connect to the PC through the USB port.)

This chapter describes specific types of Linux-supported sound cards and how you can set up a sound card after you have successfully installed Linux.

Sound Cards Supported by Linux

Linux kernel 2.6 supports a sound system called Advanced Linux Sound Architecture (ALSA) that supercedes the older Open Sound System (OSS). ALSA uses modular drivers and has support for a wide variety of sound cards as well as USB audio devices such as MIDI synthesizers that you connect to the PC through the USB port. ALSA continues to support older OSS drivers so programs that use OSS can continue to work with ALSA. To learn more about ALSA, visit the ALSA Project's home page at `www.alsa-project.org/`.

Table 5-1 lists the sound cards that Linux supports and shows the name of the driver module that supports a specific set of sound cards. To see if an ALSA driver is available for your sound, visit the ALSA Soundcard Matrix Web page at `www.alsa-project.org/alsa-doc/` and look it up using the manufacturer's name.

To see a list of all sound card vendors along with links to further information about the products and the ALSA driver type the following URL in your Web browser:

```
www.alsa-project.org/alsa-doc/index.php?vendor=All
```

Table 5-1: Supported Sound Cards

Sound Cards or Chipsets	*ALSA Driver Module*
Advanced Gravis UltraSound Classic	`snd-gus`
Advanced Gravis UltraSound Extreme	`snd-gusextreme`
Advanced Gravis UltraSound Max	`snd-gusmax`

Sound Cards or Chipsets	ALSA Driver Module
ALi M1535, M1535D, M1535+, M1535D+	snd-ali5451
AMD InterWave; Advanced Gravis UltraSound PnP; Philips PCA761AW; STB Soundrage 32	snd-interwave
Analog Devices AD1816; Aopen FX-3D Plus	snd-ad1816a
Analog Devices AD11847/848; Aztech Sound Galaxy; Cirrus Logic CS4248	snd-ad1848
ATI IXP 150/200/250	snd-atiixp
AudioTrak Prodigy 7.1; MidiMan Delta Revolution 7.1; Mad Dog Multimedia Entertainer 7.1; Terratec Aureon 5.1 Sky/Space	snd-ice1724
Aureal AU8810	snd-au8810
Aureal AU8820; Aztech PCI 338-A3D, 368-DSP; Turtle Beach Montego A3D	snd-au8820
Aureal AU8830; Diamond Multimedia MonsterSound mx300; Turtle Beach Montego II	snd-au8830
Avance Logic ALS007 (Diamond Technologies DT-019X)	snd-dt019x
Avance Logic ALS100/110/120	snd-als100
Avance Logic ALS4000; Best Union Miss Melody ALS4000; Chic Technology CoolSound 4000; Labway Xwave 4000	snd-als4000
Aztech AZT2320	snd-azt2320
Aztech AZT3328, PCI 168	snd-azt3328
Aztech AZT2320	snd-azt2320
Brooktree Bt878/878a	snd-bt87x
Cirrus Logic CS4231	snd-cs4231
Cirrus Logic CS4232/4232A	snd-cs4232
Cirrus Logic CS4235/4236/4236B/4237B/4238B/4239	snd-cs4236
Cirrus Logic CS4281	snd-cs4281
Cirrus Logic CS4280/4610/4612/4614/4615/4622/4624/4630; Aopen AW320; Hercules Game Fortissimo II and Game Theater XP; Midiman DMAN PCI; Terratec DMX XFire 1024; Turtle Beach Santa Cruz; VideoLogic SonicFury	snd-cs46xx
C-Media CMI8330	snd-cmi8330
C-Media CMI8x38; ASOUND ASONIC-8738; AudioExcel AV 510, MD Mate; Compustar WinFast CMI-8738/PCI C3DX Sound; Hercules Game Muse XML; Labway Xwave 7100; Midiman Delta DiO 2448; Terratec Aureon 5.1 Fun; Trust Sound Expert Digital Surround; Zoltrix Nightingale	snd-cmipci
Core Sound PDAudio-CF	snd-pdaudiocf
Creative Labs Sound Blaster 1.0/1.5/2.0/Pro	snd-sb8

(continued)

Table 5-1 *(continued)*

Sound Cards or Chipsets	*ALSA Driver Module*
Creative Labs Sound Blaster 16/16 ASP/16 PnP, Sound Blaster Vibra16C/16CL/16S/16X	`snd-sb16`
Creative Labs Sound Blaster 32 AWE/32 AWE PnP, Sound Blaster 64 Gold/64 Value	`snd-sbawe`
Creative Labs Sound Blaster PCI64/PCI128	`snd-ens1370`
Creative Labs Sound Blaster 16 PCI/PCI64 (newer model)/PCI128 (newer model)/PCI128 (CT5880), Sound Blaster Ensoniq AudioPCI	`snd-ens1371`
Creative Labs Sound Blaster PCI 512, SoundBlaster Live/Live Platinum/Live Value, Sound Blaster Audigy Platinum/Digital Entertainment/Gamer/ES, Sound Blaster Audigy2 ZS Platinum Pro/Value	`snd-emu10k1`
Creative Labs Sound Blaster PCI X (used by Dell)	`snd-emu10k1x`
Creative Labs Sound Blaster LS, Sound Blaster Live 24bit	`snd-ca0106`
Digigram VXpocket V2 and 440 PC Card	`snd-vxpocket`
Digigram VXpocket VX22 and VX222 V2/Mic	`snd-vx222`
Digigram miXart 8 (AES/EBU)	`snd-mixart`
Ensoniq AudioPCI (ES1370); Creative Labs Sound Blaster PCI64 and PCI128; Shuttle HOT-255	`snd-ens1370`
Ensoniq AudioPCI (ES1371/1372/1373)	`snd-ens1371`
Ensoniq SoundScape	`snd-sscape`
ESS Technology ES968	`snd-es968`
ESS Technology ES688, ES1688	`snd-es1688`
ESS Technology ES18xx	`snd-es18xx`
ESS Technology ES1938 (Solo 1), ES1946 (Solo 1E); Aopen AW180; Best Union Miss Melody Solo 1 Sound; Terratec 128i PCI	`snd-es1938`
ESS Technology ES1968 (Canyon3d, Maestro 1/2/2E/2EM); Aopen AW300; Best Union Miss Melody Maestro Sound; Diamond Multimedia MonsterSound mx400, Sonic Impact s100; Terratec DMX	`snd-es1968`
ESS Technology ES1988 (Maestro3), ES1989 (Maestro3E), ES1990 (Canyon3D-2LE), ES1992 (Canyon3D-2), ES1998/1999/199A/199B	`snd-maestro3`
Fortemedia FM801; A-trend 3DS801A; Abit AU10; Genius SoundMaker Live; Labway Xwave G7X QS3000A; Terratec 512i PCI	`snd-fm801`
IC Ensemble ICE1712 (Envy24); Digigram VX442; Hoontech Soundtrack Audio DSP 24; Midiman Delta 44/66/410/1010/1010-LT, Delta Audiophile2496, Delta DiO2496; Terratec EWS88D/88MT, EWX24/96, DMX 6Fire	`snd-ice1712`
Intel 82801AA,82901AB, i810, i810E, i820, i830, i840, i845, MX440; Ali 5455; Analog Devices AD18xx/19xx; Nvidia nForce; SiS 735/740	`snd-intel8x0`

Sound Cards or Chipsets	*ALSA Driver Module*
Korg 1212I/O	`snd-korg1212`
Labway Xwave 128	`snd-opl3sa2`
NeoMagic MagicMedia 256AV and 256ZX	`snd-nm256`
Oak Technology Mozart	`snd-opti92x-ad1848`
Philips H3600 PDA	`snd-sa11xx-uda1341`
RME Digi32, Digi32Pro, Digi 32/8; SEK'D Prodif 32/96, Prodif Gold	`snd-rme32`
RME Digi96, Digi96/8, Digi96/8 PRO/PST/PAD	`snd-rme96`
RME Hammerfall and Hammerfall Light	`snd-rme9652`
RME Hammerfall DSP Digiface/Multiface/9632/9652	`snd-hdsp`
RME Hammerfall DSP Madi	`snd-hdspm`
S3 SonicVibes; Best Union Miss Melody S3 Sound; Pine Schubert 32 PCI; Turtle Beach Daytona	`snd-sonicvibes`
SEK'D Prodif Plus	`snd-pdplus`
Shark Multimedia Predator 3D	`snd-ad1816`
Shuttle HOT-241/245	`snd-opti9xx`
STB Ultrasound 32-Pro	`snd-interwave-stb`
Tascam USB audio/MIDI US 122/224/428	`snd-usb-usx2y`
Trident 4D-Wave DX/NX; Aztech PCI 64-Q3D, PCI 288-Q3DII; Best Union Miss Melody 4DWave PCI; Chic Technology True Sound 4D Wave-DX/NX; HIS 4DWave PCI; Hoontech Soundtrack Digital-NX; SiS 630/735/745	`snd-trident`
Turtle Beach Tropez and Tropez+	`snd-wavefront`
Turtle Beach MultiSound Fiji, MultiSound Pinnacle	`snd-msnd-pinnacle`
USB audio device such as Creative Labs Sound Blaster Extigy, Sound Blaster MP3+; Evolution MK-2xx/3xx, UC-16; Midiman M-Audio USB MIDI; Edirol USB MIDI products; Yamaha synthesizers with USB interface	`snd-usb-audio`
VIA 82Cxxx chipset, Windows Sound System	`snd-via82xx`
Xitel Storm Platinum	`snd-au8330`
Yamaha OPL3-SA2, OPL3-SA3, OPL3-SAx, YMF701, YMF711, YMF715,YMF718, YMF719; Toshiba Libretto 50CT/70CT and Tecra 8000 laptops	`snd-opl3-sa2`
Yamaha Waveforce 192XG, Waveforce 192 Digital, YMF724, YMF740, YMF744, YMF754; A-trend 3DS724A; Aopen AW724, AW744, AW744 Pro; Best Union Miss Melody Samba Tornado; Chic Technology True Sound 724; Guillemot MaxiSound Fortissimo; Hoontech Digital XG, Soundtrack Digital-XG, Soundtrack i-Phone; Labway DiX, NEC PK-UG-X013; Xwave 192/320/576 /G5X/J8X/5000/5000Pro/ 6000/6000Pro; Sony VAIO N505VX and PCG-F480; Toshiba Satellite Pro 4200 laptop	`snd-ymfpci`

Configuring the Sound Card

Linux needs a driver to control the sound card. The Linux kernel should automatically load the correct sound driver after you install Linux from the companion DVD-ROM. The sound drivers are provided as loadable modules that you can also manually load or unload. You will find the sound drivers organized into several directories in the `/lib/modules/2.6.*/kernel/sound` directory. For example, the `pci` directory has driver modules for PCI sound cards. If you look at the names of the module files, you see that each filename ends with the extension `.ko` (the `.ko` extension identifies a kernel object file — a file containing binary instructions that implements the driver).

Whenever you boot Fedora Linux, it runs kudzu, a tool that detects new hardware. Whenever kudzu runs, it detects the current hardware and checks it against a list stored in a text file, `/etc/sysconfig/hwconf`. It then determines if any hardware has been added or removed. Kudzu gives the user an opportunity to configure new hardware or remove the support for hardware no longer installed on the system. Configuring new hardware includes adding appropriate lines to the `/etc/modprobe.conf` file so that the proper driver modules will be loaded when needed. Typically, a sound card should be detected by kudzu and configured during the boot sequence, but sometimes kudzu may load the incorrect driver for a card.

As Linux boots and kudzu detects hardware, kudzu displays messages about the detected hardware. The boot messages scroll by too fast to read, but you can look at them with the `dmesg` command. Type **dmesg | more** and then look for one or more lines that mention your sound card's name or model number. You can also look at the `/etc/sysconfig/hwconf` file where kudzu stores information about hardware it detects.

If you have older ISA bus plug-and-play (PnP) sound cards, look for any occurrence of lines containing the word `isapnp` in the boot messages — these lines show the result of kudzu detecting the PnP devices. On one of my PCs, for example, I have a Yamaha OPL3-SA3 PnP sound card. In this case, when I type `dmesg | grep isapnp`, I see the following messages:

```
isapnp: Scanning for PnP cards...
isapnp: Card 'OPL3-SA3 Snd System'
isapnp: 1 Plug & Play card detected total
```

For this sound card, the `/etc/modprobe.conf` file should have the following lines:

```
alias snd-card-0 snd-opl3-sa2
```

Fedora provides a sound card configuration tool (system-config-soundcard), but that tool does not work with ISA PnP cards. It can detect only PCI sound cards. Select Display ➪ System Settings ➪ Soundcard Detection. If the tool detects your sound card, it displays the information in a small window, as shown in Figure 5-1.

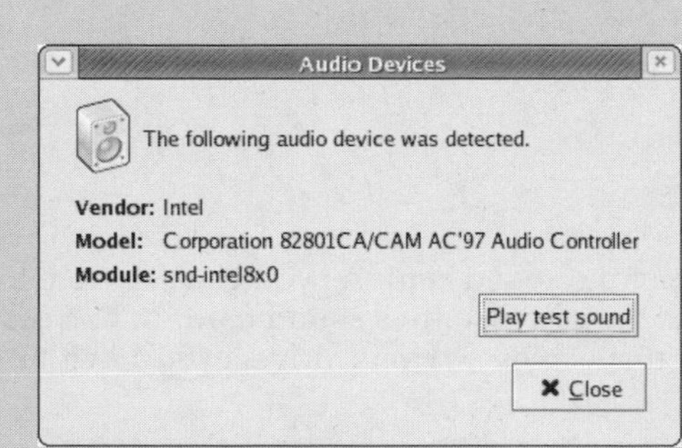

Figure 5-1: Sound Card Detected by system-config-soundcard Tool.

You can play a test sound with the sound card configuration tool, but the tool does not provide for any way to configure the sound card (for example, to load a different driver module). The bottom line is that newer PCI sound cards should work without much trouble in Linux, but for older ISA PnP sound cards you have to do some work to get sound going.

If you know your sound card type, one way to configure it is to manually load the driver and to set up information in the `/etc/modprobe.conf` file so that the correct driver is loaded.

The next few sections describe how to manually configure sound on Linux.

Checking Information about a Sound Card

Typically, you can find out information about your PC's sound card from what kudzu finds as it probes the hardware. Kudzu stores the information about all detected hardware in the following file:

```
/etc/sysconfig/hwconf
```

You can open that file in a text editor and look for a line that looks like this:

```
class: AUDIO
```

The information about the sound card is in the lines that follow, up to the next line that has a lone hyphen. For example, here is the information for an ISA bus Yamaha OPL3SA2 sound card:

```
class: AUDIO
bus: PCI
detached: 0
driver: snd-intel8x0
desc: "Intel Corporation 82801CA/CAM AC'97 Audio Controller"
vendorId: 8086
deviceId: 2485
subVendorId: 1028
```

```
subDeviceId: 00f3
pciType: 1
pcidom:    0
pcibus:  0
pcidev: 1f
pcifn:  5
-
```

The desc line tells you the name of the sound card. As you can see from the driver line, kudzu specifies snd-intel8x0 as the driver for this sound card. In this case, the driver is correct. If for some reason kudzu specifies a wrong driver, you have to do some work yourself to correct the problem.

Manually Configuring the Sound Card

When you know the sound card type and the driver that you must load, it's a simple procedure to load the driver manually. All you have to do is log in as root and use the modprobe command with the following syntax:

```
modprobe drivername
```

where *drivername* is the name of the driver module to load. Thus, you can load the snd-intel8x0 driver by typing:

```
modprobe snd-intel8x0
```

That's all you need to do. After loading the driver, you can verify that it's loaded by typing the lsmod command. For example, here are a few lines of output from the lsmod command on a PC after loading the snd_intel8x0 driver:

```
Module                  Size  Used by
... lines deleted...
snd_intel8x0           34561  1
snd_ac97_codec         71609  2 snd_intel8x0m,snd_intel8x0
snd_pcm               100937  4 snd_intel8x0m,snd_intel8x0,snd_ac97_codec,
                                snd_pcm_oss
snd_timer              33605  1 snd_pcm
snd                    56612  9 snd_intel8x0m,snd_intel8x0,snd_ac97_codec,
                                snd_pcm_oss,snd_mixer_oss,snd_pcm,snd_timer
soundcore              10913  1 snd
... rest of the lines deleted...
```

I want to point out that loading the snd_intel8x0 driver with the modprobe command causes the loading of the other modules — snd_ac97_codec, snd_pcm, snd_timer, snd, and soundcore — that snd_intel8x0 (and the supporting cast of drivers) needs.

After you load the driver manually with the modprobe command, the sound card should work. You can test it by playing an audio CD, as explained in the "Testing the Sound Card" section.

To test a sound driver, you can load it manually with the `modprobe` command, but for automatic loading you should also edit the `/etc/modprobe.conf` file and add the following line:

```
alias snd-card-0 drivername
```

where *drivername* is the sound driver you want to load. That way, when the kernel needs to load the sound driver (perhaps because you have started playing an audio CD with the CD Player application), the correct driver will be loaded.

Typically, the sound driver can probe any PnP sound card to determine its hardware parameters such as the I/O port addresses, the interrupt request numbers (IRQs), and the direct memory access (DMAs) channel. If you do not have a PnP sound card, you have to specify the I/O address, the IRQ, and the DMA channel number of the sound card. You can specify these parameters by adding options lines in the `/etc/modprobe.conf` file. For example, the following lines in `/etc/modprobe.conf` specify the parameters for a Creative Labs SoundBlaster sound card:

```
alias snd-card-0 snd-sb8
options snd-sb8 port=0x220 irq=5 dma8=1 index=0 enable=1
```

For a PnP or PCI sound card, all you have to do is have an alias line for `snd-card-0` with the correct driver name and an options line that enables the card. For example, here are the lines for a laptop with the Intel i810 Integrated AC97 Audio:

```
alias snd-card-0 snd-intel8x0
options snd-card-0 index=0 enable=1
```

Learning Sound Device Names

Like any other devices in Linux, the sound devices have files in the `/dev` directory with specific names. Table 5-2 lists the standard device files that provide sound capability in Linux (you may not have all these devices on your system).

Table 5-2: Standard Sound Device Filenames in Linux

Device Filename	*Description*
`/dev/audio`	An audio device capable of playing Sun workstation–compatible audio files (typically with a `.au` extension). The device does not support all capabilities of the Sun workstation audio device but can play Sun audio files.
`/dev/audio1`	A Sun workstation–compatible audio device for the second sound card (if any).
`/dev/dsp`	A digital signal–processing device that also can play Sun audio files.
`/dev/midi00 - 03`	MIDI ports (if you have a MIDI-capable sound card).
`/dev/mixer`	A sound-mixer device.
`/dev/mixer1`	A second sound-mixer device.
`/dev/sequencer`	A MIDI sequencer device (if sound card has MIDI sequencer).

Testing the Sound Card

To test the sound driver, you should try playing a sound file. A good way to do this is to insert an audio CD into your CD/DVD-ROM drive, and play a sound track. See the section "Playing Audio CDs" for more information about various CD Player applications.

If you don't have an audio CD handy, you can use the Helix Player to open and play a sound file. Helix Player can play many types of sound files, including MP3, OGG, and Windows WAV. You will find many OGG and WAV sound files—which usually have names that end with the .ogg and .wav extensions—in the /usr/share/sounds directory of your Fedora Linux system.

To play a sound file, start the Helix Player from the GNOME desktop by selecting Applications ➪ Sound & Video ➪ Helix Player. The Helix Player has a simple user interface. To open a sound file, select File ➪ Open File and select a .wav file from the Open dialog box. Select a file from the /usr/share/sounds directory, and then click the play button. Helix Player starts playing the sound file.

If you hear no sound, most likely the volume is turned down low. Click the Volume Control (the speaker icon) next to the clock at the right hand side of the top panel in the GNOME desktop. Then drag the slider to increase the volume. You can also adjust the volume of the sound from the volume control that appears when you select Applications ➪ Sound & Video ➪ Volume Control from the GNOME desktop.

If you have a microphone connected to your sound card, you can try recording a 10-second sound file with the following command:

```
dd bs=8k count=10 </dev/audio >test.au
```

The dd command simply copies a specified amount of data from one file to another. In this case, the input file is the audio device (which records from the microphone), and the output file is the sound file. You may have to run the volume control program to set the recording-gain level for the microphone. After recording the sound file, you can play it back by sending the data back to /dev/audio with the following command:

```
cat test.au > /dev/audio
```

Playing Audio CDs

You need a special application to play audio CDs in the CD/DVD drive. Both GNOME and KDE come with CD Players.

Before using any CD Player program, make sure you unmount any CD currently in the drive (use the umount /dev/cdrom command), remove the CD, and place an audio CD in the drive. To play the audio CD, you must also have a sound card and the appropriate sound drivers installed, as described in earlier sections of this chapter.

If you are using the GNOME desktop, you can play audio CDs by simply inserting an audio CD in the CD drive. The GNOME CD Player starts and begins playing the CD.

If the CD Player does not start automatically, you can launch the CD Player by selecting Applications ➪ Sound & Video ➪ CD Player. Figure 5-2 shows this CD Player playing a track from an audio CD. As you can see, the CD Player displays the title of the CD and the name of the current track. The CD Player gets the song titles from http://freedb.org—a free open-source CD database on the Internet (`freedb.freedb.org` at port 888). You need an active Internet connection for the CD Player to download song information from the CD database. After the CD Player downloads information about a particular CD, it caches that information in a local database for future use.

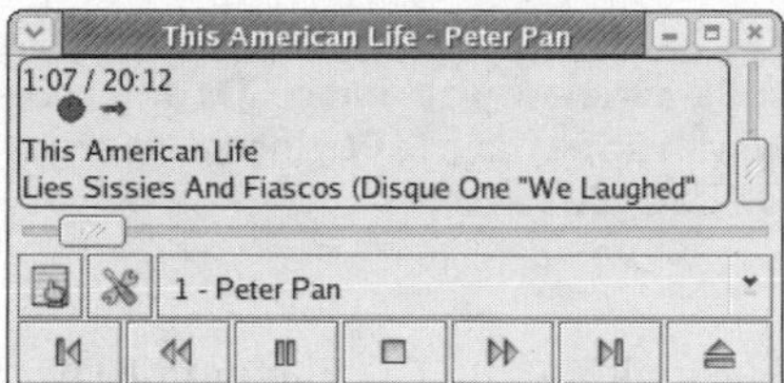

Figure 5-2: The GNOME CD Player Playing a Track from an Audio CD.

The CD Player's user interface is intuitive, and you can learn it easily. One nice feature is that you have the ability to select a track by title, as shown in Figure 5-3.

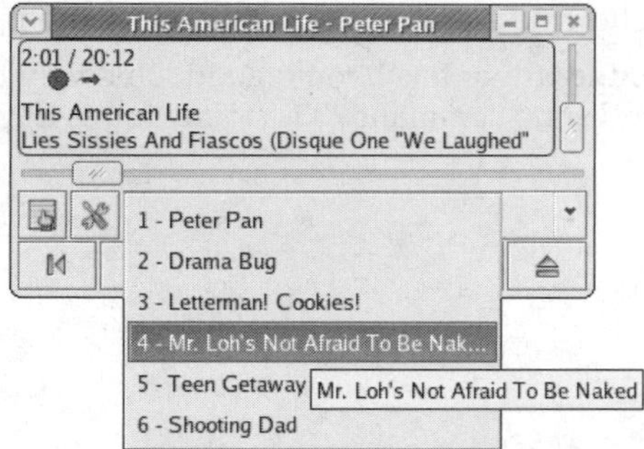

Figure 5-3: Selecting a Specific Audio Track to Play with the CD Player.

insider insight

To learn more about the freedb CD database, read the Frequently Asked Questions at `www.freedb.org/`.

If you want to log in as a normal user and play audio CDs on the CD/DVD-ROM drive, you should first log in as `root` and set the permissions settings on the CD/DVD-ROM device so that anyone can read it. (You have to set the permissions for the actual CD/DVD-ROM device, not the generic `/dev/cdrom` device.) To do this, follow these steps:

1. Log in as `root`. If you are already logged in, type **su -**, and enter the superuser's password to assume the identity of `root`.
2. Type **ls –l /dev/cdrom** and find the actual device for which `/dev/cdrom` is a symbolic link. For example, in my case, `/dev/hdc` is the physical device, as the output of the `ls -l /dev/cdrom` command indicates:

```
lrwxrwxrwx  1 root root 3 Apr  2 14:04 /dev/cdrom -> hdc
```

continued

continued

3. Make the CD/DVD-ROM device readable by all users by using the `chmod` command as follows:

```
chmod o+r /dev/hdc
```

Anyone who has access to your Linux PC can now play audio CDs and access the CD drive. Note, however, that anyone with access to the PC, including anyone who can remotely log in, can now read data CDs as well.

If you use KDE as your desktop, you can find a similar audio CD Player in KDE. Start the KDE CD Player by selecting Main Menu ➪ Sound & Video ➪ KsCD.

Troubleshooting Sound Cards

If, after you configure the sound driver, the sound card does not produce sound when you play a sound file or an audio CD, try the following steps to diagnose and fix the problem:

1. Check to see whether or not the sound driver has been loaded. One way to check is to look at the output of the `lsmod` command. The following is a typical output:

```
lsmod | more
Module                  Size  Used by
nls_utf8                2113  0
i915                   19009  1
parport_pc             28933  1
lp                     12617  0
parport                40713  2 parport_pc,lp
autofs4                26949  0
sunrpc                167941  1
dm_mod                 59989  0
md5                     4161  1
ipv6                  265089  12
uhci_hcd               33497  0
ehci_hcd               40397  0
i2c_i801                8653  0
i2c_core               22209  1 i2c_i801
snd_intel8x0           34561  3
snd_ac97_codec         71609  1 snd_intel8x0
snd_pcm_oss            52081  0
snd_mixer_oss          18497  2 snd_pcm_oss
snd_pcm               100937  4 snd_intel8x0,snd_ac97_codec,snd_pcm_oss
snd_timer              33605  1 snd_pcm
... lines deleted ...
```

   The listing should show some modules whose names begin with `snd`. If you don't see the sound drivers, the sound card may not have been detected properly.

2. Verify that kudzu detected the sound card when it was loaded. Type **more /etc/sysconfig/hwconf** to look for a section that begins with `class: AUDIO`.

3. If you know what sound card is in your PC, you can look up the name of the driver from Table 5-1 and type **modprobe drivername** to load that driver.
4. If the driver does not seem to work, you may want to read the driver's documentation. To read more about the driver, point your Web browser to `www.alsa-project.org/alsa-doc/index.php?vendor=All` and click the link to your sound card's driver.

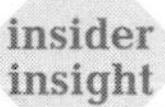

If you still cannot get the sound card to work under Linux, you may want to post a news item to one of the comp.os.linux newsgroups. Chapter 16 discusses how to connect to the Internet and access the newsgroups.

Summary

Unlike many UNIX workstations, a typical PC comes with a sound card. This chapter describes the sound cards that Linux kernel 2.6 supports and shows you how to detect and correct some common sound-card installation problems.

By reading this chapter, you learned the following:

- To use a sound card, you have to load the sound driver module. The kudzu program can detect and load the correct driver module for PCI and plug-and-play (PnP) sound cards.
- If kudzu does not load the correct driver, you can use the `modprobe` command to load the correct driver. You should also edit the `/etc/modprobe.conf` file so that the correct sound driver is automatically loaded whenever the kernel needs it.
- Both GNOME and KDE desktops come with CD Player applications that enable you to play sound tracks from audio CDs. You can use these CD Players to test your sound card.

Network Setup

Secrets in This Chapter

UNIX and networking go hand in hand; TCP/IP (Transmission Control Protocol/Internet Protocol) networking is practically synonymous with UNIX. As a UNIX clone, Linux includes extensive built-in networking capabilities. In particular, Linux supports TCP/IP networking over several physical interfaces, such as Ethernet cards, serial ports, and parallel ports.

Typically, you use an Ethernet network for your local area network (LAN) — at your office or even your home (if you happen to have two or more systems at home). TCP/IP networking over the serial port enables you to connect to other networks by dialing out over a modem. Linux supports both Serial Line Internet Protocol (SLIP) and Point-to-Point Protocol (PPP).

This chapter focuses on Linux's support for Ethernet and TCP/IP. The chapter starts with a discussion of networking in general and TCP/IP in particular; then it covers the physical setup of an Ethernet LAN, including information about specific brands of Ethernet cards. Finally, the chapter describes how to set up a TCP/IP network on a Linux system.

cross ref

Although much of this applies to TCP/IP over the serial line, this chapter does not dwell on the specific details of dial-up networking; that topic is the focus of Chapter 13. That chapter also describes how to connect to the Internet using a cable modem and DSL as well as how to configure a wireless Ethernet LAN in Linux.

Laptops often use PCMCIA cards (also called PC cards) for networking. Appendix F describes the PC cards that Linux supports.

Networking Basics

Like any other technical subject, networking is full of terminology and jargon that a newcomer might find daunting. This section introduces some basic concepts of networking, starting with a layered model of networking and proceeding to details of Ethernet and TCP/IP network protocols.

The OSI Seven-Layer Model

A widely used conceptual model of networking is the seven-layer Open Systems Interconnection (OSI) reference model, developed by the International Organizaton for Standardization (ISO). The OSI reference model describes the flow of data between the physical connection to the network and the end-user application. Each layer is responsible for providing particular functionality, as shown in Figure 6-1.

As Figure 6-1 shows, the OSI layers are numbered from bottom to top. Basic functions, such as physically sending data bits through the network cable, are at the bottom; functions that deal with higher-level abstractions of the data are at the top. The purpose of each layer is to provide services to the next-higher layer in a manner such that the higher layer does not have to know how the services are actually implemented. In fact, each layer is designed so that it does not have to know how the other layers work.

7	Application
6	Presentation
5	Session
4	Transport
3	Network
2	Data Link
1	Physical

Figure 6-1: The OSI Seven-Layer Reference Model of Networking.

The purposes of the seven layers in the OSI reference model are as follows:

- **Physical layer (Layer 1):** Transmits raw bits of data across the physical medium (the networking cable or electromagnetic waves, in the case of wireless networks). This layer carries the data generated by all the higher layers. The physical layer deals with three physical components:
  - Network topology (such as bus or star), which specifies how various nodes of a network are physically connected
  - Transmission medium (such as RG-58 coaxial cable, shielded or unshielded twisted pair, fiber-optic cable, and wireless) that carries the actual signals representing data
  - Transmission technique (such as Carrier Sense Multiple Access with Collision Detection [CSMA/CD], used by Ethernet; and token-based techniques, used by token-ring and Fiber Distributed Data Interface [FDDI]), which defines the hardware protocols for data transfer
- **Data link layer (Layer 2):** Deals with logical packets (or frames) of data. This layer packages raw bits from the physical layer into frames, the exact format of which depends on the type of network, such as Ethernet or token ring. The frames the data-link layer uses contain the physical addresses of the sender and the receiver of data.
- **Network layer (Layer 3):** Contains information about the logical network addresses and how to translate logical addresses to physical ones. At the sending end, the network layer converts larger logical packets to smaller physical data frames. At the receiving end, the network layer reassembles the data frames into their original logical packet structure.
- **Transport layer (Layer 4):** Responsible for the reliable delivery of messages that originate at the application layer. At the sending end, this layer divides long messages into several packets. At the receiving end, the transport layer reassembles the original messages and sends an acknowledgment of receipt. The transport layer also ensures that data is received in the correct order in a timely manner. In case of errors, the transport layer requests retransmission of data.

- **Session layer (Layer 5):** Enables applications on different computers to initiate, use, and terminate a connection (the connection is called a session). The session layer translates the names of systems to appropriate addresses (for example, IP addresses in TCP/IP networks).
- **Presentation layer (Layer 6):** Manages the format used to exchange data between networked computers. Data encryption and decryption, for example, are in this layer. Most network protocols do not have a presentation layer.
- **Application layer (Layer 7):** The gateway through which application processes access network services. This layer represents services (such as file transfers, database access, and electronic mail) that directly support applications.

The OSI model is not specific to any hardware or software; it simply provides an architectural framework and gives us a common terminology for discussing various networking capabilities.

A Simplified Four-Layer TCP/IP Network Model

The OSI seven-layer model is not a specification; it provides guidelines for organizing all network services. Most implementations adopt a layered model for networking services, and these layered models can be mapped to the OSI reference model. The TCP/IP networking model, for example, can be adequately represented by a simplified model.

Network-aware applications usually deal with the top three layers (session, presentation, and application) of the OSI seven-layer reference model. Thus, these three layers can be combined into a single layer called the application layer.

The bottom two layers of the OSI model — physical and data link — also can be combined into a single physical layer. These combinations result in a simplified four-layer model, as shown in Figure 6-2.

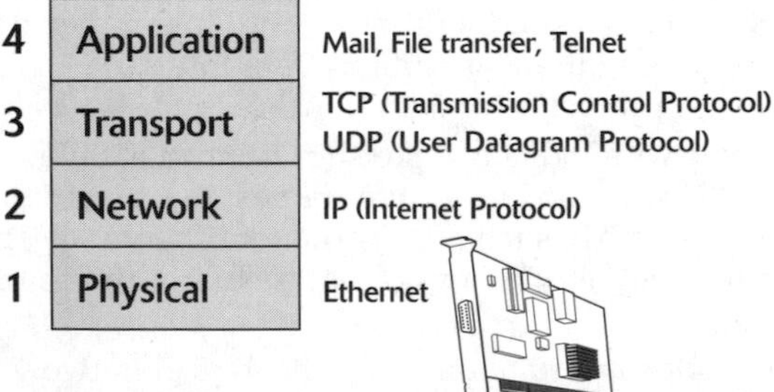

Figure 6-2: A Simplified Four-Layer TCP/IP Networking Model.

At each of these layers, information is exchanged through one of many network protocols.

Network Protocols

The term "network protocol" refers to a detailed process the sender and receiver agree upon for exchanging data at a specific layer of the networking model. Thus, you find the following protocols in the simplified four-layer network model of Figure 6-2:

- Physical-layer protocols, such as Ethernet, token ring, and FDDI
- Network-layer protocols, such as the Internet Protocol (IP), which is part of the TCP/IP protocol suite

- Transport-layer protocols, such as the Transmission Control Protocol (TCP) and User Datagram Protocol (UDP), which are part of the TCP/IP protocol suite
- Application-layer protocols, such as File Transfer Protocol (FTP), Simple Mail Transfer Protocol (SMTP), Domain Name Service (DNS), Secure Shell (SSH), Telnet, HyperText Transfer Protocol (HTTP), and Simple Network Management Protocol (SNMP), which are also part of the TCP/IP protocol suite

The term "protocol suite" refers to a collection of two or more protocols from these layers that form the basis of a network. The following are some of the well-known protocol suites:

- IPX/SPX (Internet Packet Exchange/Sequenced Packet Exchange) protocol suite, used by Novell NetWare
- NetBIOS and NetBEUI (Network BIOS Extended User Interface), used by Microsoft's operating systems
- TCP/IP protocol suite

Of these protocol suites, you are probably most interested in the TCP/IP protocol suite because that's what Linux and other UNIX systems support well.

cross ref

In addition to the TCP/IP protocol, Linux supports the IPX protocol but not the SPX protocol necessary for NetWare. Linux's support for NetBIOS comes in the form of a software package named Samba, included on the companion DVD-ROM and described in Chapter 19.

Learning More about TCP/IP

This chapter gives you an overview of TCP/IP and Ethernet networking and then moves on to Linux-specific instructions for setting up TCP/IP networking. A single chapter simply isn't enough to provide all available information about TCP/IP. For more information on TCP/IP, consult one of the following books:

- Douglas E. Comer and Ralph E. Droms, *Computer Networks and Internets, with Internet Applications, Fourth Edition*, Prentice Hall, 2003.
- Douglas E. Comer, *Internetworking with TCP/IP, Volume 1: Principles, Protocols, and Architecture, Fourth Edition*, Prentice Hall, 2000.
- W. Richard Stevens, *Unix Network Programming, Vol. 1: The Sockets Networking API*, Third Edition, Prentice Hall, 2003.

TCP/IP and the Internet

TCP/IP has become the protocol of choice on the Internet—the "network of networks" that evolved from ARPAnet, a packet-switching network that itself evolved from research the U.S. government's Advanced Research Projects Agency (ARPA) initiated in the 1970s. Subsequently, ARPA acquired a Defense prefix and became DARPA. Under the auspices of DARPA, the TCP/IP protocols emerged as a popular collection of protocols for *internetworking*—a term used to describe communication among networks.

TCP/IP has flourished for several reasons. A significant reason is that the protocol is open, which means the technical descriptions of the protocol appear in public documents, so anyone can implement TCP/IP on specific hardware and software.

Another, more important, reason for TCP/IP's success is the availability of sample implementation. Instead of describing network architecture and protocols on paper, each component of the TCP/IP protocol suite began life as a specification with a sample implementation.

Taking Stock of RFCs

The details of each TCP/IP protocol (including TCP and IP, as well as specific service protocols such as SMTP and FTP) are described in documents known as Requests for Comments (RFCs). These documents are freely distributed on the Internet. You can get RFCs from `www.rfc-archive.org/` (click the Index link for a complete index of the RFC or search by keyword). Another good site for RFCs is `www.faqs.org/rfcs/`.

In fact, the notation used to name Internet resources in a uniform manner is itself documented in an RFC. The notation, known as the Uniform Resource Locator (URL), is described in RFC 1738, "Uniform Resource Locators (URL)," written by, among others, T. Berners-Lee, the originator of the World Wide Web (WWW). A more recent RFC—RFC 3986, "Uniform Resource Identifier (URI): Generic Syntax," also written by T. Berners-Lee and others—updates RFC 1738 and introduces the general term "URI," which can be a locator such as a URL or a name such as Uniform Resource Name (URN).

You can think of RFCs as the working papers of the Internet research-and-development community. All Internet standards are published as RFCs. However, many RFCs do not specify any standards; they are informational documents only.

The following are some RFCs you may find interesting:

- RFC 768, "User Datagram Protocol (UDP)"
- RFC 791, "Internet Protocol (IP)"
- RFC 792, "Internet Control Message Protocol (ICMP)"
- RFC 793, "Transmission Control Protocol (TCP)"
- RFC 854, "TELNET Protocol Specification"
- RFC 950, "Internet Standard Subnetting Procedure"
- RFC 959, "File Transfer Protocol (FTP)"
- RFC 1034, "Domain Names: Concepts and Facilities"
- RFC 1058, "Routing Information Protocol (RIP)"
- RFC 1112, "Host Extensions for IP Multicasting"
- RFC 1155, "Structure and Identification of Management Information for TCP/IP-based Internets"
- RFC 1157, "Simple Network Management Protocol (SNMP)"
- RFC 1519, "Classless Inter-Domain Routing (CIDR) Assignment and Aggregation Strategy"
- RFC 1661, "The Point-to-Point Protocol (PPP)"
- RFC 1738, "Uniform Resource Locators (URL)"
- RFC 1796, "Not All RFCs Are Standards"
- RFC 1855, "Netiquette Guidelines"
- RFC 1918, "Address Allocation for Private Internets"
- RFC 1939, "Post Office Protocol, Version 3 (POP3)"
- RFC 1945, "HyperText Transfer Protocol—HTTP/1.0"

- RFC 2026, "The Internet Standards Process — Revision 3"
- RFC 2028, "The Organizations Involved in the IETF Standards Process"
- RFC 2045 through 2049, "Multipurpose Internet Mail Extensions (MIME)" (Parts One through Five)
- RFC 2131, "Dynamic Host Configuration Protocol (DHCP)"
- RFC 2146, "U.S. Government Internet Domain Names"
- RFC 2151, "A Primer on Internet and TCP/IP Tools and Utilities"
- RFC 2328, "Open Shortest Path First Routing (OSPF) Version 2"
- RFC 2368, "The mailto URL Scheme"
- RFC 2460, "Internet Protocol, Version 6 (IPv6) Specification"
- RFC 2616, "HyperText Transfer Protocol — HTTP/1.1"
- RFC 2660, "The Secure HyperText Transfer Protocol"
- RFC 2821, "Simple Mail Transfer Protocol (SMTP)"
- RFC 2822, "Internet Message Format"
- RFC 2853, "Generic Security Service API Version 2: Java Bindings"
- RFC 2854, "The 'text/html' Media Type"
- RFC 2865, "Remote Authentication Dial In User Service (RADIUS)"
- RFC 2870, "Root Name Server Operational Requirements"
- RFC 2871, "A Framework for Telephony Routing over IP"
- RFC 2910, "Internet Printing Protocol/1.1: Encoding and Transport"
- RFC 2911, "Internet Printing Protocol/1.1: Model and Semantics"
- RFC 3013, "Recommended Internet Service Provider Security Services and Procedures"
- RFC 3022, "Traditional IP Network Address Translator (Traditional NAT)"
- RFC 3076, "Canonical XML Version 1.0"
- RFC 3130, "Notes from the State-Of-The-Technology: DNSSEC"
- RFC 3174, "US Secure Hash Algorithm 1 (SHA1)"
- RFC 3196, "Internet Printing Protocol/1.1: Implementer's Guide"
- RFC 3275, "(Extensible Markup Language) XML-Signature Syntax and Processing"
- RFC 3330, "Special-Use IPv4 Addresses"
- RFC 3344, "IP Mobility Support for IPv4"
- RFC 3501, "Internet Message Access Protocol - Version 4rev1"
- RFC 3513, "Internet Protocol Version 6 (IPv6) Addressing Architecture"
- RFC 3965, "A Simple Mode of Facsimile Using Internet Mail"
- RFC 3596, "DNS Extensions to Support IP Version 6"
- RFC 3700, "Internet Official Protocol Standards"
- RFC 3986, "Uniform Resource Identifier (URI): Generic Syntax"
- RFC 4033, "DNS Security Introduction and Requirements"
- RFC 4034, "Resource Records for the DNS Security Extensions"
- RFC 4035, "Protocol Modifications for the DNS Security Extensions"
- RFC 4038, "Application Aspects of IPv6 Transition"

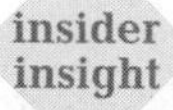

The RFCs continue to evolve as new technology and techniques emerge. If you work in networking, you should keep an eye on the RFCs to monitor emerging networking protocols. You can check up on the RFCs at `www.faqs.org/rfcs/`.

Understanding IP Addresses

When you have many computers on a network, you need a way to identify each one uniquely. In TCP/IP networking, the address of a computer is known as the IP address. Because TCP/IP deals with internetworking, the address is based on the concepts of a network address and a host address. You might think of the idea of a network address and a host address as having to provide two addresses to identify a computer uniquely:

- **Network address:** Indicates the network on which the computer is located
- **Host address:** Indicates a specific computer on that network

The IP address is a 4-byte (32-bit) value with some of the bits devoted to the network address and the rest used for the host address. The convention is to write each byte as a decimal value and to put a dot (.) after each number. Thus, you see network addresses such as 132.250.112.52. This way of writing IP addresses is known as *dotted-decimal* or *dotted-quad* notation. Each of the four decimal numbers in the dotted-decimal notation is often referred to as an octet. Note that each decimal number in the dotted-decimal notation must be between 0 and 255 because that's the range of values a byte can hold.

The bits in an IP address are organized in the following manner:

```
<Network Address, Host Address>
```

In other words, a specified number of bits of the 32-bit IP address are used as a network address, and the rest of the bits are interpreted as a host address. The network address identifies the LAN to which your PC is connected and the host address identifies your PC as one of many hosts within the LAN. Other PCs in the LAN share the same network address, but have different bits in the host address portion fo their IP addresses.

When IP addresses were initially allocated to organizations, a class system was devised to accommodate networks of various sizes. (The network size is the number of computers in that network.) Although the network classes are largely ignored nowadays, it is important to understand what the network classes are and how they work because they linger on in the backbone of the Internet. In place of predefined classes, IP networks use classless addressing schemes with network marks to separate the network address from the host address.

There are five classes of IP addresses, named class A through class E, as shown in Figure 6-3.

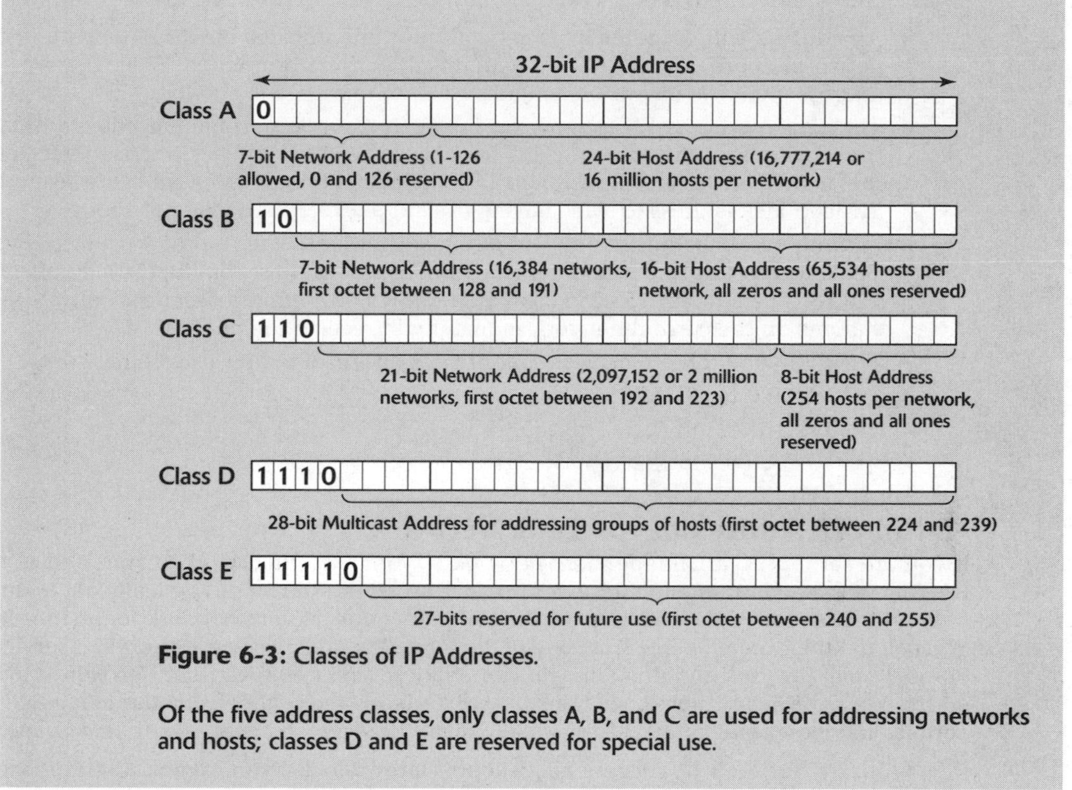

Figure 6-3: Classes of IP Addresses.

Of the five address classes, only classes A, B, and C are used for addressing networks and hosts; classes D and E are reserved for special use.

Class A addresses support 126 networks, each with up to 16 million hosts. Although the network address is 7-bit, two values (0 and 127) have special meaning; therefore, you can have only 1 through 126 as Class A network addresses. There can be approximately 2 billion class A hosts.

Class B addresses are for networks with up to 65,534 hosts. There can be at most 16,384 class B networks. All class B networks, taken together, can have approximately 1 billion hosts.

Class C addresses are meant for small organizations. Each class C address allows up to 254 hosts, and there can be approximately 2 million class C networks. Therefore, there can be at most approximately 500 million class C hosts. If you are in a small company, you probably have a class C address. Nowadays, it is customary to aggregate multiple class C addresses into a single block and use them for efficient routing.

All together, class A, B, and C networks can support at most approximately 3.5 billion hosts.

You can tell the class of an IP address by the first number in the dotted-decimal notation, as follows:

- **Class A addresses:** 1.xxx.xxx.xxx through 126.xxx.xxx.xxx
- **Class B addresses:** 128.xxx.xxx.xxx through 191.xxx.xxx.xxx
- **Class C addresses:** 192.xxx.xxx.xxx through 223.xxx.xxx.xxx

Even within the five address classes, the following IP addresses have special meaning:

- An address with all zeros in its network portion indicates the *local* network: the network where the data packet with this IP address originated. Thus, the address 0.0.0.200 means host number 200 on this class C network.
- The class A address 127.xxx.xxx.xxx is used for *loopback*: communications within the same host. Conventionally, 127.0.0.1 is used as the loopback address. Processes that need to communicate through TCP with other processes on the same host use the loopback address to avoid having to send packets out on the network.
- Turning on all the bits in any part of the address indicates a broadcast message. The address 128.18.255.255, for example, means all hosts on the class B network 128.18. The address 255.255.255.255 is known as a *limited broadcast*; all workstations on the current network segment will receive the packet.
- The following three blocks of IP addresses are reserved for private networks:
  - 10.0.0.0 to 10.255.255.255
  - 172.16.0.0 to 172.31.255.255
  - 192.168.0.0 to 192.168.255.255

Getting IP Addresses for Your Network

If you are setting up an independent network of your own that will be connected to the Internet, you need unique IP addresses for your network. You would typically get a range of IP addresses for your network from the ISP that connects your network to the Internet. You can get the domain name from one of the Internet domain name registration services. For example, for the `.com` domain, you can obtain domain names from VeriSign located on the Web at `www.networksolutions.com/`. To learn more about domain name and IP address services, point your Web browser to the InterNIC website at `www.internic.net/`.

ISPs typically get their IP address allocation in large blocks from regional Internet registries such as ARIN (American Registry for Internet Numbers, `www.arin.net/`) in the United States, RIPE (Réseaux IP Européens, `www.ripe.net/`) in Europe, and APNIC (Asia Pacific Network Information Centre, `www.apnic.net/`) for the Asia-Pacific region. For more information about IP address allocation services, visit the Internet Assigned Numbers Authority (IANA) website at `www.iana.org/ipaddress/ip-addresses.htm`.

If you don't plan to connect your network to the Internet, you really don't need a unique IP address. RFC 1918 (the "Address Allocation for Private Internets" section) provides guidance about what IP addresses you can use within private networks (the term "private Internet" refers to any network not connected to the Internet). Three blocks of IP addresses are reserved for private Internets:

- 10.0.0.0 to 10.255.255.255
- 172.16.0.0 to 172.31.255.255
- 192.168.0.0 to 192.168.255.255

You can use addresses from these blocks for your private network without having to coordinate with an organization. For example, I (and many others) use the 192.168.0.0 Class C address for a home network. Additionally, the cable/DSL routers use one of these private Class C addresses for the local network interface.

If you have only one public Internet address from your ISP, you can still use a Network Address Translation (NAT) router to connect your local network with private IP addresses to the public Internet.

Figuring Out Network Masks

The network mask is an IP address that has 1s in the bits that correspond to the network address, and 0s in all other bit positions. The class of your network address determines the network mask.

If you have a class C address, for example, the network mask is 255.255.255.0. Thus, class B networks have a network mask of 255.255.0.0, and class A networks have 255.0.0.0 as the network mask. Of course, you do not have to use the historical class A, B, or C network masks. Nowadays, you can use any other network mask that's appropriate for your network address.

Extracting Network Addresses

The network address is the bitwise AND of the network mask with any IP address in your network. If the IP address of a system on your network is 206.197.168.200, and the network mask is 255.255.255.0, the network address is 206.197.168.0. The network address is written with zero bits in the part of the address that's supposed to be for the host address.

Using Subnets

If your site has a class B address, you get one network number, and that network can have up to 65,534 hosts. Even if you work for a megacorporation that has thousands of hosts, you may want to divide your network into smaller subnetworks (or *subnets*). If your organization has offices in several locations, for example, you may want each office to be on a separate network. You can do this by taking some bits from the host-address portion of the IP address and assigning those bits to the network address. This procedure is known as defining a subnet mask.

caution **Do not confuse an IP subnet, which is a logical division of a network, with Ethernet segments, which refer to physical divisions of an Ethernet network.**

Essentially, when you define a subnet mask, you add more bits to the default network mask for that address class. If you have a class B network, for example, the default network mask would be 255.255.0.0. Then, if you decide to divide your network into 128 subnetworks, each of which has 512 hosts, you would designate 7 bits from the host address space as the subnet address. Thus, the subnet mask becomes 255.255.254.0.

Using Supernets or CIDR

There are so few class A and B network addresses that they are becoming scarce. Class C addresses are more plentiful, but the proliferation of class C addresses has introduced a unique problem. Each class C address needs an entry in the network routing tables — the tables that contain information about how to locate any network on the Internet. Too many class C addresses means too many entries in the routing tables, which causes the router's performance to deteriorate. One way to get around this problem is to ignore the predefined address classes and let the network address be any number of bits. All you need is for the network mask to figure out which part of the 32-bit IP address is the network address. Based on this idea the Classless Inter-Domain Routing (CIDR) — documented in RFC 1519 — was developed to enable routing of contiguous blocks of class C addresses with a single entry in the routing table. CIDR is used in the Internet as the primary mechanism to improve scalability of the Internet routing system.

The basis of CIDR is the idea of supernets—arbitrarily sized networks created by combining contiguous class C addresses that satisfy some criteria. For example, to create a supernet from two class C networks, the two network addresses must satisfy the following properties:

- The network addresses must be consecutive (for example, 198.41.18.0 and 198.41.19.0 are consecutive class C addresses).
- The third number of the first network address must be divisible by 2 (for example, the third number of 198.41.18.0 is 18, and 18 is divisible by 2).

Thus, you could combine 198.41.18.0 and 198.41.19.0 into a single block, but you cannot combine 198.41.15.0 with 198.41.16.0 because 15 is not divisible by 2. When you create a supernet of two class C networks, the network can have up to 512 host addresses, and the network mask becomes 255.255.254.0, which leaves 9 bits for the host address.

You can also supernet any number of class C networks in powers of two. The only requirement is that the third number (in the dotted-decimal notation) of the first address must be divisible by the number of networks you are combining. Thus, if you are supernetting eight networks, the third number of the first address must be divisible by 8. Thus, you could supernet the following eight consecutive class C networks:

```
198.41.16.0
198.41.17.0
198.41.18.0
198.41.19.0
198.41.20.0
198.41.21.0
198.41.22.0
198.41.23.0
```

The network mask of this supernet would be 255.255.248.0, which provides for 21 bits of network address and leaves 11 bits for $8 \times 256 = 2{,}048$ host addresses.

Such a network address is written with the notation /21 to indicate that there are 21 bits in the network address.

Learning about IPv6

When the 4-byte IP address was created, the number of addresses seemed to be adequate. Now, however, class A and B addresses are running out, and class C addresses are being depleted at a fast rate. The Internet Engineering Task Force (IETF) recognized the potential for running out of IP addresses in 1991, and work began then on the next-generation IP addressing scheme, named IPng, which will eventually replace the old 4-byte addressing scheme (called IPv4, for IP Version 4).

Several alternative addressing schemes for IPng were proposed and debated. The final contender, with a 128-bit (16-byte) address, was dubbed IPv6 (for IP Version 6). On September 18, 1995, the IETF declared the core set of IPv6 addressing protocols to be an IETF Proposed Standard. By now, there are many RFCs dealing with various aspects of IPv6, from IPv6 over PPP for the transmission of IPv6 packets over Ethernet.

IPv6 is designed to be an evolutionary step from IPv4. The proposed standard provides direct interoperability between hosts using the older IPv4 addresses and any new IPv6 hosts. The idea is that users can upgrade their systems to use IPv6 when they want and that network operators are free to upgrade their network hardware to use IPv6 without affecting current users of IPv4. Sample implementations of IPv6 are being developed for many operating systems, including Linux. For more information about IPv6 in Linux, consult the Linux IPv6 HOWTO at `www.tldp.org/HOWTO/Linux+IPv6-HOWTO/`.

The IPv6 128-bit addressing scheme allows for 170,141,183,460,469,232,000,000,000, 000,000,000,000 unique hosts! That should last us for a while!

Routing TCP/IP Packets

Routing refers to the task of forwarding information from one network to another. Consider the two class C networks 206.197.168.0 and 164.109.10.0. You need a routing device to send packets from one of these networks to the other.

Because a routing device facilitates data exchange between two networks, it has two physical network connections, one on each network. Each network interface has its own IP address, and the routing device essentially passes packets back and forth between the two network interfaces. Figure 6-4 illustrates how a routing device has a physical presence in two networks and how each network interface has its own IP address.

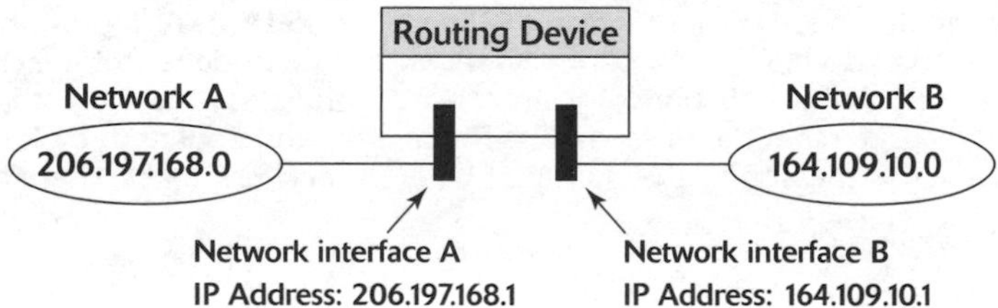

Figure 6-4: A Routing Device Allows Packet Exchange between Two Networks.

The generic term "routing device" can refer to a general-purpose computer with two network interfaces or a dedicated device designed specifically for routing. Such dedicated routing devices are known as *routers*.

insider insight

The generic term "gateway" also refers to any routing device regardless of whether the device is another PC or a router. For good performance (a high packet-transfer rate), you want a dedicated router, whose sole purpose is to route packets of data in a network.

Later, when you learn how to set up a TCP/IP network in Linux, you'll have to specify the IP address of your network's gateway. If your Linux system gets its IP address from a DHCP (Dynamic Host Configuration Protocol) server, then that DHCP server can also provide the gateway address.

A single routing device, of course, does not connect all the networks in the world; packets get around on the Internet from one gateway to another. Any network connected to another network has a designated gateway. You can even have specific gateways for specific networks. As you'll learn, a routing table keeps track of the gateway associated with an external network and the type of physical interface (such as Ethernet or Point-to-Point Protocol over serial lines) for that network. A default gateway gets packets that are addressed to any unknown network.

In your local area network, all packets addressed to another network go to your network's default gateway, except for those addresses that are explicitly directed elsewhere by static routes. If that gateway is physically connected to the destination network, the story ends there because the gateway can physically send the packets to the destination host. If that gateway does not know the destination network, however, it sends the packets to the next default gateway (the gateway for the other network on which your gateway also "lives"). In this way, packets travel from one gateway to the next until they reach the destination network (or you get an error message saying that the destination network is unreachable).

To send packets around the network efficiently, routers exchange information (in the form of routing tables), so that each router can have a "map" of the network in its vicinity. Routers exchange information by using a routing protocol from a family of protocols, known as the Interior Gateway Protocol (IGP). A commonly used Interior Gateway Protocol is the Routing Information Protocol (RIP). Another, more recent, Interior Gateway Protocol is the Open Shortest Path First (OSPF) protocol.

In TCP/IP routing, any time a packet passes through a router, it has made what is considered a hop. In RIP, the maximum size of the Internet is 15 hops. A network is considered to be unreachable from your network if a packet does not reach the destination network within 15 hops. In other words, any network more than 15 routers away is considered to be unreachable. The newer OSPF routing protocol uses a different metric for measuring the quality of different network paths; therefore, it can have hops greater than 15.

Within a single network, you don't need a router as long as you do not use a subnet mask to break the single IP network into several subnets. In that case, however, you have to set up routers to send packets from one subnet to another.

Understanding the Domain Name System

You can access any host computer in a TCP/IP network with an IP address. Remembering the IP addresses of even a few hosts of interest, however, is tedious. This fact was recognized from the beginning of TCP/IP, and the association between a host name and IP address was created. The concept is similar to that of a phone book, in which you can look up a telephone number by searching for a person's name.

In the early days of the Internet, the association between names and IP addresses was maintained in a text file named `HOSTS.TXT` at the Network Information Center (NIC), which was located in the Stanford Research Institute (SRI). This file contained the names and corresponding IP addresses of networks, hosts, and routers on the Internet. All hosts on the Internet used to transfer that file by FTP. (Can you imagine all hosts getting a file from a single source in today's Internet?) As the number of Internet hosts increased, the single file idea became unmanageable. The hosts file was becoming difficult to maintain, and it was hard for all the hosts to update their hosts file in a timely manner. To alleviate the problem, RFC 881 introduced the concept of and plans for domain names in November 1983. Eventually, in 1987 this led to the Domain Name Service (DNS) as we know it today (documented in RFCs 1032, 1033, 1034, and 1035).

DNS provides a hierarchical naming system much like your postal address, which you can read as "your name" at "your street address" in "your city" in "your state" in "your country." If I know your full postal address, I can locate you by starting with your city in your country. Then, I can locate the street address to find your home, ring the doorbell, and ask for you by name.

DNS essentially provides an addressing scheme for an Internet host that is much like the postal address. The entire Internet is subdivided into several domains, such as gov, edu, com, mil, and net. Each domain is further subdivided into subdomains. Finally, within a subdomain, each host is given a symbolic name. To write a host's fully qualified domain name (FQDN), string together the host name, subdomain names, and domain name with dots (.) as separators. Following is the full domain name of a host named ADDLAB in the subdomain NWS within another subdomain NOAA in the GOV domain: ADDLAB.NWS.NOAA.GOV. Note that domain names are not case sensitive. By the way, a single dot (.) represents the topmost level (root) of the domain-name hierarchy.

Figure 6-5 illustrates part of the Internet Domain Name System, showing the location of the host ADDLAB.NWS.NOAA.GOV.

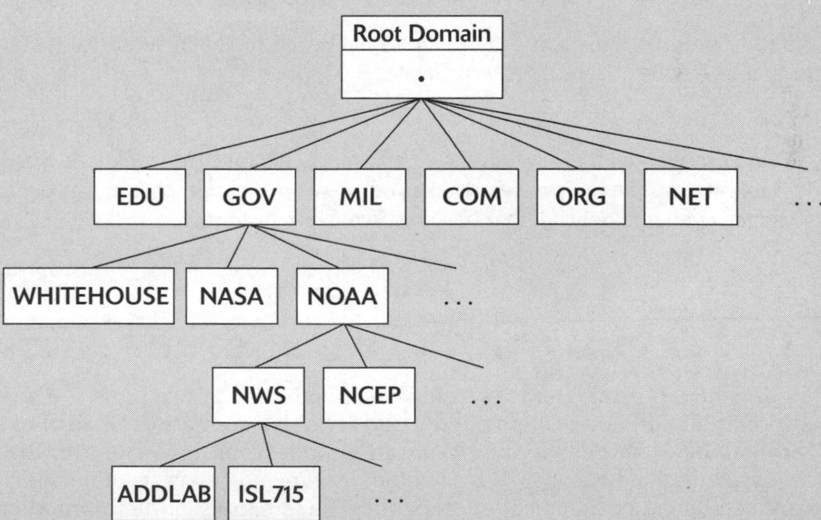

Figure 6-5: Part of the Internet Domain-Name Hierarchy.

For a commercial system in the COM domain, the name of a host might be as simple as redhat.com. Of course, within redhat.com you could have many subdomains such as ftp.redhat.com, mail.redhat.com, and so forth.

The convention for the email address of a user on a system is to append an at (@) sign to the user name (the name under which the user logs in) and then append the system's fully qualified domain name. Thus, refer to the user named webmaster at the host gao.gov as webmaster@GAO.GOV (unlike host names, user names are case sensitive).

TCP/IP network applications resolve a host name to an IP address by consulting a name server, which is another host that's accessible from your network. If you decide to use the Domain Name System (DNS) on your network, you have to set up a name server in your network or indicate a name server (by an IP address).

cross ref

Later sections of this chapter discuss the configuration files `/etc/host.conf` and `/etc/resolv.conf`, through which you specify how host names are converted to IP addresses. In particular, you specify the IP addresses of a name server in the `/etc/resolv.conf` file.

If you do not use DNS, you still can have host name–to–IP address mapping through a text file named `/etc/hosts`. The entries in a typical `/etc/hosts` file might look like the following example:

```
# Lines like these are comments
# You must have the localhost line in /etc/hosts file
127.0.0.1        localhost.localdomain localhost
192.168.0.100    lnbp933  lnbp933.local.net
192.168.0.60     lnbp600
192.168.0.200    lnbp200  lnbp200.local.net
192.168.0.40     lnbp400  lnbp400.local.net
192.168.0.25     mac      lnbmac  lnbmac.local.net
```

As the example shows, the file lists a host name for each IP address. The IP address and host names are different for your system, of course.

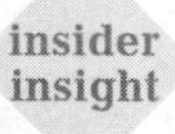

One problem with relying on the `/etc/hosts` file for name lookup is that you have to replicate this file on each system on your network. This procedure can become a nuisance even in a network that has only five or six systems.

TCP/IP Services and Client/Server Architecture

By design, a typical Internet service is implemented in two parts — a server that provides information and one or more clients that request information. Such client/server architecture has been gaining popularity as an approach for implementing distributed information systems. The client/server architecture typically consists of a collection of computers connected by a communication network. The functions of the information system are performed by processes (computer programs) that run on these computers and communicate through the network.

In recent years, the client/server architecture has become commonplace as the mechanism that brings the centralized corporate databases to desktop PCs on a network. In a client/server environment, one or more servers manage the centralized database and clients gain access to the data through the server.

Like a database server, an Internet service such as FTP or the Web also provides a service using the client/server model. A user who wants to access information uses a client (for example, a Web browser) to connect to a server and download information (for example, Web pages from a Web server). In this case, the Web server acts as a database manager — the data are the HTML files (Web pages).

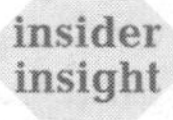

Client/server architecture requires clients to communicate with the servers. That's where TCP/IP comes in – TCP/IP provides a standard way for clients and servers to exchange packets of data. The next few sections explain how TCP/IP-based services communicate. From this discussion, you learn about the port numbers associated with many well-known Internet services.

Understanding TCP/IP and Sockets

Client/server applications such as Web servers and browsers use TCP/IP to communicate. These Internet applications perform TCP/IP communications using the Berkeley Sockets interface (so named because the socket interface was introduced in Berkeley UNIX around 1982). The sockets interface consists of a library of routines that an application developer can use to create applications that can communicate with other applications on the Internet. There is even a Windows Sockets API (application programming interface — a fancy name for a library of programming functions that can be called by C programs) modeled after the Berkeley Sockets interface. The Winsock interface, as it's known, provides a standard API that Windows programmers can use to write network applications.

Even if you do not write network applications using sockets, you have to use many network applications. Knowledge of sockets can help you understand how network-based applications work, which, in turn, helps you find and correct any problems with these applications.

Socket Definition

Network applications use sockets to communicate over a TCP/IP network. A socket is an abstraction that represents an endpoint of a connection. Because a socket is bidirectional, data can be sent as well as received through it. A socket has three attributes:

- The network address (the IP address) of the system
- The port number identifying the process (a process is a computer program running on a computer) that exchanges data through the socket
- The type of socket (such as stream or datagram) identifying the protocol for data exchange

Essentially, the IP address identifies a network node, the port number identifies a process on the node, and the socket type determines the manner in which data is exchanged — through a connection-oriented or connectionless protocol.

Connection-Oriented Protocols

The socket type indicates the protocol being used to communicate through the socket. A connection-oriented protocol works like a normal phone conversation. When you want to talk to your friend, you have to dial your friend's phone number and establish a connection before you can have a conversation. In the same way, connection-oriented data exchange requires both the sending and receiving processes to establish a connection before data exchange can begin.

insider insight

In the TCP/IP protocol suite, TCP — Transmission Control Protocol — supports a connection-oriented data transfer between two processes running on two computers on the Internet. TCP provides a reliable two-way data exchange between processes.

As the name TCP/IP suggests (and as the "Network Protocols" section indicates), TCP relies on IP — Internet Protocol — for delivery of packets. IP does not guarantee delivery of packets, nor does it deliver packets in any particular sequence. IP does, however, efficiently deliver packets from one network to another. TCP is responsible for arranging the packets in the proper sequence, detecting whether or not errors have occurred, and requesting retransmission of packets in the case of an error.

TCP is useful for applications that plan to exchange large amounts of data at a time. In addition, applications that need reliable data exchange use TCP. For example, FTP uses TCP to transfer files.

In the sockets model, a socket that uses TCP is referred to as a *stream* socket because TCP provides an illusion of a continuous stream of data.

Connectionless Protocols

A connectionless data-exchange protocol does not require the sender and receiver to explicitly establish a connection. It's like shouting to your friend in a crowded room — you can't be sure if your friend hears you, and if you can't tell whether or not he or she heard you, after a certain amount of time, you shout again to see if he or she hears you.

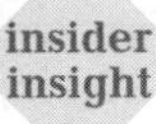

In the TCP/IP protocol suite, the User Datagram Protocol (UDP) provides connectionless service for sending and receiving packets known as datagrams. Unlike TCP, UDP does not guarantee that datagrams ever reach their intended destination. Nor does UDP ensure that datagrams are delivered in the order they have been sent.

UDP is used by applications that exchange small amounts of data at a time or by applications that do not need the reliability and sequencing of data delivery. For example, SNMP (Simple Network Management Protocol) uses UDP to transfer data. UDP is generally used by applications where each message is largely self-contained so that even if some of the messages don't get through, it's not critical.

In the sockets model, a socket that uses UDP is referred to as a *datagram* socket.

Sockets and the Client/Server Model

It takes two sockets to complete a communication path. When two processes communicate, they use the client/server model to establish the connection. The server application listens on a specific port on the system — the server is completely identified by the IP address of the system where it runs and the port number where it listens for connections. The client initiates connection from any available port and tries to connect to the server (identified by the IP address and port number). Once the connection is established, the client and the server can exchange data according to their own protocol.

The sequence of events in sockets-based data exchanges depends on whether the transfer is connection oriented (TCP) or connectionless (UDP).

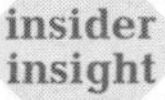

For a connection-oriented data transfer using TCP sockets, the server "listens" on a specific port, waiting for clients to request connection. Data transfer begins only after a connection is established. The server is a program that responds when a connection is attempted at a certain port.

For connectionless data transfers using UDP sockets, the server waits for a datagram to arrive at a specified port. The client does not wait to establish a connection; it simply sends a datagram to the server.

Performing Client/Server Communications with TCP/IP

Client/server applications use the following basic steps to exchange data in a TCP/IP network:

1. Create a socket. If the socket already exists, you can skip this step.
2. Bind an IP address and port to the socket.
3. Listen for connections if the application is a server using a stream socket.
4. Establish a connection if the application is a client using a stream socket.
5. Exchange data.
6. Close the socket when done.

Connectionless sockets (that implement data transfer using UDP) do not require Steps 3 and 4.

Regardless of whether it's a server or a client, each application first creates a socket. Then it associates (binds) the socket with the local computer's IP address and a port number. The IP address identifies the machine (where the application is running), and the port number identifies the application using the socket.

Servers typically listen to a well-known port number so that clients can connect to that port to access the server. For a client application, the process of binding a socket to the IP address and port is the same as that for a server, but the client can use zero as the port number — the sockets library automatically uses an unused port number for the client.

For a connection-oriented stream socket, the communicating client and server applications have to establish a connection. The exact steps for establishing a connection depend on whether the application is a server or a client.

In the client/server model, the server has to be up and running before the client can run. After creating a socket and binding the socket to a port, the server application sets up a queue of connections, which determines how many clients can connect to the server. Typically, a server listens to anywhere from one to five connections. However, the size of the listen queue is one of the parameters you can adjust (especially for a Web server) to ensure that the server responds to as many clients as possible.

After setting up the listen queue, the server waits for a connection from a client.

continues

continued

Establishing the connection from the client side is somewhat simpler. After creating a socket and binding the socket to a network address, the client establishes connection with the server. To make the connection, the client needs to know the network name or IP address of the server, as well as the port on which the server accepts connections. As the next section shows, all Internet services have well-known standard port numbers.

After a client establishes connection to a server using a connection-oriented stream socket, the client and server can exchange data by calling appropriate sockets API functions. Like a conversation between two persons, the server and client alternately send and receive data—the meaning of the data depends on the message protocol the server and clients use. Usually, a server is designed for a specific task; inherent in that design is a message protocol that the server and clients use to exchange necessary data. For example, the Web server and the Web browser (client) communicate using HTTP.

Exploring Internet Services and Port Numbers

The TCP/IP protocol suite has become the lingua franca of the Internet because many standard services are available on all systems that support TCP/IP. These services make the Internet tick by enabling the transfer of mail, news, and Web pages. These services go by well-known names such as the following:

- **DHCP (Dynamic Host Configuration Protocol)** is for dynamically configuring TCP/IP network parameters on a computer. DHCP is primarily used to assign dynamic IP addresses and other networking information such as name server, default gateway, domain names that are needed to configure TCP/IP networks. The DHCP server listens on port 67.
- **FTP (File Transfer Protocol)** enables the transfer of files between computers on the Internet. FTP uses two ports—data is transferred on port 20, while control information is exchanged on port 21.
- **HTTP (HyperText Transfer Protocol)** is a recent protocol for sending HTML documents from one system to another. HTTP is the underlying protocol of the Web. By default, the Web server and client communicate on port 80.
- **SMTP (Simple Mail Transfer Protocol)** is for exchanging email messages between systems. SMTP uses port 25 for information exchange.
- **NNTP (Network News Transfer Protocol)** is for distribution of news articles in a store-and-forward fashion across the Internet. NNTP uses port 119.
- **SSH (Secure Shell)** is a protocol for secure remote login and other secure network services over an insecure network. SSH uses port 22.
- **TELNET** enables a user on one system to log in to another system on the Internet (the user must provide a valid user ID and password to log in to the remote system: the password is sent in cleartext, which is why TELNET is not secure). Telnet uses port 23 by default. However, the TELNET client can connect to any specified port.

- **SNMP (Simple Network Management Protocol)** is for managing all types of network devices on the Internet. Like FTP, SNMP uses two ports: 161 and 162.
- **TFTP (Trivial File Transfer Protocol)** is for transferring files from one system to another (typically used by X terminals and diskless workstations to download boot files from another host on the network). TFTP data transfer takes place on port 69.
- **NFS (Network File System)** is for sharing files among computers. NFS uses Sun's Remote Procedure Call (RPC) facility, which exchanges information through port 111.

A well-known port is associated with each of these services. The TCP protocol uses this port to locate a service on any system. (A server process—a computer program running on a system—implements each service.)

Note that many applications use specific port ranges that are outside the typical list of well-known ports.

As with the /etc/hosts file, which stores the association between host names and IP addresses, the association between a service name and a port number (as well as a protocol) is stored in another text file, named /etc/services. Following is a small subset of lines from the /etc/services file in a Linux system:

```
# /etc/services:
# $Id: services,v 1.41 2004/11/05 17:01:22 notting Exp $
#
# Network services, Internet style
#
# Note that it is presently the policy of IANA to assign a single
# well-known port number for both TCP and UDP; hence, most entries
# here have two entries even if the protocol doesn't support UDP
# operations.
#
# Updated from RFC 1700, ``Assigned Numbers'' (October 1994).
# Not all ports are included, only the more common ones.
#
# The latest IANA port assignments can be gotten from
#       http://www.iana.org/assignments/port-numbers
# The Well Known Ports are those from 0 through 1023.
# The Registered Ports are those from 1024 through 49151
# The Dynamic and/or Private Ports are those from 49152
# through 65535
#
# Each line describes one service, and is of the form:
#
# service-name  port/protocol  [aliases ...]   [# comment]
tcpmux          1/tcp                           # TCP port service multiplexer
tcpmux          1/udp                           # TCP port service multiplexer
ftp-data        20/tcp
ftp-data        20/udp
# 21 is registered to ftp, but also used by fsp
ftp             21/tcp
ftp             21/udp          fsp fspd
```

```
ssh             22/tcp                  # SSH Remote Login Protocol
ssh             22/udp                  # SSH Remote Login Protocol
telnet          23/tcp
telnet          23/udp
# 24 - private mail system
lmtp            24/tcp                  # LMTP Mail Delivery
lmtp            24/udp                  # LMTP Mail Delivery
smtp            25/tcp          mail
smtp            25/udp          mail
time            37/tcp          timserver
... many lines deleted ...
```

You'll find browsing through the entries in the /etc/services file to be instructive because they show the breadth of networking services available under TCP/IP.

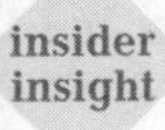

Note that port number 80 is designated for WWW service. In other words, if you set up a Web server on your system, that server listens to port 80. By the way, IANA — the Internet Assigned Numbers Authority (www.iana.org/) — is responsible for coordinating the assignment of port numbers below 1,024.

Running the xinetd Superserver

The client/server model requires that the server be up and running before a client makes a request for service. A simplistic idea would be to run all the servers and have them listen to their respective ports all the time. However, this idea is not practical because each server process would use up system resources in the form of memory and processor time. Besides, you don't really need all the services up and ready at all times. A smart solution to this problem is to run a single server, xinetd, which listens to all the ports and then starts the appropriate server when a client request comes in.

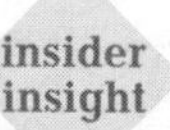

The xinetd server is a replacement for an older server named inetd but with improved access control and logging. The name xinetd stands for *extended* inetd. You can learn more about xinetd by visiting www.xinetd.org/.

Learning How xinetd Works

The xinetd server is designed to monitor the ports for the services it is configured to start. When a client requests connection to one of the monitored ports, xinetd starts the corresponding server. The client then directly communicates with that server while xinetd goes on to listening to the ports again. For example, when a client tries to connect to the Telnet port, xinetd starts the Telnet server and lets it communicate directly with the client (and the Telnet server exits when the client disconnects). xinetd also logs the connection requests in a log file based on settings in its configuration file.

The xinetd server is known as the Internet superserver because it starts various servers on demand. Typically, a Linux system starts xinetd when the system boots. The xinetd server reads a configuration file named `/etc/xinetd.conf` at startup. This file tells xinetd which ports to listen to and what server to start for each port. The file can contain instructions that include other configuration files. In Fedora Linux, the `/etc/xinetd.conf` file looks like the following:

```
#
# Simple configuration file for xinetd
#
# Some defaults, and include /etc/xinetd.d/

defaults
{
        instances                  = 60
        log_type                   = SYSLOG authpriv
        log_on_success             = HOST PID
        log_on_failure             = HOST
        cps                        = 25 30
}

includedir /etc/xinetd.d
```

Comment lines begin with the pound sign (#). The `defaults` block, enclosed in curly braces (`{ . . . }`), specifies default values for some attributes. These default values apply to all other services that xinetd is set up to start. The `instances` attribute is set to 60, which means there can be, at most, 60 servers simultaneously active for any service. The other attributes have the following meanings:

- The `log_type` attribute specifies how xinetd should log error or status information. In this case the `log_type` is `SYSLOG authpriv`, which means that xinetd will use the SYSLOG facility's `authpriv` log. The `/etc/syslog.conf` file defines the `authpriv` log as the file `/var/log/secure`. This means that the `/var/log/secure` file contains the logs for services started by xinetd.
- The `log_on_success` attribute tells xinetd what information to log when a server is started and when the server exits. In this case, the attribute is set to `HOST` and `PID`. The result is that if the startup of a service such as Telnet is successful, then xinetd logs the name of the remote host that has requested the service and the process ID of the Telnet server (that it starts). This setting for the `log_on_success` attribute results in entries in the `/var/log/secure` file of the following form:

```
Apr  3 16:44:23 localhost xinetd[2483]: START: telnet pid=3466
from=192.168.0.7
```

- The `log_on_failure` attribute tells xinetd what information to log when it cannot start a server. In this case, the attribute is set to `HOST`, which means that if xinetd cannot start a service such as Telnet, it logs the name of the remote host that requested the service.

continues

continued

- The `cps = 25 30` line tells xinetd to allow no more than 25 connections per second to a given service. If this limit is reached, the service is turned off for 30 seconds. Placing a limit such as this protects your system against denial of service attacks that attempts to overwhelm the system by requesting too many connections.

The last line in the `/etc/xinetd.conf` file uses the `includedir` directive to include all files inside the `/etc/xinetd.d` directory, excluding files whose names begin with a period (`.`). The idea is that the `/etc/xinetd.d` directory would contain all service configuration files — one file for each type of service the xinetd server is expected to manage. You should study the files in `/etc/xinetd.d` directory to see what services xinetd can start and how each service is configured. You can enable or disable a service by editing that service's configuration file in `/etc/xinetd.d` (you can also perform this task through the `chkconfig` command, as described in Chapter 22).

Here is the listing of files in the `/etc/xinetd.d` directory on a typical Fedora Linux system:

```
ls /etc/xinetd.d
chargen       daytime       echo-udp  klogin       ktalk  time-udp
chargen-udp   daytime-udp   eklogin   krb5-telnet  rsync
cvs           echo          gssftp    kshell       time
```

Each file specifies the attributes for one service. As this listing shows, there are more than two dozen services that xinetd can start. Whether all the services are enabled or not, depends on the settings in each configuration file.

Understanding the xinetd Configuration Files

For example, the following listing shows the contents of the `/etc/xinetd.d/krb5-telnet` file, which specifies the `xinetd` configuration for the `telnet` service (this version of Telnet uses Kerberos to authenticate users):

```
# default: off
# description: The kerberized telnet server accepts normal telnet
#              sessions, but can also use Kerberos 5
#              authentication.
service telnet
{
        flags           = REUSE
        socket_type     = stream
        wait            = no
        user            = root
        server          = /usr/kerberos/sbin/telnetd
        log_on_failure  += USERID
        disable         = yes
}
```

The filename (in this case, `krb5-telnet`) can be anything; what matters is the service name that appears next to the `service` keyword in the file. In this case, the line `service telnet` tells xinetd the name of the service. xinetd uses this name to look up the port number from the /etc/services file. If you use the grep command to look for telnet in the /etc/services file, here's what you'll find:

```
grep telnet /etc/services
telnet          23/tcp
telnet          23/udp
rtelnet         107/tcp                        # Remote Telnet
rtelnet         107/udp
telnets         992/tcp
telnets         992/udp
```

As the first two lines that begin with telnet show, the port number of the Telnet service is 23. This tells xinetd to listen to port 23 for Telnet service requests.

The attributes in the /etc/xinetd.d/krb5-telnet file, enclosed in curly braces, have the following meanings:

- The flags attribute provides specific instructions about how to run the servers that xinetd starts. The REUSE flag means that the service is left running even if xinetd is restarted. Note that the REUSE flag is now implicitly assumed to be set for all services.
- The socket_type attribute is set to stream, which tells xinetd that the Telnet service uses a connection-oriented TCP socket to communicate with the client. For services that use the connectionless UDP sockets, this attribute would be set to dgram.
- The wait attribute is set to no, which tells xinetd to start a new server for each request. If this attribute is set to yes, xinetd waits until the server exits before starting the server again.
- The user attribute provides the user ID that xinetd uses to run the server. In this case, the server runs the Telnet server as root.
- The server attribute specifies the program to run for this service. In this case, xinetd runs the /usr/kerberos/sbin/telnetd program to respond to requests for Telnet service.
- The log_on_failure attribute tells xinetd what information to log when it cannot start a server. In this case, the attribute appends the USERID flag to the default setting of HOST (set through the defaults block in the /etc/xinetd.conf file). The result is that if the Telnet service fails, xinetd logs the name of the remote host that requested the service as well as the user ID of the remote user.
- The disable attribute turns off the service if it's set to yes. By default the disable attribute is set to yes and Telnet is turned off.

The xinetd server uses the facilities of the libwrap library (called the *TCP wrapper*), which provides an access-control facility for Internet services. The TCP wrapper can start other services such as FTP and Telnet, but before starting the service, the wrapper consults the /etc/hosts.allow file to see if the host requesting service is allowed that service. If there is nothing in /etc/hosts.allow about that host, the TCP wrapper checks the /etc/hosts.deny file to see if the service should be denied. If both files are empty, the TCP wrapper allows the host access to the requested service. You can place the line ALL:ALL in the /etc/hosts.deny file to deny all hosts access to any Internet services, and then enable specfic hosts to access the services by listing them in the /etc/hosts.allow file (see the "/etc/hosts.allow" and "/etc/hosts.deny" sections to learn more about these access control files).

continues

continued

In addition to the access control provided by the TCP wrapper files—/etc/hosts.allow and /etc/hosts.deny—you can also control access to each service by using the following attributes in xinetd configuration files:

- The *only_from* attribute specifies a list of IP addresses that are the only ones allowed to connect to the server. To deny all connections, use the following line:

```
only_from =
```

  On the other hand, to allow access to all hosts in the 192.168.1.0 class C network, add the following line:

```
only_from = 192.168.1.0/24
```

- The *no_access* attribute specifies the IP addresses of remote hosts that are not allowed to connect to xinetd services. For example, to deny access to the host with IP address 192.168.1.64, write:

```
no_access = 192.168.1.64
```

Browse through the files in the /etc/xinetd.d directory on your Fedora Linux system to find out the kinds of services that xinetd is set up to start. By default nearly all of these services are turned off by setting the disable attribute to yes. You should leave them disabled, unless you need a service such as Telnet for your internal network.

If you need to connect to your Fedora Linux system by using telnet and you get an error message, check the appropriate Telnet file in the /etc/xinetd.d directory and make sure the disable attribute it set to no or the disable line is commented out by placing a # at the beginning of the line. You can also turn the service on or off by using the chkconfig command. For example, to turn Telnet service on, type:

```
chkconfig krb5-telnet on
```

After you make any change to the xinetd configuration files or turn a service on or off, you must restart the xinetd server by typing the following command:

```
service xinetd restart
```

Note that for a Telnet server that uses Kerberos 5 to authenticate users, you also must set up Kerberos properly. Kerberos is configured through the options stored in the /etc/krb5.conf file. To learn more about Kerberos configuration, type **man krb5.conf** and read the Kerberos Infrastructure HOWTO located at www.tldp.org/HOWTO/Kerberos-Infrastructure-HOWTO/.

Starting Standalone Servers

Although starting servers through xinetd is a smart approach, xinetd is not efficient if a service has to be started very often. The Web server typically has to be started often because every time a user clicks on a link on a Web page, a request arrives at the Web server. For such high-demand services, it's best to start the server in a standalone manner. Such standalone servers are designed to run as daemons—processes that run continuously. That means the server listens on the assigned port; whenever a request arrives, the server handles it by making a copy of itself. In this way, the server keeps running forever. A more efficient strategy, used for Web servers, is to run multiple copies of the server and let each copy handle some of the incoming requests.

To help you manage standalone servers, Fedora Linux includes scripts (called *initscripts*) in the /etc/init.d directory as well as symbolic links to enable execution of these scripts at various run levels (run levels are discussed in Chapter 20). You can log in as root and manage the standalone servers through the initscripts in the following ways:

- Use the service command to start, stop, or restart a server. The service command has the following syntax:

```
service <servicename> <action>
```

  Here, <servicename> is the name of the service such as httpd for the Web server, sendmail for the mail server, and so on. The last field, <action>, must be one of start, stop, or restart with the obvious meaning — start runs the server, stop terminates it, and restart stops the server first and then runs it again. Typically, you must restart a server after you have made changes to the server's configuration file.

- Use the chkconfig command to set up a service to start automatically when the system boots into a run level. For example, to set up httpd to run in run levels 3 and 5, type:

```
chkconfig --level 35 httpd on
```

  If a service is already set to start automatically at boot time, you can disable it with the following chkconfig command:

```
chkconfig --level 35 <servicename> off
```

  where <servicename> is the name of the service that you want to turn off.

Note that services can typically be configured to run under xinetd or on a standalone basis. For example, prior to version 9, Red Hat Linux used to start the FTP service under control of xinetd. Starting with version 9 and continuing with Fedora, however, the Very Secure FTP server (vsftpd) is set up as a standalone server. Nowadays, if you need to start the FTP service, type **service vsftpd start**. To start the FTP service automatically at boot time, type **chkconfig vsftpd on**.

TCP/IP Setup in Linux

Like almost everything else in Linux, TCP/IP setup is a matter of preparing numerous configuration files (text files you can edit with any text editor). Most of these configuration files are in the /etc directory. The Fedora installation program helps by hiding the details of the TCP/IP configuration files. Nevertheless, it's better if you know the names of the files and their purposes so that you can edit the files manually, if necessary.

The next few sections show you how to set up TCP/IP for an Ethernet LAN. Chapter 13 covers dial-up networking under Linux, including topics such as PPP. Appendix D discusses physical setup of Ethernet networks and types of Ethernet cards supported by Linux.

Before you look at TCP/IP setup, make sure your system's Ethernet card is properly installed and detected by the Linux kernel. Also, you need to know the device names for the network devices.

Learning Network-Device Names

For most devices, Linux uses files in the `/dev` directory. The networking devices, however, have names defined internally in the kernel; no files for these devices exist in the `/dev` directory. Following are the common network-device names in Linux:

- **lo:** The loopback device. This device is used for efficient handling of network packets sent from your system to itself (when, for example, an X client communicates with the X server on the same system).
- **eth0:** The first Ethernet card or 802.11b wireless network card. If you have more Ethernet cards, they get device names `eth1`, `eth2`, and so on.
- **ppp0:** The first serial port configured for a point-to-point link to another computer, using Point-to-Point Protocol (PPP). If you have more serial ports configured for PPP networking, they are assigned device names `ppp1`, `ppp2`, and so on.
- **sl0:** The first serial port configured for Serial Line Internet Protocol (SLIP) networking. SLIP is used for establishing a point-to-point link to a TCP/IP network. If you use a second serial port for SLIP, it gets the device name `sl1`. SLIP is not used much anymore; it has been superseded by PPP.

insider insight

You always have a loopback device (lo), whether or not you have a network. The loopback device passes data from one process to another without having to go out to a network. In fact, the whole point of the loopback device is to allow network applications to work, as long as the communicating processes are on the same system.

cross ref

PPP is popular in dial-up networks, in which you use a modem to dial in to an Internet host (typically, a system at your work or your ISP) and establish a connection to the Internet. Chapter 13 covers this subject in detail.

If you want to see the names of installed network devices on your system, try the following command:

```
cat /proc/net/dev
```

This command shows the network-device names, as well as statistics on the number of packets sent and received for a specific device.

Using the Network Configuration Tool

After you ensure that the Linux kernel is properly configured for TCP/IP, you have to make sure that the appropriate configuration files exist. Fedora includes a network configuration tool that enables you to configure various network interfaces on your system for TCP/IP networking. You can run the network configuration tool to add a new network interface or to alter information such as name servers and host names (you can also directly edit the configuration files listed in the "Using TCP/IP Configuration Files" section).

Log in as `root` and from the GNOME desktop, select Desktop⇨System Settings⇨Network to run the Network Configuration tool (or type **system-config-network** in a terminal window). The Network Configuration tool displays a tabbed dialog box, as shown in Figure 6-6.

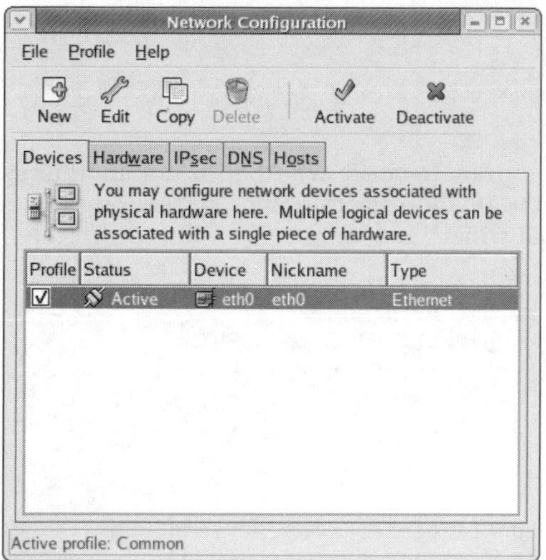

Figure 6-6: Configuring a TCP/IP Network with the Network Configuration Tool.

You can configure various aspects of your network through the four tabs that appear along the top of the dialog box:

- **Devices:** Enables you to add a new network interface, specify the IP address of the interface, and activate the interface. This information is stored in various files in the `/etc/sysconfig` directory.
- **Hardware:** Enables you to add a new hardware device such as an Ethernet card, modem, or an ISDN device. You can then provide information such as interrupt request (IRQ) and I/O port numbers, and DMA channels for the device.
- **IPsec:** Enables you to configure encrypted connections to a host or a virtual private network (VPN) for encrypted connection to a remote network.
- **DNS:** Enables you to enter the host name for your system and the IP addresses of name servers. The name server addresses are stored in the `/etc/resolv.conf` file. The host name is stored in the `HOSTNAME` variable in the `/etc/sysconfig/network` file.
- **Hosts:** Shows you the current contents of the `/etc/hosts` file and enables you to add, remove, or edit entries.

To configure the network interfaces, you need to assign IP addresses to each interface. If you are running a private network, you may use IP addresses in the range 192.168.0.0 to 192.168.255.255. (There are other ranges of addresses reserved for private networks, but this range should suffice for most needs.) For example, I use the 192.168.0.0 address for a small private network.

Testing the Network

After you run the Network Configuration tool, you may want to check whether or not the network is up and running. If you have not rebooted your system yet, you have to run `/sbin/ifconfig` to configure the Ethernet interface for your IP address. On a system whose IP address is 192.168.0.4, you type the commands shown in the code that follows.

(You have to be logged in as root to do this; type **su -** and enter the root password to become root):

```
/sbin/ifconfig eth0 192.168.0.4 netmask 255.255.255.0 broadcast 192.168.0.255
/sbin/ifconfig eth0 up
```

Now, you should use the Ping utility program to verify whether or not another system on your network is accessible. You need the IP address of another system on the network to use Ping. On my PC, I might try the following:

```
ping 192.168.0.1
PING 192.168.0.1 (192.168.0.1) 56(84) bytes of data.
64 bytes from 192.168.0.1: icmp_seq=0 ttl=63 time=0.594 ms
64 bytes from 192.168.0.1: icmp_seq=1 ttl=63 time=0.534 ms
64 bytes from 192.168.0.1: icmp_seq=2 ttl=63 time=0.587 ms
64 bytes from 192.168.0.1: icmp_seq=3 ttl=63 time=0.564 ms

--- 192.168.0.1 ping statistics ---
4 packets transmitted, 4 received, 0% packet loss, time 3000ms
rtt min/avg/max/mdev = 0.534/0.569/0.594/0.037 ms, pipe 2
```

If the ping command shows that other systems on your network are reachable, you can proceed to use other network programs, such as FTP and SSH.

Using TCP/IP Configuration Files

Running the network configuration tool may be enough to get TCP/IP configured on your system. You may want to be familiar with the configuration files, however, so that you can edit the files if necessary. For example, you can specify the name servers through the network configuration tool, but you may want to add an alternate name server directly to the configuration file. To do so, you need to know about the /etc/resolv.conf file, which stores the IP addresses of name servers.

The following sections describe the basic TCP/IP configuration files.

/etc/hosts

The /etc/hosts text file contains a list of IP addresses and host names for your local network. In the absence of a name server, any network program on your system consults this file to determine the IP address that corresponds to a host name.

Following is the /etc/hosts file from my system, showing the IP addresses and names of other hosts on my LAN:

```
# Lines like these are comments.
# You must have the localhost line in the /etc/hosts file.
127.0.0.1        localhost.localdomain localhost
192.168.0.100    lnbp933  lnbp933.local.net
192.168.0.60     lnbp600
192.168.0.200    lnbp200  lnbp200.local.net
192.168.0.40     lnbp400  lnbp400.local.net
192.168.0.25     mac      lnbmac  lnbmac.local.net
```

As the example shows, each line in the file starts with an IP address, followed by the host name for that IP address. You can have more than one host name for a given IP address.

/etc/networks

Another text file that contains the names and IP addresses of networks is /etc/networks. These network names are commonly used in the routing command (/sbin/route) to specify a network by name instead of by its IP address.

Don't be alarmed if your Linux PC does not have the /etc/networks file. Your TCP/IP network works fine without this file. In fact, the Fedora Linux installation program does not create a /etc/networks file.

/etc/host.conf

Linux uses a resolver library to obtain the IP address that corresponds to a host name. The /etc/host.conf file specifies how names are resolved. A typical /etc/host.conf file might contain the following lines:

```
order hosts, bind
multi on
```

The entries in the /etc/host.conf file tell the resolver library what services to use (and in which order) to resolve names.

The order option indicates the order of services. The sample entry specifies that the resolver library should first consult the /etc/hosts file, and then check the name server to resolve a name. In other words, this host.conf file says: "use static resolution prior to dynamic resolution."

The multi option determines whether or not a host in the /etc/hosts file can have multiple IP addresses. Hosts that have more than one IP address are called multihomed because the presence of multiple IP addresses implies that the host has several network interfaces (the host "lives" in several networks simultaneously).

/etc/resolv.conf

The /etc/resolv.conf file is another text file used by the resolver — a library that determines the IP address for a host name. Following is a sample /etc/resolv.conf file:

```
domain local.net
nameserver 164.109.1.3
nameserver 164.109.10.23
```

The first line specifies your system's domain name. The nameserver line provides the IP addresses of name servers for your domain. If you have multiple name servers, you should list them on separate lines. They are queried in the order in which they appear in the file.

If you do not have a name server for your network, you can safely ignore this file. TCP/IP should still work, even though you may not be able to refer to hosts by name. You do, however, have to make sure that you have a /etc/host.conf file that is set up to use the /etc/hosts file.

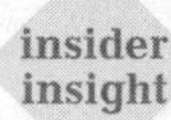

If your system gets its IP address from a DHCP server, the DHCP client also receives the IP addresses of name servers as well as the domain name from the DHCP service. In this case, the DHCP client automatically creates a /etc/resolv.conf file with the name server information it obtains from the DHCP server.

/etc/hosts.allow

This file specifies which hosts are allowed to use the Internet services such as Telnet running on your system. As explained in the section "Understanding the xinetd Configuration Files," the TCP wrapper consults the `/etc/hosts.allow` file before starting Internet services. It starts the service only if the entries in the `hosts.allow` file imply that the requesting host is allowed to use the services.

The entries in `/etc/hosts.allow` are in the form of a *`server:IP address`* format, where *`server`* refers to the name of the program providing a specific Internet service, and *`IP address`* identifies the host allowed to use that service. For example, if you want all hosts in your local network (which has the class C address 192.168.0.0) to access the Telnet service (which is provided by the in.telnetd program), add the following line in the `/etc/hosts.allow` file:

```
in.telnetd:192.168.0.
```

If you want to let all local hosts have access to all Internet services, you can use the `ALL` keyword and rewrite the line as follows:

```
ALL:192.168.0.
```

Finally, to open all Internet services to all hosts, you can replace the IP address with `ALL`, as follows:

```
ALL:ALL
```

You can also use host names in place of IP addresses.

insider insight **To learn the detailed syntax of the entries in the `/etc/hosts.allow` file, type man hosts.allow at the Linux shell prompt.**

/etc/hosts.deny

This file is just the opposite of `/etc/hosts.allow`—whereas `hosts.allow` specifies which hosts may access Internet services (such as TELNET and FTP) on your system, the `hosts.deny` file identifies the hosts that must be denied services. As explained in the section "Understanding the xinetd Configuration Files," the TCP wrapper consults the `/etc/hosts.deny` file if it does not find any rules in the `/etc/hosts.allow` file that apply to the requesting host. The TCP wrapper denies service if it finds in the `hosts.deny` file a rule that applies to the host.

The entries in `/etc/hosts.deny` file follow the same format as those in the `/etc/hosts.allow` file—they are in the form of a *`server:IP address`* format, where *`server`* refers to the name of the program providing a specific Internet service and *`IP address`* identifies the host allowed to use that service.

If you have already set up entries in the `/etc/hosts.allow` file to allow access to specific hosts, you can place the following line in `/etc/hosts.deny` to deny all other hosts access to any service on your system:

```
ALL:ALL
```

insider insight — **To learn the detailed syntax of the entries in the** `/etc/hosts.deny` **file, type man hosts.deny at the Linux shell prompt.**

/etc/nsswitch.conf

This file, known as the name service switch (NSS) file, specifies how services, such as the name resolver library, NIS, NIS+, and local configuration files such as `/etc/hosts` and `/etc/shadow`, interact. Newer versions of Linux that use GNU C Library version 2 (glibc 2) or later rely on the `/etc/nsswitch.conf` file to determine what takes precedence: a local configuration file or a service such as DNS or NIS (see Chapter 18 to learn more about DNS and NIS).

As an example, the following hosts entry in the `/etc/nsswitch.conf` file specifies that the resolver library should first try the `/etc/hosts` file, then try NIS+, and finally try DNS:

```
hosts:      files nisplus dns
```

insider insight — **You can learn more about the** `/etc/nsswitch.conf` **file by typing info libc "Name Service Switch@dp in a terminal window.**

Configuring Networks at Boot Time

You want to start your network automatically every time you boot the system. For this to happen, you have to put the appropriate commands in one or more startup scripts. The init process runs immediately after Linux boots. The process consults the `/etc/inittab` file and executes various commands (typically, shell scripts), depending on the current run level. For example, in run level 3 — the multiuser level — `/etc/inittab` specifies that init should run the script file `/etc/rc.d/rc` with the argument 3.

In run levels 3 and 5, the startup script ends up executing the `/etc/rc.d/init.d/network` **script to activate all networking interfaces. If you consult the** `/etc/rc.d/init.d/network` **file, you will notice that network initialization is done by using another set of files in the** `/etc/sysconfig` **directory. The network activation script checks the variables defined in the** `/etc/sysconfig/network` **file to decide whether or not to activate the network. In** `/etc/sysconfig/network`**, you should see a line with the** `NETWORKING` **variable as follows:**

```
NETWORKING=yes
```

The network is activated only if the `NETWORKING` **variable is set to** `yes`**. Another variable in the** `/etc/sysconfig/network` **file —** `HOSTNAME` **— defines your system's host name. The default setting of** `HOSTNAME` **is as follows:**

```
HOSTNAME=localhost.localdomain
```

continues

continued

The `/etc/rc.d/init.d/network` script, in turn, executes a number of scripts in the `/etc/sysconfig/network-scripts` directory to activate specific network interfaces. For example, to activate the Ethernet interface eth0, the `/etc/sysconfig/network-scripts/ifup` script is executed with `/etc/sysconfig/network-scripts/ifcfg-eth0` as the configuration file. Here is what a typical `/etc/sysconfig/network-scripts/ifcfg-eth0` file contains:

```
DEVICE=eth0
BOOTPROTO=dhcp
HWADDR=00:0C:76:F4:38:B3
ONBOOT=yes
TYPE=Ethernet
```

As you can see, this file contains the network device name, as well as the hardware address of the Ethernet card. The `BOOTPROTO=dhcp` line specifies that the IP address of the network interface should be obtained using the Dynamic Host Configuration Protocol (DHCP). The `ONBOOT` variable indicates whether this network interface should be activated when Linux boots. If your PC has an Ethernet card, you want to activate the interface at boot time; therefore, `ONBOOT` is set to `yes`.

The files in the `/etc/sysconfig` directory are created by the Fedora Linux installation program as you install Linux and also by the network configuration tool when you configure the network later on.

The `/etc/sysconfig/network-scripts/ifup` script essentially runs the following commands:

- `/sbin/ifconfig`, to configure the specified network interface; in this case, the Ethernet card (eth0)
- `/sbin/route`, to set up the routing table for the activated network interface

If you have PCMCIA network cards, those network interfaces are configured and activated by the `/etc/init.d/pcmcia` script, which, in turn, calls the `/etc/pcmcia/network` script. The `/etc/pcmcia/network` script then runs the `/etc/sysconfig/network-scripts/ifup` script to bring the interface up and `/etc/sysconfig/network-scripts/ifdown` script to bring the interface down.

TCP/IP Network Diagnostics

After you configure Ethernet and TCP/IP (during Fedora Linux installation or by running system-config-network later on), you should be able to use various networking applications without any problem. The TCP/IP protocol suite includes several tools that help you monitor and diagnose problems.

Looking at Network Interface Status

Use the `/sbin/ifconfig` command to view the currently configured network interfaces. The `ifconfig` command is used to configure a network interface (that is, to associate an IP address with a network device). If you run `ifconfig` without any command-line arguments, the command displays information about the current network interfaces. The following is a typical invocation of `ifconfig` and the resulting output:

```
/sbin/ifconfig
eth0      Link encap:Ethernet  HWaddr 00:0C:76:F4:38:B3
          inet addr:192.168.0.8  Bcast:192.168.0.255  Mask:255.255.255.0
          inet6 addr: fe80::20c:76ff:fef4:38b3/64 Scope:Link
          UP BROADCAST RUNNING MULTICAST  MTU:1500  Metric:1
          RX packets:11126 errors:0 dropped:0 overruns:0 frame:0
          TX packets:11376 errors:0 dropped:0 overruns:0 carrier:0
          collisions:0 txqueuelen:1000
          RX bytes:1056109 (1.0 MiB)  TX bytes:1217072 (1.1 MiB)
          Interrupt:11 Base address:0xc800

lo        Link encap:Local Loopback
          inet addr:127.0.0.1  Mask:255.0.0.0
          inet6 addr: ::1/128 Scope:Host
          UP LOOPBACK RUNNING  MTU:16436  Metric:1
          RX packets:2150 errors:0 dropped:0 overruns:0 frame:0
          TX packets:2150 errors:0 dropped:0 overruns:0 carrier:0
          collisions:0 txqueuelen:0
          RX bytes:2506375 (2.3 MiB)  TX bytes:2506375 (2.3 MiB)
```

This output shows that two interfaces—the loopback interface (lo) and an Ethernet card (eth0)—are currently active on this system. For each interface, you can see the IP address, as well as statistics on packets delivered and sent. If the Linux system had a dial-up PPP link up and running, you'd also see an item for the ppp0 interface in the output.

Viewing the IP Routing Table

The other network configuration command, `/sbin/route`, also provides status information when it is run without any command-line argument. If you are having trouble checking a connection to another host (that you specify with an IP address), check the IP routing table to see whether a default gateway is specified. Then check the gateway's routing table to ensure that paths to an outside network appear in that routing table.

A typical output from the `/sbin/route` command looks like the following:

```
/sbin/route
Kernel IP routing table
Destination     Gateway         Genmask         Flags Metric Ref    Use Iface
192.168.0.0     *               255.255.255.0   U     0      0        0 eth0
169.254.0.0     *               255.255.0.0     U     0      0        0 eth0
default         192.168.0.1     0.0.0.0         UG    0      0        0 eth0
```

As this routing table shows, the local network uses the eth0 Ethernet interface, and the default gateway is also that Ethernet interface. The default gateway is a routing device that handles packets addressed to any network, other than the one in which the Linux system resides. In this example, packets addressed to any network address other than ones that begin with 192.168.0 are sent to the gateway—192.168.0.1. The gateway forwards those packets to other networks (assuming, of course, that the gateway is connected to another network).

Checking Connectivity to a Host

To check for a network path to a specific host, use the `ping` command. Ping is a widely used TCP/IP tool that uses a series of Internet Control Message Protocol (ICMP, often pronounced as *eye-comp*) messages. (ICMP provides for an Echo message to which every host responds.) Using the ICMP messages and replies, Ping can determine whether or not the other system is alive and can compute the round-trip delay in communicating with that system.

The following example shows how I run Ping to see whether or not one of the systems on my network is alive:

```
ping 192.168.0.1
PING 192.168.0.1 (192.168.0.1) 56(84) bytes of data.
64 bytes from 192.168.0.1: icmp_seq=0 ttl=63 time=0.605 ms
64 bytes from 192.168.0.1: icmp_seq=1 ttl=63 time=0.559 ms
64 bytes from 192.168.0.1: icmp_seq=2 ttl=63 time=0.575 ms
64 bytes from 192.168.0.1: icmp_seq=3 ttl=63 time=0.568 ms

--- 192.168.0.1 ping statistics ---
4 packets transmitted, 4 received, 0% packet loss, time 3000ms
rtt min/avg/max/mdev = 0.559/0.576/0.605/0.034 ms, pipe 2
```

In Linux, Ping continues to run until you press Ctrl-C to stop it; then it displays summary statistics showing the typical time it takes to send a packet between the two systems. On some systems, Ping simply reports that a remote host is alive. However, you can still get the timing information with appropriate command-line arguments.

You can also use the `traceroute` command to check connectivity to a host and more. The `traceroute` command prints the route that packets take from your system to another system on the Internet. For example, here is an example of using `traceroute` to print the route from a system to `www.whitehouse.gov`:

```
traceroute www.whitehouse.gov
traceroute: Warning: www.whitehouse.gov has multiple addresses; using 205.161.7.118
traceroute to a1289.g.akamai.net (205.161.7.118), 30 hops max, 38 byte packets
 1  192.168.0.1 (192.168.0.1)  1.607 ms  0.792 ms  0.768 ms
 2  * * *
 3  68.87.136.37 (68.87.136.37)  11.495 ms  11.210 ms  11.781 ms
 4  68.87.129.154 (68.87.129.154)  13.428 ms  12.203 ms  12.087 ms
 5  68.87.129.158 (68.87.129.158)  11.550 ms  12.927 ms  12.028 ms
 6  68.87.136.5 (68.87.136.5)  14.534 ms  13.423 ms  14.573 ms
 7  68.87.129.34 (68.87.129.34)  15.392 ms  33.812 ms  14.613 ms
 8  68.87.16.137 (68.87.16.137)  16.797 ms  15.269 ms  16.771 ms
 9  12.118.102.5 (12.118.102.5)  21.260 ms  22.166 ms  21.027 ms
10  tbr2-p032501.n54ny.ip.att.net (12.123.3.86)  22.119 ms  21.896 ms  21.593 ms
11  ggr2-p390.n54ny.ip.att.net (12.123.3.62)  20.973 ms  22.106 ms  20.984 ms
12  sl-bb20-nyc-13-0.sprintlink.net (144.232.8.73) 22.011 ms 23.881 ms 26.592 ms
... some lines deleted ...
20  sl-bb21-sj-4-0.sprintlink.net (144.232.3.9)  92.831 ms  93.032 ms  91.066 ms
21  sl-st21-sj-13-0.sprintlink.net (144.232.20.59) 143.535 ms 118.988 ms
     232.815 ms
22  205.161.7.118 (205.161.7.118)  90.572 ms  91.919 ms  90.210 ms
```

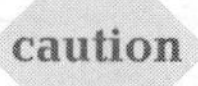

caution

The `ping` and `traceroute` commands rely on ICMP messages that many firewalls are configured to block. Therefore, `ping` and `traceroute` may not always work and are no longer reliable ways to test network connectivity. If `ping` or `traceroute` fails for a specific host, do not assume that the host is down or not connected to the network.

Checking Network Status

To check the status of the network, use the `netstat` command. This command displays the status of network connections of various types (such as TCP and UDP connections). You can view the status of the interfaces quickly with the `-i` option, as follows:

```
netstat -i
Kernel Interface table
Iface   MTU Met RX-OK RX-ERR RX-DRP RX-OVR   TX-OK TX-ERR TX-DRP TX-OVR Flg
eth0   1500   0 11824      0      0      0   12026      0      0      0 BMRU
lo    16436   0  2150      0      0      0    2150      0      0      0 LRU
```

In this case, the output shows the current status of the loopback and Ethernet interfaces. Table 6-1 describes the meanings of the columns.

Table 6-1: Columns in the Kernel Interface Table

Column	*Meaning*
`Iface`	Name of the interface
`MTU`	Maximum Transfer Unit—the maximum number of bytes that a packet can contain
`Met`	Metric value for the interface—a number indicating distance (in terms of number of hops) that routing software uses when deciding which interface to send packets through
`RX-OK, TX-OK`	Number of error-free packets received (RX) or transmitted (TX)
`RX-ERR, TX-ERR`	Number of packets with errors
`RX-DRP, TX-DRP`	Number of dropped packets
`RX-OVR, TX-OVR`	Number of packets lost due to overflow
`Flg`	`A` = receive multicast; `B` = broadcast allowed; `D` = debugging turned on; `L` = loopback interface (notice the flag on lo); `M` = all packets received; `N` = trailers avoided; `O` = no ARP on this interface; `P` = point-to-point interface; `R` = interface is running; `U` = interface is up

Another useful `netstat` option is `-t`, which shows all active TCP connections. Following is a typical result of `netstat -t` on one of my Linux PCs:

```
netstat -t
Active Internet connections (w/o servers)
Proto Recv-Q Send-Q Local Address      Foreign Address              State
tcp        0      0 192.168.0.8:53108 download.fedora.redhat.:ftp ESTABLISHED
tcp        0      0 192.168.0.8:ssh   192.168.0.7:1070            ESTABLISHED
```

In this case, the output columns show the protocol (Proto), the number of bytes in the receive and transmit queues (Recv-Q, Send-Q), the local TCP port in *hostname*:*service* format (Local Address), the remote port (Foreign Address), and the state of the connection.

insider insight

If you want netstat to display all addresses in numeric format, use the -n option of netstat, like this:

```
netstat -tn
```

Many of us prefer the numeric address format because the output looks cleaner and netstat does not have to figure out the name corresponding to each address.

Using the ip Command

The Linux kernel comes with a powerful IP routing engine together with an ip command that looks similar to the command with the same name that Cisco IOS supports (Cisco IOS is the operating system that runs on Cisco routers). You can use the ip command to manage or get information about network objects. The general syntax of the ip command is as follows:

```
ip [options] OBJECT [command [arg1 arg2 ...]]
```

where options are flags that modify the behavior of the command, OBJECT is the network object you want to manage or view, and command is the action you want to perform. The command may take zero or more arguments, as indicated by arg1, arg2, . . . in the syntax.

The objects you can manage or view with the ip command are the following:

- **link:** Refers to network devices such as eth0 and ppp0
- **address:** Refers to the IP or IPv6 address of a network device
- **neighbor:** Refers to an entry in the Address Resolution Protocol (ARP) that associates an IP address to a physical Ethernet address
- **route:** Refers to entries in the routing table
- **rule:** Refers to rules in the routing policy database
- **maddress:** Refers to a multicast address
- **mroute:** Refers to entries in the multicast routing cache
- **tunnel:** Refers to a tunnel over IP

To view information about the network interfaces, use the following ip command:

```
ip address show
1: lo: <LOOPBACK,UP> mtu 16436 qdisc noqueue
    link/loopback 00:00:00:00:00:00 brd 00:00:00:00:00:00
    inet 127.0.0.1/8 scope host lo
    inet6 ::1/128 scope host
       valid_lft forever preferred_lft forever
2: eth0: <BROADCAST,MULTICAST,UP> mtu 1500 qdisc pfifo_fast qlen 1000
    link/ether 00:0c:76:f4:38:b3 brd ff:ff:ff:ff:ff:ff
    inet 192.168.0.8/24 brd 192.168.0.255 scope global eth0
    inet6 fe80::20c:76ff:fef4:38b3/64 scope link
       valid_lft forever preferred_lft forever
```

This tells you that the eth0 interface is associated with the `inet` address `192.168.0.8/24`. The `/24` stands for the number of bits that are in the network address. There are 32 bits, of which 24 are network address, so there are 8 bits left for the hosts in this network.

To see routes, type **ip route show**. Here is a typical example of the output of that command:

```
192.168.0.0/24 dev eth0  proto kernel  scope link  src 192.168.0.8
169.254.0.0/16 dev eth0  scope link
default via 192.168.0.1 dev eth0
```

You can try out `ip` to view the other network objects, but the greatest power of `ip` is in configuring the network objects to turn your Linux system into a sophisticated router.

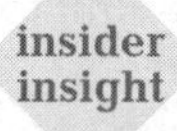

The `ip` command's capabilities are too extensive to cover in this chapter. To learn more about the `ip` command and what you can do with it, visit `www.tldp.org/HOWTO/Adv-Routing-HOWTO/` (see section 3.4 of that HOWTO document), and consult the documentation in the `/usr/share/doc/iproute*` directory of your Fedora system.

Summary

Linux has extensive built-in support for TCP/IP and Ethernet networks. This chapter explained the basics of TCP/IP networking and showed you how to set up TCP/IP networking on your Linux PC.

By reading this chapter, you learned the following things:

- The OSI seven-layer model provides a framework for making various networks work together. The OSI layered model also sets the stage for various networking protocols.
- The Transmission Control Protocol and Internet Protocol (TCP/IP) originated from research the U.S. Government's Advanced Research Projects Agency (ARPA) initiated in the 1970s. The modern Internet evolved from the networking technology developed during that time.
- All Internet protocols are documented in Requests for Comments (RFC) documents. The RFCs are available from the Internet resource `www.cis.ohio-state.edu/hypertext/information/rfc.html` or `www.faqs.org/rfcs/`. All Internet standards are in RFCs, but many RFCs simply provide information to the Internet community.
- Internetworking is at the heart of the TCP/IP protocol; that is the purpose of the Internet Protocol. The TCP/IP protocol identifies a host by using a 32-bit IP address that has two parts: a network address and a host address.
- Typically, an IP address is expressed in dotted-decimal notation, in which each byte's value is written in decimal format and separated from the adjacent byte by a dot (.). A typical IP address is 132.250.112.52.
- IP addresses are grouped in classes. Class A addresses use a 1-byte network address and 3 bytes for the host address, class B addresses use a 2-byte network and host address, and class C addresses use a 3-byte network address and a single byte for the host address. The values of the first byte indicate the type of address: 1–126 are class A, 128–191 are class B, and 192–223 are class C.

- The IP address space is filling rapidly. To alleviate this problem, the Internet Engineering Task Force has adopted a new 16-byte (128-bit) addressing scheme known as IPv6 (or IP Version 6). Hosts that use the new IPv6 addresses will work with hosts that use the older IPv4 (32-bit) addresses.
- The use of private IP addresses (as specified by RFC 1918) and Classless Inter-Domain Routing (CIDR) are interim, but proven, approaches to manage the diminishing IPv4 address pool.
- Setting up TCP/IP on Linux requires setting up various configuration files. The system-config-network tool provides a convenient way to set up these files. You need some information — such as an IP address, the address of a gateway, and the address of a name server — to set up TCP/IP networking on your system. If you do not plan to connect your local network to the Internet, you can use a range of IP addresses (such as 192.168.0.0 to 192.168.255.255) without having to coordinate with any organization.
- Linux comes with many TCP/IP utilities, such as FTP (File Transfer Protocol) and Telnet (for logging in to another system on the network).
- To diagnose TCP/IP networking problems, you can use the `ifconfig`, `ping`, `route`, and `netstat` commands. You can also use the `ip` command to view as well as manage network objects such as interfaces, addresses, and routing table entries.

Part II

Exploring Linux

Linux Basics

◆ ◆

Secrets in This Chapter

◆ ◆

Now that you have installed Linux from this book's companion DVD-ROM, you are ready to explore and learn the basics of Linux. This chapter shows you how to log in, log out, and shut down your Linux system. Then, you power up again and learn about Linux commands.

Although Linux comes with the GNOME and KDE graphical user interfaces (GUIs), you can't do everything from the graphical environment. It's not impossible to design a graphical interface that enables you to perform most chores, but sometimes you may have to perform system-administration tasks when the graphical environment is not available. You may be logged in through a terminal session, or you may have problems with X. In such cases, you have to use Linux commands to accomplish specific tasks.

This chapter also shows you how to work with files and directories in Linux. To use files and directories, you need to understand the concept of a hierarchical file system. The chapter provides a quick introduction to the Linux file system. Then, you learn to explore the file system with the Nautilus graphical shell. Finally, you learn several Linux commands that you can use to work with files and directories.

Starting Linux for the First Time

After the installation is complete, the Linux installation program automatically reboots the system. The PC goes through its normal power-up sequence and loads the GRUB boot loader. If you press any key as the GRUB loader waits to load an operating system, a graphical screen appears with the names of the partitions the boot loader can boot. You can press the up and down arrow keys to select the partition from which the system should boot. When you installed the boot loader, if you specified the Linux partition as the default one, you can simply wait; after a few seconds, Linux starts.

Controlling Linux with Boot Parameters

Before you select a partition to boot, you can get a text-mode prompt from the boot loader and enter other commands.

To provide boot parameters to the Linux kernel, press a when the GRUB screen appears. This causes GRUB to prompt you for commands to add to its default boot command (which, I assume, is set to boot Linux). Then, you can type anything else you want to add to that command. For example, to boot the system into single user mode, press the Spacebar and type:

```
single
```

You can pass many more parameters to the Linux kernel. To learn the kernel boot parameters, type **man bootparam** in a terminal window (after you boot Linux).

As the Linux kernel starts, you see a long list of opening messages, often referred to as the *boot messages.* (Because of the graphical boot screen, you may not see all the messages, but you can see these messages at any time by typing the command **dmesg** in a terminal window.) These messages include the names of the devices that Linux detects. One of the first lines in the boot messages reads (to see this message, type **dmesg | grep BogoMIPS**):

```
Calibrating delay loop... 4997.12 BogoMIPS (lpj=2498560)
```

BogoMIPS is Linux jargon for a measure of time. The number that precedes BogoMIPS depends on your PC's processor speed, whether it's an old 400 MHz Pentium II or a new 3.6 GHz Pentium 4. The kernel uses the BogoMIPS measurement when it has to wait a small amount of time for some event to occur (like getting a response back from a disk controller when it's ready).

insider insight

As you may know, MIPS is an acronym for millions of instructions per second — a measure of how fast your computer runs programs. As such, MIPS is not a very good measure of performance because comparing the MIPS of different types of computers is difficult. *BogoMIPS* is bogus MIPS, which refers to an indication of the computer's speed. Linux uses the BogoMIPS number to calibrate a delay loop, in which the computer processes some instructions repeatedly until a specified amount of time has passed.

The BogoMIPS numbers can range anywhere from 1 to 6,000 or more, depending on the type of processor (386, 486, or Pentium) and the processor's speed. An older 33 MHz 80386DX system has a BogoMIPS of about 6, whereas a 66 MHz 80486DX2/66 system shows a BogoMIPS of about 33. The BogoMIPS for newer Pentium systems is much higher. For example, on an old 200 MHz Pentium MMX system, Linux reports a BogoMIPS of 398.13. However, on a PC with a 2.53 GHz Celeron processor, the BogoMIPS is 4997.12. It's higher yet on more recent 3 GHz or better Pentium 4 systems.

Configuring for the First Time with firstboot

If you are booting Fedora Linux for the first time after installation, a server named firstboot runs and displays a welcome screen about setting up Linux. The firstboot server takes you through date and time setup, and gives you a chance to install any additional CDs.

caution

If the screen goes dark and there is no activity, the first-time configuration utility may be having trouble starting the X Window System. Unfortunately, you cannot proceed without fixing this problem. Sometimes the graphical environment fails even though the graphical interface seems to work fine during installation. There are ways to fix this problem. Go to Chapter 2 for more information on how to troubleshoot this problem.

The firstboot server takes you through the following steps (you can skip these steps if you want):

1. Read and accept the Fedora license agreement that offers the software under the GNU General Public License (GPL). Click Next to continue.
2. Set the date and time from a GUI screen. If your system is connected to the Internet, click the Network Time Protocol tab, click to Enable Network Time Protocol, and then select a server from the list of servers. This way, the system is going to get its time directly from one of the super-accurate time servers on the Internet using the Network Time Protocol (NTP). After setting the date and time, click Next.
3. firstboot then displays a GUI through which you can configure the display— change the resolution and number of colors, as well as configure the video card and the monitor. After this step is done, click Next again.
4. firstboot prompts you to define a user account. You can define a user by entering the user name, full name, and the password (you have to enter the password again to confirm). Click Next after you define a user.
5. firstboot displays information about any sound card in your PC. You can click the Play test sound button to test that the sound drivers are installed correctly. Click Next to continue.
6. firstboot displays a screen from which you can install additional CDs. If you have additional CDs to install, click Install. Otherwise, click Next.

When you're done with firstboot you're really done for good because it is set to run only once when you boot for the first time. If, for some reason, you want to go through these steps again, you can run the firstboot server again. Log in as `root`, and type the following command in a terminal window (to open a terminal window select Applications ➪ System Tools ➪ Terminal):

```
rm /etc/sysconfig/firstboot
chkconfig --level 5 firstboot on
```

That's it! Next time you reboot the PC, firstboot should run again. If you want to run firstboot interactively from GNOME or KDE, you can do so by logging in as `root` and typing the following commands in a terminal window:

```
rm /etc/sysconfig/firstboot
firstboot
```

Logging in at Graphical Login Screen

On first-time boot, you get the graphical login screen after you're through with firstboot. At other times, you would first see the boot messages, then a graphical boot screen, and then, if all goes well, you get a graphical login screen, such as the one shown in Figure 7-1.

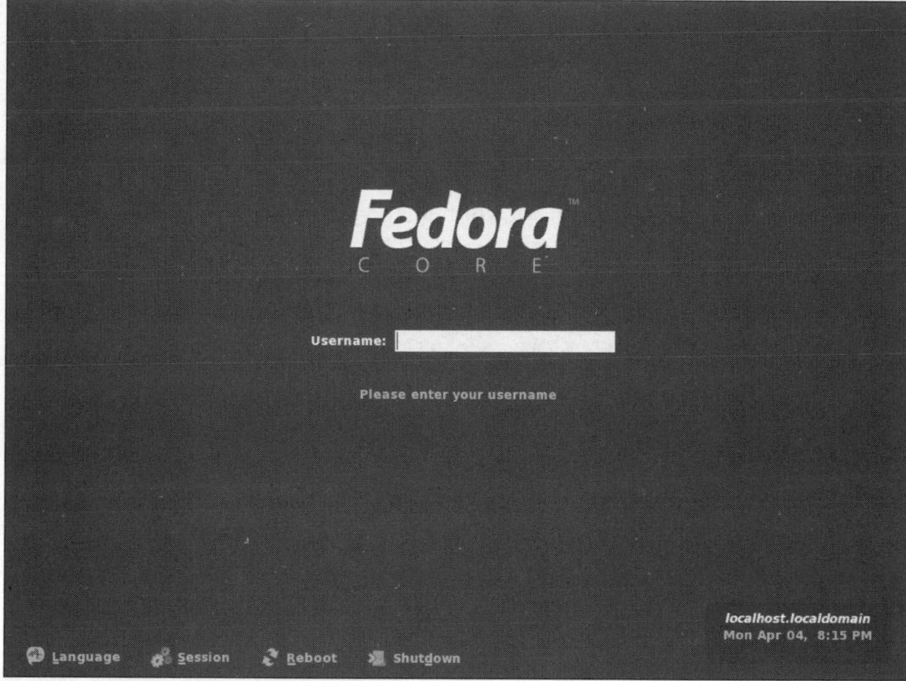

Figure 7-1: Graphical Login Screen in Fedora Linux.

You won't get a graphical login screen if your system is set for text-mode login or if there is something wrong with your X Window System setup. If you get a text-mode login screen, log in as usual and then you can configure X or switch to a graphical login. First check the runlevel with the following command:

```
runlevel
```

If you see a response with the number 3, then your system is set for text-mode login. You can enter graphical login with the following command:

```
telinit 5
```

On the other hand, if the output of runlevel contains the number 5, then there may be something wrong with the X setup. Consult Chapter 3 for more information on how to set up X.

If you get the graphical login screen, which is the login window in the middle of the screen, and your system's host name in the lower-right corner, `localhost.localdomain` is the default host name. If you use DHCP to configure the network, the DHCP server may provide a host name for your system. The login window has a text input field that prompts you for your user name.

You can log in using any of the accounts you define during the firstboot process, including `root`. However, you should not log in as `root` for routine tasks. Instead, log in as a normal user (for example, with the user name you defined when firstboot ran) and then become `root` only when needed. To become root, type **su -** in a terminal window and type the root password when prompted.

Because the default GUI is GNOME, the GNOME desktop appears, as shown in Figure 7-2. As you can see, the desktop is similar to the Windows desktop. Now, you can perform a few initial chores and learn how to shut down your Linux system.

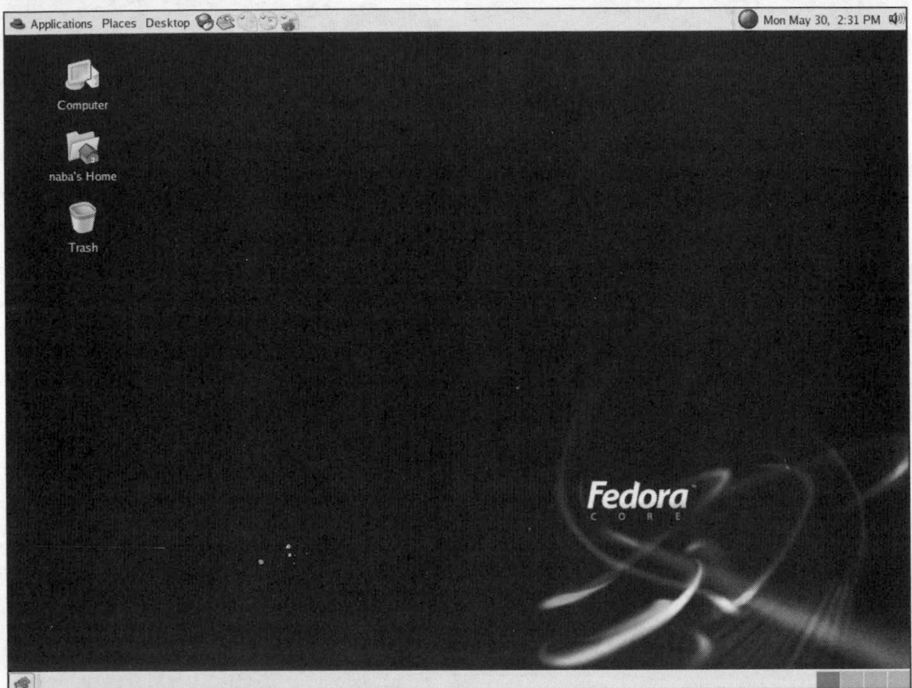

Figure 7-2: Initial GNOME Desktop.

Take a moment to look at the initial GNOME desktop as it appears in Figure 7-2. The GNOME desktop is very much like the Windows desktop except that it has two taskbars, one along the top and the other along the bottom edge of the screen. These are the GNOME panels—similar to the Windows taskbar. You can access various menus and launch applications from the top GNOME panel whereas status information, including icons for currently running applications, appear in the bottom panel. The top panel also contains such applets as the Clock, which displays the time in a small area at the right edge of the panel.

cross ref

You learn more about the GNOME desktop in Chapter 9. For now, all you need to know is that the Applications button at the left edge of the top GNOME panel is the Main Menu button. This button is like the Start button in Microsoft Windows. You can access many programs from the Main Menu button (the Applications button). You can also start some programs from the Places and Desktop menus on the top panel. Last, you can also start some programs by clicking the icons to the right of the menu buttons on the top panel. For example, to start the FireFox Web browser, click the earth-and-mouse icon on the top panel.

The following sections show you how to log out of and shut down your Linux system.

Logging Out

Now that you have seen how to log in, you should learn how to log out. To log out, select Desktop ⇨ Log Out. The screen is grayed out, and a dialog box asks you if you really want to log out. Click OK to log out.

cross ref

After a few moments, the graphical login screen (refer to Figure 7-1) appears again so that another user can log in and use the system. The graphical login window is displayed by a display manager such as xdm (X Display Manager), gdm (GNOME Display Manager), or kdm (KDE Display Manager). You learn more about the display managers and configuration of the graphical logins in Chapter 9.

Shutting Down Linux

When you are ready to shut down Linux, you should do so in an orderly manner. Even if you are the sole user of a Linux system, several other programs are usually running in the background. In addition, operating systems such as Linux try to optimize the way in which they write data to the disk. Because disk access is relatively slow (compared with the time needed to access memory locations), data usually is held in memory and written to the disk in large chunks. Therefore, if you simply turn the power off, you run the risk that some files will not be updated properly.

Any user (you do not have to be logged in as `root`) can shut down the system from the GNOME desktop. The Logout dialog box provides the options for rebooting or halting the system. To shut down the system, simply select Shutdown, and click OK. The system then shuts down in an orderly manner.

caution

Note that it does not require root access to shutdown or reboot the system in this manner. This is why you need to make sure that physical access to the console is protected adequately.

As the system shuts down, you see messages about processes being shut down. You may be surprised how many processes there are, even though no one is explicitly running any programs on the system. If your system does not automatically power off when shut down, you can manually turn the power off.

If you are already logged in as `root`, you can use the `shutdown` command to halt or reboot the system. If you are already logged in using another user name, you can become the superuser by typing the following command (your input is shown in boldface; my comments are in italic):

```
su -
Password:    (type the root password and press Enter)
```

When you become root by typing `su -` (instead of `su` alone), you also get root's environment, including settings such as the `PATH` environment variable. This enables you to run many system utilities without having to explicitly specify their path.

After you become a superuser, type the following command to halt the system:

```
shutdown -h now
```

After a few moments, you see many more messages about processes being stopped. On older systems, you see a message about the system's being halted. You can then turn the power off. On newer systems, the shutdown process also turns the power off.

If you want to reboot the system instead of halting it, use the `shutdown` command with the `-r` option, as follows:

```
/sbin/shutdown -r now
```

On the other hand, you can also simply type `reboot` to restart the system.

Looking up Online Documentation

You should familiarize yourself with an important source of information in Linux. Every so often, you see instructions that ask you to enter a Linux command. Once you've been working with Linux for a while, it's entirely possible that you'll remember a command's name but forget the exact syntax of what you're supposed to type. For such situations, the Linux online manual pages can come to your rescue.

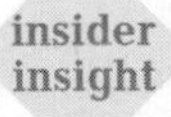

To try out the commands described in this section, you have to open a terminal window in GNOME. Select Applications ⇨ System Tools ⇨ Terminal (refer to Figure 7-2). This opens a terminal window in which you can type Linux commands.

You can view the manual page — commonly referred to as the *man page* — for a command by using the `man` command. (You do have to remember that command to access online help.) For example, to view the man page for the `modprobe` command, type the following command in a terminal window:

```
man modprobe
```

The man command then displays the help information page by page. Press the Spacebar to move to the next page. Press **b** to move backward by a page. To look for a specific word in the man page, press the forward slash, type the word, and press Enter. For example, to search for the word "debug," type **/debug**, and press Enter. When you finish reading the man page, press **q** to return to the Linux command prompt.

Having touted the usefulness of the online help pages, I must point out that the term "Linux command" refers to any executable file, ranging from a script file that contains other Linux commands to standard Linux executable programs. Although man pages exist for most standard programs, many programs do not have any online help. Nevertheless, whenever you are having difficulty recalling some command, it is worthwhile to use the man command to see whether any online help for that command exists.

If you do not want to read the full man page, you can use whatis to read a one-line summary of a command. For example, here's how you use whatis to see a brief description of the modprobe command:

```
whatis modprobe
modprobe         (8)  - program to add and remove modules from the Linux Kernel
modprobe.conf [modprobe] (5)  - Configuration file for modprobe
```

The number (8) indicates the man page section where the modprobe command is listed. You should try the whatis command to view one-line descriptions of a few other commands.

You can use the shell's wildcard feature and the whatis command to explore the files in various system directories such as /bin, /sbin, /usr/sbin, /usr/bin, and so on. Simply change the directory to one of interest and type **whatis *** to view one-line descriptions of the programs in that directory. (whatis displays information for those programs for which such information is available.) For example, here is how you can explore the /sbin directory:

```
cd /sbin; whatis * | more
MAKEDEV              (8)  - create devices
accton               (8)  - turns process accounting on or off
addpart: nothing appropriate
adsl-connect         (8)  - Shell script to manage a PPPoE link
adsl-setup           (8)  - Shell script to configure Roaring Penguin PPPoE clie
nt
adsl-start           (8)  - Shell script to bring up a PPPoE link
adsl-status          (8)  - Shell script to report on status of PPPoE link
adsl-stop            (8)  - Shell script to shut down a PPPoE link
agetty               (8)  - alternative Linux getty
alsactl              (1)  - advanced controls for ALSA soundcard driver
arp                  (7)  - Linux ARP kernel module
arp                  (8)  - manipulate the system ARP cache
arping               (8)  - send ARP REQUEST to a neighbour host
... rest of the output not shown ...
```

As you can see, the output is an alphabetic list of all programs in the current directory, along with the one-line descriptions where available. The whatis command displays a message saying nothing appropriate if there is no information available for a program.

The man and whatis commands are useful when you know the name of a command. If you do not know the exact name of a command, you can use the apropos command to search for a command by a keyword (or even a part of a word). For example, if you remember that the command contains the word probe, type the following apropos command to search:

```
apropos probe
dbus-monitor        (1)  - debug probe to print message bus messages
modprobe            (8)  - program to add and remove modules from the Linux
Kernel
modprobe.conf [modprobe] (5)  - Configuration file for modprobe
partprobe           (8)  - inform the OS of partition table changes
scanpci            (1x)  - scan/probe PCI buses
```

In this case, the search result shows several candidate commands, each with a brief description. You can then select the command that does what you want to do.

insider insight

If apropos displays a long list of commands that scroll by too fast for you to read, you can type apropos *keyword* | more to view the output one screen at a time.

Another form of online documentation you can refer to are the HOWTO files, which you can access by visiting the Linux Documentation Project (LDP) website at www.tldp.org/. (Click the earth icon on the top GNOME panel to launch the Web browser.) On that Web page, you find (among other things) links to Frequently Asked Questions (FAQs) and HOWTOs. You can click the HOWTOs main index link and read HOWTO documents online. If you click the HOWTOs main index link, the Web browser shows a list of all current HOWTOs.

Each HOWTO contains information about some area of Linux, such as the hardware it supports or how to create a boot disk. As you scroll through the list, you find over 500 HOWTOs. Table 7-1 lists and briefly describes some of these HOWTOs, especially the ones that have been kept up to date. To view any of these HOWTOs, click the name; the Web browser should display the full HOWTO document.

insider insight

Each HOWTO in the index also shows the date when it was last updated. Some of the older HOWTOs may contain some outdated information or may not cover features and capabilities that have appeared in newer versions of the Linux kernel. Please check the date and any Linux version numbers listed in the HOWTO before you use the information.

Table 7-1: Some Linux HOWTOs

HOWTO Name	*Contents*
3D-Modelling-mini-HOWTO	How to install and configure a 3D graphics modeling and rendering environment in Linux.
4mb-Laptop-HOWTO	How to put a Linux distribution on a small (4MB RAM, less than 200MB hard disk) laptop.
8021X-HOWTO	How to set up and use IEEE 802.1X Port-Based Network Access Control using Xsupplicant (available from www.open1x.org/) and using FreeRADIUS as the back-end Authentication Server.

HOWTO Name	Contents
Accessibility-HOWTO	How to use adaptive technologies – software applications and hardware devices – that can be installed to make Linux accessible to users with disabilities.
Accessibility-Dev-HOWTO	Provides software developers with information necessary for developing accessible Linux applications.
ACP-Modem-mini-HOWTO	How to build, configure, and use the ACP (Mwave) software modem found in IBM Thinkpad 600E, 600, and 770x.
ACPI-HOWTO	How to patch a kernel for Advanced Configuration and Power Interface (ACPI) support.
ADSL-Bandwidth-Management-HOWTO	How to configure a Linux router to more effectively manage outbound traffic on an ADSL modem or cable modem.
Adv-Routing-HOWTO	A guide to advanced routing and network traffic control in Linux.
Alsa-sound-mini-HOWTO	How to install the ALSA sound drivers in Linux.
Apache-Compile-HOWTO	How to compile the Apache Web server with various modules such as mod_perl, mod_jserv, and mod_php .
Apache-mods-mini-HOWTO	How to install an Apache Web server suite configured with various modules such as mod_perl, mod_ssl, and mod_php.
Apache-Overview-HOWTO	Overview of the Apache Web server and related projects.
Apache-WebDAV-LDAP-HOWTO	How to set up an Apache-based WebDAV (Web enabled Distributed Authoring and Versioning) server that can authenticate against an LDAP server.
Assembly-HOWTO	How to program in assembly language in Linux
ATA-RAID-HOWTO	How to install Linux on an Intel Pentium–compatible computer with an ATA RAID Controller and at least two hard disks.
Athlon-Powersaving-HOWTO	How to enable the power-saving functionality of the Athlon/ Duron/ AthlonXP processor on some motherboards.
Authentication-Gateway-HOWTO	How to set up an authentication gateway for wireless networks in Linux.
Autodir-HOWTO	How to install and configure Autodir, which provides a way to create directories (using the autofs protocol).
Automount-mini-HOWTO	How to configure the autofs automounter that can automatically mount and unmount file systems.
Bangla-HOWTO	How to set up and develop support for Bengali (Bangla) language in Linux.
Bash-Prog-Intro-HOWTO	How to start programming shell scripts.
Bash-Prompt-HOWTO	How to use the Bash shell (command processor).
Battery-Powered-mini-HOWTO	How to configure power management on a Linux system running on battery-powered laptops.

(continued)

Table 7-1: Some Linux HOWTOs *(continued)*

HOWTO Name	*Contents*
Belgian-HOWTO	How to configure Linux for Belgian users.
Beowulf-HOWTO	How to build a Beowulf cluster — a multi-computer architecture that can be used for parallel computations.
BogoMips-mini-HOWTO	Provides information about BogoMips — bogus MIPS, which refers to an indication of the computer's speed.
Bootdisk-HOWTO	How to create boot, root, and other utility disks for Linux.
BootPrompt-HOWTO	A list of arguments that can be passed to Linux at boot time.
BTTV-HOWTO	How to configure and use a video tuner card based on the popular Bt848 and Bt878 chipsets in Linux.
C++-dlopen-mini-HOWTO	How to dynamically load C++ functions and classes using the dlopen application programming interface (API).
Cable-Modem-HOWTO	How to configure a cable modem for Internet access.
CDServer-HOWTO	How to set up a CD server using Linux and some freely available software packages.
CD-Writing-HOWTO	How to record a CD-ROM using a CD Recorder installed in a Linux system.
CDROM-HOWTO	How to install, configure, and use CD-ROM drives with Linux.
Chroot-BIND-HOWTO	How to install and configure a BIND 9 name server in a secure manner.
Chroot-BIND8-HOWTO	How to install and configure a BIND 8 name server in a secure manner.
Clock-mini-HOWTO	How to set and keep the computer's clock on time.
Clone-HOWTO	How to boot Linux using GRUB and save partition images to and restore from a TFTP server.
Cluster-HOWTO	How to build and configure high-performance Linux computing clusters.
Conexant+Rockwell-modem-HOWTO	How to use Conexant and Rockwell chipset–based software modems in Linux.
Config-HOWTO	How to configure the most common applications in Linux.
Cryptoloop-HOWTO	How to create encrypted file systems using the Cryptoloop functionality that is part of the CryptoAPI in the 2.6 Linux kernel.
Cyrus-IMAP-HOWTO	How to install, configure, and run Cyrus Imap and Cyrus Sasl for accessing email on a remote server.
Danish-HOWTO	How to configure Linux and various Linux applications for Danish locale standards for keyboard, font, paper size, and so on.
DB2-HOWTO	How to install 32-bit IBM DB2 Universal Database Version 8.2 for Linux.

HOWTO Name	Contents
DHCP-mini-HOWTO	How to set up a Linux system to serve as a DHCP server or a DHCP client.
Disk-Encryption-HOWTO	How to encrypt a hard disk, either the whole disk or a part of it, with the encryption key stored on an external medium for increased security.
DNS-HOWTO	How to set up Domain Name Service (DNS) on a Linux system.
DocBook-Demystification-HOWTO	DocBook Demystification HOWTO Updated: Feb 2004. Attempts to clear the fog and mystery surrounding the DocBook markup system and the tools that go with it.
DocBook-Install-mini-HOWTO	How to install DocBook and use it to process SGML files into HTML, PostScript and PDF.
DocBook-OpenJade-SGML-XML-HOWTO	How to set up OpenJade to process SGML/XML DocBook documents.
DOS-Win-to-Linux-HOWTO	How to apply your DOS and Windows knowledge to the Linux environment.
DPT-Hardware-RAID-HOWTO	How to set up hardware Redundant Array of Inexpensive Disks (RAID) under Linux.
DSL-HOWTO	How to install, configure, use, and troubleshoot DSL high speed Internet access.
DVD-Playback-HOWTO	How to view DVD movies on a Linux PC with a DVD drive.
Emacs-Beginner-HOWTO	How to use the Emacs editor in Linux.
Emacspeak-HOWTO	How to install the Emacspeak audio desktop application.
Encrypted-Root-Filesystem-HOWTO	How to encrypt the Linux root file system using strong cryptography.
Enterprise-Java-for-Linux-HOWTO	How to set up an Enterprise Java environment on Linux including support for Enterprise Java Beans (EJBs).
Ethernet-HOWTO	How to configure and use Ethernet cards in Linux.
FBB-mini-HOWTO	How to install and use FBB — a popular amateur packet-radio bulletin board system (BBS) software.
Fedora-Multimedia-Installation-HOWTO	How to get various proprietary and restricted multimedia (Flash, MP3, Java, mpeg, avi, Real Media, Windows Media) working under Fedora.
Filesystems-HOWTO	How to access various file systems.
Finnish-HOWTO	How to set up Linux for the Finnish language. (Except for the initial paragraph, the HOWTO itself is in Finnish.)
Firewall-HOWTO	How to set up an Internet firewall on a Linux system.
Flash-Memory-HOWTO	How to install USB Flash Memory devices and format them for various file systems such as vfat and ext2.
Font-HOWTO	How to optimally set up and use fonts in Linux and X.

(continued)

Table 7-1: Some Linux HOWTOs *(continued)*

HOWTO Name	*Contents*
Framebuffer-HOWTO	How to use framebuffer devices (an abstraction of graphics hardware) in Linux.
Francophones-HOWTO	How to set up Linux for the French language. (This HOWTO is in French.)
From-PowerUp-To-Bash-Prompt-HOWTO	How Linux boots itself.
Game-Server-HOWTO	How to install, configure, and maintain servers for some popular multiplayer games such as Quake II and Quake III Arena.
German-HOWTO	How to use Linux with the German character set. (This HOWTO is in German.)
GIS-GRASS-mini-HOWTO	How to obtain, install, and configure a powerful public domain Geographic Information System (GIS) called the Geographic Resources Analysis Support System (GRASS).
Glibc-Install-HOWTO	How to install a new version of GNU C Library (glibc) on a Linux system.
Glibc2-HOWTO	How to install and use the GNU C Library version 2 (libc 6) on Linux systems.
Handspring-Visor-mini-HOWTO	How to use a Handspring Visor PDA with Linux and the USB port.
Hard-Disk-Upgrade	How to copy a Linux system from one hard disk to another.
Hardware-HOWTO	A list of hardware known to work with Linux; and how to locate any necessary drivers.
Hebrew-HOWTO	How to support the Hebrew character set in X Window System and text-mode screens.
Hellenic-HOWTO	How to use Linux with the Greek character set. (This HOWTO is in Greek.)
HighQuality-Apps-HOWTO	How to create Linux applications that are highly integrated with the operating system and provide security and ease of use.
Home-Electrical-Control-mini-HOWTO	How to use Linux to control home electrical devices.
Howtos-with-LinuxDoc-mini-HOWTO	How to write HOWTOs using the simple LinuxDoc markups.
HOWTO-INDEX	Index of all HOWTOs.
Indic-Fonts-HOWTO	How to install and use Indic scripts such as Devanagari using UTF-8 encoding in Linux.
Infrared-HOWTO	How to use IrDA-compliant infrared devices in Linux (IrDA is a standard for infrared wireless communication at speeds ranging from 2400bps to 4Mbps) .

HOWTO Name	Contents
IngresII-HOWTO	How to install the Ingres II Relational Database Management System on Linux.
Installation-HOWTO	How to obtain and install Linux.
Intranet-Server-HOWTO	How to use a Linux system in an intranet that ties together Unix, Novell Netware, and Windows systems.
IPCHAINS-HOWTO	How to obtain, install, and configure the IP firewall chains software for Linux (the ipchains tool).
IP-Masquerade-HOWTO	How to enable the IP Masquerading feature on a Linux system.
IPX-HOWTO	How to obtain, install, and configure various software that use the Linux support for IPX protocol (IPX is used by Novell NetWare).
IRC-mini-HOWTO	Describes Internet Relay Chat (IRC) and IRC clients and servers for Linux.
ISP-Hookup-HOWTO	How to connect a Linux system to an Internet service provider (ISP) via a dial-up modem connection .
ISP-Setup-RedHat-HOWTO	How to set up a single Red Hat Linux system for dial-ins, virtual Web hosting, virtual email, POP3, and FTP servers.
Italian-HOWTO	How to set up Linux for the Italian language. (This HOWTO is in Italian.)
Java-CGI-HOWTO	How to develop and use Java programs in Linux.
Jaz-Drive-HOWTO	How to configure and use 1GB and 2GB Iomega Jaz drives in Linux.
K7s5a-HOWTO	How to use Elite's K7s5a board with Linux.
KDE-GUI-Login-Configuration-HOWTO	How to customize the KDE GUI login screen.
Kerberos-Infrastructure-HOWTO	How to design and configure a Kerberos infrastructure for handling authentication with Linux.
KernelAnalysis-HOWTO	Description of the Linux kernel and how it works.
Keyboard-and-Console-HOWTO	How to use various Linux utilities to configure the keyboard and the console (the text-mode screen).
Kodak-Digitalcam-HOWTO	How to get a Kodak digital camera to work in Linux.
Laptop-HOWTO	How to install and use Linux on laptop computers.
Large-Disk-HOWTO	Describes disk geometry and the 1,024 cylinder limit for disks.
Latvian-HOWTO	How to localize Linux for Latvian users (written in Latvian).
LDAP-HOWTO	How to install, configure, run, and maintain a Lightweight Directory Access Protocol (LDAP) server on a Linux system.
LDAP-Implementation-HOWTO	How to configure various applications to make them LDAP-aware.

(continued)

Table 7-1: Some Linux HOWTOs *(continued)*

HOWTO Name	*Contents*
LDP-Reviewer-HOWTO	How to review Linux Documentation Project (LDP) documentation.
LILO-mini-HOWTO	Describes typical Linux Loader (LILO) installations.
Linksys-Blue-Box-Router-HOWTO	How to manage Linksys routers from a Linux system, including the firmware upgrade procedure.
Linmodem-HOWTO	How to use Winmodems (software modems) in Linux.
Linux-i386-Boot-Code-HOWTO	Describes Linux i386 boot code, serving as a study guide and commentary on the source code.
Linux-Complete-Backup-and-Recovery-HOWTO	How to back up a Linux system so as to be able to recover from a complete disk crash and how to make that recovery.
Linux-Crash-HOWTO	How to install and use the LKCD (Linux Kernel Crash Dump) package.
Linux-Gamers-HOWTO	Provides behind-the-scenes detail about games running on Linux systems.
Linux+IPv6-HOWTO	How to install, configure, and use IPv6 applications on Linux systems.
Linux-Modem-Sharing-mini-HOWTO	How to set up a Linux system to share a modem attached to this system with other systems over a TCP/IP network.
Linux+WinNT-mini-HOWTO	How to install both Linux and Windows NT on the same computer and how to boot either of them from the LILO menu.
Linux+Win9x+Grub-HOWTO	How to use the GRUB boot loader to support dual-booting of Windows and Linux.
Linux+XFS-HOWTO	How to build a Linux system that uses the SGI XFS journaling file system.
LinuxDoc+Emacs+Ispell-HOWTO	How to use Emacs and ispell to write documents such as HOWTOs for the Linux Documentation Project.
LVM-HOWTO	How to build, install, and configure Logical Volume Manager (LVM) for Linux.
Mail-Administrator-HOWTO	How to perform system-administration tasks related to electronic mail (email) systems in Linux.
Mail-User-HOWTO	Information for users of the email system.
Majordomo-MajorCool-HOWTO	How to install Majordomo Mailing List Software and the MajorCool utility to manage Majordomo lists on Linux.
Man-Page-HOWTO	How to write on-line documentation — called man pages — accessible via the man command.
Masquerading-Simple-HOWTO	How to set up IP masquerading using iptables.
Medicine-HOWTO	Description of Linux software for medical sciences.
MIDI-HOWTO	How to play and sequence using Musical Instrument Digital Interface (MIDI) in Linux.

HOWTO Name	Contents
Mobile-IPv6-HOWTO	How to set up and use mobile IPv6 in Linux.
Modem-HOWTO	How to select, connect, configure, and use modems in Linux.
Module-HOWTO	How to create and use loadable kernel modules (LKMs) in Linux.
Motorola-Surfboard-Modem	How to set up the Motorola Surfboard 4000 series of cable modems in Linux.
MP3-HOWTO	How to encode and play MP3 sound files in Linux.
MP3-CD-Burning	How to create audio CDs from MP3 files.
Multi-Disk-HOWTO	How to best use multiple disks and partitions in Linux.
Multicast-HOWTO	Information about multicasting over TCP/IP networks.
Mutt-GnuPG-PGP-HOWTO	How to configure Mutt-i, PGP, and various versions of GnuPG in order to set up a mail reader with encryption and digital-signing capabilities.
NC-HOWTO	How to hook up an IBM Netstation to the local network using a Linux system as server.
NetMeeting-HOWTO	How to make Microsoft NetMeeting work with Linux.
Network-boot-HOWTO	How to setup a Linux server capable of booting diskless Linux clients over an IP network.
Network-Install-HOWTO	How to install Linux over a Local Area Network (LAN).
Networking-Overview-HOWTO	An overview of networking capabilities of Linux.
NFS-HOWTO	How to set up an NFS (Network File System) server and client in Linux.
NFS-Root	How to set up a diskless Linux workstation that mounts its root file system via NFS.
NIS-HOWTO	How to configure Linux as a Network Information Service (NIS) or NIS+ client and how to install as an NIS server.
OLSR-IPv6-HOWTO	How to set up and use Optimized Link State Routing Protocol (OLSR) with IPv6 in Linux (OLSR is used as a routing protocol for Mobile Ad-Hoc Networks — networks that organize themselves).
Online-Troubleshooting-HOWTO	How to use resources available on the Internet to troubleshoot Linux-related problems.
openMosix-HOWTO	Describes openMosix — a software package that turns a network of Linux systems into a computer cluster.
Optical-Disk-HOWTO	How to install and configure optical disk drives in Linux (includes detailed coverage of the Panasonic LF1000 PD Phase change optical drive with the SCSI-II interface).
Oracle-8-HOWTO	How to install the Oracle 8i Enterprise Edition for Linux.
PalmOS-HOWTO	How to use your Palm OS PDA with a Linux system.

(continued)

Table 7-1: Some Linux HOWTOs *(continued)*

HOWTO Name	*Contents*
Parallel-Processing-HOWTO	How to use parallel processing approaches such as SMP (Symmetric Multiprocessing) Linux systems, clusters of networked Linux systems, and parallel execution using multimedia instructions (e.g., MMX), and attached (parallel) processors hosted by a Linux system.
Partition-HOWTO	How to plan and lay out disk space for a Linux system.
Partition-Rescue-mini-HOWTO	How to rescue a Linux partition if it has been deleted.
PCI-HOWTO	Information on Linux's support for the PCI (Peripheral Component Interconnect) bus architecture.
PCMCIA-HOWTO	How to install and use PCMCIA (Personal Computer Memory Card International Association) Card Services in Linux.
PHP-Nuke-HOWTO	Describes the PHP-Nuke content management system.
Plug-and-Play-HOWTO	How to configure a Linux system to support Plug-and-Play.
Polish-HOWTO	How to set up Linux for the Polish language. (This HOWTO is in Polish.)
Portuguese-HOWTO	How to set up Linux for the Portuguese language. (This HOWTO is in Portuguese.)
Postfix-Cyrus-Web-cyradm-HOWTO	How to install the Postfix mail transfer agent (MTA) and the Cyrus IMAP server.
PPP-HOWTO	How to set up and use Point-to-Point Protocol (PPP) networking in Linux.
ppp-ssh-mini-HOWTO	How to use PPP and SSH utilities to form an encrypted network tunnel between two hosts.
Printing-HOWTO	How to set up printing in Linux.
Printing-Usage-HOWTO	How to use the print spooling system in Linux.
Print2Win-mini-HOWTO	How to print on a Windows shared printer from Linux.
Program-Library-HOWTO	How to create and use program libraries in Linux (aimed at programmers).
Psion-HOWTO	How to use Psion palmtops with Linux (does not cover running Linux on Psion palmtops).
Qmail-ClamAV-HOWTO	How to integrate ClamAV anti-virus attachment scanner and Qmail-Scanner anti-virus message content scanner with an existing installation of a Qmail email server.
Quake-HOWTO	How to install, run, and troubleshoot Quake, QuakeWorld, and Quake II in Linux (these are 3D action games developed by id Software).
Querying-libiptc-HOWTO	How to use the libiptc library included in the iptables package.

HOWTO Name	Contents
Reading-List-HOWTO	The Linux Reading List HOWTO Updated: Feb 2004. Lists the books I think are most valuable to a person trying to learn Unix (especially Linux) top to bottom.
Remote-Serial-Console-HOWTO	How to set up Linux to support a terminal or modem attached to the serial port.
RPM-HOWTO	How to use the Red Hat Package Manager (RPM) in Linux.
RTLinux-HOWTO	How to set up and run RTLinux (real-time Linux).
Samba-Authenticated-Gateway-HOWTO	How to build a gateway for Windows PCs with a Samba Primary Domain Controller performing user authentication.
Scanner-HOWTO	How to access and use a scanner in Linux.
Scientific-Computing-with-GNU-Linux-HOWTO	How to use a Linux PC for scientific computing.
Scripting-GUI-TclTk-mini-HOWTO	How to build graphical user interface front ends for command-line utilities using Tcl and Tk.
Secure-CVS-Pserver-mini-HOWTO	How to set up a secure Concurrent Versions System (CVS) Pserver for anonymous access.
Secure-Programs-HOWTO	How to write secure programs for Linux and UNIX systems.
Security-HOWTO	An overview of security issues in a Linux system.
Security-Quickstart-HOWTO system from intrusion.	An overview of the basic steps required to secure a Linux
Security-Quickstart-Redhat-HOWTO	An overview of the basic steps required to secure a Red Hat Linux system from intrusion.
Sentry-Firewall-CD-HOWTO	How to set up a firewall using the Sentry Firewall CD (`www.SentryFirewall.com/`).
Serbian-HOWTO	How to configure Linux for Serbian users. (This HOWTO is in Serbian.)
Serial-HOWTO	How to set up serial communication devices in Linux.
Serial-Programming-HOWTO	How to program the serial port in Linux.
Shadow-Password-HOWTO	How to obtain, install, and configure the password Shadow Suite in Linux (password shadowing provides for more secure passwords than the ones stored in the `/etc/passwd` file).
Slovak-HOWTO	How to configure Linux for Slovak users. (This HOWTO is in Slovak.)
Slovenian-HOWTO	How to configure Linux for Slovenian users. (This HOWTO is in Slovenian.)
SMB-HOWTO	How to use the Server Message Block (SMB) protocol, also called the NetBIOS or LAN Manager protocol, with Linux.
SMP-HOWTO	Information on configuring Symmetric Multiprocessing (SMP) on Linux systems with multiple processors.

(continued)

Table 7-1: Some Linux HOWTOs *(continued)*

HOWTO Name	*Contents*
Snort-Statistics-HOWTO	How to configure Snort version 1.8.3, a Network Intrusion Detection System (NIDS), to gather statistics about network packets.
Software-Building-HOWTO	How to build and install UNIX software distributions in Linux.
Software-RAID-HOWTO	How to use Software RAID (software-supported virtual redundant disks) in Linux.
Software-Release-Practice-HOWTO	Describes the good software release practices of Linux Open Source projects.
Sound-HOWTO	How to enable support for sound hardware in Linux.
Sound-Playing-HOWTO	Lists many sound file formats and the applications that can be used to play sound in Linux.
Spam-Filtering-for-MX-HOWTO	How to reject junk mail received via Simple Mail Transfer Protocol (SMTP).
Spanish-HOWTO	How to configure Linux for Spanish-speaking users. (This HOWTO is in Spanish.)
Speech-Recognition-HOWTO	Description and use of automatic speech recognition software in Linux.
SquashFS-HOWTO	Describes SquashFS — a compressed file system intended for use in embedded Linux systems.
SSL-Certificates-HOWTO	How to manage a certificate authority (CA) and issue or sign certificates to be used for secure Web or secure e-mail using Secure Sockets Layer (SSL).
SSL-RedHat-HOWTO	How to build a secure Apache Web server in Red Hat Linux.
Swap-Space	How to share the Linux swap partition with Windows.
Sybase-ASE-HOWTO	How to install and configure Sybase Adaptive Server Enterprise (formerly known as SQL Server) relational database server in Linux.
Tamil-Linux-HOWTO	How to set up a working Tamil Linux environment.
TclTk-HOWTO	How to install, configure, and use the Tcl/Tk programming environment in Linux.
TeTeX-HOWTO	How to install and use the teTeX TeX (pronounced tech as in technology) and LaTeX document formatting software in Linux.
Text-Terminal-HOWTO	How to install and use text terminals (typically connected to multiport serial cards or a terminal server) with a Linux host.
Thai-HOWTO	How to set up Linux for the Thai language.
Thinclient-HOWTO	How to turn inexpensive legacy computers into fast terminals.
TimePrecision-HOWTO	How to maintain accurate date and time in Linux.

HOWTO Name	*Contents*
Tips-HOWTO	Hints and tips to make Linux more useful and fun.
Traffic-Control-HOWTO	Describes Linux's network traffic control capabilities.
Traffic-Control-tcng-HTB-HOWTO	How to implement network traffic control in Linux using tcng (Traffic Control Next Generation) with HTB (Hierarchical Token Bucket).
TransparentProxy-mini-HOWTO	How to set up a transparent caching Web (HTTP) proxy server using only squid in Linux.
Turkish-HOWTO	How to localize Linux for Turkish users (written in Turkish).
Ultra-DMA-mini-HOWTO	How to use Ultra-DMA (also known as Ultra-ATA or Ultra33) and Ultra66 hard drives in Linux.
Unicode-HOWTO	How to set up a Linux system so that it uses UTF-8 as text encoding.
Unix-and-Internet-Fundamentals-HOWTO	Nontechnical description of how PCs, UNIX-like operating systems, and the Internet work.
Unix-Hardware-Buyer-HOWTO	How to buy and configure Intel hardware for cheap, powerful Unix systems.
UPS-HOWTO	How to use an uninterruptible power supply (UPS) with Linux.
USB-Digital-Camera-HOWTO	How to use in Linux a digital camera with Universal Serial Bus (USB) mass storage capabilities.
Usenet-News-HOWTO	How to set up and access Usenet news in Linux.
User-Authentication-HOWTO	How to secure user authentication in Linux.
User-Group-HOWTO	How to establish and run a Linux User Group.
UUCP-HOWTO	How to set up and use the Unix-to-Unix Copy (UUCP) software in Linux.
VB6-to-Tcl-mini-HOWTO	A brief tour of Tcl for Visual Basic and VBScript programmers.
VCR-HOWTO	How to set up a Linux workstation as a digital VCR using the video4linux driver and a supported tuner card.
VideoLAN-HOWTO	How to use the VideoLAN video streaming software available from `www.videolan.org/`.
Virtual-Services-HOWTO	How to support virtual services on a Linux system so that a single machine can recognize multiple IP addresses without multiple network cards.
VME-HOWTO	How to run Linux on VMEbus systems (VMEbus is used in embedded systems).
VMS-to-Linux-HOWTO	How to transition from VMS to Linux. (VMS is an operating system that originally ran on VAX systems from Digital Equipment Corporation— now part of HP).
VoIP-HOWTO	Description of voice over IP (VoIP) system and software.

(continued)

Table 7-1: Some Linux HOWTOs *(continued)*

HOWTO Name	*Contents*
VPN-HOWTO	How to configure a Linux system to support a virtual private network (VPN).
VPN-Masquerade-HOWTO	How to configure a Linux firewall to masquerade IPsec and Point-to-Point Tunneling Protocol (PPTP) traffic to support a virtual private network (VPN).
Webcam-HOWTO	How to configure and use a webcam in Linux (a webcam is a video camera connected to the PC and accessible from a website).
WikiText-HOWTO	How to use the Linux Documentation Project (LDP) WikiText editing format to create DocBook documents for the LDP.
Windows-LAN-Server-HOWTO	How to use a Linux system as a Windows LAN server.
Windows-Newsreaders-under-Linux-HOWTO	How to set up and use several different Windows Usenet newsreaders under the Linux operating system using Wine.
Winmodems-and-Linux-HOWTO	How to get a Winmodem (which normally needs a Windows driver to work) working in Linux.
Wireless-HOWTO	How to set up wireless networking in Linux.
XDMCP-HOWTO	How to set up remote X terminals using X Display Manager (xdm, gdm, or kdm) and XDMCP (X Display Manager Control Protocol).
XML-RPC-HOWTO	XML-RPC HOWTO Updated: Apr 2001. Describes how to use XML-RPC to implement clients and servers in a variety of languages. Provides example code; applies to all operating systems with XML-RPC support.
Xterminals-mini-HOWTO	How to connect X Terminals to a Linux host using nfs, xfs, xdm, and xdmcp.
XWindow-Overview-HOWTO	Provides an overview of the X Window System's architecture.
XWindow-User-HOWTO	How to configure the X Window environment for a Linux user.
ZIP-Drive-mini-HOWTO	How to set up and use the Iomega ZIP drive in Linux.

Understanding the Linux File System

Like any other operating system, Linux organizes information in files and directories. The files, in turn, are contained in directories. A directory can contain other directories, giving rise to a hierarchical structure. This hierarchical organization of files is called the file system.

The Linux file system provides a unified model of all storage in the system. The file system has a single root directory, indicated by a forward slash (/). Then there is a hierarchy of files and directories. Parts of the file system can reside in different physical media, such as hard disk, floppy disk, and CD-ROM. Figure 7-3 illustrates the concept of the Linux file system and how it spans multiple physical devices.

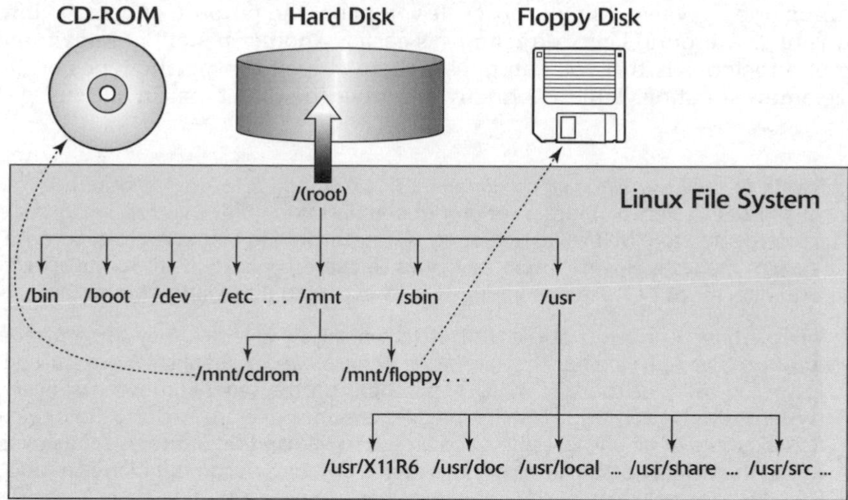

Figure 7-3: The Linux File System Provides a Unified View of Storage That May Span Multiple Drives.

If you are familiar with Windows, notice that there is no concept of a drive letter in UNIX. You can have long filenames (up to 256 characters), and filenames are case sensitive. Often, UNIX filenames have multiple extensions, such as `sample.tar.Z`. Some UNIX filenames include the following: `index.html`, `Makefile`, `kernel-devel-2.6.11-1.1177_FC4.i686.rpm`, `.bash_profile`, and `httpd_src.tar.gz`.

To locate a file, you need more than just the file's name; you also need information about the directory hierarchy. The term *pathname* refers to the complete specification necessary to locate a file — the complete hierarchy of directories leading to the file — and the filename. Figure 7-4 shows a typical Linux pathname for a file.

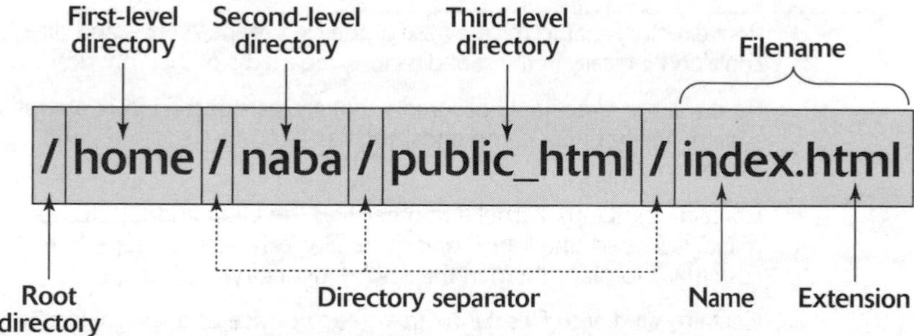

Figure 7-4: A Typical Linux Pathname.

As you can see from Figure 7-4, a Linux pathname consists of the following parts:

1. The root directory, indicated by a forward slash (/) character.
2. The directory hierarchy, with each directory name separated from the previous one by a forward slash (/) character. A / appears after the last directory name.
3. The filename, with a name and one or more optional extensions.

Many directories have specific purposes. If you know the purpose of specific directories, finding your way around Linux directories is easier. Another benefit of knowing the typical use of directories is that you can guess where to look for specific types of files when you face a new situation. Table 7-2 briefly describes the directories in a Linux system.

Linux follows the File System Hierarchy (FHS) standard for its file system layout and organization. FHS provides a set of requirements and guidelines for file and directory placement in any UNIX-like operating system, including Linux. An FHS-compliant file system makes it easy for users as well as software applications to locate specific files and directories because everything is in its expected place in the file system.

FHS is based on two basic characteristics of files—whether they are *shareable* or *unshareable* and whether they are *static* or *variable*. Shareable files are stored in one place, but may be used by many applications on the same computer or even other systems on the network. Unshareable files are ones that are exclusive to one process (an example of an unshareable file is a device lock file that indicates that a process is using the device). Static files include binaries, libraries, documentation files, and other files that are not changed by applications or users on a routine basis (static files are typically updated by the system administrator when needed). Variable files, on the other hand, are files that applications update and change. For example, error logs and mail spools are examples variable files. The idea is to organize the directories so that static and variable files are segregated because static files, unlike variable files, can be stored on read-only media and do not need to be backed up as often as variable files.

The current version of FHS is 2.3 and it was released on January 29, 2004. To learn more about the latest version of FHS, visit the Filesystem Hierarchy Standard home page at `www.pathname.com/fhs/`.

Table 7-2: Linux System Directories

Directory	*Description*
`/`	Root directory that forms the base of the file system. All files and directories are contained logically in the root directory, regardless of their physical locations.
`/bin`	Contains the executable programs that are part of the Linux operating system. Many Linux commands, such as `cat`, `cp`, `ls`, `more`, and `tar`, are located in `/bin`.
`/boot`	Contains the Linux kernel and other files the LILO and GRUB boot managers need (the kernel and other files can be anywhere, but it is customary to place them in the `/boot` directory).
`/dev`	Contains all device files. Linux treats each device as a special file; all such files are located in the device directory `/dev`.
`/etc`	Contains most system configuration files and the initialization scripts (in the `/etc/rc.d` subdirectory).
`/home`	Conventional location of the home directories of all users. User naba's home directory, for example, is `/home/naba`.
`/lib`	Contains library files, including the loadable driver modules, needed to boot the system.
`/lost+found`	Directory for lost files. Every disk partition has a `lost+found` directory.

Directory	Description
/media	A directory for mounting file systems on removable media, such as CD-ROM drives, floppy disks, and Zip drives. Contains the /media/floppy directory for mounting floppy disks and the /media/cdrom directory for mounting the CD-ROM drive. If you have a CD recorder, you'd find a /media/cdrecorder directory instead of /media/cdrom.
/mnt	A directory for temporarily mounted file systems.
/opt	Provides a storage area for large application software packages.
/proc	A special directory that contains information about various aspects of the Linux system.
/root	The home directory for the root user.
/sbin	Contains executable files representing commands typically used for system-administration tasks. Commands such as mount, halt, umount, and shutdown reside in the /sbin directory.
/srv	Contains data for services (such as Web and FTP) offered by this system.
/sys	A special directory that contains information about the devices, as seen by the Linux kernel.
/tmp	Temporary directory that any user can use as a scratch directory, meaning that the contents of this directory are considered unimportant and usually are deleted every time the system boots.
/usr	Contains the subdirectories for many important programs, such as the X Window System, and the online manual.
/var	Contains various system files (such as logs), as well as directories for holding other information, such as files for the Web server and anonymous FTP server.

The /usr and /var directories also contain a host of useful subdirectories. Table 7-3 lists a few of the important subdirectories in /usr. Table 7-4 shows a similar breakdown for the /var directory.

Table 7-3: Important /usr Subdirectories

Subdirectory	Description
/usr/X11R6	Contains the XFree86 (X Window System) software.
/usr/bin	Contains executable files for many more Linux commands, including utility programs commonly available in Linux, but is not part of the core Linux operating system.
/usr/include	Contains the header files (files with names ending in .h) for the C and C++ programming languages; also includes the X11 header files in the /usr/include/X11 directory and the kernel header files in the /usr/include/linux directory.
/usr/lib	Contains the libraries for C and C++ programming languages; also contains many other libraries, such as database libraries, graphical toolkit libraries, and so on.

(continued)

Table 7-3: *(continued)*

Subdirectory	*Description*
/usr/local	Contains local files. The /usr/local/bin directory, for example, is supposed to be the location for any executable program developed on your system.
/usr/sbin	Contains many administrative commands, such as commands for electronic mail and networking.
/usr/share	Contains shared read-only architecture-independent (this means not dependent on the processor type) data, such as default configuration files and images for many applications. For example, /usr/share/gnome contains various shared files for the GNOME desktop; and /usr/share/doc has the documentation files for many Linux applications (such as the Bash shell, mtools, and the GIMP image processing program).
/usr/share/man	Contains the online manual (which you can read by using the man command).
/usr/src	Contains the source code for the Linux kernel (the core operating system).

Table 7-4: Important /var Subdirectories

Subdirectory	*Description*
/var/cache	Storage area for cached data for applications.
/var/lib	Contains information relating to the current state of applications. (Programs modify this information when they run.)
/var/lock	Contains lock files to ensure that a resource is used by one application only.
/var/log	Contains log files organized into subdirectories. The syslogd server stores its log files in /var/log and the exact content of the files depends on the syslogd configuration file: /etc/syslog.conf. For example, /var/log/messages is the main system log file, /var/log/secure contains log messages from secure services such as sshd and xinetd, and /var/log/maillog contains the log of mail messages.
/var/mail	Contains user mailbox files.
/var/opt	Contains variable data for packages stored in the /opt directory.
/var/run	Contains data describing the system since it was booted.
/var/spool	Contains data that's waiting for some kind of processing.
/var/tmp	Contains temporary files preserved between system reboots.
/var/yp	Contains Network Information Service (NIS) database files.

Using the Nautilus Shell

Now that you know the basics of the Linux file system, you can explore it. You can access the files and directories in two ways:

- By using a graphical file manager such as the Nautilus shell in GNOME
- By typing appropriate Linux commands in a terminal window or a text console

The Nautilus graphical shell is intuitive to use — it is similar to Windows' Active Desktop — and you can perform many tasks such as navigating the file system and performing system-management tasks with Nautilus. You may want to spend a few minutes now exploring the file system by using Nautilus. (The KDE file manager — Konqueror — works in a similar manner, so it isn't covered here.)

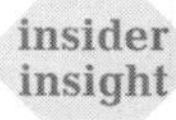

The latest version of Nautilus has changed from what you may have known in previous versions of Red Hat Linux or Fedora. Nautilus now provides a new *Object Window* view in addition to the navigation window that you know from the past. When you double-click any object on the desktop, Nautilus opens an object window that shows that object's contents. If you want the older navigation window with its Web browser–like user interface, right-click a folder icon and choose Open ⇨ Browse Folder from the pop-up menu.

When you double-click a file or a folder, Nautilus opens that object in what it calls an object window. Unlike the Nautilus windows of the past — windows that enabled you to navigate the directory hierarchy — the object window doesn't have any Back and Forward buttons, toolbars, or side panes. For example, double-click the Computer icon on the left side of the GNOME desktop, and Nautilus opens an object window where it displays the contents of the Computer object. If you then double-click an object inside that window, Nautilus opens another object window where that object's contents appear. Figure 7-5 shows the result of double-clicking some objects in Nautilus.

The Nautilus object window has a sparse user interface that has just the menu bar. You can perform various operations from the menu bar such as open an object using an application, create folders and documents, and close the object window.

If you prefer to use the familiar navigation window for browsing folders, you have to do a bit of extra work. Instead of double-clicking an icon, right-click the icon and choose Browse Folder from the context menu. Nautilus then opens a navigation window with the contents of the object represented by the icon. For example, double-click your home folder icon on the GNOME desktop. Nautilus opens a navigation window where it displays the contents of your home directory. (Think of a *directory* as a folder that can contain other files and folders.) Figure 7-6 shows a typical user's home directory in a Nautilus navigation window.

The navigation window is vertically divided into two parts. The left pane shows different views of the file system and other objects that you can browse with Nautilus. The right pane shows the files and folders in the currently selected folder in the left pane. Nautilus displays icons for files and folders. For image files, it shows a thumbnail of the image.

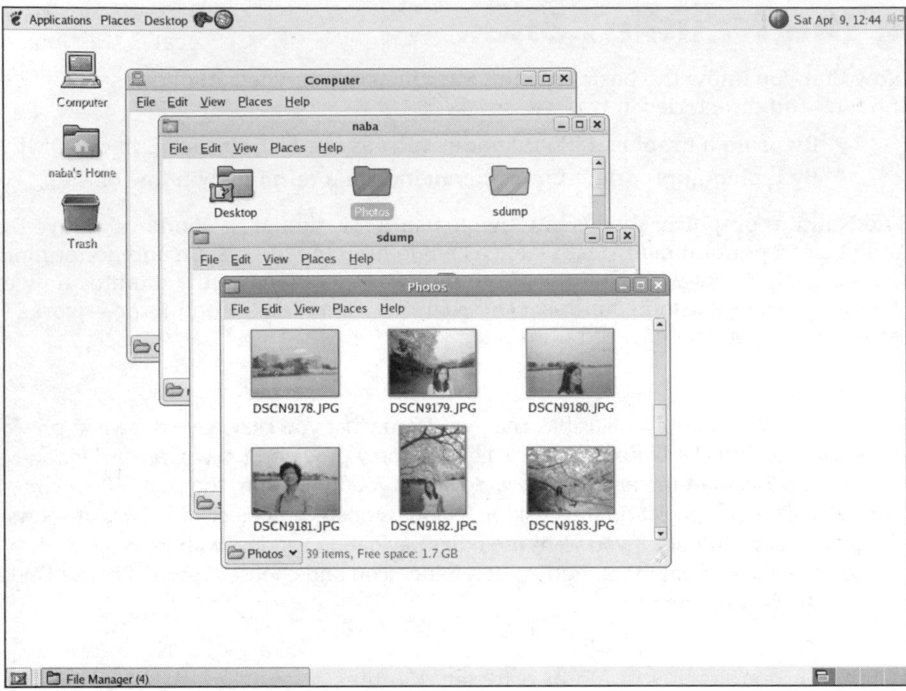

Figure 7-5: By Default, Nautilus Opens a New Object Window for Each Object.

Figure 7-6: My Home Directory, as It Appears in Nautilus.

The navigation window's user interface is similar to that of a Web browser. The window's title bar shows the name of the currently selected folder. The Location text box along the top of the window shows the full name of the current directory — for example, Figure 7-6 shows the contents of the `/home/naba` directory.

If you have used Windows Explorer, you can use Nautilus in a similar manner. Folders represent directories and you can open them by double-clicking. To move to other directories, click the up button on the toolbar as many times as necessary, and then navigate to whichever directory you want to see.

In addition to moving around the file system and viewing contents of directories, you can use Nautilus to perform tasks such as moving a file from one directory to another and deleting a file. I won't outline each step, but you can take a few moments to try the following tasks:

- To move a file to a different directory, drag and drop the file's icon on the directory where you want the file.
- To copy a file to a new location, select the file's icon and select Edit ⇨ Copy File. You can also right-click the file's icon and select Copy File from the pop-up menu. Then move to the directory where you want to copy the file, and select Edit ⇨ Paste Files.
- To delete a file or directory, right-click the icon, and select Move to Trash from the pop-up menu. To really delete the file, right-click the Trashcan icon on the desktop, and select Empty Trash from the pop-up menu.
- To rename a file or a directory, right-click the icon, and select Rename from the pop-up menu. Then, you can type the new name or edit the name.
- To create a new directory, right-click in an empty area of the right-hand window, and select New Folder from the pop-up menu. After the new folder icon appears, you can rename it by right-clicking and selecting Rename from the pop-up menu.

Navigating the File System with Linux Commands

Although graphical shells such as Nautilus are easy to use, you can use them only if you have a graphical login. Sometimes, you may not have a graphical environment to run a graphical file manager. For example, you might be logged in through a text terminal, or X might not be working on your system. In those situations, you have to rely on Linux commands to work with files and directories. Of course, you can always use Linux commands, even in the graphical environment — all you have to do is open a terminal window and type the Linux commands. Select Applications ⇨ System Tools ⇨ Terminal to start a terminal emulation program that displays a terminal window.

Using Directory Navigation Commands

In Linux, when you log in as `root`, your home directory is `/root`. For other users, the home directory is usually in the `/home` directory. My home directory (when I log in as naba) is `/home/naba`. This information is stored in the `/etc/passwd` file. By default, only you (and `root`, of course) have permission to save files in your home directory, and only you can create subdirectories in your home directory to further organize your files.

Linux supports the concept of a current directory, which is the directory on which all file and directory commands operate. After you log in, for example, your current directory is the home directory. To see the current directory, type the `pwd` command.

To change the current directory, use the `cd` command. To change the current directory to `/usr/share/doc`, type the following:

```
cd /usr/share/doc
```

Then, to change the directory to the `bash-3.0` subdirectory in `/usr/share/doc`, type this command:

```
cd bash-3.0
```

Now, if you use the `pwd` command, that command shows `/usr/share/doc/bash-3.0` as the current directory. Therefore, you can refer to a directory's name in two ways:

- An absolute pathname (such as `/usr/share/doc`), which specifies the exact directory in the directory tree
- A relative directory name (such as `bash-3.0`, which represents the `bash-3.0` subdirectory of the current directory)

If you type **cd bash-3.0** in `/usr/share/doc`, the current directory changes to `/usr/share/doc/bash-3.0`; the same command in `/home/naba` tries to change the current directory to `/home/naba/bash-3.0`.

Use the `cd` command without any arguments to change the current directory to your home directory. Actually, the lone `cd` command changes the current directory to the directory listed in the HOME environment variable; that environment variable contains your home directory by default.

Notice that the tilde character (~) also refers to the directory the HOME environment variable specifies. Thus, the command `cd ~` changes the current directory to whatever directory the HOME environment variable specifies.

You can use a shortcut to refer to any user's home directory. Prefix a user's login name with a tilde (~) to refer to that user's home directory. Therefore, `~naba` refers to the home directory of the user naba, and `~root` refers to the home directory of the root user. If your system has a user with the login name emily, you can type `cd ~emily` to change to Emily's home directory.

The directory names `.` and `..` have special meanings. A single period (`.`) indicates the current directory, whereas two periods (`..`) indicate the parent directory. If the current directory is `/usr/share/doc`, for example, you can change the current directory to `/usr/share` by typing the `cd ..` command (note that there is a space between `cd` and the two periods). Essentially, this command takes you up one level in the file-system hierarchy.

Showing the Current Directory in the Shell Prompt

Note that you can display the current directory in the shell prompt. The Bash shell uses the value of the environment variable PS1 as the primary prompt. Another variable, PS2, functions as the secondary prompt when a command requires further input from the user. You can view these variables with the `echo` command (for example, type **echo $PS1** to view the setting of PS1).

By default, the PS1 environment variable is defined in Fedora as follows:

```
[\u@\h \W]\$
```

With this setting for PS1, the prompt looks like this:

```
[username@hostname dirname]$
```

In this example, `username` is the login name of the user; `hostname` is the system's name (excluding the domain name), and `dirname` is the last part of the current working directory. Thus, if the current directory is `/usr/src/kernels`, the `dirname` is `kernels`. Thus, when a user named joe on a system with host name `mycompany.com` changes the directory to `/usr/share/doc`, the shell prompt appears as follows:

```
[joe@mycompany doc]$
```

For the root user, the `$` sign changes to a number sign (#) and the prompt looks like this:

```
[root@mycompany doc]#
```

Table 7-5 shows the character sequences you can use in the PS1 environment variable to customize your prompt.

Table 7-5: Character Sequences in the PS1 Environment

Code	*What Appears in Prompt*
`\t`	Current time in HH:MM:SS format
`\d`	Date in "Weekday Month Date" format, such as "Wed Oct 26"
`\n`	Newline
`\s`	Name of the shell, such as bash
`\w`	Full name of the current working directory, such as `/usr/share/doc`
`\W`	Basename of the current working directory, such as `doc` for `/usr/share/doc`
`\u`	User name of the current user
`\h`	Host name
`\#`	Command number of this command
`\!`	History number of this command
`\$`	# if the effective user ID is 0 (indicating the user is root); otherwise, a $
`\nnn`	Character corresponding to the octal number *nnn*
`\\`	A backslash
`\[`	Begins a sequence of nonprinting characters, which could be used to embed a terminal control sequence into the prompt
`\]`	Ends a sequence of nonprinting characters

Given this information, you can show the full directory name (enclosed in square brackets) in the prompt by using the following command:

```
export PS1="[\w]"
```

If the current directory is /usr/share/doc, the prompt appears as follows:

```
[/usr/share/doc]
```

Interpreting Directory Listings and Permissions

As you move around the Linux directories, you may want to check the contents of a directory. You can get a directory listing by using the ls command. By default, the ls command — without any options — displays the contents of the current directory in a compact, multicolumn format. For example, type the following commands to see the contents of the /etc/X11 directory. (Type the commands shown in boldface; I have omitted the command prompts from the listing):

```
cd /etc/X11
ls
X            applnk  lbxproxy      starthere  xinit             xserver
X.rpmsave    dm      prefdm        sysconfig  xkb               xsm
Xmodmap      fs      proxymngr     twm        xorg.conf
Xresources   gdm     serverconfig  xdm        xorg.conf.backup
```

From this listing, you cannot tell whether an entry is a file or a directory. To tell the directories and files apart, use the -F option with ls, as follows:

```
ls -F
X@           applnk/  lbxproxy/      starthere/  xinit/            xserver/
X.rpmsave@   dm/      prefdm*        sysconfig/  xkb@              xsm/
Xmodmap      fs/      proxymngr/     twm/        xorg.conf
Xresources   gdm/     serverconfig/  xdm/        xorg.conf.backup
```

Now, the directory names have a slash (/) appended to them. Plain filenames appear as is. The at sign (@) appended to the first filename indicates that that file is a link to another file (in other words, this filename simply refers to another file). An asterisk (*) is appended to executable files (see, for example, the prefdm file in the listing).

You can see even more detailed information about the files and directories with the -l option:

```
ls -l
```

For the /etc/X11 directory, a typical output from ls -l looks like the following:

```
lrwxrwxrwx  1 root root   24 Mar 19 16:45 X -> ../../usr/X11R6/bin/Xorg
lrwxrwxrwx  1 root root   24 Mar 19 16:22 X.rpmsave -> ../../usr/X11R6/bin/Xorg
-rw-r--r--  1 root root  547 Oct 20 18:46 Xmodmap
-rw-r--r--  1 root root  492 Oct 20 18:46 Xresources
drwxr-xr-x  2 root root 4096 Mar  9 13:41 applnk
drwxr-xr-x  3 root root 4096 Mar 19 15:49 dm
drwxr-xr-x  2 root root 4096 Mar 19 14:55 fs
drwxr-xr-x  8 root root 4096 Mar 19 18:28 gdm
drwxr-xr-x  2 root root 4096 Mar 19 15:20 lbxproxy
-rwxr-xr-x  1 root root  816 Mar  7 15:06 prefdm
drwxr-xr-x  2 root root 4096 Mar 19 15:20 proxymngr
drwxr-xr-x  2 root root 4096 Mar  9 13:41 serverconfig
... lines deleted ...
```

The detailed directory listing displayed by the `ls -l` command shows considerable information about each directory entry, which can be a file or another directory. A typical line in the detailed directory listing has the following appearance:

```
drwxr-xr-x  8 root root 4096 Mar 19 18:28 gdm
```

Looking at a line from the right column to the left, you see that the rightmost column shows the name of the directory entry. The date and time before the name show when the last modifications to that file were made. Before the date and time is the size of the file, in bytes.

The file's group and owner appear to the left of the column that shows the file size. The next number to the left indicates the number of links to the file. (A link is like a shortcut in Windows.) Finally, the leftmost column shows the file's permission settings, which determine who can read, write, or execute the file.

The first letter of the leftmost column has a special meaning, as the following list shows:

- **-** means an ordinary file
- **b** means a block special file
- **c** means a character special file
- **d** means a directory
- **l** means a symbolic link to another file
- **p** means a first-in first-out (FIFO) special file (also known as a *pipe* file)
- **s** means a local socket

After that first letter, the leftmost column shows a sequence of nine characters, which appears as `rwxrwxrwx` when each letter is present. Each letter indicates a specific permission; a hyphen (`-`) in place of a letter indicates no permission for a specific operation on the file. Think of these nine letters as three groups of three letters (`rwx`), interpreted as follows:

- The leftmost group of `rwx` controls the read, write, and execute permission of the file's owner. In other words, if you see `rwx` in this position, the file's owner can read (`r`), write (`w`), and execute (`x`) the file. A hyphen in the place of a letter indicates no permission. Thus, the string `rw-` means that the owner has read and write permission but not execute permission. Typically, executable programs (including shell programs) have execute permission. However, for directories, execute permission is equivalent to use permission—a user must have execute permission on a directory to open and read the contents of the directory.
- The middle three `rwx` letters control the read, write, and execute permission of any user belonging to that file's group.
- The rightmost group of `rwx` letters controls the read, write, and execute permission of all other users (collectively referred to as the world).

Thus, a file with the permission setting `rwx------` is accessible only to the file's owner, whereas the permission setting `rwxr--r--` makes the file readable by the group and the world.

An interesting feature of the `ls` command is that it does not list any file whose name begins with a period. To see these files, you must use the `ls` command with the `-a` option, as follows:

```
ls -a
```

Try this command in your home directory, and compare the result with what you see when you don't use the `-a` option:

1. Type **cd** to change to your home directory.
2. Type **ls -F** to see the files and directories in your home directory.
3. Type **ls -aF** to see everything, including the hidden files.

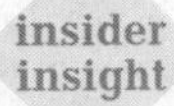

Most Linux commands take single-character options, each with a minus sign (think of this sign as a hyphen) as a prefix. When you want to use several options, type a hyphen and concatenate the option letters one after another. Therefore, `ls -al` is equivalent to `ls -a -l`. However, if an option requires a value, then you have to first list the option and then its value.

Learning the Bash Shell

If you have used MS-DOS, you may be familiar with `COMMAND.COM`, the DOS command interpreter. That program displays the infamous `C:\>` prompt. Linux provides a command interpreter that resembles `COMMAND.COM` in DOS. In UNIX, the command interpreter traditionally is referred to as a shell. The original UNIX shell was called the Bourne shell, and its executable program was named `sh`. The default Linux shell is Bash, and its program name is `bash` (found in the `/bin` directory). Bash is compatible with the original `sh`, but includes many desirable features of other well-known shells, such as the C shell and the Korn shell. For example, Bash enables you to recall commands you have entered previously, and it even completes partial commands (this is called *command completion*).

The purpose of a shell such as Bash is to display a prompt and execute the command you type at the keyboard. Some commands, such as `cd` (change directory) and `pwd` (print working directory), are built into Bash. Other commands, such as `cp` (copy) and `ls` (list directory), are separate programs (a file representing these commands resides in one of the directories on your system). As a user, however, you really do not have to know or care whether a command is built in or is in the form of a separate executable program. Note that shell built-in commands are executed before executable files with the same name.

In addition to the standard Linux commands, Bash can execute any program stored in an executable file. Bash can even execute a shell script (a text file that contains one or more commands). As you learn in Chapter 24, you can use the shell's built-in commands to write programs (also known as shell scripts). Type **help** at the shell prompt to see a list of the built-in commands.

The shell enables you to run any Linux command, but you need to know the commands before you can run them. Because Linux is a UNIX clone, all Linux commands essentially are UNIX commands. Some of the most important commands, summarized earlier in the chapter, enable you to move around the Linux file system. A large number of the Linux commands are GNU utilities — Chapter 8 provides an overview of GNU utilities.

cross ref

Consult Appendix A for a Linux command reference to learn about many more Linux commands, including most GNU utilities. Chapter 8 describes the GNU utilities and Chapter 24 shows you how to write shell programs (also called *shell scripts*).

The next few sections give you a feel for the various features of a shell, ranging from the general command syntax to defining aliases for long commands.

The discussions in this chapter assume that you use Bash as your shell because Bash is the shell you get when you install Linux from the DVD-ROM that accompanies this book.

Learning Shell Command Syntax

Because a shell interprets what you type, it is important to know how the shell processes the text you enter. All shell commands have the following general format:

```
command option1 option2 ... optionN
```

A single line of command commonly is referred to as a command line. On a command line, you enter a command followed by one or more options (or arguments), known as command-line options (or command-line arguments). Sometimes the command-line options are also called switches.

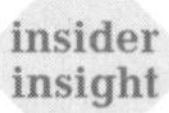

insider insight

You type shell commands at a shell prompt in a text console or a terminal window in the GUI desktop. Regardless of whether you are using GNOME or KDE you can open a terminal window by selecting Main Menu ⇨ System Tools ⇨ Terminal.

Here are the basic command-line rules:

- Use a space or a tab to separate the command from the options.
- Separate individual options with a space or a tab.
- If you use an option that contains embedded spaces, you have to put that option inside quotation marks.

To search for my name in the password file, for example, I enter the `grep` command as follows:

```
grep "Naba Barkakati" /etc/passwd
```

When `grep` prints the line with my name, it looks like this:

```
naba:x:500:500:Naba Barkakati:/home/naba:/bin/bash
```

I use shadow passwords on my system (Chapter 22 describes shadow passwords). That's why the password field (the characters between the first and second colon) is a single letter `x`. Nevertheless, this line contains some useful information; the most interesting information (for the purposes of this discussion) is the field that follows the last colon (`:`). That field shows the name of the shell I am running.

The number and the format of the command-line options, of course, depend on the actual command. When you learn more about the commands, you see that the command-line options that control the behavior of a command are of the form `-X`, in which `X` is a single character.

Because various GNU tools and utilities implement most Linux commands, you should know that GNU command-line options begin with two dashes followed by a descriptive word. Thus, the GNU options are of the form `--xxxx`, where xxxx is a word denoting the option. For example, the GNU `ls --all` command shows all directory entries, including those that begin with a period (`.`). This is the same as the `ls -a` command in all UNIX systems.

If a command is too long to fit on a single line, you can press the backslash (\) key, followed by Enter. Then continue entering the command on the next line. In addition, you can concatenate several shorter commands on a single line by using the semicolon (`;`) as a separator between the commands. For example, when rebuilding the Linux kernel (as explained in Chapter 21), you can complete three sequential tasks by typing the following commands on a single line:

```
make clean; make; make modules_install
```

Combining Commands

Linux follows the UNIX philosophy of giving the user a toolbox of many simple commands. You can, however, combine these simple commands to create a more sophisticated command. Suppose that you want to determine whether a device file named `cdrom` resides in your system's `/dev` directory because that file should have been set up as a symbolic link to your CD/DVD drive. You can use the command `ls /dev` to get a directory listing of the `/dev` directory and to see whether anything that contains `cdrom` appears in the listing. Unfortunately, the `/dev` directory has a great many entries, and it may be difficult to locate any item that has cdrom in its name. You can, however, combine the `ls` command with `grep` to come up with a command that does exactly what you want:

```
ls /dev | grep cdrom
```

The shell sends the output of the `ls` command (the directory listing) to the `grep` command, which searches for the string `cdrom`. That vertical bar (`|`) is known as a pipe because it acts as a conduit between the two programs; the output of the first command becomes the input of the second one.

For example, to see roughly how many processes are running on your system, type:

```
ps ax | wc -l
```

This sends the output of the `ps ax` command (which lists all the processes) to the `wc` command, which counts the number of lines and that count is one more than the total number of processes.

Here is another example of combining commands with pipes. Suppose you are having a meeting with a rather larger number of attendees and you have several sign-up sheets for attendees to write down their names. The attendees sign up on one or more of the sign-up sheets. Then, your assistant types each sheet into separate text files (named `list1`, `list2`, `list3`, and so on), one name per line. You can then combine the lists, sort the names, get rid of duplicates, and view the list with the following command:

```
cat list* | sort -u | more
```

The `cat` command simply turns all the names from the files into a stream of text. The `sort -u` command sorts the lines alphabetically and also removes any duplicates. Then `more` shows you the list a page at a time.

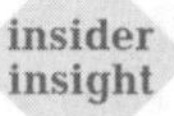

Most Linux commands are designed in a way that enables the output of one command to be fed into the input of another. To do this, simply concatenate the commands, placing pipes between them.

Using I/O Redirection

Linux commands designed to work together have a common feature — they always read from the *standard input* (usually, the keyboard) and write to the *standard output* (usually, the screen). Error messages are sent to the *standard error* (usually, the screen). These three devices often are referred to as *stdout*, *stdin*, and *stderr*.

If you want a command to read from a file, you can redirect the standard input to come from that file. Similarly, to save the output of a command in a file, redirect the standard output to a file. These features of the shell are called input and output redirection, or I/O redirection.

Using the following command, for example, you can search through all files in the `/usr/include` directory for the occurrence of the string `typedef` and save that list in a file called `typedef.out`:

```
grep typedef /usr/include/* > typedef.out
```

This command also illustrates another feature of Bash. When you use an asterisk (*), Bash replaces the asterisk with a list of all the filenames in the specified directory. Thus, `/usr/include/*` means all the files in the `/usr/include` directory.

Table 7-6 shows the syntax of common I/O redirection commands.

Table 7-6: Common Standard I/O Redirections

<table>
<tr><th>Task</th><th>Command Syntax</th></tr>
<tr><td>Send stdout to a file</td><td>command > file</td></tr>
<tr><td>Send stderr to file</td><td>command 2> file</td></tr>
<tr><td>Send stdout and stderr to file</td><td>command > file 2>&1</td></tr>
<tr><td>Read stdin from a file</td><td>command < file</td></tr>
<tr><td>Read stdin from file.in and send stdout to file.out</td><td>command < file.in > file.out</td></tr>
<tr><td>Append stdout to the end of a file</td><td>command >> file</td></tr>
<tr><td>Append stderr to the end of a file</td><td>command 2>> file</td></tr>
<tr><td>Append stdout and stderr to the end of a file</td><td>command >> file 2>&1</td></tr>
<tr><td>Read stdin from the keyboard until the character c</td><td>command <<c</td></tr>
<tr><td>Pipe stdout to command2</td><td>command | command2</td></tr>
<tr><td>Pipe stdout and stderr to command2</td><td>command 2>&1 | command2</td></tr>
</table>

Using the I/O redirection commands is fairly straightforward. For example, suppose that you want to create a new file where you want to keep storing all text until you type **ZZ**. Here is how you can accomplish that task:

```
cat <<ZZ > input.txt
```

After you type this command, you can keep typing lines and type **ZZ** on a line when done. Everything you type should be saved in the file `input.txt`.

To save the list of files in the current directory in a file named `filelist`, type:

```
ls > filelist
```

To append the listing of the `/etc/X11` directory to the same `filelist` file, type:

```
ls /etc/X11 >> filelist
```

To alphabetically sort that list of files, you can feed it to the `sort` command, like this:

```
sort < filelist
```

You should see the sorted list of files scroll by on the screen. To save that sorted list in another file named `sortedlist`, type:

```
sort < filelist > sortedlist
```

Now, the sorted list of files is saved in the `sortedlist` file.

Understanding Environment Variables

The shell and other Linux commands need information to work properly. If you type a command that isn't one of that shell's built-in commands, the shell has to locate an executable file (whose name matches the command you type). The shell needs to know which directories to search for those files. Similarly, a text editor, such as vi, needs to know the type of terminal (even if the terminal happens to be a terminal window in GNOME or KDE).

One way to provide this kind of information to a program is through command-line options. However, if you use that approach, you may have to enter many options every time you start a program. UNIX provides an elegant solution through environment variables.

When you log in as a user, you get a set of environment variables that control many aspects of what you see and do on your Linux system. If you want to see your current environment, go ahead and type the following command in a terminal window:

```
env
```

By the way, the `printenv` command also displays the environment, but `env` is shorter.

The `env` command should print a long list of lines. That whole collection of lines is the current environment and each line defines an environment variable. For example, here is a typical line displayed by the `env` command:

```
HOSTNAME=localhost.localdomain
```

This line defines the environment variable HOSTNAME as `localhost.localdomain`.

An environment variable is nothing more than a name associated with a string. On my system, for example, when I log in with the user name naba, the environment variable named PATH is defined as follows:

```
PATH=/usr/local/bin:/usr/bin:/bin:/usr/X11R6/bin:/home/naba/bin
```

The string to the right of the equal sign is the value of the PATH environment variable. By convention, the PATH environment variable is a sequence of directory names, each name separated from the preceding one by a colon (:).

When the shell has to search for a file, it simply searches the directories listed in the PATH environment variable. The shell searches the directories in PATH in the order of their appearance. Therefore, if two programs have the same name, the shell executes the one it finds first.

In a fashion similar to the shell's use of the PATH environment variable, an editor such as vi uses the value of the TERM environment variable to figure out how to display the file you are editing with vi. To see the current setting of TERM, type the following command at the shell prompt:

```
echo $TERM
```

If you type this command in a terminal window, the output is as follows:

```
xterm
```

To define an environment variable in Bash, use the following syntax:

```
export NAME=Value
```

Here, NAME denotes the name of the environment variable, and Value is the string representing its value. Therefore, you set TERM to the value vt100 by using the following command:

```
export TERM=vt100
```

You can set TERM to any of the terminal types defined in the /etc/termcap file, assuming, of course, that the terminal window or physical terminal matches the capabilities of that terminal type.

After you define an environment variable, you can change its value by simply specifying the new value with the syntax NAME=new-value. For example, to change the definition of TERM to ansi, type **TERM=ansi** at the shell prompt.

With an environment variable such as PATH, you typically want to append a new directory name to the existing definition, rather than define the PATH from scratch. The following example shows how to accomplish this task:

```
export PATH=$PATH:/sbin
```

This command appends the string :/sbin to the current definition of the PATH environment variable. The net effect is to add /sbin to the list of directories in PATH.

After you type that command, you can access programs in the /sbin directory such as ifconfig, a program that displays information about the network interfaces.

Note that you also can write this export command as follows:

```
export PATH=${PATH}:/sbin
```

PATH and TERM are only two of a handful of common environment variables. Table 7-7 lists some of the useful environment variables in Bash.

Table 7-7: Useful Bash Environment Variables

Environment Variable	*Contents*
BASH	The full path name of the Bash executable program (usually, /bin/bash).
BASH_VERSION	The version number of the Bash program.
DISPLAY	The name of the display on which the X Window System displays output (typically set to :0.0).
HOME	Your home directory.
HOSTNAME	The host name of your system.
LOGNAME	Your login name.
MAIL	The location of your mail directory.
PATH	The list of directories in which the shell looks for programs.
PS1	The shell prompt. (The default is user name and current directory followed by $ for all users except root; for root, the default prompt ends with #.)
SHELL	Your shell (SHELL=/bin/bash for Bash).
TERM	The type of terminal.

Viewing Process Information

Every time the shell acts on a command that you type, it starts a process. The shell itself is a process; so are any scripts or programs that the shell executes. Examples of such programs are the Metacity window manager and Nautilus graphical shell in GNOME. You can use the ps command to see a list of processes. When you type **ps ax**, for example, Bash shows you the current set of processes. Following is a typical report displayed when you enter the ps ax command in a terminal window. (I also include the --cols 256 option to ensure that you can see each command in its entirety.)

```
ps ax --cols 256
  PID TTY      STAT   TIME COMMAND
    1 ?        S      0:01 init [5]
    2 ?        SN     0:00 [ksoftirqd/0]
    3 ?        S<     0:00 [events/0]
    4 ?        S<     0:00 [khelper]
    9 ?        S<     0:00 [kthread]
   18 ?        S<     0:00 [kacpid]
   98 ?        S<     0:00 [kblockd/0]
... lines deleted ...
```

```
3262 ?        Sl     0:00 gnome-terminal
3263 ?        S      0:00 gnome-pty-helper
3264 pts/1    Ss+    0:00 bash
3291 ?        Ss     0:00 sshd: root@pts/2
3293 pts/2    Ss     0:00 -bash
3326 pts/2    R+     0:00 ps ax --cols 256
```

In the default output format, the `COMMAND` column shows the commands that create the processes. This list shows the Bash shell and the `ps` command as the processes. Other processes include all the programs the shell starts when I log in at the graphical login screen and start a GNOME session.

The `ps ax` form of the command is the BSD UNIX format of the `ps` command. You also can write the command as `ps -ax`—with a hyphen prefix for the options as in most other Linux commands. The Linux `ps` command accepts options both with and without a hyphen prefix. In a typical output of the `ps ax` command you should expect to see anywhere from 60 to 70 processes in the list. Quite a few processes are running in your Linux system even when you are the only user on the system. Here are the first two lines of output from `ps ax`:

```
PID TTY      STAT   TIME COMMAND
  1 ?        S      0:01 init [5]
```

In the output of the `ps` command, the first column has the heading PID and it shows a number for each process. `PID` stands for process ID (identification), which is a sequential number the Linux kernel assigns. If you look through the output of the `ps ax` command, you should see that the `init` command is the first process; it has a PID or process number of 1. That's why `init` is referred to as the mother of all processes.

The process ID or process number is useful when you have to stop an errant process forcibly. Look at the output of the `ps ax` command, and note the PID of the offending process. Then use the `kill` command with that process number. To stop process number 12318, for example, type **kill 12318**. If that does not stop the process, try **kill -9 12318**.

UNIX systems, including Linux, use signals to notify a process that a specific event has occurred. The `kill` command enables you to send a signal to a process (identified by a process number). If you don't specify any signal, kill sends a SIGTERM signal to terminate the process. To send a SIGKILL signal, which you should use only as a last resort, add a `-9` to the `kill` command. The `-9` indicates the signal to be sent is 9, which happens to be the number of the SIGKILL signal that causes a process to exit.

Running Commands in the Background or in Virtual Consoles

When using MS-DOS, you have no choice but to wait for each command to complete before you enter the next command. (You can type ahead a bit, but the MS-DOS system can hold only a few characters in its internal buffer.) Linux, however, can handle multiple tasks simultaneously. The only problem you may have is that the terminal or console is tied up until a command completes.

If you work in a terminal window and a command takes too long to complete, you can open another terminal window and continue to enter other commands. If you work in text mode, however, and a command seems to take too long, you need some other way to access your system.

Several methods enable you to continue working while your Linux system handles a lengthy task:

- You can start a lengthy command in the background, which means that the shell starts the process corresponding to a command and immediately returns to accept more commands. The shell does not wait for the command to complete; the command runs as a distinct process in the background. To start a process in the background, simply place an ampersand (&) at the end of a command line. When I want to run the convpcx shell script to convert an image file named `image1` to PCX format, for example, I run the script in the background by using the following command:

  ```
  convpcx image1 &
  ```

- If you want a command to continue running in the background after you log out, use `nohup` to start the command using the following syntax:

  ```
  nohup command
  ```

  This causes the *`command`* to run in the background and all output is redirected to a file named `nohup.out`.

- If a command (that you have not run in the background) seems to be taking a long time, press Ctrl-Z to stop it; then type **bg** to put that process in the background.
- Use the virtual-console feature of Linux. Even though your Linux system has only one physical terminal or console (the combination of monitor and keyboard is called the terminal or console), it gives you the appearance of having multiple consoles. The initial text screen is the first virtual console. Press Alt-F2 to get to the second virtual console, Alt-F3 for the third virtual console, and so on. From the GUI desktop, you have to press Ctrl-Alt-F1 to get to the first virtual console, Ctrl-Alt-F2 for the second one, and so on.

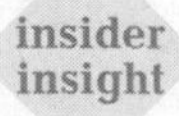

To get back to the GUI desktop, press Ctrl-Alt-F7. You can use one of the virtual consoles to log in and kill processes that may be causing your X display screen to become unresponsive (for instance, if the mouse stops responding).

Typing Less with Filename Completion

Many commands take a filename as an argument. When you want to browse through a file named `/etc/X11/xorg.conf`, for example, type the following:

```
more /etc/X11/xorg.conf
```

That entry causes the `more` command to display the file `/etc/X11/xorg.conf` one screen at a time. For commands that take a filename as an argument, Bash includes a feature that enables you to type short filenames. All you have to type is the bare minimum — usually just the first few characters — to identify the file uniquely in its directory.

To see an example, type **more /etc/X11/xo**, but don't press Enter; press Tab instead. Bash automatically completes the filename so that the command becomes `more /etc/X11/xorg.conf`. Now, press Enter to run the command.

Whenever you type a filename, press Tab after the first few characters. Bash probably can complete the filename so that you don't have to type the entire name. If you don't enter enough characters to identify the file uniquely, Bash beeps. Just type a few more characters and press Tab again.

Using Wildcards in Filenames

Another way to avoid typing too many filenames is to use wildcards, special characters, such as the asterisk (*) and question mark (?), that match zero or more characters in a string. If you were familiar with MS-DOS, you may have used commands such as `COPY *.* A:` to copy all files from the current directory to the A drive. Bash accepts similar wildcards in filenames. In fact, Bash provides many more wildcard options than MS-DOS does.

Bash supports three types of wildcards:

- The asterisk (*) character matches zero or more characters in a filename. Therefore, * denotes all files in a directory.
- The question mark (?) matches any single character.
- A set of characters in brackets matches any single character from that set. The string `[xX]*`, for example, matches any filename that starts with `x` or `X`.

Wildcards are handy when you want to perform a task on a group of files. To copy all the files from a directory named `/media/cdrom` to the current directory, for example, type the following:

```
cp /media/cdrom/* .
```

Bash replaces the wildcard character * with the names of all the files in the `/media/cdrom` directory. The period at the end of the command represents the current directory.

You can use the asterisk with other parts of a filename to select a more specific group of files. Suppose that you want to use the `grep` command to search for the string `typedef struct` in all files of the `/usr/include` directory that meet the following criteria:

- The filename starts with `s`
- The filename ends with `.h`

The wildcard specification `s*.h` denotes all filenames that meet these criteria. Thus, you can perform the search by using the following command:

```
grep "typedef struct" /usr/include/s*.h
```

The string contains a space that you want the `grep` command to find, so you have to enclose that string in quotation marks. This method ensures that Bash does not try to interpret each word in the string as a separate command-line argument.

Although the asterisk (*) matches any number of characters, the question mark (?) matches a single character. Suppose that you have four files — image1.pcx, image2.pcx, image3.pcx, and image10.pcx — in the current directory. To copy the first three of these files to the /media/floppy directory, use the following command:

```
cp image?.pcx /media/floppy
```

Bash replaces the single question mark with any single character and copies the three files — image1.pcx, image2.pcx, and image3.pcx — to /media/floppy (it leaves out image10.pcx because image? does not match image10, which has two numbers following image).

The third wildcard format — [...] — matches a single character from a specific set. You may want to combine this format with other wildcards to narrow the matching filenames to a smaller set. To see a list of all filenames in the /etc/X11/xdm directory that start with x or X, type the following command:

```
ls /etc/X11/xdm/[xX]*
```

Viewing the Command History

To make it easy for you to repeat long commands, Bash stores up to 1,000 old commands (the number of commands that Bash stores is specified by the environment variable HISTFILESIZE). Essentially, Bash maintains a command history (a list of old commands). To see the command history, type history. Bash displays a numbered list of the old commands, including those you have entered during previous logins. That list may resemble the following:

```
1  cd
2  ls -a
3  more /etc/X11/xorg.conf
4  history
```

If the command list is very long, you may choose to see only the last few commands. To see the last ten commands only, type the following:

```
history 10
```

To repeat a command from the list the history command has generated, simply type an exclamation point (!), followed by that command's number. To repeat command 3, type **!3**.

You also can repeat an old command without knowing its command number. Suppose that you typed more /usr/lib/X11/xdm/xdm-config a while ago, and now you want to look at that file again. To repeat the previous more command, type the following:

```
!more
```

Often, you may want to repeat the last command you typed, perhaps with a slight change. For example, you may have displayed the contents of the directory by using the ls -l command. To repeat that command, type two exclamation points as follows:

```
!!
```

Sometimes, you may want to repeat the previous command but add extra arguments to it. Suppose that ls -l shows too many files. Simply repeat that command, but pipe the output through the more command as follows:

```
!! | more
```

Bash replaces the two exclamation points with the previous command and appends `| more` to that command.

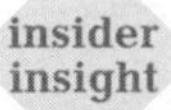

An easy way to recall previous commands is to press the up arrow key, which causes Bash to go backward in the list of commands. To move forward in the command history, press the down arrow key.

Editing Recalled Commands

After you recall a command, you do not have to use the command as is; you can edit the command. Bash supports a wide variety of command-line editing commands. These commands resemble those the Emacs and vi editors use.

Suppose that you want to look at the file `/etc/X11/xorg.conf`, but you type the following:

```
more /etc/X11/xorg.Conf
```

After you press Enter and see an error message stating that no such file exists, you realize that the `c` in `conf` should have been lowercase. Instead of retyping the entire line, you can type the following editing command to fix the problem (press the Shift key and number 6 to enter the caret character ^):

```
^Con^con
```

Bash interprets this command to mean that it should replace the string `Con` with `con` in the previous command.

By default, Bash enables you to edit the command line by using a small subset of commands that the Emacs editor supports.

Because I am already familiar with Emacs, I use Emacs commands to edit commands. To bring back a previous command line, for example, I press Ctrl-P. Then I use the following keystrokes to edit the command line:

- Ctrl-B to go backward a character
- Ctrl-F to go forward a character
- Ctrl-D to delete the character on which the text cursor rests

I can also recall previous command lines by pressing the up arrow and then edit the command line. To move about the command line, I can use the left and right arrow keys.

To insert text, I type the text. Although Emacs has a huge selection of editing commands, you can edit Bash command lines adequately with the preceding small set.

By default, the Bash shell supports Emacs-style editing of command lines. To edit the command line by using the vi editor's commands, type **set -o vi** at the shell prompt. In vi mode, you have to press Esc to enter editing commands and press i to switch back to interacting with the shell. From vi mode, you can return to Emacs editing by typing **set -o emacs** at the shell prompt.

Using Aliases

While configuring the Linux kernel, I found myself changing the directory to `/usr/src/kernels/2.6.11-1.1233_FC4-i686/arch/i386` quite a few times. After typing that directory name twice, I immediately set up a shortcut using Bash's alias feature:

```
alias gosrc='cd /usr/src/kernels/2.6.11-1.1233_FC4-i686/arch/i386'
```

I intentionally did not use any underscore characters or uppercase letters in `gosrc` because I wanted the alias to be quick and easy to type (and it had to mean something only to me). Now that I've defined the alias, I can go to that directory by typing the following at the Bash prompt:

```
gosrc
```

As you can see, an alias simply is an alternate (and usually shorter) name for a lengthy command. Bash replaces the alias with its definition and performs the equivalent command.

Many users use the alias feature to give more familiar names to common commands. If you are familiar with DOS/Windows commands and you use the `dir` command to get a directory listing, you can simply define `dir` as an alias for `ls` (the Linux command that displays the directory listing), as follows:

```
alias dir=ls
```

Now, you can type **dir** whenever you want to see a directory listing.

Another good use of an alias is to redefine a dangerous command, such as `rm`, to make it safer. By default, the `rm` command deletes one or more specified files. If you type `rm *` by mistake, `rm` deletes all files in your current directory. I learned this the hard way one day when I wanted to delete all files that ended with `.xwd`. (These files contained old screen images I no longer needed.) I intended to type `rm *.xwd`, but somehow I ended up typing `rm * .xwd`. I got the following message:

```
rm: .xwd: No such file or directory
```

At first I was puzzled by the message, so I typed `ls` to see the directory's contents again. When the listing showed nothing, I realized that I had an extra space between the `*` and `.xwd`. Of course, all the files in that directory were gone forever.

The `rm` command provides the `-i` option, which asks for confirmation before deleting a file. To make that option a default, add the following alias definition to the `.bash_profile` file in your home directory:

```
alias rm='rm -i'
```

That's it! From now on, when you use `rm` to delete a file, the command first asks for confirmation, as follows:

```
rm .bash_profile
rm: remove `.bash_profile'? n
```

Press **y** to delete the file; otherwise, press **n**.

If you type the same long command often, you should define an alias for that command. To make sure that the alias is available whenever you log in, place the definition in the `.bash_profile` file in your home directory.

To organize your aliases in one place, you could define them in a file named `.alias` in your home directory and then add the following lines to the end of the `.bashrc` file in your home directory:

```
# Add the aliases from the .alias file
if [ -f .alias ]; then
        . .alias
fi
```

Summary

Once you have installed Linux on your PC, you can begin learning how to use and operate a Linux system. Some of the basic steps are to log in, log out, and shut down the system. You also need to learn how to navigate the file system. At its heart, Linux is still UNIX, and you have to learn to use a shell — a command interpreter — to perform many common tasks. Even when you use a graphical interface, you sometimes have to open a terminal window and type commands at the shell prompt. This chapter has gotten you started with Linux operations and Bash — the Bourne Again shell — and some Linux commands for navigating the file system. You also have learned to use the Nautilus shell to explore the file system.

By reading this chapter, you learned the following:

- With graphical login enabled, you can log in, log out, and shut down a Linux system from the graphical screen. You can also use `/sbin/shutdown` to shut down the system from the shell prompt.
- Online documentation is available to help with many aspects of the Linux operating system. You can also read online HOWTO documents that describe how to perform specific tasks or use specific software in Linux.
- The Linux directory structure is organized logically as a single tree, regardless of the physical location of subdirectories. Linux includes many commands for navigating directories and manipulating files.
- GNOME includes the Nautilus graphical shell, which you can use to work with files and directories.
- Even when you stay in the graphical environment of the X Window System and GNOME (or KDE), you may have to type Linux commands in a terminal window to perform many routine tasks. This especially is true when you log in using Telnet or when you have problems with X.
- A shell is a program that runs commands for you. Bash is the default shell in Linux. Bash is compatible with the Bourne shell, which comes with all other UNIX systems.

GNU Utilities

Secrets in This Chapter

Fedora includes the Linux kernel and a large collection of utilities and applications that make it a complete operating system. Most of these utilities and applications are from the GNU Project. In a way, Linux has become a full-fledged UNIX-like operating system primarily because of the GNU software. The GNU Project provided everything from the software development tools — assembler, compiler, and make — to GNOME, the graphical user interface (GUI) desktop. This chapter gives you an overview of the GNU software and introduces you to some of the GNU utilities.

cross ref

Chapter 10 describes several applications, such as the GIMP, Ghostscript, and Ghostview. Chapter 11 describes the GNU Emacs editor, one of the most well-known software packages from the GNU Project. Other GNU software, such as the Bash shell, C/C++ compiler, the make utility, and other software packages, are described in several chapters throughout this book.

An Overview of GNU Software

As a Linux user, you may not realize the extent to which Fedora Linux (and, for that matter, all Linux distributions) relies on GNU software. Nearly all tasks you perform in a Linux system involve one or more GNU software packages. For example, the GNOME GUI and the Bash shell are both GNU software. If you rebuild the kernel or develop software, you do so with the GNU C and C++ compiler and the make utility; both are parts of the GNU software packages that accompany all Linux distributions. If you edit text files with the ed or Emacs editor, you are again using a GNU software package. The list goes on and on. It's a safe bet that when you are using any Linux system, you are running some GNU software all the time.

If you are wondering what GNU is, here's the scoop. GNU is a recursive acronym that stands for *GNU's Not Unix*. The GNU Project was launched in 1984 by Richard Stallman to develop a complete UNIX-like operating system. The GNU Project developed nearly everything needed for a complete operating system except for the operating system kernel. All GNU software was distributed under the GNU General Public License (GPL). GPL essentially requires that the software be distributed in source-code form and stipulates that any user can copy, modify, and distribute the software to anyone else in source-code form. Users may, however, have to pay for their copy of GNU software.

The Free Software Foundation (FSF) is a tax-exempt charity that raises funds for work on the GNU Project. To learn more about the GNU Project, visit its home page at `www.gnu.org/`. There you can find information about how to contact the Free Software Foundation and how you can help the GNU Project.

One way to appreciate the extent of GNU software in Linux is to take stock of various GNU software packages. Table 8-1 briefly describes some of the well-known GNU software packages that come with Linux. You can browse the table to get a feel for the types of tasks you can perform with GNU software.

Table 8-1: Some Well-Known GNU Software Packages

Software Package	*Description*
autoconf	Generates shell scripts that automatically configure source-code packages.
automake	Generates `Makefile.in` files for use with autoconf.
bash	The default shell — command interpreter — in Linux. (Bash is compatible with the UNIX sh shell and offers many extensions found in csh and ksh shells.)
bc	An interactive calculator with arbitrary precision numbers.
binutils	A package that includes several utilities for working with binary files: ar, as, gasp, gprof, ld, nm, objcopy, objdump, ranlib, readelf, size, strings, and strip.
coreutils	A package that combines three individual packages called fileutils, shellutils, and textutils and implements the following Linux commands: `chgrp`, `chmod`, `chown`, `cp`, `dd`, `df`, `dir`, `dircolors`, `du`, `install`, `ln`, `ls`, `mkdir`, `mkfifo`, `mknod`, `mv`, `rm`, `rmdir`, `sync`, `touch`, `vdir`, `basename`, `chroot`, `date`, `dirname`, `echo`, `env`, `expr`, `factor`, `false`, `groups`, `hostname`, `id`, `logname`, `nice`, `nohup`, `pathchk`, `printenv`, `printf`, `pwd`, `seq`, `sleep`, `stty`, `su`, `tee`, `test`, `true`, `tty`, `uname`, `uptime`, `users`, `who`, `whoami`, `yes`, `cut`, `join`, `nl`, `split`, `tail`, `wc`, and so on.
glibc	GNU C Library — for use with all Linux programs.
gnuchess	A chess-playing program that regularly beats many good players.
cpio	Copies file archives to and from disk or to another part of the file system.
diffutils	Compares files, showing line-by-line changes in several different formats.
ed	A line-oriented text editor.
emacs	An extensible, customizable full-screen text editor and computing environment.
findutils	A package that includes the `find`, `locate`, and `xargs` utilities.
finger	A utility program designed to enable users of UNIX systems (including Linux) on the Internet to get information about one another.
gawk	The GNU Project's implementation of the AWK programming language that conforms to the definition of the language in the POSIX 1003.2 Command Language and Utilities Standard.
GCC	Compilers for C, C++, Objective C, and other languages.
gdb	Source-level debugger for C, C++, and Fortran.
gdbm	A replacement for the traditional `dbm` and `ndbm` database libraries.
gettext	A set of utilities that enables software maintainers to internationalize a software package's user messages.
ghostscript	An interpreter for the Postscript and Portable Document Format (PDF) languages.
gimp	The GNU Image Manipulation Program (GIMP) is an Adobe Photoshop-like image-processing program.

(continued)

Table 8-1 *(continued)*

Software Package	*Description*
GNOME packages	Provides a GUI for a wide variety of tasks that a Linux user might perform.
grep package	Includes the `grep`, `egrep`, and `fgrep` commands that are used to find lines that match a specified text pattern.
groff	A document formatting system similar to `troff`.
gtk+	A GUI toolkit for the X Window System (used to develop GNOME applications).
gzip	A GNU utility for compressing and decompressing files.
indent	Formats C source code by indenting it in one of several different styles.
less	A page-by-page display program similar to `more`, but with additional capabilities.
libpng	A library for image files in the Portable Network Graphics (PNG) format.
m4	An implementation of the traditional UNIX macro processor that is commonly used to create the `sendmail` configuration file.
make	A utility that determines which files of a large software package need to be recompiled, and issues the commands to recompile them.
mtools	A set of programs that enables users to read, write, and manipulate files on a DOS file system (typically a floppy disk, but also Windows partitions of hard drives).
ncurses	A package for displaying and updating text on text-only terminals.
patch	A GNU version of Larry Wall's program to take the output of `diff` and apply those differences to an original file to generate the modified version.
rcs	The Revision Control System is used for version control and management of source files in software projects.
sed	A stream-oriented version of the ed text editor.
sharutils	A package that includes shar (used to make shell archives out of many files), unshar (to unpack these shell archives), as well as uuencode and uudecode utilities (some open source software installers need uudecode).
tar	A tape archiving program that includes multivolume support; the capability to archive sparse files, handle compression and decompression, and create remote archives; and other special features for incremental and full backups.
texinfo	A set of utilities that generates printed manuals, plain ASCII text, and online hypertext documentation (called Info), and that enables users to view and read online Info documents.
time	A utility that reports the user, system, and actual time a process uses.

The remainder of this chapter introduces you to several categories of GNU utilities.

Core Utilities

The core utilities implement basic file, shell, and text manipulation utilities. The following sections describe these three categories of utility programs.

Shell Utilities

The shell utilities are a number of shell commands you can use interactively or in shell scripts. Each utility program performs a specific task. The idea is that you can combine these commands in shell scripts to perform more complicated tasks.

Table 8-2 briefly describes each shell utility. You can try out some of these utilities by typing the program name at the shell prompt. Each program takes command-line options. You should first type **man progname**, where *progname* is the name of the utility, to learn more about the command-line options. Then try the utility with appropriate options.

cross ref

You encounter some of these shell utilities again in Chapter 24 in the section covering shell programming.

Table 8-2: GNU Shell Utilities

Program	*Description*
[	Evaluates an expression and returns zero if the result is true (same as test).
basename	Removes the path prefix from a given pathname.
chroot	Changes the root directory.
date	Prints or sets the system date and time.
dirname	Removes the last level or filename from a given pathname.
echo	Prints a line of text.
env	Prints environment variables or runs a command with modified environment variables.
expr	Evaluates expressions.
factor	Prints prime factors of a number.
false	Returns an unsuccessful exit status.
groups	Prints the names of the groups to which a user belongs.
hostid	Prints the numeric identifier for the host.
id	Prints the real and effective user and group IDs.
logname	Prints the current login name.
nice	Runs a program with specified scheduling priority.
nohup	Allows a command to continue running after the user logs out.
pathchk	Checks whether filenames are valid and portable.

(continued)

Table 8-2 *(continued)*

Program	*Description*
pinky	Prints information about users. (This is similar to the finger program; in fact, the name pinky refers to a lightweight finger.)
printenv	Prints environment variables.
printf	Formats and prints data.
pwd	Prints the working (current) directory.
seq	Prints numeric sequences.
sleep	Suspends execution for a specified time.
stty	Prints or changes terminal settings.
su	Enables the user to adopt the ID of another user, or the superuser (root).
tee	Sends output to multiple files.
test	Evaluates an expression and returns zero if the result is true.
true	Returns a successful exit status.
tty	Prints the terminal name.
uname	Prints system information.
users	Prints current user names.
who	Prints a list of all users currently logged in.
whoami	Prints the user name for the current effective user ID.
yes	Prints a string repeatedly until the process is killed.

File Utilities and the find Command

The file utilities include programs you can use to work with files and directories in your Linux system. Table 8-3 briefly describes each of these programs. You can copy and delete files, create new directories, and change file permissions and ownerships. You can also list directories and see the amount of disk space the files use.

Because you need to use the file utilities often, the next few sections show you how to use some of them. Also provided is a brief introduction to the `find` command, which enables you to locate all files that meet specified criteria.

Table 8-3: GNU File Utilities

Program	*Description*
chgrp	Changes group ownership of files.
chmod	Changes the permissions of files.
chown	Changes the ownership of files.

Program	Description
cp	Copies files.
dd	Converts a file according to a specified format and then copies the file.
df	Shows storage space (hard disk, CD-ROM, floppy, and so on) usage for the file systems.
dir	Prints a brief directory listing.
dircolors	Prints the command to set the LS_COLORS environment variable, used by the color version of the GNU ls program.
du	Shows disk space used by files and directories.
install	Copies files and sets permissions.
ln	Creates links between files.
ls	Lists the contents of a directory.
mkdir	Creates directories, if they do not already exist.
mkfifo	Creates named pipes, used for data transfer between programs. (FIFO stands for first-in first-out, which is how the named pipes transfer data.)
mknod	Creates special block or character device files (usually located in the `/dev` directory).
mv	Renames files.
rm	Deletes files.
rmdir	Deletes empty directories.
shred	Deletes a file securely by first overwriting it to make it harder to recover the data.
sync	Flushes file system buffers to disk, thereby synchronizing memory and disk.
touch	Changes the timestamps of files.
vdir	Prints detailed directory listings (similar to `ls -l`).

Working with Files

Often, you may copy files from one directory to another. Use the `cp` command to perform this task. To copy the file `/usr/X11R6/lib/X11/xinit/Xclients` to the `Xclients.sample` file in the current directory (such as your home directory), type the following:

```
cp /usr/X11R6/lib/X11/xinit/Xclients Xclients.sample
```

If you want to copy a file to the current directory and retain the same name, use a period (`.`) as the second argument of the `cp` command. Thus, the following command copies the `xorg.conf` file from the `/etc/X11` directory to the current directory (denoted by a single period):

```
cp /etc/X11/xorg.conf .
```

The `cp` command makes a new copy of a file and leaves the original intact.

If you want to copy the entire contents of a directory—including all subdirectories and their contents—to another directory, use the command `cp -ar sourcedir destdir` (this copies everything under `sourcedir` directory to `destdir`). For example, to copy all files from the `/etc/X11` directory to the current directory, type the following command:

```
cp -ar /etc/X11 .
```

Another GNU utility command, `mv`, moves a file to a new location. The original copy is gone, and a new copy appears at the specified destination. You can use `mv` to rename a file. If you want to change the name of the `today.list` to `old.list`, use the `mv` command, as follows:

```
mv today.list old.list
```

On the other hand, if you want to move the `today.list` file to a subdirectory named `saved`, use this command:

```
mv today.list saved
```

An interesting feature of `mv` is the fact that you can use it to move entire directories, with all their subdirectories and files, to a new location. If you have a directory named `data` that contains many files and subdirectories, you can move that entire directory structure to `old_data` by using the following command:

```
mv data old_data
```

Another common file operation is deleting a file. Use the `rm` command to delete a file named `old.list`, for example, by typing the following command:

```
rm old.list
```

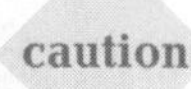

Be careful with the `rm` command—in particular, when you log in as `root`. Inadvertently deleting important files with `rm` is very common. One way to avoid problems is to add the command `alias rm='rm -i'` to the `.bash_profile` file in your home directory. With that in place, whenever you use the `rm` command to delete a file, the command first asks for confirmation.

Manipulating Directories

To organize files in your home directory, you have to create new directories. Use the `mkdir` command to create a directory. For example, to create a directory named `images` in the current directory, type the following:

```
mkdir images
```

After you create the directory, you can use the `cd images` command to change to that directory.

You can create an entire directory tree by using the -p option of the mkdir command. For example, suppose that your system has a /usr/src directory and you want to create the directory tree /usr/src/book/java/examples/applets. You can create this directory hierarchy by typing the following command:

```
mkdir -p /usr/src/book/java/examples/applets
```

When you no longer need a directory, use the rmdir command to delete it. You can delete a directory only when the directory is empty.

To remove an empty directory tree, you can use the -p option, like this:

```
rmdir -p /usr/src/book/java/examples/applets
```

This command removes the empty parent directories of applets. The command stops when it encounters a directory that's not empty.

Copying Disks with dd

The dd command is useful for copying binary data to a floppy disk or to a file. For example, you might want to back up your hard disk's master boot record (MBR) before you repartition the hard disk so that you can put things back to the original if something goes wrong.

You should do this before you edit your partition table so that you can put it back if you mess things up. To back up the MBR onto a floppy, place a formatted floppy disk in the floppy drive, and then type the following command:

```
dd if=/dev/hda of=/dev/fd0 bs=512 count=1
```

If something goes wrong, you can boot the PC with the DVD and type linux rescue at the boot prompt; then place the floppy disk in the drive and restore the MBR with the following command:

```
dd if=/dev/fd0 of=/dev/hda bs=512 count=1
```

Viewing Disk Usage Information

Two programs in the GNU file utilities — df and du — enable you to check disk-space usage. These commands are simple to use. The df command shows you a summary of disk-space usage for all mounted devices, as shown in the following example:

```
df
Filesystem          1K-blocks      Used Available Use% Mounted on
/dev/mapper/VolGroup00-LogVol00
                      7237104   4988736   1874816  73% /
/dev/hda3              101105     17250     78634  18% /boot
/dev/shm               127544         0    127544   0% /dev/shm
/dev/hdc               646896    646896         0 100% /media/cdrom
```

The output is a table that shows the device or a logical volume (if your system uses logical volume manager), the total kilobytes of storage, how much is in use, how much is available, the percentage being used, and the mount point. For example, on my system, a logical volume is mounted on the Linux file system's root directory; it has about 7.3GB of space, of which 4.9GB (or 73 percent) is being used, and 1.8GB is available. Similarly, you can see from the last line that the CD-ROM has about 646MB of storage in use.

The other command, du, is useful for finding out how much space a directory is using. For example, type the following command to view the contents of all the subdirectories in the /var/log directory (this directory contains various error logs):

```
du /var/log
8       /var/log/news/OLD
28      /var/log/news
76      /var/log/cups
16      /var/log/mail
16      /var/log/audit
56      /var/log/gdm
8       /var/log/squid
8       /var/log/samba
8       /var/log/ppp
8       /var/log/vbox
8       /var/log/httpd
2272    /var/log
```

Each directory name is preceded by a number — that number denotes the number of kilobytes of disk space that the directory uses. Thus, the /var/log directory, as a whole, uses 2272KB, or about 2.3MB, of disk space, whereas the /var/log/gdm subdirectory uses 56KB.

You can use the -h option with the du command to view the disk-space usage in human-readable format. For example, here's what you get when you type du -h /var/log to view the disk space used by the /var/log directory and its contents:

```
du -h /var/log
8.0K    /var/log/news/OLD
28K     /var/log/news
76K     /var/log/cups
16K     /var/log/mail
16K     /var/log/audit
56K     /var/log/gdm
8.0K    /var/log/squid
8.0K    /var/log/samba
8.0K    /var/log/ppp
8.0K    /var/log/vbox
8.0K    /var/log/httpd
2.3M    /var/log
```

If you simply want the total disk space a directory uses (including all the files and subdirectories contained in that directory), use the -s option together with the -h option, as follows:

```
du -sh /var/log
2.3M    /var/log
```

Notice that the -s option causes du to print just the summary information for the /var/log directory.

Learning the find Command

The find command is very useful for locating files (and directories) that meet specified search criteria. The Linux version of the find command also comes from GNU, and it has more extensive options than the standard UNIX version. I show the syntax for the standard UNIX find command, however, because its syntax works in GNU find, and you can use the same format on other UNIX systems.

I must admit that when I began using UNIX many years ago (Berkeley UNIX in the early 1980s), I was confounded by the `find` command. I stayed with one basic syntax of `find` for a long time before graduating to more complex forms. The basic syntax I learned first was for finding a file anywhere in the file system.

Suppose that you want to find any file or directory with a name that starts with "gnome". You can use `find` to perform this search, as follows:

```
find / -name "gnome*" -print
```

This command tells `find` to start looking at the root directory (/), to look for filenames that match `gnome*`, and to display the full pathname of any matching file.

You can use variations of this simple form of `find` to locate a file in any directory (as well as any subdirectories contained in the directory). If you forget where in your home directory you have stored all files named `report*` (names that start with the text string `report`), you can search for the files by using the following command:

```
find ~ -name "report*" -print
```

When you become comfortable with this syntax of `find`, you can use other options of `find`. For example, to find only specific types of files (such as directories), use the `-type` option. The following command displays all top-level directory names in your Linux system:

```
find / -type d -maxdepth 1 -print
```

To find all files that exceed 20,000KB (20MB) in size, you can use the following `find` command:

```
find / -size +20000k -print
```

You can also execute some commands on a file after you find it. For example, suppose that you want to search for the files that exceed 20,000KB in size and then print a detailed directory listing of that file. You can use the `-exec` operator of `find` to execute the `ls -l` command on each file that matches the search criteria, like this:

```
find / -size +20000k -exec ls -l {} \;
```

The `-exec` operator enables you to run any command on the files that meet whatever search criteria you use with `find`. You can type the command to execute following the `-exec` operator, then list any arguments, and end the list with a semicolon (;). However, the shell treats semicolons as command-separators, so you must place a backslash (\) in front of the semicolon to stop the shell from interpreting it. That's why every `-exec` operator ends with the characters `\;`. The curly brace pair `{}` also has special meaning. The `find` command replaces the characters `{}` with the name of the file it has found — the file that satisfies whatever search criteria you have provided.

Another good use of `find`'s `-exec` operator is to find the files with permission settings that may be too dangerous and then change the permission by using the `chmod` command. For example, suppose you want to locate any file with a group-write permission (that means the group members are allowed to alter the file) and take away that permission. Here is a `find` command that uses the `-exec` operator to accomplish this task:

```
find / -perm -20 -exec chmod g-w {} \;
```

You probably do not have to use the complex forms of `find` very often in a typical Linux system, but you can look up the rest of the `find` options by using the following command:

```
man find
```

Text Utilities

The text utilities include a large number of programs to manipulate the contents of text files. These utilities are patterned after the UNIX commands of the same name. The GNU versions of the programs usually have additional options and are optimized for speed. In general, the GNU utilities do not have any of the arbitrary limitations of their UNIX counterparts.

Table 8-4 briefly describes each text utility. The best way to learn these utilities is to try each one out. Before trying out a program, type **info progname** or **man progname** (where *progname* is the name of the program) to view the online help information.

cross ref

A few selected text utilities are described in the following sections. You can find reference pages for many of these utilities in Appendix A.

Table 8-4: GNU Text Utilities

Program	*Description*
cat	Concatenates files and writes them to standard output.
cksum	Prints the cyclic redundancy check (CRC) checksums and byte counts of files (used to verify that files have not been corrupted in transmission, by comparing the `cksum` output for the received files with the `cksum` output for the original files).
comm	Compares two sorted files line by line. (The `sort` command sorts files.)
csplit	Splits a file into sections determined by text patterns in the file and places each section in a separate file named `xx00`, `xx01`, and so on.
cut	Removes sections from each line of files and writes them to standard output.
expand	Converts tabs in each file to spaces and writes the result to standard output.
fmt	Fills and joins lines, making each line roughly the same length, and writes the formatted lines to standard output.
fold	Breaks lines in a file so that each line is no wider than a specified width, and writes the lines to standard output.
head	Prints the first part of files.
join	Joins corresponding lines of two files using a common field and writes each line to standard output.
md5sum	Computes and checks the MD5 message digest (a 128-bit checksum using the MD5 algorithm).
nl	Numbers each line in a file and writes the lines to standard output.

Program	Description
od	Writes the contents of files to standard output in octal and other formats. (This is used to view the contents of binary files.)
paste	Merges corresponding lines of one or more files into vertical columns separated by tabs, and writes each line to standard output.
pr	Formats text files for printing.
ptx	Produces a permuted index of file contents.
sort	Sorts lines of text files.
split	Splits a file into pieces.
sum	Computes and prints a 16-bit checksum for each file and counts the number of 1,024-byte blocks in the file.
tac	Writes each file to standard output, last line first.
tail	Prints the last part of files.
tr	Translates or deletes characters in files.
tsort	Performs a topological sort (used to organize a library for efficient handling by the `ar` and `ld` commands).
unexpand	Converts spaces into tabs.
uniq	Removes duplicate lines from a sorted file.
wc	Prints the number of bytes, words, and lines in files.

Counting Words and Lines in a Text File

Suppose that you want to use the `wc` command to display the character, word, and line count of a text file. Try the following:

```
wc /etc/inittab
    53  229 1666 /etc/inittab
```

This causes `wc` to display the number of lines (53), words (229), and characters (1666) in the `/etc/inittab` file. If you simply want to see the number of lines in a file, use the `-l` option:

```
wc -l /etc/inittab
     53 /etc/inittab
```

As you can see, in this case, `wc` simply displays the line count.

If you don't specify a filename, the `wc` command expects input from the standard input. You can use the pipe feature of the shell to feed the output of another command to `wc`. This can be handy sometimes. Suppose that you want a rough count of the processes running on your system. You can get a list of all processes with the `ps ax` command, but instead of manually counting the lines, just pipe the output of `ps` to `wc`, and you can get a rough count, as follows:

```
ps ax | wc -l
     85
```

That means that the `ps` command has produced 85 lines of output. Because the first line simply shows the headings for the tabular columns, you can estimate that about 84 processes are running on your system. (Of course, this count probably includes the processes used to run the `ps` and `wc` commands as well, but who's counting?)

Sorting Text Files

You can sort the lines in a text file by using the `sort` command. To see how the `sort` command works, first type **more /etc/passwd** to see the current contents of the `/etc/passwd` file. Now, type **sort /etc/passwd** to see the lines sorted alphabetically. If you want to sort a file and save the sorted version in another file, you have to use the Bash shell's output redirection feature, as follows:

```
sort /etc/passwd > ~/sorted.text
```

This command sorts the lines in the `/etc/passwd` file and saves the output in a file named `sorted.text` in your home directory.

Substituting or Deleting Characters from a File

Another interesting command is `tr` — it substitutes one group of characters for another (or deletes a selected character) throughout a file. The `tr` command is useful when you want to convert a text file from one operating system to another because different operating systems use different special characters to mark the end of a line of text.

Suppose that you occasionally have to use MS-DOS text files on your Linux system. Although you might expect to use a text file on any system without any problems, there is one catch: DOS uses a carriage return followed by a line feed to mark the end of each line, whereas Linux (and other UNIX systems) use only a line feed. Therefore, if you use the vi editor with the `-b` option to open a DOS text file (for example, type **vi -b filename** to open the file), you see `^M` at the end of each line. That `^M` stands for Ctrl-M, which is the carriage-return character.

On your Linux system, you can easily rid the DOS text file of the extra carriage returns by using the `tr` command with the `-d` option. Essentially, to convert the DOS text file `filename.dos` to a Linux text file named `filename.linux`, type the following:

```
tr -d '\015' < filename.dos > filename.linux
```

In this command, `'\015'` denotes the ASCII code in octal notation for the carriage-return character.

You can use the `tr` command to translate or delete characters from the input. When you use `tr` with the `-d` option, it deletes all occurrences of a specific character from the input data. Following the `-d` option, you must specify the character to be deleted. Like many UNIX utilities, `tr` reads the standard input and writes its output to standard output. As the sample command shows, you must employ input and output redirection to use `tr` to delete all occurrences of a character in a file and save the output in another file.

Splitting a File into Several Smaller Files

The `split` command is handy when you want to copy a file to a floppy disk but the file is too large to fit on a single floppy. You can then use the `split` command to break up the file into smaller files, each of which can fit on a floppy.

By default, `split` puts 1,000 lines into each file. The files are named by groups of letters such as `aa`, `ab`, `ac`, and so on. You can specify a prefix for the filenames. For example, to split a large file called `hugefile.tar` into smaller files that fit onto several high-density 3.5-inch floppy disks, use `split` as follows:

```
split -b 1440k hugefile.tar part.
```

This command splits the `hugefile.tar` file into 1,440KB chunks so that each can fit onto a floppy disk. The command creates files named `part.aa`, `part.ab`, `part.ac`, and so on.

To combine the split files back into a single file, use the `cat` command as follows:

```
cat part.?? > hugefile.tar
```

Binary Utilities

Just as the text utilities are meant for working with text files, the GNU binary utilities are meant for performing various tasks on binary files. Some of these utilities, such as `ar`, `as`, and `ld`, are used when building and managing object files that are generated when source files are compiled. A number of other binary utilities enable you to examine the contents of binary files. For example, the `strings` command prints all strings of printable characters in a file. Here is what the `strings` command displays for a simple C program that prints `Hello, World!` (the name of the binary executable is `a.out`):

```
strings a.out
/lib/ld-linux.so.2
_Jv_RegisterClasses
__gmon_start__
libc.so.6
puts
_IO_stdin_used
__libc_start_main
GLIBC_2.0
PTRh
QVh|
Hello, World!
```

Notice that the output includes the `Hello World!` string, as well as names of libraries (`/lib/ld-linux.so.2` and `libc.so.6`) and C functions (`puts`).

You can use the `size` command to look at the number of bytes that various sections (such as the code size, data area, and stack space) of a program would need. Here is the output of size for the `a.out` file that contains the `Hello, World!` program:

```
size a.out
   text    data     bss     dec     hex filename
    840     260       4    1104     450 a.out
```

In this case, the program requires 840 bytes for the code (called text, but it's the binary executable code of a program), 260 bytes for the data, and 4 bytes for stack. Thus, the program requires a total of 1,104 bytes of memory. Note that the actual size of the `a.out` file is about 5KB, which is much larger than 1,104 bytes because other information, such as symbols, is included in the file. Programmers would find the output of the `size` command useful because it tells them about the memory required to load and run a program.

Table 8-5 briefly describes the programs in the GNU binary utilities package. You can try some of these programs on any binary file in the system. For example, here's the result of running size on `/bin/bash` — the executable for the Bash shell:

```
size /bin/bash
   text    data     bss     dec     hex filename
 595333   22460   18720  636513   9b661 /bin/bash
```

Table 8-5: GNU Binary Utilities

Program	***Description***
addr2line	Uses debugging information in an executable file to translate program addresses into filenames and line numbers.
ar	Creates and modifies archives and extracts from archives. (An archive is a library holding the object code of commonly needed subroutines.)
as	The portable GNU assembler.
gasp	A filter program to translate encoded C++ symbols.
gprof	The GNU profiler, used to determine which parts of a program are taking most of the execution time.
ld	The GNU linker, used to combine a number of object and archive files and create executable files.
nm	Lists symbols from object files.
objcopy	Copies the contents of an object file to another (can also translate the format, if required).
objdump	Displays information from object files.
ranlib	Generates an index to the contents of an archive.
readelf	Displays information about one or more Executable and Linking Format (ELF) object files.
size	Lists the section sizes of an object or archive file.
strings	Lists printable strings from files.
strip	Discards symbols from object files.

Other Utilities

This section introduces you to a few more utilities from the GNU software packages shown in Table 8-1. The list is not exhaustive; I include only a few selected utilities. Following are the utilities summarized in the following sections:

- **GNU bc:** Arbitrary precision calculator
- **gzip:** Utility for compressing and expanding files
- **patch:** Utility for applying changes to a text file

GNU bc

GNU bc enables you to enter arbitrary precision numbers and to perform various calculations with these numbers. GNU bc implements the arbitrary precision-calculation capability the POSIX P1003.2/D11 draft standard specifies.

GNU bc is installed as part of the base operating system during the Linux installation on the companion DVD-ROM.

If you have GNU bc installed, you should be able to run it with the following command:

```
bc
bc 1.06
Copyright 1991-1994, 1997, 1998, 2000 Free Software Foundation, Inc.
This is free software with ABSOLUTELY NO WARRANTY.
For details type `warranty'.
```

After displaying the banner, bc waits for your input (there is no prompt); then you can enter numbers and expressions by using syntax similar to that of the C programming language.

Numbers are the basic elements in bc. A number is treated as an arbitrary precision number with an integral and fractional part. You can enter numbers and evaluate expressions just as you write expressions in C, as the following example shows:

```
1.000000000000000033 + 0.1
1.100000000000000033
```

As soon as you enter an expression, bc evaluates it and displays the result.

You can also define variables and use them in expressions, as follows:

```
cost=119.95
tax_rate=0.05
total=(1+tax_rate)*cost
total
125.94
```

If you check this result with your calculator, you'll notice that bc truncates the result of multiplication (it does the same with division). If you want, you can retain more significant digits by setting the scale variable, as follows:

```
scale=10
total=(1+tax_rate)*cost
total
125.9475
```

In this case, the result has more significant digits.

The bc utility supports an entire programming language with a C-style syntax. You can write loops and conditional statements and even define new functions with the `define` keyword. The following example shows how you might define a `factorial` function:

```
define factorial (n) {
  if(n <= 1) return (1);
  return (factorial(n-1)*n);
}
```

As you can see, the `factorial` function is recursive; it calls itself. Entering the lines as shown in the example is important. In particular, bc needs the open curly brace ({) on the first line because that brace tells bc to continue reading input until it comes to a closing brace (}).

After you define the `factorial` function, you can use it just as you might call a C function. Following are some examples:

```
factorial(3)
6
factorial(4)
24
factorial(10)
3628800
factorial(40)
815915283247897734345611269596115894272000000000
factorial(50)
30414093201713378043612608166064768844377641568960512000000000000
factorial(100)
933262154439441526816992388562667004907159682643816214685929638952175\
999932299156089414639761565182862536979208272237582511852109168640000\
000000000000000000000
```

As the example shows, you can use bc to represent as large a number as you want; no limit exists. When necessary, bc displays the result on multiple lines, with each continuation line ending in a backslash (\) followed by a new line.

To quit bc, type the following command:

```
quit
```

To learn more about bc, consult its man pages by using the `man bc` command. After you learn about new features of bc, try them interactively.

gzip

The gzip program is the GNU zip compression utility used to compress all Linux software distributions. When you run gzip with a filename as an argument, it reduces the file's size by using the Lempel-Ziv (LZ77) compression algorithm and stores the result in a file with the same name, but with an additional `.gz` extension. Thus, if you compress a file with the gzip `files.tar` command, the result is a compressed file with the name `files.tar.gz`.

The same gzip program can decompress any file gzip has compressed. To decompress the file `files.tar.gz`, for example, you can simply type the following:

```
gzip -d files.tar
```

Notice that you do not have to type the .gz extension explicitly; gzip automatically appends a .gz extension when it is looking for the compressed file. After decompressing, the utility creates a new file with the name files.tar.

Instead of gzip -d, you can use the gunzip command to decompress a file:

```
gunzip files.tar
```

This command also looks for a file named files.tar.gz and decompresses the file, if found.

By default, gzip stores the original filename and timestamp in the compressed file. You can decompress a file with the -N option to restore the original filename and timestamp.

Following is the basic syntax of the gzip command:

```
gzip [-cdfhlLnNrtvV19] [-S .xxx] [file ...]
```

The options have the following meanings:

- -c writes output to standard output.
- -d decompresses the file.
- -f forces compression or decompression, even if the file has multiple links or the corresponding file already exists.
- -h displays a help screen and quits.
- -l lists files sizes before and after compression.
- -L displays the gzip license and quits.
- -n stops gzip from storing the original filename in the compressed file.
- -N restores the original filename during decompression.
- -q suppresses all warnings.
- -r causes gzip to traverse the directory structure recursively and operate on all files.
- -S .xxx causes gzip to use the suffix .xxx instead of .gz.
- -t tests the integrity of a compressed file.
- -v displays the name and percentage of compression for each file.
- -V displays the version number and the compiler options used to build that version of gzip.
- -1 uses the fastest compression method (even though compression may not be as much).
- -9 uses the slowest compression method (provides the most compression).
- file ... specifies one or more filenames (the files to be compressed or decompressed).

The gzip utility is installed automatically when you install Linux from the companion DVD-ROM.

patch

The GNU patch utility is designed to apply patches, or corrections, to files. The basic idea behind patch is that when you want to distribute changes in a file, you run the standard UNIX diff command and generate a diff file that indicates how the file should be changed; then you distribute that diff file to everyone who has the original file. The recipient runs the patch utility with the diff file as input and patch makes the changes in the original files.

cross ref

The patch utility is installed automatically when you install Linux from the companion DVD-ROM. Chapter 21 discusses how to use patch to apply changes to the Linux kernel sources when you upgrade the kernel from one version to the next.

You can learn more about patch through a simple example. Assume that you have a file named original.txt that contains the following text:

```
Version: 1.0

Revision history:
  10/26/2004: Original file (NB)
```

This text file is used as an example to illustrate how to use diff and patch to update a file.

Suppose that you already distributed the original.txt file to several users. (Pretend that the file is the source file of a computer program.) After a while, you make some changes in this file. The new file, named revised.txt, looks like the following:

```
Version: 1.1

Revision history:
  10/26/2004: Original file (NB)
   4/19/2005: Added a new line (LB)
```

Now, you want to provide these changes to your users so they can use the new file. Your first task is to create a diff file that captures the changes you have made.

To create the diff file, run diff with the -u option, and specify the two filenames as arguments—the original file, followed by the revised one. Thus, the following command creates the diff file for the current example:

```
diff -u original.txt revised.txt > patch-1.1
```

This command creates the file patch-1.1, which is what you distribute to your users who are currently using the file original.txt. This diff file is also referred to as the *patch file*.

When a user receives the patch file, all he or she needs to do is put the patch file in the same directory where the file original.txt resides and type the following command:

```
patch < patch-1.1
patching file original.txt
```

The patch command applies the changes directly to the file original.txt. After patch finishes, you'll find that the content of the original.txt file matches that of revised.txt. This example should give you a good idea of how to use the patch utility to update text files.

Stream Editor — sed

The sed program is a text editor similar to ed (described in Chapter 11); unlike ed, sed is not interactive. Instead, sed is meant for editing a stream of input coming from standard input and for writing the edited text to standard output. The name sed stands for *stream editor* because it operates on a stream of text.

cross ref

To read more about standard input and standard output, consult Chapter 7.

The sed editor is typically used to edit one or more files automatically through a shell script or to simplify repetitive edits on multiple files. The following sections provide an overview of sed.

Running sed

The sed editor expects to read from the standard input and write to the standard output. You can provide a filename on the command line, but sed still writes the output to standard output. This means that sed does not change the file it edits. You can redirect the output to another file or to the original file, thereby changing that file.

By default, sed applies each editing command globally to all lines in the file. You can, however, use line addresses or patterns to restrict the lines to which the editing commands apply.

To use sed on the fly from the shell prompt, you can run it as follows:

```
somecommand | sed 'editcommand' | anothercommand
```

In this case, feed the output of `somecommand` to sed (sed applies `editcommand` to each line); sed's output goes to `anothercommand`. For example, to see all the current processes that have `gnome` in their name, you can type the following command, which uses sed to edit the stream:

```
ps ax | sed -n /gnome/p | cut -c 28-80
/usr/bin/gnome-session
/usr/bin/gnome-keyring-daemon
/usr/libexec/gnome-settings-daemon --oaf-activate-iid
gnome-panel --sm-client-id default2
gnome-volume-manager --sm-client-id default6
/usr/libexec/gnome-vfs-daemon --oaf-activate-iid=OAFI
```

In this case, each line in the output of the `ps` command is edited by sed, and a part of each line is extracted by using the `cut` command. Here, sed is invoked as follows:

```
sed -n '/gnome/p'
```

The `-n` option stops sed from printing each line to standard output. The `'/gnome/p'` part of the command line is an editing command — it means "print each line containing the string `gnome`."

If you want to apply multiple sed commands, use the -e option to specify each editing command. For example, the following sed command takes the output of ps and deletes all lines that do not contain gnome (this is the edit command -e '/gnome/!d') and then deletes any line that contains the string sed (this is done by -e '/sed/d'):

```
ps ax | sed -e '/gnome/!d' -e '/sed/d' | cut -c 28-80
/usr/bin/gnome-session
gnome-settings-daemon --oaf-activate-iid=OAFIID:GNOME
gnome-panel --sm-config-prefix /gnome-panel-9pyRb5/ -
gnome-terminal --sm-config-prefix /gnome-terminal-sHh
gnome-pty-helper
```

Of course, you typically do not type long sed commands at the shell prompt. Instead, sed is used in shell scripts. You can also place sed commands in a file and edit a text file by running sed with the -f option, as follows:

```
sed -f sedscriptfile myfile
```

This command edits myfile by using the sed commands in sedscriptfile, and writes the lines to standard output. If you want to save the output in another file, redirect the output as follows:

```
sed -f sedscriptfile myfile > editedfile
```

Learning the Basics of sed Commands

All sed commands have the following general form:

```
[address][,address][!]command[arguments]
```

The parts shown in square brackets are optional. The command is an editing command (similar to those for the ed editor) that specifies the action sed takes on a line. The address specifies the lines to which the commands apply. The exclamation mark (!) applies the command to all lines that do not match the address. The arguments are needed by some editing commands, such as the w or r command, that read a file for which you have to provide the filename as an argument.

cross ref

As you can see, the basic syntax of sed commands is simple; but the address usually includes regular expressions, which cause the sed commands to appear very cryptic. Chapter 24 describes regular expressions.

Understanding the address is the key to learning sed. A sed command can have zero, one, or two addresses. The addresses identify lines to which sed commands are to be applied. An address is a regular expression or a line number, or a symbol such as $ that refers to a line number. Use the following guidelines to understand how addresses control what gets edited:

- If there are no addresses, sed applies the command to each line. For example, if a script has the command s/UNIX/Linux/, sed changes every occurrence of UNIX to Linux.

- If there is only one address, sed applies the command to any lines matching the address. For example, `1d` deletes the first line of the stream.
- If you specify two comma-separated addresses, sed applies the command to the first matching line and to all subsequent lines up to, and including, the line matching the second address. Thus, the following command deletes everything from line 26 to the last line in the file:

```
26,$d
```

- If you add an exclamation mark (`!`) after an address, the command applies to all lines that do not match the address. For example, the command `/gnome/!d` deletes all lines that do not contain the string `gnome`.

You can use curly braces to apply more than one editing command to an address. The syntax is as follows:

```
[/pattern/][,/pattern]{
command1
command2
...other commands...
}
```

Note that the opening curly brace (`{`) must end a line, and the closing curly brace (`}`) must be on a line by itself. You should ensure that there are no blank spaces after the curly braces.

Sometimes you need to delete a line but to hold it in temporary storage and insert it elsewhere in the output stream. There are sed commands, such as `h` and `g`, for such operations. To use these commands, you need to understand the concept of pattern space and hold space. The *pattern space* is the buffer holding the current input line. The *hold space* is a separate set-aside buffer used for temporary storage. You can copy the contents of the hold space to the pattern space, and vice versa. For example, suppose that you want to extract all lines containing the string `Item:` and move them to a location later in the file (assume that the place is a line that has the string `List of items:`). You can do this with the following sed script:

```
/Item:/{
H
d
}
/List of items:/G
```

The first four lines of the script apply the commands `H` and `d` to the lines that contain `Item:`. The `H` command appends the line to the hold space; the `d` command deletes it. Then the `G` command on the last line of the script inserts the contents of the hold space after the string `List of Items:`.

Because of limited space, this section does not show you all the sed commands in detail. However, Table 8-6 provides a summary of commonly used sed commands, grouped by function.

Table 8-6: Commonly Used sed Commands

Command	*Meaning*
Editing	
`=`	Prints the line number of a line. For example, `/ORDER/=` prints the line number of the lines containing the `ORDER` string (the line number is printed before each matching line).

`a\`	Appends text after a line. For example, the following script appends a few lines to the file at the end of the output:
	`$a\`
	`This line goes at the end of the file.\`
	`Then this one.`

`c\`	Replaces text. For example, the following script replaces the first 50 lines of text with a single line that says `<50 lines deleted>`:
	`1,50c\`
	`<50 lines deleted>`

`i\`	Inserts text before a line. For example, the following script inserts text before a line containing `SKU 53055`:
	`/SKU 53055/i\`
	`*** THE FOLLOWING ITEM IS OUT OF STOCK ***`

`d`	Deletes lines. The command `1,20d` deletes the first 20 lines.
`l`	Prints the line showing nonprinting characters as ASCII codes. For example, `5l` prints the fifth line.

`n`	Skips the current line. For example, suppose a file contains section headers on a line right after a `SECTION` line. The following script extracts all section headers from the file (run this script with `sed -n -f scriptfile`, where `scriptfile` contains the following script):
	`/^SECTION/{`
	`n`
	`p`
	`}`

`p`	Prints a line. For example, the `/gnome/p` command prints the lines containing the string `gnome`. Because `sed` prints each line anyway, this causes duplicate lines to be printed. You can use the `p` command with `sed -n` to print only selected lines (`-n` stops `sed` from printing lines by default).
`q`	Quits `sed`. For example, `/Detailed Report/q` quits the editor after printing the first line that contains this string.
`s`	Substitutes one pattern with another. For example, `s/UNIX/Linux/` replaces all occurrences of `UNIX` with `Linux`.
`y`	Translates characters (similar to what the `tr` command does). For example, `/^Appendix [1-9]/y/123456789/ABCDEFGHI/` replaces Appendix 1, 2, and so on, to Appendix A, B, and so on.

Command	Meaning
Working Multiple Lines	

D	Deletes the first part of pattern space (up to a newline) created by the N command. For example, the following script deletes multiple blank lines:
	`/^$/`
	`{`
	`N`
	`/^\n$/D`
	`}`

N	Appends the next input line to the pattern space (a newline character separates the two lines). See the example for D.
Copying and Pasting	

h	Copies the pattern space to the hold space, wiping out what was in the hold space. For example, the following script finds an order number (assumed to be four digits) in a file and prints a note followed by the order number:
	`/Order/{`
	`h`
	`s/Order \#[0-9]\{4\}$/We have shipped your order:/`
	`p`
	`x`
	`}`

H	Appends the pattern space to the hold space. See example earlier in the "Learning the Basics of sed Commands" section.
g	Pastes the contents of the hold space into the pattern space, overwriting the previous contents.
G	Pastes the contents of the hold space after the current line. See example earlier in the "Learning the Basics of sed Commands" section.
x	Exchanges contents of pattern space with the contents of hold space. See example for h.
File Input and Output	
r	Reads a file into the input stream. For example, `/^Dear/r letter` inserts the contents of the `letter` file into the input stream after the line that begins with `Dear`.
w	Writes input lines to a file. For example, `/^Order/w orders` writes all lines that begin with `Order` to the file named `orders`.

Summary

Software from the GNU Project has helped make Linux a complete operating system. Many components of Linux — from the Bash shell to the GNOME GUI — come from the GNU Project. This chapter provided an overview of the GNU software packages and described some of the utility programs in those packages. Other GNU software packages are covered in other parts of this book.

By reading this chapter, you learned the following things:

- The GNU Project, supported by the Free Software Foundation, provided many software packages that make Linux a complete operating system. More information about the GNU Project is available online at `www.gnu.org/`.
- The GNU software packages include such well-known software as the Bash shell, the GNOME GUI, the GIMP image-processing program, the gzip compression/decompression utility, the tar archiving program, the Emacs editor, and a large number of other utilities that Linux users and programmers use.

GUI Desktops

Secrets in This Chapter

By now, you have installed Linux and X, and you have had your first taste of Linux. During Linux installation, the installation program configures X and gives you an option to use a graphical login screen. If you have opted for the graphical login screen, X starts automatically, and you get a graphical screen with a login dialog box.

This chapter explains how Linux automatically starts in graphics mode. If you have not enabled the graphical login screen, you can easily do so by reading this chapter. You also learn about GNOME and KDE — two graphical environments in Linux.

Turn to Chapter 2 if you have not installed Linux and X. Turn to Chapter 3 if you have installed Linux but have not configured X. Then, return to this chapter to learn how Linux automatically starts X and displays a graphical login screen.

Setting up a Graphical Login

Setting up your Linux workstation to display a graphical login screen is easy — all you have to do is make the appropriate selection during the installation. Even if you have not initially elected to have a graphical login screen, you can easily set it up once you know the details. The following sections explain how your Linux system displays the graphical login screen.

Understanding How init Starts the Display Manager

A process named init starts the initial set of processes on your Linux system. What `init` starts depends on the current run level, the contents of the `/etc/inittab` file, and the shell scripts located in the `/etc/rc.d` directory and its subdirectories. For now, you don't need to understand the details; you must know, however, that the graphical login screen starts at run level 5.

cross ref

Chapter 20 describes in detail the init process, the `/etc/inittab` file, and the Linux boot process.

The last line of the `/etc/inittab` file is responsible for starting the graphical login process with the following entry (the number 5 denotes run level 5):

```
x:5:respawn:/etc/X11/prefdm -nodaemon
```

This command runs `/etc/X11/prefdm`, a shell script that contains the following lines:

```
#!/bin/sh

PATH=/sbin:/usr/sbin:/bin:/usr/bin:/usr/X11R6/bin


# shut down any graphical boot that might exist
if [ -x /usr/bin/rhgb-client ]; then
    /usr/bin/rhgb-client -quit
fi
```

```
# We need to source this so that the login screens get translated
[ -f /etc/profile.d/lang.sh ] && . /etc/profile.d/lang.sh

# Run preferred X display manager
preferred=
if [ -f /etc/sysconfig/desktop ]; then
        . /etc/sysconfig/desktop
        if [ "$DISPLAYMANAGER" = GNOME ]; then
                preferred=gdm
        elif [ "$DISPLAYMANAGER" = KDE ]; then
                preferred=kdm
        elif [ "$DISPLAYMANAGER" = XDM ]; then
                preferred=xdm
             fi
fi

shopt -s execfail

[ -n "$preferred" ] && exec $preferred $* >/dev/null 2>&1

# Fallbacks, in order
exec gdm $* >/dev/null 2>&1
exec kdm $* >/dev/null 2>&1
exec xdm $* >/dev/null 2>&1

# catch all exit error
exit 1
```

This script starts a specific display manager — gdm, kdm, or xdm — depending on the setting of the `DISPLAYMANAGER` variable in the `/etc/sysconfig/desktop` file. The *display manager* is a program responsible for displaying the graphical login window, authenticating users who log in, running initialization scripts at the start of a session, and cleaning up after the session. The display manager process manages the display, making it available to the users and cleaning up after the user finishes a session. Note that of the three display managers — gdm, kdm, or xdm — xdm is the most generic.

If the `DISPLAYMANAGER` variable is not defined, the `/etc/X11/prefdm` script checks for gdm, kdm, and xdm — in that order — and runs whichever display manager it finds first. The end result is that you get gdm if you installed GNOME and kdm if you installed KDE as your sole desktop. If you install both GNOME and KDE, you get gdm by default because the `prefdm` script looks for gdm first. If you do have both GNOME and KDE installed on your system and you want the kdm as the display manager, define the `DISPLAYMANAGER` variable in `/etc/sysconfig/desktop` like this:

```
DISPLAYMANAGER="KDE"
```

Then, the next time you reboot the system, the kdm display manager will run.

To summarize, regardless of your choice of GUI, at run level 5 init starts a display manager. The display manager, in turn, displays the graphical login dialog box, which enables you to log in to the system.

If you have not enabled the graphical login screen during Fedora installation, you can do so by editing the /etc/inittab file. Locate the line containing initdefault, and make sure that it reads as follows:

```
id:5:initdefault:
```

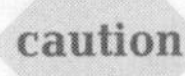

Before you edit the /etc/inittab file, you should know that any errors in this file may prevent Linux from starting up to a point at which you can log in. If you cannot log in, you cannot use your system.

After editing the default run level in /etc/inittab, you can either reboot the system or type the following command to switch to run level 5:

```
telinit 5
```

Learning the GNOME Display Manager

The gdm program is a display manager similar to xdm, the X display manager. Like xdm, gdm starts an X server for each local display, displays a login dialog box, and enables the user to log in to the system. Figure 9-1 shows a typical graphical login screen displayed by gdm.

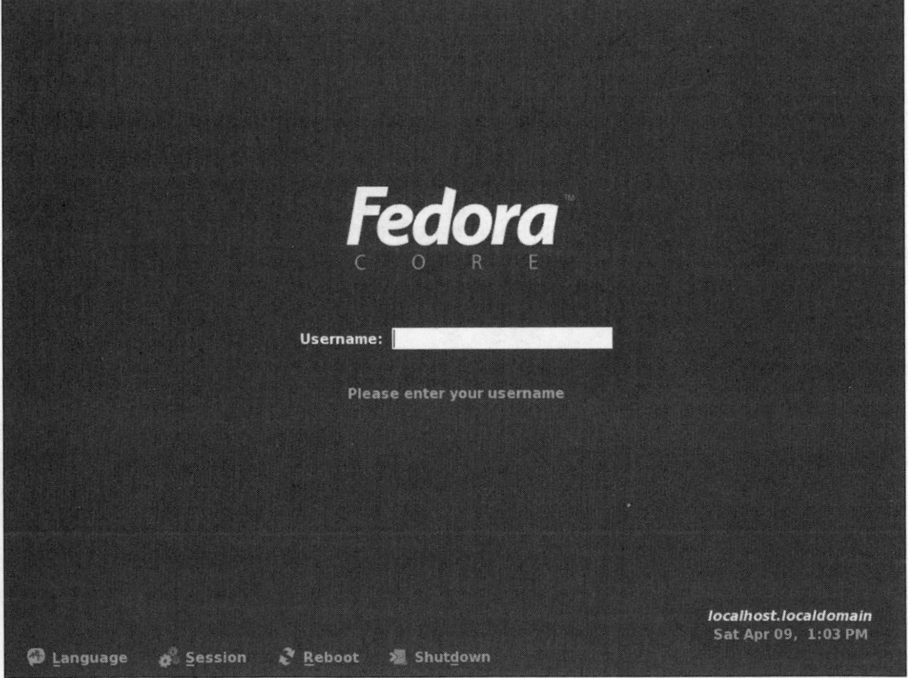

Figure 9-1: Graphical Login Screen Managed by gdm.

When gdm runs, it reads various configuration parameters from the configuration file `/etc/X11/gdm/gdm.conf`, which has a structure similar to a Windows `INI` file. For example, here is a typical `gdm.conf` file, shown without the comment lines that begin with a hash mark (#):

```
[daemon]
AutomaticLoginEnable=false
AutomaticLogin=
TimedLoginEnable=false
TimedLogin=
TimedLoginDelay=30
Greeter=/usr/bin/gdmgreeter
User=gdm
Group=gdm
LogDir=/var/log/gdm
PidFile=/var/run/gdm.pid
PostLoginScriptDir=/etc/X11/gdm/PostLogin/
PreSessionScriptDir=/etc/X11/gdm/PreSession/
PostSessionScriptDir=/etc/X11/gdm/PostSession/
DisplayInitDir=/etc/X11/gdm/Init
XKeepsCrashing=/etc/X11/gdm/XKeepsCrashing
ServAuthDir=/var/gdm
BaseXsession=/etc/X11/xdm/Xsession
InSessions/:/usr/share/xsessions/
DefaultSession=default.desktop
UserAuthDir=
UserAuthFBDir=/tmp
UserAuthFile=.Xauthority
StandardXServer=/usr/X11R6/bin/X
Xnest=/usr/X11R6/bin/Xnest -audit 0 -name Xnest

[security]
AllowRoot=true
AllowRemoteRoot=true
AllowRemoteAutoLogin=false
RelaxPermissions=0
CheckDirOwner=true

[xdmcp]
Enable=false

[gui]
GtkTheme=Bluecurve

[greeter]
TitleBar=false
ConfigAvailable=false
Browser=false
MinimalUID=500
Logo=
BackgroundColor=#20305a
ShowGnomeFailsafeSession=false
```

```
ShowLastSession=true
GraphicalTheme=Default
GraphicalThemeDir=/usr/share/gdm/themes/

[chooser]
HostImageDir=/usr/share/hosts/
Hosts=
Broadcast=true
Multicast=false

[debug]
Enable=false

[servers]
0=Standard

[server-Standard]
name=Standard server
command=/usr/X11R6/bin/X -audit 0
flexible=true
```

The `[servers]` section of the file specifies the displays on which gdm displays the login dialog box. Each line of this section starts with a display number and shows the command needed to start the X server.

You see the term `greeter` used often in the display manager configuration file. *Greeter* refers to the login screen — the user interface through which the display manager prompts the user to log in to the system.

The different sections in the configuration file control different aspects of the graphical login screen as well as the tasks the user can perform from that screen. Table 9-1 describes the gdm configuration options, organized by sections. You can configure the login screen presented by gdm by editing the `/etc/X11/gdm.conf` file or by using the GUI Login Screen Setup tool (select Desktop ➪ System Settings ➪ Login Screen from the GNOME desktop).

Add a `Welcome=` line in the `[greeter]` section of the `gdm.conf` file to display a customized welcome message on the graphical login screen. You can add a meaningful message with a line such as `Welcome=Welcome to XYZ Corp`.

Table 9-1: The gdm Configuration Options

Configuration Option	***Description***
[daemon] Section	
`AlwaysRestartServer=true` or `false`	If set to `true`, gdm always kills the existing X server and starts a new one.
`AutomaticLoginEnable=true` or `false`	If set to `true`, automatically logs in the user specified in the `AutomaticLogin` option without asking for any password.

Configuration Option	Description
[daemon] Section	
`AutomaticLogin=username`	If a user name is specified and `AutomaticLoginEnable` is `true`, that user is logged without asking for a password.
`Chooser=chooserprogram`	Full path and name of the `gdmchooser` executable file (typically, this should be `/usr/bin/gdmchooser`).
`Configurator=chooserprogram`	Full path and name of the `gdmconfig` executable file (typically, this should be `/usr/bin/gdmconfig`).
`DefaultPath=pathname`	Path (names of directories separated by colons) to be used for the user's session.
`DisplayInitDir=pathname`	Directory containing the initialization scripts (the default is `/etc/X11/gdm/Init`).
`FailsafeXServer = safex-script`	Full pathname of script that gdm should run to provide a failsafe GUI login screen.
`FirstVT =number`	The virtual terminal (VT) number where X should be run (default is 7).
`FlexibleXServers =count`	Maximum number of X servers to run.
`GnomeDefaultSession=sessionfile`	Full pathname of file that gdm should read if there are no user GNOME session files (the default is `/usr/share/gnome/default.session`).
`Greeter=greeterprogram`	Full path and name of the greeter executable file, followed by arguments (typically, this should be `/usr/bin/gdmlogin`).
`Group=groupname`	Group name under which `gdmlogin` and `gdmchooser` are run (the default is `gdm`).
`HaltCommand=haltprogram`	Full path and arguments to the commands to be executed when the user selects Halt from the System menu (typically, this should be `/sbin/shutdown -h now`).
`KillInitClients=true or false`	When set to `true`, gdm kills the X clients started by the `init` scripts after the user logs in (the default is `true`).
`LocalNoPasswordUsers =userlist`	Comma-separated list of users that are allowed to log in without a password.
`LogDir=pathname`	Directory containing the log files for the displays (the default is `/var/log/gdm`).
`PidFile=pidfile`	Name of the file where the process ID (pid) of the gdm process is stored (the default is `/var/run/gdm.pid`).

(continued)

Table 9-1 *(continued)*

Configuration Option	*Description*
[daemon] Section	
`PostSessionScriptDir= pathname`	Directory that contains the PostSession scripts — scripts run after the user logs out (the default is `/etc/X11/gdm/PostSession/`).
`PreSessionScriptDir=pathname`	Directory that contains the `PreSession` scripts — scripts run right after the user logs in (the default is `/etc/X11/gdm/PreSession/`).
`RebootCommand=rebootprogram`	Full path and arguments to the command to be executed when the user selects Reboot from the System menu (typically, this should be `/sbin/shutdown -r now`).
`RemoteGreeter =pathname`	Full pathname of the greeter executable file for remote displays.
`RootPath=pathname`	Path (names of directories separated by colons) to be used for the `root` user's session.
`ServAuthDir=pathname`	Directory (the default is `/var/gdm`) containing the X authentication files for the displays. (This directory should be owned by user `gdm`, group `gdm`, with permission 750.)
`SessionDir=pathname`	Directory containing scripts for all session types available on the system (the default is `/etc/X11/gdm/Sessions`).
`StandardXServer =pathname`	Pathname of standard X server (the default is `/usr/X11R6/bin/X`).
`TimedLogin=username`	If a user name is specified and `TimedLoginEnable` is `true`, then that user is logged in without asking for any password after the login screen is inactive for the number of seconds specified in the `TimedLoginDelay` option.
`TimedLoginDelay=N`	The number of seconds delayed before the user specified in `TimedLogin` is automatically logged in.
`TimedLoginEnable=true or false`	If set to `true`, automatically logs in the user specified in the `TimedLogin` option without asking for any password.
`User=username`	User name under which `gdmchooser` and `gdmlogin` are run (the default is `gdm`).
`UserAuthDir=pathname`	Directory where the user's `.Xauthority` file should be saved. (If this field is empty, the user's home directory is used, which is the default.)

Configuration Option	Description
[daemon] Section	
`UserAuthFBDir=pathname`	Directory where a fallback cookie (which simply refers to the small amount of authentication information) is created if gdm fails to update the user's `.Xauthority` file (the default is `/tmp`).
`UserAuthFile=filename`	Name of the file for storing the user's authentication cookies (the default is `.Xauthority`).
`VTAllocation =true or false`	If `true`, automatically allocates virtual terminal (VT) for use by X server (default is `true`).
`XKeepsCrashing=sessionfile`	Full pathname of a script that gdm should run if X keeps crashing (the default script is `/etc/X11/gdm/XKeepsCrashing`).
`Xnest = pathname`	Full pathname of the nested X server (`Xnest`) that runs as an X client, but also manages graphics on behalf of the X server (default is `/usr/X11R6/bin/Xnest -name Xnest`).
[security] Section	
`AllowRemoteAutoLogin =true or false`	When set to `true`, allows remote timed login (the default is `false`).
`AllowRemoteRoot=true or false`	When set to `true`, the root user can log in remotely (the default is `true`).
`AllowRoot=true or false`	When set to `true`, the root user can log in at the console (the default is `true`).
`RelaxPermissions=0, 1, or 2`	0 = `gdm` accepts only files and directories owned by the user; 1 = `gdm` allows group writeable files and directories; 2 = `gdm` allows world writeable files and directories (the default is `1`).
`RetryDelay=N`	Number of seconds to wait before gdm displays the login window again after a failed login (the default is 3 seconds).
`UserMaxFile=N`	Maximum size (in bytes) of files that gdm will read or write (the default is 64KB, or 65,536 bytes).
[xdmcp] section	
`DisplaysPerHost =number`	Number of displays per host (the default is `1`).
`Enable=true or false`	When set to `true`, gdm listens on port 177 and supports the X Display Manager Control Protocol (XDMCP), which enables users to log in to other hosts on the network (the default is `false`).
`HonorIndirect=true or false`	When set to `true`, gdm allows remote execution of the `gdmchooser` client on X terminals (the default is `true`).

(continued)

Table 9-1 *(continued)*

Configuration Option	*Description*
[xdmcp] section	
`MaxPending=N`	Maximum number of pending connections (the default is `4`) that gdm should allow. (This helps avoid any denial of service attacks.)
`MaxPendingIndirect=N`	Maximum number of `gdmchooser` clients that `gdm` will run simultaneously on remote displays (the default is `4`).
`MaxSessions=N`	Maximum number of remote display connections that gdm will accept (the default is `16`).
`MaxWait=N`	Maximum number of seconds that gdm waits for a response from a display before assuming that the display is not active anymore (the default is 15 seconds).
`MaxWaitIndirect=N`	Maximum number of seconds that gdm waits for a remote display to complete protocol negotiations after the display requests a chooser (the default is 15 seconds).
`Port=177`	The UDP port number where gdm listens for XDMCP requests (the default is `177`).
`Willing =pathname`	Full pathname of script to run to generate replies to XDMCP BroadcastQuery requests (the default is `/etc/X11/gdm/Xwilling`).
[gui] section	
`GtkRC=pathname`	Pathname of the file that contains the theme to be used by the gdmlogin and gdmchooser programs (the default is the file `/usr/share/themes/Default/gtk/gtkrc`).
`GtkTheme=themename`	Name of GTK+ theme to be used for the GUI (the default in Fedora Linux is the BlueCurve theme).
`MaxIconWidth=N`	Maximum width (the default is 128 pixels) of icons that the face browser will display (gdmlogin can display a face browser containing icons for all the users on a system; these icons can be installed globally by the system administrator or in the users' home directories).
`MaxIconHeight=N`	Maximum height (the default is 128 pixels) of icons that the face browser will display.
[greeter] Section	
`BackgroundColor =#colorvalue`	Background color, specified by three pairs of hexadecimal digits that specify the intensity levels of red, green, and blue colors (for example, BackgroundColor=#20305a means red level is 20, green is 30, and blue 5a, all in hexadecimal).

Configuration Option	Description
[greeter] Section	
BackgroundImage =pathname	Pathname of image to use as background (when BackgroundType=1).
BackgroundProgram =pathname	Pathname of program to run to draw the background.
BackgroundRemoteOnlyColor = true or false	When set to true, displays a solid color background for remote displays (the default is true).
BackgroundScaleToFit =true or false	When set to true, scales image to fit screen (the default is true).
BackgroundType =0, 1, or 2	Type of background for the greeter, 0 = None, 1 = Image, 2 = Color (the default is 0).
Browser=true or false	When set to true, displays a browser, called the face browser, where the faces of all system users are displayed (the default is false).
ConfigAvailable =true or false	When set to true, configuration option is available from the System menu (default is false).
DefaultFace=imagefile	A file, readable by the gdm user, containing an image that is to be displayed if a user does not have a personal picture in the ~/gnome/photo directory (which refers to the gnome/photo subdirectory of the user's home directory). The default is the /usr/share/pixmaps/nobody.png file.
Exclude=usernames	Comma-separated list of user names to be excluded from the face browser; the excluded users will still be able to log in.
GlobalFaceDir=pathname	Directory where face files (each containing an icon showing a user's face) are located (the default is /usr/share/faces/).
GraphicalTheme =themename	Name of graphical theme to use (default is BlueCurve).
GraphicalThemeDir =pathname	Directory where graphical theme files are located (the default is /usr/share/gdm/themes/).
Icon=imagefile	A file, readable by the gdm user, containing the image to be displayed when the login window is in iconified state (the default is /usr/share/pixmaps/gdm.xpm).
LocaleFile=localefile	Full pathname for the file in GNU locale format, with entries for all languages supported on the system (the default is /etc/X11/gdm/locale.alias).
LockPosition =true or false	When set to true, the user cannot move the greeter window (the default is true).

(continued)

Table 9-1 *(continued)*

Configuration Option	*Description*
[greeter] Section	
`Logo=imagefile`	A file, readable by the `gdm` user, with the image to be displayed in the logo area (the default is `/usr/share/pixmaps/gnome-logo-large.png`).
`MinimalUID =number`	Users with this user ID or higher can log in (the default is 500).
`PositionX =xpos` `PositionY=ypos`	Horizontal and vertical position of greeter window.
`Quiver=true or false`	When set to `true`, the gdmlogin program shakes the display (not physically, but by moving the graphics output) when a user enters an incorrect password (the default is `false`).
`RunBackgroundProgramAlways = true or false`	When set to `true`, runs the background program specified by `BackgroundProgram` (the default is `false`).
`SetPosition =true or false`	When set to `true`, the gdmlogin program shakes the display (not physically, but by moving the graphics output) when a user enters an incorrect password (the default is `false`).
`ShowGnomeChooserSession = true or false`	When set to `true`, shows previous GNOME sessions in the chooser (the default is `false`).
`ShowGnomeFailsafeSession = true or false`	When set to `true`, shows the GNOME failsafe session in the chooser (the default is `false`).
`ShowXtermFailsafeSession = true or false`	When set to `true`, shows the failsafe session that runs an xterm window (the default is `false`).
`SystemMenu =true or false`	When set to `true`, shows the System menu on the greeter (the default is `true`).
`TitleBar =true or false`	When set to `true`, shows a title bar on the greeter window (the default is `false`).
`Use24Clock =true or false`	When set to `true`, uses a 24-hour clock no matter what the locale (the default is `false`).
`UseCirclesInEntry =true or false`	When set to `true`, echo the typed password as circles (the default is `false`).
`Welcome=message`	The English welcome message that the gdmlogin program displays next to the logo on the login screen (the default message is `Welcome to %n`, where `%n` means the node name — the host name without the domain).
`XineramaScreen =number`	The Xinerama screen where greeter is displayed (default is `0`).

Configuration Option	Description
[chooser] Section	
Broadcast =true or false	When set to true, an XDMCP query is broadcast to get the names of all the hosts that accept login (the default is true).
DefaultHostImg=filename	File containing an image to be displayed for those hosts that do not have a unique icon file (the default is /usr/share/pixmaps/nohost.png).
HostImageDir=pathname	Directory (the default is /usr/share/hosts/) that contains host icon files; each filename matches the host system's fully qualified domain name (such as yourhost.yourdomain.com).
Hosts=hostnames	Comma-separated names of hosts to list.
ScanTime=N	Number of seconds the chooser should wait for replies to its XDMCP broadcast query (the default is 3 seconds).
[debug] Section	
Enable=true or false	When set to true, gdm saves information that can help isolate any bugs in gdm (the default is false).
[servers] section	
N=ServerName	Name of the X server to start on local display number N (if your system has a single monitor, N is 0). Default is Standard.
[server-Standard] section	
command=ServerPathName	Full pathname of the Standard X server (the default is /usr/X11R6/bin/X).
flexible=true or false	When set to true, the Standard server is considered a flexible server (the default is true).
name=servername	A descriptive name of the Standard server (default is Standard server).

For the default configuration (after you install Linux from the companion DVD-ROM), gdm manages the login session as follows:

1. **The gdm program starts the X server and looks for a script named after the local display's name (for the first display, the filename is :0) in the /etc/X11/gdm/Init directory. If it does not find that file, gdm executes the file named Default from that directory. The /etc/X11/gdm/Init/:0 script in Fedora performs some X Window System initializations and sets the background of the login screen. The gdm program runs this script as root and waits until the commands finish.**

continues

continued

2. The gdm program runs the `/usr/bin/gdmlogin` program, which displays a dialog box that contains fields in which the user can enter a name and a password.
3. After a user enters a name and password and presses Enter, gdm verifies the password and tries to execute the startup script `/etc/X11/gdm/PreSession/DisplayName`, where `DisplayName` is `:0` for the first display. If that file is not found, gdm executes the `/etc/X11/gdm/PreSession/Default` script, if it exists.
4. The gdm program runs the session script from the `/etc/X11/gdm/Sessions` directory. The exact script that gdm runs depends on the session the user selects in the Sessions menu when the login dialog box `gdmlogin` is displayed. If the user has not explicitly selected a specific type of session (GNOME or KDE), gdm runs the `/etc/X11/gdm/Default` script, which, in turn, executes the `/etc/X11/xdm/Xsession` script. This script looks for another script file, named `.xsession`, in the user's home directory and executes that script, if it exists. Next, it looks for the `.Xclients` script file in the user's home directory and executes that file, if it exists. Otherwise, `Xsession` executes the `/etc/X11/xinit/Xclients` script. When you follow through these scripts, you find that the `Xclients` script executes the `/usr/bin/gnome-session` program if the `/etc/sysconfig/desktop` file contains the line `DESKTOP="GNOME"`. The gnome-session program then starts the GNOME session (which includes a set of applications and a window manager). Initially, gnome-session uses the session file `/usr/share/gnome/default.session` (a text file) to start the applications and the window manager. Later, the GNOME session is restored to the values saved in a file in the `~/.metacity/sessions` directory (this refers to a subdirectory in the user's home directory). The default session file runs a script named `/usr/bin/gnome-wm`, which, in turn, starts an appropriate window manager. The default window manager is `metacity`, but you can specify a different window manager by defining the `WINDOW_MANAGER` environment value to the name of a window manager you want.
5. From this point on, the user can interact with the system through the X display and through the window manager (started by the gnome-session program).
6. When the user ends the GNOME session (by selecting Log out from the Desktop menu), gdm attempts to run the script `/etc/X11/gdm/PostSession/DisplayName`, where `DisplayName` is `:0` for the first display. If that file does not exist, gdm executes the `/etc/X11/gdm/PostSession/Default` script, if it exists.

Although this brief description of gdm does not show you all the details, gdm provides a user-friendly interface for user login and for starting a GNOME session. Moreover, like many other X programs, gdm is highly configurable. For example, the names of the script files in the preceding list are the typical ones, but you can specify other names through the file named `gdm.conf`, which, by default, also resides in the `/etc/X11/gdm` directory.

Switching from GNOME to KDE

GNOME and KDE are both capable GUI environments. Fedora comes with both of these GUIs, but you get GNOME as the default GUI. However, Fedora also includes the utility script `/usr/bin/switchdesk`, which enables you easily to switch from one GUI to another, and vice versa. To switch from GNOME to KDE, type **switchdesk kde** in a terminal window. When you log out and log back in, you should get the KDE GUI by default.

The `switchdesk` utility runs the `switchdesk-helper` utility, which in turn changes the default GUI by creating the appropriate scripts in your home directory. It leaves the display manager unchanged. This means that you use the GNOME display manager, gdm, for login, even when you switch to the KDE GUI. After you log in, gdm executes a session script that eventually executes the `.Xclients` script in your home directory, if that script exists.

If the switchdesk GUI is installed, the `switchdesk` script runs the program that displays the GUI from which the user can change the desktop. Otherwise, the switchdesk utility runs the switchdesk-helper utility, which, in turn, changes the default GUI by creating two scripts — `.Xclients` and `.Xclients-default` — in the home directory of the user. The `.Xclients` script contains the following lines:

```
#!/bin/bash

# Created by Red Hat Desktop Switcher

if [ -e "$HOME/.Xclients-$HOSTNAME$DISPLAY" ]; then
    exec $HOME/.Xclients-$HOSTNAME$DISPLAY
else
    exec $HOME/.Xclients-default
fi
```

The `.Xclients-default` script contains the following commands:

```
#! /bin/bash
# Created by Red Hat Desktop Switcher

WM="startkde"
WMPATH="/usr/bin /opt/bin /usr/local/bin /usr/X11R6/bin"

for p in $WMPATH ; do
        [ -x $p/$WM ] && exec $p/$WM
done

exit 1
```

continues

continued

The result of these changes is that when you log in the next time, gdm executes the `.Xclients` script in your home directory, which, in turn, executes the startkde program (`/usr/bin/startkde`) to start a KDE session.

Because the switchdesk utility changes the GUI by creating the `.Xclients` and `.Xclients-default` scripts in a user's home directory, these changes affect only that particular user.

To switch from KDE to GNOME, type **switchdesk gnome** at the shell prompt in a terminal window. After you log out of KDE and log back in, you should get GNOME as your desktop.

Note that if you want to use GNOME for one session only (as opposed to making it your default GUI), simply click Session at the bottom of the login screen, and then select Gnome from the login window menu in the initial login screen, as shown in Figure 9-2.

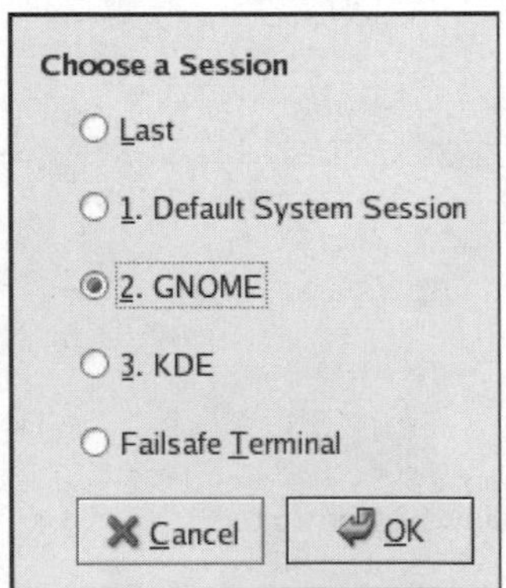

Figure 9-2: Switching to GNOME for the Current Session Only.

You should then get the GNOME desktop for this session.

Learning the KDE Display Manager

If you install only the KDE desktop or define the `DISPLAYMANAGER` variable in the `/etc/sysconfig/desktop` file as `KDE`, the kdm program starts the X server for the local display and displays the graphical login window through which you log in to the system. Figure 9-3 shows the graphical login screen that you see when you run the kdm display manager. (To change to the KDE display manager, just add the line `DISPLAYMANAGER="KDE"` to the `/etc/sysconfig/desktop` file.)

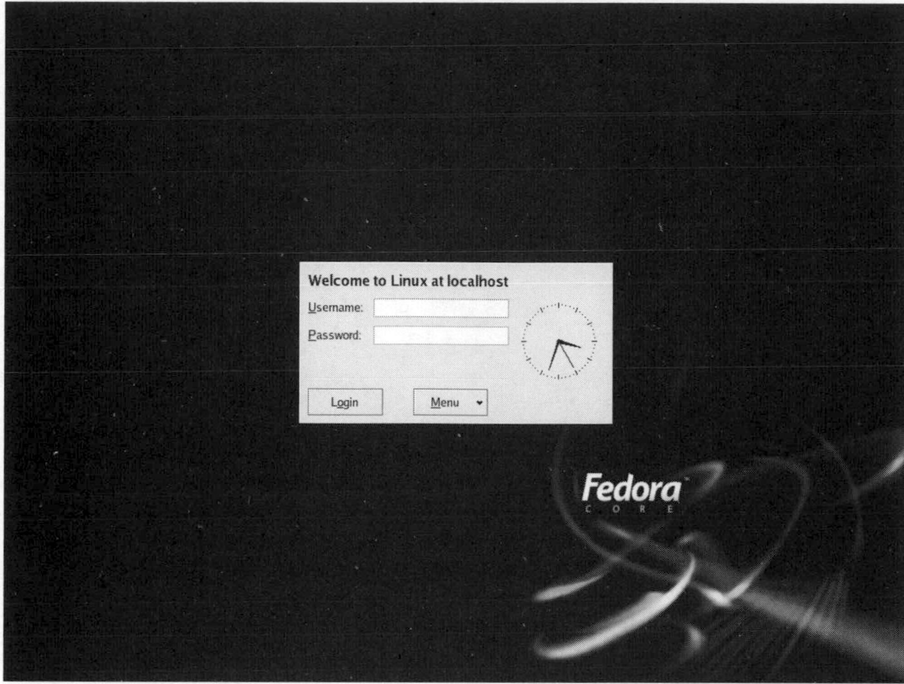

Figure 9-3: Graphical Login Screen Managed by kdm.

When kdm runs, it reads various configuration parameters from the configuration file `/usr/share/config/kdm/kdmrc`, which has a structure similar to a Windows `INI` file. For example, here is a typical `kdmrc` file (shown without most of the comment lines that begin with `#`):

```
[Desktop0]
# Background of the greeter - - the login window
BackgroundMode=VerticalGradient
BlendBalance=100
BlendMode=NoBlending
ChangeInterval=60
Color1=138,148,198
Color2=104,112,150
CurrentWallpaper=0
LastChange=0
MinOptimizationDepth=1
MultiWallpaperMode=NoMulti
Pattern=
Program=
UseSHM=false
ReverseBlending=false
Wallpaper=/usr/share/backgrounds/images/default.png
WallpaperList=
WallpaperMode=Centred
```

```
[General]
Xservers=/usr/share/config/kdm/Xservers
PidFile=/var/run/kdm.pid

[Xdmcp]
Enable=false
Xaccess=/usr/share/config/kdm/Xaccess
Willing=/usr/share/config/kdm/Xwilling

[Shutdown]
HaltCmd=/sbin/poweroff

[X-*-Core]
# Core config for all displays
Resources=/etc/X11/Xresources
Setup=/usr/share/config/kdm/Xsetup
Startup=/usr/share/config/kdm/Xstartup
Reset=/usr/share/config/kdm/Xreset
Session=/usr/share/config/kdm/Xsession
SessionsDirs=/usr/share/xsessions
AutoReLogin=false
AllowRootLogin=true
AllowNullPasswd=true
AllowShutdown=Root

[X-*-Greeter]
# Greeter config for all displays
SessionTypes=default,kde,failsafe,gnome
GUIStyle=Bluecurve
LogoArea=Clock
GreetFont=Sans,12,-1,5,75,0,0,0,0,0
StdFont=Sans,10,-1,5,50,0,0,0,0,0
FailFont=Sans,10,-1,5,75,0,0,0,0,0
AntiAliasing=true
UserList=false
HiddenUsers=adm,alias,amanda,apache,bin,bind,daemon,exim,
falken,ftp,games,gdm,gopher,halt,httpd,ident,ingres,kmem,lp,mail,mailnull,m
an,mta,mysql,named,news,nfsnobody,nobody,nscd,ntp,operator,
pcap,pop,postfix,postgres,qmaild,qmaill,qmailp,qmailq,
qmailr,qmails,radvd,reboot,rpc,rpcuser,rpm,sendmail,shutdown,
squid,sympa,sync,tty,uucp,xfs,xten
MinShowUID=500
SortUsers=true
PreselectUser=None
FocusPasswd=false
EchoMode=OneStar

[X-:*-Core]
# Core configurations for local displays
# place local display core configurations here
AllowShutdown=All
```

```
AllowRootLogin=false
AllowNullPasswd=true

[X-:*-Greeter]
# Greeter configurations for local displays
LoginMode=DefaultLocal
AllowClose=false
```

As you can see, the file is organized into sections, with each section identified by labels within square brackets. Each section specifies a related set of options that affects some aspect of the GUI login process.

You can configure the look and feel of the kdm greeter — the login dialog box — on each X display individually. The configuration of each display is specified by a section name that has the following format:

```
[X-host:number_class-subsection]
```

where `host` refers to the host name of the system to which the display is attached (can be empty for a local display), `number` is the display number (`0`, if you have only one display), `class` is a display class (it's optional and ignored in most cases), and `subsection` identifies the element of the display manager to which the options apply. For example, if the options apply to the desktop, subsection is `Desktop`. If the options are for the greeter, the subsection is `Greeter`. You can use an asterisk (*) for any of these elements — host, number, and class — as a wildcard.

Thus, to specify the options for the greeter for all displays, place the options in a section named `[X-*-Greeter]`. To change some of these greeter options for the local displays, place the changed options in the `[X-:*-Greeter]` section. On the other hand, if you want to customize some aspect of the greeter for the first local display (which is display number `0`), place those options in the section labeled `[X-:0-Greeter]`.

Table 9-2 summarizes some common kdm configuration options, organized by sections. I show the X display options for all displays. To customize these for a specific display, you can add a section with a name that reflects the X display to which the options apply.

Table 9-2: Common kdm Configuration Options

Configuration Option	*Description*
[General] section	
`LockPidFile=true or false`	If set to `true`, kdm locks the `PidFile` to prevent multiple instances of kdm from running simultaneously.
`PidFile=/var/run/kdm.pid`	File where kdm should store its process ID (ID).
`Xservers= /usr/share/config/kdm/Xservers`	File containing list of X servers to start (one per display).

(continued)

Table 9-2 *(continued)*

Configuration Option	*Description*
[Xdmcp] section	
`ChoiceTimeout=seconds`	Number of seconds to wait for display to respond after the user has selected a host from the chooser (default is 15 seconds).
`Enable=true or false`	If set to `true`, kdm listens on port 177 and supports the X Display Manager Control Protocol (XDMCP) that enables users to log in to other hosts on the network (the default is `true`).
`Port=177`	The UDP port number where kdm listens for XDMCP requests (default is `177`).
`RemoveDomainname= true or false`	If set to `true`, strips domain name from remote display names if it is equal to the local domain (default is `true`).
`SourceAddress=true or false`	Use the numeric IP address of the incoming connection instead of the host name (useful on multihomed hosts, the default is `false`).
`Willing= /usr/share/ config/kdm/Xwilling`	Program to run to generate replies to XDMCP BroadcastQuery requests (the Xwilling program is a shell script that displays the number of users and current load average).
[Shutdown] section	
`HaltCmd=/sbin/poweroff`	Full pathname of command to run to halt the system.
`RebootCmd=/sbin/reboot`	Full pathname of command to run to reboot the system (default is `/sbin/reboot`).
[X-*-Core] section (core configuration for all displays)	
`AllowNullPasswd= true or false`	If set to `true`, kdm allows users with empty passwords to log in (default is `true`).
`AllowRootLogin=true or false`	If set to `true`, kdm allows logins by `root` (default is `true`).
`AllowSdForceNow=Root or All`	Specifies who can abort all currently running programs when shutting down system; choices are `All` for anyone or `Root` for `root` user (default is `All`).
`AllowShutdown=Root or All`	Specifies who can shut down the system; possible values are `All` to enable anyone to shut down the system, `None` to prevent shutdown from the login screen, and `Root` to require `root` password for shutdown (default is `All`).
`AutoReLogin=true or false`	If set to `true`, kdm automatically restarts a session after the X server crashes or if it is killed by pressing Ctrl-Alt-Backspace (default is `false`)
`DefaultSdMode=ForceNow or TryNow or Schedule`	The default mode for shutdown; choices are `ForceNow` to shut down immediately, `Schedule` to shut down after the session exits, or `TryNow` to shut down if no session is open and do nothing otherwise (default is `Schedule`).

Configuration Option	Description
[X-*-Core] section (core configuration for all displays)	
`OpenDelay=seconds`	Number of seconds to wait before retrying to open the display after any error (default is 15 seconds).
`OpenRepeat=seconds`	Number of seconds to wait before trying to open display again (default is 5 seconds).
`OpenTimeout=seconds`	Number of seconds to wait before timing out on the attempt to open the display (default is 120 seconds).
`PingInterval=seconds`	Number of minutes between successive pinging of remote displays (ping checks if network connection is up and running; default interval is 5 minutes).
`Reset= /usr/share/config/kdm/Xreset`	Program to run after a user session ends.
`ResetSignal=1`	The signal to send to reset the local X server (default is `1`, which stands for SIGHUP).
`Session= /usr/share/config/kdm/Xsession`	Program that accepts the `SessionTypes` argument and starts an appropriate session.
`SessSaveFile=.wmrc`	Filename (in user's home directory) where the last session type is stored (default is `.wmrc`).
`Setup= usr/share/config/kdm/Xsetup`	Program to run before showing the greeter window.
`StartAttempts=number`	The maximum number of times to try opening a display before the display is disabled (default is `4`).
`StartInterval=seconds`	Number of seconds to wait before resetting the `StartAttempts` counter (default is 30 seconds).
`Startup= usr/share/config/kdm/Xstartup`	Program to run before starting a user session.
`TerminateServer= true or false`	If set to `true`, restarts the local X server instead of resetting after session ends (default is `false`).
`TermSignal=signum`	The signal to send to terminate the local X server (default is 15, which stands for SIGTERM).
[X-*-Greeter] section (greeter configuration for all displays)	
`AntiAliasing=true or false`	If set to `true`, fonts shown in the greeter should be antialiased (default is `false`).
`DefaultUser=username`	User preselected for login if `PreselectUser=Default`.
`EchoMode=OneStar or ThreeStar or NoEcho`	What to show as user types the password; choices are `NoEcho` to show nothing at all, `OneStar` to show a * for each letter typed, or `ThreeStars` to show *** for each letter typed (default is `OneStar`).
`FailFont= Sans,10,-1,5,75,0,0,0,0,0`	Font used for the "Login Failed" message.

(continued)

Table 9-2 *(continued)*

Configuration Option	*Description*
[X-*-Greeter] section (greeter configuration for all displays)	
`FocusPasswd=true` or `false`	If set to `true`, the password input line is automatically selected to receive the keyboard input (default is `false`)
`GreeterPosFixed=` `true` or `false`	If set to `true`, the position of the greeter window is fixed and specified by `GreeterPosX` and `GreeterPosY` (default is `false`).
`GreeterPosX=pixels`	Horizontal position, in pixels, of greeter window.
`GreeterPosY=pixels`	Vertical position, in pixels, of greeter window.
`GreetFont=Sans,12,-1,5,` `75,0,0,0,0,0`	The font to use for the welcome text.
`GreetString= welcometext`	Welcome text in greeter window (default is "`Welcome to %s at %n`"); use following special character strings: `%d` = current display `%h` = host name, possibly with domain name `%n` = node name, most probably the host name without domain name `%s` = operating system (`Linux`) `%r` = operating system's version `%m` = machine (hardware) type `%%` = a single `%`
`GUIStyle=Bluecurve`	The look and feel of the greeter (other choices are `Default`, `Windows`, `Motif`, `CDE`, and any other styles installed on the system).
`HiddenUsers=user1,user2,...`	List of user names not to be listed in the greeter when `ShowUsers` is `NotHidden`.
`Language=en_US`	Language to use in the greeter (default is `en_US`).
`LogoArea=Clock`	What to show in the area to the right of the text input line (other options are `Logo` to display an image specified by `LogoPixmap`, `Clock` to display an analog clock, and `None` to display nothing).
`LogoPixmap= /usr/share/` `apps/kdm/pics/kdelogo.png`	The image to show when `LogoArea` is set to Logo.
`MinShowUID=500`	Users with UID less than the specified number are not shown.
`NumLock=Off`	What to do with the Num Lock key during the time when the greeter is running; choices are `On` to turn it on, `Off` to turn it off, and `Keep` to leave it at its previous state.

Configuration Option	Description
[X-*-Greeter] section (greeter configuration for all displays)	
`PreselectUser=None` or `Previous` or `Default`	User name to be preselected for login; choices are `Previous` to preselect the previous user, `Default` to select user listed in `DefaultUser` field, or `None` to not preselect at all (default is `None`).
`SelectedUsers=user1, user2,...`	List of users to show when `ShowUsers=Selected`.
`SessionTypes= default,kde, failsafe,gnome`	Names of session types that the user can select from the GUI login window.
`ShowUsers=None`	Which user names, along with pictures, to show in the greeter; choices are `NotHidden` to show all users except those listed in `HiddenUsers`, `Selected` to show only those users listed in `SelectedUsers`, and `None` to show no users at all (default is `NotHidden`).
`SortUsers=true` or `false`	If set to `true`, sort user names alphabetically (default is `true`).
`StdFont= Sans,10,-1,5,50, 0,0,0,0,0`	Normal font used in the greeter.

Using GNOME

GNOME stands for GNU Network Object Model Environment; and GNU, as you probably know, stands for GNU's Not Unix. GNOME is a GUI and a programming environment. From the user's perspective, GNOME is like the Motif-based Common Desktop Environment (CDE) or Microsoft Windows. Behind the scenes, GNOME has many features that enable programmers to write graphical applications that work together well. The next few sections provide a quick overview of GNOME, highlighting the key features of the GNOME GUI. You can explore the details on your own.

You can always find out the latest information about GNOME by visiting the GNOME home page at `www.gnome.org`.

Taking Stock of GNOME

Although what you see of GNOME is the GUI, there is much more to GNOME than the GUI. To help you appreciate it better, note the following points and key features of GNOME:

- GNOME is officially pronounced "guh-NOME," but many people pronounce the word as "NOME." Note that "guh-NOME" stems from "guh-NU," the way people pronounce GNU.
- The latest GNOME release is 2.x, also known as GNOME 2 for short.

- GNOME runs on several UNIX systems, including Linux, BSD (FreeBSD, NetBSD, and OpenBSD), Solaris, HP-UX, AIX, and Silicon Graphics IRIX.
- GNOME uses the Gimp Tool Kit (GTK+) as the graphics toolkit for all graphical applications. GTK+ relies on X for output and supports multiple programming languages, including C, C++, Perl, and others. Users can easily change the look and feel of all GTK+ applications running on a system. GTK+ is licensed under the GNU Library General Public License (LGPL). See Chapter 23 for more information about GPL and LGPL.
- GNOME also uses Imlib, another library that supports displaying images on an X display. Imlib supports many different image formats, including XPM and PNG (Portable Network Graphics).
- GNOME uses the Object Management Group's Common Object Request Broker Architecture (CORBA) Version 2.2 to enable GNOME software components to communicate with one another regardless of where the components are located or what programming language is used to implement the components.
- GNOME applications support drag-and-drop operations.
- GNOME application developers write documentation using DocBook, which is a Document Type Definition (DTD) based on Standard General Markup Language (SGML). This means that you can view the manual for a GNOME application on a Web browser, such as Mozilla Firefox.
- GNOME supports standard internationalization (commonly referred to as I18N for the 18 letters between *i* and *n* in *internationalization*) and localization methods. This means that you can easily configure a GNOME application for a new native language.
- GNOME uses Mesa, an implementation of OpenGL (an application programming interface — API — for 3D graphics) to support 3D graphics.
- GNOME uses libxml2, a free XML library that also includes libxslt, a complete implementation of the XSLT specification (for transforming XML documents to other XML documents)

Exploring GNOME

Assuming that you have enabled a graphical login screen during Linux installation, you should get the GNOME GUI whenever you log in to your Linux system. The exact appearance of the GNOME display depends on the current session. The session is nothing more than the set of applications (including a window manager) and the state of these applications. The Metacity window manager, which is the default window manager in GNOME, stores the session information in files located in the `~/.metacity/sessions` directory (this is in your home directory). The session files are text files; if you are curious, you can browse these files with the `more` command.

Initially, when you don't yet have a session file, the GNOME session comes from the `/usr/share/gnome/default.session` file. However, as soon as the session starts, the GNOME session manager (`/usr/bin/gnome-session`) saves the current session information in the `~/.metacity/sessions` directory. A typical initial GNOME desktop produced by the session description in the default session file is shown in Figure 9-4.

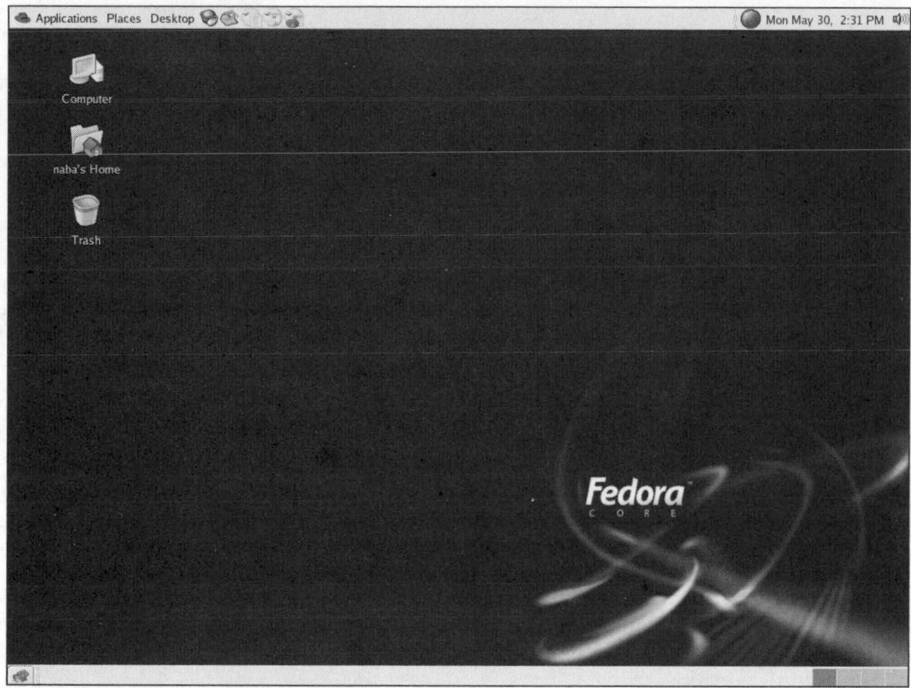

Figure 9-4: The Initial GNOME Desktop, with the Default Session File.

As you can see from the icons on the left side of the GNOME desktop, GNOME enables you to place folders and applications directly on the desktop. This is similar to the way in which you can place icons directly on the Microsoft Windows desktop.

When you are running a GUI, you need the window manager as part of your session. A window manager is a special X application that handles interactions for various applications that are displaying windows onscreen. You need a window manager to control the placement and size of each application's window. Without a window manager, you cannot change a window's location or alter its size.

To see why a window manager is necessary, consider the case of two X applications—A and B—that are displaying on the same screen. Neither application has any idea of the other's needs. Suppose that you run application B after A, and B takes over the entire screen (the root window) as its output window. At this point, A's window is obscured underneath B's, and you have no way to reach A's window.

A window manager enables you to switch from B to A, even when B is ill-behaved. (For example, if B's window fills the entire screen, you have no way of accessing A's window without a window manager). The window manager adds a decorative frame to the main window of each application. This frame enables you to move and resize the windows. You can click and drag a corner of the frame to shrink B's window. The window manager shows an outline of the window that changes in size as you move

continues

continued

the mouse. This outline enables you to make the topmost window smaller to expose windows underneath it. Additionally, the window manager adds a pull-down menu that you can get by clicking the upper-left corner of the window's frame. This menu contains options that enable you to resize the window, reduce the window to an icon, and quit the application.

As in the window frames in Microsoft Windows, the right-hand corner of the title bar includes three buttons: The leftmost button reduces the window to an icon, the middle button maximizes the window to fill up the entire screen, and the rightmost button closes the window. Unlike Windows, the locations of these buttons, as well as the appearance of the entire window frame, are configurable in GNOME.

Using the GNOME Panels

Notice the two bars along the top and bottom edges of the screen. These are the GNOME panels, or simply panels. The top panel is for launching programs whereas the bottom panel is for status information — icons for the applications that are currently running and buttons for showing the desktop and switching between desktops.

As you can see from the top edge of Figure 9-4, the top panel provides a display area for menus and small panel applets. Each panel applet is a small program designed to work inside the panel. For example, the clock applet on the top panel's far right displays the current date and time.

The top and bottom panels in GNOME include several other applets:

- Launcher applets display buttons with icons of applications. Clicking a button starts (launches) that application. For example, the top panel in Figure 9-4 shows two icons — one launches the Mozilla Firefox Web browser and the other starts the Evolution personal information manager.
- The GNOME Pager applet, at the right edge of the bottom panel, provides a virtual desktop that's larger than the physical dimensions of your system's screen. The pager displays four pages in a small display area. Each page represents an area equal to the size of the X display screen. To go to a specific page, click that page in the pager window. If you want a window to appear on a different virtual screen page, simply select Move to Another Workspace from its window menu. The window then appears in the virtual screen page you select.
- You can add other applets to either panel. For example, to add the GNOME weather applet (this displays the local weather), right-click on an unused area of the panel, and then select Add to Panel from the menu that pops up. As shown in Figure 9-5, the Add to Panel dialog box appears with a selection of applets. Scroll down and select the Weather Report applet from the list.

Figure 9-5: From This Dialog Box Select Applet to Add to the Panel.

In the Add to Panel dialog box, you will find many applets that you can add to a panel and try out.

The GNOME panel also displays a number of menu buttons that behave like the Windows Start menu.

Exploring the Menu Buttons

In Figure 9-4, the left-hand side of the top panel starts with three menu buttons—Applications, Places, and Desktop. The Applications button that I sometimes refer to as the Main Menu button is similar to the Start button in Microsoft Windows. You can launch applications from the menu that pops up when you click the left mouse button on the Applications button. Typically, this menu lists items that start an application. Most of the menu items have an arrow; another pop-up menu appears when you place the mouse pointer on an item with an arrow. Figure 9-6 shows a typical view of the Applications menu on a Fedora Linux system.

Explore all the items in the Applications menu to see all the tasks you can perform from this menu. For some menu items, pausing the mouse on the menu item displays pop-up help with information about that menu item.

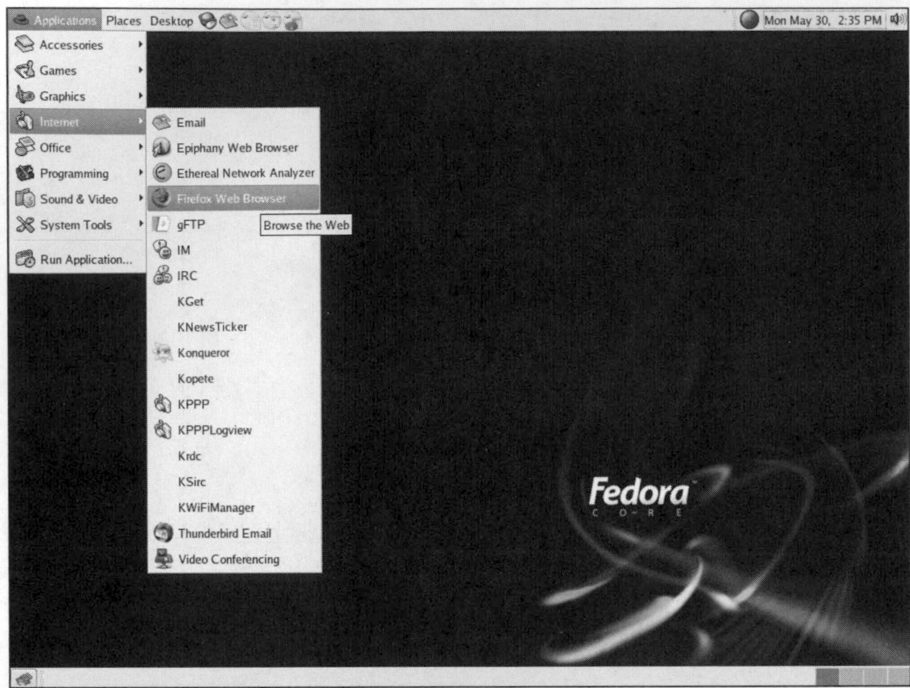

Figure 9-6: Accessing the Applications Menu in GNOME.

The other two menus — Places and Desktop — enable you to perform following categories of related tasks:

- The **Places** menu has options for opening your home folder, viewing the desktop, browsing the computer, connecting to various servers such as FTP and Windows shares, and searching for files.
- The **Desktop** menu is for editing desktop preferences, configuring system settings, getting online help, locking the screen, and logging out. Selecting Desktop ⇨ System Settings enables you to start GUI system configuration utilities for configuring, among other things, user accounts, root password, security level, display, network, printers, and date and time. To configure various Internet servers — Web, FTP, DNS, Samba, and others — go to Desktop ⇨ System Settings ⇨ Server Settings.

Setting GNOME Preferences

You can configure certain aspects of the GNOME desktop by selecting Desktop ⇨ Preferences. The resulting menu displays a number of options such as desktop background, font, keyboard, password, sound, and theme. Each option is meant for customizing one aspect of the GNOME desktop. For example, selecting Desktop ⇨ Preferences ⇨ Desktop Background enables you to customize the desktop's background.

Using KDE

KDE stands for the *K Desktop Environment*. The KDE project started in October 1996 with the intent to develop a common GUI for UNIX systems that use the X Window System. The first beta version of KDE was released a year later in October 1997. KDE version 1.0 was released in July 1998; KDE 2.0 on October 23, 2000; KDE 3.0 was released on April 3, 2002; and the latest version — KDE 3.4 — was released on March 16, 2005.

From the user's perspective, KDE provides a graphical desktop environment that includes a window manager, the Konqueror Web browser and file manager, a panel for starting applications, a help system, configuration tools, and many applications, including the OpenOffice.org office suite, image viewer, PostScript viewer, and mail and news programs.

From the developer's perspective, KDE has class libraries and object models for easy application development in C++. KDE is a large development project with many collaborators.

The following sections provide an overview of KDE, but the best way to learn about KDE is to use it for a while. Follow the instructions in the section "Switching from GNOME to KDE" to change your GUI to KDE, and then use it for a while to get a feel for KDE's capabilities.

You can always find out the latest information about KDE by visiting the KDE home page at `www.kde.org`.

Taking Stock of KDE

Like GNOME, KDE is meant to be a complete desktop environment for users and a programming environment for application developers. Here are some key features of KDE:

- KDE runs on a number of UNIX-like systems, including Linux, FreeBSD, Solaris, HP-UX, and Silicon Graphics IRIX. KDE needs the X Window System.
- The latest KDE release is 3.4, also known as KDE 3.4.
- KDE is written in C++ and uses object-oriented development.
- KDE uses the Qt Free Edition GUI toolkit from a Norwegian company, Trolltech AS (`www.troll.no/`). Qt is a C++ class library for building GUIs; it provides the widgets such as menus, buttons, and sliders used in KDE applications. Trolltech sells a commercial version of Qt, but it also licenses the Qt Open Source Edition, under an open-source license called the BSD license (see `www.opensource.org/licenses/bsd-license.php` for more details).
- KDE provides an application development framework built on DCOP (Desktop Communications Protocol) and KParts, a compound document model. DCOP and KParts are similar to Microsoft's DCOM (Distributed Component Object Model) and ActiveX controls.
- KDE includes the KOffice office application suite based on the DCOP/KParts technology. Fedora does not include the KOffice suite. You can find out more about KOffice at `www.koffice.org/`.
- KDE supports drag-and-drop operations.
- KDE supports internationalization, and most KDE applications have been translated into over 25 different languages.

Exploring KDE

Assuming that you have selected KDE as your desktop (or selected a KDE session from the Session pop-up menu), you should get the KDE desktop when you log in. Figure 9-7 shows the default KDE desktop after I log in on my Fedora Linux system.

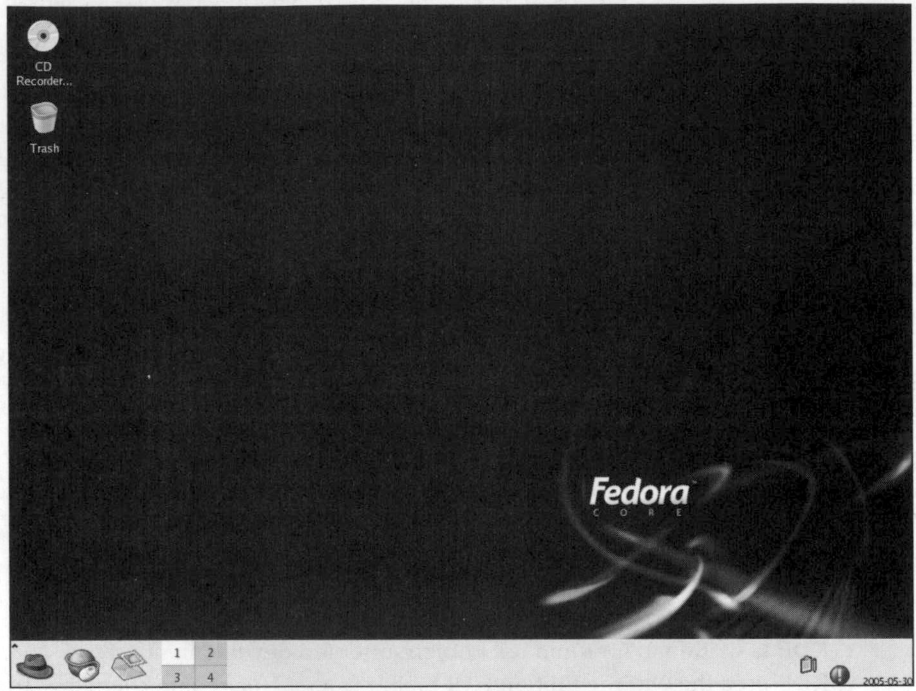

Figure 9-7: The Initial KDE Desktop.

KDE is easy to use and has many similarities with the Microsoft Windows GUI. You can start applications from a menu that's similar to the Start menu in Windows. KDE also enables you to place folders and applications directly on the desktop.

As Figure 9-7 shows, KDE provides a Windows-like desktop with a panel along the bottom edge of the screen. The most important component of the panel is the red hat button on the left-hand side. That button is like the Start button in Windows. When you click the red hat button, a pop-up menu appears. From this menu, you can get to other menus by moving the mouse over items with a right-pointing arrow. For example, Figure 9-8 shows a typical menu hierarchy for changing some desktop settings.

You can start applications from the main menu. That's why the KDE documentation calls this button the *Application Starter*. Just to keep everything simple, I will refer to the red hat button as Main Menu.

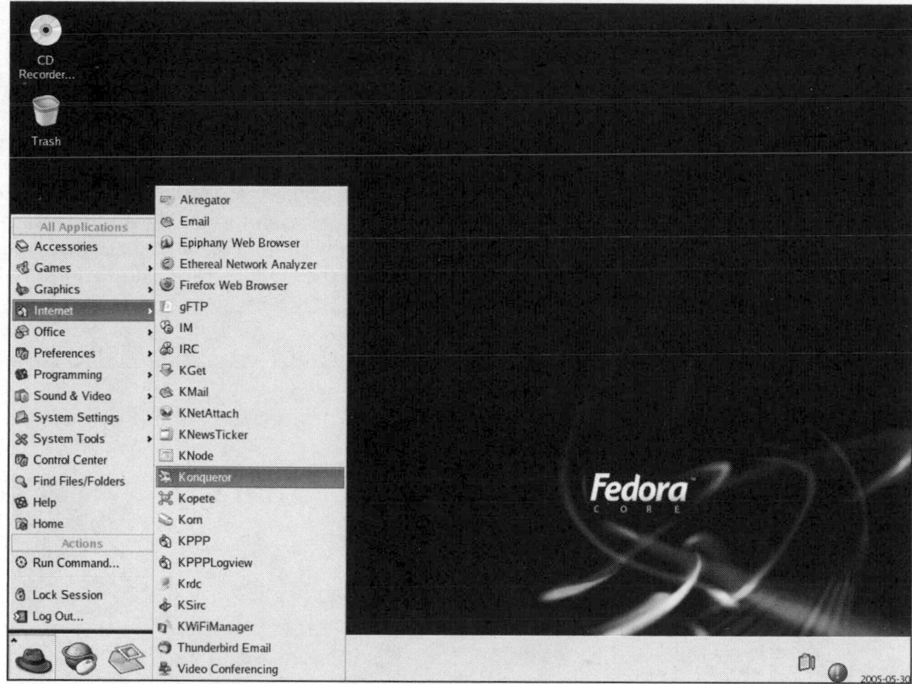

Figure 9-8: Viewing the Main Menu in KDE.

> **insider insight**
> Fedora shows the Main Menu button as a red hat icon. In a normal KDE installation, the leftmost button is a large letter *K* on top of a gear. It's sometimes called the K button for short.

Next to the red hat button (Main Menu), the panel includes several other buttons. If you don't know what a button does, simply move the mouse over the button, and a small pop-up window displays a brief message about that button.

KDE supports a virtual desktop. By default, you get four virtual desktops. You can click one of the buttons on the panel (see Figure 9-8) labeled 1, 2, 3, and 4 to switch to a specific desktop. Use the desktops to organize your application windows. You needn't clutter up a single desktop with many open windows. When a desktop gets crowded, simply switch to another desktop and open the applications there.

Sometimes you want to type Linux commands at a text prompt. Select Main Menu ⇨ System Tools ⇨ Terminal and a terminal window appears. You can then type Linux commands at the shell prompt in the terminal emulation window. Chapter 7 describes the shell and some important Linux commands.

KDE includes a KDE Control Center that you can use to customize various aspects of KDE, including the desktop background, icons, and fonts. To start the KDE Control Center, select Main Menu ⇨ Control Center or type **kcontrol** in the terminal window. The KDE Control Center main window has two parts. The left side of the window has a tree menu of items that you can control with this tool. The tree menu is organized into categories, such as Appearance & Themes, Desktop, Internet & Network, Peripherals, Security & Privacy, and so on. Click an item to view the subcategories for that item. To change an item, go through the tree menu to locate the item, and then click it. That item's configuration options then appear in a dialog box on the right side of the window. For example, Figure 9-9 shows the options for customizing the desktop background.

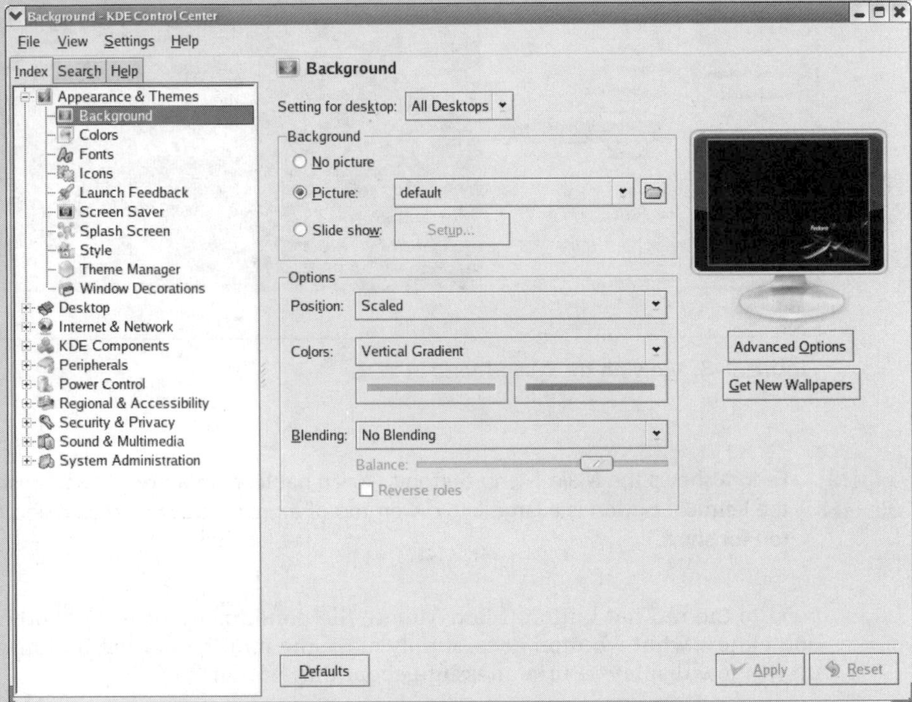

Figure 9-9: Customizing the Desktop Background with KDE Control Center.

You can choose the desktop with the background you want to customize, and then select either a solid color background or a wallpaper (an image used as a background). After making your selections, click Apply to make the change.

To log out of KDE, select Main Menu ⇨ Logout, and click the Logout button on the resulting dialog box.

Summary

Newcomers and old-timers alike can benefit from a graphical point-and-click user interface. This chapter shows you how Linux starts a graphical login screen so that you can stay in the graphical environment. This chapter also provides an overview of the GNOME and KDE graphical user interfaces and explains how to customize the appearance of X applications. The next chapter introduces you to common Linux applications.

By reading this chapter, you learned the following:

- After Linux boots, a process named init starts all the other processes. The exact set of initial processes depends on the run level, which typically is a number ranging from 0 to 6. The `/etc/inittab` file specifies the processes that start at each run level. The `/etc/inittab` file specifies that a graphical display manager starts at run level 5. In Fedora Linux, the GNOME Display Manager (gdm) provides the graphical login prompt. The Linux installation program sets up a graphical login for you.
- If you install KDE, you can opt to run the KDE Display Manager (KDM). To do so, add the line `DISPLAYMANAGER="KDE"` to the `/etc/sysconfig/desktop` file.
- You can configure the initial graphical login screen through configuration files for gdm and kdm. For gdm, the configuration file is `/etc/X11/gdm/gdm.conf` and for kdm, the file is `/usr/share/config/kdm/kdmrc`. This chapter explains both of these configuration files.
- GNOME and KDE are two popular GUIs for Linux. Fedora comes with both GNOME and KDE, but your system starts with GNOME as the default GUI. You can use the switchdesk utility to change your default GUI to KDE or simply select a GUI by clicking the Session button on the login screen.
- Both GNOME and KDE are similar to other modern desktop environments, such as Apple Mac OS and Microsoft Windows. Therefore, you can easily learn to use GNOME and KDE. Both include control centers from which you can customize various aspects of the desktop, including the appearance.

Linux Applications and Utilities

Secrets in This Chapter

The Fedora Core Linux distribution on this book's companion DVD-ROM includes many applications. The GNOME and KDE desktops come with a number of applications, such as calendars, calculators, CD players, and games. Fedora also comes with the GNU software packages, which include applications such as the GIMP (for working with images) and kghostview (for viewing PostScript files).

Many more Linux applications are available on the Internet or commercially from various Linux vendors. This chapter briefly describes some of the Linux applications included on the companion DVD-ROM. The chapter also introduces you to several prominent, commercially available office-productivity applications for Linux that are not included on the companion DVD-ROM.

Applications on the Companion DVD-ROM

Table 10-1 shows a selected set of Linux applications on the DVD-ROM, organized by category.

Table 10-1: A Sampling of Linux Applications on the DVD-ROM

Category	*Applications*
Editors	GNU Emacs, vim, GUI text editors (gedit, KWrite, Kate)
GUI desktops	GNOME, KDE
Office tools	OpenOffice.org Writer, OpenOffice.org Calc, OpenOffice.org Impress, OpenOffice.org Draw, OpenOffice.org Math, OpenOffice.org Base, calendars, calculators, spelling checker, Dictionary
Utilities	GNU bc, gzip, Midnight Commander, patch, GnuPG (GNU Privacy Guard)
Multimedia	Rhythmbox Music Player, Helix Player, CD players, gtkam, xsane, X Multimedia System (XMMS), cdrecord, growisofs, X-CD-Roast. k3b CD/DVD burner
Graphics and image manipulation	The GIMP, xfig, gnuplot, ghostscript, kghostview, ImageMagick, dia, netpbm, KView, Xpdf, Xsane, Ksnapshot, Kooka
DOS/Windows	mtools
System administration	system-config utilities for user and group management, printer configuration, network configuration, date/time setting, System Monitor
Internet	Evolution, Mozilla Firefox, Lynx, Epiphany, GFTP, Kopete, gaim, rdist, sendmail, xchat, HTTP (Web server), FTP, SSH, INN, pppd, wvdial
Serial communications	minicom, xminicom
Database	PostgreSQL, MySQL
Programming	Bison, flex, Gawk, GCC, GCJ, Perl, Python, RCS, CVS, Tcl/Tk, yacc
Text formatting	groff, TeX, docbook2dvi, docbook2html, docbook2man, docbook2ps, docbook2rtf, docbook2tex, docbook2texi, docbook2txt, docbook2pdf
Games	Blackjack, Mahjongg, GNOME Mines, FreeCell, GNOME Robots, AisleRiot, and many more

This list is by no means comprehensive. The Fedora Core Linux distribution comes with a plethora of standard GNU utilities not shown in the list.

This chapter provides a brief summary of a smaller subset of these applications. In particular, you learn about some of the programs not covered in earlier chapters. Some applications, such as GNU Emacs and vi, are covered in detail elsewhere in the book. Also, entire categories of important applications, such as Internet applications, are covered in great detail in individual chapters within the book.

Quite a few of the listed applications are automatically installed during the Linux installation process. Other applications have to be installed from the companion DVD-ROM (Chapter 21 outlines the steps for installing applications from the DVD-ROM.)

You can start many of these applications from the GNOME or KDE desktop. The menu button of each desktop provides a series of menus from which you can select the applications.

Editors

You can find the following text editors on the companion DVD-ROM:

- GNU Emacs, which is the one and only original Emacs
- Vim, which is a vi-like editor
- GUI text editors that are part of GNOME and KDE

As you can see, most of these editors aspire to be either GNU Emacs or vi. The look-alikes typically are smaller and have fewer features.

The GUI text editors are part of GNOME and KDE.

GNU Emacs

The companion DVD-ROM includes GNU Emacs version 21.2. GNU Emacs, one of the best-known GNU products, is distributed by the Free Software Foundation. The GNU Emacs binary is `/usr/bin/emacs`, which works under X and provides menus for editing operations. You must have X installed to run Emacs.

> **cross ref** Chapter 11 describes the features of GNU Emacs and how to use it for text-editing tasks.

Vim

Vim stands for Vi IMproved. As the name implies, Vim is an improved version of the standard UNIX text editor vi. The companion DVD-ROM includes version 6.3 of Vim. In addition to the standard vi commands, Vim includes many new features, including several levels of undo, command-line history, and filename completion.

> **cross ref** In Linux, when you run the vi editor, you are running Vim. Chapter 11 shows you how to use the vi editor.

GUI Text Editors

Both of the Linux graphical desktops — GNOME and KDE — come with GUI text editors (text editors that have graphical user interfaces).

To try the GNOME text editor, gedit, select Applications ⇨ Accessories ⇨ Text Editor from the GNOME desktop. You can open a file by clicking the Open button on the toolbar. This brings up the Open File dialog box. You can then change directories and select the file to edit by clicking OK.

The gedit editor then loads the file in its window. You can open more than one file and move among them as you edit the files. Figure 10-1 shows a typical editing session with gedit.

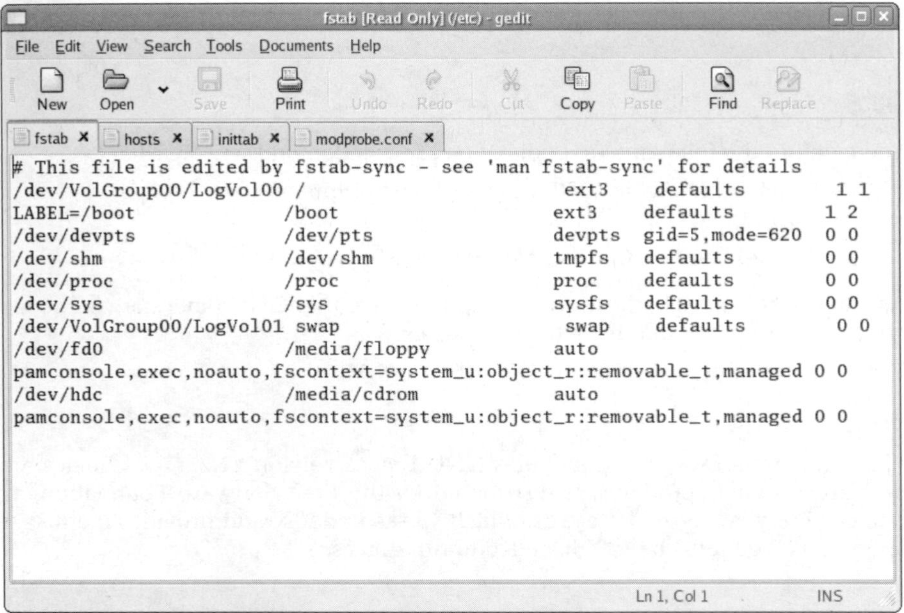

Figure 10-1: Editing Several Files with gedit.

In this case, the editor has four files open for editing: `fstab`, `inittab`, `hosts`, and `modprobe.conf` (all from the `/etc` directory). The filenames appear as tabs below the toolbar of the editor's window. You can switch among the files by clicking the tabs with the filenames.

The rest of the text-editing steps are intuitive. To enter new text, click to position the cursor and begin typing. You can select text and copy or cut it by using the buttons on the toolbar above the text-editing area. To paste the text elsewhere in the file, position the cursor, and click the Paste button.

From the KDE desktop, you can start the KDE text editor by selecting Main Menu ⇨ Accessories ⇨ Kate. To open a text file, select File ⇨ Open from the menu. A dialog box appears. From this dialog box, you can go to the desired directory, select the file to open, and click OK. The KDE text editor then opens the file and displays its contents in the window. You can then edit the file.

Office Tools

This book's companion DVD-ROM includes several office tools, such as calendars, calculators, and spell checkers. The following sections describe a few of these office tools:

- **Evolution:** A personal information manager (PIM) that includes email, calendar, contact management, and an online task list
- **OpenOffice.org Writer:** A Microsoft Word–like word processor
- **OpenOffice.org Calc:** A Microsoft Excel–like spreadsheet program
- **OpenOffice.org Impress:** A Microsoft PowerPoint–like presentation program
- **KOrganizer:** KDE calendar
- **Calculators:** GNOME calculator and KDE calculator
- **Other applications:** Commercially available office applications for Linux

Managing Your Inbox with Ximian Evolution

Fedora provides Ximian Evolution as the mail reader and organizer for appointments, contacts, and tasks. You can learn more about Evolution at Novell's website at `www.novell.com/products/desktop/features/evolution.html`.

Select Applications ⇨ Internet ⇨ Email from the GNOME or KDE desktop. If this is your first time with Evolution, the Evolution Setup Assistant starts up (see Figure 10-2).

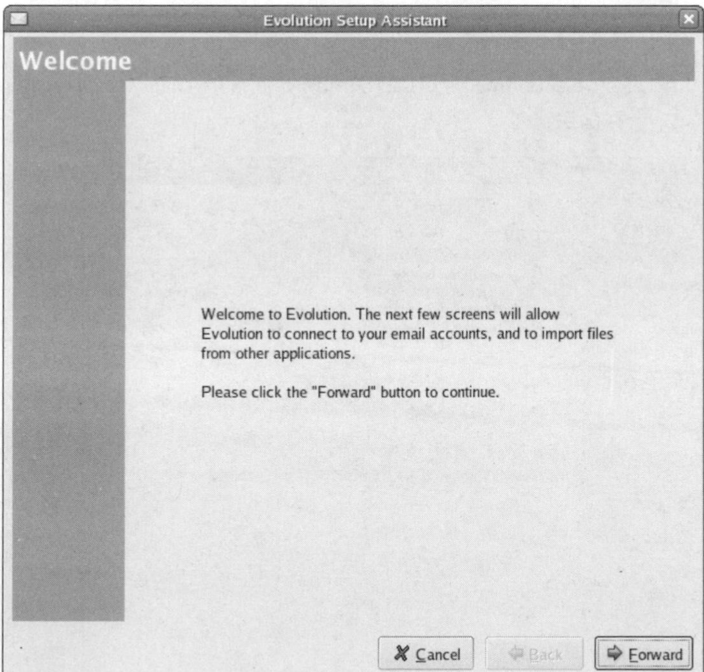

Figure 10-2: Setting Up Evolution for the First Time.

Click Forward in the Welcome screen, and the Evolution Setup Assistant guides you through the following steps:

1. Enter your name and email address in the Identity screen, and click Forward. For example, if your email address is `joe@someplace.com`, that's what you enter.
2. Set up the options for receiving email, and click Forward. Select the type of mail download protocol — POP (Post Office Protocol), IMAP (Internet Message Access Protocol), Novell Groupwise, and a few other formats. Then provide the name of the mail server (for example, `mail.comcast.net`). You don't have to enter the password for your email account right now; you will be prompted for a password when Evolution connects to the mail server the first time.
3. Provide further information about receiving email — how often to check for mail and whether to leave messages on the server — and then click Forward. Typically, you would want to download the messages and delete them on the server; otherwise, the ISP would complain after your mail piles up.
4. Set up the options for sending email. Select the server type as SMTP (Simple Mail Transfer Protocol), and then enter the name of the server such as `smtp.comcast.net`. If the server requires you to log in, click the check box that says Server requires authentication, and then enter your user name (this is the user name you need to log in to your ISP's mail server). Click Forward.
5. Enter a descriptive name for the email account. Click Forward.
6. Set your time zone by clicking on a map. Click Forward.
7. Click Apply to complete the Evolution setup and save your email settings.

After you complete the one-time setup, Evolution opens its main window, as shown in Figure 10-3.

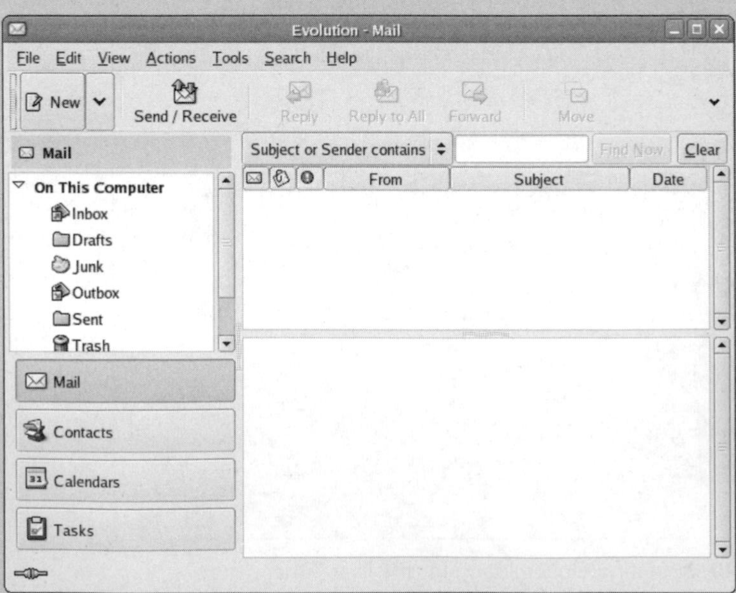

Figure 10-3: Main Window of Evolution.

Evolution's main display area is vertically divided into two windows: a narrow pane on the left with a number of shortcut buttons — Mail, Contacts, Calendars, Tasks — arranged in a column, and a bigger right pane where Evolution displays information relevant to the currently selected shortcut icon. In Figure 10-3 Evolution displays the inbox for mail.

You can click the shortcut buttons on the left-hand window to switch to different views. These buttons provide access to all the necessary components of a PIM — email, calendar, task list, and contacts. You will find all of these tasks intuitive to perform in Evolution.

To access your email in Evolution, click the Inbox icon. Evolution opens your Inbox. If you had turned on the feature to automatically check for mail every so often, Evolution would have already prompted you for your mail password and downloaded your mail. The email inbox looks very much like any other mail reader's inbox, such as the Outlook Express inbox.

To read a message, click the message in the upper window of the Inbox, and the message text appears in the lower window.

To reply to the current message, click the Reply button on the toolbar. A message composition window pops up. You can write your reply and then click the Send button on the toolbar to send the reply.

To send a new email, click the New Message button on the Evolution toolbar. A new message composition window appears, and you can type your message in that window; then click Send.

To add an appointment in Evolution, click the Calendar button. Evolution then displays the calendar. You can move to the date of the appointment and double-click the time. A new window appears where you can type in the details of the appointment. When done, click the Save and Exit buttons on that window. Evolution then shows the appointment in the calendar, as shown in Figure 10-4.

insider insight

Evolution comes with extensive online help. Select Help ➪ Contents from the Evolution menu and *Evolution User Guide* appears in a new Yelp window (Yelp is the documentation viewer for the GNOME desktop).

Writing with OpenOffice.org Writer

OpenOffice.org Writer is a word-processing program. It's part of an open-source office application suite, OpenOffice.org project (`www.openoffice.org/`). To start OpenOffice.org Writer, select Applications ➪ Office ➪ OpenOffice.org Writer from GNOME or KDE. OpenOffice.org Writer prompts you to register and displays a blank document in its main window. Using Writer is simple — it's similar to other word processors such as Microsoft Word. For example, you can type text into the blank document, format text, and save text when done.

You can also open documents that you have prepared with Microsoft Word on a Windows machine. Figure 10-5 shows a Microsoft Word document being opened in OpenOffice.org Writer.

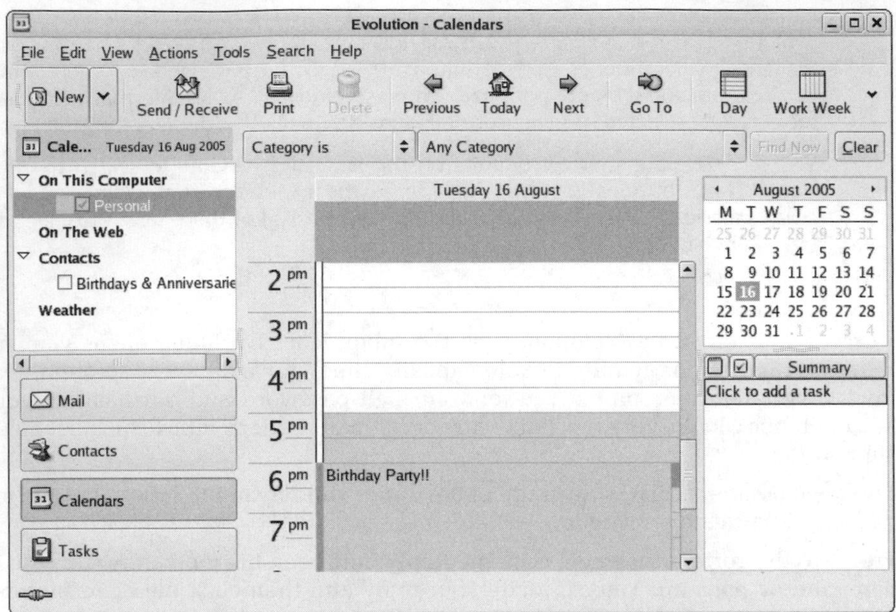

Figure 10-4: Keeping Track of Appointments in Evolution's Calendar.

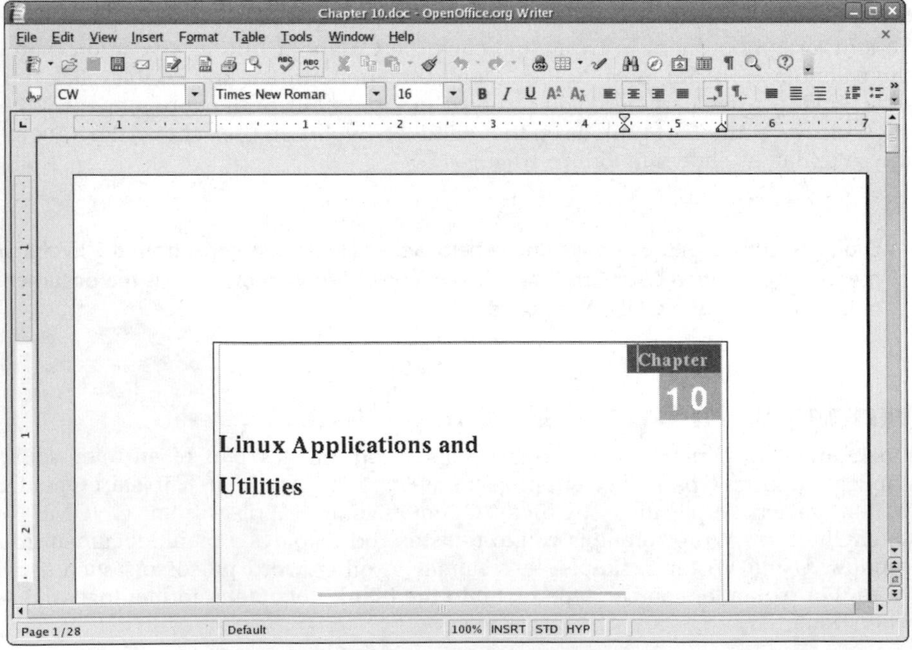

Figure 10-5: Preparing Documents in OpenOffice.org Writer.

When you save a document, by default Writer saves it in OpenDocument Text format in a file with the .odt extension.

note

OpenOffice.org version 2.0 and later uses the standard OASIS OpenDocument XML format as the default file format (the file extension is .odt). The OASIS OpenDocument format is not tied to any vendor or any specific office suite software. In addition to OpenOffice.org, StarOffice and the KDE KOffice software support the OpenDocument file format. It's also one of the formats recommended by the European Commission. For more information on Open Document format, see www.oasis-open.org/committees/tc_home.php?wg_abbrev=office.

insider insight

If you need to share OpenOffice.org Writer documents with Microsoft Word, you can save the documents in several formats, including Microsoft Word 95/97/2000/XP, Microsoft Word 6.0, and Rich Text Format (.rtf). Microsoft Word can open .rtf files. For exchanging files with users of OpenOffice.org versions prior to 2.0, save the file in StarOffice Text Document format with a .sxw extension.

I won't explain how to use Writer because it is simple and intuitive to use. If you need it, online help is available. Select Help ⇨ OpenOffice.org Help from the Writer menu (or press F1). This brings up the OpenOffice.org Help window with help information on the Writer. You can then click the links to view specific help information.

Preparing Spreadsheets with OpenOffice.org Calc

Calc is the spreadsheet program in the OpenOffice.org application suite. To start Calc, select Main Menu ⇨ Office ⇨ OpenOffice.org Calc from the GNOME or KDE panel. The Calc program displays its main window, which looks similar to Windows-based spreadsheets, such as Microsoft Excel. (In fact, Calc can read and write Microsoft Excel format spreadsheet files.)

Use Calc in the same way you use Microsoft Excel. You can type entries in cells, use formulas, and format the cells (such as specifying the type of value and the number of digits after the decimal point). Figure 10-6 shows a typical spreadsheet in Calc.

When preparing the spreadsheet, use formulas you normally use in Microsoft Excel. For example, use the formula =SUM(D2:D6) to add up the entries from cell D2 to D6. To set cell D2 as the product of the entries A2 and C2, type **=A2*C2** in cell D2. To learn more about the functions available in OpenOffice.org Calc, select Help ⇨ OpenOffice.org Help from the menu (or press F1). This opens the OpenOffice.org Help window, from which you can browse the functions by category and click a function to read more about it.

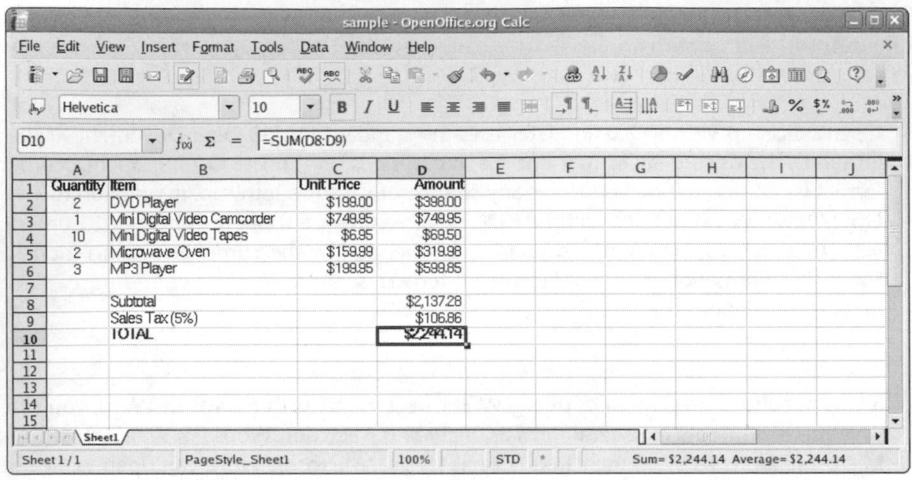

Figure 10-6: Preparing Spreadsheets Using OpenOffice.org Calc.

To save the spreadsheet, select File ➪ Save As. A dialog box appears, from which you can specify the file format, the directory location, and the name of the file. OpenOffice.org Calc can save the file in a number of formats, including Microsoft Excel 95/97/2000/XP, Microsoft Excel 5.0, and a text file with comma-separated values (CSV).

If you want to exchange files with Microsoft Excel, save the spreadsheet in Microsoft Excel format (choose an appropriate version of Excel). Then you can transfer that file to a Windows system and open it in Microsoft Excel.

Presenting Information with OpenOffice.org Impress

OpenOffice.org Impress is part of the OpenOffice.org office application suite. You can prepare briefing packages (slide presentations) using Impress. It's similar to Microsoft PowerPoint. To run Impress, select Applications ➪ Office ➪ OpenOffice.org Impress from the GNOME or KDE desktop. The Presentation Wizard appears.

To begin working, select Empty presentation and click Create. To open an existing document, select the appropriate option from the Presentation Wizard and click Open. Then select the presentation file you want to open. You can open Microsoft PowerPoint files in Impress.

Figure 10-7 shows a typical slide presentation in Impress.

The Impress window shows the first slide together with an outline view of the slides along the left side. The exact appearance depends on the document type and template you select. You can begin adding text and other graphic objects such as images, text, and lines to the slide.

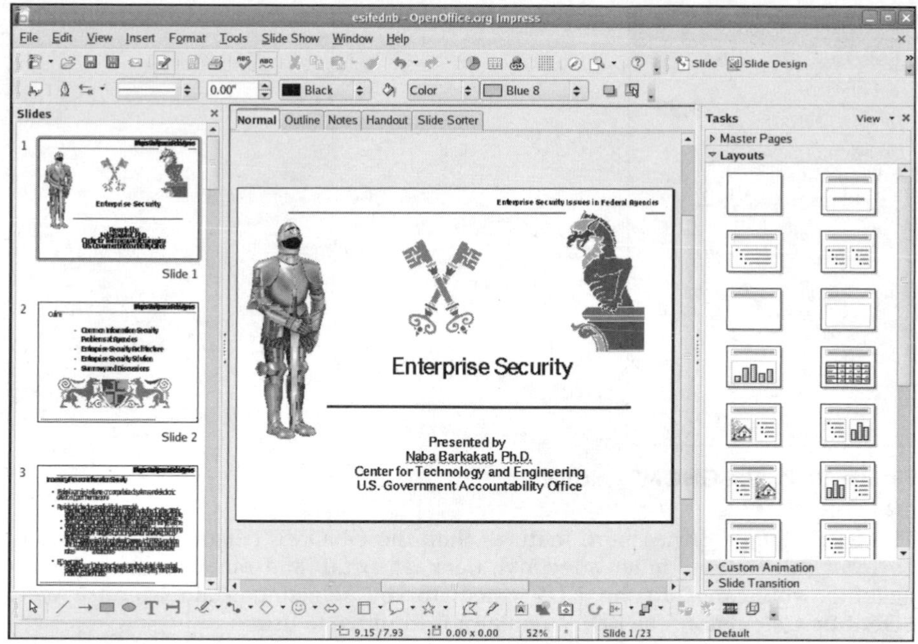

Figure 10-7: Preparing Briefing Packages in OpenOffice.org Impress.

To insert a new slide, select Insert ➪ Slide from the menu. A blank slide appears. You can then add text and graphics to that new slide.

To save a presentation, select File ➪ Save from the menu. For new documents, you have to provide a filename and select the directory in which to save the file.

insider insight If you want to share the slides with someone who uses Microsoft PowerPoint, save the presentation in Microsoft PowerPoint 97/2000/XP format.

Using Calculators

You have a choice of the GNOME calculator or the KDE calculator. Both are scientific calculators, and you can do the typical scientific calculations such as square root and inverse, as well as trigonometric functions, such as sine, cosine, and tangent.

To run the GNOME calculator, select Applications ➪ Accessories ➪ Calculator in the GNOME panel. Figure 10-8 shows the GNOME calculator.

Figure 10-8: The GNOME Calculator.

The KDE calculator has more features than the GNOME calculator. For example, it can perform calculations in hexadecimal, decimal, octal, and binary format. From the KDE desktop, you can start the KDE calculator by selecting Main Menu ⇨ Accessories ⇨ Scientific Calculator. The KDE calculator is intuitive to use.

Commercially Available Office Applications for Linux

Because office applications are important to many businesses as well as individuals, I want to briefly mention some of the commercial office applications available for Linux. These commercial offerings include Applixware Office and StarOffice. These products do cost some money, but the cost is usually less than that for Microsoft Office — the leading office application suite for Windows. (In case you don't know, Microsoft Office is a collection of several applications: Microsoft Word for word processing, Microsoft Excel for spreadsheets, Microsoft PowerPoint for presentation graphics, and Microsoft Access for databases.)

Another commercial product for Linux is CrossOver Office from CodeWeavers. With CrossOver Office, you can run your existing Microsoft Office applications such as Word, Excel, and PowerPoint under Linux and X Window System. (You need the Microsoft Office CD to install these applications under Crossover Office.)

> **note** This book's companion DVD-ROM does not include any of these commercial office applications for Linux, but I briefly describe them in the next few sections. You can visit each vendor's website for more about the products.

Running Microsoft Office in Linux with CrossOver Office

You probably have Windows and Microsoft Office installed on your PC. When you decide to install Linux on the PC, you can, for a price, continue to run the key Microsoft Office applications from the GNOME or KDE desktop. The convenience of running Microsoft Office in Linux comes in the form of a commercial product called CrossOver Office.

CrossOver Office, from CodeWeavers, is a software package that enables you to install your Microsoft Office applications (all versions of Office, including Office 97, Office 2000, and Office XP) in Linux. You do not need Microsoft Windows to run the Office applications in CrossOver Office. You simply install CrossOver Office and then install Microsoft Office from the Microsoft Office CD-ROM (CrossOver Office enables you to install many more Windows applications, including Internet Explorer, Outlook, Lotus Notes, Adobe Photoshop, Quicken, and iTunes). After you install Microsoft Office, the Office applications will be available directly from GNOME or KDE desktop.

CrossOver Office uses Wine—an open-source implementation of the Windows Win32 and Win16 application programming interfaces (APIs) using the X Window System and designed to run in UNIX and Linux systems. Wine includes the Wine loader and WineLib. Wine loader can load and run Windows applications. WineLib is used for compiling and linking Windows applications in Linux. Wine is available free of charge from `www.winehq.com`.

CodeWeavers created CrossOver Office using a customized version of Wine to make sure that the Microsoft Office applications, especially Microsoft Word, Excel, and PowerPoint, run properly on Wine. CodeWeavers charges a nominal amount for CrossOver Office—the list price is $39.95 for CrossOver Office Standard and $74.95 for CrossOver Office Professional—but all changes to Wine are returned to the Wine project. Thus, the Wine open-source project benefits from the sale of CrossOver Office.

You can learn more about CrossOver Office and purchase it at CodeWeavers' website (`www.codeweavers.com/products/cxoffice/`).

Getting Applixware Office

Applixware Office is another office application suite for all Linux distributions, including Fedora Core Linux. In April 2000, Applix, Inc., formed a separate group—VistaSource, Inc.— that focuses on Linux applications.

Like other office suites, Applixware Office includes Words (for word processing), Spreadsheets (for spreadsheets), and Graphics and Presents (for presentation graphics). In addition, it also has Mail (an email interface) and Data (an interactive relational database browsing tool). Applixware Office can also read and write documents in Microsoft Office and Corel WordPerfect formats, as well as in several other file formats. Applixware for Linux is offered for download by VistaSource's office in France; visit `www.premiumwanadoo.com/aposit/vs2/en/downloads.php` for more details.

You can learn more about Applixware at VistaSource's websites at `www.vistasource.com/` and `www.premiumwanadoo.com/aposit/vs2/en/applixware.php`.

Getting StarOffice

StarOffice is another commercial office applications suite; it was created by StarDivision of Hamburg, Germany, and purchased by Sun Microsystems in 1999. StarOffice is a cross-platform solution—it runs on Linux, Windows 95/98/Me/NT/2000/XP, Sun Solaris SPARC, and Sun Solaris x86. Also, StarOffice is available in several languages: English, French, German, Spanish, Italian, and Swedish.

StarOffice is a full-featured office productivity suite. Here's what StarOffice 7 Office Suite includes

- StarOffice Writer for word processing (Microsoft Word–compatible)
- StarOffice Calc for spreadsheets (Microsoft Excel–compatible)
- StarOffice Impress for presentations (Microsoft PowerPoint–compatible)
- StarOffice Draw for vector graphics drawing
- StarOffice Base for data management (the database functionality is provided by Software AG's Adabas D)

You can download a copy of StarOffice from `www.sun.com/staroffice/` for $59.95. You can also find the details of Sun's StarOffice licensing policy at the same URL.

In October 2000, Sun released the source code of StarOffice under open-source licenses. OpenOffice.org, an open-source project that Sun supports, released the OpenOffice.org 1.0 office productivity suite in May 2002. Presently, Fedora Core Linux comes with OpenOffice.org 2.0, including the database program—OpenOffice.org Base—that first appeared in version 2.0. To learn more about OpenOffice.org, visit `www.openoffice.org`. To download templates and sample files for the OpenOffice.org suite, visit `http://ooextras.sourceforge.net/`.

Multimedia

Linux distributions such as Fedora include a few multimedia applications—mostly music and CD players and CD burners. To play some other multimedia files (such as MP3 music or MPEG and QuickTime video), you have to download and install additional software in your Linux system. Fedora does not include decoders for various multimedia file formats because of licensing restrictions.

Here's a list of a few typical multimedia tasks and the applications you can use to perform these tasks in Fedora:

- **Accessing digital cameras:** Access the camera as a USB mass storage device in Linux so that you can download photos from your digital camera to your hard disk.
- **Playing audio CDs:** Use one of many audio CD players that come with Linux.
- **Playing sound files:** Use Rhythmbox or XMMS multimedia audio players. (You have to download some additional software to play MP3 files with Rhythmbox or XMMS. To use XMMS, you must install it first.) You can also download other players from the Internet.
- **Burning a CD:** Install a CD burner application such as K3b or X-CD-Roast and use it. You can burn data CDs with the built-in CD burning capability in Nautilus.

The following sections outline two specific tasks—accessing the digital camera as a USB storage device and burning a data CD in Nautilus.

Accessing a Digital Camera

Most digital cameras can connect to the Universal Serial Bus (USB) port. If you have such a camera, you can access its storage media (compact flash card, for example) as a USB mass storage device, provided your camera supports USB Mass Storage. To access the images on your USB digital camera, use the following steps:

1. Read the camera manual and use the menu options of the camera to set the USB mode to Mass Storage. If the camera doesn't support USB Mass Storage, you cannot use this procedure to access the photos.
2. Connect your digital camera to the USB port by using the cable that came with the camera, and then turn on the camera. This causes the Linux hotplug system to detect the camera and mount it the `/media/usbdisk` directory on the Linux file system.
3. Double-click the computer icon on the desktop, then the Filesystem folder, then media, and, finally, the `usbdisk` folder. You should see the camera's memory card contents in the Nautilus window.
4. Go through the folders on the camera's memory card to find the photos. Click to select photos and copy them to your hard disk by dragging and dropping them into a selected folder.
5. Turn off the camera and disconnect the USB cable from the PC.

Burning Data CDs from Nautilus

If you have a CD/DVD recorder attached to your system (it can be a built-in ATAPI CD recorder or an external one attached to the USB port), you can use Nautilus to burn data CDs or DVDs. From a Nautilus object window, you can access the CD Creator built into Nautilus. Just follow these simple steps:

1. In any Nautilus object window, choose Places ⇨ CD/DVD Creator. Nautilus opens a CD/DVD Creator object window. (If you don't have any Nautilus object windows open, just double-click the Computer icon on the desktop.)
2. From other Nautilus windows, drag and drop into the CD/DVD Creator window whatever files and folders you want to put on the CD or DVD. To get to files on your computer, double-click the Computer icon to open it in Nautilus and find the files you want. Then drag and drop those file or folder icons into the CD/DVD Creator window.
3. From the CD/DVD Creator window, choose File ⇨ Write to Disc. Nautilus displays a dialog box where you can select the CD/DVD recorder, the write speed, and several other options, such as whether to eject the CD when done. You can also specify the CD title.
4. Click the Write button and Nautilus burns the CD.

If you have downloaded a CD or DVD ISO image and want to burn that ISO image onto a CD or DVD, you can do so easily in Nautilus. Open the folder containing the ISO image in a Nautilus window and place a blank CD or DVD into the CD/DVD recorder. Then right-click the ISO file and select Write to Disc from the pop-up menu. Nautilus displays the Write to Disc dialog box where you can select the CD/DVD recorder device and then click Write to start burning the CD or DVD.

Graphics and Images

The applications in this category enable you to work with images, graphics (line drawings and shapes), and sound. Chapter 5 describes the CD players you can use to play audio CDs on your Linux system. The following applications, summarized in this chapter, enable you to prepare, view, modify, and print graphics and images:

- **The GIMP (the GNU Image Manipulation Program):** A program for viewing and performing image-manipulation tasks, such as photo retouching, image composition, and image creation
- **Xfig:** A drawing program capable of producing engineering drawings
- **Gnuplot:** A plotting package
- **Ghostscript:** A PostScript interpreter capable of producing output on many devices, including output in various image-file formats
- **KGhostview:** A KDE application capable of displaying PostScript and PDF files

Manipulating Images with the GIMP

The GIMP (GNU Image Manipulation Program) is an image-manipulation program written by Peter Mattis and Spencer Kimball and released under the GNU General Public License (GPL). It is installed if you select the Graphics Manipulation package when you install Linux from this book's companion DVD-ROM. The GIMP is comparable to other image-manipulation programs, such as Adobe Photoshop and Corel Photopaint.

To try out the GIMP, select Applications ⇨ Graphics ⇨ the GIMP from the GNOME desktop or the KDE desktop. The GIMP starts and displays a window with copyright and license information. Click the Continue button to proceed with the installation. The next screen shows the directories to be created when you proceed with a personal installation of the GIMP.

GIMP installation involves creating a directory called `.gimp-2.2` in your home directory and placing a number of files in that directory. This directory essentially holds information about any changes to user preferences you might make to the GIMP. Go ahead and click the Continue button at the bottom of the window. The GIMP creates the necessary directories and copies the necessary files to those directories; then it displays an installation log.

After reading the installation log and ensuring that there are no error messages, click the Continue button. The GIMP then guides you through several screens from which you are asked to specify the values of some parameters; you can accept the defaults and click the Continue button in each screen until the installation window closes. From this time on, you won't see the installation window; you have to deal with installation only when you run the GIMP for the first time.

The GIMP then loads any plug-ins — external modules that enhance its functionality. It displays a startup window that shows a message about each plug-in as it has loaded. After finishing the startup, the GIMP displays a tip of the day in a window and a number of windows, as shown in Figure 10-9. You can browse the tips and click the Close button to close the tip window.

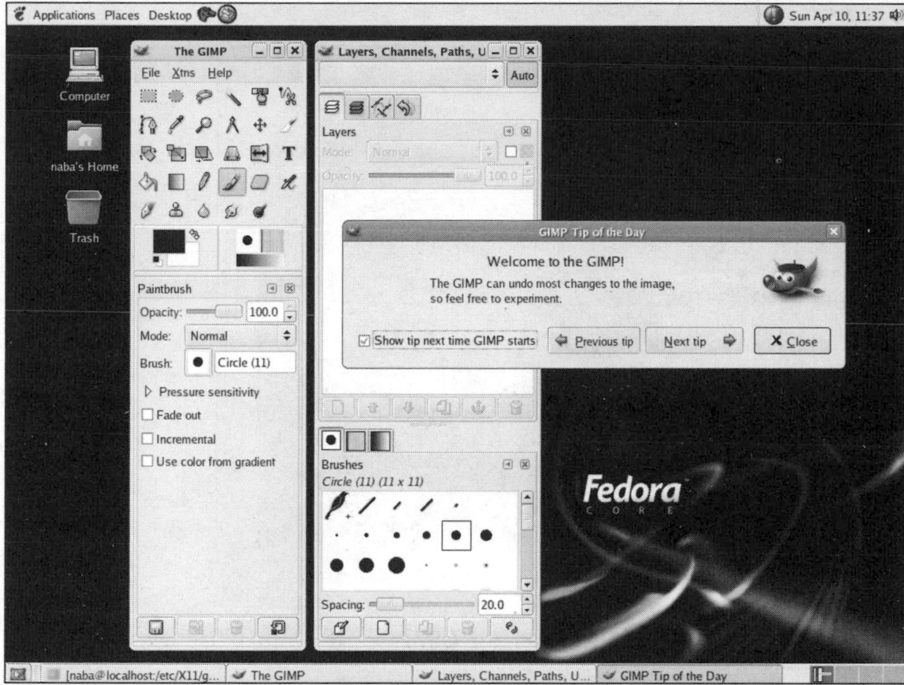

Figure 10-9: The Initial Windows Displayed by the GIMP.

The initial GIMP windows include a main toolbox window titled the GIMP, a Tool Options window and a Layers, Channels, Paths, Undo | Brushes, Patterns, Gradients window (as the window title implies, it includes lots of tools in a single window). Of these, the main toolbox window is the most important—in fact, you can close the other windows and work by using the menus and buttons in the toolbox.

The toolbox has three menus on the menu bar: File, Xtns (extensions), and Help. The File menu has options to create a new image, open an existing image, and quit the GIMP. The Xtns menu gives you access to numerous extensions to the GIMP. The exact content of the Xtns menu depends on which extensions are installed on your system. The Help menu enables you to view tips and get help on the GIMP. For example, select Help⇨Help to bring up the GIMP Help Browser with online information about the GIMP.

To open an image file in the GIMP, select File⇨Open. This brings up the Open Image dialog box from which you can select an image file. You can change directories and select the image file you want to open. The GIMP can read all common image-file formats, such as GIF, JPEG, TIFF, PCX, BMP, PNG, and PostScript. After you select the file and click OK, the GIMP loads the image into a new window. Figure 10-10 shows a JPEG image of a photograph that the GIMP has opened.

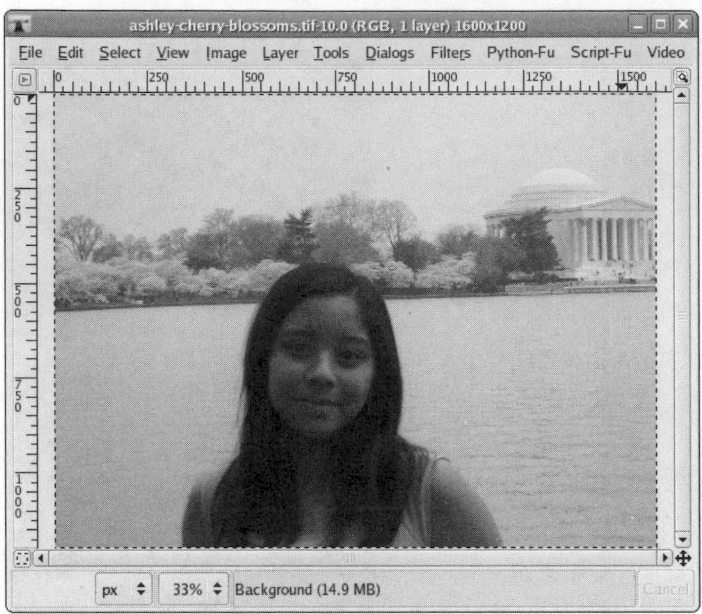

Figure 10-10: Opening an Image with the GIMP.

The GIMP's main toolbox also has many buttons that represent the tools you use to edit the image and apply special effects. You can get pop-up help on each tool button by placing the mouse pointer on the button. You can select a tool by clicking that tool's button, and you can apply that tool's effects on the image.

For your convenience, the GIMP displays a pop-up menu when you right-click your mouse on the image window. The pop-up menu has most of the options from the File and Xtns menus in the toolbox. You can then select specific actions from these menus.

You can do much more than just load and view images with the GIMP, but a complete discussion of all its features is beyond the scope of this book. If you want to try the other features of the GIMP, you should consult the GIMP User Manual (GUM), available online at `http://docs.gimp.org/en/`.

Some documentation about the GIMP is installed in the `/usr/share/doc` directory. To go to that directory, type **cd /usr/share/doc/gimp*** (the actual directory name depends on the current version of the GIMP). The README file in that directory points you to other resources on the Web, where you can learn more about the GIMP. In particular, visit the GIMP home page at `www.gimp.org/` to learn the latest news about the GIMP and to find links to other resources.

Drawing Figures with xfig

The xfig program is an interactive drawing program that runs under X and can generate encapsulated PostScript files suitable for inclusion in documents. To use xfig, you need to install three RPM files — first transfig and xpdf RPMs and then the xfig RPM.

To install xfig, log in as `root` and follow these steps:

1. Mount the DVD-ROM. Insert the DVD-ROM and wait for it to be mounted (or type **mount /media/cdrom** to mount the DVD-ROM). Then, type the following command to install the transfig program:

   ```
   cd /media/cdrom/Fedora/RPMS
   rpm -ivh transfig*.rpm
   ```

2. Install the xpdf program with the `rpm` command as follows:

   ```
   rpm -ivh xpdf*.rpm
   ```

3. Install the xfig program with the `rpm` command as follows:

   ```
   rpm -ivh xfig*.rpm
   ```

To try xfig, type **xfig &** in a terminal window. This command causes a rather large xfig window to appear. At the top edge of the window, you'll find a menu bar. To open an xfig drawing, click the File button and hold. Drag the mouse and select Open from the menu that appears. This action brings up a file-selection dialog box, through which you can change directories and locate `xfig` files (they usually have the `.fig` extension).

You will find a large number of `xfig` drawings, organized into subdirectories, in the `/usr/lib/X11/xfig/Libraries` directory of your Linux system (these files are installed when you install xfig). You can open and view some of these drawing files in xfig. For example, Figure 10-11 shows the xfig window after loading the drawing file `/usr/lib/X11/xfig/Libraries/Buildings/twostory.fig`.

As is true of any other tool, learning to use all of the features of xfig takes some practice. If you are familiar with other drawing software, such as MacDraw (Macintosh) or CorelDRAW (PC), you should be able to use xfig without much trouble.

Plotting Data with Gnuplot

Gnuplot is an interactive plotting utility. You need to run Gnuplot under the X Window System because it uses an X window as the output device. Gnuplot is a command-line-driven program; it prompts you and accepts your input commands. In response to those commands, Gnuplot displays various types of plots. The output appears in an X window.

To install Gnuplot, log in as root, mount the DVD-ROM, and type the following commands in a terminal window (change `/media/cdrom` to `/media/cdrecorder` if you are using a CD/DVD recorder):

```
cd /media/cdrom/Fedora/RPMS
rpm -ivh gnuplot*.rpm
```

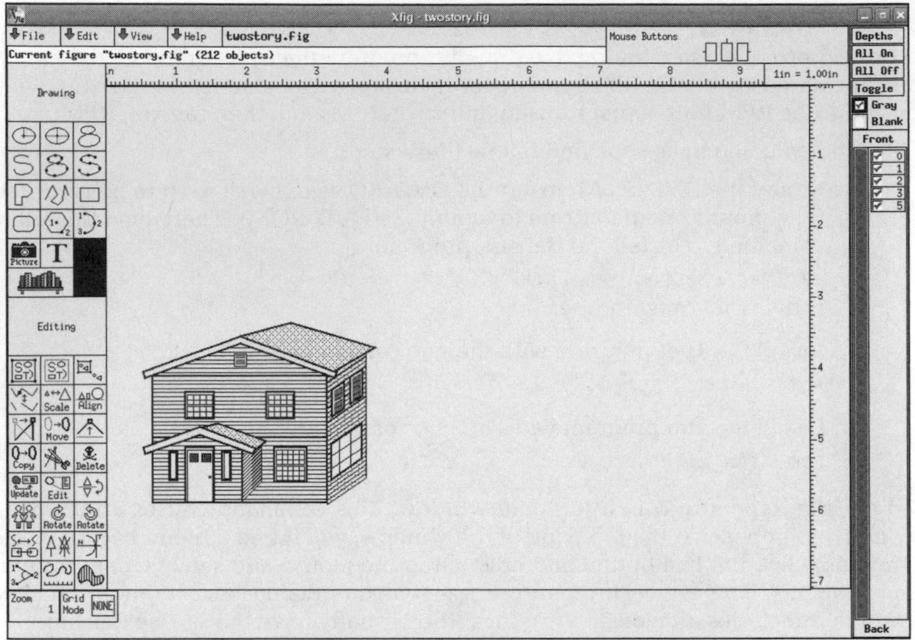

Figure 10-11: A Sample Drawing Displayed in xfig.

After installing Gnuplot, type **gnuplot** in a terminal window. Gnuplot displays an opening message and waits for further input at the prompt, as shown in Figure 10-12.

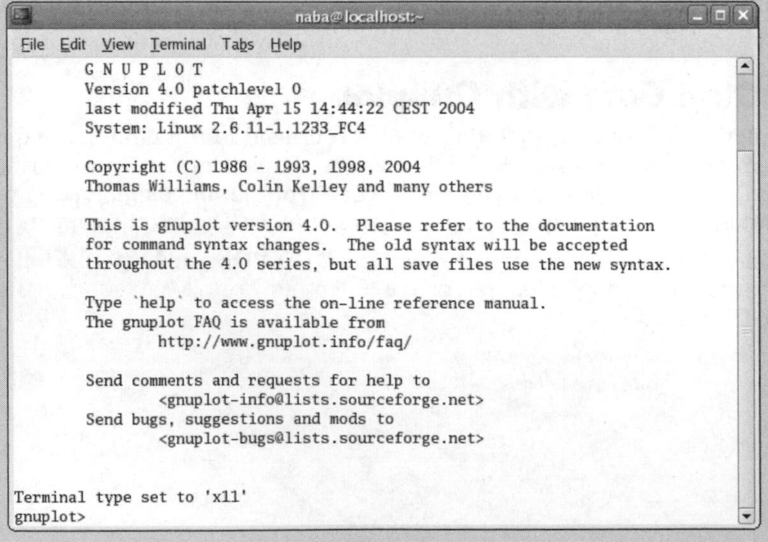

Figure 10-12: Running Gnuplot in a Terminal Window.

To see an immediate result, type the following Gnuplot command at the prompt:

```
plot sin(x)
```

Gnuplot opens an output window and displays a plot of the sine function, as shown in Figure 10-13.

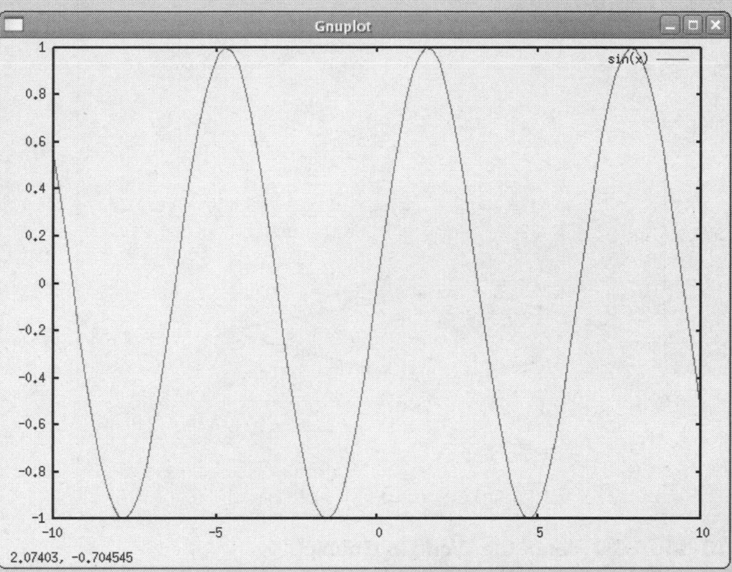

Figure 10-13: Plotting sin(x) in Gnuplot.

To quit Gnuplot, click the terminal window (where you started Gnuplot) to make it active, and then type **quit**. This example is a simple illustration of Gnuplot's capabilities.

Incidentally, although Gnuplot has "Gnu" in its name, it has nothing to do with GNU or the Free Software Foundation.

At any time in Gnuplot, you can ask for online help. The help is similar to that in the old DEC VAX/VMS system. To learn more about the `plot` command, for example, type **help plot** at the Gnuplot prompt.

Gnuplot also comes with several example files that appear in the `/usr/lib/gnuplot/demos` directory of your system. To try these demo files, type the following commands in a terminal window:

```
cd /usr/share/doc/gnuplot*
cd demo
gnuplot
```

When the Gnuplot prompt appears, load one of the demo files (the ones with the `.dem` extension) with the load command. To load the `world.dem` file, for example, type the following command at the Gnuplot prompt:

```
load "world.dem"
```

The `world.dem` Gnuplot file displays a map of the world and pauses until you press Enter (before you do so, click the terminal window where you started Gnuplot). After you press Enter, Gnuplot displays the next plot, which happens to be a view of the earth in spherical coordinates, as shown in Figure 10-14.

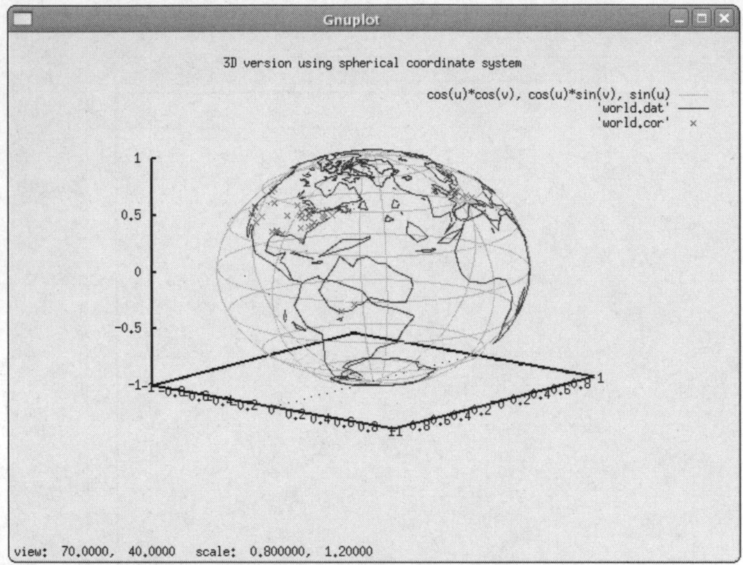

Figure 10-14: A 3D Plot of the World in Gnuplot.

If you are curious about the `world.dem` file, here's what it contains:

```
#
# $Id: world.dem,v 1.8 2003/10/28 05:35:54 sfeam Exp $
#
#
set title "Gnuplot Correspondences"
unset key
unset border
unset yzeroaxis
unset xtics
unset ytics
#
# plot world map and correspondent locations as a +
plot 'world.dat' with lines 3 4, 'world.cor' with points 1 2
set title ""
set key on
set border
set yzeroaxis
set xtics
set ytics
pause -1 "Hit return to continue"
#
# plot a '3D version using spherical coordinate system' of the world.
set angles degrees
```

```
set title "3D version using spherical coordinate system"
set ticslevel 0
set view 70,40,0.8,1.2
set mapping spherical
set parametric
set samples 32
set isosamples 9
set urange [-90:90]
set vrange [0:360]
splot cos(u)*cos(v),cos(u)*sin(v),sin(u) with lines 5 6,\
'world.dat' with lines 3 4, 'world.cor' with points 1 2
pause -1 "Hit return to continue"

# HBB 20000715: new demo:
# same plot, but with hidden3d active, plus axes through the
# poles:
set title "3D solid version through hiddenlining"
set hidden3d
set arrow from 0,0,-1.2 to 0,0,1.2 lt 5 lw 2
set arrow from -1.2, 0, 0 to 1.2, 0, 0 nohead lt 5 lw 1
set arrow from 0, -1.2, 0 to 0, 1.2, 0 nohead lt 5 lw 1
splot cos(u)*cos(v),-cos(u)*sin(v),sin(u) with lines 5 6,\
'world.dat' u 1:2:(1.001) with lines 3 4, 'world.cor' with points 1 2
pause -1 "Hit return to continue"

unset arrow
unset hidden

#
# plot a '3D version using cylindrical coordinate system' of the world.
set title "3D version using cylindrical coordinate system"
set ticslevel 0.0
set view 70,40,0.8,1.2
set mapping cylindrical
set parametric
set samples 32
set isosamples 9
set urange [-180:180]
set vrange [-90:90]
splot cos(u),sin(u),v with lines 5 6,\
'world.dat' with lines 3 4, 'world.cor' with points 1 2
pause -1 "Hit return to continue"
reset
```

As the listing shows, the `world.dem` file consists of Gnuplot commands. You can learn a great deal about Gnuplot by trying each file in the Gnuplot demo directory and by studying the commands in the file.

Working with PostScript in Ghostscript

Ghostscript is a utility for previewing and printing PostScript documents. Ghostscript enables you to print PostScript documents on many non-PostScript devices.

At its heart, Ghostscript is a nearly complete implementation of the PostScript language. Ghostscript includes the interpreter that processes PostScript input and generates output on an output device. A Ghostscript device can be a printer (or display screen), as well as an image-file format, such as BMP or PCX.

Ghostscript is distributed under the GNU GPL but is copyrighted and maintained by Aladdin Enterprises. The latest version remains under Aladdin's control for one year after its release, at which point it is transferred to the Free Software Foundation and can be distributed under GPL.

To run Ghostscript, first type **export GS_DEVICE=x11** in a terminal window and then type **gs**. Ghostscript brings up an empty window and displays the following text in the terminal window (the version number is different if you are running a later version of Ghostscript):

```
GNU Ghostscript 7.07 (2003-05-17)
Copyright (C) 2003 artofcode LLC, Benicia, CA.  All rights reserved.
This software comes with NO WARRANTY: see the file PUBLIC for
details.
GS>
```

At this point, you are interacting with the Ghostscript interpreter. Unless you know the Ghostscript language (which is like PostScript), you'll feel lost at this prompt. It's kind of like the `C:>` prompt under MS-DOS or the Linux shell prompt at a terminal.

If you have a PostScript file available, you can interactively load and view it in Ghostscript with a simple command. For example, try the following command:

```
GS> (/usr/share/ghostscript/7.07/examples/golfer.ps) run
>>showpage, press <return> to continue<<
```

You have typed a Ghostscript command that should cause Ghostscript to load the file `/usr/share/ghostscript/7.07/examples/golfer.ps` and process it. (If you are running a version of Ghostscript other than 7.07, you must change 7.07 to that version number.) The result is a picture in Ghostscript's output window. To exit Ghostscript, press Enter and type **quit**.

Fortunately, you do not have to use Ghostscript at the interpreter level (unless you know PostScript well and want to try PostScript commands interactively). Typically, you use Ghostscript to load and view a PostScript file.

Ghostscript takes several command-line arguments, including the file to be loaded. To see a list of Ghostscript options, type the `gs -h` command.

To see how Ghostscript renders a PostScript document, you can use any PostScript document you have available. You can view one of the sample PostScript files in the `/usr/share/ghostscript/`*7.07*`/examples` directory (replace *7.07* with whatever version of Ghostscript is installed on your system — Ghostscript displays its version number when you start it). Type the following command, for example, in a terminal window:

```
gs /usr/share/ghostscript/7.07/examples/golfer.ps
```

Ghostscript opens that file, processes its contents, and displays the output in another window, as shown in Figure 10-15.

Figure 10-15: Ghostscript Displaying a PostScript File.

In this case, the output happens to be a picture of a golfer. After displaying the output, Ghostscript displays the following message:

```
>>showpage, press <return> to continue<<
```

Press Enter to continue. For a multiple-page PostScript document, Ghostscript then shows the next page. After all the pages are displayed, you return to the Ghostscript prompt. Type **quit** to exit Ghostscript.

Viewing PostScript or PDF Files with KGhostview

KGhostview is a KDE application that's essentially a graphical front end to the Ghostscript interpreter. KGhostview is ideal for viewing and printing PostScript and PDF documents. For a long document, you can view and print selected pages. You can also view the document at various levels of magnification by zooming in or out.

To run KGhostview, select Applications ➪ Graphics ➪ KGhostview from the GNOME or KDE desktop (or type **kghostview** in a terminal window). This causes the KGhostview application window to appear. In addition to the menu bar and toolbar along the top edge, the main display area of the window is divided vertically into two parts.

To load and view a PostScript document in KGhostview, select File ➪ Open, or click the open folder icon on the toolbar. This action causes KGhostview to display a file-selection dialog box. Use this dialog box to navigate the file system and select a PostScript file. You can select one of the PostScript files that come with Ghostscript. For example, open the file `tiger.ps` in the `/usr/share/ghostscript/7.07/examples` directory. (If your system has a version of Ghostscript later than 7.07, you have to use the new version number in place of 7.07.)

To open the selected file, click the Open File button in the file-selection dialog box. Ghostview opens the selected file, processes its contents, and displays the output in its window, as shown in Figure 10-16.

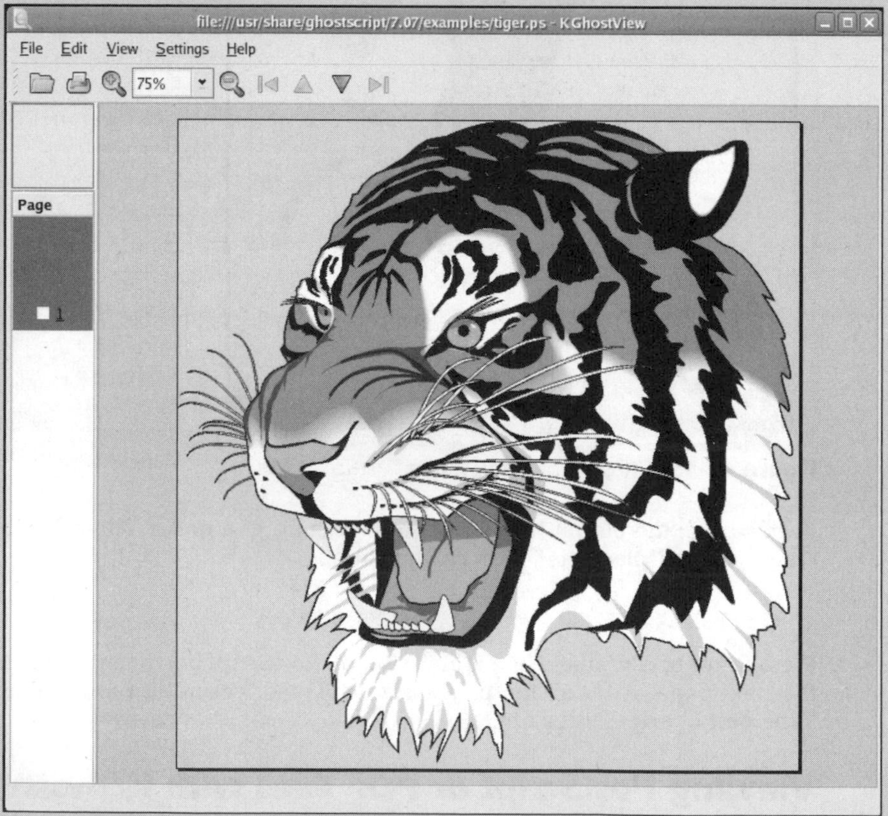

Figure 10-16: KGhostview Displaying a PostScript File.

KGhostview is useful for viewing various kinds of documentation that come in PostScript and PDF format (these files typically have the `.ps` or `.pdf` extension in their names). For example, I use Ghostview to view the documentation for the CVS program, which comes in several PostScript files you can find in the `/usr/share/doc/cvs*` directory. When viewing such documents in Ghostview, I zoom in by clicking the magnifying glass icon (with the plus sign) on the toolbar in Figure 10-16. This makes the document legible onscreen.

Summary

Linux comes with many applications and utilities. This chapter describes some of these applications, including common office tools — spreadsheet, calendars, calculators, and email programs — as well as graphics and imaging programs, such as the GIMP and KGhostview.

By reading this chapter, you learned the following:

- The companion DVD-ROM includes a variety of applications and utilities. Many of these applications are installed when you install Linux from the companion DVD-ROM, following the steps outlined in Chapter 2. You have to install some of the applications manually from the DVD-ROM.
- Evolution is a personal information manager that you can use to read and send email, manage your calendar, and keep track of your contact information.
- Linux comes with the OpenOffice.org office suite — a Microsoft Office–like suite of office applications that includes, among other components, the Writer word processor, Calc spreadsheet, and Impress presentation software.
- The GIMP, Ghostscript, and KGhostview are useful for working with image files of various formats. In particular, the GIMP is image-processing software with capabilities similar to those of commercial packages, such as Adobe Photoshop and Corel Photopaint. KGhostview is ideal for viewing and printing PostScript and PDF documents.
- There are several commercially available office application suites for Linux — Applixware Office, and StarOffice. These commercial applications are not part of Fedora Core Linux, but you can find out more about each product if you need a Linux office suite for your home or business.
- CrossOver Office from CodeWeavers is a unique commercial application that enables you to run Microsoft Office applications in Linux on the GNOME or KDE desktop.

Text Processing

Secrets in This Chapter

The term "text processing" refers to all aspects of creating, editing, and formatting textual documents. The simplest form of text processing is preparing a plaintext file, which you need to do often because most Linux configuration files are plaintext files. For this purpose, Linux offers a choice of text editors, ranging from the UNIX standard, vi, to the very powerful GNU Emacs.

To prepare formatted text in Linux, you must use a markup language such as groff or DocBook. Using a markup language, you place special formatting commands in a plaintext file, and a formatting program processes the marked-up text file to generate the formatted document for printing or viewing. You may already be familiar with a more recent markup language, HyperText Markup Language (HTML), which is the standard document format on the World Wide Web.

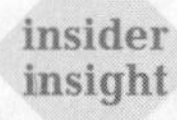

Even if you use a Microsoft Windows– or Macintosh-based "what-you-see-is-what-you-get" application (often pronounced "whizzy-whig" for its abbreviation WYSIWYG) to prepare formatted text, you must learn the rudiments of a markup language if you want to prepare a man page—online Help text available through the `man` command.

This chapter describes the text-processing facilities in Linux. The chapter starts with the ed, vi, and GNU Emacs text editors, and then it describes how to use the groff text-formatting program to prepare a man page. The chapter ends with a brief overview of the SGML- and XML-based DocBook markup language for document layout.

Text Editing with ed and vi

Text editing is an important part of all operating systems, including Linux. In Linux, you need to create and edit a variety of text files, as the following list describes:

- System configuration files, including `/etc/fstab`, `/etc/hosts`, `/etc/inittab`, `/etc/X11/xorg.conf`, and many more
- User files, such as `.newsrc` and `.bash_profile`
- Mail messages and news articles
- Shell script files
- Perl, Python, and Tcl/Tk scripts
- C or C++ programs

All Unix systems, including Linux, come with the following two text editors:

- **ed:** A line-oriented text editor
- **vi:** A full-screen text editor that supports the command set of an earlier editor by the name of ex

In Linux, another text editor, vim, emulates vi and ex, but you can invoke the editor by using the `vi` command, which is the standard UNIX name for the full-screen text editor.

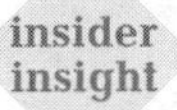

Although ed and vi may seem more cryptic than other, more graphical text editors, you should learn the basic editing commands of these two editors because at times, these editors may be the only ones available. If you run into a system problem and Linux refuses to boot from the hard disk, for example, you may need to boot from a floppy. In this case, you must edit system files by using the ed editor because that editor is small enough to fit on the floppy.

As I show in the following sections, learning the basic text-editing commands of ed and vi is easy.

Using ed

The ed text editor works by using a buffer — an in-memory storage area where the actual text resides until you explicitly store the text in a file. You must use ed only if you boot a minimal version of Linux (for example, from a boot floppy), and the system doesn't support full-screen mode.

Starting ed

To start ed, use the following command syntax:

```
ed [-] [-G] [-s] [-p<prompt-string>] [filename]
```

The arguments in brackets are optional. The following list explains these arguments:

- `-` suppresses the printing of character counts and diagnostic messages.
- `-G` forces backward compatibility with older versions of ed.
- `-s` is the same as the single hyphen.
- `-p`<*prompt-string*> sets the text that the editor displays when waiting for a command — type the prompt string immediately following `-p`. (The default is a null prompt string.)
- `filename` is the name of the file to be edited.

Learning ed

If you use the ed editor, you work in either command mode or text-input mode, as the following list explains:

- Command mode is what you get by default. In this mode, ed interprets anything that you type as a command. As you see in the section "Summarizing ed Commands," later in this chapter, ed uses a simple command set, wherein each command consists of a single character.
- Text-input mode enables you to enter text into the buffer. You can enter input mode by using the commands `a` (append), `c` (change), or `i` (insert). After entering lines of text, you can leave text-input mode by entering a period (`.`) on a line by itself.

The ed editor embodies the concept of the current line—the line to which ed applies the commands that you type. Each line has an address: the line number. You can apply a command to a range of lines by prefixing the command with an address range. The p command, for example, prints (displays) the current line. To see the first ten lines, use the following command:

```
1,10p
```

In a command, the period (.) refers to the current line, and the dollar sign ($) refers to the last line in the file. Thus, the following command deletes all the lines from the current line to the last one:

```
.,$d
```

Examining a Sample Session with ed

To try editing a file, copy the /etc/fstab file to your home directory by typing the following command:

```
cd; cp /etc/fstab .
```

Type the following command to begin editing that file in ed:

```
ed -p: fstab
867
:
```

This example uses the -p option to set the prompt to the colon character (:) and opens the fstab file in the current directory for editing. Turning on a prompt character is helpful because without the prompt, determining whether ed is in input mode or command mode is difficult.

The ed editor opens the file, reports the number of characters in the file (867), displays the prompt (:), and waits for a command.

After ed opens a file for editing, the current line is the last line of the file. To see the current line number, use the .= command, as follows:

```
:.=
10
```

The output tells you that the fstab file contains ten lines. (Your system's fstab file, of course, may contain a different number of lines.) The following example shows how you can see all these lines:

```
:1,$p
# This file is edited by fstab-sync - see 'man fstab-sync' for details
/dev/VolGroup00/LogVol00 /                 ext3    defaults        1 1
LABEL=/boot             /boot              ext3    defaults        1 2
/dev/devpts             /dev/pts           devpts  gid=5,mode=620  0 0
/dev/shm                /dev/shm           tmpfs   defaults        0 0
/dev/proc               /proc              proc    defaults        0 0
```

```
/dev/sys                /sys                   sysfs   defaults        0 0
/dev/VolGroup00/LogVol01 swap                  swap    defaults        0 0
/dev/fd0                /media/floppy          auto
pamconsole,exec,noauto,fscontext=system_u:object_r:removable_t,managed 0 0
/dev/hdc                /media/cdrom           auto
pamconsole,exec,noauto,fscontext=system_u:object_r:removable_t,managed 0 0
:
```

To go to a specific line, type the line number and the editor then displays that line. Here is an example that takes you to the second line in the file:

```
:2
/dev/VolGroup00/LogVol00 /                     ext3    defaults        1 1
```

Suppose that you want to delete the line that contains `cdrom`. To search for a string, type a slash (/) and follow it with the string that you want to locate, as follows:

```
:/cdrom
/dev/hdc                /media/cdrom           auto
pamconsole,exec,noauto,fscontext=system_u:object_r:removable_t,managed 0 0
```

That line becomes the current line. To delete the line, use the `d` command, as follows:

```
:d
:
```

To replace a string with another, use the `s` command. To replace `cdrom` with the string `cd`, for example, use the following command:

```
:s/cdrom/cd/
:
```

To insert a line in front of the current line, use the `i` command, as follows:

```
:i
    (type the line you want to insert)
.   (type a single period)
:
```

You can enter as many lines as you want. After the last line, enter a period (`.`) on a line by itself. That period marks the end of text-input mode, and the editor switches to command mode. In this case, you can tell that ed has switched to command mode because you see the prompt (`:`).

If you're happy with the changes, you can write them to the file by using the `w` command. If you want to save the changes and exit, type **wq** to perform both steps at the same time, as follows:

```
:wq
875
```

The ed editor saves the changes in the file, displays the number of characters that it saved, and exits.

If you want to quit the editor without saving any changes, use the `Q` command.

Summarizing ed Commands

The preceding sample session should give you an idea of how to use ed commands to perform the basic tasks of editing a text file. Table 11-1 lists all commonly used ed commands.

Table 11-1: Commonly Used ed Commands

Command	*Meaning*
`!command`	Execute a shell command.
`$`	Go to the last line in the buffer.
`%`	Apply the command that follows to all lines in the buffer (for example, `%p` prints all lines).
`+`	Go to the next line.
`+n`	Go to *n*th next line (*n* is a number).
`,`	Apply the command that follows to all lines in the buffer (for example, `,p` prints all lines); similar to `%`.
`-`	Go to the preceding line.
`-n`	Go to *n*th previous line (*n* is a number).
`.`	Refer to the current line in the buffer.
`/regex/`	Search forward for the specified regular expression (see Chapter 24 for an introduction to regular expressions).
`;`	Refer to a range of lines (if you specify no line numbers, the editor assumes current through last line in the buffer).
`=`	Print the line number.
`?regex?`	Search backward for the specified regular expression (see Chapter 24 for an introduction to regular expressions).
`^`	Go to the preceding line; also see the - command.
`^n`	Go to the *n*th previous line (where *n* is a number); see also the `-n` command.
`a`	Append after the current line.
`c`	Change the specified lines.
`d`	Delete the specified lines.
`e file`	Edit the file.
`f file`	Change the default filename.
`h`	Display an explanation of the last error.
`H`	Turn on verbose-mode error reporting.
`i`	Insert text before the current line.
`j`	Join contiguous lines.
`kx`	Mark the line with letter `x` (later, you can refer to the line as `'x`).
`l`	Print (display) lines.

Command	*Meaning*
`m`	Move lines.
`n`	Go to line number *n*.
`newline`	Display the next line and make that line current.
`P`	Toggle prompt mode on or off.
`q`	Quit the editor.
`Q`	Quit the editor without saving changes.
`r file`	Read and insert the contents of the file after the current line.
`s/old/new/`	Replace old string with new.
`Space n`	A space, followed by *n*; *n*th next line (*n* is a number).
`u`	Undo the last command.
`W file`	Append the contents of the buffer to the end of the specified file.
`w file`	Save the buffer in the specified file (if you name no file, ed saves it in the default file — the file whose contents ed is currently editing).

You can prefix most editing commands with a line number or an address range, which you express in terms of two line numbers that you separate with a comma; the command then applies to the specified lines. To append text after the second line in the buffer, for example, use the following command:

```
2a
(Type lines of text. End with single period on a line.)
```

To print lines 3 through 15, use the following command:

```
3,15p
```

Although you may not use ed often, much of the command syntax carries over to the vi editor. As the following section on vi shows, vi accepts ed commands if it's in its command mode.

Using vi

The vi editor is a full-screen text editor that enables you to view a file several lines at a time. Most UNIX systems, including Linux, come with vi. If you learn the basic features of vi, therefore, you can edit text files on almost any UNIX system.

As does the ed editor, vi works with a buffer. As vi edits a file, it reads the file into a buffer — a block of memory — and enables you to change the text in the buffer. The vi editor also uses temporary files during editing, but it doesn't alter the original file until you save the changes by using the `:w` command.

Setting the Terminal Type

Before you start a full-screen text editor such as vi, you must set the `TERM` environment variable to the terminal type (such as `vt100` or `xterm`). The vi editor uses the terminal type to look up the terminal's characteristics in the /etc/termcap file and then control the terminal in full-screen mode.

If you run the X Window System and a GUI, such as GNOME or KDE, you can use vi in a terminal window. The terminal window's terminal type is xterm. (To verify, type **echo $TERM** at the command prompt.) After you start the terminal window, it automatically sets the TERM environment variable to xterm. You can normally, therefore, use vi in a terminal window without explicitly setting the TERM variable.

Starting vi

If you want to consult the online manual pages for vi, type the following command:

```
man vi
```

To start the editor, use the vi name and run it with the following command syntax:

```
vi [flags] [+cmd] [filename]
```

The arguments shown in brackets are optional. The following list explains these arguments:

- flags are single-character flags that control the way that vi runs.
- +cmd causes vi to run the specified command after it starts. (You learn more about these commands in the section "Summarizing the vi Commands," later in this chapter.)
- filename is the name of the file to be edited.

The flags arguments can include one or more of the following:

- -c cmd executes the specified command before editing begins.
- -e starts in colon command mode (which I describe in the following section).
- -i starts in input mode (which I also describe in the following section).
- -m causes the editor to search through the file for something that looks like an error message from a compiler.
- -R makes the file read-only so that you can't accidentally overwrite the file. (You can also type **view filename** to start the editor in this mode to simply view a file.)
- -s runs in safe mode, which turns off many potentially harmful commands.
- -v starts in visual command mode (which I describe in the following section).

Most of the time, however, vi starts with a filename as the only argument, as follows:

```
vi /etc/hosts
```

Another common way to start vi is to jump to a specific line number right at startup. To begin editing at line 94 of the file /etc/X11/xorg.conf, for example, use the following command:

```
vi +94 /etc/X11/xorg.conf
```

This way of starting vi is useful if you edit a source file after the compiler reports an error at a specific line number.

Learning vi Concepts

If you edit a file by using vi, the editor loads the file into a buffer, displays the first few lines of the file in a full-screen window, and positions the cursor on the first line. If you type the command `vi /etc/fstab` in a terminal window, for example, you get a full-screen text window, as shown in Figure 11-1.

```
# This file is edited by fstab-sync - see 'man fstab-sync' for details
/dev/VolGroup00/LogVol00 /                    ext3    defaults        1 1
LABEL=/boot             /boot                ext3    defaults        1 2
/dev/devpts             /dev/pts             devpts  gid=5,mode=620  0 0
/dev/shm                /dev/shm             tmpfs   defaults        0 0
/dev/proc               /proc                proc    defaults        0 0
/dev/sys                /sys                 sysfs   defaults        0 0
/dev/VolGroup00/LogVol01 swap                 swap    defaults        0 0
/dev/fd0                /media/floppy        auto    pamconsole,exec,noauto,f
scontext=system_u:object_r:removable_t,managed 0 0
/dev/hdc                /media/cdrom         auto    pamconsole,exec,noauto,f
scontext=system_u:object_r:removable_t,managed 0 0
~
~
~
~
~
~
~
~
~
~
~
"/etc/fstab" [readonly] 10L, 867C
```

Figure 11-1: A File Displayed in a Full-Screen Text Window by the vi Editor.

The last line shows information about the file, including the number of lines and the number of characters in the file. (Notice that it says `[readonly]` because I am opening the `/etc/fstab` file while logged in as a normal user.) Later, vi uses this area as a command-entry area. It uses the rest of the lines to display the file. If the file contains fewer lines than the window, vi displays the empty lines with a tilde (~) in the first column.

The cursor marks the current line, appearing there as a small black rectangle. The cursor appears on top of a character. In Figure 11-1, the cursor is on the first character of the first line.

In vi, you work in one of the following three modes:

- **Visual-command mode** is what you get by default. In this mode, vi interprets anything that you type as a command that applies to the line containing the cursor. The vi commands are similar to those of ed, and I list them in the section "Summarizing the vi Commands," later in this chapter.
- **Colon-command mode** enables you to read or write files, set vi options, and quit. All colon commands start with a colon (`:`). After you enter the colon, vi positions the cursor at the last line and enables you to type a command. The command takes effect after you press Enter. Notice that vi's colon-command mode relies on the ed editor. When editing a file using vi, you can press Escape at any time to enter the command mode. In fact, if you are not sure what mode vi is in, press Escape a few times to get vi into command mode.

- **Text-input mode** enables you to enter text into the buffer. You can enter text-input mode by using the command `a` (insert after cursor), `A` (append at end of line), or `i` (insert after cursor). After entering lines of text, you must press Esc to leave text-input mode and reenter visual-command mode.

One problem with all these modes is that you can't easily determine vi's current mode. Typing text, only to realize that vi isn't in text-input mode, can be frustrating. The converse situation also is common — you may end up typing text when you want to enter a command. To ensure that vi is in command mode, just press Esc a few times. (Pressing Esc more than once doesn't hurt.)

tip

To view online Help in *vi*, type `:help` while in command mode.

Examining a Sample Session with vi

To begin editing the file `/etc/fstab`, first make a backup copy by typing the command **cp /etc/fstab /etc/fstab-saved**). Then enter the following:

```
vi /etc/fstab
```

Figure 11-1, earlier in this chapter, shows you the resulting display, with the first few lines of the file appearing in a full-screen text window. The last line shows the file's name and statistics: the number of lines and characters.

The vi editor initially positions the cursor on the first character. One of the first things that you need to learn is how to move the cursor around. Try the following commands (each command being a single letter; just type the letter, and vi responds):

- **j** moves the cursor one line down.
- **k** moves the cursor one line up.
- **h** moves the cursor one character to the left.
- **l** moves the cursor one character to the right.

You can also move the cursor by using the arrow keys.

Instead of moving one line or one character at a time, you can move one word at a time. Try the following single-character commands for word-size cursor movement:

- **w** moves the cursor one word forward.
- **b** moves the cursor one word backward.

The last type of cursor movement affects several lines at a time. Try the following commands and see what happens:

- **Ctrl-D** scrolls down half a screen.
- **Ctrl-U** scrolls up half a screen.

The last two commands, of course, aren't necessary if the file contains only a few lines. If you're editing large files, however, the capability to move several lines at a time is handy.

You can move to a specific line number at any time by using a colon command. To go to line 1, for example, type the following and then press Enter:

```
:1
```

After you type the colon, vi displays the colon on the last line of the screen. From then on, vi uses the text that you type as a command. You must press Enter to submit the command to vi. In colon-command mode, vi accepts all the commands that the ed editor accepts— and then some.

To search for a string, first type a slash (/). The vi editor displays the slash on the last line of the screen. Type the search string, and then press Enter. The vi editor locates the string and positions the cursor at the beginning of that string. Thus, to locate the string `cdrom` in the file `/etc/fstab`, type the following:

```
/cdrom
```

To delete the line that contains the cursor, type **dd**. The vi editor deletes that line of text and makes the next line the current one.

tip

To begin entering text in front of the cursor, type i. The vi editor switches to text-input mode. Now you can enter text. After you finish entering text, press Esc to return to visual-command mode.

After you finish editing the file, you can save the changes in the file by using the `:w` command. If you want to save the changes and exit, you can type **:wq** to perform both steps at the same time. The vi editor saves the changes in the file and exits. You can also save the changes and exit the editor by pressing Shift-zz (press and hold the Shift key and press z twice).

To quit the editor without saving any changes, type the **:q!** command.

Summarizing the vi Commands

The sample editing session should give you a feel for the vi commands, especially its three modes:

- Visual-command mode (the default)
- Colon-command mode, in which you enter commands, following them with a colon (:)
- Text-input mode, which you enter by typing **a**, **A**, or **i**

In addition to the few commands that the sample session illustrates, vi accepts many other commands. Table 11-2 lists the basic vi commands, organized by task.

Table 11-2: Basic vi Commands

Command	*Meaning*
Insert Text	
a	Insert text after the cursor.
A	Insert text at the end of the current line.
I	Insert text at the beginning of the current line.
i	Insert text before the cursor.

(continued)

Table 11-2 *(continued)*

Command	Meaning
Insert Text	
`o`	Open a line below the current line.
`O`	Open a line above the current line.
`Ctrl-v`	Insert any special character in input mode.
Delete Text	
`D`	Delete up to the end of the current line.
`dd`	Delete the current line.
`dG`	Delete from the current line to the end of the file.
`dw`	Delete from the cursor to the end of the following word.
`x`	Delete the character on which the cursor rests.
Change Text	
`C`	Change up to the end of the current line.
`cc`	Change the current line.
`cw`	Change the word.
`J`	Join the current line with the next one.
`rx`	Replace the character under the cursor with *x* (*x* is any character).
`~`	Change the character under the cursor to the opposite case.
Move Cursor	
`$`	Move to the end of the current line.
`;`	Repeat the last `f` or `F` command.
`^`	Move to the beginning of the current line.
`e`	Move to the end of the current word.
`fx`	Move the cursor to the first occurrence of character *x* on the current line.
`Fx`	Move the cursor to the last occurrence of character *x* on the current line.
`G`	Move the cursor to the beginning of the last line in the file.
`H`	Move the cursor to the top of the screen.
`h`	Move one character to the left.
`j`	Move one line down.
`k`	Move one line up.
`L`	Move the cursor to the end of the screen.
`l`	Move one character to the right.
`M`	Move the cursor to the middle of the screen.

Command	Meaning
Move Cursor	
`n|`	Move the cursor to column *n* on current line.
`nG`	Place cursor on line *n*.
`w`	Move to the beginning of the following word.
Mark a Location	
`'x`	Move the cursor to the beginning of the line that contains mark *x*.
`` `x ``	Move the cursor to mark *x*.
`mx`	Mark the current location with the letter *x*.
`Scroll Text`	
`Ctrl-b`	Scroll backward by a full screen.
`Ctrl-d`	Scroll forward by half a screen.
`Ctrl-f`	Scroll forward by a full screen.
`Ctrl-u`	Scroll backward by half a screen.
Refresh Screen	
`Ctrl-L`	Redraw the screen.
Cut and Paste Text	
`"xndd`	Delete *n* lines and move them to buffer *x* (*x* is any single lowercase character).
`"Xnyy`	Yank *n* (a number) lines and append them to buffer *x*.
`"xnyy`	Yank *n* (a number) lines into buffer *x* (*x* is any single uppercase character).
`"xp`	Put the yanked lines from buffer *x* after the current line.
`P`	Put the yanked line above the current line.
`p`	Put the yanked line below the current line.
`yy`	Yank (copy) the current line into an unnamed buffer.
Colon Commands	
`:!command`	Execute the shell command.
`:e filename`	Edit the file.
`:f`	Display the filename and current line number.
`:N`	Move to line *n* (*n* is a number).
`:q`	Quit the editor.
`:q!`	Quit without saving changes.
`:r filename`	Read the file and insert after the current line.
`:w filename`	Write the buffer to the file.
`:wq`	Save the changes and exit.

(continued)

Table 11-2 *(continued)*

Command	*Meaning*
Search Text	
`/string`	Search forward for string.
`?string`	Search backward for string.
`n`	Find the next string.
View File Information	
`Ctrl-g`	Show the filename, size, and current line number.
Miscellaneous	
`u`	Undo the last command.
`Esc`	End text-input mode and enter visual-command mode.
`U`	Undo recent changes to the current line.

Working with GNU Emacs

Text editors are a matter of personal preference, and many UNIX users swear by GNU Emacs. Although it's intimidating at first, GNU Emacs is one of those software packages that grows on you; it has so many features that many users and programmers often perform all their tasks directly from within GNU Emacs.

A significant advantage of GNU Emacs is its availability on nearly every computer system imaginable, from MS-DOS PCs to any UNIX system. If a system doesn't have GNU Emacs, you can get it from any one of many sites on the Internet. For your Linux system, you get GNU Emacs on the companion DVD-ROM; you can choose to install it as you install Linux on your system. If you're just getting started with UNIX text editors, I recommend that you learn to use GNU Emacs and vi. That way, you acquire a skill that's usable on any UNIX system.

Because GNU Emacs is so versatile and powerful, describing it in detail could easily take an entire book, and quite a few books about GNU Emacs are on the market. Most notably, O'Reilly & Associates publishes a GNU Emacs book, *Learning GNU Emacs, Third Edition*, by Debra Cameron, James Elliott, Marc Loy, Eric Raymond, and Bill Rosenblatt, that you may find useful.

On a text terminal, GNU Emacs runs in text-mode, full-screen display. Under X, GNU Emacs runs in a window. Either way, the basic commands remain the same. The X version also enables you to position the cursor by using the mouse.

The following sections provide a brief introduction to the text-editing features of GNU Emacs.

Starting GNU Emacs

On the Linux console, you start GNU Emacs by typing **emacs**. If you're running X, type **emacs &** in a terminal window to start GNU Emacs. This command launches GNU Emacs with its X-based interface and enables you to continue other work in the terminal window.

insider insight If you want to run Emacs in a terminal window itself—without the X-based graphical interface in a separate window—and edit a file, just type **emacs -nw *filename***.

After it first starts, GNU Emacs displays a message in a window, as shown in Figure 11-2.

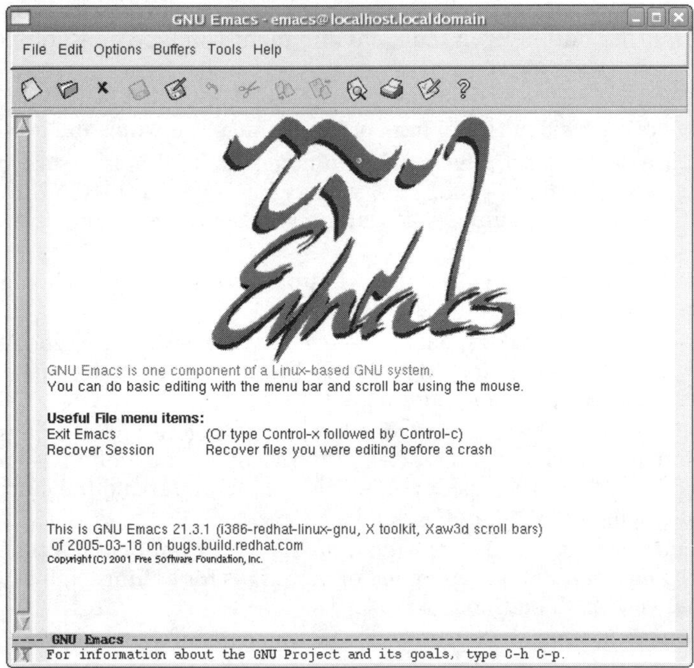

Figure 11-2: The Initial Window That the X Version of GNU Emacs Displays.

The initial GNU Emacs window also shows helpful information in the area where you normally edit the contents of a file. You can use the menus to get more help on Emacs.

Before I tell you anything else, remember that to quit GNU Emacs, you must press C-x C-c (that's Ctrl-x, followed by Ctrl-c). As you learn in the section "Typing GNU Emacs Commands," later in this chapter, all GNU Emacs command keystrokes start with a control character or Escape (which the Emacs documentation refers to as Meta and is abbreviated as M). The left Alt key also works as the Meta key.

insider insight To remain consistent with the GNU Emacs notation, I use the notation C-*x* for Ctrl-*x* and M-*x* for Esc-*x* (where *x* is any character).

Learning GNU Emacs

Although I've used GNU Emacs extensively for years, I feel that I've barely scratched the surface as far as using its full capabilities. As is true of anything else, your best bet is to start with a small subset of GNU Emacs commands. Then, as you become more proficient with the software, you can gradually add to your repertoire of GNU Emacs commands and features.

GNU Emacs employs some basic concepts that, if you learn them, are helpful. Some of those concepts include the following:

- As do other text editors (vi or ed), GNU Emacs uses a buffer to maintain the text that you enter and change. You must explicitly save the buffer to update the contents of the file.
- Unlike vi and ed, GNU Emacs doesn't require you to type any special command to enter text into the buffer. By default, anything that you type goes into the buffer.
- GNU Emacs uses a cursor to indicate the current location in the file. As you type text, GNU Emacs inserts that text in front of the character on which the cursor rests.
- GNU Emacs uses long, descriptive command names that it binds to (associates with) specific key sequences — these are the key bindings for the GNU Emacs commands. C-x C-c, for example, is bound to the GNU Emacs command `save-buffers-kill-emacs`.
- All GNU Emacs key bindings start with a control character (for which you simultaneously press Ctrl and a character) or Escape.
- GNU Emacs uses several modes, each of which provides a specific type of editing environment. (In C mode, for example, GNU Emacs indents the braces that enclose blocks of C programming language statements.)
- In the GNU Emacs window, the last screen line is the minibuffer; it displays all commands and filenames that you type. The line second to the bottom is the mode line. On this line, GNU Emacs displays the name of the buffer and the current mode (the default mode being fundamental).
- You don't need to start GNU Emacs each time that you want to edit a file. Rather, you start GNU Emacs and then open one or more files for editing. You save and close files that you finish editing.
- You can use many buffers in GNU Emacs, and you can cut and paste between buffers.

Typing GNU Emacs Commands

GNU Emacs uses an extensive set of commands in which each command has a very long descriptive name, as in the following example:

```
save-buffer save-buffers-kill-emacs scroll-up previous-line
```

Most of these commands, however, are bound to somewhat cryptic keystrokes. Otherwise, you'd need to actually type these long commands and wouldn't get much editing done.

Although you can enter any of these descriptive commands in the minibuffer (at the bottom of the GNU Emacs window), the basic means of entering the commands is through special keystrokes. These keystrokes begin with one of the following characters:

- A control character that you enter by simultaneously pressing the Ctrl key and the character. GNU Emacs documentation abbreviates each control character as `C-x` (*x* is a letter). This book uses the notation Ctrl-x to denote the control character that corresponds to the letter x. The GNU Emacs online Help writes Ctrl-v as `C-v`.
- An Escape character. GNU Emacs abbreviates the Esc key, or the Meta key, as M. Thus you write Esc v (Escape, followed by the letter v) as `M-v`. Notice that, depending on the keyboard, the Meta key may also be the Alt key or some other key, such as the Windows key, on some Windows machines.

Most of the time, you enter the control commands, which require pressing the Ctrl key together with a letter. Ctrl-v or `C-v`, for example, causes GNU Emacs to move forward one screen.

The commands with an Esc prefix are easier to enter because you press the keys in sequence: first the Escape key and then the letter. Esc v or `M-v`, for example, causes GNU Emacs to move backward one screen of text. To enter this command, press Esc first, and then press v. Although the Ctrl and Esc commands may sound complicated, you can learn a basic set very quickly.

Getting Help

The best source of information on GNU Emacs is GNU Emacs itself. For starters, GNU Emacs includes an online tutorial that teaches you its basics. To use the tutorial, press C-h t. GNU Emacs displays the initial screen of the tutorial in its window, as shown in Figure 11-3.

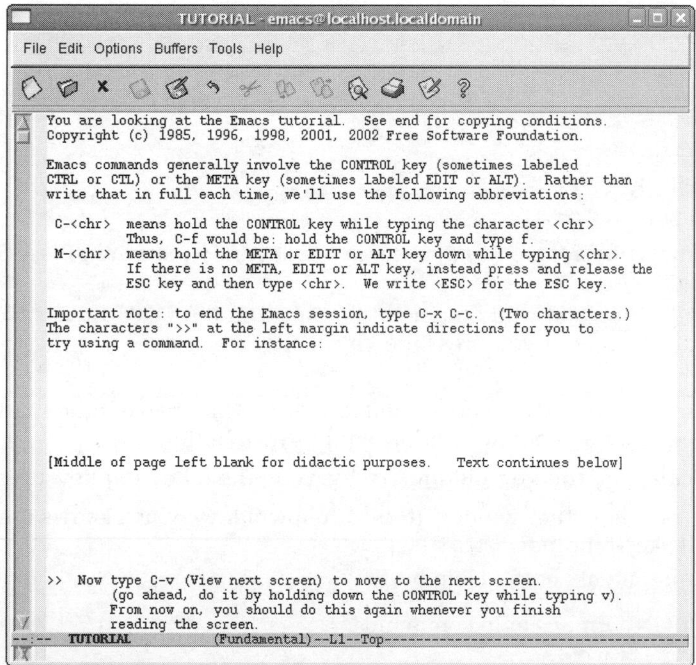

Figure 11-3: GNU Emacs Displays the Online Tutorial after You Press C-h t.

As the instructions near the bottom of Figure 11-3 show, the tutorial guides you through the steps and asks you to try GNU Emacs commands. If you're new to GNU Emacs, go through the tutorial. Because the tutorial is hands-on, it gives you a good feel for GNU Emacs.

In addition to the tutorial, you can look up the key bindings for various GNU Emacs commands. To see the key bindings, press C-h b. GNU Emacs splits the window and displays a list of key bindings in the bottom half, as shown in Figure 11-4.

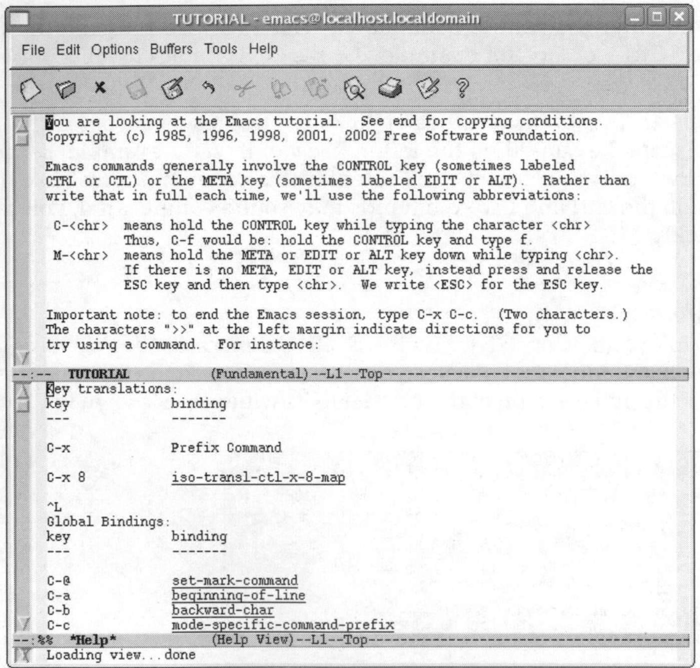

Figure 11-4: GNU Emacs Displays the Key Bindings in a Split Window after You Press C-h b.

Each line in the key binding shows the name of the key and the GNU Emacs command associated with that command. If you press the key, GNU Emacs executes the command that's bound to that key.

Figure 11-4 illustrates GNU Emacs' ability to split its window into two or more parts. After splitting, each part becomes a separate window with its own buffer.

In Figure 11-4, you can scroll the key-binding list by using the following keystrokes:

- **C-x o** switches to the other window (the bottom window, which shows the Help buffer with its key-bindings list).
- **C-v** scrolls the contents of the Help buffer.

Table 11-3 lists other GNU Emacs help commands.

Table 11-3: GNU Emacs help Commands

Command	*Meaning*
C-h c	Prompts you for a key sequence and briefly describes that sequence
C-h f	Prompts you for a GNU Emacs command name and describes that command
C-h k	Prompts you for a key sequence and describes what that sequence does
C-h l	Displays the last 100 characters typed
C-h m	Displays the current GNU Emacs mode
C-h s	Displays the syntax table for the current buffer
C-h v	Prompts for a variable name and describes that variable
C-h w	Prompts for a command and shows that command's key binding

Reading a File

After you start GNU Emacs, you can read in a file by typing the **C-x C-f** command. To open the file `/usr/share/emacs/21.3/etc/COPYING`, for example, follow these steps in GNU Emacs:

1. Press C-x C-f. GNU Emacs prompts you for a filename.
2. Type the filename — **/usr/share/emacs/21.3/etc/COPYING** — and press Enter. GNU Emacs reads the file into a buffer and displays that buffer in the window.

To open a file in the current directory, you don't need to type the full directory name; just type the filename. By default, GNU Emacs looks for the file in the current working directory.

You don't need to type the full filename in GNU Emacs; just enter the first few characters of the filename and then press Tab. If the partial name uniquely identifies a file, GNU Emacs completes the filename for you. Thus, all you need to type is the first few characters of a filename – just enough to uniquely identify the file. You can use this shortcut feature to avoid typing long filenames.

Suppose that the current working directory contains the file `Makefile`, which is the only file with a name that starts with the substring `Mak`. To load that file in GNU Emacs, press C-x C-f, type **Mak**, and press Tab. GNU Emacs completes the filename and reads the file `Makefile`.

Moving around the Buffer

One of the first things that you need to do in GNU Emacs is move around the buffer. The cursor marks the current spot in the buffer; anything that you type goes into the buffer in front of the character under the cursor. Thus, to insert text into a file, you must read in the file, move the cursor to the desired spot, and type the text.

To move around the buffer, you need to move the cursor. You must use control keys to move the cursor in any direction. Following are the six basic cursor-movement commands:

- **C-b** moves the cursor backward one character.
- **C-f** moves the cursor forward one character.
- **C-n** moves the cursor to the following line (while trying to maintain the same column position as in the current line).
- **C-p** moves the cursor to the preceding line (while trying to maintain the same column position as in the current line).
- **C-a** moves the cursor to the beginning of the current line.
- **C-e** moves the cursor to the end of the current line.

If moving one character at a time is too slow, you can move one word at a time by using the following commands:

- **M-f** moves the cursor forward one word.
- **M-b** moves the cursor backward one word.

You can move in even bigger chunks through the buffer. The following two commands enable you to move one screen at a time:

- **C-v** moves forward one screen.
- **M-v** moves backward one screen.

You can use the following two other simple cursor-movement commands for really big jumps:

- **M-<** (Esc followed by the less-than key) moves the cursor to the beginning of the buffer.
- **M->** (Esc followed by the greater-than key) moves the cursor to the end of the buffer.

A timesaving feature of GNU Emacs enables you to repeat a command a specified number of times. Suppose that you want to move 13 characters forward. You can do so by pressing C-f 13 times or by typing `C-u 13 C-f`. The `C-u` command accepts a repeat count and repeats the next command that many times. If you don't provide a count and simply type a command after `C-u`, GNU Emacs repeats the command four times. Thus, `C-u C-f` means "move forward four characters."

One exception to the behavior of the `C-u` command exists: If you use `C-u` with the `M-v` or `C-v` command, GNU Emacs doesn't repeat the screen-scrolling commands. Instead, GNU Emacs scrolls the screen up or down by the specified count. So, if you press C-u 10 C v, GNU Emacs scrolls down ten lines (not ten screens).

Inserting and Deleting Text

Because GNU Emacs doesn't have special command and insert modes as vi does, you just begin typing to insert text in GNU Emacs. GNU Emacs inserts the text in front of the cursor. GNU Emacs, of course, interprets control characters and Esc as the beginning of a command.

You can take advantage of the repeat-count feature to insert many copies of a character. I typically use the following line to separate sections of a C program:

```
/*---------------------------------------------------*/
```

I enter this line by making the following key presses:

```
/* C-u 51 - */
```

Ignore the spaces; I don't manually type them. I first type **/***, and then I press C-u and type **51**. Finally, I press the hyphen (-), following it with the ending */.

You can delete text in GNU Emacs in the following ways:

- To delete the character in front of the cursor, press Del.
- To delete the character on which the cursor rests, press C-d.
- To delete the word after the cursor, press M-d.
- To delete the word immediately before the cursor, press M-Del.
- To delete from the cursor to the end of the line, press C-k. (GNU Emacs refers to this command as "kill the line.")

insider insight Whenever you delete anything longer than one character, GNU Emacs saves it for you. Press C-y to retrieve the saved text.

You can undo a change by typing the `C-x u` command. Each time that you press C-x u, GNU Emacs performs the Undo operation for a previous command. To undo the effects of the last two commands, for example, press C-x u twice.

Searching and Replacing

Every text editor offers a search-and-replace capability, and GNU Emacs is no exception. The two most common search commands are as follows:

- **C-s string:** Incrementally searches forward for string.
- **C-r string:** Incrementally searches backward for string.

If you press C-s to search forward, GNU Emacs prompts you for a search string in the minibuffer (the last line in the GNU Emacs window). As you enter the characters for the string, GNU Emacs jumps to the first occurrence of the string that you've typed so far. As soon as you finish typing the search string, GNU Emacs positions the cursor at the end of the next occurrence of the search string (providing, of course, that GNU Emacs finds the string).

To find the next occurrence of the string, press C-s again. To end the search, press Enter. You also can halt the search by using cursor-control commands, such as C-f or C-b.

Searching in the reverse direction works similarly; just press C-r instead of C-s.

GNU Emacs also enables you to replace an occurrence of one string with another. The two basic commands for replacing strings are `replace-string` and `query-replace`. The `replace-string` command replaces all occurrences of one string with another. The `query-replace` command works similarly, but GNU Emacs prompts you each time that it's about to replace a string, enabling you to decide which strings it actually replaces.

The `query-replace` command is bound to the M-% (Esc, followed by %) key sequence. To perform a query-replace operation, first press M-%. GNU Emacs displays the following prompt in the minibuffer:

```
Query replace:
```

Enter the string that you want to replace — for example, 2004 — and then press Enter. GNU Emacs prompts you for the replacement string, as follows:

```
Query replace 2004 with:
```

Enter the replacement string — say, 2005 — and press Enter. GNU Emacs moves the cursor to the next occurrence of the string to replace and displays the following prompt in the minibuffer:

```
Query replacing 2004 with 2005: (? for help)
```

Type **y** or press the Spacebar to enable GNU Emacs to replace the string. Otherwise, press **n** or **Del** to stop GNU Emacs from replacing the string. In either case, GNU Emacs moves to the next occurrence of the string and repeats the prompt. If no more strings are left, GNU Emacs displays a message in the minibuffer informing you how many occurrences of the string it replaced.

No key binding exists for the `replace-string` command. You can type any GNU Emacs command, however, by following these steps:

1. Press M-x. GNU Emacs displays `M-x` in the minibuffer and waits for more text.
2. Type the GNU Emacs command, and press Enter. To use the `replace-string` command, for example, type **replace-string**, and then press Enter.
3. For some commands, GNU Emacs prompts you for further input; enter that input. If you use `replace-string`, for example, GNU Emacs first prompts for the string to replace and then for the replacement string.

If you type a GNU Emacs command by using M-x, you can press the Spacebar or the Tab key for command completion. To enter the `replace-string` command, for example, you may start by typing **repl** and then pressing the Spacebar. That action causes GNU Emacs to display `replace-` and then pause. Type **s** and press the Spacebar again. GNU Emacs displays `replace-string`. You then can use the command by pressing Enter. Try it to see what I mean.

Copying and Moving

Another common editing function is copying blocks of text and moving that text to another location in the buffer. The first step in working with a block of text is to define the block.

GNU Emacs defines a block as the text between a mark and the current cursor position. You can think of the mark as a physical marker that GNU Emacs places in the buffer to mark a location. To set the mark, move the cursor to the beginning of the block and then press C-@ or C-Space (pressing the Ctrl key together with the Spacebar). GNU Emacs sets the mark at the current location and displays the following message in the minibuffer:

```
Mark set
```

After the mark is set, GNU Emacs treats the text between the mark and the current cursor location as a block. To copy the block, press M-w, which copies the block to an internal storage area without deleting the block from the current buffer.

If you actually want to cut the block of text, press C-w, which deletes the block of text from the buffer and moves it to an internal storage area.

To insert the cut (or copied) text at any location, move the cursor to the insertion point, and press C-y, which causes GNU Emacs to paste the previously cut text in front of the cursor.

Between the cut and paste operations, you may switch from one buffer to another and, thereby, cut from one file and paste to another. To cut from one file and paste into another, follow these steps:

1. Open the first file by typing the **C-x C-f** command. For this exercise, assume that the first file's name is `first.txt`.
2. Open the second file by typing the **C-x C-f** command again. For this exercise, assume that the second file's name is `second.txt`.
3. Change to the first buffer by typing the **C-x b first.txt** command.
4. Move the cursor to the beginning of the text that you want to copy and press C-Space.
5. Move the cursor to the end of the block and press C-w to cut the text.
6. Change to the second buffer by typing **C-x b second.txt**.
7. Move the cursor to the location where you want to insert the text, and press C-y. GNU Emacs inserts the previously cut text from the first buffer into the second one.

Saving Changes

After you edit a buffer, you must write those changes to a file to make them permanent. The GNU Emacs command for saving a buffer to its file is `C-x C-s`. This command saves the buffer to the file with the same name.

To save the buffer in another file, type the command **C-x C-w**. GNU Emacs prompts you for a filename. Type the filename, and press Enter to save the buffer in that file. Unlike many DOS or Windows word processors, GNU Emacs doesn't automatically add a file extension. You must provide the full filename.

Running a Shell in GNU Emacs

GNU Emacs is versatile enough to enable you to access anything in Linux from within a GNU Emacs session. One way to access anything in Linux is to run a shell session. You can do so by using the GNU Emacs command shell.

To see how the shell command works in GNU Emacs, press M-x (pressing Esc, followed by x). GNU Emacs displays `M-x` in the minibuffer and waits for further input. Type **shell**, and press Enter. GNU Emacs starts a new shell process and displays the shell prompt in the GNU Emacs window. Type any shell command that you want. The output appears in the GNU Emacs window.

You can continue to use the shell for as long as you need it. All output from the commands goes into the window where the shell prompt appears. If you no longer need the shell, type **exit**. That command terminates the shell process and returns you to GNU Emacs.

If you want to run a single shell command, use the `M-!` key binding. If you press M-!, GNU Emacs displays the following prompt in the minibuffer:

```
Shell command:
```

Type a shell command (such as `ls -l`), and press Enter. GNU Emacs executes that command and displays the resulting output in a separate window. To revert to a single-window display, type **C-x 1**. (That command is Ctrl-x, followed by the number 1.) The command instructs GNU Emacs to delete the other windows (excluding the one that contains the cursor).

If you're in the mood for a lighthearted quote, type **M-x yow,** and Emacs displays a quote from Zippy the Pinhead in the minibuffer. Each time that you type this command, Emacs displays a different quote.

Writing man Pages with groff

Before the days of graphical interfaces, typesetting with the computer meant preparing a text file containing embedded typesetting commands and then processing that marked-up text file with a computer program that generated commands for the output device: a printer or some other typesetter.

As you know, such markup languages still exist. A prime example is HyperText Markup Language (HTML), which you use to prepare World Wide Web pages.

In the late 1970s and early 1980s, I prepared all my correspondence and reports on a DEC VAX/VMS system, using a program named RUNOFF. That program formatted output for a line printer or a daisy-wheel printer. That VAX/VMS RUNOFF program accepted embedded commands such as the following:

```
.page size 58,80
.spacing 2
.no autojustify
```

As you may guess, the first command sets the number of lines per page and the number of characters on each line. The second command generates double-spaced output. The last command turns off justification. Essentially, I'd pepper a text file with these commands, run it through RUNOFF, and send RUNOFF's output to the line printer. The resulting output looked as good as a typewritten document, which was good enough for most work in those days.

UNIX came with a more advanced typesetting program called troff (which stands for *typesetting runoff*) that could send output to a special device called a *typesetter*. A typesetter could produce much better output than a line printer. troff enables you to choose different fonts and to print text in bold and italic.

To handle output on simpler printers, UNIX also included nroff (which stands for *nontypesetting runoff*) to process troff files and generate output, to ignore fancy output commands, and to generate output on a line printer. troff typesetting is versatile enough that many computer books were typeset by using troff.

Now that nearly every computer offers some sort of graphical interface (Microsoft Windows, Apple Macintosh, or GNOME and KDE in Linux), most word-processing programs work in WYSIWYG (what you see is what you get) mode, in which you get to work directly with the formatted document. You probably don't have any reason, therefore, to use troff for typesetting. You still use nroff for one important task, however: preparing man pages. The remainder of this chapter focuses on that aspect of using nroff.

insider insight

The groff program is the GNU version of troff and nroff. By using appropriate flags, you can use groff to typeset for several output devices, including any typewriter-like device.

Even if you don't use groff to prepare formatted documents (because using a PC-based word processor is more convenient), you may end up using groff to write the man page for any program that you write.

Man pages are the files that contain the information that users can view by typing the command `man progname`. This command shows online Help information on progname. The subject of a man page can be anything from an overview of a software package to the programming information for a specific C function. (Try typing `man fopen`, for example, on your Linux system.)

After you go through an example, you realize that writing man pages in groff is quite simple.

note

Before reading about the man page preparation process, understand that you don't really use the groff program to prepare the man page. The man page is just a text file containing embedded commands that groff recognizes. You may use groff to view a man page during preparation, but you can prepare a man page without ever running groff.

Trying an Existing man Page

Before you write a man page, look at an existing man page. A brief example is the man page for `zless`. Figure 11-5 shows the man page for `zless` in a terminal window.

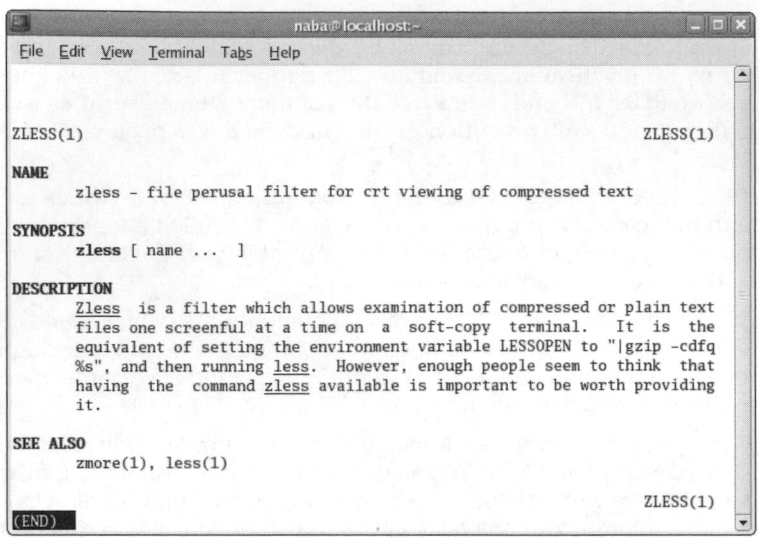

Figure 11-5: Output of the man zless Command in a Terminal Window.

The output of the `man zless` command may appear garbled if the `LANG` environment variable is set to use UTF-8 encoding for characters and the terminal window is unable to handle the UTF-8 encoding for characters such as the hyphen. To check the setting of `LANG`, type **locale** and look at the setting for `LANG`. For example, on my system (in the United States), the value of `LANG` is as follows:

```
LANG=en_US.UTF-8
```

In this case, the language is U.S. English with UTF-8 encoding. To fix the problem, I redefine `LANG` as plain U.S. English (represented by the code `en_US`):

```
export LANG=en_US
```

To reset `LANG` for the entire system, I edit the `/etc/sysconfig/i18n` file such that it contains the line:

```
LANG="en_US"
```

If the output of the `man` command is garbled on your system, try making similar changes to the `LANG` variable to correct the problem (the exact setting of `LANG` depends on your language — the garbling problem should disappear if you select a language name that does not end with `.UTF-8`).

Returning to the example of the man page for the `zless` command, you don't really need to pay attention to the exact content of the man page; all you care about is the layout. Take a moment to look at the layout and notice the following points:

- The name of the command appears at the top of the man page. The number `1` that appears in parentheses next to the command's name denotes the section of the UNIX manual where this command belongs.

- The man page contains several sections, each of which appears in boldface. The text within the section is indented.
- In this example, the sections are NAME, SYNOPSIS, DESCRIPTION, and SEE ALSO. If you try a few more man pages, you see that some man pages have many more sections. Almost all man pages, however, have these four sections.
- Some text appears in boldface.

Looking at a man Page Source

After you view a man page by using the `man` command, you should look at the original source file from which the `man` command generates the output. In your Linux system, the man page source files are in several directories. The `/etc/man.config` file defines these directory names.

The source file for the `zless` man page is `/usr/share/man/man1/zless.1.gz`. Look at this file to see how the man page appears in its final form, which is shown in Figure 11-5. This is the source file for the `zless` man page:

```
zless /usr/share/man/man1/zless.1
.TH ZLESS 1
.SH NAME
zless \- file perusal filter for crt viewing of compressed text
.SH SYNOPSIS
.B zless
[ name ...  ]
.SH DESCRIPTION
.I  Zless
is a filter which allows examination of compressed or plain text files
one screenful at a time on a soft-copy terminal.  It is the equivalent of
setting the environment variable LESSOPEN to "|gzip -cdfq %s",
and then running
.IR less .
However, enough people seem to think that having the
command
.I zless
available is important to be worth providing it.
.SH "SEE ALSO"
zmore(1), less(1)
```

One interesting feature of the marked-up text file for the man page is the haphazard manner in which lines break. The formatting program groff (the `man` command uses groff to process the marked-up text file) fills up the lines of text and makes everything presentable.

Most groff commands must appear on a line by themselves, and each such command starts with a period or a dot. You can, however, embed some groff font-control commands in the text; these embedded commands start with a backslash (\).

Following is a summary of the commands that you see in the `zless` man page source file:

- **.B** turns on boldface.
- **.I** turns on italic.
- **.SH** is the start of a new section.
- **.TH** indicates the document title.

If you use these dot commands (meaning commands that begin with a period or dot) to change the font, the man page source file tends to display many short lines because each dot command must appear on a separate line. As the following section shows, you can use embedded font-change commands to produce a more readable source file.

Writing a Sample man Page

This section shows you how to write a man page for a sample application by the name of satview. Assume that the satview program displays a satellite image in a window. The program includes some options for specifying the map projection, the zoom level, and the name of the file that contains the satellite image data.

Use a text editor to type the man page source code shown in the following listing and save it in a file named `satview.1`:

```
.TH SATVIEW 1 "April 19, 2005" "Satview Version 12.1"
.SH NAME
satview \- View satellite images.
.SH SYNOPSIS
\fBsatview\fP [-p \fIprojection\fP] [-m] [-z \fIzoomlevel\fP]
\fIfilename\fP
.SH DESCRIPTION
\fBsatview\fP displays the satellite image from \fIfilename\fP.
.SS Options
.TP
\fB-p \fIprojection\fR
Set the map projection (can be \fBL\fR for Lambert Conformal or
\fBP\fR for Polar Stereographic). The default is Lambert Conformal.
.TP
\fB-m\fP
Include a map in the satellite image.
.TP
\fB-z \fIzoomlevel\fR
Set the zoom level (can be one of: 2, 4, or 8). The default
zoomlevel is 1.
.TP
\fIfilename\fR
File containing satellite data.
.SH FILES
.TP
\fC/etc/awips/satview.rc\fR
Initialization commands for \fBsatview\fR
.SH SEE ALSO
nexrad(1), contour(1)
.SH Bugs
At zoom levels greater than 2, map is not properly
aligned with image.
```

The source file of a man page contains the following significant features:

- The `.TH` tag indicates the man page title as well as the date and a version-number string. In the formatted man page, the version and date strings appear at the bottom of each page.
- This man page has six sections — `NAME`, `SYNOPSIS`, `DESCRIPTION`, `FILES`, `SEE ALSO`, and `Bugs` — each of which starts with the `.SH` tag.
- The `DESCRIPTION` section has an `Options` subsection. The `.SS` tag indicates the beginning of a subsection.
- In the `Options` subsection, each item is listed with the `.TP` tag.
- The `\fB` command changes the font to boldface.
- `\fI` changes the font to italic.
- `\fR` changes the font to Roman.
- `\fP` changes the font to its preceding setting.

With this information in hand, you should understand the man page source listing.

Testing and Installing the man Page

As you prepare the man page file, you want to make sure that it's formatted correctly. To view the formatted output, use the following command:

```
groff -Tascii -man satview.1 | more
```

This command runs the `groff` command with the `ascii` typesetting device (which means that it produces plain ASCII output) and with the man page macro set (that's what the `-man` option does).

If you find any formatting discrepancies, check the dot commands and any embedded font-change commands, and make sure that everything looks right.

After you're satisfied with the man page format, you can make the man page available to everyone by copying the file to one of the directories in which all man pages reside. Log in as root and install the man page by using the following copy command:

```
cp satview.1 /usr/share/man/man1
```

After that, try the man page by using this command:

```
man satview
```

Figure 11-6 shows the resulting output. Compare the output with the source file listing shown in the preceding section, "Writing a Sample man Page," to see the effects of the commands on the final output. The italic command generates underlined output because the terminal window can't display an italic font.

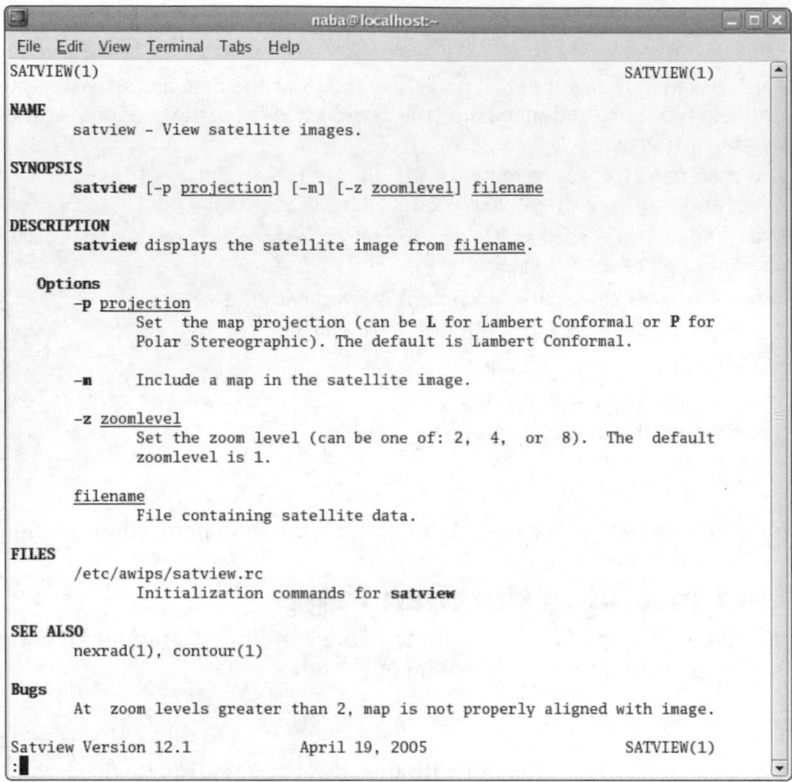

Figure 11-6: Output of the man satview Command in a Terminal Window.

Using the listing in this section as a guide, you can now write your own man pages.

Preparing Documentation with DocBook

The tradition of preparing formatted documentation using markup languages lives on. For example, the documentation for many open source software packages come in DocBook format. The remainder of this chapter briefly introduces you to DocBook and points you to sources where you can learn more about preparing documentation in DocBook.

DocBook is a vocabulary — a set of tags, kind of like HTML tags — for writing structured documents such as books and articles (anything that has chapters, sections, subsections, appendixes, and so forth). The DocBook vocabulary is defined in both Standard Generalized Markup Language (SGML) and the newer Extensible Markup Language (XML). Such vocabularies are formally known as Document Type Definition (DTD). Thus, DocBook is available as an SGML or XML DTD. You don't need to understand SGML or XML to use DocBook.

DocBook is gaining popularity as a markup language for documentation of open source projects such as GNOME and KDE. The publishing firm, O'Reilly & Associates, has also used DocBook to produce books. DocBook is edging out other markup languages such as Troff and LaTeX because the DocBook syntax is well defined and easy to parse, which means that there are automated tools available to convert from DocBook format to many different types of presentation formats such as HTML for displaying on a Web browser and PostScript for printing. Another key property of DocBook is that it only lays out the structure of a document; the final formatting and presentation of the document depend on stylesheets. This enables you to generate different output formats from the same logical DocBook document.

DocBook was created in 1991 by HaL Computer Systems and O'Reilly & Associates. The DocBook DTD is now maintained by Organization for the Advancement of Structured Information Standards (OASIS). You can find more information about DocBook at `www.oasis-open.org/committees/docbook/`.

For a good book on DocBook, consult *DocBook: The Definitive Guide* by Norman Walsh and Leonard Muellner (O'Reilly & Associates).

Getting Started with DocBook

To start using DocBook, all you need are the following:

- **A text editor** to edit the DocBook file. Although automated tools can ease the burden of preparing DocBook files, you can create a DocBook using a plain text editor.
- **DocBook DTD** that defines the XML or SGML tags used to write the DocBook.
- **DocBook stylesheets**, such as the ones written in Extensible Stylesheet Language (XSL), that enable translation of DocBook from SGML or XML into other formats such as HTML, RTF, PDF, and so on.
- **Stylesheet processor** such as xsltproc that uses the stylesheets to convert the DocBook SGML or XML into other formats such as HTML.

Linux comes with everything you need to get started with DocBook. In particular, you find both the SGML and XML DTDs for DocBook. The `/usr/share/sgml/docbook` directory contains the SGML and XML DTDs for different versions of DocBook as well as DocBook stylesheets.

Trying Out a Sample DocBook

The best way to understand DocBook is to simply try out a sample file. You can see how the same DocBook file can be used to generate different output formats.

Use a text editor and prepare the file `sample.xml` with the following lines in it:

```
<?xml version="1.0"?>
<!DOCTYPE article PUBLIC "-//OASIS//DTD DocBook XML V4.2//EN"
"http://www.oasis-open.org/docbook/xml/4.2/docbookx.dtd">
<article>
  <articleinfo>
    <title>Sample DocBook</title>
```

```
</articleinfo>
<para>This is a sample DocBook article that illustrates
     some simple DocBook XML tags.
</para>
<sect1>
  <title>Section 1</title>
  <para>Paragraph 1 of section 1</para>
  <sect2>
    <title>Section 1.1</title>
    <para>Paragraph 1 of section 1.1</para>
    <para>Paragraph 2 of section 1.1</para>
  </sect2>
  <sect2>
    <title>Section 1.2</title>
    <para>Paragraph 1 of section 1.2</para>
  </sect2>
</sect1>
<sect1>
  <title>Section 2</title>
  <para>Second high-level section in this article
  </para>
</sect1>
</article>
```

After you save the sample.xml file, you can use the xmllint utility to check if all the XML tags in the file are correct. Type the following command to check the syntax of the sample.xml file:

```
xmllint --valid --noout sample.xml
```

If everything is okay, the utility should print nothing.

Now, you can convert the sample.xml file into HTML and view it in a Web browser. To perform this task, type the following commands:

```
export DBS="/usr/share/sgml/docbook/xsl-stylesheets-1.68.1-1"

xsltproc -o sample.html $DBS/html/docbook.xsl sample.xml
```

The first command defines the DBS environment variable as the directory where the XSL stylesheets for DocBook are located in Fedora Linux. The second command runs xsltproc with appropriate options to convert the sample.xml file into sample.html.

Now, you can open the sample.html file in the Web browser and see how the document looks. Figure 11-7 shows the sample.html file in Firefox.

As Figure 11-7 shows, the DocBook is converted into a single HTML file with a table of contents at the beginning of the document. The table of contents includes links for each section and subsection.

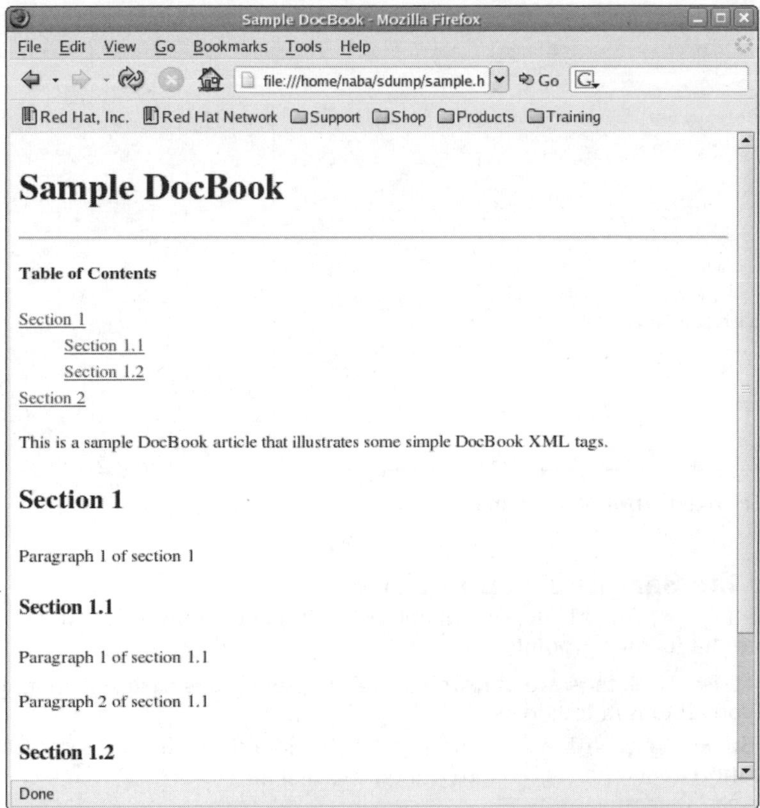

Figure 11-7: Displaying an HTML Version of a Sample DocBook in a Web Browser.

You can also create a set of linked HTML files, one for each section. This is called chunked HTML because each section becomes a chunk. To create chunked HTML files from the `sample.xml` DocBook, type the following command (I assume that you still have the DBS environment variable defined, as shown earlier in this section):

```
xsltproc $DBS/html/chunk.xsl sample.xml
```

This generates an `index.html` file and separate HTML files for the other chunks (sections). Figure 11-8 shows the HTML chunk for section 2 of the sample DocBook.

The chunked HTML output is widely used for much open source documentation, so Figure 11-8 should look familiar to you. Note that each HTML chunk contains Next, Prev, and Up links to go from section to section and go back to the first page.

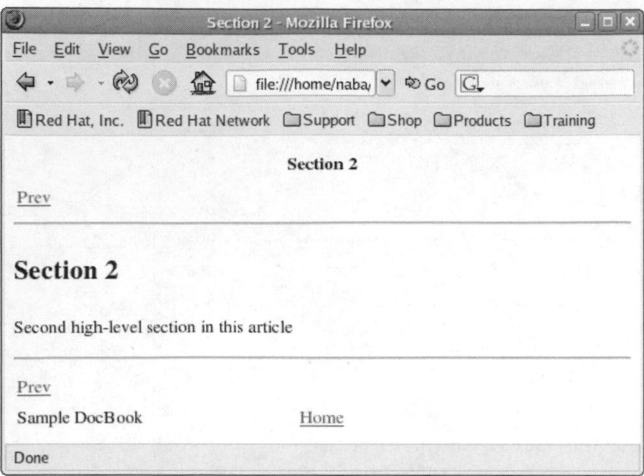

Figure 11-8: Chunked HTML Version of DocBook.

Examining the Sample DocBook File

If you examine the `sample.xml` file, shown in the "Trying out a Sample DocBook" section, you should note the following points:

- All XML DocBook tags are in lowercase. Because XML is case sensitive, you must type all tags in lowercase.
- A DocBook begins with a standard header that identifies the XML version and information about the DTD. Here is a typical header:

```
<?xml version="1.0"?>
<!DOCTYPE article PUBLIC "-//OASIS//DTD DocBook XML V4.1.2//EN"
"http://www.oasis-open.org/docbook/xml/4.1.2/docbookx.dtd">
```

- Usually the entire DocBook is a `<book>` or an `<article>`. The `sample.xml` file uses an `<article>` structure.
- An `<article>` is composed of nested section elements such as `<sect1>`, `<sect2>`, and so on.
- A `<book>` is composed of multiple `<chapter>` elements, each with section elements inside.
- As with other markup languages, all indentations and white spaces are ignored, except for some elements such as `<programlisting>` and `<literallayout>` that are meant to show verbatim text.

Using Stylesheets

DocBook documents contain only the logical layout of the document. Stylesheets define how to convert a DocBook document into various formatted output. There are two sets of stylesheets:

- **XSLT:** Stands for Extensible Stylesheet Language (XSL) Transformations, which is a language used to convert XML documents into other XML documents. XSLT can convert DocBook XML into HTML, HTML Help, Java Help, XHTML, and XSL formatting objects.
- **DSSSL:** Stands for Document Style Semantics and Specification Language. The DSSSL stylesheets can convert DocBook SGML and XML into HTML, MIF, RTF, and TeX files.

Other tools can convert some of these formats such as XSL formatting objects or TeX into other formats such as PDF and PostScript.

Linux comes with both XSL and DSSL stylesheets. These stylesheets are located in subdirectories of the `/usr/share/sgml/docbook` directory.

You can use the following stylesheet utilities to convert DocBook files into formatted output files:

- **xmllint:** Checks for correct syntax of a document. Typically, you can check the correctness of an XML file with the following command:

  ```
  xmllint --valid --noout xmlfilename
  ```

- **xsltproc:** Applies XSLT stylesheets to XML documents. A typical command line is of the following form:

  ```
  xsltproc stylesheetname xmlfilename
  ```

  Thus, if you want to apply the stylesheet `mystyles.xls` to the `mydoc.xml` file, you would use the following command:

  ```
  xsltproc mystyles.xsl sample.xml
  ```

Learning Some DocBook Elements

There are close to 400 DocBook elements in version 4.2. This chapter does not have enough space to cover them in detail. This section briefly touches upon some of the commonly used elements, especially those that you may want to use when writing documentation that you intend to convert to HTML.

insider insight For a detailed, online reference to DocBook elements, point your Web browser to www.docbook.org/tdg/en/html/ref-elements.html.

Sections

Sections are a key organizing element in a DocBook. You can define sections either through specific numbered tags `<sect1>` through `<sect5>`, or through generic `<section>` tags nested inside one another.

When you use the specific section tags `<sect1>` through `<sect5>`, the higher numbered sections are subsections of the lower numbered ones. With these tags, a complex layout of sections would be similar to the following:

```
<sect1>
   <sect2>
```

```
            <sect3>...</sect3>
            <sect3>
                <sect4>
                    <sect5>...</sect5>
                    <sect5>...</sect5>
                </sect4>
                <sect4>...</sect4>
            </sect3>
        </sect2>
        <sect2>...</sect2>
    </sect1>
    <sect1>...</sect1>
```

On the other hand, when you use generic <section> tags, the layout is written in the following form:

```
<section>
    <section>
        <section> ... </section>
        <section> ... </section>
    </section>
    <section> ... </section>
</section>
```

Itemized List

Use the <itemizedlist> element to create a bulleted list. Such lists map to the ones created with the <ul> tag in HTML. Inside the list, use <listitem> elements to define entries in the list. Here is an example:

```
<itemizedlist mark='opencircle'>
  <listitem><para>SGML</para></listitem>
  <listitem><para>HTML B</para></listitem>
  <listitem><para>XML C</para></listitem>
</itemizedlist>
```

Use the <itemizedlist> element's mark attribute to specify the appearance of the bullets. You can also have other DocBook elements inside the <listitem> elements.

Ordered List

Use the <orderedlist> element to define a numbered list that maps to the lists displayed by the <ol> tag in HTML. Use the <listitem> element to specify each entry in the ordered list, as shown in this example:

```
<orderedlist>
  <listitem><para>Step 1</para></listitem>
  <listitem><para>Step 2</para></listitem>
  <listitem><para>Step 3</para></listitem>
</orderedlist>
```

Variable List

Use the <variablelist> element to create a list of terms and their definitions. The <variablelist> maps to a list displayed by the <dl> tag in HTML. Inside the variable list, the <varlistentry> element contains the term, identified by the <term> element, and the definition, identified by a <listitem>. Here is an example:

```
<variablelist>
  <title>File Name Extensions</title>
  <varlistentry>
    <term>txt</term>
    <listitem><para>Text file.</para></listitem>
  </varlistentry>
  <varlistentry>
    <term>xml</term>
    <listitem><para>XML file</para></listitem>
  </varlistentry>
</variablelist>
```

Image and Multimedia Elements

You might want to insert screen shots or other images into the documentation. You can do so with the <mediaobject> and <imageobject> elements. You have to place the <imageobject> element inside a <mediaobject>. A simple example is as follows:

```
<mediaobject>
  <imageobject>
    <imagedata fileref="imagefile.jpg" format="JPG"/>
  </imageobject>
  <textobject>
    <phrase>Description of image</phrase>
  </textobject>
</mediaobject>
```

Use the <imagedata> element to specify the image file and format. You can associate an alternate text description of the image by adding a <textobject> element, as shown in this example.

Tables

Use the <table> element, along with <thead>, <row>, and <entry> elements to define tables in DocBook. The following example illustrates how all these elements fit together:

```
<table>
  <title>Sample Table</title>
  <tgroup cols="2">
    <thead>
      <row>
        <entry>Fruit</entry>
        <entry>Color</entry>
      </row>
    </thead>
    <tbody>
```

```
      <row>
        <entry>Apple</entry>
        <entry>Red</entry>
      </row>
      <row>
        <entry>Banana</entry>
        <entry>Yellow</entry>
      </row>
    </tbody>
  </tgroup>
</table>
```

As you can see, the table's content is inside a <tgroup> element that specifies the number of columns. Each row is defined by a <row> element that contains as many <entry> elements as there are columns.

DocBook also includes an <informaltable> element that defines a table without any title.

Figures

Use the <figure> element to add figures to documents. The figure will be numbered and have a title. You can use the <informalfigure> element for a figure that does not need a number and a title. Here is an example of a figure:

```
<figure>
  <title>AWIPS Software Architecture</title>
  <mediaobject>
    <imageobject>
      <imagedata fileref="awips-swarch.jpg" format="JPG"/>
    </imageobject>
  </mediaobject>
</figure>
```

Inside the <figure> element, you can embed the figure using a <mediaobject> and an <imageobject>, as shown in the example.

Examples

Software documentation often requires the inclusion of sample code. Use the <example> tag to show such samples. Such examples have a title and are numbered. Use the <informalexample> element for examples that do not need titles and do not have to be numbered. Here is an <example> element:

```
<example>
  <title>Sample Java Code</title>
  <programlisting>
public class HelloWorld {
    public static void main(String [] args) {
        System.out.println("Hello, World!");
    }
}
  </programlisting>
</example>
```

Enclose the program listing in a <programlisting> element, as shown in this example.

Notes, Tips, and Warnings

You may also want to include notes, tips, and warnings in documentation (just as this and many other books do). DocBook includes several elements for this purpose. Here are the relevant DocBook elements:

- **Note:** Use the `<note>` element for notes, as shown here:

  ```
  <note><para>This is a note.</para></note>
  ```

- **Tip:** Use the `<tip>` element to add a tip in the text, like this:

  ```
  <tip><para>This is a tip.</para></tip>
  ```

- **Warning:** Use the `<warning>` element to add a warning message, like this:

  ```
  <warning><para>This is a warning.</para></warning>
  ```

- **Caution:** Use the `<caution>` element to add cautionary messages, like this:

  ```
  <caution><para>This is a caution.</para></caution>
  ```

- **Important:** Use the `<important>` element to set aside any important message, like this:

  ```
  <important><para>This is important.</para></important>
  ```

Character Formatting

Within the running text in a paragraph, you may want to emphasize some text. You can do so with the `<emphasis>` element. For example, here's how you can set apart a word in a paragraph:

```
<para>
  This is the <emphasis>most important</emphasis> part of this sentence.
</para>
```

You can use the `<filename>` element to set apart filenames that occur in the text. Here is an example:

```
<para>
The XSL stylesheets for DocBook are located in the
<filename class='directory'>
  /usr/share/sgml/docbook/xsl-stylesheets-1.58.1-1
</filename> directory.
</para>
```

Software documentation also mentions commands — names of executable files — in text. To set such commands apart from the rest of the text, use the `<command>` element, as shown in the following example:

```
<para>
Type the
<command>ls -l</command> get a detailed directory listing.
</para>
```

Links

You can embed links to internal DocBook elements in a document as well as external websites and other resources. Use the <link> element to point to an internal link identified by the id attribute added to other elements. For example, suppose that you have an Introduction section, defined as follows:

```
<sect1 id="intro">
<title>Introduction</title>
<para> ... </para>
</sect1>
```

Elsewhere in the document, you can then use the <link> element to set up a link to this Introduction section, like this:

```
<para>See the <link linkend="intro">Introduction section</link>
for more information </para>
```

Use the <link> element's linkend attribute to identify the target of this link. That target should be identified by the id attribute of another element in the document.

To define an external link, use the <ulink> element. For example, here is how you can show a link to the DocBook home page:

```
<para>
To learn more about DocBook, visit the
<ulink url="http://www.docbook.org/">Docbook home page</ulink>
</para>
```

Use the <ulink> element's url attribute to specify the URL of the external link.

Summary

The configuration of many Linux features depends on settings that you store in text files. You must, therefore, know how to edit text files to set up and maintain a Linux system. Another form of text processing involves typesetting and formatting text documents. Linux includes groff for this purpose. Nowadays, you're likely to use a PC to prepare formatted documents, but you still need to prepare one kind of formatted document: the man pages that provide online help for any software that you write. Accordingly, this chapter shows you how to use several text editors. It also shows you how to prepare man pages by using groff.

By reading this chapter, you learned the following:

- Linux includes a variety of text editors. Learning the ed and vi editors is important because all UNIX systems come with these editors. Although the ed editor may seem cryptic, you may need to use it to edit files if no other editor is available.
- The ed editor works on a text file one line at a time (which is why it's called a line editor). Each command takes the form of a range of lines, followed by a one-character command that applies to that range of lines.
- The vi editor is a full-screen editor that enables you to view a file several lines at a time. The vi editor has three modes: visual-command mode, colon-command mode, and text-input mode.
- In vi's text-input mode, you can enter text. To change to text-input mode, press i, a, or A. To return to command mode, press Esc.

- In vi's colon-command mode, you enter a colon (:) followed by a command that uses the same syntax as ed commands.
- GNU Emacs is more than just an editor—it's also an environment from which you can perform most routine tasks.
- As an editor, GNU Emacs doesn't have any modes; whatever you type goes into the file. Commands begin with a control character (such as Ctrl-x) or Esc.
- To view the online tutorial, type **C-h t** in GNU Emacs.
- The groff utility is useful for formatting documents. groff provides the functionality of the standard UNIX nroff and troff utilities. You must use groff to prepare man pages.
- The best way to learn to prepare a man page is to study an existing man page and mimic its style in your own man page. This chapter provided an example of how you can prepare a typical man page.
- DocBook is a markup language for structured document layout. DocBook is defined using SGML or XML Document Type Definitions (DTDs). Linux comes with DocBook DTDs and stylesheets. This chapter showed you how to get started with DocBook.

Basic System Administration

Chapter 12

Secrets in This Chapter

This chapter introduces you to some Linux system administration tasks. You learn to perform many of these system administration tasks by using graphical tools as well as commands. You can access many of these graphical utilities from the Desktop ➪ System Settings menu in the GNOME desktop.

First, you learn how to manage users and groups by using User Manager as well as text commands. Then you explore tasks available from the Desktop ➪ System Settings menu. This overview of the Desktop ➪ System Settings menu should help you perform other system-administration tasks as the need arises.

Because you typically install Linux on a PC that previously had Microsoft Windows installed on it, a common system-administration task is to access the Windows files from Linux. This chapter shows you how to mount and access DOS/Windows disks, including floppy disks. You learn about a kernel module for the NTFS file system that enables you to read from Windows XP partitions that use the NTFS file system.

You also learn about a package by the name of mtools that enables you to access and use (copy, delete, and format) MS-DOS files (typically, on a floppy disk) in Linux.

Revisiting Linux System Administration

Chapter 1 provides an overview of the tasks involved in Linux system administration. In this chapter, you briefly revisit the key tasks that you perform as a system administrator, learning where, in this book, you can find more information about a specific task. System administration is essentially the work required to keep your Linux system working properly.

You can group the tasks into two broad categories: system administration and network administration. The first category refers to keeping the system itself up and running, while network administration focuses on the LAN and Internet services.

Typical system and network administration tasks include the following:

- **Adding and removing users:** This chapter shows you how to add or remove user accounts using User Manager and the `useradd` and `userdel` commands.
- **Managing the printing system:** You have to turn the print queue on or off, check the print queue's status, and delete print jobs if necessary. Chapter 4 describes how to set up printers and manage the print queues.
- **Installing, configuring, and upgrading the operating system and various utilities:** Chapter 2 covers how to install Linux, and Chapters 4 through 6 focus on how to configure and set up specific hardware in Linux. Chapter 21 describes how to upgrade or reconfigure the Linux kernel.
- **Installing new software:** Chapter 21 shows you how to use the Red Hat Package Manager (RPM) as well as the Package Management GUI tool to install software. In that chapter, you also learn how to unpack and build software from source archives that you can download from various Internet sites.
- **Making backups:** Chapter 20 covers backing up and restoring files and directories by using the GNU tar utility.
- **Mounting and unmounting file systems:** The `mount` and `umount` commands appear in various chapters, such as Chapters 8 and 10. This chapter shows you how to mount MS-DOS file systems. You also learn to use the mtools utilities to access Windows/DOS files.

- **Monitoring the system's performance:** This chapter describes a few utilities for monitoring system performance. I describe this topic further in Chapter 20.
- **Starting and shutting down the system:** Chapter 7 describes how to start and shut down your Linux system.
- **Maintaining the network configuration files:** Chapter 6 describes various TCP/IP configuration files.
- **Setting up PPP dialup networking:** You learn about PPP dialup networks in Chapter 13.
- **Monitoring network status:** Chapter 6 presents some utility programs that you can use as network diagnostic tools.
- **Setting up host and network security:** You have to protect the system files and your network against attacks from the outside. Chapter 22 describes how to secure your system and Internet services.
- **Monitoring security:** — You have to keep an eye on any intrusions, usually by checking the log files. Chapter 22 covers this topic.

note

As you can see from the comments next to the items in the list of system administration tasks, I cover many of these system administration topics in other chapters of this book. For topics covered elsewhere, please turn to the referenced chapter for more information.

Becoming root

You have to be logged in as `root` to perform the system administration tasks. The `root` user is the superuser and has the only account with all the privileges needed to do anything in the system.

The common wisdom is that you should not normally log in as `root`. That's because when you're `root`, one misstep and you could easily delete all the files—especially when typing commands. Take, for example, the command `rm *.html` that you may type to delete all files with the `.html` extension. Unfortunately, if you accidentally press the Spacebar after the asterisk (*), the shell takes the command to be `rm * .html` and, because `*` matches any file name, deletes everything in the current directory. That sort of thing can happen, and the damage from any mistakes is much bigger when you are logged in as `root`.

You should log in as a normal user and become `root` only when needed. Another advantage of this approach is that there will be an entry in the `/var/log/messages` file every time a user becomes `root` (only those who know the root password can become `root`). Those entries in the `/var/log/messages` file can serve as an audit trail of who became superuser when and did what.

Using the su - Command

If you are logged in as a normal user and need to become root, type the following command at a terminal window or console:

```
su -
```

Then enter the root password in response to the prompt. From this point on, you're root. Do whatever you have to do. To return back to your usual self, type:

```
exit
```

It's that easy to switch between being a normal user and root.

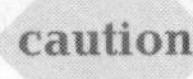

You should always type `su -` to become root rather than typing `su`. The `su -` command changes the environment to root's default environment settings whereas `su` alone retains the current user's environment, which may contain unsafe settings for environment variables.

Becoming Root for the GUI Utilities

If you use any of Fedora's GUI utilities to perform a system administration chore, it's even easier. Typically, the utility pops up a dialog box that prompts you for the root password (see Figure 12-1). Just type the root password and press Enter. The GUI utility should then start. If you don't want to use the utility, click Cancel.

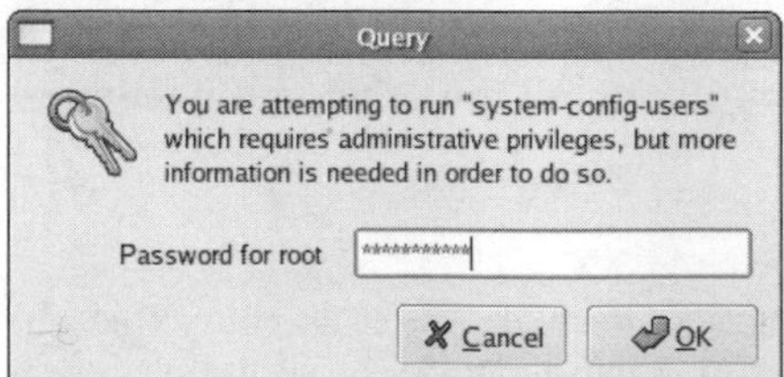

Figure 12-1: Providing the Root Password for GUI Tools That Need root Privileges.

Recovering from a Forgotten Root Password

To perform system administration tasks, you have to know the root password. What happens if you forget the root password? There is a way to recover from a forgotten root password. Just reboot the PC and you can reset the root password. Simply follow these steps:

1. Reboot the PC (select Reboot as you log out of the GUI screen) or power up as usual. Soon, you see the graphical GRUB screen with the names of operating systems you can boot. (If you have a GRUB password, press p and enter the GRUB password now.)
2. Press a (just the letter "a"). GRUB prompts you for commands to add to its default boot command.

3. Press the Spacebar, type the following word, and then press Enter:

```
single
```

This causes Linux to start up as usual, but run in a single-user mode that does not require you to log in. After Linux starts, you see the following command-line prompt:

```
sh-3.00#
```

4. Use the `passwd` command to change the root password as follows:

```
sh-3.00# passwd
Changing password for user root.
New UNIX password: (type the new root password)
```

Type the new root password that you want to use (it won't appear onscreen), and then press Enter. Linux asks for the password again, like this:

```
Retype new UNIX password:  (retype the new root password)
```

Type the password again, and press Enter. If you enter the same password both times, the `passwd` command changes the password and displays the following message:

```
passwd: all authentication tokens updated successfully.
```

5. Now, type **exit** or **reboot** to reboot the PC. After Linux starts, it displays the familiar login screen. Now, you should be able to log in as `root` with the new password.

caution

Make sure that your Linux PC is physically secure. As this procedure shows, anyone who can physically access your Linux PC can simply reboot, set a new root password, and do whatever they want with the system. Having a password for the GRUB boot loader can provide an extra level of protection, but also another password to remember.

Managing User Accounts

Adding user accounts to the system is a key system-administration function. You get the chance to add user accounts when you boot Linux for the first time. If you didn't add other user accounts at that time, you can do so now. You can use the User Manager or the `useradd` command to add a new user account to your system.

insider insight

A good idea is to create other user accounts besides root. Even if you're the only user of the system, logging in as a less-privileged user is good practice, because you can't damage any important system files inadvertently. If necessary, you can type the `su -` command to log in as `root` and perform any system-administration tasks.

Using User Manager to Add User Accounts

You can use the User Manager to add user accounts. To start the User Manager, select Desktop ➪ System Settings ➪ Users and Groups from the GNOME desktop's top panel. If you're not logged in as `root`, the User Manager prompts you for the root password. You can enter the password and click OK; then the User Manager window appears.

The window shows two tabs: Users and Groups (see Figure 12-2). The Users tab displays the current list of users from the `/etc/passwd` file. The Groups tab lists the name of groups from the `/etc/group` file. Initially, the User Manager filters out any system users and groups. However, you can turn off the filer by unchecking Preferences ➪ Filter system users and groups. Figure 12-2 shows the User Manager window with a listing of all user accounts, including the system ones.

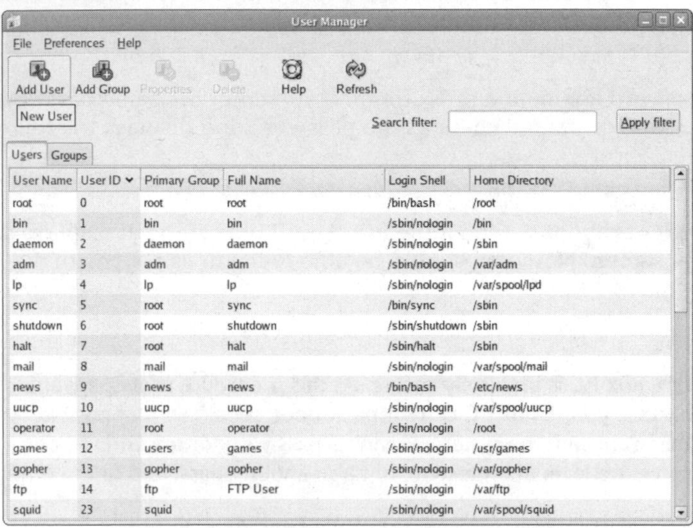

Figure 12-2: User Manager Window.

You can add new users and groups or edit existing users and groups from the User Manager. To edit the information for an existing user, click the user name in the list in the Users tab, and then click the Properties button on the toolbar. That user's information appears in a User Properties dialog box. You can then edit the information and click OK to make the changes.

To add a new user, click the New User button on the toolbar. This action opens the Create New User dialog box, as shown in Figure 12-3.

Fill in the requested information. In particular, you must enter the user name and the password. After filling in all the fields, click OK. The new user should now appear in the list on the Users tab in the User Manager window.

note

If you want to remove a user account, click the user name in the list on the Users tab that displays all user accounts (see Figure 12-2); then click the Delete button on the toolbar.

Figure 12-3: Entering Information for a New User.

Notice the checkbox labeled `Create a private group for the user` in Figure 12-3. It's checked by default, and that means each new user is in a separate private user group. However, sometimes you want a user to be in a specific group so that the user can access the files owned by that group. It's easy to add a user to another group. For example, suppose that I want to add the user name `naba` to the group called `wheel`. I can do this simply by typing the following command in a terminal window:

```
usermod -G wheel naba
```

If you simply uncheck that check box labeled `Create a private group for the user` (see Figure 12-3), the new user is assigned to the group named `users`. Type **more /etc/group** to see the group names and group ID.

Using Commands to Manage User Accounts

If you're working from a text console, you can create a new user account by using the `useradd` command. Follow these steps to add an account for a new user:

1. Log in as `root`. (If you're not already logged in as `root`, type **su -** to become root.)
2. Type the following `useradd` command with the `-c` option to create the account:

   ```
   /usr/sbin/useradd -c "Ashley Barkakati" ashley
   ```

3. Set Ashley's password by using the `passwd` command, as follows:

   ```
   passwd ashley
   Changing password for user ashley.
   New UNIX password: (Type the password and then press Enter.)
   Retype new UNIX password: (Type the password again and press Enter.)
   passwd: all authentication tokens updated successfully.
   ```

   Notice that, if you type a password that someone can easily guess, the `passwd` program rejects it.

The useradd command consults the files /etc/default/useradd and /etc/login.defs to obtain default information on various parameters for the new user account. The /etc/default/useradd file, for example, specifies the default shell (/bin/bash) and default home directory location (/home). The /etc/login.defs file provides systemwide defaults for automatic group and user IDs, as well as password expiration parameters.

You can delete a user account by using the userdel command. Simply type **userdel username** at the command prompt to delete a user's account. To wipe out that user's home directory as well, type **userdel -r username**.

To modify any information in a user account, use the usermod command. For example, if I want my user name, naba, to have root as the primary group, I would type:

```
usermod -g root naba
```

To learn more about the useradd and userdel commands, type **man useradd** or **man userdel** in a terminal window.

Understanding the /etc/passwd File

The /etc/passwd file is a list of all user accounts. It's a text file, and any user can read it; no special privileges are needed. Each line in /etc/passwd has seven fields, separated by colons (:).

Here is a typical entry from the /etc/passwd file:

```
naba:x:500:10:Naba Barkakati:/home/naba:/bin/bash
```

Figure 12-4 uses this typical entry to explain the meaning of the seven fields.

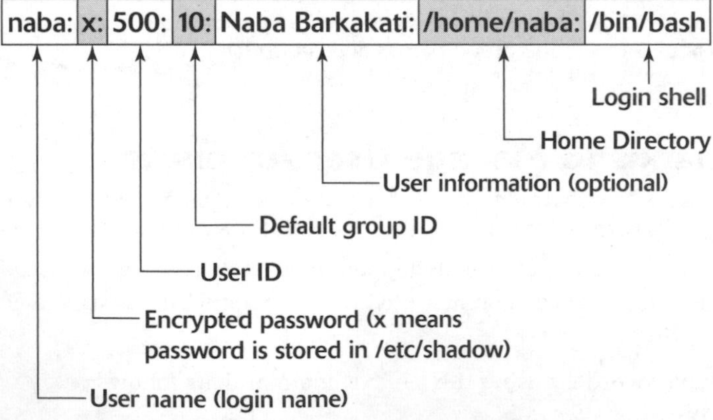

Figure 12-4: Meaning of Fields in a Typical /etc/passwd Entry.

As the example shows, the format of each line in /etc/passwd looks like this:

```
username:password:UID:GID:GECOS:homedir:shell
```

Table 12-1 explains the meaning of the seven fields in each `/etc/passwd` entry.

Table 12-1: Meaning of the Fields in the /etc/passwd File

Field	*Meaning*
`username`	An alphanumeric user name, usually eight characters long and unique. (Linux allows user names to be longer than eight characters, but some other operating systems do not.)
`password`	When present, a 13-character encrypted password. (An empty field means that no password is required to access the account; an `x` means the password is stored in the `/etc/shadow` file, which is more secure.)
`UID`	A unique number that serves as the user identifier. (`root` has a UID of 0 and usually the UIDs between 1 to 100 are reserved for nonhuman users, such as servers; it's best to keep the UID less than 32,767.)
`GID`	The default group ID (GID) of the group to which the user belongs. (GID 0 is for group root; other groups are defined in `/etc/group` and users can be and usually are in more than one group at a time.)
`GECOS`	Optional personal information about the user. (The `finger` command uses this field and GECOS stands for General Electric Comprehensive Operating System, a long-forgotten operating system that's immortalized by the name of this field in `/etc/passwd`.)
`homedir`	The name of the user's home directory.
`shell`	The command interpreter (shell) such as Bash (`/bin/bash`) that's executed when this user logs in.

Managing Groups

A group is something to which users belong. A group has a name and an identification number (GID). After a group is defined, users can belong to one or more of these groups.

You'll find all the existing groups listed in `/etc/group`. For example, here is the line that defines the group named `wheel`:

```
wheel:x:10:root,naba
```

As this example shows, each line in `/etc/group` has the following format with four fields separated by colons:

```
groupname:password:GID:membership
```

Table 12-2 explains the meaning of the four fields in a group definition.

Table 12-2: Meaning of Fields in /etc/group File

Field	*Meaning*
groupname	The name of the group (for example, wheel)
password	The group password (an x means the password is stored in the /etc/shadow file)
GID	The numerical group ID (for example, 10)
membership	A comma-separated list of users who belong to this group (for example, root,naba)

If you want to create a new group, you can simply click the Add Group button in the User Manager (see Figure 12-2). An even quicker way is to use the groupadd command. For example, to add a new group called class with an automatically selected group ID, just type the following command in a terminal window (you have to be logged in as root):

```
groupadd class
```

Then, you can add users to this group with the usermod command. For example, to add the users naba and ashley to the group named class, I type the following commands:

```
usermod -G class naba
usermod -G class ashley
```

That's it. Now I check /etc/group to find that it contains the following definition of class:

```
class:x:502:naba,ashley
```

If you want to remove a group, use the groupdel command. For example, to remove the group named class, type the following:

```
groupdel class
```

Exploring the Server Settings Menu

The Desktop ➪ Server Settings menu in the GNOME desktop provides access to options for performing many system- and network-administration tasks, including adding new users. This section provides an overview of some system-administration tasks that you can perform through the Desktop ➪ System Settings ➪ Server Settings menu (see Figure 12-5). The first two items in the Desktop menu serve the following purposes:

- **Preferences:** Displays options through which you can configure many aspects of the desktop
- **System Settings:** Enables you to perform many system-administration tasks through a number of menu options

To perform system-administration tasks, select the appropriate option from the Desktop ➪ System Settings menu.

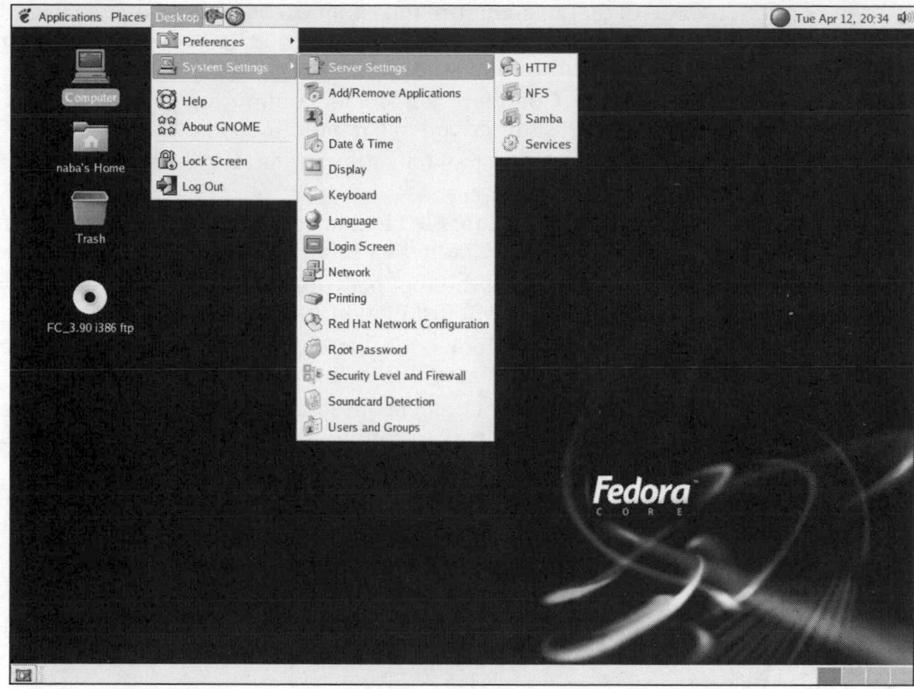

Figure 12-5: Desktop ➪ System Settings ➪ Server Settings Menu Hierarchy in GNOME.

The System Settings menu shown in Figure 12-5 enables you to perform the following system-administration tasks through easy-to-use GUI tools:

- **Server Settings:** Opens the Server Settings menu (see Figure 12-5) with options for configuring the Web server (HTTP), NFS, and Samba, and turning various services on or off.
- **Add/Remove Applications:** Package Management utility through which you can install or remove package groups (I describe this utility in Chapter 21).
- **Authentication:** GUI utility used to configure authentication (similar to what you do during Fedora installation, described in Chapter 2).
- **Date & Time:** A utility that enables you to set the date and time. You can also set the time zone and enable the use of Network Time Protocol (NTP) to automatically get the date and time from an Internet time server.
- **Display:** The system-config-display GUI tool to configure the display settings. (Chapter 3 describes the system-config-display utility.)
- **Keyboard:** GUI tool to select the keyboard layout suitable for your language (similar to the keyboard configuration that you perform during Fedora installation, as described in Chapter 2).
- **Language:** Tool to select the default language from the languages that you have installed on your system.

- **Login Screen:** GUI tool to configure the GNOME Display Manager (GDM). The tool enables you to set options in the `/etc/X11/gdm/gdm.conf` file. (Chapter 9 describes the GDM configuration options.)
- **Network:** The Network Configuration tool for configuring, activating, and deactivating network interfaces (described in Chapter 6).
- **Printing:** Printer configuration tool for setting up print queues (described in Chapter 4).
- **Red Hat Network Configuration:** GUI tool to configure options for updating the software packages in Fedora. Chapter 21 briefly describes the Red Hat Network.
- **Root Password:** GUI tool to set the root password in much the same way you set the root password during Fedora installation, as described in Chapter 2.
- **Security Level and Firewall:** Tool to disable and enable the firewall and configure mandatory access control using SELinux (described in Chapter 22).
- **Soundcard Detection:** Tool that detects the sound card and displays the information, but does not provide any way to configure the sound card (described in Chapter 5).
- **Users and Groups:** The User Manager tool, which enables you to add new users and groups and edit existing user information (as I described in the section "Managing User Accounts," earlier in this chapter).

You can explore these tools by selecting the menu options one at a time. If you're not logged in as `root`, each utility first prompts you for the root password and then proceeds to display the GUIs through which you can perform a specific set of tasks. The following section describes a few of these tools.

Managing the File System

The *file system* refers to the organization of files and directories. As a system administrator, you have to perform certain operations to manage the file system. For example, you have to learn how to mount—add a file system on a storage medium to the overall Linux file system. You also need to back up important data and learn how to restore files from a backup. Other file system operations include sharing files with the Network File System (NFS) and accessing MS-DOS files. Chapter 7 introduces you to the Linux file system, Chapter 20 describes how to back up and restore files, and Chapter 19 covers NFS. The next few sections explain how to mount file systems, and specifically, how to access DOS files in Linux.

Mounting a Device on the File System

The storage devices that you use in Linux contain Linux file systems. Each device has its own local file system, consisting of a hierarchy of directories. Before you can access the files on a device, you have to attach the device's directory hierarchy to the tree that represents the overall Linux file system.

Mounting is the operation that you perform to cause the file system on a physical storage device (a hard-disk partition or a CD-ROM) to appear as part of the Linux file system. Figure 12-6 illustrates the concept of mounting.

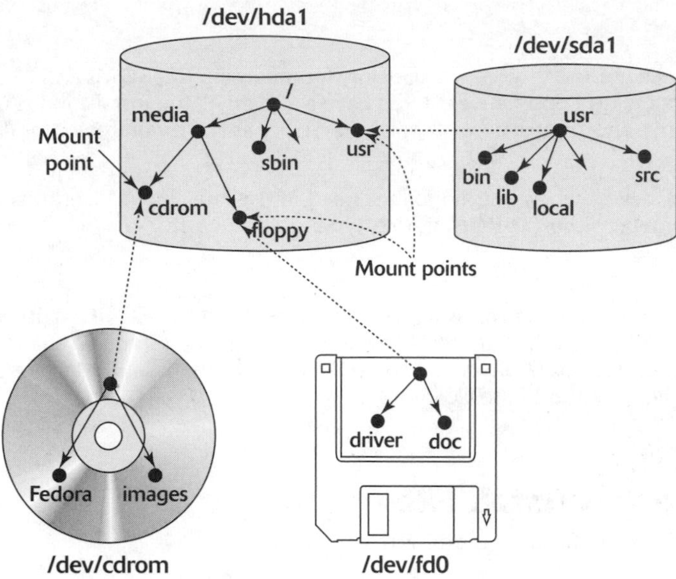

Figure 12-6: Mounting Devices on the Linux File System.

Figure 12-6 shows each device with a name that begins with `/dev`. For example, `/dev/cdrom` is the CD-ROM drive and `/dev/fd0` is the floppy drive. These physical devices are mounted at specific mount points on the Linux file system. For example, the CD-ROM drive, `/dev/cdrom`, is mounted on `/media/cdrom` in the file system. After mounting the CD-ROM in this way, the Fedora directory on the CD-ROM appears as `/media/cdrom/Fedora` in the Linux file system.

You can use the `mount` command to manually mount a device on the Linux file system at a specified directory. That directory is the *mount point*. For example, to mount the CD-ROM drive at `/media/cdrom` directory, you would type the following command (after logging in as `root`):

```
mount /dev/cdrom /media/cdrom
```

The `mount` command reports an error if the CD-ROM device is mounted already or if no CD-ROM is in the drive. Otherwise, the mount operation succeeds, and you can access the CD-ROM's contents through the `/media/cdrom` directory.

You can use any directory as the mount point. If you mount a device on a nonempty directory, however, you cannot access the files in that directory until you unmount the device by using the `umount` command. You should always, therefore, use an empty directory as the mount point.

continues

continued

Linux comes with the /media/cdrom directory for mounting CD-ROMs and /media/floppy for mounting floppy drives. If you have a Zip drive, the installation program detects that drive and creates a /media/zip directory as the mount point for the Zip drive.

To unmount a device when you no longer need it, use the umount command. For example, to unmount the CD-ROM device, type:

```
umount /dev/cdrom
```

The umount command succeeds as long as no one is using the CD-ROM. If you get an error when trying to unmount the CD-ROM, check to see if the current working directory is on the CD-ROM. If you are currently in one of the CD-ROM's directories, that also qualifies as a use of the CD-ROM.

Examining the /etc/fstab File

The mount command has the following general format:

```
mount device-name mount-point
```

However, you can mount the CD-ROM by typing one of the following commands:

```
mount /dev/cdrom
mount /media/cdrom
```

You can mount by specifying only the CD-ROM device name or the mount point name because of what's in a file named /etc/fstab. There is a line in the /etc/fstab file for the /mnt/cdrom mount point. That entry specifies the CD-ROM device name and the file system type. That's why you can mount the CD-ROM with a shorter mount command.

The /etc/fstab file is a configuration file — a text file containing information that the mount and umount commands use. Each line in the /etc/fstab file provides information about a device and its mount point in the Linux file system. Essentially, the /etc/fstab file associates various mount points within the file system with specific devices, which enables the mount command to work from the command line with only the mount point or the device as argument.

Here is a /etc/fstab file from a typical Linux system:

```
# This file is edited by fstab-sync - see 'man fstab-sync' for details
/dev/VolGroup00/LogVol00 /                      ext3    defaults        1 1
LABEL=/boot             /boot                  ext3    defaults        1 2
/dev/devpts             /dev/pts               devpts  gid=5,mode=620  0 0
/dev/shm                /dev/shm               tmpfs   defaults        0 0
/dev/proc               /proc                  proc    defaults        0 0
/dev/sys                /sys                   sysfs   defaults        0 0
/dev/VolGroup00/LogVol01 swap                   swap    defaults        0 0
/dev/fd0                /media/floppy          auto    pamconsole,
exec,noauto,fscontext=system_u:object_r:removable_t,managed 0 0
/dev/hdc                /media/cdrom           auto    pamconsole,
exec,noauto,fscontext=system_u:object_r:removable_t,managed 0 0
```

The first field on each line shows a device name, such as a hard disk partition (or it identifies a partition by the file system LABEL, which is just a name assigned to the file system and, can be changed for ext2 and ext3 file systems by the e2label command). The second field is the mount point, and the third field indicates the type of file system on the device. You can ignore the last three fields for now.

This /etc/fstab file shows that a logical volume /dev/VolGroup00/LogVol01 (which is associated with a specific hard disk partition) functions as a swap device for virtual memory, which is why both the mount point and the file system type are set to swap.

The Linux operating system uses the contents of the /etc/fstab file to mount various file systems automatically. During Linux startup, the init process executes the /etc/rc.sysinit shell script that runs the mount -a command. That command reads the /etc/fstab file and mounts all listed file systems (except those with the noauto option).

The fourth field on each line of the /etc/fstab file shows a comma-separated list of options that apply to a specific device. Typically, you find the defaults option in this field. The defaults option implies—among other things—that the device mounts at boot time, that only root can mount the device, and that the device mounts for reading and writing. If the options include noauto, the device doesn't mount automatically as the system boots.

The managed option (among others) in the fourth field of /etc/fstab entries indicates that these lines were added to the fstab file by the HAL (hardware abstraction layer) daemon that runs the fstab-sync command to add entries in the /etc/fstab file for each removable drive that it detects. You typically find that the entries for the CD-ROM (/dev/hdc in most systems) and floppy drive (/dev/fd0) have the managed option in the fourth field. On a PC with an IDE Zip drive, for instance, the /etc/fstab file should have another entry set up by the HAL daemon for the Zip drive device (/dev/hdd4).

Mounting a DOS/Windows File System

If you have Microsoft Windows 95/98/Me installed on your hard disk, you've probably already mounted the DOS partition under Linux. If not, you can easily mount DOS partitions in Linux. Mounting makes the DOS directory hierarchy appear as part of the Linux file system. To identify the DOS partitions easily, you may want to mount the first DOS partition as /dosc, the second one as /dosd, and so on.

To determine whether your DOS hard disk partitions are set up to mount automatically, type the following grep command to look for the string vfat in the file /etc/fstab:

```
grep vfat /etc/fstab
```

If the output shows one or more lines that contain vfat, your Linux system mounts DOS/Windows hard-disk partitions automatically.

If the grep command doesn't show any lines that contain the string vfat in /etc/fstab, your system is not set up to mount any DOS/Windows hard-disk partitions automatically. Of course, a very good reason may be that your hard disk doesn't have any DOS partitions.

Even if you don't have any DOS partitions on your hard disk, you should learn how to access a DOS file system from Linux because you may need to access a DOS floppy disk on your Linux system.

To mount a DOS hard disk partition or floppy, use the `mount` command but include the option `-t vfat` to indicate the file system type as DOS. For example, if your DOS partition happens to be the first partition on your IDE drive and you want to mount it on `/dosc`, use the following mount command:

```
mount -t vfat /dev/hda1 /dosc
```

The `-t vfat` part of the `mount` command specifies that the device you mount — `/dev/hda1` — has a DOS/Windows file system. Figure 12-7 illustrates the effect of this `mount` command.

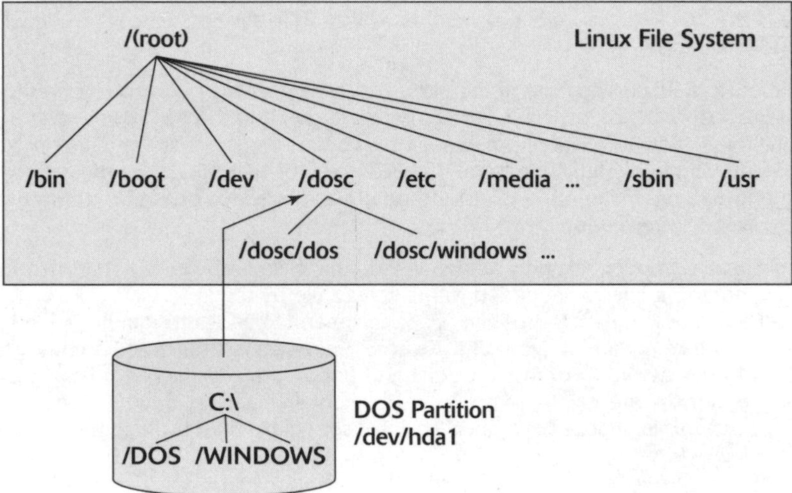

Figure 12-7: Mounting a DOS/Windows FAT Partition on the /dosc Directory.

Figure 12-7 shows how directories in your DOS partition map to the Linux file system. What was the `C:\DOS` directory under DOS becomes `/dosc/dos` under Linux. Similarly, `C:\WINDOWS` now is `/dosc/windows`. You probably can see the pattern. To convert a DOS filename to a Linux filename (after you mount the DOS partition on /dosc), perform the following steps (this does not change the file's contents; the steps show only how to derive the name of the file for use in Linux):

1. Change the DOS names to lowercase.
2. Change C:\ to /dose/.
3. Change all backslashes (\) to slashes (/).

Mounting DOS Floppy Disks

Just as you mount a DOS hard disk partition on the Linux file system, you can also mount a DOS floppy disk. You must log in as `root` to mount a floppy, but you can follow the steps shown in the latter part of this section to set up your system so that any user can mount a

DOS floppy disk. You also need to know the device name for the floppy drive. By default, Linux defines the following two generic floppy device names:

- /dev/fd0 is the A drive (the first floppy drive).
- /dev/fd1 is the B drive (the second floppy drive, if you have one).

As for the mount point, you can use any empty directory in the file system as the mount point, but the Linux system comes with a directory, /media/floppy, specifically for mounting a floppy disk.

To mount a DOS floppy disk on the /media/floppy directory, put the floppy in the drive and type the following command:

```
mount -t vfat /dev/fd0 /media/floppy
```

After you mount the floppy, you can copy files to and from the floppy by using Linux's copy command (cp). To copy the file gnome1.pcx from the current directory to the floppy, type the following:

```
cp gnome1.pcx /media/floppy
```

Similarly, to see the contents of the floppy disk, type the following:

```
ls /media/floppy
```

If you want to remove the floppy disk from the drive, first unmount the floppy drive. Unmounting removes the association between the floppy disk's file system and the mount point on the Linux file system. Use the umount command to unmount the floppy disk like this:

```
umount /dev/fd0
```

Mounting an NTFS Partition

Nowadays, many PCs come installed with Windows XP or Windows 2000. Both Windows XP and 2000, as well as Windows NT, often use the NT File System (NTFS). Linux supports read-only access to NTFS partitions, but Fedora does not come with the kernel module needed to support NTFS.

If you have installed Linux on a Windows XP system and want to access files on the NTFS partition, you can download a ready-to-run version of the NTFS kernel module from the NTFS RPMs page at http://linux-ntfs.sourceforge.net/rpm/index.html. Look for your version of Fedora Core, your kernel version (type **uname -r** to see your kernel version), and then download the RPM file for that version.

After downloading the file, log in as root, and type the following command to install the NTFS kernel module:

```
rpm -Uvh kernel-module-ntfs*.rpm
```

continues

continued

Load the module with the following command:

```
modprobe ntfs
```

Create a mount point for the NTFS partition. For example, you might create a mount point in the `/mnt` directory with the following command:

```
mkdir /mnt/windows
```

Now, you can mount the NTFS partition with the following command:

```
mount /dev/hda2 /mnt/windows -t ntfs -r -o umask=0222
```

Replace `/dev/hda2` with the device name for the NTFS partition on your system. On most PCs that come with Windows XP preinstalled, the NTFS partition is the second one (`/dev/hda2`)—the first partition (`/dev/hda1`) is a hidden partition used to hold files for Windows XP installation.

Using mtools

One way to access the MS-DOS file system is to mount the DOS hard disk or floppy disk by using the `mount` command and then use regular Linux commands, such as `ls` and `cp`, to work with the mounted DOS file system. This approach of mounting a DOS file system is fine for hard disks. Linux can mount the DOS partition automatically at startup, and you can access the DOS directories on the hard disk at any time.

If you want a quick directory listing of a DOS floppy disk, however, mounting can soon become quite tedious. First, you must mount the floppy drive. Then, you must use the `ls` or `cp` command to work with the files. Finally, you must use the `umount` command before ejecting the floppy out of the drive.

This is where the mtools package comes to the rescue. The mtools package implements most common DOS commands; the commands use the same names as in DOS, except that you add an `m` prefix to each command. Thus, the command for getting a directory listing is `mdir`, and `mcopy` copies files. The best part of mtools is the fact that you don't need to mount the floppy disk to use the mtools commands.

Trying mtools

The mtools package comes with the Linux distribution on this book's companion DVD-ROM. When you install Linux, mtools installs automatically as part of the base Linux. The mtools executable files are in the `/usr/bin` directory. To see whether you have mtools, type **ls /usr/bin/mdir** at the shell prompt. If the `ls` command shows that this file exists, mtools is available on your system.

You also can type the following `rpm` command to verify that mtools is on your system:

```
rpm -q mtools
mtools-3.9.9-13
```

If mtools is present, the output shows you the full name of the mtools package. The sample output shows that mtools version 3.9.9 is present on the system.

To try out mtools, follow these steps:

1. Log in as `root` or type **su -** and then enter the root password.
2. Place an MS-DOS floppy disk in your system's A drive.
3. Type **mdir**. You should see the directory of the floppy disk (in the standard DOS directory-listing format).

The /etc/mtools.conf File

The mtools package should work with the default setup, but if you get any errors, you should check the `/etc/mtools.conf` file. That file contains the definitions of the drives (such as A, B, and C) that the mtools utilities see. Following are a few lines from a typical `/etc/mtools.conf` file:

```
drive a: file="/dev/fd0" exclusive mformat_only
drive b: file="/dev/fd1" exclusive mformat_only

# First SCSI hard disk partition
#drive c: file="/dev/sda1"

# First IDE hard disk partition
drive c: file="/dev/hda1"
```

The pound sign (#) indicates the start of a comment. Each line defines a drive letter, the associated Linux device name, and some keywords that indicate how to access the device. In this example, the first two lines define drives A and B. The third noncomment line defines drive C as the first partition on the first IDE drive (`/dev/hda1`). If you have other DOS drives (D, for example), you can add another line that defines drive D as the appropriate disk partition.

If your system's A drive is a high-density, 3.5-inch drive, you shouldn't need to change anything in the default `/etc/mtools.conf` file to access the floppy drive. If you also want to access any DOS partition in the hard drive, uncomment and edit an appropriate line for the C drive.

Typically, you use the mtools utilities to access the floppy disks. Although you can define C and D drives for your DOS hard-disk partitions, you may want to access those partitions by using the Linux `mount` command to mount them. Because you can mount the hard-disk partitions automatically at startup, accessing them through the Linux commands is normally just as easy.

You also can access Iomega Zip drives through mtools. Simply specify a drive letter and the appropriate device's filename. For built-in IDE (ATAPI) Zip drives, try `/dev/hdd4` as the device file, and add the following line in the `/etc/mtools.conf` file:

```
drive e: file="/dev/hdd4"
```

After that, you should be able to use mtools commands to access the Zip drive (refer to it as the E drive). For example, to see the directory listing, place a Zip disk in the Zip drive and type:

```
mdir e:
```

Learning the mtools Commands

The mtools package is a collection of utilities. So far, I have been using `mdir` — the mtools counterpart of the `DIR` command in DOS. The other mtools commands are fairly easy to use.

insider insight

If you know the MS-DOS commands, using the mtools commands is very easy. Type the DOS command in lowercase letters, and remember to add `m` in front of each command. Because the Linux commands and filenames are case sensitive, you must use all lowercase letters as you type mtools commands.

Table 12-3 summarizes the commands available in mtools.

Table 12-3: The mtools Commands

mtools Utility	*MS-DOS Command (If Any)*	*Action*
`mattrib`	`ATTRIB`	Changes MS-DOS file-attribute flags.
`mbadblocks`		Tests a floppy disk and marks the bad blocks in the file allocation table (FAT).
`mcd`	`CD`	Changes an MS-DOS directory.
`mcopy`	`COPY`	Copies files between MS-DOS and Linux.
`mdel`	`DEL` or `ERASE`	Deletes an MS-DOS file.
`mdeltree`	`DELTREE`	Recursively deletes an MS-DOS directory.
`mdir`	`DIR`	Displays an MS-DOS directory listing.
`mdu`		Lists space that a directory and its contents occupy.
`mformat`	`FORMAT`	Places an MS-DOS file system on a low-level-formatted floppy disk. (Use `fdformat` to low-level-format a floppy in Linux.)
`minfo`		Gets information about an MS-DOS file system.
`mkmanifest`		Makes a list of short name equivalents.
`mlabel`	`LABEL`	Initializes an MS-DOS volume label.
`mmd`	`MD` or `MKDIR`	Creates an MS-DOS directory.
`mmove`	`MOVE`	Moves or renames an MS-DOS file or subdirectory.
`mmount`		Mounts an MS-DOS disk.
`mpartition`		Creates an MS-DOS file system as a partition.
`mrd`	`RD` or `RMDIR`	Deletes an MS-DOS directory.
`mren`	`REN` or `RENAME`	Renames an existing MS-DOS file.
`mshowfat`		Shows FAT entries for an MS-DOS file.

mtools Utility	MS-DOS Command (If Any)	Action
mtoolstest		Tests and displays the current mtools configuration.
mtype	TYPE	Displays the contents of an MS-DOS file.
mwrite	COPY	Copies a Linux file to MS-DOS.
mzip		Performs certain operations on SCSI Zip disks.

You can use the mtools commands just as you'd use the corresponding DOS commands. The mdir command, for example, works the same as the DIR command in DOS. The same goes for all the other mtools commands shown in Table 12-3.

You can use wildcard characters (such as *) with mtools commands, but you must remember that the Linux shell is the first program to see your command. If you don't want the shell to expand the wildcard character, use quotation marks around filenames that contain any wildcard characters. For example, to copy all *.txt files from the A drive to your current Linux directory, use the following command:

```
mcopy "a:*.txt" .
```

If you omit the quotation marks, the shell tries to expand the string a:*.txt with filenames from the current Linux directory. It also tries to copy those files (if any) from the DOS floppy disk.

On the other hand, if you want to copy files from the Linux directory to the DOS floppy disk, you do want the shell to expand any wildcard characters. To copy all *.jpg files from the current Linux directory to the DOS floppy disk, for example, use mcopy like this:

```
mcopy *.jpg a:
```

With the mtools utilities you can use the backslash character (\) as the directory separator, just as you would in DOS. However, when you type a filename that contains the backslash character, you must enclose the name in double quotation marks. For example, here's a command that copies a file from a subdirectory on the A drive to the current Linux directory:

```
mcopy "a:\test\sample.dat" .
```

Formatting a DOS Floppy

Suppose that you run Linux on your home PC and MS-DOS is no longer on your system, but you need to copy some files onto an MS-DOS floppy disk and take the disk to your office. If you already have a formatted MS-DOS floppy, you can simply mount that floppy and copy the file to the floppy by using the Linux cp command. But what if you don't have a formatted DOS floppy? The mtools package again comes to the rescue.

The mtools package provides the mformat utility, which can format a floppy disk for use in MS-DOS. Unlike the DOS `format` command, which formats a floppy in a single step, the `mformat` command requires you to follow a two-step process:

1. Use the `fdformat` command to low-level-format a floppy disk. The `fdformat` command uses the floppy device name as the argument; the device name includes all the parameters necessary for formatting the floppy disk. Figure 12-8 illustrates the device-naming convention for the floppy drive device. Based on the information shown in Figure 12-8, you use the following command to format a 3.5-inch, high-density floppy disk in your system's A drive:

   ```
   fdformat /dev/fd0H1440
   ```

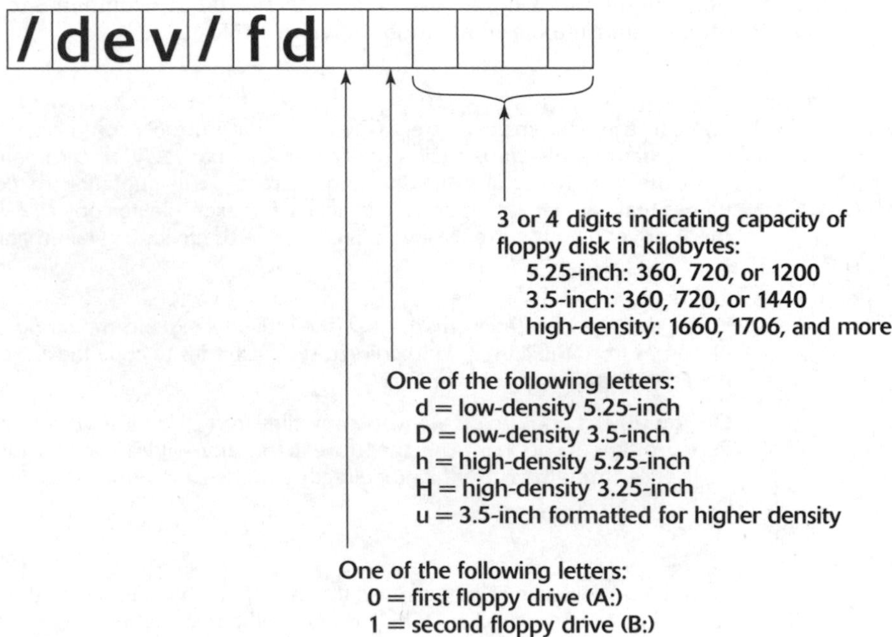

Figure 12-8: Naming Convention for the Floppy Disk Drive in Linux.

2. Use the `mformat` command to put an MS-DOS file system on the low-level-formatted floppy disk. If the floppy is in drive A, type the following command to create a formatted DOS floppy:

   ```
   mformat a:
   ```

Summary

Even if you're the only user of your Linux system, you must perform some system-administration tasks to keep the system up and running. Moreover, if your PC has a DOS partition in addition to the Linux partition, or if you work with DOS floppy disks, you may want to access the DOS files directly from Linux. This chapter provides an overview of Linux system-administration and network-administration tasks. It introduces Nautilus and shows you how to use the mtools utility programs to format and access a DOS floppy disk directly from Linux.

In this chapter, you learned the following:

- GNOME comes with a Desktop ➪ System Settings menu that enables you to perform some common system-administration tasks.
- You can add new user accounts by using the User Manager or the `useradd` command. To remove an account, you can either use User Manager or the `userdel` command.
- Linux provides built-in support for the MS-DOS file system. You can use the `mount` command to access a DOS partition or a DOS floppy from Linux. After mounting a DOS file system at a directory in your Linux system, you can use Linux commands such as `ls` and `cp` to manipulate the DOS files.
- You can download the `ntfs` kernel module and load it to enable Linux to read from NTFS partitions that are used in Windows XP, 2000, and NT.
- As you install Linux (following the directions in Chapter 2), you also install a set of utility programs known as mtools. The mtools programs provide a convenient way to access MS-DOS files, especially floppy disks, because you can use mtools commands without first needing to mount the floppy disk. The mtools utilities include commands such as `mdir` and `mcopy` that work the same as the DOS commands `DIR` and `COPY`.

Part III

Internetworking Linux

Internet Connection Setup

Secrets in This Chapter

The Internet is fast becoming a lifeline for most of us. It seems we can't get by a day without it. I know I could not write the book without it. Sometimes I wonder how we ever managed without the Internet. You'll no doubt want to connect your Linux system (and perhaps your own LAN) to the Internet. In this chapter, I show you how to connect to the Internet in several different ways — depending on whether you have DSL, a cable modem, or a dial-up network connection.

Two of the options for connecting to the Internet — DSL and cable modem — involve connecting a special modem to an Ethernet card on your Linux system. In these cases, you have to set up Ethernet networking on your Linux system. This chapter shows you how to set up a DSL and a cable modem connection. I also describe dial-up networking, which involves dialing up an Internet service provider (ISP) from your Linux system.

cross ref

As you read this chapter, consult Chapter 6 for discussions of networking, TCP/IP, and the Internet, as well as for terms such as Request for Comments (RFC).

Deciding How to Connect to the Internet

Nowadays, you have the following popular options for connecting a small office or home office to the Internet (of course, huge corporations and governments have many other ways to connect to the Internet):

- **Digital subscriber line (DSL):** Your local telephone company as well as other telecommunications companies offer DSL — a high-speed data transmission service over a regular phone line. You can use DSL to connect your Linux system to the Internet. In this case, you must connect a special DSL modem to an Ethernet card on your Linux system. When you use DSL, your Linux system is always connected to the Internet. Typically, DSL offers data transfer rates of anywhere between 128 Kbps and 1.5 Mbps. You can download from the Internet at much higher rates than when you send data from your PC to the Internet (upload). One caveat with DSL is that your home must be at most between 12,000 and 15,000 feet from your central office (this is a phone company facility where your phone lines end up). The distance limitation varies from provider to provider and depends on the specific type of DSL — ADSL, IDSL, or SDSL. In the United States, you can check out the distance limits for many providers at `www.dslreports.com/distance`.
- **Cable modem:** If the cable television company in your area offers Internet access over cable, you can use that service to hook up your Linux system to the Internet. As with DSL, connect a cable modem to an Ethernet card in your Linux system. Typically, cable modems offer higher data transfer rates than DSL for the same cost. Downloading data from the Internet is much faster than sending data from your PC to the Internet. You can expect routine download speeds of 1.5 Mbps and upload speeds of around 128 Kbps, but sometimes you may even get higher speeds than these.

- **Dial-up networking:** This is what most of us were using to connect to the Internet before DSL and cable modems came along. In this case, your Linux system uses the Point-to-Point Protocol (PPP) or Serial Line Internet Protocol (SLIP) over a dial-up link to connect to another system already on the Internet. Usually, that Internet-connected system belongs to your Internet service provider (ISP). This method of connection is referred to as dial-up networking — establishing a network connection between your Linux PC and another network (such as the Internet) through a dial-up modem. In this case, the maximum data-transfer rate is 56 Kbps. Most dial-up users connect to their ISP using PPP; SLIP is rarely used nowadays.

DSL and cable modem service connect you to the Internet and also act as your ISP — they provide you with an IP address and give you email accounts. If you use a dial-up modem to connect to the Internet, you get the phone line from the phone company and then select a separate ISP who gives you a phone number that you dial and all the other necessary goodies such as an IP address and email accounts.

Table 13-1 summarizes these three options for a small office or a home office connecting to the Internet. You can consult that table and select the type of connection that's available to you and that best suits your needs.

Table 13-1: Comparison of Dial-Up, DSL, and Cable

Feature	*Dial-Up*	*DSL*	*Cable*
Equipment	Modem	DSL modem, Ethernet card	Cable modem, Ethernet card
Also requires	Phone service and an ISP	Phone service and within 12,000 to 15,000 feet of central office	Cable TV connection
Connection type	Dial to connect	Always on, dedicated	Always on, shared
Typical speed	56 Kbps maximum	640 Kbps download, 128 Kbps upload (higher speeds cost more)	1.5 Mbps download, 128 Kbps upload
One-time costs (estimate)	None	Install = $100–200 (none for self install), Equipment = $50–100, may require activation cost	Install = $100–200 (none for self install), Equipment = $50–100
Typical monthly cost (2005)	Phone charges = $20/month, ISP charges = $15 -$30/month	$40-50/month, may require monthly modem lease	$40-50/month, may require monthly modem lease

Note: Costs vary by region. Costs shown are typical for U.S. metropolitan areas.

Connecting with DSL

DSL stands for digital subscriber line. DSL uses your existing phone line to send digital data in addition to the normal analog voice signals (analog means continuously varying whereas digital data is represented by 1s and 0s). The phone line goes from your home to a central office where the line connects to the phone company's network — by the way, the connection from your home to the central office is called the local loop. When you sign up for DSL service, the phone company has to hook up your phone line to some special equipment at the central office. That equipment can separate the digital data from the voice. From then on, your phone line can carry digital data that can then be directly sent to an Internet connection at the central office.

Understanding How DSL Works

A special box called a DSL modem takes care of sending digital data from your PC to the phone company's central office over your phone line. Your PC can connect to the Internet with the same phone line that you use for your normal telephone calls — you can make voice calls even as the line is being used for DSL. Figure 13-1 shows a typical DSL connection to the Internet.

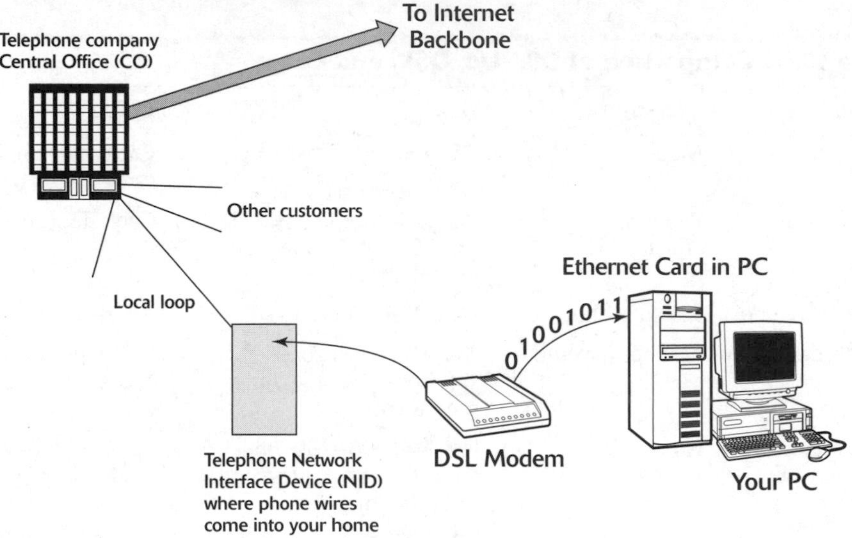

Figure 13-1: Connecting to the Internet Using DSL.

Your PC talks to the DSL modem through an Ethernet connection, which means that you need an Ethernet card in your Linux system.

Your PC sends digital data over the Ethernet connection to the DSL modem. The DSL modem sends the digital data at different frequencies than those used by the analog voice signals. The voice signals occupy a small portion of all the frequencies that the phone line can carry. DSL uses the higher frequencies to transfer digital data, so both voice and data can travel on the same phone line.

The distance between your home and the central office — the loop length — is a factor in DSL's performance. Unfortunately, the phone line can reliably carry the DSL signals only over a limited distance — typically three miles or less. This means that you can get DSL service only if your home (or office) is located within about three miles of your phone company's central office. Your phone company can tell you whether your location can get DSL or not. Often they have a website where you can type in your phone number and get a response about DSL availability. For example, try `www.dslavailability.com/` for U.S. locations.

Learning the DSL Alphabet Soup — ADSL, IDSL, SDSL

So far this chapter has used the term DSL as if there were only one kind of DSL. There are in fact three variants of DSL, each with different features, summarized as follows:

- **ADSL:** Asymmetric DSL, the most common form of DSL, has much higher download speeds (from Internet to your PC) than upload speeds (from your PC to the Internet). ADSL can have download speeds of up to 8 Mbps and upload speeds of up to 1 Mbps. ADSL works best when your location is within about 2.5 miles (12,000 feet) of your central office. ADSL service is priced according to the download and upload speeds you want. A popular form of ADSL called G.lite is specifically designed to work on the same line that you use for voice calls. G.lite has a maximum download speed of 1.5 Mbps and maximum upload speed of 512 Kbps.
- **IDSL:** ISDN DSL (ISDN, Integrated Services Digital Network, is an older technology) is a special type of DSL that works at distances of up to 5 miles between your phone and the central office. The downside is that IDSL offers downstream and upstream speeds of up to 144 Kbps only.
- **SDSL:** Symmetric DSL provides equal download and upload speeds of up to 1.5 Mbps. SDSL is priced according to the speed you want, with the higher speeds costing more. The closer your location is to the phone company's central office, the faster the connection you can get.

DSL speeds are typically specified by two numbers, like this: 1,500/384. The numbers refer to data transfer speeds in kilobits per second (Kbps, or thousand bits per second). The first number is the download speed, the second the upload. Thus, 1,500/384 means you can expect to download from the Internet at a maximum rate of 1,500 Kbps (or 1.5 Mbps) and upload to the Internet at 384 Kbps. If your phone line's condition is not perfect, you may not get these maximum rates — both ADSL and SDSL adjust the speeds to suit the line conditions.

The price of DSL service depends on which variant — ADSL, IDSL, or SDSL — you select. For most home users, the primary choice is ADSL or, more accurately, the G.lite form of ADSL with transfer speed ratings of 1,500/128.

Setting Up a DSL Connection

To get DSL for your home or business, you have to contact a DSL provider. In addition to your phone company, there are many other DSL providers. No matter who provides the DSL service, some work has to be done at your central office — the place where your phone lines connect to the rest of the phone network. The work involves connecting your phone line to equipment that can work with the DSL modem at your home or office. The central office equipment and the DSL modem at your location can then do whatever magic is needed to send and receive digital data over your phone line.

Because of the need to set up your line at the central office, it takes some time after you place an order to get your line ready for DSL.

The first step for you is to check out the DSL providers who provide service and see if you can actually get the service. Because DSL can work only over certain distances — typically less than 2.5 miles — between your location and the central office, you have to check to see if you are within that distance limit. Contact your phone company to verify this. You may be able to check this on the Web. Try typing into Google (`www.google.com`) the words **DSL**, **availability**, and your local phone company's name. You should get a website where you can type in your phone number and learn if DSL is available for your number.

If DSL is available, you can look for the types of service — ADSL versus SDSL — and the pricing. The price depends on the download and upload speeds you want. Sometimes phone companies offer a simple residential DSL that's basically the G.lite form of ADSL with 1,500/128 speed rating — meaning that you can download at 1,500 Kbps and upload at 128 Kbps. Of course, these are the maximums, and your mileage may vary.

After selecting the type of DSL service and provider, you can place an order and have the provider install the necessary equipment at your home or office. Figure 13-2 shows a sample connection diagram for typical residential DSL.

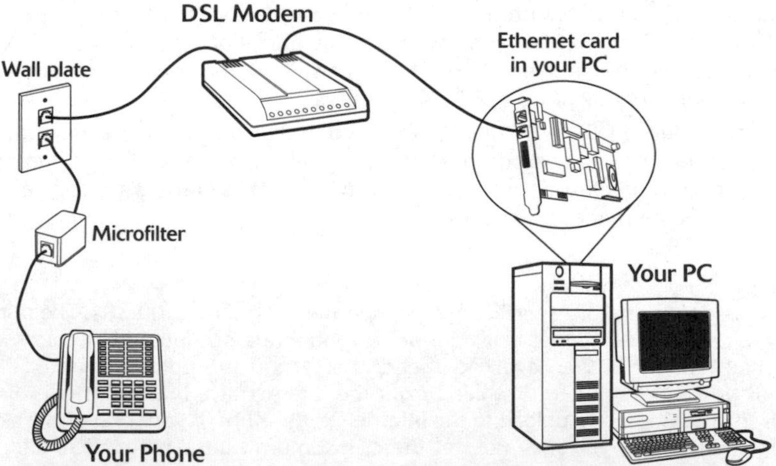

Figure 13-2: Typical Residential DSL Connection.

Here are some key points to note in Figure 13-2:

- Connect your DSL modem's data connection to the phone jack on a wall plate.
- Connect the DSL modem's Ethernet connection to the Ethernet card on your PC.
- When you connect other telephones or fax machines on the same phone line, install a microfilter between the wall plate and each of these devices.

insider insight

Because the same phone line carries both voice signals and DSL data, you need the microfilters to protect the DSL data from possible interference. You can buy them at electronic stores or from the DSL provider.

When you connect your Linux PC to the Internet using DSL, the connection is always on and there is more potential for outsiders to break into the PC. You should make sure that the Linux firewall is enabled. To configure the firewall settings, select Desktop ⇨ System Settings ⇨ Security Level and Firewall from the GNOME desktop.

There is another way to protect your Linux system from intruders and, as an added bonus, share the high-speed connection with other PCs in a local area network (LAN). To do this you need a router that can perform network address translation (NAT). The NAT router translates private Internet Protocol (IP) addresses from an internal LAN into a single public IP address and makes it possible for all the internal PCs to access the Internet. If you use a NAT router, be sure to change the administrator password from the default password after you install the router.

If you also want to set up a local area network, you need an Ethernet hub to connect the other PCs to the network. Figure 13-3 shows a typical setup that connects a LAN to the Internet through a NAT router and a DSL modem.

Here are the points to note when setting up a connection like the one shown in Figure 13-3:

- You need a NAT router with two 10Base-T Ethernet ports (the 10Base-T port looks like a large phone jack, also known as RJ-45 jack). Typically one Ethernet port is labeled Internet (or External or WAN for Wide Area Network) and the other one is labeled Local or LAN (for Local Area Network).
- You also need an Ethernet hub. For a small home network, you can buy a 4- or 8-port Ethernet hub. Basically, you want a hub with as many ports as the number of PCs you want to connect to your LAN.
- Connect the Ethernet port of the DSL modem to the Internet port of the NAT router using a 10Base-T Ethernet cable (these look like phone wires with bigger RJ-45 jacks and are often labeled Category 5 or Cat 5 wire).
- Connect the Local Ethernet port of the NAT router to one of the ports on the Ethernet hub using a 10Base-T Ethernet cable.
- Now connect each of the PCs to the Ethernet hub. Of course, you must have an Ethernet card installed in each PC.

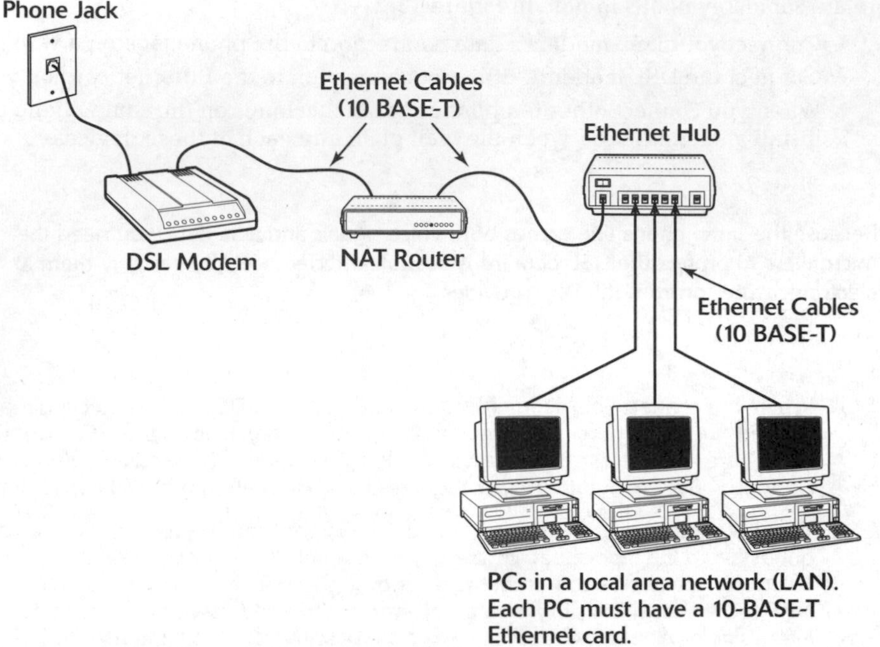

Figure 13-3: Connecting a LAN to the Internet through a NAT Router and DSL Modem.

insider insight

You can also buy a NAT router with a built-in 4- or 8-port Ethernet hub. With a combined router/hub, you need only one box to set up a LAN and connect it to the Internet with a DSL modem. These boxes are typically sold under the name Cable/DSL router because they work with both DSL and cable modem. You can even get an integrated DSL modem, NAT router, and hub—all in one box.

Connecting with a Cable Modem

Cable TV companies also offer high-speed Internet access over the same coaxial cable that carries television signals to your home. After the cable company installs the necessary equipment at their facility to send and receive digital data over the coaxial cables, customers can sign up for cable Internet service. You can then get high-speed Internet access over the same cable that delivers cable TV signals to your home.

Understanding How a Cable Modem Works

A box called a cable modem is at the heart of Internet access over the cable TV network. The cable modem takes digital data from your PC's Ethernet card and puts in an unused block of frequency (think of it as another TV channel, but instead of pictures and sound, this channel carries digital data).

The cable modem places upstream data — data that's being sent from your PC to the Internet — in a different channel from that used for the downstream data that's coming from the Internet to your PC. By design, the speed of downstream data transfers is much higher than upstream transfers. The assumption is that people download far more stuff from the Internet than they upload. Probably true for most of us.

The coaxial cable that carries all those hundreds of cable TV channels to your home is a very capable signal carrier. In particular, the coaxial cable can carry signals covering a huge range of frequencies — hundreds of megahertz (MHz). Each TV channel requires 6 MHz, and the coaxial cable can carry hundreds of such channels. The cable modem places the upstream data in a small frequency band and expects to receive the downstream data in another frequency band.

At the other end of your cable connection to the Internet is a cable modem termination system (CMTS) that your cable company installs at its central facility. The CMTS connects the cable TV network to the Internet. It also extracts the digital upstream data sent by your cable modem (and by your neighbors as well) and sends them to the Internet. The CMTS also puts digital data into the upstream channels so that your cable modem can extract that data and provide it to your PC via the Ethernet card. Figure 13-4 illustrates how cable companies provide high-speed Internet access over their cable TV network.

Cable modems can receive downstream data at the rate of about 30 Mbps and send data at around 3 Mbps upstream. However, all the cable modems in a neighborhood share the same downstream capacity. Each cable modem filters out — separates — the data it needs from the stream of data that the CMTS sends out.

In practice, with cable modems you can get downstream transfer rates of around 1.5 Mbps and upstream rates of 128 Kbps.

continues

continued

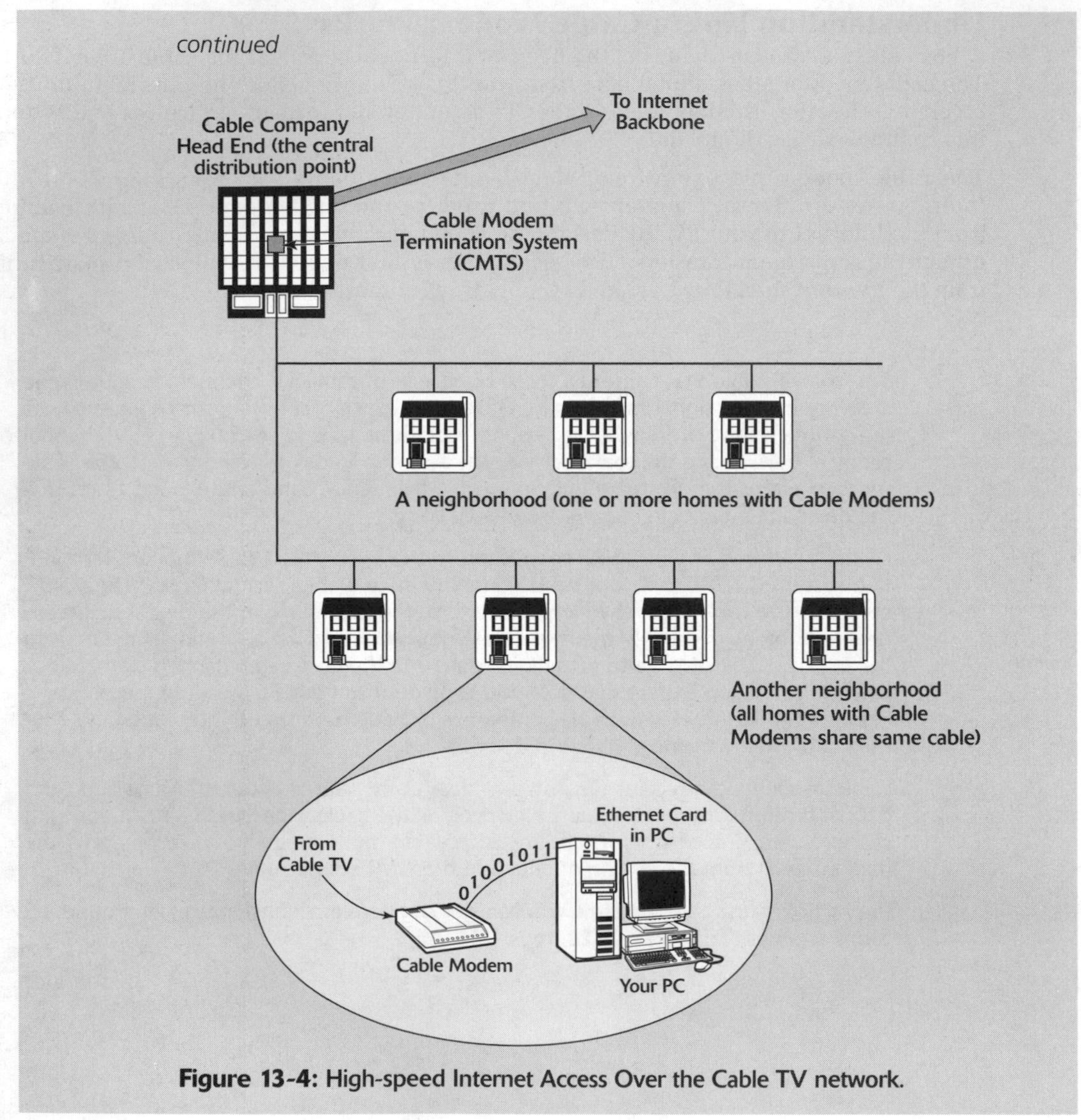

Figure 13-4: High-speed Internet Access Over the Cable TV network.

insider insight If you want to check your downstream transfer speed, go to `http://bandwidthplace.com/speedtest`, and click the link to start the test. For my cable modem connection, the tests reported a downstream transfer rate of about 1.4 Mbps on good days.

Setting Up a Cable Modem Connection

To set up cable modem access, your cable TV provider must offer high-speed Internet access. If the service is available, you can call to sign up. The cable companies often have promotional offers such as no installation fee or a reduced rate for three months. Look for these offers. If you are lucky, they may have a promotion going on just when you want to sign up.

The installation is typically done by a technician who splits your incoming cable into two — one side goes to the TV and the other to the cable modem. The technician provides information about the cable modem to the cable company's head end for setup at their end. (You can even get a self-install kit and do the installation yourself and save the technician's fee.) When all that is done, you can plug in your PC's Ethernet card to the cable modem, and you're all set to enjoy high-speed Internet access. Figure 13-5 shows a typical cable modem hookup.

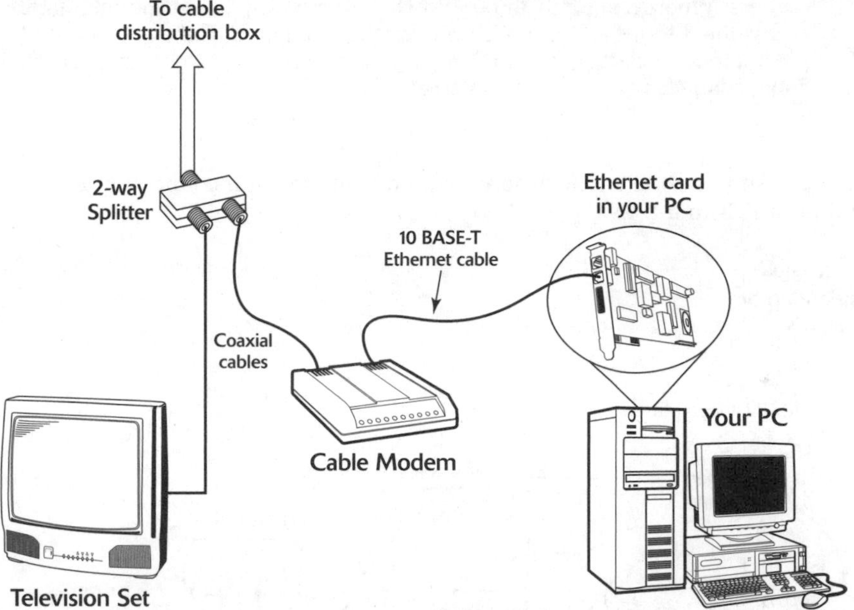

Figure 13-5: Splitting the Cable TV Signal between the TV and the Cable Modem.

The cable modem connects to an Ethernet card in your PC. So you need an Ethernet card in your PC. The cable company technician often provides an Ethernet card.

Here are some key points to note about the cable modem setup in Figure 13-5:

- Split the incoming cable TV signal into two parts by using a 2-way splitter (the cable company technician installs this). By the way, the 2-way splitter should be rated for 1 GHz; otherwise, it may not pass through the frequencies that contain the downstream data from the Internet.
- Connect one of the video outputs from the splitter to your cable modem's F-type video connector using a coaxial cable.
- Connect the cable modem's 10 Base-T Ethernet connection to the Ethernet card on your PC.
- Connect your TV to the other video output from the 2-way splitter.

caution

When you use cable modem to connect your Linux PC to the Internet, the connection is always on, so there is more chance that someone may try to break into the PC. You should enable the firewall. To configure the firewall settings, select Desktop ⇨ System Settings ⇨ Security Level and Firewall from the GNOME desktop.

You may want to add a NAT (network address translation) router between your PC and the cable modem. As an added bonus, you can even share a cable modem connection with all the PCs in your own local area network (LAN) by adding an Ethernet hub. Better yet, buy a combination NAT router and hub so you can do the job with only one box. By the way, the NAT router/hubs are typically sold under the name cable/DSL router because they work with both DSL and cable modems.

The NAT router translates private Internet Protocol (IP) addresses into a public IP address. When connected through a NAT router, any PC in the internal LAN can access the Internet as if it has its own unique IP address. The end result is that a single Internet connection is shared among many PCs. This can be an ideal solution for connecting a small LAN to the Internet.

Figure 13-6 shows what a typical setup with a cable modem connection being shared by a number of PCs in a LAN.

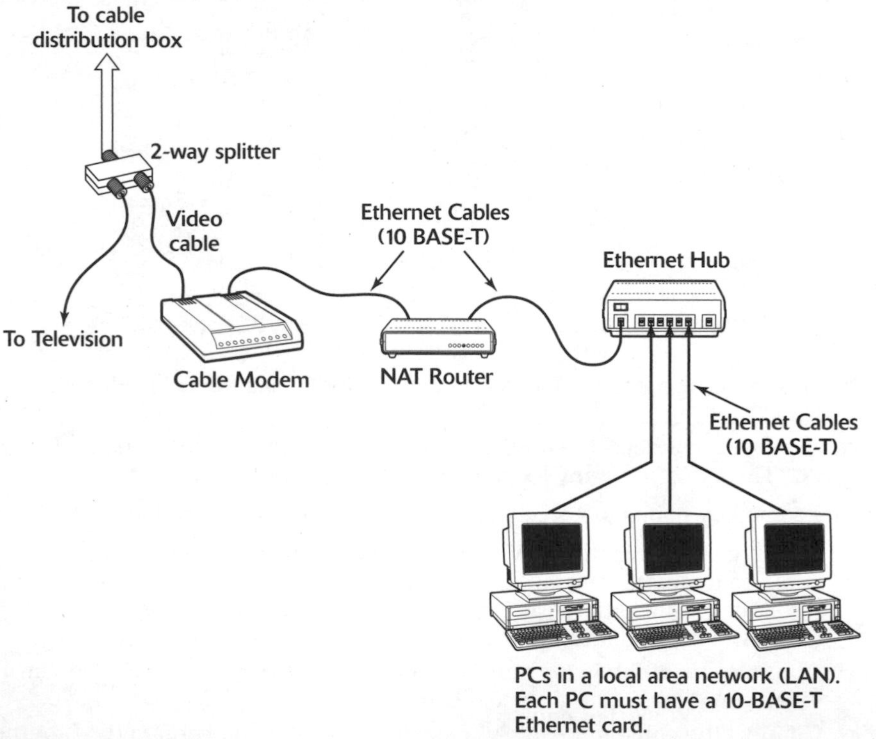

Figure 13-6: Sharing a Cable Modem Internet Connection with Several PCs in a LAN.

Here are the points to note when setting up a connection like the one shown in Figure 13-6:

- You need a cable/DSL NAT router with two 10Base-T Ethernet ports (the 10Base-T port looks like a large phone jack — it's also known as an RJ-45 jack). Typically, one Ethernet port is labeled Internet (or External or WAN for wide area network) and the other one is labeled Local.
- If you plan to set up a LAN, you also need an Ethernet hub. For a small home network, you can buy a 4- or 8-port Ethernet hub. Basically, you want a hub with as many ports as the number of PCs you want to connect to your local area network.
- Consider buying a single box that acts as a NAT router and also a hub with a number of Ethernet ports.
- Connect the video cable to the video input port of the cable modem.
- Connect the Ethernet port of the cable modem to the Internet port of the NAT router using a 10Base-T Ethernet cable (these look like phone wires, except that the Ethernet cables have bigger RJ-45 jacks and are often labeled Category 5 or Cat 5 wire).
- Connect the Local Ethernet port of the NAT router to one of the ports on the Ethernet hub using a 10Base-T Ethernet cable.
- Now connect each of the PCs to the Ethernet hub. Of course, each PC must have an Ethernet card.

Setting Up IEEE 802.11 Wireless Ethernet Networks

If you have laptop computers on your LAN or if you don't want to run wires to connect a PC to the LAN, you have the option of using a wireless Ethernet network. In a typical scenario, you have a cable modem or DSL connection to the Internet, and you want to connect one or more laptops with wireless network cards to access the Internet through the cable or DSL modem. This section shows you how to set up wireless networking for connecting to an Ethernet LAN and accessing the Internet.

Understanding Wireless Ethernet Networks

Until mid-2003, there were two popular IEEE standards — 802.11a and 802.11b — for wireless Ethernet networks, also commonly referred to Wi-Fi (for Wireless Fidelity) networks. These two standards were finalized in 1999, and they specify how the wireless Ethernet network works at the physical level. A third standard — 802.11g — was finalized by the IEEE in the summer of 2003. All these standards specify how the wireless Ethernet network works at the Physical layer. You don't have to learn all the details of all those standards to set up a wireless network, but knowing some pertinent details is good so that you can buy the right kind of equipment for your wireless network.

The three wireless Ethernet standards have the following characteristics:

- **802.11b:** Operates in the 2.4-GHz radio band (2.4 GHz to 2.4835 GHz) in up to three nonoverlapping frequency bands or channels. Supports a maximum bit rate of 11 Mbps per channel. One of the disadvantages of 802.11b is that the 2.4-GHz frequency band is crowded — many devices such as microwave ovens, cordless phones, medical and scientific equipment, as well as Bluetooth devices, all work within the 2.4-GHz frequency band. Nevertheless, 802.11b is very popular in corporate as well as home networks.
- **802.11a:** Operates in the 5-GHz radio band (5.725 GHz to 5.850 GHz) in up to eight nonoverlapping channels. Supports a maximum bit rate of 54 Mbps per channel. The 5-GHz band is not as crowded as the 2.4-GHz band, but the 5-GHz band is not approved for use in Europe. Products conforming to the 802.11a standard are available, and there are wireless access points that are designed to handle both 802.11a and 802.11b connections.
- **802.11g:** Supports up to 54 Mbps data rate in the 2.4 GHz band (the same band that 802.11b uses). 802.11g achieves the higher bit rate by using a technology called *OFDM* (orthogonal frequency-division multiplexing), which is also used by 802.11a. Equipment that complies with 802.11g is already on the market. 802.11.g has generated excitement by working in the same band as 802.11b but promising much higher data rates and by being backward compatible with 802.11b devices. Vendors currently offer access points that can support both the 802.11b and 802.11g connection standards.

In all cases, the maximum data throughput that a user sees is much less because all users of that radio channel share the capacity of the channel. Also, the data transfer rate decreases as the distance between the user's PC and the wireless access point increases.

There is a fourth standard — 802.11n — under development that would support 100-Mbps data rates in either the 2.4 GHz or the 5 GHz band, depending on which of the two proposals garner the required membership approval. Two equally matched groups of companies — known by the titles TGn Sync (Task Group n Synchronization) and WWiSE (Worldwide Spectrum Efficiency) — have each authored proposals for the 802.11n standard. TGn Sync proposes to use the 5-GHz band, the same one used by 802.11a, whereas WWiSE's proposal is for the 2.4 GHz that's used by 802.11b and g. Both groups agree that some form of multiple input multiple output (MIMO, pronounced "my-mo") antenna technology would be needed to achieve the 100-Mbps data rate. (Some MIMO access points are already becoming available on the market.) At a March 2005 balloting, the TGn Sync proposal obtained the majority votes, but it did not receive the 75 percent majority required to be the basis for the first draft. You can read the latest news about the IEEE 802.11n project at `http://grouper.ieee.org/groups/802/11/Reports/tgn_update.htm`.

If you are buying a new wireless access point, get an 802.11g. An 802.11g access point can also communicate with older (and slower) 802.11b devices. You can also consider a MIMO access point that supports multiple 802.11 standards and implements techniques for getting higher throughputs and better range.

To learn more about wireless Ethernet, visit `www.wi-fi.org/`, the home page of the Wi-Fi Alliance, a nonprofit international association formed in 1999 to certify interoperability of wireless LAN products based on IEEE 802.11 standards.

Understanding Infrastructure and Ad Hoc Modes

The 802.11 standard defines two modes of operation for wireless Ethernet networks: infrastructure and ad hoc. *Ad hoc* mode is simply two or more wireless Ethernet cards communicating with each other without an access point.

Infrastructure mode refers to the approach in which all the wireless Ethernet cards communicate with each other and to the wired LAN through an access point. For the example considered in this book, your wireless Ethernet card should be set to infrastructure mode. In the configuration files, this mode is referred to as Managed mode.

Understanding Wired Equivalent Privacy

The 802.11 standard includes the Wired Equivalent Privacy (WEP) for protecting wireless communications from eavesdropping. WEP relies on a 40-bit or 104-bit secret key that is shared between a mobile station (such as a laptop with a wireless Ethernet card) and an access point (also called a base station). The secret key is used to encrypt packets before they are transmitted and an integrity check is performed to ensure that packets are not modified in transit. The 802.11 standard does not explain how the shared key is established. In practice, most wireless LANs use a single key that is shared between all mobile stations and access points. Such an approach, however, does not scale well to an environment such as a college campus where the keys are shared with all users. Therefore, WEP is typically not used on large wireless networks such as the ones at universities. In such wireless networks, users should use other security approaches such as using SSH (Secure Shell) to log in to remote systems.

WEP uses the RC4 encryption algorithm, which is known as a stream cipher. Such a stream cipher works by taking a short secret key and generating an infinite stream of pseudorandom bits. The sending station performs an exclusive-OR operation between the pseudorandom bits and the bits representing the data packet. The receiver has a copy of the same secret key, so it generates an identical stream of pseudo-random bits. Performing an exclusive-OR between this pseudorandom stream and the received bits regenerates the original, unencrypted data packet.

Such a method of stream cipher has a few problems. If a bit is flipped (from a 0 to 1 or vice versa) in the encrypted data stream, then the corresponding bit is flipped in the decrypted output. Also, if an eavesdropper intercepts two encoded messages that were encoded with the same stream, then it is possible to generate the exclusive-OR of the original messages. That knowledge is enough to mount attacks that can eventually break the encryption.

To counter against these weaknesses, WEP uses some defenses:

- **Integrity Check (IC) Field:** To make sure that data packets are not modified in transit, WEP uses an Integrity Check field in each packet.
- **Initialization Vector (IV):** To avoid encrypting two messages with the same key stream, WEP uses a 24-bit initialization vector (IV) that augments the shared secret key to produce a different RC4 key for each packet. The IV itself is also included in the packet.

Experts say that both of these defenses are poorly implemented, making WEP ineffective. The problems with IC and IV are the following:

- The Integrity Check field is implemented using a checksum algorithm called 32-bit cyclic redundancy code (CRC-32), and that checksum is then included as part of the data packet. Unfortunately, it is possible for an attacker to flip arbitrary bits in an encrypted message and correctly adjust the checksum so that the resulting message appears valid.
- The 24-bit IV is sent in the clear. This means that there are only 2^{24} possible initialization vectors, and they have to be reused after running through all of them. In other words, after sending 2^{24}, or 16,777,216 packets, the IV has to be repeated. The number might sound like a lot, but consider the case of a busy access point that sends 1,500-byte packets at a rate of 11 Mbps. Each packet has $8 \times 1,500 = 12,000$ bits. That means each second the access point sends 11,000,000/12,000 = 916 packets. At that rate, the access point sends 16,777,216 packets in 16,777,216/916 = 18,315 seconds or 5 hours. The IV is reused after 5 hours, and the time may be less than that because many message are smaller than 1,500 bytes. Thus, there are ample opportunities for an attacker to collect two encrypted messages that are encrypted with the same key stream and perform statistical attacks to decrypt the message.

Thus, WEP has its weaknesses, but it's better than nothing. You can use it in smaller wireless LANs where sharing the same key among all wireless stations is not an onerous task.

---

insider insight

In 2003, the Wi-Fi Alliance published a specification called *Wi-Fi Protected Access* (WPA) that replaces the existing WEP standard and improves security by making some changes. For example, unlike WEP, which uses fixed keys, the WPA standard uses Temporal Key Integrity Protocol (TKIP), which generates new keys for every 10K of data transmitted over the network. This makes WPA more difficult to break.

In 2004, the Wi-Fi Alliance introduced a follow-up to WPA called the *Wi-Fi Protected Access 2* (WPA2 — the second generation of WPA security). WPA2 is based on the final IEEE 802.11i standard, which uses public key encryption with digital certificates and an authentication, authorization, and accounting RADIUS (Remote Authentication Dial-In User Service) server to provide better security for wireless Ethernet networks. WPA2 uses the Advanced Encryption Standard (AES) for data encryption.

Setting up the Wireless Hardware

To set up the wireless connection, you need a wireless access point and a wireless network card in each PC. You can also set up an ad hoc wireless network among two or more PCs with wireless network cards, but that would be a wireless LAN among those PCs only. In this section, I focus on the scenario where you want to set up a wireless connection to an established LAN that has a wired Internet connection through a cable modem or DSL.

In addition to the wireless access point, you would also need a cable modem or DSL connection to the Internet, along with a NAT router/hub, as described in the previous sections. Figure 13-7 shows a typical setup for wireless Internet access through an existing cable modem or DSL connection.

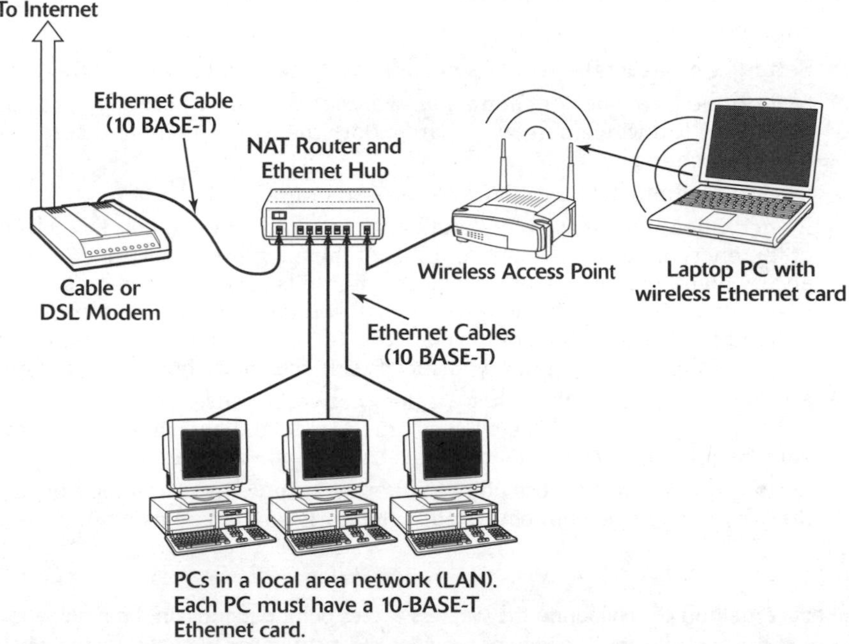

Figure 13-7: Connecting a Mixed Wired and Wireless Ethernet LAN to the Internet.

As Figure 13-7 shows, the LAN has both wired and wireless PCs. In this example, a cable or DSL modem connects the LAN to the Internet through a NAT router/hub. A wireless access point is attached to one of the RJ-45 ports on the hub. Laptops with wireless network cards connect the LAN through the wireless access point. To connect desktop PCs to the wireless network, you can use a USB wireless network card — a wireless network card that connects to a USB port.

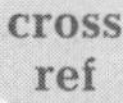

See Appendix F for a brief discussion of PCMCIA wireless network cards supported by Linux.

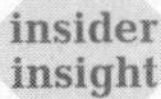

If you have not yet purchased a NAT router/hub for your cable or DSL connection, consider buying a router/hub that has a built-in wireless access point.

Configuring the Wireless Access Point

Configuring the wireless access point involves the following:

- Setting a name for the wireless network (the technical term is ESSID).
- Setting the frequency or channel on which the wireless access point communicates with the wireless network cards. Both the access point and cards must use the same channel.
- Deciding whether encryption is to be used or not.
- If encryption is to be used, the number of bits in the encryption key and the value of the encryption key. Twenty-four bits of the encryption key are internal to the access point; you specify only the remaining bits of the encryption key. Thus, for 64-bit encryption, you have to specify a 40-bit key, which comes to 10 hexadecimal digits (a hexadecimal digit is one of 0 through 9 and the letters A through F). For a 124-bit encryption key, you specify 104 bits, or 26 hexadecimal digits.
- Setting the access method that wireless network cards would use when connecting to the access point. The choices are open access and shared key. You typically use the open access method (even when you use encryption).
- Setting the wireless access point to operate in infrastructure mode because that's the way you should connect wireless network cards to an existing Ethernet LAN.

The exact method of configuring the wireless access point depends on the make and model of the access point. The vendor provides the instructions to configure the wireless access point. You would typically work through a graphical client application to configure the wireless access point. If you enable encryption, make a note of the encryption key because you have to specify the same key for each wireless network card.

Configuring Wireless Networking

On your Linux laptop, the PCMCIA or PC Card manager should recognize the wireless network card and load the appropriate driver for the card. The wireless network card is treated like another Ethernet device and assigned a device name such as `eth0` or `eth1`. If you already have an Ethernet card in the laptop, that card gets the `eth0` device name, and the wireless PC card is named the `eth1` device.

You do have to configure certain parameters to enable the wireless network card to communicate with the wireless access point. For example, you have to specify the wireless network name assigned to the access point—and the encryption settings must match those on the access point. You can usually configure everything using the graphical network configuration tool.

Follow these steps to configure and activate the wireless network connection on your Fedora Linux system:

1. Select Desktop ➪ System Settings ➪ Network from the GNOME desktop; then click New on the toolbar. The Add New Device Type window appears.
2. Click to select Wireless connection from the Device Type list and then click Forward.
3. Select the wireless device (this should be automatically detected and listed as a choice) and click Forward. The Configure Wireless Connection window appears.
4. Configure the wireless connection (see Figure 13-8). In particular, set the Mode to Managed, specify the name of the wireless network (the one you want to connect to), and set the encryption key, if any. Click Forward. The Configure Network Settings window appears.

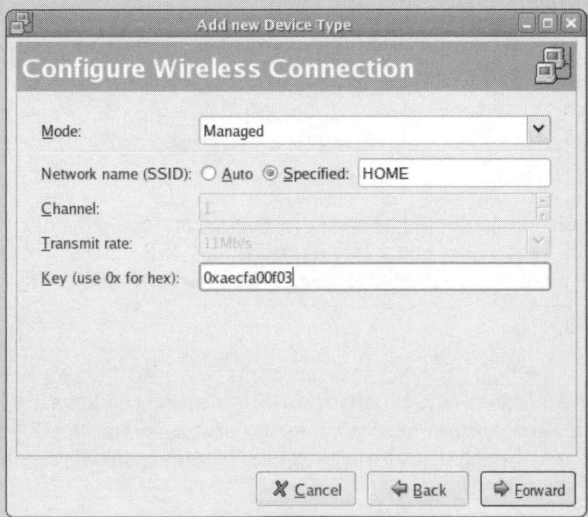

Figure 13-8: Configure the Wireless Connection from This Window.

5. Set the option for getting the IP address to DHCP (a protocol for obtaining network configuration parameters, including IP addresses from a server on the network). Click Forward. The Create Wireless Device window appears.
6. Check the configuration information and if it's correct, click Apply to complete the wireless Ethernet setup. You return to the Network Configuration tool's main window.
7. Select the new wireless device and click the Activate button. If all goes well, the wireless network should be up and running after a few moments.

continues

continued

The Network Configuration tool saves the wireless network settings in a text file whose name depends on the wireless network device name. If the wireless network device name is `eth0`, the configuration is stored in the text file `/etc/sysconfig/network-scripts/ifcfg-eth0`. If the wireless device name is `eth1`, the file is `/etc/sysconfig/network-scripts/ifcfg-eth1`. This configuration file contains various settings for the wireless network card. Table 13-2 explains the meaning of the settings. Here is a slightly edited version of the `/etc/sysconfig/network-scripts/ifcfg-eth1` file from my laptop PC running Fedora:

```
IPV6INIT=no
USERCTL=no
PEERDNS=yes
TYPE=Wireless
DEVICE=eth1
HWADDR=00:02:2d:8c:f9:c4
BOOTPROTO=dhcp
ONBOOT=no
DHCP_HOSTNAME=
NAME=
ESSID='HOME'
CHANNEL=6
MODE=Managed
RATE=auto
```

The encryption key is stored separately. For a wireless Ethernet card whose device name is `eth1`, the encryption key is stored in the `/etc/sysconfig/network-scripts/keys-eth1` file. For example, here is what this file contains for my example:

```
KEY=AECFA00F03
```

Note that the key has 10 hexadecimal digits for a 40-bit key (for example, `1fdf-3fde-fe`) or 26 hexadecimal digits for a 104-bit key. The keys are, in fact, 64-bit and 128-bit, but the encryption algorithm automatically generates 24 bits of the key, so you need to specify only the remaining bits. Needless to say, the longer the key, the more secure the encryption.

Table 13-2: Settings in the Configuration File for a Wireless Ethernet Network Interface

Parameter	*Description*
`BOOTPROTO`	The name of the protocol to use to get the IP address for the interface. Should be either `dhcp` or `bootp` for an Ethernet interface.
`CHANNEL`	Channel number (between 1 and 14 in the U.S. and Canada). Must be the same as that set for the wireless access point.
`DEVICE`	The device name for the wireless Ethernet network interface (`eth0` for the first interface, `eth1` for second, and so on)

Parameter	Description
ESSID	Extended Service Set (ESS) Identifier, also known as the wireless network name. It is case sensitive and must be the same as the name specified for the wireless access point. Provide the name within single quotes (for example, 'HOME').
HWADDR	The hardware address (also called the MAC address) of the wireless network card (six pairs of colon-separated hexadecimal numbers; for example, 00:02:2d:8c:f9:c4). The wireless card's device driver automatically detects this address.
IPV6INIT	When set to yes, this parameter initializes IPv6 configuration for the wireless interface. Set it to no if you are not using IPv6.
MODE	The mode of operation of the wireless network card. Set to Managed for a typical network that connects through a wireless access point.
NAME	A nickname for your wireless network. If you don't specify it, the host name is used as the nickname.
ONBOOT	Set to yes to activate the wireless interface at boot time; otherwise set to no.
PEERDNS	Set to yes to enable the interface to modify your system's /etc/resolv.conf file to use the DNS servers obtained from the DHCP server (this is the same server that provides the IP address for the interface). If you set this to no, the /etc/resolv.conf file is left unchanged.
RATE	Bit rate for the wireless connection (set to one of 1M, 2M, 5.5M, 11M, or auto). The M means Mbps or a million bits per second. Set to auto to use the maximum possible transmission rate.
TYPE	Set to Wireless for wireless network interface.
USERCTL	When set to yes, a non-root user can control the device. Set it to no so that only root can control the device.

Now, the wireless interface should be working properly. To check the interface status, type the following command:

```
iwconfig
```

Here's a typical output on my Linux laptop:

```
lo        no wireless extensions.

eth0      IEEE 802.11-DS  ESSID:"HOME"  Nickname:"localhost.localdomain"
          Mode:Managed  Frequency:2.437GHz  Access Point: 00:30:AB:06:2E:5D
          Bit Rate=11Mb/s   Tx-Power=15 dBm   Sensitivity:1/0
          Retry limit:4   RTS thr:off   Fragment thr:off
          Encryption key:AECF-A00F-03
          Power Management:off
          Link Quality:66/0  Signal level:-27 dBm  Noise level:-93 dBm
          Rx invalid nwid:0  Rx invalid crypt:0  Rx invalid frag:0
          Tx excessive retries:0  Invalid misc:0   Missed beacon:0
```

Here the eth0 interface refers to the wireless network card. I have edited the encryption key and some other parameters, but the sample output shows what you should see when the wireless link is working.

Learning the Basics of Dial-up Networking

Dial-up networking refers to connecting a PC to a remote network through a dial-up modem. If you are ancient enough to remember the days of dialing up with Procomm or some serial communications software, there is a significant difference between dial-up networking and the old days of serial communication. Both approaches use a modem to dial up a remote computer and to establish a communication path, but the serial communication software makes your computer behave like a dumb terminal connected to the remote computer. The serial-communication software exclusively uses dial-up connection. You cannot run another copy of the communication software and use the same modem connection, for example.

In dial-up networking, both your PC and the remote system run network-protocol (called TCP/IP) software. When your PC dials up and sets up a communication path, the network protocols exchange data packets over that dial-up connection. The neat part is that any number of applications can use the same dial-up connection to send and receive data packets. So your PC becomes a part of the network to which the remote computer belongs. (If the remote computer is not on a network, dial-up networking creates a network that consists of the remote computer and your PC.)

Chapter 6 describes TCP/IP protocol some more, but I have to use the term as well as a few concepts such as Internet Protocol (IP) address and Domain Name Service (DNS) when describing how to set up dial-up networking.

Here's what you have to do to set up dial-up networking in Linux:

- Install an internal or external modem in your PC. If your PC did not already come with an internal modem, you can buy an external modem and connect it to the PC's serial port.
- Connect the modem to the phone line. Figure 13-9 illustrates how a modem enables the PC to send digital data over the analog phone lines.

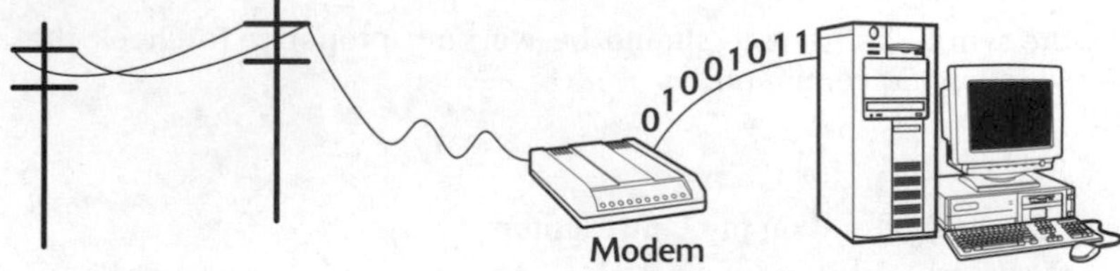

Figure 13-9: Sending Digital Data over a Modem.

- Get an account with an ISP. Every ISP provides you a phone number to dial, a user name, and a password. Additionally, the ISP should give you the domain names of servers for email and news. Typically, your system automatically gets an IP address from the ISP's server.
- Test your modem and make sure it's working. You can do this testing with a serial communication package called minicom that comes with Linux.
- Run the Internet Configuration Wizard or edit appropriate configuration files to set up a PPP connection.
- Activate the PPP connection to connect to the Internet from a GUI tool or by typing a command.

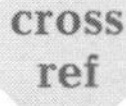

Appendix E describes how to set up and use modems to dial out from your Linux system. The following sections provide an overview of PPP and show how to set up and use a PPP connection.

Understanding SLIP and PPP

Like TCP/IP networking over Ethernet, TCP/IP networking over a dial-up link involves specifying the protocol — the convention — for packaging a network packet over the communication link. There are two popular protocols for TCP/IP networking over point-to-point serial communication links:

- **Serial Line Internet Protocol (SLIP):** This is a simple protocol that specifies how to frame an IP packet on a serial line. RFC 1055 describes SLIP.
- **Point-to-Point Protocol (PPP):** This is a more advanced protocol for establishing a TCP/IP connection over any point-to-point link, including dial-up serial links. RFC 1661 describes PPP.

I first provide an overview of SLIP and PPP; then I show you how to use PPP to set up a network connection to a remote system. SLIP is not widely used anymore, but a brief overview is useful as a context for how PPP improves upon SLIP.

Serial Line Internet Protocol

SLIP originated as a simple protocol for framing an IP packet — an Internet Protocol packet that consists of an IP header (which includes the source and destination IP addresses), followed by data (the data sent from source to destination). In RFC 1055, "A Nonstandard for Transmission of IP Datagrams over Serial Lines: SLIP," (June 1988), J. L. Romkey describes SLIP. As the title of RFC 1055 suggests, SLIP is not an official Internet standard; it's a de facto standard.

SLIP defines two special characters for framing — marking the beginning and ending — IP packets:

- SLIP-END is octal 300 (decimal 192); it marks the end of an IP packet.
- SLIP-ESC is octal 333 (decimal 219); it "escapes" any SLIP-END or SLIP-ESC characters that are embedded in the packet (for example, to ensure that a packet does not end prematurely because the IP packet happens to include a byte with decimal 192).

The protocol involves sending out the bytes of the IP packet one by one and marking the end of the packet with a SLIP-END character. The following convention handles any SLIP-END and SLIP-ESC characters that happen to appear in the IP packet:

- Replace a SLIP-END character with SLIP-ESC, followed by octal 334 (decimal 220).
- Replace a SLIP-ESC character with SLIP-ESC, followed by octal 335 (decimal 221).

That's it! Based on the most popular implementation of SLIP from Berkeley UNIX, SLIP also uses these conventions:

- Packets start and end with the SLIP-END character to ensure that each IP packet starts anew.
- The total size of the IP packet (including the IP header and data, but without the SLIP framing characters) is 1,006 bytes.

SLIP's simplicity led to its popularity (although PPP is used more widely nowadays). SLIP has several shortcomings, however:

- Each end of the SLIP connection has to know its own and the other end's IP addresses. Although some schemes permit dynamic assignment of IP addresses, the protocol does not have any provisions for address negotiation.
- Both ends of SLIP must use the same packet size because the protocol does not permit the two ends to negotiate the packet size.
- SLIP has no support for data compression. (As you learn later in this section, Compressed SLIP — CSLIP — introduces compression in SLIP.)
- There is no way to identify the packet type in SLIP. Accordingly, SLIP can carry only one protocol — the one that both ends of SLIP are hard-wired to use. A transport mechanism such as SLIP should be capable of carrying packets of any protocol type.

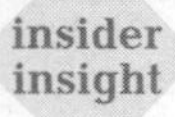

CSLIP addresses the lack of data compression in SLIP, as described in RFC 1144, "Compressing TCP/IP Headers for Low-Speed Serial Links," V. Jacobson, February 1990. CSLIP compresses TCP/IP header information, which tends to be repetitive in packets exchanged between the two ends of a SLIP connection. CSLIP does not compress the packet's data. CSLIP often is referred to as the "Van Jacobson compression" in recognition of CSLIP's author. Van Jacobson compression is also used in PPP.

Point-to-Point Protocol

PPP fixes the shortcomings of SLIP and defines a more complex protocol. Unlike SLIP, PPP is an official Internet standard. It is documented in RFC 1661, "The Point-to-Point Protocol," W. Simpson, July 1994 (updated in RFC 2153, "PPP Vendor Extensions," W. Simpson, May 1997).

PPP includes the following main components:

- A packet-framing mechanism that uses a modified version of the well-known High-Level Data Link Control (HDLC) protocol
- A Link Control Protocol (LCP) to establish, configure, and test the data link
- A family of Network Control Protocols (NCP) that enables PPP to carry more than one type of network packet — such as IP, IPX, or NetBEUI (Network BIOS Extended User Interface) — over the same connection

PPP has replaced SLIP as the protocol of choice for transporting packets over point-to-point links. In addition to the ubiquitous serial link, some versions of PPP work over several other types of point-to-point links. Some of these point-to-point links include Frame Relay, SONET/SDH (Synchronous Optical Network/Synchronous Digital Hierarchy), X.25, and ISDN (Integrated Services Digital Network).

The PPP frame has a more complex structure than SLIP has. The PPP frame structure is based on ISO (International Organization for Standardization) standard 3309, "Data Communications — High-Level Data Link Control Procedures — Frame Structure," 1979. The HDLC protocol uses a special flag character to mark the beginning and the end of a frame. Figure 13-10 shows the structure of a complete PPP frame.

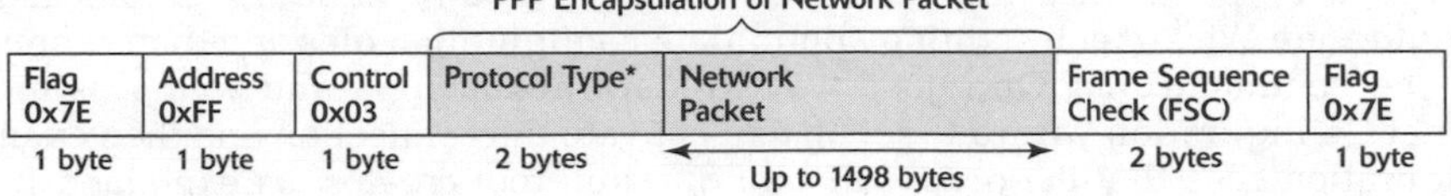

Figure 13-10: The Format of a PPP Frame.

As Figure 13-10 shows, the PPP frames begin and end with a flag character whose value is always 0x7E (7E in hexadecimal notation). The Address and Control fields come from HDLC; they have the fixed values of 0xFF and 0x03, respectively. The PPP data consists of a 2-byte protocol field. (Actually, this field can be only 1 byte; the Link Control Protocol negotiates the length of the protocol field.)

Within the encapsulated network packet, PPP uses 0x7D as the escape character. To send a byte that has a special meaning (such as 0x7E, which marks the beginning and end of a frame), PPP follows these steps:

- Embeds 0x7D in the data
- Places the data byte being escaped
- Toggles the sixth bit of that data byte

Thus, if the PPP data includes 0x7E, that byte is replaced by the 2-byte sequence 0x7D, followed by 0x5E. (If you toggle the sixth bit of 0x7E, or 0111 1110 in binary, you get 0x5E, or 0101 1110 in binary.)

When you use PPP to set up a link between your Linux PC and a remote computer, your PC first sends LCP packets to set up the data link. After the physical data link is established and any optional parameters are negotiated, your PC sends NCP packets to select one or more network protocols for use over that link. Thereafter, any of those network protocols can send packets over the PPP link.

You don't need to know the complete details of PPP to use it effectively. Later in this chapter, I describe how you can use PPP to establish a TCP/IP network connection to another computer.

Connecting to a Remote Network Using PPP

To set up a PPP networking connection between two systems, you must have PPP software running at both ends. Typically, your ISP provides you with an account already set up, so that the PPP software runs automatically upon login. In that case, simply start the PPP software on your system after you log in to the remote system. In some cases, the ISP might use another authentication protocol PAP or CHAP. Those require some additional configuration on your Linux system.

The pppd program takes care of communicating with its peer — a remote PPP server — over a dial-up line. The pppd program's name stands for Point-to-Point Protocol daemon. (In UNIX, daemon refers to a program that runs in the background and performs some useful task.) The pppd program provides an option through which you can invoke another program, such as wvdial, that actually establishes the serial communication and completes the remote login process.

You can set up and activate a PPP connection through Fedora's graphical Internet Configuration Wizard or by editing appropriate configuration files and then running pppd from the command line. One good way to learn about pppd and wvdial is to use the Internet Configuration Wizard to set up and activate the connection and then examine the configuration files that the graphical configuration tool creates, as explained further in the following sections.

Gathering Information for a PPP Connection

Most ISPs provide PPP access to the Internet through one or more systems that the ISP maintains. If you sign up for such a service, the ISP should provide you the information you need to make a PPP connection to the ISP's system. Typically, this information includes the following:

- The phone number to dial to connect to the remote system.
- The user name and password you must use to log in to the remote system.
- The names of the ISP's mail and news servers.
- The IP address for your side of the PPP connection. (This IP address is associated with your PC's PPP interface — the serial port.) The ISP does not provide this address if the IP address is assigned dynamically using DHCP (this means the IP address may change every time your system establishes a connection).
- IP addresses of the ISP's Domain Name Servers (DNS). The ISP does not provide these addresses if it assigns the IP address dynamically.

Of this information, the first two items are what you need to set up a PPP connection.

Using the Internet Configuration Wizard

Follow these steps to set up a PPP connection using the Internet Configuration Wizard:

1. Select Applications ⇨ System Tools ⇨ Internet Configuration Wizard from the GNOME desktop (if you are not logged in as `root`, you'll be prompted for the root password). The Select Device Type dialog box appears (see Figure 13-11). Click the Modem connection, and then click Forward.

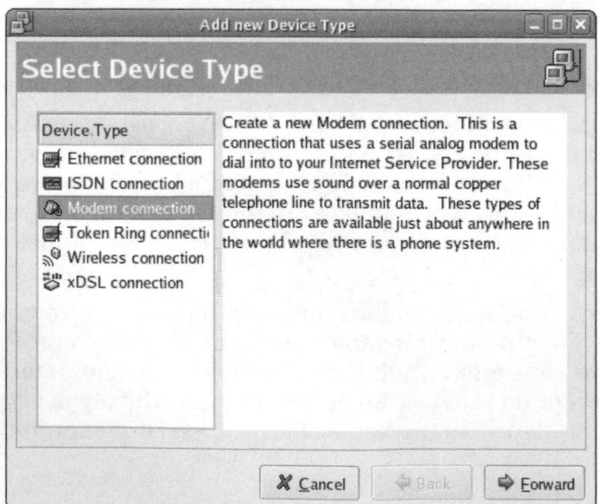

Figure 13-11: Configuring a New Modem Connection.

2. The Select Modem dialog box shows information about your modem. Click Forward to continue.
3. The Select Provider dialog box appears. Fill in the connection information — the ISP's phone number, your login name, and password — in the text boxes. Click Forward to continue.
4. The IP Settings dialog appears. Fill in the requested IP settings. Typically, you would set it to automatically obtain IP settings from the provider. However, if you have static IP address, you can enter that information in this dialog box.
5. Click Apply to save the dial-up configuration information and close the Internet Configuration Wizard.
6. The Network Configuration dialog box appears with the name of the new dial-up connection in a list (see Figure 13-12). In this case, I have configured a PPP connection with the nickname `MyISP`. Click the connection name and click Activate. You can verify the PPP connection by typing the `/sbin/ifconfig` command (and looking for the `ppp0` interface in the output) or by running a Web browser such as Firefox to access websites on the Internet.

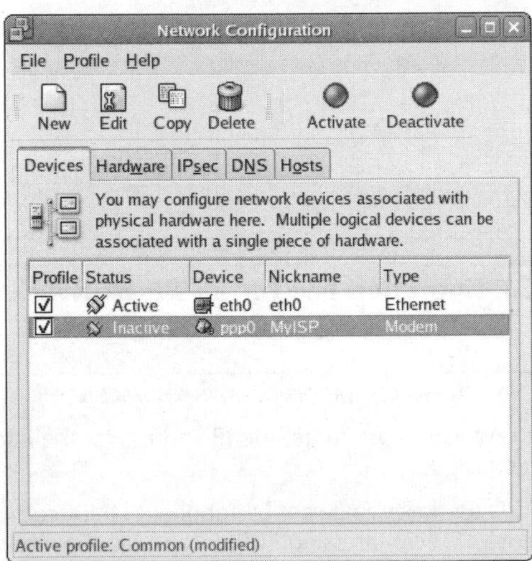

Figure 13-12: Click Activate in the Network Configuration dialog box to establish the PPP connection.

7. When you're done, click Deactivate to turn the PPP connection off.

Understanding the PPP Configuration Files

The Internet Configuration Wizard and the Network Configuration tool save configuration information in the `/etc/sysconfig/network-scripts/ifcfg-XXX` (where `XXX` is the nickname you assigned to the PPP connection in Step 5 of the configuration) and `/etc/wvdial.conf` files. In this case, I configured a PPP connection with the nickname `MyISP`. For the `MyISP` account, the contents of the `/etc/sysconfig/network-scripts/ifcfg-MyISP` file are as follows:

```
# Please read /usr/share/doc/initscripts-*/sysconfig.txt
# for the documentation of these parameters.
ONBOOT=no
USERCTL=yes
PEERDNS=yes
TYPE=Modem
DEVICE=ppp0
BOOTPROTO=dialup
AC=off
BSDCOMP=off
VJCCOMP=off
CCP=off
PC=off
VJ=off
LINESPEED=115200
MODEMPORT=/dev/ttyS1
PROVIDER=MyISP
DEFROUTE=yes
PERSIST=no
PAPNAME=naba
WVDIALSECT=MyISP
MODEMNAME=Modem0
DEMAND=no
```

Table 13-3 explains the meaning of these settings.

Table 13-3: Settings in the Configuration File for a PPP Network Interface

Parameter	*Description*
AC	Set to on to enable address compression; otherwise, set to off.
BOOTPROTO	The name of the protocol to use to get the IP address for the interface. Set to dialup for PPP interface.
BSDCOMP	Set to on if the BSD (Berkeley Software Distribution) UNIX compression protocol is to be used for compressing PPP encapsulated packets. Otherwise, set this to off.
CCP	Set to on to enable the Compression Control Protocol (CCP), which is responsible for configuring, enabling, and disabling data compression algorithms at both ends of the point-to-point link. Set to off if CCP is not being used.
DEFROUTE	Set to yes if you want the PPP connection to be the default route for your system (this is true if the PPP connection is how you connect to the Internet). Otherwise, set this option to no.
DEMAND	Set to yes if you want pppd to dial out on demand (whenever there is some application attempting a connection to the Internet). Otherwise, set to no.

Parameter	Description
DEVICE	The device name for the PPP interface (ppp0 for the first interface, ppp1 for second, and so on).
LINESPEED	Causes pppd to set the modem's data rate (often called the baud rate) to the specified number of bits per second. This is not the same as the data-transfer rate between the local and the remote modem; this simply sets the highest data rate for the UART. (See Appendix E for a discussion of UART.)
MODEMNAME	Identifies the section in /etc/wvdial.conf file that defines the characteristics of the modem (for example, Modem0).
MODEMPORT	The name of the device where the modem is connected (for example, /dev/ttyS0 for first serial port, /dev/ttyS1 for the second serial port, and so on).
ONBOOT	Set to yes to establish the PPP connection at boot time. Set to no if you want to manually activate the PPP connection when you need it.
PAPNAME	The user name to be used to log in to the remote system (this is the user name your ISP gives you).
PC	Set to on to enable protocol field compression. Otherwise, set this to off.
PEERDNS	Set to yes if you want the interface to modify your system's /etc/resolv.conf file to use the ISP's DNS servers. Set to no, if you want the /etc/resolv.conf file unchanged.
PERSIST	Set to yes if you want the PPP link to be restarted every time it goes down. Otherwise, set it to no.
PROVIDER	Name of the ISP (for example, MyISP).
TYPE	Set to Modem for dial-up PPP interface.
USERCTL	Set to yes if you want any user to control the PPP interface. Set it to no if you want only root to control the interface.
VJ	Set to on to enable Van Jacobson–style TCP/IP header compression. Otherwise, set this to off.
VJCCOMP	Set to on to enable the connection-ID compression option in Van Jacobson–style TCP/IP header compression. With this option enabled, pppd will omit the connection-ID byte from Van Jacobson–compressed TCP/IP headers and ask the other end of the PPP connection to do the same. Set the option to off if you do not want to use this compression.
WVDIALSECT	The name of the section in /etc/wvdial.conf file that should be used with /usr/sbin/wvdial to dial out (for example, MyISP refers to the [Dialer MyISP] section in /etc/wvdial.conf).

When you establish a PPP connection by clicking Activate in the Network Configuration tool, that GUI tool uses two programs — `/usr/sbin/pppd` and `/usr/bin/wvdial` — with appropriate options to dial out and set up the PPP connection. For the connection named `MyISP` PPP, the Network Configuration tool starts pppd with the following command:

```
/usr/sbin/pppd -detach lock modem crtscts asyncmap 00000000
defaultroute usepeerdns user naba remotename ppp0 /dev/ttyS1 57600
ipparam ppp0 linkname ppp0 call MyISP noauth
```

You can look up the meanings of the pppd options by reading the `pppd` man page with the `man pppd` command. A key option here is `call MyISP`. That options tells pppd to dial out using the command stored in the file `/etc/ppp/peers/MyISP`. Note that the command file is named after the nickname for the PPP connection; it's `MyISP` for my systems because that's what I assigned as the nickname when I configured the connection. For the `MyISP` connection, `/etc/ppp/peers/MyISP` contains the following line:

```
connect "/usr/bin/wvdial --remotename MyISP --chat 'MyISP'"
```

That line instructs pppd to connect by executing the command within double quotes following the connect option. In this example, pppd runs the `/usr/bin/wvdial` program with the following command line:

```
/usr/bin/wvdial --remotename MyISP --chat MyISP
```

The `--chat` option causes `/usr/bin/wvdial` to run just like the chat program, under control of pppd. Like chat, wvdial dials the modem, connects to the remote system, looks for login prompt, and sends the appropriate user name and password.

The wvdial program looks for the phone number and other details for the `MyISP` connection in the `/etc/wvdial.conf` file — in a section named `MyISP`. Here's what the `/etc/wvdial.conf` file contains:

```
[Modem0]
Modem = /dev/ttyS1
Baud = 115200
SetVolume = 0
Dial Command = ATDT
Init1 = ATZ
Init3 = ATM0
FlowControl = CRTSCTS
[Dialer MyISP]
Area Code = 301
Username = naba
Password = mypassword
Phone = 555-1212
Stupid Mode = 1
Init1 = ATZ
Init2 = ATQ0 V1 E1 S0=0 &C1 &D2 +FCLASS=0
Inherits = Modem0
```

The [Modem0] section lists information about the modem named Modem0, including any modem initialization commands (ATZ, in this example). This modem name also appears in the MODEMNAME field of the PPP configuration file such as /etc/sysconfig/network-scripts/ifcfg-ppp0.

caution

The [Dialer MyISP] section contains the information needed to dial and log in to the ISP. Notice that the password is stored in plaintext form in /etc/wvdial.conf. To protect your ISP user name and password, you should make sure that only root has read and write access to the /etc/wvdial.conf file.

Configuring CHAP and PAP Authentication

The pppd on your system has to authenticate itself to the ISP's PPP server before the PPP connection is up and running. Authentication requires proving that you have a valid account with the ISP and essentially involves providing a user name and a secret (password). PPP specifies two ways of exchanging the authentication information between the two ends of the connection:

- **CHAP:** Challenge Handshake Authentication Protocol (CHAP) requires the remote end to send a randomly generated challenge string along with the remote server's name. The local system looks up the secret using the server's name and sends back a response that includes its name and a value that combines the secret and the challenge by using a one-way hash function. The remote system then checks that value against its own calculation of the expected hash value. If the values match, the authentication succeeds; otherwise, the remote system terminates the connection. In this case, the name and secret are stored in the /etc/ppp/chap-secrets file. Note that the remote system can repeat the CHAP authentication any time while the PPP link is up.
- **PAP:** Password Authentication Protocol (PAP) is like the normal login process. When using PAP, the local system repeatedly sends a user name (name) and password (secret) until the remote system acknowledges the authentication or ends the connection. The name and secret are stored in the /etc/ppp/pap-secrets file. Note that the user name and password are sent in the clear in unencrypted plain text form so that anyone intercepting the data can read it.

The Linux pppd server supports both types of authentication. For both PAP and CHAP, the information that the pppd server needs is a name and a secret—a user-name–password pair. This authentication information is stored in the following configuration files:

- /etc/ppp/chap-secrets **stores the information for CHAP. Here's what a typical** chap-secrets **file looks like:**

```
# Secrets for authentication using CHAP
# client        server  secret                  IP addresses
"naba"  *       "mypassword"
```

continues

continued

- /etc/ppp/pap-secrets stores the information for PAP. Here's a typical pap-secrets file:

```
# Secrets for authentication using PAP
# client        server  secret                    IP addresses
"naba"  *       "mypassword"
```

As you can see, the format of entries is the same for both chap-secrets and pap-secrets. There are four fields in each line, in the following order:

1. **client:** This field contains the name to be used during authentication. This is the user name that you get from the ISP.
2. **server:** This field contains the name of the remote system to which you are authenticating the local system. If you don't know the server's name, put an asterisk to indicate any server.
3. **secret:** This field is the secret that your system's pppd has to send to the remote system to authenticate itself. This is the password you received from the ISP.
4. **IP addresses:** This optional field can contain a list of the IP addresses that the local system may use when connecting to the specified server. Typically, this field is left blank because the local system usually gets a dynamic IP address from the server and, therefore, does not know what IP address it would use.

Testing the PPP Connection

If you have PPP access to another system (such as an ISP or a system at your employer's organization), you can set up a script as described in the preceding section and enjoy the benefits of full TCP/IP network access to another system. After you run the script, and after pppd completes the initial protocol exchanges to set up the connection, you can verify that the connection is up by typing the ifconfig command. You should see the ppp0 device listed in the output. The ifconfig output also shows the IP addresses of the local and remote ends of the PPP connection. This output confirms that the PPP device is up and running.

To verify that the routing table is set up correctly, use the /sbin/route command without any arguments, as follows:

```
/sbin/route
Kernel IP routing table
Destination   Gateway       Genmask         Flags Metric Ref Use Iface
209.100.18.4  *             255.255.255.255 UH    0      0     0 ppp0
192.168.1.200 *             255.255.255.255 UH    0      0     0 eth0
192.168.1.0   *             255.255.255.0   U     0      0     0 eth0
127.0.0.0     *             255.0.0.0       U     0      0     0 lo
default       209.100.18.4  0.0.0.0         UG    0      0     0 ppp0
```

In the routing table, the first line shows a route to the remote end of the PPP connection; this one should be set to the ppp0 device. Also, the default route should be set up so that the remote end of the PPP connection serves as the gateway for your system (as the last line of the routing table shows).

After checking the interface configuration (with the `ifconfig` command) and the routing table (with the route command), verify that you can reach some well-known host. If your ISP gives you the IP address of a name server or a mail server, you can try to ping those addresses. Otherwise, try to ping the IP address of a system at your workplace or university.

The following example displays the results of the `ping` command:

```
ping 140.90.23.100
PING 140.90.23.100 (140.90.23.100): 56 data bytes
64 bytes from 140.90.23.100: icmp_seq=0 ttl=241 time=244.3 ms
64 bytes from 140.90.23.100: icmp_seq=1 ttl=241 time=200.0 ms
64 bytes from 140.90.23.100: icmp_seq=2 ttl=241 time=220.0 ms
64 bytes from 140.90.23.100: icmp_seq=3 ttl=241 time=190.0 ms

--- 140.90.23.100 ping statistics ---
4 packets transmitted, 4 packets received, 0% packet loss
round-trip min/avg/max = 190.0/213.5/244.3 ms
```

The end of each line shows the round-trip time for a packet originating at your system to reach the designated IP address (140.90.23.100, in this case) and to return to your system. For a PPP connection over dial-up lines, you can see times in hundreds of milliseconds.

Incidentally, you do not have to have an account on a system to ping its IP address. Although a system may disable the automatic response to ping messages (ping uses Internet Control Message Protocol or ICMP messages), most systems respond to ping.

Using IP Masquerading to Share an Internet Connection

Linux supports a feature called IP masquerading that enables you to connect an Ethernet LAN with a private IP address to the Internet. This occurs through a Linux PC (with an officially assigned IP address) that has a connection to the Internet as well as a connection to a LAN (for example, your home network). The Linux PC may be connected to the Internet by dial-up PPP or by a high-speed connection, such as DSL or cable modem.

With IP masquerading enabled, your Linux PC acts as a stand-in for any of the other systems on the Ethernet LAN. As with the router setup, the Linux PC is designated as the gateway for the Ethernet LAN. However, masquerading involves more than simply forwarding IP packets back and forth between the LAN and the Internet. The Linux PC acts as a network address translation (NAT) router between the LAN and the Internet.

When the Linux PC masquerades as another system on the LAN, it modifies outgoing packets so that they always appear to originate from the Linux PC. When a response to one of the outgoing packets is received, the Linux PC performs the reverse task—it modifies the packets so that they appear to come from the Internet, directly to the system that sends the outgoing packet. The result is that each system on the Ethernet LAN appears to have full access to the Internet, even though the Ethernet LAN uses a nonunique, private IP address.

To enable and use IP masquerading, perform the following steps:

1. Make sure the Linux PC has an Internet connection and a network connection to your LAN. Typically, the Linux PC has two network interfaces — an Ethernet card for the LAN and a dial-up PPP connection to the Internet (through an ISP).
2. Make sure that all other systems on your LAN use the Linux PC's local IP address (not its public, Internet-facing IP address) as the default gateway for TCP/IP networking. Use the same ISP-provided DNS addresses on all systems.
3. Enable IP forwarding in the kernel by typing the following command:

   ```
   echo "1" > /proc/sys/net/ipv4/ip_forward
   ```

   This is necessary because IP forwarding is disabled by default. To ensure that IP forwarding is enabled when you reboot your system, place this command in the `/etc/rc.d/rc.local` file.
4. Run `/sbin/iptables` — the IP packet filter administration program — to set up the rules that enable the Linux PC to masquerade for your LAN. For example, to enable masquerading for a LAN via the Linux PC's `eth0` network interface (assuming that the `eth0` interface is connected to the DSL or cable modem), you can use the following command:

   ```
   /sbin/iptables -t nat -A POSTROUTING -o eth0 -j MASQUERADE
   ```

   You can also add packet filtering to ensure that no new connections can come in through the `ppp0` interface. The following two commands turn on this packet filtering:

   ```
   /sbin/iptables -A INPUT -i eth0 -m state --state NEW,INVALID -j DROP
   /sbin/iptables -A FORWARD -i eth0 -m state --state NEW,INVALID -j DROP
   ```

   If you want the IP masquerading set up at system startup, type **service iptables save** so that iptables saves the rules in the `/etc/sysconfig/iptables` file. From then on, whenever you start the Fedora Core system, `iptables` automatically loads these rules and sets up the system as a NAT router.

You may find IP masquerading a convenient way to provide Internet access to a small LAN (for example, a LAN at home or in the office). With IP masquerading on the Linux PC, everyone in your family or small business can access the Internet from any of the other PCs on the LAN.

Setting Up a PPP Server

The preceding sections describe how your Linux PC can establish a PPP link with another system that offers PPP service. After a PPP link is set up, both ends of the PPP link behave as peers. Before a PPP link is established, you can think of the end that initiates the dial-up connection as the client because that system asks for the connection. The other end provides the PPP connection when needed, so it's the PPP server.

If you want to enable other people to connect to your Linux PC by using PPP over a dial-up modem, log in as `root` and perform these steps:

1. Insert the DVD-ROM and mount using the `mount /media/cdrom` command (or, if you are running GNOME, wait for the DVD to be automatically mounted). Then type the following commands to install the `mgetty` RPM:

   ```
   cd /media/cdrom/Fedora/RPMS
   rpm -ivh mgetty*.rpm
   ```

2. At the end of the /etc/mgetty+sendfax/mgetty.config file, add the following lines for the serial port connected to a modem for dial-in users (this example assumes that the modem is connected to the second serial port, COM2):

```
# For US Robotics Sportster 56K with speaker off
port ttyS1
init-chat "" ATZ OK AT&F1M0E1Q0S0=0 OK
answer-chat "" ATA CONNECT \c \r
```

   The AT&F1 modem command sets hardware flow-control mode on many modems. For other modems use appropriate initializations in the init-chat line. Note that the serial port device names may change depending on your serial communications hardware (for example, multiport serial boards would have their own device names).

3. Edit the text file /etc/mgetty+sendfax/login.config and search for the line that starts with /AutoPPP/. Uncomment it by deleting the # character at the beginning of the line. Edit the line so that it looks like this:

```
/AutoPPP/ - a_ppp /usr/sbin/pppd file /etc/ppp/options
```

   As the last part of that line shows, automatic PPP startup involves running pppd with the options listed in the file /etc/ppp/options.

4. Edit the file /etc/ppp/options and make sure that it contains the following lines:

```
asyncmap 0
auth
crtscts
-detach
lock
login
modem
ms-dns 192.168.0.1 #put the IP address of the DNS server here
proxyarp
refuse-chap
require-pap
```

   Here is what these options mean:

   - **asyncmap 0:** Causes pppd not to set up and use escape control sequences
   - **auth:** Causes pppd to require the peer to authenticate itself
   - **crtscts:** Causes pppd to use hardware flow control
   - **-detach:** Causes pppd not to become a background process (which pppd will do if a serial device is specified)
   - **lock:** Creates a lock file so that pppd can have exclusive access to the particular modem
   - **login:** Causes pppd to use the system password file to authenticate the peer using PAP
   - **ms-dns DNS_IP:** Specifies the IP address of the name server that pppd can send to the system that dials in
   - **modem:** Causes pppd to use modem control lines
   - **proxyarp:** Causes the other end of the PPP connection to appear as if it is on the LAN with this system
   - **refuse-chap:** Causes pppd to not use CHAP for authentication
   - **require-pap:** Causes pppd to use PAP for authentication

5. Open the /etc/ppp/pap-secrets file in a text editor and locate the following lines:

```
# Secrets for authentication using PAP
# client    server          secret          IP addresses
```

Then add the following line just below these two lines:

```
    *           *           ""          *
```

That basically says that pppd won't use any secrets (because it uses the system password file instead).

6. To set up a specific IP address for each serial port, create a file for that serial port with the name /etc/ppp/options.ttyXX where ttyXX is the serial port device name. In that file list the local IP address and the remote end's IP address, separated by a colon. For example, if for the ttyS1 serial port, the local IP address is 192.168.0.100, and the remote IP address is 192.168.0.200, then add the following line to the file /etc/ppp/options.ttyS1:

```
192.168.0.100:192.168.0.200
```

7. Open the /etc/inittab file in a text editor and add a line of the following form (this example assumes that the modem is on the second serial port, ttyS1):

```
s1:235:respawn:/sbin/mgetty -D -x 3 ttyS1
```

The -D option tells mgetty to treat the modem as a data modem, not fax. The -x 3 option turns on logging — the log file is /tmp/log_mg.ttyS1 (for modem device /dev/ttyS1).

8. Connect the modems to the serial ports, turn them on, and then make init reload the /etc/inittab file (thereby running the mgetty command) with the following command:

```
init q
```

Now, you can test this PPP server setup by dialing in from another PC. You will need to have your Linux system connected to a modem that, in turn, is connected to the phone line. You should turn on the modem, and then you or a friend can dial in to that modem and establish a PPP connection using the user name and password of any existing user on the Linux system.

Summary

Most of us do not have a direct connection to the high-bandwidth backbones of the Internet. Instead, we rely on dial-up modems, cable modems, or DSL connections to Internet service providers (ISPs), which, in turn, are connected to the backbones (typically provided by large telecommunications companies such as Sprint and AT&T). You can accomplish TCP/IP networking over serial lines with SLIP and PPP. Software for both SLIP and PPP comes with Linux. This chapter explains SLIP and PPP and shows you how to configure and use DSL, cable modem, PPP over dial-up modem, and wireless Ethernet to connect a single PC or a LAN to the Internet.

In this chapter, you learned the following:

- DSL and cable modem provides higher-speed access to the Internet than dial-up modems. You can use a network address translation (NAT) router and a hub to connect a single PC or a small LAN to the Internet through DSL or cable modem.
- If you have laptops with wireless Ethernet cards, you can bring them onto your LAN by connecting a wireless access point to the Ethernet hub and configuring wireless networking on the laptop. This chapter shows you how to configure wireless networking in Linux.
- PPP, or Point-to-Point Protocol, is a more complex protocol for packet transport over any point-to-point link. PPP can carry packets of many protocols over the same link. PPP is the preferred way to establish a dial-up TCP/IP network connection with ISPs.
- Setting up a PPP link involves two basic steps. First, you must use a utility program to dial the modem and make the connection with the remote modem; then you have to start the PPP software on your system. The wvdial program functions with the pppd program to perform these two steps.
- You can use the Internet Configuration Wizard to set up a PPP connection over a dial-up modem and you can use the Network Configuration utility to activate the PPP connection.
- You can use IP masquerading to provide Internet access to a private LAN through a Linux PC that has a PPP connection to an ISP.
- You also can set up your Linux PC as a PPP server so that others may dial in and establish a PPP connection with your system. This chapter describes the steps for setting up a PPP server.

Web Server

Secrets in This Chapter

Chapter 13 shows you how to connect your Linux PC to the Internet through an Internet service provider (ISP). This chapter addresses one of the reasons the Internet has become so popular in recent years: the World Wide Web (or simply the Web), which provides an easy graphical way to browse and retrieve information from the Internet.

As a host on the Internet, all your Linux system needs is a Web browser — an application that "knows" how to download and display Web documents — so that you can enjoy the benefits of the Web. You also can make information available to other users through Web pages — the common term for Web documents.

This chapter explains what the Web is and describes the HyperText Transfer Protocol (HTTP) — the information exchange protocol that makes the Web work. Then, it provides a brief introduction to the Firefox Web browser, which comes with Linux on this book's companion DVD-ROM.

Next, the chapter addresses the use of the Web as a popular way to publish information on the Internet. Linux includes the Apache HTTP server (HTTP server being the technical term for a Web server), which you can use simply by placing your HTML files in the appropriate directory. This chapter shows you where various files should go and how to configure the Apache Web server.

Discovering the World Wide Web

If you have used a network file server of any kind, you know the convenience of being able to access files that reside at a shared location. Using a word-processing application that runs on your computer, you can easily open a document that physically resides on the file server.

Now, imagine a word processor that enables you to open and view a document that resides on any computer on the Internet. You can view the document in its full glory, with formatted text and graphics. If the document makes a reference to another document (possibly one that resides on yet another computer), you can open that linked document by clicking the reference. That kind of easy access to distributed documents is essentially what the Web provides.

Of course, the documents have to be in a standard format, so that any computer (with appropriate Web software) can access and interpret them. In addition, a standard protocol is necessary for transferring Web documents from one system to another.

The standard Web document format is HyperText Markup Language (HTML), and the standard protocol for exchanging Web documents is HyperText Transfer Protocol (HTTP).

note

A *Web server* is the software that sends HTML documents (and other files as well) to any client that makes the appropriate HTTP requests. Typically, a Web browser is the client software that actually downloads an HTML document from a Web server and displays the contents graphically.

Learning URLs

Like the pages of real books, Web pages contain text and graphics. Unlike the pages of real books, however, Web pages can contain multimedia information such as images, video clips, digitized sound, and cross-references, called links, that can actually take the user to the page referred to.

The links in a Web page are references to other Web pages. You follow (click) the links to go from one page to another. The Web browser typically displays these links as underlined text (in a different color) or as images. Each link is like an instruction to the reader — such as "For more information, please consult Chapter 14" — that you might find in a real book. In a Web page, all you have to do is click the link, and the Web browser brings up the page referred to, even if it's on a different computer.

> **note** The term "hypertext" refers to nonlinear organization of text (as opposed to the sequential, linear arrangement of text in most books or magazines). The links in a Web page are referred to as hypertext links; by clicking a link, you can jump to a different Web page, which is an example of nonlinear organization of text.

This arrangement raises a question. In a real book, you might ask the reader to go to a specific chapter or page. How does a hypertext link indicate the location of the Web page in question? Each Web page has a special name, called a Uniform Resource Locator (URL). A URL uniquely specifies the location of a file on a computer, as shown in Figure 14-1.

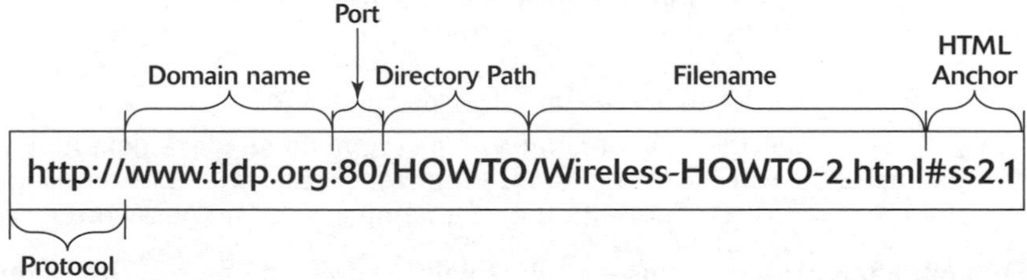

Figure 14-1: A Uniform Resource Locator (URL) Is Composed of Various Parts.

> **note** The directory path in Figure 14-1 can contain several subdirectories as indicated by the slash.

As Figure 14-1 illustrates, a URL has this sequence of components:

1. **Protocol:** This is the name of the protocol the Web browser uses to access the data that resides in the file the URL specifies. In Figure 14-1, the protocol is `http://`, which means that the URL specifies the location of a Web page. Following are the common protocol types and their meanings:
   - `file://` specifies the name of a local file that is to be opened and displayed. You can use this in your URL to view HTML files without having to connect to the Internet. For example, `file:///usr/share/doc/HTML/index.html` opens the file `/usr/share/doc/HTML/index.html` from your Linux system.

- `ftp://` specifies a file that is accessible through File Transfer Protocol (FTP). For example, `ftp://ftp.purdue.edu/pub/uns/NASA/nasa.jpg` refers to the image file `nasa.jpg` from the `/pub/uns/NASA/` directory of the FTP server `ftp.purdue.edu`. (If you want to access a specific user account by FTP, use the URL of the form `ftp://username:password@ftp.somesite.com/` with the user name and password embedded in the URL.)
- `http://` specifies a file that is accessible through the HyperText Transfer Protocol (HTTP). This is the well-known format of URLs for all websites, such as `http://www.redhat.com/` for Red Hat's home page.
- `https://` specifies a file that is to be accessed through a Secure Sockets Layer (SSL) connection, which is a protocol designed by Netscape Communications for encrypted data transfers across the Internet. This form of URL is typically used when the Web browser sends sensitive information such as credit card number, user name, and password to a Web server. For example, a URL such as `https://some.site.com/secure/takeorder.html` might display an HTML form that requests credit card information and other personal information such as name, address, and phone number.
- `mailto://` specifies an email address you can use to send an email message. For example, `mailto:webmaster@someplace.com` refers to the Webmaster at the host `someplace.com`.
- `news://` specifies a newsgroup you can read by means of the Network News Transfer Protocol (NNTP). For example, `news://news.psn.net/comp.infosystems.www.authoring.html` accesses the `comp.infosystems.www.authoring.html` newsgroup at the news server `news.psn.net`. If you have a default news server configured for the Web browser, you can omit the news server's name and use the URL `news:comp.infosystems.www.authoring.html` to access the newsgroup.
- `telnet://` specifies a user name and a system name for remote login. For example, the URL `telnet://guest:bemyguest@someplace.com/` logs in to the host `someplace.com` with the user name `guest` and password `bemyguest`.

2. **Domain name:** This contains the fully qualified domain name of the computer on which resides the file this URL specifies. You can also specify an IP address in this field (see Chapter 6 for more information on IP addresses). The domain name is not case sensitive.
3. **Port address:** This is the port address of the server that implements the protocol listed in the first part of the URL (see Chapter 6 for a discussion of port addresses). This part of the URL is optional; there are default ports for all protocols. The default port for HTTP, for example, is 80. Some sites, however, may configure the Web server to listen to a different port. In such a case, the URL must include the port address.
4. **Directory path:** This is the directory path of the file being referred to in the URL. For Web pages, this field is the directory path of the HTML file. The directory path is case sensitive.
5. **Filename:** This is the name of the file. For Web pages, the filename typically ends with .htm or .html. If you omit the filename, the Web server returns a default file (often named `index.html`). The filename is case sensitive.

6. **HTML anchor:** This optional part of the URL makes the Web browser jump to a specific location in the file. If this part starts with a question mark (?) instead of a hash mark (#), the browser takes the text following the question mark to be a query. The Web server returns information based on such queries.

Understanding HyperText Transfer Protocol

The HyperText Transfer Protocol (HTTP) — the protocol that underlies the Web — is called HyperText because Web pages include hypertext links. The Transfer Protocol part refers to the standard conventions for transferring a Web page across the network from one computer to another. Although you really do not have to understand HTTP to set up a Web server or use a Web browser, I think you'll find it instructive to know how the Web works.

Before I explain anything about HTTP, you should get some firsthand experience of it. On most systems, the Web server listens to port 80 and responds to any HTTP requests sent to that port. Therefore, you can use the Telnet program to connect to port 80 of a system (if it has a Web server) to try some HTTP commands.

To see an example of HTTP at work, follow these steps:

1. Make sure your Linux PC's connection to the Internet is up and running. (If you use SLIP or PPP, for example, make sure that you have established a connection.)
2. Type the following command:

   ```
   telnet www.gao.gov 80
   ```

3. After you see the Connected . . . message, type the following HTTP command:

   ```
   GET / HTTP/1.0
   ```

   and press Enter twice. In response to this HTTP command, the Web server returns some useful information, followed by the contents of the default HTML file (usually called `index.html`).

The following is what I get when I try the `GET` command on the U.S. General Accounting Office's website:

```
telnet www.gao.gov 80
Trying 161.203.16.2...
Connected to www.gao.gov (161.203.16.2).
Escape character is '^]'.
GET / HTTP/1.0   (type this line and then press Enter twice)

HTTP/1.1 200 OK
Date: Sat, 16 Apr 2005 19:28:52 GMT
Server: Apache
Connection: close
Content-Type: text/html; charset=ISO-8859-1

<html>
  <head>
  <title>The Government Accountability Office</title>
... (lines deleted) ...
  </head>
```

```
  <body OnUnLoad='Poll(); return true;' >
... (lines deleted) ...
  </body>
</html>

Connection closed by foreign host.
```

When you try this example with Telnet, you see exactly what the Web server sends back to the Web browser. The first few lines are administrative information for the browser. The server returns this information:

- A line that shows that the server uses HTTP protocol version 1.1 and a status code of 200 indicating success: `HTTP/1.1 200 OK`
- The current date and time. A sample date and time string looks like this:
  `Date: Sat, 16 Apr 2005 19:28:52 GMT`
- The name, version, and other details of the Web-server software. Nowadays it's common practice to show only the generic name of the software (for example, `Apache`) and not provide any other details because someone might use the version information to attack specific vulnerabilities of that version.
- The type of document the Web server returns. For HTML documents, the content type is reported as follows along with the character set used in the document:
  `Content-Type: text/html; charset=ISO-8859-1`

The document itself follows the administrative information. An HTML document has the following general layout:

```
<html>
  <head>
    <title>Document's title goes here</title>
  </head>
<body optional attributes go here >
... The rest of the document goes here.
</body>
</html>
```

You can identify this layout by looking through the listing that shows what the Web server returns in response to the `GET` command. Because the example uses a Telnet command to get the document, you see the HTML content as lines of text. If you were to access the same URL (`www.gao.gov`) with a Web browser (such as Firefox), you would see the page in its graphical form, as shown in Figure 14-2.

The example of HTTP commands shows the result of the `GET` command. `GET` is the most common HTTP command; it causes the server to return a specified HTML document.

The other two HTTP commands are `HEAD` and `POST`. The `HEAD` command is almost like `GET`: it causes the server to return everything in the document except the body. The `POST` command sends information to the server; it's up to the server to decide how to act on the information.

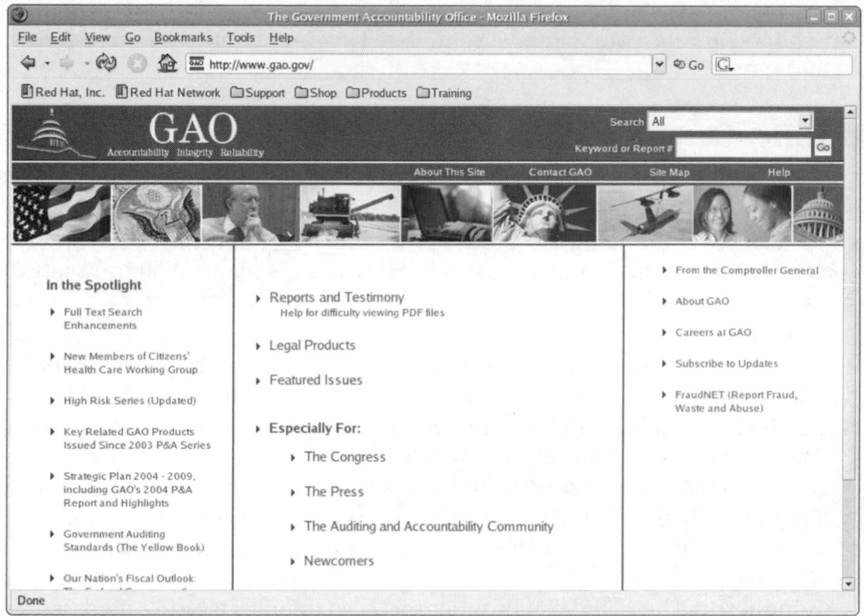

Figure 14-2: The URL www.gao.gov Viewed with the Firefox Web Browser.

Despite its widespread use on the Web since 1990, HTTP was not an Internet standard until recently. All Internet standards are distributed as Request for Comments (RFCs). The first HTTP-related RFC was RFC 1945, "HyperText Transfer Protocol—HTTP/1.0" (T. Berners-Lee, R. Fielding, and H. Frystyk, May 1996). However, RFC 1945 is considered an informational document, not a standard.

RFC 2616, "HyperText Transfer Protocol—HTTP/1.1" (R. Fielding, J. Gettys, J. Mogul, H. Frystyk, L. Masinter, P. Leach, T. Berners-Lee, June 1999) is the Draft Internet standard for HTTP.

To read these RFCs, point your Web browser to `www.faqs.org/rfcs/rfc-index.html`.

To learn more about HTTP/1.1 and other Web-related standards, use a Web browser to access `www.w3.org/pub/WWW/Protocols/`.

Surfing the Net

Like anything else, the Web is easier to understand after you have seen how it works. One of the best ways to learn about the Web is to surf it with a Web browser. Browsing Web pages is fun because the typical Web page contains both text and images. Also, browsing has an element of surprise; you can click the links and end up at unexpected Web pages. Links are the most curious aspect of the Web. You can start by looking at a page that shows today's weather; a click later, you can be reading this week's issue of *Time* magazine.

Before you can try anything, of course, you need a Web browser. (You must also have an Internet connection for your Linux system, but I am assuming you have already taken care of that part.)

Checking Out the Web Browsers in Linux

Linux comes with Mozilla and Firefox Web browsers — open-source Web browsers from the Mozilla Organization (see `www.mozilla.org/products/firefox/`).

Linux includes several other Web browsers. I briefly mention the other browsers, but I focus on Firefox in the rest of the discussions. Here are the major Web browsers that come with Linux:

- **Mozilla:** The reincarnation of that old workhorse — Netscape Communicator — only better. It includes mail and a newsreader. The Web browser is called the Mozilla Navigator, or simply Navigator (just as it was in Netscape Communicator).
- **Firefox:** Mozilla's next-generation browser that blocks popup ads, provides tabs for easily viewing multiple Web pages in a single window, and includes a set of privacy tools. You can download Firefox from `www.mozilla.org/download.html`.
- **Epiphany:** The GNOME Web browser that uses parts of the Mozilla code to draw the Web pages, but has a simpler user interface than Mozilla. Epiphany is not installed by default, but it should be on the DVDs.
- **Konqueror:** The KDE Web browser that also doubles as a file manager and a universal viewer.

In addition to these four, many other applications are capable of downloading and displaying Web pages.

Starting Firefox

From the GNOME or KDE desktop, you can start Firefox in one of two ways:

- Click the Web Browser icon on the GNOME or KDE panel.
- Select Applications ⇨ Internet ⇨ Firefox Web Browser from GNOME or KDE.

When Firefox starts, it displays a browser window with a default home page (the main Web page on a Web server is known as the home page). You can configure Firefox to use a different Web page as the default home page.

Learning Firefox's User Interface

Figure 14-3 shows a Web page from the Wiley website (`www.wiley.com`), as well as the main elements of the Firefox browser window.

The Firefox Web browser has lots in its user interface, but you can master it easily. You can turn off some of the items that make it look busy. You can also start with just the basics to get going with Firefox and then gradually expand to areas that you have not yet explored.

Starting from the top of the window, you see the standard menu bar, then a Navigation toolbar with icons such as Home and Back, followed by a thinner Bookmark toolbar with bookmark icons. The area underneath the Bookmark toolbar is where the current Web page appears.

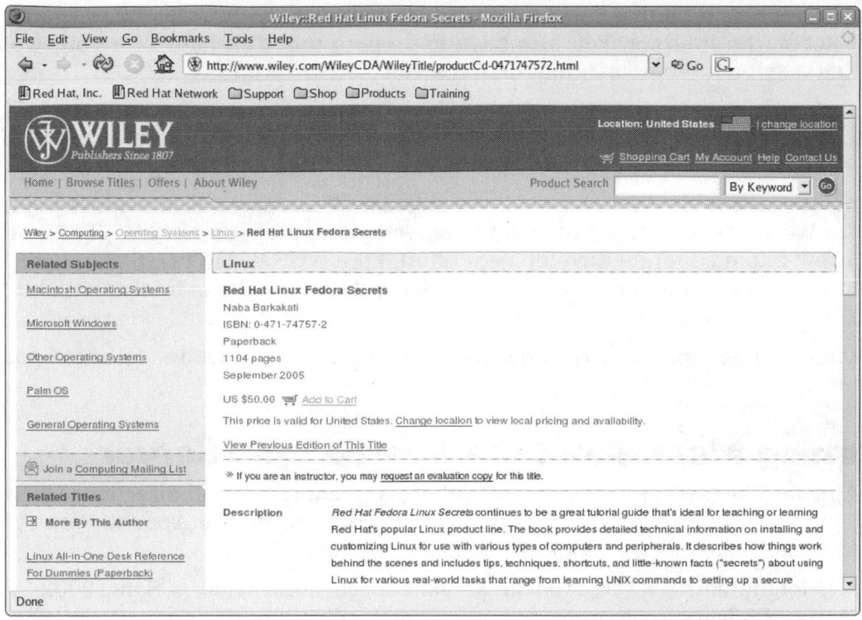

Figure 14-3: The Firefox Web Browser in Action.

Here's what you can do with the buttons on the Navigation toolbar that appears just below the menu bar (from left to right):

- **Back:** Moves to the previous Web page.
- **Forward:** Returns you to the page you left after using the Back button.
- **Reload:** Reloads the current Web page.
- **Stop:** Stops loading the current page.
- **Home:** Takes you to the home page.
- **Location text box:** Shows the URL of the current Web page (type a URL in this box to view that Web page).
- **Go:** Click to go to the URL that you have typed in the Location text box.
- **Google Search:** Type a search string and press Enter to perform a Google search.

Immediately below the Navigation toolbar comes the Bookmark toolbar with buttons that take you to Red Hat's home page or the Red Hat Network site. The rest of the links are organized into several folders. Click a folder to view the drop-down list of links, and click the link you want to visit.

You can think of the bar along the bottom edge of the Firefox window as the status bar because that area displays status information as Firefox loads a Web page.

Setting Up the Apache Web Server

You probably already know how it feels to use the Web, but you may not know how to set up a Web server so that you, too, can provide information to the world through Web pages.

To become an information provider on the Web, you have to run a Web server on your Linux PC on the Internet. You also have to prepare the Web pages for your website — a task that may be more demanding than the Web server setup.

Web servers provide information using HTTP. Web servers are also known as HTTP daemons (because continuously running server processes are called daemons in UNIX) or HTTPD for short. The Web server program is usually named httpd.

Among the available Web servers, the Apache Web server is the most popular. The Apache Web server started out as an improved version of the NCSA HTTPD server but soon grew into a separate development effort. Like NCSA HTTPD, the Apache server is developed and maintained by a team of collaborators. Apache is freely available over the Internet.

The following sections describe the installation and configuration of the Apache Web server.

Learning More about the Apache Web Server

The Apache Web server has too many options and configuration directives to describe in detail in this book. Whole books are devoted to configuring the Apache Web server. You should consult one of these books for more information:

- Mohammed J. Kabir, *Apache Server 2 Bible*, John Wiley & Sons, 2002.
- Ken Coar and Rich Bowen, *Apache Cookbook*, O'Reilly, 2003.

You can also find late-breaking news and detailed information about the latest version of Apache HTTPD from Apache's website at `http://httpd.apache.org/docs-2.0/`. In particular, you can browse a complete list of Apache directives at `http://httpd.apache.org/docs-2.0/mod/directives.html`.

Installing the Apache Web Server

Installing Linux from this book's companion DVD-ROM gives you the option to install the Apache Web server. As described in Chapter 2, simply select the Web Server package group when you are prompted for the components to install. This package group includes the Apache Web server. The Web server program is called httpd, so the Apache Web server package is called httpd.

Perform these steps to verify that the Apache Web server software is installed on your system:

1. Type **rpm -q httpd** in a terminal window to check whether or not the Apache package is installed. Here is a typical output of that command:

   ```
   httpd-2.0.53-6
   ```

   If the output shows an httpd package name, you have installed the Apache software.

2. Type the following command to check whether or not the `httpd` process is running (httpd is the name of the Apache Web server program):

   ```
   ps ax | grep httpd
   ```

If the Apache Web server is running, the output should show a number of `httpd` processes. It is common to run several Web server processes — one parent and several child processes — so that several HTTP requests can be handled efficiently by assigning each request to an `httpd` process. If there is no `httpd` process, log in as `root` and start the `httpd` service with the following command:

```
service httpd start
```

3. Use the Telnet program on your Linux system, and use the `HTTP HEAD` command to query the Web server, as follows:

```
telnet localhost 80
Trying 127.0.0.1...
Connected to localhost.localdomain (127.0.0.1).
Escape character is '^]'..
HEAD / HTTP/1.0  (press Enter twice)

HTTP/1.1 403 Forbidden
Date: Wed, 01 Jun 2005 20:33:52 GMT
Server: Apache/2.0.54 (Fedora)
Accept-Ranges: bytes
Content-Length: 3931
Connection: close
Content-Type: text/html; charset=UTF-8

Connection closed by foreign host.
```

If you get a response such as that in the preceding code, your system already has the Apache Web server installed and set up correctly. All you have to do is understand the configuration so that you can place the HTML documents in the proper directory.

Use a Web server to load the homepage from your system. For instance, if your system's IP address is 192.168.0.100, use the URL `http://192/168.0.100/` and see what happens. You should see a Web page with the title "Test Page for the Apache HTTP Server on Fedora Core."

According to the information about the Apache Web server project on `www.apache.org/`, the Apache group was formed in March 1995 by a number of people who provided patch files that had been written to fix bugs in NCSA HTTPD 1.3. The result after applying the patches to NCSA HTTPD was what they called *a patchy* server (that's how the name Apache came about).

According to the April 2005 Netcraft Web Server Survey at `http://news.netcraft.com/archives/2005/04/index.html`, the Apache Web server is the most popular — 69.32 percent of 62,286,451 sites reported using the Apache server. Microsoft Internet Information Server (IIS) is a distant second, with 20.45 percent of the sites.

Configuring the Apache Web Server

The Apache Web server software uses these files and directories:

- The Web server program — httpd — is installed in the `/usr/sbin` directory.
- The Apache Web server configuration file — `httpd.conf` — is located in the `/etc/httpd/conf` directory. The configuration file is a text file with directives that specify various aspects of the Web server (a later section describes the Apache directives).
- The Apache Web server treats files with a `.conf` extension in the `/etc/httpd/conf.d` directory as configuration files for Apache modules such as `mod_perl`, `mod_python`, `mod_ssl`, and so on. For example, the `/etc/httpd/conf.d` directory contains the configuration information that SSL needs.
- The Apache Web server is set up to serve the HTML documents from the `/var/www/html` directory. Therefore, you should place your Web pages in this directory.
- If you have any Common Gateway Interface (CGI) programs — programs the Web server can invoke to access other files and databases — you should place these in the `/var/www/cgi-bin/` directory.
- The `/var/log/httpd` directory is meant for Web server log files (access logs and error logs).
- The `/etc/init.d/httpd` script starts the httpd process as your Linux system boots. You can type the command `/etc/init.d/httpd start` to run the Web server (another way is to type **service httpd start**).

insider insight

If you want the Apache Web server to start automatically when you boot the system, log in as `root` and type the following command to enable the server:

```
chkconfig --level 35 httpd on
```

To restart Apache httpd after making changes to configuration files, type:

```
service httpd restart
```

Apache Configuration Directives

The Apache HTTPD server's operation is controlled by the directives stored in the `httpd.conf` file located in the `/etc/httpd/conf` directory as well as separate `.conf` files located in the `/etc/httpd/conf.d` directory. The directives in these configuration files specify general attributes of the server, such as the server's name, the port number and the directory in which the server's directories are located. The configuration directives also specify information about the server resources — the documents and other information the Web server provides to users — and access control directives that control access to the entire Web server as well as to specific directories.

The next few sections show you the key information about the Apache httpd configuration directives. Typically, you don't have to change anything in the configuration files to run the Apache Web server. However, knowing the format of the configuration files and the meaning of the various keywords used in them is useful.

As you study the /etc/httpd/conf/httpd.conf file, keep these syntax rules in mind:

- The configuration file is a text file that you can edit with your favorite text editor and view with the more command.
- All comment lines begin with a #.
- Each line can have only one directive.
- Extra spaces and blank lines are ignored.
- Typically, the main configuration file incorporates many other configuration files by using the Include directive.
- All entries, except pathnames and URLs, are case insensitive.

Including All Configuration Files from a Directory

The Include loads can load all configuration files from a specified directory. For example, in Fedora Core, the default /etc/httpd/conf/httpd.conf file loads all the configuration files from the /etc/httpd/conf.d directory by using the following Include directive:

```
Include conf.d/*.conf
```

This command means that you can load another set of configurations by simply adding a file to the /etc/httpd/conf.d directory. In fact, that's the directory where you find the configuration files for various Apache HTTPD modules, such as Perl, PHP, and SSL. In Fedora Core, study the configuration file in the /etc/httpd/conf.d directory to find out more about the total set of directives that affect the Apache Web server's behavior.

The following sections show the Apache directives grouped into three separate categories: general HTTPD directives, resource configuration directives, and access-control directives.

General HTTPD Directives

Many directives control the way that the Apache Web server works. The following list summarizes some of the directives you can use in the httpd.conf file. You can leave most of these directives in their default settings, but it's important to know about them if you are maintaining a Web server.

- **ServerAdmin name@host:** Specifies the email address that the Web server provides to clients in case any errors occur. The default value for ServerAdmin is root@localhost. Set this address to a valid email address that anyone on the Internet can use to report any errors that your website may contain.
- **Listen IP Address:num:** Specifies that the HTTP daemon should listen to port num (a number between 0 and 65,535) at the specified IP address for requests from clients (if you omit the IP address, HTTPD listens to all IP addresses associated with the host). The default port for HTTPD is 80. You should leave the port number at its default value; clients will assume that the HTTP port is 80. If your server does not use port 80, the URL for your server must explicitly specify the port number like this: http://www.mycompany.com:80/.

- **User name [#id]:** Specifies the user name (or ID) the HTTP daemon uses when it is running in standalone mode. You can leave this directive at the default setting (apache). If you specify a user ID, use a hash (#) prefix for the numeric ID.
- **Group name [#id]:** Specifies the group name (or ID) of the HTTP daemon when the server is running in standalone mode. The default group name is `apache`.
- **ServerRoot pathname:** Specifies the directory where the Web server is located. By default, the configuration and log files are expected to reside in subdirectories of this directory. In Fedora Linux, `ServerRoot` is set to `/etc/httpd`.
- **ServerName www.company.com:** Sets the server's host name to *`www.company.com`* instead of to its real host name. You cannot simply invent a name; the name must be a valid name from the Domain Name System (DNS) for your system.
- **StartServers num:** Sets the number of child processes that start as soon as the Apache Web server runs. The default value is 8.
- **MaxSpareServers num:** Sets the desired maximum number of idle child-server processes (a child process is considered idle if it is not handling an HTTP request). The default value is 20.
- **MinSpareServers num:** Sets the desired minimum number of idle child server processes (a child process is considered idle if it is not handling an HTTP request). A new spare process is created every second if the number falls below this threshold. The default value is 5.
- **Timeout numsec:** Sets the number of seconds that the server waits for a client to send a query after the client establishes connection. The default Timeout is 300 seconds (5 minutes).
- **ErrorLog filename:** Sets the file where httpd logs the errors it encounters. If the filename does not begin with a slash (/), the name is taken to be relative to `ServerRoot`. The default `ErrorLog` is `/var/log/httpd/error_log`. Typical error-log entries include events such as server restarts and any warning messages.
- **TransferLog filename:** Sets the file where httpd records all client accesses (including failed accesses). The default `TransferLog` is `/var/log/httpd/access_log`.
- **LogFormat formatstring formatname:** Specifies the format of log-file entries for the `TransferLog`. This format is also used by the `CustomLog` directive to produce logs in a specific format.
- **CustomLog filename formatname:** Sets the name of the custom log file where httpd records all client accesses (including failed accesses) in a format specified by *`formatname`* (which you define using a `LogFormat` directive).
- **PidFile filename:** Sets the file where httpd stores its process ID. The default `PidFile` is `/var/run/httpd.pid`. You can use this information to kill or restart the `HTTP` daemon. The following example shows how to restart `httpd`:

  ```
  kill -HUP `cat /var/run/httpd.pid`
  ```
- **MaxClients num:** Sets the limit on the number of clients that can simultaneously connect to the server. The default value is 150. The value of `MaxClients` cannot be more than 256.
- **LoadModule module modules/modfile.so:** Loads a module that was built as a Dynamic Shared Object (DSO). You have to specify the module name and the module's object file. Because the order in which modules are loaded is important, you should leave these directives as they appear in the default configuration file. Note that the `mod_ssl` module provides support for encryption using the Secure Sockets Layer (SSL) protocol.

Resource Configuration Directives

The resource configuration directives specify the location of the Web pages, as well as how to specify the data types of various files. To get started, you can leave the directives at their default settings. These are some of the resource configuration directives for the Apache Web server:

- **DocumentRoot pathname:** Specifies the directory where the HTTP server finds the Web pages. In Fedora Linux, the default `DocumentRoot` is `/var/www/html`. If you place your HTML documents in another directory, set `DocumentRoot` to that directory.
- **UserDir dirname:** Specifies the directory below a user's home directory where the HTTP server looks for the Web pages when a user name appears in the URL (in a URL such as `http://www.psn.net/~naba/`, for example, which includes a user name with a tilde prefix). The default `UserDir` is `public_html`, which means that a user's Web pages are in the `public_html` subdirectory of that user's home directory. If you do not want to allow users to have Web pages, specify `disabled` as the directory name in the `UserDir` directive. `UserDir` is disabled by default because it can open up the file system to the world. Apache documentation recommends adding the following line to the `httpd.conf` file:

  ```
  UserDir disabled root
  ```

- **DirectoryIndex filename1 filename2 ...:** Indicates the default file or files to be returned by the server when the client does not specify a document. The default `DirectoryIndex` is `index.html`. If httpd does not find this file, it returns an index (basically, a nice-looking listing of the files) of that directory.
- **AccessFileName filename:** Specifies the name of the file that may appear in each directory that contains documents and that indicates who has permission to access the contents of that directory. The default `AccessFileName` is `.htaccess`. The syntax of this file is the same as that of Apache access-control directives, which the next section discusses.
- **AddType type/subtype extension:** Associates a file extension with a MIME (Multipurpose Internet Mail Extensions) data type of the form `type/subtype`, such as `text/plain` or `image/gif`. Thus, to have the server treat files with the `.lst` extension as plaintext files, specify the following:

  ```
  AddType text/plain .lst
  ```

  The default MIME types and extensions are listed in the `/etc/mime.types` file.
- **AddEncoding type extension:** Associates an encoding type with a file extension. To have the server mark files ending with `.gz` or `.tgz` as encoded with the `x-gzip` encoding method (the standard name for the GZIP encoding), specify the following:

  ```
  AddEncoding x-gzip gz tgz
  ```

- **DefaultType type/subtype:** Specifies the MIME type that the server should use if it cannot determine the type from the file extension. If you do not specify `DefaultType`, httpd assumes the MIME type to be `text/html`. In the default `httpd.conf` file that you get from the companion DVD-ROM, `DefaultType` is specified as `text/plain`.
- **Redirect requested-file actual-URL:** Specifies that any requests for `requested-file` are to be redirected to actual URL.

- **Alias requested-dir actual-dir:** Specifies that the server use *actual-dir* to locate files in the *requested-dir* directory. (In other words, *requested-dir* is an alias for *actual-dir*). To have requests for the /icons directory go to /var/www/icons, specify the following:

```
Alias /icons/ /var/www/icons/
```

- **ScriptAlias requested-dir actual-dir:** Specifies the real name of the directory where scripts for the Common Gateway Interface (CGI) are located. For example, the following directive specifies the location of the /cgi-bin/ directory:

```
ScriptAlias /cgi-bin/ /var/www/cgi-bin/
```

  This directive means that when a Web browser requests a script, such as /cgi/bin/test-cgi, the HTTP server runs the script /var/www/cgi-bin/test-cgi.
- **DefaultIcon iconfile:** Specifies the location of the default icon that the server should use for files that have no icon information. By default, DefaultIcon is /icons/unknown.gif.
- **ReadmeName filename:** Specifies the name of a README file whose contents are added to the end of an automatically generated directory listing. The default ReadmeName is README.
- **HeaderName filename:** Specifies the name of a header file whose contents are prepended to an automatically generated directory listing. The default HeaderName is HEADER.
- **AddDescription "file description" filename:** Specifies that the file description string be displayed next to the specified filename in the directory listing. You can use a wildcard, such as *.html, as the filename. For example, the following directive describes files ending with .tgz as GZIP compressed tar archives:

```
AddDescription "GZIP compressed tar archive" .tgz
```

- **AddIcon iconfile extension1 extension2 ...:** Associates an icon with one or more file extensions. The following directive associates the icon file /icons/text.gif with the file extension .txt:

```
AddIcon /icons/text.gif .txt
```

- **AddIconByType iconfile MIME-types:** Associates an icon with a group of file types specified as a wildcard form of MIME types (such as text/* or image/*). To associate an icon file of /icons/text.gif with all text types, specify the following:

```
AddIconByType (TXT,/icons/text.gif) text/*
```

  This directive also tells the server to use TXT in place of the icon for clients that cannot accept images. (Browsers tell the server what types of data they can accept.)
- **AddIconByEncoding iconfile encoding1 encoding2 . . . :** Specifies an icon to be displayed for one or more encoding types (such as x-compress or x-gzip).
- **IndexIgnore filename1 filename2 . . . :** Instructs the server to ignore the specified filenames (they typically contain wildcards) when preparing a directory listing. To leave out README, HEADER, and all files with names that begin with a period (.), a trailing tilde (~), or a trailing hash mark (#), specify the following:

```
IndexIgnore .??* *~ *# HEADER* README* RCS CVS *,v *,t
```

- **IndexOptions option1 option2 . . . :** Indicates the options you want in the directory listing prepared by the server. Options can include one or more of the following:
  - `FancyIndexing` turns on the fancy directory listing that includes filenames and icons representing the files' types, sizes, and last-modified dates.
  - `IconHeight=N` specifies that icons are `N` pixels tall.
  - `IconWidth=N` specifies that icons are N pixels wide.
  - `NameWidth=N` makes the filename column N characters wide.
  - `IconsAreLinks` makes the icons act like links.
  - `ScanHTMLTitles` shows a description of HTML files.
  - `SuppressHTMLPreamble` does not add a standard HTML preamble to the header file (specified by the `HeaderName` directive).
  - `SuppressLastModified` stops the displaying of the last date of modification.
  - `SuppressSize` stops the displaying of the file size.
  - `SuppressDescription` stops the displaying of any file description.
  - `SuppressColumnSorting` stops the column headings from being links that enable sorting the columns.
- **ErrorDocument errortype filename:** Specifies a file the server should send when an error of a specific type occurs. You can also provide a text message for an error. Here are some examples:

```
ErrorDocument 403 "Sorry, you cannot access this directory"
ErrorDocument 403 /error/noindex.html
ErrorDocument 404 /cgi-bin/bad_link.pl
ErrorDocument 401 /new_subscriber.html
```

  If you do not have this directive, the server sends a built-in error message. The *errortype* can be one of the following HTTP/1.1 error conditions (see RFC 2616 at `www.ietf.org/rfc/rfc2616.txt` or `www.faqs.org/rfcs/rfc2616.html` for more information):
  - **400:** Bad Request
  - **401:** Unauthorized
  - **402:** Payment Required
  - **403:** Forbidden
  - **404:** Not Found
  - **405:** Method Not Allowed
  - **406:** Not Acceptable
  - **407:** Proxy Authentication Required
  - **408:** Request Timeout
  - **409:** Conflict
  - **410:** Gone
  - **411:** Length Required
  - **412:** Precondition Failed
  - **413:** Request Entity Too Large

- **414:** Request-URI Too Long
- **415:** Unsupported Media Type
- **416:** Requested Range Not Satisfiable
- **417:** Expectation Failed
- **500:** Internal Server Error
- **501:** Not Implemented
- **502:** Bad Gateway
- **503:** Service Unavailable
- **504:** Gateway Timeout
- **505:** HTTP Version Not Supported

♦ **TypesConfig filename:** Specifies the file that contains the mapping of file extensions to MIME data types. (MIME stands for Multipurpose Internet Mail Extensions, which defines a way to package attachments in a single message file.) The server reports these MIME types to clients. If you do not specify a `TypesConfig` directive, httpd assumes that the `TypesConfig` file is `/etc/mime.types`. The following are a few selected lines from the default `/etc/mime.types` file:

```
application/msword          doc
application/pdf             pdf
application/postscript      ai eps ps
application/x-tcl           tcl
audio/mpeg                  mpga mp2 mp3
audio/x-pn-realaudio        ram rm
audio/x-wav                 wav
image/gif                   gif
image/jpeg                  jpeg jpg jpe
image/png                   png
text/html                   html htm
text/plain                  asc txt
video/mpeg                  mpeg mpg mpe
```

Each line shows the MIME type (such as `text/html`), followed by the file extensions for that type (`html` or `htm`).

Access-Control Directives

Access-control directives enable you to control who can access different directories in the system. These are the global access-configuration directives. In each directory containing documents served by the Apache Web server, you can have another access-configuration file with the name specified by the `AccessFileName` directive. (That per-directory access-configuration file is named `.htaccess` by default.)

Stripped of most of the comment lines, the access-control directive has this format:

```
# First, we configure the "default" to be a
# very restrictive set of permissions.
<Directory />
  Options FollowSymLinks
  AllowOverride None
</Directory>
```

```
# The following directory name should
# match DocumentRoot in httpd.conf
<Directory /var/www/html>
    Options Indexes FollowSymLinks
    AllowOverride None
    Order allow,deny
    Allow from all
</Directory>

# The directory name should match the
# location of the cgi-bin directory
<Directory "/var/www/cgi-bin">
    AllowOverride None
    Options None
    Order allow,deny
    Allow from all
</Directory>
```

Access-control directives use a different syntax from the other Apache directives. The syntax is like that of HTML. Various access-control directives are enclosed within pairs of tags, such as `<Directory> ... </Directory>`.

The following list describes some of the access-control directives. In particular, notice the `AuthUserFile` directive; you can have password-based access control for specific directories.

- **Options opt1 opt2 . . . :** Specifies the access-control options for the directory section in which this directive appears. The options can be one or more of the following:
  - `None` disables all access-control features.
  - `All` turns on all features for the directory.
  - `FollowSymLinks` enables the server to follow symbolic links.
  - `SymLinksIfOwnerMatch` follows symbolic links, only if the same user of the directory owns the linked directory.
  - `ExecCGI` enables execution of CGI scripts in the directory.
  - `FancyIndexing` enables the display of fancy directory listings, with icons and file sizes.
  - `Includes` enables server-side include files in this directory (the term "server-side include" refers to directives, placed in an HTML file, that the Web server processes before returning the results to the Web browser).
  - `Indexes` enables clients to request indexes (directory listings) for the directory.
  - `IncludesNOEXEC` disables the `#exec` command in server-side includes.
- **AllowOverride directive1 directive2 . . . :** Specifies which access-control directives can be overridden on a per-directory basis. The directive list can contain one or more of the following:
  - `None` stops any directive from being overridden.
  - `All` enables overriding of any directive on a per directory basis.
  - `Options` enables the use of the Options directive in the directory-level file.
  - `FileInfo` enables the use of directives controlling document type, such as `AddType` and `AddEncoding`.

    - `AuthConfig` enables the use of authorization directives, such as `AuthName`, `AuthType`, `AuthUserFile`, and `AuthGroupFile`.
    - `Limit` enables the use of `Limit` directives (`allow`, `deny`, and `order`) in a directory's access-configuration file.

- **AuthName name:** Specifies the authorization name for a directory.
- **AuthType type:** Specifies the type of authorization to be used. The only supported authorization type is `Basic`.
- **AuthUserFile filename:** Specifies the file in which user names and passwords are stored for authorization. For example, the following directive sets the authorization file to `/etc/httpd/conf/passwd`:

  ```
  AuthUserFile /etc/httpd/conf/passwd
  ```

  You have to create the authorization file with the `/usr/bin/htpasswd` support program. To create the authorization file and add the password for a user named `jdoe`, specify the following:

  ```
  /usr/bin/htpasswd -c /etc/httpd/conf/passwd jdoe
  New password: (type the password)
  Re-type new password: (type the same password again)
  Adding password for user jdoe
  ```

- **AuthGroupFile filename:** Specifies the file to consult for a list of user groups for authentication.
- **order ord:** Specifies the order in which two other directives — `allow` and `deny` — are evaluated. The order is one of the following:
    - `deny,allow` causes the Web server to evaluate the `deny` directive before `allow`.
    - `allow,deny` causes the Web server to evaluate the `allow` directive before `deny`.
    - `mutual-failure` enables only hosts in the `allow` list.
- **deny from host1 host2...:** Specifies the hosts denied access.
- **allow from host1 host2...:** Specifies the hosts allowed access. To enable all hosts in a specific domain to access the Web documents in a directory, specify the following:

  ```
  order deny,allow
  allow from .nws.noaa.gov
  ```

- **require entity en1 en2...:** This directive specifies which users can access a directory. `entity` is one of the following:
    - `user` enables only a list of named users.
    - `group` enables only a list of named groups.
    - `valid-user` enables all users listed in the `AuthUserFile` access to the directory (provided that they enter the correct password).

Supporting Virtual Hosts with the Apache HTTP Server

A useful feature of the Apache HTTP server is its ability to handle virtual Web servers. This ability enables a single server to respond to many different IP addresses and to serve

Web pages from different directories, depending on the IP address. That means that you can set up a single Web server to respond to both `www.big.org` and `www.tiny.com` and serve a unique home page for each hostname. A server with this capability is known as multihomed Web server, a virtual Web server, or a server with virtual host support.

As you might guess, ISPs use virtual host capability to offer virtual websites to their customers. You must meet the following requirements to support virtual hosts:

- The Web server must be able to respond to multiple IP addresses (each with a unique domain name) and must enable you to specify document directories, log files, and other configuration items for each IP address.
- The Linux system must associate multiple IP addresses with a single physical network interface. Linux enables you to associate multiple IP addresses with a single physical interface.
- Each domain name associated with the IP address must be a unique registered domain name with proper DNS entries.

For the latest information on how to set up virtual hosts in an Apache HTTP server, consult the following website:

```
http://httpd.apache.org/docs-2.0/vhosts/index.html
```

The Apache HTTP server can respond to different host names with different home pages. You have two options when supporting virtual hosts:

- Run multiple copies of the httpd program, one for each IP address. In this case, you create a separate copy of the `httpd.conf` configuration file for each host and use the `Listen` directive to make the server respond to a specific IP address.
- Run a single copy of the httpd program with a single `httpd.conf` file. In the configuration file, set `Listen` to a port number only (so the server responds to any IP address associated with the host), and use the `VirtualHost` directive to configure the server for each virtual host.

You should run multiple HTTP daemons only if you do not expect heavy traffic on your system; the system may not able to respond well because of the overhead associated with running multiple daemons. However, you may need multiple HTTP daemons if each virtual host has a unique configuration need for the following directives:

- `UserId` and `GroupId`, which are the user and group ID for the `HTTP` daemon.
- `ServerRoot`, which is the root directory of the server.
- `TypesConfig`, which is the MIME type configuration file.

For a site with heavy traffic, you should configure the Web server so that a single `HTTP` daemon can serve multiple virtual hosts. Of course, this recommendation implies that there is only one configuration file. In that configuration file, use the `VirtualHost` directive to configure each virtual host.

Most ISPs use the `VirtualHost` capability of the Apache HTTP server to provide virtual websites to their customers. Unless you pay for a dedicated Web host, you typically get a virtual site where you have your own domain name, but share the server and the actual host with many other customers.

The syntax of the VirtualHost directive is as follows:

```
<VirtualHost hostaddr>
    ... directives that apply to this host
    ...
</VirtualHost>
```

With this syntax, you use <VirtualHost> and </VirtualHost> to enclose a group of directives that will apply only to the particular virtual host identified by the hostaddr parameter. The hostaddr parameter can be an IP address, or the fully qualified domain name of the virtual host.

You can place almost any Apache directives within the <VirtualHost> block. At a minimum, Webmasters include the following directives in the <VirtualHost> block:

- DocumentRoot, which specifies where this virtual host's documents reside
- Servername, which identifies the server to the outside world (this should be a registered domain name DNS supports)
- ServerAdmin, which is the email address of this virtual host's Webmaster
- Redirect, which specifies any URLs to be redirected to other URLs
- ErrorLog, which specifies the file where errors related to this virtual host are to be logged
- CustomLog, which specifies the file where accesses to this virtual host are logged

When the server receives a request for a document in a particular virtual host's DocumentRoot directory, it uses the configuration parameters within that server's <VirtualHost> block to handle that request.

Here is a typical example of a <VirtualHost> directive that sets up the virtual host www.lnbsoft.com:

```
<VirtualHost www.lnbsoft.com>
    DocumentRoot    /home/naba/httpd/htdocs
    ServerName   www.lnbsoft.com
    ServerAdmin   webmaster@lnbsoft.com
    ScriptAlias   /cgi-bin/   /home/naba/httpd/cgi-bin/
    ErrorLog  /usr/home/naba/httpd/logs/error_log
    CustomLog   /home/naba/httpd/logs/access_log common
</VirtualHost>
```

Here, the name "common" in the CustomLog directive refers to the name of a format defined earlier in the httpd.conf file by the LogFormat directive, as follows:

```
LogFormat "%h %l %u %t \"%r\" %>s %b" common
```

This format string for the log produces lines in the log file that look like this:

```
dial236.dc.psn.net - - [19/Apr/2005:18:09:00 -0500] "GET / HTTP/1.0" 200 1243
```

The format string contains two letter tokens that start with a percent sign (%). The meaning of these tokens is shown in Table 14-1.

Table 14-1: LogFormat Tokens

Token	*Meaning*
%b	The number of bytes sent to the client, excluding header information.
%h	The host name of the client machine.
%l	The identity of the user, if available.
%r	The HTTP request from the client (for example, GET / HTTP/1.0).
%s	The server response code from the Web server.
%t	The current local date and time.
%u	The user name the user supplies (only when access-control rules require user name/password authentication).

Configuring Apache for Server-Side Includes

"Server-side include" (SSI) refers to a feature of the Apache Web server whereby it can include a file or the value of an environment variable in an HTML document. The feature is like the include files in many programming languages such as C and C++. Just as a preprocessor processes the include files in a programming language, the Web browser reads the HTML file and parses the server-side includes before returning the document to the Web browser.

Server-side includes provide a convenient way to include date, file size, and any file into an HTML document. The SSI directives look like special comments in the HTML file. For example, you can show the size of a graphics file by placing the following SSI directive in the HTML file:

```
File size = <!--#fsize file="nbphoto.jpg"-->
```

The Web server replaces everything to the right of the equal sign with the size of the file `nbphoto.gif`.

Similarly, to display today's date, you can use the following SSI directive:

```
Today is <!--#echo var="DATE_LOCAL" -->
```

To enable SSI on the Apache Web server, place the following directive in the `/etc/httpd/conf/httpd.conf` file:

```
Options +Includes
```

Apache directives can apply to specific directories. Therefore, it's best if you place this directive in the block of directives that apply to the directory where you want to allow SSI.

You also have to tell Apache which files to parse for SSI. The convention is to use the .shtml extension for SSI files. To instruct Apache about the .shtml files, you need the following directives in /etc/httpd/conf/httpd.conf:

```
AddType text/html .shtml
AddOutputFilter INCLUDES .shtml
```

The only drawback of using the .shtml extension for SSI files is that you need to change the file extension if you decide to give SSI directives to a plain HTML file. Unfortunately, changing a file's extension requires all links to that file to be updated. A way out of this quandary is to use the XBitHack directive. To use XBitHack, add the following line to the httpd.conf file:

```
XBitHack on
```

Then, use the chmod command to make those HTML files with SSI directives executable. For example, if the file welcome.html contains SSI directives, type the following command to make that file executable:

```
chmod +x welcome.html
```

When the XBitHack is turned on, Apache parses HTML files for SSI directives if they have the execute bit set (which is what happens when you make the file executable with the chmod +x command).

From the standpoint of security, one problem of server-side includes is the ability to execute a command on the server. For example, the following line of HTML includes the contents of the /etc/passwd file in the document returned to the browser:

```
<!--#exec cmd="/bin/cat /etc/passwd"-->
```

If you want to retain some of the benefits of server-side includes but minimize the security risks, you can turn off the #exec keyword with the following directive on an Options line in httpd.conf:

```
Options IncludesNoExec
```

Supporting CGI Programs in Apache

Sometimes an HTML document's content may not be known in advance. For example, if a website provides a search capability, the result of a search depends on which keywords the user enters in the search form. To handle these needs, the Web server relies on external programs called gateways.

A gateway program accepts the user input and responds with the requested data formatted as an HTML document. Often, the gateway program acts as a bridge between the Web server and some other repository of information such as a database.

Gateway programs have to interact with the Web server. To allow anyone to write a gateway program, the method of interaction between the Web server and the gateway program has to be specified completely. Common Gateway Interface (CGI) is the standard method used by gateway programs to exchange information with the Web server. The Apache Web server supports CGI programs.

The URL specifying a CGI program looks like any other URL, but the Apache Web server can examine the directory name and determine whether the URL is a normal document or a CGI program. Typically, a directory is set aside for CGI programs, and you specify that directory through the ScriptAlias directive in the /etc/httpd/conf/httpd.conf file. You can use multiple ScriptAlias directives to specify multiple directories for CGI programs. Here's a typical ScriptAlias directive:

```
ScriptAlias /cgi-bin/ "/var/www/cgi-bin/"
```

This tells Apache that CGI URLs use the /cgi-bin/ directory name. The ScriptAlias directive also specifies that Apache should substitute the full pathname /var/www/cgi-bin/ for /cgi-bin/.

For example, if a URL specifies http://www.someplace.com/cgi-bin/dbquery, then the Apache server at www.someplace.com recognizes this as a CGI URL and invokes the dbquery program. The ScriptAlias directive in that Web server's httpd.conf configuration file indicates which directory on the server's system contains the CGI programs. In other words, for the example ScriptAlias directive, the Web server translates the CGI program name /cgi-bin/dbquery to the full pathname /var/www/cgi-bin/dbquery.

You can also permit CGI execution in specific directories by placing an explicit Options directive in that directory's configuration. For example, suppose you want to permit CGI execution in the /var/www/special directory. You could do so by adding the following block of directives to the httpd.conf file:

```
<Directory /var/www/special>
    Options +ExecCGI
... other directives for this directory...
</Directory>
```

In addition to this, you also have to indicate which files in that directory are CGI files. Suppose that the CGI files have .cgi and .pl extensions (Perl scripts are often stored in files with .pl extension and CGI programs are often written in Perl). Then, you should add the following directive to the httpd.conf file:

```
AddHandler cgi-script cgi pl
```

You also have to make sure that the CGI files are executable and have appropriate permissions.

Using Java Servlets with Apache

Servlets are Java programs that execute in a Web server in response to requests from a Web browser. Servlets are more powerful than CGI programs commonly used as gateways between Web servers and other services such as databases. One drawback of CGI programs is that the Web server has to start a new process to run a standalone CGI program whenever the server receives data from an HTML form.

Servlets provide functionality similar to that of CGI programs, but servlets avoid the overhead of new process startup. Typically, the Web server runs a Java Virtual Machine (JVM), and that JVM, in turn, loads and runs the servlets. The JVM runs a servlet in a Java thread, which is faster and requires fewer operating system resources than a new process. Additionally, the JVM can keep a servlet loaded and running so that a single instance can handle many future requests. This makes servlets more responsive than other CGI programs, especially ones written in scripting languages such as Perl. At the same time, servlets are portable to any system that supports Java, just as Perl CGI programs can run on any system with a Perl interpreter.

Many websites already use servlets extensively. While browsing the Web, you may have accessed some servlets without even realizing it. A giveaway that the Web server is using a servlet is the occurrence of `/servlet/` in the URL (in the same way that `/cgi-bin/` commonly appears in URLs that refer to CGI programs).

Many websites use another Java-based approach to generate dynamic content. That approach is based on what is known as JavaServer Pages (JSP) technology. A Web page based on JSP uses XML tags and Java scripts along with other HTML tags. Typically, a JSP page has the `.jsp` file extension, which tells the Web server that the page should be processed by a server that understands JSP.

Fedora Core comes with everything you need to support Java servlets and JSP on your Apache Web server. In particular, it comes with Apache Tomcat 5 — a server that runs servlets and can execute JSP documents. Tomcat version 5 implements the Servlet 2.4 and JSP 2.0 specifications from the Java Community Process (`www.jcp.org`). More information about Tomcat is available from the home page of the Apache Jakarta project at `http://jakarta.apache.org/tomcat/`.

To enable the Apache Web server to communicate with Tomcat, you need an Apache httpd module called `mod_jk`. Fedora includes the `mod_jk` module.

The following sections show how to install Tomcat and download and install the `mod_jk` module that connects the Apache Web server to Tomcat.

Installing Apache Tomcat 5

Tomcat 5 is included on the companion DVD-ROM. To install it, select Desktop ⇨ System Settings ⇨ Add/Remove Applications from the GNOME desktop and then select the Web Server Details link from the Package Management window that appears. From the list of RPMs in the Web Server package select the tomcat5 package; click Close, and then click Update in the Package Management window.

These installation steps should put all the Tomcat 5 files in their appropriate locations. To test the Tomcat binaries, type **su -** in a terminal window to become `root` and then type the following command to start Tomcat 5:

```
service tomcat5 start
```

After a few seconds, start a Web browser on your system or another system on the LAN. Point the browser to your system at port 8080 by using the following URL:

```
http://localhost:8080/servlets-examples/
```

If you are accessing your system from another system on the LAN, replace localhost with your system's IP address. If Tomcat is up and running, you should see a list of sample servlets that are come with Apache Tomcat 5.

Now, you can proceed to download and install the mod_jk connector module.

Downloading and Installing the mod_jk Module

To download the mod_jk module, visit http://fedora.redhat.com/download/mirrors.html and click any of the download sites for Fedora Core. Navigate the links to the latest version of Fedora Core and then go to the i386/os/Fedora/RPMS/ subdirectory. From the list of RPMs, select the one whose name begins with mod_jk- followed by a version number. Download that file and then type the following command to install it:

```
rpm -ivh mod_jk-*
```

Now you can configure both Apache httpd and Tomcat 5 so that they work with the mod_jk connector. The idea is for the Apache HTTPD server to send requests to Tomcat and get results back through the mod_jk connector.

Connecting the Apache httpd Server to Tomcat

The first step is to configure Tomcat. Make the following change in /usr/share/tomcat5/conf/server.xml:

- Look for the following line in the file:

  ```
  <Engine name="Catalina" defaultHost="localhost" debug="0">
  ```

- Insert the following line after the <Engine line:

  ```
  <Listener className="org.apache.jk.config.ApacheConfig"
  modJk="/usr/lib/httpd/mo
  dules/mod_jk.so" />
  ```

Next, type the following command to create a workers.properties file in the /etc/httpd/conf directory:

```
cp /usr/share/doc/mod_jk-1.2.6/workers.properties.sample
/etc/httpd/conf/workers.properties
```

Finally, use a text editor to create a file named mod_jk.conf in the /etc/httpd/conf directory and insert the following lines to that file and save it:

```
LoadModule      jk_module modules/mod_jk.so
JkWorkersFile   /etc/httpd/conf/workers.properties
JkLogFile       logs/mod_jk.log
JkLogLevel      error
JkMount /*.jsp ajp13
JkMount /servlet/* ajp13

Alias /examples "/usr/share/tomcat5/webapps/servlets-examples"

<Directory "/usr/share/tomcat5/webapps/servlets-examples">
    Options Indexes FollowSymLinks
</Directory>
```

```
<Location "/servlets-examples/WEB-INF/">
    AllowOverride None
    deny from all
</Location>
```

Testing Apache httpd with Tomcat 5

To test whether Apache httpd is working with Tomcat 5, perform the following steps:

1. Log in as `root` and start Tomcat with the following command:

   ```
   service tomcat5 start
   ```

2. Wait 10 seconds or so for Tomcat to start up.
3. Start Apache httpd with the following command:

   ```
   service httpd start
   ```

4. Open a Web browser on the same system and point the Web browser to the URL `http://localhost:8080/servlets-examples`. You should see a number of servlet examples and be able to execute the examples. This shows that Tomcat is working correctly.
5. Now, type the following URL in the Web browser:

   ```
   http://localhost/examples
   ```

   You should again see the same servlets as you did when you connected to port 8080. This shows that Apache `httpd` is correctly handing over the JSP and servlet requests to Tomcat.

Creating a Secure Server with SSL

You have no doubt noticed the URLs that begin with `https://` (instead of the usual `http://`)—those are HTTPS requests that use HTTP together with encryption performed using the SSL. HTTPS requests are commonly used to securely send sensitive information such as your date of birth or a credit card number to a website. The "s" in the protocol name "https" means that the Web server communicates with your Web browser using HTTP over an SSL connection.

The Apache Web server supports SSL through the `mod_ssl` module that, in turn, relies on the OpenSSL toolkit to perform the encryption function. Linux comes with everything you need to turn Apache into a secure server. The configuration file `/etc/httpd/conf.d/ssl.conf` loads the `mod_ssl` module and configures various parameters that `mod_ssl` needs. You do not have to do anything to the `ssl.conf` configuration file to enable HTTPS support, but you do have to create some additional files required for encryption using SSL.

The same Apache server can handle both HTTP and HTTPS requests because these two protocols use two different ports by default. HTTP uses port 80, whereas HTTPS uses port 443.

The following sections provide an overview of how to create a secure Apache server using SSL. In addition to the simple setup I show in the following sections, there are many different ways to configure SSL. For more information on SSL configuration of Apache, consult the online documentation at `http://httpd.apache.org/docs-2.0/ssl/`.

Secure Sockets Layer (SSL) is a client/server protocol that enables the client and server to use *public key cryptography* to authenticate each other and exchange a 40-bit or 128-bit shared secret key. That secret key is then used to encrypt and decrypt data sent between the client and the server.

Public key cryptography relies on each party having a key pair — a private key and a public key — that are related in such a way that a message encrypted with one key can be decrypted only with the other. The public and private keys are usually 1,024 bits long. The public keys are available to anyone, while the private key is kept secret, known only to the owner of the key. Then anyone can send a message securely by encrypting the message with the recipient's public key because only the recipient can decrypt the message with the corresponding private key.

A digital certificate, or simply a certificate, associates information about a recipient and the corresponding public key. It's basically a well-defined format so that the public key information can be distributed easily.

The only catch is how do you know that a public key truly belongs to your intended recipient? That's where the certificate authority (CA) comes in. The CA is the trusted third party that verifies the identity of a certificate's owner and assures that the certificate contains the public key and identifying information of that owner.

How does the CA assure the integrity of a certificate? It does so by digitally signing the certificate. The CA creates the digital signature by first computing a message digest — a short fixed-length number from a message from arbitrary length — of the certificate and then encrypting the digest with the CA's private key. Then anyone can verify the authenticity of the certificate by decrypting the digital signature with the CA's public key and computing the message digest again and comparing it with the digest in the CA's signature.

For more information about SSL, visit Netscape's website at `http://developer.netscape.com/docs/manuals/security/sslin/contents.htm`.

There are two versions of SSL:

- **SSL v2.0:** This is the original version of SSL protocol, developed by Netscape Communications. This version of SSL uses only RSA keys.
- **SSL v3.0:** A version of the SSL protocol revised to prevent certain security attacks and to support non-RSA keys and certificate chains.

SSL 3.0 is the basis for the Transport Layer Security (TLS) protocol, which is currently being developed by the Internet Engineering Task Force (IETF).

Establishing an SSL session involves a handshake sequence between the client and the server, followed by encrypted data exchange using an agreed upon secret key. The overall sequence has the following key steps:

1. The client sends a client hello message to which the server must respond with a server hello message, or else a fatal error will occur and the connection will fail. The client hello and server hello establish the following attributes: SSL protocol version, a session ID, and the cipher suite — the method to exchange the key, the secret key, and the message digest algorithm to be used to create the message authentication code that ensures integrity.

2. Optionally, the server sends its certificate to the client for authentication. The server may also send a key exchange message, and it may request a certificate from the client. The details of the exchanges between the server and the client depend on the cipher suite selected and whether the client had a digital certificate or not.
3. The client sends a change cipher message and uses the secret key to send an encrypted message indicating it's done.
4. The client and server begin to exchange encrypted data using the secret key.

To support SSL, your Apache server needs a public-private key pair and a digital certificate to provide the public key to any Web browser that connects to the server with a HTTPS request. Ideally the certificate should be signed by a well-known certificate authority so that anyone coming to your website can trust the certificate. The next section explains how to set up the keys and the certificate.

Generating Digital Certificates

To support SSL, the Apache Web server needs a public-private key pair and a digital certificate with its public key. You can perform these tasks by using the `make` command and `Makefile` in the `/etc/httpd/conf` directory.

Before you can use `Makefile`, you have to remove the keys and certificate that were generated during Apache installation. To remove the key and certificate, type the following commands while logged in as `root`:

```
cd /etc/httpd/conf
rm ssl.key/server.key
rm ssl.crt/server.crt
```

Next, generate the keys by typing the following command:

```
make genkey
```

You should see some output similar to the following that ends with a prompt for a pass phrase:

```
umask 77 ; \
/usr/bin/openssl genrsa -des3 1024 >
/etc/httpd/conf/ssl.key/server.key
Generating RSA private key, 1024 bit long modulus
........................++++++
.......++++++
e is 65537 (0x10001)
Enter PEM pass phrase:
```

Type a long pass phrase — it can be a sentence with spaces and punctuations — and press Enter. You will be prompted to re-enter the pass phrase. The new key is now in the `/etc/httpd/conf/ssl.key/server.key` file.

Generating a Certificate Request

The next step is to generate a certificate request that you can send to a Certificate Authority requesting a signed digital certificate. Typically, you have to pay an annual fee for the CA's services. Verisign, Entrust, and Thawte are some of the well-known CAs in the United States. You can find links to other CAs at the PKI Page (`www.pki-page.org/`). To generate the certificate request, type:

```
cd /etc/httpd/conf
make certreq
```

You will be prompted for the pass phrase — enter the same pass phrase you typed when creating the key. You will also be prompted for the following information:

- **Country name:** Enter the two-letter country code (for example, US for the United States). For the official list of two-letter country codes, consult `www.iso.org/iso/en/prods-services/iso3166ma/02iso-3166-code-lists/list-en1.html`.
- **State or province name:** Enter the full name (for example, Maryland).
- **Locality name:** Enter the name of your city or town (for example, North Potomac).
- **Organization name:** Enter the name of your organization.
- **Organizational unit name:** Enter the name of the division or section where you work (or type anything you want).
- **Common name:** Enter the server's host name.
- **Email address:** Enter the email address of the person responsible for the server.

When you finish entering this information, the certificate request is created and saved in the file `/etc/httpd/conf/ssl.csr/server/csr`.

After you create the certificate request, select a CA and visit its website for further instructions on how to send the certificate request and how to pay for the certificate.

After the CA is satisfied about your identity and receives payment for the certificate, it will send the signed certificate back to you by email. You should save the certificate in the file `/etc/httpd/conf/ssl.crt/server.crt` (overwrite the existing file).

Creating a Test Certificate

For the purposes of testing, you can create a self-signed certificate. To generate the test certificate, log in as `root`, and type the following commands:

```
cd /etc/httpd/conf
make testcert
```

You will see output similar to the following:

```
umask 77 ; \
/usr/bin/openssl req -utf8 -new -key /etc/httpd/conf/ssl.key/server.key -
x509 -days 365 -out /etc/httpd/conf/ssl.crt/server.crt -set_serial 0
Enter pass phrase for /etc/httpd/conf/ssl.key/server.key:
```

You have to type the same pass phrase that you used when generating the key. After you enter the pass phrase and press Enter, you have to provide the same set of information that you entered when preparing the certificate request (see the "Generating a Certificate Request" section). Provide the requested information and, at the end, a test certificate should be created and saved in the `/etc/httpd/conf/ssl.crt/server.crt` file.

Testing the Secure Server

After installing a CA-signed certificate or creating a test certificate, you can try out the secure server. Assuming that Apache is already running, log in as `root` and type the following command to restart the server:

```
service httpd restart
```

Because your server key is encrypted, you will be prompted for the pass phrase, like this:

```
Apache/2.0.53 mod_ssl/2.0.53 (Pass Phrase Dialog)
Some of your private key files are encrypted for security reasons.
In order to read them you have to provide the pass phrases.

Enter pass phrase:   type the pass phrase and press Enter

OK: Pass Phrase Dialog successful.
```

Type the pass phrase you used when creating the key and press Enter. The Apache server should now be up and running.

You can now try connecting to the secure server from a Web browser on another PC on the LAN. For example, if the IP address of your Linux system (the one running the Apache secure server) is 192.168.0.3, then type the following URL:

```
https://192.168.0.3/
```

Make sure that you type **https** and not `http`. If you are using a test certificate, the browser displays a dialog box explaining that the certificate is from an unknown certificate authority. You can view the certificate and accept it. Because this is only a test, you can accept the certificate, and the Web browser should then show you the home page on your Linux system.

Summary

The World Wide Web (WWW or the Web) has propelled the Internet into the mainstream because Web browsers make it easy for users to browse documents stored on various Internet hosts. Whether you run a small business or manage computer systems and networks for a large company, chances are good that you have to set up and maintain a Web server. Because of its built-in networking support, a Linux PC makes an affordable Web server. This chapter describes how to configure the Apache Web server on a Linux PC.

By reading this chapter, you learned:

- The Web is made possible by the standard format for documents and the standard protocol for transferring a document across the network. The document format is HyperText Markup Language, or HTML. The standard document exchange protocol is HyperText Transfer Protocol, or HTTP.
- The Web has a client/server architecture, with Web servers providing the HTML documents (often referred to as Web pages) to Web-browser clients.
- The Uniform Resource Locator (URL) syntax uniquely identifies Web pages and other network resources. A URL identifies the location of the document (machine name and directory), as well as the protocol to be used to transfer the document (such as HTTP or FTP).
- Among Web servers, the most popular is the Apache Web server. You can install the Apache Web server during Linux installation. This chapter describes the Apache Web server configuration files and some of the configuration directives.
- The Apache Web server is also referred to as the Apache HTTPD server or simply HTTPD.
- The main Apache httpd configuration file is `/etc/httpd/conf/httpd.conf`. Other configuration files are located in the `/etc/httpd/conf.d` directory, and these configuration files have filenames with the `.conf` extension.
- You can install Apache Tomcat 5 and the `mod_jk` connector to enable the Apache HTTPD server to run Java servlets (small Java applications that run on the server and usually provide access to databases or perform some computations and return a HTML document with the results). This chapter showed you the steps to install and configure Apache Tomcat 5 with Apache httpd.
- You can set up Apache for secure sockets layer (SSL) support by generating public/private key pair and obtaining a digital certificate signed by a certificate authority. This chapter showed you how to set up the secure server.

Mail Server

Secrets in This Chapter

Electronic mail (email) is the mainstay of the Internet. Email enables you to exchange messages and documents with anyone on the Internet. One of the most common ways people use the Internet is to keep in touch with friends, acquaintances, loved ones, and strangers through email. You can send a message to a friend thousands of miles away and get a reply within a couple of minutes. Essentially, you can send messages anywhere in the world from an Internet host, and that message typically makes its way to its destination within minutes — something you cannot do with paper mail, which is why paper mail is also called snail mail.

Because email can be stored and forwarded, you can arrange to send and receive email without making your Linux system a full-time host on the Internet. You won't get the benefits of nearly immediate delivery of messages, however, if your system is not an Internet host.

This chapter introduces you to the sendmail mail server for transferring mail. You learn about its configuration files and how to use its features to create mailing lists. The last part of the chapter briefly describes how to use SpamAssassin to filter out spam — unwanted email.

Installing Mail Software

During Linux installation from this book's companion DVD-ROM, you have the option to install the necessary packages for the email. As described in Chapter 2, select the Mail Server package group when you are prompted for which components to install. The mail readers such as Evolution and Thunderbird come as part of the Graphical Internet package group. The mail readers such as mutt and fetchmail are part of the Text Internet package group.

cross ref

If you install the mail software during Linux installation, you do not have to do much more to begin using the mail service. Otherwise, you can use the Red Hat Package Manager (RPM) to install individual packages. Chapter 21 describes how to use the RPM program to install new software.

To access the RPM files for mail, mount the DVD-ROM with the following command (if you have a CD recorder, change the device name to `/media/cdrecorder`):

```
mount /media/cdrom
```

Then, change the directory to `/media/cdrom/Fedora/RPMS`, where you will find the RPM files. After mounting the DVD-ROM at `/media/cdrom`, the RPMs are always in `/media/cdrom/Fedora/RPMS`. Some of the RPMs you may want to install are as follows (I show the RPM name; the actual filename starts with the RPM name, has a version number, and ends with a `.rpm` extension):

- **fetchmail:** A mail retrieval and forwarding utility
- **mutt:** A text-based email reader
- **dovecot:** An Internet Message Access Protocol — IMAP — server)

- **procmail:** A local mail-delivery package, meant to be invoked directly by sendmail or from a .forward file to process mail automatically; for example, to delete all mail from a specific address
- **sendmail:** A complex mail-transport agent
- **sendmail-cf:** Configuration files for sendmail

You probably have already installed many of these packages. For this chapter, you should install sendmail and sendmail-cf.

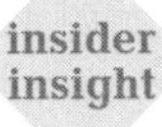

To determine whether sendmail is installed on your system, type the following command:

```
rpm -q sendmail
sendmail-8.13.4-1.1
```

If the output shows `sendmail`, it's installed. In the preceding example, sendmail version 8.13 is installed on the system.

Understanding Electronic Mail

Email is one of the most popular services on the Internet. Everyone likes the convenience of being able to communicate without having to play the game of "phone tag," in which two people leave telephone messages for each other without successfully making contact. When you send an email message, it waits in the recipient's mailbox to be read at the recipient's convenience.

Email started as a simple mechanism in which messages were copied to a user's mailbox file. That simple mechanism is still used. In Linux, your mail messages are stored in the `/var/spool/mail` directory, in a text file with the same name as your user name.

Messages are addressed to a user name. That means if John Doe logs in with the user name `jdoe`, email to him is addressed to `jdoe`. The only other piece of information needed to identify the recipient uniquely is the fully qualified domain name of the recipient's system. Thus, if John Doe's system is named someplace.com, his complete email address becomes `jdoe@someplace.com`. Given that address, anyone on the Internet can send email to John Doe.

Linux comes with all the software you need to set up and use email on your Linux system. The following sections guide you through various aspects of setting up and using email on your Linux system.

Understanding Mail Software

To set up and use email on your Linux PC, you need two types of mail software:

- **Mail user agent (MUA):** This software enables you to read your mail messages, write replies, and compose new messages. Typically, the mail user agent retrieves messages from the mail server by using the POP3 or IMAP4 protocol. POP3 is the Post Office Protocol Version 3, and IMAP4 is the Internet Message

Access Protocol Version 4. Linux comes with mail user agents such as Evolution and Thunderbird. Mozilla also includes a mail user agent and a newsreader, besides the Web browser.

- **Mail transport agent (MTA):** This software actually sends and receives mail messages. The exact method used for mail transport depends on the underlying network. In TCP/IP networks, the mail-transport agent delivers mail using the Simple Mail Transfer Protocol (SMTP). Fedora Linux includes sendmail, a powerful and popular mail-transport agent for TCP/IP networks.

Figure 15-1 shows how the MUAs and MTAs work with one another when Alice sends an email message to Bob.

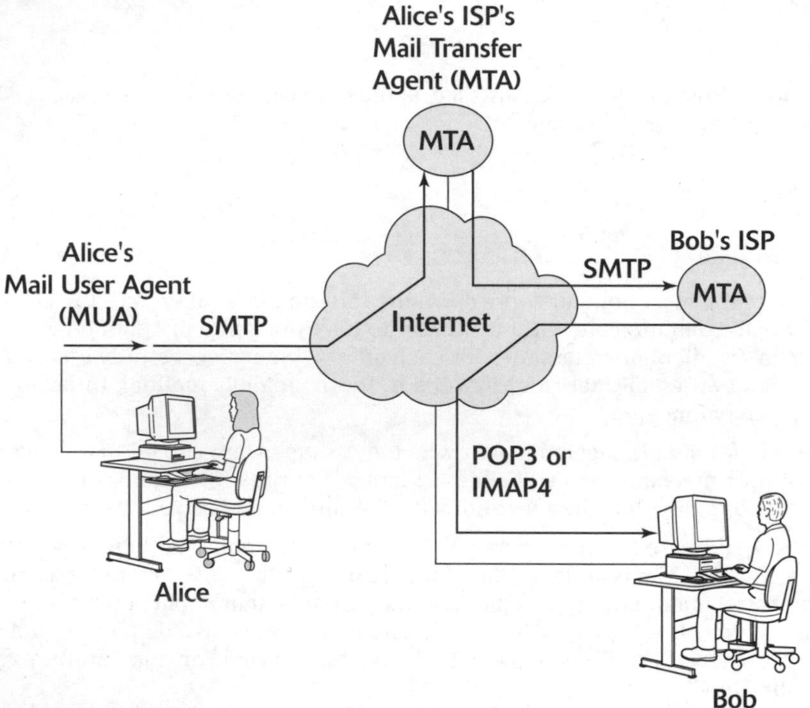

Figure 15-1: Interactions between MUAs and MTAs When Sending Email.

The scenario in Figure 15-1 is typical of email exchanges. Alice and Bob both connect to the Internet through an ISP and receive and send their email through their ISPs. When Alice types a message and sends it, her mail user agent (MUA) sends the message to her ISP's mail transfer agent (MTA) using the Simple Mail Transfer Protocol (SMTP). The sending MTA then sends that message to the receiving MTA — Bob's ISP's MTA — using SMTP. When Bob connects to the Internet, his MUA downloads the message from his ISP's MTA using the POP3 (or IMAP4) protocol. That's the way mail moves around the Internet — from sending MUA to sending MTA to receiving MTA to receiving MUA.

Most mail-transport agents run as daemons, background processes that run as long as your system is up. Because you or another user on the system might send mail at any time, the transport agent has to be there to deliver the mail to its destination. The mail user agent runs only when the user starts the mail reader and wants to check mail.

Typically, a mail-transport agent is started after the system boots. The system startup files for Fedora Linux are configured so that the sendmail mail-transport agent starts when the system is in multiuser mode. The shell script file `/etc/init.d/sendmail` starts sendmail.

Because the system is already set up to start sendmail at boot time, all you have to do is use an appropriate sendmail configuration file to get email going on your Linux system.

Learning More about sendmail

This chapter shows you how to use a predefined sendmail configuration file to get email going on your system. sendmail, however, is a very complex mail system. The book *sendmail, 3rd Edition* by Bryan Costales with Eric Allman (O'Reilly & Associates, December 2002) will help you learn to configure sendmail. For sendmail version 8.13, you can also get the *sendmail 8.13 Companion* by the same authors (O'Reilly & Associates, September 2004).

You should also visit `www.sendmail.org/` and `www.sendmail.net/` for a thorough description of sendmail features and configuration examples.

For answers to commonly asked questions about sendmail or to ask a question yourself, visit the newsgroup `comp.mail.sendmail` (see Chapter 16 for more on reading newsgroups and posting articles to them).

Using sendmail

To set up your system as a mail server, you must configure the sendmail mail-transport agent properly and start the sendmail server. If you installed sendmail, it should already be configured to run when you boot Linux. To check if this is true, type the following command:

```
chkconfig --list sendmail
sendmail        0:off   1:off   2:on    3:on    4:on    5:on    6:off
```

The output shows whether sendmail is turned on or off for each of the run levels from 1 through 6 (consult Chapter 20 to learn more about run levels). If sendmail is configured to run automatically, you should see it set to on for at least the run levels 3 and 5. If it's off for all run levels, type the following command to turn it on:

```
chkconfig --level 35 sendmail on
```

To restart sendmail after making changes to configuration files, type the following command:

```
service sendmail restart
```

sendmail has the reputation of being a complex but complete mail-delivery system. If you take a quick look at sendmail's configuration file, `/etc/mail/sendmail.cf`, you'll immediately agree that sendmail is indeed complex. Luckily, you do not have to be an expert on the sendmail configuration file. (A whole book has been written on that subject; see the "Learning More about sendmail" section.) All you need is one of the predefined configuration files from this book's companion DVD-ROM.

Your system should already have a working sendmail configuration file—`/etc/mail/sendmail.cf`. The default file assumes you have an Internet connection and a name server. Provided you have an Internet connection, you should be able to send and receive email from your Linux PC.

To ensure that mail delivery works correctly, your system's name must match the system name your ISP has assigned to you. Although you can give your system any host name you want, other systems can successfully deliver mail to your system only if your system's name is in the ISP's name server.

Testing Mail Delivery

To try out the sendmail mail-transfer agent, use the `mail` command to compose and send a mail message to an email address, as follows:

```
mail someone@someplace.com
Subject: Testing email
This is from my Linux system.
.
Cc: Press Ctrl+D
```

The `mail` command is a simple mail user agent. In the preceding example, I show the addressee—*someone@someplace.com*—in the command line (replace *someone@someplace.com* with a valid email address). The mail program prompts you for a subject line. Following the subject, you can enter your message and end it with a line that contains only a period. After you end the message, the mail user agent passes the message to sendmail—the mail-transport agent—for delivery to the specified address. If your system is already connected to the Internet, sendmail delivers the mail message immediately.

To verify the delivery of mail, the email addressee has to check his or her email. If they send a reply, you can read it on the Linux PC using the `mail` command.

Thus, the initial sendmail configuration file that comes with Fedora Linux should be adequate for sending and receiving email, provided that your Linux system has an Internet connection and a registered domain name.

Understanding the Mail-Delivery Mechanism

On an Internet host, the sendmail mail-transport agent delivers mail using the Simple Mail Transfer Protocol (SMTP). SMTP is documented in RFC 821, "Simple Mail Transfer Protocol," by Jonathan Postel, 1982.

SMTP-based mail-transport agents listen to the TCP port 25 and use a small set of text commands to interact with other mail-transport agents. In fact, the commands are simple enough that you can use them directly to send a mail message. The following example shows how I use SMTP commands to send a mail message to my account on the Linux PC from a Telnet session running on the same system:

```
telnet localhost 25
Trying 127.0.0.1...
Connected to localhost.
Escape character is '^]'.
220 localhost.localdomain ESMTP Sendmail 8.13.4/8.13.4; Mon, 18 Apr 2005
21:53:01 -0400
help
214-2.0.0 This is sendmail version 8.12.7
214-2.0.0 Topics:
214-2.0.0       HELO    EHLO    MAIL    RCPT    DATA
214-2.0.0       RSET    NOOP    QUIT    HELP    VRFY
214-2.0.0       EXPN    VERB    ETRN    DSN     AUTH
214-2.0.0       STARTTLS
214-2.0.0 For more info use "HELP <topic>".
214-2.0.0 To report bugs in the implementation send email to
214-2.0.0       sendmail-bugs@sendmail.org.
214-2.0.0 For local information send email to Postmaster at your site.
214 2.0.0 End of HELP info
HELP DATA
214-2.0.0 DATA
214-2.0.0       Following text is collected as the message.
214-2.0.0       End with a single dot.
214 2.0.0 End of HELP info
HELO localhost
250 localhost.localdomain Hello localhost.localdomain [127.0.0.1], pleased
to meet you
MAIL FROM: naba
553 5.5.4 naba... Domain name required for sender address naba
MAIL FROM: naba@localhost
250 2.1.0 naba@localhost... Sender ok
RCPT TO: naba
250 2.1.5 naba... Recipient ok
DATA
354 Enter mail, end with "." on a line by itself
Testing... 1 2 3
Sending mail by telnet to port 25
.
```

```
250 2.0.0 j3J1r1Qh029244 Message accepted for delivery
quit
221 2.0.0 localhost.localdomain closing connection
Connection closed by foreign host.
```

The `telnet` command opens a Telnet session on port 25, the port on which sendmail expects SMTP commands. The sendmail server on the Linux system immediately replies with an announcement.

I type `HELP` to view a list of SMTP commands. To get help on a specific command, I can type `HELP` *`commandname`*. The listing shows the help information sendmail prints when I type `HELP DATA`.

I type `HELO localhost` to initiate a session with the host. The sendmail process replies with a greeting. To send the mail message, I start with the `MAIL FROM:` command that specifies the sender of the message (I enter the user name on the system from which I am sending the message). sendmail requires a domain name along with the user name.

Next, I type the `RCPT TO:` command to specify the recipient of the message. If I want to send the message to several recipients, all I have to do is provide each recipient's address with the `RCPT TO:` command.

To enter the mail message, I type the `DATA` command. In response to the `DATA` command, sendmail displays an instruction that I should end the message with a period on a line by itself. I enter the message and end it with a single period on a separate line. The sendmail process displays a message indicating that the message has been accepted for delivery. Finally, I quit the sendmail session by typing the `QUIT` command.

Afterward, I log in to my Linux system and check mail with the `mail` command. The following is what I see when I display the mail message I have sent through the sample SMTP session with sendmail:

```
mail
Mail version 8.1 6/6/93.  Type ? for help.
"/var/spool/mail/naba": 1 message 1 new
>N  1 naba@localhost.local  Mon Apr 18 21:54  13/528
& 1
Message 1:
From naba@localhost.localdomain  Mon Apr 18 21:54:35 2005
Date: Mon, 18 Apr 2005 21:53:01 -0400
From: Naba Barkakati <naba@localhost.localdomain>

Testing... 1 2 3
Sending mail by telnet to port 25

& q
Saved 1 message in mbox
```

As this example shows, the SMTP commands are simple enough to understand. This example should help you understand how a mail-transfer agent uses SMTP to transfer mail on the Internet. Of course, this whole process is automated by email programs and the sendmail program (through settings in the sendmail configuration file `/etc/mail/sendmail.cf`).

Learning the sendmail Configuration File

You don't need to understand everything in the sendmail configuration file, `/etc/mail/sendmail.cf`, but you should know how that file is created. That way, you can make minor changes if necessary and regenerate the `/etc/mail/sendmail.cf` file.

To be able to regenerate the `sendmail.cf` file, you have to install the sendmail-cf package. To check whether the sendmail-cf package is installed, type **rpm -q sendmail-cf**. If the command does not print the name of the sendmail-cf package, you have to install the package. This RPM file is in the DVD-ROMs bundled with this book. To install that package, log in as `root` and mount the DVD-ROM with the following command:

```
mount /media/cdrom
```

Then change to the `/media/cdrom/Fedora/RPMS` directory and install the package by using the following code:

```
cd /media/cdrom/Fedora/RPMS
rpm -ivh sendmail-cf*
```

The sendmail-cf package installs in the `/usr/share/sendmail-cf` directory all the files needed to generate a new sendmail.cf configuration file. As you learn in the next few sections, the `sendmail.cf` file is generated from a number of m4 macro files. These macro files are organized into a number of subdirectories under `/usr/share/sendmail-cf`. You can read the `README` file in `/usr/share/sendmail-cf` to learn more about the creation of sendmail configuration files.

Now that you have taken care of the prerequisites, you can learn how to regenerate the `sendmail.cf` file.

Using the m4 Macro Processor

The m4 macro processor is used to generate the `sendmail.cf` configuration file, which comes with the sendmail package in Linux. The main macro file, `sendmail.mc`, is included with the sendmail package, but that file needs other m4 macro files that are in the sendmail-cf package. To be able to process the `sendmail.mc` file, you have to install the sendmail-cf package, as explained in the previous section. This section introduces you to the m4 macro processor.

A *macro* is a symbolic name for some action or a long string of characters. A macro processor such as m4 usually reads its input file and copies it to the output, processing the macros along the way. The processing of a macro generally involves performing some action and generating some output. Because a macro generates a lot more text in the output than merely the macro's name, the processing of macros is referred to as macro expansion.

cross ref

The m4 macro processor is the GNU implementation of the standard UNIX macro processor. Only a few simple m4 macros are described in this section, but there is much more to m4 than the simple examples shown here. It's essentially a new scripting language for generating configuration files. You can read the online manual about m4 by typing the command `info m4` at a shell prompt. Chapter 23 describes how to read online help by using `info`.

Note that m4 is stream based (like the sed editor, described in Chapter 8). That means it copies the input characters to the output, while expanding any macros. The m4 macro processor does not have any concept of lines, so it copies newline characters to the output. That's why you see the word `dnl` in most m4 macro files; `dnl` is an m4 macro that stands for *delete through newline*. The `dnl` macro deletes all characters starting at the dnl up to and including the next newline character. The newline characters in the output don't cause any harm; they merely create unnecessary blank lines. The `sendmail` macro package uses `dnl` to avoid such blank lines in the output configuration file. Because `dnl` basically means delete everything up to the end of the line, m4 macro files also use `dnl` as the prefix for comment lines.

To see a very simple use of m4, consider the following m4 macro file that defines two macros — `hello` and `bye` — and uses them in a form letter:

```
dnl #####################################################
dnl #  File: ex.m4
dnl #  A simple example of m4 macros
dnl #####################################################
define(`hello', `Dear Sir/Madam')dnl
define(`bye',
`Sincerely,


Customer Service')dnl
dnl Now type the letter and use the macros
hello,

This is to inform you that we received your recent inquiry.
We will respond to your question soon.

bye
```

Type this text using your favorite text editor, and save it in a file named `ex.m4`. You can name a macro file anything you like, but it is customary to use the `.m4` extension for m4 macro files.

Before you process the macro file by using m4, note the following key points the preceding example illustrates:

- Use the `dnl` macro to start all the comment lines (for example, the first four lines in the example).

- End each macro definition with the `dnl` macro. Otherwise, when m4 processes the macro file, it produces a blank line for each macro definition.
- Use the built-in m4 command `define` to define a new macro. The macro name and the value are both enclosed between a pair of left and right quotes (` . . . '). Note that you cannot use the plain single quote to enclose the macro name and definition.

Now process the macro file `ex.m4` by using m4 as follows:

```
m4 ex.m4
Dear Sir/Madam,

This is to inform you that we received your recent inquiry.
We will respond to your question soon.

Sincerely,


Customer Service
```

As you can see, m4 prints the form letter on standard output, expanding the macros `hello` and `bye` into their defined values. If you want to save the form letter in a file called `letter`, use the shell's output redirection feature, like this:

```
m4 ex.m4 > letter
```

What if you want to use the word `hello` or `bye` in the letter without expanding it? You can do so by enclosing these macros in a pair of left- and right-quotes (` . . . '). You have to do this for other predefined m4 macros, such as `define`. To use define as a plain word, not as a macro to expand, write `` `define' ``.

Examining the sendmail.mc File

The simple example in the preceding section should give you an idea of how m4 macros are defined and used to create configuration files such as the `sendmail.cf` file. Essentially, many complex macros are written and stored in files in the `/usr/share/sendmail-cf` directory. A top-level macro file, `sendmail.mc`, described later in this section, brings in these macro files with the `include` macro (used to copy a file into the input stream).

By defining its own set of high-level macros in files located in the `/usr/share/sendmail-cf` directory, sendmail essentially creates its own macro language. The sendmail macro files use the `.mc` extension. The primary sendmail macro file you should configure is `sendmail.mc`, located in the `/etc/mail` directory.

Unlike the `/etc/mail/sendmail.cf` file, the `/etc/mail/sendmail.mc` file is short and should be easier to work with. Here is the full listing of the `/etc/mail/sendmail.mc` file that comes with Fedora Linux:

```
divert(-1)dnl
dnl #
dnl # This is the sendmail macro config file for m4. If you make changes to
dnl # /etc/mail/sendmail.mc, you will need to regenerate the
dnl # /etc/mail/sendmail.cf file by confirming that the sendmail-cf package is
```

```
dnl # installed and then performing a
dnl #
dnl #     make -C /etc/mail
dnl #
include(`/usr/share/sendmail-cf/m4/cf.m4')dnl
VERSIONID(`setup for Red Hat Linux')dnl
OSTYPE(`linux')dnl
dnl #
dnl # default logging level is 9, you might want to set it higher to
dnl # debug the configuration
dnl #
dnl define(`confLOG_LEVEL', `9')dnl
dnl #
dnl # Uncomment and edit the following line if your outgoing mail needs to
dnl # be sent out through an external mail server:
dnl #
dnl define(`SMART_HOST',`smtp.your.provider')
dnl #
define(`confDEF_USER_ID',``8:12'')dnl
dnl define(`confAUTO_REBUILD')dnl
define(`confTO_CONNECT', `1m')dnl
define(`confTRY_NULL_MX_LIST',true)dnl
define(`confDONT_PROBE_INTERFACES',true)dnl
define(`PROCMAIL_MAILER_PATH',`/usr/bin/procmail')dnl
define(`ALIAS_FILE', `/etc/aliases')dnl
define(`STATUS_FILE', `/var/log/mail/statistics')dnl
define(`UUCP_MAILER_MAX', `2000000')dnl
define(`confUSERDB_SPEC', `/etc/mail/userdb.db')dnl
define(`confPRIVACY_FLAGS', `authwarnings,novrfy,noexpn,restrictqrun')dnl
define(`confAUTH_OPTIONS', `A')dnl
dnl #
dnl # The following allows relaying if the user authenticates, and disallows
dnl # plaintext authentication (PLAIN/LOGIN) on non-TLS links
dnl #
dnl define(`confAUTH_OPTIONS', `A p')dnl
dnl #
dnl # PLAIN is the preferred plaintext authentication method and used by
dnl # Mozilla Mail and Evolution, though Outlook Express and other MUAs do
dnl # use LOGIN. Other mechanisms should be used if the connection is not
dnl # guaranteed secure.
dnl # Please remember that saslauthd needs to be running for AUTH.
dnl #
dnl TRUST_AUTH_MECH(`EXTERNAL DIGEST-MD5 CRAM-MD5 LOGIN PLAIN')dnl
dnl define(`confAUTH_MECHANISMS', `EXTERNAL GSSAPI DIGEST-MD5 CRAM-MD5 LOGIN PLA
IN')dnl
dnl #
dnl # Rudimentary information on creating certificates for sendmail TLS:
dnl #     cd /usr/share/ssl/certs; make sendmail.pem
dnl # Complete usage:
dnl #     make -C /usr/share/ssl/certs usage
```

```
dnl #
dnl define(`confCACERT_PATH',`/usr/share/ssl/certs')
dnl define(`confCACERT',`/usr/share/ssl/certs/ca-bundle.crt')
dnl define(`confSERVER_CERT',`/usr/share/ssl/certs/sendmail.pem')
dnl define(`confSERVER_KEY',`/usr/share/ssl/certs/sendmail.pem')
dnl #
dnl # This allows sendmail to use a keyfile that is shared with OpenLDAP's
dnl # slapd, which requires the file to be readable by group ldap
dnl #
dnl define(`confDONT_BLAME_SENDMAIL',`groupreadablekeyfile')dnl
dnl #
dnl define(`confTO_QUEUEWARN', `4h')dnl
dnl define(`confTO_QUEUERETURN', `5d')dnl
dnl define(`confQUEUE_LA', `12')dnl
dnl define(`confREFUSE_LA', `18')dnl
define(`confTO_IDENT', `0')dnl
dnl FEATURE(delay_checks)dnl
FEATURE(`no_default_msa',`dnl')dnl
FEATURE(`smrsh',`/usr/sbin/smrsh')dnl
FEATURE(`mailertable',`hash -o /etc/mail/mailertable.db')dnl
FEATURE(`virtusertable',`hash -o /etc/mail/virtusertable.db')dnl
FEATURE(redirect)dnl
FEATURE(always_add_domain)dnl
FEATURE(use_cw_file)dnl
FEATURE(use_ct_file)dnl
dnl #
dnl # The following limits the number of processes sendmail can fork to accept
dnl # incoming messages or process its message queues to 12.) sendmail refuses
dnl # to accept connections once it has reached its quota of child processes.
dnl #
dnl define(`confMAX_DAEMON_CHILDREN', 12)dnl
dnl #
dnl # Limits the number of new connections per second. This caps the overhead
dnl # incurred due to forking new sendmail processes. May be useful against
dnl # DoS attacks or barrages of spam. (As mentioned below, a per-IP address
dnl # limit would be useful but is not available as an option at this writing.)
dnl #
dnl define(`confCONNECTION_RATE_THROTTLE', 3)dnl
dnl #
dnl # The -t option will retry delivery if e.g. the user runs over his quota.
dnl #
FEATURE(local_procmail,`',`procmail -t -Y -a $h -d $u')dnl
FEATURE(`access_db',`hash -T<TMPF> -o /etc/mail/access.db')dnl
FEATURE(`blacklist_recipients')dnl
EXPOSED_USER(`root')dnl
dnl #
dnl # The following causes sendmail to only listen on the IPv4 loopback address
dnl # 127.0.0.1 and not on any other network devices. Remove the loopback
dnl # address restriction to accept email from the internet or intranet.
dnl #
```

```
DAEMON_OPTIONS(`Port=smtp,Addr=127.0.0.1, Name=MTA')dnl
dnl #
dnl # The following causes sendmail to additionally listen to port 587 for
dnl # mail from MUAs that authenticate. Roaming users who can't reach their
dnl # preferred sendmail daemon due to port 25 being blocked or redirected find
dnl # this useful.
dnl #
dnl DAEMON_OPTIONS(`Port=submission, Name=MSA, M=Ea')dnl
dnl #
dnl # The following causes sendmail to additionally listen to port 465, but
dnl # starting immediately in TLS mode upon connecting. Port 25 or 587 followed
dnl # by STARTTLS is preferred, but roaming clients using Outlook Express can't
dnl # do STARTTLS on ports other than 25. Mozilla Mail can ONLY use STARTTLS
dnl # and doesn't support the deprecated smtps; Evolution <1.1.1 uses smtps
dnl # when SSL is enabled-- STARTTLS support is available in version 1.1.1.
dnl #
dnl # For this to work your OpenSSL certificates must be configured.
dnl #
dnl DAEMON_OPTIONS(`Port=smtps, Name=TLSMTA, M=s')dnl
dnl #
dnl # The following causes sendmail to additionally listen on the IPv6 loopback
dnl # device. Remove the loopback address restriction listen to the network.
dnl #
dnl DAEMON_OPTIONS(`port=smtp,Addr=::1, Name=MTA-v6, Family=inet6')dnl
dnl #
dnl # enable both ipv6 and ipv4 in sendmail:
dnl #
dnl DAEMON_OPTIONS(`Name=MTA-v4, Family=inet, Name=MTA-v6, Family=inet6')
dnl #
dnl # We strongly recommend not accepting unresolvable domains if you want to
dnl # protect yourself from spam. However, the laptop and users on computers
dnl # that do not have 24x7 DNS do need this.
dnl #
FEATURE(`accept_unresolvable_domains')dnl
dnl #
dnl FEATURE(`relay_based_on_MX')dnl
dnl #
dnl # Also accept email sent to "localhost.localdomain" as local email.
dnl #
LOCAL_DOMAIN(`localhost.localdomain')dnl
dnl #
dnl # The following example makes mail from this host and any additional
dnl # specified domains appear to be sent from mydomain.com
dnl #
dnl MASQUERADE_AS(`mydomain.com')dnl
dnl #
dnl # masquerade not just the headers, but the envelope as well
dnl #
dnl FEATURE(masquerade_envelope)dnl
dnl #
```

```
dnl # masquerade not just @mydomainalias.com, but @*.mydomainalias.com as well
dnl #
dnl FEATURE(masquerade_entire_domain)dnl
dnl #
dnl MASQUERADE_DOMAIN(localhost)dnl
dnl MASQUERADE_DOMAIN(localhost.localdomain)dnl
dnl MASQUERADE_DOMAIN(mydomainalias.com)dnl
dnl MASQUERADE_DOMAIN(mydomain.lan)dnl
MAILER(smtp)dnl
MAILER(procmail)dnl
```

As the comments (the lines that begin with `dnl`) in the beginning of the file explain, you can generate the `/etc/mail/sendmail.cf` file by using the `make -C /etc/mail` command. That command runs the `sendmail.mc` file through the m4 macro processor with the following command (you have to log in as `root`):

```
m4 /etc/mail/sendmail.mc > /etc/mail/sendmail.cf
```

The comments also tell you that you need the sendmail-cf package to process this file.

From the previous section's description of m4 macros, you can see that the `sendmail.mc` file uses `define` to create new macros. You can also see the liberal use of `dnl` to avoid inserting too many blank lines into the output.

The other uppercase words such as `OSTYPE`, `FEATURE`, and `MAILER` are sendmail macros. These are defined in the `.m4` files located in the subdirectories of the `/usr/share/sendmail-cf` directory and are incorporated into the `sendmail.mc` file with the following `include` macro:

```
include(`/usr/share/sendmail-cf/m4/cf.m4')
```

The `/usr/share/sendmail-cf/m4/cf.m4` file, in turn, includes the `cfhead.m4` file, which includes other m4 files, and so on. The net effect is that, as the m4 macro processor processes the `sendmail.mc` file, the macro processor incorporates many m4 files from various subdirectories of `/usr/share/sendmail-cf`.

Note the following key points about the `/etc/mail/sendmail.mc` file:

- The `VERSIONID(`linux setup for Red Hat Linux')` macro inserts the version information enclosed in quotes into the output.
- `OSTYPE(`linux')` specifies Linux as the operating system. You have to specify this early to ensure proper configuration. It is customary to place this macro right after the `VERSIONID` macro.
- `MAILER(smtp)` describes the mailer. According to the `/usr/share/sendmail-cf/README` file, `MAILER` declarations should always be placed at the end of the `sendmail.mc` file, and `MAILER(`smtp')` should always precede `MAILER(`procmail')`. The mailer `smtp` refers to the SMTP mailer.
- `FEATURE` macros request various special features. For example, `FEATURE(`blacklist_recipients')` turns on the capability to block incoming mail for certain user names, hosts, or addresses. The specification for what mail to allow or refuse is placed in the access database (`/etc/mail/access.db` file). You also need the `FEATURE(`access_db')` macro to turn on the access database.

- MASQUERADE_AS(`mydomain.com') causes sendmail to label outgoing mail as having come from the host *mydomain*.com (replace this with your domain name). The idea is for a large organization to set up a single sendmail server that handles the mail for many subdomains and makes everything appear to come from a single domain (for example, mail from many departments in a university would appear to come from the university's main domain name).
- MASQUERADE_DOMAIN(subdomain.mydomain.com) instructs sendmail to send mail from an address such as user@subdomain.mydomain.com as having originated from the same user name at the domain specified by the MASQUERADE_AS macro.

insider insight

The sendmail macros such as FEATURE and MAILER are described in the /usr/share/sendmail-cf/README file. Consult that file to learn more about the sendmail macros before you make changes to the sendmail.mc file.

Learning the sendmail.cf File Syntax

The sendmail.cf file's syntax is designed to be easy to parse by the sendmail program because sendmail reads this file whenever it starts. Human readability was not a primary consideration when the file's syntax was designed. Still, with a little explanation, you can understand the meaning of the control lines in sendmail.cf.

Each sendmail control line begins with a single-letter operator that defines the meaning of the rest of the line. A line that begins with a space or a tab is considered a continuation of the previous line. Blank lines and lines beginning with a pound sign (#) are comments.

Often, there is no space between the single-letter operator and the arguments that follow the operator. This makes the lines even harder to understand. For example, sendmail.cf uses the concept of a class—essentially a collection of phrases. You can define a class named P and add the phrase REDIRECT to that class with the following control line:

```
CPREDIRECT
```

Because everything is jumbled together, it's hard to decipher. On the other hand, to define a class named Accept and set it to the values OK and RELAY, write the following:

```
C{Accept}OK RELAY
```

This may be slightly easier to understand because the delimiters (such as the class name, Accept) are enclosed in curly braces.

Other more recent control lines are even easier to understand. For example, the line

```
O HelpFile=/etc/mail/helpfile
```

defines the option HelpFile as the filename /etc/mail/helpfile. That file contains help information sendmail uses when it receives a HELP command.

Table 15-1 summarizes the one-letter control operators used in sendmail.cf. Each entry also shows an example of that operator. This table should help you understand some of the lines in sendmail.cf.

Table 15-1: Control Operators Used in sendmail.cf

Operator	*Description*
C	Defines a class; a variable (think of it as a set) that can contain several values. For example, Cwlocalhost adds the name localhost to the class w.
D	Defines a macro, a name associated with a single value. For example, DnMAILER-DAEMON defines the macro n as MAILER-DAEMON.
F	Defines a class read from a file. For example, Fw/etc/mail/local-host-names reads the names of hosts from the file /etc/mail/local-host-names and adds them to the class w.
H	Defines the format of header lines that sendmail inserts into a message. For example, H?P?Return-Path: <$g> defines the Return-Path: field of the header.
K	Defines a map (a key-value pair database). For example, Karith arith defines the map named arith as the compiled-in map of the same name.
M	Specifies a mailer. The following lines define the procmail mailer:Mprocmail,P=/usr/bin/procmail,F=DFMSPhnu9,S=EnvFromSMTP/HdrFromSMTP, R=EnvToSMTP/HdrFromSMTP,T=DNS/RFC822/X-Unix, A=procmail -Y -m $h $f $u
O	Assigns a value to an option. For example, O AliasFile=/etc/aliases defines the AliasFile option to /etc/aliases, which is the name of the sendmail alias file.
P	Defines values for the precedence field. For example, Pjunk=-100 sets to -100 the precedence of messages marked with the header field Precedence: junk.
R	Defines a rule (a rule has a left-hand side and a right-hand side; if input matches the left-hand side, it's replaced with the right-hand side — this is called rewriting). For example, the rewriting rule R$* ; $1 strips trailing semicolons.
S	Labels a ruleset you can start defining with subsequent R control lines. For example, Scanonify=3 labels the next ruleset as canonify or ruleset 3.
T	Adds a user name to the trusted class (class t). For example, Troot adds root to the class of trusted users.
V	Defines the major version number of the configuration file. For example, V10/Berkeley defines the version number as 10.

Exploring Other sendmail Files

The /etc/mail directory contains other files that sendmail uses. These files are referenced in the sendmail configuration file, /etc/mail/sendmail.cf. For example, here's the result of searching for the /etc/mail string in the /etc/mail/sendmail.cf file:

```
grep "\/etc\/mail" /etc/mail/sendmail.cf
Fw/etc/mail/local-host-names
FR-o /etc/mail/relay-domains
Kmailertable hash -o /etc/mail/mailertable.db
Kvirtuser hash -o /etc/mail/virtusertable.db
Kaccess hash -T<TMPF> -o /etc/mail/access.db
#O ErrorHeader=/etc/mail/error-header
O HelpFile=/etc/mail/helpfile
O UserDatabaseSpec=/etc/mail/userdb.db
#O ServiceSwitchFile=/etc/mail/service.switch
#O DefaultAuthInfo=/etc/mail/default-auth-info
Ft/etc/mail/trusted-users
```

You can ignore the lines that begin with a hash mark or number sign (#) because sendmail treats those lines as comments. The other lines are sendmail control lines that refer to other files in the `/etc/mail` directory.

Following are brief descriptions of files in the `/etc/mail` directory that are referenced in the `sendmail` configuration file (note that not all of these files need to be present in your `/etc/mail` directory and even when present, the file may be empty):

- **/etc/mail/access:** Access list database to stop spam (unwanted mail)
- **/etc/mail/helpfile:** Help information for SMTP commands
- **/etc/mail/local-host-names:** List of alternate names for this host (the list is usually the domains for which this sendmail server accepts mail)
- **/etc/mail/mailertable:** Table that specifies routing of email for specific domains
- **/etc/mail/relay-domains:** Domains for which sendmail allows relaying (relaying refers to the process of sending mail to others by using your sendmail server as an intermediary)
- **/etc/mail/userdb.db:** User database file that specifies where a user receives incoming email
- **/etc/mail/virtusertable:** Database of incoming users

insider insight

The `/etc/mail directory` sometimes contains other files — `/etc/mail/certs` and the files with the `.pem` extension — that are meant for supporting privacy enhanced mail (PEM) in `sendmail` by using the STARTTLS extension to SMTP. The STARTTLS extension uses TLS (more commonly known as SSL — Secure Sockets Layer) to authenticate the sender and encrypt mail. RFC 2487 describes STARTTLS. (This RFC is available online at `http://ietf.org/rfc/rfc2487.txt`.)

The next few sections briefly describe a few of these sendmail configuration files in the `/etc/mail` directory.

Preparing the User Database

The user database helps sendmail deliver incoming mail when there is no centralized mail server. For example, suppose mail addressed to jdoe@someplace.net should really be sent to jd@home.someplace.net. This involves identifying a user's *maildrop* — the location where a user receives mail — to sendmail. You can accomplish this task by creating the user database.

sendmail expects to find the user database in a binary file /etc/mail/userdb.db in the Berkeley database format. Follow these steps to create the binary user database file:

1. Edit the text file /etc/mail/userdb and add lines for each user for whom you need to identify a maildrop location. The lines look like this:

   ```
   bob:mailname               robert.smith@someplace.net
   robert.smith:maildrop      bob
   ```

   In this case, outgoing mail from user name bob will go out addressed as though it is from robert.smith@someplace.net and incoming mail addressed to robert.smith will be sent to the user name bob.

2. Convert the text file /etc/mail/userdb into a Berkeley database file that sendmail can use by running the makemap with the following command:

   ```
   makemap btree /etc/mail/userdb < /etc/mail/userdb
   ```

   This creates the database file /etc/mail/userdb.db from the text file /etc/mail/userdb.

caution

You must remember to run makemap every time you change /etc/mail/userdb; otherwise sendmail will not be using your latest user database when sending mail.

Preparing the Mailer Table

The mailer table database specifies how to route email messages destined for specific domains. You specify these mail routings in a text file /etc/mail/mailertable. For example, suppose all mail meant for mydomain.net should be sent to the host mailhost.mydomain.net. You can specify this with the following entry in /etc/mail/mailertable:

```
.mydomain.net         smtp:mailhost.mydomain.net
```

The left-hand side of each line is a domain name. The right-hand side is of the form mailer:host, where mailer is a mail transfer agent and host is the host name to be provided to that mailer.

After editing the text file /etc/mail/mailertable, you have to convert it into a binary database by running makemap with the following command:

```
makemap hash /etc/mail/mailertable < /etc/mail/mailertable
```

Here is an easier way to make sure that you rebuild everything necessary after making any changes — just type the following commands while logged in as root:

```
cd /etc/mail
make
```

The first command changes the current directory to /etc/mail and the second command runs the make command, which reads a file named Makefile in /etc/mail to perform the steps necessary to rebuild everything.

cross ref

To learn more about make and Makefile, see Chapter 23.

Preparing the Access Database

The access database causes sendmail to accept or refuse mail from specified domains and also control the behavior of sendmail in various situations. The database is a list of names (user names, host names, or network addresses) and codes that specify the action sendmail performs.

You can use the access database to stop spam (unsolicited email). You prepare the access database by editing the text file /etc/mail/access. Like other sendmail databases, each line in that file has two fields. On each line, the left-hand side is an email address, a domain name, or an IP address (IPv6 addresses have to be prefixed with Ipv6:). The right-hand side is typically a code that specifies what sendmail should do.

Here is an example of a /etc/mail/access file:

```
spammer@somewhere.net            DISCARD
spam.com                         REJECT
mybuddy.com                      RELAY
192.168.15                       REJECT
IPv6:2002:c0a8:02c5              REJECT
some.unresolvable.domain.net     OK
junkmail.com                     ERROR:550 "Junk mail not allowed"
```

The codes on the right-hand side tell sendmail what to do for each case. For example, all messages from spammer@somewhere.net are discarded without any error message. On the other hand, when the action is REJECT, sendmail rejects the email with a general message. You can even use the access database to accept messages even when some errors occur. In this example, the OK keyword causes sendmail to accept messages from some.unresolvable.domain.net even though DNS could not translate that domain name to an IP address.

After editing the text file /etc/mail/access, you must convert it to a binary database with the following command:

```
makemap hash /etc/mail/access < /etc/mail/access
```

Using the .forward File

Users can redirect their own mail by placing a .forward file in their home directory. The .forward file is a plaintext file with a comma-separated list of mail addresses. Any mail sent to the user is then forwarded to these addresses. If the .forward file contains a single address, all email for that user is redirected to that single email address. For example, suppose that the following `.forward` file is placed in the home directory of a user named `emily`:

```
ashley
```

All email addressed to `emily` is automatically sent to the user name `ashley` on the same system. User `emily` does not receive mail at all.

You can also forward to a user name on another system by listing the complete email address. For example, I have added a `.forward` file with the following line to send my messages (addressed to my user name, `naba`) to the mail address `naba@comcast.net`:

```
naba@comcast.net
```

Now, suppose I want to keep a copy of the message on this system, in addition to forwarding to the address `naba@comcast.net`. I can do so by adding the following line to the `.forward` file:

```
naba@comcast.net, naba\
```

I simply append my user name and end the line with a backslash. The backslash (`\`) at the end of the line stops sendmail from repeatedly forwarding the message (because when a copy is sent to my user name on the system, sendmail processes my `.forward` file again — the backslash tells sendmail not to forward the message repeatedly).

Another use of the `.forward` file is to run procmail to handle some mail messages automatically. For example, suppose that you want to delete any email message that comes from an address containing the string `mailing_list`. Here's what you do to achieve that:

1. **Create a `.forward` file in your home directory, and place the following line in it:**

   ```
   "| /usr/bin/procmail"
   ```

   This line causes sendmail to run the external program `/usr/bin/procmail` and to send the email messages to the input stream of that program. You can run any external program this way, by invoking it in the .forward file.

2. **Create a text file named `.procmailrc` in your home directory, and place the following lines in that file:**

   ```
   # Delete mail from an address that contains mailing_list
   :0
   * ^From:.*mailing_list
   /dev/null
   ```

3. **Log in as `root` and set up a symbolic link in `/etc/smrsh` to the `/usr/bin/procmail` program with the following command:**

   ```
   ln -s /usr/bin/procmail /etc/smrsh/procmail
   ```

continues

continued

This step is necessary because sendmail uses the SendMail Restricted Shell—smrsh—to run external programs. Instead of running /usr/bin/procmail, smrsh runs /etc/smrsh/procmail. That's why you need the symbolic link. This is a security feature of sendmail that controls what external programs it can run.

That's it! Now if you receive any messages from an address containing mailing_list, the message will be deleted.

By the way, if you want only to run procmail, then you can skip the part about adding it to .forward; simply create a .procmailrc file in your home directory, and sendmail will automatically invoke procmail to process your mail using the rules you specify in the .procmailrc file.

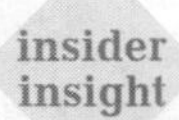

With procmail, you can perform other chores, such as automatically storing messages in a file or forwarding messages to others. All you have to do is create an appropriate .procmailrc file in your home directory. To learn more about procmail, type **man procmail**; to see examples of .procmailrc, type **man procmailex**.

Understanding the sendmail Alias File

In addition to the sendmail.cf file, sendmail also consults an alias file named /etc/aliases to convert a name into an address. The location of the alias file appears in the sendmail configuration file.

Each alias is typically a shorter name for an email address. The system administrator uses the sendmail alias file to forward mail, to create mailing lists (a single alias that identifies several users), or to refer to a user by several different names. For example, here are some typical aliases:

```
barkakati: naba
naba: naba@lnbsoft
all: naba, leha, ivy, emily, ashley
```

The first line says that mail addressed to barkakati should be delivered to the user named naba on the local system. The second line indicates that mail for naba should really be sent to the user name naba on the lnbsoft system. The last line defines all as the alias for the five users naba, leha, ivy, emily, and ashley.

As the next section explains, you can set up a mailing list simply by defining an alias in the /etc/aliases file.

Creating a sendmail Alias Mailing List

You can implement a simple mailing list through a sendmail alias. In its simplest form, all you have to do is define an alias for the addresses in the /etc/aliases file. For example, suppose a large company has several websites (one in each major department), and the

Webmasters decide to keep in touch through a mailing list. One of the Webmasters, Emily, volunteers to set up a mailing list for the group. To set up the mailing list, Emily (who logs in with the user name `emily`) adds the following alias to the `/etc/aliases` file:

```
webmasters: emily, webmaster@sales, webmaster@mktg,
        webmaster@appdev, ...,
        ...,
        webmaster@admin
```

In this case, the address list includes Emily and the Webmasters at all websites in the company (typically, mail to the Webmaster is addressed to the user name `webmaster`). If the list of addresses gets too long, end a line with a comma, and indent the next line with a tab character.

insider insight

After defining an alias in the `/etc/aliases` file, you must log in as `root` and make the new alias active by typing the following command:

```
/usr/lib/sendmail -bi
```

You can use the absolute pathname `/usr/lib/sendmail` to run sendmail because `/usr/lib/sendmail` is a symbolic link to the actual sendmail program file `/usr/sbin/sendmail`.

In addition to the `webmasters` alias, it's conventional to define two other aliases:

- The alias `listname-request` is where users send mail to subscribe to (or unsubscribe from) the list.
- The alias `owner-listname` is where errors (such as bounced messages) are sent.

In this case, because Emily sets up the Webmasters list, she might define the two aliases as follows:

```
webmasters-request: emily
owner-webmasters: emily
```

For a simple mailing list, one person is usually responsible for everything about the list.

Storing the Address List in a Separate File

Although defining an alias with all the addresses works, the drawback is that you must edit the `/etc/aliases` file whenever you want to add a new name to the list. You need to log in as `root` to edit the `/etc/aliases` file (or ask the system administrator to edit the file for you). A better solution is to store the address list in a separate file in your home directory and make sendmail read that file with the `:include:` directive in the alias definition.

For example, Emily might put the address list for the `webmasters` alias in the `/home/emily/mlist/webms` file (assuming that `/home/emily` is the login directory of user `emily`). Then the `/etc/aliases` file would reference the address list as follows:

```
webmasters: :include:/home/emily/mlist/webms
```

In the /home/emily/mlist/webms file, each address appears on a separate line:

```
emily (Emily B. -- list owner)
webmaster@appdev (Webmaster, Application Development Group)
webmaster@mktg (Webmaster, Marketing Department)
```

As you can see, you can put helpful comments in parentheses.

Every time sendmail sends a message to the webmasters alias, it reads the /home/emily/mlist/webms file. Thus, you can add a new user by simply editing this file.

If you use an address file, make sure that only the owner can modify it. Use the command chmod 644 *filename* to set the permission properly.

Ensuring That Replies Go to the List

When you set up a mailing list, you want any replies to go to everyone in the list so that discussions can take place among the group. However, when you use a sendmail alias to define a mailing list, the reply goes to the person who has sent the message instead of to the entire list. You can correct this problem by making the alias start a new sendmail process and by changing the sender's address through the -f option of sendmail.

Here's how you define the webmasters list by using this approach:

```
webmasters: "|/usr/lib/sendmail -fwebmasters -oi dist-webmasters"
dist-webmasters: :include:/home/emily/mlist/webms
```

This definition of webmasters runs sendmail with the -f option (this option sets the From address of the message) and sends mail to another alias, dist-webmasters, that points to the file containing the actual addresses. The -f option works only when a trusted user, such as root, sends mail.

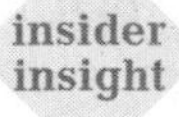

insider insight

When mail for the list arrives from another system, sendmail runs under a trusted user name. Therefore, the mail is sent out with webmasters as the return address. Unfortunately, when a user on the local system sends mail, the -f option does not work because sendmail runs under that user's name (and the user probably is not considered a trusted user). A solution to this problem is to set up the mailing list on a system where none of the list members have an account (this ensures that mail to the list always comes from a remote system).

Filtering Spam with SpamAssassin

Spam — unwanted email — can be a nuisance, especially if you get too many of these unwanted messages. They fill up your mailbox and take time to sort through. Instead of manually dealing with spam, you can use an automated tool called SpamAssassin — written in Perl — to automatically identify potential spam based on a number of rules. SpamAssassin examines the header and content of each email message and assigns a spam score.

You can set up SpamAssassin to filter mail for an entire mail server as well as using it to filter the mail in your own personal mail folder. SpamAssassin comes with Fedora Linux in the spamassassin RPM.

insider insight

SpamAssassin is a project of the Apache Software Foundation. To learn the latest information on SpamAssassin, visit `http://spamassassin.apache.org/`.

SpamAssassin comes in two parts — a client and a server:

- The spamd daemon is the server that loads the spam filtering rules and listens on port 783 for incoming requests to process mail messages.
- The spamc client application that reads a mail message from the standard input, sends the message to spamd for processing, receives the result from spamd, and sends the result to the standard output. To filter your mail messages, you can run spamc from procmail (by invoking it in the `.procmailrc` file in your home directory).

When you use sendmail as your mail server, sendmail listens at port 25 for incoming requests for mail transfer. When a request arrives, sendmail verifies that the mail is addressed to a local user account. If that user's home directory contains a `.procmailrc` file, sendmail hands the mail off to the procmail program. If the user does not have a `.procmailrc` file in the home directory, the email message is placed in the `/var/spool/mail` directory in a file with the same name as the user account (for example, my user name is `naba`, so my mail would be in the `/var/spool/mail/naba` file). If the user's home directory contains a `.procmailrc` file, the procmail program consults the rules in that `.procmailrc` file and performs the actions specified by the rules. To use SpamAssassin to filter a user's mail, you have to add a few rules in that user's `.procmailrc` file to run spamc and use the spam score to take appropriate action such as sort the mail into two folders: spam and probably spam.

Even if users don't have `.procmailrc` files in their home directories, you can configure sendmail (through the `sendmal.mc` file) to invoke procmail for every message and filter the messages using a common `.procmailrc` file — `/etc/mail/procmailrc`.

Starting SpamAssassin

To use SpamAssassin, you have to run the spamd daemon. You can start spamd manually by typing the following command (first type **su -** to become root):

```
service spamassassin start
```

To start spamd at system startup, type **chkconfig spamassassin on**.

To check if SpamAssassin is working, first run the client program — spamc — on a sample non-spam file that comes with the spamassassin RPM. Type the following command to try smapc:

```
spamc -R </usr/share/doc/spamassassin-*/sample-nonspam.txt
```

In this command's output, you should see a line that shows the following:

```
Content analysis details:   (0.0 points, 5.0 required)
```

That line indicates that the spam score was 0.0 and a score of 5.0 is needed to deem a message spam, so the message in the `sample-nonspam.txt` file is considered to be not a spam, which is correct.

Next try spamc on a sample spam message by typing the following command:

```
spamc -R </usr/share/doc/spamassassin-*/sample-spam.txt
```

In this case, you should see the following analysis details from spamc:

```
Content analysis details:   (997.2 points, 5.0 required)
```

That's a 997.2 spam score and it obviously exceeds 5.0; therefore, the sample message is a spam.

Setting Up .procmailrc

To try your hand at filtering mail through SpamAssassin, create a text file named `.procmailrc` in your home directory and then add the following lines:

```
:0fw: spamassassin.lock
| /usr/bin/spamc
```

The first line in `.procmailrc` feeds the entire mail message to the program shown after the vertical bar on the second line, `/usr/bin/spamc` — the SpamAssassin client.

Now send a message to yourself. For example, to send email to the user name `naba`, type **mail naba** and then the message and end by a single period on a line. You can check the message by typing **mail** again. You should see a number of extra lines with the X-Spam prefix right after the Subject line of the message. For example, here is a typical set of lines added to a message processed by SpamAssassin (notice the X-Spam Status line that says No because this message is not a spam):

```
X-Spam-Checker-Version: SpamAssassin 3.0.3-r122144 (2004-12-15) on
        localhost.localdomain
X-Spam-Level:
X-Spam-Status: No, score=-1.7 required=5.0 tests=ALL_TRUSTED,NO_DNS_FOR_FROM
        autolearn=ham version=3.0.3-r122144
```

You can then add additional rules to the `.procmailrc` file to move potential spam to a different folder. For example, try the following `.procmailrc` file:

```
:0fw: spamassassin.lock
| /usr/bin/spamc

:0:
* ^X-Spam-Status: Yes
maybe-spam
```

With this rule in place, any incoming message for which SpamAssassin inserts a Yes in the `X-Spam-Status` line would be moved to the file named `maybe-spam`.

Summary

The Internet has become an essential part of everyday life, as ISPs have sprung up all over the United States and in much of the world. Online services, such as AOL and Microsoft's MSN, now offer Internet mail and Web browsing, bringing even more people to the Internet. Because of its support for TCP/IP networking — the universal language of the Internet — a Linux PC is an ideal Internet host. This chapter describes the email service and shows you how to configure the sendmail server on a Linux PC.

By reading this chapter, you learned the following:

- Email is one of the important services available on Internet hosts. This chapter describes email service available on a Linux PC.
- Email software comes in two parts: a mail-transport agent (MTA), which physically sends and receives mail messages; and a mail user agent (MUA), which reads messages and prepares new messages.
- The companion DVD-ROM contains several mail-transfer agents and mail user agents. This chapter describes how to use sendmail as a mail-transport agent.
- The `sendmail` configuration is complex, but you can get it going with the configuration file that comes with Fedora Linux. All you may need to do is set your Linux PC's host name properly.
- To read email, you can use mail or Evolution. Mozilla also includes a mail reader you can use.
- You can automatically forward messages to another address by placing a `.forward` file in your home directory. The `.forward` file should contain a comma-separated list of email addresses.
- You can run the `procmail` mailer by invoking it from the `.forward` file. The typical use of procmail is to delete unwanted messages automatically and to sort messages into different files.
- You can set up a mailing list by using the `/etc/aliases` file, which stores aliases for sendmail.
- You can use SpamAssassin to filter email messages and identify potential spam (unwanted email messages).

News Server and RSS Feeds

Secrets in This Chapter

The Internet helps you communicate in many ways. With email, you generally exchange messages with people whom you already know. Sometimes, however, you may want or need to participate in group discussions. If you are looking for help in setting up the X Window System on a system with the ATI Radeon 9600 video chipset, for example, you may want to question someone who knows something about this subject. For that sort of communication, you can post a message on the appropriate Internet newsgroup; someone is likely to give you an answer.

Internet newsgroups are like the bulletin boards or forums on other online systems, such as AOL and MSN. Essentially, newsgroups provide a bulletin-board system that spans the globe. You'll find a wide variety of newsgroups — covering subjects ranging from politics to computers. For Linux-related questions, you can read and post articles to newsgroups, such as `comp.os.linux.networking` and `comp.os.linux.setup`. You can think of an Internet newsgroup as a gathering place — a virtual meeting place where you can ask questions and discuss various issues.

Linux comes with the software you need to read newsgroups and to set up your own system as a news server. This chapter introduces you to newsgroups and describes how to configure and run the InterNetNews (INN) server, a popular news server. You also learn how to set up local newsgroups for your corporate intranet.

Nowadays another popular way to read summaries of websites and weblogs is to use a program that can accept RSS feeds. At the end of this chapter, I briefly describe what an RSS feed is and how you can use a program such as the KDE Akregator to subscribe to RSS feeds and read them on your Linux system.

Using Simple News Strategies

Although using news is reasonably simple, a news server requires some effort on your part if it is to be set up and maintained properly. Newsgroups in particular need a great deal of disk space and access to a news server that provides a news feed to your server. You need a large amount of disk space because so many newsgroups exist, and the volume of messages can be quite high. In addition, the news articles must be purged periodically; otherwise, the disk becomes filled. Even if you choose a subset of newsgroups, you may need tens of gigabytes, if not hundreds, just to keep the news items on your system. Running a news server can be one of the most demanding Internet services you provide because of the bandwidth requirements, disk space, and the in-memory indexes and caches that news servers require for fast access to news articles.

If you get your Internet access from an ISP, the ISP gives you access to a mail server and a news server. Then, you can use mail software that downloads messages from the mail server and a newsreader that reads newsgroups directly from the ISP's news server. If you are the sole user of your Linux PC, I strongly recommend this strategy for reading news. That way, you get to read news and post articles without the headache of having to maintain a news server.

Another option is to read news at a website, such as Google Groups at `http://groups.google.com/`. At Google Groups, you can select a newsgroup to browse, and you can post replies to articles posted on various newsgroups. In this case, you don't even need access to a news server. Similar services are offered by InterBulletin (http://news.interbulletin.com/), Mailgate (www.mailgate.org), News2Web (http://usenet.mail2web.com/), and Usenet Replayer (www.usenet-replayer.com/)—at these sites you can read, search, and post messages to the newsgroups using a Web browser.

All these options may not be enough if you want to set up a news server for a company intranet and manage your newsgroups. You might do this to provide a forum for employees to discuss various topics and to exchange knowledge with others. Internal newsgroups can be a good way to facilitate knowledge sharing and knowledge management within a company. Internal newsgroups can provide a virtual gathering place (or what are often called *communities of practice*) for employees to share their knowledge with others. To set up your own newsgroups, you have to set up a news server, such as innd, which uses the Network News Transfer Protocol (NNTP). You will learn about the news server later in this chapter.

The next section briefly describes the news-related software packages you can install in Linux.

Installing News Software

During the installation of Linux from this book's companion DVD-ROM, you have the option to install the necessary packages for news. As described in Chapter 2, select the News Server package group when you are prompted for which package groups to install.

cross ref

If you install the mail and news software during Linux installation, you do not have to do much more to begin using the mail and news services. Otherwise, you can use the Red Hat Package Manager (RPM) to install individual packages. Chapter 21 describes how to use the RPM program to install new software.

To access the RPM files for news, mount the DVD-ROM by using the following command (if you have a DVD/CD recorder, change the device name to /media/cdrecorder):

```
mount /media/cdrom
```

Then change the directory to /media/cdrom/Fedora/RPMS. You will find the RPM files in that directory. Following are some of the RPMs you may want to install (I show the RPM name; the actual filename starts with the RPM name, has a version number, and ends with an .rpm extension):

- **inews:** An Internet news program to post news
- **inn:** InterNetNews, a TCP/IP-based news server
- **slrn:** A simple, NNTP-based newsreader

insider insight

You have probably already installed most of these packages. For this chapter, you need only inn and a newsreader such as KNode, which is installed when you install the KDE desktop. KNode is in the kdepim RPM and the executable file is /usr/bin/knode (which means that you can start KNode by typing **knode** in a terminal window).

Understanding Newsgroups

Newsgroups originated in Usenet, a store-and-forward messaging network for exchanging email and news items. Usenet works like a telegraph in that news and mail are relayed from one system to another. In Usenet, the systems are not on any network; they simply dial up and use the UNIX-to-UNIX Copy Protocol (UUCP) to transfer text messages.

Usenet is a very loosely connected collection of computers that has worked well and continues to be used because very little expense is involved in connecting to it. All you need is a modem and a site willing to store and forward your mail and news. You have to set up UUCP on your system, but you do not need a sustained network connection; just a few phone calls are all it takes to keep the email and news flowing. The downside is that you cannot use TCP/IP services, such as the Web, Telnet, or FTP.

From their Usenet origins, the newsgroups have migrated to the Internet (even though the name Usenet is still used to refer to news). Instead of UUCP, the news is transported by means of the Network News Transfer Protocol (NNTP), which is described in RFC 977, "Network News Transfer Protocol: A Proposed Standard for the Stream-Based Transmission of News," by B. Kantor and P. Lapsley, 1986.

Although the news transport protocol has changed from UUCP to NNTP (although some sites still use UUCP), the store-and-forward concept of news transfer remains. Thus, if you want to get news on your Linux system, you have to find a news server from which your system can download news.

insider insight

If you have signed up with an ISP, it should provide you with access to a news server. Such Internet news servers communicate by using NNTP. Then, you can use an NNTP-capable newsreader, such as slrn, to access the news server and read selected newsgroups. You can also read news by using newsreaders such as KNode, which comes with KDE (included with Fedora Linux). Getting newsgroups from the ISP is the easiest way to access news from your Linux system.

The following discussion about reading newsgroups assumes that you have obtained access to a news server from your ISP.

Reading News from Your ISP

To read news from your ISP, you need a newsreader — a program that enables you to select a newsgroup and view the items in that newsgroup. You also need to understand the newsgroup hierarchy and naming convention, which is described in the section "Understanding the Newsgroup Hierarchy." First, you should try reading news from a news server.

Reading Newsgroups with KNode

You can browse newsgroups and post articles from the KNode newsreader. To start KNode, type **knode** in a terminal window.

When KNode runs for the first time, it brings up the Configure KNode dialog box, shown in Figure 16-1, through which you can configure everything needed to read newsgroups and post items to newsgroups.

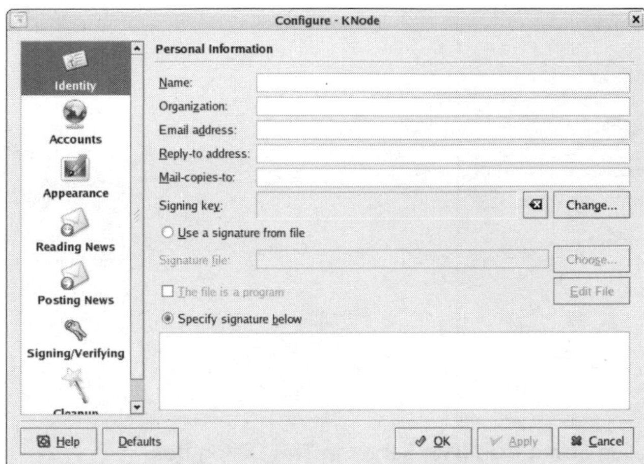

Figure 16-1: Configure the KNode Newsreader from This Dialog Box.

The left-hand side of the dialog box shows all the items that you can configure and the right-hand side is where you enter the information for the item that you have currently selected on the right-hand side.

When the Configure KNode dialog box first opens, it first prompts for your personal information. Enter your identification information such as name, email address, and organization — this information is used when you post a new item to a newsgroup.

Then, click Accounts in the left-hand side. (Refer to Figure 16-1.) Then click the Newsgroup Servers tab to set up information about the news server from which you will be reading news. Click Add in the Newsgroup Servers tab to bring up a dialog box (see Figure 16-2) where you can enter the information about the news server. Your ISP should have provided you with the information needed to access the news server. If the news server requires a login name and a password, you must enter that information as well. (If you enter a password, KNode brings up a KWallet window where you can store the password for future use, but you can simply click Cancel if you do not want KWallet to store the password.)

After you set up the news account, click OK to store the settings and close the Configure KNode dialog box. The KNode window now shows the name of the news server in its left-hand side, as shown in Figure 16-3. Right-click on the server's name and select Subscribe to Newsgroups from the pop-up menu. A dialog box appears where you can subscribe to selected newsgroups (such as `comp.os.linux.announce`).

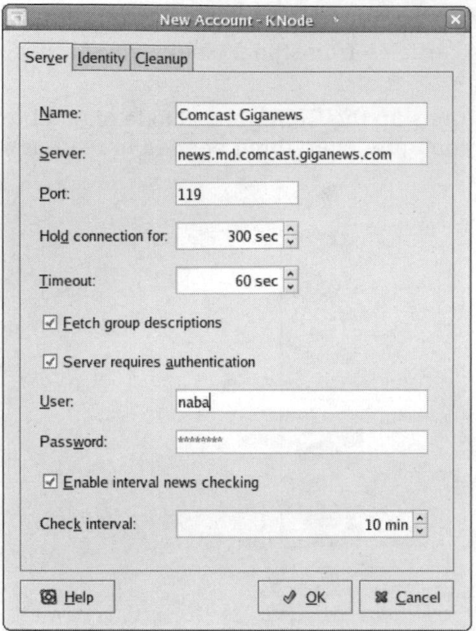

Figure 16-2: Enter Information about the News Server in This Dialog Box.

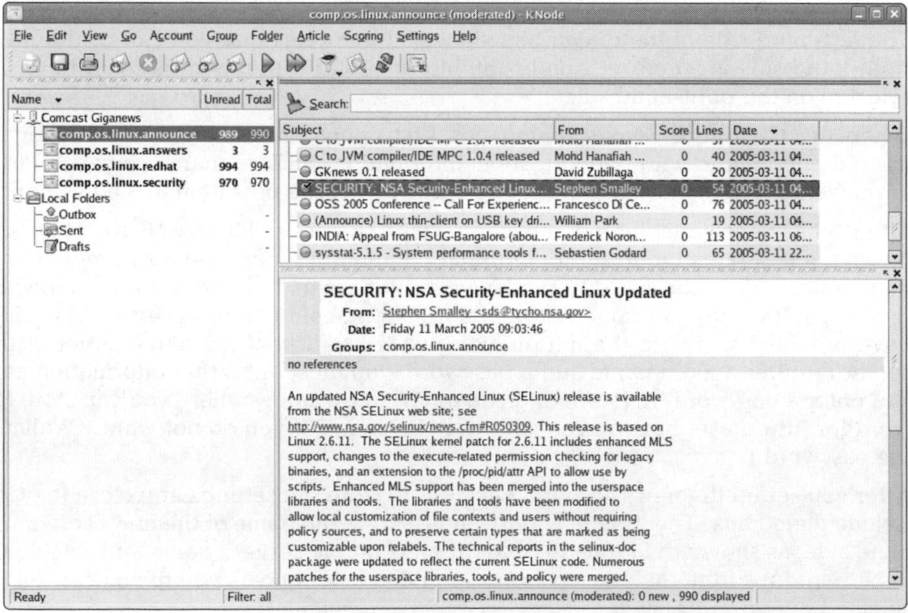

Figure 16-3: Reading Newsgroups in KNode

Figure 16-3 shows a typical view of the KNode window while reading an article from one of the subscribed newsgroups. The KNode user interface is similar to many other mail and newsreaders.

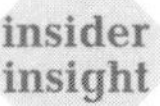

You may have to click the buttons on the toolbar in the KNode window to perform specific tasks such as followup to the newsgroup or reply by email. If you can't figure out what a button does, simply place the mouse over the button a small popup help window tells you what the button does.

Understanding the Newsgroup Hierarchy

News items are organized in a hierarchy of newsgroups for ease of maintenance as well as ease of use. A typical newsgroup name looks like the following:

```
comp.os.linux.announce
```

This name says that `comp.os.linux.announce` is a newsgroup for announcements (`announce`) about the Linux operating system (`os.linux`) and that these subjects fall under the broad category of computers (`comp`).

As you can see, the format of a newsgroup name is a sequence of words separated by periods. These words denote the hierarchy of the newsgroup.

To understand the newsgroup hierarchy, compare the newsgroup's name with the pathname of a file (such as `/usr/lib/X11/xinit/Xclients`) in Linux. Just as a file's pathname shows the directory hierarchy of the file, the newsgroup name shows the newsgroup hierarchy. In filenames, a slash (/) separates the names of directories; in a newsgroup's name, a period (.) separates the different levels in the newsgroup hierarchy.

In a newsgroup's name, the first word represents the newsgroup category. The `comp.os.linux.announce` newsgroup, for example, is in the `comp` category, whereas `alt.books.technical` is in the `alt` category.

Table 16-1 lists some of the major newsgroup categories.

Table 16-1: Major Newsgroup Categories

Category	*Subject*
`alt`	"Alternative" newsgroups (not subject to any rules), which run the gamut from the mundane to the bizarre
`bionet`	Biology newsgroups
`bit`	Bitnet newsgroups
`biz`	Business newsgroups

(continued)

Table 16-1 *(continued)*

Category	*Subject*
`clari`	Clarinet news service (daily news)
`comp`	Computer hardware and software newsgroups
`ieee`	Newsgroups for the Institute of Electrical and Electronics Engineers (IEEE)
`k12`	Newsgroups devoted to elementary and secondary education
`linux`	Newsgroups about Linux (includes a `linux.redhat` hierarchy)
`misc`	Miscellaneous newsgroups
`news`	Newsgroups about Internet news administration (`news.software.nntp` newsgroup covers INN)
`rec`	Recreational and art newsgroups
`sci`	Science and engineering newsgroups
`soc`	Newsgroups for discussing social issues and various cultures
`talk`	Discussions of current issues (such as "talk radio")

This short list of categories is deceptive because it does not really tell you about the wide-ranging variety of newsgroups available in each category. Because each newsgroup category contains several levels of subcategories, the overall count of newsgroups runs into over 50,000. The `comp` category alone has close to 1,200 newsgroups.

Typically, you have to narrow your choice of newsgroups according to your interests. If you are interested in Linux, for example, you can pick one or more of these newsgroups:

- **comp.os.linux.admin:** Information about Linux system administration.
- **comp.os.linux.advocacy:** Discussions about promoting Linux.
- **comp.os.linux.announce:** Important announcements about Linux. This newsgroup is moderated, which means that you must mail the article to the moderator, who then posts it to the newsgroup if the article is appropriate for the newsgroup.
- **comp.os.linux.answers:** Questions and answers about Linux. All the Linux HOWTOs are posted in this moderated newsgroup. (See Chapter 7 for a list of Linux HOWTOs.)
- **comp.os.linux.development:** Current Linux development work.
- **comp.os.linux.development.apps:** Linux application development.
- **comp.os.linux.development.system:** Linux operating-system development.
- **comp.os.linux.hardware:** Discussions about Linux and various types of hardware.
- **comp.os.linux.help:** Help with various aspects of Linux.
- **comp.os.linux.misc:** Miscellaneous Linux-related topics.
- **comp.os.linux.networking:** Networking under Linux.
- **comp.os.linux.redhat:** Red Hat Linux-related topics.

- **comp.os.linux.security:** Discussions about Linux security.
- **comp.os.linux.setup:** Linux setup and installation.
- **comp.os.linux.x:** Discussions about setting up and running the X Window System under Linux.
- **linux.redhat:** Discussions about Red Hat Linux.

You have to be selective about what newsgroups you read because it's impossible to keep up with all the news, even in a specific area such as Linux. When you first install and set up Linux, you might read newsgroups such as `comp.os.linux.setup`, `comp.os.linux.hardware`, and `comp.os.linux.x` (especially if you are having problems with X). After you have Linux up and running, you may want to learn only about new things happening in Linux. For such information, read the `comp.os.linux.announce` newsgroup.

Subscribing to Newsgroups

Unlike magazines or newspapers, newsgroups do not require that you subscribe to them; you can read any newsgroup that is available on the news server. The news server administrator may decide to exclude certain newsgroups, however; in that case, you cannot read them.

The only thing that you come close to "subscribing" to is the `.newsrc` file in your home directory. All newsreaders consult this file to determine which newsgroups you want to read. From inside the newsreader, you can use its menus or commands to subscribe to a newsgroup. When you subscribe to the newsgroup, the newsreader simply adds the name of that newsgroup to the `.newsrc` file.

Posting to Newsgroups

You can use any newsreader to post a news item (a new item or a reply to an old posting) to one or more newsgroups. Posting a news item to a newsgroup is basically similar to sending an email message. The exact command for posting a news item depends on the newsreader. For example, in the KNode newsreader, follow these steps to post an article:

1. Select Article ➪ Post to Newsgroup or click the Post to Newsgroup button (leftmost button on the toolbar).
2. A window appears where you can compose the message. Initially the name of the currently selected newsgroup is shown as the destination for your message. To select other newsgroups, click Browse and select the newsgroups. Then enter the subject and your message. For this test posting, type a subject line with the word `ignore` in it, and select the `misc.test` newsgroup. Otherwise, any site that receives your article replies by mail to tell you the article has reached the site; that's in keeping with the purpose of the `misc.test` newsgroup.
3. After you finish composing the message, click Send Now (the leftmost button) on the toolbar. KNode sends the message to the news server, which in turn sends it to other news servers.
4. To verify that the test message has reached the newsgroup, click Account ➪ Subscribe; then subscribe to the `misc.test` newsgroup (that's where you've recently posted the new article). Look at the latest article in `misc.test`, which should be the article you've recently posted.

Verifying Your Newsgroup Posting

If you post an article and read the newsgroup immediately, you'll see the new article, but that does not mean the article has reached other sites on the Internet. After all, your posting shows up on your news server immediately because that's where you have posted the article. Because of the store-and-forward model of news distribution, the news article gradually propagates from your news server to others around the world.

The `misc.test` newsgroup provides a way to see whether or not your news posting is really getting around. If you post to that newsgroup and do not include the word "ignore" in the subject, news servers acknowledge receipt of the article by sending an email message to the address listed in the `Reply-To` field of the article's header.

If you have your Linux host on the Internet, try posting to the `misc.test` newsgroup to verify that articles are getting out. Be prepared to receive a dozen or so replies from various sites, acknowledging the arrival of your article at those sites.

Configuring and Starting the INN Server

So far, you have seen how to read news from an existing news server. Now, you can turn to the subject of setting up an INN server on your system. Much of the InterNetNews (INN) software, bundled with Linux, is already set up for you. You need to understand the various components of INN, edit the configuration files, and start innd—the INN server. Sometimes I refer to the INN server as the *news server*.

If you want to support a selection of Internet newsgroups, you also have to arrange for a *news feed*—this is the source from which your news server gets the newsgroup articles. Typically, you can get a news feed from an ISP, for an additional monthly fee, to cover the cost of resources required to provide the feed. You need the name of the upstream server that provides the news feed, and you have to provide that server with your server's name and the newsgroups you want to receive.

Based on the newsgroups you want to receive and the number of days you want to retain articles, you have to set aside disk space for the articles. The newsgroups are stored in a directory hierarchy (based on the newsgroup names) in the `/var/spool/news` directory of your system. If you are setting up a news server, you may want to devote a large disk partition to the `/var/spool/news` directory.

In your news server's configuration files, enter the name of the server providing the news feed. At the same time, add to the configuration files the names of any downstream news servers, if any, that receive news feeds from your server. Then, you can start the news server and wait for news to arrive. Monitor the log files to ensure that the news articles are being sorted and stored properly in the `/var/spool/news` directory on your system.

Once you have news up and running, you must run news maintenance and cleanup scripts. These are run using the cron jobs (see Chapter 20 for more information about cron jobs). On Fedora Linux, a cron job is already set up to run the `/usr/lib/news/bin/news.daily` script to perform the news maintenance tasks.

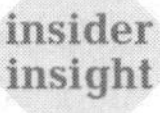

The following sections introduce you to INN setup, but you can learn more about INN from the Internet Software Consortium (ISC), a nonprofit corporation dedicated to developing and maintaining open source Internet software, such as BIND (an implementation of Domain Name Service), DHCP (Dynamic Host Configuration Protocol), and INN. Rich Salz originally wrote INN; ISC took over the development of INN in 1996. You can learn more about INN and access other resources at ISC's INN Web page (`www.isc.org/sw/inn/`).

Taking Stock of INN Components

INN includes several programs that perform specific newsgroup delivery and management tasks. It also includes a number of files that control how the INN programs work. The most important INN programs are the following:

- **innd:** The news server. It runs as a *daemon* — a background process that keeps itself running to provide a specific service — and listens on the NNTP port (TCP port 119). The innd server accepts connections from other feed sites, as well as from local newsreader clients, but it hands off local connections to the nnrpd.
- **nnrpd:** A special server invoked by innd to handle requests from local newsreader clients.
- **expire:** Removes old articles based on the specifications in the text file `/etc/news/expire.ctl`.
- **nntpsend:** Invokes the innxmit program to send news articles to a remote site by using NNTP. The configuration file `/etc/news/nntpsend.ctl` controls the nntpsend program.
- **ctlinnd:** Enables you to control the innd server interactively. The ctlinnd program can send messages to the control channel of the innd server.

Some of the important components of INN are its control files. Most of these files are in the `/etc/news` directory of your Linux system, but a few are in the `/var/lib/news` directory also. Between the two directories, there are over 30 INN control files. Some of the important files include the following:

- **/etc/news/inn.conf:** Specifies configuration data for the innd server. (To view online help for this file, type **man inn.conf**.)
- **/etc/news/newsfeeds:** Specifies what articles to feed downstream to other news servers. (The file is complicated, but you can get help by typing **man newsfeeds**.)
- **/etc/news/incoming.conf:** Lists the names and addresses of hosts that provide news feeds to this server. (To view online help for this file, type **man incoming.conf**.)
- **/etc/news/storage.conf:** Specifies the storage methods to be used when storing news articles. (To view online help for this file, type **man storage.conf**.)
- **/etc/news/expire.ctl:** Controls expiration of articles, on a per-newsgroup level, if desired. (To view online help for this file, type **man expire.ctl**.)

continues

continued

- **/var/lib/news/active:** Lists all active newsgroups, showing the oldest and newest article number for each, and each newsgroup's posting status. (To view online help for this file, type **man active**.)
- **/var/lib/news/newsgroups:** Lists newsgroups, with a brief description of each.
- **/etc/news/readers.conf:** Specifies hosts and users are permitted to read news from this news server and post news to newsgroups. The default file allows only the localhost to read news; you have to edit it if you want to allow other hosts in your local area network to read news. (To view online help for this file, type **man readers.conf**.)

The next few sections describe how to set up some of the control files.

Understanding inn.conf

This file holds configuration data for all INN programs and, as such, is the most important file. Each line of the file has the value of a parameter in the following format:

```
parameter:     value
```

Depending on the parameter, the value is a string, a number, or `true` or `false`. As in many other configuration files, comment lines begin with a number or pound sign (#).

Most of the parameters in the default `inn.conf` file in the `/etc/news` directory should not require changes. You might want to edit one or more of the parameters shown in Table 16-2.

Table 16-2: Configuration Parameters in /etc/news/inn.conf

Parameter Name	*Description*
`mta`	Set this to the mail transfer agent that will be used by innd to transfer messages. The default is to use sendmail.
`organization`	Set this to the name of your organization in the way you want it to appear in the `Organization:` header of all news articles posted from your system. Users may override this by defining the `ORGANIZATION` environment variable.
`ovmethod`	Sets the type of overview storage method (the overview is an index of the news articles in the newsgroup). The default method is `tradindexed`, which is fast for reading news, but slow for storing news items.
`pathhost`	Set this to the name of your news server as you want it to appear in the `Path` header of all postings that go through your server. If `pathhost` is not defined, the fully qualified domain name of your system is used.
`pathnews`	Set this to the full pathname of the directory that contains INN binaries and libraries. In Linux, `pathnews` is set to `/usr/lib/news`.
`domain`	Set this to the domain name for your server.

Parameter Name	Description
`allownewnews`	Set this to `true` if you want INN to support the `NEWNEWS` command from news readers. Because this command can drastically reduce your server's performance, INN documentation recommends that you set this to `false`.
`hiscachesize`	Set this to the size in kilobytes that you want INN to use for caching recently used history file entries. The default setting of `0` disables history caching. Because history caching can greatly increase the number of articles your server can process per second, you may want to set a value of 256 (for 256KB).
`innflags`	Set this to any flags you want to pass to the INN server process when it starts up.

Understanding News Feeds

The `newsfeeds` file specifies how incoming news articles are redistributed to other servers and to INN processes. If you provide news feeds to other servers, you have to list these news feeds in this file. (You also must have an entry labeled `ME`, which serves a special purpose explained later in this section.)

The `newsfeeds` file contains a series of entries, one for each feed. Each feed entry has the following format:

```
site[/exclude,exclude...]\
     :pattern,pattern...[/distrib,distrib...]\
     :flag,flag...\
     :param
```

Each entry has four fields separated by colons (`:`). Usually, the entries span multiple lines, and a backslash (\) at the end of the line is used to continue a line to the next. Following are the four fields in each entry in the `newsfeeds` file:

1. The first field, site, is the name of the feed. Each name must be unique, and for feeds to other news servers, the name is set to the host name of the remote server. Following the name is an optional slash and an exclude list (`/exclude, exclude...`) consisting of a list of names. If any of the names in this list appear in the Path line of an article, that article will not be forwarded to the feed. You can use an exclude list if you don't want to receive articles from a specific source.
2. The second field consists of a comma-separated list of newsgroup patterns, such as `*,@alt.binaries.warez.*,!control*,!local*`, followed by an optional distribution list. The distribution list is a list of comma-separated keywords, with each keyword specifying a specific set of sites to which the articles are distributed. The newsgroup patterns essentially define a subscription list of sites that receive this news feed. An asterisk (*) matches all newsgroups. A pattern beginning with an @ causes newsgroups matching that pattern to be dropped. A pattern that begins with an exclamation mark (`!`) means the matching newsgroups are not sent. By the way, the simple pattern-matching syntax used in INN configuration files is referred to as a *wildmat* pattern.

3. The third field is a comma-separated list of flags. These flags determine the feed-entry type and set certain parameters for the entry. There are numerous flags; you should type **man newsfeeds** and read the man page for more information about the flags.
4. The fourth field is for parameters whose values depend on the settings in the third field. Typically, this field contains names of files or external programs that the INN server uses. You can learn more about this field from the newsfeeds man page.

Now that you know the layout of the /etc/news/newsfeeds file, you can study that file as an example. The default file contains many sample feed entries, but all but the following two are commented out:

- ME is a special feed entry that's always required. It serves two purposes. First, the newsgroup patterns listed in this entry are preprended to all newsgroup patterns in all other entries. Second, the ME entry's distribution list determines what distributions your server accepts from remote sites.
- The controlchan feed entry is used to set up INN so that an external program is used to handle control messages (these messages are used to create new newsgroups and remove groups). For example, the following controlchan entry specifies the external program /usr/bin/controlchan to handle all control messages, except cancel messages (meant for canceling an article):

```
controlchan!\
          :!*,control,control.*,!control.cancel\
          :Tc,Wnsm:/usr/lib/news/bin/controlchan
```

In addition to these feed entries, you add entries for any actual sites to which your news server provides news feed. Such entries have the format

```
feedme.domain.com\
            :!junk,!control/!foo\
            :Tm:innfeed!
```

where feedme.domain.com is the fully qualified domain name of the site to which your system sends news articles.

Understanding incoming.conf

The incoming.conf file describes which hosts are allowed to connect to your host to feed articles (in versions of INN prior to 2.2.3, a file named hosts.nntp was used to specify remote hosts allowed to transfer articles to the local site). For a single feed, you can add an entry like

```
peer myfeed {
  hostname: myfeedsite.com
}
```

where myfeed is a label for the peer and myfeedsite.com identifies the peer — the site that feeds your site.

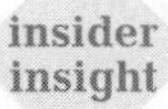

insider insight

Keep in mind that simply adding a site's name in the `incoming.conf` file does not cause that remote site to start feeding your site news—it simply enables your server to accept news articles from the remote site. At the remote site, the server must be configured to send articles to your site.

Exploring readers.conf

This file specifies the host names or IP addresses from which newsreader clients (such as Mozilla) can retrieve newsgroups from your server. For example, the following `readers.conf` file allows read access and post access (meaning you can submit articles) from localhost and any from host in the network 192.168.0.0:

```
auth "localhost" {
    hosts: "localhost, 127.0.0.1, stdin"
    default: "<localhost>"
}
access "localhost" {
    users: "<localhost>"
    newsgroups: "*"
    access: RPA
}
auth "localnet" {
    hosts: 192.168.0.0/24
    default: "<localnet>"
}
access "localnet" {
    users: "<localnet>"
    newsgroups: "*"
    access: RPA
}
```

Starting INN

In addition to the configuration files, you also need to initiate cron jobs that perform periodic maintenance of the news server. In Linux, these cron jobs are already set up. Therefore, you are now ready to start the INN server—innd.

Before you start innd, you must run `makehistory` and `makedbz` to initialize and rebuild the INN history database. Type **man makehistory** and **man makedbz** to learn more about these commands. You can use the following commands to create an initial history database and associated index:

```
/usr/lib/news/bin/makehistory -b -f history -O -l 30000 -I
cd /var/lib/news
/usr/lib/news/bin/makedbz -s `wc -l < history` -f history
chown news.news *
chown news.news /var/spool/news/overview/group.index
chmod 664 /var/spool/news/overview/group.index
```

As with any other standalone servers (these are servers that do not run under `xinetd`) in Linux, you can set up innd to start at boot time by typing the following command:

```
chkconfig --level 35 innd on
```

To start innd right now, log in as `root` and type the following command:

```
service innd start
```

If you change any configuration files (such as `inn.conf` or `newsfeeds`), restart the innd server with the following command:

```
service innd restart
```

You can type **ps ax** to see if the innd process is up and running. If all goes well, you should see two processes such as the following listed in the output of the `ps ax` command:

```
23789 ?        S      0:00 /usr/lib/news/bin/innd -p4
23794 ?        S      0:00 /usr/bin/perl /usr/lib/news/bin/controlchan
```

insider insight

The `/var/log/spooler` file contains all status and error messages from innd. Type the following command to see the last few messages in that file:

```
tail /var/log/spoolerSetting up Local Newsgroups
```

If you want to use newsgroups as a way to share information within your company, you can set up a hierarchy of local newsgroups. Then, you can use these newsgroups to create virtual communities within your company, where people with shared interests can informally discuss issues and exchange knowledge.

Defining a Newsgroup Hierarchy

The first task is to define a hierarchy of newsgroups and decide what each newsgroup will discuss. For example, if your company's name is XYZ Corporation, here's a partial hierarchy of newsgroups you might define:

- **xyz.general:** General items about XYZ Corporation
- **xyz.weekly.news:** Weekly news
- **xyz.weekly.menu:** The weekly cafeteria menu and any discussions about it
- **xyz.forsale:** A listing of items offered for sale by employees
- **xyz.jobs:** Job openings at XYZ Corporation
- **xyz.wanted:** Wanted (help, items to buy, and so on) postings by employees
- **xyz.technical.hardware:** Technical discussions about hardware
- **xyz.technical.software:** Technical discussions about software

Updating Configuration Files

Add descriptive entries for each of these newsgroups to the /var/lib/news/newsgroups file. Here are some entries from the /var/lib/news/newsgroups file:

```
control                 Various control messages (no posting).
control.cancel          Cancel messages (no posting).
control.checkgroups     Hierarchy check control messages (no posting).
control.newgroup        Newsgroup creation control messages (no posting).
control.rmgroup         Newsgroup removal control messages (no posting).
junk                    Unfiled articles (no posting).
```

Add a line for each newsgroup — type its name, followed by a brief description.

Next, edit the ME entry in the /etc/news/newsfeeds file and add the phrase !xyz.* to the comma-separated list of newsgroup patterns. This ensures that your local newsgroups are not distributed outside your site.

You must also add a storage method to be used for the local newsgroups. For example, you can add the following lines in /etc/news/storage.conf to define the storage method for the new xyz hierarchy of newsgroups (change xyz to whatever you name your local newsgroups):

```
method tradspool {
    class: 1
    newsgroups: xyz.*
}
```

After making changes to configuration files, remember to restart the news server with the command:

```
service innd restart.
```

Adding the Newsgroups

The final step is to add the newsgroups. Once you have innd running, it's very easy to add a local newsgroup. Log in as root and use ctlinnd to perform this task. For example, here's how you add a newsgroup named xyz.general:

```
/usr/lib/news/bin/ctlinnd newgroup xyz.general
```

That command adds the xyz.general newsgroup to your site. If you use the traditional storage method, the innd server creates the directory /var/spool/news/articles/xyz/general and stores articles for that newsgroup in that directory.

Once you have created all the local newsgroups, users from your intranet should be able to post news articles and read articles in the local newsgroups. If they have problems accessing the newsgroups, make sure that the /etc/news/readers.conf file contains the IP addresses or names of the hosts that should be able to access the innd server.

Testing Your Newsgroups

For example, I have added a newsgroup named `local.news` on an INN server running on my Linux system by using the instructions explained in the previous sections. Then, I start KNode (or any other newsreader) on another system on the LAN and edit the preferences so that the news server is set to my INN server. Next, I access the local.news newsgroup by typing `news:local.news` as the URL.

Reading RSS Feeds

RSS stands for Really Simple Syndication. RSS is a format for syndicating — gathering and making available — content of websites, primarily news-oriented sites and blogs. The term "blog" is short for weblog — a frequently updated journal with thoughts, comments, and opinions of the blog's creator. RSS can be used to provide any kind of information that can be broken down into discrete items and put into RSS format. Such RSS-formatted content is called an RSS feed and an RSS-aware program can check the feed periodically for changes, download new items, and make them available to the user.

The RSS format is a dialect of XML (eXtensible Markup Language). All RSS files conform to XML 1.0 specification.

There are many versions of RSS, but three versions — 0.91, 1.0, and 2.0 — are in widespread use. RSS version 0.90 was designed by Netscape for gathering and displaying headlines from news sites. A simpler version, 0.91, was proposed and UserLand Software picked up that version to use it for its blogging product. At the same time, another non-commercial group had evolved RSS 0.90 into RSS 1.0, which is based on resource description format or RDF (see `www.w3.org/RDF/`). UserLand did not accept RSS 1.0, but instead continued evolving RSS 0.91 through versions 0.92, 0.93, 0.94, and finally settled on RSS 2.0 (skipping 1.0 because that version number was already taken).

Currently many blogs and websites use RSS 0.91 for basic syndication (title, URL, and description), RSS 1.0 for readers that use RDF, and RSS 2.0 for advanced syndication with more metadata (think of metadata as "data about data," which is what the RSS format provides — it provides data about other information such as blogs and news). RSS 1.0 files have an `.rdf` extension whereas RSS 0.91 and 2.0 files have an .xml extension. However, all RSS files are text files that use XML tags.

Examining an RSS Feed

An RSS feed is a text file with XML tags that describe a website's content. You typically use an automated program to periodically generate the RSS feed file, but you can prepare the RSS feed file using a text editor. It's good to know what an RSS feed looks like, just so you can debug problems with the feed.

The specific details of an RSS feed depend on the version of RSS. The simplest feed is RSS 0.91. For example, here's a typical RSS 0.91 feed:

```
<?xml version="1.0" ?>
<!-- A comment line --->
<rss version="0.91">
  <channel> <!--- This tag specifies general information about the feed--->
    <title>Title of this feed</title>
    <link>URL of this feed, for example, http://naba.typepad.com/</link>
    <description>Brief description of feed</description>
    <language>en-us</language>
    <item>
      <title>Title of this item</title>
      <link>URL for this item</link>
      <description>Description of this item</description>
    </item>
... more items ...
  </channel>
</rss>
```

As you can see from that listing, a feed includes a channel with a title, link, description, and language, followed by a series of items, each of which has a title, link, and description.

The format is more verbose for RSS 1.0, which uses the RDF format. For example, here is a sample RSS 1.0 feed:

```
<?xml version="1.0" encoding="utf-8"?>

<rdf:RDF
  xmlns:rdf="http://www.w3.org/1999/02/22-rdf-syntax-ns#"
  xmlns:dc="http://purl.org/dc/elements/1.1/"
  xmlns:sy="http://purl.org/rss/1.0/modules/syndication/"
  xmlns:admin="http://webns.net/mvcb/"
  xmlns:content="http://purl.org/rss/1.0/modules/content/"
  xmlns:cc="http://web.resource.org/cc/"
  xmlns="http://purl.org/rss/1.0/">

<channel rdf:about="http://naba.typepad.com/nabatech/">
  <title>NabaTech</title>
  <link>http://naba.typepad.com/nabatech/</link>
  <description>A New Light on Technology, Book Writing, and All That</description>
  <dc:language>en-us</dc:language>
  <dc:creator></dc:creator>
  <dc:date>2005-04-20T20:21:37-04:00</dc:date>
  <admin:generatorAgent rdf:resource="http://www.typepad.com/?v=1.5.1" />

  <items>
  <rdf:Seq><rdf:li
rdf:resource="http://naba.typepad.com/nabatech/2005/04/is_epublishing_.html" />
  <rdf:li rdf:resource="http://naba.typepad.com/nabatech/2005/04/future_of_compu.html"
/>
```

```
... more items ...
  </rdf:Seq>
  </items>
</channel>

<item rdf:about="http://naba.typepad.com/nabatech/2005/04/is_epublishing_.html">
  <title>Is ePublishing the Future of Computer Books?</title>
  <link>http://naba.typepad.com/nabatech/2005/04/is_epublishing_.html</link>
  <description>Recently I wondered if we could publish a printed book with an online
companion. That generated quite a bit of discussion. It seems that some pioneers have
already forged ahead...</description>
  <dc:subject>Computer Books</dc:subject>
  <dc:creator>Naba</dc:creator>
  <dc:date>2005-04-20T20:21:37-04:00</dc:date>
</item>
... more items ...
</rdf:RDF>
```

RSS 1.0 essentially provides the basic information that's in RSS 0.91 and adds more details such as item-level authors, subject, and publishing dates, which RSS 0.91 does not support.

Reading RSS Feeds

There are many GUI programs available for subscribing to RSS feeds and reading items from a feed. These programs are called RSS aggregators because they can gather information from many RSS feeds and make everything available in a single place.

There are two types of RSS aggregators — Web browser plugins and standalone programs. Browser plugins such as NewsMonster (`www.newsmonster.org/`) run in a Web browser so that the feeds appear in the Web browser. Standalone programs such as GNOME Straw (`www.nongnu.org/straw/`) and KDE Akregator (`http://akregator.sourceforge.net/`) are complete GUI applications and usually look similar to other mail and newsreader programs.

Fedora Linux comes with the Akregator program that's a standalone RSS feed aggregator. The program's binary is in `/usr/bin/akregator` and it comes in the kdepim RPM, which should be installed if you install the KDE desktop. Look for a link in the Applications ⇨ Internet menu in GNOME, but if you don't see it listed, type **akregator** in a terminal window to run it.

When Akregator first runs, it displays its main window without any RSS feeds. To subscribe to a feed, select Feed ⇨ Add Feed from the menu or right-click on All Feeds in the left pane of the window (refer to Figure 16-4) and select Add Feed from the pop-up menu. Then type the URL for the feed in the Add Feed dialog box and click OK. For example, for my blog's RDF feed, I type `http://naba.typepad.com/nabatech/index.rdf`. The feed's title then appears on the left pane of the window. Click the feed title to view the items in this feed. Then you can click an item in the upper-right pane and that item appears in the lower-right pane, as shown in Figure 16-4.

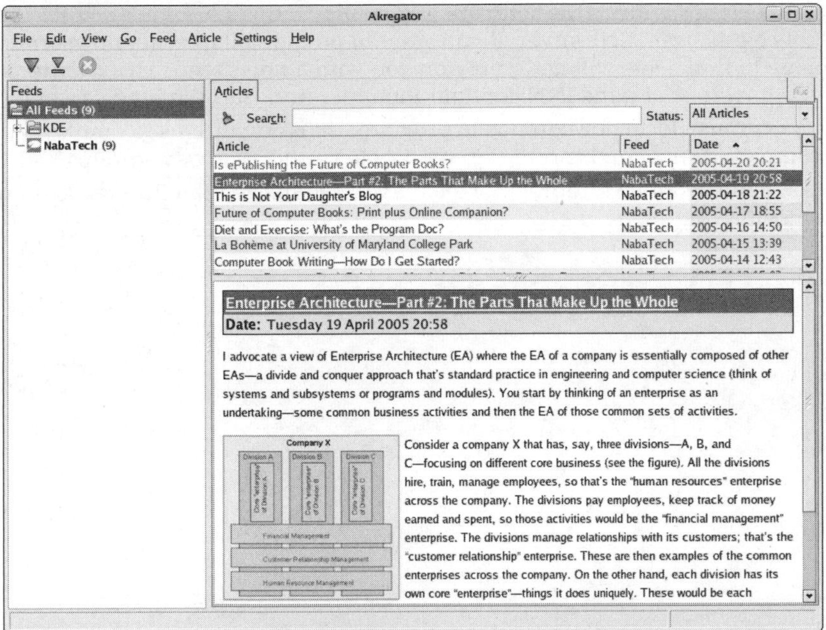

Figure 16-4: Reading RSS Feeds in Akregator.

Summary

Internet newsgroups provide a convenient way to discuss various topics and to share your knowledge with others. This chapter describes newsgroups and shows you how to set up a news server on your Linux PC. You also learn about Really Simple Syndication or RSS feeds and how to read RSS feeds in an RSS aggregator application.

In this chapter, you learned the following:

- Newsgroups originated in Usenet, which is a store-and-forward network. News items travel around the world from one system to another. Nowadays, news is transported over the Internet by means of the Network News Transport Protocol (NNTP).
- Because thousands of newsgroups exist, storing all the news articles takes a great deal of disk space. Moreover, the articles must be purged periodically or the disk becomes filled. It's best to read news from a news server maintained by an Internet service provider (ISP).
- This chapter shows you how to use KNode to read news from a designated news server.

- Linux comes with all the software and configuration files you need for the InterNetNews (INN) server. If you want to provide all Internet newsgroups, you have to find a site willing to provide you with a news feed. This chapter shows you how to set up the INN configuration files and start the innd server.
- You can use local newsgroups to provide discussion forums to employees in your company. Once innd is running, it's simple to add local newsgroups.
- You can use an RSS aggregator such as Akregator to read RSS feeds from websites and blogs.

FTP Server

Chapter 17

Secrets in This Chapter

File Transfer Protocol (FTP) is a popular client/server software for transferring files from one system to another. If you have an ISP account that provides you with a home page, you've probably used FTP to upload your Web pages to the ISP's server. Using an FTP client, you log in to your ISP account and copy the files from your home system to the ISP's server.

You can also use FTP to download other files, such as open source software from Internet hosts. In this case, you don't need an account on the remote system. You simply log in using the anonymous user name and provide your email address as the password. This is called anonymous FTP. If you want to enable others to download files from your system by using FTP, you can set up anonymous FTP on your system so that users can log in with the user name "anonymous."

Fedora Linux comes with several FTP clients and the Very Secure FTP daemon (vsftpd), written by Chris Evans. The FTP server typically includes the files you need to support anonymous FTP. This chapter introduces you to a few FTP clients and, for the command-line FTP client, describes the commands you use to work with remote directories. It also shows you how to configure the FTP server through text configuration files and how to control access to the FTP server.

Installing FTP Software

During the installation of Linux from this book's companion DVD, you have the option to install the packages necessary for FTP. As described in Chapter 2, select the FTP Server package group when you are prompted for which packages to install.

If you install the FTP Server package group during Linux installation, you do not have to do much more than start vsftpd to begin using FTP. Otherwise, you can use the Red Hat Package Manager (RPM) to install individual packages. Chapter 21 describes how to use the RPM program to install new software.

To access the RPM files for FTP, mount the DVD with the following command (if you have a CD recorder, change the second argument to `/media/cdrecorder`):

```
mount /media/cdrom
```

Then, change the directory to `/media/cdrom/Fedora/RPMS`, where you will find the RPM files. Following are some of the RPMs you may want to install. (Shown is the RPM name; the actual filename starts with the RPM name, has a version number, and ends with an `.rpm` extension.)

- **vsftpd:** The Very Secure FTP daemon — an FTP server
- **ftp:** An FTP client
- **gftp:** X Window System–based graphical FTP client
- **lftp:** Another FTP client

You have probably already installed most of these packages. For this chapter, you should install vsftpd, ftp, and gftp. If you need to install any of the packages, you can also use the graphical Package Management program (select Desktop ➪ System Settings ➪ Add/Remove Applications).

Understanding FTP

As the name implies, the File Transfer Protocol (FTP) enables users to transfer files between systems on the Internet. FTP is client/server software—you can use the FTP client on a system to access files on another Internet host. The FTP server on that host acts on commands you send via the FTP client.

The FTP clients and servers exchange information by using FTP, described in RFC 959, "File Transfer Protocol," by J. Postel and J. K. Reynolds, October 1985. FTP uses two TCP ports—data is transferred on port 20, while control information is exchanged on port 21.

With FTP, you can download files from other Internet hosts or from hosts in your local area network. Reciprocally, users on other systems also can download files from your system, typically through a feature known as anonymous FTP.

Before you can try out the FTP client, log in as `root` and start the vsftpd server on your system with the following command:

```
service vsftpd start
```

In some Linux distributions, the FTP server was run under xinetd. However, in Fedora Linux the FTP server runs as a standalone server, just like Apache httpd and the innd news server. To automatically start vsftpd when you boot the Linux system, you must turn it on with the following command:

```
chkconfig --level 35 vsftpd on
```

The next few sections introduce you to FTP for transferring files and working with remote directories. In addition to the FTP commands, you also learn about the graphical FTP clients and how to use FTP through your Web browser.

Using the Command-Line FTP Client

After you have started vsftpd, you can see how FTP works by using the command-line FTP client. You can try out the FTP commands from another system on a local area network or on your Linux system. For example, the following sample FTP session shows how I use the command-line FTP client to log in using my user name (`naba`) and browse the directories on my system (my comments appear in italics):

```
ftp localhost
Connected to localhost.localdomain.
220 (vsFTPd 2.0.3)
Name (localhost:naba):    (I press Enter)
331 Please specify the password.
Password:        (I type my password)
230 Login successful. Have fun.
Remote system type is UNIX.
Using binary mode to transfer files.
ftp> help
Commands may be abbreviated.  Commands are:
```

```
!               cr            mdir          proxy         send
$               delete        mget          sendport      site
account         debug         mkdir         put           size
append          dir           mls           pwd           status
ascii           disconnect    mode          quit          struct
bell            form          modtime       quote         system
binary          get           mput          recv          sunique
bye             glob          newer         reget         tenex
case            hash          nmap          rstatus       trace
ccc             help          nlist         rhelp         type
cd              idle          ntrans        rename        user
cdup            image         open          reset         umask
chmod           lcd           passive       restart       verbose
clear           ls            private       rmdir         ?
close           macdef        prompt        runique
cprotect        mdelete       protect       safe
ftp> cd /var/ftp (This changes directory to /var/ftp)
250 Directory successfully changed.
ftp> ls         (This command lists the contents of the directory)
227 Entering Passive Mode (127,0,0,1,128,141)
150 Here comes the directory listing.
drwxr-xr-x    2 0        0            4096 Mar 23 08:23 pub
226 Directory send OK.
ftp> bye        (This command ends the session)
221 Goodbye.
```

As the listing shows, you can start the command-line FTP client by typing the command **ftp hostname**, where *hostname* is the name of the system you want to access. Once the FTP client establishes a connection with the FTP server at the remote system, the FTP server prompts you for a user name and password. After you've supplied the information, the FTP client displays the `ftp>` prompt, and you can begin typing commands to perform specific tasks. If you can't remember a specific FTP command, type **help** to view a list of them. You can get additional help for a specific command by typing **help command**.

Many of the FTP commands are similar to UNIX commands for navigating the file system. For example, `cd` changes directory, `pwd` prints the name of the current working directory, and `ls` lists the contents of the current directory. Two other common commands are `get` and `put` — `get` downloads a file from the remote system to your system, and `put` uploads (sends) a file from your system to the remote host.

You can use the `mget` command to download multiple files. However, you cannot conveniently download entire directory hierarchies by using the command-line FTP client. Graphical FTP clients are much better at downloading entire directories and subdirectories.

Table 17-1 describes some commonly used FTP commands. Note that you do not have to type the entire FTP command. For a long command, you have to type the first characters only — enough to identify the command uniquely. For example, to delete a file, you can type `dele`, and to change the file transfer mode to binary, you can type `bin`.

Table 17-1: List of Commonly Used FTP Commands

Command	*Description*
!	Executes a shell command on the local system. For example, `!ls` lists the contents of the current directory on the remote system.
?	Displays list of commands (same as `help`).
`append`	Appends a local file to a remote file.
`ascii`	Sets the file transfer type to ASCII (or plaintext). This is the default file transfer type.
`binary`	Sets the file transfer type to binary.
`bye`	Ends the FTP session with the remote FTP server and quits the FTP client.
`cd`	Changes the directory on the remote system. For example, `cd /pub/Linux` changes the remote directory to `/pub/Linux`.
`chmod`	Changes the permission settings of a remote file. For example, `chmod 644 index.html` changes the permission settings of the `index.html` file on the remote system.
`close`	Ends the FTP session with the FTP server and returns to the FTP client's prompt.
`delete`	Deletes a remote file. For example, `delete bigimage.jpg` deletes that file on the remote system.
`dir`	Lists the contents of the current directory on the remote system.
`disconnect`	Ends the FTP session and returns to the FTP client's prompt. (This is the same as `close`.)
`get`	Downloads a remote file. For example, `get junk.tar.gz junk.tgz` downloads the file `junk.tar.gz` from the remote system and saves it as the file `junk.tgz` on the local system.
`hash`	Turns on or off hash mark (#) printing showing the progress of file transfer. When turned on, a hash mark is printed for every 1,024 bytes transferred from the remote system.
`help`	Displays a list of commands.
`image`	Same as `binary`.
`lcd`	Changes the current directory on the local system. For example, `lcd /var/ftp/pub` changes the current local directory to `/var/ftp/pub`.
`ls`	Lists the contents of the current remote directory.
`mdelete`	Deletes multiple files on a remote system. For example, `mdelete *.jpg` deletes all remote files with names ending in `.jpg` in the current directory.

(continued)

Table 17-1 *(continued)*

Command	*Description*
`mdir`	Lists multiple remote files and saves the listing in a specified local file. For example, `mdir /usr/share/doc/w* wlist` saves the listing in the local file named `wlist`.
`mget`	Downloads multiple files. For example, `mget *.jpg` downloads all files with names ending in `.jpg`. If prompt is turned on, the FTP client asks for confirmation before each file is downloaded.
`mkdir`	Creates a directory on the remote system. `mkdir images` creates a directory named `images` in the current directory on the remote system.
`mls`	Same as `mdir`.
`mput`	Uploads multiple files. For example, `mput *.jpg` sends all files with names ending in `.jpg` to the remote system. If the prompt is turned on, the FTP client asks for confirmation before each file is sent.
`open`	Opens a connection to the FTP server on the specified host. For example, `open ftp.netscape.com` connects to the FTP server on the host `ftp.netscape.com`.
`prompt`	Turns prompt on or off. When prompt is on, the FTP client prompts you for confirmation before downloading or uploading each file during a multifile transfer.
`put`	Sends a file to the remote system. For example, `put index.html` sends the `index.html` file from the local system to the remote system.
`pwd`	Displays the full pathname of the current directory on the remote system. When you log in as a user, the initial current working directory is your home directory.
`quit`	Same as `bye`.
`recv`	Same as `get`.
`rename`	Renames a file on the remote system. For example, `rename old.html new.html` renames the file `old.html` to `new.html` on the remote system.
`restart`	Restarts the next file transfer at a specified byte offset into the file (useful for restarting a failed transfer).
`rmdir`	Deletes a directory on the remote system. For example, `rmdir images` deletes the `images` directory in the current directory of the remote system.
`safe`	Sets the protection level of data transfers to `safe` so that cryptographic checksums are used to protect integrity of data.
`send`	Same as `put`.
`size`	Shows the size of a remote file. For example, `size bigfile.tar.gz` shows the size of that remote file.
`status`	Shows the current status of the FTP client.
`user`	Sends new user information to the FTP server. For example, `user naba` sends the user name `naba`; the FTP server then prompts for the password for that user name.

Using a Graphical FTP Client

GNOME comes with gFTP, a graphical FTP client. To start gFTP, select from the GNOME desktop Applications ⇨ Internet ⇨ gFTP. This starts the gFTP application to run and display its main window.

The gFTP window (see Figure 17-1) has a menu bar with menus for performing various tasks. Just below the menu bar is a toolbar with a number of buttons and text fields. Here, you can type the name of the remote host, the user name, and the password needed to log in to the remote host. After you supply the host and user information, click the button with the icon of two computers to the left of the Host field. This causes gFTP to connect to that host and to log in with the user name and password you have provided.

Figure 17-1 shows the gFTP window after you have connected to the remote FTP site and moved around the remote directories in preparation for downloading some files.

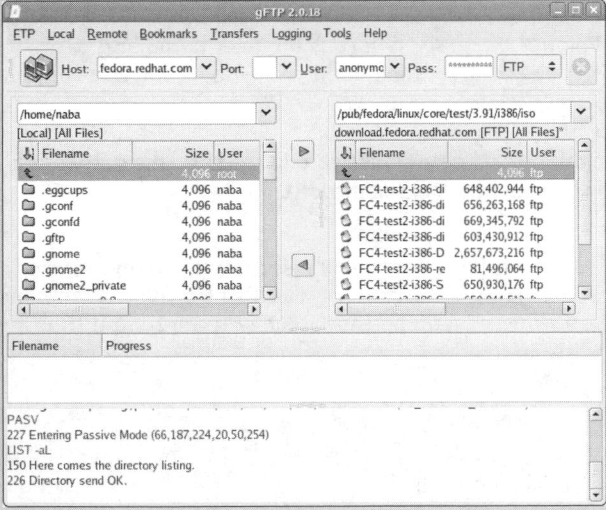

Figure 17-1: The gFTP Window after Connecting to a Remote FTP Server.

The middle part of the gFTP window is divided into two parts. The left side shows the contents of the current local directory; after establishing a connection, the right side shows the contents of the remote directory. Once the directories are listed, transferring files is simple. Simply select the desired files in the list, clicking the left arrow button to download or the right arrow button to upload.

The best part about using gFTP is that you can download entire directories by simply selecting the directories on the right-hand side window and clicking the left arrow.

To disconnect, click the computer button again. You can then quit the gFTP application by selecting FTP ⇨ Quit from the menu.

insider insight

gFTP is not for FTP transfers alone. It can also transfer files using the HTTP protocol and secure file transfers using the Secure Shell (SSH) protocol.

Using a Web Browser as an FTP Client

Any Web browser can act as an FTP client, but they are best for anonymous FTP downloads, where the Web browser can log in using the anonymous user name and any password.

In Linux, you can use the Firefox Web browser as an FTP client. Simply provide the URL that tells the Web browser to download a file using FTP. The syntax of the FTP URL is

```
ftp://username:password@hostname/pathname
```

The first part (`ftp://`) indicates that you want an FTP transfer. The *`hostname`* part should be the name of the FTP server (the name often starts with an `ftp`—for example, `ftp.beta.redhat.com`). The *`pathname`* is the full directory path and filename of the file you want to download. The *`username:password`* is the user name and password required to log in to the FTP server. You can leave them out if you want to log in as an anonymous user.

caution

When you provide the user name and password in the URL, the password is in plaintext and can be read by anyone who looks at the URL.

If the URL has only the host name for the FTP server, the Web browser displays the contents of the anonymous FTP directory. If you want to try this on your Linux system, start Firefox (click the Web browser icon on the GNOME panel), and then type the following line in the location text box:

```
ftp://localhost
```

Then press Enter. Firefox shows the contents of the anonymous FTP directory on your Linux system. You can click on folders to see their contents and download any files.

When you use the `ftp://localhost` URL, you won't get a response from your system if you are not running an FTP server or if you have set up your firewall such that no FTP connections are allowed.

The same approach for accessing anonymous FTP sites would work if you were to type the host name of some other anonymous FTP server. For example, try typing the following URL:

```
ftp://download.fedora.redhat.com
```

You should get the directory of the `download.fedora.redhat.com` server.

Configuring the FTP Server

Linux comes with the Very Secure FTP daemon (vsftpd), written by Chris Evans. The executable file for vsftpd is `/usr/sbin/vsftpd`, and it uses a number of configuration files in the `/etc` and `/etc/vsftpd` directories.

The vsftpd server is configured to run standalone and there is an initialization script (or *initscript*)—/etc/init.d/vsftpd—to start and stop the server. As explained earlier in this chapter, you can start the server with the command:

```
service vsftpd start
```

You can type the following command as root to turn vsftpd on so that it starts at system startup:

```
chkconfig --level 35 vsftpd on
```

After you start the vsftpd server, the default settings should be adequate to begin using the server. However, you should learn about the configuration files in case you need to customize them.

Learning the vsftpd Configuration Files

The vsftpd server consults a number of configuration files located in the /etc directory. These directories control many aspects of the FTP server such as whether it runs standalone, who can download files, and whether to allow anonymous FTP.

The key configuration files for vsftpd are the following:

- **/etc/vsftpd/vsftpd/conf:** Controls how the vsftpd server works. (For example, should it allow anonymous logins, should it allow file uploads, should it run standalone, and so on?)
- **/etc/vsftpd/ftpusers:** Lists the names of users who cannot access the FTP server.
- **/etc/vsftpd/user_list:** Lists the names of users who are denied access (not even prompted for password). However, if the userlist_deny option is set to NO in /etc/vsftpd/vsftpd.conf, then these users are allowed to access the FTP server.

You can usually leave most of these configuration files with their default settings. However, just in case you need to change something to make vsftpd suit your needs, the next few sections briefly explain the configuration files.

Understanding the /etc/vsftpd/vsftpd.conf File

To learn what you can have in the /etc/vsftpd/vsftpd.conf file and how these lines affect the vsftpd server's operation, start by looking at the /etc/vsftpd/vsftpd.conf file that's installed by default. The comments in this file tell you what each option does.

insider insight

By default, vsftpd allows almost nothing. Through the options in /etc/vsftpd/vsftpd.conf you can loosen the restrictions so that users can use FTP. It's up to you to decide how loose the settings should be. Note that most of the options are set to YES. That's because most of the default settings are NO. To reverse the intent of an option, just comment out that option by placing a # at the beginning of that line.

Here are the options you can set in /etc/vsftpd/vsftpd.conf:

- anon_mkdir_write_enable=YES enables anonymous FTP users to create new directories. This is a risky option and you may want to set this to NO, even if you allow anonymous users to upload files.
- anon_upload_enable=YES means anonymous FTP users can upload files. This option takes effect only if write_enable is already set to YES and the directory has write permissions for everyone. Remember that allowing anonymous users to write on your system can be very risky because someone could fill up the disk or use your disk for their personal storage.
- anonymous_enable=YES enables anonymous FTP (so users can log in with the user name "anonymous" and provide their email address as password). Comment out this line if you do not want anonymous FTP.
- ascii_download_enable=YES enables file downloads in ASCII mode. Unfortunately, a malicious remote user can issue the SIZE command with the name of a huge file and essentially cause the FTP server to waste huge amounts of resources opening that file and determining its size. This can be used by malicious users as a denial of service attack.
- ascii_upload_enable=YES enables file uploads in ASCII mode (for text files).
- async_abor_enable=YES causes vsftpd to recognize ABOR (abort) requests that arrive at any time. You may need to enable it to allow older FTP clients to work with vsftpd.
- banned_email_file=/etc/vsftpd/banned_emails specifies the file with the list of banned email addresses (used only if deny_email_enable is set to YES).
- chown_uploads=YES causes uploaded anonymous files to be owned by a different user specified by the chown_username option. Don't enable this, unless absolutely necessary and don't make the chown_username be root.
- chown_username=name specifies the user name that would own files uploaded by anonymous FTP users.
- chroot_list_enable=YES causes vsftpd to confine all users except those on a list specified by the chroot_list_file to their home directories when they log in for FTP service. This prevents these users from getting to any other files besides what's in their home directories.
- chroot_list_file=/etc/vsftpd/chroot_list is the list of users who are either confined to their home directories or not, depending on the setting of chroot_local_user.
- chroot_local_user=YES confines local users to their home directory (in other words, their home directory becomes their root directory /).
- connect_from_port_20=YES causes vsftpd to make sure that data transfers occur through port 20 (the FTP data port).
- data_connection_timeout=120 is the time in seconds after which an inactive data connection is timed out.
- deny_email_enable=YES causes vsftpd to check a list of banned email addresses and denies access to anyone who tries to log in anonymously with a banned email address as password.
- dirmessage_enable=YES causes vsftpd to display messages when FTP users change to certain directories.

- ftpd_banner=Welcome to my FTP service sets the banner that vsftpd displays when a user logs in. You can change the message to anything you want.
- idle_session_timeout=600 is the time (in seconds) after which an idle session (refers to the situation where someone connects and does not do anything) times out and vsftpd logs the user out.
- listen=YES causes vsftpd to listen for connection requests and, consequently, run in standalone mode. Set this to NO if you want to run vsftpd under xinetd.
- local_enable=YES causes vsftpd to grant local users access to FTP.
- local_umask=022 means whatever files FTP writes will have a permission of 644 (read access for everyone, but write access for owner only). You can set it to any file permission mask setting you want. For example, if you want no permissions for anyone but the owner, change this to 077.
- ls_recurse_enable=YES enables FTP users to recursively traverse directories using the ls -R command.
- nopriv_user=ftp identifies an unprivileged user that the FTP server can use.
- pam_service_name=vsftpd is the name of the Pluggable Authentication Module (PAM) configuration file that is used when vsftpd needs to authenticate a user. By default the PAM configuration files are in /etc/pam.d directory. That means vsftpd's PAM configuration file is /etc/pam.d/vsftpd.
- tcp_wrappers=YES enables support for access control through the TCP wrapper that consults the files /etc/hosts.allow and /etc/hosts.deny. (For more information about the TCP wrapper, see Chapter 22.)
- userlist_deny=YES causes vsftpd to deny access to the users listed in the /etc/vsftpd/user_list file. These users are not even prompted for a password.
- write_enable=YES causes vsftpd to allow file uploads to the host.
- xferlog_enable=YES turns on the logging of file downloads and uploads (always a good idea, but takes disk space).
- xferlog_file=/var/log/vsftpd.log specifies the full pathname of the vsftpd log file. The default is /var/log/vsftpd.log.
- xferlog_std_format=YES causes vsftpd to generate log files in a standard format used by other FTP daemons.

Understanding the /etc/vsftpd/ftpusers File

The vsftpd server uses the Pluggable Authentication Module (PAM) to authenticate users when they try to log in (just as the normal login process uses PAM to do the job). The PAM configuration file for vsftpd is /etc/pam.d/vsftpd. That PAM configuration file refers to /etc/vsftpd/ftpusers like this:

```
auth       required     pam_listfile.so item=user sense=deny
file=/etc/vsftpd/ftpusers onerr=succeed
```

continues

continued

This basically says that anyone listed in the /etc/vsftpd/ftpusers file should be denied login. The default /etc/vsftpd/ftpusers file contains the following list of users:

```
root
bin
daemon
adm
lp
sync
shutdown
halt
mail
news
uucp
operator
games
nobody
```

If you want to deny FTP access to any other user names, simply add those names to the /etc/vsftpd/ftpusers file.

Understanding the /etc/vsftpd/user_list File

If the userlist_deny option is set to YES, vsftpd does not allow users listed in the /etc/vsftpd/user_list file any access to FTP services. It does not even prompt them for a password. However, if userlist_deny is set to NO, the meaning is reversed and these users are the only ones allowed access (but the PAM configuration still denies anyone on the /etc/vsftpd/ftpusers list).

Using Anonymous FTP

Anonymous FTP refers to the use of the user name anonymous, which anyone can use with FTP to transfer files from a system. Anonymous FTP is a common way to share files on the Internet.

If you have used anonymous FTP to download files from Internet sites, you already know the convenience of that service. Anonymous FTP makes information available to anyone on the Internet. If you have a new Linux application that you want to share with the world, set up anonymous FTP on your Linux PC, and place the software in an appropriate directory. After that, all you need to do is announce to the world (probably through a posting in the comp.os.linux.announce newsgroup) that you have a new program available. Now, anyone can get the software from your system at his or her convenience.

Even if you run a for-profit business, you can use anonymous FTP to support your customers. If you sell a hardware or software product, you may want to provide technical information or software "fixes" through anonymous FTP.

Unfortunately, the convenience of anonymous FTP comes at a price. If you do not configure the anonymous FTP service properly, intruders and pranksters may gain access to your system. Some intruders may simply use your system's disk as a temporary holding place for various files; others may fill your disk with junk files, effectively making your system inoperable (this sort of attack is called a denial-of-service — DoS — attack). At the other extreme, an intruder may gain user-level (or, worse, root-level) access to your system and do much more damage.

note

If you have installed Linux from this book's companion DVD, you already have anonymous FTP on your system. The default setup also employs the necessary security precautions.

To see anonymous FTP in action, try accessing your system by using an FTP client. For example, in the following sample session, I have accessed my system from another PC on the LAN (my input appears in boldface):

```
ftp localhost
Connected to localhost.localdomain.
220 (vsFTPd 2.0.3)
Name (localhost:naba): anonymous
331 Please specify the password.
Password:       <-- I can type anything as password.
230 Login successful. Have fun.
Remote system type is UNIX.
Using binary mode to transfer files.
ftp> ls -l
227 Entering Passive Mode (127,0,0,1,114,147)
150 Here comes the directory listing.
drwxr-xr-x    2 0        0            4096 Mar 23 08:23 pub
226 Directory send OK.
ftp> bye
221 Goodbye.
```

When you successfully log in for anonymous FTP, you access the home directory of the user named `ftp` (the default directory is `/var/ftp`). Place the publicly accessible files — the ones you want to enable others to download from your system — in the `/var/ftp/pub` directory.

Learning the Key Features of Anonymous FTP

The key features of an anonymous FTP setup are as follows:

- There is a user named `ftp` whose home directory is `/var/ftp`. The user does not have a shell assigned. Here is what you get when you search for `ftp` in the `/etc/passwd` file:

```
grep ftp /etc/passwd
ftp:x:14:50:FTP User:/var/ftp:/sbin/nologin
```

continues

continued

The x in the second field means that no one can log in with the user name ftp. The login shell for this account, listed in the last field as /sbin/nologin, also ensures that the ftp user cannot log in (type **man nologin** to see what the nologin shell does).

- Here is the full permission setting and owner information for the /var/ftp directory:

```
drwxr-xr-x   3 root    root    4096 Apr 16 11:07 ftp
```

As this line shows, the /var/ftp directory is owned by root, and the permission is set to 755 (only root can read and write; everyone else can only read — the directory is however executable by everyone, which is required for accessing the directory; for more information on permission settings, see the chmod command described in Appendix A).

- To view the contents of the /var/ftp directory, type the **ls -la** command. The output of this command is as follows:

```
total 24
drwxr-xr-x   3 root root 4096 Apr 16 11:07 .
drwxr-xr-x  25 root root 4096 Apr 16 11:07 ..
drwxr-xr-x   2 root root 4096 Mar 23 03:23 pub
```

- The pub directory is where you place any files you want to enable others to download from your system through anonymous FTP.

Summary

File Transfer Protocol (FTP) is a popular Internet service for transferring files from one system to another. This chapter describes the FTP service and shows you how to configure the vsftpd server that comes with Linux.

In this chapter, you learned the following:

- FTP is an important Internet service for transferring files from one system to another. FTP is documented in RFC 959.
- You must set up and run an FTP server if you want your system's users to transfer files to and from the system. Linux comes with the Very Secure FTP daemon (vsftpd), a popular FTP server.
- The vsftpd server is set up to run standalone. You can start it with the command `service vsftpd start`. You can set the vsftpd server to start at boot time by typing the command `chkconfig --level 35 vsftpd on`.
- You can configure the vsftpd server by editing the files /etc/vsftpd/vsftpd.conf, /etc/vsftpd/ftpusers, and /etc/vsftpd/user_list.
- Anonymous FTP is another popular Internet service for distributing files. With anonymous FTP, anyone can use FTP with the anonymous user ID and can download files from your system. Although anonymous FTP is useful for distributing data, it poses a security risk if it is not set up properly.
- The default Linux installation includes everything needed to support anonymous FTP. The default anonymous FTP setup incorporates the necessary security precautions.

DNS and NIS

Chapter 18

Secret in This Chapter

Domain Name Service (DNS) is an Internet service that converts a fully qualified domain name, such as `www.redhat.com`, into its corresponding IP address. You can think of DNS as the directory of Internet hosts — DNS is what enables you to refer to a host by its name even though TCP/IP requires IP addresses for data transfers. DNS is implemented by a hierarchy of distributed DNS servers. This chapter provides an overview of DNS and shows you how to set up a caching DNS server on your Linux system.

Network Information System (NIS) is a client/server service designed to manage information shared among several host computers on a network. Typically, NIS is used on UNIX (and Linux) systems to maintain a common set of user accounts and other system files for a group of hosts. This, among other things, enables a user to log in on all hosts with the same user name and password. This chapter describes the NIS client and server software and shows you how to use them on a Linux system.

Using the Domain Name Service

In TCP/IP networks, each network interface (for example, an Ethernet card on a host computer) is identified by an IP address. Because IP addresses are hard to remember, an association is made between an easy-to-remember name and the IP address — much like the association between a name and a telephone number. For example, instead of having to remember that the IP address of Red Hat's Web server is 209.132.177.50, you can simply refer to that host by its name, `www.redhat.com`. When you type `www.redhat.com` as the URL in a Web browser, the name `www.redhat.com` has to be translated into its corresponding IP address. This is where the concept of DNS comes in.

DNS is a distributed, hierarchical database that holds information about computers on the Internet. The information includes the host name, the IP address, and mail routing information. This information resides in many DNS hosts on the Internet; that's why the DNS database is called a distributed database. The primary job of DNS is to associate host names to IP addresses and vice versa.

In ARPANET — the precursor to today's Internet, the association between host names and IP addresses was maintained in a text file named `HOSTS.TXT`, which was managed centrally and distributed to each host. As the number of hosts grew, it became clear that a static host table was unreasonable. DNS was proposed by Paul Mockapetris to alleviate the problems associated with using a static host table. As formally documented in RFCs 882 and 883 (November 1983), DNS introduced two key concepts:

- Use of hierarchical domain names, such as `www.ee.umd.edu` and `www.redhat.com`
- Distributed responsibility for managing the host database by using DNS servers throughout the Internet

DNS, as we know it today, is an Internet standard documented in RFCs 1034 and 1035. The standard has been updated and extended by several other RFCs: 1101, 1183, 1348, 1886, 1995, 1996, 2136, 2181, 2308, 2845, 2930, 2931, 3007, 3110, 3226, 3403, 3596, 3597, 3645, 3646, 4025, 4033, 4034, and 4035. The earlier updates define data encoding, whereas later ones focus on improving DNS security. To read these and other RFCs online, visit theRFC Index at `www.faqs.org/rfcs/rfc-index.html`.

DNS defines the following:

- A hierarchical domain-naming system for hosts
- A distributed database that associates a name with an IP address
- Library routines that network applications can use to query the distributed DNS database (this library is called the resolver library)
- A protocol for DNS clients and servers to exchange information about names and IP addresses

Nowadays, all hosts on the Internet rely on DNS to access various Internet services on remote hosts. As you may know from personal experience, when you obtain Internet access from an Internet service provider (ISP), the ISP provides you with the IP addresses of name servers. These are the DNS servers your system accesses whenever host names have to be mapped to IP addresses.

If you have a small LAN, you may decide to run a DNS server on one of the hosts or to use the name servers provided by the ISP. For medium-sized networks with several subnets, you can run a DNS server on each subnet to provide efficient DNS lookups. On a large corporate network, the corporate domain (such as `microsoft.com`) is further subdivided into a hierarchy of subdomains, and several DNS servers may be used in each subdomain.

The following sections provide an overview of the hierarchical domain-naming convention, and describe BIND—the implementation of DNS used on most UNIX systems, including Fedora Linux.

Understanding Hierarchical Domain Names

DNS uses a hierarchical tree of domains to organize the namespace—the entire set of names. Each higher-level domain has authority over its lower-level subdomains. Each domain represents a distinct block of the namespace and is managed by a single administrative authority. Figure 18-1 illustrates the hierarchical organization of the DNS namespace.

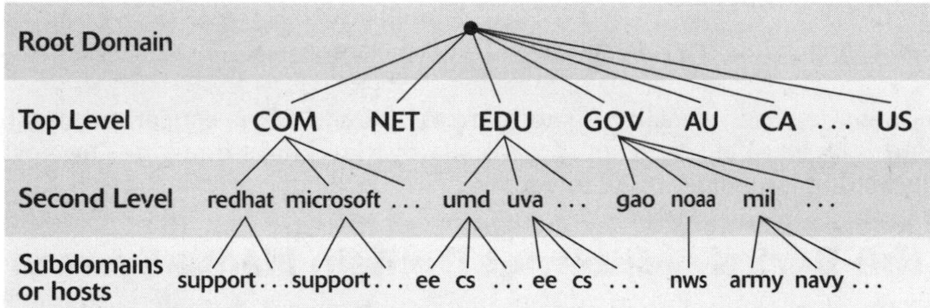

Figure 18-1: Sample Domain Names Illustrating the Hierarchical DNS Namespace.

The root of the tree is called the root domain and is represented by a single dot (.). The top-level, or root-level, domains come next. The top-level domains are further divided into second-level domains, which, in turn, can be broken into further subdomains.

The top-level domains are relatively fixed and include well-known domains such as `com`, `net`, `org`, `edu`, `gov`, and `mil`. These are the commonly used top-level domains in the United States. These top-level domains came about as the Internet became widely used in the early 1990s. More recently, however, there have been many newer top-level domains such as `aero`, `biz`, `coop`, `info`, `int`, `museum`, and `name`. To learn about these and other top-level domains, visit `www.iana.org/gtld/gtld.htm`.

There is another set of top-level domain names for the countries, called *country code domains*. These domain names use the two-letter country codes assigned by the International Organization for Standardization (abbreviated as ISO, see `www.iso.ch/`). For example, the top-level country code domain for the United States is `us`. In the United States, many local governments and organizations use the `us` domain. For example, `mcps.k12.md.us` is the domain name of the Montgomery County Public Schools in the state of Maryland in the United States. For a list of the top-level country code domain names, please see `www.iana.org/cctld/cctld-whois.htm`.

The fully qualified domain name (FQDN) is constructed by stringing together the subdomain names, from lower to higher level, using dots (`.`) as separators. For example, `redhat.com` is a fully qualified domain name; so is `ee.umd.edu`. Note that each of these may also refer to a specific host computer. Figure 18-2 illustrates the components of a fully qualified domain name.

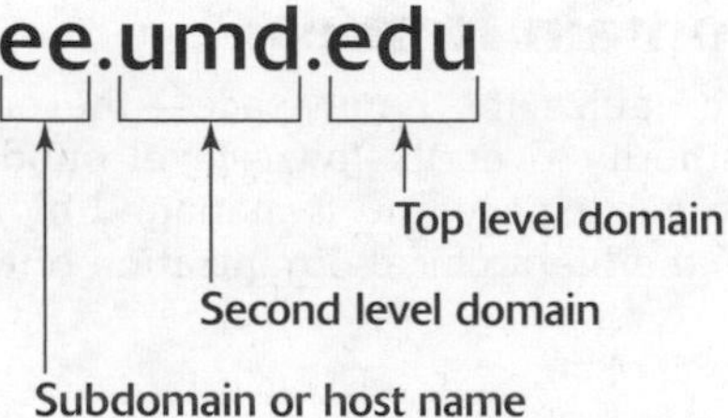

Figure 18-2: Components of a Fully Qualified Domain Name.

Domain names are case insensitive. Therefore, as far as DNS is concerned, the domains `UMD.EDU` and `umd.edu` both represent University of Maryland's domain. The norm, however, is to type domain names in all lowercase.

Using the Berkeley Internet Domain Name System

Most UNIX systems, including Fedora Linux, come with the BIND system — a well-known implementation of DNS. The BIND software is installed during Linux installation, as long as you select the DNS Name Server package group when selecting the packages for installation.

To see which version of BIND is installed on your Linux system, type the following command:

```
rpm -q bind
bind-9.3.1-2_FC4
```

As the output shows, BIND Version 9.3.1 is installed on my system.

BIND includes three major components:

- The named daemon — the name server — that responds to queries about host names and IP addresses
- A resolver library that applications can use to resolve host names into IP addresses and vice versa
- Command-line DNS utility programs (DNS clients), such as dig (Domain Internet Groper) and host, that users can use to query DNS

The next few sections describe these components of BIND. Later sections describe how to configure the resolver and the name server.

Learning More about DNS and BIND

This chapter only briefly describes DNS and BIND, but entire books have been devoted solely to them. For example, *DNS and BIND, Fourth Edition*, by Paul Albitz and Cricket Liu (O'Reilly & Associates, April 2001), can help you learn more about DNS and BIND.

BIND also comes with a lot of online documentation that's installed on your Linux system when you install the DNS Name Server package group. To read the online documentation about BIND, change the current directory with the command `cd /usr/share/doc/bind*` (the directory name depends on which version of BIND is installed on your system), and look at the files in that directory.

The Internet Software Consortium (ISC) — a nonprofit corporation — supports BIND. Visit its website at `www.isc.org/` to learn more about the latest release of BIND.

To ask questions online about DNS and BIND, or to participate in related discussions, read the following newsgroups (see Chapter 16 for more information about reading newsgroups):

- **comp.protocols.dns.bind:** Discussions about using BIND
- **comp.protocols.dns.ops:** Discussions about DNS operations
- **comp.protocols.dns.std:** Discussions about DNS standards

Understanding named — the BIND Name Server

The named daemon is the name server that responds to queries about host names and IP addresses. Based on the configuration files and the local DNS database, named either provides answers to queries or asks other servers and caches their responses. The named server also performs a function referred to as *zone transfer*, which involves copying data among the name servers in a domain.

The named name server can be configured to operate in one of three modes:

- **Primary or Master:** This is the authoritative name server that keeps the master copy of the domain's data on disk. There is one primary server for each domain or subdomain.
- **Secondary or Slave:** A secondary name server copies its domain's data from the primary server using a zone transfer operation. There can be one or more secondary name servers for a domain.
- **Caching:** A caching name server loads the addresses of a few authoritative servers for the root domain and gets all domain data by caching responses to queries resolved by contacting other name servers. Primary and secondary servers also cache responses. The Time To Live (TTL) field associated with each resource record controls the length of time for which a record may be retained in the cache of a caching name server. As you see later in this chapter, you can easily extend a caching-only name server into a primary name server.

A name server can be authoritative or not. As the term implies, the response from an authoritative name server is supposed to be accurate. The primary and secondary name servers are authoritative for their own domains, but they are not authoritative for responses provided from cached information. Caching name servers are never authoritative because all of their responses come from cached information.

To run a name server on your Linux system, you have to run named with the appropriate configuration files. Later in this chapter, you learn about the configuration files and data files that control how the name server operates.

Understanding the Resolver Library

Finding an IP address for a host name is referred to as *resolving the host name*. Network-aware applications, such as a Web browser or an FTP client, use a resolver library to perform the conversion from the name to an IP address. Depending on the settings in the `/etc/host.conf` file, the resolver library consults the `/etc/hosts` file or makes a DNS query to resolve a host name to its IP address. The resolver library queries the name servers listed in the `/etc/resolv.conf` file.

You do not need to learn much about the resolver library unless you are writing network-aware applications. To run Internet services properly, all you need to learn is how to configure the resolver. Subsequent sections in this chapter show you how to configure this and other aspects of DNS.

Using DNS Utility Programs

You can use the DNS utility programs—dig and host—to try out DNS from the shell prompt interactively. These utility programs are DNS clients. You can use them to query the DNS database and debug any name server you might set up on your system. By default, these programs query the name server listed in your system's `/etc/resolv.conf` file.

Using dig

You can use dig, the Domain Internet Groper program, to look up IP addresses for a domain name or vice versa. For example, to look up the IP address of `addlab.nws.noaa.gov`, type:

```
dig addlab.nws.noaa.gov
```

The dig program prints the results of the DNS query with a great amount of detail. Here's the output of that `dig` command on my Linux system:

```
; <<>> DiG 9.3.1 <<>> addlab.nws.noaa.gov
;; global options:  printcmd
;; Got answer:
;; ->>HEADER<<- opcode: QUERY, status: NOERROR, id: 47374
;; flags: qr rd ra; QUERY: 1, ANSWER: 1, AUTHORITY: 0, ADDITIONAL: 0

;; QUESTION SECTION:
;addlab.nws.noaa.gov.           IN      A

;; ANSWER SECTION:
addlab.nws.noaa.gov.    900     IN      A       140.90.141.131

;; Query time: 51 msec
;; SERVER: 192.168.0.1#53(192.168.0.1)
;; WHEN: Sat Apr 23 12:40:50 2005
;; MSG SIZE  rcvd: 53
```

The answer you are looking for — the IP address of the host — is in the in the part of the output labeled `ANSWER SECTION:`. Here's what that section looks like for this sample query:

```
;; ANSWER SECTION:
addlab.nws.noaa.gov.    900     IN      A       140.90.141.131
```

Thus, the IP address of `addlab.nws.noaa.gov` is `140.90.141.131`. The other sections in dig's output shows details such as the server it queried, the authoritative name servers for the host name it queried, the time it took to perform the query, and so on. In this example, the `SERVER` line near the end of dig's output shows that dig queries the name server at the IP address `192.168.0.1` — that's the first name server listed in my system's `/etc/resolv.conf` file.

Reverse lookups (finding host names for IP addresses) are also easy with dig. All you have to do is use `dig` with the `-x` option. For example, to find the host name corresponding to the IP address 140.90.141.131, type the following:

```
dig -x 140.90.141.131
```

On my system, the output from this query looks like this:

```
; <<>> DiG 9.3.1 <<>> -x 140.90.141.131
;; global options:  printcmd
;; Got answer:
```

```
;; ->>HEADER<<- opcode: QUERY, status: NOERROR, id: 42539
;; flags: qr aa rd ra; QUERY: 1, ANSWER: 1, AUTHORITY: 6, ADDITIONAL: 6

;; QUESTION SECTION:
;131.141.90.140.in-addr.arpa.   IN      PTR

;; ANSWER SECTION:
131.141.90.140.in-addr.arpa. 86400 IN   PTR     addlab.nws.noaa.gov.

;; AUTHORITY SECTION:
141.90.140.in-addr.arpa. 86400  IN      NS      netinfo.hqnoc.noaa.gov.
141.90.140.in-addr.arpa. 86400  IN      NS      ns3.noc.noaa.gov.
141.90.140.in-addr.arpa. 86400  IN      NS      merns.noaa.gov.
141.90.140.in-addr.arpa. 86400  IN      NS      mwrns.noaa.gov.
141.90.140.in-addr.arpa. 86400  IN      NS      nwrns.noaa.gov.
141.90.140.in-addr.arpa. 86400  IN      NS      serns.noaa.gov.

;; ADDITIONAL SECTION:
netinfo.hqnoc.noaa.gov. 46410   IN      A       140.90.148.33
ns3.noc.noaa.gov.       66538   IN      A       140.90.143.33
merns.noaa.gov.         75209   IN      A       192.94.173.133
mwrns.noaa.gov.         78837   IN      A       140.172.10.10
nwrns.noaa.gov.         74965   IN      A       161.55.32.3
serns.noaa.gov.         78086   IN      A       192.111.123.245

;; Query time: 84 msec
;; SERVER: 192.168.0.1#53(192.168.0.1)
;; WHEN: Sat Apr 23 13:54:25 2005
;; MSG SIZE  rcvd: 331
```

As you can see, dig prints a lot of information in addition to the result. The answer you want comes right after the label `ANSWER SECTION:`, which in this case shows the host name to be `addlab.nws.noaa.gov`.

You can use dig to query other types of DNS records than name-to-address and address-to-name lookups. For example, DNS also contains a mail exchanger (record type MX) to enable delivery of mail to a specific domain. The MX record instructs querying computers where to send messages meant for a domain. To look up an MX record for a host, simply prefix the host name with the record type. Here is an example that queries the MX record for the domain name `comcast.net`:

```
dig MX comcast.net
```

Here's the resulting output on my system:

```
; <<>> DiG 9.3.1 <<>> MX comcast.net
;; global options:  printcmd
;; Got answer:
;; ->>HEADER<<- opcode: QUERY, status: NOERROR, id: 5642
;; flags: qr aa rd ra; QUERY: 1, ANSWER: 2, AUTHORITY: 2, ADDITIONAL: 6
```

```
;; QUESTION SECTION:
;comcast.net.                   IN      MX

;; ANSWER SECTION:
comcast.net.            900     IN      MX      5 gateway-r.comcast.net.
comcast.net.            900     IN      MX      5 gateway-s.comcast.net.

;; AUTHORITY SECTION:
comcast.net.            7200    IN      NS      dns01.jdc01.pa.comcast.net.
comcast.net.            7200    IN      NS      dns02.jdc01.pa.comcast.net.

;; ADDITIONAL SECTION:
gateway-r.comcast.net.  900     IN      A       204.127.198.26
gateway-r.comcast.net.  900     IN      A       216.148.227.126
gateway-s.comcast.net.  900     IN      A       204.127.202.26
gateway-s.comcast.net.  900     IN      A       63.240.76.26
dns01.jdc01.pa.comcast.net. 7200 IN     A       68.87.96.3
dns02.jdc01.pa.comcast.net. 7200 IN     A       68.87.96.4

;; Query time: 51 msec
;; SERVER: 192.168.0.1#53(192.168.0.1)
;; WHEN: Sat Apr 23 13:55:48 2005
;; MSG SIZE  rcvd: 226
```

Again, the `ANSWER SECTION` shows the MX record, which says that mail addressed to `comcast.net` should be sent to `gateway-r.comcast.net` or `gateway-s.comcast.net`.

Using the host Command

You can also query DNS by using the `host` command. The host program produces output in a compact format. For example, here's a typical use of `host` to look up information about a host:

```
host www.gao.gov
www.gao.gov has address 161.203.16.2
www.gao.gov mail is handled by 5 listserv.gao.gov.
```

By default, host prints the IP address and any MX record (these records list the names of mail handlers for the host).

For a reverse lookup, use the `-t ptr` option, along with the IP address as an argument, as follows:

```
host -t ptr 161.203.16.2
2.16.203.161.in-addr.arpa. domain name pointer www.gao.gov.
```

In this case, host prints the PTR record that shows the host name corresponding to the specified IP address.

You can also try other types of records, such as `CNAME` (for canonical name), as follows:

```
host -t cname www.ee.umd.edu

www.ee.umd.edu is an alias for edison.eng.umd.edu.
```

This indicates that the canonical name for `www.ee.umd.edu` is `edison.eng.umd.edu`.

Configuring DNS

You configure DNS by using a number of configuration files. The exact set of files depends on whether or not you are running a name server and, if so, the type of name server — caching or primary. Some configuration files are needed whether you run a name server or not.

Configuring the Resolver

You do not need a name server running on your system to use the DNS clients — dig and host. You can use them to query one of your domain's name servers. Typically, your ISP provides you with this information. You have to list the IP addresses of these name servers in the `/etc/resolv.conf` file — the resolver library reads this file to determine how to resolve host names. The format of this file is

```
domain your-domain.com
search your-domain.com
nameserver A.B.C.D
nameserver X.Y.Z.W
```

where *`A.B.C.D`* and *`X.Y.Z.W`* are the IP addresses (dotted-decimal IP addresses, such as 192.168.0.1) of the primary and secondary name servers your ISP provides you.

The `domain` line in `/etc/resolv.conf` lists the local domain name. The `search` line specifies the domains on which a host name is searched first (usually, you put your own domain in the search line). The domain listed on the `search` line is appended to any host name before the resolver library tries to resolve it. For example, if the `search` line contains `your-domain.com`, when you look for a host named `mailhost`, the resolver library first tries `mailhost.your-domain.com`; if that fails, it tries `mailhost`. The `search` line applies to any host name you try to access. For example, if you are trying to access `www.redhat.com`, the resolver first tries `www.redhat.com.your-domain.com` and then `www.redhat.com`.

Another important configuration file is `/etc/host.conf` — this file tells the resolver what to do when attempting to resolve a host name. A typical `/etc/host/conf` file contains the following line:

```
order hosts,bind
```

This tells the resolver to consult the `/etc/hosts` file first and, if that fails, to query the name server listed in the `/etc/resolv.conf` file. As explained in Chapter 6, the `/etc/hosts` file associates IP addresses to host names. A typical line from the `/etc/hosts` file looks like the following:

```
127.0.0.1    lnbp200  localhost.localdomain  localhost
```

This line says that the IP address 127.0.0.1 is assigned to the host names `lnbp200`, `localhost.localdomain`, and `localhost`.

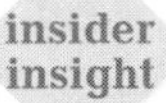

In the latest version of Linux, which uses GNU C Library version 2 (glibc 2) or later, the name service switch (NSS) file, `/etc/nsswitch.conf`, specifies how services such as the resolver library, NIS, NIS+, and local files such as `/etc/hosts` and `/etc/shadow` interact. For example, the following `hosts` entry in the `/etc/nsswitch.conf` file specifies that the resolver library should first try the `/etc/hosts` file, then try NIS+, and finally try DNS:

```
hosts:      files nisplus dns
```

To learn more about the `/etc/nsswitch.conf` file and what it does, type **info libc "Name Service Switch"** at the shell prompt in a terminal window.

Configuring a Caching Name Server

A simple but useful name server is one that finds answers to host name queries by using other name servers and then remembers the answer (by saving it in a cache) the next time you need it. This can shorten the time it takes to access hosts you have accessed recently because the answer is already in the cache.

When you install the DNS Name Server package group during Linux installation, the configuration files for a caching name server are also installed. That means you can start running the caching name server without much work on your part. This section describes the configuration files and what you have to do to start the caching name server.

Examining the /etc/named.conf File

The first configuration file you need is `/etc/named.conf`. The named server reads this configuration file when it starts. You already have this file if you have installed the DNS Name Server when you installed Linux in Chapter 2. Here's what the default `/etc/named.conf` file contains:

```
//
// named.conf for Red Hat caching-nameserver
//

options {
        directory "/var/named";
        dump-file "/var/named/data/cache_dump.db";
        statistics-file "/var/named/data/named_stats.txt";
        /*
         * If there is a firewall between you and nameservers you want
         * to talk to, you might need to uncomment the query-source
         * directive below.  Previous versions of BIND always asked
         * questions using port 53, but BIND 8.1 uses an unprivileged
         * port by default.
         */
         // query-source address * port 53;
};
```

```
//
// a caching only nameserver config
//
controls {
        inet 127.0.0.1 allow { localhost; } keys { rndckey; };
};

zone "." IN {
        type hint;
        file "named.ca";
};

zone "localdomain" IN {
        type master;
        file "localdomain.zone";
        allow-update { none; };
};

zone "localhost" IN {
        type master;
        file "localhost.zone";
        allow-update { none; };
};

zone "0.0.127.in-addr.arpa" IN {
        type master;
        file "named.local";
        allow-update { none; };
};

zone "0.0.0.0.0.0.0.0.0.0.0.0.0.0.0.0.0.0.0.0.0.0.0.0.0.0.0.0.0.0.0.0.ip6.arpa" IN
 {
        type master;
        file "named.ip6.local";
        allow-update { none; };
};

zone "255.in-addr.arpa" IN {
        type master;
        file "named.broadcast";
        allow-update { none; };
};

zone "0.in-addr.arpa" IN {
        type master;
        file "named.zero";
        allow-update { none; };
};

include "/etc/rndc.key";
```

Comments are C-style (/* ... */) or C++-style (start with //). The file contains block statements enclosed in curly braces ({...}) and terminated by a semicolon (;). A block statement, in turn, contains other statements, each ending with a semicolon.

This /etc/named.conf file begins with an options block statement with a number of option statements. The directory option statement tells named where to look for all other files that appear on file lines in the configuration file. In this case, named looks for the files in the /var/named directory.

The controls statement in /etc/named.conf contains security information so that the rndc command can connect to the named service at port 953 and interact with named. In this case, the controls statement contains the following line:

```
inet 127.0.0.1 allow { localhost; } keys { rndckey; };
```

This says the rndc can connect from localhost with the key named rndc (the file /etc/rndc.key defines the key and the encryption algorithm to be used).

The rndc (remote name daemon control) utility is a successor to the older ndc (name daemon controller) utility used to control the named server by sending it messages over a special control channel, a TCP port where named listens for messages. The rndc utility uses a cryptographic key and authenticates itself to the named server by using a fast MD5 secure hash algorithm called HMAC-MD5 (see RFCs 2085 and 2104 for more information on HMAC-MD5). The named server has the same cryptographic key so that it can decode the authentication information sent by rndc.

After the options and controls statements, the /etc/named.conf file contains several zone statements, each enclosed in curly braces and terminated by a semicolon. Each zone statement defines a zone. The first zone is named "." (root zone); it's a hint zone that specifies the root name servers.

The rest of the zone statements in /etc/named.conf are master zones. The syntax for a master zone statement for an Internet class zone (indicated by the IN keyword) is as follows:

```
zone "zone-name" IN {
        type master;
        file "zone-file";
        [...other optional statements...]
};
```

The zone-name is the name of the zone, and zone-file is the zone file that contains the resource records (RR) — the database entries — for that zone.

The /etc/named.conf file ends with an include statement:

```
include "/etc/rndc.key";
```

This statement inserts the contents of the /etc/rndc.key file into the /etc/named.conf file. This enables you to place sensitive configuration data (such as encryption keys) in a separate file with appropriate permissions to prevent nonroot users from accessing it. In this case, the /etc/rndc.key file contains the key named rndc, which was referenced in the options statement earlier in the /etc/named.conf file. Here is what the key definition looks like:

```
key "rndckey" {
        algorithm       hmac-md5;
        secret "AbigLongEncryptionKey";
};
```

The `algorithm` option specifies the type of algorithm, which can be `dsa` or `hmac-md5`. The `secret` option specifies the encryption key.

insider insight

To generate your own HMAC-MD5 key, use the `dnssec-keygen` command with the following syntax:

```
dnssec-keygen -a hmac-md5 -b 128 -n HOST yourhost.domain.
```

You should replace *`yourhost.domain`* with your host's fully qualified domain name. The `dnssec-keygen` command generates two files whose names begin with `K` followed by the host name. One of the files has a `.key` extension and the other `.private`. Use the `cat` command to look at the content of either file and copy the cryptic looking key from the file with the `.key` extension to the `secret` option of the `/etc/rndc.key` file.

Understanding the Zone File Format

The zone file typically starts with a number of directives, each of which begins with a dollar sign ($) followed by a keyword. Two commonly used directives are `$TTL` and `$ORIGIN`.

For example, the line

```
$TTL    86400
```

uses the `$TTL` directive to set the default time to live (TTL) for subsequent records with undefined TTLs. The value is in seconds, and the valid TTLs are in the range 0 to 2147483647 seconds. In this case, the directive sets the default TTL as `86400` seconds (or one day). The time specified in the time-to-live directive indicates how long the information in that record should be considered valid.

The `$ORIGIN` directive sets the domain name that will be appended to any unqualified records. For example, the following `$ORIGIN` directive sets the domain name to localhost:

```
$ORIGIN localhost.
```

insider insight

If there is no `$ORIGIN` directive, the initial `$ORIGIN` is the same as the zone name that comes after the `zone` keyword in the `/etc/named.conf` file.

After the directives, the zone file contains one or more resource records. These records follow a specific format, which is outlined in the next section.

Understanding Resource Record Format

You have to understand the format of the resource records before you can understand and intelligently work with zone files. Each resource record has the following format (the optional fields are shown in square brackets):

```
[domain] [ttl] [class] type data [;comment]
```

In a resource record the fields are separated by tabs or spaces and may contain some special characters, such as an @ symbol for the domain and a semicolon (;) to indicate the start of a comment.

The first field, which must begin at the first character of the line, identifies the domain. You can use the @ symbol to use the current `$ORIGIN` for the domain name for this record. If you have multiple records for the same domain name, leave the first field blank.

The optional `ttl` field specifies the time to live—the duration for which the data can be cached and considered valid. You can specify the duration in one of the following formats:

- *N*, where *N* is a number meaning *N* seconds
- *N*`W`, where *N* is a number meaning *N* weeks
- *N*`D`, where *N* is a number meaning *N* days
- *N*`H`, where *N* is a number meaning *N* hours
- *N*`M`, where *N* is a number meaning *N* minutes
- *N*`S`, where *N* is a number meaning *N* seconds

The letters `W`, `D`, `H`, `M`, and `S` can also be in lowercase. Thus, you can write `86400` or `1D` (or `1d`) to indicate a duration of one day. You can also combine these to specify more precise durations, such as `5w6d16h` to indicate 5 weeks, 6 days, and 16 hours.

The `class` field specifies the network type. The most commonly used value for this field is `IN` for Internet. Other values are `CH` for ChaosNet (an obsolete network used long ago by Symbolics Lisp computers), and `HS` for Hesiod (an NIS-like database service based on BIND).

Next in the resource record is the `type` field, which denotes the type of record (such as `SOA`, `NS`, `A`, or `PTR`). Table 18-1 lists many commonly used DNS resource record types. The data field comes next, and it depends on the type field.

Table 18-1: Common DNS Resource Record Types

Type	*Name*	*Description*
`A`	Address	Specifies the host address corresponding to a name
`A6`	IPv4 to IPv6 Transition Address	Specifies the IPv6 address corresponding to a name using a format suitable for transition from IPv4 to IPv6
`AAAA`	IPv6 Address	Specifies the IPv6 host address corresponding to a name

(continued)

Table 18-1 *(continued)*

Type	*Name*	*Description*
CERT	Digital Certificate	Holds a digital certificate
CNAME	Canonical Name	Defines the nickname or alias for a host name
DNAME	Delegation Name	Replaces specified domain name with another name to be looked up
HINFO	Host Info	Identifies the hardware and operating system for a host
KEY	Public Key	Stores a public key associated with a DNS name
MX	Mail Exchanger	Identifies the host that accepts mail meant for a domain (used to route email)
NS	Name Server	Identifies authoritative name servers for a zone
PTR	Pointer	Specifies the name corresponding to an address (used for reverse mapping — converting an IP address to a host name)
RP	Responsible Person	Provides the name of a technical contact for a domain
SIG	Signature	Contains data authenticated in the secure DNS (see RFC 2535 for details)
SOA	Start of authority	Indicates that all subsequent records are authoritative for this zone
SRV	Services	Lists well-known network services provided by the domain
TXT	Text	Used to include comments and other information in the DNS database

You should learn to read the resource records, at least the ones of type SOA, NS, A, PTR, and MX, which are some of the most commonly used. The next few sections briefly describe these records, illustrating each record type through an example.

SOA Record

A typical SOA record has the following format:

```
@      1D IN SOA      @ root (
                      42                  ; serial
                      3H                  ; refresh -- 3 hours
                      15M                 ; retry -- 15 minutes
                      1W                  ; expiry -- 1 week
                      1D )                ; minimum -- 1 day
```

The first field specifies the domain as @, which means the current domain (by default, the zone name, as shown in the /etc/named.conf file). The next field specifies a TTL of one day for this record. The class field is set to IN, which means that the record is for Internet. The type field specifies the record type as SOA. The rest of the fields constitute the data for the SOA record. The data includes the name of the primary name server (in this case, @, or the current domain), the email address of the technical contact, and five different times enclosed in parentheses.

NS Record

The NS record specifies the authoritative name servers for a zone. A typical NS record looks like the following:

```
.                       3600000  IN  NS    A.ROOT-SERVERS.NET.
```

In this case, the NS record lists the authoritative name server for the root zone (notice that the name of the first field is a single dot). The TTL field specifies the record to be valid for 1,000 hours (3600000 seconds). The class is `IN`, for Internet, and the record type is NS. The final field lists the name of the name server (`A.ROOT-SERVERS.NET.`), which ends with a dot.

A Record

An A record specifies the address corresponding to a name. For example, the following A record shows the address of `A.ROOT-SERVERS.NET.` as `198.41.0.4`:

```
A.ROOT-SERVERS.NET.     3600000     A     198.41.0.4
```

In this case, the network class is not specified because the field is optional, and the default is `IN`.

PTR Record

PTR records are used for reverse mapping — converting an address to a name. Consider the following example:

```
1       IN      PTR     localhost.
```

This record comes from a file for a zone named `0.0.127.in-addr.arpa`. Therefore, this record says that the name associated with the address 127.0.0.1 is `localhost`.

MX Record

An MX record specifies the name of a host that accepts mail on behalf of a specific domain. For example, here's a typical MX record:

```
naba     IN    MX    10    mailhub.lnbsoft.com.
```

This says that mail addressed to the host named `naba` in the current domain should be sent to `mailhub.lnbsoft.com` (this host is called a *mail exchanger*). The number `10` is the preference value. For a list of multiple MX records with different preference values, the ones with lower preference values are tried first.

Now that you know a bit about resource records, you can go through the zone files for the caching name server.

Understanding the /var/named/named.ca File

Information about the root name servers is in the file `/var/named/named.ca`, as specified in the `zone` statement for the root zone in the `/etc/named.conf` file. The following listing shows the `/var/named/named.ca` file from a Linux system:

```
;       This file holds the information on root name servers needed to
;       initialize cache of Internet domain name servers
;       (e.g. reference this file in the "cache  .  <file>"
```

```
;       configuration file of BIND domain name servers).
;
;       This file is made available by InterNIC
;       under anonymous FTP as
;           file                /domain/named.cache
;           on server           FTP.INTERNIC.NET
;       -OR-                    RS.INTERNIC.NET
;
;       last update:    Jan 29, 2004
;       related version of root zone:   2004012900
;
;
; formerly NS.INTERNIC.NET
;
.                        3600000  IN  NS    A.ROOT-SERVERS.NET.
A.ROOT-SERVERS.NET.      3600000      A     198.41.0.4
;
; formerly NS1.ISI.EDU
;
.                        3600000      NS    B.ROOT-SERVERS.NET.
B.ROOT-SERVERS.NET.      3600000      A     192.228.79.201
;
; formerly C.PSI.NET
;
.                        3600000      NS    C.ROOT-SERVERS.NET.
C.ROOT-SERVERS.NET.      3600000      A     192.33.4.12
;
; formerly TERP.UMD.EDU
;
.                        3600000      NS    D.ROOT-SERVERS.NET.
D.ROOT-SERVERS.NET.      3600000      A     128.8.10.90
;
; formerly NS.NASA.GOV
;
.                        3600000      NS    E.ROOT-SERVERS.NET.
E.ROOT-SERVERS.NET.      3600000      A     192.203.230.10
;
; formerly NS.ISC.ORG
;
.                        3600000      NS    F.ROOT-SERVERS.NET.
F.ROOT-SERVERS.NET.      3600000      A     192.5.5.241
;
; formerly NS.NIC.DDN.MIL
;
.                        3600000      NS    G.ROOT-SERVERS.NET.
G.ROOT-SERVERS.NET.      3600000      A     192.112.36.4
;
; formerly AOS.ARL.ARMY.MIL
;
.                        3600000      NS    H.ROOT-SERVERS.NET.
```

```
H.ROOT-SERVERS.NET.      3600000      A     128.63.2.53
;
; formerly NIC.NORDU.NET
;
.                        3600000      NS    I.ROOT-SERVERS.NET.
I.ROOT-SERVERS.NET.      3600000      A     192.36.148.17
;
; operated by VeriSign, Inc.
;
.                        3600000      NS    J.ROOT-SERVERS.NET.
J.ROOT-SERVERS.NET.      3600000      A     192.58.128.30
;
; operated by RIPE NCC
;
.                        3600000      NS    K.ROOT-SERVERS.NET.
K.ROOT-SERVERS.NET.      3600000      A     193.0.14.129
;
; operated by ICANN
;
.                        3600000      NS    L.ROOT-SERVERS.NET.
L.ROOT-SERVERS.NET.      3600000      A     198.32.64.12
;
; operated by WIDE
;
.                        3600000      NS    M.ROOT-SERVERS.NET.
M.ROOT-SERVERS.NET.      3600000      A     202.12.27.33
; End of File
```

This file contains NS and A resource records that specify the names of authoritative name servers and their addresses for the root zone (indicated by the "." in the first field of each NS record).

The comment lines in the file begin with a semicolon. These comments give you hints about the location of the root name servers. There are 13 root name servers for the Internet, most of the root servers are located in the United States. This file is a necessity for any name server because the name server has to be able to reach at least one root name server.

Understanding the /var/named/localhost.zone File

The `/etc/named.conf` file includes a `zone` statement for the `localhost` zone that specifies the zone file as `localhost.zone`. That file is located in the `/var/named` directory of your Linux system. The `/var/named/localhost.zone` file contains the following resource records:

```
$TTL    86400
$ORIGIN localhost.
@            1D IN SOA       @ root (
                             42               ; serial (d. adams)
                             3H               ; refresh
                             15M              ; retry
                             1W               ; expiry
```

```
                        1D )            ; minimum

          1D IN NS       @
             IN A           127.0.0.1
             IN AAAA        ::1
```

This zone file starts with a `$TTL` directive that sets the default TTL to one day (86400 seconds) for subsequent records with undefined TTLs. Next, a `$ORIGIN` directive sets the domain name to localhost.

After these two directives, the `/var/named/localhost.zone` file contains three resource records (RRs): an SOA record, an NS record, and an A record. The SOA and the NS record specify the `localhost` as the primary authoritative name server for the zone. The A record specifies the address of `localhost` as `127.0.0.1`. The AAAA record specifies the IPv6 address of `localhost`, in a format that's designed for transition from IPv4 to IPv6.

Understanding the /var/named/named.local File

The third zone in the `/etc/named.conf` file specifies a reverse-mapping zone named `0.0.127.in-addr.arpa`. For this zone, the zone file is `/var/named/named.local`, which contains the following:

```
$TTL    86400
@       IN      SOA     localhost. root.localhost.  (
                                    1997022700 ; Serial
                                    28800      ; Refresh
                                    14400      ; Retry
                                    3600000    ; Expire
                                    86400 )    ; Minimum
        IN      NS      localhost.

1       IN      PTR     localhost.
```

The SOA and NS records specify `localhost` as the primary name server.

insider insight

The SOA record also shows `root.localhost.` as the email address of the technical contact for the domain. Note that the DNS zone files use a `user.host.` format for the email address. When sending any email, you have to replace the first dot with @ and remove the final dot.

Starting and Testing the Caching Name Server

Now that you have studied the configuration files for the caching name server, you can start the name server and see it in operation. To start the name server, log in as `root` and type the following command at the shell prompt:

```
service named start
```

This starts named — the name server daemon.

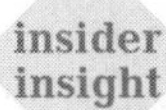

insider insight

To ensure that the server starts every time you reboot the system, log in as `root` and type the following command:

```
chkconfig --level 35 named on
```

The named server writes diagnostic log messages in the `/var/log/messages` file. After you start named, you can check the log messages by opening `/var/log/messages` in a text editor. Following are some typical log messages from named when started on my Linux system:

```
Apr 23 14:45:51 localhost named[23336]: starting BIND 9.3.1 -u named -t
/var/named/chroot
Apr 23 14:45:51 localhost named[23336]: found 1 CPU, using 1 worker thread
Apr 23 14:45:51 localhost named[23336]: loading configuration from '/etc/named.conf'
Apr 23 14:45:51 localhost named[23336]: no IPv6 interfaces found
Apr 23 14:45:51 localhost named[23336]: listening on IPv4 interface lo, 127.0.0.1#53
Apr 23 14:45:51 localhost named[23336]: listening on IPv4 interface eth0,
192.168.0.4#53
Apr 23 14:45:51 localhost named[23336]: command channel listening on 127.0.0.1#953
Apr 23 14:45:51 localhost named[23336]: zone 0.in-addr.arpa/IN: loaded serial 42
Apr 23 14:45:51 localhost named[23336]: zone 0.0.127.in-addr.arpa/IN: loaded serial
1997022700
Apr 23 14:45:51 localhost named[23336]: zone 255.in-addr.arpa/IN: loaded serial 42
Apr 23 14:45:51 localhost named[23336]: zone
0.0.0.0.0.0.0.0.0.0.0.0.0.0.0.0.0.0.0.0.0.0.0.0.0.0.0.0.0.0.0.0.ip6.arpa/IN: loaded
serial 1997022700
Apr 23 14:45:51 localhost named[23336]: zone localdomain/IN: loaded serial 42
Apr 23 14:45:51 localhost named[23336]: zone localhost/IN: loaded serial 42
Apr 23 14:45:51 localhost named[23336]: running
```

If there are no error messages from named, you can proceed to test the name server.

Now, you can use the `host` command to test the name server. For example, to look up the IP address of `www.gao.gov` by using the caching name server on `localhost`, type **host www.gao.gov localhost** at a shell prompt. Here is a typical result from that command:

```
Using domain server:
Name: localhost
Address: 127.0.0.1#53
Aliases:


www.gao.gov has address 161.203.16.2
```

As the output shows, the host command uses `localhost` as the DNS server and returns the IP address of `www.gao.gov`.

insider insight If you want to use the caching name server as your name server, you have to specify that name server as your primary one. To do this, make sure that the first line in the `/etc/resolv.conf` file is the following:

```
nameserver 127.0.0.1
```

Configuring a Primary Name Server

The best way to configure a primary name server is to start by configuring a caching name server, as explained in the previous sections. Then, add master zones for the domains for which you want this to be the primary name server. For example, suppose that I want to define a primary name server for the `naba.net` domain. Here are the steps I go through to configure that primary name server (after I log in as `root`):

1. Add the following zone statements to the `/etc/named.conf` file:

```
zone "naba.net" IN {
    type master;
    file "naba.zone";
};
zone "0.168.192.in-addr.arpa" IN {
    type master;
    file "0.168.192.zone";
};
```

2. Create the zone file `var/named/naba.zone` with the following lines in it:

```
$TTL    86400
$ORIGIN naba.net.
@           1D IN SOA       @ root.naba.net (
                            100             ; serial
                            3H              ; refresh
                            15M             ; retry
                            1W              ; expiry
                            1D )            ; minimum

            1D IN NS        @
            1D IN A         192.168.0.7

wxp    IN    A    192.168.0.2
```

3. Create the zone file `/var/named/0.168.192.zone` with the following lines in it:

```
$TTL    86400
; Remember zone name is: 0.168.192.in-addr.arpa
@       IN      SOA     naba.net. root.naba.net  (
                                  1          ; Serial
                                  28800       ; Refresh
                                  14400       ; Retry
                                  3600000     ; Expire
                                  86400 )     ; Minimum
```

```
              IN      NS      naba.net.

      7       IN      PTR     naba.net.
      2       IN      PTR    wxp.naba.net.
```

To test the new configuration, restart the named server with the following command:

```
service named restart
```

Now, use dig or host to query the DNS server. For example, here's how I use host to check the address of the host `wxp.naba.net` at the DNS server running on `localhost`:

```
host wxp.naba.net localhost
Using domain server:
Name: localhost
Address: 127.0.0.1#53
Aliases:

wxp.naba.net has address 192.168.0.2
```

If you want to use dig to check the DNS server, type the following command:

```
dig @localhost wxp.naba.net
```

That `@localhost` part specifies the DNS server that dig should contact.

Here is an example of a reverse lookup with the IP address 192.168.0.2:

```
host 192.168.0.2 localhost
Using domain server:
Name: localhost
Address: 127.0.0.1#53
Aliases:

2.0.168.192.in-addr.arpa domain name pointer wxp.naba.net
```

Using Network Information Service

Network Information Service (NIS) was developed by Sun Microsystems as a way to share information among all computers in a local area network. The types of information NIS most commonly uses include the following:

- User names and passwords from files such as `/etc/passwd` and `/etc/shadow`
- Group information from the `/etc/group` file

Normally, each system has its own copy of information in respective files, and any changes require updating the files on each system individually. Using NIS, you can maintain a single set of configuration files for a collection of computers in an NIS server. All other computers running NIS clients can then access the files. For example, if your user name and password are in the NIS password database, you will be able to log in on all computers on the network running NIS client programs.

insider insight

The NIS server is in the ypserv RPM, which is part of the Network Servers package group in Fedora. ypserv is not installed by default. To install it, use the Package Management GUI tool (select Desktop ➪ System Settings ➪ Add/Remove Applications, click Details in the Network Servers package group, and select ypserv).

NIS was originally called Sun Yellow Pages (YP), but the name Yellow Pages is a registered trademark of British Telecom in the United Kingdom, so Sun Microsystems had to change the name. However, many NIS commands, and the NIS package names, begin with the letters `yp`.

If you want to use NIS in a network, you must set up at least one NIS server. You can have multiple NIS servers in a network, each serving a different collection of computers. You can also have a master NIS server and one or more slave NIS servers that receive a copy of the master's database. The group of computers a master NIS server supports is called an NIS domain or YP domain.

The master NIS server runs the ypserv daemon (this is the NIS server daemon) that maintains the shared information in DBM databases. (DBM refers to Data Base Management, a library of functions that maintain key-value pairs in a database.) The NIS databases are called maps. You can create these NIS maps directly from the text configuration files — such as `/etc/passwd` and `/etc/group` — by using the `/usr/lib/yp/makedbm` program that comes with the NIS server software. More accurately, the ypserv daemon uses the Makefile in the `/var/yp` directory to create the maps for all shared configuration files.

The master NIS server provides the maps to all NIS client computers. The clients run the ypbind daemon through which various client programs access the master NIS server. In addition to a master server, one or more NIS slave servers may be set up to provide the NIS maps in case the master is unavailable or down. The NIS slave servers periodically copy the NIS maps from the master server (using the `/usr/lib/yp/ypxfr` command) and are able to provide these maps to clients when the master is down.

You can think of NIS as a way of distributing the same set of configuration files among all computers in an NIS domain. You get the benefits of sharing the same files (such as the same user name and password for all machines), yet you can still edit and maintain just one set of files — the files on the master NIS server.

The next few sections describe how to set up your Linux system as an NIS client and as an NIS server.

Setting Up an NIS Client

If your network uses NIS centrally to administer users and passwords, you can set up your Linux PC as an NIS client. You can enable NIS from the Authentication Configuration tool that you can start by selecting Desktop ➪ System Settings ➪ Authentication from the GNOME desktop. Then click the Enable NIS Support button in the User Information tab of the Authentication Configuration window, as shown in Figure 18-3.

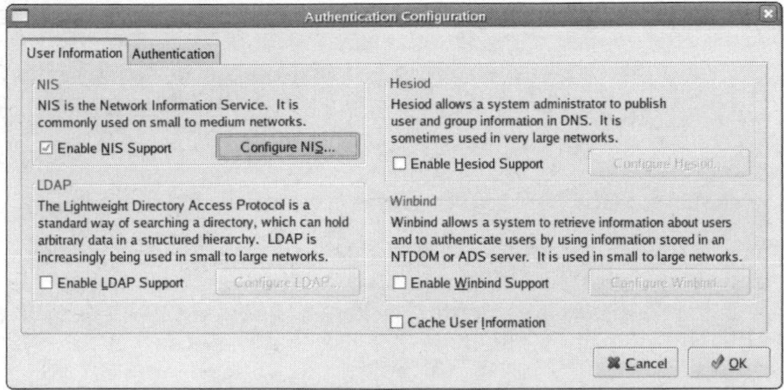

Figure 18-3: Enabling NIS through the Authentication Configuration Tool.

Of course, you should enable NIS only if your network is set up with an NIS server. If you do select the Enable NIS Support option, you should click the Configure NIS button (refer to Figure 18-3) and provide the following information in the dialog box that appears:

- Specify the NIS domain name. The domain name refers to the group of computers the NIS server serves.
- Specify the name of the NIS server.

If you want to manually configure your system as an NIS client, you can do so by performing the following tasks:

- Define your NIS domain name.
- Set up the NIS configuration file (`/etc/yp.conf`). In this file, you specify the master NIS and slave servers that provide NIS maps to your Linux PC.
- Configure the NIS client daemon — `ypbind` — to start when your system boots.

The next three sections show you how to perform these tasks.

Setting the NIS Domain Name

The NIS domain name identifies the group of computers that a particular NIS server supports. You can set the NIS domain name of your system by using the `domainname` command. For example, to set your NIS domain name to admin, log in as `root`, and type the following at the shell prompt:

```
domainname admin
```

If you type `domainname` without any arguments, the command prints the current NIS domain name.

To ensure that the NIS domain name is set as soon as your system boots, the command should be run from one of the startup scripts. You can do this by adding the following line to the /etc/sysconfig/network file on your Linux system:

```
NISDOMAIN="admin"
```

Of course, you should use the NIS domain name appropriate to your network.

The NIS domain is different from the DNS domain names discussed earlier in this chapter. It's best if you pick an NIS domain name that's not related to the DNS domain name. Doing so makes it harder for hackers to guess your NIS domain name (if they know the NIS domain name, there is a risk that they can get the NIS password database).

Preparing the /etc/yp.conf File

The ypbind daemon, described in the next section, needs information about the NIS domains and NIS servers to do its job. It finds this information in the /etc/yp.conf configuration file. The ypbind daemon reads the /etc/yp.conf file when it starts up or when it receives the SIGHUP signal (for example, when you restart ypbind with the command kill -HUP ypbind).

To specify one or more NIS servers for the local domain (which you have already set with the domainname command), all you need in /etc/yp.conf are lines such as the following:

```
ypserver nisadmin
ypserver 192.168.0.7
```

You can use a name such as nisadmin if that name is listed in the /etc/hosts file (that way, ypbind can resolve the name into an IP address without having to use NIS). Otherwise, you should specify the NIS server's IP address.

In /etc/yp.conf, you can also specify specific NIS servers for specific NIS domains, like this:

```
domain sales server nissales
domain admin server nisadmin
```

A third type of entry in the /etc/yp.conf file specifies that ypbind should use IP broadcast in the local network to find an NIS server for a specified domain. To do this, add a line such as the following to /etc/yp.conf:

```
domain admin broadcast
```

Starting the ypbind Daemon

Every computer in an NIS domain, including the server, runs the ypbind daemon. Various NIS client applications, such as ypwhich, ypcat, and yppoll, need the ypbind daemon to obtain information from the master NIS server. More precisely, the C library includes code (which is part of the client) that contacts the ypbind daemon to locate the NIS server for the domain. Then the C library code contacts the server directly to obtain administrative information. The client applications get the information through functions in the C library.

To interactively start ypbind, log in as `root` and type the following command:

```
service ypbind start
```

If you want ypbind to start when the system boots, log in as `root` and type the following commands to turn ypbind on:

```
chkconfig --add ypbind
chkconfig --level 35 ypbind on
```

Setting Up the NIS Server

To set up your Linux system as an NIS server, you should first set it up as an NIS client — set the NIS domain name, configure the `/etc/yp.conf` file, and configure the ypbind daemon. (Note that the ypbind daemon won't work until you have an NIS server up and running.) After the client configuration, you can configure the NIS server. This requires that you perform the following tasks:

- Create the NIS maps using ypinit.
- Configure the master NIS server — ypserv.
- Optionally, configure one or more slave NIS servers.

The next two sections explain these steps.

Creating the NIS Maps

Creating NIS maps involves converting the text files, such as `/etc/passwd` and `/etc/group` into DBM files by using `makedbm`. The map creation is controlled by `/var/yp/Makefile`, a file that can be used by the `make` command to perform specific tasks (see Chapter 23 for more information on `make` and `Makefile`).

You can configure what you want the NIS server to share with the clients in the NIS domain. You do so by editing the `Makefile` in the `/var/yp` directory. Open `/var/yp/Makefile` in a text editor, and locate the line that begins with `all:`. Here is a typical excerpt from the `Makefile` showing the comments before the `all:` line:

```
# If you don't want some of these maps built, feel free to comment
# them out from this list.

all:  passwd group hosts rpc services netid protocols mail \
      # netgrp shadow publickey networks ethers bootparams printcap \
      # amd.home auto.master auto.home auto.local passwd.adjunct \
      # timezone locale netmasks
```

As the comment lines (the ones that begin with #) indicate, you can comment out any maps you do not want to build. In the preceding example, the maps listed in the last three lines will not be built.

Next, you should generate the NIS map database by running the `/usr/lib/yp/ypinit` program with the `-m` option. Here is a sample session with that program:

```
/usr/lib/yp/ypinit -m
At this point, we have to construct a list of the hosts which will run NIS
servers.  localhost.localdomain is in the list of NIS server hosts.  Please continue
to add
```

```
the names for the other hosts, one per line.  When you are done with the
list, type a <control D>.
        next host to add:  localhost.localdomain
        next host to add: <Press Ctrl-D here>
The current list of NIS servers looks like this:

localhost.localdomain

Is this correct?  [y/n: y]  y
We need a few minutes to build the databases...
Building /var/yp/admin/ypservers...
Running /var/yp/Makefile...
gmake[1]: Entering directory `/var/yp/admin'
Updating passwd.byname...
...lines deleted...
```

The `/usr/lib/yp/ypinit` program automatically selects your host as an NIS server and prompts for the names of any other NIS servers. You can add the server names one at a time and press Ctrl-D when you are done. Then, you have to verify that the list of NIS servers is correct (type **y**). After that, `make` runs with the `/var/yp/Makefile` and generates the NIS maps as specified by the `all:` line in the `Makefile`. The map files are stored in a subdirectory of `/var/yp` that has the same name as the NIS domain name you have previously set for your system. For example, for the NIS domain admin, the map files are in the `/var/yp/admin` directory.

Configuring the Master NIS Server

To configure the NIS server daemon, ypserv, you have to prepare the configuration file `/etc/ypserv.conf`. You can learn about the syntax of this file by reading its man page, which you can access by typing the command **man ypserv.conf**. Among other options, you can use the following option to specify that DNS should not be used to look up host names that are not in the maps of the `/etc/hosts` file:

```
dns: no
```

You can also add other lines in `/etc/ypserv.conf` that specify access rules — which hosts can access which maps. The format of the access rules is as follows:

```
Host : Domain : Map : Security
```

The `field_to_mangle` is optional; it indicates which field in the map file should be mangled (the default is the second field because the password is in the second field of most files, such as `/etc/passwd`). To mangle a field is to replace it with an `x` if the request comes from an unprivileged host. The rest of the fields have the following meanings:

- **Host:** IP address or a wildcard (*) indicating to whom the rule applies
- **Domain:** Domain name or a wildcard (*) indicating to whom the rule applies
- **Map:** Name of the map to which the rule applies (the names of the maps are the same as those of the map files in the `/var/yp/domainname` directory, where *`domainname`* is your NIS domain name)

- **Security:** One of the following: none (to allow access always), port (to access from a port less than 1024), deny (to deny access to the map), or des (to require DES authentication — this may not be supported by all C libraries)

For example, the following lines in the /etc/ypserv.conf file restrict access to the password map to systems in the 192.168.0 network:

```
192.168.0     :     *     :     passwd.byname     : port
192.168.0     :     *     :     passwd.byuid      : port
```

If you do not specify any access rules, ypserv allows all computers to access all maps.

Once you have set up the /etc/ypserv.conf file, you can start the NIS server with the following command:

```
service ypserv start
```

insider insight

To ensure that ypserv starts whenever you reboot the system, log in as root **and type the following command to enable it:**

```
chkconfig --level 35 ypserv on
```

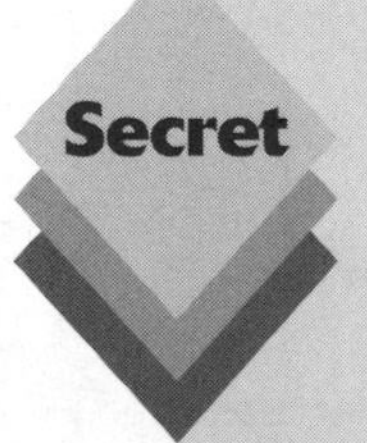

To handle password changes from clients, you must also run the rpc.yppasswdd **server on the master NIS server for the domain. The** rpc.yppasswdd **server enables users on client systems to type the** yppasswd **command and change their password in the NIS database. If you do not have the** rpc.yppasswdd **server running on the master NIS server, users will get the following error message when they type the** yppasswd **command:**

```
yppasswd: yppasswdd not running on NIS master host
```

You can correct this problem by starting rpc.yppasswdd**; log in as** root**, and type the command:**

```
service yppasswdd start
```

To start yppasswdd **automatically at run levels 3 and 5, type:**

```
chkconfig --level 35 yppasswdd on
```

Once you have the master NIS server up and running, you can test it by using various NIS client programs, such as ypwhich, yppoll, ypcat, and ypmatch, as explained in the "Testing NIS" section, later in this chapter.

Configuring a Slave NIS Server

To set up a system as a slave NIS server, first set it up as an NIS client and verify that the client works. In particular, type **ypwhich -m** and look for a list of NIS maps and the name of the master NIS server for each map (the next section shows how the ypwhich -m command works).

After you confirm that the system is configured as an NIS client, type the following command to set up the system as a slave NIS server:

```
/usr/lib/yp/ypinit -s nismaster
```

where `nismaster` is the name of the master NIS server for the domain.The ypinit program builds and installs the NIS database for the specified domain.

Testing NIS

If you do not have a master NIS server in your network, first perform the client configurations to create one, then start the master NIS server, as explained in earlier sections. Next, start the ypbind daemon as follows:

```
service ypbind start
```

Now, you can try out various NIS client programs and other utilities to see if everything is working correctly.

NIS servers and clients use Remote Procedure Call (RPC) to exchange information. Network File System (NFS), described in Chapter 19, also uses RPC. RPC requires the portmap service, which maps RPC services to TCP and UDP ports. When a server that supports RPC starts up, it registers itself with portmap and lists both the services it supports and the ports it uses. Your Linux system should already have portmap up and running. You can check for it with the following command:

```
ps ax | grep portmap
 1856 ?        Ss     0:00 portmap
 3199 pts/3    S+     0:00 grep portmap
```

You should see a line showing the portmap process and its ID in the output. In this case, the portmap process has an ID of 1856.

To see if the ypserv and ypbind processes are running on the master NIS server, use the `/usr/sbin/rpcinfo` program to check if ypserv and ypbind were able to register with the portmap service. For example, here is a sample output:

```
/usr/sbin/rpcinfo -p
   program vers proto   port
    100000    2   tcp    111  portmapper
    100000    2   udp    111  portmapper
    100024    1   udp  32768  status
    100024    1   tcp  32768  status
    100004    2   udp    794  ypserv
    100004    1   udp    794  ypserv
    100004    2   tcp    797  ypserv
    100004    1   tcp    797  ypserv
    100009    1   udp    808  yppasswdd
    100007    2   udp    820  ypbind
    100007    1   udp    820  ypbind
    100007    2   tcp    823  ypbind
    100007    1   tcp    823  ypbind
```

Each line shows the RPC program number, a version number, the protocol (TCP or UDP), the port number, and the service. As you can see, both ypbind and ypserv are registered.

To determine which NIS server your system is using, try the ypwhich command. Here is a typical example:

```
ypwhich
192.168.0.3
```

You can also use the ypwhich command to view the master NIS server for a specified map. If you want to see the master NIS server for the available maps, type the following command:

```
ypwhich -m
rpc.bynumber localhost.localdomain
ypservers localhost.localdomain
protocols.bynumber localhost.localdomain
group.bygid localhost.localdomain
hosts.byaddr localhost.localdomain
passwd.byname localhost.localdomain
mail.aliases localhost.localdomain
netid.byname localhost.localdomain
rpc.byname localhost.localdomain
hosts.byname localhost.localdomain
services.byservicename localhost.localdomain
services.byname localhost.localdomain
passwd.byuid localhost.localdomain
group.byname localhost.localdomain
protocols.byname localhost.localdomain
```

The output shows a list of the available NIS maps and, for each map, the name of the master NIS server.

To view the name of the master NIS server and information about a specific NIS map, use the yppoll command. For example, here is the result of a yppoll query for the passwd.byname map:

```
yppoll passwd.byname
Domain admin is supported.
Map passwd.byname has order number 972760603. [Sat Oct 27 15:16:43 2001]
The master server is lnbp200
```

Use the ypcat command to print the values of the keys in an NIS map. For example, here is a ypcat query for the NIS map group.byname:

```
ypcat group.byname
naba:!:500:
```

You can use ypmatch to look at the entries in an NIS map that match a specific key. For example, here is a ypmatch command line that looks for entries that match the key naba in the group.byname map:

```
ypmatch naba group.byname
naba:!:500:
```

If you compare this with the output from ypcat showing all the groups, you see that ypmatch shows the line corresponding to the group name naba.

Summary

Domain Name Service (DNS) is a key Internet service, one that enables us to use easy-to-remember names for websites and servers on the Internet, even though TCP/IP requires numeric IP addresses for data transfers. Network Information Service (NIS) is another useful service for local networks to share configuration files, such as users, groups, and passwords. Linux comes with everything needed to run the servers and clients for DNS and NIS. This chapter describes how to use DNS and NIS in Linux.

In this chapter, you learned the following:

- DNS is a distributed database that holds information about host names, IP addresses, and mail routing. Internet applications use DNS to convert host names, such as `www.redhat.com` into IP addresses.
- DNS is documented in RFCs 1034 and 1035. Many other RFCs document various updates and extensions to DNS.
- All hosts on the Internet use DNS. Each host needs a name server it can query to resolve host names into IP addresses. Typically, the ISP provides the name servers. The IP addresses of the name servers are listed in the `/etc/resolv.conf` file.
- Linux comes with the Berkeley Internet Domain (BIND) system, a well-known implementation of DNS.
- To set up a name server, you have to prepare the `/etc/named.conf` configuration files and zone files referenced in that configuration file. The zone files are usually stored in the `/var/named` directory.
- Linux comes with the configuration files for a caching name server that loads the addresses of a few authoritative servers for the root domain and gets all its data by caching responses to queries resolved by contacting other name servers. This chapter walks you through the process of setting up the caching name server and explains the configuration files the server uses.
- You can easily extend the caching name server to a primary name server for your domain by adding a master zone to the `/etc/named.conf` file and preparing the appropriate zone files.
- You can use BIND utilities such as dig and host interactively to query the DNS database interactively.
- NIS was developed by Sun Microsystems as a way of sharing configuration files among a number of computers in a local area network. The password file and group information files are typically shared by using NIS. This enables users to log in by using the same user name and password on all computers in the local network.
- NIS clients have to define their NIS domain (a name for all the computers an NIS server serves); set up the NIS configuration file `/etc/yp.conf`; and run the ypbind daemon. All NIS client applications access the NIS server through the local ypbind process.
- To set up a master NIS server, you have to create the NIS maps — the NIS databases — by running `/usr/lib/yp/ypinit`; set up the configuration file `/etc/ypserv.conf`, and start the NIS server, ypserv.
- You can test the NIS server by running NIS client applications, such as ypwhich, yppoll, ypcat, and ypmatch.
- If you want users to be able to set or change NIS passwords by using the `yppasswdd` command, you must also run the rpc.yppasswdd daemon on the master NIS server.

Samba and NFS

Chapter 19

♦ ♦

Secrets in This Chapter

♦ ♦

A low-end Pentium PC configured with Linux (from this book's companion DVD) makes a very capable workgroup (or office) server. By workgroup, I mean a small local area network (LAN) of perhaps a dozen or so PCs. You can configure the Linux PC to be the file and print server and have the other PCs be the clients. The client PCs do not have to run Linux; they can run Windows. Linux comes with the Samba package, which provides you with everything you need to set up your Linux PC as a server in a Windows network. This chapter introduces you to Samba — a software package that makes a Linux server look like a Windows server with shared drives (Samba can act as a Windows NT Primary Domain Controller and, as of version 3.0.9, it supports Active Directory). Also, you learn about file sharing through Network File System (NFS), which is built into Linux.

Sharing Files with NFS

Sharing files through NFS is simple and involves two basic steps:

- On the Linux server, export one or more directories by listing them in the `/etc/exports` file and by running the `exportfs` command. In addition, you must run the NFS server by logging in as `root` and typing the command `service nfs start`.
- On each client system, use the `mount` command to mount the directories the NFS server has exported.

The only problem in using NFS is that each client system must support it. Most Windows PCs do not come with NFS, but NFS is available on Linux and UNIX systems. That means you have to buy NFS software separately if you want to share files by using NFS between Windows and Linux systems. However, it makes sense to use NFS if all systems on your LAN run Linux (or other variants of UNIX with built-in NFS support).

caution

You should note that NFS has security vulnerabilities. Therefore, you should not set up NFS on systems directly connected to the Internet without using the RPCSEC_GSS security that comes with NFS Version 4.

The next subsections walk you through NFS setup, using an example of two Linux PCs on a LAN.

Enhancing Security with NFS Version 4 (NFSv4)

Fedora Linux comes with a Linux 2.6 kernel that has built-in support for NFS Version 4 (NFSv4). NFSv4 is built upon earlier versions of NFS, but unlike earlier versions, NFSv4 has stronger security and is designed to operate in an Internet environment. (RFC 3510 describes NFSv4; see `www.ietf.org/rfc/rfc3530.txt`.) NFSv4 uses the RPCSEC_GSS (GSS stands for Generic Security Services) protocol for security. You can continue to use the older user ID and group ID–based authentication with NFSv4, but if you want to use RPCSEC_GSS you have to run three additional services: rpcsvcgassd on the server, rpsgssd on the client, and rpcidmapd on both the client and the server. For more information about NFSv4 implementation in Linux, visit `www.citi.umich.edu/projects/nfsv4/linux/`.

Exporting a File System with NFS

Start with the server system that exports—makes available to the client systems—the contents of a directory. On the server, you must run the NFS service and also designate one or more file systems that are to be exported.

To export a file system, you have to add an appropriate entry to the `/etc/exports` file. For example, suppose that you want to export the `/home` directory and you want to enable the host named LNBP75 to mount this file system for read and write operations. You can do this by adding the following entry to the `/etc/exports` file:

```
/home LNBP75(rw, sync)
```

If you want to give access to all hosts on a LAN such as 192.168.0.0, you could change this line to:

```
/home 192.168.0.0/24(rw,sync)
```

If you are in an internal network and want to map a root user on the client to the root user on the server, you can add the `no_root_squash` option to the list of options in parentheses.

Each line in the `/etc/exports` file has this general format:

```
directory    host1(options)  host2(options)  ...
```

The first field is the directory being shared via NFS, followed by one or more fields that specify which hosts can mount that directory remotely and a number of options within parentheses. You can specify the hosts with names or IP addresses, including ranges of addresses.

The options within parentheses denote the kind of access each host is granted and how user and group IDs from the server are mapped to IDs the client (for example, if a file is owned by `root` on the server, what owner should that be on the client). Within the parentheses, the options are separated by commas. For example, if a host is allowed both read and write access and all IDs are to be mapped to the anonymous user (by default this is the user named `nobody`), then the options would look like this:

```
(rw,all_squash)
```

If you want to use RPCSEC_GSS security, then you must export the specific directories to a special client named `gss/krb5` (in other words, in the `/etc/exports` file, a line exporting the `/home/public` directory using RPCSEC_GSS security would look like this:

```
/home/public    gss/krb5(rw,sync)
```

Table 19-1 shows the options you can use in the `/etc/exports` file. There are two types of options: general options and user ID mapping options.

Table 19-1: Options in /etc/exports

Option	*Description*
General Options	
secure	Allows connections only from ports 1024 or lower (default)
insecure	Allows connections from 1024 or higher
ro	Allows read-only access (default)
rw	Allows both read and write access
sync	Performs write operations (this means writing information to the disk) when requested (default)
async	Performs write operations when the server is ready
no_wdelay	Performs write operations immediately
wdelay	Waits a bit to see if related write requests arrive and then performs them together (default)
hide	Hides an exported directory that's a subdirectory of another exported directory (default)
no_hide	Behaves exactly the opposite of hide
subtree_check	Performs subtree checking, which involves checking parent directories of an exported subdirectory whenever a file is accessed (default)
no_subtree_check	Turns off subtree checking (opposite of subtree_check)
insecure_locks	Allows insecure file locking
User ID Mapping Options	
all_squash	Maps all user IDs and group IDs to the anonymous user on the client
no_all_squash	Maps remote user and group IDs to similar IDs on the client (default)
root_squash	Maps remote root user to the anonymous user on the client (default)
no_root_squash	Maps the remote root user to the local root user
anonuid=UID	Sets the user ID of an anonymous user to be used for the all_squash and root_squash options
anongid=GID	Sets the group ID of an anonymous user to be used for the all_squash and root_squash options

After adding the entry in the /etc/exports file, manually export the file system by typing the following command in a terminal window:

```
exportfs -a
```

This command exports all file systems defined in the /etc/exports file.

Now, you can start the NFS server processes. To do this, log in as `root` and type the following command in a terminal window:

```
service nfs start
```

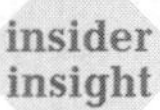

If you want the NFS server to start when the system boots, type the following command to turn it on:

```
chkconfig --level 35 nfs on
```

When the NFS service is up, the server side of NFS is ready. Now you can try to mount the exported file system from a client system and access the exported file system.

If you ever make any changes to the exported file systems listed in the `/etc/exports` file, remember to restart the NFS service. To do this, log in as `root` and type the following command in a terminal window:

```
service nfs restart
```

Mounting an NFS File System

To access an exported NFS file system on a client system, you have to mount that file system on a mount point. The *mount point* is nothing more than a local directory. For example, suppose that you want to access the `/home` directory exported from the server named LNBP200 at the local directory `/mnt/lnbp200` on the client system. To do this, follow these steps:

1. Log in as `root`, and create the directory with the command

   ```
   mkdir /mnt/lnbp200
   ```

2. Type the following command to mount the directory from the remote system (LNBP200) on the local directory `/mnt/lnbp200`:

   ```
   mount lnbp200:/home /mnt/lnbp200
   ```

After these steps, you can view and access exported files from the local directory `/mnt/lnbp200`.

To confirm that the NFS file system is indeed mounted, log in as `root` on the client system and type **mount** in a terminal window. You should see a line similar to the following one about the NFS file system:

```
lnbp200:/home/public on /mnt/lnbp200 type nfs (rw,addr=192.168.0.200)
```

note

NFS supports two types of mount operations — hard and soft. By default a mount is hard, which means that if the NFS server does not respond, the client will keep trying to access the server indefinitely until the server responds. You can soft mount an NFS volume by adding the `-o soft` option to the `mount` command. For a soft mount, the client returns an error if the NFS server fails to respond.

Setting Up a Windows Server Using Samba

If you rely on Windows for file sharing and print sharing, you probably use Windows in your servers and clients. You can move to a Linux PC as your server without losing the Windows file and printer sharing because a Linux PC can be set up as a Windows server. When you install Linux from this book's companion DVD, you also get a chance to install the Samba software package, which performs that setup. All you have to do is select the Windows File Server package group during installation.

note

After you install and configure Samba on your Linux PC, client PCs (running Windows for Workgroups or Windows 95/98/NT/2000/XP) can access disks and printers on the Linux PC by using the Server Message Block (SMB) protocol, the underlying protocol in Windows file and print sharing.

With the Samba package installed, you can make your Linux PC a Windows client, which means that the Linux PC can access disks and printers a Windows server manages. At the same time, your Linux PC can be a client to other Windows systems on the network.

The Samba software package has these major components:

- **/etc/samba/smb.conf:** The Samba configuration file the SMB server uses
- **/etc/samba/smbusers:** A Samba configuration file that shows the Samba user names corresponding to user names on the local Linux PC
- **nmbd:** The NetBIOS name server, which clients use to look up servers (NetBIOS stands for Network Basic Input/Output System — an interface that applications use to communicate with network transports, such as TCP/IP)
- **nmblookup:** A command that returns the IP address of a Windows PC identified by its NetBIOS name
- **smbadduser:** A program that adds users to the SMB password file
- **smbcacls:** A program that manipulates Windows NT access control lists (ACLs) on shared files
- **smbclient:** The Windows client, which runs on Linux and allows Linux to access the files and printer on any Windows server
- **smbcontrol:** A program that sends messages to the smbd, nmbd, or winbindd processes
- **smbd:** The SMB server, which accepts connections from Windows clients and provides file and print sharing services
- **smbmount:** A program that mounts a Samba share directory on a Linux PC
- **smbpasswd:** A program that changes the password for an SMB user
- **smbprint:** A script that enables printing on a printer on a SMB server
- **smbstatus:** A command that lists the current SMB connections for the local host
- **smbtar:** A program that backs up SMB shares directly to tape drives on the Linux system
- **smbumount:** A program that unmounts a currently mounted Samba share directory
- **testparm:** A program that ensures that the Samba configuration file is correct
- **winbindd:** A server for resolving names from Windows NT servers

The following subsections describe how to install Samba from the companion DVD and how to set up a printer on the Linux PC to print through Windows.

Checking Whether Samba Is Installed

Check whether Samba is installed, by typing the following command in a terminal window:

```
rpm -q samba
samba-3.0.14a-2
```

If the `rpm` command displays a package name that begins with `samba`, Samba is already installed on your system, and you should skip this subsection. Otherwise, follow these steps to install Samba from this book's companion DVD (replace `/media/cdrom` with `/media/cdrecorder` if your system has a CD/DVD recorder):

1. Log in as `root`, and make sure that the companion DVD is in the drive and mounted. If it is not, use the `umount /media/cdrom` command to dismount the current CD or DVD in the drive (no need for this step if there is nothing in the drive); replace it with the correct DVD, and mount that DVD with the `mount /media/cdrom` command.
2. Change the directory to the DVD—specifically to the directory where the Red Hat Package Manager (RPM) packages are located—with the following command:

   ```
   cd /media/cdrom/Fedora/RPMS
   ```

3. Use the following `rpm` command to install Samba:

   ```
   rpm -ivh samba*
   ```

   If Samba is already installed, this command returns an error message. Otherwise, the `rpm` command installs Samba on your system by copying various files to their appropriate locations.

These steps complete the unpacking and installation of the Samba software. Now, all you have to do to use Samba is configure it.

Configuring Samba

To set up the Windows file-sharing and print-sharing services, you have to provide a configuration file named `/etc/samba/smb.conf`. The configuration file is a text file that looks like a Microsoft Windows 3.1 `INI` file. You can prepare the file in any text editor on your Linux system.

Like the old Windows `INI` files, the `/etc/samba/smb.conf` file consists of sections, with a list of parameters in each section. Each section of the `smb.conf` file begins with the name of the section in brackets. The section continues until the next section begins or until the file ends.

Each line in a section specifies the value of a parameter, using the following syntax:

```
name = value
```

As in Windows `INI` files, comment lines begin with a semicolon (;). In the `/etc/samba/smb.conf` file, comments may also begin with a hash (#).

The Samba software comes with a configuration file you can edit to get started. To prepare the configuration file, log in as `root`, and use your favorite text editor to edit the file `/etc/samba/smb.conf`. Here's a sample configuration file without any comments:

```
[global]
    netbios name = LNBP200
    workgroup = LNB SOFTWARE
    server string = LNB Software-Samba Server
    hosts allow = 192.168.0.  127.
    guest ok = yes
    guest account = naba
    log file = /var/log/samba/%m.log

# Log files can be at most 50KB
    max log size = 50

    security = user
    username map = /etc/samba/smbusers

# Leave the next option as is - it's for performance
    socket options = TCP_NODELAY SO_RCVBUF=8192 SO_SNDBUF=8192

    remote browse sync = 192.168.0.255
    remote announce = 192.168.0.255/LNB SOFTWARE

    name resolve order = lmhosts bcast

    dns proxy = no
    unix password sync = no

[homes]
    comment = Home Directories
    browseable = no
    writable = yes

[printers]
    comment = All Printers
    path = /var/spool/samba
    browseable = no
    guest ok = no
    writable = no
    printable = yes

[tmp]
    comment = Temporary file space
    path = /tmp
    read only = no
    public = yes

[public]
    comment = Public Stuff
```

```
path = /home/public
browseable = yes
public = yes
guest ok = yes
writable = yes
printable = no
available = yes
guest only = no
user = naba
```

Change the user name from `naba` to your user name. Also make sure that all directories mentioned in the configuration file actually exist. For example, create the `/home/public` directory with the command `mkdir /home/public`.

After editing the Samba configuration file, add users to the `/etc/samba/smbusers` file. Here's what I have in the `/etc/samba/smbusers` file on my system:

```
# Unix_name = SMB_name1 SMB_name2 ...
root = administrator admin
nobody = guest pcguest smbguest
adm = naba
```

insider insight

After making the changes to the `/etc/samba/smb.conf file`, type the following command to verify that the file is okay:

```
testparm
```

If the command says that it loaded the files okay, you're all set to go.

Start the SMB services with the following command:

```
service smb start
```

To start the SMB services automatically when the system reboots, type the following command:

```
chkconfig --level 35 smb on
```

Accessing the Samba Server from Windows

You can try to access the Samba server on the Linux system from one of the Windows systems on your LAN. Double-click the Network Neighborhood icon on the Windows 95/98/ME desktop. On Windows XP, select Start ⇨ My Network Places, and then click View workgroup computers. You should be able to view the shared folders simply by double-clicking the icon. For the example, you should see two folders: `tmp` and `public`. You can then open these folders to explore the contents of the directories further.

Accessing Windows Resources with smbclient

You can use the smbclient program to access shared directories and printers on Windows systems on the LAN and to ensure that your Linux Samba server is working. One quick way to check is to use the `smbclient -L` command to view the list of services on the Linux Samba server itself. This is what I get when I run smbclient on my Linux Samba sever:

```
smbclient -L LNBP200
Password: (I press Enter)
Anonymous login successful
Domain=[LNB SOFTWARE] OS=[Unix] Server=[Samba 3.0.11-6]

        Sharename       Type      Comment
        ---------       ----      -------
        tmp             Disk      Temporary file space
        public          Disk      Public Stuff
        IPC$            IPC       IPC Service (LNB Software-Samba Server)
        ADMIN$          IPC       IPC Service (LNB Software-Samba Server)
Anonymous login successful
Domain=[LNB SOFTWARE] OS=[Unix] Server=[Samba 3.0.11-6]

        Server               Comment
        ---------            -------
        LNBP200              LNB Software-Samba Server
        NABA-DELL-4400

        Workgroup            Master
        ---------            -------
        LNB SOFTWARE         NABA-DELL-4400
```

The output of `smbclient` shows shared resources and lists the names of the other Windows servers on the local network.

If you have other Windows servers around, you can look at their services with the smbclient program. Here is what I get when I view the shared resources on a Windows 98 PC:

```
smbclient -L NABA-DELL-4400
Password: (I press Enter)
Domain=[NABA-DELL-4400] OS=[Windows 5.1] Server=[Windows 2000 LAN Manager]

        Sharename       Type      Comment
        ---------       ----      -------
        IPC$            IPC       Remote IPC
        print$          Disk      Printer Drivers
        SharedDocs      Disk
        Naba            Disk
        IvyOldPC        Disk
        Printer2        Printer   Brother PC-FAX
        MFC-USB         Printer   Brother MFC-9700 USB
        hplj4           Printer   HP LaserJet 4M
Domain=[NABA-DELL-4400] OS=[Windows 5.1] Server=[Windows 2000 LAN Manager]
```

You can do much more than simply look at resources with the smbclient program: you can also use it to access a disk on a Windows server or to send a file to a Windows printer. The smbclient program is like FTP—you connect to a Windows server and use commands to get or put files and to send files to the printer.

The following example shows how I use smbclient to access a disk on my Windows XP PC and view its directory:

```
smbclient //naba-dell-4400/Share naba mypassword
Domain=[NABA-DELL-4400] OS=[Windows 5.1] Server=[Windows 2000 LAN Manager]
smb: \> dir
  .                                    DR        0  Mon Dec 20 10:52:57 2004
  ..                                   DR        0  Mon Dec 20 10:52:57 2004
  Ashley                                D        0  Sun Mar  7 02:07:28 2004
  botball.ppt                           A   832000  Sun May 16 14:08:13 2004
  desktop.ini                         AHS      137  Tue Nov  9 16:52:44 2004
  DSCN3332.JPG                          A   379772  Fri Sep 17 23:00:52 2004
... lines deleted...
  Photos                                D        0  Thu Jan  6 19:54:54 2005

                34153 blocks of size 2097152. 6130 blocks available
smb: \> quit
```

To see a list of smbclient commands, type **help** at the prompt. Table 19-2 is a brief summary of commonly used smbclient commands. To familiarize yourself with smbclient, try as many of these commands as you can.

Table 19-2: Common smbclient Commands

Command	*Description*
`!`	Executes a shell command (remember that you run smbclient on Linux)
`? cmd`	Displays a list of commands or help on a specific command
`cancel id`	Cancels a print job identified by its ID
`cd dir`	Changes the remote directory
`del file`	Deletes the specified file
`dir file`	Displays the directory listing
`exit`	Logs off the Windows server
`get rfile lfile`	Copies a remote file (`rfile`) to a local file (`lfile`)
`help cmd`	Provides help on a command (or displays a list of commands)
`lcd newdir`	Changes the local directory (on the Linux PC)
`lowercase`	Toggles automatic lowercase conversion of filenames when executing the get command
`ls files`	Lists files on the server
`mask name`	Applies a mask (such as `*.c`) to all file operations
`md dirname`	Makes a directory on the server

(continued)

Table 19-2 *(continued)*

Command	*Description*
`mget name`	Gets all files with matching names (such as `*.doc`)
`mkdir dirname`	Makes a directory
`mput name`	Copies files from the Linux PC to the server
`newer file`	Gets only the files that are newer than the specified file
`print name`	Prints the named file
`printmode mode`	Sets the print mode (the mode must be text or graphics)
`prompt`	Toggles prompt mode off (similar to the command in `ftp`)
`put lfile rfile`	Copies a local file (`lfile`) to a remote file (`rfile`)
`queue`	Displays the print queue
`quit`	Logs off the Windows server
`rd dir`	Deletes the specified directory on the server
`recurse`	Toggles directory recursion during file get and put operations
`rm name`	Deletes all files with the specified name
`rmdir name`	Deletes the specified directory
`translate`	Toggles text translation (converts a line feed to a carriage return–line-feed pair).

Learning More about Samba

There is much more to Samba than what I show in this chapter. To learn more about Samba, you can consult the following resources:

- Use the documentation in the `/usr/share/doc/samba-*` directory of your system. In particular, you can consult the PDF files `Samba-Guide.pdf`, `Samba-HOWTO-Collection.pdf`, and `Samba-Developers-Guide.pdf`. The `Samba-Guide.pdf` is an electronic version of the *Samba-3 by Example* book by John Terpstra. It has examples of deploying Samba in various environments.
- To view Samba documentation online, visit `www.samba.org/samba/docs/man/Samba-HOWTO-Collection/`.
- *Using Samba, Second Edition*, by Jay Ts, Robert Eckstein, and David Collier-Brown (O'Reilly & Associates, February 2003)

You should also visit `www.samba.org/` to keep with the latest news on Samba development. That site also has links to resources for learning Samba.

Summary

Linux includes two prominent file-sharing services: NFS for sharing files with other UNIX systems (or PCs with NFS client software) and Samba for file sharing and print sharing with Windows systems. This chapter described both NFS and Samba.

In this chapter, you learned the following:

- Network File System (NFS) enables you to mount a file system from a remote computer on your local system. Linux includes everything you need to set up your system as a NFS server.
- To export a file system, add that file system in the `/etc/exports` file, and type **/usr/sbin/exportfs -a** to export the file systems. You also have to start the NFS servers by typing the command `service nfs start`. After that, other NFS client systems on the network can mount the exported file systems by using the `mount` command.
- For PC networks that use Windows networking, you can configure a Linux PC as a Windows server: all you have to do is use the Samba software package from the companion DVD. This chapter shows you how to install and use Samba.
- Samba configuration is somewhat complex — you configure using settings in the text file `/etc/samba/smb.conf`.
- You can access Windows servers and their resources from a Samba server with the smbclient program.

Part IV

Managing Linux

Advanced System Administration

Chapter 20

Secrets in This Chapter

Chapter 12 introduced the basics of systems and network administration on the Linux system. In several other chapters, you learned many other systems-administration tasks, such as configuring X, setting up printers, connecting to the Internet, and managing Internet services. This chapter introduces you to a number of other important system-administration tasks that I do not cover elsewhere in this book.

This chapter starts with a description of how Linux boots, so you know how to start and stop services automatically at boot time. Then, you learn about automating system tasks with the `at` command or the `crontab` facility of Linux. Next, this chapter focuses on another important systems-administration task—backing up and restoring files from backup storage media. Finally, the chapter discusses monitoring system performance.

Understanding How Linux Boots

It is important to learn the sequence in which Linux starts processes as it boots. You can use this knowledge to start and stop services, such as the Web server and Network File System (NFS). The next few sections provide you with an overview of how Linux boots and starts the initial set of processes. These sections also familiarize you with the shell scripts, called *initscripts*, that start various services on a Linux system.

Understanding the init Process

When Linux boots, it loads and runs the Linux kernel—the core operating-system program—from the hard disk. The Linux kernel is designed to run other programs. The kernel starts a process named init, which, in turn, starts the initial set of processes on your Linux system.

To see the processes currently running on the system, type the command **ps ax | more**. The first column in the output has the heading `PID`; that column shows a number for each process. PID stands for process ID (identification), which is a sequential number assigned by the Linux kernel. Right at the beginning of the list of processes, you notice a process with a process ID (PID) of 1:

```
PID TTY      STAT   TIME COMMAND
  1 ?        S      0:01 init [5]
```

As you can see, init is the first process, and it has a PID of 1. Also, init starts all other processes in your Linux system. That's why init is referred to as the mother of all processes.

What the init process starts depends on the following:

- The *run level*, which designates a system configuration in which only a selected group of processes exists
- The contents of the `/etc/inittab` file, a text file that specifies the processes to start at different run levels
- A number of shell scripts (called *initscripts* and located in the `/etc/rc.d` directory and its subdirectories) that are executed at a specific run level

The current run level, together with the contents of the /etc/inittab file, controls which processes init starts. Linux, for example, has seven run levels: 0, 1, 2, 3, 4, 5, and 6. By convention, some of these levels indicate specific processes that run at that level. Run level 1, for example, denotes a single-user, standalone system. Run level 0 means the system is halted, and run level 6 means the system is being rebooted. Run levels 2 through 5 are multiuser modes with various levels of capabilities, but run level 4 is not currently used.

init runs a specific sequence of shell scripts at each run level. Those scripts are often referred to as *initscripts* because they are run by init.

To check the current run level, type the runlevel command (type **/sbin/runlevel** if you are not logged in as root). Here is a typical output from runlevel:

```
N 5
```

The first character of the output shows the previous run level (N means there is no previous run level), and the second character shows the current level (5), indicating that the system is currently at run level 5.

The initial default run level is 3 for text-mode login screens and 5 for the graphical login screen. A line in the /etc/inittab file with the initdefault action indicates the default run level. Here is the line from /etc/inittab file that sets the default run level to 5:

```
id:5:initdefault:
```

If you change that 5 to a 3, the system would boot into a text-mode login screen.

Before you rush in and edit the /etc/inittab file, you should try out the run level by using the init command. For example, to switch to run level 3, log in as root and type the following command:

```
init 3
```

Examining the /etc/inittab File

The /etc/inittab file is the key to understanding the processes that init starts at various run levels. You can look at the contents of the file by using the more command as follows:

```
more /etc/inittab
```

To see the contents of the /etc/inittab file with the more command, you do not have to log in as root.

The following is a listing of the /etc/inittab file on my Linux system, which is set up for a graphical login screen:

```
#
# inittab       This file describes how the INIT process should set up
#               the system in a certain run-level.
#
# Author:       Miquel van Smoorenburg, <miquels@drinkel.nl.mugnet.org>
#               Modified for RHS Linux by Marc Ewing and Donnie Barnes
#
```

```
# Default runlevel. The runlevels used by RHS are:
#   0 - halt (Do NOT set initdefault to this)
#   1 - Single user mode
#   2 - Multiuser, without NFS (The same as 3, if you do not have networking)
#   3 - Full multiuser mode
#   4 - unused
#   5 - X11
#   6 - reboot (Do NOT set initdefault to this)
#
id:5:initdefault:

# System initialization.
si::sysinit:/etc/rc.d/rc.sysinit

l0:0:wait:/etc/rc.d/rc 0
l1:1:wait:/etc/rc.d/rc 1
l2:2:wait:/etc/rc.d/rc 2
l3:3:wait:/etc/rc.d/rc 3
l4:4:wait:/etc/rc.d/rc 4
l5:5:wait:/etc/rc.d/rc 5
l6:6:wait:/etc/rc.d/rc 6

# Trap CTRL-ALT-DELETE
ca::ctrlaltdel:/sbin/shutdown -t3 -r now

# When our UPS tells us power has failed, assume we have a few minutes
# of power left.  Schedule a shutdown for 2 minutes from now.
# This does, of course, assume you have powerd installed and your
# UPS connected and working correctly.
pf::powerfail:/sbin/shutdown -f -h +2 "Power Failure; System Shutting Down"

# If power was restored before the shutdown kicked in, cancel it.
pr:12345:powerokwait:/sbin/shutdown -c "Power Restored; Shutdown Cancelled"


# Run gettys in standard runlevels
1:2345:respawn:/sbin/mingetty tty1
2:2345:respawn:/sbin/mingetty tty2
3:2345:respawn:/sbin/mingetty tty3
4:2345:respawn:/sbin/mingetty tty4
5:2345:respawn:/sbin/mingetty tty5
6:2345:respawn:/sbin/mingetty tty6

# Run xdm in runlevel 5
x:5:once:/etc/X11/prefdm -nodaemon
```

Lines that start with a hash mark (#) are comments. The first noncomment line in the /etc/inittab file specifies the default run level as follows:

```
id:5:initdefault:
```

Even though you do not know the syntax of the `/etc/inittab file` (and you really do not have to learn the syntax), you probably can guess that the 5 in that line denotes the default run level for the graphical login screen. Thus, if you want your system to run at level 3 after startup (for a plaintext-mode login screen), all you have to do is change 5 to 3.

insider insight

Each entry in the `/etc/inittab` file specifies a process that init should start at one or more specified run levels. You simply concatenate all the run levels (for example, 235 for run levels 2, 3, and 5) at which the process should run. Each entry in the `inittab` file has four fields — separated by colons — in the following format:

```
id:runlevels:action:process
```

Type man inittab to see the detailed syntax of the entries in the `inittab` file.

The fields in each entry of the `inittab` file have the following meanings:

- The *id* field is a unique, 1- to 4-character identifier. The init process uses this field internally. You can employ any identifier you want, as long as you do not use the same identifier on more than one line. For example, `si`, `x`, and `1` are all valid identifiers.
- The *runlevels* field is a sequence of zero or more characters, each denoting a run level. The line with the identifier `1`, for example, applies to run levels 2 through 5; so the *runlevels* field for this entry is `2345`. This field is ignored if the *action* field is set to `sysinit`, `boot`, or `bootwait`.
- The *action* field tells the init process what to do with the entry. If this field is `initdefault`, for example, init interprets the *runlevels* field as the default run level. If this field is set to `wait`, init starts the process specified in the process field and waits until that process exits. Table 20-1 summarizes the valid action values you can use in the *action* field.
- The *process* field specifies the process that init has to start. Of course, some settings of the *action* field require no process field. (When *action* is set to `initdefault`, for example, you don't need a *process* field.)

Table 20-1: Valid Actions in /etc/inittab

Action	*Description*
`respawn`	Restarts the process whenever it terminates.
`wait`	Restarts the process once at the specified run level; init waits until that process exits.
`once`	Executes the process once at the specified run level.
`boot`	Executes the process as the system boots, regardless of the run level (the *runlevels* field is ignored).
`bootwait`	Executes the process as the system boots; init waits for the process to exit (the *runlevels* field is ignored).
`off`	Nothing happens for this action.

(continued)

Table 20-1 *(continued)*

Action	*Description*
ondemand	Executes the process at the specified run level, which must be one of a, b, or c.
initdefault	Starts the system at this run level after it boots. The process field is ignored for this action.
sysinit	Executes the process as the system boots before any entries with the boot or bootwait actions (the *runlevels* field is ignored).
powerwait	Executes the process when init receives the SIGPWR signal, indicating that there is something wrong with the power. Then, init waits until the process exits.
powerfail	Similar to powerwait, except that init does not wait for the process to exit.
Powerfailnow	Executes the process when init receives a signal that the battery of the external uninterruptible power supply (UPS) is almost empty and the power is failing (provided that the external UPS and the monitoring process can detect this condition).
Powerokwait	Executes the process when init receives the SIGPWR signal and the /etc/powerstatus file contains the word OK (indicating that the power is back on).
Ctrlaltdel	Executes the process when init receives the SIGINT signal, which occurs when you press Ctrl-Alt-Del. Typically, the process field should specify the /sbin/shutdown command with the -r option to reboot the PC.
kbdrequest	Executes the process when init receives a signal from the keyboard driver that a special key combination has been pressed. The key combination should be mapped to KeyboardSignal in the keymap file.

The *process* field is typically specified in terms of a shell script, which, in turn, can start several processes. The l5 entry in /etc/inittab, for example, is specified as follows:

```
l5:5:wait:/etc/rc.d/rc 5
```

This entry specifies that init should execute the file /etc/rc.d/rc with 5 as an argument. If you look at the file /etc/.rc.d/rc, you notice that it is a shell-script file. You can study this file to see how it starts various processes for run levels 1 through 5.

The last line of the /etc/inittab file starts the graphical login process with the following entry:

```
x:5:once:/etc/X11/prefdm -nodaemon
```

This command runs /etc/X11/prefdm, which is a shell script that starts the graphical display manager. The display manager, in turn, displays the graphical login dialog box that enables you to log into the system.

caution

If you want to disable the GUI and use text login, you can do so by editing the `/etc/inittab` file. Locate the line containing `initdefault`, and make sure that it reads as follows (the run level appearing between the two colons should be 3):

```
id:3:initdefault:
```

Before you edit the `/etc/inittab` file, you should know that any errors in this file may prevent Linux from starting up to a point at which you can log in. If you cannot log in, you cannot use your system. You should always try out a specific run level with the `init` command before you actually change the default run level by editing the `/etc/inittab` file. In case of errors in the `/etc/inittab` file, you can type `init 1` to enter single-user mode, and then edit the file to correct the error.

Trying Out a New Run Level with the init Command

To try a new run level, you do not have to change the default run level in the `/etc/inittab` file. If you log in as `root`, you can change the run level (and, consequently, the processes that run in Linux) with the `init` command, which has the following format:

```
init runlevel
```

Here, *`runlevel`* must be a single character denoting the run level you want. To put the system in single-user mode, for example, type the following:

```
init 1
```

Thus, if you want to try run level 5 (assuming that your system is not set up for a graphical login screen yet) without changing the `/etc/inittab` file, enter the following command at the shell prompt:

```
init 5
```

The system should end all current processes and enter run level 5. By default, the `init` command waits 20 seconds before stopping all current processes and starting the new processes for run level 5.

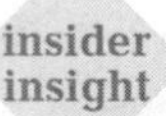

To switch to run level 5 immediately, type the command init -t0 5. The number after the `-t` option indicates the number of seconds init waits before changing the run level.

You can also use the `telinit` command, which is simply a symbolic link to init. If you make changes to the `/etc/inittab` file and want init to reload its configuration file, use the command `telinit q`.

Understanding the Linux initscripts

The init process runs a number of scripts at system startup. Notice the following lines that appear near the beginning of the `/etc/inittab` file:

```
# System initialization.
si::sysinit:/etc/rc.d/rc.sysinit
```

As the comment on the first line indicates, the second line causes init to run the /etc/rc.d/rc.sysinit script—the first Linux startup script that init runs.

The rc.sysinit script performs many initialization tasks, such as mounting the file systems, setting the clock, configuring the keyboard layout, starting the network, and loading many other driver modules. The rc.sysinit script performs these initialization tasks by calling many other scripts and reading configuration files located in the /etc/sysconfig directory.

After executing the /etc/rc.d/rc.sysinit script, the init process runs the /etc/rc.d/rc script with the run level as argument. For example, for run level 5, the following line in /etc/inittab specifies what init has to execute:

```
l5:5:wait:/etc/rc.d/rc 5
```

This says that init should execute the command /etc/rc.d/rc 5 and wait until that command completes.

The /etc/rc.d/rc script is somewhat complicated. Here is how it works:

- It changes to the subdirectory corresponding to the run level—rc0.d for run level 0, rc1.d for run level 1, and so on. For example, for run level 5, the script changes to the /etc/rc.d/rc5.d directory.
- In the directory that corresponds with the run level, /etc/rc.d/rc looks for all files that begin with a K and executes each of them with the argument stop. This kills currently running processes. Then, it locates all files that begin with an S and executes each file with an argument of start. This starts the processes needed for the specified run level.

All the scripts in run level directories—rc0.d, rc1.d, rc2.d, and so on—are symbolic links to scripts located in the /etc/rc.d/init.d directory. These scripts are called *initscripts* and they can start, stop, and restart services.

To see what is executed at a run level, look at the contents of that run level's subdirectory with the ls command. For example, to see what scripts /etc/rc.d/rc runs at run level 5, type the following command:

```
ls -l /etc/rc.d/rc5.d | cut -c41-
```

Here's a partial list of files by command (the cut command displays lines starting on the 41st character; characters before the 41st character are not displayed):

```
K01yum -> ../init.d/yum
K02NetworkManager -> ../init.d/NetworkManager
K05innd -> ../init.d/innd
... Lines Deleted ...
KK90bluetooth -> ../init.d/bluetooth
K94diskdump -> ../init.d/diskdump
S05kudzu -> ../init.d/kudzu
S08iptables -> ../init.d/iptables
S09isdn -> ../init.d/isdn
S09pcmcia -> ../init.d/pcmcia
```

```
S10network -> ../init.d/network
... Lines Deleted ...
S90crond -> ../init.d/crond
S90xfs -> ../init.d/xfs
S95anacron -> ../init.d/anacron
S95atd -> ../init.d/atd
S97messagebus -> ../init.d/messagebus
S97rhnsd -> ../init.d/rhnsd
S98cups-config-daemon -> ../init.d/cups-config-daemon
S98haldaemon -> ../init.d/haldaemon
S99local -> ../rc.local
```

As this listing of the `/etc/rc.d/rc5.d` directory shows, all files with names starting with `K` and `S` are symbolic links to scripts that reside in the `/etc/rc.d/init.d` directory—except for `S99local`, which is a link to `/etc/rc.d/rc.local`. The `K` scripts stop ("kill") servers, whereas the `S` scripts start servers. The `/etc/rc.d/rc` script executes these files exactly in the order that they appear in the directory listing. Thus, the prefixes `S05`, `S10`, `S90`, and so on have been selected judiciously to ensure that services start in the correct order.

Note that the `S99local` file is a symbolic link to the `/etc/rc.d/rc.local` script. This means that `/etc/rc.d/rc.local` is executed after all other scripts. So you can place in that script any command you want executed whenever your Linux system boots, regardless of run level.

Manually Starting and Stopping Servers

The Linux initscripts reside in the `/etc/rc.d/init.d` directory. You can manually invoke scripts in this directory to start, stop, or restart specific processes—usually servers. For example, to stop the Apache Web server (the program's name is httpd), type the following command:

```
/etc/rc.d/init.d/httpd stop
```

The `/etc/init.d` file is defined as a symbolic link to `/etc/rc.d/init.d`. Therefore, you can also execute the previous command as follows:

```
/etc/init.d/httpd stop
```

If httpd is already running and you want to restart it, all you have to do is change the `stop` to `restart`, like this:

```
/etc/init.d/httpd restart
```

insider insight

`/sbin/service` provides a more logical way to start, stop, and restart services. When you log in as root, `/sbin` is already in your `PATH` environment, so you can execute the initscripts by using the `service` command with the following syntax:

```
service servicename action
```

where *`servicename`* is the name of the service and *`action`* is one of `start`, `stop`, or `restart`. The *`servicename`* is the name of the initscript in `/etc/init.d` directory. Typically, the initscript name is the same as the name of the server. For example, the initscript for the Web server (httpd) is also named httpd. Thus, you restart the Web service by typing **service httpd restart**.

You can enhance your system-administration skills by familiarizing yourself with the initscripts in the `/etc/init.d` directory. To see its listing, type the following command:

```
ls /etc/init.d
```

Here's the output of that command on a Fedora system:

```
acpid               gdm-allow-login  mDNSResponder   postgresql    syslog
anacron             gdm-early-login  messagebus      psacct        tomcat5
apmd                gpm              mysqld          rdisc         tux
atd                 haldaemon        named           rhnsd         vncserver
auditd              halt             netdump         rpcgssd       vsftpd
autofs              hidd             netfs           rpcidmapd     winbind
bluetooth           httpd            netplugd        rpcsvcgssd    xfs
crond               innd             network         rwhod         xinetd
cups                iptables         NetworkManager  saslauthd     ypbind
cups-config-daemon  irda             nfs             sendmail      yppasswdd
dc_client           isdn             nfslock         single        ypserv
dc_server           killall          nifd            smb           ypxfrd
diskdump            kudzu            nscd            snmpd         yum
dovecot             lisa             ntpd            snmptrapd
dund                lm_sensors       pand            spamassassin
firstboot           mdmonitor        pcmcia          squid
functions           mdmpd            portmap         sshd
```

The script names give you some clue about which server the script can start and stop. For example, the `nfs` script starts and stops the processes required for NFS (Network File System) services. At your leisure, you may want to study some of these scripts to see what each one does. You don't have to understand all the shell programming; the comments should help you learn the purpose of each script.

insider insight

The servers that initscripts start are often referred to as daemons. In UNIX, *daemon* is just a term used to describe background processes that monitor and perform many critical system functions. Typically, a daemon is started when the system boots, and daemon processes run as long as the system is up. Most daemons have the capability to restart copies of themselves to handle specific tasks. Also, although this is not a rule, most daemons have names that end with *d*, such as crond, syslogd, sshd, xinetd, cupsd (the printer daemon), named, and httpd. Another characteristic of daemons is that they do not require user interaction, so no terminal devices are associated with a daemon.

Configuring Servers to Start Automatically at Boot Time

Although you can start, stop, and restart servers manually by using the scripts in the /etc/rc.d/init.d directory, you have to set up symbolic links in the scripts for an appropriate run level. For example, to start the DNS server—named—in run level 5, you need an S script in the run level 5 directory (/etc/rc.d/rc5.d). Furthermore, that S script should be a symbolic link to the /etc/rc.d/init.d/named file. You set up such symbolic links to configure servers to start automatically at boot time. Luckily, you do not have to do this job by hand. Instead, you can use the /sbin/chkconfig or /usr/sbin/ntsysv program.

Using chkconfig

The chkconfig program is a command-line utility for querying and updating the run-level scripts in Linux. I introduce you to the chkconfig utility next, but you can learn more about its options by reading the chkconfig man page with the man chkconfig command.

For example, suppose that you want to automatically start the named server at run levels 3 and 5. All you need to do is log in as root, and type the following command at the shell prompt:

```
chkconfig --level 35 named on
```

To see the status of the named server, type the following command:

```
chkconfig --list named
named    0:off  1:off  2:off  3:on   4:off  5:on   6:off
```

The output shows you the status of the named server at run levels 0 through 6. As you can see, named is set to run as run levels 3 and 5. If you now look at the directories /etc/rc.d/rc3.d and /etc/rc.d/rc5.d, you see two new S scripts that are symbolic links to /etc/rc.d/init.d/named. Both of these S scripts are symbolic links to the same script; each link looks like this:

```
lrwxrwxrwx  1 root root 15 Apr 25 19:39 S11named -> ../init.d/named
```

If you want to turn named off, you can do so with the following command:

```
chkconfig --level 35 named off
```

You can use chkconfig to see the status of all services, including the ones started through xinetd. For example, you can view the status of all services by typing the following command:

```
chkconfig --list | more
```

The output shows the standalone services started by initscripts as well as those managed by the xinetd server:

```
NetworkManager  0:off  1:off  2:off  3:off  4:off  5:off  6:off
acpid           0:off  1:off  2:off  3:on   4:on   5:on   6:off
anacron         0:off  1:off  2:on   3:on   4:on   5:on   6:off
apmd            0:off  1:off  2:on   3:on   4:on   5:on   6:off
atd             0:off  1:off  2:off  3:on   4:on   5:on   6:off
auditd          0:off  1:off  2:on   3:on   4:on   5:on   6:off
autofs          0:off  1:off  2:off  3:on   4:on   5:on   6:off
```

```
bluetooth       0:off   1:off   2:off   3:off   4:off   5:off   6:off
crond           0:off   1:off   2:on    3:on    4:on    5:on    6:off
cups            0:off   1:off   2:on    3:on    4:on    5:on    6:off
... many lines of output deleted ...
xinetd based services:
        chargen:        off
        chargen-udp:    off
        cvs:            off
        daytime:        off
        daytime-udp:    off
        echo:           off
        echo-udp:       off
        eklogin:        off
        gssftp:         off
        klogin:         off
        krb5-telnet:    off
        kshell:         off
        ktalk:          off
        rsync:          off
        telnet:         off
        time:           off
        time-udp:       off
```

The output shows the status of each service for each of the run levels from 0 through 6. For each run level, the service is either on or off. At the very end of the listing, chkconfig displays a list of the services that xinetd controls (see Chapter 6 for more information on xinetd). Each xinetd-based service is also marked on or off, depending on whether or not xinetd is configured to start the service.

Using the Service Configuration Utility

If you don't like typing the `chkconfig` commands, you can use a graphical service configuration utility program to configure the services. To run the service configuration utility, log in as root and select Desktop ➪ System Settings ➪ Server Settings ➪ Services from the GNOME desktop. You can then turn services on or off from the service configuration window (see Figure 20-1).

The service configuration utility shows the names of services in a scrolling list. Each line in the list shows the name of a service with a box in front of the name. A check mark in the box indicates that the service is already selected to start at boot time for the current run level. When the dialog box first appears, many services are already selected.

You can scroll up and down the list and click on the box to select or deselect a service. If you click the box, the check mark alternately turns on and off. To learn more about a service, click the service name and a brief description appears in the right-hand side of the window. For example, Figure 20-1 shows the help text for the atd service. Additionally, the utility also shows you whether the selected service is currently running or not.

After you select all the servers you want to start when the system boots, select File ➪ Save Changes to save the changes. Then, select File ➪ Quit to exit.

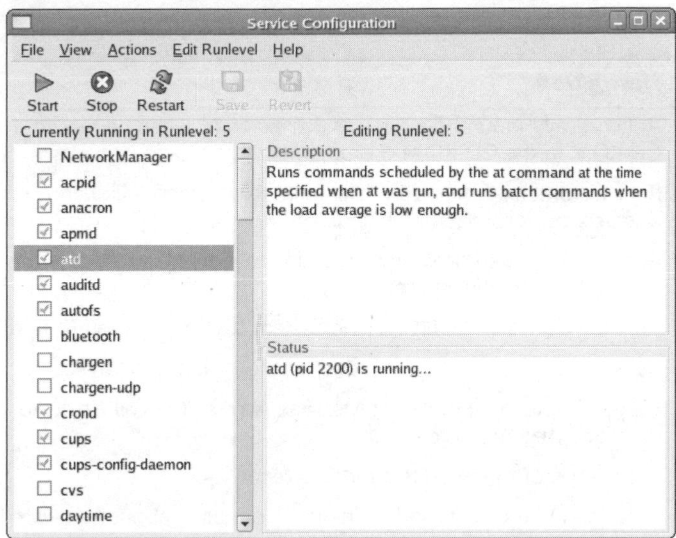

Figure 20-1: Using the Service Configuration Utility to Select the Services You Want to Start Automatically.

> caution
>
> **By default, the service configuration utility configures the selected services for the current run level. This means that if you are accessing it from the graphical desktop, the system is in run level 5 and the services you configure are set to start at run level 5. If you want to set up the services for a different level, select that run level from the Edit Run level menu.**

Table 20-2 shows a list of the services, along with a brief description of each one. The first column shows the name of the service, which is the same as the name of the program that has to run to provide the service. You may not see all of these services listed when you run the service configuration utility on your system because the exact list of services depends on what is installed on your Linux system.

Table 20-2: Some Common Services in Linux

Service Name	*Description*
acpid	Listens to Advanced Configuration and Power Interface (ACPI) events from the kernel and notifies other programs when such events occur. ACPI events can occur when the kernel puts the computer into a low-power state (for example, standby mode) to save energy.
anacron	Executes commands that are scheduled to run periodically.
apmd	Monitors the Advanced Power Management (APM) BIOS and logs the status of electric power (AC or battery backup).
atd	Runs commands scheduled by the `at` and `cron` commands.

(continued)

Table 20-2 *(continued)*

Service Name	*Description*
autofs	Automatically mounts file systems (for example, when you insert a CD-ROM in the CD-ROM drive).
bluetooth	Runs the Bluetooth host controller interface daemon (hcid) and service discovery protocol daemon (sdpd).
crond	Runs user-specified programs according to a periodic schedule the `crontab` command has set.
cups	Runs the Common UNIX Printing System (CUPS) daemon (`cupsd`).
cups-config-daemon	Runs a daemon that enables printer configuration with CUPS.
dovecot	Allows remote IMAP (Internet Message Access Protocol) clients to download mail messages.
gpm	Enables use of mouse in text-mode screens.
haldaemon	A daemon that collects and maintains information about hardware from several sources.
httpd	This is the Apache Web server.
innd	This is the InterNetNews daemon — the Internet news server you can use to support local newsgroups on your system..
iptables	Automates a packet-filtering firewall with iptables.
irda	Supports communications with IrDA-compliant infrared devices in Linux. (IrDA is a standard for infrared wireless communication at speeds ranging from 2400 bps to 4 Mbps.)
isdn	Starts and stops ISDN (Integrated Services Digital Network) services — a digital communication service over regular phone lines (enable only if you have ISDN service).
kudzu	Probes for new hardware and configures changed hardware.
messagebus	Runs the dbus-daemon that broadcasts notifications of system events and other messages to applications that subscribe.
named	This is a server for the Domain Name Service (DNS) that translates host names into IP addresses. You can run a copy on your system if you want.
netfs	Enables you to mount and unmount all network file systems (NFS, Samba, and Netware).
network	Enables you to activate or deactivate all network interfaces configured to start at system boot time.
nfs	Enables sharing of file systems specified in the `/etc/exports` file using the Network File System (NFS) protocol.
nfslock	Provides file-locking capability for file systems exported using the Network File System (NFS) protocol, so that other systems (running NFS) can share files from your system.
ntpd	This is the server for Network Time Protocol version 4 (NTPv4), which is used for synchronizing clocks on computers in a network.

Service Name	*Description*
pcmcia	Provides support for PCMCIA devices.
portmap	Server used by any software that relies on Remote Procedure Calls (RPC). For example, NFS requires the portmap service.
postgresql	Starts or stops the PostgreSQL server that handles database requests. (PostgreSQL is a free database that comes with Linux.)
rhnsd	Periodically connects to the Red Hat Network Services servers to check for updates and notifications.
rpcgssd	Server that manages RPCSEC_GSS security for NFS version 4 client.
rpcidmapd	A daemon that maps user names to user ID and group ID for NFS version 4 clients and servers.
rpcsvcgssd	Server that manages RPCSEC_GSS security for NFS version 4 server.
rsync	Server that supports remote copying of files. You have to enable `xinetd` for this service to run.
saslauthd	Supports authentication using the Cyrus-SASL (Simple Authentication and Security Layer) software.
sendmail	Moves mail messages from one machine to another. Start this service if you want to send mail from your Linux system. If you do not plan to use your Linux system as a mail server, do not start the sendmail server because it can slow down the booting process and consume unnecessary resources.
smb	Starts and stops the Samba smbd and nmbd services that support LAN Manager services on a Linux system.
snmpd	Simple Network Management Protocol (SNMP) service used for network management functions.
squid	A caching server for Internet objects — anything that can be accessed through HTTP and FTP.
sshd	Server for the OpenSSH (Secure Shell) secure remote login facility.
syslog	Service used by many other programs (including other services) to log various error and status messages in a log file (usually, the `/var/log/messages` file). You should always run this service.
talk	Server that supports chatting with users on other systems. You have to enable xinetd for this service to run.
telnet	Server that supports Telnet remote login sessions. You have to enable xinetd for this service to run.
tomcat5	This is the Apache Tomcat 5.0 Java servlet engine.
tux	This is the kernel-based HTTP server.
vsftpd	Very Secure FTP daemon for file transfers using the File Transfer Protocol (FTP).
winbind	Starts and stops the Samba winbindd server, which provides a name switch capability similar to that provided by the `/etc/nsswitch.conf` file.

(continued)

Table 20-2 *(continued)*

Service Name	Description
xfs	Server that starts and stops the X Font Server.
xinetd	This is the Internet superserver, a replacement for the older inetd. It starts other Internet services, such as Telnet and FTP, whenever they are needed.
yppasswdd	Service needed for password changes in Network Information System (NIS). You do not need to start yppasswdd unless you are using NIS.
ypserv	The server for Network Information System (NIS). You do not need to start ypserv unless you are using NIS.
ypxfrd	A server that helps ypserv. Start this service only if you are using Network Information System (NIS).
yum	Runs a nightly update of the system by using the Yellowdog Updater, Modified (Yum).

Scheduling Jobs in Linux

As a system administrator, you may need to run some programs automatically at regular intervals or execute one or more commands at a specified time in the future. Your Linux system includes the facilities to schedule jobs to run at any future date or time you want. You can set up the system to perform a task periodically or just once. Here are some typical tasks you can perform by scheduling jobs on your Linux system:

- Back up the files in the middle of the night
- Download large files in the early morning when the system is not busy
- Send yourself messages as reminders of meetings
- Analyze the system logs periodically and look for any abnormal activities

You can perform these tasks by using the `at` command or the crontab facility of Linux. The next few sections introduce these job-scheduling features of Linux.

Scheduling One-Time Jobs

You can use the `at` command to schedule the execution of one or more commands at a later time. The atd daemon — a program designed to process jobs submitted using `at` — executes the commands at the specified time, and mails the output to you.

insider insight

Before you try out the `at` command, note that the following configuration files control which users can schedule tasks using the `at` command:

- `/etc/at.allow` contains the names of the users who may submit jobs using the `at` command.
- `/etc/at.deny` contains the names of users not allowed to submit jobs using the `at` command.

If these files are not present, or if there is an empty `/etc/at.deny` file, any user can submit jobs using the `at` command. The default in Fedora Linux is an empty `/etc/at.deny` file, so anyone can use the `at` command. If you do not want some users to use `at`, simply list those user names in the `/etc/at.deny` file.

To use `at` to schedule a one-time job for execution at a later time, follow these steps:

1. Run the `at` command with the date or time when you want your commands executed. When you press Enter, the `at>` prompt appears, as follows:

   ```
   at 21:30
   at>
   ```

   This is the simplest way to indicate the time when you want to execute one or more commands — simply specify the time in a 24-hour format. In this case, you want to execute the commands at 9:30 p.m. tonight (or tomorrow, if it's already past 9:30 p.m.). You can, however, specify the execution time in many different ways (see Table 20-3 for examples).

2. At the `at>` prompt, type the commands you want to execute as if typing input at the shell prompt. After each command, press Enter and continue with the next command. When you are finished entering the commands you want to execute, press Ctrl-D to indicate the end. Here is an example showing a single command:

   ```
   at> ps
   at> <EOT>
   job 1 at 2005-01-21 21:30
   ```

   After you press Ctrl-D, the `at` command responds with a job number and the date and time when the job will execute.

Table 20-3: Specifying the Time of Execution with the at Command

Command	*When the Job Is Run*
`at now`	Immediately
`at now + 15 minutes`	15 minutes from the current time
`at now + 4 hours`	4 hours from the current time
`at now + 7 days`	7 days from the current time
`at noon`	At noontime today (or tomorrow, if already past noon)
`at now next hour`	Exactly 60 minutes from now
`at now next day`	At the same time tomorrow
`at 17:00 tomorrow`	At 5:00 p.m. tomorrow
`at 4:45pm`	At 4:45 p.m. today (or tomorrow, if already past 4:45 p.m.)
`at 3:00 Aug 16, 2005`	At 3:00 a.m. on August 16, 2005

After you enter one or more jobs, you can view the current list of scheduled jobs with the `atq` command:

```
atq
4       2005-04-19 03:00 a
5       2005-08-16 21:57 a
6       2005-10-26 16:45 a
```

The first field on each line shows the job number—the same number that the `at` command displays when you submit the job. The next field shows the year, month, day, and time of execution. The last field shows the jobs pending in the queue named `a`.

If you want to cancel a job, use the `atrm` command to remove that job from the queue. When removing a job with the `atrm` command, refer to the job by its number, as follows:

```
atrm 4
```

This deletes job 4 scheduled for 3:00 a.m., April 19, 2005.

When a job executes, the output is mailed to you. Type **mail** to read your mail and to view the output from your jobs.

Note that `at` is useful for scheduling jobs that need to run irregularly—for instance, if you want to clean up the `/var/logs` directory because the `/var` filesystem is over 85 percent full, you might use `at` to archive the old log files and then delete them to reclaim the disk space.

Scheduling Recurring Jobs

Although `at` is good for running commands at a specific time, it's not useful for running a program automatically at repeated intervals. You have to use `crontab` to schedule such recurring jobs, also called *cron jobs* because they are processed by the cron daemon (crond). You need to do this, for example, if you want to back up your files to tape at midnight every day.

Two files control who can schedule cron jobs using `crontab`:

- `/etc/cron.allow` contains the names of the users who may submit jobs using the `crontab` command.
- `/etc/cron.deny` contains the names of users not allowed to submit jobs using the `crontab` command.

If the `/etc/cron.allow` file exists, only users listed in this file can schedule cron jobs. If only the `/etc/cron.deny` file exists, users listed in this file cannot schedule cron jobs. If neither file exists or if `/etc/cron.deny` is empty, any user can submit cron jobs.

You schedule recurring jobs by placing job information in a file with a specific format and submitting this file with the `crontab` command. The cron daemon—crond—checks the job information every minute and executes the recurring jobs at the specified times.

Any output from the job is mailed to the user who submits the job. (In the submitted job-information file, you may specify a different recipient for the mailed output.)

To submit a cron job, perform the following steps:

1. Prepare a shell script (or an executable program in any programming language) that can perform the recurring task you want to perform. You can skip this step if you want to execute an existing program periodically.
2. Prepare a text file with information about the times when you want the shell script or program (from Step 1) to execute. Submit this file using `crontab`. You can submit several recurring jobs with a single file. Each line with timing information about a job has a standard format with six fields — the first five specify when the job runs, and the sixth and subsequent fields constitute the actual command that runs. For example, here is a line that executes the `myjob` shell script in a user's home directory at 5 minutes past midnight each day:

   ```
   5 0 * * * $HOME/myjob
   ```

   Table 20-4 shows the meaning of the first five fields. Note that an asterisk (*) means all possible values for that field. Also, an entry in any of the first five fields can be a single number, a comma-separated list of numbers, a pair of numbers separated by a dash (indicating a range of numbers), or an asterisk.
3. Suppose the text file `jobinfo` (in the current directory) contains the job information. Submit this information to crontab with the following command:

   ```
   crontab jobinfo
   ```

That's it! You should be set with the cron job. From now on, the cron job should run at regular intervals (as specified in the job information file), and you should receive mail messages with the output from the job.

To verify that the job is indeed scheduled, type the following command:

```
crontab -l
```

The output of the `crontab -l` command shows the cron jobs currently installed in your name. To remove your cron jobs, type **crontab –r**.

Table 20-4: Specifying the Time of Execution in crontab Files

Field Number	*Meaning of Field*	*Acceptable Range of Values*[a]
1	Minute	0–59
2	Hour of the day	0–23
3	Day of the month	0–31
4	Month	1–12 (1 means January, 2 means February, and so on) or the names of months using the first letters (Jan, Feb, Mar, Apr, May, Jun, Jul, Aug, Sep, Oct, Nov, Dec)
5	Day of the week	0–6 (0 means Sunday, 1 means Monday, and so on) or the three-letter abbreviations of the week (Sun, Mon, Tue, Wed, Thu, Fri, Sat)

[a]An asterisk in a field means all possible values for that field. For example, if an asterisk appears in the third field, the job is executed every day.

If you log in as `root`, you can also set up, examine, and remove cron jobs for any user. To set up cron jobs for a user, use this command:

```
crontab -u username filename
```

Here, *username* is the user for whom you install the cron jobs, and *filename* is the file that contains information about the jobs.

Use the following form of `crontab` command to view the cron jobs for a user:

```
crontab -u username -l
```

To remove a user's cron jobs, use the following command:

```
crontab -u username -r
```

Looking at the /etc/crontab File

The cron daemon (crond) also executes the cron jobs listed in the systemwide cron-job file `/etc/crontab`. Here's the default `/etc/crontab` file in Linux (type **cat /etc/crontab** to view the file):

```
SHELL=/bin/bash
PATH=/sbin:/bin:/usr/sbin:/usr/bin
MAILTO=root
HOME=/

# run-parts
01 * * * * root run-parts /etc/cron.hourly
02 4 * * * root run-parts /etc/cron.daily
22 4 * * 0 root run-parts /etc/cron.weekly
42 4 1 * * root run-parts /etc/cron.monthly
```

The first four lines set up several environmental variables for the jobs listed in this file. Note that the `MAILTO` environment variable specifies the user who receives the mail message with the output from the cron jobs in this file.

The line that begins with a # is a comment line. The four lines following the run-parts comment execute the `run-parts` shell script (located in the `/usr/bin` directory) at various times with the name of a specific directory as argument. Each of the arguments to run-parts — `/etc/cron.hourly`, `/etc/cron.daily`, `/etc/cron.weekly`, and `/etc/cron.monthly` — are directories. Essentially, `run-parts` executes all scripts located in the directory that you provide as an argument. This means that you can place scripts in these directories and get `crond` to execute them at the appointed time. For example, a script placed in the `/etc/cron.daily` gets executed at a certain time every day. Table 20-5 lists the directories and when they are executed. You have to look at the scripts in these directories to learn what gets executed at these periodic intervals.

Table 20-5: Script Directories for run-parts

Directory Name	*Contents*
/etc/cron.hourly	Scripts executed every hour
/etc/cron.daily	Scripts executed each day at 4:02 a.m.
/etc/cron.weekly	Scripts executed weekly on Sunday at 4:22 a.m.
/etc/cron.monthly	Scripts to be executed at 4:42 a.m. on the first day of each month

Backing Up and Restoring Files

By now, you know how to perform a number of systems-administration tasks, from automatically starting servers to scheduling periodic jobs. The next few sections introduce you to another system-administration task — backing up and restoring files. You learn about backup strategies, backup media, and how to back up and restore files by using the tape archiver (tar) program that comes with Linux. Also, you learn how to perform incremental and automatic backups on tapes.

Selecting a Backup Strategy and Media

Your Linux system's hard disk contains everything needed to keep the system running, as well as other files, such as documents and databases you need to keep your business running. You need to back up these files so that you can recover quickly and bring the system back to normal in case the hard disk crashes. Typically, you have to follow a strict regimen of regular backups because you can never tell when the hard disk might fail or the file system might get corrupted. To implement such a regimen, you need to decide which files you want to back up, how often, and what backup storage media to use. This is what I mean by selecting a backup strategy and backup media.

Your choice of backup strategy and backup media depends on your assessment of the risk of business disruption because of hard disk failure. Depending on how you use your Linux system, a disk failure may or may not have much impact on you.

For example, if you use your Linux system as a learning tool (to learn about Linux or programming), all you may need are backup copies of some system files required to configure Linux. In this case, your backup strategy can be to save important system-configuration files on one or more floppies every time you change any system configuration.

On the other hand, if you use your Linux system as an office server that provides shared file storage for many users, the risk of business disruption due to disk failure is much higher. In this case, you have to back up all the files every week and back up any new or changed files every day. You should perform these backups in an automated manner (this is where you can use the job-scheduling features from earlier in this chapter). Also, you probably need a backup storage medium that can store large amounts (multiple gigabytes) of data on a single tape. In other words, for high-risk situations, your backup strategy is more elaborate and requires additional equipment (such as a tape drive).

Your choice of backup media depends on the amount of data you have to back up. For a small amount of data, such as system-configuration files, you can use floppy disks as the backup media. If your PC has a Zip drive, you can use Zip disks as backup media; these are good for backing up a single-user directory. To back up servers, you should use a tape drive, typically a 4-mm or 8-mm tape drive that connects to a SCSI controller. Such tape drives can store several gigabytes of data per tape, and you can use them to back up an entire file system on a single tape.

When backing up files to these backup media, you have to refer to the backup device by name. Table 20-6 lists device names for some common backup devices.

Table 20-6: Device Names for Common Backup Devices

Backup Device	*Linux Device Name*
Floppy disk	`/dev/fd0`
IDE Zip drive	`/dev/hdc4` or `/dev/hdd4`
IDE floppy tape (Ftape) drive	`/dev/qft0`
SCSI Zip drive	`/dev/sda` (assuming it's the first SCSI drive; otherwise, the device name depends on the SCSI ID)
SCSI tape drive	`/dev/st0` or `/dev/nst0` (the `n` prefix means that the tape is not rewound after files are copied to the tape)

Taking Stock of Commercial Backup Utilities for Linux

This chapter describes how to back up and restore files using the tape archiver (tar) program that comes with Linux. Although you can manage backups with tar, a number of commercial backup utilities come with GUIs and other features to simplify backups. Here are some well-known backup utilities for Linux:

- **BRU:** — Backup and Restore Utility from The TOLIS Group, Inc. (`www.tolisgroup.com/`)
- **LONE-TAR:** — Tape-backup software package from Lone Star Software Corporation (`www.cactus.com/`)
- **Arkeia:** — Backup and recovery software for heterogeneous networks from Knox Software (`www.arkeia.com/`)
- **CTAR:** — Backup and recovery software for UNIX systems from UniTrends Software Corporation (`www.unitrends.com/products.php`)
- **BrightStor ARCserve Backup for Linux:** — Data protection technology for Linux systems from Computer Associates (`www3.ca.com/Solutions/Product.asp?ID=3370`)

Using the Tape Archiver

You can use the `tar` command to archive files to a device such as a floppy disk or tape. The tar program creates an archive file that can contain other directories and files and (optionally) compress the archive for efficient storage. The archive is then written to a specified device or another file. In fact, many software packages are distributed in the form of a compressed `tar` file.

The command syntax of the tar program is as follows:

```
tar options destination source
```

Here, *options* are usually specified by a sequence of single letters, with each letter specifying what tar should do. *destination* is the device name of the backup device. And *source* is a list of file or directory names denoting the files to back up. Optionally, you can add a hyphen prefix for the options.

Backing Up and Restoring a Single-Volume Archive

For example, suppose you want to back up the contents of the `/etc/X11` directory on a floppy disk. Log in as `root`, place a disk in the floppy drive, and type the following command:

```
tar zcvf /dev/fd0 /etc/X11
```

The tar program displays a list of filenames as each file is copied to the compressed tar archive on the floppy disk. In this case, the options are `zcvf`, the destination is `/dev/fd0` (the floppy disk), and the source is the `/etc/X11` directory (which implies all its subdirectories and their contents). You can use a similar `tar` command to back up files to a tape—simply replace `/dev/fd0` with the tape device—such as `/dev/st0` for a SCSI tape drive.

Table 20-7 defines a few common `tar` options.

Table 20-7: Common tar Options

Option	Definition
c	Creates a new archive
f	Specifies the name of the archive file or device on the next field in the command line
M	Specifies a multivolume archive (the next section describes multivolume archives)
t	Lists the contents of the archive
v	Displays verbose messages
x	Extracts files from the archive
z	Compresses the `tar` archive using gzip

To view the contents of the `tar` archive you create on the floppy disk, type the following command:

```
tar ztf /dev/fd0
```

You should see a list of the filenames (each begins with `/etc/X11`) indicating what's in the backup. In this `tar` command, the `t` option lists the contents of the `tar` archive.

To learn how to extract the files from a `tar` backup, try the following steps while logged in as `root`:

1. Change the directory to `/tmp` by typing this command:

   ```
   cd /tmp
   ```

   This is where you extract the files from the `tar` backup.

2. Type the following command:

   ```
   tar zxvf /dev/fd0
   ```

   This `tar` command uses the `x` option to extract the files from the archive stored on `/dev/fd0` (the floppy disk).

If you check the contents of the `/tmp` directory, notice that the `tar` command creates an `etc/X11` directory tree in `/tmp` and restores all the files from the `tar` archive into that directory. The `tar` command strips off the leading / from the filenames in the archive and restores the files in the current directory. If you want to restore the `/etc/X11` directory from the archive on the floppy, use this command:

```
tar zxvf /dev/fd0 /
```

The / at the end of the command denotes the directory where you want to restore the backup files.

As you can see, the `tar` command enables you to create, view, and restore an archive. You can store the archive in a file or in any device you specify with a device name.

Backing Up and Restoring a Multivolume Archive

Sometimes the capacity of a single storage medium is less than the total storage space needed to store the archive. In this case, you can use the `M` option for a multivolume archive — meaning the archive can span multiple tapes or floppies. Note, however, that you cannot create a compressed, multivolume archive. You have to drop the `z` option. To see how multivolume archives work, log in as `root`, place one disk in the floppy drive, and type the following `tar` command:

```
tar cvfM /dev/fd0 /usr/share/doc/ghostscript*
```

Note the `M` option in the option letters; it tells `tar` to create a multivolume archive. The `tar` command prompts you for a second floppy when the first one is filled. Take out the first floppy, and insert another floppy when you see the following prompt:

```
Prepare volume #2 for `/dev/fd0' and hit return:
```

When you press Enter, the tar program continues with the second floppy. In this example, you need only two floppies to store the archive; for larger archives, the tar program continues to prompt you for floppies if more floppies are needed.

To restore from this multivolume archive, type **cd /tmp** to change the directory to `/tmp`. Then type:

```
tar xvfM /dev/fd0
```

The tar program prompts you to feed the floppies as necessary.

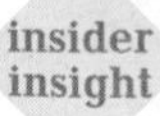

Use the `du -s` command to determine the amount of storage you need to archive a directory. For example, here's how you can get the total size of the `/etc` directory in kilobytes:

```
du -s /etc

69644   /etc
```

The resulting output shows that the /etc directory requires at least 69,644KB of storage space to back up.

Backing Up on Tapes

Although backing up on tapes is as simple as using the right device name in the tar command, you do need to know some nuances of the tape device to use it well. When you use tar to back up to the device named /dev/st0 (the first SCSI tape drive), the tape device automatically rewinds the tape after the tar program finishes copying the archive to the tape. The /dev/st0 device is called a rewinding tape device because it rewinds tapes by default.

If your tape can hold several gigabytes of data, you may want to write several tar archives — one after another — to the same tape (otherwise, much of the tape may be empty). To do this, you do not want the tape device to rewind the tape after the tar program finishes. To help you with this, there are several Linux tape devices that are nonrewinding. The nonrewinding SCSI tape device is called /dev/nst0. Use this device name if you want to write one archive after another on a tape.

After each archive, the nonrewinding tape device writes an end-of-file (EOF) marker to separate one archive from the next. You can use the mt command to control the tape — you can move from one marker to the next or rewind the tape. For example, after you finish writing several archives to a tape using the /dev/nst0 device name, you can rewind the tape with the following command:

```
mt -f /dev/nst0 rewind
```

After rewinding the tape, you can use the following command to extract files from the first archive to the current disk directory:

```
tar xvf /dev/nst0
```

After that, you must move past the EOF marker to the next archive. To do this, use the following mt command:

```
mt -f /dev/nst0 fsf 1
```

This positions the tape at the beginning of the next archive. You can now use the tar xvf command again to read this archive.

note If you save multiple archives on a tape, you have to keep track of the archives yourself.

Performing Incremental Backups

Suppose that you back up your system's hard disk on a tape by using tar. Because such a full backup can take quite some time, you do not want to repeat this task every night. (Besides, only a small number of files may have changed during the day.) You can use the find command to list those files that have changed in the past 24 hours:

```
find / -mtime -1 -type f -print
```

This command prints a list of files that have changed within the last day. The `-mtime -1` option means that you want the files that were last modified less than one day ago. You can now combine this `find` command with the `tar` command to back up only those files that have changed within the last day:

```
tar cvf /dev/st0 `find / -mtime -1 -type f -print`
```

When you place a command between single back quotes, the shell executes that command and places the output at that point in the command line. The net result is that the tar program saves only the changed files in the archive. Thus, you get an incremental backup that includes files that have changed since the previous day.

Performing Automated Backups

Earlier in this chapter, you learn to use `crontab` to set up recurring jobs (called cron jobs). The Linux system performs these tasks at regular intervals. Backing up your system is a good use of the `crontab` facility. Suppose your backup strategy is as follows:

- Every Sunday at 1:15 a.m., your system backs up the entire disk on the tape.
- Monday through Saturday, your system performs an incremental backup at 3:10 a.m. by saving only those files that have changed during the past 24 hours.

To set up this automated backup schedule, log in as `root` and type the following lines in a file named `backups` (this example assumes that you use a SCSI tape drive):

```
15 1 * * 0 tar zcvf /dev/st0 /
10 3 * * 1-6 tar zcvf /dev/st0 `find / -mtime -1 -type f -print`
```

Next, submit this job schedule by using the following `crontab` command:

```
crontab backups
```

Now, you should be set for an automated backup. All you need to do is place a new tape in the tape drive everyday. You should also give each tape an appropriate label.

Managing Devices

Everything you use to work with your computer is a device. The keyboard you use to type and the mouse you click, the hard disk where you store everything, and the printer where you get your hard copies — these are all devices. You often have to load device drivers to use the device in Linux.

To manage devices, you need to understand device drivers a bit and learn to use the tools Linux includes to help you manage devices. The next few sections provide a brief overview of device drivers and explain how to manage driver modules.

Understanding Device Drivers

The Linux kernel treats all devices as files and uses a device just as it would use a file — opens it, writes data to it, reads data from it, and closes it when done. This ability to treat every device as a file comes through the use of device drivers. A *device driver* is a special program that controls a particular type of hardware. When the kernel writes data to the device, the device driver does whatever is appropriate for that device. For example, when the kernel writes data to the floppy drive, the floppy device driver puts that data onto the physical medium of the floppy disk. On the other hand, if the kernel writes data to the parallel port device, the parallel port driver sends the data to the printer connected to the parallel port.

Thus, the device driver isolates the device-specific code from the rest of the kernel and makes a device look like a file. Any application can access a device by opening the file specific to that device. Figure 20-2 illustrates this concept of Linux device drivers.

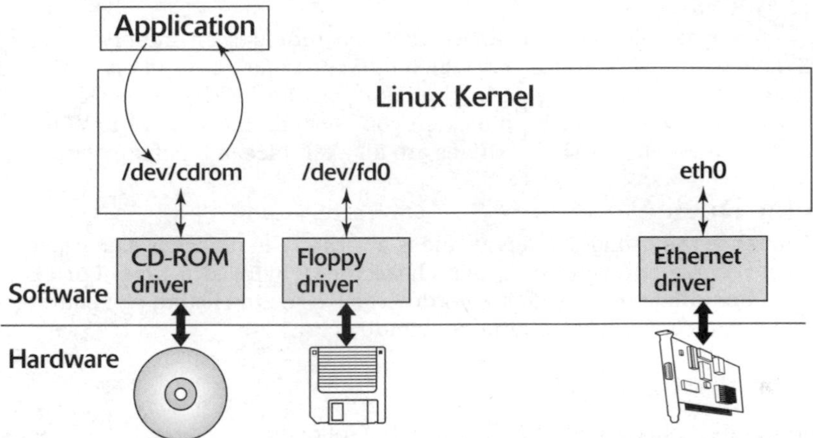

Figure 20-2: Application Accessing Devices through Device Drivers.

Device Files

As Figure 20-2 shows, applications can access a device as if it were a file. These files are special files called device files, and they appear in the `/dev` directory in the Linux file system.

If you use the `ls` command to look at the list of files in the `/dev` directory, you'll see several thousand files. This does not mean that your system has several hundred devices. The `/dev` directory has files for all possible types of devices — that's why the number of device files is so large.

So how does the kernel know which device driver to use when an application opens a specific device file? The answer is in two numbers called the major and minor device numbers. Each device file is mapped to a specific device driver through these numbers.

To see an example of the major and minor device numbers, type the following command in a terminal window:

```
ls -l /dev/hda
```

You should see a line of output similar to the following:

```
brw-r-----  1 root disk 3, 0 Apr 16 15:28 /dev/hda
```

In this line, the major and minor device numbers appear just before the date. In this case, the major device number is 3 and the minor device number is 0. The kernel selects the device driver for this device file by using the major device number.

You don't really need to learn much about the device files and the device numbers, except to be aware of their existence.

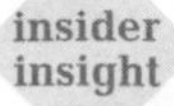

In case you are curious, all the major and minor numbers for devices are assigned according to device type. The Linux Assigned Names And Numbers Authority (LANANA) assigns these numbers. You can see the current device list at `www.lanana.org/docs/device-list/devices.txt`.

Block Devices

The first letter in the listing of a device file also provides an important clue. For the `/dev/hda` device, the first letter is a `b`, which indicates that `/dev/hda` is a *block* device—one that can accept or provide data in chunks (typically 512 bytes or 1KB). By the way, `/dev/hda` refers to the first IDE hard disk on your system (the C drive in Windows). Hard drives, floppy drives, and CD-ROM drives are all examples of block devices.

Character Devices

If the first letter in the listing of a device file is a `c`, then the device is a character device—one that can receive and send data one character (1 byte) at a time. For example, the serial port and parallel ports are character devices. To see the listing of a character device, type the following command in a terminal window:

```
ls -l /dev/ttyS0
```

The listing of this device should be similar to the following:

```
crw-rw----  1 root uucp 4, 64 Apr 16 15:28 /dev/ttyS0
```

Notice that the very first letter is a `c` because `/dev/ttyS0`—the first serial port—is a *character* device.

Network Devices

The network devices, such as Ethernet and dial-up Point-to-Point Protocol (PPP) connections, are somewhat special in that they do not have a file corresponding to the device; instead the kernel uses a special name for the device. For example, the Ethernet devices are named eth0 for the first Ethernet card, eth1 for the second one, and so on. The PPP connections are named ppp0, ppp1, and so on.

Because the network devices are not mapped to device files, there are no files corresponding to these devices in the `/dev` directory.

Persistent Device Naming with udev

Linux kernel 2.6 introduces a new approach for handling devices, based on the following features:

- **sysfs:** Kernel 2.6 provides the sysfs file system that is mounted on the `/sys` directory of the file system. The sysfs file system shows all the devices in the system as well as lots of information about each device. The information includes location of the device on the bus, attributes such as name and serial number, and the major and minor numbers of the device.
- **/sbin/hotplug:** This shell script is called whenever a device is added or removed. It can then do whatever is necessary to handle the device. This script, in turn,

calls other scripts in the /etc/hotplug directory to handle the specific device being hotplugged.

- **/sbin/udev:** This program takes care of dynamically named devices based on device characteristics such as serial number, device number on a bus, or a user-assigned name based on a set of rules that are set through the text files in the /etc/udev/udev.rules.d directory.

The udev program's configuration file is /etc/udev/udev.conf. Based on settings in that configuration file, udev creates device nodes automatically in the /dev directory.

Managing Loadable Driver Modules

To use any device, the Linux kernel must contain the driver. If the driver code is linked into the kernel as a monolithic program — a program that's in the form of a single large file — then adding a new driver would require rebuilding the kernel with the new driver code. Rebuilding the kernel means you have to reboot the PC with the new kernel before you can use the new device driver. Luckily, the Linux kernel uses a modular design that does away with all the rebooting hassles. Linux device drivers can be created in the form of modules that the kernel can load and unload without having to restart the PC.

note

Driver modules are one type of a broader category of software modules called loadable kernel modules (LKM). Other types of kernel modules include code that can support new types of file systems, modules for network protocols, and modules that interpret different formats of executable files.

Loading and Unloading Modules

You can manage the loadable device driver modules by using a set of commands. Table 20-8 summarizes these commands. You have to log in as root to use some of these commands. I explain a few of the commonly used module commands.

Table 20-8: Commands to Manage Kernel Modules

Command	*Description*
insmod	Inserts a module into the kernel.
rmmod	Removes a module from the kernel.
depmod	Determines interdependencies between modules.
lsmod	Lists all currently loaded modules.
modinfo	Displays information about a kernel module.
modprobe	Inserts or removes a module or a set of modules intelligently. For example, if module A requires B, then modprobe will automatically load B when asked to load A.

If you need to use any of these commands, log in as root or type **su -** in a terminal window to become root.

To see what modules are currently loaded, type:

```
lsmod
```

You should see a list of modules. For example, here is a list on one of my PCs:

```
Module                   Size  Used by
vfat                    13505  0
fat                     54749  1 vfat
sd_mod                  20673  0
usb_storage             72073  0
scsi_mod               148361  2 sd_mod,usb_storage
... lines deleted ...
soundcore               10913  1 snd
snd_page_alloc           9669  2 snd_intel8x0,snd_pcm
8139too                 30145  0
mii                      5441  1 8139too
floppy                  65269  0
ext3                   133449  2
jbd                     86361  1 ext3
```

As you may expect, the list of modules depends on the types of devices installed on your system.

The first column lists the names of the modules in the last-to-first order. Thus, the first module in the list is the last one to be loaded. The `Size` column shows the number of bytes that the module occupies in your PC's memory. The remaining columns show other information about each module such as how many applications are currently using the module and the names of the modules that require the module.

The list displayed by `lsmod` includes all types of Linux kernel modules, not just device drivers. For example, the last two modules — `jbd` and `ext3` — are both part of the EXT3 file system (the latest file system for Linux).

Besides `lsmod`, one commonly used module command is `modprobe`. Use `modprobe` whenever you need to manually load or remove one or more modules. The best thing about `modprobe` is that you don't need to worry if a module requires other modules to work. The `modprobe` command automatically loads any other modules that are needed by a module. For example, on my system I can manually load the sound driver with the command:

```
modprobe snd-card-0
```

This command causes `modprobe` to load everything needed to make sound work. On one of my PCs with an Intel 82801 sound card, the `modprobe snd-card-0` command loads `soundcore`, `snd`, `snd_timer`, `snd_pcm`, `snd_ac97_codec`, and `snd_intel8x0` — in that order.

You can use `modprobe` with the `-r` option to remove modules. For example, to remove the sound modules, I use the following command:

```
modprobe -r snd-card-0
```

This command gets rid of all the modules that the `modprobe snd-card-0` command has loaded.

Understanding the /etc/modprobe.conf File

How does the `modprobe` command know that it should load the `snd_intel8x0` driver module when I use a module name `snd-card-0`? The answer is in the `/etc/modprobe.conf` configuration file. That file contains a line that tells `modprobe` what it should load when it sees the module name `snd-card-0`.

To view the contents of `/etc/modprobe.conf`, type

```
cat /etc/modprobe.conf
```

On my Linux PC, the file contains the following lines:

```
alias eth0 8139too
alias snd-card-0 snd-intel8x0
options snd-card-0 index=0
install snd-intel8x0 /sbin/modprobe --ignore-install snd-intel8x0 &&
/usr/sbin/alsactl restore >/dev/null 2>&1 || :
remove snd-intel8x0 { /usr/sbin/alsactl store >/dev/null 2>&1 || : ; };
/sbin/modprobe -r --ignore-remove snd-intel8x0
alias usb-controller ehci-hcd
alias usb-controller1 uhci-hcd
```

Each line that begins with the keyword `alias` defines a standard name for an actual driver module. For example, the first line defines `8139too` as the actual driver name for the alias `eth0`, which stands for the first Ethernet card. Similarly, the second line defines `snd-intel8x0` as the module to load when I use the name `snd-card-0`.

The `modprobe` command consults the `/etc/modprobe.conf` file to convert an alias to the real name of a driver module as well as for other tasks such as obtaining parameters for driver modules. For example, you can insert lines that begin with the `options` keyword to provide values of parameters that a driver may need.

For example, to set the interrupt request (IRQ) parameter for an Yamaha OPL3SA2 sound card (the driver's name is `snd-opl3-sa2`) to 5, I would add the following line to the `/etc/modprobe.conf` file:

```
options snd-opl3sa2 irq=5
```

This line specifies 5 as the value of the parameter named `irq` in the `snd-opl3sa2` module.

If you want to know the names of the parameters that a module accepts, use the `modinfo` command. For example, to view information about the `snd-opl3sa2` driver module, I type **modinfo snd-opl3-sa2** and look in the output for lines that begin with the words `parmtype` and `parm`, like these:

```
parmtype:       irq:array of int
parm:           irq:IRQ # for OPL3-SA driver.
parmtype:       dma1:array of int
parm:           dma1:DMA1 # for OPL3-SA driver.
```

continues

continued

From the resulting output I can guess that `irq` is the name of the parameter for the Interrupt Request parameter.

Unfortunately, the information shown by the `modinfo` command can be somewhat cryptic. The only saving grace is that you may not need to do much more than use a graphical utility to configure the device, and the utility will take care of adding whatever is needed to configuration files such as `/etc/modprobe.conf`.

Managing USB Devices

Linux comes with built-in support for the Universal Serial Bus (USB) — a serial bus that's gradually replacing the functionality of the PC's serial and parallel ports, as well as that of the keyboard and mouse ports. Nowadays, many PC peripherals — such as mouse, keyboard, printer, CD burner, scanner, modem, digital camera, memory card, and so on — are designed to connect to the PC through a USB port.

USB version 1.1 supports data-transfer rates as high as 12 Mbps — 12 million bits per second or 1.5MB per second — compared with 115 Kbps or the 0.115 Mbps transfer rate of a standard serial port. You can daisy-chain up to 127 devices on a single USB bus. The bus also provides power to the devices, and you can attach or remove devices while the PC is running — a capability commonly referred to as *hot plug* or *hot swap*. USB version 2.0 (or USB 2.0 or USB2, for short) ups the ante by raising the data transfer rates to a whopping 480 Mbps, slightly faster than the competing IEEE 1394 (FireWire) bus. Nowadays many devices, such as CD burners and scanners, come with the high-speed USB2 interface. If your PC has older USB 1.1 ports, the USB2 devices can still work, albeit at lower data-transfer rates. Linux supports both USB 1.1 and USB2 interfaces.

Using USB devices in Fedora is easy. You can hot-plug a device into a USB port, and the Linux kernel can detect and load the appropriate device drivers so applications can make use of the device. To be more precise, the kernel can invoke the `/sbin/hotplug` script, which, in turn, calls the appropriate script from the `/etc/hotplug` directory to take care of the chores necessary to make the USB device accessible to applications. For USB mass storage devices, such as CD drives or hard drivers, a properly written script can also mount the device on the Linux file system. If the script does not automatically mount the device, you can do so manually.

insider insight

If Linux does not automatically mount a USB device when you plug it in, you may have to add some rules to an appropriate file in the `/etc/udev/rules.d` directory of your system. To learn more about writing udev rules, consult the online documentation at `www.reactivated.net/writing_udev_rules.html`.

To use a USB printer in Fedora, simply connect the printer to the USB port, power it up, and then follow the steps in Chapter 4 to configure a locally connected queue for the printer. The printer should show up with a device name such as `/dev/usb/lp0` (for the first USB printer), `/dev/usb/lp1` (for the second USB printer), and so on.

Using USB scanners in Fedora is as simple as using USB printers. Just plug the scanner into the USB port, power it up, and you should be able to access it by using the `xsane`—a graphical front-end for scanners that you can start by typing **xsane** in a terminal window. Of course, the USB scanner make and model must be supported by `xsane`. To quickly check whether the kernel has detected your USB scanner, log in as `root` and type **sane-find-scanner** in a terminal window.

The kernel can also automatically mount a USB mass storage device for easy access. Consider, for example, the USB keychain storage device (a USB disk). Just as the name says, these are small memory cards, capable of storing anywhere from 32MB to 1GB. You can carry them around on a keychain—in effect, taking all your data with you wherever you go. Here's how you can use a USB keychain storage device that's already formatted for use in Microsoft Windows:

1. Plug the keychain storage device to the PC's USB port. Sometimes the device plugs directly into the port, but for some devices you have to attach the keychain device to a USB cable and then plug the cable into the USB port. Some USB keychain devices have a small switch on the side that controls whether the keychain is write-protected. If you plan to write to the device, first make sure it's not write-protected or locked.
2. Linux detects the USB storage device. Depending on the hotplug script in the `/etc/hotplug` directory, the kernel may even mount the USB keychain device, but if it does not, you can mount it manually by using the device name for the USB keychain storage. For example, when I plug in a 512MB USB keychain device on my Fedora Core 4 system, the system automatically treats it as a SCSI storage device with device name `/dev/sda1` and mounts it at the `/media/usbdisk` directory. It also adds an icon for the removable media on the GNOME desktop. I can then access the USB disk by double-clicking the desktop icon or by using commands such as `ls /media/usbdisk`.
3. To mount the USB keychain storage device manually, type **mkdir /mnt/flash** to create a mount point. If this is the only USB storage device plugged in, the device name is `/dev/sda1` (USB storage devices appear as SCSI devices). The next USB storage device gets the `/dev/sda2` device name and so on. If a device file is not created for the USB device, you may need to write udev rules; see `www.reactivated.net/writing_udev_rules.html` for more information on how to perform that step.
4. Mount the device with the command

   ```
   mount /dev/sda1 /mnt/flash
   ```
5. To check that the USB device is mounted, type the following command and look for a line in the output that shows `/mnt/flash`:

   ```
   df
   ```

   For example, the following line of output is for a 512MB USB keychain drive:

   ```
   /dev/sda1              507104    198408    308696  40% /mnt/flash
   ```

Now you can access the files on the keychain at the `/mnt/flash` directory. To save a file to the USB keychain storage device, use a command of the following form:

```
cp filename /mnt/flash
```

When you're done using the device, unmount the USB keychain with this command:

```
umount /dev/sda1
```

Monitoring System Performance

A key systems-administration task is to keep track of how well your Linux system performs. You can monitor the overall performance of your Linux system by gathering information such as:

- Central Processing Unit (CPU) usage
- Physical memory usage
- Virtual memory (swap space) usage
- Hard disk usage

Fedora comes with a number of utilities you can use to monitor one or more of these performance parameters. The following sections introduce you to a few of these utilities and show you how to understand the information they present.

Understanding Load Averages

The system performance is often expressed in terms of the *load averages,* which refers to the average number of processes ready to run in the last 1, 5, and 15 minutes. You can think of the load averages as the number of processes waiting to run.

The load averages give you an indication of how busy the system is. In addition to several system monitoring programs, you can get the load averages with the `uptime` command, as follows:

```
uptime
 17:45:32 up 31 days, 22:30,  2 users,  load average: 0.29, 0.16,
0.11
```

The `uptime` command's output shows the current time, how long the system has been up, the number of users, and, finally, the three load averages. Load averages greater than one imply that many processes are competing for the CPU time simultaneously. You can then look at the top CPU processes and try to run these processes one after another rather than all at the same time.

Using top

To view the top CPU processes — the ones that use most of the CPU time — you can employ the top program. To start this program, type **top** in a terminal window (or text console). The top program then displays a text screen listing the current processes, arranged in the order of CPU usage, along with other information, such as memory and swap-space usage. Figure 20-3 shows typical output from the top program.

The top utility updates the display every 5 seconds. You can keep top running in a window so that you can continually monitor the status of your Linux system. You quit top by pressing q or Ctrl-C or by closing the terminal window.

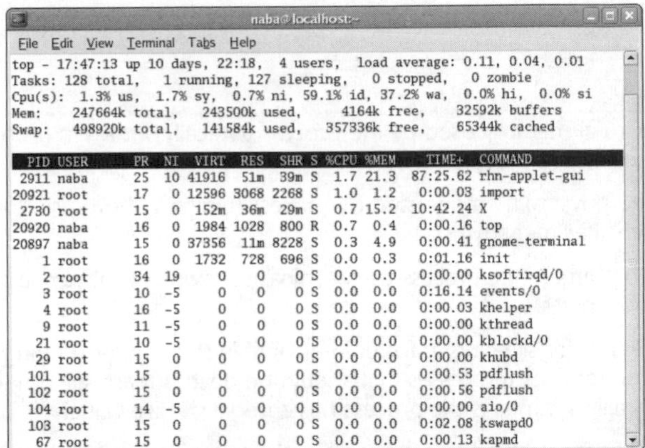

Figure 20-3: Viewing top CPU Processes.

The first six lines of the output screen provide summary information about the system. Here is what these six lines show:

- The first line shows the current time, how long the system has been up, how many users are logged in, and three load averages (the average number of processes ready to run during the last 1, 5, and 15 minutes).
- The second line lists the total number of processes and the status of these processes.
- The third line shows CPU usage—what percentage of CPU time user processes employ, what percentage of CPU time system (kernel) processes employ, and what percentage of time the CPU is idle.
- The fourth and fifth lines show how the physical memory is used—the total amount, how much is used, how much is free, how much is shared, and how much is allocated to buffers (for reading from disk, for instance).
- The sixth line shows how the virtual memory (or swap space) is used—the total amount of swap space, how much is used, how much is free, and how much is cached.

Table 20-9 lists information about the current processes arranged in decreasing order of CPU time usage. The table summarizes the meanings of the column headings in the table that top displays.

Table 20-9: Column Headings in the Top Utility's Display Screen

Heading	*Meaning*
`PID`	The process ID of the process.
`USER`	User name under which the process runs.
`PRI`	Priority of the process—the value ranges from `-20` (highest priority) to `19` (lowest priority); the default is `0`.
`NI`	Nice value of the process (same as negative PRI values).

(continued)

Table 20-9 *(continued)*

Heading	*Meaning*
VIRT	Total amount of virtual memory used by the process (typically shown in kilobytes, but an m suffix indicates megabytes).
RES	Total non-swapped physical memory used by process (typically shown in kilobytes, but an m suffix indicates megabytes).
SHR	Amount of shared memory the process uses (typically shown in kilobytes, but an m suffix indicates megabytes).
S	State of the process (S for sleeping, D for uninterruptible sleep, R for running, W for swapped out, Z for zombies (processes that should be dead but are still running), or T for stopped; a trailing < means the process has a negative nice value).
%CPU	Percentage of CPU time used since last screen update.
%MEM	Percentage of physical memory the process uses.
TIME+	Total CPU time the process has used since it started.
COMMAND	Shortened form of the command that starts the process.

insider insight

If the RES field is drastically smaller than the VIRT field for a process, the process is using too little physical memory compared with what it needs. The result is a lot of swapping as the process runs. You can use the vmstat utility (which you try later in this chapter) to find out how much your system is swapping.

You should also know that you can use combinations of other Linux commands to find the processes that are consuming the most system resources. For example, to find the top five processes that are using the most resources, type the following command line:

```
ps -A -o sz,cmd | sort -bgr | head -5
```

That command line uses ps with appropriate options to display all processes and their size, sort to sort them in decreasing numerical order of size, and, finally, head to display the first five lines of output. Here is typical output from this command line on my system:

```
29771 /usr/lib/firefox-1.0.3/firefox-bin -UILocale en-US
25367 knode
10332 eggcups --sm-config-prefix /eggcups-7f4TzK/ --sm-client-id
117f000001000111366160200000029560004 --screen 0
 9479 /usr/bin/python /usr/bin/rhn-applet-gui --sm-config-prefix
/rhn-applet-18K63w/ --sm-client-id
117f000001000111366160600000029560006 --screen 0
 9446 nautilus --sm-config-prefix /nautilus-ANHdct/ --sm-client-id
117f000001000111366160200000029560003 --screen 0 --no-default-window
```

Using the GNOME System Monitor

Like the text-mode top utility, the GNOME System Monitor tool also enables you to view the system load in terms of the number of processes currently running, their memory usage, and the free disk space on your system. To run this tool, select Main Menu ⇨ System Tools ⇨ System Monitor. The System Monitor starts and displays its output in a window (see Figure 20-4).

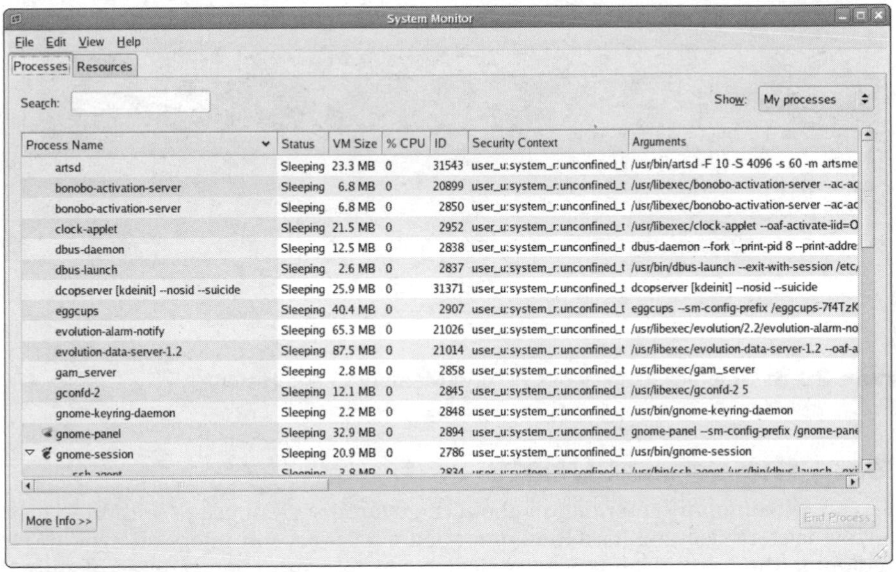

Figure 20-4: Viewing Current Processes in the System Monitor.

The output is similar to the output you see when you type `top` in a text-mode console or terminal window. In fact, the column headings in the table match what the top utility uses in its output. (See Table 20-9 for the meaning of the column headings.) As with the text-mode top utility, the display is continuously updated to reflect the current state of the system.

You can click the columns to sort the processes in different ways. You can use the drop-down list on the upper-right corner of the window to select which processes you want to see. Figure 20-4 shows a list of processes sorted in descending order of their memory usage. For each process, the GNOME System Monitor shows a number of details, including the process ID (PID), the user who starts the process, and the command used to start the process.

The GNOME System Monitor window has another tab that displays the CPU and memory usage history and the free space on the file system. To view this information, click the Resources tab. Figure 20-5 shows the typical graphical output in the Resources tab. You will find the plots easy to understand. At the bottom of the tab, you see the amount of free and used space on the file systems.

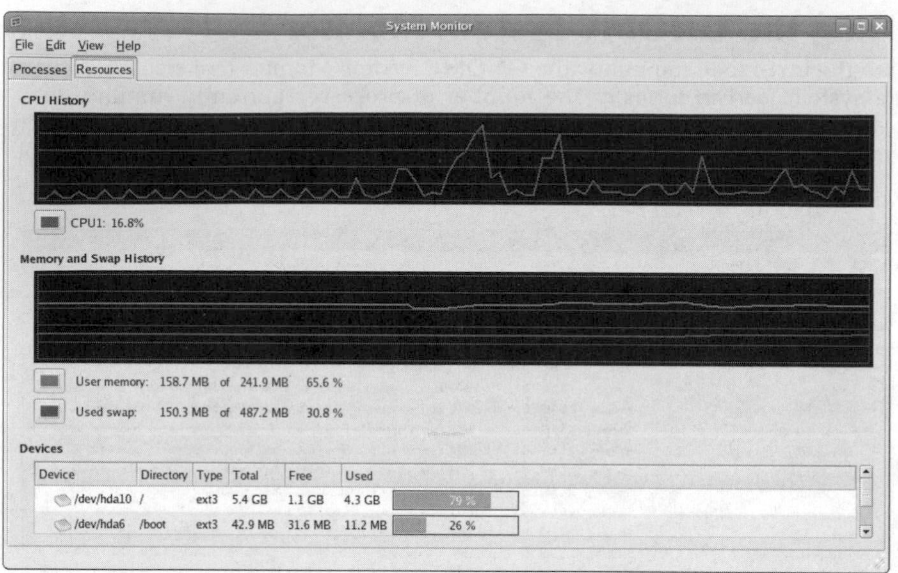

Figure 20-5: Graphical Display of CPU and Memory Usage History.

Using the vmstat Utility

You can get summary information about the overall system usage with the vmstat utility. To view system-usage information averaged over 5-second intervals, type the following command (the second argument indicates the total number of lines of output vmstat should display):

```
vmstat 5 8
procs -----------memory---------- ---swap-- -----io---- --system-- ----cpu----
 r  b   swpd   free   buff  cache   si   so    bi    bo   in    cs us sy id wa
 0  0 168868   4632    660  81208    0    0     6     5    9    33  0  0 99  0
 0  1 169120   4168    476  83980  258   65  1508    98 1245   593  8  4 41 47
 0  1 169436  21028    720  85396  818  266  2281   322 1346   837  7  6  0 87
 0  0 163084  20988   1052  90828  737    0  1913    36 1310   707 11  6 15 68
 0  0 163028  21340   1156  91500  267    0   496    66 1146   733  5  4 75 16
 0  0 160388  24976   1256  92464  202    0   480    10 1137   592  4  3 81 12
 0  0 160388  24968   1288  92524    0    0     5    22 1005   266  1  1 96  1
 0  0 160388  25004   1296  92524    0    0     0     2 1004   267  1  1 98  0
```

The tabular output is grouped into six categories of information, as the fields in the first line of output indicate. The second line shows further details for each of the six major fields. You can interpret the six major fields, as well as the detailed fields in each category, using Table 20-10.

Table 20-10: vmstat Utility Output Fields

Field Name	*Description*
`procs`	Number of processes and their types: `r` = processes waiting to run; `b` = processes in uninterruptible sleep; `w` = processes swapped out, but ready to run.
`memory`	Information about physical memory and swap space usage (all numbers in kilobytes): `swpd` = virtual memory used; `free` = free physical memory; `buff` = memory used as buffers; `cache` = virtual memory that's cached.
`swap`	Amount of swapping (the numbers are in kilobytes per second): `si` = amount of memory swapped in from disk; `so` = amount of memory swapped to disk.
`io`	Information about input and output (the numbers are in blocks per second; the block size depends on the disk device): `bi` = rate of blocks sent to disk; `bo` = rate of blocks received from disk.
`system`	Information about the system: `in` = number of interrupts per second (including clock interrupts); `cs` = number of context switches per second — the number of times the kernel changes which process is running.
`cpu`	Percentages of CPU time used: `us` = percentage of CPU time used by user processes; `sy` = percentage CPU time used by system processes; `id` = percentage of time CPU is idle.

The first line of vmstat output following the two header lines shows the averages since the last reboot. After that, vmstat displays the 5-second average data seven more times over the next 35 seconds. In the vmstat utility's output, high values in the `si` and `so` fields indicate too much swapping. High numbers in the `bi` and `bo` fields indicate too much disk activity.

Checking Disk Performance and Disk Usage

Linux comes with the `/sbin/hdparm` program, which you can use to control IDE or ATAPI hard disks common on most PCs. One feature of the hdparm program is that the `-t` option enables you to determine the rate at which data can be read from the disk into a buffer in memory. For example, here's the result of the command on my system:

```
/sbin/hdparm -t /dev/hda

/dev/hda:
 Timing buffered disk reads:  130 MB in  3.01 seconds =  43.24 MB/sec
```

As you can see, the command requires the IDE drive's device name (`/dev/hda`) as an argument. If you have an IDE hard disk, you can try this command to see how fast data can be read from your system's disk drive.

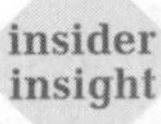

During system startup, the `/etc/rc.sysinit` script runs `/sbin/hdparm` to set the hard disk parameters based on settings in the `/etc/sysconfig/harddisks` file. Type man hdparm to learn more about the hard disk parameters you can set. To set a parameter at boot time, you can place an appropriate line in the `/etc/sysconfig/harddisks` file.

To display the space available in the currently mounted file systems, use the df command. If you want a more human-readable output from df, type the following command:

```
df -h
Filesystem            Size  Used Avail Use% Mounted on
/dev/mapper/VolGroup00-LogVol00
                      7.0G  5.0G  1.7G  75% /
/dev/hda3              99M   17M   77M  18% /boot
/dev/shm              125M     0  125M   0% /dev/shm
/dev/hda2              21G   14G  6.2G  70% /mnt/windows
/dev/hdc              619M  619M     0 100% /media/cdrom
```

As this example shows, the -h option causes the df command to show the sizes in gigabytes (G) and megabytes (M).

To check the disk space a specific directory uses, employ the du command. You can specify the -h option to view the output in kilobytes (k) and megabytes (M), as shown in the following example:

```
du -h /var/log
8.0K    /var/log/news/OLD
28K     /var/log/news
8.0K    /var/log/ppp
8.0K    /var/log/vbox
24K     /var/log/gdm
28K     /var/log/tomcat5
184K    /var/log/audit
44K     /var/log/cups
16K     /var/log/mail
116K    /var/log/samba
8.0K    /var/log/squid
100K    /var/log/httpd
1.6M    /var/log
```

The du command displays the disk space each directory uses, and the last line shows the total disk space that directory uses. If you want to see only the total space a directory uses, use the -s option, like this:

```
du -sh /var
709M    /var
```

This says that the /var directory uses 709MB of disk space.

Exploring the /proc File System

You can find out a great deal about your Linux system by consulting the contents of a special file system known as /proc. Knowing about the /proc file system is useful because it can help you monitor a wide variety of information about your system. In fact, you can even change kernel parameters through the /proc file system and thereby modify the system's behavior.

The /proc file system is not a real directory on the disk but a collection of data structures in memory, managed by the Linux kernel, that appears to the user as a set of directories and files. The purpose of /proc (also called the *process file system*) is to enable users to access information about the Linux kernel and the processes currently running on your system.

You can access the /proc file system just as you access any other directory, but you have to know the meaning of various files to interpret the information. Typically, you can use the cat or more command to view the contents of a file in /proc; the file's contents provide information about some aspect of the system.

As with any directory, you may want to start by looking at a detailed directory listing of /proc. To do so, type **ls -l /proc**. In the output, the first set of directories (indicated by the letter d at the beginning of the line) represents the processes currently running on your system. Each directory that corresponds to a process has the process ID (a number) as its name.

caution

Also notice a very large file named /proc/kcore; that file represents the entire physical memory of your system. Although /proc/kcore appears in the listing as a huge file, there is no physical file occupying that much space on your hard disk. You should not try to remove this file to reclaim disk space.

Several files and directories in /proc contain interesting information about your Linux system. The /proc/cpuinfo file, for example, lists the key characteristics of your system, such as processor type and floating-point processor information. You can view the processor information by typing **cat /proc/cpuinfo**. For example, here is what I get when I type the command on my system:

```
cat /proc/cpuinfo
processor       : 0
vendor_id       : GenuineIntel
cpu family      : 15
model           : 3
model name      : Intel(R) Celeron(R) CPU 2.53GHz
stepping        : 3
cpu MHz         : 2533.114
cache size      : 256 KB
fdiv_bug        : no
hlt_bug         : no
f00f_bug        : no
coma_bug        : no
fpu             : yes
fpu_exception   : yes
cpuid level     : 5
wp              : yes
flags           : fpu vme de pse tsc msr pae mce cx8 apic mtrr pge mca cmov
pat pse36 clflush dts acpi mmx fxsr sse sse2 ss ht tm pbe pni monitor
ds_cpl cid
bogomips        : 4997.12
```

This output is from a 2.53 GHz Intel Celeron system. The listing shows many interesting characteristics of the processor. Notice the line that starts with fdiv_bug. Remember the infamous Pentium floating-point-division bug? The bug is in an instruction called fdiv (for floating-point division). Thus, the fdiv_bug line indicates whether or not this particular Pentium has the bug (fortunately, my system's processor does not).

Table 20-11 summarizes some of the files in the /proc file system from which you can get information about your Linux system. You can view some of these files on your system to see what they contain. Note that not all the files shown in Table 20-11 are present on your system — the contents of the /proc file system depend on the kernel configuration and the driver modules loaded (which, in turn, depend on your PC's hardware configuration).

insider insight You can navigate the /proc file system just as you work with any other directories and files in Linux. Use the more or cat command to view the contents of a file.

Table 20-11: Typical Files and Directories in /proc

File Name	*Content*
/proc/apm	Information about Advanced Power Management (APM).
/proc/bus	Directory with bus-specific information for each bus type, such as PCI.
/proc/cmdline	The command line used to start the Linux kernel (for example, ro root=LABEL=/1 acpi=off rhgb quiet).
/proc/cpuinfo	Information about the CPU (the microprocessor).
/proc/devices	Available block and character devices in your system.
/proc/dma	Information about DMA (direct memory access) channels that are used.
/proc/driver	Directory with information about various drivers (for example, you will find information about the rtc driver for PC's real-time clock in this directory).
/proc/fb	Information about any frame buffer devices.
/proc/filesystems	List of supported file systems.
/proc/fs	Directory with file-system parameters.
/proc/ide	Directory containing information about IDE devices.
/proc/interrupts	Information about interrupt request (IRQ) numbers, how they are used, and how many interrupts were generated for each IRQ.
/proc/iomem	Memory map showing how various ranges of physical memory addresses are being used.
/proc/ioports	Information about input/output (I/O) port addresses and how they are used.
/proc/irq	Directory that contains subdirectories for each interrupt request (IRQ) number, with the smp_affinity file that indicates which of several CPUs should handle that interrupt (applies only to systems with multiple CPUs).
/proc/kcore	Image of the physical memory.
/proc/kmsg	Kernel messages.
/proc/kallsyms	Kernel symbol table.
/proc/loadavg	Load average (average number of processes waiting to run in the last 1, 5, and 15 minutes).

File Name	Content
/proc/locks	Current kernel locks (used to ensure that multiple processes do not write to a file at the same time).
/proc/meminfo	Information about physical memory and swap-space usage.
/proc/misc	Miscellaneous information.
/proc/modules	List of loaded driver modules.
/proc/mounts	List of mounted file systems.
/proc/net	Directory with many subdirectories that contain information about networking.
/proc/partitions	List of partitions known to the Linux kernel.
/proc/pci	Information about PCI devices found on the system.
/proc/scsi	Directory with information about SCSI devices, if any, found on the system.
/proc/stat	Overall statistics about the system.
/proc/swaps	Information about the swap space and how much is used.
/proc/sys	Directory with information about the system. (You can change kernel parameters by writing to files in this directory. This is one way to tune the system's performance, but it requires expertise to do it properly.)
/proc/sysvipc	Information about System V interprocess communication (IPC) resources such as shared memory.
/proc/tty	Information about tty drivers.
/proc/uptime	Information about how long the system has been up.
/proc/version	Kernel version number.

Using sysctl to View and Set Kernel Parameters

As the entry for /proc/sys in Table 20-11 explains, you can change kernel parameters by writing to files in the /proc/sys directory. This is one way to tune the system's performance. Linux also comes with the /sbin/sysctl program that enables you to read and write kernel parameters without having to overwrite files manually in the /proc/sys directory.

In Chapter 13, you encounter an instruction that asks you to log in as root and enable IP forwarding in the kernel by typing the following command:

```
echo "1" > /proc/sys/net/ipv4/ip_forward
```

This is the manual way to set the value of a parameter — using the echo command to copy the value into a file in the /proc/sys directory.

You can perform this same step by running sysctl as follows:

```
/sbin/sysctl -w net.ipv4.ip_forward=1
net.ipv4.ip_forward = 1
```

This sysctl command sets the value of the parameter and echoes the new value for your information. As you can see, you refer to the parameter by using the last part of the pathname excluding /proc/sys, but you use periods (.) instead of slashes (/) as separators. Note that, if you prefer, you can continue to use slashes as separators and can refer to this variable as net/ipv4/ip_forward.

You can use sysctl to both query and set the value of a parameter. To see the value of a parameter, use the parameter's name as an argument like this:

```
/sbin/sysctl dev.cdrom.info
```

The command /sbin/sysctl dev.cdrom.info displays the contents of that parameter. In this case, dev.cdrom.info is a structure that contains many different fields; sysctl shows these fields as separate lines in the output.

For a simple parameter, such as fs.file-max, sysctl displays the single value as shown in the following example:

```
/sbin/sysctl fs.file-max
fs.file-max = 24267
```

The fs.file-max variable denotes the maximum number of file handles the Linux kernel can allocate. If you get error messages about running out of file handles, you may want to increase this value with a command, such as /sbin/sysctl -w fs.file-max=65535.

To use sysctl to modify kernel variables and tune the kernel's performance, you need to know what each parameter means. You can find some documentation on these parameters in the kernel-doc RPM. If you cannot find that RPM in the Fedora/RPMS directory of the companion DVD, make sure that your Fedora system is connected to the Internet and then type **yum install kernel-doc** in a terminal window. After the kernel-doc RPM is installed, type **cd /usr/share/doc/kernel-doc*/Documentation/sysctl** and look at the files in that directory. In particular, look at the /usr/share/doc/kernel-doc*/Documentation/sysctl/kernel.txt file for information on the kernel parameters.

You can see the values of all parameters in the /proc/sys directory by typing the /sbin/sysctl -a command. It's instructive to look through the names of the parameters and their values. You should try the /sbin/sysctl -a command on your system. Table 20-12 lists some of these parameters.

Before you use sysctl to change any of the parameters listed in Table 20-12, you should know that changing some kernel parameters can adversely affect your system's performance and even cause the system to hang. You should play with these parameters only if you know what you are doing. In particular, never play around with kernel parameters on a production system.

If you have a number of parameters to alter using sysctl, you can place the parameters and their values in a file and use the command /sbin/sysctl -p filename to load the settings from that file. For example, when Linux boots, a startup script sets some parameters with the following command:

```
/sbin/sysctl -p /etc/sysctl.conf
```

On my Linux system, the /etc/sysctl.conf file contains the following lines:

```
# For binary values, 0 is disabled, 1 is enabled.  See sysctl(8) and
# sysctl.conf(5) for more details.

# Controls IP packet forwarding
net.ipv4.ip_forward = 0

# Controls source route verification
net.ipv4.conf.default.rp_filter = 1

# Do not accept source routing
net.ipv4.conf.default.accept_source_route = 0

# Controls the System Request debugging functionality of the kernel
kernel.sysrq = 0

# Controls whether core dumps will append the PID to the core filename.
# Useful for debugging multi-threaded applications.
kernel.core_uses_pid = 1

# Controls the use of TCP syncookies
net.ipv4.tcp_syncookies = 1
```

Table 20-12 describes some of the interesting kernel parameters from the /proc/sys directory, as well as the meaning of these parameters.

Table 20-12: Some Kernel Parameters in the /proc/sys Directory

Parameter Name	*Meaning*
fs.file-max	Maximum number of file handles the Linux kernel can allocate.
fs.file-nr	Three values representing the number of allocated file handles, the number of used file handles, and the maximum number of file handles.
kernel.acct	Three values specifying high, low, and frequency that control the logging of process accounting information. When free space on the file system goes below the low (percent), accounting is suspended; it resumes when free space goes above high (percent), and frequency specifies how many seconds the free space information is valid (default values are 4% for high, 2% for low, and 30 seconds for frequency).
kernel.ctrl-alt-del	When set to 0, a Ctrl-Alt-Del keypress is handled by using the init program to restart the system; when set to 1, Ctrl-Alt-Del performs an immediate reboot without even saving any dirty buffers to the disk.
kernel.domainname	The NIS domain name of the system.
kernel.hostname	The host name of the system.

(continued)

Table 20-12 *(continued)*

Parameter Name	*Meaning*
kernel.modprobe	Name of the program that the kernel uses to load one or more modules (for example, /sbin/modprobe) .
kernel.osrelease	The version number of the operating system (for example, 2.6.11-1.1233_FC4).
kernel.ostype	Name of operating system (for example, Linux for all Linux systems).
kernel.panic	Number of seconds the kernel waits before rebooting in case of a panic (default is 0).
kernel.printk	Values that affect the printing or logging of error messages by the kernel.
kernel.shmall	Total amount, in bytes, of shared memory segments that can be created.
kernel.shmmax	Maximum size, in bytes, of shared memory segments that can be created (kernel supports shared memory segments up to 1GB).
kernel.sysrq	When set to 0, the SysRq key is disabled; when set to 1, user can perform specific tasks by pressing Alt-SysRq and a command key (see the file /usr/share/doc/kernel-doc*/Documentation/sysrq.txt for more information).
kernel.version	The build number and the date the kernel was built (for example, #1 Fri Apr 8 08:56:16 EDT 2005).
net.core.netdev_max_backlog	Maximum number of packets that can be queued on input when a network interface receives packets faster than the kernel can process them (default is 300).
net.core.optmem_max	Maximum size of ancillary buffer allowed per socket (default is 10240 bytes, or 10K).
net.core.rmem_default	Default size of socket receive buffer in bytes (default is 65535 bytes, or 64K).
net.core.rmem_max	Maximum size of socket receive buffer in bytes (default is 65535 bytes, or 64K).
net.core.wmem_default	Default size of socket send buffer in bytes (default is 65535 bytes, or 64K).
net.core.wmem_max	Maximum size of socket send buffer in bytes (default is 65535 bytes, or 64K).
net.ipv4.conf.all.accept_redirects	When set to 1, the kernel accepts ICMP redirect messages (should be set to 0 for a system configured as a router)
net.ipv4.conf.all.accept_source_route	When set to 1, accepts source routed packets (should be set to 1 for a system configured as a router).
net.ipv4.conf.all.forwarding	When set to 1, enables IP forwarding for all interfaces.
net.ipv4.conf.all.hidden	When set to 1, hides network addresses from other systems.

Parameter Name	*Meaning*
net.ipv4.conf.all.log_martians	When set to 1, logs all packets with source addresses with no known route.
net.ipv4.conf.all.rp_filter	When set to 0, turns off source validation; when set to 1, performs source validation using reverse path (as specified in RFC 1812).
net.ipv4.conf.all.secure_redirects	When set to 1, accepts ICMP redirect messages only for gateways listed in default gateway list.
net.ipv4.conf.all.send_redirects	When set to 1, sends ICMP redirect messages to other hosts.
net.ipv4.conf.all.shared_media	When set to 1, assumes that different subnets share the media and can communicate directly.
net.ipv4.conf.eth0.accept_redirects	When set to 1, accepts ICMP redirect messages (must be 0 for a system used as a router).
net.ipv4.conf.eth0.forwarding	When set to 1, turns on IP forwarding for the eth0 network interface.
net.ipv4.conf.eth0.hidden	When set to 1, keeps the address hidden from other devices.
net.ipv4.conf.eth0.log_martians	When set to 1, logs packets with impossible addresses in the log file.
net.ipv4.conf.eth0.rp_filter	When set to 0, turns off source validation; when set to 1, performs source validation using reverse path (as specified in RFC 1812).
net.ipv4.icmp_echo_ignore_all	When set to 1, kernel ignores all ICMP ECHO requests sent to it.
net.ipv4.icmp_echo_ignore_broadcasts	When set to 1, kernel ignores all ICMP ECHO requests sent to broadcast or multicast addresses.
net.ipv4.ip_always_defrag	When set to 1, automatically reassembles all fragmented packets (this is enabled when masquerading is enabled).
net.ipv4.ip_autoconfig	Contains 1 if the host receives its IP address by using a mechanism such as RARP, BOOTP, or DHCP; otherwise, it is 0.
net.ipv4.ip_default_ttl	Time-to-live (TTL) for IP packets (default value is 64; this is the maximum number of routers through which the packet can travel).
net.ipv4.ip_forward	When set to 1, packets are forwarded among interfaces.
net.ipv4.ip_local_port_range	Two numbers denoting the range of port numbers used by TCP and UDP for the local port (default range 1024-4999; you can change this to 32768-61000 if you need more ports).
net.ipv4.ip_masq_debug	When set to 1, enables debugging of IP masquerading.
net.ipv4.ipfrag_high_thresh	Maximum memory for use in reassembling IP fragments (default is 262144 bytes).
net.ipv4.ipfrag_low_thresh	When maximum amount of memory net.ipv4.ipfrag_(high_thresh) is already being used to reassemble fragmented IP packets, further packets are discarded until the memory usage comes down to this value (default is 196608 bytes).

(continued)

Table 20-12 *(continued)*

Parameter Name	*Meaning*
net.ipv4.ipfrag_time	Time in seconds to keep an IP fragment in memory (default is 30 seconds).
net.ipv4.tcp_fin_timeout	Number of seconds to wait for a final FIN before the socket is closed — this occurs to prevent denial-of-service attacks (default is 180 seconds).
net.ipv4.tcp_keepalive_probes	Number of keepalive probes TCP sends out before it decides that the connection is broken (default value is 9).
net.ipv4.tcp_keepalive_time	Time in seconds between keepalive messages (default is 7200 seconds, or two hours).
net.ipv4.tcp_max_ka_probes	Maximum number of keepalive probes to send in one interval of the slow timer (default is 5).
net.ipv4.tcp_max_syn_backlog	Length of the backlog queue for each socket (default is 128).
net.ipv4.tcp_retries1	Number of times an answer to a TCP connection request is retransmitted before giving up (default is 7).
net.ipv4.tcp_retries2	Number of times a TCP packet is retransmitted before giving up (default is 15).
net.ipv4.tcp_sack	When set to 1, enables select acknowledgments as specified in RFC 2018.
net.ipv4.tcp_syn_retries	Number of times initial SYNs for a TCP connection attempt are retransmitted (default value is 10).
net.ipv4.tcp_syncookies	When set to 1, sends out SYN cookies when the SYN backlog queue of a socket overflows (this prevents the common SYN flood attack).
net.ipv4.tcp_timestamps	When set to 1, enables timestamps as defined in RFC 1323.
net.ipv4.tcp_window_scaling	When set to 1, enables window scaling as defined in RFC 1323.
vm.dirty_background_ratio	When this much of virtual memory (expressed as a percentage of main memory) is dirty, the pdflush daemon should start flushing the dirty buffers to disk; dirty indicates that a buffer's contents have changed and still remain to be written to the disk. Typical value is 10 percent.
vm.dirty_expire_centisecs	The number of "hundredths of a second" after which dirty data is considered to be old enough to be written out by the pdflush daemon (typically set to 3,000, which means every 30 seconds).
vm.dirty_ratio	When this much virtual memory (expressed as a percentage of main memory) is dirty, a process that's writing to disk will itself start writing out dirty buffers to disk without waiting for the pdflush daemon (typical value is 40 percent).

Parameter Name	Meaning
vm.dirty_writeback_centisecs	The number of "hundredths of a second" that the pdflush daemon waits between writing old dirty data to disk (typically set to 500, which means every 5 seconds).
vm.min_free_kbytes	The minimum number of kilobytes of memory that the kernel must keep free (typically set to around 2,000 kilobytes).
vm.overcommit_memory	If this value is set to 1, the system pretends that there is always enough memory; when it's 0, the kernel checks before each memory allocation request to determine if enough memory remains; when the flag is 2, the kernel never over-commits memory allocations (the default value is 0).
vm.page-cluster	If this value is n, the Linux virtual memory subsystem reads 2^n pages at once (default is 4, which means the VM subsystem reads 16 pages at a time)

Summary

If you use your Linux system for production work (to run an Internet server or an office server, for example), you have to perform some advanced systems-administration tasks. This chapter introduces you to some system-administration tasks I do not cover elsewhere in the book.

In this chapter, you learned the following:

- After Linux boots, a process named init starts all other processes. The exact set of initial processes depends on the run level, which typically is a number ranging from 0 to 6. The `/etc/inittab` file specifies the processes that start in each run level.
- The `/etc/inittab` file specifies that a graphical display manager starts at run level 5. In Linux, the display manager provides the graphical login prompt.
- The init process executes Linux startup scripts in the `/etc/rc.d` directory and its subdirectories.
- You can use the `/sbin/chkconfig` program to set up servers to start automatically at various run levels.
- You can use the `at` command to execute one or more commands at a future time and have the output mailed to you.
- You can use the `crontab` facility to set up periodic jobs (called *cron jobs*) that are executed at recurring intervals. Then, you can have the output mailed to you.
- If you use your Linux system for anything important, you have to back up your files. You should select a backup strategy and backup media based on your needs and your level of tolerance for the risk of business interruption from a hard disk failure.
- You can use the tape archiver program—tar—to back up and restore files. This chapter shows you how to set up cron jobs for automated full and incremental backups.

- Linux comes with utilities and commands you can use to keep an eye on your system's performance. You learn to use and interpret the displays produced by top, the GNOME System Monitor, and vmstat. Also, you learn some commands to check available disk space and your hard disk's performance.
- The `/proc` file system contains extensive information about the system. The `/proc` file system is not a disk-based file system; it is a collection of data structures in memory, managed by the Linux kernel, that appears to the user as a set of directories and files.
- In the `/proc/sys` directory are a number of files whose values you can set to modify the kernel's behavior at run time. You can either directly write to these files or use the `/sbin/sysctl` program to view or set the parameters. If you know what you are doing, you can tune the performance of your system by modifying the parameters in the `/proc/sys` directory.

Software Installation and Update

Secrets in This Chapter

You should know how to install or remove software packages distributed in the form of Red Hat Package Manager (RPM) files because most Fedora and Red Hat software comes in RPM files. This chapter shows you how to work with RPM files.

Many open-source software packages come in source-code form, usually in compressed archives. You have to build and install the software to use it. This chapter describes the steps you ordinarily follow when downloading, building, and installing source-based software packages.

Next, I briefly describe the Red Hat Network and how you can use the Update agent together with Yum to update specific Linux packages.

Finally, this chapter turns to the subject of configuring and rebuilding the kernel. The last part of this chapter explains how to apply a kernel patch and how to rebuild the Linux kernel.

Working with the Red Hat Package Manager

A significant innovation from the people at Red Hat is the Red Hat Package Manager (RPM) — a system for packaging all the necessary files for a software product in a single file (referred to as an RPM file or simply an RPM). Several Linux distributions including Red Hat and Fedora are distributed in the form of a lot of RPMs. In the following sections, you will learn to install, remove, and query RPMs by using Fedora's Package Management graphical tool and the `rpm` commands.

insider insight

The `rpm` commands are a must when you have to work from a text-mode command line. The graphical package management utility, however, is better than using `rpm` commands when it comes to installing or uninstalling entire package groups (a package group is a collection of related RPMs).

Using the Package Management Utility

Package Management utility is a graphical tool for installing and uninstalling RPMs. With this utility you can check what's installed on your system and also add or remove packages — as a group or individually.

To start the Package Management utility, choose Desktop ➪ System Settings ➪ Add Remove Applications. If you are not logged in as `root`, a dialog box prompts you for the root password. Enter that password, and press Enter. The Package Management utility starts and gathers information about the status of packages installed on your system. After it sorts through the information about all the installed packages, the Package Management utility displays a list of all the packages (see Figure 21-1).

The Package Management window displays information about the packages organized into package groups such as Desktops and Applications. Each package group has a graphical icon, a label such as X Window System or GNOME Desktop Environment, and a brief description as well. A check box precedes each package group's name. If the package is already installed, a check mark appears in the check box.

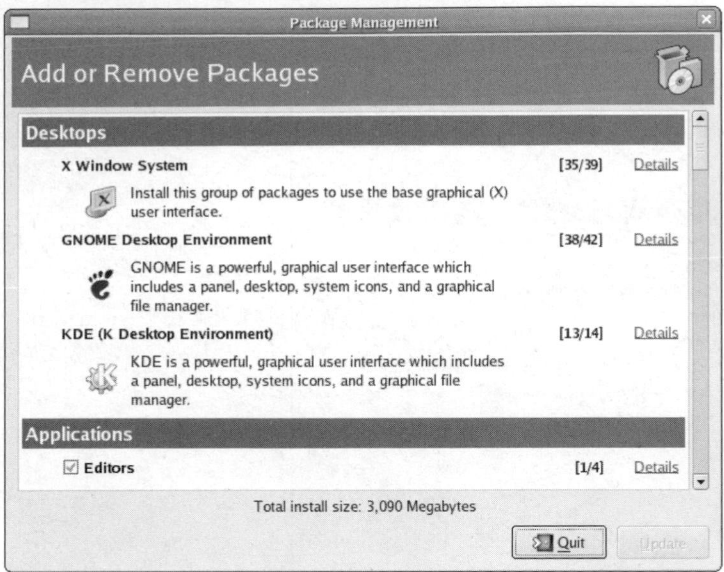

Figure 21-1: The Main Window of the Package Management Utility.

For the installed package groups (the ones with check marks), notice the hypertext link labeled Details on the right side of the package's name and description. If you click Details, the Package Management utility brings up a new window in which it displays further details about the contents of that package group. For example, Figure 21-2 displays the detailed contents of the GNOME Desktop Environment package group. Click Close after you finish examining the details of a package group.

To install an uninstalled package group, simply click the check box so that a check mark appears there. Then, click the Update button to proceed with the installation. The Package Management utility figures out what specific files have to be installed for that package group. (Because of interdependencies among package groups, installing one package group may require installing quite a few other package groups.) After it finishes gathering information, a dialog box informs you what will be installed and how much disk space will be needed For example, Figure 21-3 shows the information about package and space requirements for a selected set of packages (26 packages and about 388KB of disk space).

Click Continue to proceed. The Package Management utility then updates the system and displays the progress as it installs files. If you are installing from CD-ROMs and a new CD-ROM is needed, the Package Management utility prompts you for the next CD-ROM. Insert the requested CD-ROM, and click OK.

To remove one or more package groups, uncheck the check marks for those package groups in the Package Management window, and then click the Update button. A dialog box shows you the details of what will be removed. Click Continue, and the packages will be removed.

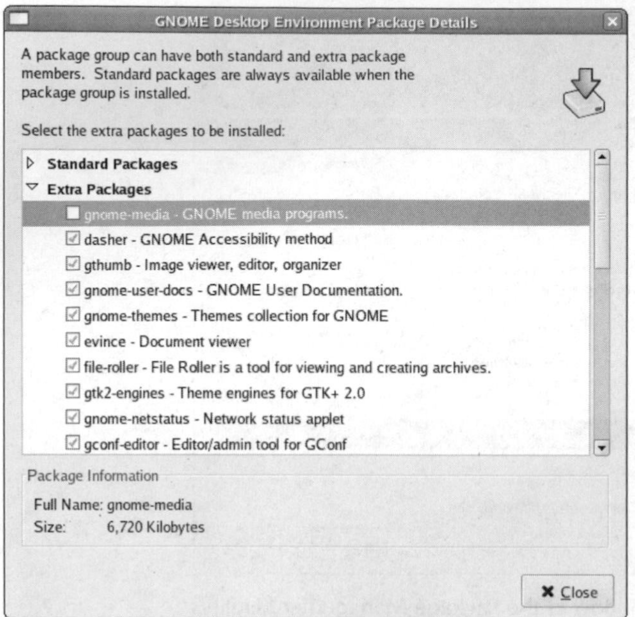

Figure 21-2: Viewing a Package Group's Detailed Contents.

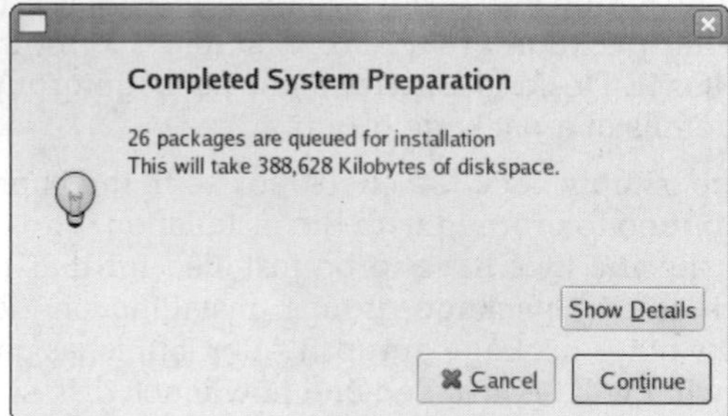

Figure 21-3: Information about Disk Space Required to Install a Package Group.

Using the RPM Commands

When you install Linux from the companion DVD-ROM, the installation program uses the `rpm` command to unpack the packages (RPM files) and to copy the contents to appropriate locations on the disk.

Although you do not need to understand the internal structure of an RPM file, you should know how to use the `rpm` command to work with RPM files. Specifically, you may want to perform one or more of the following tasks with RPMs:

- Find out the version numbers and other information about RPMs installed on your system.
- Install a new software package from an RPM. For example, you might install a package you have skipped during the initial installation. In particular, you have to install the source files for the Linux kernel before you can rebuild the kernel.
- Remove (uninstall) unneeded software you have previously installed from an RPM. You might uninstall a package to reclaim the disk space, if you find that you rarely (or never) use the package.
- Upgrade an older version of an RPM with a new one. You might upgrade after you download a new version of a package from Fedora Core download sites (listed online at `http://fedora.redhat.com/download/mirrors.html`). You must upgrade an RPM to benefit from the fixes in the new version.
- Verify that an RPM is in working order. You can verify a package to ensure that all necessary files are in the correct locations.

You can perform all of these tasks with the `rpm` command—it's just a matter of using different options. The next few subsections briefly introduce you to the `rpm` command.

insider insight

If you ever forget the `rpm` options, type the following command to see a list:

```
rpm --help | more
```

The number of options `rpm` has will amaze you!

Understanding RPM Filenames

An RPM contains a number of files, but it appears as a single file on your Linux system. By convention, the RPM filenames have a specific structure. To see the names of RPM files available on the companion DVD, use the following steps:

1. Place the DVD in the DVD drive. If you are using GNOME or KDE graphical desktops, the DVD should be mounted automatically. Otherwise, mount it by typing the following command in a terminal window (if you have a DVD recorder, use `/media/cdrecorder` as the argument for the `mount` command):

   ```
   mount /media/cdrom
   ```

2. Go to the directory in which the RPMs are located, and view the listing using the `ls` command. For example to see RPMs with names that start with `cups`, type:

   ```
   cd /media/cdrom/Fedora/RPMS
   ls cups*.rpm | more
   ```

   Here is a typical output from my system:

   ```
   cups-1.1.23-15.i386.rpm
   cups-libs-1.1.23-15.i386.rpm
   ```

As you might guess from the listing, all RPM files end with an `.rpm` extension. To understand the various parts of the filename, consider the following RPM:

```
cups-1.1.23-15.i386.rpm
```

This filename has the following parts, separated by dashes (-):

- **Package name:** `cups`
- **Version number:** `1.1.23`
- **Release number:** `15` (This is a Fedora-assigned release number.)
- **Architecture:** `i386` (This package is for Intel 80386–compatible processors.)

Usually, the package name is descriptive enough for you to guess what the RPM might contain. The version number is the same as that of the software package's current version number (even when it is distributed in some other form, such as a `tar` file). Fedora Project assigns the release number to keep track of changes. The architecture should be `i386` or `noarch` for the RPMs you want to install on a PC with an Intel x86–compatible processor.

Finding Information about RPMs

As it installs packages, the `rpm` command builds a database of installed RPMs. You can use the `rpm -q` command to query this database to find out information about packages installed on your system.

For example, to find out the version number of the Linux kernel installed on your system, type **rpm -q kernel**. Here is a typical output from that command:

```
kernel-2.6.11-1.1275_FC4
```

The response is the name of the RPM for the kernel (this is the executable version of the kernel, not the source files). The name is the same as the RPM filename, except that the last part— `.i386.rpm`—is not shown. In this case, the version part of the RPM tells you that the kernel is `2.6.11`.

You can see a list of all installed RPMs by using the following command:

```
rpm -qa
```

You will see a long list of RPMs scroll by your screen. To view the list one screen at a time, type:

```
rpm -qa | more
```

If you want to search for a specific package, feed the output of `rpm -qa` to the `grep` command. For example, to see all packages with `kernel` in their names, type:

```
rpm -qa | grep kernel
kernel-devel-2.6.11-1.1275_FC4
kernel-2.6.11-1.1275_FC4
kernel-doc-2.6.11-1.1275_FC4
```

You can query much more than a package's version number with the `rpm -q` command. By adding single-letter options, you can find out other useful information. For example, try the following command to see the files in the kernel package:

```
rpm -ql kernel | more
/boot/System.map-2.6.11-1.1275_FC4
/boot/config-2.6.11-1.1275_FC4
/boot/vmlinuz-2.6.11-1.1275_FC4
/lib/modules/2.6.11-1.1275_FC4
/lib/modules/2.6.11-1.1275_FC4/build
/lib/modules/2.6.11-1.1275_FC4/kernel
/lib/modules/2.6.11-1.1275_FC4/kernel/arch
/lib/modules/2.6.11-1.1275_FC4/kernel/arch/i386
/lib/modules/2.6.11-1.1275_FC4/kernel/arch/i386/crypto
/lib/modules/2.6.11-1.1275_FC4/kernel/arch/i386/crypto/aes-i586.ko
/lib/modules/2.6.11-1.1275_FC4/kernel/arch/i386/kernel
/lib/modules/2.6.11-1.1275_FC4/kernel/arch/i386/kernel/cpu
/lib/modules/2.6.11-1.1275_FC4/kernel/arch/i386/kernel/cpu/cpufreq
/lib/modules/2.6.11-1.1275_FC4/kernel/arch/i386/kernel/cpu/cpufreq/acpi-cpufreq.ko
/lib/modules/2.6.11-1.1275_FC4/kernel/arch/i386/kernel/cpu/cpufreq/p4-clockmod.ko
(rest of the listing deleted)
```

Following are several useful forms of `rpm -q` commands to query information about a package (to use any of these `rpm -q` commands, type the command, followed by the package name):

- **rpm -qc:** Lists all configuration files in a package.
- **rpm -qd:** Lists all documentation files in a package. These are usually the online manual pages (also known as man pages).
- **rpm -qf:** Lists the package that owns a specified file. This is a good way to find out which package installed a specific file.
- **rpm -qi:** Displays detailed information about a package, including version number, size, installation date, and a brief description.
- **rpm -ql:** Lists all the files in a package. For some packages, this can be a very long list.
- **rpm -qs:** Lists the state of all files in a package.

These `rpm -q` commands provide information about installed packages only. If you want to find information about an uninstalled RPM file, add the letter `p` to the command-line option of each command. For example, to view the list of files in the RPM file named `cups-1.1.23-15.i386.rpm`, use the following command:

```
rpm -qpl cups-*.rpm
```

Of course, this works only if the current directory contains that RPM file.

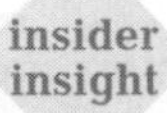

If you are curious which package installed a specific file, use the `rpm -qf` command. For example, if you notice the file `/etc/foomatic` and wonder which package installed it, you can type **rpm -qf /etc/foomatic**. The resulting display is not much of a surprise:

```
foomatic-3.0.2-18
```

Two handy `rpm -q` commands enable you to find out which RPM file provides a specific file and which RPMs need a specified package. To find out the name of the RPM that provides a file, use the following command:

```
rpm -q --whatprovides /etc/vsftpd/vsftpd.conf
```

RPM then prints the name of the package that provides the file, like this:

```
vsftpd-2.0.3-1
```

If you provide the name of a package instead of a filename, RPM displays the name of the RPM package that contains the specified package.

On the other hand, to find the names of RPMs that need a specific package, use the following command:

```
rpm -q --whatrequires packagename
```

For example, to see which packages need the `openssl` package, type

```
rpm -q --whatrequires openssl
```

The output from this command shows all the RPM packages that need the `openssl` package.

Installing an RPM

To install an RPM, use the `rpm -i` command. You have to provide the name of the RPM file as the argument. A typical example is installing an RPM from this book's companion DVD containing the Fedora Linux RPMs. As usual, you have to mount the DVD and change to the directory in which the RPMs are located. Then use the `rpm -i` command to install the RPM. If you want to view the progress of the RPM installation, use `rpm -ivh`. A series of hash marks (#) is displayed as the package is unpacked.

For example, to install the kernel-devel RPM (which contains the source files for the Linux operating system) from the companion DVD, I type the following commands:

```
mount /media/cdrom
cd /media/cdrom/Fedora/RPMS
rpm -ivh kernel-devel*
```

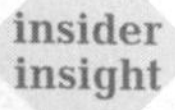

You do not have to type the full RPM filename — you can use a few characters from the beginning of the name followed by an asterisk (*). Make sure you type enough of the name to identify the RPM file uniquely.

If you try to install an RPM already installed, the `rpm` command displays an error message. For example, here is what happens when I try to install the man package on my system:

```
rpm -i man-*
package man-1.5p-4 is already installed
```

To force the rpm command to install a package even if errors are present, just add --force to the rpm -i command, as follows:

```
rpm -i --force man-*
```

Removing an RPM

You might want to remove (uninstall) a package if you realize you don't really need the software. For example, if you have installed the X Window System development package but discover you are not interested in writing X applications, you can easily remove the package by using the rpm -e command.

You need to know the name of the package before you can remove it. One good way to find the name is to use rpm -qa in conjunction with grep to search for the appropriate RPM file. For example, to locate the X Window System development RPM, you might try the following command:

```
rpm -qa | grep xorg
xorg-x11-Mesa-libGL-6.8.2-23
xorg-x11-twm-6.8.2-23
xorg-x11-font-utils-6.8.2-23
xorg-x11-xauth-6.8.2-23
xorg-x11-xdm-6.8.2-23
xorg-x11-libs-6.8.2-23
xorg-x11-devel-6.8.2-23
xorg-x11-deprecated-libs-6.8.2-23
xorg-x11-xfs-6.8.2-23
xorg-x11-tools-6.8.2-23
xorg-x11-deprecated-libs-devel-6.8.2-23
xorg-x11-6.8.2-23
xorg-x11-Mesa-libGLU-6.8.2-23
```

In this case, xorg-x11-devel happens to be the name of the package you need. To remove the package, type:

```
rpm -e xorg-x11-devel
```

Note that you do not need the full RPM filename; all you need is the package name—the first part of the filename up to the dash (-) before the version number.

The rpm -e command does not remove a package other packages need. For example, when I try to remove the vim-common package, I get the following error messages:

```
rpm -e vim-common
error: Failed dependencies:
        vim-common = 1:6.3.071-1 is needed by (installed) vim-enhanced-
6.3.071-1.i386
```

Upgrading an RPM

Use the rpm -U command to upgrade an RPM. You must provide the name of the RPM file that contains the new software. For example, if I have version 2.0.40 of Apache httpd (Web server) installed on my system but I want to upgrade to version 2.0.53, I download the RPM file `httpd-2.0.53-6.i386.rpm` from one of Fedora update sites listed at `http://fedora.redhat.com/download/mirrors.html` and use the following command:

```
rpm -U httpd-2.0.53-6.i386.rpm
```

The `rpm -U` command performs the upgrade by removing the old version of the httpd (Apache Web server) package and installing the new RPM.

You should upgrade, whenever possible, rather than remove the old package and install the new version. Upgrading automatically saves the old configuration files, which saves you the hassle of configuring the software after a fresh installation.

caution

When you are upgrading the kernel and the kernel module packages that contain a ready-to-run Linux kernel, you should install it by using the `rpm -i` command (instead of the `rpm -U` command). That way you won't overwrite the current kernel.

Verifying an RPM

You may not do this often, but if you suspect that a software package is not properly installed, use the `rpm -V` command to verify it. For example, to verify the kernel package, type the following:

```
rpm -V kernel
```

The `rpm -V` causes `rpm` to compare the size and other attributes of each file in the package against those of the original files. If everything verifies correctly, the `rpm -V` command does not print anything. If there are any discrepancies, you will see a report of them. For example, I have modified the configuration files for the Apache httpd (Web) server. Here is what I see when I verify the httpd package by typing the **rpm -V** httpd command:

```
S.5....T. c /etc/httpd/conf/httpd.conf
```

In this case, the output from `rpm -V` shows that a configuration file has changed. Each line of this command's output consists of three parts:

- The line starts with eight characters: each character indicates the type of discrepancy found. For example, `S` means the size is different, and `T` means the time of last modification is different. Table 21-1 shows each character and its meaning. A period (`.`) means that that specific attribute matches the original.
- For configuration files, a `c` appears next; otherwise, this field is blank. That's how you can tell whether or not a file is a configuration file. Typically, you shouldn't worry if a configuration file has changed; you have probably made the changes yourself.
- The last part of the line is the full pathname of the file. From this part, you can tell exactly where the file is located.

Table 21-1: Characters Used in RPM Verification Reports

Character	Meaning
S	Size has changed.
M	Permissions and file type are different.
5	Checksum computed with the MD5 algorithm is different.
D	Device type is different.
L	Symbolic link is different.
U	File's user is different.
G	File's group is different.
T	File's modification time is different.

Building Software Packages from Source Files

In the previous sections, you have seen how to install software packages distributed in the RPM format. RPM files bundle everything — all the executable binary files and configuration files — needed to install a software package. Many open-source software packages, however, are distributed in source-code form, without executable binaries. Before you can use such software, you have to build the executable binary files by compiling them, and you have to follow some instructions to install the package. This section shows you how to build software packages from source files.

Downloading and Unpacking the Software

Open-source software source files are typically distributed in compressed `tar` archives. These archives are created by the tar program and compressed with the gzip program. The distribution is in the form of a single large file with the `.tar.gz` or `.tar.Z` extension — often referred to as a *compressed tarball*. If you want the software, you have to download the compressed tarball and unpack it.

Download the compressed `tar` file by using anonymous FTP or through your Web browser. Typically, this involves no effort on your part beyond clicking a link and saving the file in an appropriate directory on your system.

To try your hand at downloading and building a software package, practice on the X Multimedia System (XMMS) — a graphical X application for playing MP3 and other multimedia files (the version that comes with Fedora does not have MP3 capability, but the version you download and build will be able to play MP3 files).

The source files for XMMS are available from `www.xmms.org/download.php` in the form of a compressed `tar` archive. Click the `http` link for the `.tar.gz` format on the `www.xmms.org/download.php` page and save the compressed source tarball in the `/usr/local/src` directory in your Linux system (be sure to log in as `root`, otherwise you cannot save in the `/usr/local/src` directory).

After downloading the compressed `tar` file, examine the contents with the following `tar` command:

```
tar ztf xmms*.gz | more
```

You should see a listing similar to the following:

```
xmms-1.2.10/
xmms-1.2.10/intl/
xmms-1.2.10/intl/ChangeLog
xmms-1.2.10/intl/Makefile.in
xmms-1.2.10/intl/config.charset
xmms-1.2.10/intl/locale.alias
xmms-1.2.10/intl/ref-add.sin
xmms-1.2.10/intl/ref-del.sin
xmms-1.2.10/intl/gmo.h
xmms-1.2.10/intl/gettextP.h
xmms-1.2.10/intl/hash-string.h
xmms-1.2.10/intl/loadinfo.h
... rest of the output not shown ...
```

The output of this `tar` command shows you what's in the archive and gives you an idea of the directories that will be created after you unpack the archive. In this case, a directory named `xmms-1.2.10` will be created in the current directory, which, in my case, is `/usr/local/src`. From the listing, you'll also learn the programming language used to write the package. If you see `.c` and `.h` files, which means that the source files are in the C programming language, they can be used to write many open-source software packages.

To extract the contents of the compressed `tar` archive, type the following `tar` command:

```
tar zxvf xmms*.gz
```

You'll again see the long list of files as they are extracted from the archive and copied to the appropriate directories on your hard disk.

Now, you are ready to build the software.

Building the Software from Source Files

After you unpack the compressed `tar` archive, all source files will be in a directory whose name is usually that of the software package with a version-number suffix. For example, the XMMS version 1.2.10 source files are extracted to the `xmms-1.2.10` directory. To start building the software, change directories with the following command:

```
cd xmms*
```

You don't have to type the entire name — the shell can expand the directory name and change to the `xmms-1.2.10` directory.

Nearly all software packages come with some sort of README or INSTALL file—a text file that tells you how to build and install the package. XMMS is no exception; it comes with a README file you can peruse by typing **more README**. There is also an INSTALL file, which contains instructions for building and installing XMMS.

Most open-source software packages, including XMMS, also come with a file named COPYING. This file contains the full text of the GNU General Public License (GPL), which spells out the conditions under which you can use and redistribute the software. If you are not familiar with the GNU GPL, read this file and show the license to your legal counsel for a full interpretation and an assessment of applicability to your business.

To build the software package, follow the instructions in the README or INSTALL file. For the XMMS package, the README file lists some of the prerequisites (such as libraries) and tells you what commands to type to build and install the package. In the case of XMMS, the instructions tell you to use the following steps:

1. Type **./configure** to run a shell script that checks your system configuration and creates a file named Makefile—a file the make command uses to build and install the package. (You can type **./configure --help** to see a list of options that configure accepts.)
2. Type **make** to build the software. This step compiles the source files in all the subdirectories (compiling source code converts each source file into an object file—a file containing binary instructions that your PC's processor can understand).
3. Type **make install** to install the software. This step copies libraries and executable binary files to appropriate directories on your system.

Although these steps are specific to XMMS, most other packages follow these steps: configure, make, and install. The configure shell script guesses system-dependent variables and creates a Makefile with commands needed to build and install the software.

note

Usually, you do not have to do anything but type the commands to build the software, but you must install the software-development tools on your system. This means that you must install the Software Development package when you install Linux. To build and run XMMS, you must also install the X Software Development package because it's an X application.

Building and Testing XMMS

To begin building XMMS, type the following command to run the configure script (you must be in the xmms-1.2.10 directory when you type this command):

```
./configure
```

The configure script starts running and prints lots of messages as it checks various features of your system—from the existence of the C compiler to various libraries needed to build XMMS. Finally, the configure script creates a Makefile you can use to build the software.

insider insight

If the `configure` script displays error messages and fails, review the `INSTALL` and `README` files to find any clues to solving the problem. You may be able to circumvent it by providing some information to the `configure` script through command-line arguments. Often the `configure` script will create a `config.log` file that should contain information about the possible causes for failure.

If the configure script complains about missing GLIB, you have to install the glib-devel and gtk+-devel packages. You can do so by typing **yum install glib-devel** and then **yum gtk+-devel**. After the configure script finishes, build the software by typing **make**. This command runs the GNU make utility, which reads the `Makefile` and starts compiling the source files according to information specified in the `Makefile`. The `make` command goes through all the source directories, compiles the source files, and creates the executable files and libraries needed to run XMMS. You'll see a lot of messages scroll by as each file is compiled. These messages show the commands used to compile and link the files. During `make`, you might get an error that references the file `ir.h` in the `General/ir` subdirectory of where you installed the XMMS source files. You can fix that error by opening the `ir.h` file in a text editor and deleting the following two lines from that file:

```
extern pthread_t irapp_thread;

extern gboolean keepGoing;
```

Save the `ir.h` file, change directory to where you installed XMMS sources, and type **make** again.

The `make` command can take 3 to 10 minutes to complete, depending on how fast your PC is. After `make` is done, you can install the XMMS software with the following command:

```
make install
```

This command also runs GNU `make`, but the `install` argument instructs GNU `make` to perform a specific set of commands from the `Makefile`. These instructions essentially go through all the subdirectories and copy various files to their final locations. For example, the binary executable files `xmms`, `wmxmms`, and `xmms-config` are copied to the `/usr/bin` directory.

To run XMMS type **xmms** in a terminal window on the GNOME or KDE desktop. From the XMMS window, press **L** to get the Load File dialog box and select an MP3 file to play. Your PC must have a sound card, and that the sound card must be configured correctly for XMMS to work.

Figure 21-4 shows a typical view of XMMS playing an MP3 music clip.

Figure 21-4: Playing MP3 Music with XMMS.

If you get an error message saying that the MPEG support has been removed, select Window menu ⇨ Options ⇨ Preferences and in the dialog box that appears select MPEG Layer 1/2/3 Placeholder Plugin. Then click off the Enable Plugin check box to disable that plug-in. The XMMS source that you downloaded builds a working MP3 plug-in.

Summarizing the Steps in Building Software from Source Code

Now, that you have tried the entire process of downloading and building a software package, here's an overview of the steps you follow to download, unpack, build, and install a typical software package:

1. Use a Web browser to download the source code, usually in the form of a `.tar.gz` file, from the anonymous FTP site or website.
2. Unpack the file with a `tar zxvf` *`filename`* command.
3. Change the directory to the new subdirectory where the software is unpacked, with a command such as `cd` *`software_dir`*.
4. Read any `README` or `INSTALL` files to learn any specific instructions you must follow to build and install the software.
5. The details of building the software may differ slightly from one software package to another, but typically you type the following commands to build and install the software:

```
./configure
make
make install
```

6. Read any other documentation that comes with the software to learn how to use the software and whether you must configure the software further before using it.

Installing SRPMS

The companion DVD provides the source RPMs for Fedora Linux. You can install the source files and build various applications directly from the source files. Fedora Project provides the sources files in RPMs and these RPMs are generally known as SRPMS (for source RPMs).

To install a specific source RPM and build the application, follow these steps:

1. Mount the CD-ROM by typing **mount /mnt/cdrom** or waiting for GNOME desktop to mount the CD.
2. Typically, source RPMs are in the SRPMS directory. Change to that directory by typing the following command:

```
cd /mnt/cdrom/SRPMS
```

3. Install the source RPM file by using the `rpm -i` command. For example, to install the Web server (`httpd`) source, type

```
rpm -ivh httpd*.src.rpm
```

The files would be installed in the `/usr/src/redhat/SOURCES` directory. A spec file with a `.spec` extension would be placed in the `/usr/src/redhat/SPECS` directory. The *spec file* describes the software and also contains information that is used to build and install the software.

4. Use the `rpmbuild` command with the spec file to build the software. You perform different tasks from unpacking the source files to building and installing the binaries by using different options with `rpmbuild` command. For example, to execute the instructions in the `%prep` section of the spec file, type:

   ```
   rpmbuild -bp packagename.spec
   ```

   where *packagename* is the name of the RPM. The `%prep` section should typically unpack the source files. The unpacked source files appear in a subdirectory in the `/usr/src/redhat/BUILD` directory. The subdirectory usually has the name of the software package, including a version number.

   If you want to run the whole spec file, type:

   ```
   rpmbuild -ba packagename.spec
   ```

   This command should typically build the software and install the binary files,

A number of single-letter options that go with `-b` are very useful. Here is a summary of these `rpmbuild -b` options:

- `rpmbuild -bp` means just run the `%prep` section of the spec file.
- `rpmbuild -bl` performs a list check that expands the `%files` section of a spec file and checks to see if all files exist.
- `rpmbuild -bc` executes the `%build` section after the `%prep`. This is equivalent to a `make` command that compiles the source code.
- `rpmbuild -bi` performs the `%prep`, `%build`, and then `%install`. This is equivalent to the `make install` command.
- `rpmbuild -bb` builds a binary package after completing the `%prep`, `%build`, and `%install` sections of the spec file.
- `rpmbuild -ba` builds both binary and source packages after completing the `%prep`, `%build`, and `%install` sections of the spec file.

Updating Fedora with the Update Agent

Fedora Core comes with Up2date — a graphical Update Agent that can download any new RPM files your system requires and install those files for you. Up2date is also known as the Red Hat Update Agent because Red Hat developed it for its Red Hat Network through which Red Hat provides services to its commercial customers.

To update Fedora Core software packages using Up2date, follow these steps:

1. Select Applications ➪ System Tools ➪ Red Hat Network. You can also type **up2date** in a terminal window. The Update Agent starts, and, if you're using Up2date for the first time, the Red Hat Network Configuration dialog box appears and guides you through the configuration steps. You can typically click OK to accept the default settings. Another dialog box then prompts you to install a public key in your GPG key ring. (GPG refers to GNU Privacy Guard or GnuPG, a program for encrypting, decrypting, and signing e-mail and other data using the OpenPGP

Internet standard.) That public GPG key verifies that the package developer has securely signed the package that Up2date has downloaded. If prompted to do so, click Yes to install the public key.

2. Up2date displays a window with a welcome message. Click the Forward button to proceed.
3. Up2date displays a list of what it calls channels — repositories from where the agent downloads package headers. Click Forward to continue. By default, the Update Agent uses a channel that works with Yum — a command-line package updater/installer that I describe later in this section. The channels are identified in the text configuration file `/etc/sysconfig/rhn/sources`. Besides Yum, Up2date can also access repositories meant for APT — the Advanced Packaging Tool used in Debian. After you click Forward, Up2date figures out what needs to be updated and retrieves a list of all headers from the specified channel.
4. After Up2date downloads the headers, it displays a list of packages. You can then scroll through the list and pick the packages you want to update; click the box to the left of a package's name to select it. Click Forward to continue. Up2date then checks for any package dependencies and begins downloading the packages. Progress bars show the status of the download.
5. After the download finishes, click the Forward button to proceed with the installation.
6. Up2date displays progress bars as it installs each package update. Click the Forward button when the installation is complete. Up2date displays a message about the package(s) it installs successfully.
7. Click the Finish button to exit Up2date.

In Fedora Core, you can also use the Yellow dog Updater, Modified (Yum) — a command-line utility for updating as well as installing and removing RPM packages. Yum downloads RPM package headers from a specified website and then uses the `rpm` utility to figure out any interdependencies among packages and what needs to be installed on your system. Then it downloads and uses `rpm` to install the necessary packages. Yum downloads just the headers to do its job and the headers are much smaller in size than the complete RPM packages. Yum is much faster than the alternative, where you manually download the complete RPM packages using the `rpm` command.

Typically, you keep your system up to date with the graphical Update Agent because it's easy to use. However, knowing how to run Yum from the command line is good, just in case you have problems with the Update Agent.

You can read more about Yum and keep up with Yum news by visiting the Yum Web page at `http://linux.duke.edu/projects/yum`.

The command line for Yum has the following syntax:

```
yum [options] command [packagenames]
```

In the preceding code, *`options`* is a list of Yum options, *`command`* specifies what you want Yum to do, and *`packagenames`* are the names of the packages on which Yum performs that action. You must provide the *`command`*, but the *`options`* and *`packagenames`* are optional. That's why I show them in square brackets in the syntax. Table 21-2 summarizes the Yum commands, and Table 21-3 lists some common Yum options.

Table 21-2: Yum Commands

Command	*What Yum Does for This Command*
`check-update`	Checks for available updates for your system.
`clean`	Cleans up the cache directory.
`info`	Displays summary information about the specified packages.
`install`	Installs latest versions of specified packages, making sure that all dependencies are satisfied.
`list`	Lists information about available packages.
`provides`	Provides information on which package provides a file.
`remove`	Removes specified packages as well as any packages that depend on the packages being removed.
`search`	Finds packages whose header contains what you specify as the package name.
`update`	Updates specified packages, making sure that all dependencies are satisfied.

Table 21-3: Some Common Yum Options

Option	*Causes Yum to Do the Following*
`--download-only`	Downloads the packages, but does not install them.
`--exclude=pkgname`	Excludes the specified package. (You can use this option more than once on the command line.)
`--help`	Displays a help message and quits.
`--installroot=path`	Uses the specified pathname as the directory under which all packages are installed.
`-y`	Assumes that your answer to any question is yes.

If you simply want Yum to update your system, just type the following (you have to be logged in as `root`):

```
yum update
```

Yum consults its configuration file, `/etc/yum.conf`, and does everything needed to update the packages installed on your system. You can specify package names to update only some packages. For example, to update the `kernel` and `xorg-x11` packages, use the following Yum command:

```
yum update kernel* xorg-x11*
```

This command updates all packages whose names begin with `kernel` and `xorg-x11`.

You may use the options to further instruct Yum what to do. For example, if you want to download the updated packages, but not install them, type the following:

```
yum --download-only update
```

Another typical option is `--exclude`, which enables you to exclude one or more packages from the update process. Suppose you want to update everything except the GNOME packages (whose names begin with `gnome`) and the `rhythmbox` package. Then you type the following Yum command:

```
yum --exclude=gnome* --exclude=rhythmbox update
```

Upgrading and Customizing the Linux Kernel

One reason that Linux is so exciting is that many programmers are constantly improving it. Some programmers, for example, write drivers that add support for new hardware, such as a new sound card or a new networking card. All these innovations come to you in the form of new versions of the Linux kernel.

Although you do not have to upgrade or modify the Linux operating system — the kernel — every time a new version is available, sometimes you need to upgrade simply because the new version corrects some problems or supports your hardware better. On the other hand, if an earlier kernel version has everything you need, there is no need to rush out and upgrade.

Sometimes you may want to rebuild the kernel even when there are no fixes or enhancements. The Linux kernel on the companion DVD is generic and uses modules to support all types of hardware. You may want to build a new kernel that *links in* (incorporates into the kernel's binary file) the drivers for only the devices installed on your system. In particular, if you have a SCSI hard disk, you may want to create a kernel that supports your SCSI adapter. Depending on your needs, you may also want to change some of the kernel-configuration options, such as creating a kernel that's specific for your Pentium processor (instead of a generic Intel 386 processor).

The rest of this chapter explains how to upgrade a kernel using a kernel RPM provided by Fedora Project as well as how to rebuild and install a new Linux kernel.

In the past it was possible to apply kernel *patches* — alterations to the kernel source code — and rebuild the kernel. You would typically download the Linux kernel patches (as well as the latest versions of the kernel sources) from the website `www.kernel.org`, decompress the files, and apply the patches by using the `patch` command. Unfortunately, these steps do not usually work with Fedora Linux because Fedora has modified some of the kernel files. In Fedora, you can still upgrade the kernel to newer versions — you just have to get the newer kernels from the Fedora FTP server. If a Fedora RPM for a newer kernel is not available yet, you can download the entire new kernel source from `www.kernel.org` and build the kernel by following the directions in the next section.

Upgrading with a Fedora Kernel RPM

Fedora distributes all software updates, including new versions of kernels, in the form of RPM files. To download and install the kernel RPMs, follow these steps:

1. Use a Web server to download the kernel RPM files from Fedora's download server (the next section explains the details). If you want to rebuild the kernel, you have to download the `kernel-devel` RPM corresponding to the new version of the kernel.
2. Install the RPMs by using the `rpm -i` command.
3. Try out the new kernel by rebooting the system.

The next few sections further describe these steps.

Downloading New Kernel RPMs

Fedora Project makes software updates available in the form of RPMs—packages—at its FTP server or one of the mirror sites listed at `http://fedora.redhat.com/download/mirrors.html`. The updates are organized in directories according to Fedora version numbers. For example, any updates for Fedora 4 for Intel x86 systems reside in the `updates/4/i386` directory. Use a Web browser (for example, Mozilla) to visit the download server and download any kernel RPMs available at that site.

Installing the Kernel RPMs

To install the kernel and the modules, follow these steps:

1. Log in as `root`.
2. Use the `cd` command to change directory to where the RPM files (the ones you downloaded from Fedora download server) are located.
3. Type the following command to install the kernel RPM:

```
rpm -ivh kernel*.rpm
```

You need to install the `kernel-devel` RPM only if you want to build a new kernel.

When you install a new kernel RPM, the installation process creates a new initial RAM disk image—a file that the kernel can copy into a block of memory and use as a memory-resident disk to load modules needed to access the hard disk. That file's name begins with initrd (initrd is shorthand for *initial RAM disk*) and has the kernel version number in the filename. The kernel RPM install also adds a description of the kernel to the GRUB configuration file—`/etc/grub.conf`. For example, here is a typical GRUB configuration file after I install a new kernel RPM:

```
title Fedora Core (2.6.11-1.1275_FC4)
        root (hd0,5)
        kernel /vmlinuz-2.6.11-1.1275_FC4 ro root=LABEL=/1 acpi=off
rhgb quiet
        initrd /initrd-2.6.11-1.1275_FC4.img
title Fedora Core (2.6.11-1.1240_FC4)
        root (hd0,5)
        kernel /vmlinuz-2.6.11-1.1240_FC4 ro root=LABEL=/1 acpi=off
rhgb quiet
        initrd /initrd-2.6.11-1.1240_FC4.img
```

Next time you reboot the system, these two kernels appear as choices in the GRUB boot screen. From that screen, you can select which kernel you want to boot.

Trying Out the New Kernel

After installing the new kernel RPM, it's time to try the new kernel. To restart the system, log in as `root` and type the following command from the Linux prompt:

```
reboot
```

You may also reboot the system as you log out of the GNOME or KDE desktop. Select Restart the computer from the dialog box, and click OK.

When the system reboots and you see the GRUB screen, press the arrow key to select the new kernel's name. Because the new kernel description appears before all other operating systems in the GRUB configuration file, that kernel should boot even if you don't do anything at the boot screen.

After Linux starts, you should see the usual graphical login screen. Log in as a user, open a terminal window, and type the `uname -sr` command to see the version number. The response should show that your system is running the new version of the kernel.

Rebuilding the Kernel

Rebuilding the kernel refers to creating a new binary file for the core Linux operating system. This binary file is the one that runs when Linux boots. You may have to rebuild the kernel for various reasons:

- After you initially install Linux, you may want to create a new kernel that includes support for only the hardware installed on your system. In particular, if you have a SCSI adapter, you may want to create a kernel that links in the SCSI driver. The kernel in the companion DVD includes the SCSI driver as an external module that the kernel loads at startup.
- If you have a system with hardware for which only experimental support is available, you have to rebuild the kernel to include that support into the operating system.
- You may want to recompile the kernel and generate code that works well on your specific Pentium processor (instead of the generic 386 processor code that comes in the standard Linux distribution).

To rebuild the Linux kernel, you need the kernel source files. The kernel source files are not normally installed. Use the following steps to install the kernel source files (the kernel source RPM) on your system:

1. Log in as `root` and insert the companion DVD into the DVD drive.
2. If the DVD does not mount automatically, type the following command to mount the DVD (if you are using a DVD/CD recorder, change `cdrom` to `cdrecorder`):

   ```
   mount /media/cdrom
   ```

   If you are using GNOME or KDE, the DVD-ROM is automatically mounted, and you should not have to perform this step manually.
3. Change the directory to the `Fedora/RPMS` directory on the DVD-ROM, and use the `rpm` command to install the kernel source files. Type the following commands:

   ```
   cd /media/cdrom/SRPMS
   rpm -ivh kernel*.src.rpm
   ```

   After the `rpm` command finishes installing the kernel source package, the source files appear in various subdirectories of the `/usr/src/redhat` directory.

4. Type the following commands to prepare the kernel source files:

```
cd /usr/src/redhat/SPECS
rpmbuild --target i586 -bp kernel*.spec
```

The `rpmbuild` command unpacks the kernel source files, places them in the `/usr/src/redhat/BUILD` directory and applies any patches included in the kernel source RPM.

5. Move the source code directory tree to the `/usr/src` directory by typing the following commands:

```
cd /usr/src/redhat/BUILD/kernel-*
mv linux-* /usr/src/kernels
```

Now the entire kernel source tree should be in `/usr/src/kernels/linux-VERSION` where *VERSION* is the current kernel version. For example, for kernel version 2.6.11, the files are in the `/usr/src/kernels/linux-2.6.11` directory. You can now go into that directory and rebuild the kernel following the steps outlined in the rest of this chapter.

note If you cannot find the kernel source RPM on this book's DVD, you have to download that file from one of the mirror sites listed at `http://fedora.redhat.com/download/mirrors.html`. Click the link to one of the listed download sites and then look in the directory corresponding to the Fedora Linux version number. For example, the source RPM (SRPM) files for Fedora 4 should be in the `4/SRPMS` directory. Use a Web browser to download the `kernel-*.src.rpm` RPM file and install it by following the steps outlined in the preceding text.

Building the kernel involves the following key phases:

- Configuring the kernel
- Building the kernel
- Building and installing the modules (if any)
- Building a new initial RAM disk (`initrd`) file
- Installing the kernel and setting up GRUB

The next section describes the use of modules versus linking hardware support directly into the kernel. Subsequent sections describe the phases of kernel building.

Creating a Monolithic versus a Modular Kernel

Before you start configuring the kernel, understand that you have two options for the device drivers needed to support various hardware devices in Linux:

- **Link in support:** You can link the drivers for all hardware on your system into the kernel. As you might imagine, the size of the kernel grows as device-driver code is incorporated into the kernel. A kernel that links in all necessary support code is called a *monolithic kernel.*

- **Use modules:** You can create the necessary device drivers in the form of modules. A module is a block of code the kernel can load after it starts running. A typical use of modules is to add support for a device without having to rebuild the kernel for each new device. Modules do not have to be device drivers; they can also serve to add new functionality to the kernel. A kernel that uses modules is called a *modular kernel*.

You do not have to create a fully monolithic or fully modular kernel. In fact, it is common practice to link some support directly into the kernel. Conversely, you can build infrequently used device drivers in the form of modules. For a Linux distribution, including a mostly modular kernel makes sense, along with a large number of modules that can support many different types of hardware. Then the Linux installer configures the system to load only modules needed to support the hardware installed in a user's system.

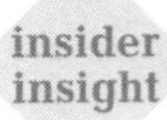

When you create a custom kernel for your hardware configuration, you may want to link all required device drivers into the kernel. In this case, you can keep the size of such a monolithic kernel under control because you link in device drivers only for the exact set of hardware installed on your system.

Configuring the Kernel

The first phase in rebuilding a kernel is configuring it. To configure the kernel, log in as `root`. Then change the kernel source directory by using the `cd` command as follows:

```
cd /usr/src/kernels/linux-*
```

To configure the kernel, you have to indicate which features and device drivers you want to include in your Linux system. In essence, you build a copy of Linux with the mix-and-match features you want.

Linux provides several ways for you to configure the kernel:

- Type **make menuconfig** to enter the kernel-configuration parameters through a text-based interface similar to the one the text-mode Linux installation program uses.
- Type **make xconfig** to use an X Window System–based configuration program to configure the kernel. You have to install the Qt development (qt-devel) package and set the QTDIR environment variable to the directory where Qt is installed (if you have installed the qt-devel package, type **export QTDIR=/usr/lib/qt-3.3** to correctly define QTDIR).
- Type **make config** to use a shell script that prompts you for each configuration option one by one. You can use this configuration program from the Linux command prompt. When you use this option, you undergo a long question-and-answer process to specify the configuration parameters.
- Type **make oldconfig** to use a shell script to reconfigure the kernel after upgrading the sources. This configuration script keeps the existing options and prompts you only for new or changed options.

The make menuconfig, make xconfig, make config, and make oldconfig commands achieve the same end result—each stores your choices in a text file named .config located in the /usr/src/kernels/* directory. Because the filename starts with a period, you don't see it when you use the ls command alone to list the directory. Instead, type **ls -a** to see the .config file in the directory listing.

The kernel-configuration step merely captures your choices in the .config file. The kernel file does not change until you compile the kernel with the make command. That means you can go through the kernel-configuration option as many times as you want. If you want to start over with default settings, type the following command before you start configuring the kernel:

```
make mrproper
```

insider insight

For an overview of the kernel configuration build steps that you can perform with the make command, type the following in a terminal window (after you type **cd /usr/src/kernels/*** to change the current directory to the correct location):

```
make help | more
```

Before starting to reconfigure the kernel, take a look at a typical .config file. For example, here are some lines of output when I type **more .config** file on a Linux system:

```
# Automatically generated make config: don't edit
#
CONFIG_X86=y
CONFIG_MMU=y
CONFIG_UID16=y
CONFIG_GENERIC_ISA_DMA=y
CONFIG_GENERIC_IOMAP=y

#
# Code maturity level options
#
CONFIG_EXPERIMENTAL=y
CONFIG_CLEAN_COMPILE=y
CONFIG_BROKEN_ON_SMP=y
CONFIG_INIT_ENV_ARG_LIMIT=32

#
# General setup
#
CONFIG_LOCALVERSION=""
CONFIG_SWAP=y
CONFIG_SYSVIPC=y
(rest of the file not shown)
```

Essentially, each configuration option has a name, and each one is assigned a value. The name begins with `CONFIG_` followed by a word that identifies the option. Each selected option has a value of `y` (to link in support for that feature) or `m` (to use a module for that feature). Lines beginning with # are comments. Comment lines list features not selected.

note

I describe the configuration process through the `make config` command. Although this approach is somewhat tedious because it walks you through each option one by one, it is ideal as a learning tool. As you step through the groups of configuration options, I provide notes explaining what most of the options mean. You can then use any configuration tool (`make xconfig`, `make menuconfig`, `make config`, or `make oldconfig`) to configure the kernel.

As you configure the kernel with the `make config` command, you have to select how to include support for specific devices. Typically, for each configuration option, you have to respond with one of the following choices:

- **y** to link support into the kernel
- **m** to use a module
- **n** to skip the support for that specific device
- **?** to get help on that kernel-configuration option

If a device does not have a modular device driver, you won't see the `m` option. For some configuration options, you may have to pick a number from a list.

Starting the Kernel Configuration

To start configuring the kernel, log in as `root`, change to the directory with the Linux kernel's source (type **cd /usr/src/kernels/***), and type **make config** in a terminal window. The configuration script then displays the first prompt:

```
*
* Linux Kernel Configuration
*
*
* Code maturity level options
*
Prompt for development and/or incomplete code/drivers (EXPERIMENTAL) [Y/n/?]
```

Press Enter to accept the default Yes answer. This causes the configuration process to show all experimental device drivers. Notice that the prompts show the names of the configuration options without the `CONFIG_` prefix that's added when they are saved in the `.config` file.

insider insight

The possible answers to each prompt appear in square brackets with the default answer in uppercase. Thus, `[Y/n/?]` means the default answer is Yes, and two other possible answers are `n` and `?`. To accept the default, press Enter. For help on this option, press `?`. If you have questions about any option, press `?` and carefully read the help text before you decide what to do. You can use this general guideline to make your choices. In the following sections, I explain only selected groups of kernel configuration options.

Configuring General Setup Options

Through this group of options you can enable support for general features such as System V Inter Process Communication (IPC), process accounting based on BSD (Berkeley Software Distribution) UNIX, and hot-pluggable devices. You can press Enter to accept the default choices.

cross ref

One of the general options is `SYSCTL`. By answering Yes to this option, you enable the necessary support in the kernel so you can use the `/sbin/sysctl` program to view or set kernel parameters. Chapter 20 shows you how to use the `sysctl` program.

Enabling Support for Loadable Modules

This group of options asks you about support for loadable modules. A loadable module is a block of code that the Linux kernel can load and execute as if it were a part of the operating system.

```
*
* Loadable module support
*
Enable loadable module support (MODULES) [Y/n/?]
  Module unloading (MODULE_UNLOAD) [Y/n/?]
    Forced module unloading (MODULE_FORCE_UNLOAD) [N/y/?]
  Module versioning support (EXPERIMENTAL) (MODVERSIONS) [Y/n/?]
  Source checksum for all modules (MODULE_SRCVERSION_ALL) [Y/n/?]
  Module signature verification (EXPERIMENTAL) (MODULE_SIG) [Y/n/?]
    Required modules to be validly signed (EXPERIMENTAL) (MODULE_SIG_FORCE) [N/y/?]
  Automatic kernel module loading (KMOD) [Y/n/?]
```

You want to include support for modules, so answer Yes to the first question. You can accept the defaults for the remaining options. Notice that a few of the options are marked EXPERIMENTAL. These questions appear only if you enabled support for EXPERIMENTAL code at the beginning of the configuration session.

Configuring Processor-Related Features

This set of options is for setting the subarchitecture type, the processor family, and support for specific processor-related features:

```
*
* Processor type and features
*
Subarchitecture Type
> 1. PC-compatible (X86_PC)
  2. AMD Elan (X86_ELAN)
  3. Voyager (NCR) (X86_VOYAGER)
  4. NUMAQ (IBM/Sequent) (X86_NUMAQ)
  5. SGI 320/540 (Visual Workstation) (X86_VISWS)
choice[1-5]:
```

The Subarchitecture Type options enable you to select from different types of fundamental system designs that make use of the Intel x86 processor family but that may differ fundamentally from the well-known PC-compatible machines. Prior to version 2.6, the Linux kernel made an implicit assumption that the system's architecture was based on the old IBM PC-AT family. Starting with kernel version 2.6, you can build the kernel for other types of Intel x86-based architectures such as SGI Visual Workstation and multiprocessor systems with non-uniform memory access (NUMA). You probably can select the default PC-compatible subarchitecture, but the other options are available if you have to build the kernel for a different type of x86-based system.

After you select the x86 PC subarchitecture, the next set of options prompts you for the processor family:

```
   1. 386 (M386)
   2. 486 (M486)
   3. 586/K5/5x86/6x86/6x86MX (M586)
   4. Pentium-Classic (M586TSC)
   5. Pentium-MMX (M586MMX)
 > 6. Pentium-Pro (M686)
   7. Pentium-II/Celeron(pre-Coppermine) (MPENTIUMII)
   8. Pentium-III/Celeron(Coppermine)/Pentium-III Xeon (MPENTIUMIII)
   9. Pentium M (MPENTIUMM)
   10. Pentium-4/Celeron(P4-based)/Pentium-4 M/Xeon (MPENTIUM4)
   11. K6/K6-II/K6-III (MK6)
   12. Athlon/Duron/K7 (MK7)
   13. Opteron/Athlon64/Hammer/K8 (MK8)
   14. Crusoe (MCRUSOE)
   15. Efficeon (MEFFICEON)
   16. Winchip-C6 (MWINCHIPC6)
   17. Winchip-2 (MWINCHIP2)
   18. Winchip-2A/Winchip-3 (MWINCHIP3D)
   19. MediaGX/Geode (MGEODE)
   20. CyrixIII/VIA-C3 (MCYRIXIII)
   21. VIA C3-2 (Nehemiah) (MVIAC3_2)
 choice[1-21]:
```

If you select 386, the compiled kernel can run on any other processor (such as a 486 or any type of Pentium). However, if you're creating a kernel specifically for your system's processor, select your processor type from the list.

Subsequent options prompt you for a host of other processor-related options, which you can leave in their default settings. If in doubt, you can read the help for each option and select the ones that apply to your system.

Enabling Power Management Options

This set of options deals with managing the system's power and includes advanced configuration and power interface (ACPI), advanced power management (APM) BIOS support, and CPU frequency scaling. You can simply accept the default settings for these options. If you don't understand what an option means, press **?** to get help on that option.

Configuring Bus Options

These options ask you about supporting specific buses: PCI, ISA, EISA, MCA, and PCMCIA. The Industry Standard Architecture (ISA) bus was once the most widely used bus (until the PCI bus came along); this bus was used in the original IBM PC-AT. The Micro Channel Architecture (MCA) bus is IBM's proprietary bus, which first appeared in the PS/2 PCs. IBM designed this bus as a high-speed bus, but its proprietary nature kept it from being widely used in PCs. The Extended Industry Standard Architecture (EISA) bus came about as an alternative to the MCA bus, with performance comparable to that of the MCA. The EISA bus is not widely used because the EISA bus peripheral cards are more expensive than their ISA bus counterparts. The Peripheral Component Interconnect (PCI) bus is the latest high-performance bus; the current crop of PCs use the PCI bus, but also offer ISA bus slots so that you can continue to use ISA cards.

PCMCIA stands for Personal Computer Memory Card International Association, a non-profit organization that standardized the interface for adding memory cards to laptop computers. Although originally conceived for memory cards, PCMCIA devices became popular for a wide variety of add-ons for laptops. The PCMCIA devices are called PC cards and the term CardBus refers to the electrical specification of PC cards.

Typically, you want to build in support for PCI and ISA and build modules for PCMCIA support. You can also add support for the PCI hot plug if your system supports adding or removing PCI cards while the system is powered up and running.

Enabling Support for Executable File Formats

Turn on the support for Executable and Linkable Format (ELF), which is the standard format for executables and libraries in Linux. Prior to ELF, the format for executables was called a.out (based on the default name of the executable generated by the C compiler). In kernel version 2.6, you can build a module to support the old a.out format.

Configuring Memory Technology Devices

This category of options provides support for file systems resident on memory technology devices, such as flash memory and random access memory. These file systems are often used in embedded devices. This category includes a number of options for building kernel modules to support various memory devices. There is no harm in building the modules because they are not loaded if your computer doesn't have the appropriate memory device.

Enabling Parallel Port Support

These options are important if you use any devices such as printers or parallel port Zip drives connected to the parallel port of your PC. Answer `m` to the Parallel port support and PC-style hardware options so the drivers are built as modules.

Enabling Plug and Play Support

These options ask if you want to enable Plug and Play (PnP) support in the kernel. If you enable PnP support, the kernel automatically configures PnP devices (just as Windows does). You should press Enter to accept the default choices for these options.

```
*
* Plug and Play support
*
Plug and Play support (PNP) [Y/n/?]
  PnP Debug Messages (PNP_DEBUG) [N/y/?]
  *
  * Protocols
  *
  ISA Plug and Play support (ISAPNP) [Y/n/?]
  Plug and Play BIOS support (EXPERIMENTAL) (PNPBIOS) [N/y/?]
  Plug and Play ACPI support (EXPERIMENTAL) (PNPACPI) [Y/n/?]
```

Configuring Block Devices

Block devices (such as disk drives) transfer data in chunks (as opposed to keyboards, which transfer data one character at a time). This set of options involves the floppy and IDE (Integrated Drive Electronics) devices connected to the PC's parallel port as well as other block devices.

```
*
* Block devices
*
Normal floppy disk support (BLK_DEV_FD) [M/n/y/?]
XT hard disk support (BLK_DEV_XD) [N/m/y/?]
Parallel port IDE device support (PARIDE) [M/n/?]
```

The first question asks if you want floppy drive support. Because many PCs do have a floppy drive, your answer generally is Yes. You should press Enter to accept the default for the third question if you have external CD-ROM or disk devices that connect through your PC's parallel port. Some IDE devices use a parallel port IDE adapter — that's what the `PARIDE` option refers to. The next set of options is for various parallel IDE drivers. You can press Enter to accept the default choice of building these drivers as modules.

Next comes another set of options for block devices. The `BLK_DEV_LOOP` option is for a loopback device. Enabling the loopback device lets the Linux kernel manipulate an entire file system image stored in a single large file. This option is useful if you want to mount a CD or DVD image (for example, a Linux ISO file) and check it out before actually burning the CD or DVD.

The RAM disk support allows the kernel to use a portion of your system's memory as a disk capable of storing a file system. Typically, a RAM disk functions only during system startup when the hard drive may not be available yet. The RAM disk is essential if you are booting a SCSI disk and you haven't compiled the SCSI drivers into the kernel.

Enabling ATA/ATAPI/MFM/RLL Support

This set of questions involves IDE devices, such as hard disks and ATAPI CD-ROM drives.

```
*
* ATA/ATAPI/MFM/RLL support
*
ATA/ATAPI/MFM/RLL support (IDE) [Y/n/m/?]
  Enhanced IDE/MFM/RLL disk/cdrom/tape/floppy support (BLK_DEV_IDE) [Y/n/m/?]
```

This set of questions has four acronyms: ATA, IDE, MFM, and RLL. All of these relate to hard disks or interface of disk drives to the PC. Here's what they mean:

- **ATA** stands for *Advanced Technology Attachment* and refers to the PC-AT style interface used to connect hard disks and CD-ROM drives to the PC's motherboard.
- **IDE** stands for *Integrated Drive Electronics* and refers to the original PC hard disks that integrated the disk controller onto the hard disk itself. The IDE interface is more accurately described as AT Attachment Packet Interface, or ATAPI. You typically see the terms IDE, ATA, and ATAPI used interchangeably.
- **MFM** stands for *modified frequency modulation* and refers to the way data was encoded on older hard drives. These hard drives can work over an IDE interface.
- **RLL** stands for *run length limited* and is also a technique for storing data on hard disk. RLL disks can work over an IDE interface.

The first question asks if you want the kernel to support IDE devices. The second question asks if you want to use the full-featured IDE device that can control up to 10 IDE interfaces. Because each IDE interface can have a master and a slave device, this enables Linux to access a total of up to 20 IDE devices, such as disks or CD-ROM drives. You can press Enter to accept the default choices of Yes for both of these options.

insider insight

The next set of options concerns various IDE drivers. The initial comment starts with a note that refers to the file `/usr/share/doc/kernel-doc*/Documentation/ide.txt`. You can find many useful help files (these are all text files) in the `/usr/share/doc/kernel-doc*/Documentation` directory. To get these files, you must install the kernel-doc RPM. If your system does not have that RPM installed, you can do so by typing yum install kernel-doc (make sure your system is connected to the Internet before you type the command).

You can accept the default answers for these options. Note that `IDE/ATAPI FLOPPY` refers to IDE floppy drives, such as Iomega Zip drive or Imation Superdisk LS-120 drive. The questions about CMD640 and RZ1000 bug fixes refer to some known problems with specific chipsets used in IDE interfaces.

Configuring SCSI Devices

This set of options has to do with SCSI devices. SCSI stands for *Small Computer Systems Interface* and refers to a type of interface through which you can connect multiple devices such as hard disks, CD/DVD drives, and scanners to the PC. If your system has a SCSI adapter, you should start by answering Yes to the `SCSI` option. After that, you have to answer questions about the types of devices (disk, tape, CD-ROM) connected to the SCSI adapter. Finally, you must enable support for the specific SCSI adapter model on your system.

Configuring IEEE 1394 Support

This set of options is for enabling IEEE 1394 support, either as a module or linked into the kernel. IEEE 1394 is a high-speed serial bus for connecting peripherals to PCs. Apple calls this bus FireWire; Sony calls it i.Link. IEEE 1394 is similar to USB, but it can transfer data at rates up to 400 Mbps, which is more than 30 times the data rate of the older USB version 1.1 (note that USB 2.0 is much faster; it can transfer data at rates of up to 480 Mbps). Because of its high data-transfer rates, IEEE 1394 is ideal for connecting high-speed peripherals such as digital audio and video devices and external hard drives to the PC.

Currently, Linux supports IEEE 1394 chipsets that are compatible with Texas Instruments PCILynx/PCILynx2 and OHCI chipsets. If your PC has an IEEE 1394 adapter, you can build the necessary drivers through these options.

```
*
* IEEE 1394 (FireWire) support
*
IEEE 1394 (FireWire) support (IEEE1394) [M/n/y/?]
```

To learn more about using IEEE 1394 peripherals in Linux, visit the website of the IEEE 1394 for Linux project at `www.linux1394.org/`.

Configuring I2O drivers

Pronounced *eye-two-oh*, I20 refers to Intelligent Input/Output—a new device driver architecture independent of the operating system and the controlled device. I2O functions by logically separating the part responsible for managing the device from the part that contains operating system-specific details. (It's called the I2O Split Driver model.) The two parts of an I2O driver are the OS Services Module (OSM), which works with the operating system, and the Hardware Device Module (HDM) that interfaces with the particular device the driver manages. The OSM and HDM communicate by passing messages to each other.

Linux comes with some I2O drivers for SCSI and PCI devices. You can build the I2O drivers through the following configuration options:

```
*
* I2O device support
*
I2O support (I2O) [M/n/y/?]
  I2O Configuration support (I2O_CONFIG) [M/n/?]
  I2O Block OSM (I2O_BLOCK) [M/n/?]
  I2O SCSI OSM (I2O_SCSI) [M/n/?]
  I2O /proc support (I2O_PROC) [M/n/?]
```

Configuring the Network

This set of options deals with networking. How you set these options depends on how you want to use your Linux system in a network. Always say Yes to the TCP/IP Networking option because the X Window System uses TCP/IP networking (even if your PC isn't on any network). You can also enable support for IPv6—the next-generation Internet Protocol.

Answer Yes to the Network packet filtering option if you want to use your Linux system as a firewall—an intermediary system that controls information flowing between a local area network (LAN) and the Internet.

Other categories in the Networking Support options include wireless LAN, Ethernet (10/100 Mpbs as well as Gigabit), ATM (Asynchronous Transfer Mode), Token ring, ARCnet, AppleTalk, wide area network (WAN), PCMCIA network devices, amateur radio, infrared, and Bluetooth. For Ethernet, you can build support for the Ethernet card installed on your system. This category also includes support for wireless networking and drivers for wireless Ethernet cards. You can also enable experimental support for SCTP—Stream Control Transmission Protocol—designed to transport public switches telephone network signaling messages over IP networks (RFC 3758 describes SCTP).

The infrared support is for infrared communication using the protocols specified by the Infrared Data Association (IrDA). IrDA communication is used by many laptops and personal digital assistants (PDAs), such as PalmOne, HP iPaq, and Dell Axim. Many IR interfaces are in the form of dongles—small adapters that typically attach to the serial port of the PC. You can use the options in this section to enable support for several common types of dongles.

Bluetooth is a low-power, short-range wireless technology for connecting devices on the 2.4 GHz frequency band. Devices that use Bluetooth can usually connect when they are within 10 meters of one another. To find out more about Bluetooth, visit `www.bluetooth.com`. Linux supports Bluetooth through a core driver and several other modules. You can answer `y` to enable Bluetooth support and then select other options specific to your Bluetooth devices.

Enabling Support for ISDN

This set of options enables you to include support for ISDN (Integrated Services Digital Network), a digital telephone line you can use to connect the Linux system to the Internet. These ISDN-related options include the configuration of specific ISDN adapters.

You should build the ISDN driver only if your PC has an ISDN card. If you anticipate adding an ISDN card and purchase ISDN service from the phone company, you can build the driver as a module. Read the file `/usr/share/doc/kernel-doc-*/Documentation/README` for more information on how to set up and use the ISDN driver in Linux.

Configuring Telephony Support

With the right hardware and software, the Telephony Support options enable you to use the Linux system for making phone calls over the Internet (also known as *voiceover IP* or *VoIP*). You can choose to build driver modules for Telephony Support if you have a Telephony card, such as the Internet PhoneJACK or Internet LineJACK manufactured by Quicknet Technologies, Inc. If you don't have a Telephony card, you can safely leave these options turned off.

Configuring Input Devices and Character Devices

The next few options deal with configuring input devices, which include devices such as keyboard, mice, joystick, and touchscreens, as well as devices connected to the serial and parallel ports. These options also include configuration of multiport serial interface cards that enable you to connect multiple terminals or other devices to your Linux system. Answer No if you do not have any such devices on your system. Near the end of the list, you see a question about parallel-printer support (`PRINTER`). If you plan to connect a printer to the parallel port, answer Yes to this option.

Configuring the Watchdog Timer

These options enable you to turn on support for the watchdog timer. Essentially, this causes the kernel to create a special file; failure to open the file and write to it every minute causes the system to reboot. Some watchdog boards can monitor the PC's status (including the temperature) and reboot the PC when necessary. You can also enable support for specific watchdog cards from this set of options.

If you want access to the PC's nonvolatile (battery-backed) memory — NVRAM — in the real-time clock, answer Yes to the `NVRAM` option. You can get access to the real-time clock by enabling the `RTC` configuration option.

Configuring Floppy Tape Drive

If you have a tape drive connected to your floppy controller, answer `y` or `m` to the next option, and select the other parameters appropriately (or accept the default choices):

```
*
* Ftape, the floppy tape device driver
*
Ftape (QIC-80/Travan) support (FTAPE) [N/m/y/?]
```

You can also enable several parameters related to floppy tape drives.

Configuring Advanced Graphics Support

This set of options configures support for advanced video cards that can perform hardware-accelerated, 3D graphics. You can enable the first option to build the AGP (Accelerated Graphics Port) driver and can answer Yes to the option for your specific chipset.

```
/dev/agpgart (AGP Support) (AGP) [Y/m/?]
```

Next, you have to configure a set of options for the *Direct Rendering Manager* (DRM), a device-independent driver that supports the XFree86 *Direct Rendering Infrastructure* (DRI). DRI is meant for direct access to 3D graphics hardware in advanced graphics cards, such as 3Dfx Banshee and Voodoo3. To learn more about DRI, use your Web browser to visit `http://dri.freedesktop.org/wiki/`.

If you have a 3D graphics card, you can answer Yes to `DRM` and build the module for the graphics card in your system. If you do not have one of the listed graphics cards, you should answer No to these options.

Configuring I2C Protocol

I2C — pronounced *eye-squared-see* — is a protocol Philips has developed for communication over a pair of wires at rates between 10 and 100 kHz. System Management Bus (SMBus) is a subset of the I2C protocol. Many modern motherboards have an SMBus meant for connecting devices such as EEPROM (electrically erasable programmable read-only memory) and chips for hardware monitoring. Linux supports the I2C and SMBus protocols. You need this support for Video for Linux. If you have any hardware sensors or video equipment that needs I2C support, answer `m` to the `I2C` option, and answer `m` to the specific driver for your hardware. For example, if you want to use a BT848 frame-grabber board (to capture video), you should answer `m` to the `I2C_ALGOBIT` option.

To learn more about the I2C, read the documentation in the `/usr/share/doc/kernel-*/Documentation/i2c` directory. In particular, the summary file briefly describes the I2C and SMBus protocols.

Configuring Multimedia Devices

The next set of options involves multimedia devices, including FM radio cards. For more information on these devices, consult the documentation in the `/usr/share/doc/kernel-doc-*/Documentation/video4linux` directory.

Enabling Frame Buffer Support

Through these options you can enable support for frame-buffer devices. A frame buffer is an abstraction for the graphics hardware so that the kernel and other software can produce graphical output without having to rely on the low-level details (such as hardware registers) of a video card. Frame buffer support is available for many video cards.

Configuring the Sound Card

Use this set of options to configure sound card support. If you have a sound card installed, start by answering `m` to the Sound Card Support option. After that, answer `m` for Advanced Linux Sound Architecture (ALSA) and the sound devices. If you don't know your PC's sound card model, you can always build the sound modules for all types of sound cards. That way, the modules needed for your system's sound card are available when needed.

Enabling USB Support

This set of options enables support for the Universal Serial Bus (USB), a serial bus that comes built into most new PCs. USB version 1.1 supports data-transfer rates as high as 12 Mbps — 12 million bits per second or 1.5MB per second — compared with 115 Kbps or the 0.115 Mbps transfer rate of a standard serial port (such as COM1). You can daisy-chain up to 127 devices on a USB bus. The bus also provides power to the devices, and you can attach or remove devices while the PC is running — a capability commonly referred to as hotplugging. USB version 2.0 (or USB 2.0 or USB2, for short) ups the ante by raising the data transfer rates to a whopping 480 Mbps, slightly faster than the competing IEEE 1394 (FireWire) bus.

USB can replace the functionality of the PC's serial and parallel ports, as well as the keyboard and mouse ports. Nowadays, many PC peripherals — such as mouse, keyboard, printer, scanner, modem, digital camera, memory card, and so on — are designed to connect to the PC through a USB port.

If your PC has a USB port, you should answer `y` or `m` to the `USB` option. Then, you have to answer `m` to the `EHCI_HCD`, `UHCI_HCD`, or `OHCI_HCD` option, depending on the type of USB interface — EHCI (for USB 2.0), UHCI (Intel) or OHCI (Compaq and others) — your PC has. To determine the type of USB interface, type **/sbin/lspci**, and look for the USB controller's make and model in the output. For example, here's the output from `/sbin/lspci` for a PC with a USB port:

```
00:00.0 Host bridge: Intel Corporation 82845G/GL[Brookdale-G]/GE/PE DRAM
Controller/Host-Hub Interface (rev 03)
00:02.0 VGA compatible controller: Intel Corporation 82845G/GL[Brookdale-G]/GE Chipset
Integrated Graphics Device (rev 03)
00:1d.0 USB Controller: Intel Corporation 82801DB/DBL/DBM (ICH4/ICH4-L/ICH4-M) USB
UHCI Controller #1 (rev 02)
00:1d.1 USB Controller: Intel Corporation 82801DB/DBL/DBM (ICH4/ICH4-L/ICH4-M) USB
UHCI Controller #2 (rev 02)
00:1d.2 USB Controller: Intel Corporation 82801DB/DBL/DBM (ICH4/ICH4-L/ICH4-M) USB
UHCI Controller #3 (rev 02)
00:1d.7 USB Controller: Intel Corporation 82801DB/DBM (ICH4/ICH4-M) USB2 EHCI
Controller (rev 02)
00:1e.0 PCI bridge: Intel Corporation 82801 PCI Bridge (rev 82)
00:1f.0 ISA bridge: Intel Corporation 82801DB/DBL (ICH4/ICH4-L) LPC Interface Bridge
(rev 02)
00:1f.1 IDE interface: Intel Corporation 82801DB (ICH4) IDE Controller (rev 02)
00:1f.3 SMBus: Intel Corporation 82801DB/DBL/DBM (ICH4/ICH4-L/ICH4-M) SMBus Controller
(rev 02)
00:1f.5 Multimedia audio controller: Intel Corporation 82801DB/DBL/DBM (ICH4/ICH4-
L/ICH4-M) AC'97 Audio Controller (rev 02)
01:0b.0 Communication controller: Agere Systems (former Lucent Microelectronics) V.92
56K WinModem (rev 03)
01:0c.0 Ethernet controller: Realtek Semiconductor Co., Ltd. RTL-8139/8139C/8139C+
(rev 10)
```

As the output shows, this PC has both USB2 EHCI controller and an Intel UHCI USB controller. Therefore, I need the driver modules for the EHCI and UHCI support (EHCI_HCD and UHCI_HCD options).

After you select the UHCI or OHCI interface support, you have to build the driver modules for specific USB devices on your system. Linux supports a huge number of USB devices. For more information on USB devices, consult the documentation in the `/usr/share/doc/kernel-doc-*/Documentation/usb` directory — especially the links in the `usb-help.txt` file.

Enabling Support for Specific File Systems

The next set of options enables you to turn on support for specific types of file systems. You can make your choices based on the guidelines shown in Table 21-4.

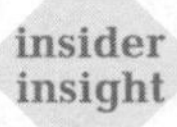

It's best to link in the support for your root partition's file system. If the support for your root partition's file system is compiled as a module, you'll have to use an initial ramdisk (initrd) to boot Linux.

Table 21-4: Common File System Configuration Options

Option	*Description*
ADFS_FS	Enables Linux to read from the ADFS — the Acorn Disc Filing System — the standard file system of the RiscOS operating system that runs on Acorn's ARM-based Risc PC systems and the Acorn Archimedes systems. Answer y if you want Linux to read from ADFS partitions on hard drives and from ADFS floppy disks.
AFFS_FS	Enables support for the Amiga Fast File System (AFFS), the file system used by Amiga systems since AmigaOS version 1.3 (34.20). Answer y if you need to read from and write to an Amiga FFS partition on your hard drive. Note that this support does not enable Linux to read from Amiga floppy disks because of an incompatibility of the floppy controller used in an Amiga and the standard floppy controller in PCs.
AFS_FS	Enables support for the Andrew File System (AFS).
BEFS_FS	Enables support for the 64-bit BeOS File System (BEFS), the file system used by Be, Inc.'s BeOS systems.
CODA_FS	Enables support for Coda, an advanced network file system that is similar to NFS but that better supports disconnected operation (for example, laptops) and is a better security model. Answer y only if you need your Linux system to act as a Coda client.
EXT2_FS	Enables support for the second extended file system. You should definitely answer y to turn on this option.
EXT3_FS	Enables support for the journaling version of the second extended file system — the current standard file system for Linux. You should definitely answer y to turn on this option. The use of journaling means that you do not have to check the file system after a crash — the journal keeps track of all changes and can keep the file system consistent even if there is a crash.
FAT_FS	Turns on support for any File Allocation Table (FAT)–based file system (including MS-DOS and Windows 95 VFAT file systems). Answer y if you want to access MS-DOS or VFAT files.
HFS_FS	Enables Linux to mount Macintosh-formatted floppy disks and hard drive partitions with full read/write access. Answer y if you want to access Macintosh file systems.
HPFS_FS	Enables your Linux system to access and read an OS/2 HPFS file system (you can read only HPFS files). Answer y if you have an OS/2 partition on your hard disk.
ISO9660_FS	Turns on support for the standard ISO 9660 file system used on CD-ROMs (this is also known as the High Sierra File System and is referred to as hsfs on some UNIX workstations). If you have a CD/DVD-ROM drive, answer y here.

(continued)

Table 21-4 *(continued)*

Option	*Description*
JFS_FS	Turns on support for IBM's Journaled File System (JFS) for Linux (for more information, see http://jfs.sourceforge.net/).
JFFS_FS	Turns on support for the Journaling Flash File System (JFFS), which was developed by Axis Communications of Sweden and is aimed at providing a safe (from crash or sudden powerdown) file system for diskless embedded devices.
JFFS_FS	Turns on support for the Journaling Flash File System version 2 (JFFS2), the second generation of JFFS for use on diskless embedded devices. You can use JFFS2 only on memory-technology devices such as compact flash memory.
MINIX_FS	Supports the Minix file system — the original file system of Linux. This simple file system still functions on floppy disks, so you should answer m to include support in the form of a module.
MSDOS_FS	Supports MS-DOS file systems. Press y if you want to read an MS-DOS partition on the hard disk or an MS-DOS floppy.
NCP_FS	Enables you to mount Netware Core Protocol (NCP) directories from Novell Netware systems on a network. Answer y if you want to access Netware directories.
NFS_FS	Enables you to mount Network File System (NFS) directories from other systems on a network. Answer y if you want to access NFS directories.
NTFS_FS	Enables Linux to read from the NT file system (NTFS), the file system used by Microsoft Windows NT. Answer y here for read-only access to an NTFS partition on the hard disk. There is also partial, but safe, write support available. To enable write support, you have to answer y to the NTFS_RW option.
PROC_FS	Turns on support for the /proc virtual file system through which you can get information about the kernel. (For example, type the cat /proc/interrupts command to list the IRQs used by the system.) The /proc file system does not exist on the disk; files are created when you access them. You should answer y to enable this option because it is useful and several Linux system utilities rely on the /proc file system.
QNX4FS_FS	Supports the file system used by the QNX 4 operating system, a popular real-time operating system (www.qnx.com/). Answer y if you intend to mount QNX hard disks or floppies for read-only access.
REISERFS_FS	Turns on support for ReiserFS, an efficient file system that stores both filenames and files in a balanced tree and uses journaling.
ROMFS_FS	Turns on support for a very small, read-only, memory-resident file system used in the initial RAM disk (initrd) during Linux installation. Answer y to include support for this file system.
SMB_FS	Enables your Linux system to access shared directories from networked PCs running Windows 95/98/NT/2000/XP or Windows for Workgroups. Answer y if you want to access shared directories on Windows systems.
SYSV_FS	Turns on support for the System V file system used by SCO, Xenix, and Coherent variants of UNIX for Intel PCs. If you need to access a System V file system, answer y here.

Option	Description
UFS_FS	Allows your Linux system to read to (but not write to) the UFS file system used by the BSD (Berkeley Software Distribution) variants of UNIX (such as SunOS, FreeBSD, NetBSD, and NeXTstep). Answer y if you need to access any UFS file system. If you also want to write to UFS file systems, answer y to the experimental UFS_FS_WRITE option.
UDF_FS	Supports the new UDF file system, which is used on some CD-ROMs and DVDs when they are written in packet mode or written by utilities such as DirectCD.
VFAT_FS	Supports Windows 95/98/NT/2000 VFAT file systems with long filenames. Answer y if your system has partitions with VFAT file systems, or you expect to read floppy disks with Windows files.
VXFS_FS	Supports a Veritas VxFS–compatible file system (VxFS is used in SCO Unixware).
XFS_FS	Supports XFS, a high-performance journaling file system that originated on the SGI IRIX system.

Linux can read and manipulate disk partitions created by many different systems. The next group of options enables you to include support for specific partition types:

```
*
* Partition Types
*
Advanced partition selection (PARTITION_ADVANCED) [Y/n/?]
  Acorn partition support (ACORN_PARTITION) [N/y/?]
  Alpha OSF partition support (OSF_PARTITION) [Y/n/?]
  Amiga partition table support (AMIGA_PARTITION) [N/y/?]
  Atari partition table support (ATARI_PARTITION) [N/y/?]
  Macintosh partition map support (MAC_PARTITION) [Y/n/?]
  PC BIOS (MSDOS partition tables) support (MSDOS_PARTITION) [Y/n/?]
    BSD disklabel (FreeBSD partition tables) support (BSD_DISKLABEL) [Y/n/?]
    Minix subpartition support (MINIX_SUBPARTITION) [Y/n/?]
    Solaris (x86) partition table support (SOLARIS_X86_PARTITION) [Y/n/?]
    Unixware slices support (UNIXWARE_DISKLABEL) [Y/n/?]
  Windows Logical Disk Manager (Dynamic Disk) support (LDM_PARTITION) [N/y/?]
  SGI partition support (SGI_PARTITION) [Y/n/?]
  Ultrix partition table support (ULTRIX_PARTITION) [N/y/?]
  Sun partition tables support (SUN_PARTITION) [Y/n/?]
  EFI GUID Partition support (EFI_PARTITION) [Y/n/?]
```

Selecting a Native Language Character Set

This set of configuration options requires you to select a native language character set. The Microsoft FAT file systems use these character sets to store and display filenames in one of several languages. The character sets are stored in files called DOS codepages. You have to include the appropriate codepages so that the Linux kernel can read and write filenames correctly in any DOS partitions in the hard disk. Note that the codepages apply only to filenames; they have nothing to do with the actual contents of files.

You can include support for as many codepages as you want. Simply answer y or m to the codepages for your selection of languages.

Enabling Support for Kernel Debugging

This set of options enables you to use the SysRq key (equivalent to pressing Alt-PrintScreen) to get important status information right after a system crash. This information is useful if you are a Linux developer who expects to debug the kernel. Most users answer No (because most users run a stable version of the kernel and do not expect to fix kernel errors) to disable these options.

Configuring Security Options

Through these options, you can include support for several security features including the Security Enhanced Linux (SELinux), which was developed by the National Security Agency (NSA), a U.S. government agency. SELinux comes with Linux, but you can turn it off during booting by providing selinux=0 as a boot option. For more information on SELinux, visit www.nsa.gov/selinux/.

Enabling Cryptography Support

This set of options is for enabling cryptography support in the kernel. You can include support for the cryptographic application programming interface (API) and then build specific algorithms as modules, as the default selections of the following options show:

```
*
* Cryptographic options
*
Cryptographic API (CRYPTO) [Y/?] y
  HMAC support (CRYPTO_HMAC) [Y/?] y
  Null algorithms (CRYPTO_NULL) [M/n/y/?]
  MD4 digest algorithm (CRYPTO_MD4) [M/n/y/?]
  MD5 digest algorithm (CRYPTO_MD5) [M/y/?]
  SHA1 digest algorithm (CRYPTO_SHA1) [Y/?] y
  SHA256 digest algorithm (CRYPTO_SHA256) [M/n/y/?]
  SHA384 and SHA512 digest algorithms (CRYPTO_SHA512) [M/n/y/?]
  Whirlpool digest algorithms (CRYPTO_WP512) [M/n/y/?]
  Tiger digest algorithms (CRYPTO_TGR192) [M/n/y/?]
  DES and Triple DES EDE cipher algorithms (CRYPTO_DES) [M/y/?]
  Blowfish cipher algorithm (CRYPTO_BLOWFISH) [M/n/y/?]
  Twofish cipher algorithm (CRYPTO_TWOFISH) [M/n/y/?]
  Serpent cipher algorithm (CRYPTO_SERPENT) [M/n/y/?]
  AES cipher algorithms (i586) (CRYPTO_AES_586) [M/n/y/?]
  CAST5 (CAST-128) cipher algorithm (CRYPTO_CAST5) [M/n/y/?]
  CAST6 (CAST-256) cipher algorithm (CRYPTO_CAST6) [M/n/y/?]
  TEA and XTEA cipher algorithms (CRYPTO_TEA) [M/n/y/?]
  ARC4 cipher algorithm (CRYPTO_ARC4) [M/y/?]
  Khazad cipher algorithm (CRYPTO_KHAZAD) [M/n/y/?]
  Anubis cipher algorithm (CRYPTO_ANUBIS) [M/n/y/?]
  Deflate compression algorithm (CRYPTO_DEFLATE) [M/y/?]
  Michael MIC keyed digest algorithm (CRYPTO_MICHAEL_MIC) [M/n/y/?]
  CRC32c CRC algorithm (CRYPTO_CRC32C) [M/n/y/?]
  Testing module (CRYPTO_TEST) [N/m/y/?]
  In-kernel signature checker (EXPERIMENTAL) (CRYPTO_SIGNATURE) [Y/?] y
    Handle DSA signatures (EXPERIMENTAL) (CRYPTO_SIGNATURE_DSA) [Y/n/?]
  Multiprecision maths library (EXPERIMENTAL) (CRYPTO_MPILIB) [Y/?] y
```

You can also enable support for some hardware cryptographic devices and build the modules for a few cyclic redundancy check (CRC) algorithms.

Building the Kernel

After configuring the kernel options, you have to build the kernel. This part can take a while. Depending on your system, making a new kernel can take anywhere from a few minutes to over an hour.

Type the following command to initiate the process:

```
make
```

The `make` command creates the new kernel as well as any modules that you have specified through the configuration step.

As the kernel is built, you see a lot of messages onscreen. When it's all over, a new kernel in the form of a compressed file named `bzImage` is in the `arch/i386/boot` subdirectory of where the kernel sources are located.

To use the new kernel, you have to copy the kernel file and the `System.map` file to the `/boot` directory under a specific name and edit the GRUB menu in `/etc/grub.conf` to set up GRUB, the boot loader. Before you proceed with the kernel installation, however, you have to install the modules and build a new initial RAM disk.

Installing the Modules

If you select any modules during the kernel configuration, the kernel building step also builds the modules. All you have to do is install them. Perform this task with the following commands:

```
cd /usr/src/kernels/linux-*
make modules_install
```

The `make modules_install` command copies all the modules to a new subdirectory in the `/lib/modules` directory. The subdirectory name should be the same as the kernel version number.

Now you can install the kernel and make it available for GRUB to boot.

Creating the Initial RAM Disk File

The new kernel needs a new initial RAM disk file that you can create by using the `mkinitrd` command. Usually, the initial RAM disk image is stored in a file whose name begins with `initrd`. As you might have guessed, `initrd` is shorthand for initial RAM disk, and the `mkinitrd` command is so named because it makes an `initrd` file.

The `mkinitrd` program is in the `/sbin` directory, and you have to log in as `root` and use a command line of the following form to create the `initrd` file:

```
/sbin/mkinitrd /boot/initrd-filename.img  module-directory
```

The `initrd` file has to be in the `/boot` directory where the kernel is also located. You can use any filename for *`initrd-filename`*. The *`module-directory`* is the name of the directory in `/lib/modules` where the module files for the new kernel are located. The `make` modules_install step places the modules in a directory whose name is the kernel version number. For example, if your kernel version (as reported by the uname -r command) is 2.6.11-1.1275_FC4, the *module-directory*, after the make modules_install step, is 2.6.11-1.1275_FC4.

Another common practice is to use an initrd filename created by appending the module directory name to the initrd- prefix. Thus, for module directory 2.6.11-1.1275_FC4, the initrd file would be initrd-2.6.11-1.1275_FC4.img.

You have to refer to the initrd file in the GRUB menu file (/etc/grub.conf) when you make the new kernel available for use.

Installing the New Kernel and Setting Up GRUB

Fedora Linux uses GRUB to load the Linux kernel from the disk. The configuration file /etc/grub.conf lists the kernel binary that GRUB runs. You can examine the contents of the GRUB configuration file by typing the following command:

```
cat /etc/grub.conf
```

Here is what I see when I try this command on one of my systems:

```
# grub.conf generated by anaconda
#
# Note that you do not have to rerun grub after making changes to this file
# NOTICE:  You have a /boot partition.  This means that
#          all kernel and initrd paths are relative to /boot/, eg.
#          root (hd0,5)
#          kernel /vmlinuz-version ro root=/dev/hda10
#          initrd /initrd-version.img
#boot=/dev/hda
default=0
timeout=5
splashimage=(hd0,5)/grub/splash.xpm.gz
hiddenmenu
title Fedora Core (2.6.11-1.1240_FC4)
        root (hd0,2)
        kernel /vmlinuz-2.6.11-1.1240_FC4 ro root=LABEL=/1 acpi=off rhgb quiet
        initrd /initrd-2.6.11-1.1240_FC4.img
title Windows XP
        rootnoverify (hd0,1)
        chainloader +1
```

You can learn more about GRUB and its configuration file (/etc/grub.conf) by typing **info grub** in a terminal window. For this discussion, you should note the following:

- The line default=0 specifies the first boot entry as the default one that GRUB should boot.
- The timeout=5 command causes GRUB to boot the default entry automatically after waiting for 5 seconds. If other boot entries are in the file, the user may select another one from a boot menu GRUB displays.
- The line hiddenmenu hides the GRUB menu that displays the partitions you can boot from. GRUB displays the menu if you press any key as GRUB waits to boot the default partition.

- The four lines that begin with `title Fedora Core` define a specific kernel file GRUB can boot. You can make GRUB boot another kernel by adding a similar section to the configuration file.
- The line `root (hd0,2)` sets the root device to the third partition of the first hard disk.
- The `kernel` line identifies the kernel GRUB loads. In this case, the kernel file is `vmlinuz-2.6.11-1.1240_FC4`, which is located in the root device — the third partition on the first hard disk. In my system, that partition is mounted on the `/boot` directory. In other words, GRUB loads the kernel file `/boot/vmlinuz-2.6.11-1.1240_FC4`. The `root=LABEL=/` part of the line specifies that the Linux root file system is on the device whose label is /. This location may differ on your system.
- The line `initrd /initrd-2.6.11-1.1240_FC4.img` specifies a file that contains an initial RAM disk (`initrd` stands for initial RAM disk) image that serves as a file system before the disks are available. The Linux kernel uses the RAM disk — a block of memory used as a disk — to get started; then it loads other driver modules and begins using the hard disk.

On systems that have a Windows partition, the GRUB configuration file typically includes another section with details for the operating system (perhaps Windows 98, Windows 2000, or Windows XP) on that partition.

To configure GRUB to boot yet another kernel (the one you just built), you need to follow these steps:

1. Copy the new kernel binary to the `/boot` directory. The new, compressed kernel file is in the `arch/i386/boot` subdirectory where the kernel source resides. The kernel filename is usually `bzImage`. I simply copy that file to the `/boot` directory with the same name:

   ```
   cp /usr/src/kernels/linux-*/arch/i386/boot/bzImage /boot
   ```

   If the kernel filename is `zImage`, make sure you use `zImage` instead of `bzImage`. You can use any other filename you want, as long as you use the same filename when referring to the kernel in the `/etc/grub.conf` file in Step 3.
2. Save the old `System.map` file in the `/boot` directory, and copy the new `System.map` file from the kernel source directory to the `/boot` directory.
3. Use your favorite text editor to edit the `/etc/grub.conf` file to add the following lines just after the `splashimage` line in the file. (If you need help with a text editor, consult Chapter 14 to learn about vi and Emacs, two popular text editors for Linux):

   ```
   title New Linux kernel
           root (hd0,2)
           kernel /bzImage ro root=LABEL=/
           initrd /initrd-VERSION
   ```

   Append to the `kernel` line any other kernel options you need for your system (for example, I need `acpi=off` on one of my systems). Remember to change *`VERSION`* on the initrd line to the version number of the new kernel that you have built.
4. Save the `grub.conf` file, and exit the editor.

caution

On your system, you should make sure the `root (hd0,2)` line is correct — instead of `(hd0,2)`, which refers to the third partition of the first hard disk, you should list the correct disk partition where the Linux `/boot` file system is located. Also, make sure that you use the correct filename for the kernel image file (for example, `/boot/vmlinuz` if the kernel file is so named).

After preparing the `/etc/grub.conf` file, you are ready to reboot the system and try out the new kernel.

Rebooting the System to Test the New Kernel

While you are still logged in as `root`, type the following command to reboot the system:

```
reboot
```

When you see the GRUB screen, select the name you have assigned to the new kernel in the `/etc/grub.conf` file.

After the system reboots with the new kernel, you should see the familiar graphical login screen. To see proof that you are indeed running the new kernel, log in as a user, open a terminal window, and type **uname -srv**. This command shows you the kernel version, as well as the date and time when this kernel was built. If you have upgraded the kernel source, you should see the version number for the new kernel. If you have simply rebuilt the kernel for the same old kernel version, the date and time should match the time when you rebuilt the kernel. That's your proof that the system is running the new kernel.

If the system *hangs* (nothing seems to happen — there is no output on the screen and no disk activity), you may have skipped a step during the kernel rebuild. You can power the PC off and on to reboot. This time, select the name of the old working kernel at the GRUB screen.

Summary

Most Red Hat and Fedora Linux software comes in Red Hat Package Manager (RPM) files, and many open-source software packages are provided in source-code form (usually in compressed archives). Therefore, you need to know how to work with RPM files and how to build software from source code. In addition, from time to time, you may have to get some updates or bug fixes and rebuild the Linux kernel. This chapter showed you how to install RPM files, download source code and build programs, and use the graphical Update Agent to update Linux packages. Also, you learned how to build and install a new kernel. Moreover, this chapter showed you how to download and install new updates from Fedora download servers in the form of Red Hat Package Manager (RPM) files.

In this chapter, you learned the following:

- Red Hat Package Manager (RPM) is a system for packaging all the necessary files for a software product in a single file. The file is referred to as an RPM file, a package, or simply an RPM. Fedora and some other Linux versions are distributed in the form of a lot of RPMs.

- You can use the rpm commands or the Red Hat Package Management graphical tool to work with RPM files. You learn to use the Package Management graphical utility with which you can install and uninstall entire package groups — collections of many related RPM files. In addition, you learn the syntax of a number of RPM commands used to query, install, upgrade, remove, and verify RPMs.
- To download and install open-source software distributed in source-code form, use a Web browser to download and tar to unpack; then read the README file for installation instructions. Typically, you have to run a configure script to create a Makefile and to run the make command to build the software. Using the X Multimedia System (XMMS) package as an example, this chapter shows you how to build the software and install it.
- You can use the graphical Update Agent to download and install any updates to various packages that make up Fedora Linux. This chapter shows you how to use the Update Agent and the yum command to update Fedora.
- The term kernel refers to the core Linux operating system, the program that makes your PC a Linux PC.
- You can upgrade to a new version of the Linux kernel from one of the mirror sites listed at http://fedora.redhat.com/download/mirrors.html. The updates are organized in directories according to Fedora version numbers. For example, any updates for Fedora 4 for Intel x86 systems appear in the updates/4/i386 directory.
- You can rebuild the Linux kernel to add support for experimental devices or build a kernel customized to include support for only devices that your PC has.
- To rebuild the kernel, install the kernel source RPM (SRPM) following instructions in this chapter, change the directory to /usr/src/kernels/linux-*, and use the make config or make xconfig command to configure the kernel. Then type **make** to build the kernel. You have also learned how to use the make modules_install command to install the modules and mkintird to build an initrd (initial RAM disk) file.
- To make a new kernel available for booting, you have to copy the new compressed kernel file to the /boot directory and edit the GRUB configuration file /etc/grub.conf so that it includes information about the new kernel file.

System and Network Security

Chapter 22

Secrets in This Chapter

As a systems administrator, you have to worry about your Linux system's security. For a standalone system, or a system used in an isolated local area network (LAN), you have to focus on protecting the system from the users and the users from one another. In other words, you do not want a user to modify or delete system files, whether intentionally or unintentionally. Also, you do not want a user destroying another user's files.

If your Linux system is connected to the Internet, you must worry about securing the system from unwanted access by outsiders over the Internet. These intruders, also known as *crackers*, typically impersonate a user, steal or destroy information, and even deny you access to your own system (this is known as a denial-of-service attack).

By its very nature, an Internet connection makes your system accessible to any other system on the Internet. After all, the Internet connects many networks across the globe. In fact, the client/server architecture of Internet information services, such as HTTP (Web) and FTP, relies on the wide-open network access the Internet provides. Unfortunately, the easy accessibility to Internet services running on your system also means anyone on the Net can easily access your system.

If you operate an Internet host that provides information to others, you certainly want everyone to access your system's Internet services, such as FTP and Web servers. However, these servers often have vulnerabilities that crackers can exploit in order to cause harm to your system. You need to know about the potential security risks of Internet services and the precautions you can take to minimize the risk of someone exploiting the weaknesses of your FTP or Web server.

You may also want to protect your company's internal network from outsiders, even though your goal is to provide information to the outside world through a Web server. You can protect your internal network by setting up an Internet firewall — a controlled access point to the internal network — and placing the Web and FTP servers on a host outside the firewall.

This chapter takes you through the basic steps you should follow in securing your Linux system. You also learn about setting up an Internet firewall and running Web and FTP servers outside the firewall, where users cannot break through and access your company's internal network. As you'll see, Linux already includes many of the tools you need to maintain system security. You can even set up a packet-filtering firewall by using the iptables software that comes with Linux.

To learn more about Linux security, consult the Linux Security HOWTO at `www.tldp.org/HOWTO/Security-HOWTO/index.html` **or** `www.ibiblio.org/pub/Linux/docs/HOWTO/Security-HOWTO`. **Another good resource is the Linux Administrator's Security Guide, which you can read online at** `www.seifried.org/lasg/`.

Establishing a Security Framework

The first step in securing your Linux system is to set up a security policy. The security policy is your guide to what you enable users (as well as visitors over the Internet) to do on the Linux system. The level of security you establish depends on how you use the Linux system and how much is at risk if someone gains unauthorized access to your system.

If you are a system administrator for Linux systems at an organization, you probably want to involve the management, as well as the users, in setting up the security policy. Obviously, you cannot create an imposing policy that prevents everyone from working on the system. On the other hand, if the users are creating or using data valuable to the organization, you have to set up a policy that protects the data from disclosure to outsiders. In other words, the security policy should strike a balance between the users' needs and the need to protect the system.

For a standalone Linux system or a home system that you occasionally connect to the Internet, the security policy can be just a listing of the Internet services you want to run on the system and the user accounts you plan to set up on the system.

For a larger organization that has one or more Linux systems on a LAN connected to the Internet — preferably through a *firewall,* a device that controls the flow of Internet Protocol (IP) packets between the LAN and the Internet — it is best to think of computer security across the entire organization systematically. Figure 22-1 shows the key elements of an organization-wide framework to computer security (some call this the *security architecture*).

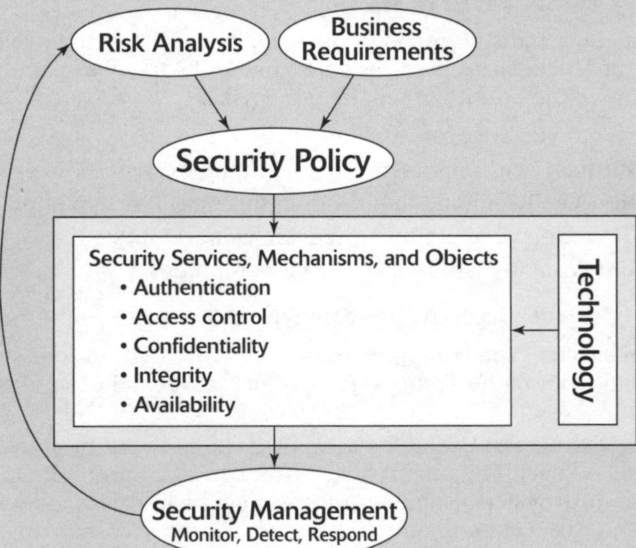

Figure 22-1: An Organization-Wide Framework for Computer Security.

Such an organization-wide computer security framework includes the following key elements:

- Determining business requirements for security
- Performing risk analysis
- Establishing a security policy
- Implementing security solutions to mitigate identified security risks
- Managing security continuously

The next few sections explain these elements of the security framework.

Determining Business Requirements for Security

The security framework outlined in Figure 22-1 starts with the development of a security policy based on business requirements and risk analysis. The business requirements identify the security needs of the business — the computer resources and information you have to protect (including any requirements imposed by applicable laws, such as the requirement to protect the privacy of some types of data). Typical security requirements might include items such as the following:

- Enable access to information by authorized users.
- Implement business rules that specify who has access to what information.
- Employ a strong user-authentication system.
- Deny malicious or destructive actions on data.
- Protect data from end to end as it moves across networks.
- Implement all security and privacy requirements that applicable laws impose.

Performing Risk Analysis

Risk analysis is all about identifying and assessing risks — potential events that can harm your Linux system. The analysis involves determining the following and performing some analysis to determine the priority of handling the risks:

- **Threats:** What you are protecting against
- **Vulnerabilities:** The weaknesses that might be exploited (these are the risks)
- **Probability:** The likelihood that a vulnerability will be exploited
- **Impact:** The effect of exploiting a specific vulnerability
- **Mitigation:** What to do to reduce the vulnerabilities

Before I describe risk analysis, here are some typical threats to your Linux system:

- **Denial of service:** The computer and network are tied up so that legitimate users cannot make use of the systems. For businesses, denial of service can mean loss of revenue.
- **Unauthorized access:** Use of the computer and network by someone who is not an authorized user. The unauthorized user can steal information or maliciously corrupt or destroy data. Some businesses may be hurt by the negative publicity from the mere act of an unauthorized user gaining access to the system, even if there is no explicit damage to any data.
- **Disclosure of information to the public:** The unauthorized release of information to the public. For example, the disclosure of a password file enables potential attackers to figure out user name and password combinations for accessing a system. Exposure of other sensitive information, such as financial and medical data, might be a potential liability for a business.

These threats come from exploitation of vulnerabilities in your organization's computer and human resources. Some common vulnerabilities are the following:

- People (divulging passwords, losing security cards, and so on)
- Internal network connections (routers, switches)
- Interconnection points (gateways — routers and firewalls — between the Internet and the internal network)

- Third-party network providers (ISPs, long-distance carriers)
- Operating-system security holes (potential holes in Internet servers, such as sendmail, named, bind, and so on)
- Application security holes (known security holes in specific applications)

To perform risk analysis, assign a numeric value to the probability and impact of each potential vulnerability. A workable approach for risk analysis is to do the following for each vulnerability or risk:

1. Assign subjective ratings of Low, Medium, and High for the probability of a risk. As the ratings suggest, Low means a lesser chance that the vulnerability will be exploited; High means there is a greater chance.
2. Assign similar ratings to the impact of a risk. What you consider impact is up to you. Businesses often assess the impact by estimating the monetary damages resulting from a risk event. If the exploitation of a vulnerability will affect your business greatly, assign it a High impact.
3. Assign a numeric value to the three levels — Low = 1, Medium = 2, and High = 3 — for both probability and impact.
4. Compute a numerical risk level by multiplying the numerical values of probability and impact. Then, make a decision to develop and implement protections for vulnerabilities that exceed a specific threshold for the risk level — the product of probability and impact. For example, you may choose to handle all vulnerabilities with a probability times impact — risk level — greater than 6.

If you want to characterize the probability and impact with a finer level of granularity, pick a scale of 1 through 5, for example, and follow the same steps as before.

Establishing a Security Policy

Based on the risk analysis and any business requirements you may need to address regardless of risk level, you can craft a security policy for the organization. The security policy typically addresses the following areas:

- **Authentication:** What method will be used to ensure that a user is the real user? Who gets access to the system? What is the minimum length and complexity of passwords? How often do users change passwords? How long can a user be idle before that user is logged out automatically?
- **Authorization:** What can different classes of users do on the system? Who can have the root password?
- **Data protection:** What data must be protected? Who has access to the data? Is encryption necessary for some data?
- **Internet access:** What are the restrictions on users (from the LAN) accessing the Internet? What Internet services (such as Web, FTP, Internet Relay Chat, and so on) can users access? Are incoming emails and attachments scanned for viruses? Is there a network firewall? Are virtual private networks (VPNs) used to connect private networks across the Internet?

- **Internet services:** What Internet services are allowed on each Linux system? Are there any file servers? Mail servers? Web servers? What services run on each type of server? What services, if any, run on Linux systems used as desktop workstations?
- **Security audits:** Who tests whether the security is adequate? How often is the security tested? How are problems found during security testing handled?
- **Incident handling:** What are the procedures for handling any computer security incidents? Who must be informed? What information must be gathered to help with the investigation of incidents?
- **Responsibilities:** Who is responsible for maintaining security? Who applies patches and upgrades system software to fix security holes? Who monitors log files and audit trails for signs of unauthorized access? Who maintains the database of security policy?

Implementing Security Solutions

After you analyze the risks — vulnerabilities — and develop a security policy, you have to select the mitigation approach: how to protect against specific vulnerabilities. This is where you develop an overall security solution based on security policy, business requirements, and available technology — a solution that consists of the following:

- Services (authentication, access control, encryption)
- Mechanisms (user name/password, firewalls)
- Objects (hardware, software)

Because it is impossible to protect computer systems from all attacks, solutions identified through the risk management process must support three integral concepts of a holistic security program: protection, detection, and reaction:

- **Protection** provides countermeasures such as policies, procedures, and technical solutions to defend against attacks on the assets being protected. For example, firewalls are used for protection against attacks over the network.
- **Detection** monitors for potential breakdowns in the protective measures that could result in security breaches. For example, intrusion detection systems can detect breaches in network security.
- **Reaction** or **Response**, which often requires human involvement, responds to detected breaches to thwart attacks before damage can be done. Disaster recovery is an example of response.

Because absolute protection from attacks is impossible to achieve, a security program that does not incorporate detection and reaction is incomplete.

Managing Security Continuously

In addition to implementing security solutions, you have to set up security management that continually monitors, detects, and responds to any security incidents.

The combination of the risk analysis, security policy, security solutions, and security management provides the overall security framework. Such a framework helps establish a common level of understanding of security and a common basis for the design and implementation of security solutions.

The remainder of this chapter shows you some of the ways in which you can enhance and maintain the security of your Linux system and any network.

Securing Linux

After you have defined a security policy, you can proceed to secure the system according to the policy. The exact steps depend on what you want to do with the system — whether it is a server or a workstation and how many users must access the system.

To secure the Linux system, you have to handle two broad categories of security issues:

- **Host security** issues that relate to securing the operating system and the files and directories on the system
- **Network security** issues that refer to the threat of attacks over the network connection

Understanding the Host Security Issues

Here are some high-level guidelines to address host security (The "Securing the Host" section covers some of these topics in detail):

- When installing Linux, select only those package groups you need for your system. Do not install unnecessary software. For example, if your system is used as a workstation, you do not need to install most of the servers (Web server, news server, and so on).
- Create initial user accounts and make sure all passwords are strong ones that password-cracking programs can't "guess." Linux includes tools to enforce strong passwords.
- Set file ownerships and permissions to protect important files and directories. In particular, understand which programs are set-UID and set-GID and remove such permissions from files where they are not needed. Use the access control lists (ACLs) to manage who gets to use which files and directories.
- Enable mandatory access control capabilities provided by Security Enhanced Linux (SELinux). Linux kernel 2.6 supports SELinux and Fedora enables SELinux by default.
- Use the GNU Privacy Guard (GnuPG) to encrypt or decrypt files with sensitive information and to authenticate files that you download from Fedora download servers. GnuPG comes with Linux, and you can use the `gpg` command to perform the tasks such as encrypting or decrypting a file and digitally sign a file.
- Regularly apply patches and upgrades that correct known security problems. When downloading and installing upgrades, check the MD5 checksums and digital signatures to ensure the integrity of the downloaded files.
- Use file-integrity checking tools, such as Tripwire, to monitor any changes to crucial system files and directories. The open source version of Tripwire(which is somewhat old) is available from `www.tripwire.org`. Visit `www.tripwire.com` for the commercial version.
- Periodically check various log files for signs of any break-ins or attempted break-ins. These log files are in the `/var/log` directory of your system.
- Install security updates from Fedora, as soon as they become available. These security updates fix known vulnerabilities in Linux.

Understanding Network Security Issues

The issue of security comes up as soon as you connect your organization's internal network to the Internet. This is true even if you connect a single computer to the Internet, but security concerns are more pressing when an entire internal network is opened to the world.

If you are an experienced system administrator, you already know that it's not the cost of managing an Internet presence that worries corporate management; their main concern is security. To get your management's backing for the website, you need to lay out a plan to keep the corporate network secure from intruders.

You may think that you can avoid jeopardizing the internal network by connecting only the external servers, such as Web and FTP servers, to the Internet. However, this simplistic approach is not wise. It is like deciding not to drive because you may have an accident. Not having a network connection between your Web server and your internal network also has the following drawbacks:

- You cannot use network file transfers, such as FTP, to copy documents and data from your internal network to the Web server.
- Users on the internal network cannot access the corporate Web server.
- Users on the internal network do not have access to Web servers on the Internet. Such a restriction makes a valuable resource — the Web — inaccessible to the users in your organization.

A practical solution to this problem is to set up an Internet firewall and to put the Web server on a highly secured host outside the firewall.

In addition to using a firewall, here are some of the other steps you should take to address network security (the "Securing the Network" section explain these further):

- Enable only those Internet services you need on a system. In particular, do not enable services that are not properly configured.
- Use secure shell (`ssh`) for remote logins. Do not use the "r" commands, such as `rlogin` and `rsh`.
- Secure any Internet services such as FTP or Telnet that you want to run on your system. You can use the TCP wrapper access control files — `/etc/hosts.allow` and `/etc/hosts.deny` — to secure some of these services.
- Promptly fix any known vulnerabilities of Internet services that you choose to run. Typically, you'd do this by downloading and installing the latest server RPM file from Fedora download sites listed at `http://fedora.redhat.com/download/mirrors.html`.

Learning Computer Security Terminology

Computer books, magazine articles, and experts on computer security use a number of terms with unique meanings. You need to know these terms to understand discussions about computer security (and to communicate effectively with security vendors). Table 22-1 describes some of the commonly used computer security terms.

Table 22-1: Commonly Used Computer Security Terminology

Term	*Description*
Application gateway	A proxy service that acts as a gateway for application-level protocols, such as FTP, Telnet, and HTTP.
Authentication	The process of confirming that a user is indeed who he or she claims to be. The typical authentication method is a challenge-response method, wherein the user enters a user name and secret password to confirm his or her identity.
Backdoor	A security weakness a cracker places on a host in order to bypass security features.
Bastion host	A highly secured computer that serves as an organization's main point of presence on the Internet. A bastion host typically resides on the perimeter network, but a dual-homed host (with one network interface connected to the Internet and the other to the internal network) is also a bastion host.
Buffer overflow	A security flaw in a program that enables a cracker to send an excessive amount of data to that program and to overwrite parts of the running program with code in the data being sent. The result is that the cracker can execute arbitrary code on the system and possibly gain access to the system as a privileged user.
Certificate	An electronic document that identifies an entity (such as an individual, an organization, or a computer) and associates a public key with that identity. A certificate contains the certificate holder's name, a serial number, expiration dates, a copy of the certificate holder's public key, and the digital signature of the Certificate Authority so that a recipient can verify that the certificate is real.
Certificate Authority (CA)	An organization that validates identities and issues certificates.
Confidentiality	Of data, a state of being accessible by no one but you (usually achieved by encryption).
Cracker	A person who breaks into (or attempts to break into) a host, often with malicious intent.
Decryption	The process of transforming encrypted information into its original, intelligible form.
Denial of Service (DoS)	An attack that uses so many of the resources on your computer and network that legitimate users cannot access and use the system.
Digital signature signature	A one-way MD5 or SHA-1 hash of a message encrypted with the private key of the message originator, used to verify the integrity of a message and ensure nonrepudiation.
Distributed Denial of Service (DDoS)	A variant of the denial-of-service attack that uses a coordinated attack from a distributed system of computers rather than a single source. It often makes use of worms to spread to multiple computers that can then attack the target.
DMZ	Another name for the perimeter network. (DMZ stands for demilitarized zone, the buffer zone separating North and South Korea.)
Dual-homed host	A computer with two network interfaces (think of each network as a home).

continued

Table 22-1 *(continued)*

Term	*Description*
Encryption	The process of transforming information so that it is unintelligible to anyone but the intended recipient. The transformation is accomplished by a mathematical operation between a key and the information.
Exploit tools	Publicly available and sophisticated tools that intruders of various skill levels can use to determine vulnerabilities and gain entry into targeted systems.
Firewall	A controlled-access gateway between an organization's internal network and the Internet. A dual-homed host can be configured as a firewall.
Hash	A mathematical function converts a message into a fixed-size numeric value known as a message digest or hash. The MD5 algorithm produces a 128-bit message digest, whereas the Secure Hash Algorithm-1 (SHA-1) generates a 160-bit message digest. The hash of a message is encrypted with the private key of the sender to produce the digital signature.
Host	A computer on any network (so called because it offers many services).
Integrity	Of received data, a state of being the same data that was sent (unaltered in transit).
IPSec (IP Security Protocol)	A security protocol for the network layer that is designed to provide cryptographic security services for IP packets. IPSec provides encryption-based authentication, integrity, access control, and confidentiality. (Visit `www.ietf.org/html.charters/ipsec-charter.html` for the list of RFCs related to IPSec.)
IP spoofing	An attack in which a cracker figures out the IP address of a trusted host and then sends packets that appear to come from the trusted host. The attacker can only send packets, but cannot see any responses. However, the attacker can predict the sequence of packets and essentially send commands that will set up a back door for future break-ins.
Logic bombs	A form of sabotage in which a programmer inserts code that causes the program to perform a destructive action when some triggering event occurs, such as terminating the programmer's employment.
Nonrepudiation	A security feature that prevents the sender of data from being able to deny ever having sent the data.
Packet	A collection of bytes that serve as the basic unit of communication on a network. On TCP/IP networks, the packet may be referred to as an IP packet or a TCP/IP packet.
Packet filtering	Selective blocking of packets based on the type of packet (as specified by the source and destination IP address or port).
Perimeter network	A network between the Internet and the protected internal network. The bastion host resides on the perimeter network (also known as the DMZ).
Port scanning	A method for discovering which ports are open (in other words, which Internet services are enabled) on a system. Performed by sending connection requests to the ports one by one. This is usually a precursor to further attacks.

Term	Description
Proxy server	A server on the bastion host that enables internal clients to access external servers (and enables external clients to access servers inside the protected network). There are proxy servers for various Internet services, such as FTP and HTTP.
Public-key cryptography	An encryption method that uses a pair of keys, a private key and a public key, to encrypt and decrypt the information. Anything encrypted with the public key can be decrypted with the corresponding private key, and vice versa.
Public Key Infrastructure (PKI)	A set of standards and services that enables the use of public-key cryptography and certificates in a networked environment. PKI facilitates tasks, such as issuing, renewing, and revoking certificates, and generating and distributing public-private key pairs.
Screening router	An Internet router that filters packets.
Setuid program	A program that runs with the permissions of the owner regardless of who runs the program. For example, if a setuid program is owned by root, that program has root privileges regardless of who has started the program. Crackers often exploit vulnerabilities in setuid programs to gain privileged access to a system.
Sniffer	Synonymous with *packet sniffer*—a program that intercepts routed data and examines each packet in search of specified information, such as passwords transmitted in clear text.
Spyware	Any software that covertly gathers user information through the user's Internet connection and usually transmits that information in the background to someone else. Spyware can also gather information about email addresses and even passwords and credit card numbers. Spyware is similar to a Trojan horse in that users are tricked into installing spyware when they install something else.
Symmetric-key encryption	An encryption method wherein the same key is used to encrypt and decrypt the information.
Threat	An event or activity, deliberate or unintentional, with the potential for causing harm to a system or network.
Trojan horse	A program that masquerades as a benign program but, in fact is a back door used for attacking a system. Attackers often install a collection of Trojan horse programs that enable the attacker to freely access the system with root privileges, yet hide that fact from the system administrator. Such collections of Trojan horse programs are called rootkits.
Virus	A self-replicating program that spreads from one computer to another by attaching itself to other programs.
Vulnerability	A flaw or weakness that may cause harm to a system or network.
War-dialing	Simple programs that dial consecutive phone numbers looking for modems.
War-driving	A method of gaining entry into wireless computer networks using a laptop, antennas, and a wireless network card that involves driving around various locations to gain unauthorized access.
Worm	A self-replicating program that copies itself from one computer to another over a network.

Securing the Host

A key aspect of computer security is to secure the host — your Linux system. The next few sections describe a few key steps you should follow in securing your Linux host. These steps include

- Installing operating system updates
- Protecting passwords
- Protecting the files and directories
- Using encryption if necessary
- Monitoring the security of the system

You can monitor host security by examining log files for any suspicious activities and by using the Tripwire tool to see if anyone has messed with important files on your system.

Installing Operating System Updates

Linux and related application updates come in RPM files. To manually download and install the updates, make sure that your system is connected to the Internet, log in as root, and type the following command:

```
yum update
```

That command causes Yum to download all currently available updates from one of the Fedora download sites. You have to respond to a few prompts from Yum and Yum takes care of the rest.

Securing Passwords

Historically, UNIX passwords are stored in the /etc/passwd file, which any user can read. For example, a typical old-style /etc/passwd file entry for the root user looks like this:

```
root:t6Z7NWDK1K8sU:0:0:root:/root:/bin/bash
```

The fields are separated by colons (:), and the second field contains the password in encrypted form. To check if a password is valid, the login program encrypts the plaintext password the user enters and compares the password with the contents of the /etc/passwd file. If there is a match, the user is allowed to log in.

Password-cracking programs work just like the login program, except that these programs pick one word at a time from a dictionary, encrypt the word, and compare the encrypted word with the encrypted passwords in the /etc/passwd file for a match. Crackers often use multiple password-cracking programs, and some of these programs also try various manipulations of the words in the dictionary. For example, password-cracking programs try obvious manipulations of words such as:

- A word with a single punctuation character at the end
- A word with punctuation character at the beginning
- A word with letters in a mix of uppercase and lowercase
- A word written backwards
- Two words with a number in between

To crack the passwords, the intruder needs the /etc/passwd file. Often, crackers use weaknesses of various Internet servers (such as mail and FTP) to get a copy of the /etc/passwd file.

Several improvements have made passwords more secure in Linux. These include shadow passwords and pluggable authentication modules, and these are installed automatically as you install Linux.

Learning the Role of Shadow Passwords

Instead of storing them in the /etc/passwd file, which any user can read, passwords are now stored in a shadow password file. In Linux, the shadow passwords are in the /etc/shadow file. Only the superuser (root) can read this file, which makes it harder for crackers to get their hands on the encrypted passwords. For example, here is the entry for root in the new-style /etc/passwd file:

```
root:x:0:0:root:/root:/bin/bash
```

In this case, the second field contains an x, instead of an encrypted password.

When you use shadow passwords, the encrypted passwords are stored in the /etc/shadow file where the entry for root is like this:

```
root:$1$AAAni/yN$uESHbzUpy9Cgfoo1Bf0tS0:12889:0:99999:7:::
```

The format of the /etc/shadow entries with colon-separated fields resembles the entries in the /etc/passwd file, but the meanings of most fields differ. The first field, however, is still the user name, and the second one is the encrypted password.

In addition to improving the password file's security by storing it in the /etc/shadow file that only root can read, Linux also improves the actual encryption of the passwords stored in the /etc/shadow file. Password encryption is now done using the MD5 message-digest algorithm that converts a plaintext password into a 128-bit fingerprint or digest. The MD5 algorithm, described in RFC 1321 (www.faqs.org/rfcs/rfc1321.html or www.ietf.org/rfc/rfc1321.txt), reduces a message of any length to a 128-bit message digest. MD5 is used to create message digests for documents so that you can digitally sign them through encryption with your private key. MD5 works quite well for password encryption, too.

Another advantage of MD5 over the older-style password encryption is that the older passwords were limited to a maximum of eight characters; new passwords (encrypted with MD5) can be much longer. Longer passwords are harder to guess, even if the /etc/shadow file falls into the wrong hands.

A clue to the use of MD5 encryption in the /etc/shadow file is the increased length of the encrypted password and the 1 prefix, as in the second field of each entry.

The remaining fields in each /etc/shadow entry control when the password expires. You do not need to interpret or change these entries in the /etc/shadow file. Instead, use the chage command to change the password-expiration information. For starters, you can check a user's password-expiration information by using the chage command with the -l option, as follows (in this case, you have to be logged in as root):

```
chage -l root
```

This command displays various expiration information, including how long the password lasts and how often you can change the password. For example, here is a typical output from the command `chage -l root`:

```
Last password change                                    : May 13, 2005
Password expires                                        : never
Password inactive                                       : never
Account expires                                         : never
Minimum number of days between password change          : 0
Maximum number of days between password change          : 99999
Number of days of warning before password expires       : 7
```

If you want to ensure that the user is forced to change his or her password every 90 days, you can use the `-M` option to set the maximum number of days the password stays valid. For example, to make sure that user `naba` is prompted to change the password in 90 days, I log in as `root` and type the following command:

```
chage -M 90 naba
```

You can do this for each user account to ensure that all passwords expire when appropriate and that all users must pick new passwords.

Understanding Pluggable Authentication Modules

A Pluggable Authentication Module (PAM) performs the actual MD5 encryption, described in the "Learning the Role of Shadow Passwords" section. PAM provides a flexible method for authenticating users on Linux systems. Through settings in configuration files, you can change the authentication method on the fly, without having to actually modify programs, such as `login` and `passwd`, which verify a user's identity.

Linux uses PAM extensively, and the configuration files are in the `/etc/pam.d` directory of your system. Check out the contents of this directory on your system by typing the following command:

```
ls /etc/pam.d
```

Each configuration file in this directory specifies how users are authenticated for a specific utility. For example, there is a file for each of `login`, `passwd`, `su`, and a whole host of the GUI redhat-config utilities. Here's what I see when I type `cat /etc/pam.d/passwd` on my system:

```
#%PAM-1.0
auth        required     pam_stack.so service=system-auth
account     required     pam_stack.so service=system-auth
password    required     pam_stack.so service=system-auth
```

These lines indicate that authentication, account management, and password checking should all be done by using the pam_stack module (`/lib/security/pam_stack.so`) with the argument `service=system-auth`. Essentially, the pam_stack module refers to another configuration file in the `/etc/pam.d` directory. In this case, the configuration file is `/etc/pam.d/system-auth`. Here's the content of the `/etc/pam.d/system-auth` file on my Linux PC:

```
#%PAM-1.0
# This file is auto-generated.
# User changes will be destroyed the next time authconfig is run.
auth        required      /lib/security/$ISA/pam_env.so
auth        sufficient    /lib/security/$ISA/pam_unix.so likeauth nullok
auth        required      /lib/security/$ISA/pam_deny.so

account     required      /lib/security/$ISA/pam_unix.so
account     sufficient    /lib/security/$ISA/pam_succeed_if.so uid < 100 quiet
account     required      /lib/security/$ISA/pam_permit.so

password    requisite     /lib/security/$ISA/pam_cracklib.so retry=3
password    sufficient    /lib/security/$ISA/pam_unix.so nullok use_authtok md5 shadow
password    required      /lib/security/$ISA/pam_deny.so

session     required      /lib/security/$ISA/pam_limits.so
session     required      /lib/security/$ISA/pam_unix.so
```

Although I won't go over all the details, here's a brief explanation of PAM configuration files.

Each line in a PAM configuration file specifies the rules to be used for a specific type of authentication service. The general syntax of each line in a PAM configuration file is the following:

```
module-type control module-path module-arguments
```

The meaning of these four fields is as follows:

- `module-type` denotes the type of service being controlled by this line. The acceptable module types are: `account` for verifying the account (for example, whether the user's password has expired or whether a user is permitted access to the requested service); `auth` for authenticating a user's claimed identity, typically by using some challenge-response method where the user is asked for a password; `password` for updating passwords; and `session` for performing tasks before the user is given access to a service and after the user is done with the service.
- `control` determines the behavior of a PAM in case the module does not succeed in the authentication task. Typically, the `control` field is set to `required` or `sufficient`. If the `control` field is set to `required`, the module must be successful for the authentication to continue. If the `control` field is set to `sufficient` and the module is successful, no other checks are needed and the authentication is considered complete.
- `module-path` specifies the pathname of a PAM module — a shared library object — that implements the service. In the pathname `/lib/security/$ISA/`, ISA refers to an environment variable that you can set to a subdirectory where you decide to organize the PAM modules for your system. Typically, ISA is not defined and the PAM modules are located in the `/lib/security` directory.
- `module-arguments` lists any module-specific options that are then passed to the module. It is up to the module to parse and interpret these options. Everything after the first three fields is interpreted as module arguments.

In the /etc/pam.d/system-auth file, the first three lines are for auth service:

```
auth      required    /lib/security/$ISA/pam_env.so
auth      sufficient  /lib/security/$ISA/pam_unix.so likeauth nullok
auth      required    /lib/security/$ISA/pam_deny.so
```

Here the first auth line loads the PAM module pam_env.so that can set or unset environment variables. The second auth line specifies an authentication module that checks the user's identity by using the PAM module pam_unix.so with the arguments likeauth nullok. The options in the argument string have the following meanings:

- **likeauth:** Returns the same value whether the module is used to set new credentials or authenticate an existing user name
- **nullok:** Allows a blank password

The third auth line in the /etc/pam.d/system-auth file uses the pam_deny.so module to deny access to the requested service if the pam_unix.so module's authentication is unsuccessful.

Following the auth lines in the /etc/pam.d/system-auth file comes an account line:

```
account    required    /lib/security/$ISA/pam_unix.so
```

The account service uses the pam_unix.so module to make sure that the user account has not expired, that the user is allowed to log in at a given time of day, and so on.

Later in the /etc/pam.d/system-auth file, you see two password lines in the /etc/pam.d/system-auth file that specify how passwords are set:

```
password    requisite    /lib/security/$ISA/pam_cracklib.so retry=3
password   sufficient  /lib/security/$ISA/pam_unix.so nullok use_authtok md5 shadow
```

The first password line uses the pam_cracklib.so module to try to crack the new password (that's what the cracklib in the module's name indicates). The retry=3 argument indicates that the user can try to enter a new password three times at most. The second password line indicates that the MD5 encryption is used to store the password in the /etc/shadow file.

The /etc/pam.d/passwd configuration file applies when you use the passwd command to change passwords. Here's an example where I am trying to change my password (the text in italic is my comment):

```
passwd
Changing password for naba
(current) UNIX password:  I type my current password
New UNIX password: I type "xyzz"
BAD PASSWORD: it is too short
New UNIX password:  I type "transport" as password
BAD PASSWORD: it is based on a dictionary word
New UNIX password:  I type "naba12" as the new password
BAD PASSWORD: it is based on your username
passwd: Authentication token manipulation error
```

In this case, the passwd program is using the PAM module to check my identity (when I first type my current password) and making sure that each of the new passwords I try are strong. Finally, the PAM modules abort the passwd program after I fail to select a good password in three tries.

Protecting Files and Directories

One important aspect of securing the host is to protect important system files and the directories that contain these files. You can protect the files through the file ownership and through the permission settings that control who can read, write, or execute (in case of executable programs) the file.

Setting File Ownership and Permissions

The default Linux file security is controlled through the following settings for each file or directory:

- User ownership
- Group ownership
- Read, write, execute permissions for owner
- Read, write, execute permissions for group
- Read, write, execute permissions for others (everyone else)

Viewing Ownerships and Permissions

You can see these settings for a file when you look at the detailed listing with the `ls -l` command. For example, type the following command to see the detailed listing of the `/etc/inittab` file:

```
ls -l /etc/inittab
```

The resulting listing should look something like this:

```
-rw-r--r--  1 root root 1663 Apr 16 17:45 /etc/inittab
```

The first set of characters describes the file permissions for user, group, and others. The third and fourth fields show the user and group that own this file. In this case, both user and group names are the same: `root`.

Changing File Ownerships

You can set the user and group ownerships with the `chown` command. For example if the file `/dev/hda` should be owned by the user root and the group disk, then you would type the following command as `root` to set up this ownership:

```
chown root.disk /dev/hda
```

To change the group ownership alone, use the `chgrp` command. For example, here's how you can change the group ownership of a file to the group named accounting:

```
chgrp accounting ledger.xls
```

Changing File Permissions

Use the `chmod` command to set the file permissions. To use `chmod` effectively, you have to learn how to specify the permission settings. One way is to concatenate one or more letters from each of the following tables in the order shown (Who/Action/Permission), as shown in Table 22-2.

Table 22-2: File Permission Codes

Who	*Action*	*Permission*
u user	+ add	r read
g group	- remove	w write
o others	= assign	x execute
a all	s set user ID	

To give everyone read and write access to all files in a directory, type **chmod a+rw ***. On the other hand, to permit everyone to execute a specific file, type **chmod a+x filename**.

Another way to specify a permission setting is to use a three-digit sequence of numbers. In a detailed listing, the read, write, and execute permission settings for the user, group, and others appear as the sequence

```
rwxrwxrwx
```

with hyphens (-) in place of letters for disallowed operations. Think of `rwxrwxrwx` as three occurrences of the string `rwx`. Now, assign the values `r=4`, `w=2`, and `x=1`. Assign zero to a hyphen. To get the value of the sequence `rwx`, simply add the values of `r`, `w`, and `x`. Thus, `rwx` = 7, `rw-`=6, and `r--=4`. Using this formula, you can assign a three-digit value to any permission setting. For example, if the user can read and write the file but everyone else can only read the file, the permission setting is `rw-r--r--` (that's how it appears in the listing), and the value is 644. Thus, if you want all files in a directory to be readable by everyone but writeable by only the user, use the command:

```
chmod 644 *
```

Setting Default File Permissions

What permission setting does a file get when you (or a program) create a new file? The answer is in what is known as the user file-creation mask that you can see and set using the `umask` command.

Type **umask**, and it prints out a number showing the current file-creation mask. The default setting is different for the `root` user and other normal users. For the `root` user the mask is set to 022 whereas the mask for normal users is 002. To see the effect of this file-creation mask and to interpret the meaning of the mask, follow these steps:

1. Log in as `root` and type the following command:

   ```
   touch junkfile
   ```

   This creates a file named `junkfile` with nothing in it.
2. Type **ls -l junkfile** to that file's permissions. You should see a line similar to the following:

   ```
   -rw-r--r--  1 root root 0 Apr 19 21:50 junkfile
   ```

Interpret the numerical value of the permission setting by converting each three-letter permissions in the first field (excluding the very first letter) into a number between 0 and 7. For each letter that's present, the first letter gets a value of 4, the second letter is 2, and the third is 1. For example, `rw-` translates to 4+2+0 (because the third letter is missing) or 6. Similarly, `r--` is 4+0+0 = 4. Thus the permission string `-rw-r--r--` becomes 644.

3. Subtract the numerical permission setting from 666 and what you get is the `umask` setting. In this case, 666 – 644 gives us a `umask` of 022.

So, a `umask` of 022 results in a default permission setting of 666 – 022 = 644. When you rewrite 644 in terms of a permission string, it becomes `rw-r--r--`.

To set a new `umask`, type **umask** followed by the numerical value of the mask. Here is how you can select a `umask` and set it:

1. Figure out what permission settings you want for new files. For example, if you want new files that can be read and written by the owner only and nothing else, then the permission setting would look like

```
rw-------
```

2. Convert the permissions into a numerical value by using the conversion method that takes the permission setting in groups of three characters each and then assigns 4 to the first field, 2 to the second, and 1 to the third. Thus, for files that are readable and writeable by owner only, the permission setting is 600.
3. Subtract the desired permission setting from 666 to get the value of the mask. For a permission setting of 600, the mask then becomes 666 – 600 = 066.
4. Use the `umask` command to set the file-creation mask, like this:

```
umask 066
```

A default `umask` of 022 is good for system security because it translates to files that have read and write permission for the owner and read permissions for everyone else. The bottom line is that you don't want a default `umask` that results in files that are writeable by the whole wide world.

Checking for the Set User ID Permission

There is another permission setting that can be a security hazard. This permission setting, called the set user ID (or *setuid* for short), applies to executable files. When the setuid permission is enabled, the file is executed under the user ID of the file's owner. In other words, if an executable program is owned by `root` and the setuid permission is set, then no matter who executes that program, it runs as if being executed by `root`. This means that that program can do a lot more (for example, read all files, create new files, and delete files) than what a normal user program could do. Another risk is that if a setuid program file has some security hole, crackers can do a lot more damage through such programs than through other vulnerabilities.

You can find all setuid programs with a simple `find` command:

```
find / -type f -perm +4000 -print
```

You should see a list of files such as the following:

```
/usr/bin/sudoedit
/usr/bin/newgrp
/usr/bin/chage
/usr/bin/crontab
/usr/bin/gpasswd
/usr/bin/lppasswd
/usr/bin/chfn
/usr/bin/sudo
/usr/bin/chsh
/usr/bin/passwd
... lines deleted ...
```

Many of the programs have the setuid permission because they need it, but check the complete list and make sure that there are no strange setuid programs (for example, setuid programs in a user's home directory).

If you want to see how these permissions are listed by the `ls` command, type **ls -l /usr/bin/passwd**, and you should see the permission settings:

```
-r-s--x--x  1 root root 18852 Mar  7 05:06 /usr/bin/passwd
```

The `s` in the owner's permission setting (`r-s`) tells you that the setuid permission is set.

To remove the setuid bit from a program's permission, type the following:

```
chmod ug-s progname
```

Using exec-shield

Buffer overflow is a major cause of many Linux security holes. When buffer overflow occurs, a cracker can overwrite data-storage areas of memory with instructions designed to execute nasty commands. The latest Linux kernel comes with a kernel setting — `exec-shield` — that enables you to stop the kernel from executing instructions from any data area. This protects against the common buffer overflow type of vulnerabilities by making many parts of a program's memory (including the stack where temporary variables are stored) not executable.

The best part about `exec-shield` is that you don't have to fix the applications that have the buffer-overflow problem. All you have to do is turn on the feature. To make the process even easier, Fedora enables `exec-shield` by default.

Some programs may have trouble working correctly when `exec-shield` is enabled. If you have to turn off `exec-shield`, log in as `root` and type the following command from a terminal window:

```
echo 0 > /proc/sys/kernel/exec-shield
```

That command sets the `exec-shield` kernel option to 0. The `exec-shield` option can take one of three values — 0, 1, and 2. Think of these values as three different levels of security. Table 22-3 summarizes the meaning of the three values of `exec-shield`. Fedora Core sets `exec-shield` to 1 by default.

Table 22-3: Four Levels of Security Using exec-shield

Value of exec-shield	*Meaning*
0	exec-shield is always disabled.
1	exec-shield is enabled for programs compiled with the newest version of gcc compiler.
2	exec-shield is always enabled.

To set `exec-shield` to its default value, type:

```
echo 1 > /proc/sys/kernel/exec-shield
```

Using SELinux

Fedora comes with Security Enhanced Linux (SELinux), which provides mandatory access control with a much finer-grained control than just user and group ownership of files and processes. The access control is determined by the SELinux policy that specifies what the users and processes (*subjects*) can do to all the *objects*—files and devices—in the system. SELinux provides role-based access control where users can perform specific tasks depending on their current roles.

cross ref

For a brief discussion of SELinux, see the "Mandatory Access Control with Security Enhanced Linux" section in Chapter 1.

Fedora comes with a default security policy that should work right out of the box. You don't have to do anything to use SELinux; it should just work behind the scenes controlling which users or processes can access various system resources such as files and devices.

insider insight

In the following sections I briefly describe how to use SELinux. You don't have to do much; SELinux is enabled by default and it should simply work in the background and enforce mandatory access control. You can use a number of commands to view or change the SELinux access control information. To learn more about SELinux in Fedora Core, see the online documentation at `http://fedora.redhat.com/docs/selinux-faq/`**.**

SELinux Configuration

In Fedora Linux, SELinux configuration information is stored in a text file: `/etc/selinux/config`. The config file controls what policy SELinux uses and how it enforces the policy. Here is the complete listing of the config file from a Fedora system:

```
# This file controls the state of SELinux on the system.
# SELINUX= can take one of these three values:
#       enforcing - SELinux security policy is enforced.
#       permissive - SELinux prints warnings instead of enforcing.
#       disabled - SELinux is fully disabled.
SELINUX=enforcing
# SELINUXTYPE= type of policy in use. Possible values are:
#       targeted - Only targeted network daemons are protected.
#       strict - Full SELinux protection.
SELINUXTYPE=targeted
```

The SELINUX parameter specifies the mode of SELinux, whether it's enforcing, permissive, or disabled. The default is enforcing, which means the policy is to be enforced. In permissive mode, SELinux prints warning messages for policy violations, but does not stop the user or processes from doing anything against the policy. You can use permissive setting when testing a new policy.

The SELINUXTYPE parameter specifies the policy that SELinux enforces. Fedora comes with only one SeLinux policy called targeted (even though the configuration file mentions another policy called strict). The files that define the targeted policy are in the `/etc/selinux/targeted` directory of your system.

The targeted policy runs selected network servers such as dhcpd, named, portmap, and syslogd—each under a server-specific protection policy, leaving everything else to an unconfined policy (indicated by the `unconfined_t` type). The rest of the system runs under standard Linux security controlled by file permissions.

You can use the Security Level Configuration GUI tool to change SELinux configurations, including the security enforced by specific network servers. To run the Security Level Configuration tool, type **system-config-securitylevel** in a terminal window in GNOME or select Desktop ➪ System Settings ➪ Security Level and Firewall from the panel. The Security Level Configuration tool's main window appears, as shown in Figure 22-2.

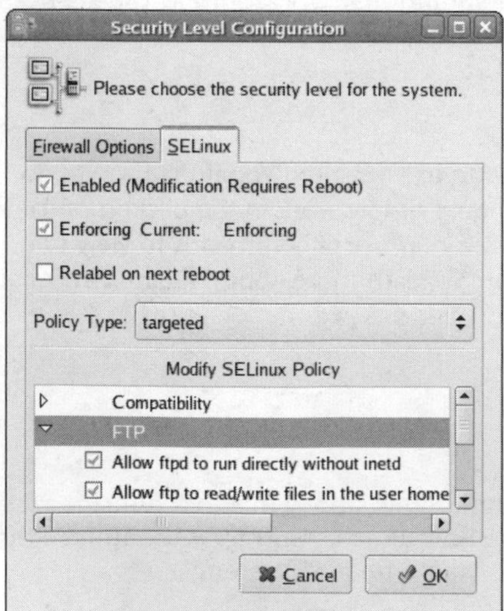

Figure 22-2: Configuring SELinux with the Security Level Configuration Tool.

The window has two tabs: Firewall Options and SELinux. Click the SELinux tab to configure SELinux (the Firewall Options tab is for configuring the firewall). You can disable SELinux and also modify SELinux policy for specific servers. To make changes to a server's policy, click the right arrow for the server in the scrolling list. The configurable options for that server then appears. You can click to toggle the check boxes and turn specific options on or off. Figure 22-2 shows the configurable options for FTP service. After making any changes, click OK. Note that if you make any changes, you must reboot your system so that all the servers can be restarted under the changed policy.

Commands and Options for SELinux

Many common Linux commands include options for viewing SELinux access control information. For example, to provide the fine-grained access control, SELinux requires that each file include a security context — think of it as the security attributes of the file or directory. Adding contexts to the files is referred to as labeling the file system. The file system should already be labeled when you install Fedora Linux and enable SELinux. You can easily check the context of a file, a user, or a process by using a new `-Z` option with the usual Linux commands such as `ls`, `id`, and `ps`. For example, to see the details of the `/etc/passwd` file including its security context, type **ls -lZ /etc/passwd**. Here is a typical output of this command:

```
-rw-r--r--  root   root    system_u:object_r:etc_t       /etc/passwd
```

Note that the context is in the form of three colon-separated fields that precede the filename — the first field is the identity, the second field is the role, and the third field is the type.

If you want to know the context of whatever user ID you are currently logged in as, type **id -Z**. For example, here is the output of the `id -Z` command when you are logged in as a `root`:

```
root:system_r:unconfined_t
```

To see the processes with their security contexts, type **ps axZ**. Here is a partial listing of output from the `ps axZ` command (the context appears in the second column):

```
LABEL                              PID TTY      STAT   TIME COMMAND
user_u:system_r:unconfined_t         1 ?        S      0:01 init [5]
user_u:system_r:unconfined_t         2 ?        SN     0:00 [ksoftirqd/0]
user_u:system_r:unconfined_t         3 ?        S<     0:24 [events/0]
user_u:system_r:unconfined_t         4 ?        S<     0:00 [khelper]
user_u:system_r:unconfined_t         9 ?        S<     0:00 [kthread]
user_u:system_r:unconfined_t        21 ?        S<     0:00 [kblockd/0]
user_u:system_r:unconfined_t        29 ?        S      0:00 [khubd]
user_u:system_r:unconfined_t       101 ?        S      0:00 [pdflush]
user_u:system_r:unconfined_t       102 ?        S      0:00 [pdflush]
user_u:system_r:unconfined_t       104 ?        S<     0:00 [aio/0]
user_u:system_r:unconfined_t       103 ?        S      0:02 [kswapd0]
user_u:system_r:unconfined_t        67 ?        S      0:00 [kapmd]
user_u:system_r:unconfined_t       197 ?        S      0:00 [kseriod]
user_u:system_r:unconfined_t       368 ?        S      0:03 [kjournald]
user_u:system_r:unconfined_t       983 ?        S<s    0:00 udevd
user_u:system_r:unconfined_t      1501 ?        S      0:00 [kjournald]
user_u:system_r:dhcpc_t           1803 ?        Ss     0:00 /sbin/dhclient -1 -q
```

```
-lf /var/lib/dhcp/dhclient-eth0.leases -pf /var/run/dhclient-eth0.pid eth0
user_u:system_r:syslogd_t        1843 ?        Ss     0:00 syslogd -m 0
user_u:system_r:initrc_t         1846 ?        Ss     0:00 klogd -x
user_u:system_r:portmap_t        1856 ?        Ss     0:00 portmap
```

There are also a number of new commands for specific SELinux-related tasks. For example, if you need to relabel a file system, you can do so with the `setfiles` or `fixfiles` command. For example, to relabel the whole file system, you would type the following command:

```
/sbin/fixfiles relabel
```

You can get more information by typing **man setfiles** or **man fixfiles**. You can also relabel the file system by checking the `Relabel on next reboot` check box in the Security Level Configuration tool (see Figure 22-2).

To relabel a directory, you can use the `restorecon` command. For example, to relabel all files in the `/home` directory, type

```
/sbin/restorecon -v -R /home
```

To change the context or type of a file, you can use the `chcon` command. For example, to change the context of all files (including any subdirectories) in a directory named `public_html` (located in your home directory) to `httpd_user_content_t`, you would type the following command:

```
chcon -R -t httpd_user_content_t ~/public_html
```

To perform some tasks such as system administration with SELinux enabled, you have to assume a specific role. You can assume a new role (provided you have access to that new role) by using the `newrole` command. For example, to change to the `sysadm_r` role (this is the system administrator role), type the following command:

```
newrole -r sysadm_r
```

Note that you can also gain the `sysadm_r` role when you become root by typing **su -** at the shell prompt.

Encrypting and Signing Files with GnuPG

Linux comes with the GNU Privacy Guard (GnuPG, or simply GPG) encryption and authentication utility. With GPG, you can create your public and private key pair, encrypt files using your key, and also digitally sign a message to authenticate that it's really from you. If you send a digitally signed message to someone who has your public key, the recipient can verify that it was you who signed the message.

Understanding Public-Key Encryption

The basic idea behind public-key encryption is to use a pair of keys — one private and the other public — that are related, but one cannot be guessed from the other. Anything encrypted with the private key can be decrypted with the corresponding public key, and vice versa. The public key is for distribution to other people, while you keep the private key in a safe place.

You can use public-key encryption for securely communicating with others. Figure 22-3 illustrates the basic idea. Suppose that Alice wants to send secure messages to Bob. Each of them generate public-private key pairs and exchange their public keys. When Alice wants to send a message to Bob, she simply encrypts the message using Bob's public key and sends the encrypted message to him. Now, the message is secure from any eavesdropping because only Bob's private key can decrypt the message, and only Bob has that key. When Bob receives the message, he uses his private key to decrypt the message and read it.

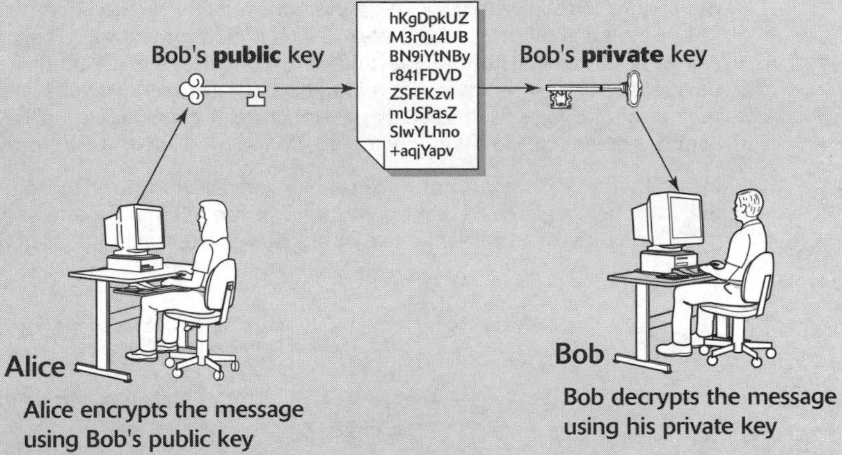

Figure 22-3: Bob and Alice Can Communicate Securely with Public-Key Encryption.

If you think about it, you realize a fundamental problem in using public key encryption. In the scenario of Figure 22-3, how does Bob know the message really came from Alice? What if someone else uses Bob's public key and sends a message as if it came from Alice? Also, how does Alice assure herself that she is indeed using Bob's public key and not some impostor's key? This is where digital signature, certificates, and certificate authority come in.

The following section describes digital signatures and then goes on to explain how to use `gpg` to digitally sign a message. I don't describe certificates, but a *certificate* is an electronic file that associates a public key with the identity of that public key's owner, which can be an individual, an organization, a computer, or an application running on a computer. The certificate is issued and digitally signed by a *certificate authority* (CA) — an organization whose public key we apparently trust. The whole purpose of a CA-issued certificate is to assure someone like Alice that before she encrypts a message for Bob's eyes only by using Bob's public key she (or a program that she uses) can verify the authenticity of Bob's public key.

Understanding Digital Signatures

The purpose of digital or electronic signatures is the same as pen-and-ink signatures, but how you sign digitally is completely different. Unlike pen-and-ink signatures, your digital signature depends on the message you are signing. The first step is to apply a mathematical function on the message and reduce it to a fixed-size message digest (also called hash).

No matter how big your message is, the message digest is always around 128 or 160 bits, depending on the hashing function.

The next step is to apply public key encryption. Simply encrypt the message digest with your private key, and you get the digital signature for the message. Typically, the digital signature is appended to the end of the message and you've got an electronically signed message.

What good does the digital signature do? Well, anyone who wants to verify that the message is indeed signed by you takes your public key and decrypts the digital signature. What they get is the message digest of the message. Then, they apply the same hash function to the message and compare the computer's hash with the decrypted value. If the two match, no one has tampered with the message. Because your public key was used to verify the signature, the message must have been signed with the private key known only to you. So the message must be from you!

In the theoretical scenario of Alice sending private messages to Bob, Alice can digitally sign her message to make sure that Bob can tell that the message is really from her. Figure 22-4 illustrates the use of digital signature along with normal public-key encryption.

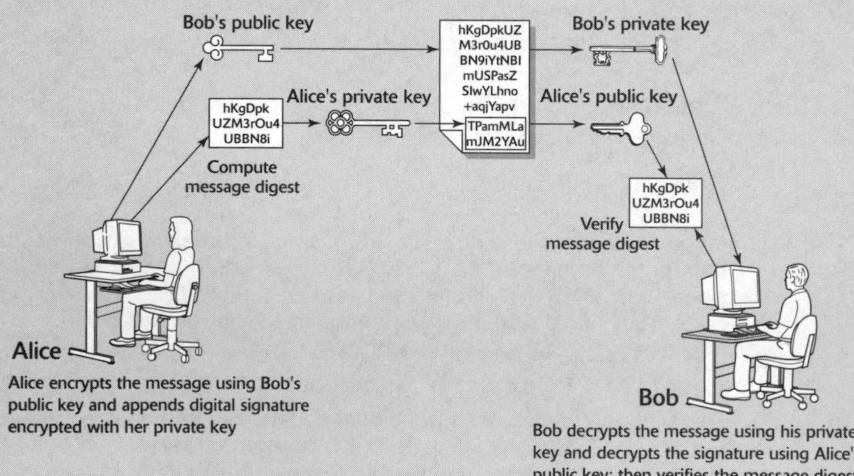

Figure 22-4: Alice Can Digitally Sign Her Message So That Bob Can Tell It's Really from Her.

Here's how Alice sends her private message to Bob with the assurance that Bob can really tell it's from her:

1. Alice uses some software to compute the message digest of the message and then encrypts the digest using her private key. This is her digital signature for the message.
2. Alice encrypts (again, using some convenient software) the message using Bob's public key.
3. She sends both the encrypted message and the digital signature to Bob.

4. Bob decrypts the messages using his private key.
5. Bob decrypts the digital signature using Alice's public key. This gives him the message digest.
6. Bob computes the message digest of the message and compares the result with what he got by decrypting the digital signature.
7. If the two message digests match, Bob can be sure that the message really came from Alice.

Using GPG

GPG includes the tools you need to use public-key encryption and digital signatures. What you'd use is the `gpg` command. You can learn to use GPG gradually as you begin using encryption. I show you some of the typical tasks you can perform with GPG.

Generating the Key Pair

The first thing you have to do is generate your own private-public key pair. Type the following command in a terminal window to generate the key pairs:

```
gpg --gen-key
```

If this is your first time with `gpg`, it creates a `.gnupg` directory in your home directory. The steps for generating the key pairs are as follows:

1. Type the **gpg --gen-key** command again. You should see a message similar to the following:
   ```
   Please select what kind of key you want:
      (1) DSA and ElGamal (default)
      (2) DSA (sign only)
      (5) RSA (sign only)
   Your selection?
   ```
2. Press Enter for the default choice because it's good enough.
3. GPG then prompts you for the key size (the number of bits). Again, press Enter to accept the default value of 1,024 bits.
4. GPG asks you when the keys should expire. The default is to never expire. If that's what you want (and why not?), press Enter.
5. GPG asks if you really want the keys to never expire. Press **y** to confirm.
6. GPG prompts you for your name, then your email address, and finally a comment so that the key pair can be associated with your name. Type the requested information and press Enter.
7. GPG gives you a chance to change the information or confirm it as is. To confirm it, type **o** and then press Enter.
8. GPG prompts you for a passphrase that will be used to protect your private key. Type a long phrase that includes lowercase and uppercase letters, numbers, and punctuation marks — the longer the better. Be sure to pick a passphrase that you can easily remember as well. Type the passphrase, and press Enter.
9. GPG generates the keys. It may ask you to perform some work on the PC so that the random number generator can generate enough random numbers for the key-generation process.

Exchanging Keys

To communicate with others, you have to give them your public key. You also have to get public keys from those who may send you a message (or to verify the signature of someone who might sign a file). GPG keeps the public keys in your key ring. To list the keys in your key ring, type

```
gpg --list-keys
```

To send your public key to someone or place it on a website, you have to export the key to a file. The best way is to put the key in what GPG documentation calls an ASCII-armored format is with a command like this:

```
gpg --armor --export naba@comcast.net > nabakey.asc
```

This command saves my public key in an ASCII-armored format (it basically looks like garbled text) in the file named `nabakey.asc`. Of course, you should replace the email address with your email address (the one you used when you created the keys) and the output filename to something different.

After you export the public key to a file, you can mail that file to others or place it on a website for use by others.

When you import a key from someone else, you typically get it in an ASCII-armored format as well. For example, if I have Red Hat's GPG public key in a file named `redhatkey.asc`, I would import it into my key ring with the following command:

```
gpg --import redhatkey.asc
```

Use the `gpg --list-keys` command to verify that the key is in your key ring.

The next step is to check the fingerprint of the new key. For example, to get the fingerprint of the Red Hat key, type the following command:

```
gpg --fingerprint security@redhat.com
```

This causes GPG to print the fingerprint:

```
pub  1024D/DB42A60E 1999-09-23 Red Hat, Inc <security@redhat.com>
     Key fingerprint = CA20 8686 2BD6 9DFC 65F6  ECC4 2191 80CD DB42 A60E
sub  2048g/961630A2 1999-09-23
```

At this point, you should verify the key fingerprint with someone at Red Hat. For a company like Red Hat, you can verify the fingerprint from a Web page (`www.redhat.com/solutions/security/news/publickey.html`). If you think the key fingerprint is good, you can sign the key and validate it. Here's the command you use to sign the key:

```
gpg --sign-key security@redhat.com
```

GPG asks for confirmation that you really want to sign the key. Press **y** and Enter. GPG then prompts you for your passphrase. After that GPG signs the key.

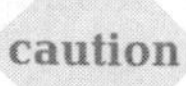

Because the key verification and signing is a potential weak link in GPG, be careful about what keys you sign. By signing a key, you basically say that you trust the key to be from that person or organization.

Signing a File

It's useful to sign files if you send out a file to someone and want to assure the recipient that no one has tampered with it and that it was you who sent the file. GPG makes it very easy to sign a file. You can compress and sign a file named message with the following command (GPG prompts you for your passphrase):

```
gpg -o message.sig -s message
```

To verify the signature, type

```
gpg --verify message.sig
```

To get back the original document, simply type

```
gpg -o message --decrypt message.sig
```

Sometimes you don't care about keeping a message secret, but simply want to sign it to indicate that the message is from you. In this case, you can generate and append a clear text signature with the following command:

```
gpg -o message.asc --clearsign message
```

This command basically appends a clear text signature to the text message. Here's a typical clear-text signature block:

```
-----BEGIN PGP SIGNATURE-----
Version: GnuPG v1.4.1 (GNU/Linux)

iD8DBQFCer/KDYFIBCP6evgRAg5MAJ4s8mAHpVMnOIVOEIFf3M+Za2fQ+wCfcUO4
L6FK2ofYG9dxBBV8SIlfw8k=
=BVoJ
-----END PGP SIGNATURE-----
```

When a message has a clear-text signature appended, you can use GPG to verify the signature with the command like this:

```
gpg --verify message.asc
```

The last line of the output should say that it's a good signature.

Encrypting and Decrypting Documents

To encrypt a message meant for a recipient, you can use the --encrypt (or -e) GPG command. Here's how you might encrypt a message for me if you had my public GPG key:

```
gpg -o message.gpg -e -r naba@comcast.net message
```

The message would be encrypted using my public key (without any signature, but you can add the signature with an -s command).

When I receive the message.gpg file, I have to decrypt it using my private key. Here's the command I would use:

```
gpg -o message --decrypt message.gpg
```

GPG then prompts me for the passphrase to unlock my private key and then decrypts the message and saves the output in the file named `message`.

If you simply want to encrypt a file and no one else has to decrypt the file, you can use GPG to perform what is called symmetric encryption. In this case, you provide a passphrase to encrypt the file with the following GPG command:

```
gpg -o secret.gpg -c somefile
```

GPG prompts you for the passphrase and asks you to repeat the passphrase (to make sure that you didn't mistype anything). Then, GPG encrypts the file using a key generated from the passphrase.

To decrypt a file encrypted with a symmetric key, type

```
gpg -o myfile --decrypt secret.gpg
```

GPG prompts you for the passphrase. If you enter the correct passphrase, GPG decrypts the file and saves the output (in this example) in the file named `myfile`.

Monitoring System Security

Even if you have secured your system, you have to monitor the log files periodically for signs of intrusion. The worst security breaches are the ones that go undetected. A savvy cracker may manage to get access to a system, replace critical system programs with Trojan horses, and hide his or her tracks by modifying the log files. (The Trojan horse programs are often called *root kits* because they allow the cracker to gain root access to your system.) Later on, the cracker may use the Trojan horse programs to access the system at will. The problem is that the system administrator may never even suspect that anything is out of the ordinary.

You may want to install the Tripwire software to monitor the integrity of critical system files and directories. Fedora does not come with the Tripwire package. To use Tripwire, you have to download it from `www.tripwire.org/downloads/index.php`. You have to download the source tarball (a compressed archive of source files) and then build Tripwire. (Chapter 21 provides more information on how to build software packages from source files.) After you build and install Tripwire, you can configure it to monitor any changes to specified system files and directories on your system.

You should also periodically examine the log files. Many Linux applications, including most servers, write log information using the logging capabilities of syslogd. On Linux systems, the log files written by syslogd reside in the `/var/log` directory. Make sure that only the `root` user can read and write these files.

insider insight **The syslogd configuration file is `/etc/syslog.conf`. The default configuration of syslogd should generate the necessary log files; however, if you want to examine and understand the configuration file, type man syslog.conf for more information.**

In Fedora Linux, the LogWatch log-monitoring system is installed by default. LogWatch goes through your system's log files and sends an email message to `root` with a report of anything worth noting such as summary of FTP transfers, invalid login attempts, mail messages transferred by `sendmail`, and current disk space information. You can read these messages by logging in as `root` and typing **mail** in a terminal window.

Securing the Network

To secure your Linux system, you have to pay attention to both host security and network security. The distinction between the two types of security is somewhat arbitrary because securing the network involves fixing up things on the host that relate to what Internet services your system offers. The next few sections explain how you can secure the Internet services (mostly by not running unnecessary services), how you can use a firewall to stop unwanted network packets from reaching your network, and how to use secure shell for secure remote logins.

Securing Internet Services

For an Internet-connected Linux system (or even one on a TCP/IP LAN that's not connected to the Internet), a significant threat is the possibility that someone will use one of many Internet services to gain access to your system. Each service — such as mail, Web, or FTP — requires running a server program that responds to client requests arriving over the TCP/IP network. Some of these server programs have weaknesses that can allow an outsider to log in to your system — maybe with root privileges. Luckily, Linux comes with some facilities that you can use to make the Internet services more secure.

caution

Potential intruders can employ a port-scanning tool — a program that attempts to establish a TCP/IP connection at a port and look for a response — to check which Internet servers are running on your system. Then, to gain access to your system, the intruder can potentially exploit any known weaknesses of one or more services.

Using the chkconfig Command to Disable Services

To provide Internet services such as Web, mail, and FTP, your Linux system has to run server programs that listen to incoming TCP/IP network requests. Some of these servers are started when your system boots, and they run all the time. We call such servers "standalone servers." The Web server and mail server are examples of standalone servers. The other servers are started on demand by another server called xinetd.

You can turn both standalone servers and the ones started by xinetd on or off using the `chkconfig` command. Here's how you should use `chkconfig` to stop unneeded services:

- Log in as `root` and type **chkconfig --list** to view all the services set to start automatically at the run levels 0 through 6. At the end of the list you see the services started by xinetd. Note that the xinetd-controlled services do not depend on the run level; they run at those run levels when xinetd itself is turned on.
- The services that are turned on for run levels 3 and 5 matter most because your Linux system is usually at run level 3 (text mode) or 5 (graphical login). Type **runlevel** to see the current run level.
- Decide which services you don't need. What you need or don't need depends on how you use your Linux system. For example, if it's just a personal workstation, you don't need to run most services.

continues

continued

- To stop a service, use the following form of the `chkconfig` command:

  `chkconfig --level 345 service_name off`

  where *`service_name`*, is the name of the service you want to turn off. For example, to prevent the `vsftpd` service (this is the FTP service) from automatically starting at run levels 3, 4, and 5, type the following command:

  `chkconfig --level 345 vsftpd off`

  You can also use `chkconfig` to turn on or off xinetd-controlled services. For example, if the Telnet service is installed, you can turn that service on by typing:

  `chkconfig telnet on`

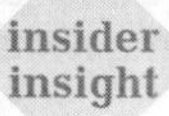

You use `chkconfig` to stop services from starting at boot time, but if you want to immediately stop a service that's currently running, use the `service` command like this:

```
service service_name stop
```

where *`service_name`* is the name of the service to stop. For example, if the mail server (`sendmail`) is already running, you can stop it with the command:

```
service sendmail stop
```

Configuring the xinetd Server to Disable Services

In addition to the stand-alone servers such as a Web server (`httpd`), mail server (`sendmail`), and domain name server (`named`), you have to configure another server separately. That other server, `xinetd` (the Internet superserver), starts a host of other Internet services, such as TELNET, POP3, and so on whenever a client makes a request over the network. The `xinetd` server includes some security features that you can use to disable the services that it can start on demand.

The `xinetd` server reads a configuration file named `/etc/xinetd.conf` at startup. This file, in turn, incorporates all the configuration files stored in the `/etc/xinetd.d` directory. The configuration files in `/etc/xinetd.d` tell `xinetd` which ports to listen to and which server to start for each port. Type **ls /etc/xinetd.d** to see a list of the files in the `/etc/xinetd.d` directory on your system. On my system, here's what the `ls /etc/xinetd.d` command lists:

```
chargen      daytime      echo-udp  klogin       ktalk  time
chargen-udp  daytime-udp  eklogin   krb5-telnet  rsync  time-udp
cvs          echo         gssftp    kshell       telnet
```

This list shows all the services `xinetd` can start. However, the configuration file for a service can also turn off a service simply by having a `disable = yes` line in the file. For example, here's the `telnet` file's content (you have this file only if you have installed the `telnet-server` RPM):

```
# default: on
# description: The telnet server serves telnet sessions;
#     it uses unencrypted username/password pairs for
#     authentication.
service telnet
{
        flags           = REUSE
        socket_type     = stream
        wait            = no
        user            = root
        server          = /usr/sbin/in.telnetd
        log_on_failure  += USERID
        disable         = yes
}
```

Notice the last line in the configuration file — that line disables the Telnet service.

I won't explain the format of the `xinetd` configuration files here (Chapter 6 covers `xinetd` configuration files), except to reiterate that you can turn off a service simply by adding the following line in the configuration file somewhere between the two curly braces `{...}`:

```
        disable         = yes
```

Conversely, to turn a service on, change that line to `disable = no` or comment it out by placing a number sign (#) at the beginning of the line.

caution

After you make any changes to any `xinetd` configuration file, you must restart the xinetd server; otherwise the changes won't take effect. To restart the xinetd server, type the following command:

```
service xinetd restart
```

This stops the xinetd server and then starts it again. When it restarts, it'll read the configuration files, and the changes will take effect.

insider insight

If you don't feel like editing the configuration file for a service in the `/etc/xinetd.d` directory, you can use the `chkconfig` command to turn these services on or off. To turn one of these services off, type chkconfig *servicename* off. There is no need to specify any run levels because these services are activated by `xinetd` and can run only when `xinetd` is running.

Depending on how you use your system, you may be able to disable many of the services. If you do not want anyone to log in remotely or download files from your system, simply disable the Telnet and FTP services. Note that to disable FTP, you have to type **chkconfig --level 35 vsftpd off** because FTP service is now a standalone service and the name of the server is vsftpd.

Another security feature of xinetd is its use of the TCP wrapper library to start various services. The TCP wrapper provides an access-control facility for Internet services. The TCP wrapper can start other services, such as FTP and Telnet, but before starting a service, it consults the /etc/hosts.allow file to see if the host requesting service is allowed that service. If nothing appears in /etc/hosts.allow about that host, TCP wrapper checks the /etc/hosts.deny file to see if it should deny the service. If both files are empty, TCP wrapper provides access to the requested service.

Follow these steps to tighten access to the services that xinetd is configured to start:

1. Use a text editor to edit the /etc/hosts.deny file, adding the following line into that file:

   ```
   ALL:ALL
   ```

   This denies all hosts access to any Internet services on your system.
2. Edit the /etc/hosts.allow file and add to it the names of hosts that can access services on your system. For example, to enable only hosts from the 192.168.1.0 network and the localhost (IP address 127.0.0.1) to access the services on your system, place the following line in the /etc/hosts.allow file:

   ```
   ALL: 192.168.1.0/255.255.255.0 127.0.0.1
   ```

3. If you want to permit access to a specific Internet service to a specific remote host, you can do so using the following syntax for a line in /etc/hosts.allow:

   ```
   server_program_name: hosts
   ```

   Here, server_program_name is the name of the server program (for example, in.telnetd for Telnet), and hosts is a comma-separated list of hosts that can access the service. You may also write hosts as a network address or an entire domain name, such as .mycompany.com. For example, here's how you can give Telnet access to all systems in the mycompany.com domain:

   ```
   in.telnetd: .mycompany.com
   ```

You should edit configuration files in the /etc/xinetd.d directory to turn off unneeded services and use the /etc/hosts.deny and /etc/hosts.allow files to control access to the services that are allowed to run on your system. After you edit the files in the /etc/xinetd.d directory, remember to type **service xinetd restart** to restart the xinetd server.

Using Open Secure Shell for Remote Logins

Linux comes with the Open Secure Shell (OpenSSH) software, a suite of programs that provides a secure replacement for the Berkeley r commands: rlogin (remote login), rsh (remote shell), and rcp (remote copy). OpenSSH uses public-key cryptography to authenticate users and to encrypt the communication between two hosts, so users can securely log in from remote systems and copy files securely.

In this section, I briefly describe how to use the OpenSSH software in Linux. To learn more about OpenSSH and read the latest news about it, visit www.openssh.com or www.openssh.org.

The OpenSSH software is installed during Linux installation. Table 22-4 lists the main components of the OpenSSH software.

Table 22-4: Components of the OpenSSH Software

Component	*Description*
`/usr/sbin/sshd`	The secure shell daemon that must run on a host if you want users on remote systems to use the `ssh` client to log in securely. When a connection from an ssh client arrives, sshd performs authentication using public-key cryptography and establishes an encrypted communication link with the ssh client.
`/usr/bin/ssh`	The secure shell client that users can run to log in to a host that is running sshd. Users can also use ssh to execute a command on another host.
`/usr/bin/slogin`	A symbolic link to `/usr/bin/ssh`.
`/usr/bin/scp`	The secure copy program that works like rcp, but securely. The scp program uses ssh for data transfer and provides the same authentication and security as ssh.
`/usr/bin/ssh-keygen`	The program you use to generate the public and private key pairs you need for the public-key cryptography used in OpenSSH. The ssh-keygen program can generate key pairs for both RSA and DSA (Digital Signature Algorithm) authentication.
`/etc/ssh/sshd_config`	The configuration file for the sshd server. This file specifies many parameters for sshd, including the port to listen to, the protocol to use (there are two versions of SSH protocols, SSH1 and SSH2, both supported by OpenSSH), and the location of other files.
`/etc/ssh/ssh_config`	The configuration file for the ssh client. Each user can also have an ssh configuration file named `config` in the `.ssh` subdirectory of the user's home directory.

OpenSSH uses public-key encryption where the sender and receiver both have a pair of keys — a public key and a private key. The public keys are freely distributed, and each party knows the other's public key. The sender encrypts data by using the recipient's public key. Only the recipient's private key can then decrypt that data.

To use OpenSSH, do the following:

- If you want to support SSH-based remote logins on a host, start the sshd server on your system. Type **ps ax | grep sshd** to see if the server is already running. If not, log in as `root`, and type the following command at the shell prompt to immediately start the sshd server:

  ```
  service sshd start
  ```

  Then type the following command to ensure that the sshd server starts when the system reboots:

  ```
  chkconfig --level 35 sshd on
  ```

- Generate the host keys with the following command:

  ```
  ssh-keygen -d -f /etc/ssh/ssh_host_key -N ''
  ```

  The `-d` flag causes the ssh-keygen program to generate DSA keys, which the SSH2 protocol uses. If you see a message saying that the file `/etc/ssh/ssh_host_key` already exists, that means that the key pairs were generated during Linux installation. You can then use the existing file without having to regenerate the keys.

A user who wants to log in using SSH can simply use the `ssh` command. For example, here is what I type on one system to log into another using SSH:

```
ssh 192.168.0.4 -l naba
```

where 192.168.0.4 is the IP address of the other Linux system. SSH then displays a message:

```
The authenticity of host '192.168.0.4 (192.168.0.4)' can't be established.
RSA key fingerprint is 7b:79:f2:dd:8c:54:00:a6:94:ec:fa:8e:7f:c9:ad:66.
Are you sure you want to continue connecting (yes/no)?
```

I type **yes** and press Enter. SSH then adds the host to its list of known hosts and prompts me for my password on the other Linux system:

```
naba@lnbp200's password: (I type my password and press Enter.)
```

After I enter my password, I have a secure login session with that system. I can also log in to this account with the following equivalent command:

```
ssh naba@192.168.0.4
```

If I simply want to copy a file securely from the `lnbp200` system, I can use `scp` like this:

```
scp 192.168.0.4:/etc/X11/xorg.conf .

naba@192.168.0.4's password: (I type my password.)
xorg.conf                          100% 2814      2.8KB/s   00:00
```

This command securely copies the `/etc/X11/xorg.conf` file from the `192.168.0.4` host to the system from which I type the `scp` command.

Setting Up Simple Firewalls

A *firewall* is a network device or host with two or more network interfaces — one connected to the protected internal network and the other connected to unprotected networks, such as the Internet. The firewall controls access to and from the protected internal network.

If you connect an internal network directly to the Internet, you have to make sure that every system on the internal network is properly secured — which can be nearly impossible because just one careless user can render the entire internal network vulnerable. A firewall is a single point of connection to the Internet: You can direct most of your efforts toward making that firewall system a daunting barrier to unauthorized external users. Essentially, a firewall is like a protective fence that keeps unwanted external data and software out and sensitive internal data and software in. (See Figure 22-5.)

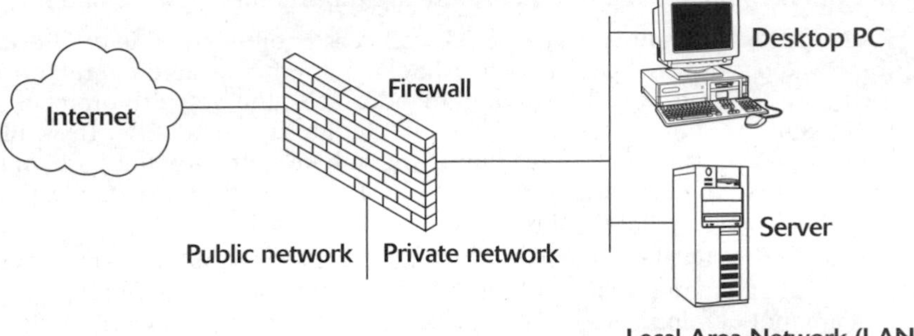

Figure 22-5: A Firewall Protects Hosts on a Private Network from the Internet.

The firewall runs software that examines the network packets arriving at its network interfaces and takes appropriate action based on a set of rules. The idea is to define these rules so that they allow only authorized network traffic to flow between the two interfaces. Configuring the firewall involves setting up the rules properly. A configuration strategy is to reject all network traffic and then enable only a limited set of network packets to go through the firewall. The authorized network traffic would include the connections necessary to enable internal users to do things such as visiting websites and receiving electronic mail.

To be useful, a firewall should have the following general characteristics:

- It must control the flow of packets between the Internet and the internal network.
- It must not provide dynamic routing, because dynamic routing tables are subject to *route spoofing* — use of fake routes by intruders. Instead, the firewall should use static routing tables (which you can set up with the `route` or `ip` command on Linux systems).
- It must not allow any external user to log in as `root`. That way, even if the firewall system is compromised, the intruder will not be able to become `root` from a remote login.
- It must be kept in a physically secure location.
- It must distinguish between packets that come from the Internet and packets that come from the internal protected network. This feature allows the firewall to reject packets that come from the Internet, but have the IP address of a trusted system on the internal network (an attack wherein packets use fake IP addresses is known as IP spoofing).
- It should act as the SMTP mail gateway for the internal network. The sendmail software should be set up so that all outgoing mail appears to come from the firewall system.
- It should not have any user accounts except for a few internal users who need access to external systems. External users who need access to the internal network should use SSH for remote login (see discussion of SSH earlier in this chapter).
- It should keep a log of all system activities, such as successful and unsuccessful login attempts.
- It should provide DNS name lookup service to the outside world to resolve any host names that should be known to the outside world.
- It should provide good performance so that it does not hinder the internal users' access to specific Internet services (such as HTTP and FTP).

A firewall can take many different forms. Here are three common forms of a firewall:

- **Packet filter firewall:** This simple firewall uses a router capable of filtering (blocking or allowing) packets according to a number of their characteristics, including the source and destination IP addresses, the network protocol (TCP or UDP), and the source and destination port numbers. Packet filter firewalls are usually placed at the outermost boundary with an untrusted network, and they form the first line of defense. An example of a packet filter firewall is a network router that employs filter rules to screen network traffic.

  Packet filter firewalls are fast and flexible, but they cannot prevent attacks that exploit application-specific vulnerabilities or functions. They can log only a minimal amount of information, such as source IP address, destination IP address, and traffic type. Also, they are vulnerable to attacks and exploits that take advantage of flaws within the TCP/IP protocol, such as IP address spoofing, which involves altering the address information in network packets in order to make packets appear to come from a trusted IP address.

- **Stateful inspection firewall:** In this case, the firewall keeps track of network connections that network applications are using. When an application on an internal system uses a network connection to create a session with a remote system, a port is also opened on the internal system. This port receives network traffic from the remote system. For successful connections, packet filter firewalls must permit incoming packets from the remote system. Opening up many ports to incoming traffic creates a risk of intrusion by unauthorized users who abuse the expected conventions of network protocols such as TCP. Stateful inspection firewalls solve this problem by creating a table of outbound network connections, along with each session's corresponding internal port. This "state table" is then used to validate any inbound packets. This stateful inspection is more secure than a packet filter because it tracks internal ports individually rather than opening all internal ports for external access.

- **Application-proxy gateway firewall:** This firewall acts as an intermediary between internal applications that attempt to communicate with external servers such as a Web server. For example, a Web proxy receives requests for external Web pages from Web browser clients running inside the firewall and relays them to the exterior Web server as though the firewall was the requesting Web client. The external Web server responds to the firewall and the firewall forwards the response to the inside client as though the firewall was the Web server. No direct network connection is ever made from the inside client host to the external Web server.

  Application-proxy gateway firewalls have some advantages over packet filter firewalls and stateful inspection firewalls. First, application-proxy gateway firewalls examine the entire network packet rather than only the network addresses and ports. This enables these firewalls to provide more extensive logging capabilities than packet filters or stateful inspection firewalls. Another advantage is that application-proxy gateway firewalls can authenticate users directly, while packet filter firewalls and stateful inspection firewalls normally authenticate users based on the IP address of the system (that is, source, destination, and protocol type). Given that network addresses can be easily spoofed, the authentication capabilities of application-proxy gateway firewall are superior to those found in packet filter or stateful inspection firewalls.

  The advanced functionality of application-proxy gateway firewalls, however, results in some disadvantages when compared with packet filter or stateful inspection firewalls. First, because of the "full packet awareness" found in application-proxy gateways, the firewall is forced to spend significant time reading and interpreting each packet. Therefore, application proxy gateway firewalls are generally not well suited to high-bandwidth or real-time applications. To reduce the load on the firewall, a dedicated proxy server can be used to secure less time-sensitive services, such as email and most Web traffic. Another disadvantage is that application-proxy gateway firewalls are often limited in terms of support for new network applications and protocols. An individual, application-specific proxy agent is required for each type of network traffic that needs to go through the firewall. Most vendors of application-proxy gateways provide generic proxy agents to support undefined network protocols or applications. However, those generic agents tend to negate many of the strengths of the application-proxy gateway architecture, and they simply allow traffic to "tunnel" through the firewall.

Most firewalls implement a combination of these firewall functionalities. For example, many vendors of packet filter firewalls or stateful inspection firewalls have also implemented basic application-proxy functionality to offset some of the weaknesses associated with their firewalls. In most cases, these vendors implement application proxies to provide better logging of network traffic and stronger user authentication. Nearly all major firewall vendors have introduced multiple firewall functions into their products in some manner.

insider insight

In a large organization, you may also need to isolate smaller internal networks from the corporate network. You can set up such internal firewalls the same way you set up Internet firewalls.

In the next few sections, I describe some common forms of network configuration with firewall — a screening router with packet filtering, a perimeter network with bastion host, and an application gateway.

Screening Router with Packet Filtering

If you were to directly connect your organization's internal network to the Internet, you would have to use a router to ensure proper exchange of packets between the internal network and the Internet. Most routers can block a packet based on its source or its destination IP address (as well as its port number). The router's packet-filtering capability can serve as a simple firewall. Figure 22-6 illustrates the basic concept of packet filtering.

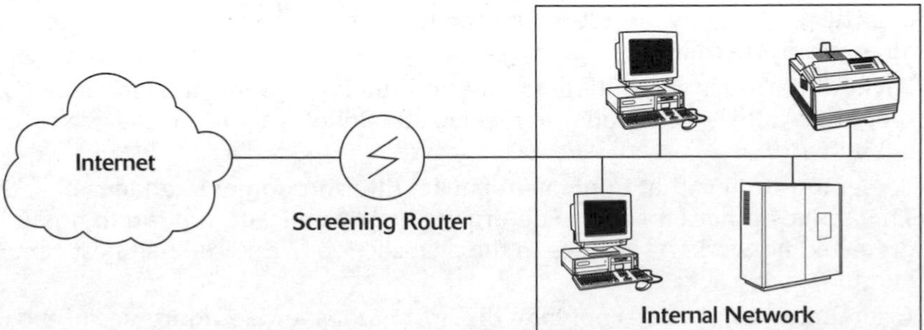

Figure 22-6: Packet Filtering with a Screening Router Provides a Simple Firewall.

Most router vendors, such as Cisco and 3Com, offer routers that can be programmed to perform packet filtering. The exact details of filtering depend on the router vendor, but all routers operate according to rules that refer to the basic attributes of an Internet packet:

- Source IP address
- Destination IP address
- Protocol (TCP, UDP, or ICMP)
- Source port number (if protocol is TCP or UDP)
- Destination port number (if protocol is TCP or UDP)
- ICMP message type

In addition, the router knows the physical interface on which the packet arrived and the interface on which the packet will go out (if it is not blocked by the filtering rules).

Most packet filters operate in the following sequence:

1. You define the rules for allowing or blocking specific types of packets based on IP addresses and port numbers. These packet-filtering rules are stored in the router.
2. The screening router examines the header of each packet that arrives for the information (such as IP addresses and port numbers) to which your rules apply.
3. The screening router applies the rules in the order in which they are stored.
4. If a rule allows the packet to be forwarded, the router sends the packet to its destination.
5. If a rule blocks the packet, the router drops the packet (stops processing it).
6. If none of the rules applies, the packet is blocked. This rule epitomizes the security philosophy that one should "deny unless expressly permitted."

Although packet filtering with a screening router is better than no security, packet filtering suffers from the following drawbacks:

- It is easy for the network administrator to introduce errors inadvertently into the filtering rules.
- Packets are filtered on the basis of IP addresses, which represent specific hosts. Essentially, packet filtering either blocks or routes all packets from a specific host. That means that anyone who breaks into a trusted host can immediately gain access to your protected network.
- Because it is based on IP addresses, packet filtering can be defeated by a technique known as IP spoofing, whereby a cracker sends packets with the IP address of a trusted host (by appropriating the IP address of a trusted host and setting up an appropriate route).
- Packet filtering is susceptible to routing-attack programs that can create a bogus route that allows an intruder to receive all packets meant for the protected internal network.
- Screening routers that implement packet filtering do not keep logs of activities. That makes it hard for you to determine if anyone is attempting to break into the protected network. As you see in the next section, a dual-homed host can provide logging.
- A screening router does not hide the host names and IP addresses of the internal network. Outsiders can access and use this information to mount attacks against the protected network.

A more sophisticated approach is to use an application gateway that controls network traffic, based on specific applications instead of on a per packet basis. You can implement an application gateway with a dual-homed host known also as a bastion host.

Perimeter Network with a Bastion Host

An Internet firewall is often more complicated than a single dual-homed host that connects to both the Internet and the protected internal network. In particular, if you provide a number of Internet services, you may need more than one system to host them. Imagine that you have two systems: one to run the Web and FTP servers and the other to provide mail (SMTP) and Domain Name Service (DNS) lookups. In this case, you place these two systems on a network that sits between the Internet and the internal network. Figure 22-7 illustrates this concept of an Internet firewall.

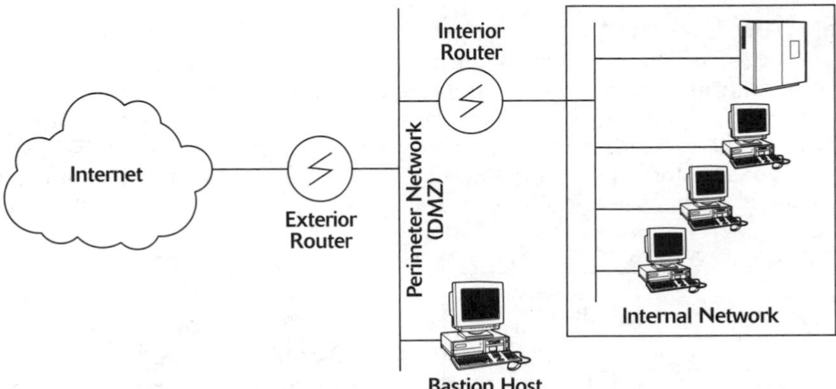

Figure 22-7: A More Complete Internet Firewall Includes a Perimeter Network and Bastion Hosts.

In this case, the firewall includes a perimeter network that connects to the Internet through an exterior router. The perimeter network, in turn, connects to the internal network through an interior router. The perimeter network has one or more hosts that run Internet services, including proxy services that allow internal hosts to access Web servers on the Internet.

insider insight

The term "bastion host" refers to any system on the perimeter network, because such a system is on the Internet and has to be well fortified. The dual-homed host is also a bastion host because the dual-homed host is also accessible from the Internet and has to be protected.

In the firewall configuration shown in Figure 22-7, the perimeter network is known as a DMZ (demilitarized zone) network because that network acts as a buffer between the Internet and the internal network (just as the real-life DMZ is a buffer between North and South Korea).

Usually, you combine a packet-filtering router with a bastion host. Your Internet service provider typically provides the external router, which means that you do not have much control over that router's configuration. But you provide the internal router, which means you can choose a screening router and employ some packet-filtering rules. For example, you might employ the following packet-filtering rules:

- From the internal network, allow only packets addressed to the bastion host.
- From the DMZ, allow only packets originating from the bastion host.
- Block all other packets.

This ensures that the internal network communicates only with the bastion host (or hosts). Like the dual-homed host, the bastion host also runs an application gateway that provides proxy services for various Internet services, such as Telnet, FTP, SMTP, and HTTP.

Application Gateway

The bastion host or the dual-homed host is the system that acts as the intermediary between the Internet and the protected internal network. As such, that system serves as the internal network's gateway to the Internet. Toward this end, the system runs software to forward and filter TCP/IP packets for various services, such as Telnet, FTP, and HTTP. The applications for forwarding and filtering TCP/IP packets for specific applications are known as proxy services. Figure 22-8 illustrates a proxy server's role in a firewall.

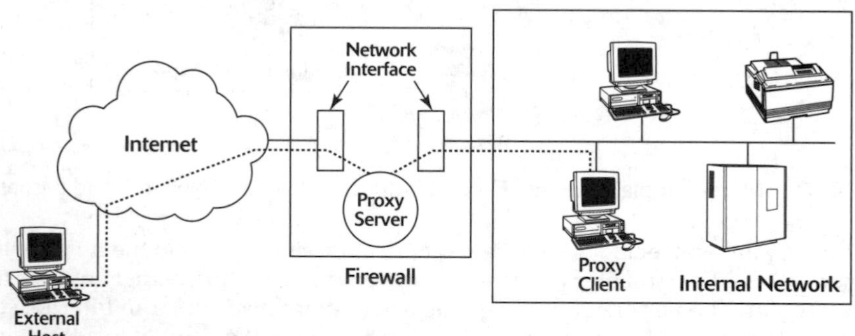

Figure 22-8: A Proxy Server Lets Internal Hosts Access Internet Servers.

A proxy server accepts a connection for a specific protocol, such as FTP, and forwards the request to another server. In other words, the proxy server acts as a proxy for an actual server. Because it acts as a gateway for a specific application (such as HTTP or FTP), a proxy server is also known as an *application gateway*.

Unlike a screening router, which blocks packets only on the basis of information in the packet header (such as source and destination IP addresses), a proxy server uses the packet's data to decide what to do. For example, a proxy server does not blindly forward packets to an Internet service. The proxy server can enforce a site's security policy and disallow certain operations, depending on the specific application. For example, an FTP proxy server may prevent users from internal networks from using the FTP `put` command to send files to the Internet.

The exact steps you take to access services through a firewall depend on the proxy software and the client program you use to access a service. With the right client program, proxies can be transparent to the user. For example, many Web browsers make it easy to access a website through an HTTP proxy. All you need to do is indicate through a menu choice the HTTP proxy you want to use.

Using NATs

Network address translation (NAT) is an effective tool that enables you to "hide" the network addresses of an internal network behind a firewall. In essence, NAT allows an organization to use private network addresses behind a firewall while still maintaining the ability to connect to external systems through the firewall.

There are three methods for implementing NAT:

- **Static:** In static NAT, each internal system on the private network has a corresponding external, routable IP address associated with it. This particular technique is seldom used because unique IP addresses are in short supply.
- **Hiding:** With hiding NAT, all systems behind a firewall share the same external, routable IP address, while the internal systems use private IP addresses. Thus, with a hiding NAT, a number of systems behind a firewall will still appear to be a single system.
- **Port Address Translation:** With port address translation, it is possible to place hosts behind a firewall system and still make them selectively accessible to external users.

In terms of strengths and weaknesses, each type of NAT — static, hiding, or port address translation — is applicable in certain situations; the variable is the amount of design flexibility offered by each type. Static NAT offers the most flexibility, but it is not always practical because of the shortage of IP addresses. Hiding NAT technology is seldom used because port address translation offers additional features. Port address translation is often the most convenient and secure solution.

Enabling Packet Filtering in Linux

Linux comes with built-in packet filtering software in the form of something called *netfilter* that's in the Linux kernel. All you have to do is use the `iptables` command to set up the rules for what happens to the packets based on the IP addresses in their header and the network connection type.

The built-in packet-filtering capability is handy when you do not have a dedicated firewall between your Linux system and the Internet. This is the case, for example, when you connect your system to the Internet through a DSL or cable modem. You can essentially have a packet-filtering firewall inside your Linux system, sitting between the kernel and the applications.

Setting the Security Level with a GUI Tool

You can turn on different levels of packet filtering through a graphical Security Level Configuration tool. To run the tool, log in as `root` and select Desktop ➪ System Settings ➪ Security Level and Firewall. The Security Level Configuration window appears (see Figure 22-9).

Figure 22-9: Setting the Firewall Options with a GUI Tool.

Click the Firewall Options tab to configure the firewall. The Security Level Configuration tool has another tab — the SELinux tab (refer to Figure 22-9) — that enables you to turn on or off and configure the mandatory access control provided by SELinux.

From the Firewall Options tab (refer to Figure 22-9), you can select two predefined levels of simple firewalling (more precisely, packet filtering) with the Security Level Configuration tool:

- **Disable Firewall:** Does not perform any filtering, and all connections are allowed. (You can still turn off Internet services by not running the servers or disabling them in the `xinetd` configuration files.) This security level is fine if your Linux system is inside a protected local area network or if you have a separate firewall device.
- **Enable Firewall:** Turns on packet filtering. You can then select the services that you want to allow and the network devices that you trust.

You can allow incoming packets meant for specific Internet services such as SSH, HTTP, and FTP. If you select a network interface such as eth0 (the first Ethernet card) as trusted, all network traffic over that interface is allowed without any filtering. After setting the firewall options, click OK to make the settings effective.

Behind the scenes, the GUI security level tool uses `iptables` rules to implement the packet filtering implied by the selections you make.

Filtering IP Packets with iptables

You can set up packet filtering manually using the `iptables` command. The `iptables` command works with the netfilter software, built into the Linux kernel, to intercept network packets and apply filtering rules to the packets. With the `iptables` command, you can set up, view, and manage tables of rules for filtering IP packets.

Packet filtering with iptables relies on the concept of a chain — a sequence of rules — to filter packets. Each rule says what to do with a packet if the header contains certain information (such as the source or destination IP address). If a rule does not apply, iptables consults the next rule in the chain. By default, there are three chains:

- **INPUT chain:** The first set of rules against which packets are tested. The packets continue to the next chain only if the input chain does not specify DROP or REJECT.
- **FORWARD chain:** Contains the rules that apply to packets attempting to pass through this system to another system (for example, when you use the Linux system as a router between your LAN and the Internet).
- **OUTPUT chain:** Includes the rules applied to packets before they are sent out (either to another network or to an application)

Figure 22-10 shows a high-level depiction of how IP packets are processed by iptables through these three chains.

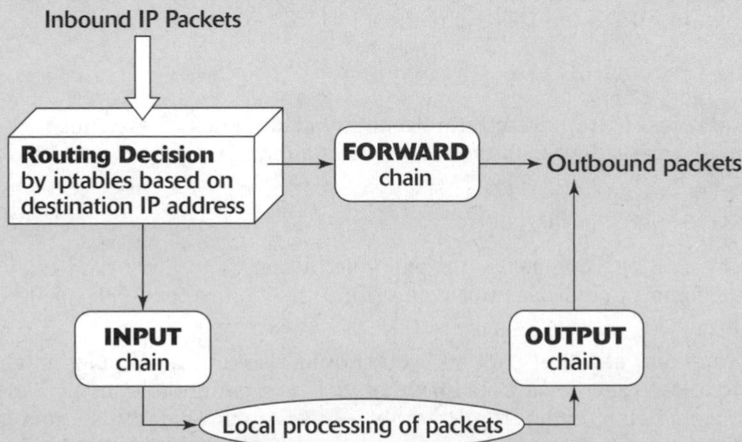

Figure 22-10: Simplified View of the iptables Processing Chains.

When an incoming packet arrives, the kernel uses iptables to make a routing decision based on the destination IP address of the packet. If the packet is for this server, the kernel passes the packet to the INPUT chain. If the packet satisfies all the rules in the INPUT chain, then the packet is processed by local processes such as an Internet server that is listening for packets of this type.

If the kernel had IP forwarding enabled and the packet has a destination IP address of a different network, the kernel passes the packet to the FORWARD chain. If the packet satisfies the rules in the FORWARD chain, it's sent out to the other network. If the kernel does not have IP forwarding enabled and the packet's destination address is not for this server, then the packet is dropped.

If the local processing programs that received the input packets want to send network packets out, then those packets pass through the OUTPUT chain. If those packets are accepted by the OUTPUT chain, they are sent out to the specified destination network.

You can view the current chains, add rules to the existing chains, or create new chains of rules by using the `iptables` command. When you view the current chains, you can also save them to a file. For example, if you have done nothing else and your system has no firewall configured, typing the `iptables -L` command should show the following:

```
Chain INPUT (policy ACCEPT)
target     prot opt source               destination

Chain FORWARD (policy ACCEPT)
target     prot opt source               destination

Chain OUTPUT (policy ACCEPT)
target     prot opt source               destination
```

In this case, all three chains — `INPUT`, `FORWARD`, and `OUTPUT` — show the same `ACCEPT` policy, which means that everything is wide open.

If you are setting up a packet filter, the first thing you do is specify the packets that you want to accept. For example, to accept packets only from the 192.168.0.0 network, add the following rule to the `INPUT` chain:

```
iptables -A INPUT -s 192.168.0.0/24 -j ACCEPT
```

Now, add rules to drop everything except local loopback (the `lo` network interface) traffic and stop all forwarding with the following commands:

```
iptables -A INPUT -i ! lo -j REJECT
iptables -A FORWARD -j REJECT
```

The first `iptables` command, for example, appends to the `INPUT` chain (`-A INPUT`) the rule that if the packet does not come from the `lo` interface (`-i ! lo`), `iptables` should reject the packet (`-j REJECT`).

Before rejecting all other packets, you should also add more rules to each of the `INPUT` chains to allow specific packets in. Otherwise, you cannot effectively use the Internet. For example, packets coming from Internet servers such as name servers and Web servers will not be accepted by your system. You can further configure the firewall by adding rules to accept or reject packets based on many different parameters such as source and destination IP addresses, protocol types (TCP, UDP), network interface, and port numbers.

You can do all sorts of specialized packet filtering with `iptables`. For example, suppose that you are setting up a Web server and you want to accept packets meant for only HTTP (port 80) and secure shell (SSH) services. The secure shell service (port 22) is for you to securely log in and administer the server. Suppose that the server's IP address is 192.168.0.10. Here is how you might set up the rules for this server:

```
iptables -P INPUT DROP
iptables -A INPUT -s 0/0 -d 192.168.0.10 -p tcp --dport 80 -j ACCEPT
iptables -A INPUT -s 0/0 -d 192.168.0.10 -p tcp --dport 22 -j ACCEPT
```

In this case, the first rule sets up the default policy of the `INPUT` chain to `DROP`, which means that if none of the specific rules match, the packet will be dropped. The next two rules say that packets addressed to 192.168.0.10 and meant for ports 80 and 22 are accepted.

caution

Don't type `iptables` commands from a remote login session. A rule that begins denying packets from all addresses can also stop what you type from reaching the system; once that happens, you may have no way of accessing the system over the network. To avoid unpleasant surprises, always type `iptables` rules at the console — the keyboard and monitor that are connected directly to your Linux PC that is running the packet filter. If you want to delete all filtering rules in a hurry, flush all the rules by typing the following command:

```
iptables -F
```

I won't provide all the details of the `iptables` commands in this section. Type **man iptables** to read a summary of the commands. You can also read about netfilter and `iptables` at `www.iptables.org`.

After you define the rules by using the `iptables` command, they are in the memory and will be gone when you reboot the system. To save them, use the `iptables-save` command to store the rules in a file. For example, you can save the rules in a file named `iptables.rules` by using the following commands:

```
iptables-save > iptables.rules
```

Here's a listing of the `iptables.rules` file, generated on a Linux system:

```
# Generated by iptables-save v1.3.0 on Sat May  7 12:17:32 2005
*filter
:FORWARD ACCEPT [0:0]
:INPUT ACCEPT [0:0]
:OUTPUT ACCEPT [32:3392]
-A FORWARD -j REJECT --reject-with icmp-port-unreachable
-A INPUT -s 192.168.0.0/255.255.255.0 -j ACCEPT
-A INPUT -i ! lo -j REJECT --reject-with icmp-port-unreachable
COMMIT
# Completed on Sat May  7 12:17:32 2005
```

In case you are curious, these rules correspond to the following `iptables` commands I used to configure the filter:

```
iptables -A INPUT -s 192.168.0.0/24 -j ACCEPT
iptables -A INPUT -i ! lo -j REJECT
iptables -A FORWARD -j REJECT
```

If you want to load these saved rules into `iptables`, use the following command:

```
iptables-restore < iptables.rules
```

On a Linux system, the process of saving and restoring firewall rules is automated by saving the `iptables` rules in the file `/etc/sysconfig/iptables` and by enabling `iptables` with the following command:

```
chkconfig iptables on
```

That should ensure that the `/etc/init.d/iptables start` command is executed at system startup. The `/etc/init.d/iptables` script then runs the `/sbin/iptables-restore` command to restore the `iptables` rules from the `/etc/sysconfig/iptables` file.

Performing Security Audits

The purpose of a computer security audit is to test your system and network security. For larger organizations, the security audit may be done by an independent auditor (much like the auditing of financial statements). If you have only a few Linux systems or a small network, you can do the security audit as a self-assessment, just to figure out if you are doing everything okay.

The following sections explain how to perform computer security audits and show you a number of free tools and resources to help you test your system's security.

Understanding Computer Security Audits

An audit is simply an independent assessment of whatever it is you are auditing. So a computer security audit is an independent assessment of computer security.

Secret

A typical computer security audit of your organization would focus on two areas:

- Independent verification of whether your organization is complying with its existing policies and procedures for computer security. This is the *nontechnical* part of the security audit.
- Independent testing of the effectiveness of your security controls, which refer to any hardware and software security mechanisms you use to secure the system. This is the *technical* part of the security audit.

You might wonder why you need security audits. You need them for the same reason an organization needs financial audits — mainly to verify that everything is being done the way it is supposed to be done. For public as well as private organizations, management may want independent security audits to assure themselves that their security is adequate. Regardless of your organization's size, you can always perform security audits on your own, either to prepare for independent security audits or simply to verify that you're doing everything right.

No matter whether you have independent security audits or perform a self-assessment, here are some of the benefits you get from security audits:

- Periodic risk assessments that consider internal and external threats to systems and data
- Periodic testing of the effectiveness of security policies, security controls, and techniques
- Identification of any significant deficiencies in your system's security (so you know what to fix)
- In case of self-assessments, preparation for any annual independent security testing that your organization might have to face

The nontechnical side of computer security audits focuses on your organization-wide security framework. The audit examines how well the organization has set up and implemented the policies, plans, and procedures for computer security. Some of the items to be verified include the following:

- Risks are periodically assessed.
- There is an entity-wide security program plan.
- A security program management structure is put in place.
- Computer security responsibilities are clearly assigned.
- Effective security-related personnel policies are in place.
- The security program's effectiveness is monitored and changes are made when needed.

As you may expect, the nontechnical aspects of the security audit involves reviewing documents and interviewing appropriate individuals to learn how the organization manages computer security. Of course, for a small organization or a home PC, it's ridiculous to expect plans and procedures to be captured in documents. In those cases, all you need to do is make sure is that you have some technical controls in place to secure your system and your network connection.

The technical side of computer security audits focus on testing the technical controls that secure your hosts and network. The testing involves determining:

- **How well the host is secured.** Are all operating system patches applied? Are the file permissions set correctly? Are user accounts protected? Are file changes monitored? Are log files monitored? And so on.
- **How well the network is secured.** Are unnecessary Internet services turned off? Is a firewall installed? Are remote logins secured with tools such as SSH? Are TCP wrapper access controls used? And so on.

Typically security experts use automated tools to perform these two security reviews — host and network.

Using a Security Test Methodology

A key element of computer security audit is the security test that checks the technical mechanisms used to secure a host and the network. The security test methodology follows these high-level steps:

1. Take stock of the organization's networks, hosts, network devices (routers, switches, firewalls, and so on), and how the network is connected to the Internet.
2. If there are many hosts and network connections, determine what are the important hosts and network devices that should be tested. The importance of a host depends on the kind of applications it runs.
3. Test the hosts individually. Typically, this involves logging in as a system administrator and then checking various aspects of host security from passwords to system log files.
4. Test the network. This is usually done by attempting to break through the network defenses from another system on the Internet. If there is a firewall, the testing checks that the firewall is indeed configured correctly.
5. Analyze the test results of both host and network tests to determine the vulnerabilities and risks.

Each of the two types of testing — host and network — focuses on three areas that comprise overall computer security:

- **Prevention:** This includes the mechanisms (nontechnical and technical) that help prevent attacks on the system and the network.
- **Detection:** This refers to techniques such as monitoring log files, checking file integrity, and using intrusion detection systems that can detect when someone is about to break into, or has already broken into, your system.
- **Response:** This includes the steps, such as reporting an incident to authorities and restoring important files from backup, that you perform when a computer security incident has occurred.

These host and network security areas have some overlaps. For example, prevention mechanisms for host security, such as good passwords or file permissions, can also provide network security. Nevertheless, it helps to think in terms of the three areas — prevention, detection, and response.

Before you can think of prevention, however, you need to know the types of problems that you are trying to prevent. In other words, what are the common security vulnerabilities? The prevention and detection steps typically depend on what these vulnerabilities are.

Understanding Common Computer Vulnerabilities

The specific tests of the host and network security depend on the common vulnerabilities. Basically, the idea is to check if a host or a network has the vulnerabilities that crackers are most likely to exploit.

Online Resources on Computer Vulnerabilities

There are several online resources that identify and categorize computer security vulnerabilities:

- **SANS Institute** publishes a list of the Top 20 most critical Internet security vulnerabilities at `www.sans.org/top20/`.
- **CVE (Common Vulnerabilities and Exposures)** is a list of standardized names of vulnerabilities. For more information on CVE, see `http://cve.mitre.org` (the list has over 9,600 names of vulnerabilities). It's common practice to use the CVE name to describe vulnerabilities.
- The **ICAT Metabase** is a searchable index of information on computer vulnerabilities, published by the National Institute of Standards and Technology (NIST), a United States government agency. The ICAT vulnerability index is online at `http://icat.nist.gov/icat.cfm`. ICAT has nearly 7,600 vulnerabilities and it provides links to vulnerability advisory and patch information for each vulnerability. ICAT also has a Top Ten List that lists the vulnerabilities that were most queried during the past year.

Typical Top 20 Computer Vulnerabilities

The SANS Top 20 vulnerabilities list includes two types of vulnerabilities — Windows vulnerabilities and UNIX vulnerabilities. Of these, the UNIX vulnerabilities are relevant to Linux. Table 22-5 summarizes the UNIX vulnerabilities that apply to Linux. The information in the table is based on past SANS Top 20 lists. You can read the complete details about these vulnerabilities at `www.sans.org/top20`.

Table 22-5: Some Common Computer Vulnerability Types

Vulnerability Type	*Description*
BIND DNS	Berkeley Internet Name Domain (BIND) is a package that implements Domain Name Service (DNS), the Internet's name service that translates a name to an IP address. Some versions of BIND have vulnerabilities.
Apache Web Server	Some Apache Web server modules (such as mod_ssl) have known vulnerabilities. Any vulnerability in common gateway interface (CGI) programs used with Web servers to process interactive Web pages can provide attackers a way to gain access to a system.
Authentication	User accounts often have no passwords or weak passwords (passwords that are easily cracked by password-cracking programs).
CVS, Subversion	Concurrent Versions System (CVS) is a popular source code control system used in Linux systems. Subversion is another version control system for Linux that is becoming popular. These version control systems have vulnerabilities that can enable an attacker to execute arbitrary code on the system.
Sendmail	Sendmail is a complex program used to transport mail messages from one system to another, and some versions of Sendmail have vulnerabilities.
SNMP	Simple Network Management Protocol (SNMP) is used to remotely monitor and administer various network-connected systems ranging from routers to computers. SNMP lacks good access control, so, if SNMP is running on your system, an attacker may be able to reconfigure or shut down your system.
Open Secure Sockets Layer (OpenSSL)	Many applications such as Apache Web server use OpenSSL to provide cryptographic security for a network connection. Unfortunately, some versions of OpenSSL have known vulnerabilities that could be exploited.
Network File System (NFS) and Network Information Service (NIS)	Both NFS and NIS have many security problems (for example, buffer overflow, potential for denial-of-service attacks, and weak authentication). Also, NFS and NIS are often misconfigured, which could allow the security holes to be exploited by local and remote users.
Databases	Databases such as MySQL and PostgreSQL are complex applications and can be difficult to correctly configure and secure. These databases have many features that can be misused or exploited to compromise the confidentiality, availability, and integrity of data. To learn more about some of the common attacks on MySQL and how to defend against them, consult this paper: `www.nextgenss.com/papers/HackproofingMySQL.pdf`.
Linux kernel	The Linux kernel is susceptible to many vulnerabilities such as denial of service, execution of arbitrary code, and root level access to the system.

Reviewing Host Security

When reviewing host security, focus on assessing the security mechanisms in each of the following areas:

- **Prevention:** Install operating system updates, secure passwords, improve file permissions, set up a password for boot loader, and use encryption.
- **Detection:** Capture log messages and check file integrity with Tripwire.
- **Response:** Make routine backups and develop incident response procedures.

I describe how to review a few of these host security mechanisms.

Operating System Updates

Fedora Project issues Fedora Linux updates as soon they learn of any security vulnerabilities, but it's up to you or a system administrator to download and install the updates. One way to keep up with the Fedora Linux security patches is to use the `yum update` command.

To assess whether the operating system updates are current, an auditor gets a current list of updates for key Fedora Linux components and then uses the `rpm` command to check if they are installed. For example, if a list shows that `glibc` version 2.3.5 is what the system should have, the auditor types the following `rpm` command to view the current `glibc` version number:

```
rpm -q glibc
```

If the version number is less than 2.3.5, the conclusion is that operating system updates are not being installed.

File Permissions

Key system files should be protected with appropriate file ownerships and file permissions. The key steps in assigning file system ownerships and permissions are to:

- Figure out which files contain sensitive information and why. Some files may contain sensitive data related to your work or business, whereas many other files are sensitive because they control the Linux system configuration.
- Maintain a current list of authorized users and what they are authorized to do on the system.
- Set up passwords, groups, file ownerships, and file permissions to allow only authorized users access to the files.

Table 22-6 lists some of the important system files in Linux. The table also shows the numeric permission setting for each file.

Table 22-6: Important System Files and Their Permissions

File Pathname	*Permission*	*Description*
`/boot/grub/grub.conf`	600	GRUB boot loader configuration file
`/etc/cron.allow`	400	List of users permitted to use cron to submit periodic jobs
`/etc/cron.deny`	400	List of users who cannot use cron to submit periodic jobs
`/etc/crontab`	644	System-wide periodic jobs
`/etc/hosts.allow`	644	List of hosts allowed to use Internet services that are started using TCP wrappers

File Pathname	Permission	Description
/etc/hosts.deny	644	List of hosts denied access to Internet services that are started using TCP wrappers
/etc/logrotate.conf	644	File that controls how log files are rotated
/etc/pam.d	755	Directory with configuration files for pluggable authentication modules (PAM)
/etc/passwd	644	Old-style password file with user account information but not the passwords
/etc/rc.d	755	Directory with system startup scripts
/etc/securetty	600	TTY interfaces (terminals) from which root can log in
/etc/security	755	Directory with policy files that control system access
/etc/shadow	400	File with encrypted passwords and password expiry information
/etc/shutdown.allow	400	Users who can shutdown or reboot by pressing Ctrl-Alt-Delete
/etc/ssh	755	Directory with configuration files for the secure shell (SSH)
/etc/sysconfig	755	System configuration files
/etc/sysctl.conf	644	Kernel configuration parameters
/etc/syslog.conf	644	Configuration file for syslogd server that logs messages
/etc/vsftpd/vsftpd.conf	600	Configuration file for the very secure FTP server
/etc/vsftpd/ftpusers	600	List of users who cannot use FTP to transfer files
/etc/xinetd.conf	644	Configuration file for the xinetd server
/etc/xinetd.d	755	Directory containing configuration files for specific services that the xinetd server can start
/var/log	755	Directory with all log files
/var/log/lastlog	644	Information about all previous logins
/var/log/messages	644	Main system message log file
/var/log/secure	400	Security related log file
/var/log/wtmp	664	Information about current logins

Another important check is to look for executable program files that have the setuid permission. If a program has setuid permission and it's owned by root, then the program runs with `root` privileges, no matter who runs the program. You can find all setuid programs with the following `find` command:

```
find / -perm +4000 -print
```

You may want to save the output in a file (just append > `filename` to the command) and then examine the file for any unusual setuid programs. For example, a setuid program in a user's home directory would be unusual.

Password Security

Verify that the password, group, and shadow password files are protected. In particular, the shadow password file should be write-protected and readable only by root. The filenames and their recommended permissions are shown in Table 22-7.

Table 22-7: Ownership and Permission of Password Files

File Pathname	*Ownership*	*Permission*
/etc/group	root.root	644
/etc/passwd	root.root	644
/etc/shadow	root.root	400

Incident Response

Incident response is the answer to the question of what to do if something does happen—in other words, what to do if someone has broken into your system.

Your response to an incident depends on how you use your system and how important it is to you or your business. For a comprehensive incident response, here are some key points to remember:

- Figure out how critical and important your computer and network are and identify who or what resources can help you protect your system.
- Take steps to prevent and minimize potential damage and interruption.
- Develop and document a comprehensive contingency plan.
- Periodically test the contingency plan and revise the procedures as appropriate.

Reviewing Network Security

Network security review focuses on assessing the security mechanisms in each of the following areas:

- **Prevention:** Set up firewall, enable packet filtering, disable unnecessary xinetd services, turn off unneeded Internet services, use TCP wrappers access control, and use SSH for secure remote logins.
- **Detection:** Use network intrusion detection and capture system logs.
- **Response:** Develop incident response procedures.

I briefly describe some key steps in assessing the network security.

Services Started by xinetd

Many Internet services such as Telnet and POP3 are started by the xinetd server. The decision to turn on some of these services depends on factors such as how the system is connected to the Internet and how the system is being used. You can usually turn off most xinetd services.

Check which xinetd services are turned on in one of the following ways:

- Check the configuration files in the `/etc/xinetd.d` directory for all the services that xinetd can start. If a service is turned off, the configuration file has a line like this:

  ```
  disable = yes
  ```

  Remember that the `disable = yes` line doesn't count if it's commented out by placing a # at the beginning of the line.
- Type the following command:

  ```
  chkconfig --list | more
  ```

  In the output, look for the lines that follow:

  ```
  xinetd based services:
  ```

  These lines list all the services that xinetd can start and whether they are on or off. For example, here are the lines showing the status of xinetd services on a system:

  ```
          chargen:        off
          chargen-udp:    off
          cvs:            off
          daytime:        off
          daytime-udp:    off
          echo:           off
          echo-udp:       off
          eklogin:        off
          gssftp:         off
          klogin:         off
          krb5-telnet:    off
          kshell:         off
          ktalk:          off
          rsync:          off
          telnet:         off
          time:           off
          time-udp:       off
  ```

  In this case, all services are off.

Also check the following files for any access controls used with the xinetd services:

- `/etc/hosts.allow` lists hosts allowed to access specific services.
- `/etc/hosts.deny` lists hosts that should be denied access to services.

Standalone Services

Many services such as HTTPD (Web server) and sendmail (mail server) start automatically at boot time, assuming that they are configured to start that way. You can use the `chkconfig` command to check which standalone servers are set to start at various run levels. Typically, your Linux system starts up at run level 3 (for text login) or 5 (for graphical login). Therefore, what matters is the setting for the servers in levels 3 and 5. To view the list of servers, type the following command:

```
chkconfig --list | more
```

Here's a partial listing of what you might see:

```
NetworkManager  0:off   1:off   2:off   3:off   4:off   5:off   6:off
acpid           0:off   1:off   2:off   3:on    4:on    5:on    6:off
anacron         0:off   1:off   2:on    3:on    4:on    5:on    6:off
apmd            0:off   1:off   2:on    3:on    4:on    5:on    6:off
atd             0:off   1:off   2:off   3:on    4:on    5:on    6:off
auditd          0:off   1:off   2:on    3:on    4:on    5:on    6:off
autofs          0:off   1:off   2:off   3:on    4:on    5:on    6:off
bluetooth       0:off   1:off   2:off   3:off   4:off   5:off   6:off
crond           0:off   1:off   2:on    3:on    4:on    5:on    6:off
cups            0:off   1:off   2:on    3:on    4:on    5:on    6:off
cups-config-daemon      0:off   1:off   2:off   3:on    4:on    5:on
dc_client       0:off   1:off   2:off   3:off   4:off   5:off   6:off
dc_server       0:off   1:off   2:off   3:off   4:off   5:off   6:off
diskdump        0:off   1:off   2:off   3:off   4:off   5:off   6:off
dovecot         0:off   1:off   2:off   3:off   4:off   5:off   6:off
gpm             0:off   1:off   2:on    3:on    4:on    5:on    6:off
haldaemon       0:off   1:off   2:off   3:on    4:on    5:on    6:off
httpd           0:off   1:off   2:off   3:off   4:off   5:off   6:off
innd            0:off   1:off   2:off   3:off   4:off   5:off   6:off
iptables        0:off   1:off   2:on    3:on    4:on    5:on    6:off
...lines deleted...
```

The first column shows the names of the servers. Look at the column of entries that begins with `3:` and the ones that begin with `5:`. These are the ones that show the status of the server for run levels 3 and 5. The ones that appear as `on` are automatically started when your Linux system starts.

If you are doing a self-assessment of your network security and you find that some servers should not be running, you can turn them off for run levels 3 and 5 with the `chkconfig` command like this:

```
chkconfig --level 35 servicename off
```

Replace `servicename` with the name of the service you want to turn off.

If you are auditing network security, make a note of all the servers that are turned on and then try to determine if they should really be on, based on what you know about the system. The decision to turn on services depends on how a system is used (as a Web server or a desktop system) and how it is connected to the Internet (through a firewall or directly).

Penetration Testing

A penetration test is the best way to tell what services are really running on a Linux system. Penetration testing involves trying to get access to your system from an attacker's perspective. Typically, you perform this test from a system on the Internet and try to see if you can break in or, at a minimum, get access to services running on your Linux system.

One aspect of penetration testing is to see what ports are open on your Linux system. The port number is simply a number that identifies specific TCP/IP network connections to the system. The attempt to connect to a port succeeds only if a server is running on that port (or put another way, if a server is "listening on that port"). A port is considered to be open if a server responds when a connection request for that port arrives.

The first step in penetration testing is to perform a port scan. The term port scan is used to describe the automated process of trying to connect to each port number and see if a valid response comes back. There are many automated tools available to perform port scanning—Linux comes with a popular port scanning tool called `nmap` (I describe it later in this chapter).

After performing a port scan, you know the potential vulnerabilities that could be exploited. Not all servers have security problems, but many servers have well-known vulnerabilities, and an open port provides a cracker a way to attack your system through one of the servers. In fact, you can use automated tools called vulnerability scanners to identify vulnerabilities that exist in your system. (I describe some vulnerability scanners next.) Whether your Linux system is connected to the Internet directly (through DSL or cable modem) or through a firewall, use the port scanning and vulnerability scanning tools to figure out if you have any holes in your defenses. Better you than them!

Exploring Security-Testing Tools

There are many automated tools available to perform security testing. Some tools are meant for finding the open ports on every system in a range of IP addresses. Others are meant to find the vulnerabilities associated with the open ports. Yet other tools can capture (or sniff) and help you analyze them so you can glean useful information about what's going on in your network.

You can browse a list of top 50 security tools (based on an informal poll of nmap users) at `www.insecure.org/tools.html`. Table 22-8 lists a number of tools by category. I describe a few of the freely available vulnerability scanners in the next few sections.

Table 22-8: Some Popular Computer Security Tools

Type	*Names of Tools*
Port scanners	nmap, Strobe
Vulnerability scanners	Nessus Security Scanner, SAINT, SARA, Whisker (CGI scanner), ISS Internet Scanner, CyberCop Scanner, Vetescan, Retina Network Security Scanner
Network utilities	Netcat, hping2, Firewalk, Cheops, ntop, ping, ngrep, AirSnort (802.11 WEP encryption cracking tool)
Host security tools	Tripwire, lsof
Packet sniffers	tcpdump, Ethereal, dsniff, sniffit
Intrusion detection system (IDS)	Snort, Abacus portsentry, scanlogd, NFR, LIDS
Password checking tools	John the Ripper, LC4
Log analysis and monitoring tools	logcolorise, tcpdstats, nlog, logcheck, LogWatch, Swatch

nmap

Network Mapper (nmap) is a port scanning tool. It can rapidly scan large networks and determine what hosts are available on the network, what services they are offering, what operating system (and the operating system version) they are running, what type of packet filters or firewalls are in use, and dozens of other characteristics. Linux comes with nmap. You can read more about nmap at www.insecure.org/nmap.

If you want to try out nmap to scan your local area network, just type a command similar to the following (replace the IP address range with addresses appropriate for your network):

```
nmap -O -sS 192.168.0.2-10
```

Here's part of a typical output listing from that nmap command:

```
Starting nmap 3.81 ( http://www.insecure.org/nmap/ ) at 2005-05-07 14:06 EDT
Interesting ports on 192.168.0.4:
(The 1660 ports scanned but not shown below are in state: closed)
PORT    STATE SERVICE
22/tcp  open  ssh
111/tcp open  rpcbind
631/tcp open  ipp
MAC Address: 00:10:5A:07:FD:BE (3com)
Device type: general purpose
Running: Linux 2.4.X|2.5.X|2.6.X
OS details: Linux 2.4.18 - 2.6.7
Uptime 1.316 days (since Fri May  6 06:32:05 2005)

... lines deleted ...

Interesting ports on 192.168.0.8:
(The 1661 ports scanned but not shown below are in state: closed)
PORT    STATE SERVICE
22/tcp  open  ssh
111/tcp open  rpcbind
MAC Address: 00:08:74:E5:C1:60 (Dell Computer)
Device type: general purpose
Running: Linux 2.4.X|2.5.X|2.6.X
OS details: Linux 2.4.18 - 2.6.7
Uptime 0.207 days (since Sat May  7 09:09:41 2005)

Nmap finished: 5 IP addresses (5 hosts up) scanned in 38.728 seconds
```

As you can see, nmap displays the names of the open ports and hazards a guess at the operating system name and version number.

Nessus

The Nessus Security Scanner is a modular security auditing tool that uses plugins written in Nessus scripting language to test for a wide variety of network vulnerabilities. Nessus uses a client/server software architecture with a server called nessusd and a client called nessus.

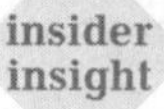

Before you try to install Nessus, you must install the sharutils RPM. That package includes the uudecode utility that the Nessaus installation script needs. For some reason, the sharutils package is no longer installed with any of the standard package groups.

To install sharutils, mount the companion DVD and install it with the following commands:

```
cd /media/cdrom/Fedora/RPMS
rpm -ivh sharutils*.rpm
```

To download and install Nessus, follow these steps:

1. Use a Web browser to go to `www.nessus.org/download/`. Then select the Nessus installer for all Unix systems and click Download. You will get a new Web page with a license agreement.
2. If you agree with the license agreement, click I accept. Otherwise, you can't download Nessus. If you accept the license agreement, you will be prompted for your email address.
3. Enter your email address and click Register. You will get a page with links to download the Nessus installer package and the MD5 checksum for the package. For version 2.2.4, the file is `nessus-installer-2.2.4.sh` and it's 6,237KB in size. The Nessus project sends you an activation code for downloading Nessus plugins (these are Nessus scripts that can test for specific vulnerabilities). You will be prompted for the activation code when you install Nessus.
4. Click the `nessus-installer-2.2.4.sh` link to download and save the file.
5. Type the following command to install Nessus (you must have the development tools, including the GIMP Toolkit, installed):

   ```
   sh nessus-installer-*.sh
   ```

   Respond to the prompts from the installer script to finish the installation. You can usually press Enter to accept the default choices. This should extract the Nessus files and build all the executables and libraries. I have had some warnings sometimes, but these steps successfully install Nessus. The final installation step, however, takes a long time to complete. Near the very end of the installation, when prompted, enter the activation code you received by email.

After the installation is complete, here are the steps to use Nessus:

1. Log in as `root` and type the following command to create the Nessus SSL certificate used for secure communication between the Nessus client and the Nessus server:

   ```
   nessus-mkcert
   ```

2. Provide the requested information to complete the certificate generation process.
3. Create a `nessusd` account with the following command:

   ```
   nessus-adduser
   ```

4. When prompted, enter your user name, password, and any rules (press Ctrl-D if you don't know what rules to enter).

5. If you want to, you can configure `nessusd` by editing the configuration file `/usr/local/etc/nessus/nessusd.conf`. If you want to try out Nessus, you can proceed with the default configuration file.
6. Start the Nessus server with this command:

   ```
   nessusd -D
   ```

   The server runs and loads all Nessus plugins, which takes a minute or two to complete.
7. Run the Nessus client by typing the following command in a terminal window:

   ```
   nessus
   ```

   The Nessus Setup window appears.
8. Type a nessusd user name and password, and then click Log In. Nessus displays the certificate used to establish the secure connection and asks if you accept it. Click Yes. After the client connects to the server, the Log in button changes to Log out, and a Connected label appears at its left.
9. Click the Target selection tab. Enter a range of IP addresses to scan all hosts in a network. For example, to scan the first eight hosts in a private network 192.168.0.0, I enter the address as:

   ```
   192.168.0.0/29
   ```

10. Click Start the Scan. Nessus starts scanning the IP addresses and checks for many different vulnerabilities. Progress bars show the status of the scan.

After Nessus completes the vulnerability scan of the hosts, it displays the result in a nice combination of graphical and text formats. The report is interactive — you can click on a host address to view the report on that host, and you can drill down on a specific vulnerability (including the CVE number that identifies the vulnerability).

SAINT

Security Administrator's Integrated Network Tool (SAINT) scans hosts for a variety of security vulnerabilities. For the vulnerabilities it finds, SAINT shows the Common Vulnerabilities and Exposures (CVE) identifier. You can download a crippled (limited to scanning two hosts only) 15-day trial version of SAINT from `www.saintcorporation.com/download.html` and see what it can do. You can decide whether to buy the full version or not.

I won't describe the steps for downloading and installing the trial version. You will find the instructions on the page from which you download the free trial version of SAINT.

SARA

Security Auditor's Research Assistant (SARA) is a vulnerability-scanning tool based on SAINT. SARA scans for known vulnerabilities, including those in the CVE list and the SANS Top 20 List (`www.sans.org/top20/`).

To try out SARA, download the latest version of SARA from `www-arc.com/sara/downloads/`. After downloading the compressed `tar` file, build and install the software using these steps:

1. Unpack the `tar` file with the command:

   ```
   tar zxvf sara*
   ```

2. To configure SARA, type the following commands:
   ```
   cd sara*
   ./configure
   ```
3. To build the software, type:
   ```
   make
   ```

After SARA is built, run it with the following command:

```
./sara
```

SARA starts a Web browser and displays its user interface in the Web browser. You can perform various tasks by clicking the links along the left-hand side of the Web browser. For example, to perform a vulnerability scan, click the Target Selection link. SARA brings up a form where you can provide information about hosts and networks to scan. You can also specify the scanning level — anywhere from light to extreme.

After filling in the information, click the Start the Scan button at the bottom of the form. SARA starts to perform the vulnerability scan. During the scan, SARA displays a data collection page that indicates progress of the scan.

After the scan is complete, you can proceed to data analysis and view the vulnerability information.

Keeping Up with Security News and Updates

To keep up with the latest security alerts, you may want to visit one or more of the following sites on a daily basis:

- CERT Coordination Center at `www.cert.org`
- Computer Incident Advisory Capability (CIAC) at `www.ciac.org/ciac/`
- United States Computer Emergency Readiness Team (US-CERT) at `www.us-cert.gov`

If you have access to Internet newsgroups, you can periodically browse the following:

- **comp.security.announce:** A moderated newsgroup that includes announcements from CERT about security.
- **comp.security.linux:** A newsgroup that includes discussions of Linux security issues
- **comp.security.unix:** A newsgroup that includes discussions of UNIX security issues, including items related to Linux

If you prefer to receive regular security updates through email, you can also sign up for, or subscribe to, various mailing lists:

- **redhat-watch-list:** Follow the directions in `www.redhat.com/mailman/listinfo/` to subscribe to this mailing list.
- **linux-security:** Follow the directions in `www.redhat.com/mailman/listinfo/` to subscribe to this mailing list.
- **FOCUS-LINUX:** Fill out the form in `www.securityfocus.com/subscribe` to subscribe to this mailing list focused on Linux security issues.

- **US-CERT National Cyber Alert System:** Follow the directions at `www.us-cert.gov` to subscribe to this mailing list. The Cyber Alert System features four categories of security information through its mailing lists:
  - Technical Cyber Security Alerts provide technical information about vulnerabilities in various common software products.
  - Cyber Security Alerts are sent when vulnerabilities affect the general public. They outline the steps and actions that non-technical home and corporate computer users can take to protect themselves from attacks.
  - Cyber Security Bulletins are bi-weekly summaries of security issues and new vulnerabilities along with patches, workarounds, and other actions that users can take to help reduce the risk.
  - Cyber Security Tips offer advice on common security issues for non-technical computer users.

Finally, you should check Fedora download mirror sites listed at `www.redhat.com/apps/support/errata/index.html` for updates that may fix any known security problems with Fedora Linux.

Summary

As the system administrator, your primary concern is the security of your Linux system and the local network. You may also have to worry about securing it from unwanted access from the Internet. This chapter introduces you to the subjects of system and network security and shows you how to use some of the security features of Linux.

In this chapter, you learned the following:

- It is helpful to think of an organization-wide security framework. In such a framework, you first establish a security policy based on business requirements and risk analysis. Then, you develop an overall security solution based on security policy, business requirements, and available technology. Finally, you put in place the management practices to continually monitor, detect, and respond to any security problems.
- Risk analysis means identifying threats and vulnerabilities. Then, you can assess the probability and impact of each vulnerability and decide to mitigate those vulnerabilities that are most likely to be exploited and whose exploitation will cause the most harm.
- To secure the Linux system, you have to secure the passwords and the network services, such as FTP, NFS, and HTTP. You can use the `chkconfig` command to disable unnecessary services. For services started by xinetd you can also edit the configuration files in `/etc/xinetd.d` directory to turn services off or on.
- Use secure shell (SSH) for secure remote logins. This chapter shows you how to use SSH.
- For a system connected to the Internet (including a local network), you can meet network security needs by setting up a firewall between the internal network and the Internet. Any publicly accessible servers, such as Web and FTP servers, should be placed outside the firewall in a perimeter network or the demilitarized zone (DMZ).

- There are many kinds of firewalls — packet filters, stateful inspection, and application gateways (or proxy servers). This chapter provides an overview of firewalls. You can implement a packet-filtering firewall by using the iptables software that comes with Linux.
- You should periodically review the log files in the `/var/log` directory of your Linux system for any signs of intrusion attempts.
- You should also perform a periodic security audit of your system and network. You can use some automated tools such as nmap and Nessus to test your network security.
- The chapter provides some online resources from which you can learn more about securing your Linux system. You can use these online resources to keep up with late-breaking security news.

Part V

Programming Linux

Software Development in Linux

Secrets in This Chapter

Many Linux users happen to be software developers. If you want to develop software as a hobby or want to add features to Linux, you'll find that Linux includes everything you need to create UNIX and X applications. You can use the GNU C and C++ compilers to write conventional programs (that you compile and link into an executable). As an alternative, you can use the Tcl/Tk scripting language to write interpreted graphical applications.

This chapter discusses software development on a Linux PC. The focus is not on any specific programming language. Instead, this chapter describes how to use various software-development tools, such as compilers, makefiles, and version-control systems.

The chapter also describes the implications of Free Software Foundation's GNU Public License on any plans you might have to develop Linux software. You need to know this because you usually use GNU tools and GNU libraries to develop software in Linux.

Also, I discuss dynamic linking and the Executable and Linking Format (ELF), which makes dynamic linking easier. These topics are of interest to Linux programmers because dynamic linking reduces the size of executables and may enable programmers to distribute software in binary form, even if software uses the GNU libraries.

Software Development Tools in Linux

As expected, as a UNIX look-alike, Linux includes these traditional UNIX software-development tools:

- A text editor, such as vi or Emacs, for editing the source code (described in Chapter 11).
- A C compiler for compiling and linking programs written in C — the programming language of choice for writing UNIX applications (although nowadays, many programmers are turning to C++). Linux includes the GNU C and C++ compilers. Originally, the GNU C Compiler was known as GCC. The acronym GCC now stands for GNU Compiler Collection (see the description in `http://gcc.gnu.org/`).
- The GNU `make` utility for automating the software build process — the process of combining object modules into an executable or a library.
- A debugger for debugging programs. Linux includes the GNU debugger `gdb`.
- A version-control system to keep track of various revisions of a source file. Linux comes with RCS (Revision Control System) and CVS (Concurrent Versions System). Nowadays, most open-source projects use CVS as the version-control system.

These tools are installed automatically if you select the *Development Tools* package group when you install Linux from this book's companion DVD, following the steps outlined in Chapter 2. The next few sections briefly describe how to use these tools to write applications for Linux.

Using info for Help on GNU Tools

You may have noticed that most of the Linux software-development tools are from the Free Software Foundation's GNU project. The online documentation for all these tools comes as `info` files. The info program is GNU's hypertext help system.

To see info in action, type **info** at the shell prompt, or type **Esc-x** followed by **info** in GNU Emacs. Typically, I access `info` from GNU Emacs; doing so enables me to use online help while editing a program. However, you can always type **info** in a separate terminal window. Figure 23-1 shows the terminal window after I type `info` at the shell prompt.

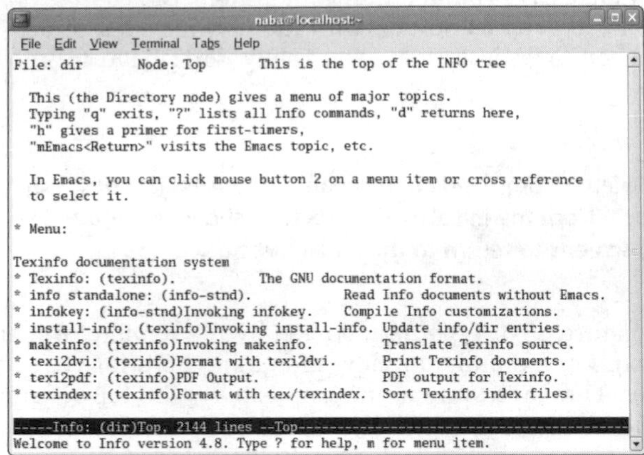

Figure 23-1: The Terminal Window after Typing info at the Shell Prompt.

In `info`, the online help text is organized in nodes; each node represents information on a specific topic. The first line shows the header for that node.

Figure 23-1 shows the initial `info` screen, with a directory of topics. This directory is an info file: `/usr/share/info/dir`, a text file that contains embedded special characters. The following are a few lines from the `/usr/share/info/dir` file that correspond to the screen shown in Figure 23-1:

```
$Id: dir,v 1.2 1996/09/24 18:43:01 karl Exp $
This is the file .../info/dir, which contains the topmost node of the
Info hierarchy.  The first time you invoke Info you start off
looking at that node, which is (dir)Top.
^_   (This is the Ctrl+_ character)
File: dir       Node: Top       This is the top of the INFO tree

  This (the Directory node) gives a menu of major topics.
  Typing "q" exits, "?" lists all Info commands, "d" returns here,
  "h" gives a primer for first-timers,
  "mEmacs<Return>" visits the Emacs topic, etc.

  In Emacs, you can click mouse button 2 on a menu item or cross reference
  to select it.

  * Menu:

Texinfo documentation system
* Standalone info program: (info-stnd).    Standalone Info-reading program.
* Texinfo: (texinfo).           The GNU documentation format.
```

```
* install-info: (texinfo)Invoking install-info. Update info/dir entries.
* makeinfo: (texinfo)makeinfo Preferred.        Translate Texinfo source.
(...Lines deleted...)
```

A comparison of this listing with the screen shown in Figure 23-1 shows that `info` displays only the lines that follow the Ctrl+_ character. In your system, the `/usr/share/info` directory contains this `info` file, as well as others, with the text for each topic. Usually, these `info` files are stored in compressed format. You really don't have to know these details to use the `info` files.

insider insight

You have to use several single-letter commands to navigate `info` files. The best way to learn the commands is to type `h` from the initial `info` directory, shown in Figure 23-1. Type `d` after reading the help screens to return to the initial directory of topics.

From the directory screen of Figure 23-1, type **m**, followed by the name of a menu item (shown with an asterisk prefix). For example, to view the online help for GCC, type **m**; then type **gcc**, and press Enter. The `info` system, in turn, displays the top-level menu of items for GCC, as shown in Figure 23-2.

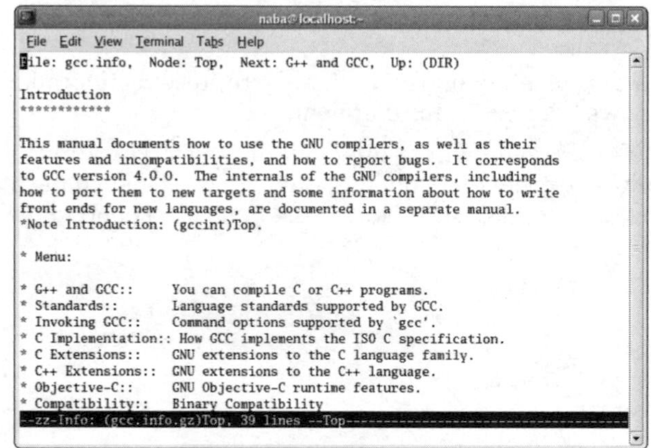

Figure 23-2: The info Window, Showing the Top-Level Help on GCC.

You can explore further by typing **m**, followed by one of the menu items shown in Figure 23-2.

While you're at it, you may want to type **m**, and then **copy**; then press Enter in the screen shown in Figure 23-2. That action displays the GNU General Public License (GPL), shown in Figure 23-3.

GPL covers Linux and the gcc compiler. GPL requires distribution of the source code (that's why all Linux distributions come with source code). In the "Implications of GNU Licenses" section, you learn that you can still use GNU tools to develop commercial applications and to distribute applications in binary form (without source code), as long as they link with selected GNU libraries only.

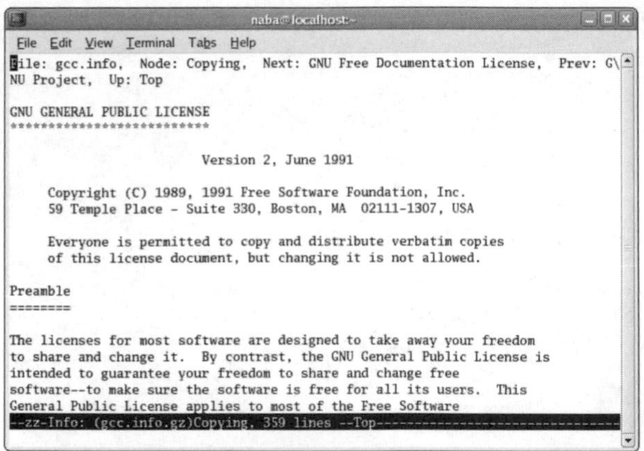

Figure 23-3: The info Window, Showing the First Page of the GNU General Public License (GPL).

At any time in `info`, you can type **d** to return to the `info` topic directory shown in Figure 23-1. From that screen, you can view help on other GNU tools, such as make and the GNU debugger.

To quit info, type **q**. If you access `info` from the Emacs editor, press Ctrl-X, followed by Ctrl-C, to quit the Emacs editor.

Running the GNU C and C++ Compilers

The most important software-development tool in Linux is GCC, which is the GNU C and C++ compiler. In fact, GCC can compile three languages: C, C++, and Objective-C (a language that adds object-oriented extensions to C). You use the same `gcc` command to compile and link both C and C++ source files. The GCC compiler supports ANSI standard C, making it easy to port any ANSI C program to Linux. In addition, if you've ever used a C compiler on other UNIX systems, you are right at home with GCC.

Running GCC

Use the `gcc` command to run GCC. By default, when you use the `gcc` command on a source file, GCC preprocesses, compiles, and links the executable. However, you can use GCC options to stop this process at an intermediate stage. For example, you might invoke `gcc` by using the `-c` option to compile a source file and to generate an object file, but not to perform the link step.

Using GCC to compile and link a few C source files is very simple. Suppose you want to compile and link a simple program made up of two source files. The following listing shows the file `area.c` (the main program that computes the area of a circle whose radius is specified through the command line):

```
#include <stdio.h>
#include <stdlib.h>

/* Function prototype */
double area_of_circle(double r);
```

```
int main(int argc, char **argv)
{
  if(argc < 2)
  {
    printf("Usage: %s radius\n", argv[0]);
    exit(1);
  }
  else
  {
    double radius = atof(argv[1]);
    double area = area_of_circle(radius);
    printf("Area of circle with radius %f = %f\n",
        radius, area);
  }
  return 0;
}
```

The following listing shows the file `circle.c`, which provides a function that computes the area of a circle.

```
#include <math.h>

#define SQUARE(x) ((x)*(x))

double area_of_circle(double r)
{
  return 4.0 * M_PI * SQUARE(r);
}
```

For such a simple program, of course, I can place everything in a single file, but this contrived example lets me show you how to handle multiple files.

To compile these two programs and to create an executable file named `area`, you might use this command:

```
gcc -o area area.c circle.c
```

This invocation of GCC uses the `-o` option to specify the name of the executable file. (If you do not specify the name of an output file, GCC creates a file named `a.out`.)

If there are too many source files to compile and link, compile the files individually, and generate object files (that have the `.o` extension). That way, when you change a source file, you need to compile only that file and to link all the object files. The following example shows how to separate the compile and link steps for the example program:

```
gcc -c area.c
gcc -c circle.c
gcc -o area area.o circle.o
```

The first two invocations of `gcc` with the `-c` option compile the source files. The third invocation links the object files into an executable named `area`.

In case you are curious, here's how you run the sample program (to compute the area of a circle with a radius of 1):

```
./area 1
Area of circle with radius 1.000000 = 12.566371
```

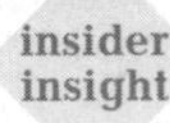

Incidentally, you have to add the ./ prefix to the program's name (area) only if the current directory is not in the PATH environment variable. There is no harm in adding the prefix, even if your PATH contains the current directory.

Compiling C++ Programs

GNU CC is a combined C and C++ compiler, so the gcc command also can compile C++ source files. GCC uses the file extension to determine whether a file is C or C++. C files have a lowercase .c extension, whereas C++ files end with .C or .cpp.

Although the gcc command can compile a C++ file, that command does not automatically link with various class libraries that C++ programs typically require. That's why it's easier to compile and link a C++ program by using the g++ command, which invokes gcc with appropriate options.

Suppose you want to compile the following simple C++ program stored in a file named hello.C (it's customary to use an uppercase C extension for C++ source files):

```
#include <iostream>

int main()
{
  using namespace std;
  cout << "Hello from Linux!" << endl;
}
```

To compile and link this program into an executable program named hello, use this command:

```
g++ -o hello hello.C
```

This command creates the hello executable, which you can run as follows:

```
./hello
Hello from Linux!
```

As you see in the following section, a host of GCC options controls various aspects of compiling C++ programs.

Exploring GCC Options

Following is the basic syntax of the gcc command:

```
gcc options filenames
```

Each option starts with a hyphen (-) and usually has a long name, such as -funsigned-char or -finline-functions. Many commonly used options are short, however, such as -c, to compile only, and -g, to generate debugging information, (needed to debug the program by using the GNU debugger).

You can view a summary of all GCC options by using info. Type **info** at the shell prompt, and type m, followed by gcc. Then follow the menu items: Invoking GCC⇨Option Summary. Usually, you do not have to specify GCC options explicitly; the default settings are fine for most applications. Table 23-1 lists some of the GCC options you might use.

Table 23-1: Commonly Used GCC Options

Option	*Meaning*
-ansi	Support ANSI standard C syntax only. (This option disables some GNU C–specific features, such as the __asm__ and __typeof__ keywords.) When used with g++, support ISO standard C++ only.
-c	Compile and generate object file only.
-DMACRO	Define the macro with the string "1" as its value.
-DMACRO=*DEFN*	Define the macro as *DEFN* where *DEFN* is some text.
-E	Run only the C preprocessor.
-fallow-single-precision	Perform all math operations in single precision.
-fpack-struct	Pack all structure members without any padding.
-fpcc-struct-return	Return all struct and union values in memory, rather than in registers. (Returning values this way is less efficient, but is compatible with other compilers.)
-fPIC	Generate position-independent code (PIC) suitable for use in a shared library.
-freg-struct-return	When possible, return struct and union values in registers.
-g	Generate debugging information. (The GNU debugger can use this information.)
-IDIRECTORY	Search the specified directory for files you include by using the #include preprocessor directive.
-LDIRECTORY	Search the specified directory for libraries.
-lLIBRARY	Search the specified library when linking.
-mtune=*cputype*	Optimize code for a specific processor (*cputype* can take many different values—some common ones are i386, i486, i586, i686, pentium, pentiumpro, pentium2, pentium3, pentium4).
-o FILE	Generate the specified output file (used to designate the name of an executable file).

Option	Meaning
`-O0`	Do not optimize.
`-O` or `-O1`	Optimize the generated code.
`-O2`	Optimize even more.
`-O3`	Perform optimizations beyond those done for `-O2`.
`-pedantic`	Generate errors if any non-ANSI standard extensions are used.
`-pg`	Add extra code to the program so that, when run, it generates information the gprof program can use to display timing details for various parts of the program.
`-shared`	Generate a shared object file (typically used to create a shared library).
`-U`*`MACRO`*	Undefine the specified macro (*`MACRO`*).
`-v`	Display the version number of GCC.
`-w`	Don't generate any warning messages.
`-Wl,`*`OPTION`*	Pass the *`OPTION`* string (containing multiple comma-separated options) to the linker. To create a shared library named libXXX.so.1, for example, use the following flag: -Wl,-soname,libXXX.so.1.

Using the GNU make Utility

When an application is made up of more than a few source files, compiling and linking the files by manually typing the `gcc` command is inconvenient. Also, you do not want to compile every file whenever you change something in a single source file. The GNU `make` utility is helpful in this situation because `make` can compile only those files that really must be compiled.

The `make` utility works by reading and interpreting a *makefile*: a text file you have to prepare according to a specified syntax. The makefile describes which files constitute a program and explains how to compile and link the files to build the program. Whenever you change one or more files, `make` determines which files should be recompiled and issues the appropriate commands for compiling those files and rebuilding the program.

The `make` utility is, in fact, specified in Section 6.2 of the POSIX.2 standard (IEEE Standard 1003.2-1992) for shells and tools. GNU make conforms to the POSIX.2 standard.

Learning makefile Names

By default, GNU `make` looks for a makefile that has one of the following names, in the order shown:

- `GNUmakefile`
- `makefile`
- `Makefile`

In UNIX systems, using Makefile as the name of the makefile is customary because it appears near the beginning of directory listings where the uppercase names appear before the lowercase names.

When you download software from the Internet, you usually find a Makefile, together with the source files. To build the software, you have only to type **make** at the shell prompt; make takes care of all the steps necessary to build the software.

If your makefile does not have a standard name, such as Makefile, you have to use the -f option to specify the makefile's name. If your makefile is called webprog.mak, for example, you have to run make using the following command line:

```
make -f webprog.mak
```

GNU make also accepts several other command-line options, which are summarized in the "Running make" section of this chapter.

Understanding the makefile

For a program that consists of several source and header files, the makefile specifies the following:

- The items make will create — usually the object files and the executable. The term "target" is used for an item to be created.
- The files or other actions required to create the target.
- Which commands should be executed to create each target.

Suppose you have a C++ source file named form.C that contains the following preprocessor directive:

```
#include "form.h"  // Include header file
```

The object file form.o clearly depends on the source file form.C and the header file form.h. In addition to these dependencies, you must specify how make should convert the form.C file to the object file form.o. Suppose you want make to run g++ (because the source file is in C++) with these options:

- -c (compile only)
- -g (generate debugging information)
- -O2 (optimize some)

In the makefile, you can express this with the following rule:

```
# This a comment in the makefile
# The following lines indicate how form.o depends
# on form.C and form.h and how to create form.o.

form.o: form.C form.h
        g++ -c -g -O2 form.C
```

In this example, the first noncomment line shows form.o as the target and form.C and form.h as the dependent files.

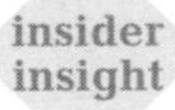

The line following the dependency indicates how to build the target from its dependents. This line must start with a Tab; otherwise make will not work. Make would exit with an error message and you'd be left scratching your head because when you look at the makefile in a text editor you can't tell the difference between a tab and a space. Now that you know the secret, the fix is to replace the spaces at the beginning of the offending line with a single tab.

The benefit of using make is that it prevents unnecessary compilations. After all, you can invoke g++ (or gcc) in a shell script to compile and link all the files that make up your application, but the shell script compiles everything, even if the compilations are unnecessary. GNU make, on the other hand, builds a target, only if one or more of its dependents have changed since the last time the target was built. make verifies this change by examining the time of the last modification of the target and the dependents.

make treats the target as the name of a goal to be achieved; the target does not have to be a file. You can have a rule such as this:

```
clean:
        rm -f *.o
```

This rule specifies an abstract target named clean that does not depend on anything. This dependency statement says that to make clean, GNU make should invoke the command rm -f *.o, which deletes all files that have the .o extension (these are the object files). Thus, the net effect of creating the target named clean is to delete the object files.

Using Variables (or Macros)

In addition to the basic service of building targets from dependents, GNU make includes many nice features that make it easy for you to express the dependencies and rules for building a target from its dependents. If you need to compile a large number of C++ files by using GCC with the same options, for example, typing the options for each file is tedious. You can avoid this task by defining a variable or macro in make as follows:

```
# Define macros for name of compiler
CXX= g++

# Define a macro for the GCC flags
CXXFLAGS= -O2 -g -mcpu=i686

# A rule for building an object file
form.o: form.C form.h
        $(CXX) -c $(CXXFLAGS) form.C
```

In this example, CXX and CXXFLAGS are make variables. GNU make prefers to call them variables, but most UNIX make utilities call them macros.

To use a variable anywhere in the makefile, start with a dollar sign ($) followed by the variable within parentheses. GNU make replaces all occurrences of a variable with its definition; thus, it replaces all occurrences of $(CXXFLAGS) with the string -O2 -g -mcpu=i686.

GNU make has several predefined variables that have special meanings. Table 23-2 lists these variables. In addition to the variables listed in Table 23-2, GNU make considers all environment variables predefined.

Table 23-2: Some Predefined Variables in GNU make

Variable	*Meaning*
$%	Member name for targets that are archives. If the target is libDisp.a (image.o), for example, $% is image.o, and $@ is libDisp.a.
$*	Name of the target file without the extension.
$+	Names of all dependent files with duplicate dependencies, listed in their order of occurrence.
$<	The name of the first dependent file.
$?	Names of all dependent files (with spaces between the names) that are newer than the target.
$@	Complete name of the target.
$^	Names of all dependent files, with spaces between the names. Duplicates are removed from the dependent filenames.
AR	Name of the archive-maintaining program. (Default value: ar)
ARFLAGS	Flags for the archive-maintaining program. (Default value: rv)
AS	Name of the assembler program that converts the assembly language to object code. (Default value: as)
ASFLAGS	Flags for the assembler.
CC	Name of the C compiler. (Default value: cc)
CFLAGS	Flags to be passed to the C compiler.
CO	Name of the program that extracts a file from RCS. (Default value: co)
COFLAGS	Flags for the RCS co program.
CPP	Name of the C preprocessor. (Default value: $(CC) -E)
CPPFLAGS	Flags for the C preprocessor.
CXX	Name of the C++ compiler. (Default value: g++)
CXXFLAGS	Flags to be passed to the C++ compiler.
FC	Name of the FORTRAN compiler. (Default value: f77)
FFLAGS	Flags for the FORTRAN compiler.
GET	Name of the program to extract a file from SCCS. (Default value: get)
GFLAGS	Flags for the SCCS get program.
LDFLAGS	Flags for the compiler when it is supposed to invoke the linker ld.
LEX	Name of the program to convert Lex grammar to C program. (Default value: lex)
LFLAGS	Flags for Lex.

Variable	Meaning
MAKEINFO	Name of the program that converts Texinfo source files to info files. (Default value: makeinfo)
RM	Name of the command to delete a file. (Default value: rm -f)
TEX	Name of the program to generate TeX DVI files from TeX source files. (Default value: tex)
TEXI2DVI	Name of the program to generate TeX DVI files from the Texinfo source. (Default value: texi2dvi)
YACC	Name of the program to convert YACC grammars to C programs. (Default value: yacc -r)
YFLAGS	Flags for yacc.

Taking Stock of Implicit Rules

GNU make also includes built-in, or implicit, rules that define how to create specific types of targets from various dependencies. An example of an implicit rule is the command that make should execute to generate an object file from a C source file.

GNU make supports two types of implicit rules:

- **Suffix rules:** Suffix rules define implicit rules for make. A suffix rule defines how to convert a file that has one extension to a file that has another extension. Each suffix rule is defined with the target showing a pair of suffixes (file extensions). The suffix rule for converting a .c (C source) file to a .o (object) file, for example, might be written as follows:

```
.c.o:
$(CC) $(CFLAGS) $(CPPFLAGS) -c -o $@ $<
```

  This rule uses the predefined variables CC, CFLAGS and CPPFLAGS. For filenames, the rule uses the variables $@ (the complete name of the target) and $< (the name of the first dependent file).

- **Pattern rules:** These rules are more versatile because you can specify more complex dependency rules by using pattern rules. A pattern rule looks just like a regular rule, except that a single percent sign (%) appears in the target's name. The dependencies also use % to indicate how the dependency names relate to the target's name. The following pattern rule specifies how to convert any file X.c to a file X.o:

```
%.o: %.c
$(CC) $(CFLAGS) $(CPPFLAGS) -c -o $@ $<
```

GNU make has a large set of implicit rules, defined as both suffix and pattern rules. To see a list of all known variables and rules, run make by using the following command:

```
make -p -f/dev/null
```

The output includes the names of variables, as well as implicit rules.

Writing a Sample makefile

You can write a makefile easily if you use GNU make's predefined variables and its built-in rules. Consider, for example, a makefile that creates the executable xdraw from three C source files (xdraw.c, xviewobj.c, and shapes.c) and two header files (xdraw.h and shapes.h). Assume that each source file includes one of the header files. Given these facts, here is what a sample makefile might look like:

```
#####################################################################
# Sample makefile
# Comments start with '#'
#
#####################################################################

# Use standard variables to define compile and link flags

CFLAGS= -g -O2
# Define the target "all"
all: xdraw

OBJS=xdraw.o xviewobj.o shapes.o

xdraw: $(OBJS)

# Object files
xdraw.o: Makefile xdraw.c xdraw.h

xviewobj.o: Makefile xviewobj.c xdraw.h

shapes.o: Makefile shapes.c shapes.h
```

This makefile relies on GNU make's implicit rules. The conversion of .c files to .o files uses the built-in rule. Defining the variable CFLAGS passes the flags to the C compiler.

The target named all is defined as the first target in a makefile for a reason — if you run GNU make without specifying any targets in the command line (see the make syntax described in the following section), it builds the first target it finds in the makefile. By defining the first target all as xdraw, you can ensure that make builds this executable file, even if you do not explicitly specify it as a target. UNIX programmers traditionally use all as the name of the first target, but the target's name is immaterial; what matters is that it is the first target in the makefile.

If you have a directory that contains the appropriate source files and header files, you can try the makefile. Here are the commands that get executed when I type make to try the sample makefile:

```
cc -g -O2  -c xdraw.c -o xdraw.o
cc -g -O2  -c xviewobj.c -o xviewobj.o
cc -g -O2  -c shapes.c -o shapes.o
cc  xdraw.o xviewobj.o shapes.o  -o xdraw
```

As the output of make shows, make uses the cc command (which happens to be a symbolic link to GCC in your Linux system) with appropriate options to compile the source files and, finally, to link the objects to create the xdraw executable.

Running make

Typically, you run make with a single command in the command line; that is, you run make by typing make. When run this way, GNU make looks for a file named GNUmakefile, makefile, or Makefile—in that order. If make finds one of these makefiles, it builds the first target specified in that makefile. However, if make does not find an appropriate makefile, it displays the following error message and exits:

```
make: *** No targets.  Stop.
```

If your makefile happens to have a different name from the default names, you have to use the -f option to specify the makefile. The syntax of this make option is the following:

```
make -f filename
```

where filename is the name of the makefile.

Even when you have a makefile with a default name such as Makefile, you may want to build a specific target out of several targets defined in the makefile. In that case, you have to run make by using this syntax:

```
make target
```

If the makefile contains the target named clean, you can build that target with this command:

```
make clean
```

Another special syntax overrides the value of a make variable. For example, GNU make uses the CFLAGS variable to hold the flags used when compiling C files. You can override the value of this variable when you invoke make. Here is an example of how you can define CFLAGS to be the option -g -O2:

```
make CFLAGS="-g -O2"
```

In addition to these options, GNU make accepts several other command-line options. Table 23-3 lists the GNU make options.

Table 23-3: Options for GNU make

Option	*Meaning*
-b	Ignore but accept for compatibility with other versions of make.
-C *DIR*	Change to the specified directory before reading the makefile.
-d	Print debugging information.
-e	Allow environment variables to override definitions of similarly named variables in the makefile.
-f *FILE*	Read *FILE* as the makefile.

(continued)

Table 23-3 *(continued)*

Option	Meaning
-h	Display the list of make options.
-i	Ignore all errors in commands executed when building a target.
-I DIR	Search specified directory for included makefiles (the capability to include a file in a makefile is unique to GNU make).
-j NUM	Specify the number of commands that make can run simultaneously.
-k	Continue to build unrelated targets, even if an error occurs when building one of the targets.
-l *LOAD*	Don't start a new job if load average is at least *LOAD* (a floating-point number).
-m	Ignore but accept for compatibility with other versions of make.
-n	Print the commands to be executed, but do not execute them.
-o *FILE*	Do not rebuild the file named *FILE*, even if it is older than its dependents.
-p	Display the make database of variables and implicit rules.
-q	Do not run anything, but return zero if all targets are up-to-date; return 1 if anything needs updating and 2 if an error occurs.
-r	Get rid of all built-in rules.
-R	Get rid of all built-in variables and rules.
-s	Work silently (without displaying the commands as they are executed).
-t	Change the timestamp of the files.
-v	Display the version number of make and a copyright notice.
-w	Display the name of the working directory before and after processing the makefile.
-W FILE	Assume that the specified file has been modified (used with -n to see what happens if you modify that file).

The GNU Debugger

Although make automates the process of building a program, that task is the least of your worries when a program does not work correctly or when a program suddenly quits with an error message. You need a debugger to find the cause of program errors. This book's companion DVD includes gdb — the versatile GNU debugger with a command-line interface.

Like any debugger, gdb lets you perform typical debugging tasks, such as the following:

- Set the breakpoint so that program execution stops at a specified line.
- Watch the values of variables in the program.
- Step through the program one line at a time.
- Change variables in an attempt to fix errors.

The gdb debugger can debug C and C++ programs.

Preparing a Program for Debugging

If you want to debug a program by using gdb, you have to ensure that the compiler generates and places debugging information in the executable. The debugging information contains the names of variables in your program and the mapping of addresses in the executable file to lines of code in the source file. gdb needs this information to perform its functions, such as stopping after executing a specified line of source code.

insider insight

To ensure that the executable is properly prepared for debugging, use the -g option with GCC. You can do this by defining the variable CFLAGS in the makefile as:

```
CFLAGS= -g
```

Running gdb

The most common way to debug a program is to run gdb by using the following command:

```
gdb progname
```

In the preceding code, progname is the name of the program's executable file. After it runs, gdb displays the following message and prompts you for a command:

```
GNU gdb Red Hat Linux (6.3.0.0-1.12rh)
Copyright 2004 Free Software Foundation, Inc.
GDB is free software, covered by the GNU General Public License, and you are
welcome to change it and/or distribute copies of it under certain conditions.
Type "show copying" to see the conditions.
There is absolutely no warranty for GDB.  Type "show warranty" for details.
This GDB was configured as "i386-redhat-linux-gnu".
(gdb) help
List of classes of commands:

aliases -- Aliases of other commands
breakpoints -- Making program stop at certain points
data -- Examining data
files -- Specifying and examining files
internals -- Maintenance commands
obscure -- Obscure features
running -- Running the program
stack -- Examining the stack
status -- Status inquiries
support -- Support facilities
tracepoints -- Tracing of program execution without stopping the program
user-defined -- User-defined commands

Type "help" followed by a class name for a list of commands in that class.
Type "help" followed by command name for full documentation.
Command name abbreviations are allowed if unambiguous.
(gdb) q
```

When you type **help**, gdb displays the classes of gdb commands. You can get further help on a specific class of commands or a specific command by following the instructions. To see the list of commands you use to run the program you are debugging, type **help running** at the gdb prompt.

To quit gdb, type **q**, and press Enter.

gdb has a large number of commands, but you need only a few to find the cause of an error quickly. Table 23-4 lists the commonly used gdb commands.

Table 23-4: Commonly Used gdb Commands

Command	*Description*
`break` *NUM*	Set a breakpoint at the specified line number (the debugger stops at breakpoints).
`bt`	Display a trace of all stack frames. (This command shows you the sequence of function calls so far.)
`clear` *FILENAME*`:`*NUM*	Delete the breakpoint at a specific line in a source file. For example, `clear xdraw.c:8` clears the breakpoint at line 8 of file `xdraw.c`.
`Continue`	Continue running the program being debugged. (Use this command after the program has stopped because of a signal or breakpoint.)
`display` *EXPR*	Display value of expression (consisting of variables defined in the program) each time the program stops.
`file` *FILE*	Load specified executable file for debugging.
`help` *NAME*	Display help on the command named *NAME*.
`info break`	Display a list of current breakpoints, including information on how many times each breakpoint has been reached.
`info files`	Display detailed information about the file being debugged.
`info func`	Display all function names.
`info local`	Display information about local variables of the current function.
`info prog`	Display the execution status of the program being debugged.
`info var`	Display all global and static variable names.
`Kill`	End the program you are debugging.
`List`	List a section of the source code.
`Make`	Run the `make` utility to rebuild the executable without leaving gdb.
`Next`	Advance one line of source code in the current function without stepping into other functions.
`print` *EXPR*	Show the value of the expression *EXPR*.
`Quit`	Quit gdb.
`Run`	Start running the currently loaded executable.
`set variable` *VAR*`=`*VALUE*	Set the value of the variable *VAR* to *VALUE*.
`shell` *CMD*	Execute a Linux command *CMD*, without leaving gdb.

Command	Description
Step	Advance one line in the current function, stepping into other functions, if any.
watch *VAR*	Show the value of the variable named *VAR* whenever the value changes.
Where	Display the call sequence. Use this command to locate where your program died.
x/F *ADDR*	Examine the contents of the memory location at address *ADDR* in the format specified by the letter F, which can be o (octal); x (hex); d (decimal); u (unsigned decimal); t (binary); f (float); a (address); i (instruction); c (char); or s (string). You can append a letter indicating the size of data type to the format letter. Size letters are b (byte); h (halfword, 2 bytes); w (word, 4 bytes); and g (giant, 8 bytes). Typically, *ADDR* is the name of a variable or pointer.

Finding Bugs by Using gdb

To understand how you can find bugs by using gdb, you need to see an example. The procedure is easiest to show with a simple example, so I start with a rather contrived program that contains a typical bug.

This is the contrived program, which I store in the file dbgtst.c:

```
#include <stdio.h>

static char buf[256];
void read_input(char *s);

int main(void)
{
  char *input = NULL; /* Just a pointer, no storage for string */

  read_input(input);

/* Process command. */
  printf("You typed: %s\n", input);

/* ... */
  return 0;
}

void read_input(char *s)
{
  printf("Command: ");
  gets(s);
}
```

This program's main function calls the read_input function to get a line of input from the user. The read_input function expects a character array in which it returns what the user types. In this example, however, main calls read_input with an uninitialized pointer—that's the bug in this simple program.

Build the program by using gcc with the -g option:

```
gcc -g -o dbgtst dbgtst.c
```

Ignore the warning message about the gets() function being dangerous; we are trying to use the shortcoming of the gets() function to show how gdb can be used to track down errors.

To see the problem with this program, run it:

```
./dbgtst
Command: test
Segmentation fault
```

The program dies after displaying the Segmentation fault message. For this small program, you can find the cause by examining the source code. In a real-world application, however, you may not immediately know what causes the error. That's when you use gdb to find the cause of the problem.

To use gdb to locate a bug, follow these steps:

1. **Load the program under gdb.** To load a program named dbgtst in gdb, type the following:

   ```
   gdb dbgtst
   ```

2. **At the (gdb) prompt, type run.** When the program prompts for input, type some input text. The program should fail as it has previously. Here's what happens with the dbgtst program:

   ```
   (gdb) run
   Starting program: /home/naba/apps/dbgtst
   Reading symbols from shared object read from target memory...done.
   Loaded system supplied DSO at 0x753000
   Command: test

   Program received signal SIGSEGV, Segmentation fault.
   0x00915160 in gets () from /lib/libc.so.6
   (gdb)
   ```

3. **Type the where command to determine where the program died.** For the dbgtst program, this command yields this output:

   ```
   (gdb) where
   #0  0x00915160 in gets () from /lib/libc.so.6
   #1  0x0804841c in read_input (s=0x0) at dbgtst.c:22
   #2  0x080483de in main () at dbgtst.c:10
   (gdb)
   ```

   The output shows the sequence of function calls. Function call #0 — the most recent one — is to a C library function, gets. The gets call originates in the read_input function, which in turn is called from the main function.

4. **Type the list command with the name of a file and line number to inspect the lines of suspect source code.** In dbgtst, you might start with line 22 of the dbgtst.c file, as follows:

```
(gdb) list dbgtst.c:22
17      }
18
19      void read_input(char *s)
20      {
21        printf("Command: ");
22        gets(s);
23      }
24
(gdb)
```

After looking at this listing, if you have some experience writing C programs, you should be able to tell that the problem might be the way `read_input` is called. Then you list the lines around line 10 in dbgtst.c (where the `read_input` call originates):

```
(gdb) list dbgtst.c:10
5
6       int main(void)
7       {
8         char *input = NULL; /* Just a pointer, no storage for string
*/
9
10        read_input(input);
11
12      /* Process command. */
13        printf("You typed: %s\n", input);
14
(gdb)
```

At this point, you should be able to narrow the problem to the variable named `input`. That variable should be an array, not a NULL pointer.

Fixing Bugs in gdb

Sometimes you can try a bug fix directly in `gdb`. For the example program in the preceding section, you can try this fix immediately after the program dies after displaying an error message. Because the example is contrived, I have an extra buffer named `buf` defined in the dbgtst program, as follows:

```
static char buf[256];
```

I can fix the problem of the uninitialized pointer by setting the variable `input` to `buf`. The following session with `gdb` corrects the problem of the uninitialized pointer (this example picks up immediately after the program has run and died because of the segmentation fault):

```
 (gdb) file dbgtst
A program is being debugged already.  Kill it? (y or n) y

Load new symbol table from "/home/naba/apps/dbgtst"? (y or n) y
Reading symbols from /home/naba/apps/dbgtst...done.
(gdb) list
```

```
1       #include <stdio.h>
2
3       static char buf[256];
4       void read_input(char *s);
5
6       int main(void)
7       {
8         char *input = NULL; /* Just a pointer, no storage for string */
9
10        read_input(input);
(gdb) break 9
Breakpoint 1 at 0x80483d3: file dbgtst.c, line 9.
(gdb) run
Starting program: /home/naba/apps/dbgtst
Reading symbols from shared object read from target memory...done.
Loaded system supplied DSO at 0x7e7000

Breakpoint 1, main () at dbgtst.c:10
10        read_input(input);
(gdb) set var input=buf
(gdb) cont
Continuing.
Command: test
You typed: test

Program exited normally.
(gdb) q
```

As the previous listing shows, if I stop the program just before `read_input` is called and set the variable named `input` to `buf` (which is a valid array of characters), the rest of the program runs fine.

After trying in `gdb` a fix that works, you can make the necessary changes to the source files and can make the fix permanent.

Implications of GNU Licenses

You have to pay a price for the bounty of Linux—to protect its developers and users, Linux is distributed under the GNU GPL (General Public License), which stipulates the distribution of the source code.

This does not mean, however, that you cannot write commercial software for a Linux application that you want to distribute (either for free or for a price) in binary form only. You can follow all the rules and still sell your Linux applications in binary form.

When writing applications for Linux, be aware of two licenses:

- The GNU General Public License (GPL), which governs many Linux programs, including the Linux kernel and GCC
- The GNU Library General Public License (LGPL), which covers many Linux libraries

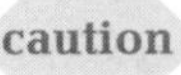

caution The following sections provide an overview of these licenses and some suggestions on how to meet their requirements. Because I am not a lawyer, however, you should not take anything in this book as legal advice. The full text for these licenses is in text files on your Linux system; show these licenses to your legal counsel for a full interpretation and an assessment of applicability to your business.

Understanding the GNU General Public License

The text of the GPL is in a file named `COPYING` in various directories in your Linux system. For example, type **cd /usr/share/doc/gdb***, and type **more COPYING** to read the GPL.

The GPL has nothing to do with whether you charge for the software or distribute it for free; its thrust is to keep the software free for all users. GPL does this by requiring that the software is distributed in source-code form and by stipulating that any user can copy and distribute the software in source-code form to anyone else. In addition, everyone is reminded that the software comes with absolutely no warranty.

The software that GPL covers is not in the public domain; such software is always copyrighted, and the GPL spells out the restrictions on the software's copying and distribution. From a user's point of view, of course, GPL's restrictions are not really restrictions; they are benefits because the user is guaranteed access to the source code.

caution If your application uses parts of any software the GPL covers, your application is considered a derived work; because the GPL covers it, you must distribute the source code to your application.

Although the GPL covers the Linux kernel, the GPL does not cover your applications that use the kernel services through system calls. Those applications are considered normal use of the kernel.

If you plan to distribute your application in binary form (as most commercial software is distributed), you must make sure your application does not use any parts of any software the GPL covers. Your application may end up using parts of other software when it calls functions in a library. Most libraries, however, are covered by a different GNU license, which is described in the following section.

You have to watch out only for a few library and utility programs the GPL covers. The GNU `dbm (gdbm)` database library is one of the prominent libraries GPL covers. The GNU bison parser-generator tool is another utility the GPL covers. If you allow bison to generate code, the GPL covers that code.

Other alternatives for the GNU dbm and GNU bison are not covered by GPL. For a database library, you can use the Berkeley database library db in place of gdbm. For a parser-generator, you might use yacc instead of bison.

Understanding the GNU Library General Public License

The text of the GNU LGPL is in a file named `COPYING.LIB`. If you have the kernel source installed, a copy of `COPYING.LIB` file is in one of the source directories. To locate a copy of the `COPYING.LIB` file, use this `find` command:

```
find /usr/share/doc -name "COPYING*" -print
```

This command lists all occurrences of `COPYING` and `COPYING.LIB` in your system. The `COPYING` file contains the GPL, whereas `COPYING.LIB` has the LGPL.

The LGPL is intended to allow use of libraries in your applications, even if you do not distribute source code for your application. The LGPL stipulates, however, that users must have access to the source code of the library you use and that users can make use of modified versions of those libraries.

The LGPL covers most Linux libraries, including the C library (`libc.a`). Thus, when you build your application on Linux by using the GCC compiler, your application links with code from one or more libraries the LGPL covers. If you want to distribute your application in binary form only, you need to pay attention to LGPL.

One way to meet the intent of the LGPL is to provide the object code for your application and a makefile that relinks your object files with any updated Linux libraries the LGPL covers.

A better way to satisfy the LGPL is to use dynamic linking, in which your application and the library are separate entities, even though your application calls functions in the library when it runs. With dynamic linking, users immediately get the benefit of any updates to the libraries without ever having to relink the application.

Version Control

When you write applications with a few files, it is simple enough to prepare a makefile to automate the software-build process and to avoid worrying about keeping track of changes. Typically, for small projects, you might keep track of changes through comments at the beginning of a file.

This approach works well for a small project, but for larger software projects, you should use some tools that help manage different versions of your applications. In fact, you can benefit from version-control tools even if you are the sole author of a small application. Eventually, you may have trouble remembering what changes you have made. Software version control can help you track these changes.

The Linux software distribution comes with RCS and CVS. Both of these products are collections of tools that help you control software revisions.

The next few sections provide an overview of RCS through some simple examples. A later section briefly discusses CVS and lists some other sources of information about CVS.

Controlling Source Files Using RCS

Source control refers to saving a version of the source code so you can recover a specific version or revision of a file whenever you need it. Essentially, when you modify a source file, the sequence goes something like this:

1. When you have an initial version of the source file, you archive it — place it under source control.
2. When you want to make changes in the file, you first get a copy of the current revision. (When you get it this way, the tools should ensure that no one else can modify that revision.)
3. You make the changes in the source file, test the code, and store the modified file as a new revision.
4. The next time you want to make changes in the file, you start with the latest revision of the file.

RCS provides the tools that enable you to archive file revisions and update them in a controlled manner. Table 23-5 lists the tools.

Table 23-5: RCS Tools

Tool	*Purpose*
`ci`	Creates a new revision of a file, or adds a working file to an RCS file (`ci` stands for check in).
`co`	Gets a working version of a file for reading. (`co -l` provides a working file and locks the original so you can modify the working file.) `co` stands for check out.
`ident`	Searches for identifiers in a file.
`merge`	Incorporates changes from two files into a third file.
`rcsdiff`	Compares a working file with its RCS file.
`rcsmerge`	Merges different revisions of a file.
`rlog`	Views the history of changes in a file.

Suppose you have just finished developing the initial working version of an application and want to use RCS to manage the revisions from now on. The following sections outline the steps to follow to use RCS for your development effort.

Creating Initial RCS Files

The first step in managing source-file revisions by using RCS is to enable RCS to archive the current revision of your files. Follow these steps to put the source file under the control of RCS:

1. In the directory where you keep your application's source files, create a subdirectory named RCS by typing **mkdir RCS**. If the RCS subdirectory exists, RCS archives file revisions in this directory.
2. In each file you plan to place under revision control, add a comment by adding the following RCS identification keyword:

   ```
   $Id$
   ```

   In a C source file, for example, add the following:

   ```
   /*
    * $Id$
    */
   ```

In a makefile, on the other hand, use the following (you would typically put this near the beginning of the file although it works no matter where you put it in the file):

```
# $Id$
```

Later, RCS expands these identifier keywords to include information about the file revision and date.

3. Check in each file with RCS; use the `ci` command, and provide a brief description of each file as prompted by `ci`. Following is how you might check in Makefile:

```
ci Makefile
RCS/Makefile,v  <--  Makefile
enter description, terminated with single '.' or end of file:
NOTE: This is NOT the log message!
>> Makefile for sample programs.
>> .
initial revision: 1.1
done
```

When a file is checked in, the `ci` command creates a corresponding RCS file in the RCS subdirectory. The RCS file's name is the same as the original file, except a `,v` is appended to the name. Thus, the RCS file for `Makefile` is `Makefile,v`. Also, `ci` deletes the original source file after it creates the RCS file. To use or edit the file again, you have to extract it by using the `co` command.

After you follow these steps, all your files are safely stored in RCS files in the RCS subdirectory.

Using the Archived Files

Now suppose you want to edit one of the files (for example, to add a new feature) and rebuild the application. For starters, you need all the source files and the makefile for the compile and link step.

You should extract all these files by using the `co` command for read-only access (except for the file you want to change). Using the `co` command is straightforward. To get a working copy of `Makefile` for read-only use, for example, I type `co Makefile`, which produces the following output from RCS:

```
RCS/Makefile,v --> Makefile
revision 1.1
done
```

By default, this command looks for an RCS file named `RCS/Makefile,v` and creates a read-only working copy of it named `Makefile`.

A copy of `Makefile` is in the directory. Examine that copy of `Makefile` to see what happens to the `$Id$` keyword that you add as a comment. Here's what my example `Makefile` shows:

```
# $Id: Makefile,v 1.1 2005/05/08 16:01:00 naba Exp $
```

As this example shows, RCS expands each identifier keyword into a string with information. The exact information depends on the identifier.

If you want to modify a file, you have to check it out by using the `-l` option. If you want to check out a copy of the file `xmutil.c` for editing, type **co -l xmutil.c** and RCS should show the following output:

```
RCS/xmutil.c,v --> xmutil.c
revision 1.1 (locked)
done
```

Compare this output with that from the previous example of `co`; the current output confirms that the RCS file is locked. No one else can modify the archived file until you check in the copy you have checked out for editing.

When you check out a file and put a lock on it, no one else can check out the same file for editing. However, anyone can get a copy of the file for read-only use.

After you make changes in a file, you can check it in again by using the `ci` command, just as you do when you create the RCS file.

Using RCS Identification Keywords

You can use RCS identification keywords — each of which is a string delimited by dollar signs (`$...$`) — to record information in source files. RCS expands the `$Id$` keyword, for example, into summary information about the file, including the filename, revision number, date, and author. All you have to do is put the keyword in the file; RCS takes care of expanding that keyword into the appropriate information. Table 23-6 lists the identification keywords RCS supports.

Table 23-6: Identification Keywords RCS Supports

Keyword	*Purpose*
`$Author$`	Login ID of the user who checked in the revision.
`$Date$`	Date and time when the revision was checked in.
`$Header$`	Expands to summary information, including full pathname of the RCS file, revision number, date, author, and the state of file revision.
`$Id$`	Same as `$Header$`, except the RCS filename does not have a directory prefix.
`$Locker$`	Login ID of the user who locked the file (empty if the file is not currently locked).
`$Log$`	Expands to a log of changes made in the file.
`$RCSfile$`	Name of the RCS file without the directory names.
`$Revision$`	Revision number of the RCS file.
`$Source$`	Expands to the full pathname of the RCS file.
`$State$`	Indicates the state of the file revision (whether it is locked or not).

insider insight

At minimum, you may want to use the `$Id$` keyword in your files to include summary information about the latest revision.

RCS expands the identifier keywords anywhere in a file. Thus, you might mark an object file (and the executable that uses that object file) by placing the identifier keyword in a string variable. A common practice is to define a string named `rcsid` as follows:

```
static const char rcsid[] = "$Id";
```

Defining the `rcsid` string causes the object and executable file to contain a string such as the following:

```
$Id: xmutil.c,v 1.1 2005/05/08 16:04:00 naba Exp naba $
```

Viewing the Changes Made So Far

Most of the time, the `ci` and `co` commands are used to maintain file revisions with RCS. RCS, however, includes several other tools for managing various aspects of version control, such as comparing two revisions, viewing the history of changes, and examining identifiers in files.

If you have checked out a file for modification, you might want to know what changes you have made thus far. You can use the `rcsdiff` program to see a list of changes. If you've been editing a file named `xmutil.c`, for example, you can compare the working file against its RCS file, by using this command:

```
rcsdiff xmutil.c
```

The `rcsdiff` program runs the UNIX diff utility to find the differences between the working file and the RCS file.

If necessary, you can even find the differences between two specific revisions of a file by using a command such as the following:

```
rcsdiff -r1.1 -r1.2 xmutil.c
```

This command lists the differences between revision 1.1 and 1.2 of the file `xmutil.c`.

Discarding Changes Made So Far

Sometimes after making changes in a file, you realize the changes are either wrong or unnecessary. In such a case, you want to discard the changes you have made so far.

To discard changes, all you have to do is unlock the RCS file and delete the working copy of the file. To unlock an RCS file, use the `rcs` command with the `-u` (unlock) option. The following command discards the current changes in the file named `xmutil.c`:

```
rcs -u xmutil.c
```

Another, more convenient, way to discard changes is to overwrite the current working file with a copy of the former RCS file. To do this, use the `co` command with `-u` and `-f` flags:

```
co -f -u xmutil.c
```

The `-u` option unlocks the checked-out revision, and `-f` forces `co` to overwrite the working file with the former revision of that file.

Viewing the Change Log

As you make changes in a file and keep checking in revisions, RCS maintains a log of changes. You can view this log by using the `rlog` command. The following example shows how to view the log of changes for the file `xmutil.c`:

```
rlog xmutil.c

RCS file: RCS/xmutil.c,v
Working file: xmutil.c
head: 1.2
branch:
locks: strict
access list:
symbolic names:
keyword substitution: kv
total revisions: 2;     selected revisions: 2
description:
Motif utilities
----------------------------
revision 1.2
date: 2005/05/08 01:16:47;  author: naba;  state: Exp;  lines: +10 -6
Added new header file
----------------------------
revision 1.1
date: 2004/10/26 01:10:27;  author: naba;  state: Exp;
Initial revision
=============================================================================
```

The first part of the `rlog` output displays some summary information about the RCS file. The lines following the `description:` line show the description I enter when I create the RCS file. Following this description is an entry for each revision, with the most recent revision appearing first. Each revision's entry shows the date, the author, and a brief description the author has entered.

Examining Identifier Keywords

If any identifier keywords are embedded in a file, you can view them by using the `ident` command. If `Makefile` contains the `$Id$` keyword, you can type **ident Makefile** to examine the keyword; here's a typical output of that command:

```
Makefile:
     $Id: Makefile,v 1.1 2005/05/08 01:06:26 naba Exp $
```

If you define a string variable with a keyword that eventually gets embedded in a binary file (an object file or an executable file), `ident` displays those identifiers as well. You can try `ident` in any binary file to see whether it contains any embedded keywords. This is what I find when I try `ident` on the file `/usr/bin/ident` (the executable program for the `ident` command itself):

```
ident /usr/bin/ident
/usr/bin/ident:
     $Id: rcsbase.h,v 5.20 1995/06/16 06:19:24 eggert Exp $
     $Id: ident.c,v 5.9 1995/06/16 06:19:24 eggert Exp $
     $Id: rcsmap.c,v 5.3 1995/06/16 06:19:24 eggert Exp $
```

From this output, you can tell the exact versions of source files that are used to build this version of the `ident` program.

Performing Concurrent Version Control with CVS

CVS is another source-control tool designed to keep track of changes made by a group of developers working on the same set of files. CVS keeps track of collections of files in a shared directory. An entire collection of files is given a module name; a developer can check out an entire collection of files by using the module name.

CVS uses RCS to save the version-control information in RCS files stored in a directory hierarchy called the repository, which is separate from the developer's working directory. Unlike RCS, CVS does not lock the files when they are checked out. In fact, CVS enables multiple developers to check out an entire collection of files. When developers commit the files back to the repository, CVS tries to merge the changes various developers have made. If CVS cannot successfully merge the changes, the developers are notified, and they have to resolve any conflicting changes manually.

To use an existing CVS repository, first set the `CVSROOT` environment variable to that repository. The repository can even be on a different system. For example, to work on GNOME as a developer, set `CVSROOT` as follows:

```
export CVSROOT=':pserver:anonymous@anoncvs.gnome.org:/cvs/gnome'
```

You also must log in to the CVS server by using this command:

```
cvs login
Logging in to :pserver:anonymous@anoncvs.gnome.org:2401/cvs/gnome
CVS password:  (There is no password, simply press Enter)
```

You will be back at the shell prompt, but you are now logged in and can use the `cvs` command to access this CVS repository. Use the `cvs checkout` command to extract the packages you need from the repository. When extracting files from a remote CVS server, you can specify a compression level with the `-z` option (the recommended level is `-z3`). Thus, you might use the following command to get the `gnome-xml` package from the GNOME CVS repository:

```
cvs -z3 checkout gnome-xml
```

You see a number of messages as the copy of CVS on your system downloads from the repository the latest version of each file in the gnome-xml module, creates a directory named `gnome-xml` in the current directory, and places the files in that directory. You can simply type **cd gnome-xml** to change the directory and begin working on these files.

If you have checked out a module to a working directory, you can use the `cvs update` command to bring your copy current. The `cvs update` command essentially merges the changes in the repository with whatever changes you may have made in the working directory. If conflicting changes exist, you have to resolve the problem manually.

After you work on these files, you can use the `cvs commit` command to incorporate your changes to the files in the repository. You can either commit specific files or commit the entire module.

When you no longer want your working copy of a module, use the `cvs release` command to indicate that you no longer need the module. To remove the files, use the `cvs release -d` command; the `-d` flag means you want to delete the files.

When you are done working with a CVS repository, type **cvs logout** to log out of that repository.

That, in short, is how CVS works. To learn more about CVS, consult these resources:

- Type **info cvs** to browse help information on CVS.
- Type **cd /usr/share/doc/cvs*** to change to the CVS documentation directory. In that directory is a file named FAQ (Frequently Asked Questions) and several PostScript files about CVS. The FAQ file may be a bit out of date, but you can still use it as a source of information about CVS.
- Visit one of these websites to read the latest online information about CVS:
  - `www.cvshome.org/`
  - `www.gnu.org/software/cvs/`
  - `www.gnu.org/software/cvs/manual/`

Linux Programming Topics

Developing software under Linux is quite similar to developing software under any UNIX system. Most C and UNIX programming issues are generic and apply to all UNIX systems. There are, however, a few topics you want to know about if you are developing software for Linux.

This section covers the most significant topic: the Executable and Linking Format (ELF) binary in Linux. The other topic — the use of dynamic linking in applications — is related to ELF. Also, I describe how you can exploit dynamic linking and how you can create a dynamically linked library in Linux.

Understanding the Executable and Linking Format

If you have programmed in UNIX, you probably know that when you compile and link a program, the default executable file is named `a.out`. What you may not have realized is that a file format is associated with the `a.out` file. The operating system has to know this file format so it can load and run an executable. In the early days, Linux used the `a.out` format for its binaries.

Although the `a.out` format has served its purpose adequately, it has two shortcomings:

- Shared libraries are difficult to create.
- Dynamically loading a shared library is cumbersome.

Using shared libraries is desirable because a shared library enables many executable programs to share the same block of code. Also, the dynamic loading of modules is becoming increasingly popular because it enables an application to load blocks of code only when needed, thus reducing the memory requirement of the application.

The UNIX System Laboratories (USL) had developed the Executable and Linking Format or ELF, a new binary format, for use in System V Release 4 (SVR4). The ELF format is much more flexible than the `a.out` format. In particular, ELF has these advantages over the old `a.out` format in Linux:

- Shared libraries for the ELF format are simpler to create. You compile all source files with the `gcc -fPIC -c` command and link them by using a command such as the following, which creates the library `libXXX.so.1.0`:

  ```
  gcc -shared -Wl,-soname,libXXX.so.1 -o libXXX.so.1.0 *.o
  ```

- Dynamic loading (wherein a program loads code modules at runtime) is simpler. With dynamic loading, you can design an application to be extensible so that users can add new code in the form of shared libraries.

Because of ELF's increased flexibility, Linux developers (in particular, the GCC developers) decided to move to ELF as the standard binary-format Linux. By default, the new GCC compilers — `gcc` version 2.7 and later — generate ELF binaries.

Note that GCC continues to use `a.out` as the default name of the executable file (used only if you do not specify an output filename by using the `-o` option). Although the executable may be named `a.out`, the binary format is ELF, not the old `a.out` format.

If you want to check the binary format of an executable file, use the `file` command. The following example shows how to check the file type of `/bin/ls` (the executable file for the `ls` command):

```
file /bin/ls
/bin/ls: ELF 32-bit LSB executable, Intel 80386, version 1 (SYSV), for GNU/Linux
 2.2.5, dynamically linked (uses shared libs), stripped
```

On the other hand, the `file` command reports the following for an older `a.out` format executable (the default name of executable files is still `a.out`, but the format is ELF):

```
file a.out
a.out: Linux/i386 demand-paged executable (QMAGIC)
```

Using Shared Libraries in Linux Applications

Most Linux programs use shared libraries. At minimum, most C programs use the C shared library `libc.so.X`, wherein `X` is a version number. When a program uses one or more shared libraries, you need the program's executable file, as well as all the shared libraries, to run the program. In other words, your program won't run if all shared libraries are not available on a system.

If you sell an application, you need to make sure all necessary shared libraries are distributed with your software.

Examining Shared Libraries That a Program Uses

Use the ldd utility to determine which shared libraries an executable program needs. The following is what ldd reports for a typical C program that uses the ELF binary format:

```
ldd a.out
        linux-gate.so.1 =>  (0x0021a000)
        libc.so.6 => /lib/libc.so.6 (0x008bf000)
        /lib/ld-linux.so.2 (0x008a2000)
```

For a more complex program, such as gimp (ELF version), ldd shows more shared libraries:

```
ldd /usr/bin/gimp
        linux-gate.so.1 =>  (0x00be8000)
        libgimpwidgets-2.0.so.0 => /usr/lib/libgimpwidgets-2.0.so.0 (0x06eae000)
        libgimpcolor-2.0.so.0 => /usr/lib/libgimpcolor-2.0.so.0 (0x0085e000)
        libgimpmodule-2.0.so.0 => /usr/lib/libgimpmodule-2.0.so.0 (0x00869000)
        libgimpbase-2.0.so.0 => /usr/lib/libgimpbase-2.0.so.0 (0x0084e000)
        libgimpthumb-2.0.so.0 => /usr/lib/libgimpthumb-2.0.so.0 (0x00c14000)
        libgimpmath-2.0.so.0 => /usr/lib/libgimpmath-2.0.so.0 (0x00c0d000)
        libgtk-x11-2.0.so.0 => /usr/lib/libgtk-x11-2.0.so.0 (0x0028a000)
        libgdk-x11-2.0.so.0 => /usr/lib/libgdk-x11-2.0.so.0 (0x001e7000)
        libatk-1.0.so.0 => /usr/lib/libatk-1.0.so.0 (0x001b6000)
        libgdk_pixbuf-2.0.so.0 => /usr/lib/libgdk_pixbuf-2.0.so.0 (0x001cf000)
        libm.so.6 => /lib/libm.so.6 (0x009e9000)
... lines deleted ...
        libc.so.6 => /lib/libc.so.6 (0x008bf000)
        libX11.so.6 => /usr/X11R6/lib/libX11.so.6 (0x00a29000)
... lines deleted ...
        /lib/ld-linux.so.2 (0x008a2000)
        libexpat.so.0 => /usr/lib/libexpat.so.0 (0x00b8d000)
```

In this case, the program uses several shared libraries, including the X11 library (`libX11.so.6`), the GIMP toolkit (`libgtk-x11-2.0.so.0`), the General Drawing Kit (GDK) library (`libgdk-x11-2.0.so.0`), the Math library (`libm.so.6`), and the C library (`libc.so.6`).

Thus, almost any Linux application requires shared libraries to run. In addition, the shared libraries must have the same binary format an application uses.

Creating a Shared Library

With ELF, creating a shared library for your own application is simple enough. Suppose you want to implement an object in the form of a shared library. A set of functions in the shared library represents the object's interfaces. To use the object, load its shared library, and invoke its interface functions (you learn how to do this in the following section).

Here is the C source code for this simple object, implemented as a shared library (you might also call it a dynamically linked library) — save this in a file named `dynobj.c`:

```
/*-------------------------------------------------*/
/* File: dynobj.c
 *
 * Demonstrate use of dynamic linking.
 * Pretend this is an object that can be created by calling
 * init and destroyed by calling destroy.
 */
#include <stdio.h>
#include <stdlib.h>
#include <string.h>
```

```
/* Data structure for this object */
typedef struct OBJDATA
{
  char *name;
  int version;
} OBJDATA;

/*-------------------------------------------------------*/
/* i n i t
 *
 * Initialize object (allocate storage).
 *
 */
void* init(char *name)
{
  OBJDATA *data = (OBJDATA*)calloc(1, sizeof(OBJDATA));
  if(name)
    data->name = malloc(strlen(name)+1);
  strcpy(data->name, name);

  printf("Created: %s\n", name);

  return data;
}
/*-------------------------------------------------------*/
/* s h o w
 *
 * Show the object.
 *
 */
void show(void *data)
{
  OBJDATA *d = (OBJDATA*)data;
  printf("show: %s\n", d->name);
}
/*-------------------------------------------------------*/
/* d e s t r o y
 *
 * Destroy the object (free all storage).
 *
 */
void destroy(void *data)
{
  OBJDATA *d = (OBJDATA*)data;
  if(d)
  {
    if(d->name)
    {
      printf("Destroying: %s\n", d->name);
      free(d->name);
```

```
        }
        free(d);
    }
}
```

The object offers three interface functions:

- init to allocate any necessary storage and initialize the object
- show to display the object (here, it simply prints a message)
- destroy to free any storage

To build the shared library named libdobj.so, follow these steps:

1. Compile all source files with the -fPIC flag. In this case, compile the dynobj.c file by using this command:

   ```
   gcc -fPIC -c dynobj.c
   ```

2. Link the objects into a shared library with the -shared flag, and provide appropriate flags for the linker. To create the shared library named libdobj.so.1, use the following:

   ```
   gcc -shared -Wl,-soname,libdobj.so.1 -o libdobj.so.1.0 dynobj.o
   ```

3. Set up a sequence of symbolic links so that programs that use the shared library can refer to it with a standard name. For the sample library, the standard name is libdobj.so, and the symbolic links are set up by using these commands:

   ```
   ln -sf libdobj.so.1.0 libdobj.so.1
   ln -sf libdobj.so.1 libdobj.so
   ```

4. When you test the shared library, define and export the LD_LIBRARY_PATH environment variable by using the following command:

   ```
   export LD_LIBRARY_PATH=`pwd`:$LD_LIBRARY_PATH
   ```

After you test the shared library and are satisfied that the library works, copy it to a standard location, such as /usr/local/lib, and run the ldconfig utility to update the link between libdobj.so.1 and libdobj.so.1.0. These are the commands you use to install your shared library for everyone's use (you have to be root to perform these steps):

```
cp libdobj.so.1.0 /usr/local/lib
/sbin/ldconfig
cd /usr/local/lib
ln -s libdobj.so.1 libdobj.so
```

Dynamically Loading a Shared Library

ELF makes it simple to load a shared library in your program and to use the functions within the shared library. The header file <dlfcn.h> declares the functions for loading and using a shared library. Four functions are declared in the file dlfcn.h for dynamic loading:

- **void *dlopen(const char *filename, int flag);** Loads the shared library specified by filename and returns a handle for the library. The flag can be RTD_LAZY (resolve undefined symbols as the library's code is executed); or RTD_NOW (resolve all undefined symbols before dlopen returns and fail if all symbols are not defined). If dlopen fails, it returns NULL.

- **const char *dlerror (void);** If `dlopen` fails, call `dlerror` to get a string that contains a description of the error.
- **void *dlsym (void *handle, char *symbol);** Returns the address of the specified symbol (function name) from the shared library identified by the handle (that was returned by `dlopen`).
- **int dlclose (void *handle);** Unloads the shared library if no one else is using it.

Here is the `dlfcn.h` file with the appropriate function declarations:

```
/*-------------------------------------------------------*/
/* File: dlfcn.h
 *
 * Header file with function prototypes.
 */
void *dlopen(const char *filename, int flag);
const char *dlerror (void);
void *dlsym (void *handle, char *symbol);
int dlclose (void *handle);
```

When you use any of these functions, include the header file `<dlfcn.h>` with this preprocessor directive:

```
#include <dlfcn.h>
```

The following is a simple test program—`dltest.c`—that shows how to load and use the object defined in the shared library `libdobj.so`, which you created in the preceding section:

```
/*-------------------------------------------------------*/
/* File: dltest.c
 *
 * Test dynamic linking.
 *
 */
#include <dlfcn.h>  /* For the dynamic loading functions */
#include <stdio.h>

int main(void)
{
  void *dlobj;
  void * (*init_call)(char *name);
  void (*show_call)(void *data);
  void (*destroy_call)(void *data);

/* Open the shared library and set up the function pointers */
  if(dlobj = dlopen("libdobj.so.1",RTLD_LAZY))
  {
    void *data;

    init_call=dlsym(dlobj,"init");
    show_call=dlsym(dlobj,"show");
    destroy_call=dlsym(dlobj,"destroy");
```

```
/* Call the object interfaces */
    data = (*init_call)("Test Object");
    (*show_call)(data);
    (*destroy_call)(data);
  }
  return 0;
}
```

The program is straightforward: it loads the shared library, gets the pointers to the functions in the library, and calls the functions through the pointers.

You can compile and link this program in the usual way, but you must link with the `-ldl` option so you can use the functions declared in `<dlfcn.h>`. Here is how you build the program dltest:

```
gcc -o dltest dltest.c -ldl
```

To see the program in action, run dltest:

```
./dltest
Created: Test Object
show: Test Object
Destroying: Test Object
```

Although this demonstration is not exciting, you now have a sample program that uses a shared library.

To see the benefit of using a shared library, return to the preceding section, and make some changes in the `dynobj` shared library (print some other message in a function, for example). Rebuild the shared library alone by typing the following commands:

```
gcc -fPIC -c dynobj.c
gcc -shared -Wl,-soname,libdobj.so.1 -o libdobj.so.1.0 dynobj.o
```

Then run dltest again. The resulting printout should show the effect of the changes you make in the shared library, which means you can update the shared library independently of the application. You should also note that a change in a shared library can affect many applications installed on your system. Therefore, you should be careful when making changes to any shared library.

Summary

Your Linux system comes loaded with all the tools you need to develop software. In particular, it has all the GNU software-development tools, such as GCC, the GNU debugger, GNU make, and the RCS version-control utility. This chapter describes these software-development tools and shows you how to use them.

In this chapter, you learned the following:

- The GNU tools compose the software-development environment on your Linux PC. These tools include GNU Emacs for text editing; GCC for compiling C and C++ programs; GNU make for automating software builds; the GNU debugger for debugging; and the RCS for version control.

- A utility named info provides online help information on the GNU tools. You can run info alone in a terminal window or under GNU Emacs by using the Ctrl-h i command.
- GCC is the GNU C and C++ compiler. You can use the `gcc` command to compile and link C programs. Use g++ to compile and link C++ programs.
- GCC has a plethora of options, but you need to use only a few. Some of the common options are `-c` (for compiling only) and `-o` (for specifying the name of the output executable file).
- The GNU make utility enables you to automate the build process. You specify the modules that compose an executable, as well as any dependencies; make takes care of compiling only files that need recompilation. The input file for make is known as a *makefile* and is commonly named `Makefile`.
- The GNU debugger enables you to locate errors in your programs. Use the `gdb` command to run the debugger. You have to compile the program by using GCC's `-g` option to generate debugging information the GNU debugger can use.
- When you use GNU tools to develop software (as you do in Linux), you should be aware of the GNU licenses: the GNU General Public License (GPL) and the GNU Library General Public License (LGPL). The LGPL covers GNU libraries. If you distribute your software in binary form, you should use dynamic linking to comply with the terms of the LGPL. You should not take anything in this book as legal advice, of course; always consult your own legal counsel for a definitive answer.
- Version control is an important aspect of software development. In Linux, you get the RCS (Revision Control System) to manage revisions of source files.
- Concurrent Versions System (CVS) is a versatile RCS-based, version-control system that manages multiple directories of files. CVS enables multiple developers to work simultaneously on the same set of files. Open-source projects, such as GNOME, use CVS to enable many developers to work on various parts of the project.
- Shared libraries are commonly used in Linux applications to reduce the memory requirements of executables. Applications are dynamically linked with a shared library at runtime, and many applications can share a single library.
- The Linux development community has adopted the Executable and Linking Format (ELF) for binaries. ELF makes dynamic linking simpler to program. This chapter shows an example of how to use dynamic linking in your own applications.

Shell and Perl Scripting

Secrets in This Chapter

The fundamental philosophy of UNIX, which Linux continues to follow, is to give the user many small and specialized commands, along with the plumbing necessary to connect these commands. By plumbing, I mean the way in which one command's output functions as a second command's input. Bash, the default shell in Linux, provides this plumbing in the form of I/O redirection and pipes. Bash also includes features such as the `if` statement, which runs commands only when a specific condition is true, and the `for` statement, which repeats commands a specified number of times. You can use these features of Bash when writing interpreted programs called shell scripts.

This chapter shows you how to write simple shell scripts: a collection of shell commands stored in a file. Shell scripts are used to automate various tasks. For example, when Linux boots, many shell scripts stored in various subdirectories in the `/etc` directory (for example, `/etc/init.d`) perform many initialization tasks.

When it comes to writing scripts, the Perl language is also popular among UNIX system administrators. Because you probably are the system administrator of your Linux system, this chapter also introduces you to Perl scripting.

cross ref

Chapter 25 covers Tcl/Tk, another popular scripting language you can use to build applications with a graphical interface.

Looking at Some Shell Scripts

If you are not a programmer, you may feel apprehensive about programming. But shell scripting (or programming) can be as simple as storing a few commands in a file. In fact, you can have a useful shell program that has a single command.

While writing this book, for example, I have captured screens from the X Window System and have used the screenshots in figures. I have used the X screen-capture program, xwd, to store the screen images in the X Window Dump (XWD) format. The book's production team, however, wanted the screenshots in TIFF format. Therefore, I used the Portable Bitmap (PBM) toolkit to convert the XWD images to TIFF format. To convert each file, I run two programs and delete a temporary file, by using the following commands:

```
xwdtopnm < file.xwd > file.pnm
pnmtotiff < file.pnm > file.tif
rm file.pnm
```

These commands assume that the xwdtopnm and pnmtotiff programs are in the `/usr/bin` directory, one of the directories listed in the PATH environment variable. By the way, xwdtopnm and pnmtotiff are two programs in the PBM toolkit.

After converting a few XWD files to TIFF format, I get tired of typing the same sequence of commands for each file, so I prepare a file named `totif` and save the following lines in it:

```
#!/bin/sh
xwdtopnm < $1.xwd > $1.pnm
pnmtotiff < $1.pnm > $1.tif
rm $1.pnm
```

Then, I make the file executable by using this command:

```
chmod +x totif
```

The chmod command enables you to change the permission settings of a file. One of those settings determines whether the file is executable or not. The +x option means that you want to mark the file as executable. You need to do this because Bash runs only executable files. (See the chmod command reference in Appendix A for more information on permission settings for files.)

Finally, I convert the file figure1.xwd to figure1.tif by using the following command:

```
./totif figure1
```

The ./ prefix indicates that the totif file is in the current directory—you don't need the ./ prefix if the PATH environment variable includes the current directory. The totif file is called a *shell script* or *shell program*. When you run this shell program with the command totif figure1, the shell substitutes figure1 for each occurrence of $1.

That, in a nutshell, is why you might create shell programs—to have your Linux shell perform repetitive chores.

Here is another interesting example of a shell program. Suppose that you occasionally have to use MS-DOS or Windows text files on your Linux system. Although you might expect to use a text file on any system without any problems, there is one catch: Windows and DOS uses a carriage return followed by a line feed to mark the end of each line, whereas Linux (and other UNIX systems) use only a line feed. As a result, if you use the vi editor with the -b option to open a Windows/DOS text file (for example, type **vi -b filename** to open the file), you see ^M at the end of each line. That ^M stands for Ctrl-M, which is the carriage-return character.

On your Linux system, you can easily rid the Windows/DOS text file of the extra carriage returns by using the tr command with the -d option. Essentially, to convert the Windows/DOS text file filename.dos to a Linux text file named filename.linux, type the following:

```
tr -d '\015' < filename.dos > filename.linux
```

In this command, '\015' denotes the ASCII code for the carriage-return character in octal notation. In this command, the < symbol is used to read from a file and > is used to save output to a file.

insider insight

You can use the tr command to translate or delete characters from the input. When you use tr with the -d option, it deletes all occurrences of a specific character from the input data. Following the -d option, you must specify the character to be deleted. Like many UNIX utilities, tr reads the standard input and writes its output to standard output. As the sample command shows, you must employ input and output redirection to use tr to delete all occurrences of a character in a file and save the output in another file.

If you don't want to remember all this information every time you convert a Windows/DOS file to UNIX, store the following in a file named `txt2unix`:

```
tr -d '\015' < $1 > $2
```

Then, make the file executable by using this command:

```
chmod +x txt2unix
```

That's it! Now you have a shell program named `txt2unix` that converts a Windows/DOS text file to a UNIX text file. If you have the MS-DOS partition mounted as `/dosc`, you can try the `dos2unix` shell program with the following command:

```
txt2unix /dosc/autoexec.bat aexec.bat
```

The preceding command creates a file named `aexec.bat` in the current directory. If you open this file with the `vi -b aexec.bat` command, you should not see any `^M` characters at the ends of lines.

insider insight

If you are familiar with MS-DOS, you may notice that shell scripts closely resemble MS-DOS batch files, except for some syntax differences. Shell scripts, however, are much more powerful.

Shell scripts are popular among system administrators. If you are a system administrator, you can build a collection of custom shell scripts that help you automate tasks you perform often. If a disk seems to be getting full, for example, you may want to find all files that exceed some size (say, 10MB) and that have not been accessed in the past 30 days. In addition, you may want to send an email message to all users who have large files, requesting that they archive and clean up those files. You can perform all these tasks with a shell script. You might start with the following `find` command to identify large files:

```
find / -type f -atime +30 -size +10000k -exec ls -l {} \; >
/tmp/largefiles
```

This command creates a file named `/tmp/largefiles`, which contains detailed information about the old files taking up too much space. After you get a list of the files, you can use a few other Linux commands—such as `sort`, `cut`, and `sed`—to prepare and send mail messages to users who have large files that they should clean up. Instead of typing all these commands manually, place them in a file, and create a shell script. That, in a nutshell, is the essence of shell scripts—to gather shell commands in a file so that you can easily perform or even automate repetitive systems-administration tasks.

Learning the Basics of Shell Scripting in Bash

Now that you have seen examples of simple shell scripts, the next few sections provide an overview of Bash programming.

As you try out simple shell programs, don't name your sample programs test. Linux includes an important program named test (/usr/bin/test). This program tests for various conditions in shell scripts, such as whether or not a file exists and whether or not a file is readable. If you create a sample program named test, some scripts may end up calling your program instead of calling the system's test program.

Writing a Simple Shell Script

Earlier in this chapter, you learn how to place frequently used commands in a file and use the chmod command to make the file executable. *Voilà*—you have a shell script. Just as most Linux commands accept command-line options, a Bash script accepts command-line options. Inside the script, you can refer to the options as $1, $2, and so on. The special name $0 refers to the name of the script itself.

Consider the following Bash script:

```
#!/bin/sh
echo "This script's name is: $0."
echo Argument 1: $1
echo Argument 2: $2
```

The first line causes Linux to run the /bin/sh program, which subsequently processes the rest of the lines in the script. The name /bin/sh traditionally refers to the Bourne shell—the first UNIX shell. In Linux, /bin/sh is a symbolic link to /bin/bash, which is the executable program for Bash. Therefore, in Linux, Bash runs Bourne shell scripts (Bash happens to be compatible with the Bourne shell).

If you save this simple script in a file named simple, and you make that file executable with the command chmod +x simple, you can run the script as follows:

```
./simple
This script's name is: ./simple.
Argument 1:
Argument 2:
```

The script file's name appears relative to the current directory, which is represented by a period. Because you have run the script without arguments, the script does not display any arguments.

Now, try running the script with a few arguments, as follows:

```
./simple "This is one argument." second-argument third
This script's name is: ./simple.
Argument 1: This is one argument.

Argument 2: second-argument
```

As this example shows, the shell treats the entire string within double quotation marks as a single argument. Otherwise, the shell uses spaces as separators between arguments on the command line.

Note that this sample script ignores the third argument because the script is designed to print only the first two arguments. The script ignores all arguments after the first two.

Getting an Overview of Bash Programming

Like any programming language, Bash includes the following features:

- Variables that store values, including special built-in variables for accessing command-line arguments passed to a shell script and other special values.
- The capability to evaluate expressions.
- Control structures that enable you to loop over several shell commands or to execute some commands conditionally.
- The capability to define functions that can be called in many places within a script. Bash also includes many built-in commands that you can use in any script.

The next few sections illustrate some of Bash's programming features through simple examples. Because you are already running Bash, you can try the examples by typing them at the shell prompt in a terminal window.

Understanding Bash Variables

You define variables in Bash just as you define environment variables. Thus, you might define a variable as follows:

```
count=12  # note no embedded spaces allowed
```

To use a variable's value, prefix the variable's name with a dollar sign (`$`). `$PATH`, for example, is the value of the variable `PATH` (yes, the famous `PATH` environment variable that contains the list of directories to search for any commands the user types). To display the value of the variable `count`, use the following command:

```
echo $count
```

Bash has some special variables for accessing command-line arguments. In a shell script, `$0` refers to the name of the shell script. The variables `$1`, `$2`, and so on refer to the command-line arguments. The variable `$*` stores all the command-line arguments as a single variable, and `$?` contains the exit status of the last command the shell executes.

In addition, you can prompt the user for input and use the `read` command to read the input into a variable. Following is an example:

```
echo -n "Enter value: "
read value
echo "You entered: $value."
```

insider insight

The `-n` option prevents the `echo` command from automatically adding a new line at the end of the string that it displays.

Writing Shell Functions

You can group a number of shell commands into a function and assign it a name. Later, you can execute that group of commands by using the single name assigned to the function. Here is a simple script that illustrates the syntax of shell functions:

```
#!/bin/sh

hello() {
        echo -n "Hello, "
        echo $1 $2
}

hello Jane Doe
```

When you run this script, it displays the following output:

```
Hello, Jane Doe
```

This script defines a shell function named `hello`. The function expects two arguments; in the body of the function, these arguments are referenced by `$1` and `$2`. The function definition begins with `hello()`—the name of the function, followed by parentheses. The body of the function is enclosed in curly braces—`{...}`. In this case, the body uses the echo built-in command (see Table 24-1 for a list of built-in commands).

Using Bash Control Structures

In Bash scripts, the control structures—such as `if`, `case`, `for`, and `while`—depend on the exit status of a command to decide what to do next. When any command executes, it returns an exit status: a numeric value that indicates whether or not the command has succeeded. By convention, an exit status of zero means the command has succeeded. (Yes, you read it right: zero indicates success.) A nonzero exit status indicates that something has gone wrong with the command.

As an example of using control structures, consider the following script, which makes a backup copy of a file before opening it with the vi text editor:

```
#!/bin/sh
if cp "$1" "#$1"
then
    vi "$1"
else
    echo "Failed to create backup copy"
fi
```

This script illustrates the syntax of the `if-then-else` structure and shows how the exit status of the `cp` command is used by the if structure to determine the next action. If `cp` returns zero, the script invokes vi to edit the file; otherwise, the script displays a message and exits. By the way, the script names the backup file the same as that of the original, except for a number sign (#) added at the beginning of the filename.

insider insight **Don't forget the final `fi` that terminates the `if` structure. Forgetting `fi` is a common source of errors in Bash scripts.**

Bash includes the `test` command to enable you to evaluate any expression and to use the expression's value as the exit status of the command. Suppose that you want a script that enables you to edit a file only if it exists. Using `test`, you might write such a script as follows:

```
#!/bin/sh
if test -f "$1"
then
    vi "$1"
else
    echo "No such file"
fi
```

A shorter form of the `test` command omits `test` and places the `test` command's options in square brackets (`[ . . . ]`). Using this notation, you can write the script that enables you to edit only existing files, as follows:

```
#!/bin/sh
if [ -f "$1" ]
then
    vi "$1"
else
    echo "No such file"
fi
```

The left square bracket (`[`) is in fact a symbolic link to `/usr/bin/test`. You can confirm this fact by typing `ls -l /usr/bin/[`.

Another common control structure is the `for` loop. The following script adds the numbers 1 through 10:

```
#!/bin/sh
sum=0
for i in 1 2 3 4 5 6 7 8 9 10
do
    sum=`expr $sum + $i'
done
echo "Sum = $sum"
```

This example also illustrates the use of the `expr` command to evaluate an expression.

The `case` statement is used to execute a group of commands based on the value of a variable. For example, consider the following script:

```
#!/bin/sh
echo -n "What should I do -- (Y)es/(N)o/(C)ontinue? [Y] "
read answer
case $answer in
    y|Y|"")
      echo "YES"
    ;;
    c|C)
      echo "CONTINUE"
    ;;
    n|N)
      echo "NO"
```

```
        ;;
        *)
          echo "UNKNOWN"
        ;;
  esac
```

Save this in a file named confirm, and type **chmod +x confirm** to make it executable. Then, try it out like this:

```
./confirm
What should I do -- (Y)es/(N)o/(C)ontinue? [Y] c
CONTINUE
```

The script displays a prompt and reads the input you type. Your input is stored in a variable named answer. Then the case statement executes a block of code based on the value of the answer variable. For example, when I type c, the following block of commands is executed:

```
        c|C)
          echo "CONTINUE"
        ;;
```

The echo command causes the script to display CONTINUE.

From this example, you can see that the general syntax of the case command is as follows:

```
case $variable in
    value1 | value2)
    command1
    command2
    ...other commands...
    ;;

    value3)
    command3
    command4
    ...other commands...
    ;;
esac
```

Essentially, the case command begins with the word case and ends with esac. Separate blocks of code are enclosed between the values of the variable, followed by a right parenthesis and terminated by a pair of semicolons (;;).

insider insight **Don't forget the final esac that terminates the case structure. Forgetting esac is a common source of errors in Bash scripts.**

Taking Stock of Built-in Commands in Bash

Bash has more than 50 built-in commands, including common commands such as cd and pwd, as well as many others that are used infrequently. You can use these built-in commands in any Bash script or at the shell prompt. Appendix A describes many of the built-in commands that you typically use at the shell prompt.

Although this chapter does not have enough space to cover all built-in Bash commands, Table 24-1 describes most of these commands and their arguments. After looking through this information, type **help cmd** (where *cmd* is a command's name) to read more about a specific built-in command. For example, to learn more about the built-in command `test`, type the following:

```
help test | more
test: test [expr]
    Exits with a status of 0 (true) or 1 (false) depending on
    the evaluation of EXPR.  Expressions may be unary or binary.  Unary
    expressions are often used to examine the status of a file.  There
    are string operators as well, and numeric comparison operators.

    File operators:

        -a FILE        True if file exists.
        -b FILE        True if file is block special.
        -c FILE        True if file is character special.
        -d FILE        True if file is a directory.
        -e FILE        True if file exists.
        -f FILE        True if file exists and is a regular file.
        -g FILE        True if file is set-group-id.
        -h FILE        True if file is a symbolic link.
        -L FILE        True if file is a symbolic link.
        -k FILE        True if file has its `sticky' bit set.
        -p FILE        True if file is a named pipe.
        -r FILE        True if file is readable by you.
        -s FILE        True if file exists and is not empty.
        -S FILE        True if file is a socket.
        -t FD          True if FD is opened on a terminal.
... Lines deleted ...
```

Where necessary, the online help from the `help` command includes a considerable amount of detail.

Note that some external programs may have the same name as Bash built-in commands. If you want to run any such external program, you have to specify explicitly the full pathname of that program. Otherwise, Bash executes the built-in command of the same name.

Table 24-1: Summary of Built-in Commands in the Bash Shell

Function	*Description*
`. filename [arguments]`	Reads and executes commands from the specified file using the optional arguments (same as source).
`: [arguments]`	Expands the arguments but does not process them.
`[ expr ]`	Evaluates the expression *expr* and returns zero status if *expr* is true.
`alias [name[=value] ...]`	Defines an alias or lists all aliases if no arguments are provided.

Function	Description
`bg [job]`	Puts the specified job in the background. If no job is specified, it puts the currently executing command in the background.
`bind [-m keymap] [-lvd] [-q name]`	Binds a key sequence to a macro.
`break [n]`	Exits from a for, while, or until loop. If n is specified, the *n*th enclosing loop is exited.
`builtin builtin_command [arguments]`	Executes a shell built-in command.
`cd [dir]`	Changes the current directory to `dir` or to the user's home directory if no arguments provided.
`command [-pVv] cmd [arg ...]`	Runs the command `cmd` with the specified arguments (ignoring any shell function named `cmd`).
`continue [n]`	Starts the next iteration of the for, while, or until loop. If n is specified, the next iteration of the *n*th enclosing loop is started.
`declare [-frxi] [name[=value]]`	Declares a variable with the specified `name` and, optionally, assigns it a value.
`dirs [-l] [+/-n]`	Displays the list of currently remembered directories.
`echo [-neE] [arg ...]`	Displays the arguments on standard output.
`enable [-n] [-all] [name ...]`	Enables or disables the specified built-in commands.
`eval [arg ...]`	Concatenates the arguments and executes them as a command.
`exec [command [arguments]]`	Replaces the current instance of the shell with a new process that runs the specified command.
`exit [n]`	Exits the shell with the status code n.
`export [-nf] [name[=word]] ...`	Defines a specified environment variable and exports it to future processes.
`fc -s [pat=rep] [cmd]`	Re-executes the command after replacing the pattern `pat` with `rep`.
`fg [jobspec]`	Puts the specified job in the foreground. If no job is specified, it puts the most recent job in the foreground.
`getopts optstring name [args]`	Gets optional parameters (called in shell scripts to extract arguments from the command line).
`hash [-r] [name]`	Remembers the full pathname of a specified command.
`help [cmd ...]`	Displays help information for specified built-in commands.
`history [n]`	Displays past commands or past n commands, if you specify a number n.

(continued)

Table 24-1 *(continued)*

Function	*Description*
`jobs [-lnp] [ jobspec ... ]`	Lists currently active jobs.
`kill [-s sigspec | -sigspec] [pid | jobspec] ...`	Sends a specified signal to one or more processes.
`let arg [arg ...]`	Evaluates each argument and returns `1` if the last *arg* is `0`.
`local [name[=value] ...]`	Creates a local variable with the specified *name* and *value* (used in shell functions).
`logout`	Exits a login shell.
`popd [+/-n]`	Removes entries from the directory stack.
`pushd [dir]`	Adds a specified directory to the top of the directory stack.
`pwd`	Prints the full pathname of the current working directory.
`read [-r] [name ...]`	Reads a line from standard input and parses it.
`readonly [-f] [name ...]`	Marks the specified variables as read-only, so that the variables cannot be changed later.
`return [n]`	Exits the shell function with the return value n.
`set [--abefhkmnptuvxldCHP] [-o option] [arg ...]`	Sets various flags.
`shift [n]`	Makes the n+1 argument `$1`, the n+2 argument `$2`, and so on.
`source filename [arguments]`	Reads and executes commands from a file.
`suspend [-f]`	Stops execution until a `SIGCONT` signal is received.
`test expr`	Evaluates the expression *expr* and returns zero if *expr* is true.
`times`	Prints the accumulated user and system times for processes run from the shell.
`trap [-l] [cmd] [sigspec]`	Executes *cmd* when the signal *sigspec* is received.
`type [-all] [-type | -path] name [name ...]`	Indicates how the shell interprets each name.
`ulimit [-SHacdfmstpnuv [limit]]`	Controls resources available to the shell.
`umask [-S] [mode]`	Sets the file creation mask — the default permission for files.
`unalias [-a] [name ...]`	Undefines a specified alias.
`unset [-fv] [name ...]`	Removes the definition of specified variables.
`wait [n]`	Waits for a specified process to terminate.

Perl as a Scripting Language

Perl stands for Practical Extraction Report Language. Larry Wall created Perl to extract information from text files and to use that information to prepare reports. Programs written in Perl, the language, are interpreted and executed by perl, the program. This book's companion DVD includes Perl, and you can install it at the same time as you install Linux (simply select the Development Tools package group).

Perl is available on a wide variety of computer systems because, like Linux, Perl can be distributed freely. In addition, Perl is popular as a scripting language among many users and system administrators, which is why I introduce Perl and describe its strengths. In Chapter 25, you learn about another scripting language (Tcl/Tk) that provides the capability to create GUIs for the scripts.

The term "script" is simply a synonym for program. Unlike programs written in languages such as C and C++, you do not have to compile Perl programs; the perl program simply interprets and executes the Perl programs. The term "script" often is used for such interpreted programs written in a shell's programming language or in Perl. (Strictly speaking, perl does not interpret a Perl program; it converts the Perl program to an intermediate form before executing the program.)

If you are familiar with shell programming or the C programming language, you can pick up Perl quickly. If you have never programmed, becoming proficient in Perl may take a while. I encourage you to start with a small subset of Perl's features and ignore anything you do not understand. Then, slowly add Perl features to your repertoire.

Determining Whether You Have Perl

Before you proceed with the Perl tutorial, check whether you have Perl installed on your system. Type the following command:

```
which perl
```

The `which` command tells you whether it finds a specified program in the directories listed in the `PATH` environment variable. If perl is installed, you should see the following output:

```
/usr/bin/perl
```

If the `which` command complains that no such program exists in the current `PATH`, this does not necessarily mean you do not have perl installed; it may mean that you do not have the `/usr/bin` directory in `PATH`. Ensure that `/usr/bin` is in `PATH`; either type **echo $PATH** or look at the message displayed by the `which` command (that message includes the directories in `PATH`). If `/usr/bin` is not in `PATH`, use the following command to redefine `PATH`:

```
export PATH=$PATH:/usr/bin
```

Now, try the `which perl` command again. If you still get an error, you may not have installed Perl. You can install Perl from the companion DVD by performing the following steps:

1. Log in as `root`.
2. Insert the companion DVD into the DVD drive. If you are working in GNOME or KDE graphical desktop, the DVD should mount automatically. If it does not or if you are working at a text console, type **mount /media/cdrom** to mount the DVD (if you are using a DVD recorder, type **mount /media/cdrecorder**).
3. Type the following command to change the directory to the location of the RPM files:

   ```
   cd /media/cdrom/Fedora/RPMS
   ```
4. Type the following `rpm` (Red Hat Package Manager) command to install Perl:

   ```
   rpm -ivh perl*
   ```

After you have perl installed on your system, type the following command to see its version number:

```
perl -v
```

Following is typical output from that command:

```
This is perl, v5.8.6 built for i386-linux-thread-multi

Copyright 1987-2004, Larry Wall

Perl may be copied only under the terms of either the Artistic License or the
GNU General Public License, which may be found in the Perl 5 source kit.

Complete documentation for Perl, including FAQ lists, should be found on
this system using `man perl' or `perldoc perl'.  If you have access to the
Internet, point your browser at http://www.perl.com/, the Perl Home Page.
```

This output tells you that you have Perl Version 5.8, patch Level 6, and that Larry Wall, the originator of Perl, holds the copyright. Perl is distributed freely under the GNU General Public License, however.

You can get the latest version of Perl by pointing your World Wide Web browser to the Comprehensive Perl Archive Network (CPAN). The following address connects you to the CPAN site nearest to you:

```
www.cpan.org/
```

Writing Your First Perl Script

Perl has many features of C, and, as you may know, most books on C start with an example program that displays `Hello, World!` on your terminal. Because Perl is an interpreted language, you can accomplish this task directly from the command line. If you enter:

```
perl -e 'print "Hello, World!\n";'
```

the system responds

```
Hello, World!
```

This command uses the `-e` option of the `perl` program to pass the Perl program as a command-line argument to the Perl interpreter. In this case, the following line constitutes the Perl program:

```
print "Hello, World!\n";
```

To convert this line to a script, simply place the line in a file, and start the file with a directive to run the perl program (as you do in shell scripts, when you place a line such as `#!/bin/sh` to run the Bourne shell to process the script).

To try a Perl script, follow these steps:

1. Use a text editor, such as vi or Emacs, to save the following lines in the file named `hello`:

   ```
   #!/usr/bin/perl
   # This is a comment.
   print "Hello, World!\n";
   ```

2. Make the `hello` file executable by using the following command:

   ```
   chmod +x hello
   ```

3. Run the Perl script by typing the following at the shell prompt:

   ```
   ./hello
   Hello, World!
   ```

That's it! You have written and tried your first Perl script.

The first line of a Perl script starts with `#!`, followed by the full pathname of the perl program. If the first line of a script starts with `#!`, the shell simply strips off the `#!`, appends the script file's name to the end, and runs the script. Thus, if the script file is named `hello` and the first line is `#!/usr/bin/perl`, the shell executes the following command:

```
/usr/bin/perl hello
```

You can also add other perl options on the first line of the Perl script. For example, the `-w` option causes the Perl interpreter to print warning messages about any bad constructs in the Perl script. It's a good idea to include the `-w` option on the line that invokes the Perl interpreter. Thus, you should use the following line as the first line of your Perl scripts:

```
#!/usr/bin/perl -w
```

Learning More about Perl

I devote a few sections of this chapter to giving you an overview of Perl and to showing a few simple examples. However, this discussion does not do justice to Perl. If you want to use Perl as a tool, consult one of the following books:

- Larry Wall, Tom Christiansen, and Jon Orwant, *Programming Perl, Third Edition* (O'Reilly & Associates, 2000)
- Randal L. Schwartz and Tom Phoenix, *Learning Perl, Third Edition* (O'Reilly & Associates, 2001)
- Paul E. Hoffman, *Perl For Dummies, Fourth Edition* (John Wiley & Sons, 2003)

Programming Perl, Third Edition, is the authoritative guide to Perl (although it may not be the best resource for learning Perl). The book by Randal Schwartz focuses more on teaching Perl programming. Paul Hoffman's book is a good introduction for nonprogrammers wanting to learn Perl.

Getting an Overview of Perl

Most programming languages, including Perl, have some common features:

- **Variables** to store different types of data. You can think of each variable as a placeholder for data — kind of like a mailbox, with a name and room to store data. The content of the variable is its value.
- **Expressions** that combine variables by using operators. One expression might add several variables; another might extract a part of a string.
- **Statements** that perform some action, such as assigning a value to a variable or printing a string.
- **Flow-control statements** that enable statements to be executed in various orders, depending on the value of some expression. Typically, flow-control statements include for, do-while, while, and if-then-else statements.
- **Functions** (also called *subroutines* or *routines*) that enable you to group several statements and give them a name. This feature enables you to execute the same set of statements by invoking the function that represents those statements. Typically, a programming language provides some predefined functions.
- **Packages and modules** that enable you to organize a set of related Perl subroutines that are designed to be reusable. (Modules were introduced in Perl 5.)

The next few sections provide an overview of these major features of Perl and illustrate the features through simple examples.

Learning Basic Perl Syntax

Perl is free-form, like C; no constraints exist on the exact placement of any keyword. Often, Perl programs are stored in files with names that end in `.pl`, but there is no restriction on the filenames you use.

As in C, each Perl statement ends with a semicolon (`;`). A number sign or hash mark (#) marks the start of a comment; the perl program disregards the rest of the line beginning with the number sign.

Groups of Perl statements are enclosed in braces (`{...}`). This feature also is similar in C.

Using Variables in Perl

You don't have to declare Perl variables before using them, as you do in C. You can recognize a variable in a Perl script easily, because each variable name begins with a special character: an at symbol (@), a dollar sign (`$`), or a percent sign (`%`). These special characters denote the variable's type.

The three variable types in Perl are as follows:

- *Scalar* variables represent the basic data types: integer, floating-point number, and string. A dollar sign ($) precedes a scalar variable. Following are some examples:

```
$maxlines = 256;
$title = "Red Hat Fedora Linux Secrets";
```

- *Array* variables are collections of scalar variables. An array variable has an at symbol (@) as a prefix. Thus, the following are arrays:

```
@pages = (62, 26, 22, 24);
@commands = ("start", "stop", "draw", "exit");
```

- *Associative arrays* are collections of *key-value* pairs, in which each *key* is a string and the *value* is any scalar variable. A percent-sign (%) prefix indicates an associative array. You can use associative arrays to associate a name with a value. You might store the amount of disk space each user occupies in an associative array, such as the following:

```
%disk_usage = ("root", 147178, "naba", 28547, "emily", 55);
```

Because each variable type has a special character prefix, you can use the same name for different variable types. Thus, `%disk_usage`, `@disk_usage`, and `$disk_usage` can appear within the same Perl program.

Using Scalars

A scalar variable can store a single value, such as a number, or a text string. Scalar variables are the basic data type in Perl. Each scalar's name begins with a dollar sign ($). Typically, you start using a scalar with an assignment statement that initializes it. You even can use a variable without initializing it; the default value for numbers is zero, and the default value of a string is an empty string. If you want to see whether a scalar is defined, use the defined function as follows:

```
print "Name undefined!\n" if !(defined $name);
```

The expression `(defined $name)` is 1 if `$name` is defined. You can "undefine" a variable by using the `undef` function. You can undefine `$name`, for example, as follows:

```
undef $name;
```

Variables are evaluated according to context. Following is a script that initializes and prints a few variables:

```
#!/usr/bin/perl
$title = "Red Hat Fedora Linux Secrets";
$count1 = 650;
$count2 = 425;

$total = $count1 + $count2;

print "Title: $title -- $total pages\n";
```

When you run the preceding Perl program, it produces the following output:

```
Title: Red Hat Fedora Linux Secrets -- 1075 pages
```

As the Perl statements show, when the two numeric variables are added, their numeric values are used; but when the `$total` variable is printed, its string representation is displayed.

Another interesting aspect of Perl is that it evaluates all variables in a string within double quotation marks ("..."). However, if you write a string inside single quotation marks ('...'), Perl leaves that string untouched. If you write

```
print 'Title: $title -- $total pages\n';
```

with single quotes instead of double quotes, Perl displays

```
Title: $title -- $total pages\n
```

and does not generate a new line.

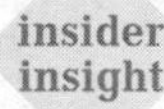

A useful Perl variable is `$_` (the dollar sign followed by the underscore character). This special variable is known as the default argument. The Perl interpreter determines the value of `$_` depending on the context. When the Perl interpreter reads input from the standard input, `$_` holds the current input line; when the interpreter is searching for a specific pattern of text, `$_` holds the default search pattern.

Using Arrays

An array is a collection of scalars. The array name begins with an at symbol (@). As in C, array subscripts start at zero. You can access the elements of an array with an index. Perl allocates space for arrays dynamically.

Consider the following simple script:

```
#!/usr/bin/perl
@commands = ("start", "stop", "draw" , "exit");

$numcmd = @commands;
print "There are $numcmd commands.\n";
print "The first command is: $commands[0]\n";
```

When you run the script, it produces the following output:

```
There are 4 commands.
The first command is: start
```

Equating a scalar to an array sets the scalar to the number of elements in the array. The first element of an array is referenced by changing the `@` sign to `$` and then appending the index 0 in square brackets. Thus, the first element of the `@commands` array is referenced as `$commands[0]` because the index starts at zero. Thus, the fourth element in the `@commands` array is `$commands[3]`.

Two special scalars are related to an array. The `$[ variable` is the current base index (the starting index), which is zero by default. The scalar `$#arrayname` (in which `arrayname` is the name of an array variable) has the last array index as the value. Thus, for the `@commands` array that has three elements, `$#commands` is 3.

You can print an entire array with a simple `print` statement like this:

```
print "@commands\n";
```

When Perl executes this statement for the `@commands` array used in this section's examples, it displays the following output:

```
start stop draw exit
```

Using Associative Arrays

Associative array variables, which are declared with a percent sign (%) prefix, are unique features of Perl. Using associative arrays, you can index an array with a string, such as a name. A good example of an associative array is the `%ENV` array, which Perl automatically defines for you. In Perl, `%ENV` is the array of environment variables you can access by using the environment-variable name as an index. The following Perl statement prints the current PATH environment variable:

```
print "PATH = $ENV{PATH}\n";
```

When Perl executes this statement, it prints the current setting of PATH. In contrast to indexing regular arrays, you have to use braces to index an associative array.

Perl has many built-in functions — such as `delete`, `each`, `keys`, and `values` — that enable you to access and manipulate associative arrays.

Listing the Predefined Variables in Perl

Perl has several predefined variables that contain useful information you may need in a Perl script. Following are a few important predefined variables:

- `@ARGV` is an array of strings that contains the command-line options to the script. The first option is `$ARGV[0]`, the second one is `$ARGV[1]`, and so on.
- `%ENV` is an associative array that contains the environment variables. You can access this array by using the environment-variable name as a key. To access each element in the array, change the percent sign to a dollar sign and enclose the key in parentheses. For example, `$ENV{HOME}` is the home directory, and `$ENV{PATH}` is the current search path that the shell uses to locate commands.
- `$_` is the default argument for many functions. If you see a Perl function used without any argument, the function probably is expecting its argument in the `$_` variable.
- `@_` is the list of arguments passed to a subroutine.
- `$0` is the name of the file containing the Perl program.
- `$]` is the version number of Perl you are using (for example, if you use Perl Version 5.8.6, `$]` will be `5.008006`).
- `$<` is the user ID (an identifying number) of the user running the script. This is useful on UNIX and Linux, where each user has an ID.
- `$$` is the script's process ID.
- `$?` is the status the last system call has returned.

Using Operators and Expressions

Operators are used to combine and compare Perl variables. Typical mathematical operators are addition (+), subtraction (-), multiplication (*), and division (/). Perl and C provide nearly the same set of operators. When you use operators to combine variables, you end up with expressions. Each expression has a value.

Following are some typical Perl expressions:

```
error < 0
$count == 10
$count + $i
$users[$i]
```

These expressions are examples of the comparison operator (the first two lines), the arithmetic operator, and the array-index operator.

In Perl, don't use the == operator to determine whether two strings match; the == operator works only with numbers. To test the equality of strings, Perl includes the FORTRAN-style eq operator. Use eq to see whether two strings are identical, as follows:

```
if ($input eq "stop") { exit; }
```

Other FORTRAN-style, string-comparison operators include ne (inequality), lt (less than), gt (greater than), le (less than or equal), and ge (greater than or equal). Also, you can use the cmp operator to compare two strings. The return value is -1, 0, or 1, depending on whether the first string is less than, equal to, or greater than the second string.

Perl also provides another unique operator. C lacks an exponentiation operator, which FORTRAN includes; Perl uses ** as the exponentiation operator. Thus, you can enter the following:

```
$x = 2;
$y = 3;
$z = $x**$y;  # z should be 8 (2 raised to the power 3)
$y **= 2;     # y is now 9 (3 raised to the power 2)
```

You can initialize an array to null by using ()—the null-list operator—as follows:

```
@commands = ();
```

The dot operator (.) enables you to concatenate two strings, as follows:

```
$part1 = "Hello, ";
$part2 = "World!";
$message = $part1.$part2;  # Now $message = "Hello, World!"
```

The repetition operator, denoted by x=, is curious but useful. You can use the x= operator to repeat a string a specified number of times. Suppose that you want to initialize a string to 65 asterisks (*). The following example shows how you can initialize the string with the x= operator:

```
$marker = "*";
$marker x= 65;  # Now $marker is a string of 65 asterisks.
```

Another powerful operator in Perl is range, which is represented by two periods (..). You can initialize an array easily by using the range operator. Following are some examples:

```
@numerals = (0..9); # @numerals = 0, 1, 2, 3, 4, 5, 6, 7, 8, 9
@alphabet = ('A'..'Z'); # @alphabet = capital letters A through Z
```

Learning Regular Expressions

If you have used Linux (or any variant of UNIX) for a while, you probably know about the `grep` command, which enables you to search files for a pattern of strings. Following is a typical use of `grep` to locate all files that have any occurrences of the string `Linux` or `linux`—on any line of all files with names that end in `.h`:

```
cd /usr/include
grep "[Ll]inux"  *.h | more
```

Here are some lines of output that the preceding commands produce on my system:

```
apm.h:#include <linux/apm_bios.h>
bfd.h:/* Linux shared library support routines for the linker.  */
bfd.h:extern bfd_boolean bfd_i386linux_size_dynamic_sections
bfd.h:extern bfd_boolean bfd_m68klinux_size_dynamic_sections
bfd.h:extern bfd_boolean bfd_sparclinux_size_dynamic_sections
bfdlink.h:     wrap_hash.  Used by PowerPC Linux for 'dot' symbols.  */
elf.h:#define ELFOSABI_LINUX          3       /* Linux.  */
expat.h:/* Expat follows the GNU/Linux convention of odd number minor version fo
r
gpm.h: * Copyright 1994,1995   rubini@linux.it (Alessandro Rubini)
idn-int.h:/* generated using gnu compiler i386-redhat-linux-gcc (GCC) 4.0.0 2005
0314 (Red Hat 4.0.0-0.34) */
iwlib.h:#include <linux/version.h>
iwlib.h:#include <linux/if_arp.h>       /* For ARPHRD_ETHER */
iwlib.h:#include <linux/socket.h>       /* For AF_INET & struct sockaddr */
```

As you can see, `grep` has found all occurrences of `Linux` and `linux` in the files with names ending in `.h`.

The `grep` command's `"[Ll]inux"` argument is known as a *regular expression*, a pattern that matches a set of strings. You construct a regular expression with a small set of operators and rules that resemble the ones for writing arithmetic expressions. A list of characters inside brackets (`[...]`), for example, matches any single character in the list. Thus, the regular expression `"[Ll]inux"` is a set of two strings, as follows:

```
Linux   linux
```

Perl supports regular expressions, just as the `grep` command does. Many other UNIX programs, such as the vi editor and sed (the stream editor), also support regular expressions. The purpose of a regular expression is to search for a pattern of strings in a file. That's why editors support regular expressions.

Perl enables you to construct complex regular expressions. The rules, however, are fairly simple. Essentially, the regular expression is a sequence of characters in which some characters have special meaning. Table 24-2 describes the basic rules for interpreting the characters.

continues

continued

If you want to match one of the characters $, |, *, ^, [,], \, and /, you have to place a backslash before them. Thus, you type these characters as \$, \|, *, \^, \[, \], \\, and \/. Regular expressions often look confusing because of the preponderance of strange character sequences and the generous sprinkling of backslashes. As with anything else, however, you can start slowly and use only a few of the features in the beginning.

Table 24-2: Rules for Interpreting Regular Expression Characters

Expression	*Meaning*
.	Matches any single character except a newline
x*	Matches zero or more occurrences of the character x
x+	Matches one or more occurrences of the character x
x?	Matches zero or one occurrence of the character x
[...]	Matches any of the characters inside the brackets
x{n}	Matches exactly n occurrences of the character x
x{n,}	Matches n or more occurrences of the character x
x{,m}	Matches zero or, at most, m occurrences of the character x
x{n,m}	Matches at least n occurrences, but no more than m occurrences of the character x
$	Matches the end of a line
\0	Matches a null character
\b	Matches a backspace
\B	Matches any character not at the beginning or end of a word
\b	Matches the beginning or end of a word—when not inside brackets
\cX	Matches Ctrl-X (where X is any alphabetic character)
\d	Matches a single digit
\D	Matches a nondigit character
\f	Matches a form feed
\n	Matches a newline (line-feed) character
\ooo	Matches the octal value specified by the digits ooo (where each o is a digit between 0 and 7)
\r	Matches a carriage return
\S	Matches a non–white space character
\s	Matches a white space character (space, tab, or newline)
\t	Matches a tab
\W	Matches a nonalphanumeric character

Expression	Meaning
\w	Matches an alphanumeric character
\x*hh*	Matches the hexadecimal value specified by the digits *hh* (where each *h* is a digit between 0 and f)
^	Matches the beginning of a line

So far, this section has summarized the syntax of regular expressions. But, you have not seen how to use regular expressions in Perl. Typically, you place a regular expression within a pair of slashes and use the match (=~)or not-match (!~) operators to test a string. You can write a Perl script that performs the same search as the one done with grep earlier in this section. The following steps help you complete this exercise:

1. Use a text editor to type and save the following script in a file named lookup:

```
#!/usr/bin/perl

while (<STDIN>)
{
    if ( $_ =~ /[Ll]inux/ ) { print $_; }
}
```

2. Make the lookup file executable by using the following command:

```
chmod +x lookup
```

3. Try the script by using the following command:

```
cat /usr/include/*.h | ./lookup
```

My system responds with this:

```
#include <linux/apm_bios.h>
/* Linux shared library support routines for the linker.  */
extern bfd_boolean bfd_i386linux_size_dynamic_sections
extern bfd_boolean bfd_m68klinux_size_dynamic_sections
extern bfd_boolean bfd_sparclinux_size_dynamic_sections
     wrap_hash.  Used by PowerPC Linux for 'dot' symbols.  */
#define ELFOSABI_LINUX        3       /* Linux.  */
/* Expat follows the GNU/Linux convention of odd number minor version
for
 * Copyright 1994,1995   rubini@linux.it (Alessandro Rubini)
/* generated using gnu compiler i386-redhat-linux-gcc (GCC) 4.0.0
20050314 (Red
Hat 4.0.0-0.34) */
#include <linux/version.h>
#include <linux/if_arp.h>       /* For ARPHRD_ETHER */
#include <linux/socket.h>       /* For AF_INET & struct sockaddr */
```

The cat command feeds the contents of a specific file (which, as you know from the grep example, contains some lines with the regular expression) to the lookup script. The script simply applies Perl's regular expression-match operator (=~) and prints any matching line.

The $_ variable in the script needs some explanation. The <STDIN> expression gets a line from the standard input and, by default, stores that line in the $_ variable. Inside the while loop, the regular expression is matched against the $_ string. The following single Perl statement completes the lookup script's work:

```
if ( $_ =~ /[Ll]inux/ ) { print $_; }
```

This example illustrates how you might use a regular expression to search for occurrences of strings in a file.

After you use regular expressions for a while, you can better appreciate their power. The trick is to find the regular expression that performs the task you want. Following is a search that looks for all lines that begin with exactly seven spaces and end with a right parenthesis:

```
while (<STDIN>)
{
    if ( $_ =~ /\)\n/ && $_ =~ /^ {7}\S/ )  { print $_; }
}
```

Using Flow-Control Statements

So far, you have seen Perl statements intended to execute in a serial fashion, one after another. Perl also includes statements that enable you to control the flow of execution of the statements. You already have seen the if statement and a while loop. Perl includes a complete set of flow-control statements just like those in C, but with a few extra features.

In Perl, all conditional statements take the following form:

```
conditional-statement
{ Perl code to execute if conditional is true }
```

Notice that you must enclose within braces ({...}) the code that follows the conditional statement. The conditional statement checks the value of an expression to determine whether to execute the code within the braces. In Perl, as in C, any nonzero value is considered true, whereas a zero value is false.

The following sections briefly describe the syntax of the major conditional statements in Perl.

Using if and unless Statements

The Perl if statement resembles the C if statement. For example, an if statement might check a count to see whether the count exceeds a threshold, as follows:

```
if ( $count > 25 ) { print "Too many errors!\n"; }
```

You can add an else clause to the if statement, as follows:

```
if ($user eq "root")
{
    print "Starting simulation...\n";
}
else
{
    print "Sorry $user, you must be \"root\" to run this program.\n.";
    exit;
}
```

If you know C, you can see that Perl's syntax looks quite a bit like that in C. Conditionals with the `if` statement can have zero or more `elsif` clauses to account for more alternatives, such as the following:

```
print "Enter version number:"; # prompt user for version number
$os_version = <STDIN>;          # read from standard input
chop $os_version;  # get rid of the newline at the end of the line
# Check version number
if ($os_version >= 10 ) { print "No upgrade necessary\n";}
elsif ($os_version >= 6 && $os_version < 9)
                                     { print "Standard upgrade\n";}
elsif ($os_version > 3 && $os_version < 6) { print "Reinstall\n";}
else { print "Sorry, cannot upgrade\n";}
```

The `unless` statement is unique to Perl. This statement has the same form as `if`, including the use of `elsif` and `else` clauses. The difference is that `unless` executes its statement block only if the condition is false. You can, for example, use the following:

```
unless ($user eq "root")
{
    print "You must be \"root\" to run this program.\n";
    exit;
}
```

In this case, unless the string user is `"root"`, the script exits.

Using the while Statement

Use Perl's `while` statement for *looping*, the repetition of some processing until a condition becomes false. To read a line at a time from standard input and to process that line, you might use the following:

```
while ($in = <STDIN>)
{
# Code to process the line
    print $in;
}
```

If you read from the standard input without any argument, Perl assigns the current line of standard input to the `$_` variable. Thus, you can write the `while` loop to read lines from the standard input, as follows:

```
while (<STDIN>)
{
# Code to process the line
    print $_;
}
```

continues

continued

Perl's `while` statements are more versatile than those of C because you can use almost anything as the condition to be tested. If you use an array as the condition, for example, the `while` loop executes until the array has no elements left, as in the following example:

```
# Assume @arglist has the current set of command arguments
while (@arglist)
{
    $arg = shift @arglist;  # this extracts one argument
# Code to process the current argument
    print $arg;
}
```

The `shift` function removes the first element of an array and returns that element.

You can skip to the end of a loop with the `next` keyword; the `last` keyword exits the loop. The following `while` loop adds the numbers from 1 to 10, skipping 5:

```
while (1)
{
    $i++;
    if($i == 5) { next;}  # Jump to the next iteration if $i is 5
    if($i > 10) { last;}  # When $i exceeds 10, end the loop
    $sum += $i;           # Add the numbers
}
# At this point $sum should be 50.
```

Using for and foreach Statements

Perl and C's `for` statements have similar syntax. Use the `for` statement to execute a statement any number of times, based on the value of an expression. The syntax of the `for` statement is as follows:

```
for (expr_1; expr_2; expr_3) { statement block }
```

`expr_1` is evaluated one time, at the beginning of the loop; the statement block is executed until expression `expr_2` evaluates to zero. The third expression, `expr_3`, is evaluated after each execution of the statement block. You can omit any of the expressions, but you must include the semicolons. In addition, the braces around the statement block are required. Following is an example that uses a `for` loop to add the numbers from 1 to 10:

```
for($i=0, $sum=0; $i <= 10; $sum += $i, $i++) {}
```

In this example, the actual work of adding the numbers is done in the third expression, and the statement the `for` loop controls is an empty block (`{}`).

The `foreach` statement is most appropriate for processing arrays. Following is the syntax of the `foreach` statement:

```
foreach Variable (Array) { statement block }
```

The `foreach` statement assigns to `Variable` an element from the `Array` and executes the statement block. The `foreach` statement repeats this procedure until no array elements remain. The following `foreach` statement adds the numbers from 1 to 10:

```
foreach $i (1..10) { $sum += $i;}
```

Notice that I declare the array with the range operator (`..`). You also can use a list of comma-separated items as the array.

If you omit the `Variable` in a `foreach` statement, Perl automatically uses the `$_` variable to hold the current array element. Thus, you can use the following:

```
foreach (1..10) { $sum += $_;}
```

Using the goto Statement

The `goto` statement transfers control to a statement label. Following is an example that prompts the user for a value and repeats the request, if the value is not acceptable:

```
ReEnter:
print "Enter offset: ";
$offset = <STDIN>;
chop $offset;
unless ($offset > 0 && $offset < 512)
{
    print "Bad offset: $offset\n";
    goto ReEnter;
}
```

Accessing Linux Commands

You can execute any Linux command from Perl in several ways:

- Call the `system` function with a string that contains the Linux command you want to execute.
- Enclose a Linux command within backquotes (`` `command` ``), which also are known as grave accents. You can run a Linux command this way and capture its output.
- Call the `fork` function to copy the current script and process new commands in the child process. (If a process starts another process, the new one is known as a child process.)
- Call the `exec` function to overlay the current script with a new script or Linux command.
- Use `fork` and `exec` to provide shell-like behavior. (Monitor user input, and process each user-entered command through a child process.) This section presents a simple example of how to accomplish this task.

The simplest way to execute a Linux command in your script is to use the `system` function with the command in a string. After the system function returns, the exit code from the command is in the `$?` variable. You can easily write a simple Perl script that reads a string from the standard input and processes that string with the `system` function. Follow these steps:

1. Use a text editor to enter and save the following script in a file named `rcmd.pl`:

```
#!/usr/bin/perl
# Read user input and process command

$prompt = "Command (\"exit\" to quit): ";
print $prompt;

while (<STDIN>)
{
    chop;
    if ($_ eq "exit") { exit 0;}

# Execute command by calling system
    system $_;
    unless ($? == 0) {print "Error executing: $_\n";}
    print $prompt;
}
```

2. Make the `rcmd.pl` file executable by using the following command:

```
chmod +x rcmd.pl
```

3. Run the script by typing `./rcmd.pl` at the shell prompt in a terminal window. The following listing shows some sample output from the `rcmd.pl` script (the output depends on what commands you enter):

```
Command ("exit" to quit): ps
  PID TTY          TIME CMD
 3575 pts/2    00:00:00 bash
 3629 pts/2    00:00:00 vsftpd
 2075 pts/2    00:00:00 rcmd.pl
 2076 pts/2    00:00:00 ps
Command ("exit" to quit): exit
```

Also, you can run Linux commands by using `fork` and `exec` in your Perl script. Following is an example script—`psh.pl`—that uses `fork` and `exec` to execute commands the user enters:

```
#!/usr/bin/perl

# This is a simple script that uses "fork" and "exec" to
# run a command entered by the user

$prompt = "Command (\"exit\" to quit): ";
print $prompt;

while (<STDIN>)
{
```

```
    chop;     # remove trailing newline
    if($_ eq "exit") { exit 0;}

    $status = fork;
    if($status)
    {
# In parent... wait for child process to finish...
        wait;
        print $prompt;
        next;
    }
    else
    {
        exec $_;
    }
}
```

Type **chmod +x psh.pl** to make the script executable and then type **./psh.pl** to run the script. The following example shows how the `psh.pl` script executes the `ps` command:

```
Command ("exit" to quit): ps
  PID TTY          TIME CMD
 3575 pts/2    00:00:00 bash
 3629 pts/2    00:00:00 vsftpd
 2079 pts/2    00:00:00 psh.pl
 2080 pts/2    00:00:00 ps
Command ("exit" to quit): exit
```

Linux shells, such as Bash, use the `fork` and `exec` combination to run commands.

Working with Files

You may have noticed the `<STDIN>` expression in various examples in this chapter. That's Perl's way of reading from a file. In Perl, a file handle, also known as an identifier, identifies a file. Usually, file handles are in uppercase characters. `STDIN` is a predefined file handle that denotes the standard input — by default, the keyboard. `STDOUT` and `STDERR` are the other two predefined file handles. `STDOUT` is used for printing to the terminal, and `STDERR` is used for printing error messages.

To read from a file, write the file handle inside angle brackets (<>). Thus, `<STDIN>` reads a line from the standard input.

You can open other files by using the `open` function. The following example shows you how to open the `/etc/passwd` file for reading and how to display the lines in that file:

```
open (PWDFILE, "/etc/passwd");  # PWDFILE is the file handle
while (<PWDFILE>) { print $_;}  # By default, input line is in $_
close PWDFILE;                  # Close the file
```

By default, the `open` function opens a file for reading. You can add special characters at the beginning of the filename to indicate other types of access. A > prefix opens the file for writing, whereas a >> prefix opens a file for appending. Following is a short script that reads the `/etc/passwd` file and creates a new file, named `output`, with a list of all users who lack shells (the password entries for these users have `:` at the end of each line):

```
#!/usr/bin/perl
# Read /etc/passwd and create list of users without any shell

open (PWDFILE, "/etc/passwd");
open (RESULT, ">output");                    # open file for writing

while (<PWDFILE>)
{
    if ($_ =~ /:\n/) {print RESULT $_;}
}

close PWDFILE;
close RESULT;
```

After you execute this script, you should find a file named `output` in the current directory. Following is what the `output` file contains when I run this script on a Linux system:

```
news:x:9:13:news:/etc/news:
```

One interesting filename prefix is the pipe character — the vertical bar (|). If you call `open` with a filename that begins with |, the rest of the filename is treated as a command. The Perl interpreter executes the command, and you can use `print` calls to send input to this command. The following Perl script sends a mail message to a list of users:

```
#!/usr/bin/perl
# Send mail to a list of users.

foreach ("root", "naba")
{
    open (MAILPIPE, "| mail -s
 Greetings $_");
    print MAILPIPE "Remember to
send in your weekly report
today!\n";
    close MAILPIPE;
}
```

If a filename ends with a pipe character (|), that filename is executed as a command; you can read that command's output with the angle brackets (<. . .>) as shown in the following example:

```
open (PSPIPE, "ps ax |");
while (<PSPIPE>)
{
# Process the output of the ps command here.
# This example simply echoes each line.
    print $_;
}
```

Writing Perl Subroutines

Although Perl includes a large assortment of built-in functions, you can add your own code modules in the form of subroutines. In fact, the Perl distribution comes with a large set of subroutines. Following is a simple script that illustrates the syntax of subroutines in Perl:

```
#!/usr/bin/perl
sub hello
{
# Make local copies of the arguments from the @_ array.
    local ($first,$last) = @_;

    print "Hello, $first $last\n";
}

$a = Jane;
$b = Doe;

&hello($a, $b);     # Call the subroutine.
```

When you run the preceding script, it displays the following output:

```
Hello, Jane Doe
```

Note the following points about subroutines:

- The subroutine receives its arguments in the array @_ (the at symbol, followed by an underscore character).
- Variables used in subroutines are global by default. Use the `local` function to create a local set of variables.
- Call a subroutine by placing an ampersand (&) before its name. Thus, subroutine `hello` is called by typing `&hello`.

If you want, you can put a subroutine in its own file. The hello subroutine, for example, can reside in a file named `hello.pl`. When you place a subroutine in a file, remember to add a return value at the end of the file—just type **1**; at the end to return 1. Thus, the `hello.pl` file appears as follows:

```
sub hello
{
# Make local copies of the arguments from the @_ array.
    local ($first,$last) = @_;

    print "Hello, $first $last\n";
}
1;     # return value
```

continues

continued

Then, you can write a script that uses the hello subroutine, as follows:

```
#!/usr/bin/perl
require 'hello.pl';   # Include the file with the subroutine.
$a = Jane;
$b = Doe;
&hello($a, $b);     # Call the subroutine.
```

This script uses the `require` function to include the `hello.pl` file that contains the definition of the `hello` subroutine.

Taking Stock of the Built-in Functions in Perl

Perl has nearly 200 built-in functions (also referred to as Perl functions), including functions that resemble the ones in the C Run-Time Library, as well as functions that access the operating system. You really need to go through the list of functions to appreciate the breadth of capabilities available in Perl. Table 24-3 briefly describes each of the Perl functions.

insider insight

This chapter does not have enough space to cover these functions, but you can learn about the Perl functions by pointing your Web browser to the following address:

```
http://perldoc.perl.org/index-functions.html
```

This address connects you to the Perl Functions page at the Perl 5.8.6 documentation site. On that page, click a function's name to view more detailed information about that function.

Table 24-3: A Quick Reference Guide to Perl Functions

Function Call	*Description*
`abs(VALUE)`	Returns the absolute value of the argument
`accept(NEWSOCKET, GENERICSOCKET)`	Waits for a connection on a socket
`alarm(SECONDS)`	Sends an alarm signal after a specified number of seconds
`atan2(Y,X)`	Returns the arctangent of Y/X
`bind(SOCKET,NAME)`	Associates a name to an already opened socket
`binmode(FILEHANDLE)`	Arranges for a file to be treated as binary
`bless(REF,PACKAGE)`	Makes a referenced item an object in a package
`caller(EXPR)`	Returns information about current subroutine calls
`chdir(EXPR)`	Changes the directory to the directory specified by EXPR

Function Call	*Description*
`chmod(LIST)`	Changes the permissions of a list of files
`chomp(VARIABLE)`	Removes trailing characters that match the current value of the special variable `$/`
`chop(VARIABLE)`	Chops off the last character (useful for removing the trailing newline character in a string)
`chown(LIST)`	Changes the owner of a list of files
`chr(NUMBER)`	Returns the character whose ASCII code is NUMBER
`chroot(FILENAME)`	Changes the root directory to the specified FILENAME
`close(FILEHANDLE)`	Closes the specified file
`closedir(DIRHANDLE)`	Closes the directory that had been opened by `opendir`
`connect(SOCKET,NAME)`	Initiates a connection to another system using a socket
`cos(EXPR)`	Returns the cosine of the angle EXPR (radians)
`crypt(PLAINTEXT, SALT)`	Encrypts a string
`dbmclose(ASSOC_ARRAY)`	Disassociates an associative array from a DBM file. (DBM, or data base manager, is a library of routines that manages *DBM files*, data files that contain key/data pairs.)
`dbmopen(ASSOC, DBNAME,`	Associates an associative array with a DBM file `MODE)`
`defined(EXPR)`	Returns `true` if EXPR is defined
`delete $ASSOC{KEY}`	Deletes a value from an associative array
`die(LIST)`	Prints LIST to standard error and exits the Perl program
`do SUBROUTINE (LIST)`	Calls a subroutine
`dump(LABEL)`	Causes a core dump
`each(ASSOC_ARRAY)`	Returns the next key-value pair of an associative array
`endgrent`	Closes the `/etc/group` file in UNIX
`endhostent`	Closes the `/etc/hosts` file in UNIX
`endnetent`	Closes the `/etc/networks` file in UNIX
`endprotoent`	Closes the `/etc/protocols` file in UNIX
`endpwent`	Closes the `/etc/passwd` file in UNIX
`endservent`	Closes the `/etc/services` file in UNIX
`eof(FILEHANDLE)`	Returns `true` if end of file is reached
`eval(EXPR)`	Executes the EXPR as if it were a Perl program
`exec(LIST)`	Terminates the current Perl program by running another program (specified by LIST) in its place
`exists($ASSOC($KEY))`	Returns `true` if the specified key exists in the associative array

(continued)

Table 24-3 *(continued)*

Function Call	*Description*
`exit(EXPR)`	Exits the Perl program and returns EXPR
`exp(EXPR)`	Returns *e* raised to the power EXPR
`fcntl(FILEHANDLE, FUNCTION, SCALAR)`	Performs various control operations on a file
`fileno(FILEHANDLE)`	Returns the file descriptor for a file handle
`flock(FILEHANDLE, OPERATION)`	Locks a file so other processes cannot change the file (useful when multiple processes need to access a single file)
`fork`	Creates a child process and returns the child process ID
`format NAME = picture line value list`	Defines an output format to be used by the write function
`formline(PICTURE, LIST)`	Formats a list of values according to the contents of PICTURE
`getc(FILEHANDLE)`	Reads the next character from the file
`getgrent`	Returns group information from `/etc/group`
`getgrgid(GID)`	Looks up a group file entry by group number
`getgrnam(NAME)`	Looks up a group file entry by group name
`gethostbyaddr(ADDR, ADDRTYPE)`	Translates a network address to a name
`gethostbyname(NAME)`	Translates a network host name to corresponding addresses
`gethostent`	Gets entries from the `/etc/hosts` file on UNIX
`getlogin`	Returns current login information in UNIX
`getnetbyaddr(ADDR, ADDRTYPE)`	Translates a network address to its corresponding network name
`getnetbyname(NAME)`	Translates a network name to its corresponding network address
`getnetent`	Gets entries from the `/etc/networks` file (or equivalent on non-UNIX systems)
`getpeername(SOCKET)`	Returns the socket address of the other end of a socket connection
`getpgrp(PID)`	Returns the current process group for the specified process ID
`getppid`	Returns the process ID of the parent process
`getpriority(WHICH, WHO)`	Returns the current priority of a process
`getprotobyname(NAME)`	Translates a protocol name into a number
`getprotobynumber(NUMBER)`	Translates a protocol number into a name
`getprotoent`	Gets networking protocol information from the `/etc/networks` file in UNIX

Function Call	Description
getpwent	Gets entry from the password file (/etc/passwd in UNIX)
getpwnam(NAME)	Translates a user name into the corresponding entry in the password file
getpwuid(UID)	Translates a numeric user ID into the corresponding entry in the password file
getservbyname(NAME, PROTO)	Translates a service (port) name into the corresponding port number
getservbyport(PORT, PROTO)	Translates the service (port) number into a name
getservent	Gets entries from the /etc/services file in UNIX
getsockname(SOCKET)	Returns the address of this end of a socket connection
getsockopt(SOCKET, LEVEL, OPTNAME)	Returns the requested socket options
glob(EXPR)	Returns filenames corresponding to a wildcard expression
gmtime(EXPR)	Converts binary time into a nine-element list corresponding to Greenwich Mean Time (GMT)
goto(LABEL)	Jumps to the statement identified by the LABEL
grep(EXPR, LIST)	Searches LIST for occurrences of the expression
hex(EXPR)	Returns the decimal value corresponding to hexadecimal EXPR
index(STR, SUBSTR, POSITION)	Returns the position of the first occurrence of a string (the search begins at the character location specified by POSITION)
int(EXPR)	Returns the integer portion of EXPR
ioctl(FILEHANDLE, FUNCTION, SCALAR)	Controls various aspects of FILEHANDLE
join(EXPR, LIST)	Returns a single string by joining list elements
keys(ASSOC_ARRAY)	Returns an array of keys for an associative array
kill(LIST)	Sends a signal to a list of processes
last(LABEL)	Exits the loop identified by LABEL
lc(EXPR)	Returns the lowercase version of EXPR
lcfirst(EXPR)	Returns EXPR, after changing the first character to lowercase
length(EXPR)	Returns length in number of characters
link(OLDFILE, NEWFILE)	Creates NEWFILE as a link to OLDFILE
listen(SOCKET, QUEUESIZE)	Waits for incoming connections on a socket
local(LIST)	Makes a list of variables local to a subroutine

(continued)

Table 24-3 *(continued)*

Function Call	*Description*
`localtime(EXPR)`	Converts binary time into a nine-element list corresponding to local time
`lock SHAREDVAR`	Locks a shared variable
`log(EXPR)`	Returns the logarithm (to base *e*) of EXPR
`lstat(FILEHANDLE)`	Returns file statistics for a file (if the file refers to a symbolic link, returns information about the symbolic link)
`m/PATTERN/gimosx`	Performs pattern matching
`map(EXPR, LIST)`	Evaluates the expression EXPR for each item of LIST
`mkdir(FILENAME, MODE)`	Creates the directory specified by FILENAME
`msgctl(ID, CMD, ARG)`	Performs message control operations on message queues
`msgget(KEY, FLAGS)`	Gets a message queue identifier corresponding to KEY
`msgrcv(ID, VAR, SIZE, TYPE, FLAGS)`	Receives a message from the message queue identifier ID
`msgsnd(ID, MSG, FLAGS)`	Sends a message-to-message queue identifier ID
`my(EXPR)`	Declares one or more private variables that exist in a subroutine or a block enclosed in curly braces (`{...}`)
`next(LABEL)`	Starts the next iteration of the loop identified by LABEL
`no(Module LIST)`	Stops using a Perl module
`oct(EXPR)`	Returns the decimal equivalent of an octal number in EXPR
`open(FILEHANDLE, EXPR)`	Opens a file whose name is in EXPR, and associates that file with FILEHANDLE
`opendir(DIRHANDLE, EXPR)`	Opens a directory whose name is in EXPR, and associates that directory with DIRHANDLE
`ord(EXPR)`	Returns the numeric ASCII code of the first character in EXPR
`our EXPR`	Declares the listed variables in EXPR as valid global variables within the enclosing block (similar to `my`, but does not create any local variables)
`pack(TEMPLATE, LIST)`	Takes a list of values and returns a string containing a packed binary structure (TEMPLATE specifies the packing)
`package PACKAGENAME`	Declares the current file to be part of the specified package
`pipe(READHANDLE, WRITEHANDLE)`	Opens a pipe for reading and writing
`pop(ARRAY)`	Removes and returns the last element of an array
`pos(SCALAR)`	Returns the position where the last pattern match occurred (applies when a global search is performed with `/PATTERN/g`)

Function Call	*Description*
`print(FILEHANDLE LIST)`	Prints a list of items to a file identified by FILEHANDLE
`printf(FILEHANDLE LIST)`	Prints formatted output to a file
`prototype FUNCTION`	Returns the prototype of a function as a string (the *prototype* shows the declaration of the function, including its arguments)
`push(ARRAY, LIST)`	Appends values in LIST to the end of ARRAY
`q/STRING/`	Quotes a STRING, without replacing variable names with values (similar to a single quoted string)
`qq/STRING/`	Quotes a STRING, but replaces variable names with values (similar to a double-quoted string)
`quotemeta(EXPR)`	Returns the value of EXPR, after adding a backslash prefix for all characters that take on special meaning in regular expressions
`qw/STRING/`	Quotes a word list (similar to parentheses used in patterns)
`qx/STRING/`	Quotes a command (similar to backquotes)
`rand(EXPR)`	Returns a random value between 0 and EXPR
`read(FILEHANDLE, SCALAR, LENGTH)`	Reads a specified number of bytes from the file
`readdir(DIRHANDLE)`	Reads directory entries from a directory handle
`readlink(EXPR)`	Returns the filename pointed to by a symbolic link
`readpipe(EXPR)`	Returns the output after executing EXPR as a system command
`recv(SOCKET, SCALAR, LEN, FLAGS)`	Receives a message from a socket
`redo(LABEL)`	Restarts the loop identified by LABEL
`ref(EXPR)`	Returns `true` if EXPR is a reference (a reference points to an object)
`rename(OLDNAME, NEWNAME)`	Changes the name of a file from OLDNAME to NEWNAME
`require(FNAME)`	Includes the file specified by FNAME, and executes the Perl code in that file
`reset(EXPR)`	Clears global variables
`return(LIST)`	Returns from subroutine with the specified values
`reverse(LIST)`	Reverses the order of elements in LIST
`rewinddir(DIRHANDLE)`	Sets the current position to the beginning of the directory identified by DIRHANDLE
`rindex(STR, SUBSTR)`	Returns the last position of a substring in a string
`rindex(STR, SUBSTR, POSITION)`	Returns the position of the last occurrence of a substring in a string

(continued)

Table 24-3 *(continued)*

Function Call	***Description***
`rmdir(FILENAME)`	Deletes the directory specified by FILENAME
`s/PATTERN/REPLACEMENT/ egimosx`	Replaces PATTERN (a regular expression) with REPLACEMENT
`scalar(EXPR)`	Evaluates the expression EXPR in a scalar context
`seek(FILEHANDLE, POSITION, WHENCE)`	Moves to a new location in a file
`seekdir(DIRHANDLE, POS)`	Moves to a new position in a directory
`select(FILEHANDLE)`	Returns the currently selected file handle, and sets FILEHANDLE as the default file handle for output
`select(RBITS, WBITS, EBITS, TIMEOUT)`	Checks if one or more files are ready for input or output
`semctl(ID, SEMNUM, CMD, ARG)`	Controls the semaphores used for interprocess communication
`semget(KEY, NSEMS, FLAGS)`	Returns the semaphore ID corresponding to a key
`semop(KEY, OPSTRING)`	Performs a semaphore operation (semaphores are used for interprocess communications in UNIX System V)
`send(SOCKET, MSG, FLAGS, TO)`	Sends a message to a socket
`setgrent`	Sets group information in `/etc/group`
`sethostent(STAYOPEN)`	Opens the host database (the `/etc/hosts` file in UNIX)
`setnetent(STAYOPEN)`	Opens the network database (the `/etc/networks` file in UNIX)
`setpgrp(PID,PGRP)`	Sets the current process group of a process
`setpriority(WHICH, WHO, PRIORITY)`	Sets the priority for a process
`setprotoent(STAYOPEN)`	Opens the protocol database (the `/etc/protocols` file in UNIX)
`setpwent`	Opens the `/etc/passwd` file in UNIX
`setservent(STAYOPEN)`	Opens the `/etc/services` file in UNIX
`setsockopt(SOCKET, LEVEL, OPTNAME, OPTVAL)`	Sets the specified socket options
`shift(ARRAY)`	Removes the first value of the array and returns it
`shmctl(ID, CMD, ARG)`	Controls shared memory settings, such as permissions
`shmget(KEY, SIZE, FLAGS)`	Allocates a shared memory segment
`shmread(ID, VAR, POS, SIZE)`	Reads from the shared memory segment identified by ID
`shmwrite(ID, STRING, POS, SIZE)`	Writes to the shared memory segment identified by ID

Function Call	Description
shutdown(SOCKET, HOW)	Shuts down a socket connection
sin(EXPR)	Returns the sine of the angle specified by EXPR (in radians)
sleep(EXPR)	Sleeps for EXPR seconds
socket(SOCKET, DOMAIN, TYPE, PROTOCOL)	Opens a socket for a specified type and attaches it to the file handle SOCKET
socketpair(SOCKET1, SOCKET2, DOMAIN, TYPE, PROTOCOL)	Creates an unnamed pair of sockets
sort(LIST)	Sorts a list and returns the sorted list in an array
splice(ARRAY, OFFSET, LENGTH, LIST)	Replaces some ARRAY elements with LIST
split(/PATTERN/, EXPR, LIMIT)	Splits EXPR into an array of strings
sprintf(FORMAT, LIST)	Returns a string containing formatted output consisting of LIST elements formatted according to the FORMAT string
sqrt(EXPR)	Returns the square root of EXPR
srand(EXPR)	Sets the seed for random number generation
stat(FILEHANDLE)	Returns a 13-element list with statistics for a file
study(STRING)	Examines STRING in anticipation of doing many pattern matches on the string
substr(EXPR, OFFSET, LEN)	Returns a substring from the string EXPR
symlink(OLDFILE, NEWFILE)	Creates NEWFILE as a symbolic link to OLDFILE
syscall(LIST)	Calls the system function specified in the first element of LIST (and passes to that call the remaining list elements as arguments)
sysopen(FILEHANDLE, FILENAME, MODE, PERMS)	Opens a file named FILENAME and associates it with FILEHANDLE
sysread(FILEHANDLE, SCALAR, LENGTH, OFFSET)	Reads a specified number of bytes from a file
sysseek(FILEHANDLE, POSITION, WHENCE)	Sets FILEHANDLE's position to the specified POSITION in bytes (WHENCE refers to the reference point for setting the position and it can be one of SEEK_SET, SEEK_CUR, and SEEK_END)
system(LIST)	Executes the shell commands in LIST
syswrite(FILEHANDLE, SCALAR, LENGTH, OFFSET)	Writes a specified number of bytes to a file
tell(FILEHANDLE)	Returns the current file position in bytes from the beginning of a file

(continued)

Table 24-3 *(continued)*

Function Call	*Description*
`telldir(DIRHANDLE)`	Returns the current position where the `readdir` function can read from a directory handle
`tie(VARIABLE, PACKAGENAME, LIST)`	Associates a variable to a package that implements the variable
`time`	Returns the number of seconds since 00:00:00 GMT 1/1/1970
`times`	Returns time in seconds for this process
`tr/SEARCHLIST/REPLACE_LIST/cds`	Translates a search list into a replacement list
`truncate(FILEHANDLE, LENGTH)`	Truncates the file FILEHANDLE to a specified LENGTH
`uc(EXPR)`	Returns the uppercase version of EXPR
`ucfirst(EXPR)`	Returns EXPR after changing the first character to uppercase
`umask(EXPR)`	Sets the permission mask to be used when creating a file (this specifies what operations are not allowed on the file)
`undef(EXPR)`	Undefines EXPR
`unlink(LIST)`	Deletes a list of files
`unpack(TEMPLATE, EXPR)`	Unpacks a string into an array and returns the array
`unshift(ARRAY, LIST)`	Prepends LIST to the beginning of ARRAY
`untie(VARIABLE)`	Breaks the binding between a variable and a package
`use(MODULE)`	Starts using a Perl module
`utime(LIST)`	Changes the access and modification time of a list of files
`values(ASSOC_ARRAY)`	Returns an array containing all values from an associative array
`vec(EXPR, OFFSET, BITS)`	Treats the string EXPR as a vector of integers, and returns a specified element of the vector
`wait`	Waits for a child process to terminate
`waitpid(PID, FLAGS)`	Waits for a specific child process (identified by PID) to terminate
`wantarray`	Returns if the current subroutine has been called in an array context
`warn(LIST)`	Produces a warning message (specified by LIST) on the standard error
`write(FILEHANDLE)`	Writes a formatted record to a file
`y/SEARCHLIST/REPLACE_LIST/cds`	Translates a search list into a replacement list

Understanding Perl Packages and Modules

A Perl package is a way to group together data and subroutines. Essentially, it's a way to use variable and subroutine names without conflicting with any names used in other parts of a program. The concept of a package has existed in Perl since version 4.

A Perl package provides a way to control the *namespace* — a term that refers to the collection of variable and subroutine names. Although you may not be aware of this, when you write a Perl program, it automatically belongs to a package named main. Besides main, there are other Perl packages in the Perl library (these packages are in the `/usr/lib/perl5` directory of your Linux system, under a subdirectory whose name is the same as the Perl version you are running), and you can define your own package, as well.

Perl modules, as you'll learn soon, are packages that follow specific guidelines.

You can think of a Perl package as a convenient way to organize a set of related Perl subroutines. Another benefit is that variable and subroutine names defined in a package do not conflict with names used elsewhere in the program. Thus, a variable named `$count` in one package remains unique to that package and does not conflict with a `$count` used elsewhere in a Perl program.

A Perl package is in a single file. The package statement is used at the beginning of the file to declare the file as a package and to give the package a name. For example, the file `ctime.pl` defines a number of subroutines and variables in a package named `ctime`. The `ctime.pl` file has the following package statement in various places:

```
package ctime;
```

The effect of this package declaration is that all subsequent variable names and subroutine names are considered to be in the `ctime` package. You can put such a package statement at the beginning of the file that implements the package.

What if you are implementing a package and you need to refer to a subroutine or variable in another package? As you might guess, all you need to do is specify both the package name and the variable (or subroutine) name. Perl 5 provides the following syntax for referring to a variable in another package:

```
$Package::Variable
```

Here `Package` is the name of the package, and `Variable` is the name of the variable in that package. If you omit the package name, Perl assumes you are referring to a variable in the main package. Note that C++ happens to use a similar syntax when referring to variables in another C++ class (a class is basically a collection of data and functions — a template for an object).

To use a package in your program, you can simply call the `require` function with the package filename as an argument. For instance, there is a package named `ctime` defined in the file `ctime.pl`. That package includes the `ctime` subroutine that converts a binary time into a string. The following simple program uses the `ctime` package from the `ctime.pl` file:

```
#!/usr/bin/perl -w

# Use the ctime package defined in ctime.pl file.
require 'ctime.pl';
```

```
# Call the ctime subroutine.
$time = ctime(time());

# Print the time string.
print $time;
```

As you can see, this program uses the `require` function to bring the `ctime.pl` file into the program. When you run this program, it should print the current date and time formatted, as shown in the sample output:

```
Sun May  8 15:30:12 2005
```

Perl 5 takes the concept of a package one step further and introduces the module, a package that follows certain guidelines and is designed to be reusable. Each module is a package that is defined in a file with the same name as the package but with a `.pm` extension. Each Perl object is implemented as a module. For example, the `Shell` object is implemented as the `Shell` module, stored in the file named `Shell.pm`.

Perl 5 comes with a large number of modules. You'll find these modules in the `/usr/lib/perl5` directory under a subdirectory corresponding to your Perl version. For Perl Version 5.8.6, the Perl modules are in the `/usr/lib/perl5/5.8.6` directory (the last part of the pathname is the Perl version number). Look for files with names that end in `.pm` (for Perl module).

Using a Perl Module

You can call the `require` function, or the `use` function, to include a Perl module in your program. For example, a Perl module named `Cwd` (defined, as expected, in the `Cwd.pm` file) provides a `getcwd` subroutine that returns the current directory. You can call the `require` function to include the `Cwd` module and call `getcwd` as follows:

```
require Cwd;  # You do not need the full filename.
$curdir = Cwd::getcwd();
print "Current directory = $curdir\n";
```

The first line brings the `Cwd.pm` file into this program — you do not have to specify the full filename; the `require` function automatically appends `.pm` to the module's name to figure out which file to include. The second line shows how you call a subroutine from the `Cwd` module. When you use `require` to include a module, you must invoke each subroutine with the `Module::subroutine` format.

If you were to rewrite this example program with the `use` function in place of `require`, it would take the following form:

```
use Cwd;
$curdir = getcwd(); # no need for Cwd:: prefix
print "Current directory = $curdir\n";
```

The most significant difference is that you no longer need to qualify a subroutine name with the module name prefix (such as `Cwd::`).

You can call either `require` or `use` to include a module in your program. You need to understand the following nuances when you use these functions:

- When you include a module by calling `require`, the module is included only when the `require` function is invoked as the program runs. You must use the `Module::subroutine` syntax to invoke any subroutines from a module you include with the `require` function.
- When you include a module by calling `use`, the module is included in the program as soon as the use statement is processed. Thus, you can invoke subroutines and variables from the module as if they were part of your program. You do not need to qualify subroutine and variable names with a `Module::` prefix.

You may want to stick to the `use Module;` syntax to include modules in your program because this lets you use a simpler syntax when you call subroutines from the module.

Using Perl Objects

An *object* is a data structure that includes both the data and the functions that operate on that data. Each object is an instance of a class that defines the object's type. For example, a rectangle class may have the four corners of the rectangle as data, and functions such as one that computes the rectangle's area and another that draws the rectangle. Then, each rectangle object can be an instance of the rectangle class, with different coordinates for the four corners. In this sense, an object is an instance of a class.

The functions (or subroutines) that implement the operations on an object's data are known as *methods*. That's terminology borrowed from Smalltalk, one of the earliest object-oriented programming languages.

Classes also suggest the notion of inheritance. You can define a new class of objects by extending the data or methods (or both) of an existing class. A common use of inheritance is to express the *is a* relationship among various classes of objects. Consider, for example, the geometric shapes. Because a circle *is a* shape and a rectangle *is a* shape, you can say that the circle and rectangle classes inherit from the shape class. In this case, the shape class is called a parent class or base class.

The basic idea behind *object-oriented programming* is that you can package the data and the associated methods (subroutines) of an object as a black box. Programmers access the object only through advertised methods, without having to know the inner workings of the methods. Typically, a programmer can create an object, invoke its methods to get or set attributes (that's another name for the object's data), and destroy the object. This section shows you how to use objects in Perl 5. With this knowledge in hand, you'll be able to exploit objects as building blocks for your Perl programs.

Perl 5 implements objects by using modules, which package data and subroutines in a file. Perl 5 presents the following simple model of objects:

continues

continued

- An **object** is denoted by a reference (objects are implemented as references to a hash).
- A **class** is a Perl module that provides the methods to work with the object.
- A **method** is a Perl subroutine that expects the object reference as the first argument.

Object implementers have to follow certain rules and provide certain methods in a module that represents a class. However, you really don't need to know much about an object's implementation to use it in your Perl program. All you need to know are the steps you have to follow when you use an object.

Creating and Using Perl Objects

A useful Perl object is a `Shell` object, which is implemented by the Perl module `Shell.pm`. That module comes with the Perl distribution and is in the `/usr/lib/perl5/5.8.6` directory (for Perl Version 5.8.6).

As the name implies, the `Shell` object is meant for running shell commands from within Perl scripts. You can create a `Shell` object and have it execute commands.

To use the `Shell` object, follow these general steps:

1. Place the following line to include the Shell module in your program:

   ```
   use Shell;
   ```

   You must include this line before you create a `Shell` object.
2. To create a `Shell` object, use the following syntax:

   ```
   my $sh = Shell->new;
   ```

   where `$sh` is the reference to the `Shell` object.
3. Run Linux commands by using the `Shell` object and capture any outputs by saving to an appropriate variable. For example, to save the directory listing of the `/usr/lib/perl5/5.8.6` directory in an array named `@modules`, write the following:

   ```
   @modules = $sh->ls("/usr/lib/perl5/5.8.6/*.pm");
   ```

   Then you can work with this array of Perl module filenames (that's what `*.pm` files are) any way you want. For example, to simply go through the array and print each string out, use the following `while` loop:

   ```
   while(@modules)
   {
     $mod = shift @modules;
     print $mod;
   }
   ```

How do you know which methods of an object to call and in what order to call them? You have to read the object's documentation before you can use the object. The method names and the sequences of method invocation depend on what the object does.

Using the English module

Perl includes several special variables with strange names, such as `$_` for the default argument and `$!` for error messages corresponding to the last error. When you read a program, it can be difficult to guess what a special variable means. The result is that you may end up avoiding a special variable that could be useful in your program.

As a helpful gesture, Perl 5 provides the English module (`English.pm`), which enables you to use understandable names for various special variables in Perl. To use the English module, include the following line in your Perl program:

```
use English;
```

After that, you can refer to `$_` as `$ARG` and `$!` as `$ERRNO` (these "English" names can still be a bit cryptic, but they're definitely better than the punctuation marks).

The following program uses the `English` module and prints a few interesting variables:

```
#!/usr/bin/perl -w
# File: english.pl

use English;
print "Perl executable = $EXECUTABLE_NAME\n";
print "Script name = $PROGRAM_NAME\n";
```

When I run this script, the output appears as follows:

```
Perl executable = /usr/bin/perl
Script name = ./english.pl
```

The `English` module is handy because it lets you write Perl scripts in which you can refer to special variables by meaningful names. To learn more about the Perl special variables and their English names, type **man perlvar** at the shell prompt.

Summary

Scripts or interpreted programs are often used to automate various tasks in Linux. This chapter focused on writing scripts in Bash — the Bourne Again shell — as well as in the scripting language Perl.

In this chapter, you learned the following:

- A shell script is nothing more than a sequence of Linux commands in a file. Typically, you have to place a special line at the beginning of the script file and make it executable. Then you can run the script by typing its name at the shell prompt.
- When your Linux system boots, shell scripts stored in various subdirectories in the `/etc` directory (for example, `/etc/init.d`) perform many initialization tasks.
- There are many built-in shell commands you can use in shell scripts. You already know some of the built-in commands, such as `cd` and `pwd`, but this chapter describes many more built-in shell commands.
- Perl is a popular scripting language that appears on this book's companion DVD. You can use Perl to write powerful scripts on your Linux system.

- Perl contains features comparable to those of other programming languages, such as C. A powerful feature of Perl is its capability to use regular expressions and to search files for occurrences of a search pattern.
- Perl 5, the latest version of Perl (and the one that comes with Linux), includes a number of helpful features. A key feature is the Perl module, a package of subroutines that follows certain guidelines. Modules make it possible to implement objects in Perl.
- You can download the latest version of Perl (as well as Perl documentation) from the Comprehensive Perl Archive Network (CPAN) at `www.cpan.org/`.

Tcl/Tk Scripting

Chapter 25

Secrets in This Chapter

If you are already a C and X Window System programmer, you will be surprised by the ease with which you can create graphical applications with *Tcl (Tool Command Language)* and its associated X toolkit, and *Tk*—collectively referred to as Tcl/Tk (pronounced "tickle/tee kay"). Tcl is a scripting language like Perl. The biggest strength of Tcl is its X toolkit, Tk, which enables you to develop scripts with GUIs.

When I started using Tcl/Tk, I was pleasantly surprised by how few lines of Tcl/Tk it takes to create a functioning graphical interface. To a newcomer, a Tcl/Tk script still looks rather complicated, but if you have used C-based toolkits, such as Xt and Motif, to write programs, you can appreciate the high-level abstractions of Tk. Creating a user-interface component such as a button is much simpler in Tk than in Motif. In Tk, you still have to tend to many details, such as how to lay out the components of the user interface, but you can see results faster than you can with a C program that calls the Motif library.

If you have never programmed, don't avoid this chapter out of fear. The examples in this chapter teach you the basics of Tcl and Tk. You are bound to become a believer in Tcl/Tk after you see how quickly you can use Tcl/Tk's interpreter to create applications with graphical interfaces.

Introducing Tcl

The creator of Tcl, John Ousterhout, intended it to be a simple, embeddable scripting language whose interpreter could be linked with any C program, so that the C program could use Tcl scripts. The term *embeddable* refers to this property of Tcl—the capability of any C program to use the Tcl interpreter and run Tcl scripts.

John Ousterhout created Tcl and Tk when he was at the University of California at Berkeley. Tcl first appeared in 1989; Tk followed in 1991. Tcl/Tk are freely available for unrestricted use, including commercial use. At the time of this writing, the current Tcl version is 8.4; Tk is also 8.4. Linux comes with Tcl/Tk.

The following sections provide an overview of Tcl, its syntax, and some of its important commands. Because Tcl underlies the Tk toolkit, you should become familiar with Tcl before jumping into Tk, although Tk undoubtedly is more fun because you can use it to create graphical interfaces.

Writing Your First Tcl Script

In Chapter 24, you learned how to write shell scripts and Perl scripts. You write Tcl scripts the same way. Unlike Perl, Tcl includes a *shell*, an interactive interpreter of Tcl commands. The Tcl shell program's name is tclsh; it should be in the `/usr/bin` directory.

When you log in, the `PATH` environment variable should include the `/usr/bin` directory. Thus, you can start the Tcl shell by typing `tclsh` at a text console or in a terminal window in GNOME or KDE. A percent sign (`%`) appears on the next line; this is the Tcl shell program's prompt. To see which version of Tcl you have, type **info tclversion** at the Tcl shell prompt. The Tcl shell program responds by printing the version of Tcl. Here is an example of how you interact with the Tcl shell:

```
tclsh
% info tclversion
8.4
%
```

Now you can interactively try the following Tcl program, which prints `Hello, World!` on the standard output (the display screen or the terminal window):

```
% puts "Hello, World!"
Hello, World!
% exit
```

Type **exit** to quit the Tcl shell.

> **note** Note that I don't show the shell prompt in previous chapters, but I show the Tcl prompt (%) in many of this chapter's code listings. That's because the Tcl prompt looks different from the Bash prompt, which should tell you that you aren't working in Bash.

The Tcl shell immediately processes the Tcl command you enter and displays the results, then it prompts you for the next input. At this point, you can type **exit** to quit the Tcl shell (`tclsh`).

To prepare and run a Tcl script, follow these steps:

1. Use a text editor to enter and save the following lines in a file named `hellotcl` (this file will be the Tcl script):

   ```
   #!/usr/bin/tclsh
   # A simple Tcl script
   puts "Hello, World!"
   ```

2. Type the following command at the shell prompt to make the `hellotcl` file executable (that's what the `+x` in the `chmod` command means):

   ```
   chmod +x hellotcl
   ```

3. To run the `hellotcl` script, type the following at the shell prompt:

   ```
   ./hellotcl
   Hello, World!
   ```

Use these basic steps to create and run any Tcl script. You still have to learn the nuances of Tcl syntax, of course — as well as many rules. This section gets you started with an overview of Tcl.

Getting More Information on Tcl/Tk

This chapter provides an overview of Tcl and Tk, highlights many key points, and shows simple examples. However, there isn't enough room in this chapter to list all the information you need to fully exploit the power of Tcl and Tk. Because of Tcl/Tk's popularity, you can find quite a few resources about it, ranging from books to Internet sites. Following is a short list of Tcl/Tk resources:

- **Books:** Two prominent books on Tcl/Tk are available. The first book is *Tcl and the Tk Toolkit* (Addison-Wesley, 1994) by John K. Ousterhout, the originator of Tcl and Tk. John's book provides a broad overview of Tcl and Tk, including an explanation of the way that Tcl command strings are parsed. The other book is *Practical Programming in Tcl and Tk, Fourth Edition* (Prentice Hall, 2003) by Brent B. Welch and Ken Jones. This book provides more Tcl and Tk examples.

- **Internet resources:** Several FTP sites and websites contain the latest Tcl/Tk distributions and information about Tcl/Tk development. Following are the URLs for two key sites:
  - **ftp://ftp.scriptics.com/pub/tcl/:** (Tcl/Tk master distribution site)
  - **www.tcl.tk/:** (Tcl developer site)

Getting an Overview of Tcl

True to its name (Tool Command Language), Tcl consists of a set of commands you can combine according to a set of rules. To write Tcl scripts, you have to understand two broad subjects:

- **Tcl syntax:** Tcl syntax is the set of rules the Tcl command interpreter follows when it interprets a command string (a line that contains a command and its arguments).
- **Tcl commands:** Although the syntax is the same for all commands, each Tcl command is meant to perform a specific task. To exploit Tcl fully, you have to know what commands are available and what each command does. The Tcl command set can be extended by applications. In fact, Tk itself is an extension of Tcl; Tk adds commands that manipulate components of GUIs.

Start by learning the Tcl syntax, a handful of rules that determine the way each Tcl command is parsed. Because Tcl has many commands, learning all of them can take a while. Even after you become proficient in the Tcl syntax and a small set of commands, you may need to keep a reference manual nearby so that you can check the exact format of the arguments that each command requires.

Tcl commands include the following basic programming facilities that you expect from any programming language:

- **Variables**, which store data. Each variable has a name and a value. Tcl also allows you to define arrays of variables.
- **Expressions**, which combine values of variables with operators. An expression might add two variables, for example. Tcl uses the `expr` command to evaluate expressions.
- **Control-flow commands**, which enable commands to be executed in various orders, depending on the value of some expression. Tcl provides commands such as `for`, `foreach`, `break`, `continue`, `if`, `while`, and `return` to implement flow control in Tcl scripts.
- **Procedures**, which enable you to group several commands and give them a name. Procedures also accept arguments. Tcl provides the `proc` command to enable you to define procedures. You can use a procedure to execute the same set of commands (usually with different arguments) by invoking the procedure that represents those commands.

The next few sections provide an overview of the Tcl syntax and the core Tcl commands.

Learning the Basic Tcl Syntax

To understand the basic Tcl syntax, you have to know a bit about how the Tcl interpreter processes each command string. The steps are as follows:

1. The Tcl interpreter parses (breaks down) the command string into words — the constituent parts, including variables and operators.
2. The Tcl interpreter applies rules to substitute the values of variables and replace certain commands with their results.
3. The Tcl interpreter executes the commands, taking the first word as the command name and calling a command procedure to execute the command. The command procedure receives the rest of the words as strings.

When writing Tcl command strings, you have to use *white space* (a space or a tab) to separate a command's name from its arguments. A new line or a semicolon (;) marks the end of a command string. You can put two commands on the same line if you insert a semicolon after the first command. Thus, you can use the following:

```
% puts Hello, ; puts World!
Hello,
World!
```

The resulting output appears on separate lines because the `puts` command adds a new line by default.

Use a backslash (\) at the end of a line to continue that command string on the next line (this is a standard convention in UNIX). Thus, you can write a command string to print Hello, World! as follows:

```
puts "Hello, \
World!"
```

This Tcl command produces the following output:

```
Hello,  World!
```

Substitutions

The Tcl interpreter replaces certain parts of the command string with an equivalent value. If you precede a variable's name with a dollar sign ($), for example, the interpreter replaces that word with the variable's value. As you learn in the "Variables" section, you can define a variable in a Tcl script by using the `set` command, as follows:

```
set count 100
```

This command defines a variable named `count` with the value 100. Suppose that you type the following:

```
puts $count
```

The interpreter first replaces `$count` with its value, 100. Thus, that command string becomes:

```
puts 100
```

When the interpreter executes the `puts` command, it prints 100. This is an example of *variable substitution*.

In all, the Tcl interpreter supports three kinds of substitutions:

- **Variable substitution:** As the preceding example shows, if the Tcl interpreter finds a dollar sign ($), it replaces the dollar sign as well as the following variable name with that variable's value.
- **Backslash substitution:** You can embed special characters, such as the newline and tab, in a word by using backslash substitution. Type a backslash, followed by one or more characters; the interpreter replaces that sequence with a nonprintable character. These sequences are patterned after ANSI Standard C's escape sequences. Table 25-1, which follows this list, summarizes the backslash sequences that the Tcl interpreter understands.
- **Command substitution:** This type of substitution refers to the mechanism that enables you to specify that a command be evaluated and replaced by its result before the interpreter processes the command string. The command `string length "Hello, World!"`, for example, returns 13, the length of the string. To set a variable named `len` to the length of this string, type the following:

  ```
  set len [string length "Hello, World!"]
  ```

  The interpreter processes the command inside the square brackets and replaces that part of the command string with the value of the command. Thus, this command becomes

  ```
  set len 13
  ```

  and the `set` command sets the `len` variable to 13.

Table 25-1: Backslash Sequences and Their Meanings in Tcl

Sequence	*Replacement Character*[a]
`\a`	Bell character (0x7)
`\b`	Backspace (0x8)
`\f`	Form feed (0xc)
`\n`	New line (0xa)
`\r`	Carriage return (0xd)
`\t`	Horizontal tab (0x9)
`\v`	Vertical tab (0xb)
`\<newline>`	Replace the newline and white space on the next line with a single space
`\\`	Interpret as a single backslash (\)
`\"`	Interpret as double quotation marks (")
`\ooo`	Use the value specified by the octal digits *ooo* (up to three)
`\xhh`	Use the value specified by the hexadecimal digits *hh* (up to two)

[a]Hexadecimal values are shown in parentheses (for example, 0xd means hexadecimal d)

Comments

A pound sign (#) marks the start of a comment; the Tcl interpreter disregards the rest of the line, beginning with the pound sign. Tcl does, however, have a peculiar requirement for comments: you cannot start a comment within a command. The command string must end before you start a comment.

To understand this problem, try the following Tcl command at the `tclsh` prompt:

```
% puts "Hello, World!" # This is a comment
wrong # args: should be "puts ?-nonewline? ?channelId? string"
%
```

Essentially, the `puts` command processes the remainder of the line and complains about the number of arguments. The solution is to put a semicolon just before the pound sign (#), as follows:

```
% puts "Hello, World!" ;# This is a comment
Hello, World!
```

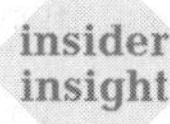

If you put comments at the end of a Tcl command, remember to precede the pound sign (#) with a semicolon (;). The semicolon terminates the preceding command and enables you to start a comment.

Braces and Double Quotation Marks

You can use braces ({...}) and double quotation marks ("...") to group several words. Use double quotes to pass arguments that contain an embedded space or a semicolon, which otherwise ends the command. The quotes are not part of the group of words; they simply serve to mark the beginning and end of a group of words. Following are some examples of using double quotes to group words:

```
% puts "Hello, World!"
Hello, World!
% puts "Enter 1; otherwise file won't be saved!"
Enter 1; otherwise file won't be saved!
```

When you group words with double quotes, all types of substitutions still take place, as the following example illustrates:

```
% puts "There are [string length hello] characters in 'hello'"
There are 5 characters in 'hello'
```

The Tcl interpreter replaces everything inside the brackets with the result of the `string length hello` command, whose return value is the number of characters in `hello` (5). In the expression `[string length hello]`, you can replace the string `hello` with any variable to determine the length of that variable's value.

Also, you can use braces to group words. The Tcl interpreter does not perform any substitutions when you group words with braces (if you enclose words in double quotes, the interpreter does perform a substitution). Consider the preceding example with braces instead of double quotes:

```
% puts {There are [string length hello] characters in 'hello'}
There are [string length hello] characters in 'hello'
```

As the result shows, the Tcl interpreter simply passes everything, unchanged, as a single argument.

insider insight

Use braces as a grouping mechanism when you have to pass expressions to control commands, such as `while` loops, `for` loops, or procedures.

Understanding Tcl Variables

Everything is a string in Tcl. Variable names, as well as values, are stored as strings. To define a variable, use the built-in Tcl command `set`. The following commands, for example, define the variable `book` as `"Red Hat Fedora Linux Secrets"`; the variable `year` as `2003`; and the variable `price` as `$49.99`:

```
set book "Red Hat Fedora Linux Secrets"
set year 2005
set price \$49.99
```

To refer to the value of a variable, add a dollar sign (`$`) prefix to the variable's name. Therefore, to print the variable `book`, use the following format:

```
% puts $book
Red Hat Fedora Linux Secrets
```

If you use set with a single argument, set returns the value of that argument. Thus, set book is equivalent to `$book`, as the following example shows:

```
% puts [set book]
Red Hat Fedora Linux Secrets
```

Writing Expressions

You can write expressions by combining variables with mathematical operators, such as + (add), - (subtract), * (multiply), and / (divide). Here are some examples of expressions:

```
set count 1
$count+1
$count + 5 - 2
2 + 3.5
```

You can use numbers, as well as variable names, in expressions. Use white space to enhance readability. Use parentheses to specify how you want an expression to be evaluated.

In addition to the basic mathematical operators, Tcl includes several built-in mathematical functions, such as `sin`, `cos`, `tan`, `log`, and `sqrt`. Call these functions just as you do in C, with arguments in parentheses, as follows:

```
set angle 1.5
2*sin($angle)
```

In addition, you can use Boolean operators, such as ! (not), `&&` (and), and `||` (or). Comparison operators — such as < (less than), > (greater than), <= (less than or equal to), == (equal to), and != (not equal to) — also are available. Expressions that use Boolean or comparison operators evaluate to 1 if true and 0 if false. You can write expressions, such as the following:

```
count == 10
angle < 3.1415
```

Expressions are not commands by themselves. You can use expressions as arguments only for commands that accept expressions as arguments. The `if` and `while` commands, for example, expect expressions as arguments.

Tcl also provides the `expr` command to evaluate an expression. The following example shows how you might evaluate an expression in a Tcl command:

```
% set angle 1.5
1.5
% puts "Result = [expr 2*sin($angle)]"
Result = 1.99498997321
```

Although Tcl stores everything as a string, you have to use numbers where numbers are expected. If `book` is defined as `"Red Hat Fedora Linux Secrets"`, for example, you cannot write an expression `$book+1`, because it does not make sense.

Using Control-Flow Commands in Tcl

Tcl's control-flow commands enable you to specify the order in which the Tcl interpreter executes commands. You can use the `if` command to test the value of an expression; and if the value is true (nonzero), you can make the interpreter execute a set of commands. Tcl includes control-flow commands similar to those in C, such as `if`, `for`, `while`, and `switch`. This section provides an overview of the control-flow commands.

A Tcl control-flow command typically has a *command block* (a group of commands) that the control-flow command executes after evaluating an expression. To avoid substitutions (such as replacing variables with their values), you must enclose the entire command block in braces. The following `if-else` control-flow commands illustrate the style of braces that works properly:

```
if { expression } {
# Commands to execute when expression is true
  command_1
  command_2
} else {
# Commands to execute when expression is false
# ...
}
```

You should follow this style of braces religiously in Tcl scripts. In particular, remember to include a space between the control-flow command (such as `if`) and the left brace (`{`) that follows the command.

Using the if Command

In its simplest form, Tcl's `if` command evaluates an expression and executes a set of commands if that expression is nonzero (true). You might compare the value of a variable with a threshold as follows:

```
if { $errorCount > 25 } {
    puts "Too many errors!"
}
```

You can add an `else` clause to process commands if the expression evaluates to zero (false). Following is an example:

```
if { $user == "root" } {
    puts "Starting system setup ..."
} else {
    puts "Sorry, you must be \"root\" to run this program!"
}
```

Tcl's `if` command can be followed by zero or more `elseif` commands if you need to perform more complicated tests, such as the following:

```
puts -nonewline "Enter version number: "  ;# Prompt user
set version [gets stdin]                  ;# Read version number

if { $version >= 10 } {
   puts "No upgrade necessary"
} elseif { $version >= 6 && $version < 9} {
   puts "Standard upgrade"
} elseif { $version >= 3 && $version < 6} {
    puts "Reinstall"
} else {
    puts "Sorry, cannot upgrade"
}
```

Using the while Command

The `while` command executes a block of commands until an expression becomes false. The following `while` loop keeps reading lines from the standard input until the user presses Ctrl-D:

```
while { [gets stdin line]  != -1 } {
    puts $line
# Do whatever you need to do with $line.
}
```

Although this `while` command looks simple, you should realize that it has two arguments inside two sets of braces. The first argument is the expression; the second argument contains the Tcl commands to be executed if the expression is true. You must always use braces to enclose both of these arguments. The braces prevent the Tcl interpreter from evaluating the contents; the `while` command is the one that processes what's inside the braces.

If you use a variable to keep count inside a `while` loop, you can use the `incr` command to increment that variable. You can skip to the end of a loop by using the `continue` command; the `break` command exits the loop. The following Tcl script uses a `while` loop to add all the numbers from 1 to 10, except 5:

```
#!/usr/bin/tclsh

set i 0
set sum 0
```

```
while { 1 } {
    incr i                     ;# Increment i
    if {$i == 5} { continue }  ;# Skip if i is 5
    if {$i > 10} {break }      ;# End loop if i exceeds 10
    set sum [expr $sum+$i]     ;# Otherwise, add i to sum
}
puts "Sum = $sum";
```

When you run this script, it should display the following result:

```
Sum = 50
```

Using the for Command

Tcl's `for` command takes four arguments, which you should type in the following manner:

```
for {expr1} { expr2} { expr3} {
    commands
}
```

The `for` command evaluates `expr1` once at the beginning of the loop and executes the commands inside the final pair of braces, until the expression `expr2` evaluates to zero. The `for` command evaluates the third expression — `expr3` — after each execution of the commands. You can omit any of the expressions, but you must use all the braces. The following example uses a `for` loop to add the numbers from 1 to 10:

```
#!/usr/bin/tclsh
for {set i 0; set sum 0} {$i <= 10} {set sum [expr $sum+$i]; incr i} {
}
puts "Sum = $sum";
```

When you run this script, it displays the following result:

```
Sum = 55
```

Using the foreach Command

You have not seen a command like `foreach` in C, but `foreach` is handy when you want to perform some action for each value in a list of variables. You can add a set of numbers with the `foreach` command as follows:

```
set sum 0
foreach i { 1 2 3 4 5 6 7 8 9 10} {
    set sum [expr $sum+$i]
}
puts "Sum = $sum"
```

When you run this script, this one also prints `Sum = 55` because the script is adding the numbers 1 through 10.

If you have a list in a variable, you can use that variable's value in place of the list shown within the first pair of braces. Following is a `foreach` loop that echoes the strings in a list:

```
set users "root naba"
foreach user $users {
    puts "$user"
}
```

Using the switch Command

Tcl's `switch` command is different from C's `switch` statement. Instead of evaluating a mathematical expression, Tcl's `switch` command compares a string with a set of patterns and executes a set of commands, depending on which pattern matches. Often, the pattern is expressed in terms of a regular expression.

cross ref

See Chapter 24 for an introduction to regular expressions.

The following script illustrates the syntax and a typical use of the `switch` command:

```
#!/usr/bin/tclsh
# This script reads commands from the user and processes
# the commands using a switch statement.

set prompt "Enter command (\"quit\" to exit): "

puts -nonewline "$prompt"; flush stdout

while { [gets stdin cmd]  != -1 } {
    switch -exact -- $cmd {
        quit    { puts "Bye!"; exit}
        start   { puts "Started"}
        stop    { puts "Stopped"}
        draw    { puts "Draw.."}
        default { puts "Unknown command: $cmd" }
    }
# Prompt user again
    puts -nonewline $prompt; flush stdout
}
```

Following is a sample session with this script (user input is in boldface):

```
Enter command ("quit" to exit): help
Unknown command: help
Enter command ("quit" to exit): start
Started
Enter command ("quit" to exit): stop
Stopped
Enter command ("quit" to exit): quit
Bye!
```

As this example shows, the `switch` statement enables you to compare a string with a set of other strings and to activate a set of commands, depending on which pattern matches. In this example, the string is `$cmd` (which is initialized by reading the user's input with a `gets` command), and the patterns are literal strings: `quit`, `start`, `stop`, and `draw`.

When you want the switch statement to compare a string with a set of other strings and look for an exact match, use the -exact flag on the first line of the switch command, as follows:

```
switch -exact -- $cmd {
  ...
}
```

The two hyphens (--) immediately after the -exact flag mark the end of the flags. When you use the switch command, you should always use the double hyphens at the end of the flag to prevent the test string (in this example, the test string is $cmd) from matching a flag inadvertently.

You can use the switch command with the -regexp flag to compare a string with a regular expression, as in the following example:

```
# Assume that $cmd is the string to be matched.

switch -regexp -- $cmd {
    ^q.*     { puts "Bye!"; exit}
    ^x.*   { puts "Something x..."}
    ^y.*   { puts "Something y..."}
    ^z.*   { puts "Something z..."}
    default { puts "Unknown command: $cmd" }
}
```

In this example, each regular expression has a similar form. The pattern ^z.* means any string that starts with a single z, followed by any number of other characters.

Writing Tcl Procedures

You can use the proc command to add your own commands. Such commands are called *procedures*; the Tcl interpreter treats them just as though they were built-in Tcl commands. The following example shows how easy it is to write a procedure in Tcl:

```
#!/usr/bin/tclsh

proc total items {
    set sum 0
    foreach i $items {
        set sum [expr $sum+$i]
    }
    return $sum
}

set counts "5 4 3 5"
puts "Total = [total $counts]"
```

When you run the preceding script, it prints the following:

```
Total = 17
```

In this example, the procedure's name is `total`, and it takes a list of numbers as the argument. The procedure receives the arguments in the variable named `items`. The body of the procedure extracts each item and returns a sum of the items. Thus, to add numbers from 1 to 10, you have to call the `total` procedure as follows:

```
set sum1_10 [total {1 2 3 4 5 6 7 8 9 10}]
```

In a Tcl procedure, the argument name `args` has special significance; if you use `args` as the argument name, you can pass a variable number of arguments to the procedure. For example, write the `total` procedure with the argument name `args`, as follows:

```
proc total args {
     set sum 0
     foreach i $args {
         set sum [expr $sum+$i]
     }
     return $sum
 }
```

Now, you can call `total` in the following manner:

```
set sum1_10 [total 1 2 3 4 5 6 7 8 9 10]    ;# Variable arguments
```

This should set `sum1_10` to the sum of the numbers from 1 through 10.

If you want to access a global variable (a variable defined outside a procedure) in the Tcl procedure, you have to use the `global` command inside the procedure. The `global` command makes a global variable visible within the scope of a procedure. If a variable named `theCanvas` holds the current drawing area in a Tk (Tcl's X toolkit) program, a procedure that uses `theCanvas` must include the following command:

```
global theCanvas
```

Taking Stock of Built-in Tcl Commands

You have seen many Tcl commands in the preceding examples. Knowing the types of commands that are available in Tcl helps you decide which commands are most appropriate for the task at hand. Although this chapter does not have enough room to cover all Tcl commands, Table 25-2 summarizes Tcl's built-in commands.

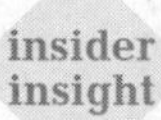

To get online help about any Tcl command listed in Table 25-2, type **man n**, followed by the command name. To get online help about Tcl's `file` command, for example, type **man n file**.

Table 25-2: Built-in Tcl Commands

Command	*Action*
`append`	Appends an argument to a variable's value.
`array`	Performs various operations on an array variable.
`break`	Exits a loop command (such as `while` and `for`).
`catch`	Executes a script and traps errors to prevent errors from reaching the Tcl interpreter.
`cd`	Changes the current working directory.
`close`	Closes an open file.
`concat`	Joins two or more lists in a single list.
`continue`	Immediately begins the next iteration of a `for` or `while` loop.
`eof`	Checks to see whether end-of-file is reached in an open file.
`error`	Generates an error.
`eval`	Concatenates lists (as `concat` does), and then evaluates the resulting list as a Tcl script.
`exec`	Starts one or more processes that execute the command's arguments.
`exit`	Terminates the Tcl script.
`expr`	Evaluates an expression.
`file`	Checks filenames and attributes.
`flush`	Flushes buffered output to a file.
`for`	Implements a `for` loop.
`foreach`	Performs a specified action for each element in a list.
`format`	Formats output and stores it in a string (as the `sprintf` function in C does).
`gets`	Reads a line from a file.
`glob`	Returns the names of files that match a pattern (such as `*.tcl`).
`global`	Accesses global variables.
`history`	Provides access to the *history list* (the list of past Tcl commands).
`if`	Tests an expression and executes commands if the expression is true (nonzero).
`incr`	Increments the value of a variable.
`info`	Returns internal information about the Tcl interpreter.
`join`	Creates a string, by joining all items in a list.
`lappend`	Appends elements to a list.
`lindex`	Returns an element from a list at a specified index. (Index 0 refers to the first element.)
`linsert`	Inserts elements into a list before a specified index.
`list`	Creates a list composed of the specified arguments.
`llength`	Returns the number of elements in a list.

(continued)

Table 25-2 *(continued)*

Command	Action
`lrange`	Returns a specified range of adjacent elements from a list.
`lreplace`	Replaces elements in a list with new elements.
`lsearch`	Searches a list for a particular element.
`lsort`	Sorts a list in a specified order.
`open`	Opens a file and returns a file identifier.
`pid`	Returns the process identifier (ID).
`proc`	Defines a Tcl procedure.
`puts`	Sends characters to a file.
`pwd`	Returns the current working directory.
`read`	Reads a specified number of bytes from a file. (You can read the entire file in a single read.)
`regexp`	Matches a regular expression with a string.
`regsub`	Substitutes one regular expression pattern for another.
`rename`	Renames or deletes a command.
`return`	Returns a value from a Tcl procedure.
`scan`	Parses a string, using format specifiers patterned after C's `sscanf` function.
`seek`	Changes the *access position* (where the next input or output operation occurs) in an open file.
`set`	Sets a variable's value or returns its current value.
`source`	Reads a file and processes it as a Tcl script.
`split`	Breaks a string into a Tcl list.
`string`	Performs various operations on strings.
`switch`	Processes one of several blocks of commands, depending on which pattern matches a specified string.
`tell`	Returns the current access position for an open file.
`time`	Returns the total time needed to execute a script.
`trace`	Executes a specified set of Tcl commands whenever a variable is accessed.
`unknown`	Handles any unknown command. (The Tcl interpreter calls this command whenever it encounters any unknown command.)
`unset`	Removes the definition of one or more variables.
`uplevel`	Executes a script in a different context.
`upvar`	References a variable outside a procedure. (This is used to implement the pass-by-reference style of procedure call, in which changing a procedure argument changes the original copy of the argument.)
`while`	Implements a `while` loop that executes a set of Tcl commands repeatedly, as long as an expression evaluates to a nonzero value (true).

Manipulating Strings in Tcl

If you browse through the Tcl commands listed in Table 25-2, you find quite a few — such as `append`, `join`, `split`, `string`, `regexp`, and `regsub` — that operate on strings. This section summarizes a few string-manipulation commands.

When you set a variable to a string, the Tcl interpreter considers that string to be a single entity, even if that string contains embedded spaces or special characters. Sometimes you need to access the string as a list of items. The `split` command is a handy way to separate a string into its components. The lines in the `/etc/passwd` file, for example, look like the following:

```
root:x:0:0:root:/root:/bin/bash
```

The line is composed of fields separated by colons (`:`). Suppose that you want to extract the first field from each line (because that field contains the login name). You can read the file one line at a time, split each line into a list, and extract the first element (the item at index 0) of each list. Following is a Tcl script that does this:

```
#!/usr/bin/tclsh

set fid [open "/etc/passwd" r]     ;# Open file for read-only access

while { [gets $fid line] != -1 } {
    set fields [split $line ":"]  ;# Split the string into a list
# Just print out the first field
    puts [lindex $fields 0]       ;# Extract item at a index 0
}
```

When you run this script, it prints all the login names from your system's `/etc/passwd` file.

The `join` command is the opposite of `split`; you can use it to create a single string from the items in a list. Suppose that you have a list of six items, defined as follows:

```
set x {1 2 3 4 5 6}
```

When you join the elements, you can select what character you want to use between fields. To join the elements without anything in between them, use the following format:

```
set y [join $x ""]
```

Now the y string is `"123456"`.

The string command followed by arguments constitutes a group of commands for working with strings; the first argument of `string` specifies the operation to be performed. The `string compare` command, for example, compares two strings, returning zero when the two strings are identical. A return value of `-1` indicates that the first string argument is lexicographically less than the second one, which means it appears before the second one in a dictionary. Similarly, a `1` return value indicates that the first string is lexicographically greater than the second one. Thus, you might use `string compare` in an `if` command as follows:

```
if { [string compare $command "quit"] == 0} {
    puts "Exiting..."
    exit 0
}
```

Table 25-3 lists the operations you can perform with Tcl's `string` command.

Table 25-3: Operations You Can Perform with string in Tcl

String Command	*Description*
`string compare` *`string1 string2`*	Returns `-1`, `0`, or `1` after comparing strings
`string first` *`string1 string2`*	Returns the index of the first occurrence of *`string1`* in *`string2`*
`string index` *`string charIndex`*	Returns the character at index *`charIndex`*
`string last` *`string1 string2`*	Returns the index of the last occurrence of *`string1`* in *`string2`*
`string length` *`string`*	Returns the length of the *`string`*
`string match` *`pattern string`*	Returns `1` if the *`pattern`* matches the *`string`*, and `0` if it does not
`string range` *`string first last`*	Returns a range of characters from *`string`*
`string tolower` *`string`*	Returns the *`string`* in lowercase characters
`string toupper` *`string`*	Returns the *`string`* in uppercase characters
`string trim` *`string chars`*	Returns the *`string`* after trimming the leading or trailing characters
`string trimleft` *`string chars`*	Returns the *`string`* after trimming the leading characters
`string trimright` *`string chars`*	Returns the *`string`* after trimming the trailing characters

Using Arrays

In Tcl, an *array* is a variable with a string index. An array contains elements; the string index of each element is called the element name. In other words, you can access an element of an array by using its name. Internally, Tcl implements arrays with an efficient data structure known as a *hash table*, which enables the Tcl interpreter to look up any array element in a relatively constant period of time.

Declare an array variable by using the `set` command. The following example shows how you might define the `disk_usage` array that holds the amount of disk space a system's users consume:

```
set disk_usage(root)        147178
set disk_usage(naba)        28574
set disk_usage(emily)       73
set disk_usage(ivy)         61
set disk_usage(ashley)      34
```

After you define the array, you can access its individual elements by element name, as in the following example:

```
set user "naba"
puts "Disk space used by $user = $disk_usage($user)K"
```

Accessing Environment Variables in Tcl

Tcl provides the environment variables in a predefined global array named env, with the environment-variable names used as element names. In other words, you can look up the value of an environment variable by using the variable name as an index. The following command prints the current PATH:

```
puts "$env(PATH)"
```

You can manipulate the environment variable array, env, just as you do any other variables. You can add a new directory to PATH, for example, as follows:

```
set env(PATH) "$env(PATH):/usr/sbin"
```

Any changes to the environment variable do not affect the parent process (for example, the shell from which you start the Tcl script). Any new processes the script creates by means of the exec command, however, inherit the altered environment variable.

Performing File Operations in Tcl

Most of the examples presented so far in this chapter use Tcl's puts command to display output. By default, puts writes to the standard output, the terminal window or text console, when you use X. You can write to a file, however, by providing a file identifier as the first argument of puts. To get a file identifier, you first have to open the file by using Tcl's open command. The following example shows how you open a file, write a line of text to the file, and close the file (in this example fid is a variable that stores the file identifier):

```
set fid [open "testfile" w]  ;# Open "testfile" for writing
puts $fid "Testing 1..2..3"  ;# Write to this file
close $fid                   ;# Close the file
```

When you use puts to display a string on the standard output, you do not have to provide a file-identifier argument. In addition, puts automatically appends a newline character to the end of the string. If you do not want the newline, use puts with the -nonewline argument, as follows:

```
puts -nonewline "Command> "  ;# This is good for command prompts.
flush stdout ;# Make sure output appears right away
```

You have seen the use of the gets command to read a line of input from the standard input. The following invocation of gets, for example, reads a line from the standard input (the command returns when you press Enter):

```
set line [gets stdin]  ;# Read a line from standard input.
```

The keyword stdin is a predefined file identifier that represents the standard input, which by default is your keyboard. Other predefined file IDs are stdout, for the standard output; and stderr, for the standard error-reporting device. By default, both stdout and stderr are connected to the display screen.

Following is a different way to call gets and read a line of input into a variable named line:

```
gets stdin line  ;# Read a line of input into the line variable
```

To read from another file, you should open the file for reading and then use gets with that file's ID. To read all lines from /etc/passwd and display them on the standard output, for example, use the following:

```
set fpass [open "/etc/passwd" r]      ;# Open /etc/passwd.
while { [gets $fpass line] != -1} {   ;# Read the lines one by one
    puts $line                        ;# and print each line.
}
```

The gets command is good for reading text files because it works one line at a time; in fact, it looks for the newline character as a marker that indicates the end of a line of text. If you want to read binary data, such as an image file, use the read command instead. To read and process a file in 2,048-byte chunks, you might use read in the following manner:

```
# Assume fid is the file ID of an open file.
while { ![eof $fid]} {           ;# Until end-of-file is reached
    set buffer [read $fid 2048] ;# read 2048 bytes into buffer
# process the data in buffer    ;# and process the buffer.
}
```

The second argument of the read command is the maximum number of bytes to be read. If you omit this argument, the read command reads the entire file. You can use this feature to process entire text files. After reading the contents of the file, use the split command to separate the input data into lines of text. Following is an example:

```
set fid [open "/etc/passwd" r] ;# Open file for reading
set buffer [read $fid 100000]  ;# Read entire file into buffer
split $buffer "\n"             ;# Split buffer into lines
foreach line $buffer {
    puts $line                 ;# Process each line.
}
```

If you want to process several files (such as all files whose names end with .tcl), use the glob command to expand a filename, such as *.tcl, into a list. Then, you can use the open command to open and process each file in the following manner:

```
foreach filename [glob *.tcl] { ;# Create list of filenames
    puts -nonewline $filename   ;# Print the filename.
    set file [open $filename r] ;# Open that file.
    gets $file line             ;# Read the first line
    puts $line                  ;# and print it (for testing).
# process rest of the file as necessary
    close $file                 ;# Remember to close the file.
}
```

This is a good example of how to use the glob command in a script.

Executing Linux Commands in Tcl

Instead of duplicating the large number of Linux commands, Tcl simply provides the mechanism to run any Linux command. If you know Linux commands, you can use them directly in Tcl scripts.

Use the `exec` command to execute a Linux command in a Tcl script. In the command's simplest form, you provide the Linux command as an argument of `exec`. To show the current directory listing, for example, type the following:

```
exec ls
```

The output appears on the standard output (the monitor), just as it does when you enter the `ls` command at the shell prompt.

When you run Linux commands from the shell, you can redirect the input and output by using special characters, such as < (redirect input), > (redirect output), and | (pipe). These options are available in Tcl as well; the `exec` command accepts a complete command line, including any input or output redirections. Thus, you can send the directory listing to a file named `dirlist` as follows:

```
exec ls > dirlist
```

Tcl's `exec` command does not expand wildcard characters (such as an asterisk or a question mark) in filenames passed to a Linux command. If you use wildcards in filenames, you have to perform an additional step: You must process the filename specification through the `glob` command to expand it properly before providing the command to `exec`. In addition, you must pass the entire `exec` command to `eval` as an argument. To see a list of all files with names that end in `.tcl`, for example, you have to use the `exec` command with `glob` and feed the entire command to `eval` as follows:

```
eval exec ls [glob *.tcl]    ;# this is equivalent to "ls *.tcl"
```

Introducing Tk

Tk (pronounced *tee-kay*) is an extension of Tcl. Tk provides an X Window system–based toolkit you can use in Tcl scripts to build GUIs. As you might expect, Tk provides a set of Tcl commands beyond the core built-in set. You can use these Tk commands to create windows, menus, buttons, and other user-interface components and to provide a GUI for your Tcl scripts.

Tk uses the X Window System for its graphic components, known as *widgets*. A widget represents a user-interface component, such as a button, scroll bar, menu, list, or even an entire text window. Tk widgets provide a Motif-like, three-dimensional appearance.

If you are familiar with the Motif widgets, you may know that Motif relies on Xt Intrinsics — an X toolkit used to build widgets. Unlike Motif, the Tk toolkit is not based on any other toolkit; it uses only Xlib, which is the C-language library for the X Window system. The upshot is that you need only the freely available X Window System to use Tk.

As with anything new, you can best learn Tk through examples, which the following sections provide.

Saying "Hello, World!" in Tk

Tk is a major-enough extension to Tcl to warrant its own shell, called `wish` (the *windowing shell*). The `wish` shell interprets all built-in Tcl commands, as well as the Tk commands. You must start X before you can run `wish`; after all, `wish` enables you to use X to create graphical interfaces.

The wish program should be in the `/usr/bin` directory, which should be in your `PATH` environment variable by default. To start `wish`, all you have to do is type the following at the shell prompt in a terminal window:

```
wish
%
```

The wish program displays its prompt (the percent sign) and a small window, as shown in the upper-right corner of Figure 25-1.

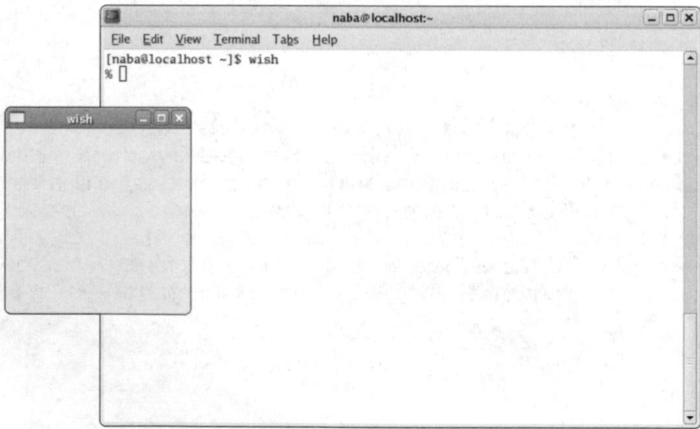

Figure 25-1: The Result of Running wish from a Terminal Window.

Therefore, `wish` provides an interactive prompt from which you can enter Tk commands to create a graphical interface. As `wish` interprets the commands, it displays the resulting graphical interface in the window.

To see how this interactive creation of graphical interface works, try the following commands at the `wish` prompt):

```
% label .msg -text "Hello, World!"
.msg
% button .bye -text "Bye" -command { exit }
.bye
% pack .msg .bye
%
```

Figure 25-2 shows the result of these commands; wish displays a `Hello, World!` label with a `Bye` button below it.

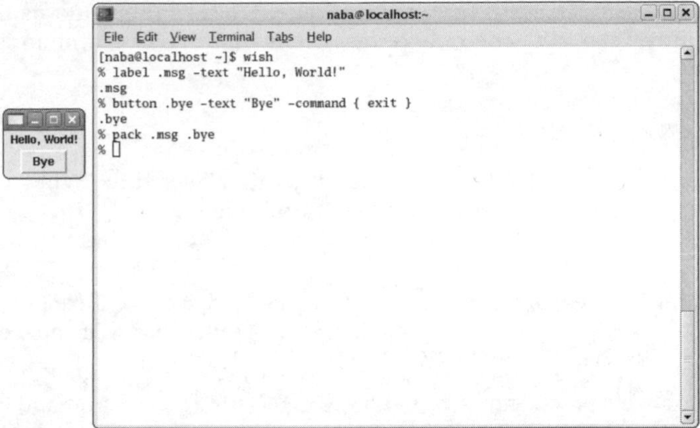

Figure 25-2: Interactively Creating a Label and a Button in wish.

Notice that the label and the button do not appear until you enter the `pack` command. In addition, the `wish` window shrinks to a size just large enough to hold the label and the button.

Click the `Bye` button; the `wish` program exits. This is because the `-command { exit }` argument of the `button` command associates the Tcl command `exit` with a click of the `Bye` button.

To create a Tk program or script that displays the `Hello, World!` label and the `Bye` button, all you have to do is place the Tk commands in a file and add a special line at the beginning to ensure that the `wish` shell processes the file. To do so, follow these steps:

1. Use a text editor to enter and save the following lines in a file named `hellotk`:

   ```
   #!/usr/bin/wish
   # A simple Tk script
   label .msg -text "Hello, World!"
   button .bye -text "Bye" -command { exit }
   pack .msg .bye
   ```

2. Type the following command at the shell prompt to make the `hellotk` file executable (that's what the `+x` in the `chmod` command means):

   ```
   chmod +x hellotk
   ```

3. To run the `hellotk` script, type the following at the shell prompt in a terminal window:

   ```
   ./hellotk
   ```

Figure 25-3 shows the window with a `Hello, World!` label and the `Bye` button that should appear when you run the `hellotk` script. Click the `Bye` button to close the window and end the script.

Figure 25-3: The Result of Running the hellotk Script.

As this example shows, the basic steps for writing a Tk script are the same as those for creating and running any Tcl script. The only difference is that the Tk commands generate graphical output.

Learning Tk Widget Basics

Now that you have been exposed to Tcl, you can begin writing Tk scripts. What you need to know are the Tk commands used to create and configure widgets.

The term *widget* has the same meaning in Tk as it does in an X toolkit, such as Motif — a widget is a user interface component, such as a push button, list box, or dialog box.

As the examples in the preceding section show, you use the `label` command to create a label and the `button` command to create a button widget. This is a general guideline for working with all Tk widgets — the command for creating a widget is the same as the widget's name. Table 25-4 lists the names of Tk's widgets, which are also the widget-creation commands.

Table 25-4: Tk Commands for Creating Widgets

Command	*Action*
`button`	Creates a button widget
`canvas`	Creates a canvas widget on which you can display text, bitmaps, lines, boxes, polygons, and other widgets
`checkbutton`	Creates a toggle button and associates it with a Tcl variable
`entry`	Creates a one-line text-entry widget
`frame`	Creates a frame widget that is capable of holding other widgets
`label`	Creates a read-only, one-line label widget
`listbox`	Creates a list-box widget that is capable of scrolling lines of text
`menu`	Creates a menu
`menubutton`	Creates a menu-button widget that pops up an associated menu when clicked
`message`	Creates a read-only, multiple-line message widget
`radiobutton`	Creates a radio-button widget that is linked to a Tcl variable
`scale`	Creates a scale widget that can adjust the value of a variable
`scrollbar`	Creates a scroll bar widget that you can link to another widget
`text`	Creates a text widget where the user can enter and edit text
`toplevel`	Creates a top-level widget (a widget whose window is a child of the X Window System's root window)

As you create a widget, you can specify many of its characteristics as arguments of the command. You can, for example, create a blue button with a red label (`test`) and display the button by using the following commands:

```
button .b -text test -fg red -bg blue
pack .b
```

The `pack` command does not create a widget; rather, it positions a widget in relation to others. Table 25-5 lists all the widget-manipulation commands.

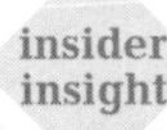

For online help about any Tk command listed in Tables 25-4 and 25-5, type **man n**, followed by the command name. To get online help about the `bind` command, for example, type **man n bind**.

Table 25-5: Tk Commands for Manipulating Widgets

Command	*Action*
`after`	Executes a command after a specified amount of time elapses.
`bind`	Associates a Tcl command with an X event, so that the Tcl command is automatically invoked whenever the X event occurs.
`destroy`	Destroys one or more widgets.
`focus`	Directs keyboard events to a particular window (gives that window the input focus).
`grab`	Confines pointer and keyboard events to a specified widget and its children.
`lower`	Lowers a window in the stacking order. (The stacking order refers to the order in which various windows overlap one another on the display screen.)
`option`	Provides access to the X resource database.
`pack`	Automatically positions widgets in a frame, based on specified constraints.
`place`	Allows manual positioning of a widget relative to another widget.
`raise`	Raises a window's position in the stacking order.
`selection`	Manipulates the X PRIMARY selection (the standard name of a selection in X).
`send`	Sends a Tcl command to a different Tk application (used for interprocess communications).
`tk`	Provides information about the internal state of the Tk interpreter.
`tkerror`	Handles any error that occurs in Tk applications (the interpreter calls this command when errors occur in Tk applications).
`tkwait`	Waits for an event, such as the destruction of a window, or a change in the value of a variable.
`update`	Processes all pending events and updates the display.
`winfo`	Returns information about a widget.
`wm`	Provides access to the window manager. (You can send commands to the window manager, requesting a size for your top-level window, for example.)

Defining Widget Hierarchies in Tk

From the example that creates a label and a button, you may have guessed that the argument that follows the widget-creation command is the widget's name. If you are wondering why all the names start with a period, which is required at the beginning of a widget's name, it is because widgets are organized in a hierarchy.

Suppose that you have a main window that contains a menu bar, a text area, and a scroll bar. The menu bar has two buttons, labeled File and Help. Figure 25-4 shows this widget hierarchy as it appears onscreen; it also shows how the widget names relate to this hierarchy.

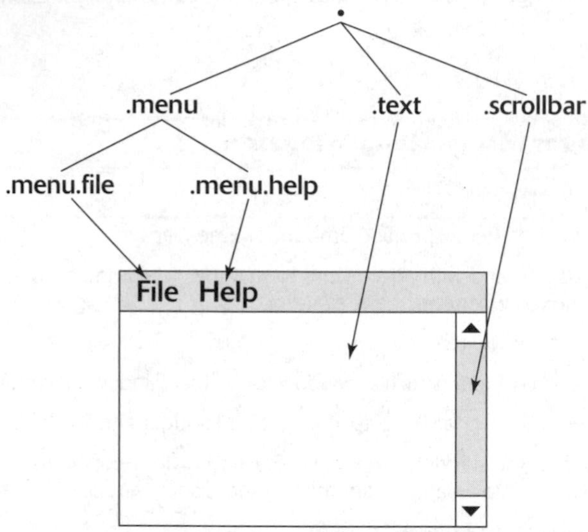

Figure 25-4: Relationship between Widget Names and the Widget Hierarchy.

The root of the widget hierarchy is the main window of the application; a single period (dot) is used to denote the main window. This main window is a child of the root window of the X display. Each child of the main window has a name that begins with a dot. Thus, `.menu` is a child of the main window.

The names of other widgets depend on their positions in the hierarchy. The buttons in the menu bar have names — `.menu.file` and `.menu.help` — that indicate that they are child widgets of the `.menu` widget. As you create widgets, you specify the name of each widget, in turn defining the widget hierarchy.

If you think about it, you can see that the widget-naming scheme is similar to the pathname of a file in Linux. The period (.) in a widget's name is analogous to the slash (/) in a file's pathname. In fact, the Tk documentation and online manual pages use the term "Tk pathname" to indicate the widget hierarchy.

All widget names must start with a lowercase letter or a number. The name cannot include a period because the period indicates the widget's location in the hierarchy. Names that start with an uppercase letter denote a class used in specifying resources; the meaning of the term "resources" is the same as in X.

Configuring Widgets

Tk treats each widget name as a command name. You can perform operations on a specific widget by using that widget's name, followed by arguments that make sense for that widget. If you have a button named .b, for example, use the following command to set that button's background to blue:

```
.b config -fg blue
```

You can change the button's label to Goodbye! by using the following command:

```
.b config -text Goodbye!
```

The arguments -fg blue and -text Goodbye! specify the attributes of a widget. Each attribute name begins with a hyphen (-), as in -text. The next argument is that attribute's value.

Displaying Widgets

Tk does not display a widget, until you use a command to position the widget in the main window. To display the widgets, you have to use a *geometry manager*—a Tk procedure that arranges one or more child widgets in a parent widget.

Tk provides two geometry-management commands for organizing and displaying widgets:

- The place command enables you to position a widget at a fixed location in the window of a designated master widget (which does not necessarily have to be a parent widget). The master widget is used as a reference—other widgets are positioned relative to the master widget. Also, you can specify relative positions, such as a horizontal position half the width of the master widget.
- The pack command arranges child widgets around the edges of the master window. You can specify the side of the parent on which the child widget is placed, as well as any extra space you want to use around the child. As the name suggests, the pack command packs widgets together as tightly as possible.

Although the pack and place commands take many different options, their basic use is straightforward. I suggest you start wish, create a few widgets, and try the place and pack commands to see their effects.

insider insight

The pack and place commands have a form—pack forget and place forget—that you can use to hide a widget. If you want to hide a button named .btn1, for example, use the command pack forget .btn1. To make the button reappear, use the pack .btn1 command again.

Using the pack Command

The pack command is the most commonly used geometry-management command in Tk. As some of the simple examples in this chapter show, to make a button named .btn1 appear, use pack as follows:

```
pack .btn1
```

You can specify several widget names on the same `pack` command line. To display the buttons `.btn1`, `.btn2`, and `.btn3`, arranged in a vertical line in that order, use the following:

```
pack .btn1 .btn2 .btn3
```

On a menu bar, for instance, this type of `pack` command makes the most efficient use of the available space.

Table 25-6 summarizes the `pack` command's syntax. As Table 25-6 shows, you can use the `pack` command to position widgets and get information about the widget hierarchy.

Table 25-6: Different Forms of the pack Command

Command	*Description*
`pack` *`widgetNames options`*	Packs the listed widgets according to the specified *`options`* (same as `pack configure`). Table 25-7 shows the list of available options.
`pack configure` *`widgetNames options`*	Packs the listed widgets according to the specified options.
`pack forget` *`widgetNames`*	Hides (unpacks) the specified widgets.
`pack info` *`widget`*	Returns the packing configuration (a list of options and values) of the specified *`widget`*.
`pack propagate` *`widget boolean`*	If *`boolean`* is `1`, this enables geometry propagation for the specified widget; otherwise, this command disables propagation. (When geometry propagation is enabled, the size of a widget's window is determined by the sizes of the widgets contained in that window.)
`pack slaves` *`widget`*	Returns the list of widgets managed by a specified widget.

If you want a more complicated layout of widgets, you have to use the packing options shown in Table 25-7.

Table 25-7: Options for Packing Widgets

Option	*Description*
`-after` *`widgetName`*	Places the widget that is being packed after the widget specified by *`widgetName`*.
`-anchor` *`anchorPos`*	Determines where the managed widget is placed. (This applies only when the containing widget is larger than the managed widget.) The *`anchorPos`* value can be `center`, `e`, `n`, `ne`, `nw`, `s`, `se`, `sw`, or `w`; the default is `center`.
`-before` *`widgetName`*	Places the widget that is being packed before the widget specified by *`widgetName`*.

Option	Description
`-expand` *boolean*	If *boolean* is `1`, the contained widget expands to use any space left over in the containing widget.
`-fill` *style*	Indicates how to expand the containing widget, if it becomes bigger than what the widgets contained in it require. The *style* value can be `both`, `none`, `x`, or `y`.
`-in` *widgetName*	Indicates the widget in which the widgets specified in the pack command line are placed. If you do not use this option, widgets are packed in their parent widget (`.f.b` is packed in `.f`).
`-ipadx` *amount*	Specifies extra horizontal space inside the widget being packed (in addition to the space that it already needs). The *amount* value is a number, in screen units.
`-ipady` *amount*	Specifies extra vertical space inside the widget being packed (in addition to the space it already needs). The *amount* value is a number, in screen units.
`-padx amount`	Specifies extra horizontal space outside the border of the widget that is being packed. The *amount* value is a number, in screen units.
`-pady` *amount*	Specifies extra vertical space outside the border of the widget being packed. The *amount* value is a number, in screen units.
`-side` *sideName*	Packs against the specified side. The *sideName* value is `bottom`, `left`, `right`, or `top`; the default is `top`.

insider insight

If you are wondering how to remember all these options, my advice is that you not remember them. Usually, you can get by with just a few of these options, and you will begin to remember them after a while. To become familiar with what each option does, start `wish`, create a few widgets, and try packing them with different options. From then on, whenever you need the exact syntax of an option, consult the online manual by typing man n pack or simply man pack.

Using the place Command

The `place` command is a simpler way to specify the placement of widgets as compared to the `pack` command, but you have to position all the windows yourself. It is simpler than `pack` because the `place` command gives you direct control of the widget positions. On the other hand, direct control of widget placement is fine for a few windows, but it can get tedious in a hurry when you have many widgets in a user interface.

Using `place`, you can position a widget at a specific location. For example, to place `.btn1` at the coordinate (100, 50) in its parent widget, use the following command:

```
place .btn1 -x 100 -y 50
```

A good use of `place` is to center a widget within its parent widget. For this purpose, use the `-relx` and `-rely` options of place. If `.f` is a frame widget (a widget that contains other widgets), you can display it at the center of the parent window by using the following commands:

```
frame .f
button .f.b1 -text Configure
button .f.b2 -text Quit
pack .f.b1 .f.b2 -side left
place .f -relx 0.5 -rely 0.5 -anchor center
```

As the code fragment shows, the buttons inside the frame are packed with the `pack` command. Only the frame, `.f`, is positioned with the `place` command. The `-relx` and `-rely` options enable you to specify the relative positions in terms of a fraction of the containing widget's size. A zero value for `-relx` means the left edge; 1 is the right edge; and 0.5 means the middle.

Like `pack`, the `place` command has several forms, listed in Table 25-8.

Table 25-8: Forms of the place Command

Command	*Description*
`place` *`widgetNames options`*	Positions the listed widgets according to the specified *`options`* (same as `place configure`). Table 25-9 shows the list of available options.
`place configure` *`widgetNames options`*	Positions the listed widgets according to the specified options.
`place forget` *`widgetNames`*	Stops managing the specified widgets and unpacks (hides) them.
`place info` *`widget`*	Returns the list of options and their values for the specified widget.
`place slaves` *`widget`*	Returns the list of widgets managed by the specified widget.

In addition, `place` takes several options, summarized in Table 25-9. Use these options with the plain `place` command or the `place configure` command.

Table 25-9: Options for Placing Widgets

Option	*Description*
`-anchor` *`anchorPos`*	Specifies which point of the managed widget is placed in the specified position in the managing window. The *`anchorPos`* value can be `center`, `e`, `n`, `ne`, `nw`, `s`, `se`, `sw`, or `w`; the default is `nw` (upper-left corner).
`-bordermode` *`bmode`*	Indicates how the managing widget's borders are used when the managed widgets are positioned. The `bordermode` value must be `ignore`, `inside`, or `outside`.

Option	Description
`-height` *size*	Specifies the height of the managed widget.
`-in` *widgetName*	Indicates the widget relative to which the positions of the widgets specified in the place command line are specified. If you do not use this option, widgets are placed relative to their parent widgets (`.f.b` is positioned relative to `.f`).
`-relheight fraction`	Specifies the height of the managed widget as a fraction of the managing widget. The fraction is a floating-point value.
`-relwidth` *fraction*	Specifies the width of the managed widget as a fraction of the managing widget. The fraction is a floating-point value.
`-relx` *fraction*	Specifies the horizontal position of the managed widget as a fraction of the managing widget's width. The *fraction* is a floating-point value; `0.0` means the left edge, and `1.0` means the right edge.
`-rely` *fraction*	Specifies the vertical position of the managed widget as a fraction of the managing widget's height. The *fraction* is a floating-point value; `0.0` means the top edge, and `1.0` means the bottom edge.
`-x` *coord*	Specifies the horizontal position of the managed widget's anchor point in the managing widget. The *coord* value is specified in screen coordinates.
`-y` *coord*	Specifies the vertical position of the managed widget's anchor point in the managing widget. The *coord* value is specified in screen coordinates.
`-width` *size*	Specifies the width of the managed widget.

Binding Actions to Events

When you write a program that has a graphical user interface, various program actions are initiated by events, such as the user clicking a button in the user interface. In a Tk script, you indicate what the program does by associating actions with events. In this case, an action is simply a Tcl script that performs some task. In the case of a Quit button, for example, a logical action is the Tcl command `exit`, which ends the Tk script.

For buttons, a click of the button is a simple way to form this association. Use the `command` option of the button command to specify a Tcl command to be executed when the user clicks the button. The `exit` command is associated with the Quit button as follows:

```
button .b -text Quit -command { exit }
```

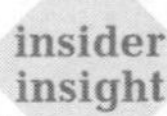

The curly braces are not necessary when you have only one Tcl command, but you must enclose multiple commands inside braces.

The `bind` command is the most common way to associate an action with an event. Following is the general syntax of the `bind` command:

```
bind widgetName <eventSpecification> TclCommand
```

The `widgetName` argument is usually the pathname of a widget, although you can bind an event to a class of widgets, such as all buttons. Typically, you have to consult online help to specify eventSpecification. (In this section, I show you an example and explain event specifications.) The last argument — `TclCommand` — refers to the Tcl commands you want to execute when the specified event occurs. These Tcl commands can be any Tcl script, ranging from a simple `puts` command to a complete Tcl script stored in a separate file.

To see a more detailed example of how to bind an action to an event, consider this scenario. You may have noticed that many Microsoft Windows applications, as well as GNOME and KDE applications, sport a toolbar — essentially, a collection of buttons, each of which is meant to perform a specific task. Typically, each button bears an icon that indicates its purpose. To help users learn the meaning of a button quickly, many Windows applications have a feature called *tool help*. If you place the mouse pointer on a button, a small window pops up, displaying a short help message that tells you what the button does.

You can use Tk to implement a similar tool-help feature. Follow these steps:

1. Create the button.
2. Prepare the help message as a label (preferably with a bright background, such as yellow).
3. When the mouse pointer enters a button, an Enter event occurs. Bind the Enter event to a command that makes the help label visible. Use the `place` command to position the label relative to the button, so that the tool help label always appears near the associated button. The following example shows how `bind` is used to associate the `place` command (shown within braces) with the Enter event:

   ```
   bind .f.q <Enter> { place .bh -in .f.q -relx 0.5 -rely 1.0 }
   ```

4. When the mouse pointer leaves the button, a Leave event occurs. Bind the Leave event to the `place forget` command to hide the help message, as follows:

   ```
   bind .f.q <Leave> { place forget .bh }
   ```

The following sample toolhelp script demonstrates how to implement tool help in Tk:

```
#!/usr/bin/wish -f
# Demonstrates a "tool help" window that appears when you
# place the mouse pointer inside the Quit button.

wm geometry . 180x60

frame .f
button .f.b -text File
```

```
label .bh -text "Quit program"
.bh config -bg yellow
button .f.q -text Quit -command { exit }

bind .f.q <Enter> { place .bh -in .f.q -relx 0.5 -rely 1.0 }
bind .f.q <Leave> { place forget .bh }


pack .f.b .f.q -side left
pack .f -fill x
```

Make the toolhelp script file executable by using the `chmod +x toolhelp` command. Then run that script by typing **./toolhelp** at the shell prompt in a terminal window. Figure 25-5 shows the window that results after you place the mouse pointer on the Quit button.

Figure 25-5: A Tk Script That Demonstrates How to Implement Toolhelp Messages.

When you use `bind` to associate a Tcl script with an event, you need to know how to specify the event. Most events are either keyboard events or mouse events. A smaller number of events are related to the state of a widget's window. `<Map>` and `<Unmap>` events, for example, occur when a widget is managed or unmanaged (when you use `pack forget` or `place forget`).

Understanding Keyboard Events

There are two keyboard events:

- `<KeyPress>` occurs when you press a key.
- `<KeyRelease>` occurs when you release a key.

You can specify a keyboard event for a specific key by appending that key's *keysym* (which is the X Window System's standard name for a key) to the string `KeyPress-` and enclosing everything in angle brackets. The event associated with pressing the `q` key, for example, is specified by `<KeyPress-q>`. Tk provides a shorter format for keyboard events. You can simply place the keysym inside angle brackets, as follows:

```
<q>
```

For most key presses, the event specification is straightforward. If you want to exit when the user presses Ctrl-C inside a widget named `.text`, use the `bind` command as follows:

```
bind .text <Control-c> exit
```

Table 25-10 shows some other commonly used keysyms. To view a list of all kyesyms, visit `www.tcl.tk/man/tcl8.4/TkCmd/keysyms.htm`.

Table 25-10: Some Commonly Used Keysyms

Keysym	*Name of Key*
`BackSpace`	Backspace
`comma`	Comma
`Down`	Down arrow
`dollar`	Dollar sign ($)
`Escape`	Escape
`exclam`	Exclamation mark
`Left`	Left arrow
`numbersign`	Number sign (#)
`period`	Period
`Return`	Enter
`Right`	Right arrow
`Tab`	Tab
`Up`	Up arrow

Inside the Tcl commands that are bound to a key event, use the `%A` keyword to refer to the printable character the user presses. For any nonprintable character, `%A` is replaced by `{}` (a pair of empty braces). The `%W` keyword is replaced by the name of the widget that receives the keypress. Thus, you can use the following code to insert text into a text widget named `.text1`:

```
# Assume .text1 is a text widget
bind .text1 <KeyPress> {
    if { "%A" != "{}"} { %W insert insert %A}
}
```

Remember that a widget's name itself is a command and that the command's argument depends on the type of widget. For a text widget, the command `%W insert insert %A`, as shown in the example, inserts the character into the text widget.

Understanding Mouse Events

Use `<ButtonPress>` and `<ButtonRelease>` to denote mouse-button click and release events, respectively. You have to append the button number to make the event specific. Thus, clicking the left mouse button (which is button 1 in X terminology) is denoted by `<ButtonPress-1>`. A shorthand notation for button presses is to omit `Press`; thus, you can write `<Button-1>` to denote the event generated by clicking the left mouse button.

In the Tcl commands that are bound to a mouse event, the keywords `%x` and `%y` denote the `x` and `y` coordinates of the mouse pointer (relative to the widget's window) at the time of the mouse event. Thus, you can track the position of mouse clicks on a widget `.text1` as follows:

```
bind .text1 <Button-1> { puts "Click at (%x, %y) on widget: %W"}
```

Other mouse events include the Enter and Leave events, which occur when you move the mouse pointer into or out of a widget, respectively. These two events are denoted by `<Enter>` and `<Leave>`. The toolhelp example shown in "Binding Actions to Events," earlier in this chapter, illustrates a way to use the `<Enter>` and `<Leave>` events.

Another event related to the mouse pointer is `<Motion>`, which occurs when you move the mouse pointer within a widget.

Understanding Window Events

In addition to keyboard and mouse events, X includes many events that occur when a window is manipulated. The X server generates `<Map>` and `<Unmap>` events, for example, when a widget is displayed or hidden (by the `pack` or `place` command).

A `<Configure>` event occurs when the user resizes a window. Thus, you can bind a `<Configure>` event to a redisplay procedure that redraws the contents of a widget based on the new size.

A `<Destroy>` event occurs when a window is about to be destroyed. Bind a procedure to the `<Destroy>` event, and intercept requests to delete a window.

Summary

The combination of Tool Command Language (Tcl) and its X Window System–based graphical toolkit, Tk, is ideal for quickly developing applications with a graphical interface. This chapter introduces Tcl/Tk through simple examples.

In this chapter, you learned the following:

- Tcl is an interpreted language with a set of commands you can combine, according to a set of rules. Tcl comes with the Linux distribution on the companion DVD.
- You can learn the Tcl syntax and develop Tcl scripts interactively by running the Tcl command interpreter, `tclsh`, and entering Tcl commands at the `tclsh` prompt.
- Tcl includes built-in commands for most routine tasks, such as reading and writing files, manipulating strings, and running any Linux command. Also, Tcl includes control-flow commands—such as `if`, `for`, and `while`—that enable you to control the sequence of commands the interpreter processes. Finally, you can use Tcl's `proc` command to write new Tcl commands that use combinations of existing commands.
- Tk, the Tcl toolkit, is an extension of Tcl that uses the X Window System to enable you to build graphical user interfaces. Tk provides the three-dimensional

appearance of Motif, but Tk does not require the Motif toolkit or any other X toolkit. Tk is built on Xlib, which is the C-language Application Programming Interface (API) for X.

- Tk includes commands for creating many common widgets (user-interface elements), such as buttons, labels, list boxes, and scrollbars. A widget-naming convention specifies the widget hierarchy (the organization of the widgets).
- To make the graphical interface active, you have to use the `bind` command to associate Tcl commands with specific keyboard events and mouse events.
- You can interactively experiment with and create Tk programs by running `wish`, the windowing shell that can interpret all Tcl and Tk commands.

Java Programming

Chapter 26

Secrets in This Chapter

Java is an object-oriented programming language that began life as a language for embedded systems — small computers that control electronic devices. Java became popular as a way of embedding small application programs called *applets* into the HTML code of Web pages. When the browser downloads a Web page with an applet, the browser also downloads the applet and executes that application program. To be more precise, these Java applets are transmitted as sequences of bytes that can be executed by a Java Virtual Machine (JVM) embedded in a Web browser. Thus, a Java program can be executed anywhere a JVM and the Java libraries are available.

Java's use has extended beyond applets to general-purpose applications that do not have to run inside a Web browser. Many organizations now use Java for developing mission-critical applications, including three-tiered Web applications that provide access to the corporate databases that often reside on older mainframe systems. These three-tiered Web applications use Java *servlets* — Java code that runs on the Web server and provides access to corporate databases through Java Database Connectivity (JDBC) application programming interface (API).

This chapter provides you an overview of the Java language and shows you a few simple examples. As you might guess, a single chapter cannot do justice to Java; all this chapter can do is get you started. With that goal in mind, this chapter focuses immediately on the tools you need to create Java applications and shows you several small examples to illustrate specific Java programming techniques.

insider insight

The latest version of Fedora includes Eclipse, a graphical interactive development environment (IDE) for building Java applications. To try Eclipse, select the Eclipse package group when you install Fedora. You can start Eclipse by selecting Applications ➪ Programming ➪ Eclipse from the GNOME desktop. You can then explore the Eclipse environment and try your hand at writing Java applications in Eclipse. There is online help to guide you through the steps involved in writing an application. Eclipse comes with the Standard Widget Toolkit (SWT), which is a basic graphics and widget toolkit for Java applications. Instead of the Java Swing (described later in this chapter), you can use SWT to develop GUI Java applications in Eclipse.

Getting Ready for Java Programming

Like any programming language, the best way to learn Java is to begin writing some programs. Of course, you need an overview of the language as well, but if you already know C++ and understand the basics of object-oriented programming, you can quickly become proficient in Java.

This section gets you started with the hands-on aspects of Java programming by briefly describing *GCJ* — the GNU Java compiler that comes with Linux.

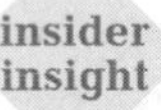

Fedora Linux comes with everything you need to develop Java applications — applets, client-side applications, and server-side applications (servlets). The Java development tools should be installed provided you installed the Java Development package group when you installed Fedora. You can do almost everything without having to download the Java 2 Software Development Kit (SDK) from Sun's website. However, I still show you how to download and install the Java 2 SDK.

Using GCJ

Fedora Linux comes with GCJ — the GNU Compiler for the Java Programming Language. GCJ should be installed if you selected the Development Tools package during Fedora installation.

You can use the GCJ to compile and run Java programs. For example, to build a simple Java program that prints `Hello, World!`, follow these steps from a text console or a terminal window (I explain Java programming further in the latter part of this chapter):

1. Use a text editor such as vi or Emacs to create a file named `HelloWorld.java` and add the following lines to that file:

```
public class HelloWorld {
    public static void main(String [] args) {
        System.out.println("Hello, World!");
    }
}
```

2. Compile and create an executable program named `HelloWorld` by running `gcj` (that's the name of the GNU Java compiler's executable) with the following command line:

```
gcj --main=HelloWorld -o HelloWorld HelloWorld.java
```

3. Run the program with the following command:

```
./HelloWorld
```

The program should display the following line of output:

```
Hello, World!
```

You can compile more complex Java programs using GCJ, but you run into a roadblock because GCJ does not yet include all the Java libraries.

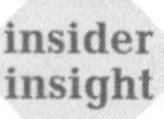

Although Java code can theoretically run wherever a JVM is available, all but the simplest Java applications also require one or more of the Java libraries that may not necessarily be available in a JVM. The Java libraries provide the application programming interfaces (APIs) that Java programs use to perform tasks such as displaying graphical output or exchanging data over the network. Fedora comes with the necessary libraries to run typical Java programs. You can also use the libraries that come with Sun's Java 2 Standard Edition (J2SE). You can download the latest J2SE by following the links at Sun's Java home page (`http://java.sun.com/`).

Downloading and Installing Java 2 SDK

To develop Java applications, you can use Sun's Java 2 Software Development Kit. You can download the latest version of this kit by following the links at the following website:

```
http://java.sun.com/j2se/downloads/index.html
```

Sun has two Java development products — Java 2 Standard Edition (J2SE) and Java 2 Enterprise Edition (J2EE). The J2SE Software Development Kit (SDK) — also known as Java 2 SDK — includes the Java compiler, APIs, and other tools you need to develop Java applications and applets.

J2EE is meant for developing Java applications that run on Web servers. Such server-side applications include *servlets* — Java applications that run under the control of a Web server and perform computations or provide access to databases. J2EE includes the servlet APIs as well the APIs needed to support Web services and application servers. *Web services* refer to software systems with public interfaces defined in the Extensible Markup Language (XML). Other applications can discover information about a Web service by using well-defined protocols and then make use of whatever services the Web service provides. *Application servers* refer to the tools and utilities that can be used on a Web server to run Java servlets, maintain session and state information, access databases, perform database transactions, process new content such as XML, and generate dynamic HTML documents. J2EE relies on J2SE.

You should download the J2SE SDK because it has all the tools you need to develop Java applications. If you also plan to develop servlets and other server-side Java applications, you need the J2EE as well.

At its J2SE download website (`http://java.sun.com/j2se/downloads/index.html`), Sun Microsystems provides J2SE SDK versions 1.3.1, 1.4.2, and 5.0 for the following systems:

- Linux (32-bit Intel processors)
- Linux (64-bit AMD processors)
- Microsoft Windows 95/98/Me/200/NT/XP
- Sun Solaris SPARC — both 32 bit and 64 bit
- Sun Solaris x86
- Solaris for AMD 64-bit processors

For Fedora Linux, you should download the 32-bit Linux version of the J2SE SDK.

To download and install J2SE SDK for Linux, follow these steps from your Fedora Linux system:

1. Make sure that your system is connected to the Internet. Start the Web browser and point the Web browser to the following URL:

   ```
   http://java.sun.com/j2se/downloads/index.html
   ```

   Click the link for the latest version of J2SE SDK. You have to read and accept the license agreement before you can proceed. Click Continue when you are ready,
2. Select the SDK download link for the item labeled "Linux RPM in self-extracting file." Read the license agreement and, if you agree, click Accept.

3. Click the link for the J2SE SDK file, and save it a convenient directory on your Linux system (for example, `/usr/local`). The SDK is typically close to 45MB in size, so the download can take a while if you have a slow dial-up Internet connection. After the download is completed, you end up with a file whose name ends in `.rpm.bin`. This file is a shell script that you must execute to extract the RPM file for J2SE SDK.
4. From a terminal window, change to the directory where you saved the J2SE SDK file and type the following command to make that file executable:
   ```
   chmod +x jdk*.bin
   ```
5. Execute the file by typing the following command:
   ```
   ./jdk*.bin
   ```
   This displays the license agreement a page at a time. After reading each page, press Enter to move forward. After the last page, you see the following prompt:
   ```
   Do you agree to the above license terms? [yes or no]
   ```
6. Type **yes**, and press Enter. This unpacks and installs the Java 2 SDK in the `/usr/java` directory under a subdirectory whose name depends on the version you are installing. For example, when I installed J2SE SDK version 1.5.0_02, everything was installed in the following directory:
   ```
   /usr/java/jdk1.5.0_02
   ```

Set the `PATH` environment variable to include the directory where the Java 2 SDK binaries are located. For example, if you install the Java 2 SDK in the `/usr/java/jdk1.5.0_02` directory, use a text editor to create a `java.sh` file in the `/etc/profile.d` directory and add the following line in that file :

```
PATH=/usr/java/jdk1.5.0_02/bin:$PATH
```

Performing this step ensures that the PATH environment variable includes the JAVA2 SDK directory every time you log in. Type **source /etc/profile.d/java.sh** to update the PATH environment variable for the current login session.

Taking Stock of the Java 2 SDK

The Java 2 SDK comes with a number of files organized into several directories. The top-level directory contains the files and subdirectories shown in Table 26-1.

Table 26-1: Java 2 SDK Content Summary

Name	*Description*
`LICENSE`	The license agreement under which Sun Microsystems is providing you the Java 2 SDK. You should read this file before using the Java 2 SDK.
`COPYRIGHT`	The copyright information for this release of the Java 2 SDK.
`README.html`	HTML file that provides information about the Java 2 SDK contents with links to Sun's websites.

(continued)

Table 26-1 *(continued)*

Name	*Description*
src.zip	JDK source code in a ZIP archive. You don't need the source files to write Java applets or applications.
bin	Directory containing the executable programs. You should add the full pathname of this directory to your PATH environment variable.
demo	Directory with many sample Java programs with source code .
include	Directory with the header files for the Java 2 SDK source (you don't need these to write Java programs).
lib	Directory with Java class libraries.
man	Directory with man pages for Java 2 SDK tools such as the javac compiler and java — the Java interpreter.

The tools you'll use most are in the `bin` subdirectory. Here are some of the tools that you'll use when creating Java applications:

- **appletviewer:** Java applet viewer program to load and run Java applets that are designed to be embedded in an HTML document (you can also load applets in a Java-capable browser by embedding the applet in an HTML document using the `<applet>` tag).
- **java:** Java interpreter that runs standalone Java programs specified by a class name (it expects to find the class in a file with same name as the class, but with a `.class` extension). Standalone Java applications are Java classes with a `main` method (in Java, functions are called *methods*).
- **javac:** Java compiler that converts Java source code into "byte code" (that's the instruction set of the Java Virtual Machine). The compiler takes source code in a `.java` file and generates compiled code in a `.class` file.
- **jdb:** Java debugger with a command syntax like that of the Linux gdb debuggers.
- **javadoc:** Java API documentation generator that extracts documentation from source files with special comments that begin with /** and ends with a */.
- **javah:** Java C file generator that generates C `.h` and `.c` files for a Java class. Such C files are needed to implement the native methods that make the APIs work on a particular operating system.
- **javap:** Java class file disassembler that takes a class name and prints a human-readable description of the class.

Of these programs, the three that you'll use most are the following:

- You'll use `javac` a lot because that's the Java compiler program. The `javac` program converts a Java source file (you'll see some examples in the next section) into a binary file that contains Java byte code — the instruction set of the Java Virtual Machine.
- If you write a standalone Java application — one that can run without being embedded in a Web browser — you'll use the Java interpreter program, java, to run the application.

- If you write Java *applets* — miniapplications that run inside a Web browser — you'll use the appletviewer program to test the applets. Of course, you can also test applets using a Java-capable Web browser such as Mozilla (after you install the Java plug-in).

Writing Your First Java Program

In the grand old tradition of C programming books, I'll begin by showing you how to display `"Hello, World!"` from a Java program. However, before I proceed, I should point out the difference between three types of Java programs:

- **Standalone Java application:** This is a Java program that can be executed by a Java interpreter. A Java standalone application is just like the standalone C or C++ programs that you might know. The application has a main method and the java interpreter can run the application. General-purpose Java applications take the form of standalone applications.
- **Java applet:** This is a Java class that can be loaded and executed by the appletviewer program or by a Java-capable Web browser. You have to first embed the applet inside an HTML document using the `<applet>` tag and then load that HTML document to activate the applet. As a Webmaster, you'll mostly write Java applets.
- **Java servlet:** This is a Java class loaded and executed by a Web server (or a server that helps the Web server such as the Apache Tomcat server). To develop servlets, you need the Java 2 Enterprise Edition.

Whether you write a standalone application or an applet or a servlet, the basic steps are similar except for the last step when you execute the program. You use the java interpreter to run standalone programs and appletviewer to test applets. For servlets, you simply place them in a specific directory and insert HTML code to refer to the servlets. These development steps are as follows:

1. Use a text editor to create the Java source file. A Java application is a class (a type of object — collection of data and methods). The source file's name must be the class name with a `.java` extension.
2. Process the source file with javac (the Java compiler) to generate the class file with a `.class` extension.
3. If it's a standalone application, run the class with the java interpreter with the following command:

   ```
   java classname
   ```

4. If the program is an applet, create an HTML document and embed the applet using the `<applet>` tag. Then, load that HTML document using appletviewer or a Java-capable Web browser. When the browser loads the HTML document, it also activates all embedded Java applets.

Writing a Standalone "Hello, World!" Program

The classic C-style `"Hello, World!"` application is easy to write in Java. That's because many of Java's syntactical details are similar to that of C and C++. The following code implements a simple `"Hello, World!"` program in Java (you have seen this in an earlier section, but it's so short that I'll just show you again):

```
public class HelloWorld
{
    public static void main(String[] args)
    {
        System.out.println("Hello, World!");
    }
}
```

Even this simple Java program illustrates some key features of Java:

- Every Java program is a public class definition.
- A standalone application contains a `main` method that must be declared `public static void`. The interpreter starts execution at the `main` method.

Save this program in a file named `HelloWorld.java`. Then, compile it with the following command:

```
javac HelloWorld.java
```

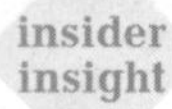

If you get an error saying "command not found," then you need to add the Java 2 SDK binary directory to the `PATH` environment variable. If you installed the Java2 SDK in `/usr/java/jdk1.5.0_02`, then type the following command to add the binary directory to `PATH`:

```
PATH=/usr/java/jdk1.5.0_02/bin:$PATH
```

You need the Java 2 SDK directory at the beginning of `PATH` because Fedora includes its own java and javac commands, but for this chapter, you should use the java and javac commands that come with Sun's Java 2 SDK.

The `javac` compiler creates a class file named `HelloWorld.class`. To run the application, use the Java interpreter and specify the class name as a parameter, like this:

```
java HelloWorld
```

The program prints the following output:

```
Hello, World!
```

Writing a Simple Java Applet

The other model of a Java program is the applet that runs inside the appletviewer program or a Java-capable Web browser. Specifically, a Java applet is a class in the Java Abstract Windowing Toolkit (AWT). In an applet, you do not have to provide a `main` method. Instead, you provide a `paint` method where you place code to draw in an area of a window. You can use the applet model to implement GUIs and other graphical programs.

For a `"Hello, World!"` applet, I'll do the following:

- Instead of displaying the message in a default font, pick a specific font to display the message.
- Use the information about the font sizes to center the message within the area where the applet is required to display its output.
- Draw the text in red instead of the default black color.

Listing 26-1 shows the Java code that implements the "Hello, World!" applet.

Listing 26-1: The HelloWorld Java Applet

```
//--------------------------------------------------------------
// File: HelloWorld.java
//
// Displays "Hello, World!" in Helvetica font and in red color.
//--------------------------------------------------------------

import java.applet.*;
import java.awt.*;

//--------------------------------------------------------------
// H e l l o W o r l d
//
// Applet class to display "Hello, World!"

public class HelloWorld extends Applet
{
    private String hellomsg = "Hello, World!";
    private static final long serialVersionUID = 1L;
//--------------------------------------------------------------
// p a i n t
//
// Method that paints the output

    public void paint(Graphics gc)
    {
// Draw a rectangle around the applet's bounding box
// so we can see the box.
        gc.drawRect(0, 0, getSize().width-1,
                          getSize().height-1);

// Create the font to be used for the message.
        Font helv = new Font("Helvetica", Font.BOLD, 24);

// Select the font into the Graphics object.
        gc.setFont(helv);

// Get the font metrics (details of the font size).
        FontMetrics fm = gc.getFontMetrics();
        int mwidth = fm.stringWidth(hellomsg);
        int ascent = fm.getAscent();
        int descent = fm.getDescent();
```

(continued)

Listing 26-1 *(continued)*

```
// Compute starting (x.y) position to center string
// The size() method returns size of the applet's
// bounding box.
        int xstart = getSize().width/2 - mwidth/2;
        int ystart = getSize().height/2 + ascent/2 - descent/2;

// Set the color to red.
        gc.setColor(Color.red);

// Now draw the string.
        gc.drawString(hellomsg, xstart, ystart);
    }
}
```

By browsing through this code, you can learn a lot about how to display graphics output in Java. Here are the key points to note:

- The `import` statement lists external classes that this program uses. The name that follows the `import` statement can be the name of a class or can be a name with a wildcard (*), which tells the Java compiler to import all the classes in a package. This example uses the `Applet` class as well as a number of graphics classes that are in the java.awt package.
- The `HelloWorld` applet is defined as an extension of the `Applet` class. That's what the statement `public class HelloWorld extends java.applet.Applet` means.
- An applet's `paint` method contains the code that draws the output. The `paint` method receives a `Graphics` object as an argument. You have to call methods of the `Graphics` object to display output.
- The `getSize` method returns the size of the applet's drawing area.
- To use a font, you have to first create a `Font` object and then call the `setFont` method of the `Graphics` object.
- To draw text in a specific color, invoke the `setColor` method of the `Graphics` object with an appropriate `Color` object as argument.
- If you know C++, you'll notice that Java's method invocation is similar to the way you call the member function of a C++ object. Indeed, there are many similarities between C++ and Java.

Save the listing in a file named `HelloWorld.java`. Then, compile it with the command:

```
javac HelloWorld.java
```

This step creates the applet class file: `HelloWorld.class`. To test the applet, you have to create an HTML document and embed the applet in that document, as shown in the following example:

```
<html>
<head>
<title>Hello, World! from Java</title>
```

```
</head>

<body>

<h3>"Hello, World!" from Java</h3>

A Java applet is given an area where it displays
its output. In this example, the applet draws a
border around its assigned area and then displays
the "Hello, World!" message centered in that box.
<br>

<applet code=HelloWorld width=200 height=60>
If you see this message, then you do not have a
Java-capable browser.
</applet>

Here is the applet!
</body>
</html>
```

As this HTML source shows, you have to use the `<applet>` tag to insert an applet in an HTML document.

You can use two tools to test the applet. The first one is appletviewer, which comes with JDK. To view the `HelloWorld` applet, you have to run the appletviewer program and provide the name of the HTML document that includes the applet. Suppose that the HTML document is in the file named `hello.html`. Then, you'd run appletviewer with the following command:

```
appletviewer hello.html
```

Figure 26-1 shows how the appletviewer displays the applet.

Figure 26-1: Running the "Hello, World!" Java Applet in appletviewer.

Notice that appletviewer displays only the applet; the rest of the text in the HTML document is ignored. However, the appearance is quite different in a Java-capable Web browser.

To view the applet in a Web browser, start the Firefox Web browser and select File ⇨ Open File from the menu. From the Open File dialog box, go to the directory where you have the `hello.html` file and the `HelloWorld.class` file (for the applet). Then, select the `hello.html` file, and click Open. Firefox then renders the HTML document containing the `HelloWorld` applet.

Unlike the appletviewer, Firefox should display the entire HTML document and the Java applet appears embedded in the document just like an image. The applet draws inside the rectangle assigned to it through the width and height attributes of the `<applet>` tag.

If Firefox fails to display the applet when you load an HTML document with an embedded applet, the most likely cause is that you have not yet installed Sun's Java plug-in for Firefox. The Java plug-in comes with the Java 2 SDK that you have already downloaded. To install the plug-in, you have to set up a symbolic link (shortcut) from the Firefox plug-in directory to the plug-in located in the Java 2 SDK directory. Here are the commands I type (after logging in as `root`) to install the Java plug-in file for J2SE version 1.5.0_02:

```
cd /usr/lib/firefox-1.0.3/plugins
ln -s /usr/java/jdk1.5.0_02/jre/plugin/i386/ns7/libjavaplugin_oji.so
```

To check that the plug-ins are loaded, start Firefox, type **about:plugins**, and press Enter. Firefox then displays information about the installed plug-ins in its window. In particular, you should see plug-ins that can handle the MIME data types `application/x-java-vm` and `application/x-java-applet` because those are needed to run a Java applet.

For the latest information about the Java plug-in, point your Mozilla browser to `http://java.sun.com/products/plugin/`.

Learning Java

Now that you have seen some examples of Java programming, this section provides an overview of Java. Previous examples show that Java can be used to create both standalone applications and applets that can be embedded in an HTML document. As you learn the features of Java, you'll notice that Java has everything you need from a general-purpose programming language. Although Java has been associated mostly with the creation of applets to be embedded in Web pages, many people have come to realize that Java is also ideal for developing general-purpose applications. Nowadays, Java is also extensively used for server-side programs such as Java servlets that work with Web servers.

One of the reasons for Java's popularity is the portability of Java code. The compiled Java code runs on any system for which a Java interpreter and the Java libraries are available. It's not trivial to build the Java libraries, but once the Java interpreter and libraries are available on an operating system, you can run most Java applications unchanged on that system.

Objects in Java

Java is an object-oriented language. So much so that Java does not allow any standalone procedures at all; all data and procedures must be inside an object. In fact, the entire Java application is an object as well.

The basic concepts of object-based programming are the same as those of other object-oriented programming languages such as Smalltalk or C++. There are three underlying concepts:

- Data abstraction
- Inheritance
- Polymorphism

Data Abstraction

To understand data abstraction, consider the file input/output (I/O) routines in the C run-time library. These routines allow you to view the file as a stream of bytes and allow you to perform various operations on this stream by calling the file I/O routines. For example, you can call `fopen` to open a file, `fclose` to close it, `fgetc` to read a character from it, and `fputc` to write a character to it. This abstract model of a file is implemented by defining a data type named `FILE` to hold all relevant information about a file. The C constructs `struct` and `typedef` are used to define `FILE`. You can think of this definition of `FILE`, together with the functions that operate on it, as a new data type just like C's `int` or `char`.

To use the `FILE` data type in C, you do not have to know the data structure that defines it. In fact, the underlying data structure of `FILE` can vary from one system to another. Yet, the C file I/O routines work in the same manner on all systems. This is possible because you never access the members of the `FILE` data structure directly. Instead you rely on functions and macros that essentially hide the inner details of `FILE`. This is known as *data hiding*.

Data abstraction is the process of defining a data type, often called an abstract data type (ADT), together with the principle of data hiding. The definition of an ADT involves specifying the internal representation of the ADT's data as well as the functions to be used by others to manipulate the ADT. Data hiding is used to ensure that the internal structure of the ADT can be altered without any fear of breaking the programs that call the functions provided for operations on that ADT. Thus, C's `FILE` data type is an example of an ADT (see Figure 26-2).

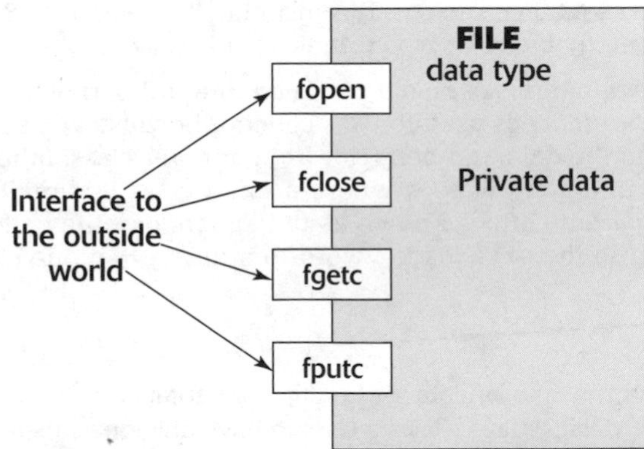

Figure 26-2: C's FILE Data Type as an Example of Abstract Data Type (ADT).

In object-oriented languages, you create an object from an ADT. Essentially, an ADT is a collection of variables together with the procedures necessary to operate on those variables. The variables represent the information contained in the object while the procedures define the operations that can be performed on that object. You can think of the ADT as a template from which specific instances of objects can be created as needed. The term "class" is often used for this template; consequently "class" is synonymous with an ADT. In fact, Java provides the class keyword precisely for the purpose of defining an ADT—the template from which objects are created. The ADT is a template for objects in the sense that creating an object involves setting aside a block of memory for the variables of that object.

In Java, the procedures that operate on an object are known as *methods*. This term comes from the object-oriented language Smalltalk. The methods define the behavior of an object. Another common term of object-oriented programming also originated in Smalltalk—the idea of sending messages to an object causing it to perform an operation by invoking one of the methods. In Java, you do this by calling the appropriate method of the object.

In Java, you use the `class` keyword to define the blueprint of an object. That means a class defines the data and methods that constitute a type of object. Then, you can create instances of the object by using the new keyword. For example, you might create an instance of a `Circle` class as follows:

```
Circle c1 = new Circle(100.0, 60.0, 50.0);
```

This example invokes the `Circle` class constructor that accepts three floating-point numbers as an argument (presumably, the coordinates of the center and the radius of the circle). You'll see a complete example of classes in the "Geometric Shapes in Java: An Example" section, later in this chapter.

Inheritance

Data abstraction does not cover an important characteristic of objects. Real-world objects do not exist in isolation. Each object is related to one or more other objects. In fact, you can often describe a new kind of object by pointing out how the new object's characteristics and behavior differ from those of a class of objects that already exists. This is what you do when you describe an object with a sentence such as: B is just like A, except that B has . . . and B does . . . . Here you are defining objects of type B in terms of those of type A.

This notion of defining a new object in terms of an old one is an integral part of object-oriented programming. The term *inheritance* is used for this concept because you can think of one class of objects as inheriting the data and behavior from another class. Inheritance imposes a hierarchical relationship among classes where a child class inherits from its parent. In Java terminology, the parent class is known as the *superclass*; the child is the *subclass*. In a Java program, you use the `extends` keyword to indicate that one class is a subclass of another.

Unlike C++, Java does not support multiple inheritance (multiple inheritance allows a class to inherit from multiple superclasses). Java allows a class to have only one superclass. In Java, all classes inherit from a single root class named `Object`. (The Smalltalk programming language also provides a class hierarchy of this type). Here the term "root class" refers to a class that does not have any superclass.

Polymorphism

In a literal sense, *polymorphism* means the quality of having more than one form. In the context of object-oriented programming, "polymorphism" refers to the fact that a single operation can have different behavior in different objects. In other words, different objects react differently to the same message. For example, consider the operation of addition. For two numbers, addition should generate the sum. In a programming language that supports object-oriented programming, you should be able to express the operation of addition by an operator, say, +. When this is possible, you can use the expression x+y to denote the sum of x and y, for many different types of x and y integers, floating-point numbers, and, even strings (for strings the + operation means the concatenation of two strings).

Similarly, suppose a number of geometrical shapes all support a method, draw. Each object reacts to this method by displaying its shape on a display screen. Obviously, the actual mechanism for displaying the object differs from one shape to another, but all shapes perform this task in response to the same method.

Polymorphism helps by allowing you to simplify the syntax of performing the same operation on a collection of objects. For example, by exploiting polymorphism, you can compute the area of each geometrical shape in an array of shapes with a simple loop like this:

```
// Assume "shapes" is an array of shapes (rectangles, circles,
// etc.) and "computeArea" is a function that computes the
// area of a shape.

for(int i=0; i < shapes.length; i++)
{
    double area = shapes[i].computeArea();
    System.out.println("Area = "+area);
}
```

This is possible because regardless of the exact geometrical shape, each object supports the computeArea method and computes the area in a way appropriate for that shape.

Geometric Shapes in Java: An Example

For a concrete illustration of object-oriented programming in Java, consider the following example. Suppose that you want to write a computer program that handles geometric shapes such as rectangles and circles. The program should be able to draw any shape and compute its area.

Shape Class

The first step in implementing the geometric shapes in Java is to define the classes. I'll start with an abstract class that simply defines the behavior of the shape classes by defining the common methods. The following listing shows the abstract Shape class, which you should save in the Shape.java file:

```
//-------------------------------------------------------------
// File: Shape.java
//
// Abstract class for Shape objects

abstract public class Shape
{
    abstract public void draw();
    abstract public double computeArea();
}
```

As this listing shows, you use the abstract keyword to indicate that a class cannot be instantiated because it does not implement all the methods.

caution

If you know C++, you'll notice some superficial similarities between C++ and Java class definitions. Note, however, that the similarities are really superficial. As an experienced C++ programmer, I would say that you'll be better off if you approach Java as a brand-new, object-oriented language rather than as a mutation of C++. You can still use your knowledge of C syntax, but when it comes to the object-oriented features of Java, you should not try to extrapolate from your knowledge of C++.

Circle Class

After you define the abstract Shape class, you can create concrete versions of Shape classes such as a Circle and Rectangle. Here is a simple implementation of the Circle class that you should save in a file named Circle.java:

```
//--------------------------------------------------------------
// File: Circle.java
//
// Circle class

public class Circle extends Shape
{
    double x, y;
    double radius;

    public Circle(double x, double y, double r)
    {
        this.x = x;
        this.y = y;
        this.radius = r;
    }

    public double computeArea()
    {
        return Math.PI * radius * radius;
    }

    public void draw()
    {
        System.out.println("Circle of radius "+radius+
                           " at ("+x+", "+y+")");
    }
}
```

As this definition of the Circle class shows, this shape class implements the computeArea and draw methods that were declared as abstract in the Shape class. The Circle class also defines three double variables—x, y, and radius—that denote the coordinates of the center and the radius of the circle. Such variables are referred to as *instance variables* of the class.

The extends keyword in the Circle class definition indicates that Circle is a subclass of the Shape class. The public qualifier specifies that the Circle class is accessible from other packages (in Java, a *package* is a collection of classes).

Rectangle Class

Following the pattern of the Circle class, I defined the Rectangle class as shown in the following code:

```
//----------------------------------------------------------------
// File: Rectangle.java
//
// Rectangle class

public class Rectangle extends Shape
{
    double x1, y1;
    double x2, y2;

    public Rectangle(double x1, double y1,
                     double x2, double y2)
    {
        this.x1 = x1;
        this.y1 = y1;
        this.x2 = x2;
        this.y2 = y2;
    }

    public double computeArea()
    {
        return Math.abs((x1-x2)*(y1-y2));
    }

    public void draw()
    {
        System.out.println("Rectangle with corners "+
                           "("+x1+", "+y1+") and "+
                           "("+x2+", "+y2+")");
    }
}
```

Just as the Circle class is saved in the Circle.java file, the Rectangle class should be saved in the Rectangle.java file—at least that's how Sun's Java 2 SDK expects the class definitions.

insider insight

The computeArea method of the Rectangle class calls the Math.abs method to get the absolute value of an argument. Although this looks like the invocation of an object's method, there is no object named Math; instead Math is the name of a class. The abs method is a static method in the Math class. You can invoke a static method without having to create an instance of the class.

MakeShape Class — The Test Program

Now that I have defined the Circle and Rectangle classes, it's time to test them with a simple program. In Java, the program itself must be another class, and for a standalone Java program, the class must include a public static void method called main (this is akin to the main function in a C program).

The following code shows the MakeShape class (in a file named MakeShape.java), which includes a main method to test the geometric shapes:

```
//---------------------------------------------------------------
// File: MakeShape.java
//
// Java application to try out various shapes

public class MakeShape
{
    public static void main(String args[])
    {
        Shape shapes[] = new Shape[2];

        shapes[0] = new Circle(100.0, 100.0, 50.0);
        shapes[1] = new Rectangle(80., 40., 120., 60.);

        System.out.println("\n"+shapes.length+" shapes\n");

        for(int i=0; i < shapes.length; i++)
        {
            double area = shapes[i].computeArea();
            System.out.println("Shape #"+i);
            shapes[i].draw();
            System.out.println("Area = "+area);
            System.out.println("-----------");
        }
    }
}
```

The main method creates an array of Shape objects and initializes the array with different shapes. Then, the computeArea and draw methods of each shape are invoked.

insider insight

You use the new keyword to create instances of objects in Java. There is no corresponding delete or free keyword to get rid of objects when you no longer need them. Instead, Java supports a technique called *garbage collection* to automatically destroy objects that are no longer needed. (Java keeps track of all references to an object and removes the object when there are no more references to it.) That means you never have to worry about freeing memory in Java. Because memory management is a source of many errors in C and C++ programs, Java's support for garbage collection helps eliminate a major source of potential errors in your applications.

In this example, the MakeShape class is the Java application. To compile the program, type the following command:

```
javac MakeShape.java
```

This step takes care of compiling the MakeShape.java file and all the related classes (the Shape.java, Circle.java, and Rectangle.java files). In other words, the Java compiler (javac) acts a bit like the make utility in UNIX—javac determines the dependencies among classes and compiles all necessary classes.

To run the MakeShape program, use the Java interpreter, as follows:

```
java MakeShape
```

The following code shows the result of running the MakeShape program in a terminal window in Linux:

```
2 shapes

Shape #0
Circle of radius 50.0 at (100.0, 100.0)
Area = 7853.981633974483
-----------
Shape #1
Rectangle with corners (80.0, 40.0) and (120.0, 60.0)
Area = 800.0

-----------
```

Java Program Structure

A Java program consists of one or more classes. For standalone applications, you must have a class with a public void static main method. Applets require only a subclass of the Applet class.

The Java 2 SDK expects the source files to have the same name as the class, but with a .java extension (thus, a class named Circle is defined in the file Circle.java). Within each source file, the parts of the program are laid out in the following manner:

1. The file starts with some comments that describe the purpose of the class and provide other pertinent information such as the name of author and revision dates. Java supports both C and C++-style comments. As in ANSI C, comments may start with a /* and end after a */ pair. Or, you may simply begin a line of comment with a pair of slashes (//). A special type of comment, known as *doc comment*, begins with a /** and ends with */. The doc comments can be extracted by the javadoc utility program to create online documentation for classes.
2. One or more import statements that allow you to use abbreviated class names. For example, if you use the java.applet.Applet class, you can refer to that class by the short name Applet provided you include the following import statement in the source file:
   ```
   import java.applet.*;
   ```

Note that the `import` statement does not really bring in any extra code into a class; it's simply a way to save typing so you can refer to a class by a shorter name (for example, `Applet` instead of `java.applet.Applet`).

3. The class definition that includes instance variables and methods. All variables and methods must be inside the class definition.

Primitive Data Types in Java

Java supports the standard C data types of `char`, `short`, `int`, `long`, `float`, and `double`. Additionally, Java introduces the `byte` and `boolean` types. Unlike C, however, Java also specifies the exact size of all primitive data types (in C, the size of the `int` type varies from one system to another). Table 26-2 summarizes Java's primitive types.

Table 26-2: Java's Primitive Data Types

Type	*Description*
`boolean`	A 1-bit value that contains `true` or `false`. A `boolean` value is not an integer.
`byte`	An 8-bit signed integer with values between −128 and 127.
`char`	A 16-bit unsigned integer value representing a Unicode character (Unicode is a character encoding system designed to support storage and processing of written texts of many diverse languages). You can initialize a `char` variable with the notation `\u`*xxxx*, where *xxxx* is a sequence of hexadecimal digits (for example, `char c = \u00ff;`).
`double`	A 64-bit, double-precision floating-point value in the IEEE 754 format (a standard format that expresses a floating-point number in binary format).
`float`	A 32-bit, single-precision floating-point value in IEEE 754 format.
`int`	A 32-bit signed integer with values between −2,147,483,648 and 2,147,483,647.
`long`	A 64-bit signed integer with values between −9,223,372,036,854,775,808 and 9,223,372,036,854,775,807.
`short`	A 16-bit signed integer with values between −32,768 and 32,767.

Although most of the primitive types should be familiar to C programmers, the following C-style usage is not allowed in Java:

- There is no `unsigned` keyword in Java; all integer values are signed.
- You cannot write `short int` or `long int` (these combinations are often used in C programs).

Nonprimitive Data Types in Java

The nonprimitive data types in Java are objects and arrays. All nonprimitive types are handled by *reference*—that means when you pass a nonprimitive type to a method, the address of the object is passed to the method. The primitive types, however, are passed by *value*, which means a copy of the data is passed to the method.

Unlike C, Java does not have any pointer type. So, you cannot work with addresses of variables with the &, *, and -> operators. By eliminating pointers, Java gets rid of a common source of bugs and also prevents programmers from performing tricks with pointers that bypass Java's security mechanisms.

Instead of pointers, you have to work with references to objects (a *reference* is the address of an object). You need to understand the following implications of the fact that you have to handle objects through references:

- When you assign one object to another, Java does not actually copy the value of the object. All that happens is that you end up with two references to the same object. Consider the following example:

```
Circle c1 = new Circle(0., 0., 20.);
Circle c2 = new Circle(100.0, 60.0, 20.0);
c1 = c2; // c1 now refers to the same Circle as does c2.
```

  Here, both `c1` and `c2` end up referring to the same `Circle` object. The `Circle` object that `c1` originally referred to is lost after you assign `c2` to `c1`. (The Java garbage collector automatically reclaims the memory allocated to the lost object.)

- To actually copy an object's value into another, you have to call the `clone` method of the object (this assumes that the object supports the `clone` method). Here is an example:

```
Vector x = new Vector();
Vector y = x.clone();  // Vector y is a copy of Vector x.
```

- When you use the == operator, you check whether two variables refer to the same object. In other words, the == operator checks whether two objects are identical. To check if two separate objects contain the same value, you must use a special method for that object type. For example, many Java classes provide an `equals` method to check for equality of object values.

String Type

Java includes a built-in `String` type, and the compiler treats a `String` almost like a primitive type. Java's `String` class is a part of the java.lang package, which the Java compiler uses by default.

The Java compiler automatically converts text within double quotes ("...") into a `String`. Also, the + operator concatenates `String` objects. For example, you can write code such as the following:

```
String welcome = "Welcome to " + "Java.";
int numchars = welcome.length();
System.out.println("There are "+numchars+
                   " characters in: "+welcome);
```

When executed, this code prints the following:

```
There are 16 characters in: Welcome to Java.
```

The String class supports a number of other methods that provide the functionality of the C's string manipulation functions (that are defined in the C header file <string.h>). Java includes two related classes for handling text strings:

- String to hold a string of characters that cannot be individually manipulated (in other words, you cannot insert or replace characters in the string).
- StringBuffer to represent a string of characters that may be manipulated as necessary. You can append, insert, and replace characters in a StringBuffer object.

Table 26-3 summarizes the methods of the String class.

Table 26-3: Methods of the String Class

Method	*Description*
`char charAt(int index);`	Returns character at a specified index.
`int compareTo(String s);`	Compares this String with another String s.
`String concat(String s);`	Concatenates this String with another String.
`String copyValueOf(char[] ca);`	Returns a String equivalent to the specified array of characters. This is a static method of the String class.
`boolean endsWith(String suffix);`	Returns true if String ends with suffix.
`boolean equals(String s);`	Returns true if this String matches another String s (case-sensitive comparison).
`boolean equalsIgnoreCase(String s);`	Returns true if this String matches another String s regardless of case (case-insensitive comparison).
`byte[] getBytes();`	Copies characters from a String into a new byte array (uses the default character-encoding of the system).
`byte[] getBytes(String encodingName);`	Copies characters from a String into a new byte array according to the character encoding specified by a name such as US-ASCII, ISO-8859-1, UTF-8, UTF-16, and so on.
`void getChars(int srcBegin, int srcEnd, char[] dest, int destBegin);`	Copies characters from a String into a char array.
`int hashcode();`	Returns hash code for the String.
`int indexOf(int c);`	Returns index of first occurrence of a character.
`int indexOf(String s);`	Returns index of first occurrence of String s in the current String.

Method	Description
`String intern();`	Returns a unique instance of `String` from a global shared pool of `String` objects.
`int lastIndexOf(int c);`	Returns index of the last occurrence of a character.
`int lastIndexOf(String s);`	Returns index of last occurrence of `String` `s` in the current `String`.
`int length();`	Returns the length of the `String` (the number of characters in the `string`).
`boolean regionMatches(int offset, String s, int soffset, int length);`	Returns true if a region of the `String` matches the specified region of another `String s`.
`String replace(char old, char new);`	Replaces all occurrences of old characters with new.
`boolean startsWith(String prefix);`	Returns `true` if `String` starts with specified prefix.
`String substring(int begin, int end);`	Returns a substring of this `String`.
`char[] toCharArray();`	Returns a character array from the `String`.
`String toLowerCase();`	Converts `String` to lowercase.
`String toString();`	Returns another `String` with the same contents.
`String toUpperCase();`	Converts `String` to uppercase.
`String trim();`	Removes any leading and trailing white space from `String`.
`String valueOf(type obj);`	Returns the `String` representation of an object's value (type may be any object of primitive type such as `boolean`, `char`, `int`, `long`, `float`, and `double`). This is a static method of the `String` class.

insider insight

The `String` class is defined with a `final` keyword. That means you cannot subclass `String`. The Java compiler can optimize a final class so that the class can be used as efficiently as possible. To declare a class as `final`, use the following syntax:

```
public final class ClassName extends SuperClassName
{
// Body of class
}
```

Arrays in Java

An *array* is an ordered collection of one or more elements. Java supports arrays of all primitive as well as nonprimitive data types. As in C, you can declare an array variable by appending square brackets to the variable name, as follows:

```
byte buffer[] = new byte[256]; // Create an array for 256 byte variables.

Shape shapes[] = new Shape[10];  // Create an array to hold 10 Shape objects.
```

In Java creating an array for a specific type of object does not actually create the objects that are stored in the array. All that Java creates is an array capable of holding references to objects of a specified type. All array elements are initialized with the value `null` (which is a Java keyword that means a variable that does not refer to any object). You must individually create the objects that you want to store in the array.

Here is how you might create and initialize an array of `String` objects:

```
String language[] = new String[4];
language[0] = "C";
language[1] = "C++";
language[2] = "Java";
// language[3] == null (the default value)
```

As this example illustrates, you access array elements the same way you use arrays in C—by putting an integer-values expression within square brackets after the array's name. The array indexes start at 0.

You can always get the length of an array—the number of elements the array can hold—by accessing the length instance variable of the array. Here is an example:

```
String names[] = new String[5];
int len = names.length; // len = 5
```

Exception-Handling in Java

Exceptions refer to unusual conditions in a program. They can be outright errors that cause the program to fail or conditions that can lead to errors. Typically, you can always detect when certain types of errors are about to occur. For instance, when indexing an array with the `[]` operator, you could detect if the index is beyond the range of valid values. Although you could check for such an error, it's tedious to check for errors whenever you index into an array. Java's exception-handling mechanism allows you to place the exception-handling code in one place and avoid having to check for errors all over your program.

Java's exception-handling mechanism is similar to that in C++. The basic features are as follows:

- When a block of code generates an error, it uses the `throw` keyword to throw an exception. When an exception is thrown, the Java interpreter stops executing that block of code and transfers control to a block that is designated as the handler for that exception (there are many types of exceptions).
- Enclose inside a `try` block any code that may throw an exception.
- Immediately following the `try` block, place one or more `catch` blocks that handle specific exceptions thrown by the code inside the `try` block.
- Inside a `finally` block place any code that should be executed to clean up before exiting the `try` block (regardless of whether there is an exception or not). In the `finally` block, you may include code to close files and network connections before the program exits.

The following code fragment illustrates the syntax of `try`, `catch`, and `finally` blocks in Java:

```
try
{
    // Code that may generate exceptions of type AnException and
    // AnotherException
}
catch(AnException e1)
{
    // Handle exception of type AnException
}
catch(AnotherException e2)
{
    // Handle exception of type AnotherException
}
finally
{
    // This block of code is always executed after exiting the try block
    // regardless of how the try block exits.
}
```

Interfaces

Java does not support multiple inheritance, so each class can have only one superclass. However, sometimes you may want to inherit other types of behavior. For example, you may want to support a specific set of methods in a class (this is akin to saying that your class can do x, y, and z). Java provides the interface keyword that allows a class to implement a specific set of capabilities.

An interface looks like an abstract class declaration. For example, the `run` method is used by the `Thread` class (see the "Threads in Java" section) to start a thread of execution in a Java program. The `Runnable` interface specifies this capability through the following interface declaration:

```
public interface Runnable
{
    public abstract void run();
}
```

If you implement all the methods of an interface, you can declare this fact by using the `implements` keyword in the class definition. For example, if a class defines the `run` method (which constitutes the `Runnable` interface), the class definition specifies this fact as follows:

```
import java.applet.*;
public class MyApplet extends Applet implements Runnable
{
// Must include the run() method
    public void run()
    {
// This can be the body of a thread.
    }

// Other methods of the class
// ...
}
```

Threads in Java

Java includes built-in support for threads. A *thread* refers to a single flow of control — a single sequence of Java byte codes being executed by the Java Virtual Machine. Just as an operating system can execute multiple processes (by allocating short intervals of processor time to each process in turn), the Java Virtual Machine can execute multiple threads within a single application. You can think of threads as "multitasking within a single process."

Threads can be very useful because you can turn individual threads loose on different sets of tasks. For example, one thread might monitor all user inputs to an applet, while another thread periodically updates the display. The problem with threads is that they all share the same set of variables within the program. That means, each thread must be careful when accessing and updating any variable. As a thread changes parts of an object, it may lose its time slice and another may become active and use the partially updated object. Java includes the `synchronized` keyword that allows you to mark objects and methods that should not be accessed simultaneously by multiple threads. For example, you'd write the following code to ensure that a thread acquires a lock on `myObject` before executing the statements within the curly braces (`{ . . . }`):

```
synchronized(myObject)
{
// Some task that needs to be synchronized among threads
// ...
}
```

Using Threads in an Applet

The best way to understand threads is to go through a simple example. The following code shows the `DigitalClock` applet that uses a thread to display the current date and time:

```
//----------------------------------------------------------------
// File: DigitalClock.java
//
// Displays a digital clock using a thread.

import java.util.*;
import java.awt.*;
import java.applet.*;

public class DigitalClock extends Applet implements Runnable
{
    private volatile Thread clockThread;
    private int interval = 1000;
    private static final long serialVersionUID = 1L;

// The run method is required by the Runnable interface.
    public void run()
    {
        Thread curThread = Thread.currentThread();
        while(curThread == clockThread)
        {
            try
            {
                Thread.sleep(interval);
            }
            catch(InterruptedException e) {}
// Repaint the clock.
            repaint();
        }
    }

    public void start()
    {
// Create and start the clock thread.
        clockThread = new Thread(this);
        clockThread.start();
    }

    public void stop()
    {
// Get rid of the clock thread.
        clockThread = null;
    }

// The paint method displays the date and time.
    public void paint(Graphics gc)
```

```
        {
            Font helv = new Font("Helvetica", Font.ITALIC, 16);
            gc.setFont(helv);
            gc.drawString(new Date().toString(), 4, 20);
        }
    }
```

Save this listing in the `DigitalClock.java` file and compile the applet with the following command:

```
javac DigitalClock.java
```

Next, create an HTML document, `DigitalClock.html`, and embed the applet as follows:

```
<html>
<body>

<applet width=200 height=24 code=DigitalClock>
A Java clock applet.
</applet>

</body>

</html>
```

Now, type the following command to run the applet using the appletviewer:

```
appletviewer DigitalClock.html
```

Figure 26-3 shows the resulting appletviewer window with the output from the Clock applet.

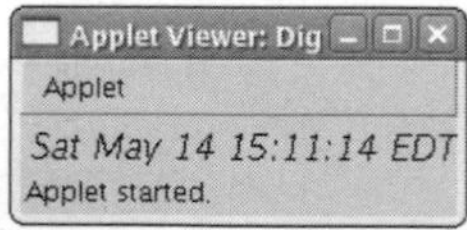

Figure 26-3: Running the Clock Applet in the appletviewer.

As the applet runs, it should update the clock display every second.

Understanding Thread Usage in an Applet

After you have seen the `DigitalClock` applet in action, you should go through its listing to see how a thread works. When going through the `DigitalClock` applet's code, you should note the following:

- To create a thread, you need an instance of a class that implements the `Runnable` interface. Typically, you would implement the `Runnable` interface in your applet by providing a `run` method. Then, you can create the `Thread` object by calling its constructor as follows:

  ```
  myThread = Thread(this);
  ```

- The Java Virtual Machine (JVM) calls the `start` method of the applet when the applet should run and the JVM calls the `stop` method when the applet should stop running. Thus, the applet's `start` method is a good place to create the `Thread` object.

- After you create the `Thread` object, you must call that `Thread` object's `start` method (note that this is different from the `start` method of the applet) to start running the thread.
- When started, the `Thread` executes the body of the `run` method. Thus, the `run` method should include code to perform whatever task you want the thread to perform.
- When you want to stop the thread, set the `Thread`'s reference to `null`, as follows:

```
myThread = null;
```

The Java garbage collection mechanism would clean up the `Thread` at an appropriate time.

Writing GUI Applications in Java

You can also write standalone GUI applications in Java. Unlike applets, you do not need a Web browser to run standalone applications. Also, these applications are not burdened by the strict security restrictions that are imposed on applets. Like other applications on your system, these Java applications can perform all operations. For example, standalone Java applications can read and write files and establish a TCP/IP connection with any Internet host.

Java GUI applications use the Swing GUI components that are part of Java 2 SDK. The applet example shown in the "Writing a Simple Java Applet" section uses GUI components from the older Abstract Windowing Toolkit (AWT). The AWT includes a limited selection of components that may have been adequate for applets, but standalone GUI applications require many more user interface components, such as menu bars and tables, that the older AWT lacks. Swing extends AWT by adding an extensive collection of GUI components that are on a par with other popular windowing systems. Additionally, the Swing architecture supports what is known as *pluggable look-and-feel* that allows users to change the appearance of the user interface without having to restart the application.

insider insight **You will see the word `plaf` in the package name of `Swing` classes. That word is an acronym for "pluggable look-and-feel."**

The next few sections briefly introduce the `Swing` GUI components, including a description of the modified Model-View-Controller (MVC) architecture of the `Swing` classes. Then a sample GUI application illustrates how to use many `Swing` GUI components. The sample GUI application shown is designed to run either as an applet or a standalone application.

An Overview of Swing

To understand the `Swing` class library, you need to know a bit about how Java's GUI classes came about. Java 1.0 came with the Abstract Windowing Toolkit, or AWT for short. AWT is a set of classes that allows you to build GUIs for applets and applications. AWT classes include the basic components such as buttons, labels, check boxes, frames, text-input areas, scrollbars, and panels. AWT also provides graphics classes to handle drawing and image rendering.

Each of the GUI components in AWT has two parts: a Java class representing the component and a peer object that renders the component using the capabilities of the native windowing system on which the Java Virtual Machine is running. For example, in Microsoft Windows, AWT's `Button` component is drawn using a button from a Microsoft Windows library. This means that the button should look the same as other buttons in Microsoft Windows. On the other hand, the `Button` on a Macintosh will look like other buttons in the Macintosh user interface. The AWT components are known as heavyweight components because each component has a platform-specific implementation that is directly supported by a user interface component of the underlying windowing system. Typically, each component is rendered in a window from the windowing system.

The `Swing` components are a high-level collection of GUI components, implemented entirely in Java. (Swing was the name of the project that developed these components.) `Swing` renders components such as buttons and labels in a container such as a frame or a dialog box. The container is a heavyweight component that does rely on the underlying windowing system, but the components themselves do not make use of any user interface components from the underlying windowing system. The container provides the drawing area where various `Swing` components render themselves. `Swing` components are called lightweight because they do not have any representation in the underlying windowing system. For example, on a Microsoft Windows system, a `Swing` button does not use a Windows button. Instead, the button is drawn using graphics primitives such as lines and rectangles. This means that a `Swing` component should look the same on any system. In fact, as you will see later in this section, `Swing` allows you to change the look and feel of the user interface (UI) on the fly.

The following sections summarize the `Swing` classes, describe the modified Model-View-Controller architecture used in `Swing`, and provide some `Swing` programming tips.

Java Foundation Classes and Swing

Java Foundation Classes (JFC) is a collection of classes that provide everything you need to develop GUI applications. Swing happens to be a part of JFC, and JFC itself is incorporated into Java 2.

JFC includes the following major components:

- `Swing` GUI components are lightweight GUI components for Java applications and applets. For the latest information on `Swing` classes and some programming tips, see *The Swing Connection*, an online newsletter at `http://java.sun.com/products/jfc/tsc/`. `Swing` does not replace AWT. Rather, `Swing` extends AWT by adding more class libraries that support all aspects of GUI programming.
- Accessibility APIs allow developers to create GUI applications that can support people with disabilities such as limited sight or the inability to operate a mouse. For more information on the accessibility features, visit Sun's website at `http://java.sun.com/products/jfc/jaccess-1.2.2/doc/` and browse the online accessibility documentation.

- Java 2D API is a set of classes for two-dimensional (2D) graphics and imaging. In particular, Java 2D API provides more control over the image rendering process. For more information on Java 2D API, visit the Java 2D API home page at `http://java.sun.com/products/java-media/2D/`. If you have JDK 1.2 installed, you can see what Java2D offers by running the Java2Demo program, which should be in the `demo/jfc/Java2D` subdirectory of the location where you installed JDK 1.2. (Use the command `java Java2Demo` to start the demo program.)
- "Drag and drop" refers to the ability to cut and paste text and images between Java applications (as well as other applications running on your system). You can download the latest Drag and Drop specification from `http://java.sun.com/j2se/1.5.0/docs/guide/dragndrop/spec/dnd1.html`. In Java 2, the java.awt.dnd package includes the interfaces and classes for supporting drag-and-drop operations.

`Swing` happens to be the largest part of JFC. Originally, `Swing` was released as a separate class library that could be used with Java 1.1 class libraries. However, when Java 2 was officially released in December 1998, the `Swing` classes were included in it. The `Swing` classes are in various packages with names that begin with `javax.swing`.

JFC is essentially layered on the AWT, which, in turn, relies on the native windowing system (such as Microsoft Windows or Motif) to render the user interface on the display. Figure 26-4 illustrates the layered model of JFC. As the figure shows, the `Swing` components rely on parts of the AWT but not all of it. AWT components use the native windowing system to display output and receive user input from the mouse and keyboard. AWT components such as buttons, labels, panels, and frames are still available for use. The Accessibility APIs are closely tied to `Swing` components, but the Java2D API and Drag and Drop also rely on the native windowing system. Finally, Java GUI applications rely on the `Swing` components and they can also use the AWT components, if necessary.

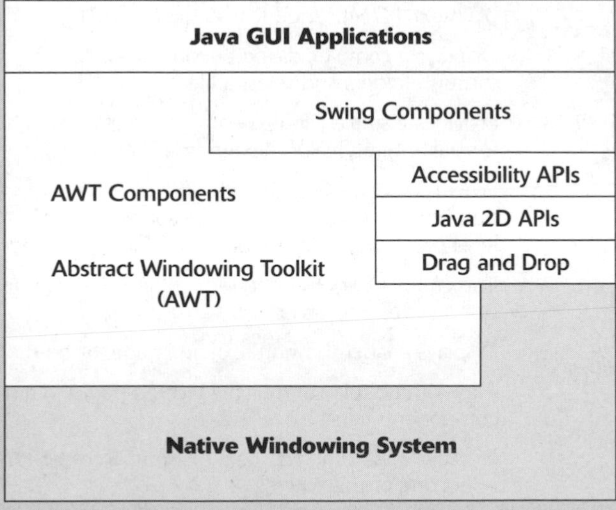

Figure 26-4: The Layered Model of Java Foundation Classes (JFC).

Swing Classes

Because this book focuses on explaining Java programming through sample programs, you may not encounter all of the Swing classes here. Only the most commonly used Swing components show up in the various examples. However, it's useful to know the names of the various components, so you know what's available in Swing. Accordingly, Table 26-4 summarizes the Swing classes.

Table 26-4: Summary of Some Swing Component Classes

Class	*Description*
JApplet	Implements a Java applet capable of using Swing components. Any applet that uses Swing classes must be a subclass of JApplet.
JButton	Displays a button with some text and, optionally, an icon.
JCheckBox	Displays a check box.
JCheckBoxMenuItem	Displays a menu item that can be selected or deselected.
JColorChooser	Displays a complex dialog box from which the user can select a color.
JComboBox	Displays a combo box that includes a text field and a button to view a drop-down list of items.
JComponent	Represents the superclass of most Swing classes.
JDesktopPane	Implements a Desktop Manager object that can be plugged into a JInternalFrame object.
JDialog	Provides a container in which Swing components can be laid out to create custom dialog boxes.
JEditorPane	Provides a text component to edit various types of content such as plaintext, HTML, and Rich Text Format (RTF).
JFileChooser	Displays a complex dialog box in which the user can browse through folders and select a file.
JFormattedTextField	Provides a single-line text entry and editing area, with the ability to format arbitrary values (extends JTextField).
JFrame	Provides a container in which other Swing components can be laid out. Most standalone GUI applications use a JFrame as the top-level container for laying out other Swing components.
JInternalFrame	Implements a lightweight frame object that can be placed inside a JDesktopPane object.
JLabel	Displays a label showing text, an image, or both.
JLayeredPane	Allows the display of multiple layered panes in a frame so that components can be overlaid.
JList	Displays a list of objects (text or icons) from which the user can select one or more items.
JMenu	Implements a drop-down menu that can be attached to a menu bar (the menu can show text, images, or both).

Class	Description
JMenuBar	Implements a menu bar.
JMenuItem	Implements a menu item that appears in a JMenu.
JOptionPane	Displays a dialog box that prompts the user for input and then provides that input to the program.
JPanel	Provides a lightweight container for arranging other components such as JButton, JLabel, and JComboBox.
JPasswordField	Displays a text field in which the user can type a password (the characters typed by the user are not displayed).
JPopupMenu	Implements a pop-up menu.
JProgressBar	Displays a progress bar that can be used to indicate the progress of an operation.
JRadioButton	Implements a radio button that can display text, an image, or both.
JRadioButtonMenuItem	Implements a menu item that is part of a group of menu items, only one of which can be selected at any time.
JRootPane	Creates an object with a glass pane, a layered pane, an optional menu bar, and a content pane.
JScrollBar	Displays a scrollbar.
JScrollPane	Implements a scrolled pane that can scroll objects placed inside the pane.
JSeparator	Implements a separator that can be placed in a JMenu to separate one group of menu items from another.
JSlider	Displays a slider bar from which the user can select a value.
JSpinner	Displays a single line input field with a pair of tiny arrow buttons that enable the user to step through a sequence of values and select one (functionality is similar to that of JComboBox, but without a drop-down list).
JSplitPane	Implements a pane that can be split horizontally or vertically.
JTabbedPane	Implements tabbed pane components that allow the user to view different pages by clicking on tabs (much like the tabs on file folders).
JTable	Implements a table that can display tabular data (ideal for displaying the results of database searches).
JTableHeader	Implements the column header part of a JTable (shares the same TableColumnModel with the JTable).
JTextArea	Implements a multiline text area that can be used to display read-only or editable text.
JTextField	Provides a single-line text entry and editing area.
JTextPane	Provides a text component that can be marked up with attributes that are represented graphically.

(continued)

Table 26-4 *(continued)*

Class	*Description*
`JToggleButton`	Implements a button that can display text or an image and that can be in one of two states (on or off).
`JToolBar`	Implements a toolbar that can either be attached to a frame or stand alone.
`JToolTip`	Displays a short help message (attached to a component to provide help when the user moves the mouse onto that component).
`JTree`	Displays a set of hierarchical data in the form of a tree (similar to the directory structure in Windows Explorer).
`JViewport`	Displays a clipped view of a component (used by `JScrollPane`).
`JWindow`	Implements a container that can be displayed anywhere on the user's desktop (`JWindow` does not have the title bar and window-management buttons that are associated with a `JFrame`).

The Model-View-Controller Architecture and Swing

Swing components use a modified form of the Model-View-Controller (MVC) architecture. The classic MVC architecture of Smalltalk-80 breaks an application up into three separate layers:

- **Model:** This is the application layer that implements the application's functionality. All application-specific code is in this layer.
- **View:** This is the presentation layer that implements whatever is needed to present information from the application layer to the user. In a GUI, the view provides the windows.
- **Controller:** This is the virtual terminal layer that handles the user's interactions with the application. This is a graphics library that presents a device-independent interface to the presentation layer.

Figure 26-5 illustrates this classic MVC architecture of Smalltalk-80.

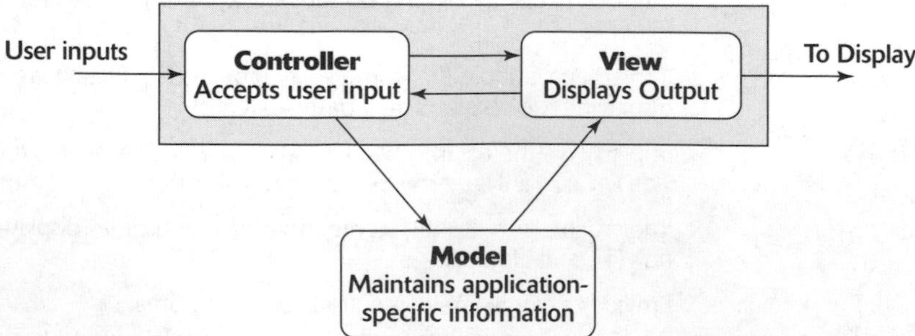

Figure 26-5: The Model-View-Controller (MVC) architecture of Smalltalk-80.

Smalltalk's MVC architecture does an excellent job of separating the responsibilities of the objects in the system. The application-specific details are insulated from the user interface. Also, the user interface itself is broken down into two parts, with the presentation handled by the view and the user interaction (mouse and keyboard input) handled by the controller.

Each Smalltalk-80 application consists of a model and an associated view-controller pair. Figure 26-5 shows the usual interactions in Smalltalk-80's MVC architecture. The controller accepts the user's inputs and invokes the appropriate methods from the model to perform the task requested by the user. When the work is done, the method in the model sends messages to the view and controller. The view updates the display in response to this message, accessing the model for further information, if necessary. Thus, the model has a view and a controller, but it never directly accesses either of them. The view and controller, on the other hand, access the model's functions and data when necessary. The shaded box enclosing the view and controller in Figure 26-5 is meant to emphasize that in actual implementations, the view and controller are tightly coupled and typically treated as a single view-controller pair.

`Swing` uses a modified form of Smalltalk's MVC model. Each `Swing` component collapses the view and controller into a single user interface (UI) object but retains the model as a separate entity. The model maintains state information such as the maximum, minimum, and current values of a scrollbar. The UI object handles the view and controller responsibilities by rendering the component and processing user input in the form of mouse and keyboard events. Additionally, `Swing` introduces a UI manager that handles the look-and-feel characteristics of each component. Figure 26-6 depicts the Model-UI object-UI manager architecture of `Swing` components.

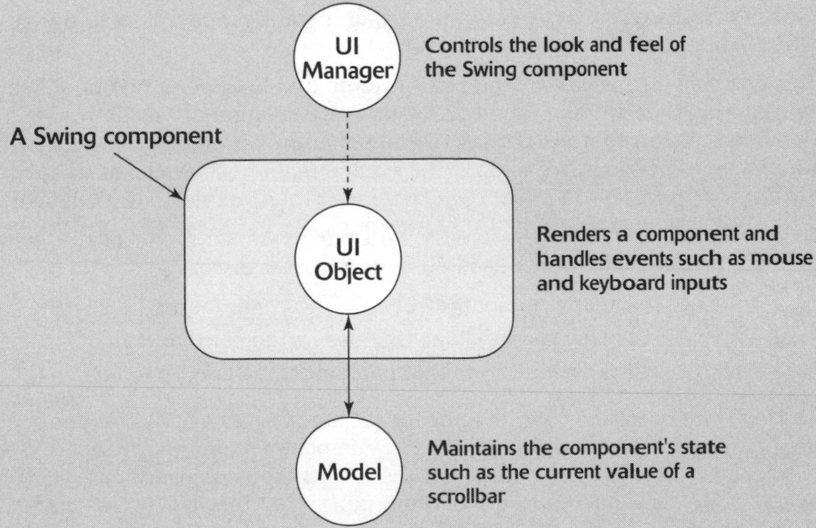

Figure 26-6: The Modified MVC Architecture Used by Swing Components.

The UI manager controls the look-and-feel capabilities of a `Swing` component by communicating with the component's UI object, as shown in Figure 26-6.

If you think about look and feel, *look* refers to how the component appears on the display, and *feel* refers to how the component reacts to user inputs. In other words, look and feel are the responsibilities of the view and controller components of the MVC architecture. In each `Swing` component, the UI object handles the look and feel of the component. Because the class representing the component delegates the look-and-feel responsibilities to the UI object, that object is also referred to as the UI delegate.

You should remember that all `Swing` components use a separate model. Many simple components provide a default model that maintains the information you provide when you create the `Swing` component. For more complex `Swing` components, such as `JTable`, you have to provide a model that represents the tabular data and implements the interface expected by `JTable`.

Swing Programming Tips

When you use AWT components to create a user interface, you place AWT components such as buttons, labels, and check boxes inside various AWT containers such as frames and panels. Typically, you end up with a hierarchical containment structure, grouping several components in a panel and then placing several panels inside another panel. You do not have to worry much about how the components paint themselves, because the AWT components are heavyweight components that rely on the underlying windowing system for rendering themselves.

The situation changes when you create a user interface with the lightweight `Swing` components. `Swing` components rely on Java code (as opposed to the underlying windowing system) to support the windowing features such as showing, hiding, moving, and resizing the components. The upshot is that you have to follow certain rules when constructing user interfaces with `Swing` components, and you have to follow a few key rules to ensure that the user interface is painted properly.

The first rule is to avoid mixing heavyweight and lightweight components when they may overlap. In other words, do not place an AWT component inside a `Swing` component and vice versa. When these two types of components overlap, they are not painted correctly. (If you must use both AWT and `Swing` components, the article at `http://java.sun.com/products/jfc/tsc/articles/mixing/index.html` explains the rules for doing so.)

To use `Swing` components properly, you must start with one of the container classes in `Swing`. The most commonly used container classes are

- `JApplet` for any applet that uses `Swing` components
- `JFrame` for GUI applications that use `Swing` components
- `JDialog` for dialog boxes that contain `Swing` components

These `Swing` containers use an appropriate heavyweight AWT component to create the display area where the lightweight `Swing` components can be arranged. Each of these containers has a content pane in which the rest of the components are placed. You must add other `Swing` components to the content pane. Call the `getContentPane()` method of the `Swing` container to get the content pane and then add the components to that pane. For example, here is how you would create a `JFrame` and add a `JDesktopPane` to that frame:

```
JFrame frame = new JFrame("Main Application Frame");
JDesktopPane jdp = new JDesktopPane();
frame.getContentPane().add(jdp);
```

To add lightweight components to other lightweight components, such as JPanel, you simply need to call the add() method of the JPanel object.

Whenever you want to redraw any Swing component, call that component's repaint() method. As with AWT components, do not call paint() directly. For example, here's how the repaint() method of a JButton is called in a mouse listener to repaint the button as the user presses and releases the button:

```
MouseListener l = new MouseAdapter()
{
    public void mousePressed(MouseEvent ev)
    {
        JButton b = (JButton)ev.getSource();
        b.setSelected(true);
        b.repaint();
    }
    public void mouseReleased(MouseEvent ev)
    {
        JButton b = (JButton)ev.getSource();
        b.setSelected(false);
        b.repaint();
    }
};
```

When you define any class as a subclass of the Swing container classes (JApplet, JFrame, or JDialog) and override the paint() method, you must insert a call to super.paint(), as shown in the following example:

```
public class MyApplet extends JApplet
{
    public void paint(Graphics g)
    {
        // Paint my applet's contents first. Then make sure
        // lightweight Swing components are painted.
            super.paint(g);
    }
}
```

If you do not call super.paint(), the lightweight Swing components inside the container won't show up. This is a common problem with beginners to Swing programming.

Additionally, each Swing component breaks down the paint() processing into three distinct parts by calling three methods in the following sequence:

1. paintComponent() to draw this component
2. paintBorder() to draw this component's border
3. paintChildren() to draw this component's children

When you define any class as a subclass of a lightweight Swing component such as JPanel , you should override the paintComponent() method to perform any additional painting you want done. You should first call super.paintComponent() to properly draw the component, as shown in the following example:

```
public class MyPanel extends JPanel
{
    protected void paintComponent(Graphics g)
    {
        // First call the superclass' paintComponent() to
        // ensure correct painting of the component
        super.paintComponent(g);
        // Now paint anything MyPanel needs ...
    }
}
```

Because Swing components draw themselves in a *pane* — a drawing area — provided by a container, Swing uses double buffering to avoid flickering when components are drawn. This means that the user interface is drawn in an off-screen buffer and then the off-screen image is copied to the screen. The doubleBuffered property of the JComponent class controls whether double buffering is enabled. By default, the doubleBuffered property is set to true. Although you can change this property by calling the setDoubleBuffered() method, you should leave double buffering enabled for all Swing components.

Displaying a Calendar Using Swing

This section presents ViewCal, a GUI application that displays a calendar for any selected month of a year. You can run ViewCal in two ways — as an applet inside an HTML document or as a standalone application by typing a command from a terminal window. By studying this application, you will learn how to use a number of different Swing components. You will also learn how to convert an applet to an application by providing a static main() method that creates the frame necessary to display the calendar.

Listing 26-2 shows the ViewCal.java file that implements the ViewCal application. I describe the code in the section that follows the listing.

Listing 26-2: A GUI Application to Display the Calendar for Any Month

```
//---------------------------------------------------------------
// ViewCal.java
//
// A calendar applet that you can run as a standalone
// application. Uses a GUI built with the Swing classes in
// Java 2. Shows how you can convert an applet into a
// standalone GUI application.
//---------------------------------------------------------------
import java.awt.*;
import java.util.*;
import java.awt.event.*;
import javax.swing.*;
/** ViewCal is an applet that includes a main() method so it
 *  can run as a standalone application. Use the command
 *  "java ViewCal" to run the application. Note that ViewCal
 *  is a subclass of JApplet because it uses Swing components.
 */
public class ViewCal extends JApplet implements ActionListener,
                                                ItemListener
```

```
{
    private static final long serialVersionUID = 1L;
    private JComboBox   monthChoice;
    private JTextField  year;
    private JButton     previousButton;
    private JButton     nextButton;
    private int         currentMonth;
    private int         currentYear;
    private String      currentDayString;
    private String      currentDateString;
    private Font helvB16 =
            new Font("Helvetica", Font.BOLD, 16);
    private String days[] = {"SUN", "MON", "TUE", "WED", "THU",
                             "FRI", "SAT"};
    private String months[] = {"January", "February", "March",
                   "April", "May", "June", "July",
                   "August", "September", "October",
                   "November", "December"};
    private int daysInMonth[] = {31, 28, 31, 30, 31, 30, 31, 31,
                                 30, 31, 30, 31};
    private JButton[][] monthButtons = new JButton[6][7];
    private JButton highlightedBtn = null;
    private JLabel[] dayLabels = new JLabel[7];
    /** Initializes the calendar's user interface */
    public void init()
    {
        Calendar today = new GregorianCalendar();
        currentMonth = today.get(Calendar.MONTH);
        currentYear = today.get(Calendar.YEAR);
        currentDayString = ""+today.get(Calendar.DAY_OF_MONTH);
        // In JApplet everything is inside a ContentPane
        Container cp = this.getContentPane();
        cp.setLayout(new BorderLayout());

        JPanel pTop = new JPanel();
        pTop.setLayout(new GridLayout(1, 4));
        previousButton = new JButton("<-Prev");
        previousButton.addActionListener(this);
        previousButton.setToolTipText("Previous month");
        pTop.add(previousButton);
        monthChoice = new JComboBox();
        for(int i = 0; i < months.length; i++)
            monthChoice.addItem(months[i]);
        monthChoice.setSelectedIndex(currentMonth);
        monthChoice.setMaximumRowCount(6);
        monthChoice.addItemListener(this);
        pTop.add(monthChoice);
        year = new JTextField("" + currentYear, 4);
        year.setFont(helvB16);
```

(continued)

Listing 26-2 *(continued)*

```
        year.setBackground(Color.lightGray);
        year.setHorizontalAlignment(JTextField.CENTER);
        year.addActionListener(this);
        year.setToolTipText("Enter number, then press <Enter>.");
        pTop.add(year);
        nextButton = new JButton("Next->");
        nextButton.addActionListener(this);
        nextButton.setToolTipText("Next month");
        pTop.add(nextButton);
        cp.add("North", pTop);

        JPanel pButtons = new JPanel();
        pButtons.setLayout(new GridLayout(7,7));
        for(int i=0; i < days.length; i++)
        {
            dayLabels[i] = new JLabel(days[i], JLabel.CENTER);
            pButtons.add(dayLabels[i]);
        }
        for(int i=0; i < 6; i++)
            for(int j=0; j < 7; j++)
            {
                monthButtons[i][j] = new JButton("");
                monthButtons[i][j].setBackground(Color.lightGray);
                monthButtons[i][j].addActionListener(this);
                pButtons.add(monthButtons[i][j]);
            }
        cp.add("Center", pButtons);
        validate();
        repaint();
    }
    /** Returns true if the year is a leap year */
    public boolean isLeapYear(int year)
    {
        if((year % 400) == 0) return(true);
        if((year > 1582) && ((year % 100) == 0)) return(false);
        if((year % 4) == 0) return(true);
        return(false);
    }
    /** Displays the calendar for a specific month of a year */
    public void displayMonth(int month, int year)
    {
        int day = 1; // first of the month
        //  Compute firstWeekday =>  0=Sun, 1=Mon, 2=Tue, ...
        Calendar cal = new GregorianCalendar(year, month, 1);
        int firstWeekday = cal.get(Calendar.DAY_OF_WEEK)-1;

        // Now draw the dates on the buttons in the calendar
        int maxDate = daysInMonth[month];
```

```
    if(month == 1 && isLeapYear(year)) maxDate += 1;
    int dateNow = 1;
    if(highlightedBtn != null)
        highlightedBtn.setBackground(Color.lightGray);
    String ds;
    for(int i=0; i < 6; i++)
    {
        for(int j=0; j < 7; j++)
        {
            if(dateNow == 1 && j < firstWeekday)
                monthButtons[i][j].setText("");
            else if(dateNow > maxDate)
                monthButtons[i][j].setText("");
            else
            {
                ds = ""+dateNow;
                monthButtons[i][j].setText(ds);
                if(ds.equals(currentDayString))
                {
                    monthButtons[i][j].setBackground(
                                       Color.gray);
                    highlightedBtn = monthButtons[i][j];
                }
                dateNow++;
            }
        }
    }
}
/** Processes the year entered by the user */
public int processYear(String yearString)
{
    if((yearString.length() == 4))
    {
        try
        {
            int year = Integer.parseInt(yearString);
            return year;
        }
        catch(NumberFormatException e)
        {
            return currentYear;
        }
    }
    return -1;
}
/** Calls displayMonth() to display the calendar */
public void paint(Graphics g)
{
    g.setColor(Color.black);
```

(continued)

Listing 26-2 *(continued)*

```
        Dimension d = getSize();
        g.drawRect(0, 0, d.width-1,d.height-1);
        displayMonth(currentMonth, currentYear);
        super.paint(g);   // Important step for Swing components
    }
   /** Handles mouse clicks in the buttons and drop-down menus*/
    public void actionPerformed(ActionEvent ev)
    {
        if(ev.getSource().equals(previousButton))
        {
            if((currentYear > 1) || (currentMonth > 0))
            {
                currentMonth--;
                if(currentMonth < 0)
                {
                    currentMonth = 11;
                    currentYear--;
                }
                monthChoice.setSelectedIndex(currentMonth);
                year.setText(""+currentYear);
                currentDayString = "1";
                repaint();
            }
        }
        else if(ev.getSource() == nextButton)
        {
            if((currentYear < 9999) || (currentMonth < 11))
            {
                currentMonth++;
                if(currentMonth > 11)
                {
                    currentMonth = 0;
                    currentYear++;
                }
                monthChoice.setSelectedIndex(currentMonth);
                year.setText(""+currentYear);
                currentDayString = "1";
                repaint();
            }
        }
        else if(ev.getSource() == year)
        {
        // Called when user presses Enter in text field
            int y = processYear(year.getText());
            if((y > 0) && (y != currentYear))
            {
                currentYear = y;
                currentDayString = "1";
```

```
                repaint();
            }
        }
        else
        {   // Check for click on a day of the month
            String ds;
            for(int i=0; i < 6; i++)
            {
                for(int j=0; j < 7; j++)
                {
                    if(ev.getSource() == monthButtons[i][j])
                    {
                        ds = ev.getActionCommand();
                        if(!ds.equals(""))
                        {
                            highlightedBtn.
                                setBackground(Color.lightGray);
                            highlightedBtn = monthButtons[i][j];
                            monthButtons[i][j].setBackground(
                                                    Color.gray);
                            currentDayString = ds;
                        }
                    }
                }
            }
        }
    }
    /** Handles selections from the month list */
    public void itemStateChanged(ItemEvent ev)
    {
        if(ev.getSource() == monthChoice)
        {
            int m = monthChoice.getSelectedIndex();
            year.setText(""+currentYear);
            if(m != currentMonth)
            {
                currentMonth = monthChoice.getSelectedIndex();
                currentDayString = "1";
                repaint();
            }
        }
    }
    /** Makes room for a 1-pixel border */
    public Insets getInsets()
    {
        return new Insets(1,1,1,1); // 1-pixel border
    }
    /** Provides a frame so ViewCal can run standalone */
    public static void main(String s[])
```

(continued)

Listing 26-2 *(continued)*

```
        {
            WindowListener l = new WindowAdapter()
            {
                public void windowClosing(WindowEvent e)
                {System.exit(0);}
            };

            JFrame frame = new JFrame("Calendar");
            frame.addWindowListener(l);
            ViewCal c = new ViewCal();
            c.init();
            frame.getContentPane().add("Center", c);
            frame.pack();
            frame.setVisible(true);
        }
    }
```

To compile and run ViewCal, type the following commands (I assume that you have the Java 2 SDK binary directory in the `PATH` environment variable):

```
javac ViewCal.java
java ViewCal
```

You should see the ViewCal application's window, as shown in Figure 26-7.

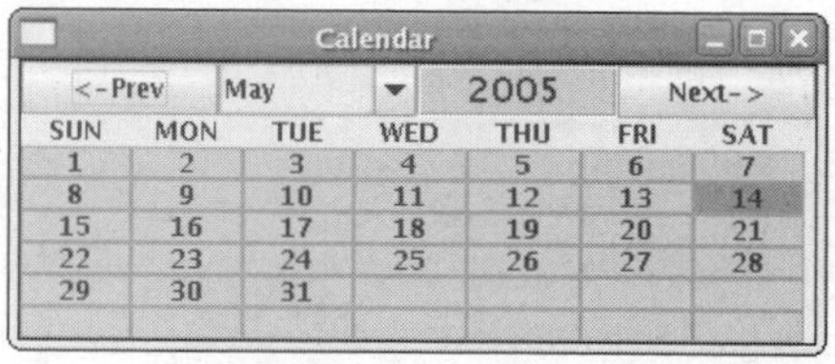

Figure 26-7: The ViewCal Application Displaying a Monthly Calendar.

Here is how you can interact with the ViewCal application's user interface:

- Clicking on the drop-down menu (implemented using a `Choice` component) displays a list of months from which you can select a specific month. That month's calendar is then displayed.
- You can type in a year (such as `2006`) in the text field next to the drop-down menu for selecting a month. After you press Enter, ViewCal updates the monthly calendar to reflect the change in year.
- Clicking the Prev and Next buttons changes the calendar to the previous or next month.

The ViewCal application's user interface is organized using `Panel` objects, where each panel holds other components such as `Label`, `Choice`, and `Button` objects. Typically, each panel uses a `GridLayout` layout manager to arrange its components into rows and columns. The `Panel` objects, in turn, are placed in the applet using a `BorderLayout` layout manager.

To display the calendar, the application needs the day of the week for the first day of any month. The ViewCal application uses the `GregorianCalendar` class to create a Gregorian calendar. Then it calls the `get(Calendar.DAY_OF_WEEK)` method of the `GregorianCalendar` object to get the day of the week for a specific date.

Recall that ViewCal is designed to be an applet as well as a standalone GUI application. Essentially, ViewCal is an applet first. That's why Listing 26-2 shows the `ViewCal` class as a subclass of `JApplet` (any applet that uses `Swing` components must be defined as a subclass of `JApplet`):

```
public class ViewCal extends JApplet implements ActionListener,
                                                ItemListener
```

ViewCal also implements the `ActionListener` and `ItemListener` interfaces to handle mouse clicks on various GUI components. The `ViewCal` class implements these interfaces by providing the required `actionPerformed()` and `itemStateChanged()` methods.

As is typical in an applet, the `init()` method in Listing 26-2 lays out the user interface. Because `ViewCal` is a subclass of `JApplet`, you must add all GUI components to its content pane. The following lines of code from Listing 26-2 show how to get the content pane (which is a `Container` object) and set the layout manager for the content pane:

```
Container cp = this.getContentPane();
cp.setLayout(new BorderLayout());
```

Later on, other high-level containers are added to the content pane named `cp`. For example, here is a line that adds a `JPanel` named `pTop` to the north position of the content pane (in the `BorderLayout` manager, the north position is the top edge of the container):

```
cp.add("North", pTop);
```

To enable ViewCal to run as a standalone application, you need a `static main()` method that prepares a frame and provides the context where the applet can run. The following lines show the `main()` method:

```
public static void main(String s[])
{
    WindowListener l = new WindowAdapter()
    {
        public void windowClosing(WindowEvent e)
        {System.exit(0);}
    };

    JFrame frame = new JFrame("Calendar");
    frame.addWindowListener(l);
    ViewCal c = new ViewCal();
    c.init();
    frame.getContentPane().add("Center", c);
    frame.pack();
    frame.setVisible(true);
}
```

As these lines of code show, the `main()` method accepts an array of `String` objects as arguments — these are the arguments that the user might have specified on the command line. For example, if the user were to start the application with a command such as `java`

ViewCal arg1 arg2, the String array would contain arg1 and arg2. (Although ViewCal does not make any use of command-line arguments, the main() method must be declared with a String array for the arguments.)

The main() method defines a WindowListener of type WindowAdapter and provides the windowClosing() method, which handles a window closing event by exiting the application. The rest of main() creates a JFrame object that provides the window where ViewCal's user interface is displayed. The WindowListener object is associated with the JFrame so that the application exits when the user closes the JFrame.

Then main() creates an instance of ViewCal and initializes it by calling the init() method. It then adds the applet to the center of the JFrame (notice that you have to add the applet to the JFrame's content pane). Finally, the main() method makes the JFrame visible (this causes the ViewCal user interface to appear on the display screen).

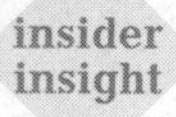

You can use the technique of providing a main() method to convert any applet to a standalone application. In the main() method, create a frame. Then, create an instance of the applet and call its init() method. Add that instance to the frame. You should also provide a WindowListener that handles the window closing event that occurs when the user closes the frame.

Writing Java Servlets

In concept, servlets are analogous to applets. Both applets and servlets reside on a server, but an applet runs in a Java-capable Web browser after the browser downloads the applet from the Web server. Because the Web browser is a client to the Web server, applets are referred to as client-side applications. A servlet, on the other hand, runs in a Java Virtual Machine (JVM) on the Web server. Thus, servlets are server-side applications.

Another difference between applets and servlets is that an applet typically produces some visible output, whereas servlets do not display anything. Instead, servlets perform specific tasks for the Web server. They are commonly used at websites to support interactive and dynamic Web pages, which are then displayed by the Web browser that downloads the pages.

A Web search engine such as Google (www.google.com/) is a good example of an interactive Web page; the user enters one or more keywords, and the Google search engine returns an HTML document containing links to other Web pages that contain the search words. The HTML document returned by the search engine is dynamic because the contents of that page depend on what search words the user types; it's not a predefined, static document.

To create an interactive Web page, you have to use certain HTML codes (to display the form that solicits user input) and implement special computer programs on the Web server. These programs process the user input (sent by the Web browser) and return requested information to the user, usually in the form of a dynamic Web page — a page that is constructed on the fly by a computer program. Such programs are known as gateways because they typically act as a conduit between the Web server and an external source of information such as a database (even if the database is simply a collection of files).

Traditionally, websites have used gateway programs that are started by the Web server and that exchange information with the Web server using a standard protocol known as Common Gateway Interface (CGI). These standalone CGI programs can be written in any language (C, C++, Perl, PHP, Tcl/Tk, and even Java). One drawback of CGI programs is that the Web server has to start a new process to run a standalone CGI program whenever the server receives data from an HTML form.

Servlets provide functionality similar to that of CGI programs, but servlets avoid the overhead of new process startup. Typically, the Web server runs a JVM, and that JVM, in turn, loads and runs the servlets. The JVM runs a servlet in a Java thread, which is faster and requires fewer operating system resources than a new process. Additionally, the JVM can keep a servlet loaded and running so that a single instance can handle many future requests. This makes servlets more responsive than other CGI programs, especially ones written in scripting languages such as Perl. At the same time, servlets are portable to any system that supports Java, just as Perl CGI programs can run on any system with a Perl interpreter.

Many websites already use servlets extensively. While browsing the Web, you may have accessed some servlets without even realizing it. Typically, a giveaway that the Web server is using a servlet is the occurrence of `/servlet/` in the URL (in the same way that `/cgi-bin/` commonly appears in URLs that refer to CGI programs). The next few sections explain how Java servlets work and what you need to develop servlets.

The Role of Java Servlets

A servlet performs specific tasks for a Web server and typically returns the results formatted as an HTML document (if necessary, servlets can also return images and other multimedia content). Often, the servlet program acts as a bridge between the Web server and some other repository of information such as a database. Typically, you use a servlet engine such as Apache Tomcat in conjunction with a Web server such as Apache httpd to set up a Java-capable Web server. Figure 26-8 highlights the interrelationships among the Web browser, Web server, servlets, database, and HTML documents, using the Apache httpd and Apache Tomcat as examples. Web servers also serve images and other multimedia content, but the figure does not show these.

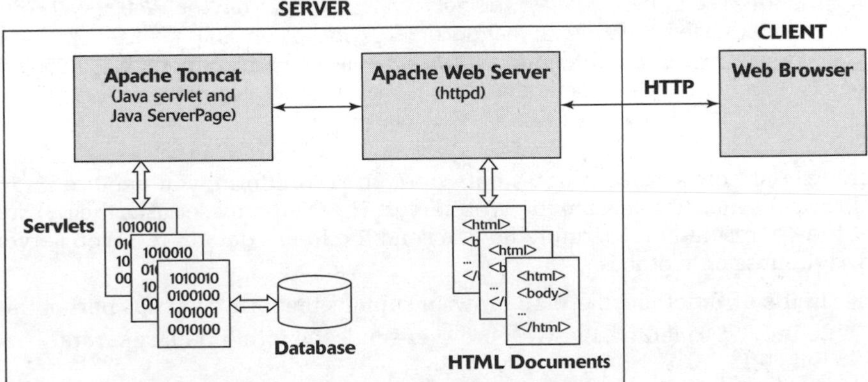

Figure 26-8: The Interrelationships among the Web Browser, Web Server, and Servlets.

As Figure 26-8 shows, the Web browser running on the user's system uses the HyperText Transfer Protocol (HTTP) to exchange information with the Web server. The Web server (also called the HTTP daemon or httpd) has access to the HTML documents and other content. Depending on the type of request from the browser, the Web server either serves an HTML document or passes the request to run a servlet thread to its Java servlet engine. The servlets run in the servlet engine and results are communicated to the Web server. If necessary, the servlets may access other system resources such as disk files or databases. Typically, a servlet generates a dynamic HTML document that the Web server sends back to the Web browser.

In a typical scenario, the user interacts with an HTML form that, in turn, contains a reference to a servlet that processes whatever the user enters into the form. Here is the basic sequence of events:

1. The user clicks on some link on a Web page, and that causes the Web browser to request an HTML document that contains an online form.
2. The Web server sends the HTML document with the form, which the browser displays.
3. The user fills in the fields of the form and clicks the Submit button. The browser, in turn, sends the form's data using the `GET` or `POST` method (as specified by the `<form>` tag in the HTML form). In either method, the browser sends to the Web server the URL specified in the `<form>` tag's `action` attribute. That URL refers to the servlet that should process the form's data.
4. From the URL the Web server determines that it should pass along the form's data and the URL for the servlet to the Java servlet engine.
5. The servlet engine runs the servlet listed in the URL and sends the form's data to that servlet.
6. The servlet processes the form's data and returns a new MIME document to the Web browser through the servlet engine. (MIME refers to Multipurpose Internet Mail Extension, an Internet standard described in RFC 1521 for attaching any type of data to a mail message. It is also used by Web servers when sending documents back to the Web browser.)
7. The Web browser displays the document received from the Web server. The information contained in that document depends on what the user entered in the HTML form. (Often the information may be nothing more than a confirmation from the server that the user's input has been received.)

To understand how servlets process data from an HTML form, you need to know how a Web browser sends form data to the Web server. The Web browser uses the `method` attribute of the `<form>` tag to determine how to send the form's data to the Web server. There are two submission methods:

- In the `GET` method, the Web browser submits the form's data as part of the URL.
- In the `POST` method, the Web browser sends the form's data separately from the URL.

The `GET` and `POST` methods are so called because the browser uses the HTTP `GET` and `POST` commands to submit the data. The `GET` command sends a URL to the Web server.

This means that to send a form's contents to the server using the GET method, the browser must include all data in the URL. Because there is typically an upper limit on the length of a URL, the GET method cannot be used to transfer large amounts of form data from the browser to the server. The POST command, on the other hand, sends the form's data in a separate stream. Therefore, the POST method can send much larger amounts of data to the server.

Regardless of which method — GET or POST — is specified in the HTML form, a servlet can get the form's data by overriding specific methods in the HttpServlet class and calling other servlet API methods to retrieve specific parameters from the HTML form.

Because you, as the developer, design the form as well as the servlet that will process the form's data, you can select the method that best suits your needs. The basic guidelines for choosing a data submission method are as follows:

- Use GET to transfer a small amount of data, and use POST to send potentially large amounts of data. For example, GET is appropriate for a search form that solicits a few keywords from the user. On the other hand, you'd want to use POST for a feedback form with a free-form text-entry area because the user might enter considerable amounts of text.
- Use the GET method if you want to access the servlet without using a form. For example, if you want to access a servlet at the URL www.someplace.com/servlet/dbquery with a parameter named keyword as input, you could invoke the servlet with a URL such as www.someplace.com/servlet/dbquery?keyword=Linux. In this case, Linux is the value of the keyword parameter. If a servlet is designed to receive data with the POST method only, you cannot activate that servlet with a URL alone.

Tools to Develop Servlets

Fedora Linux comes with everything you need to try out Java servlets and learn how to write a servlet. Specifically, it includes

- The Java servlet application programming interface (API) in the /usr/share/java/servletapi5.jar file
- The Tomcat 5 Web server that supports Java servlets as well as Java Server Pages (JSP)

The Java servlet API includes the servlet classes in the javax.servlet and javax.servlet.http packages. You also need the Java compiler and the Java virtual machine and you should have them installed if you selected the Java Development package group when you installed Fedora.

cross ref

If you are installing a production Web server that can run Java servlets, your best bet is to use Apache Tomcat along with the Apache HTTPD server. Chapter 14 shows you how to download, install, and configure Apache Tomcat to work with the Apache HTTPD server. If you plan to try out some servlets, you can use Apache Tomcat alone, as I explain later in this chapter. For this chapter, you can test the examples with the Apache Tomcat 5 that comes with Fedora.

Linking HTML Forms to Servlets

Before you jump into servlet programming, you need to understand how to associate servlets to an HTML form. A key relationship between servlets and HTML forms is that the servlet processes the data that users enter on the form. One of the attributes of the form specifies the name of the servlet that receives the input from the form. Additionally, each element of the form has an identifying name that helps the servlet isolate the user's input for that element. This section highlights the aspects of an HTML form that are important when you are writing a servlet to handle the form's data.

Consider a typical book order form that lets the user sign in using an ID and password, select one or more books, select the payment option, fill out the credit card information, and submit the order. Figure 26-9 shows a simple book order form.

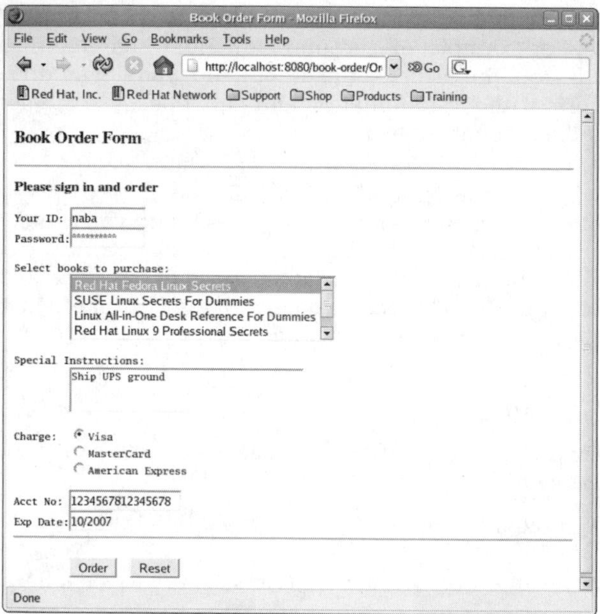

Figure 26-9: A Book Order Form in HTML.

Listing 26-3 shows the HTML text used to display the book order form. You should save this HTML text in a file named `OrderBooks.html`.

Listing 26-3: The OrderBooks.html File, Which Displays the Book Order Form

```
<html>
<head>
<title>Book Order Form</title>
</head>
<body>
<form action="servlet/OrderBooks" method=post>
<h3> Book Order Form</h3>
```

```
<hr>
<b>Please sign in and order</b>
<pre>
Your ID: <input type=text size=10 name=id>
Password:<input type=password size=10 name=passwd>

Select books to purchase:
        <select name=books size=4 multiple>
          <option>Red Hat Fedora Linux Secrets
          <option>SUSE Linux Secrets For Dummies
          <option>Linux All-in-One Desk Reference For Dummies
          <option>Red Hat Linux 9 Professional Secrets
          <option>Discover Perl 5
          <option>X Window System Programming
          <option>Object-oriented programming in C++
          <option>Visual C++ Developer's Guide
          <option>Borland C++ Developer's Guide
          <option>Turbo C++ Bible
          <option>UNIX Webmaster Bible
          <option>Microsoft Macro Assembler Bible
        </select>

Special Instructions:
        <textarea name=instructions rows=2 cols=35></textarea>

Charge: <input type=radio checked name=card value="Visa">Visa
        <input type=radio name=card value="MC">MasterCard
        <input type=radio name=card value="Amex">American Express

Acct No: <input type=text name=acct size=16>
Exp Date:<input type=text name=expire size=5>
<hr>
        <input type=submit value="Order">  <input type=reset>
</pre>
</form>
</body>
</html>
```

This is a good example of the typical HTML elements that you can use in interactive forms. You can also see how the `<form>` element associates a servlet URL with a form. Here are the key points to note in this HTML sample:

- The entire form is enclosed within `<form>` and `</form>` tags. The `action` attribute of the `<form>` tag specifies the URL of the servlet that processes this form's data. The `method` attribute specifies how the Web browser sends the form's data to the Web server.
- The `<input>` tag defines a number of common form elements, such as single-line text fields, password fields, radio buttons, and submit buttons.
- The `<select>` element defines menus. An `<option>` tag defines each menu item.
- The `<textarea>` element allows the user to enter multiple lines of text.

- Most importantly, each of the tags — `<input>`, `<select>`, and `<textarea>` — has a `name` attribute that identifies that input parameter. In the servlet that handles this form's data, you have to use the value of the `name` attribute to indicate which input parameter's value you want to retrieve.

At the heart of the HTML form is the `<form>` tag whose attributes specify the servlet that processes this form's input and how the Web browser sends the user's input to the Web server. A typical `<form>` element definition has the following structure:

```
<form method="post" action="servlet/servletName">
...(other form elements appear here)
</form>
```

The `<form>` tag's `action` attribute specifies a URL for the servlet that you have designed to handle the form's input. You can use an absolute URL that specifies the full server name as well as the pathname for the servlet. Often, however, you'd use a relative URL that identifies the directory on your Web server where the servlets reside.

The exact directory where you must place the Java servlets depends on the Web server. In Apache Tomcat, you have to place the servlets in the `WEB-INF/classes` subdirectory of the server's root directory and define the mapping of servlet name to the URL in the `WEB-INF/web.xml` file. The exact location of servlet classes depends on the package name of the class and how Apache Tomcat is configured.

The `method` attribute indicates how the Web browser sends form input back to the server. You can specify one of the following submission methods:

- `POST` causes the browser to send the data in a two-step process. First the browser contacts the server specified in the action attribute. Then, after a successful connection is established, the browser sends the form's data to the server, which in turn provides the data to the servlet.
- `GET` causes the browser to append the form's data to the URL specified in the action attribute and send everything to the Web server in a single step. A question mark (`?`) separates the data from the URL.

If you don't specify a method, the browser uses the `GET` method by default.

A Servlet That Reads an HTML Form

The previous sections explain how servlets work, what you need to use and develop servlets, and how HTML forms are linked to servlets. This section shows you a simple Java servlet that retrieves the parameters that the user enters in the book order form shown in the section "Linking HTML Forms to Servlets" (see Figure 26-9).

The book order form uses a `<form>` tag that begins with the following:

```
<form action="servlet/OrderBooks" method=post>
```

This tells you that you need a servlet named OrderBooks to process the data sent by this form. Listing 26-4 shows the `OrderBooks.java` file that implements the servlet.

Listing 26-4: The OrderBooks Servlet, Which Processes a Book Order Form

```
//---------------------------------------------------------------
// File: OrderBooks.java
// A servlet that demonstrates how to process data from
// a form.
//---------------------------------------------------------------
import java.util.*;
import java.io.*;
import javax.servlet.*;
import javax.servlet.http.*;
public class OrderBooks extends HttpServlet
{
    private static final long serialVersionUID = 1L;

    public void doPost(HttpServletRequest  request,
                       HttpServletResponse response)
                            throws ServletException, IOException

    {
        StringBuffer buffer = new StringBuffer();
        String title = "Received book order";
        // Set content type to HTML
        response.setContentType("text/html");
        // Write the response using HTML tags.
        PrintWriter out = response.getWriter();
        buffer.append("<html><head><title>");
        buffer.append(title);
        buffer.append("</title></head><body bgcolor=\"#ffffff\">");
        buffer.append("<h2>" + title + "</h2>");
        buffer.append("Customer ID: ");
        buffer.append(request.getParameter("id"));
        buffer.append("<br>");
        buffer.append("Password: ");
        buffer.append(request.getParameter("passwd"));
        buffer.append("<br>");
        buffer.append("Books Ordered: ");
        String books[] = request.getParameterValues("books");
        if(books == null)
            buffer.append("NONE<br>");
        else
        {
            buffer.append("<ul>");
            for(int i = 0; i < books.length; i++)
            {
                buffer.append("<li>");
                buffer.append(books[i]);
            }
            buffer.append("</ul>");
        }
```

(continued)

Listing 26-4 *(continued)*

```
            buffer.append("Charge to: ");
            buffer.append(request.getParameter("card"));
            buffer.append("<br>");
            buffer.append("Account Number: ");
            buffer.append(request.getParameter("acct"));
            buffer.append("<br>");
            buffer.append("<br>");
            buffer.append("Expiration Date: ");
            buffer.append(request.getParameter("expire"));
            buffer.append("<br>");
            buffer.append("Special Instructions = ");
            buffer.append(request.getParameter("instructions"));
            buffer.append("<hr>");
            buffer.append("<em>Order received at: ");
            buffer.append(new Date().toString());
            buffer.append("</em>");
            buffer.append("</body></html>");
            out.println(buffer.toString());
            out.close();
        }
    }
```

A real-life OrderBooks servlet would use the customer's ID and password to authenticate the customer and retrieve the customer record from a database. Then, the servlet should probably display all of the information that will be used to process the order and allow the customer to confirm that information. Only then should the servlet actually record the order in the database. In this case, the OrderBooks servlet simply sends back the parameters received from the order form in another HTML document.

As Listing 26-4 illustrates, to use the servlet classes, you need to include the following import statements in a servlet:

```
import javax.servlet.*;
import javax.servlet.http.*;
```

Like everything else in Java, a servlet is also a class. Listing 26-4 defines OrderBooks as a subclass of the HttpServlet class (from the javax.servlet.http package):

```
public class OrderBooks extends HttpServlet
```

This is how you declare a servlet that is designed to work with the HTTP protocol (which is how the Web server communicates with the Web browser).

You implement the servlet by overriding the appropriate methods of the HttpServlet class. If you are designing the servlet to handle HTML form data, the method of form data submission — GET or POST — determines the method you have to override. If the form's data is submitted using the GET method, you should override the doGet() method. On the other hand, if the method attribute of the <form> tag is POST, you should override the doPost() method.

The OrderBooks servlet expects the form data to be sent by the POST method, so it overrides the doPost() method of the HttpServlet class. The doPost() declaration is as follows:

```
public void doPost(HttpServletRequest  request,
                   HttpServletResponse response)
                        throws ServletException, IOException
```

As this declaration shows, the doPost() method receives two arguments: an HttpServletRequest and an HttpServletResponse. The doPost() method throws two exceptions: ServletException and IOException. Apart from declaring the function like this, there is no need to handle any exceptions in the method.

In the body of the doPost() method, you use the HttpServletRequest interface to access HTTP-protocol-specified header information and any parameters sent by the Web browser. In particular, you would call this interface's getParameter() method to obtain the value of a parameter whose name matches the name assigned with the name attribute in the HTML tag. Recall from the discussion in the section "Linking HTML Forms to Servlets" that the name attribute of the <input>, <select>, and <textarea> HTML tags identifies the input parameter. You have to use the name of each as an argument when retrieving the parameter value with the getParameter() method. For example, to get the value that the user had entered for the HTML form element <input type=text size=10 name=id>, you would call request.getParameter("id").

The HttpServletResponse interface is used to send data back to the Web browser. You would set the MIME type of the servlet response by calling a method of this interface. For example, the following line of code sets the response type to text/html (this means that the servlet sends back a text file with HTML tags):

```
response.setContentType("text/html");
```

To actually send the response to the Web browser, you would get an output stream by calling a method of the HttpServletResponse interface, and then you would write the servlet's response to that output stream. For example, the OrderBooks servlet calls the getWriter() method of the HttpServletResponse interface named response to get a PrintWriter stream for formatted text output:

```
PrintWriter out = response.getWriter();
```

You can send HTML text to the Web browser client by calling the println() or print() method of this PrintWriter class. However, instead of writing text a line at a time, it's better to accumulate the text in a StringBuffer and then send the accumulated text with a single call to the println() method. The OrderBooks servlet illustrates this approach. For example, here is a line that initializes a StringBuffer named buffer:

```
StringBuffer buffer = new StringBuffer();
```

The servlet's response is then accumulated in this buffer through calls to the append() method of StringBuffer. For example, the following lines of code append the HTML <head> and <body> tags to the buffer:

```
buffer.append("<html><head><title>");
buffer.append(title);
buffer.append("</title></head><body
              bgcolor=\"#ffffff\">");
```

If a parameter can have multiple values, you have to call the `getParameterValues()` method. In the book order form, the customer may select multiple books from the selection menu (in the HTML form that menu is assigned the name "books"). For example, the following code shows how to get the values of the books parameter and format them in an unnumbered list enclosed in the HTML tags `<ul>` and `</ul>`:

```
String books[] = request.getParameterValues("books");
if(books == null)
    buffer.append("NONE<br>");
else
{
    buffer.append("<ul>");
    for(int i = 0; i < books.length; i++)
    {
        buffer.append("<li>");
        buffer.append(books[i]);
    }
    buffer.append("</ul>");
}
```

The first line calls `getParameterValues()` to get the values in a `String` array named `books[]`. If the return value is `null`, the string `NONE` is appended to the buffer. Otherwise, the `for each` returned value is appended to the buffer as an entry in an unnumbered list.

After everything has been appended to the `StringBuffer`, the `println()` method of the `PrintWriter` class is used to send the response to the client:

```
out.println(buffer.toString());
```

After the response has been written to the `PrintWriter`, you should close the stream like this:

```
out.close();
```

Testing a Java Servlet with Sun Java System Application Server

To test the `OrderBooks` servlet, you need a Web server capable of running Java servlets. In the steps that follow, I test the servlet by using the Apache Tomcat 5 server that comes with Fedora. I log in as `root` and follow these steps to compile and test the `OrderBooks` servlet shown in Listing 26-4:

1. Create the directories in the Tomcat 5 server's installation directory where the new Web application will be installed. Here are the commands I typed to install the new application in the `book-order` directory:

```
cd /usr/share/tomcat5/webapps
mkdir book-order
mkdir WEB-INF
cd WEB-INF
mkdir classes
```

2. Change directory to where you have edited the `OrderBooks.java` file and copy it to the `book-order/WEB-INF/classes` directory. Here's the command I type:

```
cp OrderBooks.java /usr/share/tomcat5/webapps/book-order/
WEB-INF/classes
```

3. Compile the `OrderBooks.java` file with the following commands:

```
cd /usr/share/tomcat5/webapps/book-order/WEB-INF/classes
javac -cp /usr/share/java/servletapi5.jar OrderBooks.java
```

4. Copy the HTML file shown in Listing 26-3 — `OrderBooks.html` — to the Web application's top-level directory. In my case, I type the following command to copy the HTML file to the correct location:

```
cp OrderBooks.html /usr/share/tomcat5/webapps/book-order
```

5. Use a text editor to create the file `/usr/share/tomcat5/webapps/book-order/WEB-INF/web.xml` and place the following lines in that file:

```
<?xml version="1.0" encoding="ISO-8859-1"?>

<!DOCTYPE web-app
    PUBLIC "-//Sun Microsystems, Inc.//DTD Web Application 2.3//EN"
    "http://java.sun.com/dtd/web-app_2_3.dtd">

<web-app>
    <display-name>Book Order Form Example</display-name>
    <description>
        Demonstrates a book order form servlet.
    </description>

    <servlet>
        <servlet-name>OrderBooks</servlet-name>
        <servlet-class>OrderBooks</servlet-class>
    </servlet>

    <servlet-mapping>
        <servlet-name>OrderBooks</servlet-name>
        <url-pattern>/servlet/OrderBooks</url-pattern>
    </servlet-mapping>
</web-app>
```

6. Restart Apache Tomcat 5 with the following command:

```
service tomcat5 restart
```

7. Start the Web browser and point the Web browser to the following URL:

```
http://localhost:8080/book-order/OrderBooks.html
```

This causes the HTML form that was shown in Figure 26-9 to appear.

8. I fill in some information in the form and click Order. The Web browser displays some dialog boxes about sending unencrypted information. I click OK, and the Web browser displays the HTML document returned by the `OrderBooks` servlet. Figure 26-10 shows the servlet's response to what I entered on the book order form.

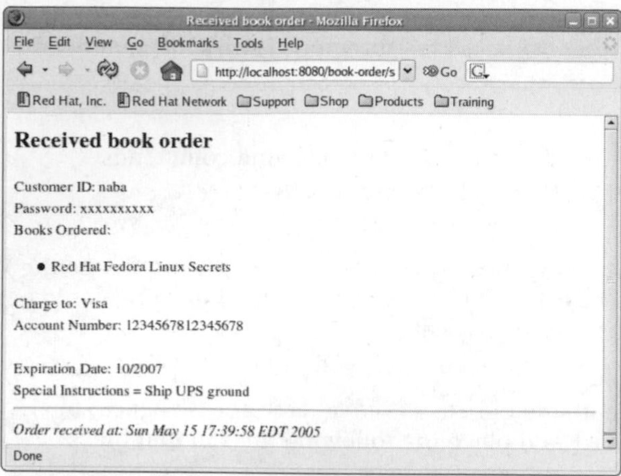

Figure 26-10: The OrderBooks Servlet Displays What the User Entered in the Book Order Form.

Becoming Proficient in Java

To become a proficient Java programmer, you have to become familiar with the Java language as well as the classes and methods available in various Java APIs. The best way to do so is to begin using some of these classes in your Java programs — whether you are writing applets, servlets, or standalone programs. Unfortunately, this chapter simply does not have enough room to cover all of the Java APIs in detail. It really takes an entire book (maybe more) to cover Java programming in detail. Because Java is very popular, there is no shortage of reference material on Java. In fact, the problem is in deciding which one of the many Java books best suits your needs. Here are a few suggestions for reference books on Java programming:

- **Ken Arnold, James Gosling, and David Holmes, The Java Programming Language, 3rd Edition (Addison-Wesley, 2000):** You may want a copy of this book for the very reason that C++ programmers may want a copy of *The C++ Programming Language* by Bjarne Stroustrup (Addison-Wesley, 1997) — James Gosling is the originator of Java. This book provides a concise and precise presentation of how Java works and why. It's not a tutorial guide, but professional Java developers will find this book worthwhile.
- **Barry Burd, Java 2 For Dummies, 2nd Edition (John Wiley & Sons, 2004):** This is a good introduction to Java 2 in the popular and well-known Dummies style.

For Java APIs, look for API documentations, tutorials, and code samples at Sun's Java website at the following URL:

```
http://java.sun.com/reference/
```

Summary

Java is an object-oriented programming language that you can use to develop applets, servlets, and standalone applications. This chapter provides an overview of Java and gets you started with a few simple programming examples.

In this chapter, you learned the following:

- To write Java programs, you need a Java development environment. Fedora comes with a Java development environment. You can also use the freely available Java 2 Standard Edition Software Development Kit (Java 2 SDK or J2SE SDK) from Sun Microsystems. You can download the Java 2 SDK from `http://java.sun.com/j2se/downloads/`.
- Fedora also includes the tools — Java servlet API and Tomcat 5 application server — that you need to develop servlets. The tools are installed when you select the Java Development package during Fedora installation.
- The compiled Java code is known as Java byte code.
- There are several types of Java programs — standalone Java applications, applets, and servlets. Standalone applications can be executed using the Java interpreter that comes with the Java 2 SDK. Java applets must be embedded in an HTML document and run under the appletviewer (a program that comes with the Java 2 SDK) or a Java-capable Web browser. Java servlets run on the Web server and typically perform tasks such as process HTML forms, access a database, and prepare dynamic HTML documents.
- To embed a Java applet in an HTML document, you use the `<applet>` tag.
- Java has a syntax that's similar to that of C and C++. Like C++, Java is an object-oriented programming language. Everything in Java must be an object. Unlike C and C++, Java does not allow any standalone functions.
- Java supports both C-style comments (enclosed within `/*...*/`) and C++-style comments (comment begins with `//`). Additionally, Java also supports a third-style comment that begins with `/**` and ends with `*/` (this style of comment is called a *doc comment*).
- A Java class defines an object type. The class is the template from which an object can be created (or instantiated). The class includes data and procedures that operate on the data. These procedures are referred to as methods.
- A class can inherit from another class thereby establishing a parent-child relationship. The parent class is referred to as the superclass, and the child class is called the subclass. Unlike C++, Java supports single inheritance only — that means a subclass can inherit from at most one superclass.
- Java supports the primitive C data types (such as `int`, `char`, `float`, `double`) as well as the basic programming C constructs (such as `for`, `while`, `if...else`). Java introduces two new primitive types: `boolean` and `byte`.
- Java does not include any pointers. Unlike C and C++, you cannot manipulate pointers to access blocks of memory.
- Java introduces the `interface` keyword, which is a set of methods that any class may implement. The `interface` keyword defines a set of capabilities.
- Java supports multiple threads, where each thread is an independent sequence of execution. That means a single application or applet may have multiple independent threads of execution — it's multitasking at the individual process level.

You can have a thread download data from the server while another thread updates the applet's display.

- Like the run-time library in C, Java comes with a number of class packages — these are the foundation classes on which you build a Java application. For example, Java applets are subclassed from the Applet class in the java.applet package. Applets display user interfaces (such as buttons and menus) and generate graphics output by using classes from the java.awt package.
- Java Foundation Classes (JFC), included in the Java 2 SDK, includes the Swing classes that enable you to create more complex GUIs in Java.

Part VI

Appendixes

Linux Commands

This appendix presents alphabetically arranged reference entries for the most important Linux commands. The goal here is to provide you with an overview of all commands needed to manage files and directories, start and stop processes, find files, work with text files, and access online help.

If you are looking for a command for a specific task, but don't know which command to use, you may find it helpful to browse through the commands by category. Table A-1 shows the Linux commands organized by categories.

Table A-1: Linux Commands

Command Name	*Action*
Getting Online Help	
`apropos`	Finds man pages for a specified keyword
`info`	Displays online help information about a specified command
`man`	Displays online help information
`whatis`	Similar to `apropos`, but searches for complete words only
Making Commands Easier	
`alias`	Defines an abbreviation for a long command
`type`	Shows the type and location of a command
`unalias`	Deletes an abbreviation defined using `alias`

(continued)

Table A-1 *(continued)*

Command Name	*Action*
Managing Files and Directories	
`cd`	Changes the current directory
`chattr`	Changes file attributes in Linux ext2 and ext3 file systems
`chgrp`	Changes group ownership of file
`chmod`	Changes file permissions
`chown`	Changes file owner and group
`cp`	Copies files
`ln`	Creates symbolic links to files and directories
`ls`	Displays the contents of a directory
`mkdir`	Creates a directory
`mv`	Renames a file as well as moves a file from one directory to another
`rm`	Deletes files
`rmdir`	Deletes directories
`pwd`	Displays the current directory
`touch`	Updates a file's time stamp
Finding Files	
`find`	Finds files based on specified criteria such as name, size, and so on
`lsof`	Lists open files
`locate`	Finds files using a periodically updated database
`whereis`	Finds files based in the typical directories where executable (also known as binary) files are located
`which`	Finds files in the directories listed in the `PATH` environment variable
Processing Files	
`cat`	Displays a file on standard output (can be used to concatenate several files into one big file)
`cut`	Extracts specified sections from each line of text in a file
`dd`	Copies blocks of data from one file to another (used to copy data from devices)
`diff`	Compares two text files and finds any differences
`expand`	Converts all tabs into spaces
`file`	Displays the type of data in a file
`fold`	Wraps each line of text to fit a specified width
`grep`	Searches for regular expressions within a text file
`less`	Displays a text file, one page at a time (can go backward also)

Command Name	Action
lpr	Prints files
more	Displays a text file, one page at a time (goes forward only)
nl	Numbers all nonblank lines in a text file and prints the lines to standard output
paste	Concatenates corresponding lines from several files
patch	Updates a text file using the differences between the original and revised copy of the file
sed	Copies a file to standard output while applying specified editing commands
sort	Sorts lines in a text file
split	Breaks up a file into several smaller files with specified size
tac	Reverses a file (last line first and so on)
tail	Displays the last few lines of a file
tr	Substitutes one group of characters for another throughout a file
uniq	Eliminates duplicate lines from a text file
wc	Counts the number of lines, words, and characters in a text file
zcat	Displays a compressed file (after decompressing)
zless	Displays a compressed file one page at a time (can go backwards also)
zmore	Displays a compressed file one page at a time
Archiving and Compressing Files	
bzip2	Compresses files using an algorithm called the Burrows-Wheeler block-sorting text-compression algorithm and Huffman coding
bunzip2	Decompresses files compressed by `bzip2` (same as `bzip2 -d`)
compress	Compresses files
cpio	Copies files to and from an archive
gunzip	Decompresses files compressed with GNU ZIP (`gzip`) or `compress`
gzip	Compresses files (more powerful than `compress`)
tar	Creates an archive of files in one or more directories (originally meant for archiving on tape)
uncompress	Decompresses files compressed with `compress`
Managing Processes	
bg	Runs an interrupted process in the background
fg	Runs a process in the foreground
free	Displays the amount of free and used memory in the system
halt	Shuts down Linux and halts the computer

(continued)

Table A-1 *(continued)*

Command Name	*Action*
`kill`	Sends a signal to a process (usually used to terminate a process)
`ldd`	Displays the shared libraries needed to run a program
`nice`	Runs a process with lower priority (referred to as *nice mode*)
`ps`	Displays a list of currently running processes
`printenv`	Displays the current environment variables
`pstree`	Similar to `ps`, but shows parent-child relationships clearly
`reboot`	Stops Linux and then restarts the computer
`shutdown`	Shuts down Linux
`top`	Displays a list of most processor- and memory-intensive processes
`uname`	Displays information about the system and the Linux kernel
Managing Users	
`chsh`	Changes the shell (command interpreter)
`groups`	Prints the list of groups that includes a specified user
`id`	Displays the user and group ID for a specified user name
`passwd`	Changes the password
`su`	Starts a new shell as another user or `root` (when invoked without any argument)
Managing the File System	
`df`	Summarizes free and available space in all mounted storage devices
`du`	Displays disk usage information
`fdformat`	Formats a diskette
`fdisk`	Partitions a hard disk
`fsck`	Checks and repairs a file system
`mkfs`	Creates a new file system
`mknod`	Creates a device file
`mkswap`	Creates a swap space for Linux in a file or a disk partition
`mount`	Mounts a device (for example, the CD-ROM) on a directory in the file system
`swapoff`	Deactivates a swap space
`swapon`	Activates a swap space
`sync`	Writes buffered data to files
`tty`	Displays the device name for the current terminal
`umount`	Unmounts a device from the file system

Command Name	Action
Working with Date and Time	
`cal`	Displays a calendar for a specified month or year
`date`	Shows the current date and time or sets a new date and time

The rest of this appendix covers individual reference entries for each command shown in Table A-1. Each reference entry is organized as follows:

- **Purpose** tells you when to use the command.
- **Syntax** shows the syntax of the command with a few common options. Also, typical option values are shown. All optional items are shown in square brackets.
- **Options** lists most options, along with a brief description of each option. For many commands, you will find all options listed in this section. However, some commands have too many options to cover here. For those commands, I describe the most commonly used options.
- **Description** describes the command and provides more details about how to use it.

alias

Purpose Define an abbreviation for a long command or view the current list of abbreviations.

Syntax `alias [abbrev=command]`

Options None

Description If you type **alias** alone, you get a listing of all currently defined abbreviations. Typically, you use `alias` to define easy-to-remember abbreviations for longer commands. For example, if you type **ls -l** often, you might add a line with `alias ll='ls -l'` in the `.bashrc` file in your home directory. Then, you can type **ll** instead of **ls -l** to see a detailed listing of a directory. `alias` is a built-in command of the Bash shell and is described in Chapter 7.

apropos

Purpose View a list of all man pages that contain a specific keyword.

Syntax `apropos keyword`

Options None

Description The `apropos` command looks up the keyword in a database (known as the `whatis` database) the `/usr/sbin/makewhatis` program creates. The `whatis` database is an index of keywords contained in all of the man pages in the system. Unfortunately, when you try `apropos` with a simple keyword such as `find`, you may end up with a long listing of man pages because the word "find" appears in many man pages.

bg

Purpose Run an interrupted process in the background.

Syntax `bg`

Options None

Description After you type a command that takes a long time to finish, you can press Ctrl-Z to interrupt the process. Then, you can type **bg** to continue that command in the background while you type other commands at the shell prompt. `bg` is a built-in command of the Bash shell.

bzip2, bunzip2

Purpose Compress file using block-sorting file compression.

Syntax `bzip2 [-cdfktvVL] files`

Options
`-c` sends output to the standard output.
`-d` decompress files (equivalent to `bunzip2` command).
`-f` overwrites existing output files of the same name.
`-k` keeps input files.
`-t` tests the integrity of a compressed file.
`-v` runs in verbose mode, which shows more information.
`-L` displays license information.
`-V` displays version information.

Description Use `bzip2` to compress files using the Burrows-Wheeler block-sorting text-compression algorithm and Huffman coding. To decompress, use `bzip2 -d` or `bunzip2`. The compressed file names have a `.bz2` extension.

cal

Purpose View the calendar of any month in any year.

Syntax
`cal`
`cal [-jy] [[month_number] year]]`

Options
`-j` displays Julian dates (days numbered between 1 and 366).
`-y` displays the calendar for all months of the current year.

Description If you type **cal** without any options, it prints a calendar for the current month. If you type **cal** followed by a number, `cal` treats the number as the year and prints the calendar for that year. To view the calendar for a specific month in a specific year, provide the month number (1 = January, 2 = February, and so on) followed by the year. Thus, to view the calendar for April 2006, type the following:

```
cal 4 2006
     April 2006
Su Mo Tu We Th Fr Sa
                   1
 2  3  4  5  6  7  8
 9 10 11 12 13 14 15
16 17 18 19 20 21 22
23 24 25 26 27 28 29
30
```

cat

Purpose Copy contents of a file to standard output (the screen).

Syntax `cat [-benstvA] files`

Options
`-b` numbers nonblank lines.
`-e` shows each end-of-line (as `$`) and all nonprinting characters.
`-n` numbers all output lines starting with number 1.
`-s` replaces multiple blank lines with a single blank line.
`-t` shows tabs as `^I`.
`-v` shows nonprinting characters.
`-A` shows all characters (including nonprinting ones).

Description Typically, `cat` is used to display the contents of a file or to concatenate several files into a single file. For example, `cat file1 file2 file3 > all` combines three files into a single file named `all`.

cd

Purpose Change the current directory.

Syntax `cd [`*`directory`*`]`

Options None

Description Typing `cd` without a directory name changes the current directory to your home directory. Otherwise, `cd` changes to the specified directory. `cd` is a built-in command of the Bash shell.

chattr

Purpose Change file attributes in Linux ext2 and ext3 file systems.

Syntax `chattr [ -RV ] [ -v `*`version`*` ] [ `*`mode`*` ] `*`files...`*

Options `-V` verbosely displays permission changes.

`-v` *`version`* sets the version number of the file to *`version`*.

Description The attribute is defined by the *`mode`* argument and mode is of the form `+-=[ASacdisu]`, where the `+` causes the specified attributes to be added to the existing attributes of the files, `-` causes them to be removed from the existing attributes, and `=` causes the file attributes to be set to only the specified attributes. The letters `ASacdisu` specify the attributes for the files: `A` means do not update `atime` (`atime` is the time when the file was accessed); `S` means synchronous updates; `a` means append only; `c` means compressed, `i` means immutable (file cannot be changed); `d` means no dump; `s` means secure deletion (file contents are completely wiped out when it is deleted); and `u` means undeletable (file cannot be removed).

chgrp

Purpose Change the group ownership of one or more files.

Syntax `chmod [-cfvR] `*`group files`*

Options `-c` lists only files whose permissions have changed.

`-f` stops any error message displays.

`-v` verbosely displays permission changes.

`-R` recursively changes the permissions of files in all subdirectories.

Description To change the group ownership of one or more files, invoke `chgrp` with the group name followed by the filenames (you can also change the group ownership by using the `chown` command).

chmod

Purpose Change the permission settings of one or more files.

Syntax `chmod [-cfvR] `*`permission files`*

Options `-c` lists only files whose permissions have changed.

`-f` stops any error message displays.

`-v` verbosely displays permission changes.

`-R` recursively changes permissions of files in all subdirectories.

Description To use `chmod` effectively, you have to learn how to specify the permission settings. One way is to concatenate one letter from each of the following tables in the order shown (*Who/Action/Permission*):

Who	*Action*	*Permission*
u user	+ add	r read
g group	- remove	w write
o others	= assign	x execute
a all	s set user ID	

To give everyone read access to all files in a directory, type **chmod a+r ***. On the other hand, to permit everyone to execute a specific file, type **chmod +x *filename***.

Another way to specify a permission setting is to use a three-digit sequence of octal numbers. In a detailed listing, the read, write, and execute permission settings for the user, group, and others appear as the sequence `rwxrwxrwx` (with dashes in place of letters for disallowed operations). Think of `rwxrwxrwx` as three occurrences of the string `rwx`. Now, assign the values `r`=4, `w`=2, and `x`=1. To get the value of the sequence `rwx`, simply add the values of `r`, `w`, and `x`. Thus, `rwx` = 7. Using this formula, you can assign a three-digit value to any permission setting. For example, if the user can read and write the file but everyone else can only read the file, the permission setting is `rw-r--r--` (that's how it appears in the listing), and the value is 644. Thus, if you want all files in a directory to be readable by everyone but writeable by only the user, use the command `chmod 644 *`.

chown

Purpose Change the user and group ownership of a file.

Syntax `chown [cvfR] username.groupname files`

Options `-c` lists only those files whose ownership has changed.

`-f` stops any error message displays.

`-v` verbosely displays ownership changes.

`-R` recursively changes the ownership of files in all subdirectories.

Description To make a user the owner of one or more files, invoke `chown` with the user name followed by the filenames. To change the group ownership as well, append the new group name to the user name with a period as separator. For example, to make user `naba` the owner of all files in a directory, type **chown naba ***. To change both the owner and group to naba, type **chown naba.naba ***. Note that you have to be logged in as `root` to change the ownership of files.

chsh

Purpose Change the default shell started at login.

Syntax `chsh [-s shell] [username]`

Options `-s` shell specifies the name of the shell executable to use (shell can be any program listed in the `/etc/shells` file, such as `/bin/bash` and `/bin/csh`).

Description A user's default shell is stored in the `/etc/passwd file`. The `chsh` command lets you change the default shell to any of the shells listed in the `/etc/shells` file. If you type `chsh` without any arguments, `chsh` prompts you for the name of a shell.

compress

Purpose Compress one or more files by using Lempel-Ziv compression.

Syntax `compress [-cdrvV] files`

Options

`-c` writes the compressed file to the standard output and retains the original file.

`-d` decompresses the file.

`-r` recursively compresses the files in all subdirectories.

`-v` displays a message as each file is compressed.

`-V` prints the version number and exits.

Description The `compress` command compresses each specified file and replaces the original with the compressed version (with a `.Z` suffix appended to the name). You can decompress the file with the `compress -d` command or the `uncompress` command.

cp

Purpose Copy files and directories.

Syntax

`cp [options] source_files destination_directory`
`cp [options] source_file destination_file`

Options

`-a` preserves all file attributes.

`-b` makes a backup copy before copying.

`-d` copies a link but not the file pointed to by the link.

`-i` asks for confirmation before overwriting files.

`-l` creates hard links instead of copying files.

`-p` preserves ownership, permissions, and the file time stamp.

`-R` recursively copies files in all subdirectories.

`-s` creates soft links instead of copying files.

`-u` copies a file only when the file being copied is newer than the destination.

`-v` displays verbose messages as copying progresses.

`--help` displays a Help message about `cp`.

Description The `cp` command copies one file to another. You can also copy several files from one directory to another.

cpio

Purpose Copy files in from, or out to, an archive that can be on a storage medium such as tape or a file on the disk.

Syntax

`cpio [-icdv] pattern`
`cpio [-ocBv] pattern`
`cpio [-padm] pattern`

Options

`-i` extracts files whose names match the *pattern*.

`-o` copies files to archive files whose names are provided on standard input.

`-p` copies files to another directory on the same system.

`-a` resets access times of input files.

`-B` copies files using 5,120 bytes per record (the default is 512 bytes per record).

`-c` reads or writes header information as ASCII characters.

`-d` creates directories as needed.

`-m` retains the previous file-modification time.

`-v` prints a list of filenames.

Description The `cpio` command copies files in from, and out to, archives. There are three distinct variants of the `cpio` command: `cpio -o` creates an archive, `cpio -i` extracts from an archive, and `cpio -p` copies from one directory to another. `cpio` is not that popular among Linux users; `tar` is much more commonly used. However, some installation programs use `cpio` during the installation process.

cut

Purpose Copy selected parts of each line of text from a file to standard output.

Syntax `cut [options] file`

Options `-b list` extracts the characters at positions specified in the *list*.

`-f list` extracts the fields (assumed to be Tab-separated) specified in *list*.

`-d char` specifies the character that delimits the fields (the default is Tab).

`-s` skips lines that do not contain delimited fields (see the `-f` option).

Description The `cut` command extracts specified parts from each line of text in a file and writes those lines out to standard output. You can extract either a range of characters (specified by their positions) from each line or specific fields, where the fields are separated by a special character such as the Tab. For example, to extract characters 1 through 11 and the 48th character onward from a detailed directory listing, use the following command:

```
ls -l /etc| cut -b 1-11,48- | more
total 3660
drwxr-xr-x 4Suite
-rw-r--r-- a2ps.cfg
-rw-r--r-- a2ps-site.cfg
drwxr-xr-x acpi
-rw-r--r-- adjtime
drwxr-xr-x alchemist
-rw-r--r-- aliases
-rw-r----- aliases.db
drwxr-xr-x alsa
drwxr-xr-x alternatives
(... lines deleted)
```

date

Purpose Display the current date and time or set a new date and time.

Syntax `date [options] [+format]`
`date [-su] [MMDDHHMM[[CC]YY][.SS]]`

Options `-u` displays or sets the time using Greenwich Mean Time (GMT).

Description The `date` command alone displays the current date and time. Using the `+format` argument, you can specify a display format for the date and time. For a complete listing of the format specification, type **man date**.

To set the date, use `date` followed by the date and time in the `MMDDHHMM` format, where each character is a digit (`MM` is the month, `DD` is the day, `HH` the hour, and `MM` the minutes). You can optionally specify the year (`YY`) and century (`CC`) as well.

dd

Purpose Copy blocks of data from standard input to standard output (and optionally convert the data from one format to another).

Syntax `dd option1=value1 option2=value2 option3=value3 ...`

Options

`if=file` reads from the specified file instead of standard input.

`of=file` writes to the specified file instead of standard output.

`ibs=nbytes` reads blocks of *nbytes* bytes at a time.

`obs=nbytes` writes blocks of *nbytes* at a time.

`bs=nbytes` reads and writes blocks of *nbyte* bytes at a time.

`cbs=nbytes` converts *nbytes* bytes at a time.

`skip=nblocks` skips *nblocks* input blocks from the beginning of the input file.

`seek=nblocks` skips *nblocks* output blocks in the output file.

`count=nblocks` copies *nblocks* blocks from input to output.

`conv=code` performs conversion; *code* can be one of following:

- `ascii` converts EBCDIC to ASCII.
- `ebcdic` converts ASCII to EBCDIC.
- `lcase` converts to lowercase.
- `ucase` converts to uppercase.
- `swab` swaps every pair of input bytes.
- `noerror` continues after read errors.

(Note: EBCDIC is a character-encoding format used in IBM mainframes.)

Description The `dd` command copies blocks of data from standard input to standard output, optionally converting the data as the copying proceeds. Typically, `dd` is used to copy data directly from one device to another. For example, you can copy the Linux kernel (`/boot/vmlinuz`) to a diskette with the following command: `dd if=/boot/vmlinuz of=/dev/fd0`.

df

Purpose Display the amount of free and used storage space on all mounted file systems.

Syntax `df [options] [filesystem]`

Options

`-a` displays information for all file systems.

`-h` displays size information in human-readable format.

`-i` displays inode information (the disk is organized into inodes).

`-T` prints the type of file system.

`-t type` displays information about specified types of file systems only.

`-x type` excludes specified types of file systems from the output.

`--help` displays a Help message.

Description The `df` command shows the amount of free and used space on a specified file system. If you want to know how filled up all of your disks are, use the `df` command without any arguments. The `df` command then displays information about used and available storage space on all currently mounted file systems.

diff

Purpose Show the difference between two text files (or all files with the same names in two directories).

Syntax `diff [options] from_file to_file`

Options

`-a` treats all files as text even if they aren't text files.

`-b` ignores blank lines and repeated blanks.

-c produces output in a different format.

-d tries to find a smaller set of changes (this makes diff slower).

-e produces a script for the ed editor to convert from_file to to_file.

-f produces output similar to that of -e, but in reverse order.

-i ignores case.

-l passes the output to the pr command to paginate it.

-n works like -f, but counts the number of changed lines.

-r recursively compares files with the same name in all subdirectories.

-s reports when two files are the same.

-t expands tabs to spaces in the output.

-u uses the unified output format.

-v displays the version of diff.

-w ignores spaces and tabs when comparing lines.

Description The diff command compares *from_file* with *to_file* and displays the lines that differ. The output is in a format the patch command can use to convert *from_file* to *to_file*.

du

Purpose Displays summary information about disk usage (in kilobytes).

Syntax du [options] [*directories_or_files*]

Options

-a displays usage information for all files (not just directories).

-b displays usage in bytes (instead of kilobytes).

-c displays a grand total of all usage information.

-h displays size information in human-readable format.

-k displays usage information in kilobytes (default).

-s displays total disk usage without per directory details.

Description The du command displays the disk space (in kilobytes) the specified files or directories use. By default, du displays the disk space that each directory and subdirectory uses. A common use of du is to view the total space the current directory uses. For example, here is how you might check the details of disk space the /var/log directory uses:

```
du /var/log
8       /var/log/httpd
8       /var/log/news/OLD
28      /var/log/news
8       /var/log/ppp
36      /var/log/cups
16      /var/log/mail
116     /var/log/audit
24      /var/log/gdm
8       /var/log/vbox
8       /var/log/samba
56      /var/log/tomcat5
8       /var/log/squid
1064    /var/log
```

expand

Purpose Write files to standard output after expanding each tab into an appropriate number of spaces.

Syntax `expand [options] [files]`

Options `-n` (where *n* is a number) sets the tabs *n* spaces apart.

`-n1 [n2, ...]` (where *n1*, *n2*,... are numbers) specifies the tab stops.

`-i` converts only the initial tab into spaces.

Description The `expand` command reads from the specified files (or standard input, if no files are specified) and writes them to standard output, with each tab character expanded to an appropriate number of spaces. By default, `expand` assumes that the tab positions are eight spaces apart (equivalent to the `-8` option).

fdformat

Purpose Format a diskette specified by device name (such as `/dev/fd0H1440` for a 3.5-inch, high-density diskette in drive A).

Syntax `fdformat [-n] device_name`

Options `-n` disables the verification performed after formatting.

Description The `fdformat` command formats a diskette. Use an appropriate device name to identify the diskette drive (see Chapter 12 for naming conventions for diskette drives). After formatting a diskette with `fdformat`, you can use `mkfs` to install a Linux file system or `tar` to store an archive.

fdisk

Purpose Partition a disk or display information about existing partitions.

Syntax `fdisk [options] [device_name]`

Options `-l` displays partition tables and exits.

`-s device` displays the size of the specified partition.

`-v` displays the version number of the `fdisk` program.

Description The `fdisk` command partitions a specified hard disk (see Appendix B for disk-drive naming conventions). You can also use `fdisk` to display information about existing partitions. You should never run `fdisk` and alter the partitions of a hard disk while one or more of its partitions are mounted on the Linux file system. Instead, you should boot from an installation CD or DVD (or a boot CD) and perform the partitioning. Remember that partitioning typically destroys all existing data on a hard disk.

fg

Purpose Continue an interrupted process in the foreground.

Syntax `fg`

Options None

Description After you interrupt a process by pressing Ctrl-Z, you can continue that process in the foreground by typing the `fg` command. Note that `fg` is a built-in command of the Bash shell.

file

Purpose Display the type of data in a file based on rules defined in the `/usr/lib/magic` file (this is known as the *magic file*).

Syntax `file [options] files`

Options

`-c` displays a parsed form of a magic file (or the default one) and exits.

`-m file1[:file2 : . . .]` specifies other magic files.

`-v` displays the version number and exits.

`-z` looks inside compressed files.

Description The `file` command uses rules specified in the `/usr/lib/magic` file to determine the type of data in the specified files. For example, you can use the `file` command to check the type of each file in the `/usr/lib` directory, as shown here:

```
file * | more
4Suite:                              directory
alchemist:                           directory
anaconda-runtime:                    directory
ao:                                  directory
aspell:                              directory
autofs:                              directory
bonobo:                              directory
bonobo-2.0:                          directory
cracklib_dict.hwm:                   symbolic link to `../../
                                     usr/share/cracklib/
                                     pw_dict.hwm'
cracklib_dict.pwd:                   symbolic link to `../../
                                     usr/share/cracklib/
                                     pw_dict.pwd'
cracklib_dict.pwi:                   symbolic link to `../../
                                     usr/share/cracklib/
                                     pw_dict.pwi'
crt1.o:                              ELF 32-bit LSB relocatable,
                                     Intel 80386, version 1
                                     (SYSV), not stripped
(. . . lines deleted)
```

find

Purpose Display a list of files that match a specified set of criteria.

Syntax `find [path] [options]`

Options

`-depth` processes the current directory first, then subdirectories.

`-maxdepth n` restricts searches to *n* levels of directories.

`-follow` processes directories included through symbolic links.

`-name pattern` finds files whose names match the *pattern*.

`-ctime n` matches files modified exactly *n* days ago.

`-user uname` finds files the specified user owns.

`-group gname` finds files the specified group owns.

`-path pattern` finds files whose pathname matches the *pattern*.

`-perm mode` finds files with the specified permission setting.

`-size +nK` finds files bigger than *n* kilobytes.

`-type x` finds files of a specified type, where *x* is one of the following:

f matches files.

d matches directories.

l matches symbolic links.

-print displays the names of the files found.

-exec *command [options]* {} \; executes the specified command by passing it the name of the file that was found.

Description The find command is useful for finding all files that match a specified set of criteria. If you type **find** without any arguments, the output is a listing of every file in all subdirectories of the current directory. To view all files whose names end with .gz, type **find . -name "*.gz"**.

fold

Purpose Wrap lines of text to a specified width (the default is 80 characters).

Syntax fold [options] [*files*]

Options -b counts bytes instead of columns, so backspaces and tabs are counted.

-s breaks lines at word boundaries.

-w *N* (where *N* is a number) sets line width to *N* characters.

Description The fold command wraps each input line to a specified number of characters and displays the results on the screen (standard output). If you do not specify any filename, fold reads lines from the standard input.

free

Purpose Display the amount of free and used memory in the system.

Syntax free [options]

Options -b displays memory in number of bytes.

-k displays memory in kilobytes (default).

-m displays memory in megabytes.

-s *n* repeats the command every *n* seconds.

-t displays a line containing a summary of the total amounts.

Description The free command displays information about the physical memory (RAM) and the swap area (on the disk). The output shows the total amount of memory, as well as the amount used and the amount free.

fsck

Purpose Check and repair a Linux file system.

Syntax fsck [options] *device_name*

Options -A checks all file systems listed in the /etc/fstab file.

-R skips the root file system (when checking all file systems).

-T does not show the title on startup.

-N shows what might be done but does not actually do anything.

-V produces verbose output.

-t *fstype* specifies the file-system type (such as ext2).

-n answers all confirmation requests with no (only for the ext2 file system).

-p carries out all repairs without asking for confirmation (for ext2).

-y answers all confirmation requests with yes (only for the ext2 file system).

Description The `fsck` command checks the integrity of a file system and carries out any necessary repairs. Depending on the type of file system, `fsck` runs an appropriate command to check and repair the file system. For example, to check an `ext2` file system, `fsck` runs the `e2fsck` program. You have to run `fsck` when you power down your system without running the `shutdown` command. Typically, `fsck` is automatically run during system startup.

grep

Purpose Search one or more files for lines that match a regular expression (a search pattern).

Syntax `grep [options]` *`pattern files`*

Options `-`*`N`* (where *`N`* is a number) displays *`N`* lines around the line containing *`pattern`*.

`-c` shows the number of lines that contain the search pattern.

`-f` *`file`* reads options from a specified file.

`-i` ignores case.

`-l` displays the filenames that contain *`pattern`*.

`-n` displays a line number next to lines that contain *`pattern`*.

`-q` returns a status code but does not display any output.

`-v` displays the lines that do not contain *`pattern`*.

`-w` matches only whole words.

Description The `grep` command searches the specified files for a pattern. The pattern is a regular expression that has its own rules. Typically, you use `grep` to search for a specific sequence of characters in one or more text files.

groups

Purpose Show the groups to which a user belongs.

Syntax `groups [`*`username`*`]`

Options None

Description The `groups` command displays the names of groups to which a user belongs. If you do not specify a user name, the command displays your groups.

gunzip

Purpose Decompresses files the `gzip` or the `compress` command compresses.

Syntax `gunzip [options]` *`files`*

Options See the options for `gzip`.

Description The `gunzip` command decompresses compressed files (these files have the `.gz` or `.Z` extension). After decompressing, `gunzip` replaces the compressed files with their decompressed versions and removes the `.gz` or `.Z` extension in the filenames. The `gunzip` command is the same as `gzip` with the `-d` option.

gzip

Purpose Compress one or more files.

Syntax `gzip [options]` *`files`*

Options `-c` writes output to standard output and retains the original file.

`-d` decompresses the file (same as `gunzip`).

`-h` displays a Help message.

`-l` lists the contents of a compressed file.

`-n` does not save the original name and time stamp.

-r recursively compresses files in all subdirectories.

-v displays verbose output.

-V displays the version number.

Description The gzip command compresses files using Lempel-Ziv (LZ77) coding, which produces better compression than the algorithm the compress command uses. After compressing a file, gzip replaces the original file with the compressed version and appends a .gz to the filename.

halt

Purpose Terminate all processes and halt the system (you must log in as root).

Syntax halt [options]

Options -n does not flush out in-memory buffers to disk before halting the system.

-f forces a halt without calling the /sbin/shutdown command.

-i shuts down all network interfaces before halting the system.

Description The halt command lets the superuser (root) terminate all processes and halt the system. The halt command invokes /sbin/shutdown with the -h option.

id

Purpose List the user ID, group ID, and groups for a user.

Syntax id [options] [*username*]

Options -g displays group ID only.

-n displays group name instead of ID.

-u displays user ID only.

-Z displays the SELinux security context.

Description The id command displays the user ID, the group ID, and the groups for a specified user. If you do not provide a user name, id displays information about the current user.

info

Purpose View online help information about any Linux command.

Syntax info [options] *command*

Options -d *dirname* adds a directory to a list of directories to be searched for files.

-f *infofile* specifies the file to be used by info.

-h displays usage information about info.

Description The info command displays online help information about a specified command in a full-screen text window. You can use Emacs commands to navigate the text displayed by info. To learn more about info, type **info** without any arguments.

kill

Purpose Send a signal to a process.

Syntax kill [options] *process_id*

Options -*signum* (where *signum* is a number or name) sends the specified signal.

-l lists the signal names and numbers.

Description The kill command sends a signal to a process. Typically, the signal is meant to terminate the process. For example, kill -9 123 terminates the process with ID 123. To see process IDs, use the ps command. To see a list of signal names and numbers, type **kill -l** (that's a lowercase "L").

ldd

Purpose Display the names of shared libraries required to run a program.

Syntax `ldd [options] programs`

Options `-v` prints the version number of `ldd`.

`-V` prints the version number of the dynamic linker (`ld.so`).

`-d` relocates functions and reports missing functions.

`-r` relocates both data and functions and reports missing objects.

Description The `ldd` command lets you determine which shared libraries are needed to run the specified programs. For example, to determine what you need to run the Bash shell (`/bin/bash`), type the following:

```
ldd /bin/bash
        linux-gate.so.1 =>  (0x0026f000)
        libtermcap.so.2 => /lib/libtermcap.so.2 (0x00981000)
        libdl.so.2 => /lib/libdl.so.2 (0x007aa000)
        libc.so.6 => /lib/libc.so.6 (0x00658000)
        /lib/ld-linux.so.2 (0x0063a000)
```

less

Purpose View text files one screen at a time (and scroll backward if necessary).

Syntax `less [options] filenames`

Options `-?` displays a list of commands you can use in `less`.

`-p text` displays the first line where *text* is found.

`-s` reduces multiple blank lines to a single blank line.

Description The `less` command displays the specified files one screen at a time. Unlike when you use `more`, you can press `b`, Ctrl-B, or Esc-V to scroll backward. To view the commands you can use to interact with `less`, press `h` while you are viewing a file in `less`.

ln

Purpose Set up a hard or symbolic link (shortcut or pseudonym) to files and directories.

Syntax `ln [options] existing_file new_name`

Options `-b` makes backup copy of files about to be removed.

`-d` creates a hard link to a directory (only root can do this).

`-f` removes the existing file with *new_name*.

`--help` displays a Help message.

`-s` creates a symbolic link.

`-v` displays verbose output.

Description The `ln` command assigns a new name (shortcut) to an existing file. With the `-s` option, you can create symbolic links that can exist across file systems. Also, with symbolic links, you can see the link information with the `ls -l` command. Otherwise, `ls -l` shows two distinct files for a file and its hard link.

locate

Purpose From a periodically updated database, list all files that match a specified pattern.

Syntax `locate pattern`

Options `-u` updates the database of files.

Description The `locate` command searches a database of files for any name that matches a specified pattern. Your Linux system is set up to update the file database periodically. If you are not sure about the location of a file, just type **locate** followed by a part of the filename. For example, here's how you can search for the `xorg.conf` file:

```
locate xorg.conf
/usr/X11R6/man/man5/xorg.conf.5x.gz
/etc/X11/xorg.conf
```

lpr

Purpose Print one or more files.

Syntax `lpr [options] [files]`

Options

`-Pprinter` prints to the specified printer (the name appears in `/etc/printcap`).

`-#N` (where *N* is a number) prints that many copies of each file.

`-h` suppresses the burst page (the first page, with user information).

`-m` sends mail upon completion of a print job.

`-r` removes the file after printing.

`-J jobname` prints this job name on the burst page.

`-U username` prints this user name on the burst page.

Description The `lpr` command prints the specified files by using your system's print-spooling system. If no filenames are specified, `lpr` reads input from the standard input. You can print to a specific printer with the `-P` option.

ls

Purpose List the contents of a directory.

Syntax `ls [options] [directory_name]`

Options

`-a` displays all files, including those that start with a period (`.`).

`-b` displays unprintable characters in filenames with octal code.

`-c` sorts according to file creation time.

`-d` lists directories like any other file (rather than listing their contents).

`-f` lists directory contents without sorting (exactly as they are in the disk).

`-i` shows the inode information.

`-l` shows the file listing in the long format, with detailed information.

`-p` appends a character to a filename to indicate its type.

`-r` sorts the listing in reverse alphabetical order.

`-s` shows the size (in kilobytes) of each file next to the filename.

`-t` sorts the listing according to the file's time stamp.

`-1` displays a one-column listing of filenames.

`-R` recursively lists the files in all subdirectories.

Description The `ls` command displays the listing of a specified directory. If you omit the directory name, `ls` displays the contents of the current directory. By default, `ls` does not list files whose names begin with a period (`.`); to see all files, type **ls -a**. You can see full details of files (including size, user and group ownership, and read-write-execute permissions) with the `ls -l` command.

lsof

Purpose List open files and network connections.

Syntax `lsof [options] [names]`

Options

`-h` displays a Help message.

`-c X` displays files for commands that begin with letter *X*.

`-i IP` shows network connections whose IP address matches *IP*.

`-s` shows the file size (when available).

`-t` displays terse output.

`-u names` lists the open files for the specified users.

`-R` lists the parent process ID.

Description The `lsof` command displays a list of all the open files for a user. An open file may be a regular file, a directory, a device file, a library, or a network file (Internet socket, NFS file, or UNIX domain socket). You can use this command to see who is using a specific file. You can also use `lsof` as an intrusion detection tool to browse the current Internet connections and see if there are any unexpected connections.

man

Purpose View online manual pages (also called *man pages*).

Syntax `man [options] [section] command`

Options

`-C cfile` specifies the man configuration file (the default is `/etc/man.config`).

`-P pager` specifies the program to use to display one page at a time (for example, `less`).

`-a` displays all man pages matching a specific *command*.

`-h` displays a Help message and exits.

`-w` shows the location of the man pages to be displayed.

Description The `man` command displays the man pages for the specified command. If you know the section for a man page, you can provide the section as well or simply use the -a option to view all man pages in all sections matching a command.

mkdir

Purpose Create a directory.

Syntax `mkdir [options] directory_name`

Options

`-m mode` assigns the specified permission setting to the new directory.

`-p` creates the parent directories if they do not already exist.

Description The `mkdir` command creates the specified directory.

mkfs

Purpose Create a Linux file system on a hard-disk partition or a diskette.

Syntax `mkfs [-V] [-t] [options] device_name [blocks]`

Options

`-V` produces verbose output needed for testing.

`-t fstype` specifies the file system type (such as `ext2`).

`-c` checks the device for bad blocks before creating the file system.

`-l filename` reads the bad-block list from specified file.

Description The `mkfs` command creates a Linux file system on a specified device. The device is typically a hard-disk partition or a diskette (that has been formatted with `fdformat`).

mknod

Purpose Create a device file with specified major and minor numbers.

Syntax `mknod` *`device_file`* `{b|c}` *`major minor`*

Options None

Description The `mknod` command creates a device file (such as the ones in the `/dev` directory) through which the operating system accesses physical devices, such as hard disk, serial port, keyboard, and mouse. To create a device file, you have to log in as root, and you have to know the major and minor numbers of the device for which you are creating the device file. In addition, you must specify either `b` or `c` to indicate whether the device is block oriented or character oriented. Typically, you perform this step following specific instructions in a HOWTO document.

mkswap

Purpose Create a swap space for Linux.

Syntax `mkswap [options]` *`device_or_file numblocks`*

Options `-c` checks the device for bad blocks before creating the swap space.

`-f` forces creation of swap space even if there are errors, such as the requested size being greater than space available on the device.

`-P` *`NNN`* uses *`NNN`* as the page size for the swap space.

`-v`*`N`* (where *`N`* is 0 or 1) creates an old-style swap space if *`N`* is 0; if *`N`* is 1, creates a new-style swap space.

Description The `mkswap` command creates a swap space for use by the Linux kernel. If you are creating swap space in a disk partition, specify the partition's device name (such as `/dev/hda2`) as the second argument to `mkswap`. If you want to use a file as swap space, create the file with a command such as `dd if=/dev/zero of=swapfile bs=1024 count=16384`. Then, type **mkswap swapfile 16384** to create the swap space. You have to use the `swapon` command to activate a swap space.

more

Purpose View text files one screen at a time.

Syntax `more [options]` *`filenames`*

Options +*`N`* (where *`N`* is a number) displays the file starting at the specified line number

+/*`pattern`* begins displaying two lines before the *`pattern`*.

`-s` reduces multiple blank lines to a single blank line.

Description The `more` command displays the specified files one screen at a time. To view the commands you can use in `more`, press h while you are viewing a file using `more`. For more advanced file viewing, use the `less` command.

mount

Purpose Associate a physical device to a specific directory in the Linux file system.

Syntax `mount [options]` *`device directory`*

Options `-a` mounts all devices listed in the `/etc/fstab` file.

`-h` displays a Help message and exits.

`-r` mounts the device for read-only (no writing allowed).

`-t` *`fstype`* specifies the file system type on the device.

`-v` displays verbose messages.

`-V` displays the version number and exits.

Description The `mount` command attaches the contents of a physical device to a specific directory on the Linux file system. For example, you may mount a CD-ROM at the `/media/cdrom` directory. Then, you can access the contents of the CD-ROM at the `/media/cdrom` directory (in other words, the root directory of the CD-ROM appears as `/media/cdrom` after the mount operation). To see the listing of the `Fedora` directory on the CD-ROM, type **ls /media/cdrom/Fedora**.

mv

Purpose Rename files and directories or move them from one directory to another.

Syntax `mv [options]` *`source destination`*

Options `-b` makes backup copies of files being moved or renamed.

`-f` removes existing files without prompting.

`-i` prompts before overwriting any existing files.

`-v` displays the name of the file before moving it.

Description The `mv` command either renames a file or moves it to another directory. The command works on either plain files or directories. Thus, you can rename the file `sample` to `sample.old` with the command `mv sample sample.old`. On the other hand, you can move the file `/tmp/sample` to `/usr/local/sample` with the command `mv /tmp/sample /usr/local/sample`.

nice

Purpose Run a program at a lower or higher priority level.

Syntax `nice [options]` *`program`*

Options +*n* (*n* = number) adds *n* to the nice value (positive values are lower priority).

-*n* (*n* = number) subtracts *n* from the nice value (negative nice value indicates a higher priority).

Description The `nice` command enables you to run a program at lower or higher priority. By default, programs run at the nice value of zero. Adding to the nice value decreases the priority, whereas subtracting from the nice value increases the program's priority. Only `root` can decrease the nice value.

nl

Purpose Add line numbers to nonblank lines of text in a file and write to standard output.

Syntax `nl [options] [`*`file`*`]`

Options `-ba` numbers all lines.

`-bt` numbers text lines only (the default).

`-s`*`c`* separates text from line numbers with the character *c* (the default is tab).

`-w`*`n`* uses *n* columns to show the line numbers.

Description The `nl` command adds a line number to each nonblank line of text from a file and writes the lines to standard output. Suppose the file `sample.txt` has the following lines:

```
A line followed by a blank line and

then another non-blank line.
```

The `nl` command applied to this file produces the following result:

```
nl sample.txt
     1  A line followed by a blank line and

     2  then another non-blank line.
```

passwd

Purpose Change password.

Syntax `passwd [username]`

Options None

Description The `passwd` command changes your password. It prompts for the old password, followed by the new password. If you log in as root, you can change another user's password by specifying the user name as an argument to the `passwd` command.

paste

Purpose Write to standard output corresponding lines of each file, separated by a tab.

Syntax `paste file1 file2 [. . .]`

Options `-s` pastes the lines from one file at a time, instead of one line from each file.

`-d delim` uses delimiters from the list of characters, instead of a tab.

`-` causes paste to use standard input as a file.

Description The `paste` command takes one line from each of the listed files and writes them out to standard output, separated by a tab. With the `-s` option, the `paste` command can also concatenate all lines from one file into a single gigantic line.

patch

Purpose Apply the output of the `diff` command to an original file.

Syntax `patch [options] < patch_file`

Options `-c` causes the patch file to be interpreted as a context `diff`.

`-e` forces `patch` to interpret the patch file as an `ed` script.

`-f` forces patch to be applied regardless of any inconsistencies.

`-n` causes the patch file to be interpreted as a normal `diff`.

`-pn` strips everything up to *n* slashes in the pathname.

`-R` indicates that patch file has been created with new and old files swapped.

`-u` causes the patch file to be interpreted as a unified `diff`.

`-v` displays the version number.

Description The `patch` command is used to update an original file by applying all the differences between the original and a revised version. The differences are in the form of an output from the `diff` command, stored in the `patch_file`. Changes to Linux kernel source code are distributed in the form of a patch file. Chapter 21 discusses how to apply patches to the kernel source.

printenv

Purpose View a list of environment variables.

Syntax `printenv`

Options None

Description The `printenv` command displays a list of all current environment variables.

ps

Purpose Display status of processes (programs) running in the system.

Syntax `ps [options]`

Options Note that unlike other commands, `ps` options do not have a - prefix.

`a` displays processes of other users.

`e` displays all processes.

`f` displays a family tree of processes.

`j` displays output using jobs format.

`l` displays in long format, with many details for each process.

`m` displays memory usage information for each process.

`u` displays the user name and start time.

`x` displays processes that are not associated with any terminal.

`Z` displays SELinux security context.

Description The `ps` command displays the status of processes running in the system. Typing `ps` alone produces a list of processes you are running. To see a list of all processes in the system, type **ps ax** (or **ps aux**, if you want more details about each process).

pstree

Purpose Display all running processes in the form of a tree.

Syntax `pstree [options] [`*`pid`*`]`

Options `-a` shows command-line arguments.

`-c` does not compact subtrees.

`-l` displays long lines.

`-n` sorts processes by process ID (instead of by name).

`-p` shows process IDs.

Description The `pstree` command shows all of the processes in the form of a tree, which makes it easy to understand the parent-child relationships among the processes.

pwd

Purpose Display the current working directory.

Syntax `pwd`

Options None

Description The `pwd` command prints the current working directory. `pwd` is a built-in command of the Bash shell.

reboot

Purpose Terminate all processes and reboot the system (you must log in as `root`).

Syntax `reboot [options]`

Options `-n` reboots the system without flushing out in-memory buffers to disk.

`-f` forces a halt without calling the `/sbin/shutdown` command.

`-i` shuts down all network interfaces before rebooting the system.

Description The `reboot` command lets the superuser (`root`) terminate all processes and reboot the system. The `reboot` command invokes `/sbin/shutdown` with the `-r` option.

rm

Purpose Delete one or more files.

Syntax `rm [options] files`

Options `-f` removes files without prompting.

`-i` prompts before removing a file.

`-r` recursively removes files in all subdirectories, including the directories.

`-v` displays the name of each file before removing it.

Description The `rm` command deletes the specified files. To remove a file, you must have write permission to the directory that contains the file.

rmdir

Purpose Delete a specified directory (provided that the directory is empty).

Syntax `rmdir [options] directory`

Options `-p` removes any parent directories that become empty.

Description The `rmdir` command deletes empty directories. If a directory is not empty, you should use the `rm -r` command to delete the files, as well as the directory.

sed

Purpose Copy a file to standard output after editing according to a set of commands.

Syntax `sed [options] [editing_commands] [file]`

Options `-e'instructions'` applies the editing instructions to the file.

`-f scriptfile` applies editing commands from *scriptfile*.

`-n` suppresses default output.

Description The `sed` command is known as the stream editor — it copies a file to standard output while applying specified editing commands. If you do not specify a file, it reads from the standard input. To use the stream editor, you have to learn its editing commands, which are very similar to the ones the `ed` editor uses (described in Chapter 11).

shutdown

Purpose Terminate all processes and shut down (or reboot) the system.

Syntax `shutdown [options] time [messages]`

Options `-t seconds` specifies the time between the message and the kill signal.

`-h` halts the system after terminating all the processes.

`-r` reboots the system after terminating all the processes.

`-f` performs a fast reboot.

`-k` sends warning messages but does not shut down the system.

`-c` cancels a shutdown that's in progress.

Description The `shutdown` command (the full pathname is `/sbin/shutdown`) brings down the Linux system in an orderly way. You must specify a time when shutdown begins; use the keyword `now` to shutdown immediately. You must be logged in as `root` to run the `shutdown` command.

sort

Purpose Sort or merge lines from a file, and write to standard output.

Syntax `sort [options] [files]`

Options -c checks if files are already sorted and prints error message if not.

-m merges files by sorting them as a group.

-b ignores leading blanks.

-d sorts in phone directory order (using only letters, digits, and blanks).

-f treats lowercase letters as equivalent to uppercase letters.

-k *pos1*[,*pos2*] specifies the sort field as characters between the two positions *pos1* and *pos2*.

-o *file* writes output to the specified file instead of standard output.

-r sorts in reverse order.

-g sorts numerically after converting the prefix of each line into a floating-point number.

-i ignores unprintable characters.

-n sorts numerically (used when a number begins each line).

-t*c* specifies the separator character.

+*n* considers characters only from position *n* onward (0 = first position).

Description The sort command sorts the lines in one or more files and writes them out to the standard output. The same command can also merge several files (when used with the -m option) and can produce an appropriately sorted and merged output.

split

Purpose Split a file into several smaller files.

Syntax split [options] *file* [*prefix*]

Options -l *n* (where *n* is a number) puts *n* lines in each file.

-*n* (where *n* is a number) puts *n* lines in each file.

-b *n*k (where *n* is a number) splits the file every *n* kilobytes.

-c *n*k (where *n* is a number) puts as many lines as possible in a split file without exceeding *n* kilobytes per file.

Description The split command breaks up a large file into smaller files. By default, split puts 1,000 lines into each file. The files are named by groups of letters such as aa, ab, ac, and so on. You can specify a prefix for the filenames. For example, to split a large archive into smaller files that fit into several high-density, 3.5-inch diskettes, use split as follows:

split -C 1440k bigfile.tar disk.

This creates files named disk.aa, disk.ab, and so on.

su

Purpose Become another user.

Syntax su [options] [*username*]

Options -c *command* passes the *command* to the shell.

-f prevents reading the startup file (.cshrc) when the shell is csh or tcsh.

-l or - makes the new shell a login shell by reading the user's startup file.

-p preserves the environment variables HOME, USER, LOGNAME, and SHELL.

-s *shell* runs the specified *shell* instead of the user's default shell.

Description The su command lets you assume the identity of another user. You have to provide the password of that user before you can continue. If you do not provide a user name, su assumes you want to change to the root user.

swapoff

Purpose Deactivate the specified swap device or file.

Syntax swapoff *device*

Options None

Description The swapoff command stops Linux from using the specified device or file as a swap space.

swapon

Purpose Activate the specified swap device or file.

Syntax swapon [-a] *device*

Options -a enables all swap devices listed in the /etc/fstab file.

Description The swapon command activates the specified device or file as a swap space. During system startup, all swap spaces are activated by the swapon -a command, which is invoked by the script file /etc/rc.d/rc.sysinit.

sync

Purpose Write buffers to disk.

Syntax sync

Options None

Description When you cannot shut down your Linux system in an orderly manner (for example, when you cannot execute shutdown, halt, or reboot commands), you should type **sync** before switching off the computer.

tac

Purpose Copy a file, line by line, to the standard output in reverse order (last line first).

Syntax tac *file*

Options -b places the separator at the beginning of each line.

-r treats the separator string specified by -s as a regular expression.

-s *sep* specifies a separator (instead of the default newline character).

Description The tac command displays the specified text file in reverse order, copying the lines to standard output in reverse order. By default, tac treats each line as a record and uses the newline character as the record separator. However, you can specify a different separator character, in which case tac copies those records to standard output in reverse order.

tail

Purpose View the last few lines of a file.

Syntax tail [options] *file*

Options -*N* (where *N* is a number) displays last *N* lines.

-n *N* (where *N* is a number) displays last *N* lines.

-f reads the file at regular intervals and displays all new lines.

Description The `tail` command displays lines from the end of the specified file. By default, `tail` displays the last 10 lines from the file. To view the last 24 lines from a file named `/var/log/messages`, type **tail -24 /var/log/messages**.

tar

Purpose Create an archive of files or extract files from an archive.

Syntax `tar [options]` *`files_or_directories`*

Options

`-c` creates a new archive.

`-d` compares files in an archive with files in the current directory.

`-r` extends the archive with more files.

`-t` lists the contents of an archive.

`-x` extracts from the archive.

`-C` *`directory`* extracts files into the specified directory.

`-f` *`file`* uses the specified file as the archive, instead of a tape.

`-L` *`n`* specifies the capacity of the tape as *`n`* kilobytes.

`-N` *`date`* only archives files newer than the specified date.

`-T` *`file`* archives or extracts the filenames specified in *`file`*.

`-v` displays verbose messages.

`-z` compresses or decompresses the archive with `gzip`.

Description The `tar` command creates an archive of files, or extracts files from an existing archive. By default, `tar` assumes the archive to be on a tape. However, you can use the `-f` option to specify a file as the archive.

top

Purpose List currently running processes, arranged in order by their share of CPU time.

Syntax `top [q] [d` *`delay`*`]`

Options

`q` causes top to run with the highest possible priority (you have to be logged in as `root`).

`d` *`delay`* specifies the delay between updates, in seconds.

Description The `top` command produces a full-text screen with the processes arranged according to their share of the CPU time. By default, `top` updates the display every five seconds. Press `q` or Ctrl-C to quit `top`.

touch

Purpose Change a file's time stamp.

Syntax `touch [options]` *`files`*

Options

`-c` stops `touch` from creating a file that does not exist.

`-d` *`time`* uses the specified time.

`-r` *`file`* uses the time stamp from the specified file.

`-t` *`MMDDhhmm`*`[[`*`CC`*`]`*`YY`*`][.`*`ss`*`]` uses the specified date and time.

Description The `touch` command lets you change the date and time of the last modification of a file (this information is stored with the file). If you use `touch` without any options, the current date and time are used as the time stamp for the file. If the specified file does not exist, `touch` creates a new file of size 0 bytes.

tr

Purpose Copies from standard input to standard output, while substituting one set of characters with another.

Syntax `tr [options] string1 [string2]`

Options `-c` complements characters in *`string1`* with ASCII codes 001–377.

`-d` deletes from the input all characters specified in *`string1`*.

`-s` replaces repeated sequences of any character in *`string1`* with a single character.

Description The `tr` command substitutes all characters in *`string1`* in the input with the corresponding characters in *`string2`*. For example, to convert the file `sample.lc` to all uppercase and store in `sample.uc`, type the following:

```
tr [a-z] [A-Z] < sample.lc > sample.uc
```

To replace repeated occurrences of newlines in a file with a single newline character, type the following:

```
tr -s '\n' < infile > outfile
```

tty

Purpose Display the device name of the terminal.

Syntax `tty`

Options None

Description The `tty` command displays the name of the terminal connected to the standard input. This is useful in shell scripts that may need the terminal name.

type

Purpose Display the type of a command (whether it is a built-in shell command or a separate executable program).

Syntax `type` *`command`*

Options None

Description The `type` command tells you the type of a command—whether it is a built-in shell command, an alias, or an executable program. For example, I use `alias ll='ls -l'` to define the alias `ll`. Here is what I get when I check the type of the command `ll`:

```
type ll
ll is aliased to `ls -l'
```

umount

Purpose Disassociate a device from the Linux file system.

Syntax `umount` *`device`*

Options None

Description The `umount` command removes the association between a device and a directory in the Linux file system. Only the root can execute the `umount` command.

unalias

Purpose Delete an abbreviation defined earlier with `alias`.

Syntax `unalias` *`abbreviation`*

Options None

Description The `unalias` command removes an abbreviation defined earlier with the `alias` command. `unalias` is a built-in command of the Bash shell.

uname

Purpose Display system information, such as type of machine and operating system.

Syntax `uname [options]`

Options
`-a` displays all information.
`-m` displays the hardware type (for example, `i586`).
`-n` displays the machine's host name.
`-p` displays the processor type (this appears as `unknown`).
`-r` displays the operating system release (for example, 2.4.0-0.43.12).
`-s` displays the operating system name.
`-v` displays the operating system version (shown as date of compilation).

Description The `uname` command displays a variety of information about your machine and the operating system (Linux).

uncompress

Purpose Decompress one or more files that have been compressed using the `compress` command.

Syntax `uncompress [-cdrvV] files`

Options
`-c` writes the result to the standard output and retains the original.
`-r` recursively decompresses files in all subdirectories.
`-v` displays a message as each file is decompressed.
`-V` prints the version number and exits.

Description The `uncompress` command decompresses each specified file and replaces the compressed version with the original (also removes the `.Z` suffix appended to the name of the compressed file). Using the `uncompress` command yields the same result as running `compress` with the `-d` option.

uniq

Purpose Write all unique lines from an input file to standard output.

Syntax `uniq [options] file`

Options
`-n` (where *n* is a number) ignores the first *n* fields on each line.
`+n` (where *n* is a number) ignores the first *n* characters on each line.
`-c` writes the number of times each line occurred in file.
`-d` writes only duplicate lines.
`-u` writes only unique lines (the default).

Description The `uniq` command removes duplicate lines from an input file and copies the unique lines to the standard output. If you do not specify an input file, `uniq` reads from standard input.

wc

Purpose Display the byte, word, and line count of a file.

Syntax `wc [options] [files]`

Options
`-c` displays only the byte count.
`-w` displays only the word count.
`-l` displays only the line count.

Description The `wc` command displays the byte, word, and line count of a file. If you do not specify an input file, `wc` reads from standard input.

whatis

Purpose Search the `whatis` database (see `apropos`) for complete words.

Syntax `whatis` *`keyword`*

Options None

Description The `whatis` command searches the `whatis` database (see the entry for `apropos`) for the specified keyword and displays the result. Only complete word matches are displayed.

whereis

Purpose Find the source, binary, and man page for a command.

Syntax `whereis [options]` *`command`*

Options `-b` searches only for binaries.

`-m` searches only for man pages.

`-s` searches only for sources.

Description The `whereis` command searches the usual directories (where binaries, man pages, and source files are located) for binaries, man pages, and source files for a command. For example, here is the result of searching for the files for the `rpm` command:

```
whereis rpm
rpm: /bin/rpm /etc/rpm /usr/lib/rpm /usr/include/rpm
/usr/share/man/man8/rpm.8.gz
```

which

Purpose Search the directories in the `PATH` environment variable for a command.

Syntax `which` *`command`*

Options None

Description The `which` command searches the directories in the `PATH` environment variable for the file that will be executed when you type the command. This is a good way to check what will be executed when you type a specific command.

zcat, zless, zmore

Purpose View the contents of a compressed text file without having to first decompress the file.

Syntax

```
zcat filename
zless filename
zmore filename
```

Options None

Description The `zcat`, `zless`, and `zmore` commands work the same way as `cat`, `less`, and `more`. The only difference is that the z-commands can directly read files compressed with `gzip` or `compress` (without having to first decompress the files with `gunzip`). These commands are particularly useful for reading compressed text files, such as the ones in the `/usr/info` directory.

Disk Drives

When it comes to disk drives and Linux, what matters is whether or not Linux supports the *disk controller*, the card that connects the disk drive to your PC's motherboard. Linux supports most common disk controllers. This appendix gives you information about various disk controllers and some operations you can perform on disks.

Disk Controller Types

The disk controller is the adapter card that acts as an intermediary between your PC's motherboard and one or more hard disk drives. Typically, you can connect up to two hard drives and two floppy drives to a single disk controller. The Small Computer System Interface (SCSI) controller is an exception to this norm; you can connect as many as 7 or 15 SCSI devices (anything that has a SCSI interface, such as a disk drive, CD-ROM drive, tape drive, or scanner) in a series.

Over the years, several types of hard disk controllers have appeared for the PC. Following are some of the disk controllers you may find in a PC:

- **ST-506** disk controllers, which originally appeared in IBM XT and AT computers, became the common disk controller of the PC industry in its early years (remember that the IBM PC-AT came out in 1984). Many PCs have disk controllers that are compatible with the ST-506. Seagate's ST-506 was the original hard drive for PCs; Western Digital's WD1003 was the controller card. Thus, these controllers are often referred to as WD1003-compatible controllers. The original ST-506 drives used a recording method known as modified frequency modulation (MFM). Many ST-506 disk controllers also support drives that use another type of data-recording technique known as run length limited (RLL). This technology is outdated and not used in new PCs anymore.

- The **Integrated Drive Electronics (IDE)** or **AT Attachment Packet Interface (ATAPI)** emulates the ST-506 interface. IDE drives, however, have the necessary controller circuitry built into them. The motherboard typically contains an IDE interface for connecting the drive to the motherboard. For many years now, IDE drives have been the most widespread in PCs. Nowadays, the term "AT Attachment" (ATA) is used to refer to IDE. The original IDE interface could support only two drives, and it limited the maximum disk size to approximately 500MB. You needed third-party drivers to use disks larger than 500MB. Today's PCs with large disk drives use the Enhanced IDE interface (described next). You can learn more about ATA standards at `www.t13.org/`.
- The **Enhanced IDE (EIDE)** interface supports up to four internal IDE devices (which include hard drives as well as CD-ROM drives), higher-capacity drives, and higher speeds of data transfer. Typical EIDE interfaces consist of two IDE interfaces: primary and secondary, each of which is capable of supporting up to two drives. EIDE interfaces are popular because of their low cost. Many PCs use the EIDE interface to connect both the hard disk and the CD-ROM drive to the PC's motherboard.
- The **Ultra ATA** or **Ultra DMA (UDMA)** interface is a newer version of the IDE interface that utilizes bus direct memory access (DMA) techniques to provide much faster data transfer rates, as much as 33 or 66MB per second, depending on the mode of operation. These data transfer rates are two to four times that of EIDE. Many new PCs come with Ultra ATA interfaces.
- The **Enhanced Small Device Interface (ESDI)** controllers emulate the ST-506 interface but provide higher data-transfer rates. This technology is outdated and not used in new PCs anymore.
- The **Serial AT Attachment (SATA)** controllers are a relatively new interface for connecting hard drives to the PC's motherboard. SATA can support data transfer rates of up to 150MB per second. SATA uses a serial data transfer mechanism as opposed to the parallel transfer — many bits simultaneously on separate wires — used by the IDE (or ATAPI) interface. This means that the SATA cables are thinner (only 7 conductors) than the ribbon cables (40 conductors) used by IDE. Because of the serial-parallel distinction between the new SATA and older IDE interfaces, the IDE interface is nowadays also referred to as parallel ATA or PATA. You can learn more about SATA at `www.serialata.org/`.
- **Small Computer System Interface (SCSI)** controllers provide a separate bus onto which you can connect up to seven SCSI devices. You can find hard drives, CD-ROM drives, tape drives, and scanners that support SCSI. You can connect multiple SCSI devices to the computer by daisy-chaining (connecting first to second, second to third, and so on) the devices with a SCSI cable. All UNIX workstations (such as the ones from Hewlett-Packard, IBM, and Sun Microsystems) use SCSI. Lately, SCSI is becoming popular on PCs as well. The only drawback is that SCSI controllers are relatively expensive compared with EIDE controllers. There are many variants of the SCSI bus, as summarized in the following list:
  - **SCSI 1:** The original SCSI standard (ANSI specification X3.131-1986) specifies an 8-bit parallel bus that can transfer data asynchronously at 1.5 Mbps and synchronously at 5 Mbps.
  - **Fast SCSI:** The SCSI 2 standard (ANSI specification X3.131-1994) increased the maximum synchronous data transfer rate to 10 Mbps and defined a differential bus that enables cable lengths to increase to 25 meters.

- **Wide SCSI:** SCSI 2 standard increased the width of the bus allowing 16-bit and 32-bit parallel data transfers. Typical wide SCSI buses use 16-bit data transfers. Wide SCSI buses enable up to 16 SCSI devices to be connected to the bus (at least one of these device is the host adapter, so you can attach only 15 more devices to the controller). The letter W in SCSI controller names reflects the use of wide bus.
- **Ultra SCSI:** Uses a technique to double the maximum data transfer rate from 10 Mbps to 20 Mbps. SCSI controllers that support ultra SCSI often have the letter U as a qualifier in their name.
- **Ultra Wide SCSI:** Combines the ultra technique to 16-bit wide SCSI bus, resulting in a maximum data transfer rate of 40 Mbps. This bus is abbreviated as UW in many SCSI controller names.
- **Ultra 2 Wide SCSI:** Uses a technology called "low voltage differential (LVD) signaling" that further doubles the data transfer rate of Ultra Wide SCSI to support rates of 80 Mbps when using a 16-bit wide bus. In this case, the maximum SCSI bus length is 12 meters. Ultra 2 Wide SCSI controllers often have the U2W designation in their names.
- **Ultra 160 SCSI:** Doubles the data transfer rate, raising it to 160 Mbps. Uses cyclic redundancy check (CRC) to improve data integrity and adjusts transfer rates if the error rate is too high.
- **Ultra 320 SCSI:** Further doubles the data transfer rate to 320 Mbps. You can find more information about Ultra 320 SCSI at the SCSI Trade Association website (`www.scsita.org`). That website mentions Ultra 640 SCSI, capable of 640 Mbps data transfer rates, which should be appearing on the market soon.

note

Linux supports all these common disk controllers. Even though several disk controllers appear in the preceding list, there are essentially three types: IDE or ATA (where IDE refers to all ST-506-compatible interfaces), SATA, and SCSI.

Most Pentium systems use a motherboard that supports the Peripheral Component Interconnect (PCI) bus. Both IDE and SCSI controllers can connect to the PCI bus. Linux supports the PCI bus. The PCI bus is now dominant in the PC marketplace, replacing the outdated ISA bus.

Disk Drive Concepts

When you read about disk drives, you run into some terms and concepts unique to the world of hard disks. The following sections explain some of these concepts.

Cylinders, Heads, and Sectors

The physical organization of the disk is expressed in terms of cylinders, heads, and sectors. A hard disk consists of several platters of magnetic material. In physical terms, you can think of cylinder, head, and sector as follows:

- A *cylinder* is a set of matching tracks on both sides of all the platters in the disk drive, where each track is one of a series of concentric rings on one side of a disk platter.
- The total number of *heads* is the number of sides of all the magnetic platters.
- A *sector* is a pie-shaped wedge on the platter. Each cylinder is divided into sectors.

Any location on the disk can be expressed in terms of the cylinder, the head, and the sector. Identifying a disk location in terms of cylinder (C), head (H), and sector (S) is known as CHS addressing.

The physical geometry of a hard disk usually is expressed in terms of cylinders, heads, and sectors (CHS). A disk may have a geometry of CHS = 5,169/240/63, which means that the disk has 5,169 cylinders, 240 heads, and 63 sectors. Usually, each sector can store 512 bytes (or half a kilobyte) of data. Thus, the capacity of this disk is (5,169 × 240 × 63) × 2 kilobytes, or 39,077,640 kilobytes (about 39GB).

note

PC hard disk controllers include a read-only memory (ROM) basic input/output system (BIOS) on the controller. By convention (and for compatibility with the original IBM PC architecture), the BIOS uses CHS addressing to access the hard disk. The disk BIOS, however, uses a 10-bit value as the cylinder address. Because 10 bits can hold numbers between 0 and 1,023, the BIOS can address, at most, 1,024 cylinders. Nowadays, the BIOS supports what are called Int 13h (that's interrupt number 13 in hexadecimal) extensions that use logical block address to get around the 1,024 cylinder limitation.

Logical Block Address

Many large disks have more than 1,024 cylinders. To accommodate the 1,024-cylinder limit, the disk controllers as well as newer BIOS use what is known as logical block address (LBA) to handle disks with more than 1,024 cylinders.

Instead of thinking of in terms of cylinder, head, and sector — CHS addresses — for each block, the idea behind LBA is to address each 512-byte block sequentially and not think of any artificial limit on the number of cylinders. In fact, with LBA, you do not have to think of a physical cylinder, head, sector model for the hard disk; a disk can simply be some storage medium organized into same-size blocks and the blocks are numbered sequentially.

Master Boot Record

The first sector of the hard disk (cylinder 0, head 0, sector 1) is called the master boot record (MBR). This 512-byte storage area contains important information about the disk, such as the partition table, and a small amount of code that the PC's BIOS loads and runs when you boot the PC.

The small program in the MBR reads the partition table; determines which partition is active (that's just an attribute of a partition), reads the active partition's first sector, or boot sector, and runs whatever program resides in that boot sector. The program in a partition's boot sector usually loads whatever operating system is installed on that partition.

When you install a boot loader such as GRUB on the hard disk, the GRUB program resides on the hard disk's MBR or the boot sector of the partition on which the Linux root directory (/) is located.

Partitions

Partitions are a way of dividing up a hard disk and treating each part separately. By dividing your PC's hard disk into partitions, you can install different operating systems in different partitions. Even if you use the entire disk for Linux, you need, at minimum, a partition Linux can use as swap space — an extension of memory, so that you can have more virtual memory than the physical memory on your system. The Fedora Linux installer creates three partitions: a swap partition, a small (100MB) partition for `/boot` file system that holds the Linux kernel files, and the remaining disk space is assigned to a large partition that holds the main Linux file system (/).

Although you can set up a Linux system with a swap partition and a single large partition for the entire Linux file system, there are circumstances in which you may want to place specific parts of the file system in their own partitions to limit their growth or for performance reasons. When you place a file system such as `/var` in a partition by itself, that file system cannot grow beyond the physical size of the partition and fill up the entire file system.

In practice, most production Linux installations use quite a few partitions. Here's a typical example of the file systems that could be placed in their own disk partitions:

- **swap:** Used as virtual memory (typically twice the amount of physical memory or at least 64MB).
- **/:** Is the root file system and provides the mount points for all other file systems. When there are no other partitions, the root partition also holds the entire Linux file system.
- **/boot:** A primary partition to hold the Linux kernel files (typically around 100MB). In cases where the BIOS can access only the first 1,024 cylinders, you can place this small `/boot` partition within the first 1,024 cylinders (this constraint does not affect new PCs that access disks using logical block address).
- **/var:** Contains the spool directories for mail and print scheduler as well as error logs. The Web server and anonymous FTP directories are also in `/var`. You could place this in its own partition to ensure that the entire file system does not get filled up by too many error messages (in case something goes wrong).
- **/usr:** Contains most executable files (binaries).
- **/tmp:** Holds temporary files for many programs. Any process and any user can write to this directory, so it is wise to keep `/tmp` in a different partition than /.
- **/home:** Contains the home directories of the users. Placing `/home` in a separate partition ensures that users do not inadvertently fill up the whole file system and bring the system down.

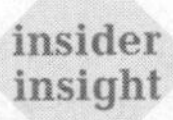

The master boot record contains the partition table, starting at byte number 446 (or 0x1be, which means 1be in hexadecimal). The partition table can have up to four 16-byte entries at bytes 446, 462, 478, 494, respectively, followed by a signature in the two bytes with offset 510 and 511. The signature has the hexadecimal value 0x55 in byte 510 and 0xaa in byte 511.

Each 16-byte value in the partition table defines a partition. Each partition is specified by a starting and ending cylinder number. The partition entry also includes a type that identifies the operating system that creates the partition. The concept of partitions is a convention that all PC-based operating systems, ranging from MS-DOS to Linux, follow.

In MS-DOS, you use the FDISK program to manipulate the partitions. In Windows XP/2000, use the DISKPART program (located in the `\WINDOWS\SYSTEM32` directory) to work with disk partitions. Linux includes a program with the same name — `fdisk` (lowercase) — to alter the disk partitions. In addition to `fdisk`, Linux includes another disk-partitioning program called `sfdisk`.

The partitions described in the partition table in the MBR are the primary partitions. Because there is room for only four entries, there can be at most four primary partitions on a hard disk. However, a primary partition can be marked as an extended partition and then the first sector of that extended partition will contain another partition table that subdivides the extended partition. The partitions in the extended primary partition are called *logical* partitions.

Linux Device Names for Disks

In Linux, each device is represented by a device file in the `/dev` directory. The device name for the hard disk depends on the type of disk controller. For IDE and EIDE drives, the device name is `/dev/hda` for the first disk, `/dev/hdb` for the second disk, and so on.

On an IDE interface, if you have a hard disk on the primary interface and a CD-ROM drive as the first device on the secondary interface, the device names are `/dev/hda` for the hard disk drive and `/dev/hdc` for the CD-ROM drive.

The Linux disk drivers treat each disk partition as a separate device. The first primary partition in the first IDE disk is `/dev/hda1`, the second partition is `/dev/hda2`, the third one is `/dev/hda3`, and so on. The first logical partition is `/dev/hda5`, the second one `/dev/hda6`, and so on. Similarly, the device names for the partitions on the second IDE drive are `/dev/hdb1`, `/dev/hdb2`, and so on.

The SCSI disk devices are named `/dev/sda`, `/dev/sdb`, and so on. If a SCSI device is a hard disk, its partitions are named by appending the partition number to the device name. Thus, the partitions of the first SCSI hard disk are named `/dev/sda1`, `/dev/sda2`, `/dev/sda3`, and so on.

External USB CD/DVD drives are also treated as SCSI devices, but use device names such as `/dev/scd0` and `/dev/scd1`. The first external USB CD/DVD drive is named `/dev/scd0`, the second one is `/dev/scd1`, and so on.

Floppy Disks in Linux

Chapter 12 describes several ways to access MS-DOS floppy disks under Linux; you can mount the floppy and use Linux commands, or use the mtools utility programs to read from or write to the floppy. You also can create a Linux file system on a floppy disk. In fact, you'll find Linux file systems on the boot and root floppies that you use to install Linux.

Formatting and creating a Linux file system on a floppy is a straightforward process. To format a 3.5-inch high-density floppy in the A drive, for example, use the following command (for more on floppy drive naming conventions, see the "How to Format a DOS Floppy" section in Chapter 12):

```
fdformat /dev/fd0H1440
```

If you have an old PC with a 5.25-inch high-density floppy as the A drive, you can access that floppy with the device name /dev/fd0h1200. On the B drive, change the first 0 in the device name to 1.

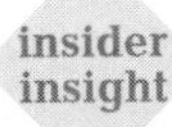

After you format the floppy, use the following command to create a Linux file system on the floppy:

```
mke2fs -m 0 /dev/fd0H1440 1440
```

The -m option is used to specify what percentage of blocks should be reserved for the use of super user (root). By specifying the -m 0 option, you ensure that mke2fs does not reserve space on the floppy disk for the super user. If you do not explicitly specify the -m option, mke2fs reserves 5 percent of the disk space for the superuser.

After you create the file system on the floppy drive, you can mount the floppy at a mount point (an empty directory) in the Linux file system. The following example shows how you mount the floppy drive at the /mnt/floppy directory:

```
mount /dev/fd0H1440 /mnt/floppy
```

Now you can use Linux commands, such as cp and mv, to copy or move files to the floppy disk. Before you eject the floppy disk from the drive, use the following command to dismount the floppy:

```
umount /dev/fd0H1440
```

Hard Disk Operations in Linux

You must perform some disk operations to install and use Linux on your system. Chapter 2 explains some of the disk operations you perform when you set up Linux. The next few sections provide some additional information about these disk operations.

When you first get a PC, the hard disk usually is set up as one huge partition, and DOS and Windows are already installed on it. (If you have bought your PC recently, it probably comes with Windows 2000 or Windows XP preinstalled.) To install Linux, you have to start by creating at least three partitions for Linux: one for the swap space, a /boot partition for the Linux kernel files, and a / partition for the Linux file system.

If you want to retain the existing Windows operating system, you have to resize the Windows partition and create disk space for Linux. When you install Linux, you can use the unused disk space for all the Linux partitions.

Resizing Partitions

If you do not want to go through the trouble of reinstalling Windows, you have to alter the existing partition somehow. FIPS, which can split an existing FAT or FAT32 partition into two separate partitions, enables you to perform this task. By the way, FAT and FAT32 partitions were used in MS-DOS and Windows 95/98/Me. Windows NT, 2000, and XP also support FAT and FAT32, but they typically use the NT file system (NTFS). Chapter 2 describes how to use FIPS. You can also use one of the following utilities to repartition your hard disk:

- **PowerQuest's PartitionMagic:** This commercial utility enables you to resize, split, merge, delete, undelete, and convert partitions without destroying existing data. PartitionMagic works on Windows XP and can resize partitions containing FAT, FAT32, NTFS, and Linux ext2 file systems. For more information, visit `www.powerquest.com`.
- **Acronis Disk Director Suite:** This commercial utility enables you to resize, copy, and move partitions without losing data. It can resize partitions containing FAT, FAT32, and NTFS, and Linux `ext2` file systems, among others. For more information, visit `www.acronis.com`.
- **GNU parted:** Linux includes the GNU parted utility that can manipulate FAT, FAT32, and Linux `ext2` partitions. Using parted, you can resize partitions from within Linux. For more information, visit `www.gnu.org/software/parted/`.

Partitioning Using fdisk

Partitioning the disk involves creating several smaller logical devices within a single hard disk. In Linux, you can use the partitioning program fdisk to view and alter a disk's partition table.

Even if you have already partitioned your hard disk, you can always run fdisk just to see the current partition table of a hard disk. If you have an IDE disk drive with the device name `/dev/hda`, for example, you can look at its partition table with fdisk as follows:

```
/sbin/fdisk /dev/hda
The number of cylinders for this disk is set to 5169.
There is nothing wrong with that, but this is larger than 1024,
and could in certain setups cause problems with:
1) software that runs at boot time (e.g., old versions of LILO)
2) booting and partitioning software from other OSs
   (e.g., DOS FDISK, OS/2 FDISK)
Command (m for help): m
Command action
   a   toggle a bootable flag
   b   edit bsd disklabel
   c   toggle the dos compatibility flag
   d   delete a partition
   l   list known partition types
   m   print this menu
   n   add a new partition
   o   create a new empty DOS partition table
   p   print the partition table
```

```
   q   quit without saving changes
   s   create a new empty Sun disklabel
   t   change a partition's system id
   u   change display/entry units
   v   verify the partition table
   w   write table to disk and exit
   x   extra functionality (experts only)

Command (m for help): p

Disk /dev/hda: 40.0 GB, 40020664320 bytes
240 heads, 63 sectors/track, 5169 cylinders
Units = cylinders of 15120 * 512 = 7741440 bytes

   Device Boot      Start         End      Blocks   Id  System
/dev/hda1               1         566     4278928+   b  W95 FAT32
/dev/hda2   *         567        2694    16087680    7  HPFS/NTFS
/dev/hda3            2695        5169    18711000    5  Extended
/dev/hda5            2695        2700       45328+  83  Linux
/dev/hda6            2701        2706       45328+  83  Linux
/dev/hda7            2707        2712       45328+  83  Linux
/dev/hda8            2713        2778      498928+  82  Linux swap /
Solaris
/dev/hda9            2779        3553     5858968+  83  Linux
/dev/hda10           3554        4328     5858968+  83  Linux
/dev/hda11           4329        5169     6357928+  83  Linux

Command (m for help): q
```

The m command shows you a list of the single-letter commands that fdisk accepts. You can see the current partition table with a p command. This example's IDE disk has three partitions, all for Linux.

The Id field in the table of partitions the fdisk program prints (when you type **p** at the fdisk prompt) is a number that denotes a partition type. That partition ID is a hexadecimal number. If you want to see a list of all known partition IDs, type **l** (a lowercase L) at the fdisk prompt, as follows:

```
Command (m for help): l
 0  Empty           1e  Hidden W95 FAT1 80  Old Minix       be  Solaris boot
 1  FAT12           24  NEC DOS         81  Minix / old Lin bf  Solaris
 2  XENIX root      39  Plan 9          82  Linux swap / So c1  DRDOS/sec (FAT-
 3  XENIX usr       3c  PartitionMagic  83  Linux           c4  DRDOS/sec (FAT-
 4  FAT16 <32M      40  Venix 80286     84  OS/2 hidden C:  c6  DRDOS/sec (FAT-
 5  Extended        41  PPC PReP Boot   85  Linux extended  c7  Syrinx
 6  FAT16           42  SFS             86  NTFS volume set da  Non-FS data
 7  HPFS/NTFS       4d  QNX4.x          87  NTFS volume set db  CP/M / CTOS / .
 8  AIX             4e  QNX4.x 2nd part 88  Linux plaintext de  Dell Utility
 9  AIX bootable    4f  QNX4.x 3rd part 8e  Linux LVM       df  BootIt
 a  OS/2 Boot Manag 50  OnTrack DM      93  Amoeba          e1  DOS access
 b  W95 FAT32       51  OnTrack DM6 Aux 94  Amoeba BBT      e3  DOS R/O
```

```
 c  W95 FAT32 (LBA) 52  CP/M            9f  BSD/OS           e4  SpeedStor
 e  W95 FAT16 (LBA) 53  OnTrack DM6 Aux a0  IBM Thinkpad hi eb  BeOS fs
 f  W95 Ext'd (LBA) 54  OnTrackDM6      a5  FreeBSD          ee  EFI GPT
10  OPUS            55  EZ-Drive        a6  OpenBSD          ef  EFI (FAT-12/16/
11  Hidden FAT12    56  Golden Bow      a7  NeXTSTEP         f0  Linux/PA-RISC b
12  Compaq diagnost 5c  Priam Edisk     a8  Darwin UFS       f1  SpeedStor
14  Hidden FAT16 <3 61  SpeedStor       a9  NetBSD           f4  SpeedStor
16  Hidden FAT16    63  GNU HURD or Sys ab  Darwin boot      f2  DOS secondary
17  Hidden HPFS/NTF 64  Novell Netware  b7  BSDI fs          fd  Linux raid auto
18  AST SmartSleep  65  Novell Netware  b8  BSDI swap        fe  LANstep
1b  Hidden W95 FAT3 70  DiskSecure Mult bb  Boot Wizard hid ff  BBT
1c  Hidden W95 FAT3 75  PC/IX
```

Booting from the Hard Disk

To automatically boot Linux from a hard disk, you need a boot loader. Fedora Linux comes with the GNU Grand Unified Bootloader (GRUB). The boot loader program usually resides in the master boot record of a disk and is the first to be loaded. The boot loader program, in turn, prompts you for the operating system to start (which typically means a disk partition from which to boot). Starting an operating system basically involves loading that operating system's main program into memory and running it. For Linux, this step involves loading the Linux kernel into memory and giving control to the kernel.

cross ref

Chapter 21 describes how to configure GRUB to install a new kernel. You can consult that chapter to learn more about GRUB.

If, during installation, you forget to assign a label to the Windows XP partition in the Boot Loader Installation screen, GRUB will not show the Windows XP partition as an option when it starts. That leaves with you with the problem that you cannot boot Windows XP anymore, even though the XP partition is intact. To recover from this problem, you have to edit the GRUB configuration file, `/etc/grub.conf`.

insider insight

Assuming that the XP partition is `/dev/hda2`, here's what you add to the end of the `/etc/grub.conf`: to enable GRUB to boot the Windows XP partition:

```
title Windows XP
        root (hd0,1)
        makeactive
        chainloader +1
```

For most PCs that come with Windows XP preinstalled, the second disk partition (`/dev/hda2`) is the one with the Windows XP file system; the first disk partition is a hidden one used to store files needed to install Windows XP. You do not have to restart GRUB or do anything special for these changes to take effect. Simply save the `/etc/grub.conf` file and reboot. This time GRUB should display a menu that includes Windows XP as an option. To boot Windows XP, all you have to do is select that option.

If your PC has Windows NT/2000/XP installed and you want to leave the MBR untouched, you can choose to install GRUB on the first sector of the Linux boot partition (`/boot` in the file system) when you install Fedora following the instructions in Chapter 2. In that case, you have to perform the following steps to ensure that you can start GRUB from the Windows boot loader (otherwise the Windows boot loader does not see GRUB and you cannot boot Fedora even though it's installed on the hard drive):

1. Remember the Linux boot partition from when you installed Linux. If there is a separate boot partition, it's mounted on `/boot`. You can see this in the disk partition step as you install Fedora (see Chapter 2).
2. Boot from the Fedora DVD and type **linux rescue** at the `boot:` prompt (remember to add other options such as `acpi=off` if you need them to boot Linux on your PC). This starts Linux in rescue mode. When you get the shell prompt, type the following command:

   ```
   chroot /mnt/sysimage
   ```

3. Place an MS-DOS–formatted floppy into the floppy drive and type the following command (here I assume that the boot partition is `/dev/hda3`; replace it with whatever the boot partition is on your PC):

   ```
   mount -t msdos /dev/fd0 /media/floppy
   dd if=/dev/hda3 of=/mnt/floppy/linux.bin bs=512 count=1
   ```

   This creates a file named `linux.bin` on the floppy and that file contains the 512-byte boot sector from the Linux boot partition.
4. Take the floppy disk out and reboot the PC to start Windows.
5. Place the floppy in the drive and type **copy a:\linux.bin c:** and after the command finishes, take the floppy out of the drive.
6. Type **attrib -R -S -H c:\boot.ini** to make the `c:\boot.ini` file writeable (otherwise you cannot edit the file).
7. Select Start ➪ Run, and then type **c:\boot.ini** in the Run dialog box and click OK to open the `c:\boot.ini` file in Notepad. At the end of the file, add the following line:

   ```
   c:\linux.bin="Linux"
   ```

   Save the file and quit Notepad.
8. Type **attrib +R +S +H c:\boot.ini** to set the file attributes back to what they were before you edited `c:\boot.ini`.
9. Reboot the PC. You should see options for Windows and Linux. Selecting Linux should start GRUB and then GRUB can boot your Linux partition.

Creating Swap Space

Swap space is a disk partition Linux uses as an extension of its memory. When some memory-resident data is not needed immediately, Linux stores that data in the swap space. To create the swap space, you have to create a disk partition using fdisk. Make sure that you set the type of that disk partition to Linux swap (partition ID 82 in hexadecimal). Typically, you set up the swap partition and turn on swapping as you install Linux from this book's DVD-ROM.

If you have to set up the swap space outside the installation program, you have to use the `mkswap` command to initialize the swap partition. You need the size of the swap partition (in number of blocks) before you use the mkswap command. Use the Linux fdisk program, and type the p command at the fdisk prompt to find the size of the swap partition.

For example, to initialize /dev/hda4 as a swap partition, type the following command:

```
/sbin/mkswap -c /dev/hda4 192772
```

In this case, 192772 is the block size of the swap partition. You can skip the size parameter because the mkswap command can determine the size from the partition table.

The size of the swap partition depends on the amount of virtual memory you need. To Linux, the total amount of memory in your PC is the combined total of the swap partition's size and the amount of physical RAM. Although there is no formula to tell you how much virtual memory you need, the conventional wisdom is that you should have at least as much swap space as physical memory.

You can have a swap partition as large as 2GB, and you can have up to eight swap partitions. All you have to do is run the mkswap command for each swap partition you create.

After mkswap finishes, use the /sbin/swapon command to turn on swapping. Linux then begins to use the swap space.

The /proc/swaps file contains information about the swap spaces your Linux system is using. For example, here's what I get when I check /proc/swaps on my system:

```
cat /proc/swaps
Filename                        Type          Size     Used     Priority
/dev/hda8                       partition     514820   114360   -1
```

The output shows the current swap spaces. Although it is customary to use a disk partition as the swap space, you can also use a file as swap space. The first column in the list of swap spaces is labeled Filename because the swap space can be a file. If you want to use a file as swap space, create the file with a command, such as the following:

```
dd if=/dev/zero of=swapfile bs=1024 count=131072
```

This creates a file named swapfile of size 131,072. Type **/sbin/mkswap -c swapfile** to initialize that file, and then type **/sbin/swapon swapfile** to use the file for swapping.

To ensure that Linux uses the swap space every time it boots, you need a line in the /etc/fstab file that indicates the swap partition's name. If the swap partition is /dev/hda8, for example, add the following line to /etc/fstab:

```
/dev/hda8        swap        swap    defaults      0 0
```

If you create a swap space when you install Linux, the installation program adds the appropriate line in the /etc/fstab file. You may need to add such a line if you create additional swap spaces later.

If you put a partition's name in /etc/fstab but forget to run mkswap on that partition, Linux displays the following error message:

```
Unable to find swap-space signature
```

The fix is to run mkswap to initialize the swap partition.

Creating File Systems

To use a disk partition in Linux, you have to create a file system on that partition. You can think of this procedure as formatting the partition for Linux. When you install Linux by following the steps described in Chapter 2, one of the steps creates the file system; the setup program asks you whether or not you want to format a partition. For a Linux partition, the setup program uses the `mke2fs` command to create a Linux file system.

Linux supports several types of file systems, including the following:

- **MS-DOS file system:** This DOS file system is based on the file allocation table (FAT). This file system type is designated by the keyword `msdos`.
- **Microsoft Windows file system with support for long filenames:** This is a DOS-compatible FAT file system with support for long filenames. This file type is identified by the keyword `vfat`. You should use this file system to access all DOS/Windows disks from Linux.
- **Minix file system:** Minix is the original UNIX clone that inspired the creation of Linux. Linux started by using the Minix file system, which limits filenames to 14 or 30 characters. The `minix` keyword identifies this file-system type.
- **Extended file system:** This old Linux file system goes by the keyword `ext`. You should not use this file system anymore.
- **Second extended file system:** This is the latest and greatest Linux file system. The keyword `ext2` refers to this file-system type. You can use longer filenames in this file system.
- **Third extended file system:** This is an enhancement of the `ext2` file system with journaling to enable rapid recovery in case of any errors. The keyword `ext3` refers to this file-system type.

The Fedora Linux installation program automatically creates an `ext3` file system on the Linux partition. To create an `ext3` file system manually, you have to use the `mke2fs` command as follows:

```
/sbin/mke2fs -c -j /dev/hda3
```

This command creates an `ext3` file system on the `/dev/hda3` partition. The `mke2fs` command automatically figures out the size of the partition and uses it to size the file system. The `-c` option forces `mke2fs` to check for bad blocks (using a fast read-only test) before creating the file system. The `-j` option causes `mke2fs` to create the file system with an ext3 journal.

When you install Linux on a hard disk that uses standard IDE, MFM, or RLL controllers, always install the ext3 file system and use the bad-block-checking options when you create the file system.

SCSI Disk Controllers and Linux

SCSI (pronounced "scuzzy") is an increasingly popular interface for connecting up to seven different devices on the SCSI bus. Each device, and the SCSI controller, has a unique SCSI identifier (ID) in the range 0 through 7. The controller usually is set to SCSI

ID 7; the other devices use numbers between 0 and 6 (that means you can connect up to seven devices to a SCSI controller). Typically, a SCSI hard disk is set to SCSI ID 0.

Table B-1 lists the SCSI controllers that the version of Linux kernel on the companion CD-ROMs supports. The table also shows the name of the driver module that supports each specific set of controllers. If necessary, you can manually load the driver for your SCSI controller with the command `/sbin/modprobe` *modname*, where *modname* refers to the name of the driver module.

Table B-1: Supported SCSI Controllers

SCSI Controller	*Linux Driver Module*
3ware 9000 Storage Controller	`3w-9xxx`
3ware Storage Controller	`3w-xxxx`
ACARD ATP870U, ATP876, ATP885	`atp870u`
Acer MegaRAID ROMB-2E	`megaraid_mbox`
Adaptec AHA-460 (AHA152X-compatible) PCMCIA SCSI card	`aha152x_cs`
Adaptec AHA-1510/152x (ISA)	`aha152x`
Adaptec AHA-154x (ISA) (all models)	`aha1542`
Adaptec AHA-274x/274xT (EISA), AHA-284x (VLB), AHA-2910B (PCI), AHA-2920C (PCI), AHA-2930/U/U2/CU, AHA-2940/U/W/AU/UW/U2W (PCI), AHA-294160M, AHA-2944D/WD/UD/UWD (PCI), AHA-2950U2/U2W/U2B, AHA-39160M, AHA-3940/U/W/UW (PCI), AHA-3950U2D, AHA-3960D, AHA-398x/U/W/UW (PCI)	`aic7xxx`
Adaptec AHA-2920A (PCI) with Future Domain chipset	`fdomain`
Adaptec AVA-1502E (ISA/VLB), AVA-1505/1515 (ISA), AVA-282x— all are Adaptec AHA-152x compatible	`aha152x`
Adaptec RAID Controllers (2020S, 2025S, 2120S, 2200S, 2230S, 2240S, 2410SA, 2610SA, 2810SA, 21610SA, 3230S, 3240S, 4000SAS, 4005SAS, 4800SAS, 4805SAS, 5400S), Dell PERC 2 Quad Channel, Dell PERC 2/Si, Dell PERC 3/Si, Dell PERC 3/Di, Dell CERC 2, HP NetRAID-4M, Legend S220, Legend S230	`aacraid`
Adaptec I2O RAID	`dpt_i2o`
AdvanSys ABP510/5150 Bus-Master ISA, ABP5140 Bus-Master ISA PnP (Plug and Play), ABP5142 Bus-Master ISA PnP with floppy, ABP542 Bus-Master ISA with floppy (single channel), ABP742 Bus-Master EISA (single channel), ABP752 Dual Channel Bus-Master EISA (dual channel), ABP842 Bus-Master VL (single channel), ABP852 Dual Channel Bus-Master VL (dual channel), ABP920 Bus-Master PCI, ABP930/U Bus-Master PCI/Ultra, ABP940/U/UA/UW and 3940UA/UW Bus-Master PCI/Ultra (single channel), ABP 3940U2W Bus-Master PCI Ultra2-Wide (single channel), ABP950/UW Dual Channel Bus-Master PCI/Ultra-Wide (dual channel), ABP960/U Bus-Master PCI/ULTRA MAC/PC, ABP970/U Bus-Master PCI/Ultra MAC/PC (single channel), ABP980/U/UA and 3980UA Bus-Master PCI/Ultra (four channel), ABP3950U2W/U3W Bus-Master PCI Ultra2-Wide/Ultra3-Wide	`advansys`

SCSI Controller	*Linux Driver Module*
Advanced Host Control Interface (AHCI) Serial ATA (SATA) controllers	ahci
AIC-7901, AIC-7901A, and AIC-7902 chipsets	aic79xx
AIC-777x, AIC-785x, AIC-786x, AIC-787x, AIC-788x, AIC-789x, and AIC-3860 chipsets	aic7xxx
Always IN2000 (ISA)	in2000
AMI Fast Disk VLB/EISA (BusLogic-compatible), BusLogic FlashPoint LT/DL/LW/DW PCI	BusLogic
Compaq 64-bit/66Mhz PCI Fibre Channel Host Bus Adapter	cpqfc
Domex DMX3191D	dmx3191d
DPT SmartRAID V I2O	dpt_i2o
DPT PM2001, PM2012A (EATA-PIO)	eata_pio
Data Technology Corp DTC 3180/3280	dtc
DTC 329x (EISA) (Adaptec 154x–compatible)	aha1542
Enterprise Fibre Channel Host Bus Adapter	lpfc
FSC MegaRAID PCI Express ROMB	megaraid_mbox
Future Domain TMC-1800, TMC-18C50, TMC-18C30, TMC-36C70, TMC-16x0, TMC-3260 (PCI)	fdomain
Future Domain TMC-8xx, TMC-950	seagate
Future Domain–compatible PCMCIA SCSI card	fdomain_cs
IBM ServeRAID controller	ips
ICP-Vortex GDT ISA and EISA SCSI Controllers, GDT PCI SCSI Disk array Controllers (many RAID levels supported)	gdth
IDE/ATAPI adapters (SCSI emulation for IDE devices, so SCSI driver can be used to access IDE devices such as CD-ROM drives)	ide-scsi
Initio INI-9X00U/UW SCSI host adapters	initio
Initio INI-A100U2W SCSI host adapters	a100u2w
Intraserver ITI-6200U2 Dual Channel Ultra2 SCSI Host Adapter (uses the NCR53C896 chipset)	ncr53c8xx
Iomega Match Maker parallel-port SCSI Host Bus Adapter embedded in ZIP Plus drive	imm
Iomega PPA3 parallel-port SCSI Host Bus Adapter embedded in ZIP drive	ppa
Intel parallel and serial ATA controllers	ata_piix
Intel RAID Controller SRCU42X, SRCS16, SRCU42E, SRCZCRX, SRCS28X, SROMBU42E, SROMBU42E, SRCU51L	megaraid_mbox
LSI Logic MegaRAID 418, 428, 438, 466, 762, 467, 471, 490, 493, 518, 520, 531, and 532	megaraid

(continued)

Table B-1 *(continued)*

SCSI Controller	*Linux Driver Module*
LSI Logic MegaRAID SCSI 320-0, 320-1, 320-2, 320-0X, 320-2X, 320-4X, 320-1E, 320-2E, 150-4, 150-6, 300-4X, 300-8X	`megaraid_mbox`
Mylex (formerly BusLogic) A Series (ISA/EISA), C Series (ISA/EISA/VLB/PCI), S Series (ISA/EISA/VLB), W Series (PCI)	`BusLogic`
NCR 5380 and 53C400 generic cards	`sim710`
NCR 53C406a (Acculogic ISApport / Media Vision Premium 3D SCSI)	`NCR53c406a`
NCR5380 (generic driver)	`g_NCR5380`
NCR NCR (or Symbios) 53c700 and 53c700-66	`53c700`
NCR 53C8xx chipsets	`ncr53c8xx`
NEC MegaRAID PCI Express ROMB	`megaraid_mbox`
NinjaSCSI-32Bi PCMCIA SCSI Host Adapter	`nsp32_cs`
NinjaSCSI-32UDE PCI/CardBus SCSI controllers	`nsp32`
NVIDIA nForce SATA	`sata_nv`
OnStream SCSI Tape	`osst`
Perceptive Solutions PCI-2000 IntelliCache	`pci2000`
Perceptive Solutions PCI-2220I EIDE RAID	`pci2220i`
Perceptive Solutions PSI-240I EIDE	`psi240i`
Pro Audio Spectrum/Studio 16 (ISA)	`pas16`
Promise SATA SX4	`sata_sx4`
Promise SATA TX2/TX4	`sata_promise`
QLogic QLA1280 (Ultra2) and QLA12160 (Ultra3)	`qla1280`
Qlogic ISP2100	`qla2100`
Qlogic ISP2200	`qla2200`
Qlogic ISP2300	`qla2300`
Qlogic ISP2322	`qla2322`
Qlogic ISP6312	`qla6312`
Qlogic Fast SCSI FAS408 family of chips (ISA/VLB/PCMCIA)	`qlogicfas`
QLogic ISP1020 Intelligent SCSI cards IQ-PCI, IQ-PCI-10, IQ-PCI-D (PCI)	`qlogicisp`
QLogic PCMCIA SCSI card	`qlogic_cs`
QStor SATA	`sata_qstor`
Quantum ISA-200S, ISA-250MG	`fdomain`
Seagate ST-01/ST-02 (ISA)	`seagate`

SCSI Controller	Linux Driver Module
ServerWorks / Apple K2 SATA	sata_svw
Silicon Image SATA	sata_sil
Silicon Integrated Systems SATA	sata_sis
SoundBlaster 16 SCSI-2 (Adaptec 152x–compatible) (ISA)	aha152x
Symbios Logic SYM53C416 Chip	sym53c416
Symbios Logic 53c500 PCMCIA SCSI	sym53c500_cs
Symbios Logic SYM53C896 (also supports the 538XX controller family, except 53C815 and versions lower than 16 of the 53C810 and 53C825 controllers)	sym53c8xx
Tekram DC-390, DC-390W/U/F (AMD53C974A chipset)	tmscsim
Trantor T128/T128F/T228 (ISA)	t128
Trantor T130B (NCR 53C400 chipset)	g_NCR5380
ULi Electronics SATA	sata_uli
UltraStor 14F (ISA), 24F (EISA), 34F (VLB)	u14-34f
VIA SATA	sata_via
Vitesse VSC7174 4 port DPA SATA	sata_vsc
Western Digital WD7000-FAST, WD7000-FASST2, WD7000-ASC, WD7000-AX/MX/EX	wd7000

Cable and Termination Problems

The SCSI bus needs terminators at both ends to work reliably. A terminator is a set of resistors that indicate the end of the SCSI bus. One end is the controller card itself, which typically has the terminator on it. Often, a SCSI device has two SCSI connectors, so that you can daisy-chain several external SCSI devices. You are supposed to place a terminator on the last connector on the chain.

Some SCSI controllers — such as Adaptec AHA 154xC, 154xCF, and 274x (x is any digit) — are sensitive to the type of cable and terminator you use. If the cables are not perfect or the terminator is not used properly, these SCSI cards may fail intermittently or may not work at all.

To avoid problems with overly sensitive SCSI cards, use cables that come from a reputable vendor, and use cables from the same vendor to connect all SCSI devices. The cables should be SCSI 2–compliant and should have an impedance of 132 ohms (a characteristic of the cable; all you have to do is make sure the specified value is 132 ohms).

Most SCSI problems are caused by bad cables or improper termination. You should check the cables and the terminator before trying anything else.

SCSI Device at All SCSI IDs

If a SCSI device shows up at all possible SCSI IDs, you must have configured that device with the same SCSI ID as the SCSI controller (usually, 7). Change the ID of that device to another value. (Many devices have a simple switch for setting the SCSI ID; on others, you have to change a jumper.)

SCSI Device at All LUNs

If a SCSI device shows up at all possible SCSI logical unit numbers (LUNs), the device probably has errors in the *firmware*, the built-in code in the device's SCSI interface. To verify these errors, use the following command line during boot:

```
max_luns=1
```

If the device works with this option, you can add it to the list of blacklisted SCSI devices in the array of structures named `scsi_static_device_list` in the file `drivers/scsi/scsi_devinfo.c`, located wherever you have installed the kernel source code (you have to then rebuild the kernel). The definition of that structure and some parts of the array are as follows:

```
static struct {
    char *vendor;
    char *model;
    char *revision; /* revision known to be bad, unused */
    unsigned flags;
} scsi_static_device_list[] __initdata = {
    /*
     * The following devices are known not to tolerate a lun != 0 scan
     * for one reason or another. Some will respond to all luns,
     * others will lock up.
     */
    {"Aashima", "IMAGERY 2400SP", "1.03", BLIST_NOLUN},     /* locks up */
    {"CHINON", "CD-ROM CDS-431", "H42", BLIST_NOLUN},       /* locks up */
    {"CHINON", "CD-ROM CDS-535", "Q14", BLIST_NOLUN},       /* locks up */
    {"DENON", "DRD-25X", "V", BLIST_NOLUN},                 /* locks up */
    {"HITACHI", "DK312C", "CM81", BLIST_NOLUN},  /* responds to all lun */
    {"HITACHI", "DK314C", "CR21", BLIST_NOLUN},  /* responds to all lun */
    {"IMS", "CDD521/10", "2.06", BLIST_NOLUN},      /* locks up */
... lines deleted ...
    {"TOSHIBA", "CDROM", NULL, BLIST_ISROM},
    {"TOSHIBA", "CD-ROM", NULL, BLIST_ISROM},
    {"USB2.0", "SMARTMEDIA/XD", NULL, BLIST_FORCELUN | BLIST_INQUIRY_36},
    {"WangDAT", "Model 2600", "01.7", BLIST_SELECT_NO_ATN},
    {"WangDAT", "Model 3200", "02.2", BLIST_SELECT_NO_ATN},
    {"WangDAT", "Model 1300", "02.4", BLIST_SELECT_NO_ATN},
    {"WDC WD25", "00JB-00FUA0", NULL, BLIST_NOREPORTLUN},
    {"XYRATEX", "RS", "*", BLIST_SPARSELUN | BLIST_LARGELUN},
    {"Zzyzx", "RocketStor 500S", NULL, BLIST_SPARSELUN},
    {"Zzyzx", "RocketStor 2000", NULL, BLIST_SPARSELUN},
    { NULL, NULL, NULL, 0 },
};
```

From this list, you can get an idea of the types of SCSI devices that have the problem of showing up at all LUNs. If you have the same problem with a SCSI device, you can add that device's name to this list before the last line before rebuilding the kernel. You may not want to do this, however, if you are not familiar with the C programming language.

Sense Errors on an Error-Free SCSI Device

The cause of this problem usually is bad cables or improper termination. Check all cables, and make sure the SCSI bus is terminated at both ends.

Networking Autoprobe Conflicts with a SCSI Device

If a Linux kernel with networking support does not work with SCSI devices, the problem may be the autoprobe function of the networking drivers. The autoprobe capability is meant to detect the type of networking hardware automatically; the network drivers read from and write to specific I/O addresses during autoprobing. If an I/O address happens to be the same as that a SCSI device uses, the system may have a problem. In this case, you have to check the I/O address, IRQ, and DMA values of the network cards and of the SCSI controller and make sure no conflicts exist. Most SCSI controllers (and even network adapters) allow you to configure these parameters (I/O address, IRQ, and DMA) through setup software that comes with the adapter.

SCSI Lockup

If the SCSI system locks up, check the SCSI controller card, using any diagnostic software that came with the card (usually, the diagnostic software runs under DOS). Look for conflicts in I/O address, IRQ, or DMA with other cards. Some sound cards, for example, use a 16-bit DMA channel in addition to an 8-bit DMA; make sure you have not inadvertently used the same 16-bit DMA for the SCSI card.

The Linux SCSI driver for some SCSI cards supports only one outstanding SCSI command at a time. With such a SCSI card, if a device such as a tape drive is busy rewinding, the system may not be able to access other SCSI devices (such as a hard disk or a CD-ROM drive) that are daisy-chained with that tape drive. A solution to this problem is to add a second SCSI controller to take care of the tape drives.

SCSI Devices Not Found

If the Linux kernel does not detect your SCSI devices at startup, but you know that the SCSI devices are there (and that they work under Windows), the problem may be the lack of a BIOS on the SCSI controller; the autoprobe routines that detect SCSI devices rely on the BIOS.

This problem occurs for the following SCSI cards:

- Adaptec 152x, 151x, AIC-6260, and AIC-6360
- Future Domain 1680, TMC-950, and TMC-8xx
- Trantor T128, T128F, and T228F
- Seagate ST01 and ST02
- Western Digital 7000

insider insight

Even if a SCSI controller has a BIOS, jumpers often are available for disabling the BIOS. If you have disabled the BIOS for some reason, you may want to reenable it (read the documentation of your SCSI controller for directions) so that Linux can detect the SCSI devices automatically.

For a SCSI card, such as the Adaptec 151x, that does not have any BIOS, use the following command line during boot to force detection of the card:

```
aha152x=0x340,11,7,1
```

CD and DVD Drives

If you have installed or are planning to install Fedora Linux from this book's companion DVD-ROM, chances are good that your system already has a CD/DVD drive. You are probably reading this appendix because you have questions about using your CD/DVD drive in Linux. In this appendix, you can find answers to some common questions about CD/DVD drives. In particular, this appendix describes specific types of Linux-supported CD/DVD drives, categorized by interface type.

CD and DVD as Storage Media

Typically each CD-ROM can hold up to 700MB of data (the equivalent of over 450 high-density 3.5-inch floppy disks) and does not cost much to produce. DVD-ROMs can store even more data — up to 4.7GB for single layer DVDs and up to 8.54GB for double-layer DVDs. Single-layer DVDs are called DVD-5 and double-layer ones are called DVD-9; the number denotes the approximate storage capacity in gigabytes. The huge storage capacity makes DVD-ROM an attractive medium for distributing data and programs. In fact, many Linux books (including this one) bundle a DVD with a complete Linux distribution that includes the operating system and lots of popular software. Although CDs and DVDs can store lots of information, the data-transfer rates of CD/DVD drives are not as fast as those of hard disk drives.

Typically software is distributed in read-only CD and DVD discs (CD-ROM and DVD-ROM), but there are recordable CDs and DVDs that you can use with appropriate CD/DVD recorders to burn your own CDs and DVDs. For CDs, the recordable disc can be a write-once CD-R or a rewriteable CD-RW that can be erased and rewritten. Recordable DVDs come in several different flavors:

- DVD-R and DVD+R discs are write-once discs with different formats, but same capacity. You cannot write copy-protected content to these discs.
- DVD-RW and DVD+RW discs are rewriteable discs that you can erase and rewrite.
- DVD-RAM discs are rewriteable discs meant to be used to archive data although some DVD video recorders also support this format.

note

Most CD/DVD-ROMs contain information in an ISO-9660 file system (formerly known as High Sierra). This file system supports only the MS-DOS–style 8.3 filenames, such as `README.TXT`, which have names up to eight characters and optional three-character filename extensions, such as `.DOC` or `.TXT`. An extension to the ISO-9660 file system, called the Rock Ridge Extensions, uses unused fields to support longer filenames and additional UNIX-style file attributes, such as ownership and symbolic links.

Most CD/DVD drives—whether they are recordable or read-only—enable you to play audio CDs via an external headphone jack. With the appropriate video decoders you can also play DVD videos on a DVD drive.

Supported CD/DVD Drives

As with hard disks, Linux's support for a CD or DVD drive depends on the interface through which that CD drive connects to the PC's motherboard. CD and DVD drives come with four types of interfaces:

- **IDE or AT Attachment Packet Interface (ATAPI):** ATAPI is a recent specification for accessing and controlling a CD/DVD drive connected to the PC through the AT Attachment (ATA). ATAPI is gaining popularity because it is built on the cheaper IDE interface. (ATA is the new name for IDE.)
- **Small Computer System Interface (SCSI):** SCSI is popular because of its relatively high data rates and because it can support multiple devices. The only drawback is that you need a relatively expensive SCSI controller card for the PC.
- **Universal Serial Bus (USB):** USB is a popular interface for attaching various devices from printers to scanners to PCs. There are CD/DVD drives as well as CD-R (recordable CD), CD-RW (rewriteable CD), and different types of recordable DVD (DVD-R, DVD+R) and rewriteable DVD (DVD-RW, DVD+RW) drives that attach to USB ports. USB CD/DVD recordable and rewriteable drives are popular because they can be quickly and easily moved between systems. To support USB CD/DVD drives, all you need is to enable USB mass storage support in the kernel. This causes the USB CD/DVD drives to appear as SCSI drives, but with different device names such as `/dev/scd0` and `/dev/scd1`.
- **Proprietary CD-ROM interfaces:** In the early days of CD-ROM drives, many CD-ROM vendors provided their own proprietary interfaces between the CD-ROM drive and the PC's motherboard. Many sound cards included a built-in CD-ROM–drive interface, which is typically proprietary. The problem with proprietary interfaces is that someone has to develop a Linux driver specifically for each interface, whereas with a SCSI or IDE interface you can use a SCSI or IDE driver to access any SCSI or IDE device.

ATAPI CD/DVD Drives

ATA (AT Attachment) is the official ANSI (American National Standards Institute) standard name for the commonplace IDE interface, which is commonly used to connect hard-disk drives to the PC. ATAPI (ATA Packet Interface) is a protocol (similar to SCSI) for controlling storage devices, such as CD and DVD drives and tape drives. ATAPI is the most popular type of interface for CD and DVD drives because ATAPI is based on the ATA (or IDE) interface and does not need any expensive controller card or cable. Also, an ATAPI CD/DVD can simply be connected as the second drive on the same interface on which the PC's hard drive is connected. That means that the ATAPI CD/DVD drive does not require a separate interface card.

The Linux kernel includes an ATAPI driver that should work with any ATAPI CD/DVD drive. ATAPI CD/DVD drives are available from many vendors, such as Memorex, NEC, Philips, Pioneer, Panasonic, Sony, and Toshiba. Most new PCs (such as those from Gateway and Dell) come configured with ATAPI CD-ROM drives.

SCSI CD/DVD Drives

Linux supports a SCSI CD/DVD drive connected to one of the supported SCSI controller cards (see Appendix B for more information). The only restriction is that the block size (for data transfers) of the SCSI CD/DVD drive should be 512 or 2,048 bytes, which covers all CD/DVD drives on the market.

Some CD/DVD drives include a controller with a modified interface that's not fully SCSI-compatible. These interfaces are essentially proprietary, and you cannot use such CD-ROM drives with the SCSI driver.

SCSI CD/DVD drives are available from many vendors, such as HP, Plextor, Sanyo, Teac, and Toshiba.

Proprietary CD-ROM Drives

Although the ATAPI and SCSI CD/DVD drives fall into neat categories and work well in Linux, the situation is much more confusing when it comes to older CD-ROM drives with a proprietary interface. Following are two of the biggest sources of confusion:

- Some vendors, such as Creative Labs (of SoundBlaster fame), have sold CD-ROM drives with all types of interfaces: ATAPI, SCSI, and proprietary interfaces on a sound card. Thus, the vendor's name alone does not mean anything; you have to know what type of interface the CD-ROM drive uses.
- PC vendors sometimes categorize the CD-ROM–drive interface as IDE, even though the interface is really proprietary. Like the IDE (or ATAPI) interface, the proprietary CD-ROM–drive interface is cheap and popular.

As you may have guessed, proprietary CD-ROM–drive interfaces were popular because they tend to be much simpler than SCSI interfaces, which were the primary alternative to proprietary interfaces before ATAPI came along. Because of the popularity of the relatively inexpensive ATAPI, most new PCs do not use proprietary interfaces for CD-ROM drives.

insider insight

If you have a choice, avoid proprietary CD-ROM–drive interfaces. They're more trouble than they're worth. Of course, if you have an older PC with a proprietary CD-ROM interface, you may be stuck with it.

Table C-1 lists CD-ROM drives with proprietary interfaces and the drivers you need to support those drives.

Table C-1: CD-ROM Drives with Proprietary Interfaces

Driver	*CD-ROM Drive*
`aztcd`	Aztech CDA268-01A (other models are ATAPI drives), Orchid CDS-3110, Okano/Wearnes CDD-110, Conrad TXC, CyCDROM CR520ie/CR940ie
`cdu31a`	Sony CDU31A/CDU33A
`cm206`	Philips/LMS CM 206
`gscd`	GoldStar R420 (may be sold as part of the Reveal Multimedia kit)
`isp16`	CD-ROM drives attached to the interface on an ISP16, MAD16, or Mozart sound card
`mcdx`	Mitsumi CRMC LU005S, FX001
`optcd`	Optics Storage Dolphin 8000AT, Lasermate CR328A
`sbpcd`	Matsushita/Panasonic (Panasonic CR-521, CR-522, CR-523, CR-562, and CR-563), Kotobuki, Creative Labs (CD-200), Longshine LCS-7260, Teac CD-55A
`sjcd`	Sanyo H94A
`sonycd535`	Sony CDU-535/CDU-531

Linux uses a unique device name for each type of CD-ROM interface. The CD-ROM devices are block devices like the disk devices, such as `/dev/hda` and `/dev/sda`. Table C-2 lists the CD-ROM device names for the CD/DVD interfaces, including the proprietary ones.

Table C-2: CD/DVD Device Names

Device Name	*CD-ROM Type*
`/dev/aztcd0`	Aztech CD-ROM drive interface
`/dev/cdu31a`	Sony CDU31A/CDU33A CD-ROM drive interface
`/dev/cm206cd`	Philips/LMS CD-ROM drive interface
`/dev/gscd0`	GoldStar CD-ROM interface
`/dev/hdc`	ATAPI CD/DVD drive on the secondary IDE interface on an EIDE controller
`/dev/mcd`	Mitsumi CD-ROM drive interface
`/dev/optcd0`	Optics Storage CD-ROM drive interface
`/dev/sbpcd0`	Sound Blaster Pro CD-ROM drive interface
`/dev/scd0`	First SCSI CD/DVD drive
`/dev/scd1`	Second SCSI CD/DVD drive, if any
`/dev/sjcd`	Sanyo CD-ROM drive interface
`/dev/sonycd535`	Sony CDU-535/CDU-531 CD-ROM drive interface

CD-ROM Troubleshooting

The initial Linux kernel comes with driver modules for all supported CD/DVD drives; therefore, you should not have any problem as long as Linux supports your CD/DVD. Remember that the CD/DVD drive's interface is what counts, not the brand name. For example, any CD/DVD drive with the IDE interface works under Linux because Linux supports the IDE interface.

If Linux does not seem to recognize the CD-ROM drive after you reboot the system, try the following steps to fix the problem:

1. If Linux has not loaded the CD-ROM driver module, you can manually load the driver by logging in as `root` and typing the command **modprobe cdrom**. Then check if the CD-ROM drive works by typing **eject /dev/cdrom** — the CD/DVD drive door should open if it's working. You can then try to mount a CD or DVD.
2. If you have rebuilt the kernel with support for your CD/DVD drive, verify that you are indeed running the new kernel. To see the kernel's version number, type the **uname -srv** (or **uname -a**) command. This output from the `uname` command shows the kernel's version number, as well as the date on which the kernel was built. If that date does not match the date on which you rebuilt the kernel, you may not be running the new kernel. Go through the steps outlined in Chapter 21, and make sure you have really installed the new kernel. One common problem is forgetting to reboot, so try that as well.
3. Look at the contents of the `/proc/devices` file to verify that the CD/DVD device is present. Use the following procedure to view the contents of a `/proc/devices` file:

```
cat /proc/devices | more
Character devices:
  1 mem
  4 /dev/vc/0
  4 tty
  4 ttyS
  5 /dev/tty
  5 /dev/console
  5 /dev/ptmx
  6 lp
  7 vcs
 10 misc
... lines deleted ...
Block devices:
  1 ramdisk
  2 fd
  3 ide0
  9 md
 22 ide1
253 device-mapper
254 mdp
```

This listing corresponds to the devices on one of my Linux PCs. It shows two lists of devices — *character devices*, such as serial ports that transfer data one or more characters at a time, and *block devices*, such as hard disks that transfer data in fixed-size blocks. You should look for the CD/DVD device in the list of block devices. I know my CD/DVD drive is connected to the secondary IDE interface. The two IDE interfaces correspond to the devices `ide0` and `ide1` in `/proc/devices`. Because `ide1` appears in the listing, I know that the CD/DVD driver is in the kernel.

If you have an old PC with a CD-ROM drive connected to a Sound Blaster Pro or compatible interface, look for a device number of 25 and the device name `sbpcd`.

If you don't see a device that corresponds to your CD/DVD drive, you have not configured the kernel properly to include the CD/DVD driver. Reconfigure and rebuild the kernel, making sure that you include support for your CD/DVD drive.

4. Verify that the CD/DVD driver detected the CD/DVD drive when the system started. Type the **dmesg | more** command to look at the boot messages and to see whether a line reports that the CD/DVD drive has been found. On my system, which has an ATAPI CD/DVD drive, the message looks like this:

```
hdc: SAMSUNG CDRW/DVD SM-352F, ATAPI CD/DVD-ROM drive
```

If you find no boot message about the CD/DVD drive, make sure that the CD/DVD is physically installed. For an external CD/DVD drive, make sure that the drive is powered on and the cables are connected. Check any drive ID or jumpers, and make sure that they are set correctly. You may want to first make sure that the CD/DVD drive works under Windows; if you see the CD-ROM work under Windows, you can be sure that the drive is physically sound. Next, verify that you have rebuilt the kernel with support for the correct CD/DVD-drive interface.

5. Verify that you can read from the CD/DVD drive. Try the following command, and see whether the drive's activity light comes on (it should) and whether any error messages are present (they shouldn't be):

```
dd bs=1024 count=5000 < /dev/cdrom > /dev/null
5000+0 records in
5000+0 records out
```

The `/dev/null` device is what you might call the bit bucket. Output directed to `/dev/null` simply vanishes.

If the `dd` command does not work, the device file for the CD-ROM device may not be set properly. Type the **ls -l /dev/cdrom** command to view detailed information about your CD/DVD device. The Linux installation program sets up `/dev/cdrom` as a symbolic link to the actual CD-ROM device. For an ATAPI CD/DVD drive on the secondary IDE interface, for example, I look at the `/dev/cdrom` symbolic link to make sure that it points to the real CD/DVD device (`/dev/hdc` in this case), as follows:

```
ls -l /dev/cdrom
lrwxrwxrwx  1 root root 3 May 21 09:35 /dev/cdrom -> hdc
```

6. Verify that you can mount the CD or DVD (depending on your drive type; on DVD drives, you can mount both CDs and DVDs). Place a good CD-ROM in the CD/DVD drive, and try to mount it by using the following command (for a CD/DVD recorder, change `/media/cdrom` to `/media/cdrecorder`):

```
mount -t iso9660 -r /dev/cdrom /media/cdrom
```

The `-t iso9660` option specifies that the CD-ROM has an ISO-9660 file system, and the `-r` option says you want to mount the file system as read-only.

If you can read from the CD-ROM drive with the dd command but cannot mount the CD-ROM, you may have configured the kernel without support for the ISO-9660 file system. To verify the currently supported file systems, use the following command:

```
cat /proc/filesystems
```

If you do not see iso9660 listed in the output, you have to rebuild the kernel and add support for the ISO-9660 file system.

7. If nothing works, you may want to read the latest CDROM-HOWTO document. To read the HOWTO documents, point your Web browser to http://tldp.org/HOWTO/CDROM-HOWTO/ (your Linux system must be connected to the Internet for this to work).

If you still cannot get the CD-ROM drive to work under Linux, you may want to post a news item to one of the comp.os.linux newsgroups. Chapter 16 describes how to post to newsgroups.

The following sections suggest solutions for a few more common problems.

Kernel Configuration for Specific CD-ROM Drives

If you are rebuilding the kernel and you have an ATAPI CD-ROM drive, you should answer yes to the following questions as you configure the kernel (see Chapter 21 for more on configuring the kernel):

```
ATA/ATAPI/MFM/RLL support (IDE) [Y/n/m/?]
  Enhanced IDE/MFM/RLL disk/cdrom/tape/floppy support (BLK_DEV_IDE) [Y/n/m/?]
   Include IDE/ATAPI CDROM support (CONFIG_BLK_DEV_IDECD) [Y/m/n/?] y
```

The possible responses are shown in brackets: y means yes (that means include support in the kernel); m means use a driver module, and n means no.

For SCSI CD-ROM drives, answer yes to the following questions:

```
*
* SCSI support
*
SCSI device support (SCSI) [Y/m/n/?]
*
* SCSI support type (disk, tape, CD-ROM)
*
SCSI CDROM support (BLK_DEV_SR) [Y/m/n/?]
```

Of course, you must specify your SCSI controller type; otherwise, the SCSI CD-ROM won't work. If you have an Adaptec AHA1542 SCSI controller, for example, answer yes to the following question:

```
Adaptec AHA1542 support (SCSI_AHA1542) [M/n/y/?]
```

If your CD-ROM drive has a proprietary interface, you must enable support for that specific CD-ROM drive interface. Start by answering yes to the following question during kernel configuration:

```
*
* Old CD-ROM drivers (not SCSI, not IDE)
*
Support non-SCSI/IDE/ATAPI CDROM drives (CD_NO_IDESCSI) [Y/n/?]
```

After that, answer yes to the question about the specific CD-ROM drive in your PC. If you have a Mitsumi CD-ROM drive (with a proprietary interface, not ATAPI), for example, answer yes to the line that starts with Mitsumi.

Newer versions of the Linux kernel may support other types of proprietary CD-ROM–drive interfaces. Check the prompts carefully before answering the questions the kernel-configuration program has posted.

Because most CD-ROMs use the ISO-9660 file system, you must enable support for this file system in the kernel. To do this, answer yes to the following question during kernel configuration:

```
ISO 9660 CDROM filesystem support (ISO9660_FS) [Y/m/n/?]
```

IDE (ATAPI) CD-ROM Troubles

A PC's ATA (IDE) adapter has two interfaces, primary and secondary, each of which is capable of supporting two drives. In Linux, the two primary devices are `/dev/hda` and `/dev/hdb`, typically used for hard disk drives. The secondary IDE devices are `/dev/hdc` and `/dev/hdd`. Thus, if you have an IDE hard drive connected to the primary interface and an IDE CD/DVD drive connected to the secondary interface, the hard drive will be `/dev/hda` and the CD/DVD drive will be `/dev/hdc`.

insider insight

Often, of the two devices on an IDE interface, one is designated the master and the other the slave. When only one IDE device is attached to an interface, it must be designated the master (or single). Typically, the IDE device has a jumper (a connector that connects a pair of pins) to indicate whether the device is a master or a slave.

If Linux refuses to recognize your IDE CD/DVD drive, however, you should check the CD/DVD drive's parameters, making sure the drive uses the secondary IDE interface (IRQ 15 and I/O address 170H) and is set to be the master.

Some interface cards support more than two IDE interfaces. In such a case, you should know that the Linux IDE CD/DVD driver might not recognize anything but the primary and secondary IDE interfaces. The Creative Labs Sound Blaster 16 CD-ROM interface is, by default, set to be the fourth IDE interface. If you are connecting a CD-ROM drive to a Sound Blaster 16 for use in Linux, you have to set the jumpers on the Sound Blaster 16 so that the IDE interface is the secondary interface instead of the fourth interface.

Boot-Time Parameters for CD-ROM Drives

Usually, Linux drivers find CD-ROM drives (and other peripherals) by probing — reading from and writing to various I/O addresses. Linux drivers also use any available information from the PC's CMOS memory. CMOS stands for complementary metal-oxide semiconductor — a type of semiconductor. Each PC has a small amount of battery-backed, nonvolatile CMOS storage, where vital pieces of information about the PC, such as the number of types of disk drives, are stored. The real-time clock is also stored in the CMOS.

One problem with probing is that it involves reading from or writing to specific I/O addresses. Depending on what device uses that I/O address, probing can cause the system to hang (become unresponsive). When the Sound Blaster Pro CD driver, `sbpcd`, probes for a CD-ROM drive, it may access an I/O address used in an NE2000 Ethernet card; if this happens, the system hangs.

To avoid probing at boot time, you can pass specific device parameters for the device corresponding to your CD-ROM drive.

If you have a CD-ROM drive with the Sound Blaster Pro CD interface, the device name is `sbpcd`, and you can provide settings at boot loader's prompt as follows:

```
sbpcd=0x230,SoundBlaster
```

This command tells the `sbpcd` driver that the I/O address of the CD-ROM drive is 230H. The exact boot-time parameters for a device depend on that device driver.

As you boot the system with GRUB, you can add options such as `sbpcd=0x230,SoundBlaster` to the `kernel` line in the `/etc/grub.conf` file.

Ethernet Cards

Ethernet is a good choice for the physical data-transport mechanism in local area networks (LANs) for the following reasons:

- Ethernet is proven technology (it has been in use since the early 1980s).
- Ethernet provides good data-transfer rates: typically 10 million bits per second (10 Mbps), although there is now 100-Mbps Ethernet and Gigabit Ethernet (1,000 Mbps).
- Ethernet runs on many different media from copper to fiber to wireless media.
- Ethernet hardware is relatively low-cost (PC Ethernet cards cost about $20).

Typically, Linux effectively supports affordable hardware, and Ethernet is no exception. This appendix describes the physical setup of an Ethernet LAN and summarizes the Ethernet cards Linux supports.

Ethernet Basics

Ethernet is a standard way to move packets of data between two or more computers connected to a single cable. (Larger networks are constructed by connecting multiple Ethernet segments with gateways.) Because a single wire is used, a protocol has to be used for sending and receiving data because only one data packet can exist on the cable at any time. An Ethernet LAN uses a data-transmission protocol known as Carrier Sense Multiple Access/Collision Detection (CSMA/CD) to ensure that multiple computers can share the single transmission cable. Ethernet controllers embedded in the computers follow the CSMA/CD protocol to transmit and receive Ethernet packets.

The idea behind the CSMA/CD protocol is similar to the way in which you have a conversation at a party. You listen for a pause (carrier sense) and talk when no one else is speaking. If you and another person begin talking at the same time, both of you realize the problem (collision detection) and pause for a moment; then one of you starts speaking again. As you know from experience, everything works out.

In an Ethernet LAN, each Ethernet controller checks the cable for signals — that's the carrier-sense part. If the signal level is low, a controller sends its packets on the cable; the packet contains information about the sender and the intended recipient. All Ethernet controllers on the LAN listen to the signal, and the recipient receives the packet. If two controllers send out a packet simultaneously, the signal level in the cable rises above a threshold, and the controllers know a collision has occurred (two packets have been sent out at the same time). Both controllers wait for a random amount of time before sending their packets again.

Ethernet was invented in the early 1970s at the Xerox Palo Alto Research Center (PARC) by Robert M. Metcalfe. In the 1980s, Ethernet was standardized by the cooperative effort of three companies: Digital Equipment Corporation (DEC), Intel, and Xerox. Using the first initials of the company names, that Ethernet standard became known as the DIX standard. Later, the DIX standard was included in the 802-series standards developed by the Institute of Electrical and Electronics Engineers (IEEE). The final Ethernet specification is formally known as IEEE 802.3 CSMA/CD, but people continue to call it Ethernet.

Ethernet sends data in packets (also known as *frames*) with a standard format that consists of the following sequence of components:

- 8-byte preamble
- 6-byte destination address
- 6-byte source address
- 2-byte length of the data field
- 46- to 1,500-byte data field
- 4-byte frame-check sequence (used for error checking)

You don't need to know much about the innards of Ethernet packets except to note the 6-byte source and destination addresses. Each Ethernet controller has a unique 6-byte (48-bit) address. At the physical level, packets must be addressed with these 6-byte addresses.

Address Resolution Protocol

In an Ethernet LAN, two Ethernet controllers can communicate only if they know each other's 6-byte physical Ethernet address. You may wonder how IP addresses are mapped to physical addresses. This problem is solved by the Address Resolution Protocol (ARP), which specifies how to obtain the physical address that corresponds to an IP address. Essentially, when a packet has to be sent to an IP address, the TCP/IP protocol uses ARP to find the physical address of the destination.

When the packet is meant for an IP address outside your network, that packet is sent to the gateway that has a physical presence on your network. Therefore, that gateway can respond to an ARP request for a physical address.

Ethernet Cables

The original Ethernet standard used a thick coaxial cable, nearly half an inch in diameter. That wiring is called *thickwire* or *thick Ethernet*, although the IEEE 802.3 standard calls it 10Base5. That designation means several things: The data-transmission rate is 10 megabits per second (10 Mbps); the transmission is baseband (which simply means that the cable's signal-carrying capacity is devoted to transmitting Ethernet packets only); and the total length of the cable can be no more than 500 meters. Thickwire was expensive, and the cable was rather unwieldy.

Nowadays, two other forms of Ethernet cabling are more popular. The first alternative to thick Ethernet cable is *thinwire*, or 10Base2, which uses a thin, flexible coaxial cable. A thinwire Ethernet segment can be, at most, 185 meters long. The other, more recent, alternative is Ethernet over unshielded twisted-pair cable (UTP), known as 10BaseT and 100BaseT. The Electronic Industries Association/Telecommunications Industries Association (EIA/TIA) defines the following categories of shielded and unshielded twisted pair cables:

- **Category 1 (Cat 1):** Traditional telephone cable.
- **Category 2 (Cat 2):** Cable certified for data transmissions up to 4 Mbps.
- **Category 3 (Cat 3):** Cable that can carry signals up to a frequency of 16 MHz. Cat 3 is the most common type of wiring in old corporate networks and it normally contains four pairs of wire. Considered obsolete nowadays.
- **Category 4 (Cat 4):** Cable that can carry signals up to a frequency of 20 MHz. Cat 4 wires are not that common. Considered obsolete nowadays.
- **Category 5 (Cat 5):** Cable that can carry signals up to a frequency of 100 MHz. Cat 5 cables normally have four pairs of copper wire. Cat 5 UTP is the most popular cable used in new installations today. This category of cable is being superseded by Category 5e (enhanced Cat 5).
- **Category 5e (Cat 5e):** Similar to Cat 5, but with improved technical parameters such as near-end cross talk and attenuation. Cat 5e cables support 10BaseT, 100BaseT4, 100BaseT2, 100BaseTX, and 1000BaseT Ethernet. Nowadays, Cat 5e is the minimum acceptable wiring.
- **Category 6 (Cat 6):** Similar to Cat 5e, but capable of carrying signals up to a frequency of 250 MHz. Cat 6 cables can support all existing Ethernet standards and is expected to support Gigabit Ethernet standard 1000BaseTX that will use two pairs of wires in each direction as opposed to all four pairs for 1000BaseT Ethernet over Cat 5e cables.

To set up a 10BaseT or 100BaseT Ethernet, you need an Ethernet *hub* — a hardware box with RJ-45 jacks. You build the network by running twisted-pair wires (usually, Category 5, or Cat 5, cables) from each PC's Ethernet card to this hub. You can get a 4-port 10BaseT hub for about $50 U.S. Figure D-1 shows a typical small 10BaseT Ethernet LAN that you might set up at a small office or your home. 100BaseT networks work the same way and nowadays most LANs are set up for 100BaseT Ethernet.

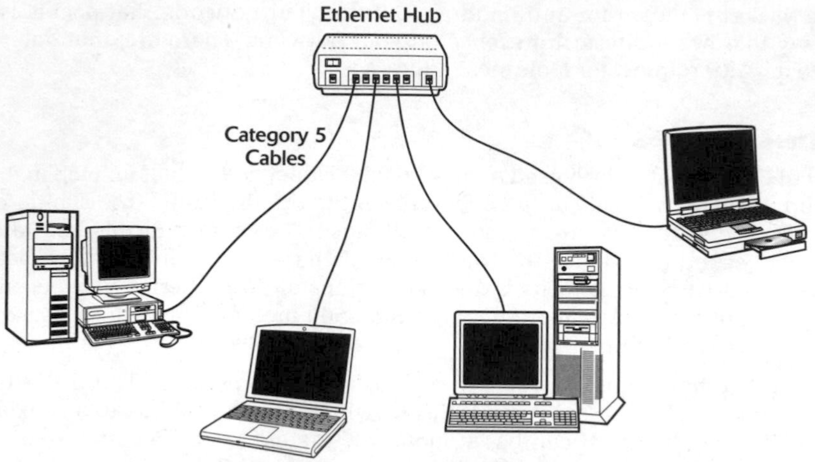

Figure D-1: A 10BaseT Ethernet LAN Using a Hub.

Supported Ethernet Cards

To set up an Ethernet LAN, you need an Ethernet card for each PC. Linux supports a wide variety of Ethernet cards for the PC. Table D-1 lists the supported Ethernet cards and their Linux drivers. The table includes wireless Ethernet cards as well as PCMCIA Ethernet cards. The driver name is useful when you load the Ethernet driver module (log in as `root` and type **modprobe drivername** to load a driver module).

Table D-1: Ethernet Cards and Their Linux Drivers

Ethernet Card	*Driver Name*
3Com 3C359 Tokenlink Velocity XL PCI	`3c539`
3Com 3C501 (obsolete and very slow)	`3c501`
3Com EtherLink II, 3C503, 3C503 (16-bit)	`3c503` and `8390`
3Com Etherlink Plus 3C505	`3c505`
3Com Etherlink-16 3C507	`3c507`
3Com Etherlink III, 3C509 / 3C509B (ISA), 3C529 9MCA bus equivalent of 3C509), 3C579 (EISA version of 3C509)	`3c509`
3Com 3C515 Fast EtherLink Ethercard (ISA)	`3c515`
3Com 3C574TX, 3CCFE574BT, 3CXFE574BT, 3CCSH572BT, 3CXSH572BT PCMCIA Card	`3c574_cs`
3Com 3C562 B/C/D, 3C563 B/C/D, 3C589 B/C/D, Megahertz 3CXE589 D/EC, 3CCE589EC/ET PCMCIA Card	`3c589_cs`

Ethernet Card	*Driver Name*
3Com Etherlink III Vortex (3C590, 3C592, 3C595, 3C597) (PCI)	`3c59x`
3Com 3C689 TokenLink III (PCMCIA) token ring card	`ibmtr_cs`
3Com Etherlink XL Boomerang Ethercards (3C900, 3C905), 3C905B Cyclone, 3C905C Tornado (PCI)	`3c59x`
3Com 3C985 3Com	`acenic`
3Com 3CR990 family	`typhoon`
Accton MPX	`ne` and `8390`
Accton EN1203, EN1207, EtherDuo-PCI	`de4x5`, `tulip`
Adaptec DuraLAN (also known as Starfire) ANA-6915, 62022, and 62044	`starfire`
Aironet 4500 and 4800 series wireless Ethernet PCI	`airo`
Aironet 4500 and 4800 series wireless Ethernet PCMCIA	`airo_cs`
Aironet Arlan 655	`arlan`
Allied Telesis AT1500	`lance`
Allied Telesis AT1700	`at1700`
Allied Telesis AT2450	`pcnet32`
Allied Telesis AT2540FX	`eepro100`
Alteon AceNIC Gigabit Ethernet card and other Tigon-based cards	`acenic`
AMD LANCE (7990, 79C960/961/961A, PCnet-ISA)	`lance`
AMD 79C965 (PCnet-32), 79C970/970A (PCnet-PCI), 79C971 (PCnet-FAST), 79C972 (PCnet-FAST+), 79C974 (PCnet-SCSI)	`pcnet32`
AMD 8111E	`amd8111e`
Ansel Communications AC3200 (EISA)	`ac3200`
Apricot 82596 bus-master Ethernet	`lp486e`
Asix AX88190–based PCMCIA Ethernet	`axnet_cs`
Atmel at76c502, at76c504, and at76c506 wireless Ethernet	`atmel_cs`
Atmel at76c502, at76c504, and at76c506 PCI Ethernet	`atmel_pci`
Boca BEN (ISA, VLB, PCI)	`lance`
Broadcom 4400	`b44`
Broadcom BCM570x (Tigon3) Gigabit Ethernet controller	`tg3`
Cabletron E21xx	`ne` and `8390`
Cabletron E2100	`e2100` and `8390`
Cabletron E22xx	`lance`

(continued)

Table D-1 *(continued)*

Ethernet Card	*Driver Name*
Cirrus Logic (previously Crystal Semiconductor) CS89x0	`cs89x0`
Cogent EM100 ISA/EISA	`smc9194`
Cogent eMASTER+, EM100-PCI, EM400, EM960, EM964	`de4x5`, `tulip`
Compaq Deskpro / Compaq XL (Embedded AMD Chip)	`pcnet32`
Compaq Fast Ethernet Server Adapter	`e100`
Compaq Nettelligent/NetFlex (Embedded TI ThunderLAN Chip)	`tlan`
Compex RL100-ATX	`winbond-840`
Danpex EN9400	`de4x5`, `tulip`
D-Link DE-100, DE-200, DE-220-T, DE-250	`ne` and `8390`
D-Link DE-520	`pcnet32`
D-Link DE-528	`ne`, `ne2k-pci`, and `8390`
D-Link DE-530	`de4x5`, `tulip`
D-Link DE-600	`de600`
D-Link DE-620	`de620`
D-Link DFE-550 and DFE-580 with Sundance ST201 Alta and Kendin KS8723	`sundance`
D-Link DL2000–based Gigabit Ethernet Adapter	`dl2k`
DEC DEPCA, DE100/1, DE200/1/2, DE210, DE422	`depca`
DEC EtherWorks 3 (DE203, DE204, DE205)	`ewrk3`
DEC FDDIcontroller (EISA and PCI)	`defxx`
DEC DE425 EISA, DE434, DE435, DE500	`de4x5`, `tulip`
DEC 21040, 21041, 2114x, Tulip	`de4x5`, `tulip`
DFINET-300 and DFINET-400	`ne` and `8390`
Digi RightSwitch SE-X	`dgrs`
Farallon Etherwave	`3c509`
Fujitsu FMV-181/182/183/184	`fmv18x`
Fujitsu FMV-J18x series PCMCIA Ethernet	`fmvj18x_cs`
HP 27245A	`hp` and `8390`
HP EtherTwist, PC LAN+ (27247, 27252A)	`hp-plus` and `8390`
HP-J2405A	`lance`
HP-Vectra On Board Ethernet	`lance`
HP 10/100 VG Any LAN (27248B, J2573, J2577, J2585, J970, J973)	`hp100`

Ethernet Card	Driver Name
HP NetServer 10/100TX PCI (D5013A)	eepro100
IBM Thinkpad 300 built-in adapter	znet
IBM Token Ring PCMCIA	ibmtr_cs
ICL EtherTeam 16i/32 (EISA)	eth16i
Intel EtherExpress	eexpress
Intel EtherExpress PRO/10	eepro
Intel EtherExpress PRO/100	eepro100
Intel PRO/100, 8255x-based Ethernet Adapter, 82559 Fast Ethernet LAN on Motherboard, 82562-based Fast Ethernet Connection	e100
Intel PRO/1000	e1000
Intel PRO/10GbE	ixgb
Intel PRO/Wireless 2100	ipw2100
Intel PRO/Wireless 2200/2915	ipw2200
Intersil Prism54 802.11 Wireless LAN adapter	prism54
Kingston - KNE100TX (Fast EtherRx PCI)	de4x5 or tulip
LinkSys Etherfast 10/100 cards	tulip
LinkSys Pocket Ethernet Adapter Plus	de620
LinkSys WMP11 (Prism II) PCI wireless Ethernet	orinoco_pci
Mylex LNE390A, LNE390B	lne390 and 8390
Mylex LNP101, LNP104	de4x5 or tulip
Myson MTD-8xx 100/10 Mbps PCI	fealnx
Novell Eagle NE1000, NE2000	ne and 8390
National Semiconductor 83820 chip (10/100/1000 Mbps 64-bit PCI Ethernet)	ns83820
National Semiconductor NS8390–based PCMCIA Ethernet	pcnet_cs
National Semiconductor DP8381x series	natsemi
NE2000-PCI (RealTek/Winbond/Compex)	ne, ne2k-pci and 8390
NE1500, NE2100	lance
NE/2 (MCA bus)	ne2
NE3210	ne3210 and 8390
NE5500	pcnet32
NVIDIA nForce media access controller	forcedeth
Orinoco wireless Ethernet cards (based on Hermes chipset)	orinoco_cs

(continued)

Table D-1 *(continued)*

Ethernet Card	*Driver Name*
Orinoco Ethernet card connected to PCI bus via PLX9052	`orinoco_plx`
Orinoco Ethernet card connected to PCI bus via TMD7160	`orinoco_tmd`
Packet Engines Yellowfin G-NIC Gigabit Ethernet	`yellowfin`
Packet Engines GNIC-II PCI Gigabit Ethernet	`hamachi`
Proteon P1370-EA	`ne` and `8390`
Proteon P1670-EA	`de4x5`, `tulip`
Pure Data PDUC8028, PDI8023	`wd` and `8390`
Racal-Interlan ES3210	`es3210`
Racal-Interlan NI5010	`ni5010`
Racal-Interlan NI5210	`ni52`
Racal-Interlan NI6510 (not EB)	`ni65`
Racal-Interlan EtherBlaster (also known as NI6510EB)	`lance`
Raytheon Raylink Wireless LAN card	`ray_cs`
RealTek RTL8002/8012 (AT-Lan-Tec) Pocket adaptor	`atp`
RealTek 8009, 8019	`ne` and `8390`
RealTek 8029	`ne`, `ne2k-pci` and `8390`
RealTek RTL-8139C+ series 10/100 PCI Ethernet	`8139cp` and `8139too`
RealTek RTL-8169 Gigabit Ethernet	`r8169`
RedCreek Communications PCI	`rcpci`
Sager NP943	`3c501`
Schneider & Koch SK G16	`sk_g16`
SEEQ 8005	`seeq8005`
SMC SMC91c92-based PCMCIA Ethernet cards (Megahertz, Motorola, Ositech, and Psion Dacom)	`smc91c92_cs`
SMC Elite Ultra/EtherEZ (ISA)	`smc-ultra` and `8390`
SMC Elite Ultra32 EISA	`smc-ultra32` and `8390`
SMC PCI EtherPower 10/100	`de4x5`, `tulip`
SMC EtherPower II PCI	`epic100`
SMC-9000 / SMC 91c92/4, 91c100	`smc9194`
Sparc HME/BigMac 10/100BaseT (also known as Happy Meal Ethernet)	`sunhme`
Sun GEM Gigabit Ethernet	`sungem`
Texas Instruments ThunderLAN	`tlan`
Toshiba TC35815CF PCI 10/100 Mbps Ethernet	`tc35815`

Ethernet Card	Driver Name
VIA 86C926 Amazon	ne, ne2k-pci and 8390
VIA 86C100A Rhine I, 6102 Rhine II, and 6105/6105M Rhine III	via-rhine
VIA Velocity Family Gigabit Ethernet	via-velocity
WaveLAN 2.4 GHz Wireless Ethernet PCMCIA card (version 2.0)	wavelan_cs
Western Digital WD8003 (SMC Elite) and WD8013 (SMC Elite Plus)	wd and 8390
Winbond W89c840 PCI Ethernet chip	winbond-840
WL3501 Wireless LAN PCMCIA Card	wl3501_cs
Xircom Cardbus Ethernet card	xircom_cb
Xircom Cardbus Ethernet CBE-100	xircom_tulip_cb
Xircom CreditCard Ethernet Adapter (CE2, CE IIps, RE-10, CEM28, CEM33, CE33, CEM56, CE3-100, CE3B, RE-100, REM10BT, and REM56G-100)	xirc2ps_cs
Zenith Z-Note built-in adapter	znet
Znyx ZX342 (DEC 21040 based)	de4x5, tulip

If you have upgraded the Linux kernel, the new kernel may support even more cards than the ones shown in this list.

If you have not bought an Ethernet card yet, you want to buy a 16-bit card, not an 8-bit card. A 16-bit card transfers data faster and has a larger onboard buffer. The cards come with different types of connectors, as follows:

- A DB-15 connector for thick Ethernet. (You need an additional transceiver to connect thickwire to other types of Ethernet, such as thinwire or 10BaseT.)
- A thinwire BNC connector.
- An RJ-45 connector for 10BaseT. (The RJ-45 connector looks like a common RJ-11 phone jack, but the RJ-45 version has eight positions instead of six.)

Nowadays, most Ethernet cards come with a 10BaseT connector. If you have more than one PC with 10BaseT Ethernet cards, you can easily set up a small LAN — all you need is a 10BaseT Ethernet hub. A wire goes from each PC's Ethernet card to the hub, and the hub sets up the proper connections for Ethernet.

You can use Ethernet cards with a DB-15 thick Ethernet connector in a thinwire or 10BaseT network. All you need is a transceiver that attaches to the DB-15 port and provides the right type of connector (BNC for thinwire, and RJ-45 for 10BaseT).

Ethernet Driver Modules

Linux ships with most drivers, including Ethernet drivers, in the form of dynamically loadable modules. When you set up networking during Fedora Linux installation, the installation program adds appropriate entries to the text file `/etc/modprobe.conf`. These entries tell the `modprobe` command what modules to load. For Ethernet drivers, the important entries are lines that define the driver aliases eth0, eth1, and so on. If you have only one Ethernet card, the alias eth0 should be set to the name of the driver for your Ethernet card (refer to Table D-1 for a list of cards and their corresponding drivers).

For example, my PC has a 3Com 3C905C PCI Ethernet card. For this card, the installation program adds the following alias entry in the `/etc/modprobe.conf` file:

```
alias eth0 3c59x
```

For some older Ethernet cards, you may need another entry in the `/etc/modprobe.conf` file to specify various options, such as I/O port address and interrupt request (IRQ) for your Ethernet card. For example, the following line in `/etc/modprobe.conf` specifies an IRQ of 5 and an I/O port address of 0x300 (hexadecimal 300) for the 3Com 3C503 card:

```
options 3c503 irq=5 io=0x300
```

For PCI and EISA Ethernet cards, it is safe to let the driver probe for various parameters of the card. To find information about the options an Ethernet driver module accepts, type modinfo followed by the driver's name (look up the driver in Table D-1).

Ethernet Autoprobing

At boot time, a kernel with Ethernet support or an Ethernet driver module (being loaded by `modprobe`) attempts to probe and detect the Ethernet card. The probing involves reading from and writing to specific I/O port addresses.

Although you specify a single I/O port address for a device, most devices use a block of I/O addresses for their operation. The I/O address you specify is the base address; the rest of the I/O addresses are consecutive I/O ports, starting at the base address.

note

Depending on the number of I/O addresses a device uses, two devices may end up with overlaps in the range of I/O addresses they use. The NE2000 card, for example, uses 32 I/O ports (that's 0x20 in hexadecimal notation). If you select 0x360 as the base I/O address for a NE2000 card, the card uses the ports from 0x360 to 0x37F. Unfortunately, the PC's parallel port (LPT1) uses the base I/O address of 0x378, and the secondary IDE controller uses the addresses 0x376–0x376. Thus, the NE2000 configured at 0x360 now has an overlap with the I/O addresses the first parallel port and the secondary IDE controller use. In this case, you can prevent any problems by configuring the NE2000 card at a different I/O address, such as 0x280.

Overlapping I/O port addresses cause problems; during autoprobing, the kernel may perform operations that might be harmless for some devices, but that may cause another device to lock up the system. Typically, however, if your Ethernet card and other devices are working under DOS or Windows, you should have no problem with them under Linux (assuming, of course, that your Ethernet card is supported under Linux).

If your system hangs during autoprobing, you can exclude a specific range of I/O addresses from being probed. To exclude a range of addresses during autoprobing, use the `reserve` command during the boot loader boot prompt. The `reserve` command has the following syntax:

```
reserve=BASE-IO-PORT1,NUMPORTS1[,BASE-IO-PORT2,NUMPORTS2,...]
```

Here, BASE-IO-PORT1 is an I/O port address in hexadecimal notation (for example, 0x300), and NUMPORTS1 is the number of ports (for example, 32) to be excluded when autoprobing. The arguments in brackets are optional; they are used to specify additional exclusion regions.

If you prevent a range of I/O addresses from being autoprobed, a device that may be at that address may not be detected. Thus, you must specify that device's parameters explicitly on the boot command line.

For Linux kernels with Ethernet support linked into the kernel, the boot command for specifying device parameters is `netdev`, which takes the following format:

```
netdev=IRQ,BASE-IO-PORT,PARAM-1,PARAM-2,NAME
```

Table D-2 explains the meanings of the arguments. All arguments are optional. The Ethernet driver takes the first nonnumeric argument as `NAME`.

Table D-2: Arguments for netdev

Argument	*Meaning*
IRQ	The IRQ of the Ethernet card. Specify a zero IRQ to make the driver autodetect the IRQ.
BASE-IO-PORT	The base I/O port address of the Ethernet card. Specify a zero BASE-IO-PORT to make the driver autodetect the base I/O port address.
PARAM-1	The meaning depends on the Ethernet driver. Some drivers use the least significant 4 bits of this value as the debug message level. The default is `0`; set this argument to a value of `1` to `7` to indicate how verbose the debug messages should be (`7` means most verbose). A value of `8` stops debug messages. The AMD LANCE driver uses the low-order 4 bits as the DMA channel.
PARAM-2	The meaning depends on the Ethernet driver. The 3Com 3c503 drivers use this value to select between an internal and external transceiver — `0` means the internal transceiver, and `1` means that the card uses an external transceiver connected to the DB-15 thick Ethernet port.
NAME	The name of the Ethernet driver (eth0, eth1, and so on). By default, the kernel uses eth0 as the name of the first Ethernet card it autoprobes. The kernel does not probe for more than one Ethernet card; that would increase any chance of conflicts with other devices during autoprobing.

If you have an Ethernet card at the I/O address 0x300 and do not want this card to be autoprobed, use a command line such as the following at the boot prompt:

```
reserve=0x300,32 ether=0,0x300,eth0
```

The `reserve` command prevents 32 I/O ports starting at 0x300 from being autoprobed, whereas the `ether` command specifies the base I/O port address for the Ethernet card. The exact I/O addresses depend on your Ethernet card and the range of addresses for which an overlap with some other device exists. Most of the time, you should not have to use these commands.

note

The I/O addresses and IRQs of PCI cards are assigned by the PCI BIOS when the system powers up. Thus, you cannot set the I/O address or IRQ of any PCI card through the boot commands. Even if you specify these parameters through boot commands, they are ignored for a PCI device.

Multiple Ethernet Cards

You might use a Linux PC as a gateway between two Ethernet networks. In that case, you might have two Ethernet cards in the PC. The Linux kernel can support more than one Ethernet card; however, it does not detect multiple cards automatically. The kernel looks for only the first Ethernet card. If you happen to have two Ethernet cards, you should specify the parameters of the cards on the boot command line. (The two cards must have different IRQs and I/O addresses, of course.) Following is a typical boot command line for two Ethernet cards:

```
ether=10,0x220,eth0 ether=5,0x300,eth1
```

If you happen to have two Ethernet cards, you can place the necessary boot parameters in the `/etc/grub.conf` file so that you don't have to enter the arguments every time you boot Linux. For the preceding example, you can append the `kernel` line in `/etc/grub.conf` so it looks like the following:

```
ether=10,0x220,eth0 ether=5,0x300,eth1
```

You can use a Linux PC with two network interfaces as a TCP/IP gateway.

Modems and Terminals

If you have installed Linux on your home PC, you may want to use a modem to dial out to your Internet service provider (ISP) and connect to the Internet. To use a modem, you have to learn how Linux works with the PC's serial ports — the ports through which the modem communicates with the PC. You need also to get cables to connect the modem to the PC, to select the proper serial device to use in Linux, and to set up configuration files that control the communication parameters for the serial port.

Terminals — devices that have a display screen and a keyboard — also connect to the PC through serial ports. In that sense, terminals are similar to modems. Terminals are ideal for simple data-entry tasks and are often used in point-of-sale systems. Linux also supports multiport serial boards that enable you to connect many terminals or modems to your PC running Linux.

This appendix explains how to connect, set up, and use modems and terminals. Much of the information applies to any device connected to the serial port, but some information is specific to modems. This appendix focuses primarily on modems because modems are more popular than dumb terminals connected to a Linux system.

Serial Ports

If you have used communications software, such as Procomm or Crosstalk, under MS-DOS or Windows, you have used your PC's modem and serial port. These communications programs transfer bytes of data from the PC to the modem over the serial port. The serial port is so named because each byte of data is sent serially — one bit at a time. Serial data communication comes with its own set of terminology. To understand how to set up the serial port, you need to understand the terminology.

UART

A chip named the universal asynchronous receiver/transmitter (UART), which is at the heart of all serial communication hardware, takes care of converting each byte to a stream of ones and zeros. That stream of ones and zeros is then sent over the communications medium (for example, the telephone line). At the receiving end, another UART reconstitutes bytes of data from the stream of ones and zeros.

The original IBM PC's motherboard did not include serial communication capabilities. Instead, the serial communication function was provided through a separate serial adapter card (or *serial board*) called the IBM Asynchronous Communications Adapter. This serial board used National Semiconductor's INS8250 UART chip.

Later, PCs began including the serial communication hardware on the motherboard, but the same 8250 or compatible UART was used for a long time. Still later, an improved version of the 8250 — the 16450 — was introduced, but the improvements were in the chip's fabrication details, not in its basic capability.

A problem with the 8250 and 16450 UARTs is that they do not have any way to buffer received characters. If the PC cannot keep up with the character stream, some characters may be lost. At high data-transfer rates (more than 9,600 bits per second), the PC may have trouble keeping up with the arrival of characters, especially with operating systems that keep the PC busy (such as Microsoft Windows).

The solution was to add a first in, first out (FIFO) buffer on the UART, enabling the PC to fall behind occasionally, without losing any incoming characters. The newer 16550A UARTs have send and receive buffers, each of which is capable of storing up to 16 characters. The 16550A UART is compatible with the old 8250 and 16450, but it can support higher data-transfer rates because the built-in buffers can store incoming and outgoing characters directly on the UART.

On a historical note, National Semiconductor's original 16550 UART had the FIFO buffers, but the FIFO circuits had some bugs. The 16550A (and later versions of that UART) fixed the problems of the original 16550. By now, however, the 16550 name is often used to refer to any UART with an onboard receive and transmit buffer. You don't have to worry about the distinctions between the 16550 and 16550A, except in the case of the original 16550 UARTs from National Semiconductor; those chips are marked NS16550 (without an A).

note

Linux supports PC serial ports and serial I/O boards that use a 8250, 16450, 16550, 16550A, or compatible UART. However, you really need a 16550A or better UART to keep up with today's high-speed modems, which can transfer data at rates of up to 56,000 bits per second. Most new Pentium PCs should already have 16550A UARTs. If you are buying a new PC to run Linux, you should check with the vendor and make sure that the serial interface uses 16550A UARTs. Newer UARTs, such as the 16654 and 16750, come with a 64-byte buffer. These UARTs should also work with Linux.

Communications Parameters

In serial communications, the transmission medium (such as the telephone line) is kept at a logical 1 when it is idle (1 is represented by the presence of a signal on the line). In this case, the line is said to be marking. On the other hand, when the line is at a logical 0, it is said to be spacing. Thus, logical 1 and 0 are also referred to as *mark* and *space*, respectively.

A sequence of ones and zeros makes up a single 8-bit character. A change in the condition of the line from mark to space indicates the start of a character. That change in line condition is referred to as the *Start* bit. Following the Start bit is a pattern of bits that represents the character and then a bit known as the *Parity* bit. Finally, the line reverts to its idling mark condition, which represents the *Stop* bit and indicates the end of the current character. The number of bits used to represent the character is known as the word length and is usually either seven or eight.

The Parity bit is used to perform rudimentary error detection. When even parity is selected, for example, the Parity bit is set so that the total number of ones in the current word is even (the logic is similar for odd parity). At the receiving end, the parity is recalculated and compared with the received parity bit. If the two disagree, the receiver declares a parity error. One problem of error detection with the parity check is that it can detect only errors that affect a single bit. The bit pattern 0100 0001 0 (the ASCII code for the letter A), for example, transmitted with an 8-bit word length and even parity, may change (because of noise in the telephone line) to 0100 0111 0 (ASCII G); the receiver, however, does not see the error, because the parity is still even. Thus, parity error detection is rarely used nowadays.

In serial communications, the transmitter and the receiver both must have some knowledge of how long each bit lasts; otherwise, they cannot detect the bits correctly. The duration of each bit is determined by data clocks at the receiver and the transmitter. Notice, however, that although the clocks at the receiver and the transmitter must have the same frequency, they do not have to be synchronized. The Start bit signals the receiver that a new character follows; the receiver then begins detecting the bits until it sees the Stop bit.

A particular condition of the line is sometimes used to gain the attention of the receiver. The normal state of the line is mark (1), and the beginning of a character is indicated by a space (0). If the line stays in the space condition for a period of time longer than it would have taken to receive all the bits of a character, a *break* is assumed to have occurred. When the receiver sees the break condition, it can get ready to receive characters again.

The selection of the clock frequency depends on the *baud rate* (or simply baud), which refers to the number of times that the line changes state every second. Typically, the serial I/O hardware uses a clock rate of 16 times the baud rate so that the line is sampled often enough to detect reliably.

Baud versus BPS

The data-transfer rate is expressed in terms of bits per second, or bps. In the early days of modems, the data-transfer rate was the same as the *baud rate* — the rate of change of the line's state — because each line state carried a single bit of information. Nowadays, modems use different technology that can send several bits of information each time the line state changes. In other words, you can get a high bps with a relatively low baud rate. The fastest modems today use a baud rate of 2,400, even though the bits per second can be as high as 56,000.

Thus, baud and bits per second are not the same. Most of us, however, ignore the exact definition of baud rate and simply use baud to mean bits per second. Even though I'll stick to bps when I speak of data-transfer rates, you'll run across Linux settings that use baud rate to mean bps.

Serial-Port IRQs and I/O Addresses

The PC typically has two serial ports, called COM1 and COM2 in MS-DOS/Windows parlance. The PC can also support two more serial ports: COM3 and COM4. Because of these port names, the serial ports are often referred to as COM ports.

Like other devices, the serial ports need interrupt request (IRQ) numbers and I/O port addresses. Two IRQs — 3 and 4 — are shared among the four COM ports. Table E-1 lists the IRQs and I/O port addresses assigned to the four serial ports.

Table E-1: IRQ and I/O Port Addresses Assigned to Serial Ports

Port	*IRQ*	*I/O Address*
COM1	4	0x3f8
COM2	3	0x2f8
COM3	4	0x3e8
COM4	3	0x2e8

Modems

Modem is a contraction of modulator/demodulator, and is a device that converts digital signals (string of 1s and 0s) into continuously varying analog signals that can be transmitted over telephone lines and radio waves. Thus, the modem is the intermediary between the digital world of the PC and the analog world of telephones. Figure E-1 illustrates the concept of a modem.

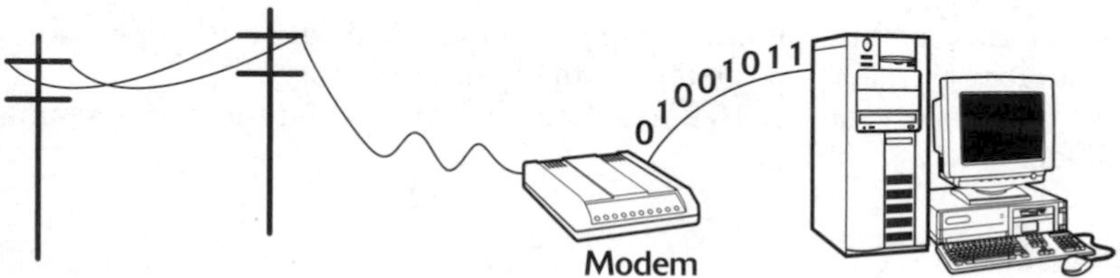

Figure E-1: A Modem Bridges the Digital World of PCs and the Analog World of Telephones.

Inside the PC, 1s and 0s are represented with voltage levels, but signals carried over telephone lines are usually tones of different frequencies. The modem sits between the PC and the telephone line and makes data communication possible over the phone lines. The modem converts information back and forth between the voltage/no voltage representation of digital circuits and different frequency tones that are appropriate for transmission over phone lines.

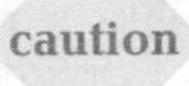

A quick word of caution about Winmodems that come with many new PCs and laptops. These are largely software-based internal modems and totally different from the traditional hardware modems. Winmodems work only with special software, so they are often called software modems. See the "Winmodems and Linux" section for more on Linux support for Winmodems.

The communication between the PC and the modem follows the RS-232C standard (often stated as RS-232, without the C). The communications protocol established between two modems also follows one of several international modem standards. The next few sections briefly describe these standards.

RS-232C Standard

The RS-232C standard, set forth by the Electronic Industries Association (EIA), specifies a prescribed method of information interchange between the modem and the PC's serial-communication hardware.

note

In EIA terminology, the modem is data communications equipment (DCE), and the PC is data terminal equipment (DTE). You'll see references to DCE and DTE in discussions of the RS-232C standard.

A modem can communicate in one of two modes:

- **Half-duplex mode:** Data transmission can occur in only one direction at a time.
- **Full-duplex mode:** Enables independent two-way communications.

Most modems communicate in full-duplex mode.

RS-232C Cables

The RS-232C standard also provides control signals, such as Request to Send (RTS) and Clear to Send (CTS), that can be used to coordinate the transmission and reception of data between the PC and the modem. Handshaking refers to the coordination of the data exchange.

Handshaking signals, as well as data transmission and reception, occur through wires in the cable that connects the PC to the modem. The RS-232C specifies a 25-pin connector, with a specific function assigned to each pin.

A typical modem has a female 25-pin, D-shell connector (called the DB-25 connector), whereas the PC's serial port provides a male 9-pin, D-shell (DB-9) connector. Thus, to connect a PC's serial port to a modem, you need a cable with a female DB-9 connector at one end and a male DB-25 connector at the other end. The typical PC-to-modem cable is often sold in computer stores as an *AT Modem Cable*.

Some PCs have a DB-25 connector for the serial port. For these machines, you need a cable that has DB-25 connectors on both ends.

Of the 25 pins available in a DB-25 connector, only 9 are used in the PC's serial port. In the Serial/Parallel Adapter card for the PC-AT, IBM decided to save space by introducing a DB-9 connector.

Using Modem Cables (DTE to DCE)

When you connect a PC (DTE) to a modem (DCE), the cable should connect the like signals at both ends. A cable that has such connections is often called a straight-through cable, as it connects like signals to each other.

Using Null Modem Cables (DTE to DTE)

If you want to connect two PCs through the serial port, you cannot use a straight-through cable like the one that connects the PC to a modem. The reason is that each PC expects to send data on the TD line and receive data on the RD line. If both PCs send data on the same line, neither PC can hear the other. A solution is to create a cable that connects one PC's output (TD) to the other one's input (RD), and vice versa. Such a cable is known as a null modem cable.

Choosing Serial Cables

When you connect two devices that support RS-232C serial communications, the choice of cable depends on the type of each device: DTE or DCE. As I mentioned previously, the PC is a DTE, and a modem is a DCE. Many printers and terminals are DTEs.

Use a straight-through modem cable to connect a DTE to a DCE. To connect a DTE to a DTE, you need a null modem cable. Many computer stores sell null modem adapters. You can connect two DTE devices by using a modem cable with a null modem adapter.

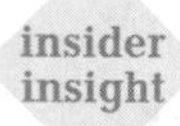

Notice that the serial interface on the Hewlett-Packard LaserJet family of printers is configured as a DTE. Thus, you need a null modem–style cable to connect a PC's serial port to a LaserJet printer. Unfortunately, serial printer cables (for connecting a printer to the serial port) introduce a further complication. Printer manufacturers interpret some of the RS-232C signals in a printer-specific way. Thus, you may have to connect various signals in a specific way to use a printer with a serial interface.

Flow Control

The RS-232C standard includes the RTS/CTS signals for hardware handshaking between the communicating devices (such as the PC and the modem). In addition to this hardware flow control, special ASCII control characters (Ctrl-Q/Ctrl-S, or XON/XOFF) are typically used to implement flow control in software. Flow control is necessary because sometimes the receiver may not be able to keep up with the rate of data arrival and should be able to inform the sender to stop data transmission while it catches up.

Suppose that a receiver has a buffer to store incoming characters. As the buffer gets full, the receiver can send the XOFF character (Ctrl-S) to the transmitter, indicating that transmission should stop. If the transmitter understands the meaning of the XOFF character, it can stop sending data.

Then, when the receiver empties the buffer, it can send an XON character (Ctrl-Q) to indicate that transmission can resume. This scheme of flow control is used in many communications programs because it is simple. This is unfortunate; when the XON/XOFF protocol is used, the XON and XOFF characters cannot be part of the data because of their special meaning.

note

The software-based XON/XOFF flow control is not used with modem speeds faster than 9,600 bps because it slows down data transfers. Most high-speed modem connections use hardware flow control only.

Modem Standards

As the Internet and online services have grown in popularity, the demand for modems that offer high data-transfer rates has grown accordingly. Early modems transferred data at the rate of 300 bits per second (bps), whereas the latest modems can transfer at rates of up to 56,000 bps — which represents an increase of more than a hundredfold in modem performance. To achieve these high data-transfer rates, modems use many tricks, including compressing the data before sending it. As you might expect, two modems can communicate successfully only if both modems understand how to interpret the signal being exchanged between the two. This is where the standard modem protocols come into play.

note

The International Telecommunications Union (ITU) has ratified several modem standards in use today. These standards have names that start with V. The latest standard is V.90, which supports data-transfer rates of 56,000 bps (more precisely, 56,000 bps downstream and up to 33,600 bps upstream). The V.90 standard is also called V.PCM because it uses a technique known as pulse code modulation (PCM). Table E-2 lists some of the common modem standards used today.

If you need the exact text of the ITU Series V recommendations, as these data communication standards are called, you can purchase copies from ITU's website at `www.itu.int/rec/recommendation.asp?type=products&lang=e&parent=T-REC-V`. The site offers the files in English, French, and Spanish, and in a number of file formats, including Microsoft Word for Windows and Adobe's Portable Document Format (PDF).

Table E-2: Modem Standards

Standard Name	*Maximum Data-Transfer Rate (bps)*
Bell 103	300
Bell 212A	1,200
V.17 (Group III Fax)	14,400
V.21	300
V.22	1,200
V.22bis	2,400
V.23	1,200
V.27ter (Group III Fax)	4,800
V.29 (Group III Fax)	9,600

(continued)

Table E-2 *(continued)*

Standard Name	*Maximum Data-Transfer Rate (bps)*
V.32	9,600
V.32bis	14,400
V.34	28,800
V.90	56,000 downstream and up to 33,600 bps upstream
V.91 and V.92	Up to 64,000 bps for use on a 4-wire circuit-switched connection and on leased point-to-point 4-wire digital circuits

When you buy a modem, make sure that it conforms to these international standards. Currently, the ITU V.92–compliant 56K modems are the norm.

Modem Commands (AT Commands)

The now-famous AT command set first appeared in the 300-baud Hayes Smartmodem, a name coined and trademarked by Hayes Microcomputer Products, Inc. The Smartmodem worked in two distinct modes:

- **Command mode:** Characters sent from the PC (DTE) are interpreted as commands for the modem.
- **Online mode:** After receiving a dial command and establishing a connection, the modem sends all received data out on the phone lines.

The Hayes Smartmodem commands start with the characters AT (for attention). The initial command set included those to dial a number, turn the modem's speaker on or off, and set the modem to answer an incoming call.

Modern manufacturers have widely copied the AT command system, making it a de facto standard. Although virtually all modems use a core command set, each modem manufacturer has its own proprietary commands that control some of the exotic and advanced features of the modem.

The AT Command Line

I have found it very helpful to know at least a few of the AT commands for controlling a modem. Although many communications programs hide the details of the AT commands, you can end up in a situation in which the communications software is primitive — all the software does is send the other modem whatever you type. In such situations, you can enter AT commands to set up the modem, dial out, and establish a connection. The following sections briefly cover the AT command set.

As the name implies, each command in the AT command set starts with the letters AT. Following these letters, you can enter one or more valid commands and end the command line with a carriage return (press Enter on the PC's keyboard). Thus, the command line has the following format:

```
AT[command1][command2]...<CR>
```

In the preceding line of code, `[command1]` and `[command2]` denote optional commands, each of which has appropriate arguments. The ending `<CR>` is a required carriage return (the Enter key).

Suppose that you want to use the following commands:

- The `E` command with an argument of 1 to force the modem to echo the commands
- The `V` command with 1 as the argument to make the modem provide verbose result codes (instead of numeric codes)

You can send these commands to the modem with the following AT command line:

```
ATE1V1
```

As with any AT command line, of course, you have to end this command by pressing Enter. If you enter this command through a communications software package, you see that the modem replies with the string `OK`.

note

All modems accept at least 40 characters per command line, in which the character count includes the AT and the final carriage return. Many modems, however, can accept up to 255 characters on an AT command line.

If an internal modem stops responding to the AT commands, you may have to shut down the system and power it off to reset the modem.

The A/ Command

The `A/` command is an exception to the AT command syntax. If you enter `A/` as the only command on a line by itself (no need to press Enter), the modem immediately repeats the last command line it has received.

Configuration Commands

These commands specify how the modem should operate and how it responds to commands. Following are some useful configuration commands:

- **Echo commands:** `ATE1` causes the modem to display a command as you type it; ATE0 disables the display of the command.
- **Speaker volume:** The `ATLn` (`n` being a number between 0 and 3) command sets the volume of the modem's built-in speaker. `ATL0` and `ATL1` set the volume to low, `ATL2` sets it to medium, and `ATL3` sets it to high.
- **Speaker control:** `ATMn` (`n` being a number between 0 and 2) controls whether and when the modem's speaker is turned on. `ATM0` turns the speaker off, `ATM1` turns it on until a call is established, and `ATM2` turns it on always.
- **Quiet mode:** When quiet mode is enabled, the modem does not acknowledge commands or report call status. `ATQ0` disables quiet mode and causes the modem to respond to commands and show call status. `ATQ1` enables quiet mode.
- **Verbose mode:** When verbose mode is enabled, the modem acknowledges commands and reports call status with words. Otherwise, it responds with numeric codes (which may be more suitable for communications software than for humans). The `ATV1` command turns on verbose mode; `ATV0` turns it off. A typical modem generates the nine responses listed in Table E-3.

Table E-3: Responses[a] from a Typical Modem

Numeric Response	*Word Response*
0	OK
1	CONNECT
2	RING
3	NO CARRIER
4	ERROR
5	CONNECT 1200
6	NO DIALTONE
7	BUSY
8	NO ANSWER

[a]Most modems include several other responses for reporting successful connections at higher data rates.

- **Result code selection:** The ATXn command selects the type of reports the modem should send back. The argument n can be one of the following:

  0 CONNECT

  1 CONNECT bits-per-sec

  2 CONNECT bits-per-sec, NO DIALTONE

  3 CONNECT bits-per-sec, BUSY

  4 CONNECT bits-per-sec, NO DIALTONE, BUSY
- **View stored profiles:** The AT&V command causes the modem to display the current values of a selected set of configuration parameters and the values of internal registers. Some modems have nonvolatile memory to store groups of settings, known as profiles. On such modems, AT&V displays the stored profiles.

Action Commands

Each action command causes the modem to perform some action immediately. The most important action command is the dial command: ATDT*number*. Two other useful action commands are ATZn and AT&Fn, which reset the modem's configuration. Following are some of the important action commands:

- **Pulse dial:** The ATDP*number* command causes the modem to use the pulse-dialing system to dial a specified phone number. The pulse-dialing system was used by rotary telephones. Nowadays, you typically use the ATDT command to dial a number by using the tone-dialing system.
- **Tone dial:** Use the ATDT*number* command to dial a specified phone number by using the tone-dialing system. To dial the number 555-1234, for example, use the command ATDT555-1234. You should enter whatever other digits you may need to dial the number you want to reach. If you need to dial 9 for an outside line,

simply use ATDT9,555-1234. The comma introduces a slight pause (typically, two seconds), which may be necessary to get an outside line.

- **Dial last number:** The ATDL command causes the modem to execute the last dial command.
- **Hook control:** The ATH command simulates lifting or putting down the handset of a regular telephone. ATH0 hangs up the phone; ATH1 makes the modem go online (as though you have picked up the handset).
- **Answer call:** Use the ATA command to make the modem answer the phone. You can put the modem in answer mode (by setting register S0 — a storage area in the modem — to a nonzero value), so that it answers the phone when someone calls. With the ATA command, you can force the modem to answer the phone even if register S0 is set to 0 (which means the modem won't answer the phone).
- **Return to online:** The ATO command returns the modem to online mode. Use this command after you press **+++** (rapidly enter three plus signs in sequence with some pause before and after the sequence) to take the modem offline.
- **Software reset:** If the modem stores configuration profiles in nonvolatile memory, you can recall one of the configuration profiles with the ATZn command (n being the number of the configuration profile). If you enter ATZ without any argument, the modem is reset. The ATZ command terminates any existing connection.
- **Factory-default setting:** The AT&F command causes the modem to restore the factory-default settings. Some modems take a numeric argument with AT&F; consult your modem's documentation for more information on the meaning of the numeric arguments.

The ATSr=n Commands

In addition to the AT command set, Hayes Smartmodem pioneered the use of internal modem registers to configure the modem. All current modems have registers, called the S registers, that control many aspects of the modem (including features that may be unique to a specific brand of modem).

note

A typical modem has anywhere from 30 to 60 S registers, denoted by S0, S1, S2, and so on. The ATSr=n command sets the S register numbered r to the value n. To view the current contents of the S register numbered r, use the ATSr? command.

Register S0, for example, contains the number of rings after which the modem answers the phone. When S0 is 0, the modem does not answer the phone at all. The following listing shows how you might query and set the S0 register with the ATS command:

```
ATS0?
000
OK
ATS0=1
OK
ATS0?
001
```

The exact set of S registers varies from one brand of modem to another, but most modems seem to provide and interpret the following 13 S registers consistently, as follows:

- **S0, ring to answer on:** The number of rings after which the modem answers the phone. When S0 is 0, the modem does not answer the phone.
- **S1, counts number of rings:** The count of incoming rings. When S1 equals S0, the modem answers the phone (assuming that S0 is nonzero). The modem resets S1 to 0 a few seconds after the last ring.
- **S2, escape code character:** The character used as the escape sequence to switch the modem from online mode to command mode. The default value is 43, which is the ASCII code for the plus (+) character. To go from online mode to command mode, enter this escape character three times in rapid succession.
- **S3, carriage-return character:** The ASCII code of the character used as the carriage return (this character terminates the AT command lines). The default value is 13.
- **S4, line-feed character:** The ASCII code of the character used as the line-feed character when the modem generates word responses to commands. The default value is 10.
- **S5, backspace character:** The ASCII code of the character used as the backspace. The modem echoes this character to implement the "erase preceding character" function. The default value is 8.
- **S6, wait time for dial tone (seconds):** The number of seconds to wait before dialing the first digit in a dial command. The default value is 2.
- **S7, wait time for carrier (seconds):** The number of seconds the modem waits for a carrier. If the modem does not detect a carrier after waiting for this many seconds, it displays the `NO CARRIER` message. The default value depends on the modem. Typically it will be anywhere from 30 to 60.
- **S8, comma time (seconds):** The number of seconds to pause when the modem finds a comma in the phone number to dial. The default value is 2.
- **S9, carrier detect time (tenths of a second):** The amount of time, in tenths of a second, that the carrier must be present before the modem declares that a carrier has been detected. The default value is 6, which means the carrier must be present for 0.6 seconds before the modem detects it.
- **S10, carrier loss time (tenths of a second):** The amount of time, in tenths of a second, that the carrier must be lost before the modem disconnects. The default value is anywhere from 7 to 15, which means the carrier must be lost for 0.7 to 1.5 seconds before the modem disconnects.
- **S11, dial-tone spacing (milliseconds):** The duration of each dial tone and the spacing between adjacent tones. The default value is typically somewhere between 50 and 100 milliseconds (50 is considered the minimum necessary for dial tones to be recognized by the phone system).
- **S12, escape sequence guard time (fiftieths of a second):** The amount of guard time, in fiftieths of a second, that must occur before and after the escape-code sequence (the default sequence is +++) that switches the modem from online mode to command mode. The default value is 50, which means the guard time is one second.

Online Help

In response to the `AT$` command, U.S. Robotics modems display online help information on the basic modem command sets. You'll find the help information instructive because it shows you the breadth of commands that a typical modem accepts. You can enter the command in a serial communication program such as Minicom, which I describe briefly later in the "Dialing Out with a Communication Program" section of this appendix.

Linux and Modems

If you're using Linux at home or in a small office, you probably want to use the modem for one or more of the following reasons:

- To dial out to another computer, an online service (such as America Online), or another UNIX system, perhaps at your university or company.
- To enable other people to dial in and use your Linux system. If your home PC runs Linux and you have a modem set up, you might even dial in to your home system from work.
- To use dial-up networking with Serial Line Internet Protocol (SLIP) or Point-to-Point Protocol (PPP) to connect to the Internet (typically through an Internet service provider).

cross ref

The following sections describe how to use a modem to dial out from your Linux PC. Dial-up networking with SLIP or PPP is an important topic in itself: Chapter 13 covers that subject in detail.

Winmodems and Linux

Many PCs and laptops come with Winmodems that turn over much of the modem's signal-processing functions to the main CPU. These modems work only with special software that performs the necessary parts of the modem's functions. For this reason, they are often called software modems. Initially, such software modems came with special driver software for Microsoft Windows only; hence the name Winmodem (for Windows modem). Lately, Linux software necessary to operate these modems has become available. If your system has a Winmodem, you should visit the Linux Winmodem Support homepage at `www.linmodems.org/` to learn more about Linux support for various models of Winmodems. For a list of Linux-compatible Winmodems — or Linmodems, as they are often called — visit the Web page at `www.idir.net/~gromitkc/winmodem.html`.

USB Modem Support in Linux

You should be able to use USB modems in Linux provided that you load the `acm` module that supports the Abstract Control Model (ACM) of the USB Communication Device Class (CDC) specification. The USB modem must also comply with the CDC specification; otherwise, it will not work with the `acm` driver module.

You also must set up the device node entries for the modems. You can use up to 32 modems with the `acm` driver. For example, the following commands set up the first four modem devices:

```
mknod /dev/usb/ttyACM0 c 166 0
mknod /dev/usb/ttyACM1 c 166 1
mknod /dev/usb/ttyACM2 c 166 2
mknod /dev/usb/ttyACM3 c 166 3
```

After you set up the devices and load the `cdc-acm` driver (type the command **modprobe cdc-acm** while logged in as `root`), you should be able to use a serial communication program such as minicom to dial out of a USB modem by specifying `/dev/usb/ttyACM0` as the device name for the modem.

Dialing Out with a Modem

When you install Linux from this book's companion DVD-ROM, you automatically install some tools you can use to dial out from your Linux system with a modem. Before you can dial out, however, you have to make sure you have a modem properly connected to one of the serial ports of your PC and that the Linux devices for the serial ports are set up correctly.

Examining a Modem's Hardware Setup

Make sure that your modem is properly connected to the power supply and the telephone line.

Buy the right type of cable to connect the modem to the PC. As explained in earlier sections of this chapter, you need a straight-through serial cable to connect the modem to the PC. The types of connectors at the ends of the cable depend on the type of serial connector on your PC. The modem end of the cable needs a male DB-25 connector. The PC end of the cable often is a female DB-9 connector, but, in addition, some PCs need a female DB-25 connector at the PC end of the cable.

You can buy modem cables at most computer stores. In particular, the DB-9 to DB-25 modem cables are often sold as AT modem cables.

note

If your PC's serial port is a DB-25, the connector at the back of the PC (not the one on the cable) is a male DB-25 connector. Don't confuse this connector with the parallel port's DB-25 connector, which is female. If you use the wrong connector, no damage should occur, but serial communication won't work.

If your PC has an internal modem, all you have to do is make sure the IRQ and I/O addresses are set properly (assuming that the modem card has jumpers for setting these values). For COM1, set the IRQ to 4 and the I/O address to 0x3f8; for COM2, set the IRQ to 3 and the I/O address to 0x2f8. You also have to connect the phone line to the phone jack at the back of the modem card.

Checking Linux's Serial Devices

When you install Linux from this book's DVD-ROM, following the directions in Chapter 2, the necessary Linux serial devices are automatically created for you. You should have the `/dev/ttyS*` devices for dialing in and out through the modem.

The installation process creates the `/dev/ttyS*` files with a permission setting that does not enable everyone to read the device. If you want any user to be able to dial out with the modem, type the following command while you are logged in as `root`:

```
chmod o+rw /dev/ttyS*
```

This command gives all users access to the dial-out devices.

Another approach is to create a group named ppp and to make it the owner of the /dev/ttyS* files. Then, you can add to the ppp group those users you trust to use the dial-out capability.

To verify that the Linux kernel has detected the serial port correctly, check the boot messages by typing dmesg | grep ttyS in a terminal window. If you see a message about the serial driver being loaded, the next few lines should show information about one or more serial ports on your system. On one of my PCs, for example, I get the following message for the first serial port (COM1):

```
ttyS0 at 0x03f8 (irq = 4) is a 16550A
```

You can also check for the serial ports with the setserial command. Type **setserial -g /dev/ttyS?** to see detailed information about the serial ports. A telltale sign of a problem is a message from setserial of the form:

```
/dev/ttyS0, UART: unknown, Port: 0x03f8, IRQ: 4
```

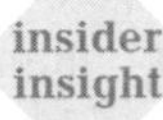

If the UART is shown as unknown, this means the serial port was not detected. This usually occurs because your PC's BIOS is set up to expect a Plug and Play (PnP) operating system. You should reboot your PC and, as it powers up, press a key (typically you have to press a function key such as F2, but the exact key depends on your PC's BIOS) to enter BIOS setup. In the setup screen, locate the option for PnP operating system (often labeled "Plug & Play O/S") and turn that option off. Then, save the BIOS settings and exit. This causes the PC to reboot. This time, when Linux boots again, the kernel should be able to detect the PC's serial port correctly.

Dialing Out with a Communication Program

After you complete the physical installation of the modem and verify that the necessary Linux device files exist, you can try to dial out through the modem. The best approach is to use the Minicom serial communications program included in the Linux distribution on this book's DVD-ROM and installed in the /usr/bin directory. The Minicom program is a serial communication program with a text-based interface that emulates a VT102 terminal. Minicom is similar to other communication software, such as Procomm or Crosstalk, which you may have used under MS-DOS or Windows.

To run Minicom, type **minicom** at the shell prompt in a terminal window or in a virtual console. If you run Minicom as a normal user (not root), Minicom may display the following error message and exit:

```
minicom
minicom: there is no global configuration file /etc/minirc.dfl
Ask your sysadm to create one (with minicom -s).
```

Log in as root, and type:

```
minicom -s
```

Minicom starts and displays a dialog box that lets you configure various aspects of Minicom, including serial-port commands and the modem-dialing commands. Make any changes you want, and then use the up and down arrow keys to highlight the item labeled `Save as dfl` (meaning "save as default"); then, press Enter. Minicom saves the settings in the `/etc/minirc.dfl` file — the default configuration file for Minicom. After that, you can exit Minicom by selecting Exit from Minicom and pressing Enter.

You also need to do the following before any user can run Minicom:

- Make sure that the text file `/etc/minicom.users` has a line containing the word `ALL`. (This enables all users to access Minicom's default configuration file.)
- Assuming that you want all users to be able to dial out using the modem, enable any user to read from and write to the serial port where the modem is connected. For example, if the modem is on COM1 (`/dev/ttyS0`), type **chmod o+rw /dev/ttyS0** to give everyone write permission for that device.
- Establish a link between the `/dev/modem` and the serial port device where the modem is connected. If the modem is on COM1 (`/dev/ttyS0`), you should type the following command:

  ```
  ln -s /dev/ttyS0 /dev/modem
  ```

After that, you can run Minicom as an ordinary user. When Minicom first runs, it resets the modem.

The Minicom program is similar to an older shareware communication program named Telix. As in that program, you can press Ctrl-A to get the attention of the Minicom program. After you press Ctrl-A, if you press Z, a help screen appears in the form of a text window.

In the help screen, you can get information about other Minicom commands. From the help screen, press Enter to return to online mode. In online mode, you can use the modem's AT commands to dial out. In particular, you can use the `ATDT` command to dial the phone number of another modem (for example, your Internet service provider's computer or a system at work). Once you get the login prompt, you can log in as usual and use the remote system.

When you log out of the other system and want to exit Minicom, press Ctrl-A, and then type **X** to exit the program. Press Enter again in response to the Minicom prompt.

Setting Up Linux for Dial-in

You can set up the same modem for dial-in use as well as dial-out use (only one operation is allowed at any one time, of course). Setting up a modem for dial-in use involves setting up a program that monitors the serial port for any incoming calls; this program provides the login prompt. You can use the `mgetty` program for this purpose.

Chapter 13 describes how to set up Linux as a dial-in PPP server. That description also tells you how to set up the `mgetty` program for dial-in. You can learn more about setting up dial-in modems by reading the latest Modem-HOWTO at `www.ibiblio.org/pub/Linux/docs/HOWTO/Modem-HOWTO`. You should also read the `mgetty` manual — just type **kghostview /usr/share/doc/mgetty*/mgetty.ps** in a terminal window from the GUI screen to read the PostScript manual that comes with the `mgetty` software distribution. If mgetty is not installed on your system, you'll find the `mgetty` RPM on the DVD-ROM (see Chapter 21 for information on how to install RPMs).

Terminals and Multiport Serial Boards

The previous sections show you how to set up and use a modem in Linux for dialing out. The rest of this appendix briefly describes the steps involved in setting up terminals connected to the PC's serial port. You'll also find a list of multiport serial boards Linux supports.

You can learn more about connecting terminals to Linux systems by reading the Text-Terminal-HOWTO, available online at `www.tldp.org/HOWTO/Text-Terminal-HOWTO.html`.

> **note** Note that you might want to use other x86 PCs (especially older Pentium PCs) as terminals connected to your Linux system. To convert a PC to a terminal, all you need on the PC is a serial-communications package, such as Procomm Plus or Telix.

Setting Up a Terminal on a Serial Port

To set up a terminal on a serial port, you have to set up a getty process, just as you do when you set up a dial-in modem. Follow these steps:

1. Make sure that you use the correct serial cable to connect the terminal to the serial port. Most terminals need a null modem cable in which the TD (transmit data) and RD (receive data) signal lines are reversed in going from one end of the cable to the other. (See earlier sections of this chapter for further discussions of serial cables.)
2. Set up the terminal's communication parameters. The exact steps depend on the terminal type.
3. Log in as `root` and edit the `/etc/inittab` file, and add a line to start the `agetty` process on the line connected to the terminal. If you have a VT102-compatible terminal on the line `ttyS1` (COM2), you might add the following line to your system's `/etc/inittab`:

   ```
   S1:23:respawn:/sbin/getty -L 9600 ttyS1 vt102
   ```

   This assumes that the terminal operates at a baud rate of 9,600. If the terminal is set to some other rate, change 9600 to that number.
4. Force the init process to reexamine the `/etc/inittab` file, as follows:

   ```
   init q
   ```
5. A login prompt should appear on the terminal's screen, and you should be able to log in using an existing user name.

Setting Up Multiport Serial Boards in Linux

If you plan to support a small business with a Linux PC and dumb terminals (terminals are cheaper than complete PCs, although you can also use old PCs as terminals), you want more than two serial ports. With another serial board, the PC can support four serial ports. If you want more than four serial ports, you have to buy special serial I/O boards known as multiport serial boards. These boards typically support anywhere from 4 to 32 serial ports. The serial ports share one IRQ, but each port has a unique I/O address.

> **note** Many multiport serial boards use the 16450 or 16550A UARTs. When you buy a board, you may want to make sure the UART is 16550A-compatible.

To add support for a specific multiport serial board, you have to add appropriate commands in the `/etc/rc.serial` file. That file is automatically executed by the `/etc/rc.sysinit` script as your Linux system boots. For specific information on what to place in the `/etc/rc.serial` file, consult the multiport serial board's documentation or contact the vendor. The Linux kernel's serial port driver supports the following 16450 or 16550A UART–based multiport serial boards:

- Accent Async-4 (4 ports)
- Arnet Multiport-8 (8 ports)
- AST FourPort and clones (4 ports)
- Bell Technologies HUB6 (6 ports)
- Boca BB-1004 (4 ports), BB-1008 (8 ports), BB-2016 (16 ports)
- Boca IOAT66 (6 ports)
- Boca 2by4 (four serial and two parallel ports)
- Byte Runner
- Computone ValuePort V4-ISA (AST FourPort-compatible)
- Digi PC/8 (eight ports)
- Dolphin
- Globetek
- GTEK BBS-550 (eight ports)
- Hayes ESP
- Longshine LCS-8880, Longshine LCS-8880+ (AST FourPort-compatible)
- Moxa C104, Moxa C104+ (AST FourPort-compatible)
- National Instruments NI-SERIAL
- PC-COMM (four ports)
- Sealevel Systems COMM-2 (two ports), COMM-4 (four ports), and COMM-8 (eight ports)
- SIIG I/O Expander 2S IO1812 (four ports)
- STB-4COM (four ports)
- Twincom ACI/550
- Usenet Serial Board II (four ports)
- VScom (same driver as Byte Runner)

The Boca BB-1004 and BB-1008 boards do not support the Carrier Detect (CD) and Ring Indicator (RI) signals necessary to make dial-in modems work. Thus, you cannot use the BB-1004 and BB-1008 boards with dial-in modems.

Some multiport serial boards use special processors instead of the 16450 or 16550A UART. Table E-4 lists some intelligent multiport serial boards Linux supports. It also shows the name of the driver module you must load to add support for a specific type of multiport serial board. These driver modules are located in the `/lib/modules/`*`VERSION`*`/kernel/drivers/char` directory of your Linux system, *`VERSION`* being the Linux kernel version. Thus, for kernel version 2.6.11-1.1286_FC4, these driver modules are in the `/lib/modules/2.6.11-1.1286_FC4/kernel/drivers/char` directory.

Table E-4: Linux Drivers for Intelligent Multiport Serial Boards

Multiport Serial Board	*Linux Driver Module*
3780i Advanced Communications Processor (Mwave)	`mwave`
Computone IntelliPort II	`ip2main`
Comtrol RocketPort	`rocket`
COSA or SRP synchronous serial card	`cosa`
Cyclades Cyclom-Y and Cyclades-Z series multiport serial boards	`cyclades`
Digi International PC/Xe, PC/Xi, PC/Xr, and PC/Xem	`epca`
Hayes ESP serial card	`esp`
ISI series of cards by MultiTech	`isicom`
Microgate SyncLink ISA and PCI high-speed, multiprotocol serial adapters	`synclink`
MOXA Intellio family of multiport serial cards	`moxa`
MOXA Smartio family of multiport serial cards	`mxser`
SDL RISCom/8	`riscom8`
Specialix IO8+	`specialix`
Stallion Intelligent Multiport Serial Boards	`istallion`
Stallion Multiport Serial Driver	`stallion`
Winbond W83977AF Super I/O chip multiport boards	`w83977af_ir`

note

To learn more about setting up a multiport serial board, you may want to read the latest Serial-HOWTO document. To read the Serial-HOWTO document, go to `www.ibiblio.org/pub/Linux/docs/HOWTO/Serial-HOWTO`.

PC Cards

Laptop computers typically include PCMCIA slots for attaching peripherals. PCMCIA stands for Personal Computer Memory Card International Association, a nonprofit organization that has standardized the interface for adding memory cards to laptop computers. Although originally conceived for memory cards, PCMCIA devices became popular for a wide variety of add-ons for laptops. Today, laptop computers use many PCMCIA devices, such as modems, network cards, SCSI controllers, and sound cards. Using Linux on a laptop means having to use the PCMCIA devices, or *PC Cards*, as the popular press calls them nowadays. Thanks to the efforts of David Hinds, you can now use PCMCIA devices under Linux with his PCMCIA Card Services for Linux. This appendix briefly describes PC Cards that use the PCMCIA interface and the PCMCIA support package for Linux.

note I refer to the actual cards as PC Cards because that's the proper name for the devices. PCMCIA refers to the industry organization that specifies the standard for PC Cards. However, I use the term PCMCIA Card in one context — when referring to PCMCIA Card Services for Linux (or Card Services, for short), the software that supports PC Cards under Linux.

PC Card Basics

PC Cards originated as static random access memory (SRAM) and flash RAM cards used to store data on small laptop computers. The credit card–sized cards fit into a slot on the side of the laptop. The flash memory cards used electrically erasable programmable read-only memory (EEPROM) to provide laptop storage capability that might have been too small for other conventional storage media.

Vendors soon realized the convenience of the memory-card slot as a general-purpose expansion slot for laptop computers. The Personal Computer Memory Card International Association (PCMCIA) standardized various aspects of PC Cards, including the electrical interface, card dimensions, and card-slot sizes. This standardization has contributed to the proliferation of PC Cards in the laptop market.

By now, PCMCIA slots are a feature of almost all laptops, and the memory card is a small part of the overall PC Card market. Most laptops provide PCMCIA slots so that users can add hardware, such as fax/modems, sound cards, network cards, SCSI cards, and even hard disks.

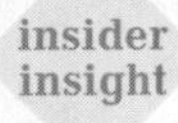

To learn more about PCMCIA (the association) and PC Card specifications, point your favorite Web browser to `www.pcmcia.org/faq.htm`**. For information about PCMCIA support in Linux, visit the Linux PCMCIA Information page at** `http://pcmcia-cs.sourceforge.net/`.

PC Card Physical Specifications

PC Cards are divided into three different classifications, according to the thickness of the card. Following are the standard physical dimensions for each type of PC Card, in terms of width by length by thickness:

- **Type I PC Card:** 54 mm by 85.6 mm by 3.3 mm
- **Type II PC Card:** 54 mm by 85.6 mm by 5 mm
- **Type III PC Card:** 54 mm by 85.6 mm by 10.5 mm

All three types of PC Cards have the same length and width—the size of a standard credit card, except that credit card corners are rounded. The cards, however, are thicker than credit cards, and the card types are differentiated by thickness.

The term *form factor* is often used to refer to the dimensions of PC Cards.

All PC Cards use the same 68-pin connector. Because of this connector, a thinner card (Type I, for example) can be used in a thicker slot (Type II, for example). As you might guess, a thicker card cannot be used in a thinner slot because you cannot physically insert a thick card into a thin slot.

Typical PC Card Applications

Each type of PC Card is used for a specific type of application. Following are the typical applications of PC Cards, by card type:

- **Type I PC Card:** These thin cards are used for memory devices, such as static RAM (SRAM) and flash RAM.
- **Type II PC Card:** These cards are used for input and output (I/O) devices, such as fax/modems, network adapters, and sound cards.
- **Type III PC Card:** These cards are used for devices that need the added thickness, such as hard disks with rotating components (hard to believe, isn't it?).

A PC Card can have a maximum length of 135.6 mm (slightly longer than 5.25 inches), meaning the card can extend outside the host. Such extended cards are used for devices such as removable media, transceivers, and antennas.

PCMCIA Standards

All these specifications are described in the PCMCIA Standard, of which there have been three major releases:

- **PCMCIA Standard Release 1.0 (June 1990):** The initial standard defined the 68-pin connector and Type I and Type II PC Cards. This standard also defined the Card Information Structure (CIS) that has been the basis for interoperability of PC Cards. The first release of the PCMCIA Standard did not account for any I/O cards; only memory cards were considered.
- **PCMCIA Standard Release 2.0, 2.01, 2.1 (1991–94):** The second release of the standard defined an I/O interface for the 68-pin connector. Release 2.01 added the PC Card AT Attachment (ATA) specification and provided an initial version of the Card and Socket Services (CSS) Specification. Release 2.1 further enhanced the CSS Specification.
- **PC Card Standard (February 1995):** The current release of the standard has a new name: it is called the *PC Card Standard*, instead of the PCMCIA Standard. This release of the standard adds information to improve compatibility among different types of PC Cards and includes support for features such as 3.3-volt operation, DMA support, and 32-bit CardBus bus mastering.

PC Card Terminology

As all laptop vendors have adopted PC Card slots, the PC Card market has experienced explosive growth. Thanks to the PCMCIA Standards, the PC Card devices can be used in any PC Card slot. As you use PC Cards, you'll run into some special terms, including the following:

- **Card information structure (CIS):** Describes the characteristics and capabilities of a PC Card, so that the operating system or driver software can configure the card.
- **CardBus:** An electrical specification that describes the use of 32-bit bus mastering technology and enables PC Cards to operate at up to 33 MHz.
- **Direct Memory Access (DMA):** Has the same meaning as in other peripherals; now PC Cards can use DMA technology.
- **Execute in Place (XIP):** Enables operating-system and application software to run directly from the PC Card without having to be loaded into the system's RAM, which eliminates the need for too much system RAM.
- **Low-voltage operation:** The ability of PC Cards to operate at 3.3 volts (as well as at 5 volts). The connector has a physical key to ensure that you do not inadvertently insert a 3.3-volt card into a 5-volt slot.
- **Multifunction capability:** Enables a PC Card to support several functions. 3Com's 3C562, for example, is a 10Base-T Ethernet card and a 28,800-bps modem in a Type II form-factor PC Card.
- **Plug and Play:** Enables you to insert or remove a PC Card while the system is turned on (this is known as *hot-swapping*). You can hot-swap PC Cards by

making the power-connection pins the longest, so that the data lines disconnect before the power.

- **Power management:** The capability of PC Cards to interface with the Advanced Power Management (APM) capabilities of laptops through the Card Services Specification.
- **Zoomed video (ZV):** A connection between a PC Card and the system's video controller that enables the card to write video data directly to the video controller.

PCMCIA Card Services for Linux

The standardization of PC Cards means Linux developers can get their hands on the programming information they need to write device drivers for PC Cards. In particular, the Card Services Specification provides an application programming interface (API) that's independent of the hardware that controls the PC Card sockets — the receptacles or slots for PC Cards.

The Socket Services Specification, a related specification, also provides an API that enables software applications to access the hardware that controls the sockets for PC Cards.

You do not have to learn about the PC Card and Socket Services APIs. David Hinds has already done the work in his PCMCIA Card Services for Linux, a software package that you can use to access PC Card devices under Linux. All you need to do is turn on the PCMCIA support when you need it.

Activating Card Services

PCMCIA Card Services software will be installed on your system when you install Linux. The PCMCIA software is in the `pcmcia-cs` RPM.

Assuming that PCMCIA support is installed, the following files control the activation of the Card Services:

- `/etc/init.d/pcmcia` is the shell script that starts the PCMCIA Card Services. Essentially, the command `/etc/init.d/pcmcia start` (or `service pcmcia start`) activates the Card Services when you boot the system. The script loads the appropriate PCMCIA driver modules by using the `modprobe` command. Then the script runs the `/sbin/cardmgr` program, which handles all card-insertion and card-removal events. Running the `cardmgr` program enables you to hot-swap PC Cards so that you can insert or eject a card at any time. To stop Card Services, type **/etc/init.d/pcmcia stop** or **service pcmcia stop**.
- `/etc/sysconfig/pcmcia` contains a number of variables the `/etc/init.d/pcmcia` script uses. In particular, the Card Services are not activated unless the line `PCMCIA=yes` appears in the `/etc/sysconfig/pcmcia` file. Lines such as the following specify the name of the PC Card Interface Controller (PCIC) as well as any options that the PCIC may need:

  ```
  PCMCIA=yes
  PCIC=yenta_socket
  PCIC_OPTS=
  CORE_OPTS=
  ```

  If your system does not have any PCMCIA interface, you will find the line `PCMCIA=no` in the `/etc/sysconfig/pcmcia` file.

You can activate the Card Services at system startup by ensuring that the line `PCMCIA=yes` appears in the `/etc/sysconfig/pcmcia` file. Of course, you want to do this only if your PC has a PCMCIA slot (most laptop PCs do).

Using the cardctl Program

If you have PCMCIA Card Services running, you can use the `/sbin/cardctl` program to monitor and control a PCMCIA socket. To view the status of a PCMCIA slot, type:

```
/sbin/cardctl status
```

The output should show the current socket-status flags.

The `cardctl` program takes many more arguments. With different arguments, you can suspend a card, resume it, or view the configuration parameters, such as interrupts and configuration registers. To learn more about `cardctl` from the online manual, type **man cardctl** to view the manual page.

Using Supported PC Cards

In the PCMCIA Card Services documentation directory, you'll find a file named `SUPPORTED.CARDS`. (You can change to that directory by typing **cd /usr/share/doc/pcmcia***.) That file lists some of the PCMCIA Cards that are known to work with at least one system. The same list is available online at `http://pcmcia-cs.sourceforge.net/ftp/SUPPORTED.CARDS`. You can also read about the various types of supported cards at `www.pcmcia.org/faq.htm#devices`.

The list of supported cards has become too numerous to include here. Some of the common categories of cards supported by the Card Services are as follows:

- **Ethernet cards:** More than one hundred different models of Ethernet cards are supported, including popular models such as 3Com 3c589/B/C/D; and Xircom CreditCard CE2, CE IIps, and RE-10.
- **Fast Ethernet (10/100BASET) cards:** Over 70 cards are supported, including 3Com 3c574TX, 3c575TX, 3CCFE575B, and 3CXFE575B; Linksys EtherFast 10/100; NetGear FA410TXC and FA411; and Xircom CreditCard CE3-100, CE3B, RE-100, R2E-100BTX, and XE2000.
- **Token Ring cards:** IBM Token Ring Adapter and 3Com 3c689 TokenLink Velocity and Tokenlink III cards are supported.
- **Wireless network cards:** Over 50 cards are supported, including Lucent Orinoco WaveLAN/IEEE 802.11b; Dell TrueMobile 1150 Series; D-Link DE-650, DE-660, and DWL-650; Intel EtherExpress PRO/100 Mobile Adapter; Linksys WPC11; and Xircom CreditCard Netwave.
- **Modem and serial cards:** All modem and serial-port cards should work. The only exceptions are modems such as Compaq 192, New Media WinSurfer, Megahertz XJ/CC2560, 3Com 3CXM356/3CCM356 and 3CXM656/3CCM656, and other WinModems that require special Windows drivers. The Trimble Mobile GPS card is supported through the serial/modem driver.
- **Memory cards:** All static RAM (SRAM) memory cards should work.
- **SCSI adapter cards:** Over 30 different models of SCSI cards are supported, including models such as Adaptec APA-1460, APA-1460A, APA-1450A, and

APA-1460B SlimSCSI; IBM SCSI; Iomega Zip and Jaz Cards; NEC PC-9801N-J03R; and Toshiba NWB0107ABK and SCSC200B.

- **ATA/IDE disk drive cards:** All ATA/IDE disk-drive PC Cards are supported.
- **ATA/IDE CD-ROM and DVD adapter cards:** Many ATA/IDE CD-ROM and DVD adapters are supported, including Argosy EIDE CD-ROM, Caravelle CD-36N, Creative Technology CD-ROM, IBM Max 20X CD-ROM, Sony PCGA-CD5 CD-ROM, Digital Mobile Media CD-ROM, some EXP models, and several IO-DATA models.
- **IEEE 1394 (FireWire) cards:** A number of cards are supported, including Belkin F5U512, Orange Micro OrangeLink, and Western Digital 1394 Adapter.
- **Multifunction cards:** —Over 30 multifunction Ethernet/Modem cards are supported, including 3Com 3c562, 3c562B/C/D, and 3c563B/C/D; IBM Home and Away Card; Linksys LANmodem 28.8, 33.6; Intel EtherExpress PRO/100 CardBus LAN/Modem; Megahertz EM1144, EM3288, and EM3336; Motorola Mariner and Marquis; Ositech Jack of Diamonds; and Xircom CreditCard CEM28, CEM33, CEM56 models.

Further Reading

To learn more about the PCMCIA Card Services software, consult the PCMCIA-HOWTO. To read this HOWTO document, type **cd /usr/share/doc/pcmcia*** to change to the directory where that HOWTO file is located. (If you cannot find the file, type **locate PCMCIA-HOWTO** to find it.) Then, type **more PCMCIA-HOWTO** to view the PCMCIA-HOWTO file. This file contains the latest information about the Card Services software, including common problems and suggested fixes. (You can also read the PCMCIA-HOWTO online at `www.tldp.org/HOWTO/PCMCIA-HOWTO.html`.)

In particular, you should look through the PCMCIA-HOWTO file for any information that applies to your specific PC Card.

Linux Resources

This appendix lists some resources where you can get more information about specific topics. Most of the resources are on the Internet because that's where you can get the latest information on Linux. Often, you'll be able to download the files necessary for a specific task.

Some Internet resources appear in the standard Uniform Resource Locator (URL) syntax — Chapter 14 explains URLs. If you have used a Web browser, you are probably already familiar with URLs.

Instead of providing a long listing of URLs, this appendix describes a few key websites you can use as a starting point for your search.

Web Pages

If you browse the Internet, you may notice that there are quite a few Web pages with Linux-related information. A good starting point for locating information about Fedora Linux is the Fedora Project home page at:

```
http://fedora.redhat.com/
```

You can click the buttons to access more information about the topic that button's label identifies. At this page, you also find an organized collection of information about Fedora.

For another good guide to Fedora with lots of useful tips, consult the unofficial Fedora FAQ at:

```
www.fedorafaq.org/
```

To browse recent news about Linux, visit the Linux Resources page at:

```
www.linuxjournal.com/xstatic/community
```

Specialized Systems Consultants, Inc. (SSC), the publisher of *Linux Journal*, maintains this page. You can scan the articles in the latest issue of *Linux Journal* and find out other information, such as the latest version of the kernel and links to other Linux resources.

Another popular and definitive source of Linux information is the home page of The Linux Documentation Project (LDP):

```
www.tldp.org/
```

On this website, you can find many more pointers to other Linux resources on the Internet. In particular, you can browse and download the latest HOWTO documents from this website:

```
www.tldp.org/HOWTO/HOWTO-INDEX/howtos.html.
```

For older Fedora and Red Hat Linux distributions you can continue to get security and bug fix packages from the Fedora Legacy Project. To learn more about the Fedora Legacy Project and make use of their services, visit:

```
http://fedoralegacy.org/
```

The Fedora Legacy Project is a community-supported open source project whose goal is to enable a longer life for Fedora and Red Hat Linux distributions. Although it's not a Red Hat project, Red Hat provides some support for the Fedora Legacy project.

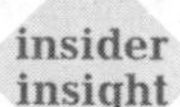

If you are interested in open source development, including Linux, a good resource is the SourceForge.net website at `http://sourceforge.net/`.

Newsgroups

To keep up with Linux developments, you need access to the Internet, especially to the newsgroups. You can find discussions on specific Linux-related topics in the newsgroups listed in Table G-1.

Table G-1: Linux Newsgroups on the Internet

Newsgroup	*Provides the Following*
`comp.os.linux.admin`	Information about Linux system administration.
`comp.os.linux.advocacy`	Discussions about promoting Linux.
`comp.os.linux.announce`	Important announcements about Linux. (This is a moderated newsgroup, which means you must mail an article to the moderator, who then posts it to the newsgroup.)

Newsgroup	Provides the Following
comp.os.linux.answers	Questions and answers about Linux. (All the Linux HOWTOs are posted in this moderated newsgroup.)
comp.os.linux.development	Current Linux development work.
comp.os.linux.development.apps	Linux application development.
comp.os.linux.development.system	Linux operating system development.
comp.os.linux.hardware	Discussions about Linux and various hardware.
comp.os.linux.help	Help with various aspects of Linux.
comp.os.linux.misc	Miscellaneous topics about Linux.
comp.os.linux.networking	Networking under Linux.
comp.os.linux.redhat	Discussions about Red Hat's Linux products.
comp.os.linux.setup	Linux setup and installation.
comp.os.linux.x	Discussions about setting up and running the X Window System under Linux.
linux.redhat	Discussions about Red Hat's Linux products.

You can typically use a Web browser or a special newsreader such as KNode to read the newsgroups. To read a newsgroup in a Web browser, use a URL of the form news://*my.newsserver.com*/*newsgroup*, in which *my.newsserver.com* is the fully qualified domain name of your news server (your Internet service provider should give you this name), and *newsgroup* is the name of the newsgroup you want to read. For example, assuming that your news server is *news.myisp.net*, you can browse the comp.os.linux.setup newsgroup by typing the following URL in the Location field of the Netscape Web browser:

```
news://news.myisp.net/comp.os.linux.setup
```

note

You can also use the Google Groups page at http://groups.google.com/ **to search for specific items in the** comp.os.linux **newsgroups or browse that newsgroup.**

Fedora Download Sites

You can download Fedora Linux and other Linux distributions from one of several servers around the world. In addition to the Fedora Core distribution itself, these sites also contain many other software packages that run under Linux.

For the latest list of Fedora download sites worldwide, visit the following Web page maintained by the Fedora Project:

```
http://fedora.redhat.com/download/mirrors.html
```

This page displays a list of URLs of sites that maintain the Fedora distribution for downloading. You can click a link near your geographical location and then locate what you want to download. You can download CD or DVD ISO image files or individual RPM files.

cross ref

Appendix H explains how to download the latest ISO images of Fedora and burn a DVD that you can use to install Fedora Linux.

Magazines

Linux Journal is a monthly magazine devoted entirely to Linux. On the Web, the magazine's home page can be found at `www.linuxjournal.com/`. There, you can find information about how to subscribe.

Linux Magazine is another monthly magazine that covers everything about Linux. Visit its home page at `www.linux-mag.com/` to learn more about the magazine and to how to subscribe.

Fedora Upgrade Procedure

Fedora Project releases new versions of Fedora quite frequently, so the chances are good that there might be a newer version available than what's on this book's DVD. There is no need to despair, however. Nearly everything in this book (except perhaps the screen shots) should apply to the new version of Fedora. All you need is a DVD (or multiple CDs) containing the latest Fedora distribution to upgrade your system. That's easy to do provided you have a DVD or CD recorder. This appendix shows you how to download Fedora DVD or CD ISO image files and burn your own DVD or CD.

I have organized the instructions into two separate projects. The first project shows you how to join BitTorrent and help the community get its Fedora download while you get yours as well. In the second project, you find out how to burn the DVD from the downloaded ISO images. If you don't have a DVD burner, you can download the CD ISO files and burn CDs instead.

cross ref

After you download and burn a new Fedora DVD, turn to Chapter 2 and follow the installation instructions in that chapter. Even though the screen shots may not match, the installation steps remain about the same from one version of Fedora to the next.

Downloading Fedora Using BitTorrent

BitTorrent is a protocol for distributing files. You don't really need to understand the protocol to use BitTorrent. All you need to know is that as you download a file, your machine also uploads the file to others who want the same file. So you are not just taking something; you are also giving something back — you are helping others get that file without overloading the server from which you started getting the file. That communal spirit of sharing in an equitable manner is what makes BitTorrent an appealing way to distribute software such as Fedora Core. In fact, once you try it, you'll find that it's easier to download Fedora Core by joining the BitTorrent than getting it through FTP from a central server. You do have to do a few things before you can start using BitTorrent. It's a neat little project to download the CD or DVD image of Fedora Core and burn the DVD (or CDs). The first step is to join the BitTorrent and download the necessary files.

insider insight

If you do not want to use BitTorrent and want to download Fedora ISO files using FTP or HTTP, visit `http://fedora.redhat.com/download/mirrors.html` and click a link for a site near your geographical location. Then you can locate the ISO image file for the latest version of Fedora and download it through the Web browser. After downloading the ISO image, skip to the "Burning the Fedora Core DVD" section.

Things You Need

Here's what you need to join the BitTorrent:

- A PC running Linux (this can be an older Fedora system)—you use this system to run the BitTorrent client and download the Fedora DVD or CD image. If you are running Microsoft Windows on your PC, you can still use BitTorrent; just check out the information at `www.bittorrent.com/`. In fact, if you have not yet installed any Linux, you should download the Windows client for BitTorrent and use that.
- Python version 2.2 or later already installed on your Linux system. If you want to use the BitTorrent GUI, you also need Python 2.3, GTK 2.2 or greater, and pygtk 2.4 or greater. For Windows systems, all you need is the EXE file offered at the BitTorrent site.
- A connection to the Internet, the higher the bandwidth the better.

Steps to Follow

You have three high-level steps to complete:

1. Download and install the BitTorrent client software on your system.
2. Adjust your system's firewall settings to open up TCP ports 6881 through 6999 that are used by BitTorrent to send files to others.
3. Run the BitTorrent client to start the file transfers.

I describe these three high-level steps in detail in the following sections.

Download and Install the BitTorrent Client

Make sure your system's Internet connection is up. Then follow these steps:

1. Run the Web browser and visit `www.bittorrent.com/` and click the Linux RPM link to download the BitTorrent software. Save the downloaded RPM file in a directory on your system and make note of where you saved it.
2. Open a terminal window and change the directory to where you saved the BitTorrent RPM file and then install the BitTorrent software. Type the following command to install BitTorrent:

```
rpm -ivh BitTorrent*.rpm
```

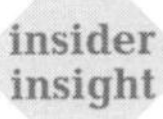

If your Linux system is running a different version of Python from what the BitTorrent RPM assumes, then you must also set up a symbolic link for the BitTorrent package. First, type **rpm -q python** and make note of your system's Python version. Now type **rpm -qpl BitTorrent* | more** and see the Python version in the listed filenames. For example, if BitTorrent is using Python version 2.3, you see `/usr/lib/python2.3` in the filenames. If your system is using Python 2.4, then type the following commands to set up the symbolic link:

```
cd /usr/lib/python2.4/site-packages

ln -s /usr/lib/python2.3/site-packages/BitTorrent BitTorrent
```

If you do not perform this step, the BitTorrent download command fails with an error message saying that it cannot find any BitTorrent modules.

For Windows systems, click the Windows Client link at `www.bittorrent.com/` and run the downloaded EXE file to install BitTorrent.

Open Incoming TCP Ports Used by BitTorrent

Typically, your system runs a firewall that restricts access to many of the ports. BitTorrent, however, requires that you open up the TCP ports numbered 6881 through 6999 so that other BitTorrent clients can contact your system and request uploads. To open TCP ports 6881 through 6999, type the following command in a terminal window:

```
iptables -I RH-Firewall-1-INPUT --protocol tcp --dport 6881:6899 -i eth0 -j
ACCEPT
```

This command assumes that your system connects to the Internet through its Ethernet interface and that interface is eth0 (the first Ethernet card). Change eth0 to the name of the external network interface of your system. For example, if it's the second Ethernet card, the interface is eth1. For a dial-up PPP connection, the interface is ppp0.

Start BitTorrent Transfers

To download using BitTorrent, you have to run the BitTorrent client. You use a URL to identify the *torrent*, which refers to the collection of files that you want to download. The URL also identifies the tracker — the server that hooks up your system's BitTorrent client with others that can provide parts of the files you want. In turn, the tracker also lets other clients begin requesting the torrent from your system.

On Windows systems, open a Web browser and visit `http://torrent.dulug.duke.edu`. You'll see a list of ISO image files for different Fedora distributions. Find and click the link for the latest distribution and the format (DVD or multiple CDs) that you want. That starts the BitTorrent client and gets the download going.

On Linux systems, you can use a command-line client to start the BitTorrent download. Type the following command where *`tfile`* is the name of the torrent file that you want:

```
btdownloadcurses.py --url http://torrent.dulug.duke.edu/tfile
```

For example, to download the Fedora Core 4 test 3 DVD ISO image for i386 systems — provided in a torrent named `FC4-test3-DVD-i386.torrent` — I type the following command:

```
btdownloadcurses.py --url http://torrent.dulug.duke.edu/FC4-test3-DVD-
i386.torrent
```

A text screen shows you the status of the BitTorrent download as well as any uploads that are going on at the same time.

note After BitTorrent finishes the download, leave the BitTorrent client running for as long as possible. This time enables your system to provide the file to others who are also joining BitTorrent. After all, this sharing is what makes BitTorrent such an efficient way to distribute files.

Burning the Fedora Core DVD

Typically, the binary Fedora Core distribution takes four CDs, but a single DVD with its 4.7GB capacity can easily hold all 2.5GB of binary files. The DVD even has room for all the source files. (By the way, that's why my publisher bundles a Fedora Core DVD with this book.)

note A word of caution about DVD capacity — when marketing people talk about the 4.7GB capacity of a DVD, they mean 4,700,000,000 bytes. However, for technology purists, that number translates to about 4,482MB or only 4.377GB because 1,024 bytes are in each KB and 1,024 × 1,024 = 1,048,576 bytes in a MB, and so on. The bottom line is that you can fit only about 4,482MB of data onto a DVD.

If you want to burn your own Fedora Core DVD, it's easy enough to do, provided you have a DVD recorder. This project guides you through the steps in burning a Fedora Core DVD.

Things You Need

Here's what you need to burn the Fedora Core DVD:

- A PC running Red Hat or Fedora Linux. Note that you need Linux kernel version 2.4 or higher so that you can create a DVD ISO file that's larger than 2GB.
- An internal or external DVD recorder.
- Blank DVD recordable media in a format compatible with your DVD recorder — the media can be one of DVD-R, DVD-RW, DVD+R, or DVD+RW.
- The downloaded Fedora Core DVD ISO file. If you have not done so already, complete the BitTorrent project and download the Fedora Core DVD ISO image.

Burn the DVD ISO File onto DVD Media

I explain the step assuming that the DVD ISO file is named `fedora-core-dvd.iso`. When you burn the DVD, use the name of the ISO image file you downloaded with BitTorrent. Follow these steps to burn the DVD ISO file onto the DVD:

1. Use the cd command to change the current directory to where the DVD ISO file is located.
2. Place a blank DVD media into the DVD recorder.
3. Type the following growisofs command to start burning the DVD:

   ```
   growisofs -dvd-compat -Z /dev/scd0=fedora-core-dvd.iso
   ```

   Remember to change the DVD recorder device name from /dev/scd0 to whatever is appropriate for your PC's DVD recorder. Use the /dev/scd0 device name for an external DVD recorder. For internal DVD recorders, use /dev/hdc as the device name.

Label the DVD with the Fedora version number and follow the instructions in Chapter 2 to install the latest Fedora from the DVD.

About the DVD-ROM

The companion DVD-ROM contains Fedora Core 4 with the Linux 2.6.11 kernel, which is the latest version of Linux available as of this writing. Linux is a complete UNIX-like operating system for your PC. The Fedora Linux distribution includes over 2GB of files. The companion DVD, which accompanies this book, contains the Fedora Linux software — both binary files as well as all the source code. By installing Linux on a PC, you can turn that PC into a full-fledged UNIX workstation.

note

Please note that the software contained in the DVD-ROM is distributed under a variety of license agreements. Some of the software (such as the Linux kernel) is distributed in full source and binary format under the GNU General Public License. In all cases, the software is copyrighted by the respective authors. After installing Fedora Linux, you should consult the `README.*` files (or files with names such as `COPYING` and `COPYRIGHT`) in various subdirectories of the `/usr/share/doc` directory for information on the licensing terms for each software package.

This appendix provides you with information on the contents of the DVD-ROM that accompanies this book. (For late-breaking information, please see the `README-en` and `RELEASE-NOTES-en` files located at the root of the DVD-ROM.) Here is what you'll find in this appendix:

- System requirements
- DVD-ROM installation instructions
- What's on the DVD-ROM
- Troubleshooting

System Requirements

Make sure that your computer meets the minimum system requirements listed in this section. If your computer doesn't match up to most of these requirements, you may have a problem using the contents of the DVD-ROM.

- A PC with a Pentium processor running at 400 MHz or faster for graphical installation
- At least 192MB of total RAM for graphical installation (256MB recommended)
- At least 5GB of free space on your hard drive
- A DVD-ROM drive
- Ethernet network interface card (NIC) or modem with a speed of at least 56 Kbps

DVD-ROM Installation Instructions

To install the Fedora Linux distribution from the companion DVD, follow these steps. (Consult Chapter 2 for details.)

1. Gather information about your PC's hardware, such as the graphics card, network card, and SCSI card before you install Linux.
2. Use a partitioning program such as PartitionMagic to create room on your hard drive for Linux by reducing the size of the existing Windows partition. Skip this step if you plan to use Linux as the sole operating system or if you plan to install Linux on an empty second hard drive.
3. Boot your PC from the DVD-ROM. This procedure automatically runs the Fedora Linux installer. From this point on, you must respond to a number of dialog boxes as the installer takes you through the steps. Here are some of the key installation steps:
   - Let the installer automatically create partitions for Linux by using the free space you created by shrinking the existing Windows partition.
   - Configure the Ethernet network, if any. Typically, you configure the network automatically by using DHCP.
   - Specify the local time zone and set the root password.
   - Install the GRUB boot loader program on your hard disk's master boot record (MBR) so that you can boot Linux when you power up your PC after shutting it down.
   - Select the specific software package groups that you want to install, such as the X Window System, the GNOME Desktop Environment, and Open Office.org.

To install specific items from the DVD-ROM to your hard drive, follow these steps:

1. Log in as `root`.
2. Insert the DVD-ROM into your computer's DVD drive.
3. If you are using GNOME or KDE GUI, wait for the DVD to mount. Otherwise, open a terminal window and at the command prompt type (if you are using a DVD recorder, change `/media/cdrom` to `/media/cdrecorder`):

   ```
   mount /media/cdrom
   ```

4. Browse the DVD-ROM and follow the instructions in Chapter 21 to install individual software packages either by using the `rpm` command or the GUI Package Management tool accessible from the GNOME desktop by selecting Desktop ⇨ System Settings ⇨ Add/Remove Applications.
5. To remove the DVD-ROM from your DVD-ROM drive, type the following command in a terminal window:

   ```
   umount /mnt/cdrom
   ```

   You can also right-click on the DVD-ROM icon on the desktop and choose Eject from the selections. This will unmount your DVD-ROM and eject it.

What's on the DVD-ROM

You can find the following software on the Fedora Core 4 DVD-ROM:

- Linux kernel 2.6.11 with driver modules for all major PC hardware configurations, including IDE/ATA and SCSI drives, PCMCIA devices, and CD-ROMs
- A complete set of installation and configuration tools for setting up devices and services
- A graphical user interface based on the X.Org X11 6.8.2 package, with GNOME 2.10 and KDE 3.4.0 graphical desktops
- Full TCP/IP networking for Internet, LANs, and intranets
- Tools for connecting your PC to your Internet service provider (ISP) using DSL, cable modem, or dial-up serial communications programs
- A complete suite of Internet applications, including electronic mail (sendmail and mail), news (inn), SSH, FTP, DNS, and NFS
- Apache HTTPD (Web) server 2.0.54, to turn your PC into a Web server; and Mozilla Firefox 1.0.4, to surf the Net
- Evolution 2.2.2 email and calendar application
- OpenOffice.org 1.9 office suite with word processor, spreadsheet, presentation software, and more
- Samba 3.0.14a LAN Manager software for Microsoft Windows connectivity and to incorporate Linux systems into a Windows network
- Several text editors (for example, GNU Emacs 21.4; vim)
- Graphics and image manipulation software, such as the GIMP, XPaint, Xfig, Gnuplot, Ghostscript, Ghostview, and ImageMagick
- Programming languages (GNU C and C++ 4.0.0, Perl 5.8.6, PHP 5.0.4, Tcl/Tk 8.4.9, Python 2.4.1, GNU AWK 3.1.4), and software development tools (GNU Debugger 6.3, CVS 1.11.19, RCS 5.7, GNU Bison 2.0, flex 2.5.4a, and TIFF and JPEG libraries)
- Support for industry standard Executable and Linking Format (ELF) and Intel Binary Compatibility Specification (iBCS)
- A complete suite of standard UNIX utilities from the GNU project
- Tools to access and use DOS files and applications (mtools 3.9.9)
- Text-formatting and typesetting software (DocBook, groff, TeX, and LaTeX)

Troubleshooting

If you have difficulty installing or using any of the materials on the companion DVD-ROM, consult the detailed installation and troubleshooting instructions in Chapter 2.

If you still have trouble with the DVD-ROM, please call the Wiley Product Technical Support phone number: (800) 762-2974. Outside the United States, call (317) 572-3994. You can also contact Wiley Product Technical Support through the Internet at `www.wiley.com/techsupport`. Wiley Publishing will provide technical support only for installation and other general quality control items; for technical support on the applications themselves, consult the program's vendor or author.

To place additional orders or to request information about other Wiley products, please call (800) 225-5945.

Index

Symbols and Numerics

A

continued

B

C

continued

E

F

H

J

K

continued

L

M

N

O

continued

continued

Q

R

continued

T

U

V

W

X

Y

Z

Wiley Publishing, Inc.
End-User License Agreement

READ THIS. You should carefully read these terms and conditions before opening the software packet(s) included with this book "Book". This is a license agreement "Agreement" between you and Wiley Publishing, Inc. "WPI". By opening the accompanying software packet(s), you acknowledge that you have read and accept the following terms and conditions. If you do not agree and do not want to be bound by such terms and conditions, promptly return the Book and the unopened software packet(s) to the place you obtained them for a full refund.

1. **License Grant.** WPI grants to you (either an individual or entity) a nonexclusive license to use one copy of the enclosed software program(s) (collectively, the "Software") solely for your own personal or business purposes on a single computer (whether a standard computer or a workstation component of a multi-user network). The Software is in use on a computer when it is loaded into temporary memory (RAM) or installed into permanent memory (hard disk, CD-ROM, or other storage device). WPI reserves all rights not expressly granted herein.
2. **Ownership.** WPI is the owner of all right, title, and interest, including copyright, in and to the compilation of the Software recorded on the disk(s), CD-ROM or DVD "Software Media". Copyright to the individual programs recorded on the Software Media is owned by the author or other authorized copyright owner of each program. Ownership of the Software and all proprietary rights relating thereto remain with WPI and its licensers.
3. **Restrictions on Use and Transfer.**
   - **(a)** You may only (i) make one copy of the Software for backup or archival purposes, or (ii) transfer the Software to a single hard disk, provided that you keep the original for backup or archival purposes. You may not (i) rent or lease the Software, (ii) copy or reproduce the Software through a LAN or other network system or through any computer subscriber system or bulletin-board system, or (iii) modify, adapt, or create derivative works based on the Software.
   - **(b)** You may not reverse engineer, decompile, or disassemble the Software. You may transfer the Software and user documentation on a permanent basis, provided that the transferee agrees to accept the terms and conditions of this Agreement and you retain no copies. If the Software is an update or has been updated, any transfer must include the most recent update and all prior versions.
4. **Restrictions on Use of Individual Programs.** You must follow the individual requirements and restrictions detailed for each individual program in the About the DVD appendix of this Book. These limitations are also contained in the individual license agreements recorded on the Software Media. These limitations may include a requirement that after using the program for a specified period of time, the user must pay a registration fee or discontinue use. By opening the Software packet(s), you will be agreeing to abide by the licenses and restrictions for these individual programs that are detailed in the About the DVD appendix and on the Software Media. None of the material on this Software Media or listed in this Book may ever be redistributed, in original or modified form, for commercial purposes.

5. **Limited Warranty.**
   - **(a)** WPI warrants that the Software and Software Media are free from defects in materials and workmanship under normal use for a period of sixty (60) days from the date of purchase of this Book. If WPI receives notification within the warranty period of defects in materials or workmanship, WPI will replace the defective Software Media.
   - **(b)** WPI AND THE AUTHOR OF THE BOOK DISCLAIM ALL OTHER WARRANTIES, EXPRESS OR IMPLIED, INCLUDING WITHOUT LIMITATION IMPLIED WARRANTIES OF MERCHANTABILITY AND FITNESS FOR A PARTICULAR PURPOSE, WITH RESPECT TO THE SOFTWARE, THE PROGRAMS, THE SOURCE CODE CONTAINED THEREIN, AND/OR THE TECHNIQUES DESCRIBED IN THIS BOOK. WPI DOES NOT WARRANT THAT THE FUNCTIONS CONTAINED IN THE SOFTWARE WILL MEET YOUR REQUIREMENTS OR THAT THE OPERATION OF THE SOFTWARE WILL BE ERROR FREE.
   - **(c)** This limited warranty gives you specific legal rights, and you may have other rights that vary from jurisdiction to jurisdiction.
6. **Remedies.**
   - **(a)** WPI's entire liability and your exclusive remedy for defects in materials and workmanship shall be limited to replacement of the Software Media, which may be returned to WPI with a copy of your receipt at the following address: Software Media Fulfillment Department, Attn.: RED HAT FEDORA LINUX SECRETS, Wiley Publishing, Inc., 10475 Crosspoint Blvd., Indianapolis, IN 46256, or call 1-800-762-2974. Please allow four to six weeks for delivery. This Limited Warranty is void if failure of the Software Media has resulted from accident, abuse, or misapplication. Any replacement Software Media will be warranted for the remainder of the original warranty period or thirty (30) days, whichever is longer.
   - **(b)** In no event shall WPI or the author be liable for any damages whatsoever (including without limitation damages for loss of business profits, business interruption, loss of business information, or any other pecuniary loss) arising from the use of or inability to use the Book or the Software, even if WPI has been advised of the possibility of such damages.
   - **(c)** Because some jurisdictions do not allow the exclusion or limitation of liability for consequential or incidental damages, the above limitation or exclusion may not apply to you.
7. **U.S. Government Restricted Rights.** Use, duplication, or disclosure of the Software for or on behalf of the United States of America, its agencies and/or instrumentalities "U.S. Government" is subject to restrictions as stated in paragraph (c)(1)(ii) of the Rights in Technical Data and Computer Software clause of DFARS 252.227-7013, or subparagraphs (c) (1) and (2) of the Commercial Computer Software - Restricted Rights clause at FAR 52.227-19, and in similar clauses in the NASA FAR supplement, as applicable.
8. **General.** This Agreement constitutes the entire understanding of the parties and revokes and supersedes all prior agreements, oral or written, between them and may not be modified or amended except in a writing signed by both parties hereto that specifically refers to this Agreement. This Agreement shall take precedence over any other documents that may be in conflict herewith. If any one or more provisions contained in this Agreement are held by any court or tribunal to be invalid, illegal, or otherwise unenforceable, each and every other provision shall remain in full force and effect.

GNU General Public License

Version 2, June 1991

Preamble

The licenses for most software are designed to take away your freedom to share and change it. By contrast, the GNU General Public License is intended to guarantee your freedom to share and change free software—to make sure the software is free for all its users. This General Public License applies to most of the Free Software Foundation's software and to any other program whose authors commit to using it. (Some other Free Software Foundation software is covered by the GNU Library General Public License instead.) You can apply it to your programs, too.

When we speak of free software, we are referring to freedom, not price. Our General Public Licenses are designed to make sure that you have the freedom to distribute copies of free software (and charge for this service if you wish), that you receive source code or can get it if you want it, that you can change the software or use pieces of it in new free programs; and that you know you can do these things.

To protect your rights, we need to make restrictions that forbid anyone to deny you these rights or to ask you to surrender the rights. These restrictions translate to certain responsibilities for you if you distribute copies of the software, or if you modify it.

For example, if you distribute copies of such a program, whether gratis or for a fee, you must give the recipients all the rights that you have. You must make sure that they, too, receive or can get the source code. And you must show them these terms so they know their rights.

We protect your rights with two steps: (1) copyright the software, and (2) offer you this license which gives you legal permission to copy, distribute and/or modify the software.

Also, for each author's protection and ours, we want to make certain that everyone understands that there is no warranty for this free software. If the software is modified by someone else and passed on, we want its recipients to know that what they have is not the original, so that any problems introduced by others will not reflect on the original authors' reputations.

Finally, any free program is threatened constantly by software patents. We wish to avoid the danger that redistributors of a free program will individually obtain patent licenses, in effect making the program proprietary. To prevent this, we have made it clear that any patent must be licensed for everyone's free use or not licensed at all.

The precise terms and conditions for copying, distribution and modification follow.

Terms and Conditions for Copying, Distribution and Modification

0. This License applies to any program or other work which contains a notice placed by the copyright holder saying it may be distributed under the terms of this General Public License. The "Program", below, refers to any such program or work, and a "work based on the Program" means either the Program or any derivative work under copyright law: that is to say, a work containing the Program or a portion of it, either verbatim or with modifications and/or translated into another language. (Hereinafter, translation is included without limitation in the term "modification".) Each licensee is addressed as "you".

Activities other than copying, distribution and modification are not covered by this License; they are outside its scope. The act of running the Program is not restricted, and the output from the Program is covered only if its contents constitute a work based on the Program (independent of having been made by running the Program). Whether that is true depends on what the Program does.

1. You may copy and distribute verbatim copies of the Program's source code as you receive it, in any medium, provided that you conspicuously and appropriately publish on each copy an appropriate copyright notice and disclaimer of warranty; keep intact all the notices that refer to this License and to the absence of any warranty; and give any other recipients of the Program a copy of this License along with the Program.

You may charge a fee for the physical act of transferring a copy, and you may at your option offer warranty protection in exchange for a fee.

2. You may modify your copy or copies of the Program or any portion of it, thus forming a work based on the Program, and copy and distribute such modifications or work under the terms of Section 1 above, provided that you also meet all of these conditions:

a) You must cause the modified files to carry prominent notices stating that you changed the files and the date of any change.

b) You must cause any work that you distribute or publish, that in whole or in part contains or is derived from the Program or any part thereof, to be licensed as a whole at no charge to all third parties under the terms of this License.

c) If the modified program normally reads commands interactively when run, you must cause it, when started running for such interactive use in the most ordinary way, to print or display an announcement including an appropriate copyright notice and a notice that there is no warranty (or else, saying that you provide a warranty) and that users may redistribute the program under these conditions, and telling the user how to view a copy of this License. (Exception: if the Program itself is interactive but does not normally print such an announcement, your work based on the Program is not required to print an announcement.)

These requirements apply to the modified work as a whole. If identifiable sections of that work are not derived from the Program, and can be reasonably considered independent and separate works in themselves, then this License, and its terms, do not apply to those sections when you distribute them as separate works. But when you distribute the same sections as part of a whole which is a work based on the Program, the distribution of the whole must be on the terms of this License, whose permissions for other licensees extend to the entire whole, and thus to each and every part regardless of who wrote it.

Thus, it is not the intent of this section to claim rights or contest your rights to work written entirely by you; rather, the intent is to exercise the right to control the distribution of derivative or collective works based on the Program.

In addition, mere aggregation of another work not based on the Program with the Program (or with a work based on the Program) on a volume of a storage or distribution medium does not bring the other work under the scope of this License.

3. You may copy and distribute the Program (or a work based on it, under Section 2) in object code or executable form under the terms of Sections 1 and 2 above provided that you also do one of the following:

   a) Accompany it with the complete corresponding machine-readable source code, which must be distributed under the terms of Sections 1 and 2 above on a medium customarily used for software interchange; or,

   b) Accompany it with a written offer, valid for at least three years, to give any third party, for a charge no more than your cost of physically performing source distribution, a complete machine-readable copy of the corresponding source code, to be distributed under the terms of Sections 1 and 2 above on a medium customarily used for software interchange; or,

   c) Accompany it with the information you received as to the offer to distribute corresponding source code. (This alternative is allowed only for noncommercial distribution and only if you received the program in object code or executable form with such an offer, in accord with Subsection b above.)

The source code for a work means the preferred form of the work for making modifications to it. For an executable work, complete source code means all the source code for all modules it contains, plus any associated interface definition files, plus the scripts used to control compilation and installation of the executable. However, as a special exception, the source code distributed need not include anything that is normally distributed (in either source or binary form) with the major components (compiler, kernel, and so on) of the operating system on which the executable runs, unless that component itself accompanies the executable.

If distribution of executable or object code is made by offering access to copy from a designated place, then offering equivalent access to copy the source code from the same place counts as distribution of the source code, even though third parties are not compelled to copy the source along with the object code.

4. You may not copy, modify, sublicense, or distribute the Program except as expressly provided under this License. Any attempt otherwise to copy, modify, sublicense or distribute the Program is void, and will automatically terminate your rights under this License. However, parties who have received copies, or rights, from you under this License will not have their licenses terminated so long as such parties remain in full compliance.

5. You are not required to accept this License, since you have not signed it. However, nothing else grants you permission to modify or distribute the Program or its derivative works. These actions are prohibited by law if you do not accept this License. Therefore, by modifying or distributing the Program (or any work based on the Program), you indicate your acceptance of this License to do so, and all its terms and conditions for copying, distributing or modifying the Program or works based on it.

6. Each time you redistribute the Program (or any work based on the Program), the recipient automatically receives a license from the original licensor to copy, distribute or modify the Program subject to these terms and conditions. You may not impose any further restrictions on the recipients' exercise of the rights granted herein. You are not responsible for enforcing compliance by third parties to this License.

7. If, as a consequence of a court judgment or allegation of patent infringement or for any other reason (not limited to patent issues), conditions are imposed on you (whether by court order, agreement or otherwise) that contradict the conditions of this License, they do not excuse you from the conditions of this License. If you cannot distribute so as to satisfy simultaneously your obligations under this License and any other pertinent obligations, then as a consequence you may not distribute the Program at all. For example, if a patent license would not permit royalty-free redistribution of the Program by all those who receive copies directly or indirectly through you, then the only way you could satisfy both it and this License would be to refrain entirely from distribution of the Program.

If any portion of this section is held invalid or unenforceable under any particular circumstance, the balance of the section is intended to apply and the section as a whole is intended to apply in other circumstances.

It is not the purpose of this section to induce you to infringe any patents or other property right claims or to contest validity of any such claims; this section has the sole purpose of protecting the integrity of the free software distribution system, which is implemented by public license practices. Many people have made generous contributions to the wide range of software distributed through that system in reliance on consistent application of that system; it is up to the author/donor to decide if he or she is willing to distribute software through any other system and a licensee cannot impose that choice.

This section is intended to make thoroughly clear what is believed to be a consequence of the rest of this License.

8. If the distribution and/or use of the Program is restricted in certain countries either by patents or by copyrighted interfaces, the original copyright holder who places the Program under this License may add an explicit geographical distribution limitation excluding those countries, so that distribution is permitted only in or among countries not thus excluded. In such case, this License incorporates the limitation as if written in the body of this License.

9. The Free Software Foundation may publish revised and/or new versions of the General Public License from time to time. Such new versions will be similar in spirit to the present version, but may differ in detail to address new problems or concerns.

Each version is given a distinguishing version number. If the Program specifies a version number of this License which applies to it and "any later version", you have the option of following the terms and conditions either of that version or of any later version published by the Free Software Foundation. If the Program does not specify a version number of this License, you may choose any version ever published by the Free Software Foundation.

10. If you wish to incorporate parts of the Program into other free programs whose distribution conditions are different, write to the author to ask for permission. For software which is copyrighted by the Free Software Foundation, write to the Free Software Foundation; we sometimes make exceptions for this. Our decision will be guided by the two goals of preserving the free status of all derivatives of our free software and of promoting the sharing and reuse of software generally.

NO WARRANTY

11. BECAUSE THE PROGRAM IS LICENSED FREE OF CHARGE, THERE IS NO WARRANTY FOR THE PROGRAM, TO THE EXTENT PERMITTED BY APPLICABLE LAW. EXCEPT WHEN OTHERWISE STATED IN WRITING THE COPYRIGHT HOLDERS AND/OR OTHER PARTIES PROVIDE THE PROGRAM "AS IS" WITHOUT WARRANTY OF ANY KIND, EITHER EXPRESSED OR IMPLIED, INCLUDING, BUT NOT LIMITED TO, THE IMPLIED WARRANTIES OF MERCHANTABILITY AND FITNESS FOR A PARTICULAR PURPOSE. THE ENTIRE RISK AS TO THE QUALITY AND PERFORMANCE OF THE PROGRAM IS WITH YOU. SHOULD THE PROGRAM PROVE DEFECTIVE, YOU ASSUME THE COST OF ALL NECESSARY SERVICING, REPAIR OR CORRECTION.
12. IN NO EVENT UNLESS REQUIRED BY APPLICABLE LAW OR AGREED TO IN WRITING WILL ANY COPYRIGHT HOLDER, OR ANY OTHER PARTY WHO MAY MODIFY AND/OR REDISTRIBUTE THE PROGRAM AS PERMITTED ABOVE, BE LIABLE TO YOU FOR DAMAGES, INCLUDING ANY GENERAL, SPECIAL, INCIDENTAL OR CONSEQUENTIAL DAMAGES ARISING OUT OF THE USE OR INABILITY TO USE THE PROGRAM (INCLUDING BUT NOT LIMITED TO LOSS OF DATA OR DATA BEING RENDERED INACCURATE OR LOSSES SUSTAINED BY YOU OR THIRD PARTIES OR A FAILURE OF THE PROGRAM TO OPERATE WITH ANY OTHER PROGRAMS), EVEN IF SUCH HOLDER OR OTHER PARTY HAS BEEN ADVISED OF THE POSSIBILITY OF SUCH DAMAGES.

END OF TERMS AND CONDITIONS